D0607292

Masterpieces of Christian Literature

IN SUMMARY FORM

Masterpieces of Christian Literature

IN SUMMARY FORM

EDITED BY

Frank N. Magill

WITH

Ian P. McGreal

ASSOCIATE EDITOR

Harper & Row, Publishers

New York, Evanston, and London

K—N

LIBRARY OF CONGRESS CATALOG CARD NUMBER: 63-10622

ACKNOWLEDGMENTS

The articles describing the following works were prepared in whole or in part by reference to the editions indicated. The editors and staff gratefully acknowledge the use of these editions.

The First Epistle of Clement to the Corinthians; The Epistle of Barnabas; The Seven Epistles of Ignatius, The Shepherd by Hermas, and *The Epistle to Diognetus.* From *The Apostolic Fathers.* Translated by Kirsopp Lake. Published by William Heinemann, Ltd. and Harvard University Press, and by The Macmillan Company.

The First Apology and *The Second Apology* by Saint Justin Martyr. From *The Writings of Saint Justin Martyr* in *Fathers of the Church* (Volume 6). Translated by Thomas B. Falls. Published by Christian Heritage.

The Apology of Athenagoras. From *Ancient Christian Writers.* Translated by J. H. Crehan, S.J. Published by The Newman Press.

The Apostolic Tradition by Hippolytus. Translated by B. S. Easton. Published by The Macmillan Company.

Against Celsus by Origen. Translated by Henry Chadwick. Published by The Cambridge University Press.

The Incarnation of the Word of God by Athanasius. Translated by a Religious of the C.S.M.V.S. S.Th. Published by The Macmillan Company.

Ecclesiastical History by Eusebius of Caesarea. Translated by Kirsopp Lake. Published by Loeb Classical Library, Harvard University Press.

The Life of Antony by Athanasius in *Ancient Christian Writers* (Volume 10). Translated by R. T. Meyer. Published by The Newman Press.

The Longer Rules and *The Shorter Rules* by Saint Basil of Caesarea. From *The Ascetic Works of Saint Basil.* Translated by W. K. L. Clarke. Published by The Society for Promoting Christian Knowledge.

The *City of God* by Saint Augustine. Translated by Gerald G. Walsh and others. Published by Fathers of the Church, Inc.

Seven Books of History Against the Pagans by Paulus Orosius. Translated by Irving Woodworth Raymond. Published by Columbia University Press.

The Enchiridion on Faith, Hope, and Love by Saint Augustine. From *The Basic Writings of Saint Augustine.* Published by Random House, Inc.

Tome by Saint Leo I. Translated by E. H. Blakeney. Published by The Society for Promoting Christian Knowledge and by The Macmillan Company.

The Bazaar of Heraclides by Nestorius. Translated by G. R. Driver and Leonard Hodgson. Published by The Oxford University Press.

The Divine Names by Dionysius, the Pseudo-Areopagite. Translated by C. E. Rolt. Published by The Society for Promoting Christian Knowledge.

On the Holy Trinity by Boethius. From *The Theological Tractates.* Translated by H. F. Stewart and E. K. Rand. Published by William Heinemann, Ltd. and G. P. Putnam's Sons.

Pastoral Care by Saint Gregory I. From *Ancient Christian Writers.* Translated by Henry Davis. Published by The Newman Press.

The Ladder of Divine Ascent by Saint John Climacus. Translated by A. L. Moore. Published by Harper & Brothers.

Ecclesiastical History of the English Nation by Saint Bede. From *Baedae Opera Historica.* Translated by J. E. King. Published by Harvard University Press.

The Fountain of Wisdom by Saint John of Damascus. From *The Writings of Saint John of Damascus.* Translated by Frederic H. Chase. Published by Fathers of the Church, Inc.

The Steps of Humility by Saint Bernard. Translated by G. B. Burch. Published by Harvard University Press.

Soliloquy on the Earnest Money of the Soul by Hugh of St. Victor. Translated by K. Herbert. Published by The Marquette University Press.

Know Thyself by Peter Abelard. From *Abailard's Ethics.* Translated by J. Ramsay McCallum. Published by Basil Blackwell.

Policratus by John of Salisbury. From *The Statesman's Book of John of Salisbury.* Translated by J. Dickinson. Published by Alfred A. Knopf, Inc.

Benjamin Minor by Richard of St. Victor. From *Richard of Saint-Victor: Selected Writings on Contemplation.* Translated by Clare Kirchberger. Published by Faber and Faber, Ltd.

Retracing the Arts to Theology by Saint Bonaventura. From *Saint Bonaventure's De Reductione Artium Ad Theologiam.* Translated by Sister E. R. Healy. Published by The Franciscan Institute.

The Journey of the Mind to God by Saint Bonaventura. Translated by George Boas. Published by The Liberal Arts Press.

Ordinatio: Oxford Commentary on the Sentences of Peter Lombard by Johannes Duns Scotus. From *Duns Scotus: Philosophical Writings.* Translated by Allan Wolter. Published by Thomas Nelson and Sons, Ltd.

The Divine Comedy by Dante Alighieri. Translated by H. R. Huse. Published by Rinehart and Company.

The Little Flowers of St. Francis. Translated by Leo Sherley-Price. Published by Penguin Books.

De Corpore Christi by William of Ockham. From *The De Sacramento Altaris of William of Ockham.* Published by The Lutheran Literary Board.

The Adornment of the Spiritual Marriage by John of Ruysbroeck. Translated by C. A. Wynschenk, Dom. Published by J. M. Dent and Sons, Ltd.

The Revelations of Divine Love by Lady Julian of Norwich. Translated by James Walsh, S.J. Published by Harper and Brothers.

The Cloud of Unknowing. Edited by Justin McCann. Published by The Newman Press.

The Following of Christ by Gerhard Groote. Translated by Joseph Malaise. Published by The American Press.

Treatise on the Church by John Huss. Translated by David S. Schaff. Published by Charles Scribner's Sons.

The Imitation of Christ by Thomas a Kempis. Translated by Leo Sherley-Price. Published by Penguin Books.

Of Learned Ignorance by Nicholas of Cusa. Translated by G. Haron. Published by Rutledge and Kegan Paul.

The Scale of Perfection by Walter Hilton. Translated by Evelyn Underhill. Published by John M. Watkins.

An Open Letter to the Christian Nobility of the German Nation; The Babylonian Captivity of the Church; and *A Treatise on Christian Liberty by* Martin Luther. From *Works of Martin Luther.* Published by The Muhlenberg Press.

The Bondage of the Will by Martin Luther. Translated by Henry Cole and Edward Thomas Vaughan. Published by Sovereign Grace Union.

On the Errors of the Trinity by Michael Servetus. Translated by Earl Morse Wilbur. Published by Harvard University Press.

A Short and Clear Exposition of the Christian Faith by Ulrich Zwingli. From *Zwingli and Bullinger* in *The Library of Christian Classics* (Volume XXIV). Translated by G. W. Bromiley. Published by SCM Press and The Westminster Press.

Foundation of Christian Doctrine by Menno Simons. Translated by Leonard Verduin. Published by The Herald Press.

The Life of St. Teresa of Ávila by Saint Teresa of Ávila. Translated by David Lewis. Published by The Newman Press.

A Treatise of Reformation Without Tarrying for Any by Robert Browne. Published by George Allen and Unwin, Ltd.

The Dark Night of the Soul by Saint John of the Cross. Translated by K. F. Reinhardt. Published by Frederick Ungar Publishing Company.

The Declaration of Sentiments by Jacobus Arminius. Translated by James Nichols and W. R. Bagnall. Published by Baker Beck House.

Introduction to the Devout Life by Saint Francis of Sales. Translated by Allan Ross. Published by Burns, Oates and Washbourne, Ltd.

De Religione Laici by Edward Herbert, First Lord of Cherbury. Translated by Harold Randolph Hutcheson. Published by The Yale University Press.

Didactica Magna by Johannes Amos Comenius. Translated by M. W. Keatinge. Published by A & C Black, Ltd.

Pensées by Blaise Pascal. Translated by W. F. Trotter. Published by P. F. Collier and Son.

The Practice of the Presence of God by Brother Lawrence (Nicholas Herman). Translated by Sister Mary David, S.S.N.D. Published by The Newman Book Shop.

The Creed of a Savoyard Priest by Jean Jacques Rousseau. Translated by Barbara Foxley. Published by J. M. Dent and Sons, Ltd., and by E. P. Dutton and Company.

The Journals of Henry Melchior Mühlenberg. Translated by Theodore G. Tappert and John W. Doberstein. Published by The Muhlenberg Press.

Religion Within the Limits of Reason Alone by Immanuel Kant. Translated by Theodore M. Greene and Hoyt H. Hudson. Published by Open Court Publishing Company.

Early Theological Writings by Georg Wilhelm Friedrich Hegel. Translated by T. M. Knox. Published by The University of Chicago Press.

On Religion: Speeches to its Cultured Despisers by Friedrich Schleiermacher. Translated by John Oman. Published by Harper and Brothers.

The Phenomenology of Spirit by George Wilhelm Friedrich Hegel. Translated by J. B. Baillie. Published by Allen and Unwin, Ltd.

The Christian Faith by Friedrich Schleiermacher. Translated by H. R. Mackintosh and J. S. Stewart. Published by T. & T. Clark.

The Essence of Christianity by Ludwig Feuerbach. Translated by George Eliot. Published by Harper and Brothers.

Concluding Unscientific Postscript by Søren Kierkegaard. Translated by David F. Swenson and Walter Lowrie. Published by The Princeton University Press.

Christian Discourses by Søren Kierkegaard. Translated by Walter Lowrie. Published by The Oxford University Press.

Training in Christianity by Søren Kierkegaard. Translated by Walter Lowrie. Published by The Princeton University Press.

The Attack on Christendom by Søren Kierkegaard. Translated by Walter Lowrie. Published by The Princeton University Press.

The Christian Doctrine of Justification and Reconciliation by Albrecht Ritschl. Translated by H. R. Mackintosh and A. B. Macauley. Published by T. & T. Clark.

Lectures on Godmanhood by Vladimir Solovyev. Translated by Peter Zouboff. Published by Dennis Dobson, Ltd.

The Grand Inquisitor by Fyodor Dostoevski. From *The Brothers Karamazov*. Translated by Constance Garnett. Published by Random House, Inc.

Systematic Theology by Augustus Hopkins Strong. Published by The American Baptist Publication Society.

Practical Christianity by Rufus M. Jones. Published by The John C. Winston Company.

What is Christianity? by Adolf Harnack. Translated by Thomas Bailey Saunders. Published by Harper and Brothers.

The Philosophy of Religion by Harald Höffding. Translated by B. E. Meyer. Published by Macmillan and Company, Ltd.

The Quest of the Historical Jesus by Albert Schweitzer. Translated by W. Montgomery. Published by A. & C. Black, Ltd.

Personalism by Borden Parker Bowne. Published by Houghton, Mifflin and Company.

The Person and Place of Christ by Peter Taylor Forsyth. Published by The Independent Press.

The Meaning of God in Human Experience by William Ernest Hocking. Published by The Yale University Press.

The Social Teaching of the Christian Churches by Ernst Troeltsch. Translated by Olive Wyon. Published by The Macmillan Company.

The Problem of Christianity by Josiah Royce. Published by The Macmillan Company.

The Idea of the Holy by Rudolf Otto. Translated by John W. Harvey. Published by The Oxford University Press.

A Theology for the Social Gospel by Walter Rauschenbusch. Published by The Abingdon Press and The Macmillan Company.

The Plan of Salvation by Benjamin B. Warfield. Published by The William B. Eerdmans Publishing Company.

The Epistle to the Romans by Karl Barth. Translated by Sir Edwyn C. Hoskyns. Published by The Oxford University Press.

Theology as an Empirical Science by Douglas Clyde Macintosh. Published by The Macmillan Company.

On the Eternal in Man by Max Scheler. Translated by Bernard Noble. Published by Harper and Brothers.

Christianity and Liberalism by J. Gresham Machen. Published by The William B. Eerdmans Publishing Company.

The Faith of the Christian Church by Gustaf Aulén. Translated by Eric H. Wahlstrom. Published by The Muhlenberg Press.

I and Thou by Martin Buber. Translated by Ronald Gregor Smith. Published by T. & T. Clark.

Love, the Law of Life by Toyohiko Kagawa. Translated by J. F. Gressitt. Published by The John C. Winston Company.

Religion in the Making by Alfred North Whitehead. Published by The Macmillan Company.

Freedom and the Spirit by Nikolai Berdyaev. Translated by Oliver Fielding Clarke. Published by Geoffrey Bles: The Centenary Press.

Philosophical Theology by Frederick Robert Tennant. Published by The Cambridge University Press.

Selected Letters by Baron Friedrich von Hügel. Published by J. M. Dent and Sons, Ltd.

Christ and Society by Charles Gore. Published by Charles Scribner's Sons.

Agape and Eros by Anders Nygren. Translated by Philip S. Watson. Published by The Society for Promoting Christian Knowledge.

Christus Victor by Gustaf Aulén. Translated by A. G. Herbert. Published by The Society for Promoting Christian Knowledge, and The Macmillan Company.

The Faith of a Moralist by Alfred Edward Taylor. Published by Macmillan and Company, Ltd.

The Destiny of Man by Nikolai Berdyaev. Translated by Natalie Duddington. Published by Geoffrey Bles.

The Growth of the Idea of God by Shailer Mathews. Published by The Macmillan Company.

Lectures on Calvinism by Abraham Kuyper. Published by The William B. Eerdmans Publishing Company.

The Natural and the Supernatural by John Oman. Published by the Syndics of The Cambridge University Press.

The Vision of God: The Christian Doctrine of the Summum Bonum by Kenneth E. Kirk. Published by Longmans, Green, and Company.

Church Dogmatics by Karl Barth. Translated by G. T. Thomson. Published by T. & T. Clark.

The Divine Imperative by Emil Brunner. Translated by Olive Wyon. Published by The Lutterworth Press.

The Two Sources of Morality and Religion by Henri Bergson. Translated by R. Ashley Audra and Cloudesley Brereton. Published by Henry Holt and Company.

The Living God by Nathan Söderblom. Published by The Oxford University Press.

Nature, Man and God by William Temple. Published by Macmillan and Company, Ltd.

Being and Having by Gabriel Marcel. Translated by Katharine Farrer. Published by The Beacon Press.

Jesus the Lord by Karl Heim. Translated by D. H. van Daalen. Published by The Muhlenberg Press.

The Parables of the Kingdom by Charles Harold Dodd. Published by Nisbet and Company.

A New Critique of Theoretical Thought by Herman Dooyeweerd. Translated by David H. Freeman and William Young. Published by H. J. Paris and The Presbyterian and Reformed Publishing Company.

True Humanism by Jacques Maritain. Translated by Margot Adamson. Published by Charles Scribner's Sons.

Worship by Evelyn Underhill. Published by Harper and Brothers.

The Cost of Discipleship by Dietrich Bonhoeffer. Translated by R. H. Fuller. Published by The Macmillan Company.

The Philosophical Bases of Theism by G. Dawes Hicks. Published by The Macmillan Company.

The Wisdom of God by Sergius Bulgakov. Published by The Paisley Press, Inc. and Williams and Norgate, Ltd.

The Christian Message in a Non-Christian World by Hendrik Kraemer. Published by Kregel Publications.

The Idea of a Christian Society by Thomas Stearns Eliot. Published by Faber and Faber, Ltd.

A Philosophy of Religion by Edgar Sheffield Brightman. Published by Prentice-Hall, Inc.

Christian Doctrine by J. S. Whale. Published by The Macmillan Company.

The Meaning of Revelation by H. Richard Niebuhr. Published by The Macmillan Company.

The Nature and Destiny of Man by Reinhold Niebuhr. Published by Charles Scribner's Sons.

Prayer by George Arthur Buttrick. Published by Whitmore and Stone.

The Screwtape Letters by Clive Staples Lewis. Published by The Macmillan Company.

Christ and Time by Oscar Cullmann. Translated by Floyd V. Filson. Published by The Westminster Press.

Dogmatics by Emil Brunner. Translated by Olive Wyon. Published by The Lutterworth Press.

The Idea of Christ in the Gospels by George Santayana. Published by Charles Scribner's Sons.

The Source of Human Good by Henry Nelson Wieman. Published by The University of Chicago Press.

The Divine Relativity by Charles Hartshorne. Published by The Yale University Press.

God Was in Christ by Donald M. Baillie. Published by Charles Scribner's Sons.

Theology of the New Testament by Rudolf Bultmann. Translated by Kendrick Grobel. Published by Charles Scribner's Sons.

Ethics by Dietrich Bonhoeffer. Translated by Eberhard Bethge. Published by The Macmillan Company.

Faith and History by Reinhold Niebuhr. Published by Charles Scribner's Sons.

God's Grace and Man's Hope by Daniel Day Williams. Published by Harper and Brothers.

The Living Word by Gustaf Wingren. Translated by Victor C. Pogue. Published by The Muhlenberg Press.

Basic Christian Ethics by Paul Ramsey. Published by Charles Scribner's Sons.

Christ and Culture by H. Richard Niebuhr. Published by Harper and Brothers.

The Christian Understanding of God by Nels F. S. Ferré. Published by Harper and Brothers.

Introduction to the Philosophy of Religion by Peter Anthony Bertocci. Published by Prentice-Hall, Inc.

Systematic Theology by Paul Tillich. Published by The University of Chicago Press.

Time and Eternity by Walter T. Stace. Published by The Princeton University Press.

Natural Religion and Christian Theology by Charles E. Raven. Published by the Syndics of The Cambridge University Press.

Christian Theology: An Ecumenical Approach by Walter Marshall Horton. Published by Harper and Brothers.

The Divine Milieu by Pierre Teilhard de Chardin. Published by Harper and Brothers.

Faith and Knowledge by John Hick. Published by The Cornell University Press.

The Form of the Personal by John Macmurray. Volume I, *The Self as Agent,* published by Faber and Faber, Ltd. Volume II, *Persons in Relation,* published by Harper and Brothers.

The Reality of Faith by Friedrich Gogarten. Translated by Carl Michalson, and others. Published by The Westminster Press.

Christianity and Paradox by Ronald W. Hepburn. Published by C. A. Watts and Company, Ltd.

Christians and the State by John Bennett. Published by Charles Scribner's Sons.

Commentary on Galatians by Ragnar Bring. Translated by Eric Wahlstrom. Published by The Muhlenberg Press.

The Nature of Faith by Gerhard Ebeling. Translated by Ronald Gregor Smith. Published by The Muhlenberg Press.

Our Experience of God by H. D. Lewis. Published by George Allen and Unwin, Ltd. and The Macmillan Company.

ALPHABETICAL LIST OF TITLES

PREFACE

MAN'S most disturbing intellectual problem is his relationship to the infinite and the eternal. For as long as he has had a rational intellect, he has pondered over the mystery of birth and death, the whence and whither of his existence. Alone and in ignorance yet sensing a kinship with nature and the rhythm of the seasons, he has in the past chosen as the object of his reverence such diverse images as the sun, the sea, mountain peaks, even gods and goddesses he himself had to invent.

About two thousand years ago Jesus Christ appeared on the earth, representing man's first visual, physical contact with the Deity his senses told him surely existed. This book is a survey of the historical, philosophical, and devotional literature that has grown out of Christ's divine revelation, an event that has already affected the lives of billions of people and will unquestionably influence billions to come.

MASTERPIECES OF CHRISTIAN LITERATURE IN SUMMARY FORM, which examines this body of literature from the Protestant viewpoint, is one of two works dealing with the subject. The Roman Catholic interpretation is entitled MASTERPIECES OF CATHOLIC LITERATURE IN SUMMARY FORM. Obviously, the books selected for review are somewhat the same for both works up to the time of the Reformation, but with different interpretations, the emphasis oriented toward the separate doctrines established by these two divergent groups. Such differences do not affect the basic structure of Christianity, however, founded as it is on the towering faith of the early Church Fathers, the passionate dedication of the early martyrs, and the great conviction of Church leaders in the Middle Ages.

Included in MASTERPIECES OF CHRISTIAN LITERATURE are two-thousand-word essay-reviews of three hundred books dealing with the Christian movement, beginning with THE FIRST EPISTLE OF CLEMENT TO THE CORINTHIANS, written near the end of the first century. Approximately thirty percent of the titles included appeared prior to the Reformation, an indication of the honor and reverence in which these early works are held by Christians everywhere.

Because of the vast number of books under consideration for inclusion in MASTERPIECES OF CHRISTIAN LITERATURE, the co-operation of scores of professors of Christian literature at many leading universities and divinity schools was sought in connection with the final selection of the three hundred titles to be reviewed. These scholars were asked to name the three hundred books in the entire range of Protestant literature which, in their opinions, had been most influential in the development of Protestantism. I wish to acknowledge with thanks the generous response of these individuals, whose suggestions have helped to broaden the scope of our work.

Assisting the editors in interpreting the three hundred books under consideration was a writing staff of forty scholars and specialists, whose names and academic affiliations appear elsewhere in this volume. In addition to the writing staff, we have had the invaluable assistance of eight special consultants in various fields of Protestant scholarship, and the untiring aid of Dr. Jean Faurot, Professor of Philosophy at Sacramento State College, whose many helpful suggestions reflected his years in the pulpit as well as on the university campus. To all these scholars I wish to express my appreciation for the dedicated way in which they turned to the task of making this book as useful a Protestant reference as possible for the historian, the student, the minister, and the serious layman.

All the articles in MASTERPIECES OF CHRISTIAN LITERATURE were written expressly for this book. While every effort has been made to interpret the original book in the light of the best current scholarship, each article is animated by the insight of the individual scholar who undertook to interpret the particular book under discussion. The main points to be elaborated upon are listed in italics at the beginning of the article under the heading PRINCIPAL IDEAS ADVANCED.

Arrangement of the articles is chronological rather than alphabetical by book title, so that the orderly development of Christian thought will be clearly evident. However, two indexes enable the user to locate any article promptly without regard to chronology: a title index at the front of the book, an author index at the end. For those who wish to consider certain types or groupings from the literature available, such as Church History or Existential Theology, for example, a Category Index is included that lists seventy-five classifications under which the various articles fall.

I am sure that Associate Editor Ian P. McGreal and all staff members share my hope that MASTERPIECES OF CHRISTIAN LITERATURE will serve a useful purpose for those who wish to examine, or review, the great expressions of Christian thought that have sprung from the hearts and minds of Protestantism's most revered leaders.

FRANK N. MAGILL

SPECIAL CONSULTANTS IN PROTESTANT SCHOLARSHIP

GLANVILLE DOWNEY
Professor of Byzantine Literature, Dumbarton Oaks Research Library and Collection of Harvard University
Eastern Orthodox Church
Apostolic Fathers and Early Christian Church
New Testament

HELMUT H. KOESTER
Associate Professor of New Testament Studies, Harvard Divinity School
Early Christian Church
New Testament

SAMUEL LAEUCHLI
Professor of Church History, Garrett Theological School
Church History

DONALD A. LOWRIE
Formerly of the University of Paris
Eastern Orthodox Church
Russian Spiritual Classics

JOHN MACQUARRIE
Professor of Systemic Theology, Union Theological Seminary
Modern Christian Thought
Contemporary Theology

JOHN T. McNEILL
Professor Emeritus, Union Theological Seminary
Reformation Writings

HEIKO A. OBERMAN
Associate Professor of Church History, Harvard Divinity School
Church History
Medieval Christian Thought

PAUL RAMSEY
Professor of Christian Ethics, Princeton University
Christian Ethics
American Church History

PROJECT STAFF MEMBERS

	Graduate School	Present Affiliation
Gregory T. Armstrong, Th.D.	Heidelberg University	Vanderbilt University
Walter F. Bense, B.D.	Western Conservative Baptist Theological Seminary	Harvard University Divinity School
Peter Bertocci, Ph.D.	Boston University	Boston University
Ernest Cassara, Ph.D.	Boston University	Crane Theological School, Tufts University
Kenneth Cauthen, Ph.D.	Vanderbilt University	Crozer Theological Seminary
John W. Chandler, Ph.D.	Duke University	Williams College
Gerald R. Cragg, Ph.D., Litt.D.	McGill University; University of Cambridge	Andover Newton Theological School
Frank B. Dilley, Ph.D.	Columbia University	Smith College
Bernhard Erling, Ph.D., Th.D.	Yale University; University of Lund	Gustavus Adolphus College
Jean Faurot, Ph.D.	University of Toronto	Sacramento State College
Robert L. Ferm, Ph.D.	Yale University	Pomona College
Frederick Ferré, Ph.D.	University of St. Andrews	Dickinson College
A. Durwood Foster, Th.D.	Union Theological Seminary	Pacific School of Religion
David H. Freeman, Ph.D.	University of Pennsylvania	University of Rhode Island
John D. Godsey, Th.D.	University of Basel	Theological School, Drew University
Robert B. Hannen, Ph.D.	University of Glasgow	Berkeley Baptist Divinity School
Howard Hunter, Ph.D.	Boston University	Boston University School of Theology

John A. Hutchison, Ph.D.	Columbia University	Claremont Graduate School
William A. Johnson, Ph.D.	Columbia University	Trinity College
W. Paul Jones, Ph.D.	Yale University	Princeton University
John H. Lavely, Ph.D.	Boston University	Boston University
Clarence L. Lee, B.Th.	Lutheran Theological Seminary	Lutheran Theological Seminary at Philadelphia
Robert Lee, Ph.D.	Columbia University	San Francisco Theological Seminary
Edward L. Long, Jr., Ph.D.	Columbia University	Oberlin College
Ian P. McGreal, Ph.D.	Brown University	Sacramento State College
Clyde Manschreck, Ph.D.	Yale University	Methodist Theological School
Louis Martyn, Ph.D.	Yale University	Union Theological Seminary
Carol Morris, B.D.	Crane Theological School, Tufts University	State College at Framingham
John Pemberton, B.D.	Duke University	Amherst College
Catherine Rau, Ph.D.	University of California	Moorhead State College
Theodore Runyon, Th.D.	University of Goettingen	Candler School of Theology, Emory University
Calvin O. Schrag, Ph.D.	Harvard University	Purdue University
Frederick Sontag, Ph.D.	Yale University	Pomona College
Robert B. Tapp, Ph.D.	University of Southern California	Scripps College
Theodore G. Tappert, D.D.	University of Western Ontario	Lutheran Theological Seminary at Philadelphia
Kenneth Thompson, Jr., B.D.	Union Theological Seminary	Southern Methodist University
Hugh Vernon White, Ph.D.	Stanford University	(Emeritus) Pacific School of Religion
E. David Willis, B.D.	Princeton Theological Seminary	Harvard University
William Young, Th.D.	Union Theological Seminary	University of Rhode Island

CATEGORY INDEX

THE FIRST EPISTLE OF CLEMENT TO THE CORINTHIANS

Author: Saint Clement of Rome (fl. c.96)
Type of work: Epistle on Church practice
First transcribed: c.96

Principal Ideas Advanced

Disorder and strife in the Church are caused by jealousy.

The way to peace and concord is through obedience to established authorities, the elders (presbyteroi).

Christ rules the churches through the Apostles, the bishops appointed by them, and the approved successors of the bishops.

The epistle entitled "First Clement" is traditionally attributed to Clement, the third or fourth bishop of Rome. It is formally a communication from the Church in Rome to the Church in Corinth which had sought its help and counsel. Controversy had arisen in the Church of Corinth, and some of its members had rebelled against the authority of its leaders, called sometimes elders (*presbyteroi*) and sometimes bishops (*episcopoi*). The letter begins with a testimony to the godliness and peace that had formerly prevailed in the Church, and special mention is made of "obedience to your rulers, and fitting honor paid to the older among you (*presbyterois*)." Humility and wisdom had protected the Church from "sedition and schism." But now all this is changed. "Thus 'the worthless' rose up 'against those who were in honor,' those of no reputation against the renowned, the foolish against the prudent, the 'young against the old.'" Faith and virtue have suffered accordingly.

The root causes of such disruption are set forth step by step, and the Corinthian Church is called to repentance and a return to humility, order, and peace. This summons is developed in terms of God's dealing with the nation Israel and with individuals. It concludes with a declaration of the divine ordering of the Church and the establishment of authorities for its government. The virtues involved and illustrated are obedience, concord, and humility. It is pointed out that the source of enmity between brethren is jealousy. This is illustrated by the stories of Cain and Abel, of Jacob and Esau, of David and Saul, and others. Both Peter and Paul were persecuted and opposed through jealousy, but they triumphed over it by their endurance and won spiritual victory. This lesson is driven home and then the greatness of repentance is praised, and examples of it are found in Noah and Jonah. Both men preached repentance, and those who repented were accepted by God even though they were aliens.

God's call to repentance in the Psalms and through the prophets is put before the Church in Corinth.

The letter then dwells on the need for obedience. Enoch and Noah are examples of obedience, as is also Abraham, whose obedience reaches its high point in his offering up of Isaac. Lot also was obedient, but his wife shows the doom of the double-minded. Even the harlot Rahab was approved of God for her faithfulness in the face of danger. So the brethren in Corinth are summoned to a life of obedience, and urged to hold fast to those who truly seek peace and to shun the hypocrisy of those who only profess to do so. There follows a call to be humble and to follow Christ, who Himself fulfilled the ideal of Isaiah 53. The prophets are praised for their humility, as are also Job, Abraham, and Moses. Finally, the fifty-first Psalm is quoted at length to show David the king humbling himself before God, and the Corinthians are urged to follow such great figures in this necessary virtue.

The writer then shows how God calls His flock to concord through the orderliness of creation, and in the succession of day and night and of the seasons. We should be faithful to Him even though we offend proud and foolish men. The Holy Spirit calls us to righteousness and peace. God blesses the sincere and obedient, and judges the evil. The demand for reverence and obedience toward God is supported and sanctioned by the evidence of His power, seen in the Resurrection, which appears both in the raising of Christ and in nature. The story of "the bird called the Phoenix" is narrated by Clement and is applied as an aid to the understanding and acceptance of the Resurrection. God knows all things; we are His portion and we should seek His blessing, as did men of ancient times. Let us do good, for we are made in His image. He will accept and reward all who do His will. God's gifts are righteousness, truth, holiness, faith, and immortal life. But doom awaits the sinner. All these gifts come through Christ.

After this weighty background of religious and moral exposition, the exposure of the causes of conflict among brethren, and the requirement of humility, repentance, and obedience to God, the letter turns to the issue of authority in the Church. An analogy is found in the chain of authority in an army with its lower and higher officers, and with generals themselves subject to the Emperor. The head and the body also represent the fact of rule and subordination. In all this order of higher and lower each serves the other. The rich really serve the poor, the wise the simple. Each serves in his place. God's wrath will destroy those who are foolish and conceited and who do not respect the order of authority. There is such an order in Israel's service of God. The High Priests and the Levites have their duties; "the layman is bound by ordinances for the laity. . . . Let each one of us, brethren, be well pleasing to God in his own rank, and have a good conscience, not transgressing the appointed rules of his ministration, with all reverence."

The government of the Church is now declared in terms of its origin: "The Apostles received the Gospel for us from the Lord Jesus Christ; Jesus the Christ was sent from God. The Christ therefore is from God and the Apostles from Christ . . . in accordance with the appointed order of God's will." The Apostles preached "and they appointed their first converts, testing them by the Spirit, to be bishops, and deacons of the future believers." They anticipated strife over succession to the office of bishop and "added the codicil that if they should fall asleep, other approved men should succeed to their ministry." It is therefore not right to remove any thus appointed "with the consent of the whole Church," and who have served faithfully and well. This is the offense which had been committed in the Church of Corinth: "For we see that in spite of their good service you have removed some from the ministry which they fulfilled blamelessly."

This judgment on the wrong done in the Church of Corinth is followed by an exhortation to return to the former state of concord. The appeal of Paul against partisanship is invoked. The brethren in Corinth are in fact disloyal to the presbyters "on account of one or two persons." They should put an end to all this and obey the commands of Christ, especially His command to love. All should pray for forgiveness, especially the leaders of sedition, as Moses prayed for those who made the golden calf. The offenders should offer to depart and leave the flock in peace. Many noted and innocent persons have left their cities to put an end to strife. So pray that the present transgressors may be given a spirit of meekness and humility. Deliverance is promised for them in Scripture if they repent. To the troublemakers themselves is addressed a direct injunction to "submit to the presbyters, and receive the correction of repentance, bending the knees of your hearts." And a final appeal is made to all to be obedient to Christ: "Receive our counsel, and there shall be nothing for you to regret."

THE EPISTLE OF BARNABAS

Author: Unknown, but attributed to the Apostle Barnabas
Type of work: Christian exegesis of the Old Testament
First transcribed: Unknown, but probably between 70 and 100

Principal Ideas Advanced

Christians must be warned against a Judaic conception of the Old Testament.

Any literal interpretation of the commands of the Law should be avoided and a symbolic exegesis is rather to be followed.

An evil angel used the device of the literal interpretation of the ceremonial law to deceive the Jews, and Christians must give the Old Testament an entirely different interpretation, one in keeping with their belief in Jesus Christ as the true revealer of God.

The *Epistle of Barnabas,* although anonymous, is ascribed by tradition to the Apostle Barnabas, who was a companion of St. Paul, and it was obviously intended for a community in which Alexandrian ideas prevailed.

Early authors, such as Clement of Alexandria (c.150-c.215), actually quote it as Scripture, but it was never accepted into the canon. Origen (c.185-c.254) refers to it as a Catholic epistle, and it was included in the Codex Sinaiticus, the manuscript of the Greek Bible. Despite the fact that the *Epistle* is not accepted as part of the Scriptures, its influence is beyond question.

It begins, as do many of the epistles which are included in the New Testament, with a greeting to the community addressed. The reason given for the sending of the letter is that the author—who does not identify himself by name—has an interest in strengthening Christian conviction through correct teaching. Immediately the author sets forth the three doctrines of the Lord: the hope of life makes Him the beginning and the end of faith; His righteousness is the beginning and the end of judgment, and love and joy are the testimony of the works of righteousness.

The writer of the letter views his own days as evil, and for this reason, he writes, these ordinances of the Lord must be sought out diligently. Fear and patience will help faith, while long-suffering and continence are its allies. The author then begins his searching and his exposition of these ordinances, beginning, as is so often the case in the epistles, with a consideration of the Jewish law and of the Christian's release from it. God abolished the law for Christians and set forth a new law in Jesus Christ, one which is without the yoke of necessity. This new law has its obligation from God and is not made by man. The writer fears that the final trial is at hand, which means that it is all the more important for man to seek out those things which are able to save him.

The author admonishes his readers not to live alone but to come together and to seek out a common good. Be spiritual, he writes; be a temple consecrated to God. Christ endured too, offering up even His flesh, and because He did we are sanctified by the remission of sins, by His sprinkled blood. Nor are we left alone to understand the times. The Lord has also given us knowledge of the past, and wisdom for the present, together with understanding for the future. A man deserves to perish if he has knowledge of the way of righteousness and still turns away to darkness. God's Son came in flesh so that we might have a way of beholding Him in order to be saved. He has opened the way for men, through His death, by completing the total of the sins begun by those who persecuted God's prophets.

Turning to the Old Testament, the author begins to expound passages there to indicate that the prophets anticipated the coming of Christ. The Christians, for instance, are actually the ones whom God brings into the good land; they have been made perfect as heirs of the covenant of the Lord.

Christians are fortunate, the author of the letter tells his readers, in that the good Lord has made all things plain beforehand, so that we can know Him to whom we ought to give thanks and praise for everything. All we need to do is to learn to read the signs, to interpret the Scriptures figuratively and not literally.

Since the Old Testament contains passages which are apparently in conflict, one of the important jobs of interpretation is that of reconciling inconsistencies. The Old Testament reports the Christian message in an indirect, not a direct, fashion, and, consequently, a Christian reader must learn to discern hidden meanings in what he reads. Christ is present in the Old Testament, writes the author, just as He is in the New, but since Christ is mentioned only symbolically in the Old Testament, a Christian reader must learn to understand symbolism. When the Old Testament speaks of the sacrificial calf, for example, the Christian reader must realize that the reference is to the sacrifice of Christ.

The author of the *Epistle of Barnabas* then asks why it is that the Jews were not able to understand the Christian symbolism which runs through the Old Testament. The answer is that the Lord's voice was not clear to the Jews. The coming of Christ could have been recognized even in the practice of circumcision, had the Jews been enlightened enough to understand the symbolism of what they believed.

"Barnabas" especially concerns himself with the allegorical and Christological interpretation of the ritual law of the Old Testament and of details from the Old Testament narrative; he does not discuss truly prophetical passages or the ethical law of the Old Testament.

The distinctive character of the author's mode of allegorical interpretation is provided by his analysis of the number 318, found in the following passage (Genesis 14:14): "And when Abram heard that his brother was taken captive, he led forth his trained men, born in his house, three hundred and eighteen. . . ." The number is interpreted to mean "Jesus crucified," since the numerals of this number in Greek, taken in their letter value, are the two first letters of the name "Jesus" together with the letter "T," which is taken to symbolize the Cross of Christ.

Everywhere in the original message of the prophets the new message of the Cross is to be found, a message which can be discerned symbolically by the enlightened eye of the Christian. Did the prophets understand that they were actually foretelling the Cross and the Crucifixion of Christ? No, God acted through the prophets to conceal in their message a significance which could be discerned only after Christ's coming. Passage after passage is examined, and the author of the *Epistle* concludes that God wished to reveal in the Old Testament everything concerning His Son. The Old Testament could not be understood before Christ, but now every facet of Christ's life can be discerned beneath the literal meaning of the Old Testament stories.

Jesus inherits the covenant, the central Jewish religious concern, and He does what it cannot do; namely, redeem its followers from their sin. But what is one to do with apparently literal facts? The world, the book of Genesis tells us, was created in six days. The author understands this passage to mean that the Lord will make an end to everything in six thousand years, since each day is a thousand years to God. Everything, then, will be completed in six thousand years. The Sabbath must no longer be celebrated as the day upon which God rested after creation; Christians celebrate the eighth day upon which Jesus rose from the dead. Every factor of Jewish observance is thus altered and transformed, and new meanings are read into old.

What about such a central doctrine of Judaism as that of the Temple? Christians may now take passages referring to the Temple as signifying the new man created through the Resurrection of Christ. The doctrine of the Temple could not have had such a meaning to the pre-Christian Jews, but now it can be seen that the meaning of the Temple was symbolical, hidden there by God in order that it might be revealed later. God dwelt in the Temple; God dwells in Christians now created anew.

The Jews had a literal temple; the Christians now have a spiritual Temple; thus, the author indicates the pattern for all reinterpretation of the Old Testament. Since Christianity is a spiritual religion, it has spiritual meaning, and thus all Old Testament statements are to be interpreted spiritually, not literally. Christians must learn to read everything anew, giving to what formerly had only a literal meaning a new spiritual meaning, thus demonstrating that their eyes have been opened through God's revelation. Giving a spiritual rendering to literal passages is itself a proof that one understands the spiritual nature of Christianity and the revealed truth in Christ.

The author, then, having demonstrated how the Old Testament is to be given a spiritual reinterpretation, begins a summary of an idea drawn from the traditional Jewish-Christian catechism, also to be found in the *Didache*. There are two ways of teaching and power, one of Light and one of Darkness. By the Light the Lord rules from eternity to eternity, but the way of Darkness prevails in the present time of iniquity. The way of Light demands that one be zealous in one's works, and that each man demonstrate a love of the Maker and a fear of the Creator. Furthermore, the way of Light involves glorifying Him who redeemed men from death; it requires that all men be simple in heart and rich in spirit, that they hate all that is not pleasing to God, that they hate all hypocrisy, and that they hold fast to the commandments of the Lord.

Having made this introduction to the way of Light, the author of the letter provides a long explanation of the characteristics of the Christian life, drawn from the tradition of exhortative writings to be found in late Judaism and early Christianity.

The way of the Black One, he continues, is crooked and full of cursing, a way of death and of eternal punishment. Along this path are the sins which destroy men's souls: idolatry, adultery, murder, pride, and other offenses against God.

The ordinances of the Lord have been given to us for good reason, the author writes, and he who does what God requires will be glorified in the Kingdom of God, whereas he who chooses the other path will perish with his works. Since there are two paths from which men may choose, there is a resurrection and an eventual recompense for choosing properly. Moreover, the day of accounting is near at hand, when all things will perish with the Evil One and only those who have followed the way of Light will be saved from this destruction.

The letter closes, then, on an urgent note. The author pleads with his readers: Be taught by God and seek out what the Lord requires of you, in order that you may be found faithful in the day of Judgment. While yet you occupy a body, do not fail in any of God's commandments, but seek them out and fulfill them. The hour of destruction and of reckoning is at hand and nothing else could possibly be more important. The matter is desperate, but the way has been made clear by God's revelation, even in the Old Testament, once it is read through enlightened eyes.

THE SEVEN EPISTLES OF IGNATIUS

Author: Saint Ignatius, Bishop of Antioch (c.35-c.107)
Type of work: Pastoral letters
First transcribed: c.107

Principal Ideas Advanced

The authority of Christ is present in the churches through the Apostles and the leaders appointed by them.

Unity and peace in the Church and the validity of the Church are acquired through faithful adherence to the bishop, and to the presbyters and deacons.

True Christian life and fellowship, together with the hope of immortality and eternal life, are based on the real earthly existence of Jesus Christ, and on His death and bodily resurrection.

These letters were written by Ignatius, Bishop of Antioch, on his way to martyrdom in Rome. While at Smyrna he wrote to the churches at Ephesus, Magnesia, Tralles, and Rome. Later at Troas he wrote to those at Philadelphia and Smyrna, and to Polycarp, bishop of Smyrna. The letters all show the elevation of spirit of one who regarded himself as "theophorus," a God-bearer, and who voluntarily and even eagerly went to his death as a martyr to the faith. They are full of warm expressions of love for the churches and of prayers and exhortations for their faithfulness, unity, and peace. Frequent mention is made of individuals, and of the bishop's gratitude for their prayers for him and for their blameless lives. Ignatius constantly refers to the purpose of his journey, protesting his unworthiness for such a role, praying for strength, and asking for the prayers of the churches. Ignatius shows great concern for his own church in Antioch which he has been compelled to leave, and he asks the other churches to choose worthy representatives and to send them to the Antioch brethren to comfort and encourage them in their trial.

The dominating theme of the letters is the bishop's concern for the unity of the church in each place, its purity of doctrine, and its faithfulness in life and worship. These virtues of unity, purity, and faithfulness are grounded in the leadership and authority of the bishop, the presbyters, and the deacons. A typical and inclusive statement of this position is found in Smyrneans VIII: "I. See that you all follow the bishop, as Jesus Christ follows the Father, and the presbytery as if it were the Apostles. And reverence the deacons as the command of God.

Let no one do any of the things appertaining to the Church without the bishop. Let that be considered a valid Eucharist which is celebrated by the bishop, or by one whom he appoints. 2. Wherever the bishop appears let the congregation be present; just as wherever Jesus Christ is, there is the Catholic Church. It is not lawful either to baptise or to hold an 'agape' without the bishop; but whatever he approve, this is also pleasing to God, that everything which you may do may be secure and valid."

The epistles are not systematic treatises. Rather, they are composed of brief and often disjointed paragraphs written apparently under pressure both of time and of emotion. The main theme is clearly the divinely bestowed authority of the bishop, presbyters, and deacons, and the fact that the integrity and validity of the churches rest upon this foundation. There is no New Testament canon yet; hence, the Church depends completely on the successors and the Apostles.

Frequent warnings against false doctrine reveal primarily the danger of Docetism, which denies the real earthly life, ministry, suffering, and the death and resurrection of Christ. There is no charge that this heresy actually exists in any of the churches, but Ignatius is very much conscious of such a possibility. Over against the false doctrine of "semblance" he lays great emphasis upon the full reality of flesh and spirit, the visible and the invisible. This simple dualism runs through the whole conception of Christ, the Church, and the Christian life. Not only did Christ live and suffer and die in the flesh, but He also arose from the dead: "After his resurrection he ate and drank with them as a being of flesh, although he was united in spirit with the Father." So Ignatius prays for the churches "that in them there may be a union of the flesh and the spirit of Jesus Christ, who is our everlasting life, a union of faith and love, to which is nothing preferable, and (what is more than all) a union of Jesus and the Father." This "flesh and spirit" reality of the Church is based on the presence of Christ in spirit, but also upon the visible authority which He has delegated through the Apostles to the bishop, presbyters, and deacons. The "dispensation of the new man Jesus Christ" is found in this fellowship and obedience and in "breaking one bread, which is the medicine of immortality, the antidote that we should not die, but live for ever in Jesus Christ."

The life of the Christian also is a life in the spirit and in the flesh. It is first obedience to the bishop; "do nothing without the bishop." But it is also a pure moral life, a life of honesty and uprightness, and of faithfulness in marriage. The Christian life is "in the flesh," but it is not a carnal life. "But even what you do according to the flesh is spiritual," writes Ignatius, "for you do all things in Jesus Christ." Moreover, this faithfulness in moral living wins the favor of God just as unrighteousness incurs His condemnation. By faithfulness the Christian "attains to God." He is "full of God," and he is thereby assured of resurrection and eternal life. The bishop does not seem to fear or even to be aware of a "doctrine of works"; moral purity appears as direct obedience to God and in full participation in the life of the Church. Thus is conceived as of one piece the saving work and power of Christ, the Church united with the bishop and the presbyters, the sacramental efficacy of the Eucharist, the moral life of the Christian believer, and the hope of resurrection and eternal life. The theological basis for all this is the Incarnation: "Wait for him who is above seasons, timeless, invisible, who for our sakes became visible, who cannot be touched, who cannot suffer, who for our sakes accepted suffering, who in every way endured for our sakes."

Ignatius shows a lesser but real concern for the Judaizers. He warns that those who listen to them will be led astray. The prince of this world has hidden from the Jews the Virgin Birth of Christ. One should not listen to the Jews; one cannot be a Christian and live as a Jew.

Ignatius writes as a pastor. His care for his own church is frequently expressed. He counsels Polycarp to foster the fellowship of the church by frequent meetings, by personal humility and interest in the members, by care for the widows, and by positive teaching which will make the people less subject to any influence of false doctrine. He lovingly charges Polycarp to "Be sober as God's athlete," for "The prize is immortality and eternal life."

The "care of all the churches" occupies the greater part of all the letters. But the suppressed and often openly expressed theme of martyrdom is climactic. The bishop's vivid conception of resurrection and of the unity of flesh and spirit, his faith in the risen Christ, and his deep assurance of his own resurrection cannot remove the emotional tension and spiritual exhilaration with which he contemplates his own death. He writes especially to the Romans about this, for they are to be his immediate Christian companions before he goes to death: "Suffer me to be eaten by the beasts, through whom I can attain to God. I am God's wheat, and I am ground by the teeth of wild beasts that I may be found pure bread of Christ. Rather entice the wild beasts that they may become my tomb, and leave no trace of my body, that when I fall asleep I be not burdensome to any." As he approaches Rome he lives through this trial in anticipation. The ten soldiers that guard him already test and prepare him by their harsh treatment. He sees in this physical suffering a figure of the attacks upon his spirit of temptations, and his fight for faithfulness to his Lord. Now, he lives no longer for this world but for the higher world of the spirit. Thus he wins the victory in advance and prepares for the time when the flesh as well as the spirit must face the moment of violent death. The letters provide a powerful support for all Christians who are called upon to face a similar trial—and triumph.

THE APOLOGY OF ARISTIDES

Author: Aristides (fl. second century)
Type of work: Christian apologetics
First transcribed: c.124

Principal Ideas Advanced

There is one true living God, the creator of Heaven and earth, who is worshiped by the Christians, whereas the barbarians and the Greeks have given themselves to the folly of worshiping many gods which are merely subjective creations of their own imagination, and which are unfitting examples for human conduct.

The Christians possess the true knowledge of a holy and just God and live exemplary lives modeled after His precepts so that the very continuance of the world is due to their intercession, and they are, therefore, unjustly harassed by their persecutors.

The *Apology of Aristides* is of importance as a witness to the character of early Christianity. The history of Eusebius mentions Aristides as one of the early Christians who defended Christianity before the Roman emperor Hadrian (117-138). Aristides is one of the foremost apologists of the second century. Like Justin Martyr (c.100-c.165), Tatian (fl. c.160), Melito (d. c.190), Athenagoras (second century), Theophilus (later second century), and others, Aristides sought to win recognition for Christianity throughout the Roman Empire by putting an end to the false rumors against the Christians. The Apologists tried to make known the true nature of Christianity and to put an end to the persecutions. They appealed to the cultured members of society by arguing that Christianity is the highest wisdom, the true answer to the questions of the philosophers, and by attacking the error of polytheism and its effects on morality.

The work of Aristides was lost for centuries. The first two chapters were rediscovered in 1878 when the monks of St. Lazarus of Venice published a Latin translation of an Armenian text. The authenticity of the Armenian fragment remained in dispute until 1889, when a Syriac version of the *Apology* was discovered at the Convent of St. Catherine on Mount Sinai. The publication of the Syriac text led to the discovery that the greater part of the Greek text is contained in the widely-circulated medieval romance, *The Life of Barlaam and Josaphat.*

The original date of Aristides' *Apology*, according to Eusebius, is 124, when the *Apology* was presented to Hadrian. A second superscription in the Syriac version causes some scholars to assign the work to the time of Antonius Pius (138-161), but it is most likely that Eusebius's early date is correct.

Aristides' argument may be divided into three parts. The first seeks to demonstrate the existence of God; the second, the foolishness of polytheism; and the third, the truth that Christians alone possess the purest knowledge of God and live a life in keeping with God's holiness.

Aristides begins by claiming that philosophical contemplation of the beauty and the majesty of the world discloses that God is the power that moves the world and what it contains. As the cause of motion God is greater than the world, and although His nature is not fully comprehensible, it is reasonable that a philosopher should stand in awe of Him.

God is not born, nor made; His nature is unchangeable and without end. He is perfect and without defect; all things are in need of Him, but He is in need of nothing.

Mankind is divided into four classes, Aristides writes; there are the Greeks, the Barbarians, the Christians, and the Jews. The barbarians trace the origin of their religion to many gods, to Kronos and Rhea; they worship things, mere images or idols made in honor of the elements, rather than their creator. The earth, the waters, fire, the winds, the sun, the moon, and the stars are not gods. Only God is imperishable, invisible, and unvarying, holy, blessed, and immortal. The earth and the waters were created for man, and put under his rule. The winds of themselves have no authority; they too serve man by transporting his ships, and scattering seeds. Man is able to keep the winds in check so that they may be of service to him. Nor does man himself have the nature of a God, for man is born and dies; he has defects, and he is destroyed by animals and the elements.

The Greeks have gone even further than the barbarians in their error concerning God, Aristides continues, for the Greeks have introduced numerous fictitious gods, some females, others males; some are adulterers, others murderers. Their gods are wrathful, passionate, and envious; some are thieves, or cripples; some are sorcerers, some insane; they are kidnaped, struck by lightning, and seduced by other gods; they are perverted, incestuous, and vain. By worshiping such false gods the Greeks accepted folly and absurdity, and in emulating the gods they committed the same foul practices themselves, thereby bringing wars, famines, captivity, and desolation upon themselves.

Aristides writes that the Greeks sacrifice their children to Kronos; they burn them alive in honor of a god who has children, who went mad, and was bound and mutilated by his son Zeus. The latter is made king of the gods, a god who changes himself into men and animals, into a swan, and an eagle.

Such tales cause wickedness in men, Aristides argues, for by imitating their gods, men practice adultery, defile themselves with their sisters and mothers, have sexual relations with other men, and kill their parents. Such gods are worse than demons.

A god such as Hephaistos is lame and needy, Aristides points out; Hermes is a thief, greedy for gain, a maimed magician; Asklepios is a physician that was killed by lightning; Ares is a jealous warrior who covets sheep, commits adultery with Aphrodite; Dionysus arranges nocturnal orgies, teaches drunkenness, abducts women, eats snakes while mad; Herakles kills his own children while insane, casts himself into a fire and dies; and Apollon utters oracles for men so that he can be rewarded.

Such gods lead to corruption, delusion, and the defilement of nations, Aristides maintains. To believe in such gods is unworthy of the philosopher. The true God is not in need of sacrifices. The gods of the Greeks are based on myths, idle tales, and superficial speculations; the very deeds of such gods are at variance with the righteous laws of men.

The Jews approach the truth more than any other nation, Aristides concedes, for they recognize that God is one, the omnipotent Creator; they worship God and not His works; they show compassion to the poor, and they are just; but they, too, err in their worship of angels, their ritualism, and their rejection of the truth which the Christians have found. From its beginning the Christian religion has centered about Jesus the Messiah, the Son of the most high God, who descended from Heaven, born of a Hebrew virgin. The teachings of Christianity can be read by all in the Gospel. This same Jesus, God incarnate, was pierced by the Jews, buried, rose again after three days, and ascended to Heaven. The Christian religion grew because of the preaching by Jesus' twelve disciples.

Aristides continues his zealous arguments by claiming that the Christians trust and know the God who created the heavens and the earth, in whom are all things and from whom are all things come; the true and living God, besides whom there is no other. From this God the Christians have received commandments as to how they should live, and because of their hope in the world to come, their lives are at present exemplary. Christians do not commit fornication, nor adultery; they do not lie, steal, or covet what is not theirs. They honor their parents, are kind to those near to them, are upright and honest in their judgments. They do not worship idols; they do to others what they would have others do to them. They comfort their oppressors and do good to their enemies; their women are pure and modest, and their bondsmen are treated as brethren; they love one another, are charitable to widows and orphans, hospitable to strangers, solicitous of the well-being of prisoners, observing the teachings of their Messiah with care, and living justly and soberly as their Lord has commanded them. Each day and every hour the Christians praise and give thanks to God for their food and drink; they rejoice at the birth of a child, and give thanks when a righteous man passes from the world to be with God, but when one of them dies in his sins, they grieve bitterly.

Aristides contends that the teachings of the Christians are readily available in their writings, the study of which is able to give full assurance of their veracity. The very earth abides through the supplication of the Christians, who are innocent of the monstrous impurity attributed to them by their persecutors. The Christians are just and good; their spirit is long suffering and they have compassion for those who revile them.

Aristides concludes his apology by stating that the Christians pray that those who wrong them in ignorance may come to purity of heart and receive the forgiveness of their own sins, thus becoming members of the most blessed race—the "new . . third race"—of men upon the face of the earth, and thereby escaping the final judgment that will come upon those who are without the knowledge of God. Aristides' faith that "Verily this is a new people, and there is something divine in it" illuminates his work.

THE SHEPHERD

Author: Hermas (second century)
Type of work: Account of revelations
First transcribed: c.130

Principal Ideas Advanced

Revelations are made to Hermas by the Church, which appears in the form of a woman; by a shepherd, the angel of repentance; and by the great angel, who is in charge of all Christians.

Sin and baptism are the main themes of the revelations.

It is possible to live a sinless life after baptism, but for those who sin after baptism, the message given Hermas offers a final opportunity of forgiveness for those who repent and do penance.

The *Shepherd,* the most voluminous writing among the works produced by the Apostolic Fathers, achieved almost canonical standing, together with the New Testament Book of Revelation. The book was written in Rome by a man who had no particular office in the Church. The author writes with the self-consciousness of a prophet (as does the author of the book of Revelation), but the book nevertheless contains a great deal of traditional material. The message of the book is presented in the form of various "Visions," "Mandates," "Similitudes," and "Parables," to which detailed instructions for proper interpretation are appended.

As the work begins, Hermas is described as walking along a road. He becomes sleepy. Led by a spirit, he crosses a stream and kneels to pray. Then the heavens open, and a woman whom Hermas once secretly desired appears and greets him. She accuses him of having sinned by desiring her in his heart, and she tells him that he must repent. When the vision ends, Hermas ponders the question as to how he can be saved, and he reconsiders his overt actions, for even his unuttered desires have been shown to be sinful.

While he is reflecting, a great white chair appears before him and a woman in shining garments comes to occupy it. Hermas tells her the reason for his grief, and they discuss sin and the means for its restitution. The lady reads to him, speaking of the glory and the power of God, and then she is borne away as the first vision closes.

The second vision comes a year later, when he is again walking near the same spot. Again the ancient lady whom he had seen the year before appears. This time she has a little book, which she tells him to take away and copy. He does this, and only later does he begin to understand the things written there. The message is primarily concerned with Hermas's relationship to his family, and with his duties as a Christian toward them. At the close of this vision it is revealed to Hermas that the Lady who appeared to him was the Church. She is old because she was created first of all things, and for the sake of the Church the world was established.

Hermas's third vision comes after a

period of fasting, when the Lady appears to him in response to his desire to know fully the meaning of his previous revelations. This time six young men come with her, and they listen to Hermas as he recites his sins. She explains the glory which is due to one who is a martyr for the faith, and then Hermas has a vision of a great tower being built on water by a company of young men. It is so built of shining square stones that the tower appears to be of one stone. On his demand, the Lady begins to explain the vision to Hermas. The tower is the Church, and it is built upon water because the lives of those who comprise it have been saved through the water of baptism. The best stones which go into it are the Apostles, bishops, and teachers—men who served God in reverence and holiness. The other stones used represent those who have suffered for the Lord, those who are upright and preserve His commandments; but the stones thrown away represent those who did not repent. Stones with cracks represent those with malice in their hearts. Round stones, which must be cut before they can be used, signify those who have faith but also riches. Hermas and the lady then discuss how those who are rejected may repent so as finally to be fitted into the tower.

Seven women, representing faith and the other central Christian virtues, then appear, and Hermas is told to follow them in order of importance, faith being first. Hermas demands to know why the Lady appears different at different times, sometimes young, sometimes old. A long explanation is given which concerns the various types of people who make up the Church through repentance, and which calls attention to the Church's antiquity and to its continual renewal.

In Hermas's fourth vision he sees the type of the persecutions to come. A great beast comes to threaten him, and again he meets the ancient Lady. She explains to him that he escaped destruction from the beast because he was not double-minded; his singularity of faith preserved him from the beast's destruction.

The shepherd, who inspires the title, appears in the fifth revelation; he tells Hermas that he has come to dwell with him the rest of his days, Hermas having been handed over to his care. The shepherd, who is the angel of repentance, commands Hermas to write down the commandments and parables which the shepherd gives him.

The second part of the book contains the twelve mandates which the shepherd gives to Hermas, and their detailed explanation.

The first mandate is to believe that God is one, that He has made all things and contains all things and is Himself alone uncontained. Simplicity is the theme of the second mandate, since the innocence of simplicity keeps one from evil-speaking and encourages one to live according to God. Love truth: this is the injunction of mandate three, since by doing so one receives a spirit free from lies. One who loves truth abstains from the sin of lying and thus shall live with God. Purity is commanded in mandate four. Healing can be given to the one who sins here, although it can come only from the One who has the power over all. He who sins and is given repentance in baptism, Hermas is told, ought not to sin again but ought to live in purity. There is no second repentance given. Remission of sins is available only if the commandments are kept.

Mandate five tells Hermas that he should be long-suffering and prudent, and that if he is, he shall have power over all evil deeds and shall do all righteousness. The Lord dwells in long-suffering, but the Devil dwells in ill-temper. Temper destroys the servants of God and leads them away from righteousness. It cannot, of course, lead astray those who are filled with faith, but it does mislead those who are vain and double-minded. Long-suffering dwells with those who have faith in perfectness, and it turns out to be the chief virtue. Hermas is told that if he is able to master this commandment, he will be strong enough to keep all the other commandments given to him.

Mandate six explains the first mandates. Hermas is further told to believe only the righteous and not to believe the unrighteous. Two angels are with all men, one of righteousness and the other of unrighteousness. The angel of righteousness is delicate, modest, meek, and gentle, whereas the angel of wickedness is ill-tempered, bitter, and foolish.

Fear is the theme of mandate seven, for the fear of the Lord is the means for keeping His commandments. However, do not fear the Devil, Hermas is told, for by fearing the Lord you are given power over the Devil and need have no fear of him. Temperance, the quality of mandate eight, is said to be two-fold: it causes one to refrain from evil, and it also causes one not to refrain from the good but to do it. Hermas is then given a specific list of acts to be avoided and acts to be performed.

Mandate nine enjoins Hermas not to be double-minded. He is directed to purify his heart from all the vanities of this world. Doubt is the worst enemy of faith and causes double-mindedness. Unless he repents, every double-minded man will have trouble being saved. Grief, mandate ten tells Hermas, is the sister of double-mindedness. Grief is more evil than all the other spirits and is more terrible to the servants of God because it corrupts man more than any of the other spirits, wearing out the Holy Spirit. However, grief can also bring salvation. For if a man grieves over an ill-tempered act, grief may lead to repentance and salvation; but if a man fails in his work because of double-mindedness, and if he grieves over this, then the Holy Spirit is grieved also and worn out. Therefore, to combat grief, put on joyfulness, which always is acceptable to God, since the joyful man does good deeds, has good thoughts, and despises grief. But the mournful man is wicked. If grief is mixed with intercession at the altar, it does not permit the intercession to ascend in purity.

Mandate eleven reveals a man sitting on a bench, and Hermas is told that the man is a false prophet, one who corrupts the understanding of the children of God. Hermas naturally asks how one can discern the false from the true prophet, and he is told: Test a man by his life. A true prophet will be meek, gentle, and lowly minded, whereas the false prophet will exhalt himself, be impudent and shameless, and lead a life of great luxury. Most important, if a person accepts rewards for his prophecy, then he is a false prophet. The vision ends as Hermas is told to have faith in the Divine Spirit.

Mandate twelve, the last of the mandates, concerns desire. The same man continues to instruct Hermas.

Hermas is to put away from himself every evil desire and to put on only desires which are good and holy. A wicked desire is cruel and hard to tame, and it destroys men. Carnal desires are the worst; serving only good desires will enable one to overcome wicked desires. To serve good desires, Hermas is told, means to work righteousness and virtue, to fear the Lord, and to have both faith and meekness.

The angel of repentance has been speaking to Hermas, and the angel concludes the last mandate by saying that these commandments are given so that one may continue pure after repentance by following the commandments. Hermas is not sure that a man is able to keep such commandments simply from his own power, but he is told that whoever believes that the commandments can be kept will be able to keep them; and this assurance is important since without keeping the commandments there is no salvation. Man, after all, is the lord of all creatures and should be able also to be the lord of the commandments. If you have only the name of the Lord on your lips, Hermas is told, that will not do; but if you have the Lord in your heart, then you will be able to master these commandments. If you purify your heart from the vain desires of the world, and if your heart is pure towards the Lord, then these commandments can be kept, the angel of repentance assures Hermas.

The third part of the work presents ten parables, or similitudes, some quite brief and direct, some quite long and involved. On the whole they are rather simple and straightforward in their meaning. For each parable or vision, Hermas is given a detailed and allegorical translation of its meaning. They are not mere stories but elaborately constructed illustrations. The first parable points up the fact that since Christians are like strangers in a foreign land, they ought not to secure for themselves more than the bare minimum of what they need for temporary living.

The second parable describes the two types of servants of God, the rich and the poor, who may complement each other and thus aid each other in achieving salvation. The rich man rests upon the poor and gives him what he needs; the poor man is rich in intercession and confession. The third parable explains that in this world righteous men and sinners appear to be the same and cannot easily be distinguished. Parable four continues this theme, explaining that the righteous will be known in the world to come through their fruits. The acceptable and proper mode of fasting is the subject of parable five; true fasting involves serving the Lord with a pure heart and keeping His ordinances.

Parable six begins by considering Hermas's perplexity over the previous parables and his concern to understand them properly. The angel of repentance appears again and attempts to calm Hermas's perplexity, assuring him that he can both understand and keep the commandments. Then Hermas is presented with a vision of different types of shepherds. One represents the shepherd of luxury and deceit, another the shepherd of punishment; it is luxury which provides the main stumbling block to the good life. In parable seven Hermas continues to express his uncertainty concerning the punishment given to those who have not repented, but parable eight turns to a new theme and concerns a great willow tree and the various kinds of branches which Hermas sees being cut from it. These represent various kinds of lives, and some are so fruitful that they are sent directly to become part of a tower, which represents the Kingdom of God. Useless branches are those who have not observed God's law. Some whose lives were not acceptable on first inspection are given a second chance and through repentance are made acceptable for entrance.

Parable nine is the longest parable; it is a vision of twelve mountains, each with a different appearance. Twelve maidens and six men are building a tower with stones taken from these mountains. The tower is built upon a rock which contains a gate. In elaborate detail the different stones are described, and they are pictured as representing various kinds of lives. And, again, some stones are immediately acceptable for inclusion in the tower, the Kingdom of God, and others must first be reshaped through repentance. Others are never fit to be used and are rejected. Again the message is, repent while there is still time.

The tenth and final parable promises every good thing to Hermas if he keeps the commandments given to him. All the lusts of the world will be made subject to him, so that nothing will impede him. Whoever keeps the commandments has life and honor from the Lord; whoever does not is delivering himself to death. To keep the commandments means to minister to others. If anyone sees another person laboring under the yoke of the lusts of the world, he should help him in his distress and thus gain great joy. Whoever does not rescue another from such distress incurs sin and becomes guilty. The building of the tower, which is the Church, has been broken off so that, through such actions as that of obeying the commandments and ministering to others, each man might have the opportunity to prove his worth and to gain inclusion for himself in the tower. With this injunction to Hermas to obey and to transmit the commandments, the visions of Hermas abruptly end.

EPISTLE TO THE PHILIPPIANS

Author: Saint Polycarp of Smyrna (c.69-c.155)
Type of work: Pastoral letter
First transcribed: c.135

Principal Ideas Advanced

The fruit of faith in Christ is a life of love and purity; Christ Himself provides the example which all Christians should imitate.

Christians are citizens of a heavenly Kingdom and will reign with Christ if they are obedient to His commandments.

Christians are to pray for civil authorities even when the authorities persecute and hate the Church.

The letter of Polycarp of Smyrna to the church at Philippi is one of the documents belonging to the corpus of early Christian literature known as the works of the Apostolic Fathers. Of all the writers whose works are included in this group, Polycarp has probably the most impressive credentials for being considered an "Apostolic" writer, since it is quite possible that he had some personal associations with the Apostle John during Polycarp's youth (see, Eusebius's *Ecclesiastical History*).

Polycarp must have been a central figure in the Church of Asia as early as the first decade of the second century. He was a significant Church leader for more than half a century. Ignatius, Bishop of Antioch, while on his way to his martyrdom in Rome, visited Polycarp, and the letters which Ignatius wrote to the church at Smyrna and to Polycarp himself show the affection he felt for Polycarp and the faith he had in Polycarp's importance to the advancement of Christianity. The fact that there is a somewhat larger body of knowledge about Polycarp than about most figures from the second century is itself evidence in support of the claim that Polycarp played an important and creative part in the building of the early Church.

Two incidents from Polycarp's life, recorded in Irenaeus's *Against the Heresis* (182-188), throw valuable light upon Polycarp's character and temperament. One concerns a trip which Polycarp made to Rome about the year 155. During his stay in Rome he became involved in the problem of determining the correct date for the celebration of Easter, and although he and Anicetus, the leader of the Roman Church, were unable to agree on the same practice, they nevertheless remained in friendly communion with each other; Bishop Anicetus, as a sign of friendship and recognition, permitted Polycarp to celebrate the Eucharist in the Church of Rome. The other incident concerns a meeting which took place between Polycarp and the arch-heretic Marcion (d.c.160). In this meeting Polycarp exhibited none of the charity and tolerance which he had shown in his disagreement with Anicetus. Rather, he firmly denounced Marcion as the "first-born of Satan."

These same two attitudes—charity and tolerance in matters of Church practice and discipline, and implacable opposition to every distortion of the essentials of the Christian faith—are strongly reflected in the Epistle to the Philippians.

The occasion for the writing of the letter was a scandal which had developed in the church at Philippi. A presbyter by the name of Valens had evidently used his position in the church for financial profit and thus had violated the strong feelings of the church against the accumulation of wealth. Polycarp wrote in a spirit of fraternal concern for the church and the wayward presbyter, urging the church to be moderate and understanding and Valens to be truly repentant.

The over-all tone of the letter, therefore, is one of gentleness and restraint. Yet flashes of anger do show forth when Polycarp considers those "who bear in hypocrisy the name of the Lord, who deceive empty-headed people." What Polycarp had in mind here were the heretics who denied the reality of Christ's incarnation and consequently rejected the Apostolic accounts of the Crucifixion and the Church's teachings concerning the resurrection of the body. It is possible that he had

Marcion and his followers specifically in mind when he wrote these words, since he used the same expression he had used of Marcion—"first-born of Satan"—to describe these hypocrites and deceivers.

One obvious fact which emerges from a reading of this letter is that the writer can hardly be called an original thinker. For the most part, Polycarp was content to express his thoughts by means of a patchwork of Scriptural quotations. It is not necessary to conclude from this technique, however, that Polycarp was incapable of originality. Rather, it would seem that he deliberately adopted the technique because it was consistent with his own theological point of view. The entire message of Polycarp can be summed up in the words "Stand fast in the faith delivered to you." His purpose in writing to the Philippians was not to advance new and original ideas, but to remind the church at Philippi of the faith which it had been taught. In short, Polycarp's chief concern was for the preservation of the Church's tradition—a tradition which he clearly identified with the message of the Apostles.

Closely related to this emphasis on the preservation of pure doctrine in the Church is the emphasis on pure living. Again, in the area of morals and conduct, Polycarp showed no interest in presenting his readers with novel arguments and sophisticated expositions, but rather encouraged them to pattern their conduct after the life of Christ. By imitating Christ's example—particularly his purity, patient endurance, and forbearance—the church at Philippi could be assured of an exalted position in the Kingdom of God when the saints would reign with Christ and judge the world.

Behind the oft-repeated encouragement, "Be steadfast," must be seen the constant threat of persecution which faced Christians in the early centuries. Polycarp would one day prove his own steadfastness by his heroic martyrdom. Perhaps the clearest indication of the charitable spirit of this man is to be found in his plea that Christians pray for those who persecute and hate them.

THE FIRST APOLOGY and THE SECOND APOLOGY

Author: Saint Justin Martyr (c.100-c.165)
Type of work: Apologetics
First transcribed: c.150; c.160

Principal Ideas Advanced

Truth and right are equal for all men, and all men should be treated equally.

Christians should be treated justly and should not be unlawfully condemned by prejudice, malicious gossip, and false accusations, for in killing Christians, the ruler does them no harm but condemns himself to everlasting perdition.

Christians are loyal citizens, for they have been instructed by God to obey the government in secular matters; there is nothing in Christian belief or practice that is detrimental to the welfare of the state.

The First Apology and *The Second Apology* are the works of Justin Martyr, the second century apologist, and the first outstanding defender of Christianity against the attacks of non-Christians. Justin Martyr was born at the beginning of the second century (c.100-110) in Samaria. Before his conversion to Christianity (c.130), he frequented the schools of the Stoics, the Peripatetics, the Pythagoreans, and the Platonists. After his conversion, Justin opened a school of philosophy at Rome, where he openly and fearlessly engaged in apologetic controversy until his martyrdom about 165.

The First Apology was written at Rome about the year 150. The petition is directed to the Emperor Antoninus Pius, to the Emperor's sons, to the Senate, and to the Roman people as a whole. *The Second Apology* is assigned by critics to the latter part of Antoninus Pius's reign (147-161), although in his *Ecclesiastical History*, Eusebius states that it was addressed to Marcus Aurelius (121-180). It is most likely that *The Second Apology* is not an appendix to the first, but an independent petition, written at Rome between 155 and 160.

The First Apology can be divided into three main divisions. The first twenty chapters deal with the proper relationship between the authorities of the State and Christians; Chapters 21 to 60 seek to demonstrate the superiority of Christianity over paganism, and Chapters 61-68 offer explanations of Christian practices. At a time when the Christian religion was grossly misunderstood, such explanations were significant features of the Christian apology.

Justin Martyr first asks the rulers of the state for justice, for fair treatment to Christians, based upon facts, not prejudice. As citizens, Christians can rightly be called upon to give an account of their life and doctrine; they in turn can expect to be judged in accordance with philosophy and piety, not by force and tyranny. To inflict injustice is more detrimental to the tyrant than to his victim. In fact, the Emperor may be able to kill Christians, but he is unable to harm them, unless he can convict them of being sinful persons or criminals.

To punish Christians simply because they call themselves Christians, without showing they have done evil is, says Justin, to act unjustly. To call Christians atheists because they refuse to worship pagan idols is to overlook the fact that Christians do worship the most true God, the God who is alien to all evil and is the Father of all virtue. Christians worship God the Father and the Son who came forth from Him and the Prophetic Spirit, and they pay homage to Him in reason and truth, and teach His doctrine to anyone who wishes to learn it.

If some Christians have been arrested and convicted of crimes, writes Justin, this is no reason for condemning other Christians. Whoever is convicted of a crime ought to be punished as a criminal, not as a Christian.

Christians do not wish to live by lying; they desire to make their abode with God, the Father and Creator of all, and they make haste to confess their faith in the belief that the righteous will be rewarded, and that the wicked will be assigned to eternal torment.

Christians do not worship idols made with human hands, Justin asserts; such practice is both stupid and disrespectful to God, who is of ineffable glory and form. God has no need of the material gifts of men, but is Himself the giver of all things. God approves only of those who imitate his inherent virtues; namely, justice, temperance, and the love of man.

To the accusation against the Christians that they owe allegiance to another kingdom and are thus guilty of treason and are unable to be good citizens, Justin Martyr replies that the Kingdom of which Christians speak is not of this world but is a Kingdom that is with God.

Christians, more than all other men, are good citizens and allies in fostering peace, since they believe that it is impossible for the wicked to hide from God, and that each man receives eternal punishment or salvation according to the merits of his actions.

As citizens Christians have been instructed by their Lord and Savior, Jesus Christ, to pay their taxes to the officials of the state. While the Christian worships God alone, in other things he joyfully obeys the powers that be and acknowledges the rulers of this world, praying that they may have sound judgment, lest by their wickedness they incur in the everlasting fire the penalty of their misdeeds.

Christianity is indeed superior to pagan religion; for what Christians believe, they learned from Christ and the Prophets who spoke the truth. Jesus Christ alone is properly the Son of God, since He alone is the first begotten of the Father, and having become man by His will, He taught Christians their doctrines for the conversion and restoration of mankind.

To hate Christians because of the name of Christ, writes Justin, and to execute them as criminals, although they have committed no crime, while others are left unmolested in spite of their bizarre and divergent beliefs and practices, is to be grossly unfair. Christians are accused of cannibalism, incest, and sexual orgies, whereas in fact such charges are false, while others who allow newly born children to be raised in prostitution or to perish remain unpunished.

To refute the charge that Christ was a worker of magic rather than of miracles, Justin points to the prophecies which predicted that events were to happen before they actually took place. The books of the Prophets foretold that Jesus Christ would come to us born of a virgin, that He would reach manhood, that He would heal the sick and raise the dead to life, that He would be hated and crucified, that He would rise from the dead and ascend into Heaven as the very Son of God. It was further predicted that the Gentiles rather than the Jews would believe in Him.

The fact that prophecies have been fulfilled does not mean that everything happens by fate and that man does not have the power of choice. Without the free faculty to shun evil and to choose good, a man is not responsible for his actions no matter what they may be. Men were created with the ability to choose good of their own accord, and thus they are responsible when they freely choose what is evil.

Christians do not hold that men who lived before the birth of Christ were unaccountable for their actions. As the first-begotten of God the Father, Christ is the Logos of whom all mankind partakes. Anyone who lived by reason (*logos*), such as Socrates and Heraclitus, even though he may have been considered an atheist, is a Christian. All those who have lived *reason-*

ably, in accordance with the Logos, are in fact Christians.

A reasonable man must be persuaded that since so much of what the Prophets have predicted has already come to pass, those things which were likewise foretold, but are yet to happen, shall with certainty happen. Two comings of Christ have been foretold by the Prophets; the first, which has already occurred, was that of a suffering servant; the second, which will take place, is when He shall come gloriously from Heaven with His angelic army. He shall then raise to life the bodies of all men, and He shall separate the righteous from the wicked, condemning the latter to sensible pain for all eternity and to eternal fire together with the evil demons.

The myths that have been fabricated by the pagan poets are taught to the young without any proof of their truth, says Justin. Such myths were first related through the instigation of evil demons and were designed to seduce and to deceive men. For when the demons heard the Prophets predict the coming of Christ, they produced tales, thinking that they would thereby arouse the suspicion that those things foretold of Christ were on a par with the fabulous tales of the poets. The demons were unable to convince men that there will be no Hell fire to punish sinners, nor could they keep Christ unknown after His appearance on earth. They were able, however, to cause Christians to be hated and to be executed by unreasonable men, who indulged their passions in evil ways. Christians do not hate their persecutors, but pity them and desire their conversion. The Christian has no fear of death, for death is but the beginning of eternal life, free from pain and want.

Christian practices have been slandered and distorted, Justin insists. The rulers of Rome should understand that a Christian who is regenerated through Christ consecrates himself to God. Those who believe pledge themselves to live righteously, and they are taught in prayer and fasting to ask God to forgive their past sins. The new convert is baptized with the washing of water, in the name of God, the Father and Lord of all, and of Jesus Christ, and of the Holy Ghost. Christians are baptized to obtain in the water the forgiveness of past sins, and to be regenerated. Christians do not indulge in sexual orgies or cannibalism; their worship is simple and pure. Newly baptized persons gather with other believers for prayer. They partake of bread and wine mixed with water, the Eucharist, of which only he can share who has accepted the truth of Christianity, who has been baptized for the remission of his sins and for his regeneration, and who lives according to the principles of Christ. The bread and wine which Christians eat and drink is regarded as the flesh and blood of Christ, who died for man's salvation.

Christians come together each Sunday to remind one another of the truths of their faith, to partake of the Eucharist, to read the writings of the Apostles and the Prophets, to pray, and to show their gratitude to God by collecting gifts to take care of all those in need, such as the orphans and widows.

The beliefs of the Christians ought to be respected if they are in accordance with reason and truth; they are to be despised if they are deemed erroneous; but in no case ought death to be inflicted on those who have done no wrong. Those who continue to be unjust shall not escape the future judgment of God. In the words of the Emperor Hadrian, justice demands: "If anyone accuses the Christians and proves that they broke the law, you must assign the punishment in accordance with the gravity of the crime. . . . If anyone shall accuse these persons [the Christians] merely to calumniate them, you arrest him for villainy and inflict penalties against his guilt."

The Second Apology consists of fifteen short chapters written in protest against the unjust execution of three Christians by Urbicus, the prefect of Rome, solely because they dared to confess that they were Christians.

Justin reports that Christians are sarcastically asked why they do not kill themselves and go immediately to God, thereby saving the state the trouble. Why do they confess to being Christians? The answer is simply that man is not the master of his own life. God created the world for the sake of mankind; God is pleased with those who follow His perfections and are displeased with evil. If Christians were to commit suicide, no one would be instructed in the divine doctrines, and they would be acting in opposition to the will of God. Christians confess their faith on being interrogated because they have done no wrong and they believe that it is wicked to lie.

The further question as to why God permits Christians to be persecuted when He has the power to help them is answerable in terms of man's free will and in terms of the hatred of demons who are permitted to persuade men to do evil.

Justin concludes by suggesting that a wise ruler will for his own sake judge the case of the Christian with justice, lest he condemn himself in the eyes of God by convicting the innocent.

THE DIDACHE
or
THE TEACHING OF THE TWELVE APOSTLES

Author: Unknown
Type of work: Code of Christian ethics (first part); manual of Church order (second part)
First transcribed: Probably the middle of the second century

Principal Ideas Advanced

The way of life is marked out by two commandments and their implications: (1) Love God and your neighbor, and refrain from doing to people what you do not want done to you; and (2) commit neither murder nor adultery.

The way of death is by violation of these two commandments.

There are definite rules by which churches should: (1) celebrate baptism, the Eucharist, weekly services of worship; (2) test the genuineness of visiting teachers, apostles, and prophets; and (3) elect bishops and deacons.

Every Christian should always stand ready for the Lord's coming "on the clouds of the sky."

It will help preclude misunderstanding to state at the outset, and in brief compass, what we do *not* know about the *Didache*. We know neither the author's name nor where he lived. We cannot be certain whether he borrowed "The Two Ways" from the *Epistle of Barnabas* (written about 100), or whether both depend upon an earlier Jewish-Christian catechism, itself derived from stoical philosophy, possibly the *Cebetis tabula*. Within tolerable limits we can fix the date of composition, as indicated above; but we do not know, at every point, whether the author is quoting an old document representing first century thought and practice, or whether he is speaking about Church morals and Church orders which were actually followed in his own day.

Other factors which are more certain enable us to read the *Didache* intelligently and help us to see in this document one of the most important pieces of early Christian literature. We may be quite sure that the longer title (*The Teaching of the Twelve Apostles*) is not to be taken literally. In their own time the original Apostles were active in forming and transmitting teaching materials. It is quite obvious, however, that in its present form the *Didache* comes from the second century. In the first instance it must, therefore, be read and interpreted against the background of what we know about life in the second century Church. Such an approach does not exclude one's finding first century customs preserved in the *Didache,* as we shall presently see.

With some degree of probability we may assume that the author employed not only a Christian catechism stating "The Two Ways," but also a late first century document stating regulations for ordering Church life. The latter source was very probably written in Syria—it contains quotations from Matthew's Gospel—and it may be that the *Didache* itself found its origin in that country, though a case may also be made for Alexandria.

The image of two ways is a very old device, employed by the ancient Hebrews for imparting moral instruction: "Thus says the Lord: Behold, I set before you the way of life and the way of death." (Jeremiah 21:8). Use of the same device extends well down into the Christian era, examples being found in Rabbinic literature (*Pirge Aboth* 2:1) and in the New Testament (Matthew 7:13-14; II Peter 2:15). Indeed, when the Christian Church was still a sect within Judaism, it was natural enough for it to be known as "The Way" (Acts 9:2, for example). Thus, the form itself of the *Didache* 1:1-6:2 is an index of its *Jewish*-Christian character. It is not completely fanciful to compare it with the Rabbinic tractate *Pirge Aboth* (*Sayings of the Fathers*), with the understanding that in the *Didache* one hears the voice not of many rabbis, but of only one: Jesus.

The author's method is, in part, to give two or three maxims, then to explicate these basic statements in specific exhortations. Love for God and neighbor, and the "golden rule" (in its negative form) mean in practical terms to pray for our enemies, to turn the other cheek, and to give to everyone who begs. It is important to see that the author works out his explication by quotations from Jesus' words in most instances, but without clear reference to the highly eschatological note which permeated Jesus' teaching. Thus the injunction, "If someone deprives you of your property, do not ask for it back . . . ," is followed by the practical comment: "You could not get it back anyway!" And the exhortation to make donations is qualified in a practical way by a saying of unknown origin: "Let your donation sweat in your hands until you know to whom to give it." Thus the author of "The Two Ways" has assembled words of moral exhortation from various sources—chiefly Jesus' sayings, but also Old Testament verses and even unknown sayings which are merely practical and may have been in general use. He obviously believes that these exhortations convey the true meaning inherent in the basic maxims of the Way of Life; they are also eminently practical suggestions.

The Way of Death is explicated in a similar manner, though in much shorter compass. Persons who follow this way are guilty of all kinds of immorality, they hate truth, they "have no pity for the poor, . . . and are thoroughly wicked." The author of the *Didache* shares with the unknown author of "The Two Ways" a keen interest in *practical* instruction. For he summarizes this first part of his writing with the eminently sensible statement: "If you can bear the Lord's full yoke, you will be perfect. But if you cannot, then do what you can."

In the second part of the *Didache* the reader is provided with advice about food, baptism, prayer, the Eucharist, the Apostles and prophets, the Lord's Day, the election of bishops and deacons, and true eschatology.

Baptism is to be preceded by the moral instruction contained in "The Two Ways." The candidate is to be baptized in running water, if such is available. If not, other arrangements may be made, including affusion.

The Christian is to pray the Lord's Prayer (the text given by the Didachist is similar to that of Matthew 6:9-13) three times each day.

In his directions for celebrating the Eucharist, the author allows the cup to precede the loaf. The Eucharistic prayers which he gives for recitation bear marks of an early age and may have originated in Judea. The one for the cup reads: "We thank you, our Father, for the holy vine of David, your child, which you have revealed through Jesus, your child. To you be glory forever." According to the author, the Eucharist is to be celebrated as a real supper.

Perhaps most interesting are the regulations pertaining to prophets. We know from the New Testament not only that there were prophets in the early Church, but also that they were known by the title "prophet" (I Corinthians 12:28). From what we find about prophets in the *Didache*, we may conclude that this itinerant office continued into the second century and that it soon became necessary to distinguish genuine from false prophets: "If he stays three days, he is a false prophet." "If he asks for money, he is a false prophet." ". . . not everybody making ecstatic utterances is a prophet, but only if he behaves like the Lord." ". . . if someone says in the Spirit, 'Give me money,' or something else, you must not heed him."

True prophets are, however, greatly

to be venerated, "for they are your high priests." Whereas others are to follow the set prayers in celebrating the Eucharist, "in the case of prophets, . . . you should let them give thanks in their own way." Genuine prophets and teachers have a right to be supported by the church members. They are to receive the members' first fruits. (This reflects a rural setting).

The ministry of bishops and deacons "is identical with that of the prophets and teachers." This affirmation points toward a period when the monarchical episcopate had not yet been established. Indeed, the author must adjure his readers to value bishop and deacon as highly as prophet and teacher.

The final chapter presents the Didachist's summation of eschatological teaching. New Testament quotations are again employed. "Be ready, for you do not know the hour when our Lord is coming." Thus the primitive Christian belief in the coming of the Lord is still alive, yet it is necessary for the faithful to persevere in the remaining time. At the end, "The Lord will come, and all his saints with him. Then the world will see the Lord coming on the clouds of the sky."

Thus, the *Didache* is an invaluable source for our understanding of Christian ethics and Church order in the late first and early second centuries. A modified kind of Jewish-Christian ethics evidently sufficed for the Didachist's church and others. It is true that in his final chapter the Didachist penned an eloquent plea for the maintenance of the Christian eschatological hope, but he did not feel compelled to relate that hope to the ethical teaching of the two ways which he propounded in the first six chapters. With regard to Church order, the *Didache* shows that it had become necessary formally to regulate celebration of the sacraments and to lay down definite rules governing the authority of Church officials.

ADDRESS OF TATIAN TO THE GREEKS

Author: Tatian (c.110-c.172)
Type of work: Christian apologetics
First transcribed: Second century

Principal Ideas Advanced

The wisdom of Christianity is the true philosophy in comparison with which the philosophy of the Greeks is mere idle quibbling, a collection of conflicting human opinions which lack both credibility and profoundity.

The pride of the Greeks in their inherent superiority is unfounded, for by wisdom they know not God, and they have given themselves to the worship of their own conceit; thus, they shall suffer for their ignorance when the Judge of all mankind holds them accountable for their wickedness.

Tatian belongs to the Christian apologists of the second century, although toward the end of his life he apparently accepted the Gnostic heresy and advocated the practice of extreme asceticism. Little of his life is known other than that he was an Assyrian who embraced Christianity in Rome, where he was instructed by Justin Martyr (c.100-c.165). In addition to his attack on the enormities of paganism, in his *Address to the Greeks*, Tatian is credited with an early *Harmony of the Four Gospels*, a very valuable testimony to the early recognition of the Gospels by the primitive churches.

The *Address to the Greeks* is Tatian's only extant work. It is a biting attack on the Greek claim to superiority, as well as a persuasive argument to show that the Gospel of Christ is the highest wisdom.

The Greeks, writes Tatian, are vainly proud in their superior attitude toward barbarians, when in fact they owe their own institutions to foreign invention. For astronomy, they are indebted to the Babylonians; for alphabetic writings, to the Phoenicians; for the writing of history, to the Egyptians. Furthermore, the Greek pursuit of philosophy has produced nothing noble; the Greeks gather in rather solemn assemblies of dogmatic philosophers, each of whom gives vent to the crude fancies of the moment. The Greeks hate the opinion of others, and they vie for fame, wise in their own conceited arrogance.

The Christian, on the other hand, obeys the ruler in civil matters; he honors his fellow men, but he fears only God, and he will obey no man who orders him to deny the living God. The Christian will never adore what God has made; he will never worship the sun or moon, nor speak of the stones as gods. God alone is to be worshiped, and He is a spirit, not pervading matter, but the maker of the forms that are in matter.

God, says Tatian, is the invisible creator of sensible and invisible things. God in the beginning was the necessary ground of all being; no creature was then in existence. The Logos came forth from Him as the first-begotten work of the Father, and the Logos then begat our world, after first creating matter, which, unlike God, had a beginning and was brought into existence by the framer of all things.

After the consummation of all things, there will be a resurrection of bodies, but not because of a cyclical return, as the Stoics affirm. The periods of mortal existence will be completed once for all, and judgment will be passed upon man by the creator God. The Christian is not troubled by the ridicule of the Greeks, for the Christian believes that after death he will live again. Although his body may be destroyed, he will be restored by the Sovereign God.

The heavenly Logos has made man an image of immortality; thus, since incorruption is with God, man too shares in the principle of immortality, with the freedom of choice to do good or evil. Man is not determined by fate, but is responsible for his deeds. Man is superior to fate, and he is free from the need to obey arbitrary deities or wandering demons.

To believe in the Greek deities is absurd, Tatian insists. Who can wisely believe in a God who becomes a tree, a dragon, a swan, or an eagle? Who can reverence gods who eagerly await presents, and who become angry when they do not receive any?

Man was not created to die, but he destroys himself by the wrong exercise of his freedom and thus he becomes the slave of sin. In itself the soul is mortal, but it is possible for it not to die. When the soul does not know the truth, it is dissolved with the body for a time, but it is to be resurrected with the body at the end of the world, and the soul will then receive punishment. If, however, the soul has acquired knowledge of God, it dies not, although it is dissolved for a time. When it enters into a union with the divine spirit, the soul ascends to heavenly regions. The Spirit of God abides with those who live justly, but not with those who follow demons and false appearances.

Man is not merely a rational animal; only croaking philosophers could believe such an absurdity. Man is made in the image and likeness of God. The human soul consists of many parts; it manifests itself through the body, and it never appears by itself without the body. Man ought to seek what he once had: unity of the soul with the Holy Spirit. By repentance and faith man has conquered death, and the Spirit of God dwells within him.

According to Tatian, the demons are inspired with frenzy against men and they pervert the minds of men so that men are unable to ascend the path to Heaven. Demons turn men from the pious acknowledgment of God, and the demons make use of the productions of nature for evil purposes; they deceive instead of heal. At the bottom of demon worship, Tatian insists, lies human depravity.

The world was excellently constructed, Tatian claims, but men have corrupted their world. Men should remember that death is not to be feared and that if anyone is healed of an illness, God alone is to be credited with the cure. Everything that hinders man in his attainment to perfection is to be put aside.

When the Christian announces that God was born in the form of a man, the Christian utters no myth. The Incarnation is in no way comparable to the mythical tales in which Athene assumes the form of Deiphobus in order to please Hector; nor is the Christian belief like those Greek stories in which a goddess becomes an old woman.

The philosophy of the Christians, says Tatian, is older than that of the Greeks. The Egyptians themselves bear witness to the claim that the Jews left Egypt under the leadership of Moses, who is more ancient than the heroes of Greece. Many of the philosophers altered what they learned from Moses, and whatever they could not understand they misrepresented as if it were a fable.

The Christian is interested solely in the truth, not in vain glory; nor does the Christian allow a variety of conflicting beliefs. Popularity and temporal fame, together with everything that rests upon human opinion, are renounced by the Christian. The Christian's sole interest is in obeying the commands of God and following the law of the Father of immortality, for what comes from God surpasses all earthly gifts. The Christian philosophy is not the possession of a few idle rich; it is taught to the poor without fee. Anyone can hear, the old and the young, male and female. Those who laugh at Christians now will weep hereafter, writes Tatian.

Those who would learn the Christian philosophy are readily admitted for instruction, no matter what their appearance or previous faith. All are invited to inspect the sober character of Christian institutions, and to discover the Christian freedom from all forms of lewdness and impropriety.

Tatian concludes his fervent apology by insisting that the Christian knows who God is, and he lives the life that is according to God, always prepared to submit his doctrines to examination, never fearful that they shall be found wanting in wisdom, but ever certain that his philosophy is the wisdom of God and the power of salvation.

THE APOLOGY OF ATHENAGORAS

Author: Athenagoras (fl. second century)
Type of work: Christian apologetics
First transcribed: c.177

Principal Ideas Advanced

Christians are not atheists because, although they do not worship gods, they worship the God who created the world.

While pagan thinkers have sometimes come by means of reason to believe in God, Christians have this faith through prophecy.

Christians regard God as Father, Son, and Holy Spirit; God is therefore powerful in unity and rich in diversity.

The world was created good, and the evil that is in it is due to the defection of some of the ministering spirits whom God placed in control over it.

Christians, far from being guilty of the immoral practices charged against them, obey higher ethical principles than do the pagans.

Athenagoras's *Presbeia peri Christianōn,* sometimes referred to by its Latin title, *Legatio pro Christianis,* is commonly known in English by the name *Apology,* in spite of the fact that this term does not appear in the Greek title. It is also known as the *Embassy for Christians,* and as *A Supplication for Christians.* But by whatever name, the work belongs to the same general class as the celebrated apologies of Justin Martyr (c.100-c.165) and Tertullian (c.160-c.220). Addressed to emperor Marcus Aurelius and his son Commodus, the *Apology* is a defense of Christians against the familiar charges of atheism, cannibalism, and incest.

In reply to the charge that Christians are atheists, Athenagoras explains that Christians do not worship gods of wood and stone, because they believe that God is entirely separate from matter, being "unbegotten and invisible, beheld only by mind and thought." Christians also believe that there is but one God, the maker of all things. But they ought not to be charged with atheism for this, because many of the poets and philosophers also believed in one god, and yet they were not atheists.

Athenagoras says that pagan thinkers came to believe by guesswork in one God, for they were inspired to seek the truth by the divine breath that is present in all men. The Christian belief has a surer foundation, resting on teachings of the prophets, who spoke not by their own understanding, but as God moved their lips. Athenagoras supposes that his readers will agree that it is entirely reasonable to put one's faith in prophecy. Nevertheless, he produces a logical demonstration designed to prove that there can be only one God if God is understood to be the maker and ruler of the universe.

In the course of his explanation Athenagoras gives one of the most complete accounts of the Christian doctrine of God to come down to us from these early times. Christians, he says, "hold God to be one, unbegotten, eternal, invisible, suffering nothing, comprehended by none, circumscribed by none, apprehended by mind and reasoning alone, girt about by light and beauty and spirit and power indescribable, creator of all things by His Word, their embellisher and master." He explains that, while Christians say that God has a Son, their teaching is not to be confused with that of pagan myth. Every notion that the Son had a beginning must be put away, for God is "eternal mind," and the Son of God is "the Word of the Father in thought and power." Father and Son are one God, he says, "the Son being in the Father and the Father in the Son by the wonderful union of the Spirit." He describes the Holy Spirit as "an outflow from God, flowing out and returning like a ray of the sun." Is it not astonishing, he asks, to hear Christians called atheists "who call God Father and Son and Holy Spirit, proclaiming their power in unity and in rank their diversity?"

Athenagoras argues that "goodness" is included in the nature of God, and he suggests that the material world, which owes its being to Him, is naturally good also. But he maintains that when God created the world, He also created "a multitude of angels and ministers" whom He set in charge of his handiwork. Angels are pure spirits, endowed with free choice, he argues; and while some angels were faithful to the task appointed to them, others became "heedless and wicked." The latter, says Athenagoras, are responsible for the irrational elements in the world. Furthermore, these evil spirits enslave the minds of men, who worship them under "the fancies of idol-madness."

As to the second and third charges, that Christians devour the flesh of children and engage in illicit unions, Athenagoras says that Christians do not consider themselves besmirched by the unproven calumnies which their enemies circulate. He points to "some kind of divine law and sequence," which seems to determine evil men to fight against the good, and he cites the persecution of Pythagoras, Heraclitus, Democritus, and Socrates. He expresses his conviction that the philosophical persons to whom his *Apology* is addressed will realize that because Christians desire above all things to live blamelessly in the sight of God, they will not fall short when measured by human laws. However, Athenagoras answers the charges against the Christians, and in doing so he preserves to posterity a clear account of Christian ethics in his day. Furthermore, his work provides a thoughtful consideration of the problem of evil.

Sexual morality among second century Christians was governed by the principle that even a lustful thought is evil. Recognizing that the "kiss of salutation" might be abused, the law of the Church warned specifically against "a second kiss for the motive of pleasure," since "if any one of us was even in the least stirred to passion in thought thereby, God would set him outside eternal life." Athenagoras points out that among the Christians virginity was recommended in both sexes, married persons indulged their passions only for the purpose of begetting children, and second marriages were forbidden.

A similar principle governed the Christian attitude toward taking human life. Christians, writes Athenagoras, will not even attend gladiatorial spectacles because they consider it "nigh unto murder itself" even to look at these shows. They do not even defend themselves when others strike them or plunder their goods. As for murdering children, they do not countenance the practice of exposing infants, and they consider abortion to be murder.

Athenagoras explains the Christians' adherence to this severe moral code on the grounds of their conviction that man is a spiritual being who must appear before God in judgment for the deeds done in the body. Christians do not consider it a great calamity when they suffer malice in this world, because they are assured that the divine Judge will repay them more than they have lost "in the shape of a gentle, humane, and equitable way of life on the other side." "We shall then abide with God as heavenly spirits," he says, "not as fleshly creatures, even if we have bodies, and by His aid shall be changeless and free from suffering in our souls."

The Christian belief in the resurrection of the body, mentioned briefly in the *Apology,* is the subject of a further discourse by Athenagoras, called *The Resurrection of the Dead.* For apologetic purposes, at least, Athenagoras did not find it necessary to appeal to the Resurrection of Christ as evidence for the Christian belief, but he based the belief upon God's purpose in creating man, His justice, and man's composite nature. In contrast to the dualistic tendency of the Greek mystery religions, the Christian religion, Athenagoras insists, contends that man was created "neither for the soul by itself nor for the body in isolation," but to achieve "one harmony and concord of the whole living being." Thus, if man is to endure beyond the grave in his integrity, the body must be resurrected and reunited with the soul. Athenagoras proves that man was made to live eternally, from the fact that man, of all God's creatures, has been endowed with rational judgment for the contemplation of eternal truth. Here, indeed, Athenagoras is more in agreement with Greek modes of thought. "One would not be far wrong," he writes, "in describing the end of a life of understanding and reasoning judgment as a perpetual and inseparable companionship with those realities for which the natural reason is principally and primarily adapted, in the unceasing and exultant contemplation of our Benefactor, and of all that He has decreed."

Almost nothing is known of Athenagoras personally. One source says that he was born in Athens; another, that he was the first head of the catechetical school in Alexandria, and that he had Clement of Alexandria (c.150-c.215) as one of his students. Scholars disagree as to the value of these notices. It is abundantly clear from his writings themselves that Athenagoras was well-schooled in Greek literature and philosophy, and disciplined in the art of dialectic. In the *Apology* he does not content himself with stating the Christian position, but he carries the argument onto pagan ground and shows the absurdity and immorality of those religious practices which Christians were censured for omitting. Athenagoras's repudiation of Greek polytheism does not, however, diminish his appreciation for Greek poetry and philosophy.

One is tempted to say that Athenagoras is more Greek than Christian, because there is no mention in either of his surviving works of such central Christian teachings as the Incarnation and the sacrificial death of Christ, and of man's sin and his need for redemption. It would be a mistake, however, to minimize the Christian content of his work. Some parts of the Christian teaching were more pertinent than other parts to the accusations against which the Christians had to defend themselves, and, at the same time, some Christian ideas were more intelligible than others to the Hellenistic mind. In the interests of his apologetic, Athenagoras advanced only the relevant parts of the Christian faith, and he kept back such ideas as might complicate his task of defending Christianity. "These thoughts," he writes, addressing Marcus Aurelius, "are but a few out of many, and trivial rather than lofty, but we do not wish to trouble you with more. Those who taste honey and whey can tell if the whole be good by tasting even a small portion."

THEOPHILUS TO AUTOLYCUS

Author: Theophilus of Antioch (d. 181 or 188)
Type of work: Apologetics
First transcribed: Latter half of second century

Principal Ideas Advanced

The inspired Scriptures provide mankind with the true account of the nature of God, the origin of the world, and mankind, for they have been given by the Holy Spirit of God, and are sufficient to persuade the intelligent pagan that his own gods are but absurd fantasies.

The highest wisdom is not to be found in the follies of the poets and the speculations of the philosophers but in the truth of God possessed by Christians.

Theophilus of Antioch was a second century apologist, a kindred spirit to Justin and Irenaeus, and the successor of Ignatius as bishop of Antioch, a position he occupied from 168 until his death in 181 or in 188. Theophilus was one of the first commentators on the Gospels, if not the first; he was probably the first Christian historian of the Old Testament, and was the founder of the science of Biblical chronology. Little is known of his personal history. From his writings it is apparent that he was born a pagan and was converted by studying the Scriptures.

The three books now entitled *Theophilus to Autolycus* are the only remaining works of Theophilus. They are characterized by a gentleness and a contempt for paganism and cover the same material treated by Justin Martyr and the other early apologists. Their purpose is to convince Autolycus, an intelligent pagan who scorned Christianity, that the Scriptures are superior in every way to pagan philosophy and poetry and ought therefore to be accepted and believed.

Theophilus does not consider it a reproach to be called a Christian, for a Christian is a lover of truth who would be serviceable to the true God, not to idols, which are the works of human hands, and which neither see nor hear.

The true God can be seen by the eyes of the soul and the ears of the heart, after first casting away all manner of sin and evil deeds. God's appearance is indescribable and ineffable; it cannot be seen by the eye of flesh, for His glory is incomprehensible, His power incomparable, and His goodness inimitable. For the true God is without beginning, unchangeable in nature, the ruler and creator of the universe; He is known by His works and can be beheld through them. From observing a ship sailing into a harbor, we infer that a pilot is steering it; likewise, we can perceive that God is the pilot, the governor of the universe. When the mortal is put off, and incorruption, immortality, put on, God will then be seen in all His glory.

Faith in God is necessary, Theophilus writes, if eternal happiness is to be obtained. After the resurrection it will be too late to repent. In all matters faith is the leading principle. The farmer must trust the earth; the traveler, the pilot of his ship; the patient, the physician. It is not difficult to believe that the God who has once brought mankind into existence will again bring man back from the dead.

God has exhibited much evidence that enables man to believe in the resurrection. Analogies can be found in the dying of the seasons, in planting and harvesting, in the cycles of the moon, and in recovery from sickness.

The Scriptures are able to produce trust in their own veracity, for they contain accounts written by holy Prophets who by the Spirit of God foretold events that were to happen before they occurred, predictions that have been and continue to be fulfilled. Those that put their trust in the truth of God will receive everlasting life, peace, joy, rest, good things in abundance, and such happiness as neither eye hath seen, nor ear heard. For unbelievers and despisers, who are obedient to unrighteousness rather than truth, there is in store wrath, anger, anguish, tribulation, and everlasting fire.

Deities of the pagans, such as Saturn, Jupiter, Bacchus, and Venus, are simply representations of human sinners. Their deeds of incest, adultery, lust, drunkenness, and wanton revelry are unworthy of imitation and lead to the absurdity of idolatry.

The pagan practice of worshiping the king is also foolishness, for the king is not a god. The Christian is, however, a loyal citizen who honors his king, not by worshiping him but by praying for him, by giving him the honor that is his due. The king is subservient to the true and living God, and is a man appointed by God, not to be worshiped but to rule justly. To honor and to obey a just king, to pray for him, and to be subject to him is to do the will of God, who has established the governments of the earth.

It is the height of folly and absurdity to worship men as gods, and to worship statuaries and carvings, which when made are of no value, but which on being purchased become objects of worship. When one reads of the birth of the gods, they are reminded of men, and only afterwards of gods. It is certainly strange that the gods who once lived on Mount Olympus can no longer be found anywhere now that the mountain lies deserted.

The philosophers and poets of the pagans are in disagreement with themselves, Theophilus writes. The Epicureans deny the existence of God, and hold that the world is uncreated and nature is eternal, while still others regard matter as being coeval with God, who formed the world out of the material at hand as an artist plies his craft. Others describe the origin of the world and the gods in speculative terms.

The truth is to be found in the writings of the Prophets, men of God, who were moved by the spirit of God and hence were God-taught; since they were made wise by God Himself, whatever they wrote is the wisdom of God. With one accord the Prophets teach that all things were made by the Word of God out of nothing, for nothing was coeval with God. The world was created that man might dwell therein in obedience to God's commandments. Instead of living happily in paradise, man yielded to temptation by freely disobeying his creator, thereby incurring God's wrath and curse, which can be removed solely by a new obedience to the will and commandments of God.

Secular history gives no account of the matters disclosed in the Scriptures because the poets and historians were born much later and did not possess the Spirit of God. They had no means of knowing the truth, which is possessed by Christians alone, not because the Christians are of any inherent virtue, but because they have been taught by the Holy Spirit, who spoke through holy men of old.

The Christian learns from God Himself that all things are arranged by His providence, that He is a holy lawgiver who would have each man act righteously and be pious, refraining from all wickedness and uncleanliness, doing good to every man, and loving all, even his enemies.

The Christians are innocent of the many false charges brought against them, insists Theophilus. They lead a quiet and peaceful life, submissive to the powers that be in secular matters, rendering honor to whom honor is due. It is unthinkable that they should eat human flesh; they are forbidden even to be spectators at gladiatorial spectacles. It is inconceivable that they participate in sexual orgies, "for with them temperance dwells, self restraint is practiced, monogamy is observed, chastity is guarded, iniquity exterminated, sin extirpated, righteousness exercised, law administered, worship performed, God acknowledged: truth governs, grace guards, peace screens them; the holy word guides, wisdom teaches, life directs, God reigns."

Theophilus concludes by writing

that reason and wisdom demand that Christians who are zealous in the pursuit of truth and who practice a holy life should not be subjected to savage tortures and persecutions by those who in their folly have themselves lost the wisdom of God and have failed to find the truth.

AGAINST HERESIES

Author: Saint Irenaeus (c.130-c.200)
Type of work: Systematic theology
First transcribed: c.182-188

Principal Ideas Advanced

The teachings of the Gnostic heretics are refuted by reason, by the Scriptures, and by the teaching of the Church.

God created the world out of nothing, by His Word and Spirit, and made man a free agent.

When, by disobeying his Maker, man lost the gift of divine fellowship, the Son of God became man in order to restore that which was lost.

Men become partakers of immortality through Christ's gift of the Holy Spirit; and, in the last day, their bodies shall be raised up to participate, with nature itself, in incorruptible glory.

Irenaeus's most important work, commonly known by the short title, *Against Heresies,* was called by its author *The Detection and Overthrow of False Gnosis.* Polemic rather than didactic in its design, the work first gives a detailed exposition of the various Gnostic systems, then patiently marshals logic, the Scriptures, and Church doctrine in an assault against particular Gnostic claims. *Against Heresies* is an indispensable historical source for the student of Gnosticism, but to most readers Irenaeus's book is chiefly interesting for its mature and competent statement of Christian doctrine.

That Irenaeus develops his positive theology in opposition to the rival teachings of the Gnostics instead of treating it topically is no great disadvantage. Irenaeus was in possession of a fully articulated system of doctrine; and the reader has no trouble in recovering his doctrines of the Godhead, Creation, Man, the Incarnation, Salvation, and Last Things. In fact, because Irenaeus's theology is confessional rather than speculative, its worth is more apparent in a controversial setting than it would be if stated in a more schematic form.

As the term "Gnostic" indicates, the early heretical groups were chiefly distinguished by their claims to be possessors of superior knowledge. They maintained that in the nature of things there are three kinds of men: carnal men, animal or psychic men, and spiritual men. The Gnostics, of course, claimed to be of the spiritual variety, and they boasted that they had a special knowledge which had been handed down orally from Christ by those who were able to receive it. The public teaching of Christ, together with His death and resurrection, was, they said, for the benefit of animal men, who, lacking the element of spirit, must always be subject to authority. The Gnostics denied that Christ was truly man; the divine Christ, they said, merely simulated manhood in order to lead men godward. The Gnostics used Scripture when it suited their purposes, but their doctrines were mostly fanciful constructions modeled on Greek theogonic myths. They had elaborate explanations concerning the emanation from an unnamable primal Being of a celestial hierarchy consisting of Aeons, Principalities, and Powers; and they traced the origin of the physical world to an indiscretion on the part of one of the Aeons, by the name of Sophia. The whole scheme of redemption was, in their view, an attempt to compensate for this indiscretion, and, by saving a spiritual heritage out of the world, make it possible for Sophia to achieve reunion with the Highest.

In *Against Heresies,* Irenaeus employs three kinds of arguments to overthrow the Gnostic teachings. First, he appeals to reason, and to the *consensus gentium.* A simple exercise in dialectic enables him to show that if there is any reason to believe that there must be a Being above the highest Aeon, the same reason requires us to believe in a still higher Being, and so on *ad infinitum.* The plain fact is, says Irenaeus, all nations of the world, whether by tradition handed down from their first progenitors, or by reasoning from the evidences in nature, are convinced that there is one God, and that He is the Creator of the world.

But Irenaeus rests his arguments mostly on the teachings of Scripture, devoting the greater part of his work to exposition of the key passages from the Old Testament, the Gospels, and the Epistles. In opposition to the arbitrary use which the Gnostics made of the Bible, he laid down the principle that each passage must be interpreted in harmony with all the remainder of Scripture, and he urged at the same time that men bring a "sound mind" to the study of these writings, and that they interpret the obscure parts in the light of those which are clear and unambiguous, rather than follow the contrary practice.

In the third place, Irenaeus put great store by the authority of the Church as the interpreter of Scripture and as the depository of the teachings of Christ. As offering a contrast to the endless diversity that was to be found among the Gnostic doctrines, Irenaeus could point to the uniform confession of the Church. He refutes the Gnostics' claim to possess a secret oral tradition by pointing out that the bishops of the Church in every city are direct successors of the Apostles. He cites his own case as an example: in his youth, he had been a hearer of Polycarp (c.69-c.155), Bishop of Smyrna, who in turn had been taught by the Apostle John and by other of the Lord's disciples. Irenaeus further argues, against those Gnostics who were disposed to pick and choose among the Scriptures, that all the four Gospels were of Apostolic origin; and he reasons that Paul could not have delivered a separate gospel, as some of them claimed, otherwise Luke, who traveled with him, would have dropped some hints of it in The Acts of the Apostles.

It is evident, says Irenaeus, that the Gnostics are late-comers, by comparison with the Church's bishops, and that they can only be understood as deviating from the right way. What that "right way" is, the confession of the Church makes clear. Irenaeus cites, on several occasions, a confessional formulary which, he says, was used by churches in all parts of the world. Obviously, it is an early form of what we know as the Apostles' Creed. "The path," he says, "of those belonging to the Church circumscribes the whole world, as possessing the sure tradition from the apostles, and gives unto us to see that the faith of all is one and the same, since all receive one and the same God the Father, and believe in the same dispensation regarding the incarnation of the Son of God, and are cognizant of the same gift of the Spirit, and are conversant with the same commandments, and preserve the same form of ecclesiastical constitution, and expect the same advent of the Lord, and await the same salvation of the complete man, that is, of the soul and body."

Drawing upon Scriptures for proof, Irenaeus seeks to show that there is but one God, the Father of all, and that, far from there being an interminable succession of divine personages emanating from the One, there was with God before the creation of the world only "the Word and Wisdom, the Son and the Spirit." It is characteristic of Irenaeus not to enter upon any investigation of the internal relations of these three, nor to inquire what was happening before God created the world. God, he says, has revealed to us all that is profitable for us to know; notably, that He had need of nothing outside of Himself when He brought the world into existence, but that He devised it in his own Mind and created it by his own Power. "For God did not stand in need of these [intervening Aeons], in order to the accomplishing of what He had Himself determined with Himself beforehand should be done, as if He did not possess His own hands. For with him were always present the Word and Wisdom, the Son and the Spirit, by whom, and in whom, freely and spontaneously, He made all things."

In discussing the creation of man, Irenaeus recounts that God the Father consulted with the Son and with the Spirit, saying, "Let us make man in our image and in our likeness." In opposition to the Gnostic contention that some men are naturally carnal, some animal, and some spiritual, Irenaeus maintains that the essential characteristic of all men is that, being made in God's image, they are free to determine what they will make of themselves. Irenaeus introduces the distinction between "image" and "likeness," which has become official Roman doctrine. God's image, according to this view, is the free and rational constitution which is inalienable from man; God's likeness is the gift of incorruptibility which man lost as a result of disobedience.

Irenaeus holds that the plan for man's salvation is clearly taught both in the Old and the New Testament. In discussing the question why man was not made perfect and thereby prevented from falling into sin, he cites, by way of illustration, the story of Jonah. Just as Jonah learned through trial the justice and the goodness of God, so man, having been permitted to follow his own devices to the brink of destruction, is taught by his undeserved deliverance to love God with all his heart and to seek his good in God alone.

Man fell into sin by following Satan. In this way, he lost his "likeness" to God and became liable to judgment. But, says Irenaeus, God sent His Son into the world in order that those who follow Him may recover their lost inheritance and be reunited with God in their resurrected bodies. Irenaeus is careful to oppose the Gnostic view that Christ did not become truly man. While holding firmly to the teaching that Christ is "truly God," present everywhere in His creation, Irenaeus insists that He was "united to and mingled with His own creation, . . . and thus took up man into Himself, the invisible becoming visible, the incomprehensible being made comprehensible, the impassible becoming capable of suffering, and the Word being made man, thus summing up all things in Himself."

Irenaeus accepts the teaching of Scripture and of the Church that Christ was born of a virgin, that He suffered, rose from the dead, and ascended bodily to Heaven. A characteristic feature of his theology is the doctrine that Christ, as the new Adam, "sums up" or "recapitulates" in Himself all that man is and can become. By his victory over temptation, Christ accomplishes the obedience which Adam failed to perform; by His suffering and death, He redeems those who have been led into captivity by Satan; by the gift of His Spirit, He restores to men their likeness to God.

Irenaeus stresses the continuity between the Old and the New Covenants, insisting that believers under the former are just as much members of Christ's body, the Church, as those under the latter. He further teaches that Christ did not repudiate the Ten Commandments, which, he says, merely reaffirm those natural precepts which God, from the first, implanted in mankind. In opposition to Gnostic antinomianism, he maintains that no one can be saved who does not obey the commandments.

Those who accept salvation in Christ, says Irenaeus, all become spiritual men; but they are such not by nature but by Christ's gift of the Spirit to them. By the Spirit dwelling in them, believers are joined to Christ and to each other in the Church. The Spirit also makes them partakers of eternal life, by restoring the bond between man and God which our first parents lost by their disobedience. While emphasizing man's spiritual inheritance, however, Irenaeus is careful not to lose sight of man's physical constitution. The mystery by which bread and wine are, by the Word of God, made the body and blood of Christ is, he says, a pledge that our bodies, nourished by Christ, shall, by God's Word, rise at the appointed time, and receive the gift of immortality. Nor, according to Irenaeus, shall man be alone in his glorification. A diligent student of Daniel and the Apocalypse, Irenaeus argues that, after the overthrow of Antichrist, the earth itself shall be renewed in the likeness of paradise, and believers of all generations shall be raised up, to live forever with Christ. Irenaeus is no universalist. Christ's coming, which will be for the resurrection of believers, also will be for the damnation of those who have not agreed to follow Him. For, says Irenaeus, God has given men free choice in these matters; and knowing that some will despise his dispensation, God has prepared a place for them, although, as far as Irenaeus cares to indicate, their punishment is simply the loss of those goods from which they have voluntarily excluded themselves.

With Irenaeus, Western Christendom found its characteristic theological stance. Distrustful of speculation, he purchased certitude by limiting the scope of man's investigation into divine things. He did not repudiate reason, maintaining that God's plan for man's salvation is completely rational. He insisted, however, that love, rather than knowledge, is necessary to lead men's souls to their perfection. It was, in his view, no little thing that Gnosticism had no martyrs, whereas the Church numbered its martyrs by thousands.

THE APOLOGY OF TERTULLIAN

Author: Tertullian (Quintus Septimius Florens Tertullianus) (c.160-c.220)
Type of work: Apologetics
First transcribed: c.197

Principal Ideas Advanced

Roman justice is outraged when Christians are persecuted; if Christians are enemies of the state, it is wrong to encourage them to deny their affiliation; if there is some doubt whether they are enemies of the state, their alleged crimes should be inquired into.

The charge that Christians deny the Roman gods is true; but Romans ought to refute the denial rather than persecute those who make it.

The charges that Christian worship is immoral and that the Christians are disloyal citizens is false; Christians are the best supporters of imperial government, but they are enemies of pagan civilization.

Born in North Africa, the son of a Roman centurion, Tertullian was educated at Rome in rhetoric and philosophy, and he probably practiced law there. After being converted to Christianity in 195 or 196, he was ordained a presbyter, and he served the Church in Carthage. He is considered the father of Latin Christianity, not merely because he is the first theologian to employ the Latin tongue, but also because of his influence on Cyprian, Augustine, and Jerome. The *Apology* is the best known of his numerous writings because it gives the most comprehensive statement of the Christian position, and because it is free from certain extravagances found in his other writings; the work reflects both Tertullian's mastery of his subject and his legal competence.

The *Apology* was written against the background of the imperial persecution of the Church, and it was intended to instruct the Romans concerning the true nature of the Christian faith. With the logic of a trained pleader and with a minimum of passion, Tertullian criticizes imperial edicts and the manner in which they have been implemented by the courts; in effect, he pleads for freedom of religion. He mentions the famous correspondence (c.112) between Pliny the Younger (62-113) and the emperor Trajan (c.53-117), in which the latter replied that, although Christians were not to be sought out, they should be punished if any informed on them. "O miserable deliverance,—under the necessities of the case, a self-contradiction!" Tertullian cries; "It forbids them to be sought after as innocent, and it commands them to be punished as guilty." In the same connection, he points to the use made of torture. Ordinary offenders, he says, are tortured to make them confess their crimes; but Christians are tortured to make them deny their beliefs. The whole judicial procedure thus becomes a farce. Instead of pressing the inquiry, to be certain that only the guilty are punished, judges offer the defendants every opportunity to escape what the law demands—provided they recant. At the same time, the defendant is denied the securities which Roman law guarantees a common criminal; for, if a man is charged with murder or incest, the court insists on evidence that a specific crime has been committed; but if a man is charged with being a Christian, all sorts of rumors and prejudices (for example, that in the Lord's Supper a child is sacrificed and his flesh and blood eaten, and that in the Love Feast incest is committed) are assumed to be true, but never proved.

Tertullian's argument has a positive and a negative side. On the one hand, the author gives a careful, detailed exposition of the beliefs and practices of the Church of his day; on the other hand, as a former pagan, well-placed for observing Roman society, he gives a telling exposé of the immorality and irreligion of those who put the Christians to death.

Christians are charged with not believing in the gods of the Romans. This is true, says Tertullian, but it is no scandal. There are tribes throughout the Empire which do not believe in the Roman gods, yet they have permission to practice their religion. Moreover, philosophers, such as Socrates, are held in honor, in spite of the fact that they deny the gods. In any case, when matters of this sort are in dispute, arguments ought to be heard; if their beliefs are false, they should be refuted; if simply ridiculous, they should be laughed to scorn. Nothing is accomplished by killing those who hold unconventional beliefs. As a matter of fact, Tertullian reminds his readers, it often happens that persons who scorned the Christian teaching when they were ignorant of it were converted to Christianity once they learned what it is.

According to Tertullian, Christians worship "the One God" who by His word and power has created and sustains the world. Although He is not visible, every man has some notion of Him because He is manifest both in the works of nature and in the native testimony of the soul itself. In evidence of the latter, Tertullian cites such pagan expressions as "God is great and good," "May God give!", and "I commend myself to God." But, says Tertullian, for our better knowledge of Him, God has also given us a written revelation of Himself. Tertullian stresses the antiquity of this revelation, which was given to the Hebrews. It antedates Homer, the tragic poets, and the philosophers, who, in Tertullian's opinion, probably drew upon it. Then, in the reign of Tiberius, God bestowed His grace in ampler measure, when "He appeared among us, whose coming to renovate and illuminate man's nature was pre-announced by God—I mean Christ, that Son of God." The prophecies had said that Christ would come twice, once to suffer, and once to reign. The Jews, among whom he made His appearance, did not adequately distinguish these two comings; therefore, they rejected Him, delivered Him to death, and tried to conceal the truth when He arose from the grave. Tertullian is convinced that these were matters of public knowledge. He alleges that Pilate became a Christian and reported everything to Tiberius, who actually presented the claim of Christ's divinity to the Roman senate, which, however, refused to consider the claim on the grounds that the senate must originate business of this sort.

As to the pagan divinities, Tertullian holds the view, known anciently as euhemerism, that the gods are men who, after their death, were made objects of worship. There are, then, in actuality, no gods other than God. But, according to Tertullian, there are devils, which take advantage of men's idolatrous propensities and appear to them as gods in order to enslave their souls to darkness.

Another charge which had to be met was that Christians gathered secretly for immoral and criminal purposes. Tertullian shows great patience in dealing with this report, which he regards as absurd. He points out the well-known characteristics of rumor, and shows that, if one's knowledge of religious practices is limited to paganism, it is easy for him to imagine all sorts of sordid things about the new religion, because human sacrifice and temple prostitution have played a prominent part in many ancient cults. He also notes that for the Romans of his day feasting was connected with all sorts of unbridled acts; so that when the Romans heard of a Christian "love feast," their imaginations fed upon their own excesses. Still, he maintains, it is difficult to reconstruct these orgies in the manner in which they are supposed to take place. Try to conceive of the Christians, who will not even permit the practice of abortion, plunging the knife into an infant's breast! Or, try to imagine the confusion of the banquet scene in which, after the lights have been extinguished, each one present is under obligation to commit incest. Each one would have to take careful note while the lights were on where his relations were sitting! And pity the person who has no mother or sister, because he cannot be a true follower of Christ!

The simplicity of Christian worship must be difficult for those to grasp who are accustomed to the florid festivals of Gaia or of Bacchus, writes Tertullian. The service of Christ consists in reading the Scriptures, in prayer, in exhortation and censure. Once a month, Christians gather donations for the poor and the unfortunate. They call one another "brethren," not in the hypocritical manner of those who curry favor of one another, but because of their common mother, Nature. Thus, Christians think of pagans as their brothers and sisters; but they feel special kinship toward those who have been led to the common knowledge of God. They have all things in common, says Tertullian, except their wives, which is the opposite of what is the case among their neighbors. Their modest supper, called *agape,* that is, "affection," stands in sharp contrast to the Roman feast. The measure of their eating and drinking is evidenced by the fact that after the meal, each participant is asked to sing a hymn to God, either one from Scripture or one of his own composition. As the ritual commences, so it closes, with prayer. If the noninitiate needs a model to help him imagine it, let him think of a Roman lawcourt instead of a Roman banquet.

More serious, perhaps, was the charge that Christians were disloyal to Caesar, inasmuch as they refused to offer sacrifice to him as to a god. (Here, Tertullian's argument against sacrifice becomes an attack on the ideological basis of the Roman Empire.) Tertullian insists on the distinction made in the Gospels between that which is Caesar's and that which is God's. Christians are even willing to call Caesar "lord," so long as it is understood that this is not a title of divinity. They also pray for Caesar and for the preservation of Roman rule. This they are instructed to do, as part of their duty to God, from whom rulers receive their authority. Moreover, because of the prophecy that when the Empire is overthrown the Antichrist will come, Christians have special interest in strengthening the existing order.

The same kind of reply is brought to the charge that, in causing the sacrifices to be neglected, Christians are responsible for various natural calamities. The charge had better be turned against the heathen themselves, says Tertullian, considering the hypocritical and perfunctory manner in which they perform their religious rites. If the well-being of the Empire depended on the gods, as is maintained, then the pagans should take it that disasters are a warning to themselves. But since, in reality, it depends upon the one God, whom Christians serve, such prosperity as Rome continues to enjoy must be the result of the prayers of Christians. In any case, says Tertullian, there were natural catastrophies before there were Christians.

Writing at a time when it was not even dreamed that Christianity might become the imperial religion, Tertullian saw no possibility of compromise between Christianity and secular culture. The civil disabilities imposed by the government upon Christians were, in his opinion, the manifestation of "a certain system" which is opposed to God and His truth, and he was determined to fight this injustice. The existence of organized opposition to Christianity did not surprise Tertullian or particularly disturb him; but in his apology he challenges the assumption that government must serve this pagan outlook. Tracing the mischief to the Greek and Roman practice of deifying civic values, he argues for the complete secularization of the political order, and for complete religious toleration. He insists that by paying taxes and obeying the laws, as well as by their prayers, Christians do fulfill their obligations as citizens. Tertullian can boast that no Christian is ever hailed before the court for any crime except that of bearing the name "Christian," and he maintains that because the Christians obey a higher law than Caesar's, they contribute more than any other group to the welfare and stability of the empire. There is, therefore, no political argument for requiring Christians to worship Caesar, or for persecuting them to death.

But if there is nothing in his obedience to God that prevents the Christian from fulfilling the duties of a citizen, there is much, according to Tertullian, which prevents him from making peace with the civilization which the Caesars represent. In spite of what Tertullian calls man's "naturally Christian soul," which continues to witness to the existence and perfection of the one God while he offers his sacrifice to idols, mankind has fallen under the power of demons, and it has systematically ordered its existence in enmity against God. Here Tertullian anticipates the theme of Augustine's *City of God,* even outdoing his illustrious successor in the rigor with which he sets the community of God over against the community of this world. What, he asks, has Jerusalem in common with Athens? What concord is there between the Christian and the philosopher? All the world's wisdom is folly in God's sight; its righteousness, shame; its boasting, vanity. The Christian is falsely accused of undermining the government, but he is rightly understood to have stripped himself of all the ambition and pride of the world, and to have turned his face away from the amusements and delights in which the pagans rejoice. That is why Christians are willing, if necessary, to go to death rather than compromise.

Asked why, then, he complains because they are persecuted, Tertullian replies that the Christian attitude is that of a soldier who, without courting death, is prepared to meet it without flinching, or of the hero who endures torture without betraying his cause. If such sacrifice is glorious when endured for the cause of city or empire, how much more so when it is for the cause of God!

THE STROMATA or MISCELLANIES

Author: Saint Clement of Alexandria (Titus Flavius Clemens) (c.150-c.215)
Type of work: Spiritual instruction
First transcribed: c.200

Principal Ideas Advanced

Faith in the Gospel is necessary and sufficient for salvation, but knowledge is also necessary for Christian perfection; Christianity is the true Gnosticism.

The Divine Logos is the author of the Jewish Law and of Greek philosophy, both of which were given to prepare men for the teaching of Christ.

Christ is the Logos manifest in the flesh to bring men into union with God; through faith, Christ leads men to knowledge, and to the unitive love in which they find perfection.

The title *Stromata,* given by Clement to his main work, is sometimes translated "Miscellanies." Literally, it means "Carpets," and in late Hellenistic times the term was a characteristic designation for a composition which sacrifices system for wealth and variety of contents. Clement stated that his purpose in writing *The Stromata* was to preserve the doctrinal tradition which he had been privileged to hear from his teachers. There was, in Clement's opinion, something dubious about committing to writing for the many what had hitherto been communicated only orally to selected hearers. An author, because he has no control over the reading of his book, may well be casting pearls before swine. To avoid this result, Clement adopted the stratagem of hiding the spiritual seed in a vast amount of erudition, confident that such a procedure would effectively conceal the secret tradition from unworthy readers while taking away nothing of value from those who were able to receive it.

Clement had traveled widely and studied under several teachers before coming at last to one whose teaching impressed him as being truly divine. This was Pantaenus (died c.190), who was at that time head of the Christian catechetical school in Alexandria. Clement became Pantaenus's associate, and he later succeeded Pantaenus as head of the school.

In this center of Hellenistic culture, the Christian teacher was compelled to take some sort of stand with respect to pagan learning. The average Christian in Alexandria was inclined to hold that no reconciliation was possible between the Gospel and Greek philosophy. But Alexandria was also a hotbed of that synthesis of Christian teaching and Greek speculation known as Gnosticism. As between these two positions, Clement stood firmly on the side of Catholic teaching. He maintained that faith in the teaching of the Scriptures is both necessary and sufficient for man's salvation. But, in opposition to the popular attitude, he taught that Greek philosophy has its legitimate uses, both as preparing men's minds to receive the Gospel and as edifying their minds after they have believed. Clement's own learning is impressive, prompting one modern historian to speak of him as "the pioneer of Christian scholarship," and the seven books of *The Stromata,* in addition to their importance in Christian thought, are a treasure-trove for antiquarians interested in reconstructing pagan civilization.

Clement justifies his use of pagan learning on the ground that every good thing comes from God, including craftsmanship and knowledge. The Christian has no more reason to turn away from poetry, geometry, rhetoric, and dialectic than from agriculture, or architecture, or medicine. They are all diverse expressions of the same Wisdom, which, in another context, is the object of faith. On the level of sense experience, Wisdom is called "right opinion"; on that of manual dexterity, it is called "art" (*techne*); when concerned with first causes, it is called "reason" (*noesis*); and when based on proof, it is called "knowledge" or "science" (*gnosis*). The same Wisdom, however, "when it is occupied in what pertains to piety, and receives without speculation the primal Word," is called "faith."

In Clement's opinion, there is no basis for setting knowledge in opposition to faith. Faith is a "voluntary preconception," that disposition of the mind to receive and assent to truth, without which knowledge of any sort is impossible. This is the teaching of Isaiah,

"Unless ye believe, neither will ye understand." Heraclitus was merely paraphrasing the Hebrew prophet when he wrote, "If a man hope not, he will not find that which is not hoped for, seeing it is inscrutable and inaccessible." Faith is assent and an act of the will; for, says Clement, "the intellectual powers are ministers of the will."

Clement's discussion of faith and knowledge must be considered in relation to the gnostic controversies of that day. Alexandrian Gnostics claimed that faith is for the simple, and that Christians who advance to higher stages of spirituality possess knowledge "which is as far removed from faith as the spiritual is from the animal." Clement, for his part, not only asserts that there is no knowledge which does not rest on faith; he also goes on to say that those who believe in the revelation of God through Christ are the true Gnostics. On the other hand, Clement gives small comfort to those who, having confessed their faith in the Gospel, think they can neglect their spiritual growth. Viewed in this light, faith is the foundation (spoken of by the Apostle) upon which some build with wood, hay, and stubble, while others build with gold, silver, and precious stones. Or, again, it is that milk which suffices for babies, but is not adequate food for mature men and women. As the true Gnosis, Christianity demands mental as well as moral discipline. Speaking and acting, says Clement, are rational work, and can be done well only by one who is trained in intellectual matters.

Clement accepts the widely popular Platonic and Pythagorean world-view, according to which God the Father, the Unbegotten Being, transcends the possibility of knowledge; but the Son of God, who is Wisdom, Knowledge, and Truth, manifests the Father, and is therefore the proper object for gnosis. The Son, as the author of creation, is the first principle both of action and of thought, of morals and of philosophy: "Whence also He alone is Teacher, who is the only Son of the Most High Father, the Instructor of men." Because of His love for men, the Son clothed himself with human nature in order to communicate His Wisdom to the Apostles and, through them and their successors, to all who have the will to achieve perfection. But He is also the Lord of Providence, who inspired Moses and the Prophets of Israel, and revealed the truth to those Greeks "who have philosophized accurately."

Himself a convert from paganism, Clement made the conversion of the Greeks his special concern. His earliest work, entitled *The Exhortation to the Heathen* (*ho protreptikos*), employed the art of rhetoric in the effort to persuade pagans to forsake their former religion and embrace the benefits conferred through Christ. His second work, *The Instructor* (*paedagogus*), has the practical aim of counseling converts in fundamental Christian morality. Both works were thought of as preparatory, in the sense that they were intended to bring men to the position where they could profit from the Teacher, who would "guide the soul to all requisite knowledge." Some scholars think that Clement intended to write a third book with the title, "The Teacher," forming a trilogy. Others hold that *The Stromata* fills the place indicated in this outline. What is illuminating, in either case, is Clement's underlying conception of Christianity as the authentic regimen by which the Divine Logos labors to bring men to perfection: "Eagerly desiring to perfect us by a gradation conducive to salvation, suited for efficacious discipline, a beautiful arrangement is observed by the all-benignant Word, who first exhorts, then trains, and finally teaches."

Clement insists that God's revelation to Abraham, to Moses, and to the prophets of the Old Testament was an important stage in Christ's endeavor for man's salvation. In opposition to the followers of Marcion (died about 160), who held that the Jehovah of the Jews was an inferior deity and that the Law of Moses is evil because it appeals to fear and not to love, Clement argues that insofar as fear turns men away from evil and sets them on the path of Wisdom, it is good. "Such a fear," says Clement, "leads to repentance and hope." But it is a distortion to hold that the teachings of the Old Testament are servile and degrading. On the contrary, says Clement, they are superior to the vaunted teachings of the Greeks who, Clement holds, borrowed their best sayings from the Hebrews. Moses, according to Clement, was the greatest of moralists, legislators, and philosophers; he could have received his pre-eminent wisdom only through "the first expounder of the divine commands, who unveiled the bosom of the Father, the only-begotten Son."

But just as the religion of the Old Testament was a means used by the Son of God to prepare the Jews for accepting the Gospel, so, according to Clement, philosophy was ordained to bring the Greeks to Christ. Clement is professedly an eclectic where philosophy is concerned, using the term to stand for no particular sect but for "whatever has been well said by each of those sects, which teach righteousness along with a science pervaded by piety." Hellenistic philosophy had many religious overtones, and the wisdom which it professed to love could fairly be described as "rectitude of soul and purity of life." For Clement, this was nothing else but "the knowledge of the Son of God" which the Apostles proclaimed in its fullness; and he could say to them what Paul said to the worshipers of the Unknown God, "Whom ye ignorantly worship, him declare I unto you." Clement does not admit that philosophy is itself sufficient for man's salvation but that, like the Law, it "shut up unbelief to the Advent." Those devotees of philosophy who died before Christ's coming had their chance to believe when Christ preached in Limbo, but those who live in the dispensation of the Gospel must turn from philosophy and believe the teaching of the Apostles.

Clement's teaching concerning the person and work of Christ has never entirely satisfied orthodox theologians. He makes the Logos central to his doctrine of creation and providence, as well as to his doctrine of salvation; and he seems to regard the manifestation of the Logos in the flesh as necessary for man's salvation. But his account of Christ's human nature does not agree with that which the Church has come to affirm. For example, Clement agrees that Christ partook of food, but he explains that He did so not because His body required sustenance, but in order that the disciples might not be misled into supposing that they were seeing a phantasm. Moreover, says Clement, Christ was "inaccessible to any movement of feeling—either pleasure or pain"; and, although He underwent death, yet He "suffered no harm."

Clement's teaching about the Savior is, however, quite consistent with his teaching concerning the plan of salvation. As Clement sees it, God's purpose in making the world was to bring into existence complete or perfect men. But a complete man is one whose soul is at one with God. It is by faith, and then by knowledge, that man rises to this union. Indeed, knowledge, when it is perfect, becomes love—not the love of desire, but the love of fruition and peace. In our earthly life, says Clement, it is impossible for men to get rid of certain appetites which are essential to the maintenance of the body, but these are the only desires which need to remain. For the rest, the advanced Christian, the true Gnostic, the high-souled man, is free from every passion, having "obtained the affinity to the impassible God which arises from love."

Such being the salvation which Christ came to make possible, it is scarcely to be expected that the perfect humanity of the Savior would exhibit those very weaknesses which men must overcome. The problem of saving man from sin, as Clement views it, does not consist in freeing him from the guilt of past sins but, rather, in converting, disciplining, and instructing his soul. By assuming our nature in its perfection, the Son of God brought humanity and God for the first time into effective union. By His life and teaching, Christ instructs others how to achieve this goal.

Clement concedes that the Scriptures open salvation to the many, who experience the "first saving change" when they pass from heathenism to faith, or from law to Gospel. But these are saved only in the first degree. Besides his public teaching, Christ also taught his Apostles the gnosis which leads to perfection. This knowledge, Clement claims, "has descended by transmission to a few, having been imparted unwritten by the apostles." Great preparation and previous training are necessary to receive it. But those who can obey it achieve here and now a foretaste of eternal bliss, and, in the world to come, will take their places with the Apostles in the highest sphere. "Such an one," writes Clement, "is wholly a son, passionless, gnostic, perfect, formed by the teaching of the Lord; in order that in deed, in word, and in spirit itself, being brought close to the Lord, he may receive the mansion that is due to him who has reached manhood thus."

While holding that perfection involves turning away from the world toward God, Clement does not advocate the kind of asceticism which requires a person to mortify the flesh and to relinquish all his belongings. On the contrary, Clement says that men who have not attained to perfection are likely to be harmed by poverty and suffering, and prevented from carrying out their spiritual endeavors. He therefore enjoins his readers to make the necessary provisions for their bodies "to keep the soul free and unimpeded." In opposition to the teaching of the Marcionites and other Gnostic groups, Clement affirms the goodness of the material world. On this ground, he commends the married state. Not everyone ought to marry, he says, "but there is a time in which it is suitable, and a person for whom it is suitable, and an age up to which it is suitable." Celibacy is good, but marriage is better. It opens the way to higher attainment, providing "more varied preparatory exercise" through the temptations arising from wife and children, domestics, and possessions. Still, the aim of all Christian striving is to get rid of all desire, not simply to get the better of our passions. Thus, the family man (or woman, for Clement says that the way of perfection is open to both) achieves the Christian ideal only if he conducts the affairs of his household "without pleasure or pain" and preserves his soul "inseparable from God's love." Such a man is mild, beneficent, magnanimous. Having put to death the old man, with his passions and lusts, he holds himself above both pleasure and pain. Thus Clement writes, "If the Word, who is Judge, call; he having grown inflexible, and not indulging a whit the passions, walks unswervingly where justice advises him to go; being very well persuaded that all things are managed consummately well, and that progress to what is better goes on in the case of souls that have chosen virtue, till they come to the Good itself, to the Father's vestibule, so to speak, close to the great High Priest. Such is our Gnostic."

THE EPISTLE TO DIOGNETUS

Author: Unknown
Type of work: Christian apologetics
First transcribed: Unknown, probably second or third century

Principal Ideas Advanced

Neither the pagan religions, with their worship of idols, nor the Jewish religion, which ignores Christ, can be tolerated.

The beliefs which Christians hold must be understood if they are to be effective; Christian character at its best must be held up as an example, and the benefits which this life offers should be explained to converts.

What the soul is to the body, Christians are to the world.

Both the author and the one addressed are unknown in the *Epistle to Diognetus,* but the letter clearly stands out as one of the early classics in Christian apologetics, the art and practice of explaining Christianity and its practices to nonbelievers. Diognetus, who is addressed in the letter, is taken as one exceedingly zealous to learn the religion of the Christians, as one who has been asking clear and careful questions about them. Who is the God, he wants to know, in whom these Christians believe? How is He worshiped, and what is the love which Christians have for one another? Diognetus has obviously been impressed by the way Christians disregard the world, by the way in which they despise death, and particularly by the fact that they do not accept the Greek gods. These observed facts have made him anxious to know more about these Christians and their beliefs.

The writer, in replying to Diognetus, first asks him to clear himself of all prejudice, for undoubtedly he has heard many false reports about the Christians, their practices, and their beliefs. If he is to learn about Christianity profitably, he must become a new man; he must prepare himself to listen to a new story. Concerning the gods of the day, the writer tells him: look with your eyes; idols are made of ordinary stone and clay like any perishable vessel. These idols are dumb and blind, without souls, lacking feeling, and they can be made by men into other forms if men wish. The idols do not move, and they decay. Are these things to be called gods? How can it possibly be that because Christians cannot acknowledge such material objects as gods, they should be hated? These pagan idols need to be protected from harm themselves; they do not protect men. How can Christians be expected to pay heed to such fragile gods?

The writer, then, takes it as almost obvious that the pagan idols are not worthy of worship. The Jewish God, however, is not such a series of perishable objects. He is a mighty spirit Who protects His people. Why, then, since the Christian religion began among the Jews, are the Christians not worshipers of the Jewish God? Jews worship the one God, master of the universe. The author then refers to the Jewish law, to their food regulations and their custom of sacrifice. In brief compass the author gives the Christian argument against observance of Jewish law, describing it as encouraging silliness, fussiness, and pride. The Christian cannot accept the Jewish belief that the religious life consists in complete observance of the letter of the law, particularly since men take pride in mere obedience to law. Law is a matter of human observance, whereas the mystery of the Christian's religion cannot be learned from men.

The distinction between Christians and other men, actually, is neither in country nor language nor custom. Their teaching has not, they believe, been discovered by the intellect or by the thought of busy men. Christians are not advocates of any human doctrine. They live in Greek and barbarian cities, and they follow local customs, yet still they exhibit their wonderful and admittedly strange character as sojourners in their own fatherland. Christians share all things as citizens and yet suffer all things as strangers. Every foreign country is their fatherland, and every fatherland is nevertheless a foreign country to them. They must conform to the flesh, but their lives are not patterned after the flesh. Their time is spent on earth, but their real citizenship is in Heaven.

The irony of Christians' lives is that their Gospel directs them to love all men and yet they are persecuted by all men. Their belief teaches them that even when they are put to death they gain eternal life. Christians may be dishonored, but they are glorified in their dishonor. When a Christian does a good deed and is treated as an evildoer, he rejoices in his ill-treatment as does a man who receives life.

Given such a reception, warred upon by Jews and persecuted by Greeks, how does the Christian look upon his role in the world? It can be stated very simply: What the soul does for the body, Christians do for the world. The soul is spread to all parts of the body; Christians are found throughout the cities of the world. The soul dwells in the body but is not of the same substance as the body; Christians are recognized in the world but their religion remains as invisible as the soul. The soul has been shut up in the body but actually sustains the body; Christians are confined in the world as in a prison but actually sustain the world.

Although this position in the world is not a pleasant one, God has appointed Christians to it and they must not decline to serve in this way. It is no earthly discovery which has been given to men. What Christians believe, in truth, is that the almighty, all-creating, and invisible God Himself has founded among men the truth from Heaven. They believe nothing less than that the holy and incomprehensible Word has been established in their hearts. No angel or intermediary has been sent to do this. The very framer and creator of the universe Himself has come to do this. He who ordered the world in the beginning and sustains it now has been sent to men to establish the religion the Christians hold. Did such a world-creator come in sovereignty and fear and terror, as one might suppose? No, what the Christians assert is that even such a mighty one as this came in gentleness and meekness. He was sent as God and yet He was sent as Man to men. He came saving and persuading, not compelling, since Christians do not believe that compulsion is an attribute of God.

Such actions do not seem to be the works of man, the author of the letter continues. Such an unexpected event in such unexpected form is a miracle of God. Christians are punished for their beliefs, but the more they are punished the more they seem to multiply, a proof that God Himself came as a man to men. The Christians are thrown to wild beasts and asked to deny their Lord, but they do not, and they are not put down but multiply instead. Such a coming of God as the Christians announce was a calling, not a pursuing. The creator of the world was sent in love, not as a judge, and the proof of this lies in the Christian's increase of power in the face of treatment that might otherwise put an end to the religion. In dealing with Christian beliefs, the oppressors of the Christians are dealing with God Himself and not with the inventions of men.

The Christians claim, then, for their revelation nothing less than the true knowledge of God revealed. In Christ, what God is was revealed, and before His coming no man knew or could discern what God is like. Foolish philosophers have thought God to be fire or water, but such views are unacceptable. Now God has manifested Himself, and He is revealed by Himself, not by men. Yet He is revealed through faith, by which alone it is possible to see God. Before the coming of Christ, God seemed to neglect us and to be careless, but then He revealed His true nature through His beloved Child. Now we know that God alone is good, kindly, long-suffering, free from wrath, and true.

All of this was planned from the beginning, the author writes, but it was revealed at a particular time through God's Child. We lived as men before this time—governed by unruly impulses, carried away by pleasures and lusts—and the coming of God's Son was planned in order to prove to us that it is impossible for us by ourselves to enter into the Kingdom of God. We are able to do so only by the power of God, and His revelation demonstrates this to us and enables us now to enter God's Kingdom. God Himself took pity on our sin, gave His Son as ransom for us, the Holy for the wicked, the innocent for the guilty. Nothing else could cover our sins but God's own righteousness. We were convinced of our own inability to attain life, and now we have a Savior who is able to save.

What does the Christian do now, believing as he does in this divine act for his salvation? The author answers Diognetus: By love he should imitate this example of God's goodness. It is possible for man to imitate God's goodness if God wills. Happiness now for the Christian is not domination over his neighbors; it is not in wishing to have more than the weak, nor is it in the possession of wealth or power. Rather, the imitator of God is the man who takes up the burden of his neighbor, who wishes to help others, and who ministers to others.

If a man does this, if he imitates God after the example given by God's sacrifice in Christ, then even while he is occupied on earth such a man will see that God lives in Heaven, and he will begin to speak of the mysteries of God. Anyone who understands this way will begin to admire those who are persecuted; no one can deny such a God, and He will condemn the conceit and error of the world. When one learns the true life of Heaven and despises the apparent death of this world, then he comes to fear the death that is real, the loss of eternal life.

The writer of the epistle concludes by declaring that, as a disciple of the Apostles, he is becoming a teacher of the heathen. If one speaks with pain, commanded by the will of God to do so, then he becomes a sharer through love of all the things revealed by God. Knowledge does not kill, the writer asserts; only disobedience kills. Thus, Christians claim to possess a new knowledge through their revelation, and it gives them life. They die only if they are disobedient to God by not proclaiming and sharing the message given.

OCTAVIUS

Author: Minucius Felix (Second or third century)
Type of work: Christian apologetics
First transcribed: Latter half of second century, or first half of third century

Principal Ideas Advanced

To the pagan accusation that Christianity is foolishness, destitute of reason, and filled with obscene and lustful practices, the answer is given that reason itself discloses that the contents and constitution of the world are determined and governed by God; Christ was God in the world.

Pagan religion rather than Christianity is filled with foolish and obscene practices, for the moral practices of the Christians are above reproach; they do not worship monsters, devour infants, or hold incestuous banquets.

Minucius Felix, author of the *Octavius,* was a master of Latin style. He stands at the very fountainhead of Latin Christianity, and he demonstrated by his writing that Christians were not illiterate or devoid of learning. Prior to his conversion, Minucius Felix is said to have been an advocate at Rome. Little is known of his personal history or of his writings other than the *Octavius.* The date of his celebrated apology is a matter of dispute. The question is whether Minucius borrowed from Tertullian or whether Tertullian borrowed from Minucius. If the latter alternative is the case, then the *Octavius* was probably written around 166, and Minucius flourished during the reign of Marcus Aurelius. If, on the other hand, Minucius borrowed from Tertullian, he must have flourished at the beginning of the third century, and the book could not have been written before 205.

The *Octavius* is a Christian apology written in the traditional Roman form of an imaginary dialogue. The disputants are the pagan Caecilius and the Christian Octavius. The author Minucius (who gives evidence of a thorough acquaintance with Cicero and other Latin writers) plays the role of arbitrator between the disputants.

The argument opens with Caecilius's assertion that all things are uncertain and doubtful in human affairs, and that everything is probable rather than true. It is therefore to be deplored that Christians, who are generally illiterate, should dare to be certain concerning the nature of God. The world shows no sign of being governed by divine providence.

Caecilius continues by arguing that every nation, especially the Roman, has paid homage to its own deities in order that it might gain dominion over the earth. When the Roman auguries have been observed, good fortune has resulted; whereas, when they have been neglected, the consequences have been unfortunate. The impiety of the Christians toward the gods exceeds that of all others, for they despise the temples, reject the gods, and, while fearing to die, after death are indifferent to the torments of the present. Furthermore, the religion of the Christians is a foolish superstition, a conspiracy that ought to be rooted out and execrated, a religion of lust and incest. Christians adore the head of an ass, worship the virilia of their priest, worship a crucified man, and initiate young novices by having them eat an infant covered with meal. They strive in every way to conceal their worship, for they have no altars, temples, or images.

Continuing his indictment of the Christians, Caecilius charges that their one God is unknown to every nation; the Christians can neither show Him nor behold Him, and yet they threaten the whole world with conflagration and assert that the conflagration will be followed by the resurrection of the body and by rewards and punishments. Such old women's fables are spread abroad.

Such religion, says Caecilius, is to be repudiated, for what is above us is nothing to us, and things which are as uncertain as is religion ought not to be disturbed, lest superstition be introduced and all religion be overthrown.

On behalf of the Christians Octavius replies that Christians are not to be reproached because they talk about heavenly things, for wisdom is implanted by nature. The poor are not to be despised, for intelligence is not given to the rich alone. When a person utters his thoughts about divine things, what is most important is not the position of the speaker, but the truth of what he says.

It is of course true, says Octavius, that man ought to know himself and to see what he is, whence he is, and why he is. His reason will then show him that the constitution of the world and everything in it is governed and administered by a Deity of most excellent intelligence, who takes care not only of the world as a whole but also of its individual parts.

The Lord and Creator of the universe is far more glorious than the stars and the parts of the world, says Octavius. The Lord orders everything by His word; He can neither be seen nor fully understood, and yet when all His titles are laid aside, His glory is most fully seen.

Poets and philosophers have attained a glimpse of the unity of God, Octavius concedes, but men have been carried away by fables and have believed in monstrous falsehoods; they have worshiped their own kings and the inventors of the arts, and thus they have adopted men as gods. Men of antiquity fell into ridiculous and absurd practices which have been elaborated by the poets, so that even Plato wanted to banish the poets from the state.

Gods cannot be made from dead people, Octavius argues, since a god cannot die, nor can a piece of metal or wood become a god simply because men consecrate it and pray to it. The rites associated with many religions are truly cruel and obscene, comic and pitiable: "Naked people run about in the raw winter. . . . Some sacred places are crowned by a woman having one husband, some by a woman with many; and she who can reckon up most adulteries is sought after with most religious zeal. . . ." During pagan rites, Octavius charges, men castrate themselves, but if God wished for eunuchs, he would have caused men to be born as such.

The Romans did not gain power from observing superstitions, Octavius suggests. On the contrary, the Romans began with crime, and they grew by the terror of their own fierceness, by their irreligious audacity and violence. They grew rich from pillage, from the spoils of the gods and the murder of priests. They became great not because they were religious but because they were irreligious with impunity.

Demons fly from Christians and then introduce hatred and fear of the Christians in the minds of the ignorant, who then unjustly charge them with horrid crimes which no one has ever proved against them. The gentiles do themselves engage in infanticide, incest, and monstrous acts of worship. They expose their newborn children to the elements, and they perform abortions, whereas Christians regard such practices as wicked and sinful.

The Egyptians worship a mere man whom they propitiate and consult in all things, and to whom they slaughter victims, whereas the Christ that was crucified was innocent of all crime; in truth, He was God.

The banquets of the Christians, says Octavius, are modest and temperate; incestuous love is unheard of, and even modest association between the sexes causes some to blush.

The worship of the Christians is not concealed, he continues; Christians build no temples because they realize that God cannot be enclosed in limits made by man, and no likeness can be made of Him; He is present everywhere. To cultivate innocence is to supplicate God; to cultivate justice is to make offerings unto Him; to abstain from fraud is to propitiate Him. God is beheld in all His works; He is near to us and infused within us, so that we live in Him, and our most secret thoughts are known to Him.

God does not forsake those who follow Him, Octavius declares; it is man who first foresakes God. Nor is it to be wondered at if this world is to come to an end, since what has a beginning also has an end. Yet the God who made man from nothing can raise him up unto life eternal. The pious and the righteous shall then be rewarded with everlasting happiness, while the unrighteous shall receive the eternal punishment which is their due and just reward.

Christians now suffer as a discipline, not as a penalty. The tortures they endure for the sake of Christ are spectacles worthy of the name they bear, and their suffering in the name of God is a fitting testimony to the truth they profess.

The dialogue ends with Caecilius's being convinced of the truth of the Christian faith. His objections are answered, and the pagan world is shown that Latin prose can be utilized in the service of the Christian faith.

The *Octavius* is important as one of the most charming and elegantly styled apologies of the early Christian period. As a work directed at cultivated pagans, the *Octavius* exhibits a remarkable impartiality in its treatment of pagan beliefs and practices, and its dignity and literary excellence made it widely influential.

THE APOSTOLIC TRADITION

Author: Hippolytus (c.170-c.236)
Type of work: Church manual
First transcribed: c.217

Principal Ideas Advanced

Laws for Church organization and for the conduct of worship are taken from the practices in Rome; the Roman practice is truly Apostolic.

The Apostolic tradition concerns ordination by bishops, the routine for new converts, the rules for fasting, and the procedures for instruction and prayer.

Hippolytus's *Apostolic Tradition* is the oldest and most important of the ecclesiastical constitutions, and it is one of the most important sources of information concerning the development of Church practice during the first three centuries. The work played a major part in the development of the liturgy in the East, as well as in the development of Canon Law. In particular, the description of baptismal procedures is important as constituting the first distinctively Roman creed.

For Hippolytus, tradition is the most important source of Church practice. In his work he addresses the churches, urging them to hold fast to the Apostolic tradition. Ignorance of the tradition causes lapses into error, he claims, and he suggests that with careful instruction liturgical errors could be avoided.

The instructions which Hippolytus gives are simple injunctions with no explanations appended; the instructions are directives, handed down as authoritative, and they need no support, the author claims, other than their existence as expressions of the tradition of the Church, as means by which true doctrine and correct observance are conserved.

To ordain a bishop, Hippolytus advises, the people, with the presbytery, must assemble on a Sunday. Such other bishops as are already present are to lay their hands upon him, while the presbytery and the people stand by in silence. Together they are to pray in their hearts for the descent of the Holy Spirit. Hippolytus then gives verbatim a prayer which one of the bishops present is to recite. The prayer calls upon God, the Father of our Lord Jesus Christ, to pour forth His Spirit. Then God's blessing is asked upon the servant being consecrated, so that he may serve his flock well. As he is being made bishop, all offer him the kiss of peace, after which the deacons bring him the offering and he blesses it with a prayer.

When the consecration is concluded, the new bishop recites what amounts to a catechism, a short version of the essential beliefs of Christianity. If oil, cheese, or olives are offered, he gives a prayer of sanctification. However, if it is a presbyter who is being ordained, the procedure is somewhat different. Those who are already presbyters touch him, while the bishop lays on hands, and offers a shorter prayer. When a deacon is ordained, the bishop alone lays on his hands, since a deacon is ordained not to the priesthood but to serve the bishop and to carry out his commands. Therefore, the deacon does not receive the Spirit that is possessed by the presbytery; he receives only what is confided to him under the bishop's authority.

Although the presbyter does receive the Spirit, in common with the clergy, the presbyter has only the power to receive but not to give the Spirit, Hippolytus declares. For this reason a presbyter does not ordain the clergy. At an ordination, a presbyter merely seals while the bishop ordains. On the other hand, if one has been in bonds for the Lord or has been insulted for defending the name of the Lord, then this in itself gives him special status, and he is dealt with differently.

Although Hippolytus gives the specific words of the prayers to be recited, he says that it is not necessary for everyone to say the exact words prescribed. Each may pray according to his own ability. Widows, readers, and virgins all follow under various special rules. Anyone with the gift of healing may be considered as having already made his gifts manifest.

Part Two begins with a discussion of new converts, who are first to be admitted as hearers of the Word. First they are brought to the teachers in front of the assembled people and examined as to their reasons for embracing the faith. Testimony must be furnished that each convert is competent to hear the Word. Whether the person is a slave, the wife of a believer, an unmarried man, each situation involves slightly different rules for his reception and for his disposition after reception. Next the convert must be asked his trade, since not all trades are acceptable, some not at all, and others only if modified. A heathen priest, for instance, must be rejected, says Hippolytus, but a concubine who has reared her children and been faithful to her master may become a hearer. Each catechumen, after such examination and specification, must spend three years as a hearer of the Word. However, Hippolytus admits, if a man is zealous and perseveres well in the work, his character, and not the time spent as a catechumen, is the decisive factor.

When the teacher finishes his instruction, the catechumens pray by themselves, after which the teacher prays over them, lays his hands upon them, and dismisses them. Baptism, which is a further step, can only come after the life of the person has been investigated. Each person desiring baptism must have a sponsor, who must testify that the candidate lives soberly and is active in well-doing. When those who are to be baptized have been chosen, they are to fast on Friday and then to assemble on Saturday, to kneel before the bishop in prayer. After the bishop has exorcised all evil spirits, the chosen ones are to spend the night in vigil, listening to reading and instruction.

At dawn a prayer shall be made over the water to be used for baptism. Then, as each one presents himself for baptism, a presbyter shall take hold of him and command him to renounce Satan and his works. Then, while standing in the water, the deacon questions the one to be baptized about his beliefs: Does he believe in God, the Father Almighty? Does he believe in Christ Jesus, the Son of God, and the Holy Church, and the resurrection of the flesh? When the one to be baptized answers that he believes, he is baptized three times. He is then brought to the bishop for the laying on of hands and anointing with oil, with an appropriate prayer for each act given by the bishop. Water, milk, and wine are brought and each consumed, with the symbolism explained to the one newly baptized.

Part Three begins with a discussion of the rules for fasting. Others may fast more frequently, but the bishop may fast only when all the people do, since his office of breaking bread requires that he eat of it when it is brought to him to be blessed. The next important ceremony to be discussed and described is that of the Lord's Supper. No catechumen is allowed to sit at the Lord's Supper during his period as a hearer. Others are admonished to eat silently, attending such instruction as the bishop may give during the meal. Each one eats in the name of the Lord.

The balance of Part Three gives a series of similar minor regulations. For example, in the paschal season no one is to eat before the offering is made, with certain exceptions outlined. The deacons are to assemble daily before they go to their duties. The closing injunction is that burial shall be provided at a modest cost. By the end of Part Three Hippolytus has left behind the major doctrines and ceremonies of the Church and has begun on the minor regulations, points which need to be covered, about which controversy can arise, but which do not concern major Church doctrines.

Part Four is actually quite short. In fact, the whole of the reporting of the tradition is very brief and is done in abbreviated style. Some specifications concern the central practices of Christianity, and it is obvious that if such tradition were not preserved, the Church would become quite different. However, mixed with these major specifications are minor regulations, so that it is sometimes difficult to tell where the essential points leave off and the noncrucial ones begin. When regulations are specifically fixed, there is an unfortunate tendency to place all of them on a similar level, to make the most obscure point seem as important as the crucial doctrine.

The first point for Part Four concerns the beginning of the day. Before work, hands should be washed, and prayer should be said to God. If instruction in God's Word is to be given on that day, each one should go willingly to that first. One should be zealous in desiring to go to the church for instruction, since that is the place where the Holy Spirit abounds. However, if there is to be no instruction at the church on any given day, then each one shall take home a Bible and read what he finds profitable. At the third hour of the day, public or private prayer is to be made, since it is that hour at which Jesus was nailed to the cross. In like manner all should pray at the sixth hour during the day, since that is the hour at which there was great darkness during the Crucifixion. At the ninth hour of the day each person, wherever he is, is to offer a prayer of thanksgiving for the Resurrection. Prayer is to be given again at night, just before going to bed, and the final prayer of the day is to be given at midnight, when the instructions are to rise from bed. Why this midnight prayer? Because, our author tells us, all creation rests for a moment at this hour. Then, at dawn, the next day begins with another prayer.

This accounting of the tradition of the Church, which has been received and is to be transmitted to each new group, closes with the assertion that if these ways are accepted with thanksgiving and right faith, they will give edification in the Church and eternal life to believers. If this Apostolic tradition is kept, Hippolytus writes, then heretics cannot prevail to lead the members of the Church astray. Heresy, he feels sure, is increased when Church leaders do not follow the tradition, do not learn the purposes of the Apostles, but instead follow their own ways. Thus it is no small matter whether these specifications for observances are followed or not. The traditional rules are not incidental rules, to be changed if they are not found convenient. In observing these traditional practices, it is thought, the very heart of the Christian faith is preserved and protected. Tradition is not accidental, and, if it is Apostolic, directly descending from Jesus and His Apostles, and their instruction, then keeping the traditional observances is the very path to religious health and purity of belief.

ON FIRST PRINCIPLES

Author: Origen (c.185-c.254)
Type of work: Systematic theology
First transcribed: c.220-230

Principal Ideas Advanced

The source of all Christian doctrine is in the Scriptures of the Old and New Testaments and in the Apostolic tradition of the Church.

The Church has clear teachings on God, the Creator; Jesus Christ, His incarnate Son; and the Holy Spirit; but some points such as the origin of the Spirit and of the good angels are unclear.

Both God and the Devil are active in the created world, but man is given a rational soul and free will to direct himself in the ascent to God.

The Scriptures are filled with mysteries which are understood by any man who shares the mind of Christ and uses the threefold method of interpretation to discover the literal, moral, and spiritual senses of Scripture.

Origen has the distinction of having written the first textbook of systematic theology in his *On First Principles*. Although incomplete by modern standards or even by those of the fifth century, the work represents a great achievement in the history of Christian thought. Origen himself recognized that there were not clear teachings on every subject, but so far as possible he set forth the fundamentals of Christian doctrine as he knew them. As models or analogies he had the works of pagan Platonists, and he too was informed and influenced by the philosophy of middle Platonism. No doubt his experience as a student of philosophy and as a teacher of catechetical classes revealed to him the need for such a Christian handbook of theology.

This work was written while he was serving as the head of the Christian school in Alexandria before his exile in 230-231 to Palestine. It has survived the later purges of Origen's writings only in a Latin translation by Rufinus (c.345-410), an Italian churchman who tried to correct the controversial or unorthodox passages of Origen. The remaining excerpts and fragments of Origen in other Greek authors indicate that Rufinus translated Origen rather freely. *De principiis* is, nevertheless, a tolerably accurate statement of Origen's thought in his middle years. Especially to be observed are his own frequent warnings and qualifications that many points were still speculative and had not then been clarified by the Church.

On First Principles consists of four books which treat the following themes: God and the spiritual beings, the material world and man, free will and morality, and the Holy Scriptures. The long preface to the first book discusses the derivation of Christian doctrine from the inspired Scriptures and the tradition of the Apostles and the Church. Origen distinguishes here between clear and unclear teachings. In the former category are the basic doctrines of the trinitarian God, the soul, the Resurrection, and the creation of the world. Unclear are such matters as the origin or generation of the Holy Spirit and the origin of the good angels. In acknowledging this uncertainty Origen reflects faithfully the position of the Bible on these points.

The doctrine of God is taken essentially from the Bible. God is an incomprehensible Spirit who reveals

Himself to the pure in heart. He is a simple intellectual nature. The Second Person of the Trinity, Jesus Christ, has two natures and many titles. He is the only-begotten Son, without any beginning, the eternal Word of God. A long discourse on the significance of such titles as Wisdom, Truth, and Light follows. It is from the goodness of God that the Son is born and the Spirit proceeds. The Holy Spirit is also known from the Scriptures where He exercises great authority. The Spirit reveals God to man and works with the other two Persons in the regeneration of man. Although Father and Son work in saints as well as sinners, the Holy Spirit is given only to the worthy; for God gives existence, Christ provides reason, and the Holy Spirit is the source of holiness.

The first book goes on to discuss the defection or fall of men, rational natures, the coming consummation or perfection of all rational creatures, and the origin of incorporeal and corporeal beings. It is here that we note some of the concepts for which Origen could later be accused of heresy. He considers the stars to be living beings with souls implanted from without by God. He also discusses the angels and ranks them according to merit.

The material world is as much under God as the spiritual or heavenly, but it is much more diverse. No creature in the material world is privileged to enjoy an incorporeal life. There is always a body even when the corruptible puts on incorruption. The world, of course, has a beginning, and it has many ages without repeating itself. So for example, there are the Old and New Covenants, but only one God.

We detect in this first book the traditional anti-Gnostic, anti-Marcionite polemic against separating or differentiating between the God of the Old Testament and the God of the New. This line of thought is continued in a chapter on justice and goodness, two qualities of God that must go together.

It is in the second book's treatment of the incarnation of Christ that we find the best-known errors of Origen. He is, naturally, orthodox in his acknowledgment of Christ's majesty and divinity and of the miracle of the Incarnation, but his concept of pre-existent souls, one of which was found worthy to become the soul of Christ by union with the Logos, was quite naturally fated to be rejected by the Church. Even Origen admits that his ideas are speculative. He shows no intention, however, of abandoning the doctrine of pre-existent souls, for he goes on to declare that the souls, when cooling, fall away into sin. On the mysterious doctrine of the Holy Spirit or the Comforter, Origen was hesitant to make pronouncements. It follows from the pre-existence of souls, he argues, that there can be only a fixed number of rational beings to inhabit the earth, but he holds that their number is sufficient. He defends the free will of these beings and sees them rewarded according to merit, because God is just. At another place, however, Origen anticipates a universal salvation. Certainly there will be a general resurrection of the body if simply because it is the body which dies and therefore must be raised. (Such an argument is by no means new with Origen although it fits very well with his teaching on the soul.)

Book III of *De principiis* turns to the question of free will and its consequences. Origen recognizes the shortcomings of men, particularly their need for self-knowledge and the knowledge of God. He believes, however, that God is perfecting man, that men are vessels who prepare themselves by being purged. The human soul is engaged in an ascent to the highest good or God, who is reached in eternity. There are, on the other hand, opposing powers, such as the Devil and his demons, but these powers are the cause of only part of man's sin. Many transgressions are due to man's free choice. Man is confronted by a variety of human temptations which seem inseparable from his having a body.

From this discussion of free will and sin, Origen turns rather abruptly to the problem of the creation of the world. In conforming to the Genesis account, he maintains that the world had a beginning in time, but he goes on to assert that there is a logical need for several worlds because a new heaven and earth is promised in Scripture. If a new world is coming, it is likely that others have preceded this one, but never more than one world can exist at any given time. Scripture points most clearly, however, to the end of this world. It is then that God's image in man will be perfected. Man will complete his ascent and be glorified in the likeness of God. All vice will be purged, and God will dwell in every man. Man will receive a spiritual body, and death will be destroyed.

The fourth book on the Holy Scriptures is an especially valuable account of Origen's handling of the Bible. It is almost a description of his hermeneutics. Fundamental is, of course, the fact that the Scriptures are inspired books. The traditional evidence for this inspiration is presented, in particular the fulfillment of prophecy. However, when Origen considered the proper way to read the Bible, he found it necessary to deal with prophecies which had not been visibly fulfilled. At this point, he argues, the need for a spiritual or allegorical interpretation of Scripture is obvious. He points out that many previous misunderstandings of the Bible arose from literal readings, and he would correct this error. He cites the importance of sharing the mind of Christ when reading the Scriptures, a principle that appears repeatedly throughout the history of Christian exegesis.

The doctrine of the threefold interpretation of Scripture is based on Proverbs 22:20ff., as found in the Septuagint text. The three steps or aspects are the flesh, soul, and spirit, corresponding to the nature of man. Not all passages of the Bible contain all three forms of wisdom, but since most do, there is often a three-fold meaning of the Bible. The literal meaning is sometimes offensive or a stumbling-block, but God's intent is to keep us from stopping at the literal meaning and thereby missing the heavenly meaning. The anthropomorphisms in the Old Testament descriptions of God are not to be understood literally, and the absurdities of the law, Origen writes, are to be interpreted allegorically. On the other hand, many historical passages are true and consequently are to be accepted as written. It is typical of Origen that he claims the entire written Gospel is but a shadow of the coming heavenly and everlasting Gospel. Thus, one sees the need for the wisdom of the Holy Spirit in the reading of the Scriptures.

In concluding the final book of *On First Principles* Origen gives a summary of the doctrine of God. Even here he touches on new problems such as the nature and origin of matter. Characteristically, his summary of doctrine is generously documented with Scripture.

Although the later judgment of the Church on Origen was unfavorable, we cannot overlook the recognition he received in his own day nor the influence he exerted for over a century on the theologians of East and West. He produced the first great synthesis of Christian teaching and provided his successors with a method of Biblical interpretation which, if sometimes artificial and arbitrary, was at least consistent and thorough. He was an intellectual who applied all his powers to the teaching office of the Church, in defense of the Gospel and in opposition to the heresies of his day. It is especially to his credit that he dealt with the whole of theology and not merely with one doctrine. Origen represents the coming of age of Christianity as an intellectual force in the ancient world.

THE EXTANT WRITINGS OF JULIUS AFRICANUS

Author: Sextus Julius Africanus (c.160-c.240)
Type of work: Biblical chronology
First transcribed: Third century

Principal Ideas Advanced

By studying the genealogies given in the Old Testament in conjunction with Greek and Babylonian Sources, the age of the world from Adam to the advent of Jesus Christ can be accurately set at 5500 years.

The apparent discrepancy between the genealogies of Jesus recorded in Matthew and in Luke is explicable in terms of a twofold manner of recording generations in Israel, the one by nature, the other by law, so that in effect there is no real disparity between the two accounts.

Sextus Julius Africanus, a pupil of Heraclas of Alexandria sometime between 228 and 232, contributed to the Biblical science of chronology in his *Five Books of Chronology* and in his letter to Aristides.

The main facts of his life are known from the *Chronicle* of Eusebius and from his own writings, in which he states that he was attracted to Alexandria by the fame of the teacher Heraclas.

The works ascribed to Africanus, besides the ones already mentioned, are a letter to Origen, in which he sought to prove, by ingenious critical argument, that the story of Susanna in Daniel was forgery; *The Acts of Symphorosa and her Seven Sons,* which is attributed to him in the manuscript, although no other ancient author makes mention of his authorship; and the *Cesti,* ascribed to him by Eusebius, but which may have been written by someone else of the same name.

In the *Five Books of Chronology,*

Julius Africanus undertakes to summarize the events from the cosmogony of Moses to the advent of Christ, and from the advent of Chirst to the reign of the Emperor Macrinus. The chief interest in the fragments that we possess arises from the treatment of the difficult questions of the genealogies of Jesus contained in the Gospels.

The extant fragments of the *Five Books of Chronology* deal first of all with the mythical chronology of the Chaldeans and Egyptians who, according to Julius, in their boastful manner inflate their antiquity and appeal to their astrologers to establish countless cycles and myriad years in their past.

The truth of the matter, writes Julius, is to be found in the writings of the Jews, the descendants of Abraham who, with a modesty and sobriety appropriate to those who were taught the truth of Moses, have correctly informed us that the number of years up to the advent of Jesus Christ is 5500. This figure can be arrived at by adding the ages of those mentioned in the Old Testament genealogies. It then becomes apparent that 2262 years transpired from Adam to Noah and the flood, and that Abraham entered the promised land of Canaan in the 3277th year of the world. From Adam until the death of Joseph, a total of 3563 years transpired. From Daniel 9:24 and other Biblical passages, it is possible to determine that the world will end 6000 years from its creation, in the year 500.

Among the Greeks there is no certain history until the time of the Olympiads, before which time dates are confused and inconsistent. By correlating Hebrew, Greek, and Persian history, it is possible to further ascertain the course of events, and to set the date of the exodus from Egypt, and the date of the exile, as well as the subsequent course down to the very coming of Jesus Christ, the Savior of all.

Such an attempt at chronology, while historically interesting, overlooks the fact that Biblical genealogies are never used in Scripture itself as a basis for chronological calculations. In fact, modern scholarship has noted the fact, overlooked by Julius Africanus, that genealogies have symmetrical forms which suggests the omission of links. They are cast in forms easy to remember and give only such information as is useful to the reader.

Julius Africanus overlooked the fact that many Old Testament genealogies are abridged, and the word "son" frequently means descendant. In spite of the errors that he made, however, the attempt at tracing the history of the world is understandable, at a time when there was no reason to believe that the world is older. His efforts to understand historical sequences by comparing various source materials provided a model for subsequent historical research.

Of further interest is the example of Biblical exegesis in which he suggests the hermeneutic principle that Scripture is to be interpreted by Scripture. In commenting upon Genesis 6:4, where the sons of God are depicted as marrying the daughters of men, Julius Africanus appears to suggest that while it is possible to interpret the expression "sons of God" as referring to angels, it is more likely that it refers to the descendants of Seth, who are called the sons of God because of the righteous men and the patriarchs who descended from him, whereas the descendants of Cain are named the daughters of men, as being destitute of the divine because of their wickedness, which stirred God's indignation.

Julius's letter to Aristides is a famous attempt to reconcile the apparent discrepancies in the genealogies given by Luke and Matthew. Modern scholarship recognizes that the genealogy in Matthew is an arbitrary arrangement in three groups of fourteen, in order to make the divisions come with David and the captivity. In the second group four kings are omitted and Jechonias is mentioned twice. The expression "so all the generations" refers to the generations given in these lists. In the summary statement the generations are reduced to three and Jesus Christ is called the Son of David, who is called the son of Abraham, so that it is readily seen that the word "son" refers to descendant.

The solution to the problem of the apparent discrepancies between Luke and Matthew is worked out in detail by Julius. He rejects the notion that the discrepant enumeration is a mixing of royal and priestly names given in order to show that Christ holds both a kingly and priestly office. Such a device would be both false and unnecessary since every Christian knows that Christ is the high priest of His Father, that Christ presents our petitions to Him, and that Christ is also a supramundane King, who rules by the Spirit those whom He has delivered.

The real reason for the discrepancies, according to Julius, is that the names of the generations in Israel were enumerated in a twofold manner, by nature or according to law. When the enumeration is given by nature, the succession is that of physical offspring; it is given according to law whenever another raised up children to the name of a brother dying childless. Thus neither of the Gospel writers is in error, since the one reckons by nature, and the other by law. Both of the accounts are true, and they come down to Joseph quite accurately, although with considerable intricacy. The same persons are quite justly reckoned as belonging either to their actual fathers or to their legal fathers. Thus, both the genealogies of Matthew and Luke are those of Joseph, since Joseph was the Son of Jacob or of Heli, either by adoption, or simply because Heli and Jacob were either half brothers or brothers. At the death of one of the brothers who was childless, the surviving brother married the widow, who then became Joseph's mother by marriage, so that Joseph was reckoned the son of Heli and of Jacob.

A further work ascribed to Julius, the *Passion of St. Symphorosa and Her Seven Sons,* is of interest in shedding light upon the life of the early Christians in their experience of martyrdom, and although the events portrayed occurred under the persecutions of Hadrian around the year 120, there is no ground to doubt its genuineness, even if it cannot be asserted with certainty that Julius is its author.

The widow Symphorosa and her seven sons refused to sacrifice to the gods in honor of a newly built palace, although they had been given the choice of sacrificing to the gods or themselves becoming sacrifices. When they refused to comply with Hadrian's demands, Symphorosa, whose husband had previously died a martyr's death, was beaten, suspended by the hair, and finally thrown into a river with a stone tied to her neck. Her sons fared no better; they were fastened to stakes, stretched on blocks around the temple of Hercules, and either stabbed to death or cleft in twain from the head downward.

A DECLARATION OF FAITH
(and Other Writings)

Author: Saint Gregory Thaumaturgus (c.213-c.270)
Type of work: Theology, Church practice
First transcribed: c.240-270

Principal Ideas Advanced

God is a triune being, Father, Son, and Holy Spirit, a perfect Trinity which in neither glory, eternity, nor dominion is ever divided from itself.

The Church of Christ is to exercise proper judgment in the readmission of members who have committed offenses in times of persecution; the Church recognizes the distinction between offenses committed under duress and those voluntarily committed because of an evil and covetous heart.

Willful violators of God's commandments whose offenses are particularly heinous are not to be permitted into the public congregation until such time as the Holy Spirit guides the saints in their common judgment concerning them.

Gregory Thaumaturgus, also known by the name Theodorus, was a native of Neocaesarea, one of the most important towns of Pontus. He was born into a wealthy pagan family and was educated in law at such centers of learning as Alexandria, Athens, Berytus, and Palestinian Caesarea. He studied logic, geometry, physics, ethics, philosophy, ancient literature, and theology with Origen, under whose influence he accepted Christianity. In 240 he became Bishop of Neocaesarea and faithfully served the Christian cause until his death about 270.

Gregory was an extremely gifted bishop, deeply versed in pagan learning, and richly imbued with Christian wisdom. His accredited extant writings include a creed on the doctrine of the trinity, *A Declaration of Faith;* a *Metaphrase of the Book of Ecclesiastes;* a *Panegyric to Origen,* in which he expresses his indebtedness to his teacher; and a *Canonical Epistle,* containing penances to be performed by Christians who were unfaithful during the barbarian invasion.

In *A Declaration of Faith,* Gregory affirms his belief in a single God, the Father of the living Word. God the Father is subsistent wisdom and power, the Father of the only-begotten Son, the perfect begetter of the perfect-begotten. There is a single Lord, God of God, the efficient Word, the Power which formed the whole creation. This one Lord is the true Son of the true Father, the Invisible of the Invisible, and the Incorruptible of the Incorruptible, the Eternal of the Eternal. There is also one Holy Spirit, who has his subsistence from God, and is made manifest to men by the Son. The Holy Spirit is the image of the Son, the perfect image of the perfect, the life and cause of the living, the supplier of sanctification, the one in whom God the Father is manifested. God the Son is through all; God the Father is above all and in all; and yet the Father, the Son, and the Holy Spirit are neither divided nor estranged but together constitute a perfect Trinity in sovereignty, eternity, and glory. In the Trinity there is nothing created or in servitude, nor is anything superinduced. There is nothing that was formerly nonexistent. The Son was never wanting to the Father, nor was the Spirit ever wanting to the Son, but without change and variation the same Trinity endures forever.

A Declaration of Faith is significant as a creed in that it is concerned solely with the Trinity.

In his *Canonical Epistle,* written about 258 or 262, Gregory writes of those Christians who ate things sacrificed to idols or offended in other matters during the time of the barbarian invasion. The epistle is addressed to an anonymous bishop who asks Gregory's advice concerning what transpired during the ravage of the Goths in the time of Gallienus (259-267).

Whatever was forced upon Christians while they were in captivity cannot be charged against them. Externals do not corrupt a man, but a believer is corrupted because of what issues from his heart.

Women who were forcibly defiled in their bodies while in captivity are to be received again among the faithful, unless their past lives give evidence that they willingly submitted to such outrage. The damsel in Deuteronomy who was forcibly violated serves as an example for the manner in which the penitent is to be received. Nothing is to be done to punish such a person, since anyone overcome by violence has committed no sin. If in the past a violated woman has lived in utmost chastity, in a manner free of suspicion and purity, she is not to be blamed for falling into wantonness through force or necessity.

In normal times, Gregory continues, the Church of Christ is to bear no one in her midst who is covetous, for covetousness is a great evil. The Scriptures declare that it is not robbery alone that is to be abhorred, but the grasping mind. The disposition to meddle with what belongs to others in order to satisfy the sordid love of gain is sufficiently wicked to give cause to the Church of God to excommunicate such persons from her number. In times of persecution, only the impious, those who hate God, and are of unsurpassable iniquity, would in the midst of woeful sorrow be audacious enough to consider the crisis which brought destruction to all to be the very moment for aggrandizing their private coffers. It seems good, therefore, writes Gregory, that such heinous offences be punished with excommunication, lest God's wrath descend upon the whole people and first of all upon those who bear the responsibility of an office. Unpunished covetousness is such a crime that the wrath of God may descend upon the righteous. The Christian is to have nothing to do with such persons, for he can have no fellowship with such as do the work of darkness. For, if in time of peace it is unlawful to reap gain at the expense of another, whether an enemy or brother, it is even a more heinous crime when adversity strikes, and one steals from another who has been forced to abandon his possessions. Nor is it lawful to retain the property of others on the pretext that it is but just compensation for one's own property that has been lost.

Those who have descended to such depths as to detain by force certain captives who have made their escape are to be treated as men who know not the name of the Lord, says Gregory. And such sinners as have freely enrolled among the barbarians, committing acts of treason against their fellow countrymen, putting members of their own race to death, are to be debarred from the congregation of the Lord, even as listeners, at least until some common decision has been reached by the saints with respect to them.

Those who have invaded the houses of others, or who have taken what the barbarians left behind, and have been tried and convicted, ought not to be permitted into the congregation even as listeners, but if they themselves voluntarily make restitution, they should be put in the rank of the repentant.

Christians who have been faithful ought to demand no reward, nor recompense, nor any acknowledgment. For their behavior was no more than fitting for one who knows the Lord.

Certain other writings attributed to Gregory, *A Sectional Confession of Faith, A Discourse on the Trinity, Twelve Topics on the Faith,* a discourse *On the Soul, Four Homilies, On the Saints,* and *On the Gospel of Matthew* are generally regarded as belonging to other authors of a later date.

The reputation of Gregory made him the subject of legendary lore that was propagated long after his death, and his surname Thaumaturgus, "wonder-worker," testifies that miracles were then regarded as rare.

His address in honor of Origen sheds further light on Origen's character, for Origen is described as one who disclaims any virtue on his own part and extols true piety and faith in the living God as the parent of all justice, temperance, courage, and prudence. The panegyric is one of the most important sources concerning Origen's personality and teaching, and it is a document of the first importance for Christian education in this period.

Gregory's works are of importance, for they show the early attempts of all the Ante-Nicene doctors to work out the formulas of orthodoxy. That they used inept theological phrases, which lack skill and precision, is to be expected when the immensity of their labors and the variety of their works is taken into consideration.

AGAINST CELSUS

Author: Origen (c.185-c.254)
Type of work: Christian apologetics
First transcribed: c.246-249

Principal Ideas Advanced

Christianity is its own best witness or proof, refuting by its practice the arguments of its opponents.

The antiquity of the Old Testament with its prophecies of Christ provides a ground for refuting all charges that the Bible borrowed from pagan religions, and it rules out dependence on the Greek philosophers.

Most philosophical arguments against Christianity can be neutralized by opposing arguments from other schools of philosophy.

The mass appeal of Christianity should not obscure the fact that the leaders of the Church are educated and that the Church requires a long period of catechetical training.

The Holy Scriptures properly interpreted provide a more than adequate defense of Christianity against paganism and philosophy.

Origen's eight books *Against Celsus* rank as the outstanding apologetic work of the first three centuries. The work is the intellectual equal of Augustine's *City of God.* With Origen the Church met the pagan philosophers on fully equal terms. Indeed Origen seems better acquainted with the different schools and systems of Greek philosophy than was his opponent, Celsus.

Celsus wrote his attack on Christianity under the title, *True Discourse* or *True Doctrine* in about 178. The attack was little noticed at the time, and we would probably know nothing of its contents had not Origen preserved a substantial part of it in citations throughout his *Contra Celsum.* It was, moreover, only at the request of his patron, Ambrose, that Origen took note of Celsus and prepared his great defense of Christianity. Indeed, the preface suggests that in the face of false accusations Christianity has always done best to remain silent, for the lives of Christ's disciples are a sufficient witness of Christian truth. The doctrines of Celsus can be recognized as false doctrines by anyone who knows Christianity, Origen argues. Still, for the sake of the unknowledgeable and the weak in faith, Origen overcame his reluctance and went on to produce eight long books, each averaging seventy-five sections or chapters in length.

The reader of *Against Celsus* is struck immediately by Origen's extensive use of Scripture, both Old Testament and New. Most other apologists made little appeal to Scripture because their pagan audiences were not willing to credit the Bible with authority. Thus, most other apologetic appeals were made to reason and morality. Origen, however, was a Biblical theologian, and he found answers to every question in the Holy Scriptures. He usually interpreted the Bible in three senses, literal, moral, and allegorical, and thus he achieved a great deal of freedom of interpretation.

Besides relying on Scriptures, Origen also made use of his predecessors, the second century apologists, Justin Martyr (c.100-c.165), Theophilus (later second century), and Athenagoras (fl.177). These early apologists used many of the arguments of Hellenistic Judaism in defense of monotheism and the antiquity of Old Testament prophecy. Origen showed a marked advance beyond them, however, in his wide use of the arguments of the philosophers. This use was possible because of the many rivalries among the latter. The Stoics, for example, believed in providence, and their arguments could be used against the Epicureans and Peripatetics who did not. Whatever school of philosophy Celsus turned to, Origen could employ the teachings of its opponents, in all of whom he was well-versed. An incidental result is that *Against Celsus* is a valuable source of information about early philosophy.

Among the general charges against Christianity to which Celsus continually returned were that Christianity is barbarian in origin and a newcomer among religions, that it is for the uneducated and irrational, and that it is disloyal to the Emperor and therefore dangerous to the Empire. It is noteworthy that Celsus did not dwell at length on the old charges of immorality and vice. In fact, he recognized the worth of Christian morals and also that of the Logos doctrine.

The first book of *Contra Celsum* responds to the fairly common accusation that the Christians formed a secret society which engaged in magical and barbarous practices. This charge, Origen writes, reflects an outsider's point of view and is easily enough dismissed. The simplicity of the Christian faith, which offends some philosophers, is really a virtue when this faith is placed in God and not in some man. The person of Jesus serves as an example of wisdom, power, and leadership arising from humble origins, and together with the traditional arguments from prophecy and the Virgin Birth it points to His divinity. At this point in Book I, Origen is considering the objections made by an imaginary Jew whom Celsus introduced in his treatise to present certain traditional Jewish objections to Christianity, but Origen was too skillful an interpreter of the Old Testament to let any literary convention upset his careful analysis and refutation of the arguments advanced by Celsus. Origen employs interpretations developed by his predecessors to meet Jewish polemics, as, for example, that of a double advent, which accounts for the differences between those prophecies which describe Christ as a suffering servant and those which describe Him as a glorious king.

Book II deals further with the arguments of Celsus' Jew. Origen refers to the Jewish-Christians who have not abandoned the Law and the Prophets in any sense. He considers also the Jews' rejection of Christ and denies that this act in any way invalidates Christ, especially since it was already prophesied in the Old Testament. The fulfillment of prophecy becomes the main defense of Christianity in this book. The difficulties presented to the non-Christian mind by the accounts of the Passion of Christ, always a problem for Greeks, are met in this way as well as by comparisons with the Greek myths. The Resurrection also comes under discussion as a traditional difficulty for philosophic minds. As if finally to silence Celsus' spokesman, Origen observes that Jews had a long record of disbelief in God even before Christ and so it is no surprise that they rejected Him.

With Book III the defense against the arguments presented by Celsus on his own commences. Celsus held that the disagreements between Jews and

Christians militate against both. Origen's reply is a summary consideration of the question as to which religion better understands the prophets. The argument that the Church is divided against itself in numerous sects is refuted by reference to the differences among philosophers. Such disputes do not prevent Celsus from trusting in philosophy. Origen is able, moreover, to compare the unity and dignity of the Church to the divisions among pagan religious groups and their unseemly practices and beliefs. The honor paid to Jesus, which Celsus protested, can be shown to be fully deserved by His miraculous works, which excel anything done by pagan deities. The charges that Christianity is for the ignorant and foolish or for the masses, especially for women and boys, are met by reference to the Scriptures where such examples as Solomon and Daniel reveal the greatest wisdom and where Paul's description of a bishop's qualifications shows the true meaning of worldly foolishness and divine wisdom. Nor does the Church appeal to the public indiscriminately. It seeks all men but seeks to educate them in its doctrines and way of life. The Church accepts sinners because sinners are the very ones who need to be saved, but Celsus seems to object to the practice, notes Origen, mainly on the ground that the sinners thereby lose the counsel of philosopher-physicians.

The attack of Celsus which Origen answers in Book IV of *Against Celsus* centers around the Incarnation. How or why should God come down to men? Both Jews and Christians are wrong in expecting such an unreasonable event. This line of thought gives Origen occasion to expand on the divine plan and the gracious nature of God. The use of punishments or terrors to reform men, to which Celsus objects, is justified for the sake of improving the race. Origen explains certain of the actions of God such as the Incarnation as the necessary adaptation of spiritual food for the conditions of men. A considerable discussion of the narratives in Genesis is found in this book, perhaps because Genesis was the Biblical book most familiar to the pagans. Origen uses allegorical interpretation freely, especially for the anthropomorphical descriptions of God. He argues that the legends of the Greeks are more to be scorned than those of the Old Testament. In the end he exposes the irrationality of Celsus in exalting the powers of animals in respect to divination and knowledge of God's ways.

The fifth book opens with a discussion of the worship of heavenly bodies. Celsus argued that since the Christians worshiped God in Heaven, they might as well worship the stars. Origen replies that it is wrong to worship the objects of the Creator which themselves worship Him. The refutation turns next to the doctrine of the resurrection of the body, a doctrine which seemed unreasonable and even undesirable to Celsus; but all things are possible for God, Origen counters, and it is He who determines what is good. To the objection that the Christians depart from the traditional customs of the Jews, which are tolerable because traditional, Origen replies that such customs may often be both impious and evil. Tradition is, or at least can be, simply superstition, which would be unphilosophical to follow. Other topics for discussion are the names of God and the activity of the angels.

Origen demonstrates that names do make a difference and that even some Greeks have believed in angels. He also attributed many of the ideas objected to by Celsus to Gnostic and Jewish-Christian sects; and thus he protected orthodox Christianity.

Book VI of *Contra Celsum* returns again to the problem of education. Origen observes that many of the leaders of the Church have in fact been educated men. Moreover, Christian teaching is not simply Plato misunderstood. Thereafter follows a lengthy discourse on the meaning of numbers and symbols as used in the diagrams of the cosmos by the Gnostics. Out of this discourse emerges the problem of evil and Satan, a problem which is solved, Origen argues, by the New Testament. Origen goes on to explain the relationship of Jesus, the Son, to God, the Father. He follows up this discussion, occasioned by Gnostic cosmogonies which made places for both Satan and Jesus, with an explanation of the creation of the world according to Scripture. Celsus had, however, presented all these matters in order to question the possibility of knowing God, and it is with this question that the next book is concerned.

Book VII looks first at oracles and prophetic spirits that claim to know the will of God. Origen argues that the pagan oracles cannot be compared to the Christian prophets, nor can the latter be judged on the basis of false prophets who have arisen. The Holy Scriptures alone are authoritative. It is these that have prophesied the incarnation of the Word.

At this point Origen expounds his ante-Nicene Christology with its distribution of Christ's activities among the two natures. He tends to equate the soul with the Logos in Christ. He also takes the occasion to clarify the doctrine of the Resurrection again. He argues that Celsus attributed inappropriate ideas and statements to the Christians and that he was not even consistent in his picture of them. The Christians have in effect a direct source of knowledge of God in the Scriptures, and they do not need the philosophical approaches to this knowledge. God has, in addition, spoken to men through Jesus Christ. Origen concludes this book with an attack on images and demon worship.

The final book of *Against Celsus* is essentially a defense of monotheism. Christians cannot serve two masters, Origen argues, and it is misleading of Celsus to describe Christ and God as two gods. The witness of the Bible is that they are one. Naturally any worship of demons is excluded even if they are subordinate to God. Thus, Christians properly honor God when they scorn demons, magic, astrology, and emperor-worship. Nonetheless, Christians are loyal to the state even when they decline to accept public office because their divine services and prayers benefit all mankind.

Origen wrote his apology not merely to refute Celsus but primarily to convert the learned pagans of his acquaintance at Alexandria and Caesarea. It was to such persons that Celsus' arguments against Christianity probably appealed. Origen wanted to prove to them that Christianity was a sound philosophy as well as a sound religion, and that it was not only moral and patriotic but also intellectually respectable. We cannot say who read this work, but the very fact that it has come down to us in its original Greek text would indicate that many copies were in circulation. Certainly no better apology had been prepared for the educated classes prior to this one; and, as it turned out, not many more apologies were to be needed to aid in bringing about, in the next century, the granting of official status to Christianity.

INSTRUCTIONS IN FAVOR OF CHRISTIAN DISCIPLINE

Author: Commodianus (Commodian, fl. c.250)
Type of work: Apologetics
First transcribed: Third century

Principal Ideas Advanced

The worship of pagan gods is foolish, for what came into existence and what passes away cannot truly be a god.

Man's salvation is to be found in the keeping of the law of Christ, for He alone has redeemed mankind and will return as the conqueror of the Antichrist, as the judge of the wicked, and as the rewarder of those who have diligently served Him by their works of righteousness.

Little is known about the life of Commodianus, except that he was apparently a North African bishop in the third century. His extant work (which is in Latin verse) reflects the earnestness and piety—and, at the same time, the paucity of learning and theological skill—of a practical Christian whose *Instructions in Favor of Christian Discipline* was written against the pagans. The work is a series of eighty poems, each on a different subject and combined in no particular order.

Commodianus writes that he seeks to instruct those who worship pagan gods; his desire is to supplant ignorance by the truth which he himself found by reading God's word. Eternal life is to be found only in the law of God, which forbids the worship of idols made with human hands. When the Jews were delivered from Egypt, God enjoined them to serve Him alone. The law teaches of the Resurrection and gives hope of happiness in the world.

The many gods that pagans pray to are not gods at all, Commodianus writes. To beautify nature, the true God decreed that angels visit the earth. But the angels that were sent down were contaminated by beautiful women, and hence they were not allowed to return to Heaven. Their descendants, who were said to be giants, made known the arts upon the earth; and when the descendants died, images were erected to them. Since God did allow the demons to be brought back from death, their spirits wander to and fro perverting those who worship them as gods.

The worship of such gods as Saturn, Jupiter, the Stars, the Sun and Moon, Neptune, Hercules, and numerous other gods and goddesses, is sheer folly. Men are seduced by the stories of the poets. Saturn grew old on earth and died. The sun and moon are not to be worshiped; they do not run of their own accord, but were placed in the heavens on the fourth day of creation by the omnipotent Creator who, in His law, commanded that none should worship them.

Man shares the nature of whatever god or goddess he worships. Bacchus, for example, is honored in the midst of drunken orgies. Man is mad to worship the gods of the heavens, gods who were born, who grow old and die. To believe tales about such gods is to believe the lies of a few wicked and empty poets; it is to be the victim of deceit and abominable superstition. A prudent man, says Commodianus, cannot worship a log and call it a deity. To seek what is healthy is to seek the righteousness of the law that brings eternal salvation. To rise again with Christ, man must abandon the wickedness and blindness of the world. The Lord God has permitted demons to wander in the world for man's discipline, but He has ordered that those who forsake the altars of demons shall become dwellers in Heaven.

God will judge those who have chosen the wrong path and who live in wanton gluttony, outside the law, turning their backs upon the God of life, whose desire it is that man will live, not perish in an evil place.

It is mere foolishness, Commodianus writes, to delay in acknowledging Christ, for those who believe in Him will live forever. Whoever believes in Him who was dead will rise again and live for all time, but those who do not believe will undergo a second death; their present joy and luxury will be short-lived; they will suffer the torments of Hell forever. The life of this world is not the true one, Commodianus insists; it is an error to believe that the soul dies with the body. A cruel Hell has been prepared for the wicked. A man does not escape from God when he dies; the dead are not extinct; death is not a mere vacuity. Mortal man is separated from his body, but he is brought back for judgment, to be punished according to his deeds.

Goodness, righteousness, peace, and true patience end in happiness with Christ; an evil mind ends in terrible punishments, in burning fire. Those who are rich in the things of this world ought therefore to humble themselves and to become grateful to God. It is foolish to cling to material possessions and to neglect God's holy law. Whatever a man possesses belongs to God alone, for He made the world and now rules it by His power.

The foolish rich man does not know the time of his departure from this world; he is proud and haughty, and he is uncharitable to the poor; he dishonors God and his fellows. But such an evildoer shall not escape the wrath to come, for his god is his belly, and he is lover of gold.

Both Jews and gentiles should desist from their rejection of Christ, Commodianus writes, for the time will soon come when it will no longer be possible to repent. God Himself has died for us, and Christ will again appear, after the time of the Antichrist. The end of the world will witness the resurrection of Nero, who shall be brought up from Hell. He will reconquer Rome and rage against the Christians. Nero, however, will be conquered by the Antichrist from the East, who will burn Rome, then return to Judea, perform false miracles, and deceive many. Finally, when Christ returns, He will destroy the armies of the Antichrist and convert all nations. Judgment will then take place and the earth will be destroyed by fire.

Commodianus advises that every true believer should live a godly life. Catechumens who fall into error should, when admonished, return to the true faith, leaving all for Christ. The newly converted believer must guard against falling into his old sins and consequently into despair.

The faithful are not to hold their brethren in hatred, Commodianus writes, but are to walk in love, free from strife, shunning all great sins and all evil deeds. The Christian is not to meet force with force. He should even willingly accept martyrdom. Worldly things are to be avoided absolutely; neither the world nor anything in it is to be loved. A believing man is not to live in the pleasures of the world as do the gentiles; his joy is in Christ, and his refreshment is found in giving help and encouragement to the martyr.

The Christian on the path to martyrdom ought to live a godly life, for martyrdom is suited to the blessed and is to be desired only by those who first live well. It is an error to believe that our blood overcomes the wicked one. Only good deeds conquer Satan; if the Christian performs good deeds, he is already a martyr, and he can feel secure.

The true Christian is to labor in the Lord, to wage a daily war in which he restrains all lust, lives temperately, represses rage. He must be peaceable to all men, a protector of all, a man free from jealousy, without envy, and charitable to everyone.

Ministers are to be an example to the people, Commodianus writes; they are to be submissive to the commands of their Master, always looking upward to the supreme God.

The sick are to be cared for, and food is to be shared with the needy; the hungry and the thirsty are not to be dismissed with mere words. The Christian is to live soberly before his Lord; the women are to conduct themselves in all modesty and chastity, avoiding pomp and vain apparel; men, in meekness and faith, are to serve God in all things. As the servant of God, the Christian has no end other than to please God by doing that of which the Lord approves. Simplicity and meekness are to dwell in his body. When six thousand years have passed, Commodianus predicts, the world will come to an end; the thousand years during which Christ is the ruler will terminate, and Christ will finally judge the wicked and reward the faithful.

ON THE UNITY OF THE CATHOLIC CHURCH

Author: Saint Cyprian of Carthage (c.200-258)
Type of work: Ecclesiology
First transcribed: c.251

Principal Ideas Advanced

The true Church of Jesus Christ was founded upon one man, Peter, in order that its essential unity might be clearly demonstrated; later, all the Apostles were given powers and honors equal to those originally bestowed upon Peter, and they in turn passed on the one office which each possessed in its fullness to the bishops.

The episcopate, therefore, is a single whole which binds the Church into a visible unity, each bishop bearing a responsibility for the entire Church, since the entire Church is present in the one office in which he has a share.

There can be no salvation apart from the Church presided over by the unity of bishops; schismatics and heretics can inherit none of the promises made to the Church, for they have deserted the Church.

The treatise *De ecclesiae unitate* is unquestionably the best known and most important of all the works of the great African martyr-bishop Cyprian. Few attempts to define the nature of the Church have proved to be as widely read and influential as this one. Much of the credit for the popularity which the *De unitate* has enjoyed down through the centuries must be given to the aphoristic style which Cyprian employed with great effectiveness. Such statements as "You cannot have God for your father unless you have the church for your mother" and "He who rends and divides the church cannot possess the garment of Christ" probably account for much of the abiding fame of the treatise as a whole.

In addition to being his most important and best-known work, the *De unitate* is also the most controversial of all of Cyprian's writings. The controversy is due to the fact that the text of the treatise exists in two different forms. In one version—generally called the "episcopalian" or *Textus receptus* —the emphasis is clearly upon the equality of all bishops within the Church. According to the other version, however, the primacy of Peter is stressed in such a way as to suggest that Cyprian recognized the supremacy of the Roman bishop.

In the past, scholarship has tended to divide along denominational lines on this issue, Roman Catholics claiming that the "primacy" text was the original and Protestants claiming that the primacy phrases had been interpolated into the original "episcopalian" text by later champions of papal authority.

More recent scholarship, however, has demonstrated rather convincingly that both versions are genuine, and that historical circumstances in the life of Cyprian were responsible for his issuing the same treatise in two different forms.

The circumstances, briefly, were these: in the year 251, Cyprian was moved to write a treatise on the unity of the Church because of schisms which had occurred not only in his own Church at Carthage, but also in the Church of Rome. The Roman schism, in particular, seems to have been in his mind as he attempted to define the meaning and nature of the Church's unity. In Rome, the presbyter Novatian had had himself consecrated as bishop in opposition to the legitimate bishop Cornelius. For Cyprian it was unthinkable that the same Church could be divided and presided over by two bishops, since the bishop, according to Cyprian, was meant to be the visible symbol of the unity of the Church. Although he seems to have wavered for a time in deciding which of the two men he should recognize as the legitimate occupant of the episcopal office in Rome, he finally decided in favor of Cornelius and then turned all his energies to healing the schism.

In order to impress upon the Romans the necessity for submitting to the one lawful bishop of that city, Cyprian appealed to the Petrine origins of the Church. Peter was chosen as the founder of the Church, he insisted, in order that the essential unity of the Church might be clearly demonstrated. This unity was later represented by the entire apostolic college and then by the successors of the Apostles, the bishops, all of whom were made to share in the one episcopal authority bestowed upon Peter. In every church, therefore, there should be a recognition and zealous preservation of the unity which the bishop personifies, but especially in the Church of Rome where the bishop actually sits upon the *Cathedra* or chair once occupied by Peter, the symbol of the Church's oneness.

It is in this context that the famous statement in the "primacy" text must be understood— "He who deserts the chair of Peter on whom the church was founded, does he trust that he is in the church?" Cyprian's intention in this passage was not to bestow upon the Roman bishop a jurisdiction wider than his own See, but rather to claim for the legitimate occupant of the chair of Peter an exclusive authority over all the Christians in Rome.

A later development in the relations between Cyprian and the Roman Church caused the African to reconsider some of the expressions which he had used in the original version of the *De unitate.* The Church of Rome and the Church of North Africa had different practices with respect to the admission of former heretics and schismatics. Cyprian and his African colleagues insisted upon their rebaptism, whereas the Roman Church did not. Stephan, who succeeded to the Roman episcopate in 254, tried to force the Roman practice upon the North Africans, but he was firmly resisted by Cyprian. To prevent the inference that he himself had previously recognized the right of the Roman bishop to interfere in the affairs of other churches in the original version of the *De unitate,* Cyprian removed the so-called primacy phrases from the treatise about the year 256. The removal of these passages from the text in no way changed Cyprian's basic point of view on the nature of the Church but simply removed the possibility of a papalistic exploitation of the strong Roman orientation of the original version.

In spite of the fact that the *De unitate* was written during one of the most severe persecutions which the Church has ever undergone, Cyprian showed himself to be more concerned about the problems of internal subversion than about external attack. Since the Devil had failed to destroy the Church through persecution, Cyprian noted, he had devised a new method of assault in which the Christians themselves accomplished his purposes by causing dissensions and schisms in the Church.

In addition to schismatics like Novatian (fl. c. 250), one of the most frequent sources of discord and dissension in the Church was the group known as Confessors. These were the Christians who had witnessed to their faith in the face of persecution, many of them undergoing severe torture but without actually being put to death. It was natural that the Confessors should be accorded an exalted position in the Church, but often, as Cyprian discovered, the honors and powers which were bestowed upon them—particularly the power to grant pardon to those who had apostatized during the persecutions—interfered with the established order and discipline of the Church. Cyprian regarded any usurpation of clerical prerogatives by the Confessors as a breach of the unity of the Church and refused to consider the conventicles which formed around the Confessors as expressions of the true Church. The Confessors, like all Christians, were expected to submit to the established authorities and officials of the Church rather than cause discord by presuming to possess powers which belonged only to the clergy.

The passages in the *De unitate* which deal with the Confessors are particularly significant, for they indicate that for Cyprian the unity which he was so anxious to preserve depended mainly upon submission to the visible authorities and officials of the Church. A heroic witness to the faith was completely meaningless unless it was made by one who belonged to the visible organization presided over by a legitimate bishop. Even if a schismatic should be put to death confessing the name of Christ, he could not be saved, for nothing could atone for the great sin of breaking the unity of the Church except a return to the organization which embodied that unity.

For Cyprian, any refusal to conform to the established episcopal structure of the Church was construed as an act of apostasy or adultery. There could be no possible justification for deserting the Church which was presided over by legitimate bishops, since Cyprian held it to be axiomatic that the presence of a legitimate bishop meant the presence of Christ. It was, of course, equally axiomatic that to be separated from the bishop and the unity which he personified was to be separated from Christ.

The motives for leaving the Church which Cyprian most frequently imputed to the schismatics were pride and greed. If the schismatics had been motivated by charity rather than by personal ambition, they would have been willing to submit themselves to the Church and thus preserve its unity. From what we know about the schismatic groups which sprang up in North Africa and Rome in the third century there is no reason to dispute the unworthy and basically selfish motives which Cyprian imputed to them. Thus, it is possible to sympathize, to a degree, with the rigid attitude which he took toward these particular groups. It is not so easy, however, to sympathize with Cyprian's complete identification of the unity of the Church with its visible organization and his conclusion that every protest against and departure from its organization places one outside the saving purpose of the Lord of the Church.

EXTANT FRAGMENTS OF THE WORKS OF DIONYSIUS

Author: Dionysius the Great (c.200-c.265)
Type of work: Theology of the early Church
First transcribed: Third century

Principal Ideas Advanced

The notion of an earthly, thousand-year reign of Christ is not supported by Scripture; however, the canonicity of the book of Revelation is not to be rejected, since its deeper meaning is found in a nonliteral sense which underlies its words.

The author of the book of Revelation was not the Apostle John, but an inspired person called John, as can be ascertained by a comparison between the style of both the gospel and the epistles of the Apostle John and the style of Revelation.

It is further alleged that the universe in which we live is not the result of the chance collision of atoms moving in space but is ordered by the providential power of the omnipotent Deity that brought it into being.

For our knowledge of the career of Dionysius the Great, Bishop of Alexandria, we are indebted to the sixth and seventh books of Eusebius's *Historia ecclesiastica* and the fourteenth book of his *Praeparatio evangelica,* as well as to other references in Jerome, Athanasius, and Basil. Only fragments remain of Dionysius's many theological treatises. What remains, however, is of importance to us in that the *Extant Fragments of the Works of Dionysius* provides the historian of Christianity with a valuable account of the life of the Church in the third century.

Dionysius was born of heathen parents. He studied pagan philosophy and later embraced Christianity under the influence of Origen's teaching. In about 232, Dionysius succeeded Heracles as the head of the catechetical school in Alexandria, and he later became the Bishop of that city in about 247, an office which he held until his death, about 265. His tenure as Bishop was far from tranquil, for the period in which he held office was marked by persecution and theological controversy. Dionysius was himself arrested during the Decian persecution and was freed by a fortunate uprising of the populace of a rural district through which he was being transported. During the persecution under Valerian, which began in 257, Dionysius was driven into exile for two or three years. On other occasions he was forced to deal with pestilence and famine as well as civil conflicts.

Dionysius also played a prominent role in the ecclesiastical controversy of his day. He served as arbitrator in a dispute concerning the rebaptism of heretics, and he zealously opposed the Sabellian heresy, although in a manner which later led him to acknowledge his own errors. In all his activities Dionysius displayed an independent spirit of investigation which won him the respect of his contemporaries. He was held in the highest esteem for his learning, moderation, and remarkably productive pen.

The most important of his writings

are his *Treatise on the Promises, A Book on Nature,* and *A Work Against the Sabellians.* Two large abstracts of the *Treatise on the Promises,* written in two books against Nepos, have been preserved by Eusebius.

Nepos was an Egyptian bishop who interpreted certain promises of the Scriptures in such a manner as to lend support to a literal thousand year period on earth that would be replenished with corporeal pleasures. His work entitled the *Refutation of the Allegorists* sought to establish his view of the millennial period on the basis of the New Testament book of Revelation.

Dionysius sharply attacked Nepos's opinion that Christ will establish a temporal reign on earth; at the same time, in a spirit of Christian love, Dionysius expressed his appreciation of Nepos's faith and labors.

The situation in the Church was such, Dionysius declared, that errors had to be opposed, for truth is the primary concern of those who follow Christ. Certain teachers, he contended, held that the law and the prophets are of no importance; they disparaged the gospels and the epistles, and did not concede that the simpler brethren had any conceptions of Christ's appearing in His glory and true divinity, or of our own resurrection from the dead and of our being united to Him at the last day. Such teachers led the people to hope only for what is trivial and corruptible.

Christians ought to be satisfied to accept only that which can be established by the demonstrations and teachings of the Holy Scriptures, Dionysius wrote. What cannot be so established ought neither to be discussed, taught, nor mentioned, if the harmony of the brethren is to be maintained.

The book of Revelation had been the cause of much dissension, and Dionysius, writing in the third century, mentions that some had set it aside, repudiated it entirely, and criticized it chapter by chapter. The critics of the book, Dionysius reports, denied that John the Apostle was its author and held that it could not be revelation because it is too difficult to understand. It is alleged that Cerinthus, the founder of a heretical sect, sought to give authority to his own notion that Christ will establish an earthly reign, a sensuous kingdom in which bodily pleasures are satisfied. Cerinthus, therefore, attributed his own opinions to the Apostle John, so that in fact the book of Revelation was not written by an Apostle but by a heretic.

Dionysius was, however, unwilling to reject the canonicity of Revelation, although he acknowledged that he was himself unable to comprehend its full import. Many brethren value it highly, Dionysius writes, and it undoubtedly contains much hidden and wonderful intelligence, with a deeper meaning underlying the words. Its authorship is not the work of the Apostle John, the Son of Zebedee and the brother of James, as is evident from a study of its style when compared with the Gospel and epistles of John the Apostle. It was, rather, written by a holy and inspired writer whose name was John. The Apostle John nowhere affixes his name to his writings. Which John wrote the book of Revelation is uncertain, but the fact that its author is unknown in no way disparages its authority or makes it the object of ridicule.

In his *Book on Nature,* preserved in part by Eusebius in his *Praeparatio evangelica,* Dionysius opposes the school of Epicurus, which denied the existence of Providence and insisted that the universe is made up of atomic bodies.

Dionysius argued that it is folly to attribute the universe to an infinite unoriginated matter that holds sway without the aid of divine Providence. To make the constructions of the universe the work of a chance combination of an infinite number of atoms jostling one another in a space of infinite vastness overlooks the analogies even of the small familiar things which come under observation. For no object of any utility, which is fitted to be serviceable, is made by mere chance, but comes into being by design, and is wrought by the skill of the hand, so as to serve its proper use. The notion of chance combinations of atoms is unable to explain the design and order of the world that is experienced by the senses. It is an idle speculation, beyond all observable experience and conception. The Christian is far wiser who confesses to God that the order of the world must be attributed to God Himself. Referring to the atomists, Dionysius writes, "But when they assert now that those things of grace and beauty, which they declare to be textures finely wrought out of atoms, are fabricated spontaneously by these bodies without either wisdom or perception in them, who can endure to hear them talk in such terms of those unregulated atoms, than which even the spider, that plies its proper craft of itself, is gifted with more sagacity."

The body of man and of the universe in all its parts was composed by the providence of an all-wise Father and maker, not by a blind deified nature, Dionysius concludes; the very heavens declare God's glory and show forth his handiwork.

The remaining works of Dionysius that we possess have been handed down to us by Athanasius and Basil and consist for the most part of certain unguarded statements made during the Sabellian controversy, together with letters and a few exegetical fragments.

THE DIVINE INSTITUTES

Author: Lucius Caecilius Firmianus Lactantius (c.240-c.320)
Type of work: Christian apologetics
First transcribed: 304-313

Principal Ideas Advanced

The chief sources of error in human life are pagan polytheism, which ignores or denies the true God, and philosophy, which is undermined by its own contradictions.

True wisdom is found in the religion derived from God the Lord and Father and from Jesus Christ, and this religion rewards man for virtue with the highest good, immortality.

Justice, or true equity, which, together with the true worship of God, was banished under paganism, has been restored by Jesus Christ.

The world looks now toward its own destruction and the judgment of Christ over the virtuous and the wicked in His thousand-year Kingdom.

Lactantius was one of several pagan teachers and writers who became important spokesmen for Christianity after conversion in later life. As an apologist, he employed all the skills acquired as a teacher of rhetoric in the preparation of one of the longest and most eloquent treatises on Christianity up to his day. The *Divine Institutes* was directed to the Emperor Constantine (c.288-337) whom Lactantius later (c.317) served as tutor for Constantine's son Crispus. The work, in seven books, was intended to inform the emperor of the errors of paganism, the injustices done to Christianity, and the nature of true religion and worship. It is really the first systematic account in Latin of the Christian attitude toward life, although it stands in a tradition shaped by the earlier Latin-speaking fathers Tertullian (c.160-220), Minucius Felix (fl.195), Cyprian (c.200-258), and Lactantius' own teacher, Arnobius of Sicca (fl.300). Its distinctive aim was to use a high level of style and language and classical erudition to appeal to literate readers. The success of Lactantius in achieving this aim brought him the epithet, the Christian Cicero, and was to make him very popular among the humanists of Renaissance Italy.

The first two books of the *Divinae institutiones* form a concentrated attack on the errors of paganism. Polytheism is the root of all these errors. It is obvious, writes Lactantius, that there can, logically speaking, be only one God, and the prophets, poets, philosophers, Sibylline Oracles, and Hermes Trismegistus (the Egyptian god Thoth) may be adduced as evidence. Homer and Hesiod show us how unworthy the lives of the gods are, and the Stoic interpretations fail to make them more acceptable. If the gods are merely apotheosized men, as seems often to be the case, they do not deserve to be worshiped. Indeed there is nothing about the pagan deities deserving of worship. Their images are made by men, and, if anyone, man should be worshiped as their maker. Since everything in nature and the universe points to God, a right exercise of reason would lead men away from polytheism.

In all this discussion of paganism some reference is made to the Bible in regard to the creation of the world and the fallen angels, but the main body of references is to classical literature and philosophy, of which Lactantius has an excellent command. He openly acknowledges his preference for authorities that will convince an unconverted audience. At the same time he does not hesitate to chastise the pagan writers for leading men into error.

The third book of the *Institutes* takes up the "false wisdom" of the philosophers, another significant source of error. Lactantius stresses, as does the Bible, that truth is superior to eloquence, although he does not hesitate to employ eloquence where appropriate. Insofar as philosophy seeks the truth, it is made up of "knowledge" and conjecture, but the latter is, of course, to be dismissed outright. When the "knowledge" of philosophy is then examined, it is found that the different systems of philosophy contradict or deny one another, thereby disproving themselves completely. Only one philosopher, Arcesilas (c.315-c.240 B.C.), recognized that all other philosophers know nothing. He therefore changed the character of philosophy into complete skepticism by denying even the possibility of knowledge; but here he went too far, Lactantius claims, for truth is possible in dependence on God.

Turning next to moral philosophy, Lactantius maintains that the chief good, the *summum bonum,* must be something peculiar to man and the human soul. It must be something which requires knowledge and virtue to be achieved. He concludes that man's chief good is therefore the immortality promised by religion, and not any physical pleasures or even virtue as such. In respect to achieving this good, philosophy generally errs, and philosophers themselves set bad examples in their lives. (Even his beloved Cicero comes in for Lactantius' censure.) Only divine instruction bestows true wisdom, Lactantius insists. To depend on nature or fortune is simply another mistake of the philosophers, for neither nature nor fortune can reward virtue with immortality as God can. (One should note that Lactantius, in rebuking the philosophers, condemns the foolishness of those who believe that the earth is round.)

With the fourth book the emphasis turns to the positive statement of Christian teaching; namely, "true wisdom" and religion. These two, wisdom and religion, are one harmonious whole for Lactantius. They spring as two streams from one fountain; namely, God the Father and Lord. As proof of this argument Lactantius adduces the antiquity of the Old Testament Prophets, who are also witnesses to God's Son, Jesus Christ, through whom true religion is revealed. The Sibylline Oracles and Hermes Trismegistus are again impartial witnesses to Christ. There follows a discussion of the birth of Jesus as the Word of God and then of the preparations in the history of Israel for His earthly birth. The Incarnation receives a good deal of explanation, for the work is being presented to a pagan audience. The life, miracles, passion, death, resurrection, and ascension of Jesus are also narrated and related to prophecy. In the conclusion to the fourth book, Lactantius explains the union of Father and Son and the dangers of heresies.

The two books that follow, on justice and true worship, are often considered the finest of the entire *Institutes.* In Book V the fundamental argument is that Christianity has suffered unjustly under paganism but that true justice will emerge victorious under Christ. After paying tribute to his predecessors, Tertullian, Minucius Felix, and Cyprian, Lactantius sets forth a general defense against all anti-Christian writings. He recounts the decline of justice under the pagan gods, who gave free reign to all sorts of vices. With Jesus, however, justice is being restored because the real origin of justice is in the true religion or piety which Jesus taught. Since only God by His eternal reward can sustain justice, all men must trust Him. The basic principle of justice for Lactantius is equity. Since equity is no respecter of persons or earthly compensations, the Christians alone can remain just and pious despite afflictions. They alone can practice full equity because they alone trust in God, who rewards them.

A similar moralistic emphasis on rewards is found in Lactantius' discussion of true worship. Religion or worship or service to God is the way of virtue. It is the chief duty of man and leads him to Heaven. The way of vice leads, of course, to Hell. All these things are worked out under the unchangeable divine law. Indeed, virtue apart from God is in vain because there is no reward of immortality attached to it.

There is a second aspect of worship or religion; namely, that directed toward one's fellow man. Here the principle is mercy or kindness which forms the bond of human society. Without mercy, vice and error prevail. Yet even acts of mercy are predicated in large measure on God's rewards. Lactantius appeals to the rich at this point with the argument that the greatest advantage of riches is the ability to do deeds of charity.

The sixth book closes with a discussion of human affections and passions and their right use or application. Above all others, patience is exalted as a Christian virtue. In this connection too, the pleasures of the senses are considered and very nearly condemned as a form of earthly recompense that is enjoyed only at the expense of the heavenly. The note of revulsion at the excesses of pagan society, a revulsion which characterizes most early Christian writers, is sounded quite forcefully by Lactantius. Thus, this sixth book seems less a discussion of worship than an extension of the discussion of religion begun in the fifth book and entitled, "Justice." True and complete religion is just and pious and consist in devoted service to God.

The motif of immortality is continued and expanded in the final book of the *Divine Institutes* on the happy life. The end of the world, toward which Lactantius looks, will bring heavenly rewards for the blessed and hellish punishments for the condemned. After demonstrating that the world must have an end and after exposing the errors of the philosophers in this matter, Lactantius discourses on the immortality of the soul of man, for whom the whole creation exists. Man, in turn, exists or, more correctly, was made to acknowledge and worship God, and for this worship he is rewarded. The pattern of creation is based on the six days of Genesis I, and so the world will come to an end after 6000 years and the 1000-year Kingdom of Christ will begin. The end of the world will be marked, of course, by wars, natural disasters, and false prophets. It will also see a loosing of the Devil and, in effect, two judgment days. One of the most unworthy concepts of Lactantius appears in this book when he declares that the wicked will receive indestructible bodies so that they can endure the torments of eternal fire forever. The *Institutes* closes with an exhortation to virtue.

However eloquent a spokesman for Christianity Lactantius may have been, he was clearly not a theologian. He is obviously ante-Nicene in his Christology. He has no doctrine of or place for the Holy Spirit in his writings. The Church and the Sacraments are hardly mentioned at all. Nor is it surprising that he never occupied an official ecclesiastical position, for he was perhaps sixty years old at the time of his conversion. His zeal to do something for Christianity must, however, be admired. The special talents which, as a layman, he did possess, he gave freely to the writing of the *Institutes.* If this work is often moralistic and theologically superficial, nonsacramental, and even unorthodox, it nevertheless reveals what many people took to be the general intent of the Christian faith. That such a work found a place in the Church of the fourth century is indicated by the preparation of an *Epitome of the Institutes* a few years after its completion. It remains true, on the other hand, that the need for apologetics was lessened after recognition of the Church by the Empire, and the writings of Lactantius do not figure in the great theological controversies of the following generations.

THE INCARNATION OF THE WORD OF GOD

Author: Saint Athanasius (c.296-373)
Type of work: Christology
First transcribed: c.318

Principal Ideas Advanced

Contrary to the opinions of unbelievers, the Incarnation of the divine Word (Logos) was entirely plausible and fitting.

Out of love for men, and in order to uphold the divine purpose, salvation has been accomplished by the same One who created in the beginning.

Through the Incarnation, the progressive sinful degeneration of mankind has been checked, human nature has been restored to the image of God, and the knowledge of God has spread abroad in the world, awakening faith, hope, and love.

The crucifixion of the Incarnate Word was necessary to preserve the consistency of the divine judgment upon man's willful disobedience, but in the Word's death and resurrection, death itself was destroyed.

Athanasius is revered in the history of the Church as the saintly orthodox champion in the long, hard, and eventually successful fourth century struggle against Arianism. The latter maintained that Christ was the incarnation of an intermediate, secondary deity, "like," but not one with, the Highest. The teaching that prevailed was that of the Nicene Creed, that the God united with man in Christ is the same as—"of one substance with"—the ultimate and only God. But between the Council of Nicea in 325, and the Council of Constantinople in 381, the issue was often in grave doubt. During these critical decades Athanasius gave the orthodox party decisive intellectual and moral leadership. Exiled five times, he was by 366 at last triumphant and died seven years later as Patriarch of Alexandria, his native city. From earliest youth Athanasius was no stranger to persecution, having lived through the severe one launched in 303 by the Roman emperor Diocletian. The behavior of Christians facing death made a deep impression on him, as *The Incarnation of the Word of God* shows. Most scholars believe that Athanasius wrote it about 318, when he was barely twenty, and before the outbreak of the Arian conflict.

One of two small treatises (the other being the *Contra gentes*) prepared for the instruction of a recent convert, *The Incarnation of the Word of God* undertakes a "brief statement of the faith of Christ and of the manifestation of His Godhead to us." This purpose, drawing upon what fellow Christians could take for granted, enhances its value as an expression of what the faith was in the Alexandria of that time. The work is not a systematic treatise on all aspects of the Incarnation; the main theme is the redemption of the world by the Incarnate Word; redemption is *theiosis,* deification.

In the companion treatise (the *Contra gentes*), after discussing heathen idol worship and how it arose, Athanasius had sketched the rudiments of the Christian belief in the divinity of the Word (Logos), through whom God the Father creates and governs the universe. Now, he tells Marcarius, the convert whom he is instructing, they must take the further step of considering the Word's becoming man. This mystery, which "the Jews traduce, the Greeks deride, but we adore," was indeed the center of the Christian faith. The belief in a creative, all-governing Word was not exclusively Christian. The uniqueness and the scandal of the Christian claim was that this Word had taken flesh and appeared among us as Jesus Christ, that He had been crucified, had died and been buried, and had risen in the body. It is these things, decried by unbelievers as impossible, unfitting, and ridiculous, which Athanasius sets out to explain as altogether possible, appropriate, and necessary.

The indispensable backdrop of the Incarnation is the Christian doctrine of creation. Against the Epicurean theory of purposelessness, the limiting matter of Plato, and the intervening, evil artificer of the Gnostics, Athanasius stresses that the universe was created "out of non-existence absolute and utter," according to the unimpeded purpose of the one sovereign God, acting through His Word, or Image, the Son. Thus, *"the renewal of creation has been wrought by the Self-same Word Who made it in the beginning."* This is a crucial step in the argument, since it establishes the ground for regarding the Incarnation as a rectifying and conserving action, undertaken upon the basis of the original divine purpose. From the beginning, the creation, and man in particular, is God's business. Therefore it is not implausible, but entirely appropriate, that God should undertake to reclaim and restore, by whatever means necessary, that which is originally His.

Created to know and worship God, man's natural mortality was in abeyance so long as he remained centered upon God. But ". . . the will of man could turn either way . . ." and, at the Devil's tempting, turned to violation of the divine commandment. God had warned concerning the forbidden fruit, "in the day that ye do eat, ye shall surely die." (Genesis 2:17). Thus, "men, having turned from the contemplation of God to evil of their own devising, had come inevitably under the law of death. . . . In process of becoming corrupted entirely . . . ," the human race faced extinction. Athanasius' thought is not that God takes vindictive action, but that man, having forfeited the divine presence, deprives himself of the sources of his being. The Author of all being could have replenished man's being, but the irrevocability of the divine judgment stood in the way. Yet what was happening was contrary to God's loving purpose. "It would . . . have been unthinkable that God should go back upon His word, and that man, having trespassed, should not die. But it was equally monstrous that beings which had once shared the nature of the Word should die." In this dilemma is the rationale of the Incarnation.

Three things were needed. First, the divine judgment must be upheld; death must occur in consequence of sin. Second, there must be a renewal of man's being, to reverse the progressive deterioration and to restore the divine image. Third, the knowledge of God must be taught throughout the world. Only the Creator Logos could meet these needs. "For He alone, being Word of the Father and above all, was able . . . to recreate all, and worthy to suffer on behalf of all. . . ." And only He "Whose ordering of the universe reveals the Father . . . [could] renew the same teaching." Since in His divine nature the Word could not suffer or die, He fashioned, from the virgin, a human and mortal body. This assumption of corporeal humanity not only enabled Him to meet the sentence of death in man's stead but also to renew life and health where it was needed, in man's actual, bodily existence. At the same time, the teaching or revealing purpose was served, in that the invisible and universal truth became visibly centered in His personal concreteness.

Athanasius was mindful of the paradox in the thought that the omnipresent Word has become incarnate at a particular place. He explains that the universality of the Word is not diminished by special presence in a human body, nor are the world-governing operations of the Word suspended. The Incarnation does not entail an adulteration of the divine; the Word was in no way changed by the virgin birth. Nor does being in the body defile Him; rather He sanctifies it. It is the same as with His cosmic immanence: "For His being in everything does not mean that He shares the nature of everything, only that he gives all things their being and sustains them in it." Sunlight is not tainted by, but purifies, what it touches. The Word's divinity was not in fact, even within His incarnate existence, held to human limits. By His *ordinary* acts He showed that He was truly in the body, as was necessary. But, Athanasius maintains, by His *extraordinary* acts—miracles showing power over nature, demons, sickness, and death—He proved His divinity.

After explaining its general purpose, Athanasius turns to a more detailed consideration of the death of Christ. It is clear that Christ died for *all*—to pay the debt of the whole race. But two components mingle in the conception of how the Cross accomplishes its result. On the one hand, Athanasius brings into view the surpassing *worth* of Christ as the Incarnate Word, whereby the one death, as it were, has the value of all. On the other hand, we are to think of death itself as being expended and destroyed by union with the Word. Christ, by virtue of His human body, could and really did die; that is, He absorbed death into Himself and swallowed it up: "Thus it happened that two opposite marvels took place at once: the death of all was consummated in the Lord's body; yet, because the Word was in it, death and corruption were in the same act utterly abolished." The death of our bodies still occurs, but no longer under condemnation. Like seeds cast into the earth, we shall rise again in God's good time, and we shall partake in the general resurrection. Meanwhile, we already experience the renewal of life in Christ.

Addressing the circumstances of Christ's death, Athanasius attempts to render plausible even the details. Violence was necessary, because Christ would not have died naturally. The public crucifixion forestalled the ready doubt that might have arisen concerning a resurrection after a private death. The shamefulness was to show that the victory encompassed all, not merely better, kinds of death. It would have been unbecoming for Christ to die by His own hand, nor would it have been fitting for Him to flinch from the aggression of His foes. The fact that His purpose was also to teach by words and deeds explains why the atoning death did not occur earlier in His life. As for the entombment, it was just long enough to establish that natural corruption *should* have set in, and yet not so long as to allow the scattering of the witnesses or the fading of vivid memory. In such reasonings, Athanasius mixes the small and the large; every item of the Gospel story is precious to him.

Special attention is given also to the Resurrection. The Word itself, of course, could not die. Nor, in Athanasius' view, did the mortal body experience corruption. As the instrument through which the sting of death was suffered and overcome, the body lay for a time under death's sway. But the infinite life of the Word resurged, as it were, through the body; in a mighty demonstration of victory over death, Christ's body was raised as the first-fruits of the general resurrection still to come: "How could the destruction of death have been manifested at all, had not the Lord's body been raised?" But now the fact that death's power has been broken is plain to see in the fearlessness of Christian martyrdom. Men, women, and children who previously shrank from danger now mock at death's impotence. In such valiant faith, Athanasius feels the living presence of the triumphant Christ. "Dead men cannot take effective action. . . ." But "the Saviour is working mightily among men. . . ."

The last third of the book deals with refutation of the Jews and the gentiles. Against the Jews, the basis of argument is the Old Testament. Their own Scriptures show that the characteristics of the expected Messiah correspond to Jesus alone. The Jews say they are still waiting. But for what? What more could they ask than what Jesus has already accomplished? As for the gentiles, Athanasius first focuses upon objections to the idea of incarnation, restating earlier arguments for its plausibility. He stresses the analogy of the Word using the world as His instrument—a thought acceptable to Greeks. But if the whole world, why not a specialized organ in the world? It scandalizes no one that a personality, immanent in the whole body, confers on the tongue a unique expressive role. Should God have used sun or moon for a grander demonstration? But He accommodated himself to our weakness; and, besides, nothing had erred but man. Beyond such considerations, Athanasius appeals finally to what is actually happening. Formerly, every place was full of fraud, magic, madness, and savagery. But now, "where the Saviour is named, every demon is driven out." Christ brings peace, unity, joy, and love throughout the world. He proves his Lordship in that He reigns. In this context occurs the famous utterance: "He, indeed, assumed humanity, that we might become God." It implies, not that essences were blended, but that Christ's victory created a new situation for all mankind.

From the perspective of later thought, it may appear that Athanasius does not do justice to the full manhood of Christ. Some of his ideas are not fully defined, and his discussion of the Bible is, of course, precritical. But the claim of this small book to a place in the classic literature of the faith is unimpeachable. Besides its immense value as an epitome of the Patristic period, there is an assurance and an enthusiasm about it which illuminates Christ for every age.

ECCLESIASTICAL HISTORY

Author: Eusebius of Caesarea (c.260-c.339)
Type of work: Church history
First transcribed: 324

Principal Ideas Advanced

Christianity proclaims the truth of the divine Logos, who was present in creation, who revealed Himself to Israel through the prophets, and who was incarnated in the person of Jesus Christ.

Satan has opposed this truth by hardening the hearts of the Jews, by raising up heresies and schisms, and by stirring up persecutions.

God has defeated the efforts of Satan; the Jews have been punished; heretics have been refuted; and persecutors have been overthrown.

The Church has preserved the truth unchanged from the time of the Apostles.

The recognition of the Christian religion by Constantine marks the beginning of a universal reign of righteousness and peace.

Eusebius explains at the beginning of his *Ecclesiastical History* the method and scope of his work. It is his purpose to bring together memoirs, letters, and various other writings (including state papers) which will preserve a record of the Church's struggles from its beginnings until its official recognition by the Emperor Constantine (c.288-337). Materials are included which record the succession of bishops, important transactions of the Church, the work of evangelists and apologists, and the heroism of martyrs. To round out the story, an account is also given of the opposition which the Church received from the Jews, from heretics, and from kings and emperors. Although Eusebius does not say so, an important part of his purpose was apologetic: to prove by means of historical events that the Church is indeed a divine foundation, and that it is God's providence which has guided it to victory over paganism.

Eusebius begins by pointing out that Christianity is not a novelty. The divine Logos which was incarnated in Jesus Christ was present at the creation of the world, and He revealed His will from ancient times to the people of Israel through Moses and the prophets. The name "Christian" is new, as is also the "new race" which that name signifies. But, he says, "Even if we are clearly new, and this really fresh name of Christians is recently known among all nations, nevertheless our life and method of conduct, in accordance with the precepts of religion, has not been recently invented by us, but from the first creation of man, so to speak, has been upheld by the natural concepts of the men of old who were the friends of God." Eusebius views the story of God's work among men in much the same way as does the author of the Fourth Gospel. He writes, "The light of the truth and the divine Logos himself, which has shown from God upon men by growing up on the earth and dwelling among his own Apostles, was overcoming all things in the might of victory."

But, as John also records, "the light shineth in darkness, and the darkness comprehended it not." From the beginning, says Eusebius, Satan, out of envy, has blinded the hearts of men and stirred up enmity in them against God's truth and against those in whom it is revealed. Thus, the Jews, who in the first dispensation often put to death their prophets, demanded the death of Christ, and afterwards persecuted his followers. Eusebius quotes at length from the writings of the Jewish historian Josephus (c.37-c.95), to show both the wickedness of latter-day Jews and the horrible punishment that was visited upon them as a reward for their iniquity and "their impiety against the Christ of God." God did not permit Jerusalem to be destroyed for a whole generation after the death of Christ because, during that time, James, the Lord's brother, and many other disciples still resided in Jerusalem. But the crime of the Jews against James, when they threw him from the pinnacle of the temple and then clubbed him to death, was the final critical act; and God gave the city over to the horrors of famine, which Josephus so graphically describes.

"Like brilliant lamps," says Eusebius, "the churches were now shining throughout the world, and faith in our Savior and Lord Jesus Christ was flourishing among all mankind, when the Devil who hates what is good, as the enemy of truth, ever most hostile to men's salvation, turned all his devices against the church." The opposition of the Jews had not noticeably slowed down the Church's advance. Therefore, Satan employed "sorcerers and deceivers" in an effort to turn men away from the truth. The first of these mentioned by Eusebius is Simon Magus, who, having professed Christianity in his native Samaria, went to Rome and claimed that he was himself a god. Simon, according to Eusebius, was the "first author of all heresy." From him "there proceeded a certain snake-like power with two mouths and a double head," the gnostic heresies of Saturninus and Basilides. But God's grace "quickly extinguished the flames of the Evil One." Peter's advent at Rome sufficed to bring an end to Simon Magus's pretensions; and against the Gnostics there came into being a band of apologists "fighting with great eloquence" for the glory of the Church, and providing by their writings a permanent refutation of these particular heresies. There were, of course, other heresies besides Gnosticism, and Eusebius records them all, together with the refutations which Christian writers brought against them. In these parts, as elsewhere, Eusebius has rendered an invaluable service for the historian of dogma, preserving extracts and fragments of numerous works which have since been lost.

The third major kind of opposition to the Church was the recurrent persecution of believers at the hands of Roman authorities. Eusebius, who, through his friendship with Constantine, had access to government archives, preserves an accurate record of the state's fluctuating policy toward the Church, and he includes moving accounts written by Christians of the faithfulness and courage of their own martyrs. It is to Eusebius, for example, that we owe the preservation of the record of the Gallic martyrs, most celebrated of whom is the slave girl Blandina. Eusebius contrasts the Church's warfare with that recorded in other kinds of history where men are honored who stained themselves with the blood of countless murders for the sake of patriotism, wealth, and posterity. Our wars, he says, are waged peacefully for peace of soul, for truth, and piety; and our histories are glorious for struggles won over demons and unseen adversaries.

Eusebius suggests that the last and most furious of persecutions against the Church was, in some measure, a punishment drawn by the Church upon itself. Prior to the time of Diocletian (245-313) and Galerius (?-311), the Church had enjoyed unprecedented prosperity; but as a result of greater freedom, pride and sloth entered the Christian fellowship, and envy and strife divided it into factions. Then it was that "the divine judgment" descended. At first the persecutions were mild and sporadic; but when the Church was heedless of these chastisements, God permitted the persecutions to increase, as he did in the time of the prophet Jeremiah. For ten years, persecution raged, rising to unprecedented degrees, until God changed the minds of the rulers and suddenly brought it to an end by afflicting the person of the Emperor Galerius.

Eusebius lived through the final era of the Church's persecutions, and he seems to have been imprisoned at Caesarea, but to have escaped torture. It is believed by scholars that his *Ecclesiastical History* was written during the final years of the Galerian persecution, and that the work was originally intended to end with Book VIII, which records Galerius's Edict of Toleration (311). When persecutions were revived under Maximin (?-314), and later by Licinius (250-324), the work was extended through two further books. In its final form, *The Ecclesiastical History* concludes with Constantine's victory over Licinius, in 323. Constantine, in Eusebius's opinion, was the human embodiment of all that is regal and humane. The *Ecclesiastical History* omits the story, told by Eusebius in his *Life of Constantine,* of the vision in which Constantine saw the shining cross inscribed with the words

"In this Sign Conquer"; but it relates that, after the victory over Maxentius (?-312), a victory which the vision heralded, Constantine erected in the Roman Forum a statue of himself bearing the cross and the words, "By this salutary sign, the true proof of bravery, I saved and delivered your city from the yoke of the tyrant!"

Although Eusebius was inferior to Origen and Augustine in his speculative power, he was nevertheless a competent scholar whose learning was matched by a fine sense of balance and perspective. Through the favor of Constantine he was in a unique position to get from all parts of the Empire whatever materials he needed, and he made good use of his opportunities. It is noteworthy that, while he occasionally cites from sources in which accounts of miracles abound (for example, the apocryphal account of the Apostle Thaddaeus, which was found in the royal archive of Edessa), reports of miracles are almost completely absent from his own work and from the authentic materials which he cites; this is in striking contrast to the practice in the writing of medieval histories and chronicles.

Eusebius was interested, on the one hand, in establishing strict continuity in the development of the Church through the centuries, and, on the other, in preserving the unity of the Christian fellowship in his own day. He was further persuaded that there is no inherent conflict between Christianity and creation, that Christian history represents a victory of Christ over the powers of darkness, and that the Church need not be at odds with society or the state, for the Church continues in this world to insure Christ's victory.

As a historian, Eusebius had no wish to trace any developments within Christianity. From his point of view, Christian truth is eternal, and any alteration of the revelation handed down by the Apostles is the work of the Devil. Eusebius's motive for establishing the succession of bishops in Jerusalem, Rome, Antioch, Alexandria, and other leading centers was mainly to show that the Church in his day was the same as that founded by Christ. For similar reasons, Eusebius was interested in establishing the canon of the New Testament, and he cites the opinions of second and third century writers wherever they bear upon this subject. In Eusebius's day, the four Gospels, the Acts of the Apostles, the fourteen epistles of Paul (including Hebrews, which, however, was sometimes said not to be Paul's), and the first epistles of Peter and of John were admitted without dispute. The remainder were contested by some teachers. It was uniformly agreed, however, that none of the other early writings (such as the *Shepherd of Hermas* and the *Epistle of Barnabus*) was apostolic.

Eusebius's interest in establishing the New Testament canon led him to cite Papias (c. 60-130), whose testimony to the authorship of the four Gospels is of great importance to modern Biblical scholars. Papias relates that he heard from the lips of men who heard it from the Apostles themselves that Mark based his Gospel on the preaching of Peter, and that Matthew "collected the oracles in the Hebrew language." Papias mentions, as one of the sub-apostolic Fathers, the presbyter John of Ephesus. This suggests to Eusebius, as it does to some modern students, the hypothesis that tradition confused this John with the Apostle John, who is also supposed to have resided at Ephesus, and that some of the writings attributed to the Apostle may have been written by the presbyter. Little is known of Papias except what Eusebius records of him, and Eusebius would probably not have mentioned him were it not for the light Papias sheds on Biblical origins. Eusebius describes Papias as "a man of very little intelligence," mainly because Papias took literally the teaching of the Apocalypse that the Resurrection would precede a millennial reign of Christ on earth.

The millenarianism of Papias, the enthusiasm of Montanus, the innovations of Paul of Samasota and Sabellius, and the "puritanism" of Novatian were all regarded by Eusebius as threats to the unity of the Church and its mission in the world. As a bishop of Caesarea (after 313), and as a confidant of the Emperor Constantine, Eusebius labored throughout his life to keep peace and harmony in the Church. The Arian controversy was just beginning at the time when the *Ecclesiastical History* was being completed. In the ecclesiastical counsels which decided the fate of Arius, Eusebius inclined toward a mediating position. Another issue which divided the Church in his day was the question whether those could be readmitted to Christian fellowship who had denied Christ during the persecutions. From the time of Cyprian, this question had been a lively one. Eusebius, as we may suppose, favored the inclusivist position.

Eusebius owed his theological position very largely to the followers of Origen, notably Dionysius of Alexandria (d.c. 264), sometimes called Dionysius the Great. Of his writings, much esteemed in ancient times, only fragments remain, chiefly from his epistles as quoted by Eusebius. These deal mostly with the issue raised by Novatian, who, with his followers, refused fellowship to Christians who had apostatized during the Decian persecutions, and with the more general question as to whether, as Cyprian (c.200-258) had recommended, apostates be rebaptized before they were readmitted. Dionysius was in favor of tolerance, and he advised that, so far as baptism was concerned, local tradition should be the rule. In Africa, where rebaptizing heretics was a tradition, he advised that it be allowed, for, he says, "I do not dare to overturn their decisions and involve them in strife and contention." Dionysius is also remembered for opposing Sabellius, who, in the third century, brought into controversy the Trinitarian belief concerning God, which was to loom so large in the fourth and fifth centuries. Sabellius taught that the three "persons" of the Godhead are merely three ways in which God reveals himself to men. Against this view, Dionysius not merely insisted on the essential distinction between the Father, Son, and Holy Spirit within the Godhead, but he subordinated the Son to the Father in a way which suggests the opposite heresy of Arianism. However, when Dionysius of Rome protested against the Alexandrian Dionysius' statement, and insisted that the Son is of the same substance with the Father (*homoousios*), the latter agreed to this formulation.

Eusebius closes the *Ecclesiastical History* on a panegyrical note, praising God the King and Christ the Redeemer that the enemies of righteousness have been removed and the whole human race freed from the oppression of tyrants. The major part of the tenth book consists of an oration delivered by Eusebius at Tyre on the occasion of the rebuilding of one of the Christian basilicas which had been destroyed during the late persecutions. In it he draws copiously from the Scriptures, mainly the Old Testament, which prophesy the final triumph of righteousness over iniquity. It seemed to him, as no doubt it did to the majority of Christians in his day, that the new imperial favor which Constantine had shown toward the Church was indeed the goal toward which mankind had been moving since the beginning of time. For Eusebius, the basilica at Tyre, originally built to worship God, but laid low by God's enemies, only to be raised up again more magnificently than before by God's grace and the munificence of Constantine, was a parable of mankind, and indeed of the whole universe. He writes: "Such is the great temple which the Word, the great Creator of the Universe, hath builded throughout the whole world beneath the sun, forming again this spiritual image upon earth of those vaults beyond the vaults of heaven; so that by the whole creation and by the rational, living creatures upon earth His Father might be honored and revered."

THE CATECHETICAL LECTURES

Author: Saint Cyril, Bishop of Jerusalem (c.315-386)
Type of work: Catechetical instruction
First transcribed: c.347

Principal Ideas Advanced

The candidate for baptism is to present himself before God in true repentance and humility, making sincere confession of his sins, and in the knowledge that there is one God, the Father of the Lord Jesus Christ, who together with the Holy Spirit, is the rewarder of those who diligently seek Him.

At baptism the sins of the believer are remitted; he receives the regeneration of the Holy Spirit, and symbolically he shares in the burial and Resurrection of the Lord.

Cyril, Archbishop of Jerusalem, played an important role in the life of the Church in the fourth century. His writings include the *Catechetical Lectures,* which exemplifies the care bestowed by the early Christian Church upon the instruction and training of converts before admitting then to baptism. The work consists of a series of twenty-three lectures delivered extemporaneously and probably transcribed by one of the audience. The lectures are divided into two groups; the first eighteen are addressed to persons desirous of receiving baptism, while the last five lectures are addressed to the newly baptized. This work is an important source of information concerning the early liturgy and the local creed of Jerusalem.

Before receiving baptism, Cyril writes, the candidate, being duly registered and admitted, was required to take a course of instruction and begin a course of penitential discipline. The length of the instruction and training varied. Baptism was to be the completion and seal of a spiritual illumination. The candidate was required to confess his past sins and to be truly repentant. Before being baptized he was exorcised, or cleansed of evil spirits. Exorcism, very important in the ancient Church, was applied to all catechumens. The candidate renounced the Devil and his works, made profession of faith, and then was baptized in the name of the Father, the Son, and the Holy Ghost. It was then customary to anoint the baptized with consecrated ointment, and for the baptized then to receive first communion.

Baptism promised the candidate a new birth of the soul, a remission of offences, and the death of sin. The grace of baptism is not bestowed by God upon the hypocrite, Cyril writes, but solely upon the true believer who has put off the bondage of sin. God sees the heart of the candidate and rejects the hypocrite as unfit for His service, but when He finds someone worthy, God readily gives His grace and the seal of salvation. The catechumen is henceforth to be called a believer, for he is now made a partaker of the truth of God.

To be properly prepared to receive the sacrament of baptism, the catechumen must make a sincere confession. The communion of the Holy Ghost is then bestowed in proportion to each man's faith. True confession of sin is followed by forgiveness and pardon, for God is merciful to those who repent. The Scriptures afford numerous examples of those who have sinned and repented and been saved. The candidate is to take heart and make confession unto the Lord in order that he may receive the forgiveness of his former sins, be found worthy of the heavenly gift, and, together with all the saints, inherit the Kingdom of Jesus Christ.

To be baptized is to be enrolled in the army of the divine King. He that is baptized with water and is not found worthy by the Spirit does not receive the grace in perfection, nor does the virtuous man who does not receive the seal of water enter into the Kingdom of Heaven. With the exception of martyrs, who even without water receive the Kingdom, every man must be baptized to attain salvation.

True godliness, advises Cyril, consists of virtuous practices and pious doctrines. The latter are not acceptable to God without good works, nor does God accept works which are not perfected by pious doctrines. The candidate for baptism must therefore receive instruction in the faith so that he is not spoiled by false doctrine. It is necessary that he understand that God is one, alone unbegotten, the Father of our Lord Jesus Christ, who was begotten God of God, who is in all things equal to Him who begat, and was before all ages eternally and incomprehensibly begotten of the Father. The candidate is to believe that the only-begotten Son took upon Himself a human nature, was born of a virgin, was of two natures, man in what was seen, and God in what was not seen. He was truly crucified for our sins, was buried, rose again from the dead, ascended into Heaven, and will come again to judge the quick and the dead. The candidate is also to believe in the Holy Spirit, the sanctifier of all. He is to keep the faith and thus to be free of condemnation.

Through belief in one God, all polytheism is excluded; by confessing God's triune nature, every heresy is avoided. God cannot be seen with the eye of flesh; His nature is incomprehensible, but it is possible to attain some comprehension of His power from His works. From the Scriptures we know that there is an only-begotten Son of God, a son by nature, not by adoption. It suffices for devotion, writes Cyril, that we know that God is living, that He is good and just, holy and almighty.

The Church glories in the Cross of Christ, Cyril emphasizes, for by the Cross the blind are led into light, sinners are loosed from bondage, and the whole world is ransomed. On the cross the only-begotten Son of God died in man's behalf. The cross was no illusion, Cyril insists; Jesus' passion was real, and He came to it willingly, rejoicing in the salvation of mankind. His Resurrection from the dead was also real, as is attested by many witnesses.

The Christian does not believe in three Gods, but one. The Trinity is not to be separated, Cyril claims, nor is it to be confused. For we know three persons in one Godhead.

The true believer at baptism receives the remission of sins, and the Holy Spirit abides with him. The Christian strives for life eternal, believes virtuously, and receives instruction so that his soul may be prepared for reception of heavenly gifts. When he partakes of baptism, the believer is enlightened by the power of God.

The newly baptized are to be sober and vigilant, Cyril advises, for they are thereafter true-born children of the Church. Once they are baptized, they are ready to receive the more sacred mysteries, for, having renounced Satan and all sin, they have been found worthy of divine and life-giving baptism. The paradise of God is now open to them.

Baptism is not merely the grace of remission of sins, Cyril remarks, nor does it simply minister to us the gift of the Holy Ghost; baptism is also the counterpart of the sufferings of Christ and represents His true sufferings. The candidate is stripped naked to imitate Christ, who was naked on the cross; he is then anointed with exorcised oil, so as to be made a partaker of the olive tree, Jesus Christ, and to ward off the invisible powers of the evil one. The candidate is then led to the holy pool of divine baptism, as Christ was carried from the cross to the sepulcher, and after making the saving confession that he believes in the name of the Father, of the Son, and of the Holy Ghost, he descends thrice into the water and ascends again; this act is a symbol of Christ's burial and Resurrection.

As Christ was in reality crucified, buried, and raised from the dead, so the believer in baptism, if worthy, is crucified, buried, and raised together with Him. And as Christ was anointed with the ideal oil of gladness, with the Holy Spirit, so the believer is anointed with ointment, having been made a partaker and follower of Christ. The ointment with which the believer is anointed is Christ's gift of grace, and it is made fit to impart His divine nature. While the body is anointed with the visible ointment, the soul is sanctified by the Holy Spirit.

The believer is now ready, writes Cyril, to partake of the body and blood of Christ, for after the invocation of the Holy Ghost, the elements of the Eucharist are no longer bread and wine, but the body and blood of Christ.

When the service is near completion, those who have given their lives to Christ, namely, the patriarchs, prophets, Apostles, and martyrs, are commemorated, "that at their prayers and intercessions God should receive our petitions. . ." The Lord's Prayer is then recited and the benediction pronounced.

Although Cyril's *Catechetical Lectures* is primarily concerned with the preparation for baptism, his declarations of faith in the efficacy of baptism as a result of the divine presence give his work a power of sincerity and dedication which continues to impress the Christian spirit.

THE LIFE OF ANTONY

Author: Saint Athanasius (c.296-373)
Type of work: Hagiography
First transcribed: 357

Principal Ideas Advanced

The ascetic life is prescribed by the Scriptures.
Christ commanded men to forsake all and follow Him.
Those who follow Christ must mortify the flesh and fight with demons.
Christ has broken the power of Satan, and those who trust in Christ's name can achieve victory over sin and so attain to peace and joy.

The Life of Antony was written by Athanasius at the request of "brethren in foreign parts," probably persons in the West whom the author met during his exile there. Athanasius, who had known Antony personally and embraced many of his ascetic principles, expresses his own satisfaction in being able to pass on some part of what he has heard of the great man and encourages his readers to make inquiries of others. If everyone who has recollections of Antony tells what he knows, says Athanasius, "an account will be had that does approximate justice to him."

Antony was born in Middle Egypt about the middle of the third century of well-to-do Christian parents. As a boy he avoided attending school because he did not enjoy the companionship of other children; hence, he never learned to read or write. He attended church, however, and paid close attention to lessons that he heard. Thus it happened that, when he was about twenty years old, the words of Jesus to the Rich Young Ruler, "If thou wilt be perfect, go sell all thou hast, and give to the poor," impressed him with such force that he disposed of his property, gave his younger sister, who had been left to his care, to be brought up by Christian virgins, and devoted his life to the practice of asceticism.

At that time ascetics were content to practice their discipline within the vicinity of towns and villages, for, as Athanasius notes, "there were not yet so many monasteries in Egypt, and no monk even knew of the faraway desert." Antony profited from what he could learn by visiting these hermits; but in time his peace of mind required him to seek greater solitude, first in tombs which lay at some distance from the village, and later in an abandoned fort in the desert. There he immured himself for twenty years seeing no one and receiving his store of bread only twice a year.

In his absence Antony's reputation grew. There were reports that he fought with demons in bodily form, and that persons who camped beside his cell were healed of their diseases. Finally men forced their way into his cell and brought him out. It was the first time any had seen him since he had come to the desert; but his body appeared healthy, and the state of his soul appeared to be pure. "He had himself completely under control," says Athanasius, "a man guided by reason and stable in his character."

From this time on Antony did not hesitate to assume the role of a teacher and servant of men; he counseled and healed not only the monks who came to him, but also the general public. He possessed unusual power in prayer, and was gifted with "charm in speaking." As a result of his exhortations, many took up the monastic life, and, in Athanasius' words, "the desert was populated with monks who left their own people and registered themselves for citizenship in Heaven." In 311, during the persecution by Maximin, Antony went to Alexandria and ministered to Christians in prisons and in the mines. He even appeared in the court room, encouraging those who were on trial. Antony wanted to suffer martyrdom, says Athanasius, but "the Lord was guarding him for our own good and for the good of others, that to many he might be a teacher of the ascetic life."

Now it became impossible for Antony to find solitude. He therefore followed a caravan of Arabs eastward almost to the Gulf of Akaba, where he found an oasis at the foot of a high mountain, and "fell in love with the place." Here he made a small garden and raised his own grain, together with a few vegetables which he served to occasional visitors. Respecting his solitude, his disciples were nevertheless solicitous for his welfare, because he was now an old man. Thus, each month someone made the three-day journey to his hermitage to make sure that he was well.

Once Antony made the journey again to visit the cells of those who had taken up their abode in the desert. "As he came to the outer cells, all gave him a hearty welcome, regarding him as a father. And he, for his part, as though bringing them provisions from his mountain, entertained them with his stories and gave them of his practical experience." A new enthusiasm swept the region and Antony rejoiced in the zeal that he found. Again he saw his sister, now grown old in virginity, "herself the guiding spirit of other virgins."

Such, in outline, is the story of Antony's life. A person of ordinary physique, he nevertheless exercised "a great and indescribable charm" over all whom he met. He was never agitated or gloomy, but seemed to radiate in his countenance the joy and imperturbability of his soul. He conversed freely, asking questions as often as he answered them, and he profited from the replies he received. When he was in Alexandria, the multitudes, both pagan and Christian, wanted to touch him, confident that he had power to heal them. He became the national hero of the Egyptians, the "physician of Egypt," (and a forerunner of the religious nationalism which reached massive proportions in the Monophysite controversy during the sixth century). Pagan philosophers who went to see him were astonished at what they found. "For he did not have the rough manner of one who had lived and grown old in the mountains, but was a man of grace and urbanity. His speech was seasoned with divine wisdom so that no one bore him ill-will, but rather all rejoiced over him who sought him out."

Athanasius knew Antony well enough to preserve some of the monk's actual sayings: "He used to say that one should give all one's time to the soul rather than to the body"; ". . . he used to say to himself that the life led by the great Elias should serve the ascetic as a mirror in which always to study his own life." He experienced visions and trances, but spoke of these with reluctance, and only to those who sat with him during his ecstasy and afterwards pressed him to tell them what he had seen. The visions which Athanasius reports do not suggest that Antony was a great mystic. On one occasion he heard a voice bidding him go out and look at the skies. Looking up, he saw a frightful, towering figure, whose body reached to the clouds. With his hands the monster knocked down the souls of men as they endeavored to rise to Heaven. He exulted over those who fell, but some passed through his grasp. On another occasion, Antony seemed to see himself carried aloft by angels, but stopped by demons who charged him with faults; these, however, they could not prove, so that the way opened and he proceeded unhindered. Miracles were reported; but Athanasius is careful to say that Antony healed "not by giving out commands, but by praying and by calling upon Christ's name." Thus, when a soldier knocked at his cell and begged him to heal his child, Antony replied, "Man, why do you make all this clamor to me? I am a man just as you are. If you believe in Christ whom I serve, go, and, as you believe, pray to God and it will come to pass."

Unfortunately, Athanasius' first-hand reports on Antony were not sufficient to compose a full-length portrait of the monk; or, perhaps, Antony's sayings were too dry and puzzling to satisfy literary fashions and to serve the purposes of popular edification. In any case, *The Life of Antony* is, in certain respects, Athanasius' own invention.

In order to make some kind of story out of Antony's dreary years in the desert, Athanasius relates them as a kind of *Pilgrim's Progress*, with many exciting episodes in which the saint contended with demons and monsters. Once the Devil masqueraded as a woman; another time he came with his demons and lashed Antony's body so that his friends took him up for dead; again, Antony was surrounded by phantoms of lions, bears, serpents, and wolves; when he first moved to the desert, the Enemy scattered gold along the way in an effort to corrupt him. On each occasion, Antony cited

Scripture verses and pointed to Christ's victory upon the cross, and in this way overcame his tempters. Certainly, there is nothing improbable in the supposition that Antony had such temptations to contend with; but even his Roman Catholic editor concedes that "there is quite too much of it in the *Vita*."

Athanasius makes abundant use of the ancient literary practice of putting speeches into the mouth of his hero. One of these purports to be the speech which Antony made to the monks on the occasion of his coming back to civilization after twenty years in the fort where he had retired. It is a plausible apology for the ascetic life, concentrating especially on ways of overcoming demonic assaults. Another speech is addressed by Antony to the Neoplatonists and contrasts religious truth with philosophical reasoning in a manner which shows considerably more knowledge of Greek thought than Antony is likely to have had. However, it seems fairly probable that Antony was opposed to the influence of Greek ideas on Christian apologetics and theology.

Finally, Athanasius represents Antony as a zealous opponent of Manicheanism and Arianism, heresies that presumably provoked the Bishop of Alexandria more than they did the monk of the Outer Desert. Antony is reported as having said that Arianism was the worst heresy of all, and was the forerunner of Antichrist. "He taught the people," says Athanasius of Antony, "that the Son of God is not a creature nor has He come into being 'from non-existence'; but 'He is the eternal Word and Wisdom of the substance of the Father.'" But obviously these are Athanasius' views; and while Antony may very well have been zealous against the Arians, there is little reason to suppose that he entered intelligently into the debates to which it gave rise.

Antony could neither read nor write. Still, as Athanasius portrays him, he found in the Bible the rule of his life. If, as most Protestants would probably maintain, his was a one-sided and distorted understanding of what the Scriptures require, one need only run through *The Life of Antony* and mark the numerous Biblical citations which Athanasius puts in Antony's mouth to be convinced that the ascetic ideal is, nonetheless, deeply ingrained in New Testament Christianity. "If thou wilt be perfect, go sell all that thou hast. . . . Be not solicitous for the morrow. . . . He that is lazy, neither let him eat. . . . I die daily. . . . Our wrestling is not against flesh and blood, but against principalities and powers. . . ." Such are the principles which guided Antony at each step of his life, sustained him in anxiety, and brought him joy and peace.

Antony's monasticism, as the reader of *The Life* easily observes, was of the hermit variety, and his immediate followers were content so far to emulate him as to live each in his own cell, yet near enough to others that fellowship was possible. It was St. Pachomius (c. 290-346), another Egyptian, who developed the communal monastery surrounded by a wall and ruled over by a superior.

No other monk, however, caught the popular imagination in the same way as Antony did, a fact for which Athanasius' book is largely responsible. The work was translated into Latin almost immediately and made a striking impression in decadent Roman circles, as Augustine remarks in his *Confessions. The Life of Antony* continued to be read throughout the Middle Ages. It was influential, not only in helping form Catholic ideals of piety and in fostering asceticism as a religious alternative to martyrdom, but also in providing a model for medieval hagiography. Meanwhile, the story of Antony's temptations became a perennial source of inspiration to artists and poets.

"The fact that he became famous everywhere and that he found universal admiration," says Athanasius, "betokens his virtue, and a soul beloved of God. For Antony gained renown not for his writings, nor for worldly wisdom, nor for any art, but solely for his service of God. . . that those who hear of him may realize that the commandments can lead to perfection, and may take courage in the path to virtue."

THE LONGER RULES and THE SHORTER RULES

Author: Saint Basil of Caesarea (c.330-379)
Type of work: Ascetical theology
First transcribed: c.358-364

Principal Ideas Advanced

The underlying motivation of the monastic and ascetic life is the love of Christ and obedience to Him through the fulfillment of the Biblical command to love God and neighbor.

One sets himself free to fulfill this double commandment by renouncing the world and its distractions, including property and family, and by joining in a common life with other similarly dedicated persons under a common discipline.

Continence or temperance is the guiding principle for all the regulations of monastic life in harmony with the Scriptures.

The community life of the monastery is oriented around regular public and private prayer and useful work.

Although Basil, Archbishop of Caesarea in Cappadocia (modern Kayseri in central Turkey), is most often remembered as a dogmatic theologian, the influence of his *Longer Rules* and *Shorter Rules* has probably been more widespread than that of his doctrinal writings. The importance of the *Rules* lies in the fact that in them a great theologian supplies the monastic movement with a sound theological basis.

The son of a distinguished family, whose sister had entered upon the monastic life before him and whose younger brother, Gregory of Nyssa (c.330-c.395), became the great mystical theologian among the Cappadocian fathers, Basil the Great was qualified by his classical education, by his travels as a young man among the monks of Syria, Egypt, and Palestine, and by later experience as monk and bishop to set forth the first formal and comprehensive rules for monastic communities.

At the time of his birth Christian monasticism was still in its beginnings, although there had been individual ascetics since New Testament times. The growth of a distinctive monastic way of life came with the end of the persecutions and the formal recognition of Christianity by the Roman empire under Constantine the Great (c.288-337). The earliest form of monasticism seems to have been eremitic, as exemplified by the Egyptian hermit-monk Antony (c.251-356). The communal or cenobitic form appeared, also in Egypt, under the leadership of Pachomius (c.290-346), and the monastery founded by Pachomius at Tabennisi was among those which Basil visited before settling down on the family estate in 356 to found a monastic community. Pachomius and Eustathius of Sebaste (c.306-c.377), a close friend and teacher of Basil who led a monastic movement in lower Armenia, had both given some brief rules to their followers but nothing complete or systematic and nothing firmly based on the teachings of the Bible. The *Longer Rules* of Basil thus met a felt need and came to have a far-reaching influence on the development of monasticism in West and East.

Both the *Longer Rules* and the *Shorter Rules* seem to have been first compiled in that period while Basil and Gregory of Nazianzus (329-389), the orator and preacher among the three Cappadocians, were together at the monastery on the River Iris between 358 and 364, when Basil was elected bishop of nearby Caesarea. The *Longer Rules* is composed of fifty-five discourses, perhaps *extempore* addresses, in question and answer form. The headings or questions do not in every case seem to be original. The first twenty-three chapters form a unit stating the basic principles of monastic life and community organization. Chapters 24-36 deal with more specific aspects of community life such as types of discipline and duties of officers. Chapters 37-42 and 43-55 deal with worship and work, and with the office of the Superior, respectively. It is quite possible that these later sections were added by Basil after he had had more experience in leading the community and sensed the need for them. There are some references which imply that he was already bishop at the time they were written. In any case no doubt has been cast on the genuineness of the *Rules*.

It is especially characteristic of the *Regulae fusius tractatae* that the principles of monastic organization are drawn wherever possible from Scripture. There is a strong emphasis on discipleship, on the love of Christ, as the motive behind monasticism. The primary commandments are the love of God and the love of neighbor. All else is subordinated to the fulfillment of this double commandment. It is for the sake of pleasing God and loving the neighbor that Basil warns against absolute solitude and comes out strongly in favor of communal organization. There is also the need of mutual discipline and correction. This advocacy of the communal life was especially influential on the development of monasticism in the West, and it was essential to the integration of monasticism into the total life of the Church.

Renunciation of the world, which includes the relinquishing of property and complete separation from family and friends, is not an end in itself, nor is it a simple rejection of the world. All the monasteries founded by Basil showed a remarkable concern for the sick and poor in the communities around them. In fact, many of these monasteries were established in the midst of cities or towns and not in the wilderness as in Egyptian monasticism. Renunciation is a release, a setting free from material concerns in order to perform spiritual duties and acts of love. It is the same freedom from material concerns which the guiding principle of continence seeks. All things are to be taken temperately: food, clothing, laughter, and even work. Basil saw the wisdom of moderating the excesses, in particular the abuses of the body, which typified much of Syrian and Egyptian monasticism both then and later. He recognized the different needs of different men in regard to food and other physical necessities, but in regard to the vices of the soul all harmful pleasures were naturally excluded. His rule is a strict one; simplicity and uniformity mark the monastic life.

Many of the *Rules* reveal Basil's great insight into human nature. He warns, for example, against fighting over the lowest seat at the table out of misconceived humility. He recommends distinctive clothing as a means of keeping the brothers up to the standard of a godly life when out in public and faced with temptations. He likewise urges the avoidance of journeys and of contact with relatives from the outside world. All work and duties should be assigned by the Superior according to individual abilities but without respect to individual preferences. The products of the community may be sold outside the monastery, but not for large profits and if possible in the immediate vicinity. In no case are the products of the monastery to be sold at religious gatherings or synods. One of the chapters also discusses the proper relationships with the sisters in the case of double monasteries for men and women. More detailed questions about all these points appear in the *Shorter Rules*.

One of the historically most significant chapters of the *Longer Rules* is the thirty-seventh, which describes the hours or times for prayer. We find here one of the earliest accounts of the eight canonical hours; namely: prime, tierce, sext, nones, vespers, compline, nocturns, and lauds. Each has its particular place and value in the monks' day, and only in the most urgent instances should prayers be missed. At the same time they are not an excuse for idleness and neglect of assigned work, most of which was manual, such as building, carpentry, and agriculture, and could be interrupted for prayers during the day.

One other important aspect of the monastic life is the regular confession of sins to the Superior, often called a physician of souls, or to one of the senior brothers who is suitably qualified by character and experience. With confession goes, of course, correction.

The *Shorter Rules* or *Regulae brevius tractatae* consists of 313 chapters, also in question and answer form, but here the questions are almost certainly original. The questions are of considerable variety, and the whole is not especially well arranged. Some questions may have been submitted to Basil in writing from different monasteries, others may have come from catechism classes, and still others may have been taken down in shorthand at conferences of monastic leaders or Superiors with Basil. In any case, the collection does not seem to have been edited, and it was probably added to over the years of Basil's administration as bishop and founder of monasteries. Among the general concerns dealt with are pastoral care, monastic administration, Biblical exegesis, and liturgical practice. In almost every case we see real situations and practical concerns reflected in the questions and answers, and altogether the many brief chapters of the *Shorter Rules* form a larger work than the *Longer Rules*. Yet they do not set forth a comprehensive system of principles or rules proper as do the more polished chapters of the *Longer Rules*.

The preface of the *Shorter Rules* refers to an all-night meeting of Superiors and thus points to one source of the questions. The first group of chapters deals primarily with questions of repentance, conversion, and the forgiveness of sins, but other chapters near the end of the *Rules* also deal with these topics. The chapters on sin in general and on particular sins and their remedies, which follow, make up a large section, as might be expected. Many of the questions could apply to any Christian, but some arise obviously from the monastic situation. There is one, for example, about being cross or angry when awakened at midnight or before dawn to say prayers. Attention is also given to property, clothing, food, and taxes. One answer is rather amusing. When asked what a brother with nothing of his own except the garment on his back should do for a naked beggar, Basil replies with Scripture, "Let each man abide in that wherein he was called." This verse from I Corinthians 7:20 and one like it from 7:24 are cited several times as a counsel to contentment with one's lot in life.

A great many questions deal with the learning and interpretation of the Bible. These questions often cite for Basil's opinion difficult verses from both the Old and New Testaments. As one would expect, the problems of administering a monastery, especially the double monasteries for men and women, appear repeatedly. In general Basil gives sound and conservative directions, emphasizing always the absolute authority of the Superior. Indeed obedience is the very center of monastic living and takes specific form in self-discipline, in regulated fasting and use of food (one meal a day was customary), and in proper conduct in the workshops, kitchen, and cellar. A central section of the *Shorter Rules* discusses disposition and attitude toward God, others, oneself, and the duties imposed by the community. In all the *Rules* there is only brief reference to priests and to the sacraments, but there is no question that Basil the bishop recognized the place of both.

The lasting contributions of Basil to the development of Christian monasticism emerge clearly from the *Longer Rules* and the *Shorter Rules*. He gave it a foundation of organized asceticism with stated rules. He moderated the extreme austerity and extreme enthusiasm of monasticism in other lands. There was no place for special visions and miracles, but spiritual gifts were not excluded. Although not the first to establish communities of monks, he made the common life the unalterable basis of monastic living. Finally, he brought monasticism into the service of the Church and the larger community. He was the first great monk *and* bishop.

The *Rules* of Basil were taken during his lifetime to the newly organized monasteries of the West and were translated very soon into Latin by Tyrannius Rufinus (c.345-410), a widely traveled churchman from Italy, who either abridged them or used a shorter early version of them. In his translation they were known and used by Benedict of Nursia (c.480-c.550), the father of monasticism in the West and the founder of Monte Cassino. The influence of Basil's *Rules* may be seen in Eastern monasticism to this day, although there was never a Basilian order as such.

THE HYMNS OF EPHRAEM THE SYRIAN

Author: Saint Ephraem the Syrian (c.306-373)
Type of work: Hymnody
First transcribed: c.360

Principal Ideas Advanced

The Lord chastens those He loves, is merciful to His children, and is greatly to be praised, for He is exceedingly just, long-suffering, and kind, by whose glory we are healed and brought into His marvelous salvation.

At the birth of the Lord, the glory and majesty of God was revealed; sin and death were conquered, and the doors of Paradise were thrown open.

Saint Ephraem, the Syrian, is one of the earliest Syriac authors whose works remain to any considerable extent. His work is characteristic of Syrian Christianity and was thus little affected by outside influences. Not much is known of Ephraem's life, for there is hardly any trustworthy biographical evidence. He was born in Nisibis in Mesopotamia during the reign of Constantine the Great, was a disciple of St. Jacob of Nisibis, and finally settled in a cell at the Mount of Edessa as a "Solitary." Here he gained a reputation as a saint, an ascetic, a teacher, and a champion of orthodoxy. He wrote voluminously and left a large body of *Sermons, Commentaries,* and *Hymns,* of which many are extant.

The *Hymns* of Ephraem did more than provide the Syrian churches with devotional literature, although the whole of public worship was animated by them. Many of his hymns were controversial and polemical; they were the chosen means by which Ephraem sought to combat error and to teach the truth. Many of the hymns are songs of exhortation, of praise, and of thanksgiving and triumph, but others sought to combat the errors of heretics, errors which had won popularity through expression in attractive tunes that caught the ear and inclined the people to receive false doctrine. The *Hymns* of Ephraem were set to the same tunes, and they superseded the rival hymnody of heresy, so that the day was carried by an orthodox hymnody.

Syriac hymnody is constructed, as is the Hebrew, on the principle of parallelism, in which one thought answers another; but unlike the Hebrew, the clauses of the Syriac are regulated by an equivalence of syllabic measure. A systematic rhyme is missing. The literary value of Ephraem's *Hymns* is not to be compared with the Psalms of David; nevertheless, some do display devotional fervor and human pathos. They differ from the Psalms of David, however, in that whereas the latter render the inner feelings of man in words of simplicity, and rise without effort to utter the things of God, the *Hymns* of Ephraem reflect the somberness of the ascetic, the gloom of the recluse; they express self-reproach, mortification, fears, and sorrow.

Some of the hymns were written about the year 350 during the siege of Nisibis by Sapor, King of Persia. The songs call upon the God who had delivered Noah from the waters of the flood to deliver those oppressed within the walls of the city. The God who gave rest in the haven of a mountain is supplicated to relieve the distressed within besieged walls. The affliction of oppression is recognized as the chastening of guilt and unrighteousness, and yet God is merciful to the wicked, and greatly to be praised. For the Lord is merciful, the hymns declare; He smites the enemy, and rescues the Church from mockery. The Lord forgives us even though our evil deeds outweigh our repentance; the Lord delivers us although we deserve destruction. We ought to sing praises to the One Being, that is unsearchable to us.

No man can complain against the Creator, writes Ephraem, for it is our offenses which cause our troubles. The medicine of salvation is applied to our afflictions. The Son of God heals us, even if our afflictions are like those of Job. The justice of the Lord is to be praised, for He chastises us as a mother rebukes her child; He restrains us from folly, and makes us wise.

Jesus has triumphed over the Evil One and his hosts, Ephraem writes; He resisted the temptations of sin and the Devil and conquered death. He is man and God; His manhood is intermingled with His Godhead. Holy men of old awaited His birth. On the day of His birth the words of the prophets were fulfilled. Immanuel was brought forth by the Virgin in Bethlehem. The True One who came from the Father of truth is blessed; He was sent for our propitiation. He let himself be born, crucified, and buried for our salvation. He sealed our soul, adorned it, and espoused it to himself. He sowed his light in darkness. The clothing of our filthiness was stripped from us; His leaven was mixed in our souls, and our deadness was quickened. Our minds have been enlightened by His doctrine. Our curse has been taken away by His stripes.

Ephraem sings of the Lord: "His Birth flowed on and was joined to His Baptism; and His Baptism again flowed on even to His death; His death led and reached to His Resurrection, a fourfold bridge unto His Kingdom, and lo! His sheep pass over in His footsteps."

Baptism is the wellspring of life which the Son of God has opened, the Father has sealed, and the Spirit has stamped, says Ephraem. The poor are invited to descend to the fountain of life and to be enriched, for the unsearchable Trinity has laid up treasures in baptism.

Besides the hymns of praise and adoration, the controversial hymns by Ephraem are of great interest. The following are typical:

"I have chanced upon the tares, my brethren,
That wear the color of wheat, to choke the good seed;
Concerning which the husbandmen are commanded,
Take them not away nor root them out;
And though the husbandmen needed not,
The seed waxed stronger than they,
Grew and multiplied and covered and choked them."

"I have chanced upon a book of Bardaisan,
And I was troubled for an hour's space;
It tainted my poor ears,
And made them a passage
For words filled with blasphemy.
I hastened to purge them
With the goodly and pure reading
Of the Scriptures of truth."

Further insight into the character and theology of Ephraem and the nature of the verses that he wrote can be gained from his own testament which he wrote in anticipation of his death:

"By him who came down on Mount Sinai and by him who spake on the rock,
By that Mouth which spake the "Eli" and made the bowels of creation tremble,
By him who was sold in Judah and by him who was scourged in Jerusalem,
By the Might which was smitten on the cheek and by the Glory which endured spitting,
By the threefold Names of fire and by the one Assent and will, I have not rebelled against the Church, nor against the might of God.
If in my thought I have magnified the Father above the Son, Let Him have no mercy on me!
And if I have accounted the Holy Spirit less than God, let mine eyes be darkened!
If as I have said, I confessed not, let me go into outer darkness!
And if I speak in hypocrisy, let me burn with the wicked in fire!"

Ephraem sought no special honor at burial, for he despised all pomp and vulgar ceremony. He wished no luxurious tomb, but counted his body as without import. He declares that he desires to be laid in the cemetery with the broken in heart, "That when the Son of God comes: He may embrace me and raise me among them." His sole hope in this life, he says, and in that which is to come lies in that Firstborn who was begotten according to His nature, and was born in another birth that we may know that after our natural birth, we must undergo a rebirth so that we may become spiritual.

Death has been trampled on by the Lord, Ephraem declares. On the Cross death slew and was itself slain. A bridge has been built across Sheol. The precious pearl of victory awaits the saints. The gates of paradise are open. The Cross has opened them, and the gates of Hell are shut forever!

So Ephraem—like Prudentius (348-c.410), the Latin poet and hymn-writer; like St. Ambrose (c.339-397); and, finally, like Martin Luther (1483-1546)—expressed his Christian faith through his hymnody, and in so doing he exerted a lasting influence on both the content and the expression of the Christian faith.

ON THE TRINITY

Author: Saint Hilary of Poitiers (c.315-367)
Type of work: Theology
First transcribed: Fourth century

Principal Ideas Advanced

The true faith as taught in Scripture is opposed to heretical notions which deny the persons of the Godhead and which assert that since the Son was created, He is not God in the true sense.

Christ is the true and perfect God, neither identical in person with the Father, nor severed from the Godhead; in Christ the fullness of the Godhead dwells.

Hilary of Poitiers exerted an important influence on the growth of Christian doctrine. His work *On the Trinity* was written primarily against Arianism in the Church. The treatise is divided into twelve books which seek to set forth the true faith on the basis of Scripture, in opposition to the interpretations of heretics.

Hilary writes that heretics vary in their errors, whereas the true faith is one. Under the cloak of being loyal to the true God, some tamper with the Gospel by denying the birth of God the only-begotten. Such persons assert that there was an extension of God into man, and that He who took our flesh was the Son of Man, but was not then, nor had previously been, the Son of God. They maintain that there is an identity of begetter and begotten, that in the Incarnation the Father simply extended Himself into the Virgin and was born as His own Son. The Son and the Father are thought to be mere names or aspects of one divine person, so that there was no true birth of the Son.

Other heretics, Hilary reports, hold that the Son was merely created. They deny that Christ was, even in the beginning, God the Word with God. They cut Christ off from the divine unity, so that, as a mere creature called into being, He could not be said to possess the fullness of the Godhead.

The primary objective of Hilary's work is to refute by the clear assertion of the evangelists and prophets the false opinions of those who deny either that God was born in Christ, or that Christ is God. The true Christian faith does not confess two Gods, Hilary insists, nor yet a solitary God. It holds firmly to the confession that God the Father and God the Son are united, but not confounded. It refuses to allow that Christ is God in some imperfect sense, or that the Father and the Son are identical persons. The very center of saving faith is the faith in God as the Father, and in Christ, the Son of God; faith in Him, not as a creature, but as God the Creator.

The analogies that can be adduced in support of the true doctrine are incomplete and imperfect, Hilary concedes, for there can be no adequate comparison between God and earthly things. The truth is to be found in Scripture. Heresy results when the latter is misunderstood and given some arbitrary interpretation in defiance of the clear meaning of the words. Heresy is found not in the words as they are written, but in the sense assigned; the guilt belongs to the expositor, not to the text. To make the Son an extension of the Father is to make one and the same person both Son to Himself and also Father.

The Church has been commanded to baptize in the name of the Father, the Son, and the Holy Ghost, Hilary continues. All existence owes its origin to the Father. Through Christ, the Father is the source of all; He is self-existent, infinite, eternally anterior to time, which is a dimension of creation. Only the Son knows God. Each of the divine persons has complete and perfect knowledge of the other.

The Son is the offspring of the Father; the Only-begotten of the Unbegotten. There is a distinction, Hilary agrees, for they are Father and Son; but their divinity is not different in kind: both are One, God is God, One God only, begotten of One God unbegotten. Christ and the Father are not two Gods. There is no diversity in nature, for in the living Christ is the life of the living God. The generation of the Son is mysterious. The proper service of faith, Hilary insists, is to confess the truth, as taught by the Gospels and the Apostles. The Christian answer to heresy is that ". . . there is One Unbegotten God the Father, and One Only-begotten Son of God, perfect Offspring of perfect Parent; that the Son was begotten by no lessening of the Father or subtraction from His Substance, but that He Who possesses all things begat an all-possessing Son; a Son not emanating nor proceeding from the Father, but compact of, and inherent in, the whole Divinity of Him Who wherever He is present is present eternally. . . ."

Hilary emphasizes the belief that the son of God was born of the Virgin and of the Holy Ghost, for the sake of mankind. Since the Holy Spirit proceeds from the Father and the Son, the existence of the Holy Spirit as a person is not to be doubted. In the Christian confession of faith the Spirit is joined to the Father and to the Son. True wisdom believes what it cannot comprehend. Man cannot comprehend God's nature; he can apprehend it only as it is set forth in the Scriptures. The ineffable cannot be set forth in the limits and bounds of a definition, Hilary affirms.

God the Father and God the Son are one altogether, as Israel had been taught, not by confusion of person, but by unity of substance, writes Hilary. Scripture testifies that God is not a solitary person. God the Son is not God by adoption, or by gift of the name. He is God, equal with true God in power. Unity is to be recognized among the persons. The Arians would make Christ a creature; they are propagators of blasphemy, who deny the words, "This is my beloved Son in whom I am well pleased." Christ is

Son by birth, not by adoption, as is attested by the witness of the Apostles and by the witness of those for whom He performed miracles.

The Arians are blind to the true meaning of Scripture, Hilary insists. In Christ and the Father there is neither one person, nor two Gods. We are given full assurance of the divinity of Jesus Christ, by His name, His birth, His nature, His power, and His own assertions with respect to Himself. The prologue of John's Gospel assures us that in the beginning was the Word, and the Word was with God, and the Word was God. The very essence of the Godhead exists in the Word and is expressed in the very name.

For Christ, to be is to be in God; and it is not to be in God as one thing is in another. Hilary claims that the life and subsistence of Christ is of such a nature that although Christ is within the subsisting God, Christ has a subsistence of His own. Only one divine nature exists. The words, "I and the Father are one, and he that hath seen me hath seen the Father," indicate that the Son who is born is not inferior to the Father. He possesses the divine nature and is therefore nothing other than God. The union between the persons is perfect; it is a unity of nature, an indwelling of the Son in the Father and of the Father in the Son. Christ is one in nature with the Father, but He is not a creature, and He is one in will with the Father. The Godhead is one in nature, although it consists of three Persons.

According to Hilary, the Christian confesses that the only-begotten Son of God was born before times eternal and that He eternally contains in Himself the form and image of the invisible God.

The conclusion reached by faith and by argument, Hilary concludes, is that the Lord Jesus was born and always existed. For God the Father is eternally Father, and God the Son is eternally begotten.

THE LETTERS OF ST. JEROME

Author: Saint Jerome (c.345-420)
Type of work: Pastoral epistles
First transcribed: 370-419

Principal Ideas Advanced

When social morality is on the verge of collapse, Christians must undergo rigorous self-discipline in order to save their souls.

Those who wish to undertake the ascetic life should enter a convent instead of attempting to live as hermits.

Work and study, as well as acts of charity and mercy, are as much a part of the ascetic life as are prayer and fasting.

Even after he had undertaken an ascetic life, Jerome could not throw off his passion for literature; but, because of a dream in which he saw himself rejected at the Throne of Judgment for loving Cicero more than Christ, he made a strong resolution to attend more to sacred authors than to profane. Jerome's zeal for languages and learning never abated; and, while his energies were chiefly devoted to translating and commenting upon the Scriptures, he indulged his flair for literary invention by composing and publishing his celebrated *Letters.*

The collection of Jerome's *Letters* which has come down to posterity includes several letters written to Jerome as well as some in which he is merely mentioned. But 117 of Jerome's letters have been preserved, many of which are personal letters, while others are what we should call "open letters."

Ordained a priest, but with no specific priestly responsibilities, Jerome became a spiritual director to a wide circle of devout Romans, especially of the leisure class, during the period of Italy's hastening decline. The *Letters,* which in part are written in the manner of the Latin satirists, give a sorry picture of a society which, though nominally Christian, was really a pagan society in the last stages of disintegration. Jerome's opinion, obviously shared by many of his correspondents, is that serious Christians must undergo rigorous spiritual discipline if they are to save their own souls. He recommends that they break sharply with the customs of the society in which they live, that if possible they remove with their families to the country, and, if they are free from family responsibilities, that they take up the monastic life.

Jerome did not introduce monasticism into Italy. On the contrary, he was one of great numbers who were caught up into the movement, the seeds of which had been planted there by Athanasius (c.296-373). Inspired by the example of the Egyptian hermits, he went to Antioch in the year 374, and he spent five years in the Syrian desert. His purpose was to subdue his youthful passions; but he discovered that physical hardship by itself is not sufficient to discipline the flesh, and that one must find something important to occupy the mind. Having no talent for mystical exercises, Jerome set himself the task of improving his knowledge of Greek and of learning Hebrew, and he spent much time in the study of Scriptures. Upon returning to Rome, he was enthusiastically received into a circle of ascetically-minded Christians, whom he taught to sing psalms in Hebrew and guided in the study of the Scriptures. Then, in 385, with a number of his friends, he left Rome for Bethlehem, where the little community built a monastery and a convent. Here he spent the rest of his life, helping with the community, translating and commenting on the Scriptures, and entertaining a constant stream of visitors from all over the western world.

Like many another seeker after perfection (for example, the English clergyman William Law, in *A Serious Call to a Devout and Holy Life,* 1728), Jerome takes seriously the Scriptural injunctions about the world, the flesh, and the Devil. But, for all his rigor, Jerome is no fanatic, and he does not lose the capacity to suit his advice to the needs of the person at hand. Indeed, he takes his place, along with Benedict of Nursia (c.480-c.547), as one who has helped regulate and moderate the ascetic life.

Jerome's views concerning monasticism, like those of Benedict, are the product of first-hand experience. He requires both monks and nuns to work with their hands, to care for the sick and the poor, to memorize the Scriptures, and to observe stated hours of prayer. He sometimes praises austerities in persons notable for their charity and zeal; but he recommends modest fare and cleanliness as ministering more to a useful life. Knowing the irregularities which overtake most anchorites, he maintains that the discipline of a monastery is preferable for most people. "Do I condemn a solitary life?" he writes to a young man who was contemplating a religious profession; "By no means: in fact I have often commended it. But I wish to see the monastic schools turn out soldiers who have no fear of the rough training of the desert, who have exhibited the spectacles of a holy life for a considerable time, who have made themselves last that they might be first, who have not been overcome by hunger or satiety, whose joy is in poverty, who teach virtue by their garb and mien, and who are too conscientious to invent—as some silly men do—monstrous stories of struggles with demons. . . ."

The most characteristic of Jerome's *Letters* are addressed to members of the circle of Christian friends whom he left behind him in Rome. The reader soon makes the acquaintance of the aristocratic widow, Marcella, who was one of those influenced by Athanasius to profess the monastic life. Her home on the Aventine was a shelter for Christian virgins and widows and the center of the circle in which Jerome was most at home. Many of the *Letters* are in response to Marcella's requests for help in the study of the Bible. Another remarkable woman was Fabriola, the Magdalene of the group, who, as penance for her youthful folly, sold her lands and gave the money to the poor. Jerome writes: "She was the first person to found a hospital, into which she might gather sufferers out of the streets, and where she might nurse the unfortunate victims of sickness and want." But most celebrated of all was the impetuous Paula, mother of five remarkable children, who led a company of virgins to Bethlehem and established the convent there. Her unmarried daughter, Eustochium, accompanied her in her travels and took her place at the head of the convent upon the death of her mother, to be succeeded in turn by a second Paula, granddaughter of the first. Of the mother, Jerome says, "So lavish was her charity that she robbed her children; and, when her relatives remonstrated with her for doing so, she declared that she was leaving to them a better inheritance in the mercy of Christ." Jerome's letters to these friends are unfailingly kind and courteous, whether he is counseling or consoling, instructing in the Scriptures, or eulogizing departed saints.

Jerome's courtesy sometimes fails him when he is engaged in controversy with other theologians and ecclesiastics. Augustine of Hippo (354-430) wrote in the year 397 to question Jerome concerning the latter's interpretation of the rebuke administered by Paul to Peter, according to Galatians 2:11. Taking the accounts of Paul given in The Acts, Jerome had charged Paul with the same kind of tergiversation with which Paul had charged Peter. Augustine's letter questioning Jerome's interpretation did not get to Jerome, but was transcribed and circulated in the West so that to Jerome it seemed that Augustine was attacking him behind his back. Not for several years were the two great Latin churchmen able to make up their quarrel.

Jerome was even more violent in attacking those with whom he disagreed on principle, notably the partisans of Origen (c.185-c.254), and of Pelagius (c.355-c.425). In theological matters, Jerome may not have had the insight that characterized his work in Biblical exegesis. At any rate, he seems at first not to have detected anything heretical in either of these writers; and when at last he joins issue with them, he does so along established lines. One important issue, however, comes out of these disputes; namely, a clarification of the Church's doctrine concerning the origin of the soul. Jerome distinguishes three possible positions: that men's souls were "created long since" and "kept in God's storehouse"; that "they are formed by God and introduced into bodies day by day"; and that "they are transmitted by propagation." The followers of Origen held to the first of these views; Tertullian and most of the Western writers held to the third; but Jerome argued for the second view, and the Western Church has generally followed Jerome, in spite of the authority of Augustine, who was inclined toward the third view as better securing the doctrine of original sin.

Many of Jerome's letters were concerned with theological questions, as was, for example, his correspondence with Pope Damasus (c.304-384). Jerome had definite opinions about the proper procedure for translating the Bible. But for the most part he dedicated himself to stressing the value of the ascetic life and the duties of the clergy. His letters are a reflection of the spiritual and intellectual turmoil of his times, and they reveal a passionately spiritual man who demanded as much of himself as he did of others.

PANARION

Author: Saint Epiphanius of Salamis (c.315-403)
Type of work: Heresiology
First transcribed: c.377

Principal Ideas Advanced

Heresy is as old as creation and consists primarily of man's tendency to render divine honors to the creature rather than to the creator.

The Church alone has received the genuine tradition of Christ and the Apostles.

The tradition of Christ is contained in the Church's teachings and comprises the only effective antidote against the poison of heresy.

The title which Epiphanius chose for his lengthy work against heresies is suggestive of his conception of the nature of heresy and the means by which it could be overcome. The Greek word *panarion* means "medicine chest."

Epiphanius, in other words, regarded heresy as a deadly poison which would result in spiritual death unless treated by an effective antidote. The "medicine" which Epiphanius held out as antidote was the orthodox tradition of the Church, which, by its very nature, was life-giving and therapeutic.

Few figures in the history of the Church have dedicated themselves so thoroughly to the study of heresy as did Epiphanius. The obvious enjoyment which he derived from identifying and attacking heretical ideas prompted him to see heresies and heretics virtually everywhere he looked. In a number of instances, it would seem that he actually invented heresies and provided them with a history in order that he might further indulge his passion for heresy-hunting. In other instances, he included under the label of heresy certain movements and ideas which, for someone with a more open mind than Epiphanius possessed, would have no place in a Christian catalogue of heresies.

The *Panarion* is generally regarded as the most important treatise written by Epiphanius. It was written in response to a request by two monks for a more detailed study of the heresies which Epiphanius had earlier set forth in his doctrinal treatise, the *Ancoratus*. The *Panarion* is divided into three major sections and considers a total of eighty heresies. The first section deals with pre-Christian heresies and is subdivided, in turn, in accordance with the scheme suggested by Colossians 3:11, into the heresies of Barbarism, Scythianism, Hellenism, Samaritanism and Judaism. Most of what he has to say about Barbarism, Scythianism, and Samaritanism is of little value, reflecting more of a concern for schematization than for historical accuracy.

Epiphanius's identification of the heresies within Hellenism provides an interesting insight into his own intellectual and theological bias, since, for him, the philosophical schools—Platonism, Pythagoreanism, Stoicism, Epicureanism—were the chief transmitters of heresy within Hellenism. At this point, it might be argued, Epiphanius succeeds in displaying not so much the heresy of the philosophical schools, as his own suspicion of classical Greek philosophy. With respect to Judaism, there were, according to Epiphanius, seven distinct heretical sects—the Sadducees, Scribes, Pharisees, Hemerobaptists, Nazarenes, Essenes, and Herodians. Epiphanius's treatment betrays a lack of historical perspective, although the recent discoveries of the *Dead Sea Scrolls* have shown that in some respects Epiphanius's knowledge of first century Judaism was not as deficient as once was supposed.

The second division of the *Panarion* deals with the heretical sects of the second and third centuries, chiefly those of the Judeo-Christians and the Gnostics. Here, Epiphanius is both confused and unfair. Like most of the early Fathers, Epiphanius imputed the basest of motives and a complete lack of moral principles to the leaders of the heretical sects. The chief value of the second division of the *Panarion* is that it preserves the works of earlier writers such as Justin Martyr (c.100-c.165) and Hippolytus (c.170-c.236), whose testimony concerning the heresies of their times is far more reliable than that which resulted from Epiphanius's own independent investigations. A number of writings by some of the early heretics themselves, which otherwise would have been completely lost, are also included in this section and add considerably to its value.

The third section brings Epiphanius's study of heresy down to his own day and includes discussion of such important groups as the Arians, Semi-Arians, Apollinarians, and Pneumatomachi. The fact that he knew these heretical groups intimately makes this part of the *Panarion* much more valuable and reliable than the earlier sections, where his knowledge was often based on nothing more than his own imagination. If the quality of his scholarship improves in this section, however, his narrow-mindedness does not. His attack against the theology associated with the great Alexandrian scholar Origen (c.185-c.254) is particularly indicative of his uncharitable spirit. Epiphanius was incapable of appreciating the rich philosophical orientation of Origen's thought, an orientation which occasionally resulted in some rather bold conjectures on Origen's part. Rather than acknowledge the great debt of the Church to Origen, Epiphanius chose to concentrate on certain peripheral aspects of Origen's thought and thereby to force Origen into the gallery of heretics. It is important to note in this connection that Epiphanius was not at all an armchair heresiologist. His opposition to Origenism—an opposition prompted by a meeting with St. Jerome in Rome in 392—led him to make a relentless search throughout the Eastern churches for traces of Origen's thought, and he condemned in the most unreasonable fashion anyone who admitted a debt to Origen.

The *Panarion,* sometimes called the "Refutation of all the Heresies," is positively dedicated to the proposition that spiritual health is established and preserved only by correct opinions and beliefs. These correct opinions and beliefs are to be found, Epiphanius claimed, only within the doctrinal tradition of the Church.

FIVE THEOLOGICAL ORATIONS

Author: Saint Gregory of Nazianzus (329-389)
Type of work: Theology
First transcribed: c.380

Principal Ideas Advanced

Because God is its subject, theological discourse can be carried on only within the limits of what is proper for man to say and what is possible for man to know; the mystery may not be treated lightly, and God's nature ultimately remains beyond man's comprehension.

By visible signs and natural law men may know that God exists; but who God is, that which is described by the doctrine of the Trinity, is known only through Scripture and illumination.

The Father, Son, and Holy Spirit, eternally one God, are equal in nature; but they are distinguished in that the Father is unbegotten, the Son is begotten, and the Spirit proceeds.

When we consider the Godhead, or the divine monarchy, what we conceive of is one; but when we consider the Persons of the Godhead, there are three whom we worship.

The *Five Theological Orations* of St. Gregory of Nazianzus earned for him, more than did any other of his works, the honorific title of "Theologian" in the Eastern Orthodox Church. He was noted for his polished style as a writer and orator, his dislike for unrestrained theological speculation, his aversion to the tumultuous life of a bishop, and above all for his contribution to the definition of the doctrine of the Trinity which was accepted at the Second Ecumenical Council held at Constantinople in 381.

Like his two great contemporary compatriots, St. Basil of Caesarea (c.330-379) and Basil's brother, St. Gregory of Nyssa (c.330-c.395), St. Gregory of Nazianzus came from a leading aristocratic family of Cappadocia, a district of Asia Minor. The son of a bishop of Nazianzus, Gregory was educated in Caesarea of Palestine and Alexandria of Egypt. When he was about thirty he was baptized either in Athens, where he was a student with St. Basil, or upon his return to his own country. Much of Gregory's life was spent alternating between able work as a priest or bishop and retreat to the solitude he so dearly loved. Gregory found himself in the center of theological controversy when he was called in 379 to Constantinople to lead the minority of Christians there who held to the faith as set forth by the Council of Nicaea (325). The following year, the Emperor Theodosius installed Gregory in the imperial Church of Santa Sophia in place of the rival bishop Demophilus. Although the Second Ecumenical Council confirmed him as the patriarch of Constantinople, Gregory resigned his office there to administer once again the diocese of Nazianzus before retiring (384) to his estate in Arianzum, where he remained until his death.

The *Five Theological Orations* (*Orationes* 27-31) were delivered as sermons in Constantinople in 380. The first of the five is introductory and posits, against the excesses of the Eunomians, the limits within which genuine theological discourse may take place. The Eunomians taught a special form of Arianism (which said that Christ was not of the same nature as the Father but was an intermediary between the Father and creation) to the effect that the Son was unlike the Father. The Eunomians were also known for the boldness with which they discussed the most intimate features of God's being. Gregory complains that these talkative dialecticians so delight in strife over words that every marketplace buzzes with profane babblings about that which is most sacred. He maintains that the subject of God is not so cheap that everyone can philosophize about it: discussion about God is only for certain occasions, before certain men, and within certain limits. As in dress and diet, and laughter and demeanor, there is a certain decorum in speech and silence, especially so for Christians because of their reverence for the Word as a title of God. Systematic reflection about God is permitted only to those who have been duly trained, who are skilled in meditation, and who have been or are being purified. Gregory adds that it is necessary to be truly at leisure to know God, for then we have an appropriate time to discern the straight road of divine matters. He says he is not against continual remembrance of God, which is desirable, nor does he want to hinder all talking about God; his objection is to a lack of proper moderation. The reason for Gregory's insistent warning is that ultimately God's nature is incomprehensible to us in this life, and that without these limits in theological discourse ". . . our great mystery is in danger of being made a thing of little moment." (First Theological Oration).

In the second of these orations, Gregory considers how we may know God, whose inscrutability imposes the boundaries explained in the first oration. At the outset, Gregory discloses the method controlling his theological deliberation: ". . . being molded and molding others by Holy Scripture . . . let us now enter upon theological questions, setting at the head thereof the Father, the Son, and the Holy Ghost, of whom we are to treat; that the Father may be well pleased, and the Son may help us, and the Holy Ghost may inspire us; or rather that one illumination may come upon us from the one God, one in diversity, diverse in unity, wherein is a marvel." (Second Theological Oration). Drawing on Exodus 32, Gregory likens the theologian's experience to that of ascending a mount and drawing aside the cloudy curtain by going away from materiality and withdrawing within oneself. Sheltered by the rock which is the Word made flesh for us, the theologian sees only the back parts of God: not the primary and unmingled nature, known exclusively to the Trinity itself, but only ". . . that nature, which at last even reaches to us. And that is, as far as I can learn, the majesty, or, as holy David calls it, the glory which is manifested among the creatures, which it has produced and governs." (Second Theological Oration). The darkness of this world and of the flesh prevents a full understanding of the truth in this life.

Gregory's admonition is not to be used as a starting-point for a quibbling denial of God. For him, we can know by reason that God *is* but not *Who* He is. Our eyes, seeing the beautiful stability and progress of visible things as ordered by natural law and reasoning back from the order of these things to their author, teach us that God exists and that He is their efficient and maintaining cause. Every rational nature longs for God but is unable to grasp Him. Impatient at this disability, the rational creature either fabricates idols out of visible things or attains through the visible order that which is above sight. In the latter case reason, which proceeds from God and is implanted in all from the beginning, enables this ascent. Relying upon all the approximations of reason, however, man still cannot comprehend God: "For how is he an object of worship if he be circumscribed?" (Second Oration).

In the third and fourth theological orations, Gregory sets out to refute his opponents and to state his position on the equality and distinction of the Son in relation to the Father. Some of his adversaries ascribed the name of God only to the Father; others bestowed on the Son a name equal to the one they applied to God but in practice denied

His deity by denying exact equality. Gregory's position is that among the three ancient opinions concerning God, namely, anarchy, polyarchy, and monarchy, the first two were the favorites of the Greeks and led to disorder and dissolution, while the third is the one honored by Christians. However, monarchy, the rule by the one God, is not limited to any one of the Persons of the Trinity: "The Father is the begetter and the emitter; without passion, of course, and without reference to time, and not in a corporeal manner. The Son is the begotten, and the Holy Ghost the emission; for I know not how this could be expressed in terms altogether excluding visible things." (Third Theological Oration). We are not to think of this generation, this begetting of the Son, as an involuntary and natural overflow of goodness. Nor are we to think of the "when" of this generation since it is above all time. The only answer to the question "when" the Father came into being is that "There never was a time when he was not." (Third Oration). (This crucial formula, which is a repudiation of the slogan of Arius, "There was when he was not," is not accurately rendered into English by the phrase used here. The Greek expresses an important subtlety and says literally, "There never was when he was not." Gregory uses this formula so as not to concede the possibility of "time" as a category applicable to the Godhead.) The same is the case with the begetting of the Son and the proceeding of the Spirit. The Son and the Holy Spirit originate from the Father, yet are co-eternal with him since the Father is everlastingly the cause and therefore is not "prior" to the effects. The generation of the Son is without passion because it is incorporeal, yet it is voluntary since will is not passion.

While all this points to the distinctiveness of the Persons, it also describes their full equality. Countering the viewpoint which insists the uncreated and the created are not the same any more than begetting and being begotten are the same, Gregory preaches that the begetter and the begotten are nonetheless of the same nature, that therein lies the object of the "Father-Son" terminology: the offspring is of the same nature as the parent. The term "Father" does not refer to essence or action; it is a name of relationship indicating an identity of nature. Should "Father" be taken as a term of essence, a Son of the same nature is implied anyway, and if it be taken as a term of action, a Son who is *homoousios* (of the same nature) with the Father is also included.

Gregory recognizes two kinds of Biblical passages about Christ: those witnessing to His divinity and those suggesting His inequality with the Father. The correct interpretation of both sorts, he says, is to apply what is lofty to the Godhead and to that nature in Him which is incorporeal and above all suffering, and to apply what is lowly to the composite condition of Him who for our sakes made Himself of no reputation, who was incarnate, and indeed who was made man and was afterwards exalted. He was incarnate for a cause, and the cause was that we might be saved.

In the fifth theological oration, an oration of particular significance for Greek Orthodoxy, Gregory turns to the campaign against the doctrine of the Trinity waged by another group, the Macedonians. These men rejected the divinity of the Holy Spirit, maintaining instead that He was a creature of the Son. Gregory holds that the Holy Spirit is no strange or interpolated God, as those Macedonians imagine who are so literal in their exposition of Scripture. If ever there was a time when the Father or the Son did not exist, there was also a time when the Spirit did not exist. But if one was from the beginning, then the three were from the beginning. It will not do to call the Spirit God in such a way as to deny His equality in nature with the Father and the Son. If the Spirit is God, then He is consubstantial with the Father and the Son; He is not a creature, nor a fellow servant, nor is any such lowly designation appropriate to Him. The Holy Spirit's distinctiveness lies in His procession, His eternal going forth from the Father by a process of generation which, like the generation of the Son, is beyond human comprehension. The very fact of being unbegotten, of being begotten, and of proceeding gives the name of Father to the first, Son to the second, and Holy Spirit to the third, so that the distinction of the three Persons may be preserved in the one nature and dignity of the Godhead. "When, then, we look at the Godhead, or the first cause, or the monarchia, that which we conceive is one; but when we look at the Persons in whom the Godhead dwells, and at those who timelessly and with equal glory have their being from the first cause, there are three whom we worship." (Fifth Theological Oration).

A final complication dealt with by Gregory is the Macedonian allegation that Scripture is silent about the divinity of the Spirit. On this, he teaches that by God's gracious dispensation the Old Testament proclaims the Father openly and the Son more obscurely, that the New Testament manifests the Son and suggests the deity of the Spirit, and that now the Spirit Himself dwells among us and supplies us with a clear demonstration of Himself. The Holy Spirit's divinity is so marvelous that men could not have believed it without the marvelous precedent of Christ's Resurrection. Of the many things the Savior promised that the Spirit would manifest to His followers, none was greater than the Spirit's divinity. Even if Scripture were silent in this matter, these arguments would still support this doctrine. Yet Gregory goes on to say that in fact Scripture does provide a wealth of testimonies for the divinity of the Spirit.

In the end, Gregory concludes that all images fall short of the subject and that it is best for him, using few words, to abide by the reverent conceptions, to keep as his comrade the enlightenment of the Holy Spirit, and to pass through this world persuading others to worship Father, Son, and Holy Ghost, the one Godhead and power.

HOMILIES ON THE STATUES

Author: Saint John Chrysostom (c.347-407)
Type of work: Sermons on Christian Practice
First transcribed: 387

Principal Ideas Advanced

In a time of civic danger, the Church, like a mother, comforts and strengthens those who turn to her.

Christians need have no fear of loss, not even loss of life itself.

The Christian should lead a life of austerity and mortification; the true ascetic is one who is pure in heart, reverent toward God, and charitable toward all men.

The Christian priest ministers redemption through the sacraments, and persuades men to do the will of God by means of the art of preaching.

Of the extensive body of Chrysostom's writing to be preserved, the most permanently valuable are his commentaries on Biblical books, and his sermons or homilies. Especially celebrated are the collection of twenty-one *Homilies on the Statues,* delivered when Chrysostom was a priest at his native city, Antioch, prior to being made Archbishop of Constantinople.

The series takes its name from a serious political incident which developed during the Lenten season in which the sermons were preached, an incident which, to a considerable degree, determined the character of the sermons. Certain elements in Antioch, stirred by resentment over a new tax levy, stormed the Prefect's palace, and, when repulsed, vented their anger by overthrowing the public statues of the Emperor Theodosius (346-395) and his late Empress, and dragging them through the streets. The Prefect imprisoned a large number of leading citizens and brought them to trial. Meanwhile, the entire population awaited fearfully the judgment of the Emperor. Rumor ran wild, and many inhabitants fled the city under the impression that the whole population would be slain and the buildings razed. The incident, however, came to a relatively happy conclusion when, on Easter, it was announced that the Emperor had granted full pardon.

Chrysostom did not take the pulpit on account of the disturbances. It was his practice, during Lent, to preach three or four times a week. Indeed, the first homily of this series was given a few days before the seditious acts were committed. But since the fear that emptied the forums and marketplaces filled the churches, it could not be ignored. Chrysostom spoke of the matter at hand, particularly in homilies two through six. For the rest, he dealt very much in his ordinary manner with Lenten topics, giving only incidental attention to the civic concern, until he came to the final sermon, which, falling on Easter, coincided with the news of the city's deliverance. Various incidents, however, provide topical interest. Flavian, Bishop of Antioch, though an old man, traveled to Constantinople, and was largely influential in moving Theodosius to clemency. Great numbers of Christian monks left their cloisters in the desert and returned to Antioch in order to share whatever punishment should be visited upon the citizens. These sacrificial acts, says Chrysostom, demonstrate the love which the Church has toward men. He points, by way of contrast, to the pagan philosophers, who, he says, forsook the city and hid themselves in caves as soon as danger appeared. The *Homilies* also contain vivid and moving descriptions of the brutality of soldiers, the devotion of wives and sisters, and the odd and unpredictable sorts of conduct, sometimes pathetic, sometimes heroic, which sudden stress produces among a people unaccustomed to danger and hardship.

Chrysostom roundly condemns those who overthrew the statues, and he places the Church solidly on the side of Imperial authority. The Church, he says, stands to the Emperor in the same relation as a mother does to the schoolmaster: when the child is punished, she comforts him, and she tries to show him the necessity for the master's severity. His main point, however, is that Christians ought not fear any penalty which the Emperor may choose to impose. As an ascetic moralist, who has himself spent several years in the desert as a monk, Chrysostom argues against the vanity of wealth and position. "We do not live with the austerity that becometh Christians," he says. The Christian, he maintains, should have no fear of what man can do to him: "He who by the aid of virtue leads a life of austerity, and mortification, earnestly longs for death in order that he may be freed from his present labours, and may be able to have full assurance in regard to the crowns laid up in store." Chrysostom presses home his teaching with the aid of such Old Testament stories as that of the destruction of Sodom, Esther's intercession for the Jews, Jonah's mission to Nineveh, the temptation of Job, and the trial of the three young men in Nebuchadnezzar's fiery furnace. To the Socratic (and Stoic) persuasion that no harm can happen to the good man, and the Hebraic confidence that temporal loss and gain are tokens of divine judgment, he adds the Christian conviction that life on earth is merely preparatory to an eternity of condemnation or blessedness.

The more general topics which Chrysostom deals with in these Lenten sermons are fasting, swearing, and forgiving one's neighbor. Chrysostom is an intrepid expounder of Scripture, as might be expected from the impressive list of commentaries which he wrote, but he uses Scripture to enforce practical, not theological, lessons.

Speaking of fasting, he takes as his text Paul's words to Timothy: "Drink a little wine for thy stomach's sake, and thine often infirmities." Timothy was, on the witness of this text, an abstainer, says Chrysostom; that is, he knew the dangers of indulging fleshly appetites. But Paul assures him that there is nothing wrong in partaking of wine as such, the evil lying in the abuse of a thing that is good. Nevertheless, Paul enforces the need for mastering our desires, inasmuch as he says, "Drink a little."

The practice of swearing is treated more frequently than any other subject. In sermon after sermon, Chrysostom reproaches his hearers with their bad habit of using oaths. We may take this as a commentary on the customs of the times, but it is also a lesson in moral pedagogy, for if a people are severely taken in a fault, it is not enough to preach a single sermon against it; one must preach sermon after sermon, repeating as much as is necessary until a sufficient impression has been made. If one has the wit and imagination of a Chrysostom (whose surname, meaning The Golden Mouth, was given to him because of his eloquence), repetition need never become stale. Chrysostom's most striking text against swearing is that which tells of the curse which King Saul pronounced in the heat of battle against any who should partake of food before victory, and of his son Jonathan's unwitting violation of his father's oath. Another is that of the oath of Herod which led to the death of John the Baptist. Let each of you, Chrysostom enjoins, "taking the head of John, just cut off, and the warm blood yet dripping from it, . . . go home, and think that you saw it before your eyes, while it emitted a voice, and said, 'Abhor my murderer, the oath!' "

Chrysostom takes up the subject of forgiveness in the next to last homily. As the time for Holy Communion approaches, it behooves each one to consider what fault remains that will prevent his participating in the Feast with a good conscience, especially whether he is at odds with his fellow man. "Let no one who hath an enemy draw near the sacred Table, or receive the Lord's body!" the preacher warns; "Let no one who draws near have an enemy! Hast thou an enemy? Draw not near! Wilt thou draw near? Be reconciled, and then draw near, and touch the Holy thing!" He proceeds to give a profound analysis of the violence which resentment does, not to the man toward whom it is directed, but to the man who nourishes it in his breast. "For thou supposest that thou art paying him back the injury; but thou art first tormenting thyself, and setting up thy rage as an executioner within thee in every part, and tearing up thine own bowels." But does someone suppose that it is a weakness to be reconciled to those who have done wrong, and that it will make the wicked man worse? On the contrary, says Chrysostom, he will become far worse if you remain unreconciled toward him, while if you offer to forgive him, his heart may be touched. "For although he were the vilest of men; although he might neither confess nor publish it openly; yet he will silently approve thy Christian wisdom, and in his own conscience will respect thy gentleness."

Chrysostom's preaching consists mainly in exhorting men to live according to the righteousness of God and to forsake the ways of the world and of their great adversary, the Devil. Protestants will miss in the *Homilies* any pronounced evangelical emphasis, but this does not mean that Chrysostom was lacking in appreciation of the redemptive work of Christ; rather, he stood in the sacerdotal tradition and held that the grace of God is communicated objectively through the sacraments. Readers who are interested in Chrysostom's own reflections on the office of preaching are advised to turn to his *Treatise on the Priesthood,* where, besides magnifying the office of the priest in the Eucharistic sacrifice, where Christ is "laid upon the altar," and the priest stands "praying over the victim," he also places great stress on the "ministry of the Word." Preaching, says Chrysostom, who was trained as a rhetorician before he became a Christian, does not come by nature, but by study and practice. It is an art to be judged by strict canons like any other art, and not by the applause of the masses. The preacher, in Chrysostom's view, is a workman responsible to God, committed with the task of bringing the multitudes to know and obey the will of their Sovereign. It is a particularly difficult task, because the multitudes only half listen, and consequently they readily distort what they hear, for their own purposes. Hence, the preacher must never be swayed by their praise or blame, but must labor in his sermons with a view to pleasing God.

ON THE DUTIES OF THE CLERGY

Author: Saint Ambrose (c.339-397)
Type of work: Christian ethics
First transcribed: c.391

Principal Ideas Advanced

Christian virtue is living according to Christ and, consequently, according to what is most in harmony with nature and reason.

The Christian life is balanced and observes due measure; it is not given to the pursuit of extremes in either external affairs and possessions, or in internal states of character.

Whatever is virtuous and whatever is useful to our final happiness are identical.

When *On the Duties of the Clergy* was written about 391 by Ambrose, Bishop of Milan, the Christian Church enjoyed a favored status in Roman imperial policy and was active in formulating its internal discipline. A startling illustration of what could happen in the provision of leadership was the experience of Ambrose himself. He was chosen to be Bishop of Milan in 374 while he was as yet unbaptized (although he had been converted, of course), and only eight days intervened between his baptism and his elevation to the bishopric (at which time he was a catechumen). In addition, his predecessor had been an advocate of Arianism, a theological position which Ambrose vigorously opposed. This change in the doctrinal allegiance of the occupant of the bishop's chair was not a considered product of formal discussion, but a matter of personal perspective on the part of the incumbent.

Clearly, much had yet to be done in the ordering of the ministry when such happenings were possible, and Ambrose's book, *De officiis ministrorum*, was produced as a contribution to one area of concern; namely, the kind of Christian morality that should govern the life of the clergy and, in turn, that of their congregations. The book was written as a practical guide for the young men whom Ambrose was preparing for ordination.

The significance of the work is both in what it has to say and in the time and circumstances in which it was said. Ambrose had had no training in Christian theology or ethics, and he confesses that he had to teach and learn at the same time. His education was that of the Roman governing classes, and, in his case, fortunately, his studies included Greek. With this background it is not surprising that Ambrose turned to Stoic literature for a model when he proposed to discuss the obligations of the clergy. Cicero had written a book, *De officiis,* and this provided a basis from which to work, although the actual occasion on which Ambrose decided to write on the theme was a meditation on Psalm 39.

The work is divided into three books, the first dealing with what is virtuous, the second with what is useful, and the third with a comparison of the two. The fact is, however, that this plan is only loosely adhered to, and there are topics in all the books that do not fit the scheme, and, again, topics that recur throughout the entire work.

Even though the debt to Cicero is obvious, Ambrose did not simply repeat Stoic maxims on moderation, self-control, manly virtue, and self realization. Although by later standards of Christian ethics the book as a whole has its limitations and leaves much to be desired, it is nevertheless a Christian work directed toward "the blessing of eternal life" and not simply toward worldly happiness. Allusions to Scripture are copious, the work of God in history is everywhere emphasized, and the authority of Christ for life-direction is explicitly confessed.

The first duty of any man, Ambrose asserts, is to do what is seemly or suitable, especially with regard to speech. A note of "due measure" recurs again and again; virtue is rewarded. Such an idea seems to be contrary to much of our experience, however, for evil men are often found to be prosperous, and the innocent, like Job, are left in want. But if the conscience of wicked men is taken into account, the picture is different, for the soul of an evil man "is more foul than any sepulchre" and his end is in Hell. Nothing escapes the knowledge of God, the just judge of all, and the end will vindicate the righteous.

The duties of youth are next enumerated in traditional terms; namely, the fear of God, subjection to parents, respect for age, preservation of purity, and, especially, modesty in word and deed. "The movement of the body is a sort of voice of the soul," Ambrose writes. He recalls that he refused to accept among his clergy a person who was arrogant in his gestures. Even the way we walk reveals our disposition. "We ought to be humble, gentle, mild, serious, patient," Ambrose continues; "We must keep the mean in all things, so that a calm countenance and quiet speech may show that there is no vice in our lives."

The principle of due measure has a clear contextual reference. What is virtuous will vary with the occasion in which we act, for we must act suitably and not with a rigid conformity to rules, all of which is abundantly illustrated by Abraham, Jacob, Joseph, Job, and David. These men followed the four virtues of prudence, justice, fortitude, and temperance.

Ambrose then develops the classical quartet of virtues, and he attempts to subsume the many qualities of the good life under these key categories, showing that they are interdependent and all united in piety. He is insistent that good will is as necessary as good external action and that this inner motivation will greatly affect the specific behavior of the Christian man.

His treatment of fortitude, however, reveals the latent difficulty of handling a Christian ethic under a pagan formula. Examples of courage are plentiful in the Old Testament, but the Christian martyrs are eulogized. Again, courage in withstanding temptations of the mind is duly delineated and praised; but love and humility do not fit easily into the Roman admiration for the military virtues, and in Book III Ambrose denies that a Christian should defend himself when attacked "lest in defending his life he should stain his love toward his neighbour."

The second book opens with the thesis, "So great is the splendour of a virtuous life that a peaceful conscience and a calm innocence work out a happy life"; that is, it is most useful to achieve the truly blessed life. Happiness has been variously defined by philosophers in terms of freedom from pain, knowledge, or pleasure, but the Scriptures clearly associate it with "divine things and . . . the fruit of good works." It is a mistake to base happiness on good fortune or to tie it to external possessions. Indeed, some things, such as riches, which are counted good, can be a hindrance to the blessed life; on the other hand, things such as pain, blindness, exile, hunger, slavery, which are thought to be bad, can promote it. What is truly useful is truly godly and serves Christ.

Love is outstanding in its relation to utility. We should labor to be loved by showing moderation, courtesy, honor, and modesty, as Moses and David showed gentleness and affection even to those who had wronged them. Ambrose writes, "It gives a very great impetus to mutual love if one shows love in return to those who love us and proves that one does not love them less than oneself is loved, especially if one shows it by the proofs that a faithful friendship gives."

Utility is also closely allied to the four cardinal virtues. The man who practices the virtues inspires the confidence of others so that his counsel is sought and he is then able to do the most good.

How wonderful it is "to gain the love of the people by liberality," Ambrose exclaims. This remark is especially pertinent to the clergy, who have opportunity to influence liberality by the feeding of the poor, the redemption of captives, and many other forms of kindness. Due measure, however, has to be observed in liberality for, Ambrose advises, it must be "neither too freely shown to those who are unsuitable, nor too sparingly bestowed upon the needy." Professional beggars, for example, have to be watched: "If anyone were to trust their tale too readily, he would quickly drain the fund which is meant to serve the sustenance of the poor." Ambrose, obviously, had had experience in handling the importunate, and he offers sage advice at considerable length on the administration of church funds. Generosity is a virtue only when it is wise and unostentatious.

If one would learn true wisdom, he must seek the company of wise men, for we become like our companions. Especially ought the young to improve themselves by friendship with the old, as did Joshua with Moses, Elisha with Elijah, Mark with Barnabas, and Timothy with Paul. This is the direct way to be worthy of esteem and to avoid extravagance, dissipation, and destruction. We must study hospitality, defend the weak, and shun avarice, pretense, and adulation.

In one of the most eloquent passages in *De officiis ministrorum,* Ambrose discourses on the occasion when he sold the gold vessels of the church to redeem some captives: "So I once brought odium on myself because I broke up the sacred vessels to redeem captives." But his memorable act, he believed, was according to the spirit of Christ: "It is far better to preserve souls than gold for the Lord." In so acting he followed, he claims, the example of the martyr Lawrence who, when the treasures of the church were demanded from him, brought the poor together: "When asked where the treasures were which he had promised, he pointed to the poor, saying, 'These are the treasures of the church.' "

In the third book the comparison between virtue and utility is discussed. The two are not opposed if they are understood as identical when informed by the Christian spirit. To emphasize this point, Ambrose draws a distinction between ordinary levels of duty and the perfection which the Christian obligation imposes. This distinction led in later ethical theory to the double standard by which one set of duties (the commandments) was expected of laymen and a higher standard of poverty, obedience, and chastity (the counsels) was demanded of the clergy. At this stage, however, the division is at the more elementary level of a comparison between what "the many" count as good, such as saving money or enjoying a banquet, and the self-sacrifice and other-centered ideals of those who are dedicated to Christ. The distinction had been noted in Book I, but it is repeated in Book III, preparatory to an expansion of the "primary" duties of the many. Ambrose is not altogether clear as to the significance of this duality in duty, for he notes Paul's sayings about being not yet perfect and being already perfect, and he concludes that "There is a twofold form of perfection, the one having but ordinary, the other the highest worth. The one availing here, the other hereafter." What develops in the discussion that follows is little more than a commendation of conduct that serves others rather than the self. To act in such a manner is to be conformed to Christ. We are to be concerned for all who need our help, knowing that we are in a relation of interdependence after the manner of an organism. To act thus is to follow also the law of nature, for "a man who guides himself according to the ruling of nature, so as to be obedient to her, can never injure another." Thus, conscience rebukes us when we are unjust, cruel, and self-centered. Even if we could make ourselves invisible, the upright man will live according to the example of Christ. He will "not hide his person by putting on a ring, but his life by putting on Christ."

By this standard a Christian will never injure another for self-advantage, defraud others in the market, expel strangers in time of famine, or be a party to financial trickery. If a person binds himself with a promise which is subsequently seen to involve what is dishonorable, he is not under any obligation to keep such a commitment. Better that Herod should have perjured himself, than keep his promise to murder John the Baptist. Even for the sake of friendship, which is the guardian of virtue, no one should betray his integrity. It is with a eulogy on friendship that Ambrose concludes his work *On the*

Duties of the Clergy. He has, he says, spoken what will be to the advantage of his readers, and supported his reflections with many illustrations from the past, "So that, although the language may not be graceful, yet a succession of old-time examples set down in such a small compass may offer much instruction."

THE GREAT CATECHISM

Author: Saint Gregory of Nyssa (c.330-c.395)
Type of work: Spiritual instruction
First transcribed: c.395

Principal Ideas Advanced

The Christian must avoid not only polytheism but also any monotheism which leads to a rejection of the Trinity.

The doctrine of the Incarnation is central to Christian teaching and may be understood through analogy.

The sacrament of baptism is the first and necessary step in a resurrection to a new, immortal life.

Unless they be followed by righteousness in living, the sacraments are without value.

In *The Great Catechism* by Gregory, Bishop of Nyssa, are found those qualities which caused him to be held in high esteem by his contemporaries and have earned for him an enduring place in the history of the Christian Church as one of its honored founders. The combination of personal sanctity, theological erudition, and zealous defense of Nicene creedal orthodoxy, apparent here as throughout his works, understandably brought to Gregory high praise, leading to his being termed the Father of Fathers and to his being elevated to sainthood. Moreover, Gregory's passionate concerns for the fruit of orthodoxy in righteous living and for the conversion of those outside the faith through carefully balanced and discriminating explanations of Christian beliefs, add to the work an appeal which overcomes the limitations of his historical period and give it an abiding value.

The third son of ten children born to a Christian family of wealth and distinction in the important bishopric of Cappadocia, Gregory, because of delicate health, was educated at home. It is noteworthy that his older sister was extremely devout and established a religious society, and that his brother, Basil, who had studied in Athens and was a student of the great Christian apologist, Origen, was Gregory's most influential teacher. Termed shy and retiring, Gregory remained at home and chose no profession. His religious awakening occurred in a vision which came during a religious service at which he had fallen asleep through fatigue. His sister persuaded him to abandon all secular pursuits and to retire to his brother's monastery, where he devoted himself to prayer and the study of Scripture and of Origen. From his thirtieth year he became increasingly involved in the affairs of the Church. His brother, who had been appointed Bishop of Caesarea in Cappadocia, appointed Gregory bishop in the small town of Nyssa, in western Cappadocia.

Because of his personality and his theological convictions, Gregory found the life of a bishop very trying—so much so, in fact, that he became the object of intrigue and was eventually brought to trial, deposed from his episcopal throne, and banished. With the restoration of the orthodox bishops, Gregory returned to Nyssa but not to happiness, for within a year both his brother and his sister died. From that time onward Gregory enlarged the scope of his labors and received increasingly wider appreciation for his gifts as a teacher and as a great religious spirit. He had been assigned an obscure post, but at his death, about 395, he left it ennobled by his name.

It was not until the end of the nineteenth century that the treatises of Gregory were translated from their original Greek. Among the dogmatic, ascetic, and philosophical works translated and collected in the series edited by Philip Schaff and Henry Wace as *A Select Library of Nicene and Post-Nicene Fathers of the Christian Church,* it is perhaps the apologetic work entitled *The Great Catechism* which reveals Gregory most adequately for the contemporary reader. It is in this manual of instruction for catechizers, this text for teachers, that Gregory advances his defense and theory of Christianity in terms not so much of the historic arguments based on prophecy or moral considerations as in terms of its truth in the metaphysical sense. In good pedagogic fashion Gregory supplies his readers with a summary of his work, and he indicates the three main topics: the Trinity, the reasonableness of the Incarnation, and the Sacraments.

Gregory begins his discussion of the Trinity by developing the arguments for God based on the presence of design in the world and for God's perfection in unity on the basis of the incompatibility of any notion of imperfection with the notion of deity. The Christian, in combating polytheism, must not so emphasize the unity of God as to fall into the opposite error of Judaism, with its strict monotheistic rejection of the Trinity. In closely reasoned passages which are often intricate and subtle, Gregory undertakes the difficult task of demonstrating both the better logic of Christian belief and the ultimate mystery to which true (Christian) use of logic leads. Gregory meets his logical opponents on their own ground and shows them their errors, yet he does not proceed to present Christianity as a logical system. Careful to insist upon the inherent imprecision of arguing by analogy, and stressing the inability of man to reason by analogy directly to deity, Gregory nevertheless employs this means of argument: "As in our own case we say that the word is from the mind, and no more entirely the same as the mind, than altogether other than it . . . in like manner, too, the Word of God by its self-subsistence is distinct from Him from whom it has its subsistence; and yet by exhibiting in itself those qualities which are recognized in God it is the same in nature with Him who is recognizable by the same distinctive marks."

Here is right reason leading to the point at which the ineffable depth of mystery is reached and for which the doctrine of the Trinity, illogical on a lower level, is the most logical, although paradoxical, expression.

Closely reasoned as they are, Gregory's arguments appear to the critical contemporary reader as open to the criticism that they proceed from premises whose validity has been taken for granted rather than established through careful analysis. When, for example, Gregory proves that God created the world by His reason and wisdom because He could not have proceeded irrationally in that work, the "proof" seems to be nothing more than a statement of what God ought to be. God is defined so as to make it both absurd and impious to "install unreason and unskillfulness on the throne of the universe."

In the section dealing with the reasonableness of the Incarnation, similar lines of argument are developed showing that the Word of God is "a power essentially and substantially existing, willing all good, and being possessed of strength to execute all its will." Gregory explores the implication of the theory of man's having been created from God's superabounding love and in His image as immortal and with the gifts of freedom, independence, and self-determination. Man is thus free to choose against God, as did Adam, who disturbed the divinely ordered harmony between man's sensuous and intellectual natures. Since evil is deprivation of good and has no existence of its own, God, maker of all substantial things, is not maker of evil. "He who formed the sight did not make blindness," Gregory writes.

Gregory refutes the argument of those who oppose the Incarnation on the ground that the finite cannot contain the Infinite, by referring to the relationship of the human soul to its body. Characteristically he asks "Why may we not, by examples of which we are capable of understanding, gain some reasonable idea of God's plan of salvation?" The question of Incarnation requires a prior consideration of the mind-body problem, which is itself grounded in mystery.

It is the figure of the ransom that Gregory employs to explain the death of the Son of God. The death proves that God's justice impelled Him to offer one who exceeded in value that which was to be ransomed (sinful man). That a description of this sort involves conceiving of God as engaging in a deception upon Satan is candidly acknowledged by Gregory, who sees God's deception as just. God's deception is for good since even Satan will at last recognize God's justice and experience the benefits of the Incarnation.

With strong emphasis on baptism as essential to the sacramental system of salvation, Gregory teaches that in baptism God as Holy Spirit is truly given. Baptism is the first and necessary step in a resurrection to a new, immortal life. Gregory then develops a view of the sacrament of the Eucharist as a transformation of the elements of bread and wine into the body and blood of Christ. Gregory's view is credited as being the first such among the Fathers and as forming the basis for the doctrine of transubstantiation of later medieval theology. Bread and wine are sanctified by the word of God and prayer and become at once, not gradually, the body of God. It is the Eucharist which unites the body of the Christian to God just as baptism unites the soul to God. Bread and wine are thus the antidotes to the poison which human bodies inherited from the Fall.

Gregory ends his treatise to the catechetical leaders with a reminder that for true regeneration it is essential to believe that the Son and the Spirit are not created spirits of like nature with God the Father. The necessity of this emphasis is clear when one realizes that to make one's salvation dependent on anything created would be to trust an imperfect nature which itself needs a savior. The Gospel releases man from the vicious circle of dependence upon other dependents, for it tells us "that the birth of the saved is from above."

For all his insight into the ineffable nature of Christian truth and his emphasis upon the centrality of the sacraments, Gregory's final exhortation reveals a most practical side of his nature and shows how far he was from permitting his high sacramentalism to degenerate into mere magic. If a person is baptized and yet shows no indication that his soul has been washed through better living, Gregory asserts, "though it may be a bold thing to say, yet I will say it and will not shrink; in these cases the water is but water, for the gift of the Holy Ghost in no way appears in him who is thus baptismally born. . . ." Let no one be mistaken, he adds: "If you continue with the characteristic marks of vice in you, it is in vain that you babble to yourself of your birth from above." The seriousness of this condition is made clear when one remembers that the fire of punishment for sin is only a pale suggestion of that torment for which no equivalent may be found in earthly experience.

THE CONFESSIONS OF SAINT AUGUSTINE

Author: Saint Augustine (354-430)
Type of work: Spiritual autobiography
First transcribed: c.397

Principal Ideas Advanced

Man's love finds its proper object in God, yet man's temptation is to give his love to finite objects.

Through conversion to faith in God and Jesus Christ, a unification of the self is possible; man acquires insight and power through Christian faith.

The self finds God not through memory or other exercises of the mind but through preparing itself for God's revelation of Himself.

God is the creator; He is not to be identified with His creation.

Time is God's creation; in God Himself there is an eternal present.

The *Confessions,* completed about 397, is surely the best known of Saint Augustine's many works, and it is also perhaps the most synoptic statement of his many-sided mind and life. The title calls attention to the form of the work, which is Augustine's personal address to God. In the presence of God, Augustine discovered his own human personality. His account of his spiritual development is the first of a long tradition of such confessions. Since the book contains accounts of many events of Augustine's life it has often been termed a spiritual autobiography, a characterization which calls for the qualification that the *Confessions* omits many events of Augustine's life and also contains much which is not biography. Yet, the important fact is that the personality of Augustine is clearly delineated in the pages of the *Confessions.*

As the reader reads through the thirteen books of the *Confessions,* he follows Augustine through the changing scenes of his life from his birth and childhood in Tagaste, to his college days in Carthage, to professional posts in Carthage, Rome, and Milan. He also follows Augustine's wanderings among the faiths and philosophies of his time to his baptism into Catholic Christianity in 387. He witnesses Augustine's passionate heart seeking an object worthy of its allegiance. He observes Augustine's adventurous mind seeking an adequate philosophy, probing Manicheanism, Platonism, skepticism, and finally finding truth in Christianity. Yet, most of all, he watches Augustine probing the depths of his anxious and restless self, and coming finally to rest in God.

Augustine's ideas in the *Confessions* are a synthesis of Neoplatonic and Hebraic or Biblical elements. His view of God is similar to the idea of the Absolute One in Neoplatonism, yet the ideas of sovereign will and love are clearly Biblical. Similarly, with respect to man, Augustine's view of the inward depths of personality owes much to Plotinus, yet man for Augustine is basically volitional in nature, and here, once more, his view is Biblical. Again, his view of evil is a synthesis of the Neoplatonic conception of nonbeing and the Biblical conception of rebellion against the sovereign God. As a mortal or finite being, man's love finds its proper object in God. Yet man's temptation is to give this love to objects short of God; it is, in other words, the inordinate love of finite goods. But such objects are unable to sustain this allegiance or love, and so man falls into confusion and nonbeing.

The curtain is raised in Book I upon Augustine's stormy dialogue with God by a characteristic quotation from Psalms 145 and 147: "Great art thou, O Lord and greatly to be praised; great is thy power, and infinite is thy wisdom," which elicits from Augustine the response that ". . . thou hast made us for thyself and our hearts are restless until they rest in thee." These reflections in turn lead onward to the question, so characteristic of Augustine, as to how the finite mind of man can contain the infinite God. The answer here and throughout the work is that only through a paradoxically articulated divine grace and human faith can man know the divine.

Turning to autobiography, Augustine reflects upon his own infancy and childhood. Supplementing recollection and introspection with observation of other human beings and reports of other observers, he speaks of such matters as the origin of speech and the grasping selfishness of infants. In a similar spirit, Augustine recalls the games and pranks of childhood, finding in them an expression of original sin and wickedness as well as the guiding, providential grace of God. He alludes to the austerities of his schooling with its beatings and its full lessons, to his dislike of Greek, and to his intense love of Latin and Roman literature.

Book II continues these juvenile recollections, concentrating attention on the famous prank in which, at the age of sixteen, Augustine and some friends pilfered and then wantonly wasted some pears. Augustine's analysis of this deed emphasizes its wanton and sinful character, leading him to the sort of deep, though often morbid, probing of the self which is recurrent in the *Confessions,* and which is also a salient feature of Augustine's view of the human self.

Book III describes the author's student days in Carthage where, as he put it, "a caldron of unholy loves was seething and bubbling around me." He studied literature and went to the theater. During this period he also encountered Cicero's *Hortensius,* which impressed him deeply as a call to the intellectual and contemplative life. He records his first contact with the Manicheans, who were to hold his attention for the next nine years and to defer his full entrance into Catholic Christianity. Manicheanism was a widely popular faith and philosophy of the ancient world which emphasized both a cosmic and psychological dualism of spirit and matter. The explanation of evil as rooted in matter was attractive to Augustine.

Upon completion of his studies, Augustine took up a career in the teaching of literature and rhetoric, as he tells us in Book IV. His first post was in his home town of Tagaste. During this time he took a mistress who remained with him until shortly before his conversion. He reports also an interest in astrology. A friend's death plunged him into intense grief, leading in the *Confessions* to reflections upon the inordinate love of finite goods, such as human friends. During this time he reports the reading of Aristotle's *Categories* and the writing of his first book, entitled *Concerning the Beautiful and the Apt.*

Book V deals with the year of decision in which Augustine became disenchanted with Manicheanism. Bishop Faustus, a Manichean leader, visited Carthage, and Augustine found the answers to his questions evasive and unimpressive. Renouncing Manicheanism, Augustine moved in the direction of orthodox Christianity, but the way led through skepticism and Neoplatonism. He went to Rome to take a teaching post, only to become the victim of illness. From Rome, with its gay and stimulating life, as well as its disorderly students, he made his way in a year's time to a teaching post in Milan.

Augustine's mother, Monica, followed him to Milan. Here, as elsewhere, his relations to his mother are deeply significant for Augustine's personality and life. These relations constitute a recurrent theme of the *Confessions.* It was she who persistently sought his conversion to Christianity, yet it had been she who had counseled deferring baptism in the fear of postbaptismal sins. It was she who wept on the African shore as his ship departed for Europe, and who subsequently followed him there. It was she who, presumably seeking a more desirable match for her son, led him to break with his faithful mistress.

Surrounded in Milan by a group of friends, Augustine pondered the step of becoming a catechumen of the Catholic Church. One factor of great importance in this step was the eloquent and fervent bishop of Milan, Ambrose. Augustine's admiration for Ambrose was unfeigned and enthusiastic. Still another factor leading to his conversion was his Neoplatonism, which enabled him to think of God as spiritual in nature, in contrast to the corporeal notions of deity characteristic of many faiths of the time. Speaking of the Neoplatonists, Augustine says, "There I read, In the beginning was the word, but I read not the Word was made flesh. . . ." From Neoplatonism Augustine acquired several features of his own system of thought, including notably his penchant for mysticism.

Book VIII describes the event of conversion which, as the *Confessions* clearly asserts, was the climax of Augustine's life. Two of his devoted friends had decided to turn to Catholic Christianity. His own heart in a torment of indecision, Augustine found his way to a Milanese garden where he pondered the course of his life. All at once he heard a voice saying "Take and read." Seeing a Bible, he turned at random to Romans 13:13f., "Not in rioting and drunkenness, not in chambering and wantonness, not in strife and envying, but put on the Lord Jesus Christ, and make no provision for the flesh to fulfill the lusts thereof." Taking this as divine direction, his course was clear. Conversion meant to Augustine, as it has meant to many others before and since, a new unification of a hitherto unintegrated life, together with new insight and new power.

Augustine resigned his professorship at the end of the following term and retired with several friends to a villa at Cassiciacum, where their days were devoted to contemplation, study, and preparation for baptism. Augustine was baptized April 25, 387, by Ambrose. Soon afterward he turned homeward toward Africa with his mother and his son Adeodatus, presumably to undertake some sort of comtemplative or monastic life. As they paused at Ostia, waiting for passage, Monica became ill and died.

In the shadows of his mother's impending death, Augustine records in Book IX an experience of particularly vivid and personal communion between mother and son. He tells of their exalted and intimate conversation concerning life and death, of her satisfaction that her wandering son had at last come home to Catholic Christianity, as well as of her intimation of impending death. This mystical experience may be characterized as the consummation of the lifelong relation of mother and son.

It is also the end of the autobiographical section of the *Confessions.* Ahead of him, and thus unrecorded in the *Confessions,* lay his years in Africa as monk, priest, and then bishop, and his stormy struggles with the Donatists and Pelagians. Nevertheless, it may safely be said that all the ideas developed in subsequent works are sketched or at least intimated in the *Confessions.*

In Books X-XIII Augustine turns to

reflection on philosophical and theological issues which never ceased to fascinate him, such as the nature and depth of the self, the nature of creation and time, and the relation of God to the world. While his subjects were among the most abstract and technical of all theological study, he continues throughout these books the devotional, confessional style of the earlier books. Also, he continues the deft turn of phrase so characteristic of the *Confessions* and indeed of all his writing, as well as the intensely autobiographical nature of his theological reflection. For Augustine, here as elsewhere, life and thought were bound together in seamless unity. It is worth noting in passing that in this section occurs the famous line which triggered Pelagius's reaction and the Pelagian controversy: "Give what thou commandest and command what thou wilt."

In Book X Augustine turns first to the relation of memory to selfhood, and thence of self to God. Augustine enters what he terms "the fields and spacious halls of memory where are stored as treasures the countless images that have been brought into them from all manner of things by the senses." There follows a notable passage in which these fields and halls of memory are explored in all their vastness and variety and in all their endless spontaneity. Memory becomes a hall of mirrors where, as Augustine says, "I meet myself and recall myself." This analysis of the memory and imagination of man in its depth and transcendence emphasizes once again Augustine's debt both to Neoplatonism and to the Bible.

It is significant to note that Augustine, having plumbed the depths of mind or self, does not simply find deity there, as would be expected on Neoplatonic assumptions. Rather, he remarks, "I will pass even beyond this power of mine that is called memory — I will pass beyond it that I may come to thee, O lovely Light. And what art thou saying to me?" In this view of the self as being addressed by a God who is beyond the self, the reader sees the victory of the Bible over Neoplatonism in Augustine's thinking.

Earlier in the same book, Augustine, in an often quoted passage, celebrates the transcendence of God. He asks, "And what is this God? I asked the earth and it answered 'I am not he'; and everything in the earth made the same confession." In a similar manner he moves through the whole created universe and receives the same reply, "We are not God, but he made us." So it is that, deeply influenced by the Absolute One of Neoplatonism, Augustine acknowledges as God the Sovereign Will and Love which the Bible celebrates.

According to the Bible, the God who rules the world created it in the beginning. Augustine adds a philosophic idea which translates the Genesis creation story into the language of metaphysics; namely, the concept of creation *ex nihilo,* out of nothing. God also providentially guides the whole course of creation and will eventually bring it consummation. Hence, the themes of beginning and end never ceased to attract Augustine's thought.

Book XI is devoted to an extraordinarily subtle analysis of the nature of time and the relation of time to creation. "What then is time? If no one asks me, I know what it is. If I wish to explain it to him who asks me, I do not know." His analysis of time arrives at the conclusion that time is an aspect of created being, and that, consequently, in the uncreated being of God time has no effective reality. In God and God's consciousness there is no change, no before or after, but only an eternal present. This is, in effect, Augustine's response to the question, What was God doing before He made Heaven and earth? The question turns out to be meaningless for the good reason that, according to Augustine, time was created with the rest of creation. Time or change and the relations of before and after were created when God called the world into being; they have no reality apart from this context.

Yet, as Augustine points out, it is man's mind that perceives and measures time. Indeed, Augustine's treatment of the subject is noteworthy alike for its perception of time's manifold nature and for the candor with which he faces its enigmatic and mysterious aspects.

From time, Augustine moves in Books XII and XIII to the Biblical story of creation and to the philosophic idea which he constructs out of the Biblical story. Augustine's Platonism is apparent in his notions of the unformed matter and primal possibility, which God created first, and out of which he formed all else. In other passages Augustine equates Heaven, which God made, with the Platonic world of intelligible or ideal forms, which subsequently finds embodiment or illustration in the visible or experienced world. Yet Augustine realizes that these interpretations are not the only possible meanings which the Genesis story will bear.

Once the doctrine of creation is raised as a problem, Augustine cannot put it down. The final book of the *Confessions* develops further Augustine's allegorical interpretation of the Genesis story. In his use of allegorical exegesis Augustine was a child of his age. He finds allegories of the Trinity in the Genesis creation story, and he ponders the activity of the Spirit as it broods upon the original chaos. In the firmament he discovers an allegory of the Holy Scripture; in the dry land and bitter sea he finds the division between the people of God and the unfaithful nations, — a theme which was to receive definitive statement a decade or more later in the *City of God.*

The *Confessions* is concluded by a meditation upon the goodness of creation, a goodness which is expressed in the peace which God gives to His people. Truly, the mysteries of God's goodness and power are manifested in His creation, and among His many creatures, most of all in man. St. Augustine's *Confessions* not only summarizes the Christian thought of the ancient or patristic period, but also points ahead to the medieval period, and indeed to the whole subsequent development of Christian thought.

ON THE TRINITY

Author: Saint Augustine (354-430)
Type of work: Philosophical theology
First transcribed: c.400-428

Principal Ideas Advanced

Father, Son, and Holy Spirit are one and the same substance and essence; the persons of the Trinity are equal, and God is one.

God is the source of whatever is good.

The trinitarian nature of God is not rare and esoteric; it has myriad counterparts in ordinary experience.

The mind, in having memory, understanding, and will as components, provides a model for understanding the Trinity.

Perhaps no figure dominated medieval philosophy and theology more, or continues to influence contemporary theology so much, as the towering figure of Aurelius Augustinus, Bishop of Hippo. If the *Confessions* is a classic of the religious life and the *City of God* a massive landmark in philosophy of history, then *On the Trinity* is certainly his longest and most important work in philosophical theology. A full appreciation of the brilliance of mind which Augustine exhibits in the work can come only from a reading of the treatise itself, but even a summary examination of his ideas is enough to suggest the remarkable character of Augustine's theological creation.

It is a matter of dispute as to whether the concept of the triune nature of God is actually Biblical or is not really a part of primitive Christian thinking, but there is no question about the fact that after Augustine the problem of the Trinity became a central philosophical and theological issue.

No one can begin theological thought or investigate the nature of God without running into the doctrines Augustine developed here. There is some dispute about the exact origin of trinitarian concepts, but it seems clear that, whatever Augustine did with the ideas, he did not originate them. Trinities are commonplace in Neoplatonic thought and in the *Enneads* of Plotinus, which Augustine probably read, although trinities there are usually characteristic of the lower orders and not of the First Principle. After Augustine the Trinitarian concept is a central part of Christian theological thought.

The work itself is typically Augustinian; that is, it contains a vast collection of philosophical doctrines, interwoven with Scriptural exegesis. To understand *On the Trinity* means to grasp Augustine's blend of psychology, Neoplatonism, theological speculation, Biblical commentary, and philosophical elaboration. Since the work was composed over a long period of time, it is not surprising, particularly in view of its monumental length, that it contains so many doctrines. It is perhaps the best single work upon which to base an understanding of Augustine, since almost every facet of his philosophical, theological, and religious thought is brought to bear upon the central problem of understanding what is apparently a contradictory assertion; namely, that the One is three.

Following the traditional plan of beginning with an exegesis of the relevant Scriptural passages, Augustine, in the first half of the work, attempts to establish (upon a Biblical basis) the crucial point of the *equality* and *unity* of the parts of the Supreme Trinity. Of course, the whole point which makes this lengthy procedure necessary is that the Scriptural passages neither agree with one another nor are clear in their meaning. Some texts are used to argue against the equality of the Son, and Augustine was forced to establish a framework within which to deal with these difficult passages. Philosophical issues are involved in such a discussion, for rational consistency and interpretive standards must be brought *to* the Bible. Since the Bible is not theologically adequate as it stands, philosophy is the catalyst needed to make it so.

Like much of Augustine's work, *On the Trinity* has a polemical quality about it. Augustine begins by arguing against and attempting to refute those who attack the doctrine of the Trinity. Although it is characteristic of Augustine, it is not peculiar to him to have his systematic work generated by a polemical purpose. Religious beliefs, such as the trinitarian doctrine, would not be turned into technical theology if divergent views did not arise within the community of the faithful. Almost all early creeds and much early Christian theology developed in response to philosophical issues involved in religious disputes.

Holy Scripture, Augustine reminds his reader, does not hesitate to use words drawn from actually existing things to describe God and yet He is ineffable. Discussion about Him is difficult and requires that we purge our minds in order to see ineffably that which is ineffable. His thesis is: the Trinity is the one and only true God; Father, Son, and Holy Spirit are one and the same substance or essence. There is an indivisible equality, and yet it is true that the Father has "begotten" the Son. The problem is to understand the unity of the Trinity; that is, how three different forms can be a single being.

Augustine begins his proof by establishing the divinity of the Son. Using the assumption that there is but one God and that what is not creature is divine (there being no ground in between), he argues that since the Son as the agent of all creation is not Himself created He must be uncreated, thus necessarily of the same substance with the Father. The Son, therefore, is equal with the Father, and the working of the Father and the Son is indivisible. Such argument is made necessary, of course, by the accounts in the Scriptures which portray Jesus as born to Mary. This leads Augustine from the issue of the Trinity on to the specific Christian doctrine of the Incarnation, the dual nature of Jesus, so that Augustine can ascribe the creaturely qualities of Jesus to His human nature and thus can preserve the fully divine status of the Trinity's second person.

Since the Son appeared "in the form of a servant" Augustine had to explain how the numerous Biblical passages, most of which portray the human side of Jesus, do not essentially deny the Son's fully divine status. The bulk of his concern is to establish Jesus as fully divine, and all the proof is bent to this aim, His human nature being assumed as evident. Yet the ways of God are so much opposed to those of men that Augustine attempts at great length to explain how Jesus serves as a mediator between man and God, while yet preserving His fully divine status as Son. Nevertheless, Augustine acknowledges that human understanding will always fall at least a little short in any attempt to understand the Trinity, its nature being beyond full rational grasp.

There is no change or accident in God, and yet the Trinity as one substance and three persons must have each person share fully in that substance without losing its personal identity. As individual persons, the Son and the Holy Spirit seem subject to change and relation, but as of one substance with God they are not so subject. The relations between the various persons of the Trinity are difficult to describe, and Augustine admits that there are no terms which accurately express these relations. Every direct statement requires qualification: "Person" seems to be the most desirable term for the constituents of the Trinity, but the three "persons" together are equal to each singly. They are of one essence, with no bulk or interval or unlikeness or inequality. If, however, after this explanation we cannot understand the doctrine of the Trinity, then we must hold it by faith.

As far as the description of any member of the Trinity goes, what is difficult to understand is that whenever each is spoken of in respect to itself, then the persons of the Trinity are not spoken of as three in the plural number, but as one. This leads Augustine on to a discussion of the difficulties of reasoning about God, and of the necessity for the use of the negative method (understanding first what God is *not*), and he recommends trying to understand God through the concept of good, as that Being through which all things are good. There would be no changeable goods unless there were an unchangeable Good, and thus the mind can be led to grasp unchangeableness. The Good, then, is not far from every one of us.

We know what a mind is because we too have a mind, Augustine argues in a manner suggestive of Berkeley and Descartes. Within our own understanding of our self we have the basis for understanding pure concepts, such as righteousness. Where should a man discern himself except within himself? The attempt to understand a difficult aspect of the nature of God drove Augustine back to a search for self-knowledge, in the hope that in this way he could understand both himself and God more fully through the analogies to be found there. Man understands external things through the truth which he discerns and understands within himself. In accordance with Platonic theories of knowledge, Augustine asks: How can you recognize what you find externally if you cannot in some sense know it from within?

Love is a good example. No one can say that he does not know what love is. When a man loves his brother, Augustine argues, he knows the love with which he loves more intimately than he knows the brother whom he loves. And if one knows love he knows the Trinity, since God is love. Love involves three factors: he that loves, that which is loved, and love itself. In love, accordingly, there is a trace of the

Trinity. A kind of trinity also exists in man, who is the image of God: the mind, the knowledge whereby the mind knows itself, and the love with which it loves both itself and its knowledge. Since these three are mutually equal and of one essence, in explaining himself psychologically a man can discover the best mode for understanding the relationships which exist in the Trinity.

When the mind goes further and examines the basis upon which it judges corporeal things, it discovers that particular things are judged according to a form of the eternal Trinity and that this form is discerned by the intuition of the rational mind. Thus, the mind knows God as the source of such truth, and in so far as we know God we are like Him, but not to the extent of becoming equal to Him. An examination of the mind, of its knowing and its judging powers, shows the mind to be like divinity, at least in its trinitarian aspect. For that reason an attempt to understand the Trinity is not an impossibility, since there is a kind of image of the Trinity discoverable in the mind itself.

Since it is absolutely impossible to love things which are unknown, the discovery of man's love for God indicates that at least to some extent man has knowledge of Him. The mind seems to understand itself and to discover, as Descartes insisted, certain truths about itself which it cannot doubt. The mind, we discover, has memory, understanding, and will as its primary components, so that in understanding the unitary action of these capacities we have a mental model for understanding the divine Trinity. In sight also it is possible to distinguish three things; namely, the visible object, the act of seeing, and the attention of the mind. Everywhere he turns, particularly in considering psychological phenomena, Augustine finds images of trinitarian action. Since the mind recognizes its natural affinity to the divine, only the intellectual cognizance of *eternal* things should be called "wisdom," whereas "knowledge" shall mean the rational cognizance of *temporal* things. In rightly understanding and loving its best part, the mind actually loves and understands God in His trinitarian nature. Starting with the creature, Augustine discovered certain trinities, until at last he came to the mind of man and found traces there of the highest trinity which we seek when we seek God. Understanding the human mind means recognizing certain trinities in its action, and understanding the functioning of a trinity is identical with a grasp of God's nature. The undeniable threefold but unified truth—I exist, I love, I understand—leads to as much comprehension of the Trinity as the mind of man, since it is human, although partly divine, can possibly achieve.

THE LIFE OF ST. MARTIN

Author: Sulpicius Severus (c.363-c.420)
Type of work: Hagiography
First transcribed: c.410

Principal Ideas Advanced

St. Martin's life is an inspiring example for all Christians who would draw close to God.

The saint was a virtuous man, able to raise the dead, heal the sick, and give courage and strength to the poor and needy.

He showed his spiritual strength when he resisted the temptations of the Devil, who appeared to him in many disguises.

Sulpicius Severus was born about 363 in Aquitania, and he lived until about 420; thus, he was a contemporary of Augustine and Jerome, and he was acquainted with St. Martin, whose life Sulpicius recounts. The biography of St. Martin is interesting because it contributes to knowledge about the period of which Sulpicius writes, and the work provides an example of one of the most popular forms of Christian literature—the pious biography, in which didactic edification is as important as factual information.

In the biography Sulpicius extols the virtues of Martin, for whom Sulpicius had the greatest affection and the highest respect.

In addition to writing the biography of St. Martin, Sulpicius published a *Sacred History,* which aimed at presenting a compendious history of the world from creation to the year 400. The first part is an abridgment of the Scriptural narrative, but unfortunately it is not without error; the second part deals with events that are not recorded in Scripture, but which are of some value to the historian.

Sulpicius wrote the *Life of St. Martin* so that the life of a most holy man—whom he himself had met—might serve as an example to others who would then also be aroused to divine virtue and to the pursuit of truth, while enlisted in the army of Heaven. Sulpicius claims to have written nothing of his hero except that for which he had certain evidence and knowledge; he claims that he would rather be silent than write anything false.

Martin was born about the year 315 of pagan parents in Sabaria, which was in Pannonia, and he was brought up in Italy in Ticinum. His father pursued a military career, and he opposed his son's service to God. At the age of ten Martin endeavored to become a catechumen; at twelve he desired to live the life of a hermit, and he was already a professed servant of Christ. The government issued an edict, however, which forced the young Martin, as the son of a veteran, to take the military oath, so that for three years prior to his baptism he served in the army. His fellow soldiers held him in the highest esteem, and even in the military service Martin was more a monk than a soldier. He was exceedingly kind, patient, humble, and free of the vices usually associated with the military life; he behaved as a candidate for baptism, was given to good works, aided those in trouble, supported the needy, and kept nothing for himself.

On one occasion, during a severe winter in which he himself had nothing but a cloak, Martin cut his sole remaining garment in two in order to clothe a poor man destitute of clothing. His act of charity was followed by a vision in which Christ appeared to him, arrayed in that part of the cloak which Martin had given to the poor man, and Christ commended Martin for his act of love. The vision did not fill Martin with pride but caused him to acknowledge God's goodness and to seek baptism at the age of twenty.

For two years after his baptism Martin remained in the military. He was released from service only after he offered to face the enemy in battle unarmed, an act which proved unnecessary since, to spare Martin the pain of witnessing the death of others, God caused the enemy to surrender without bloodshed. According to Sulpicius, victory was won because of the piety of a saint.

Upon leaving the military service, Martin sought the company of Hilarius, Bishop of Pictava, who instituted Martin in the office of a diaconate, and appointed him to be an exorcist. After a time Martin was warned in a dream that he should visit his native land in the religious interests of his parents, who were still pagans. Waylaid by robbers along the way, he was set free after his courageous witness to evangelical truth wrought conversion in the heart of the robber who guarded him. As Martin continued his journey, the Devil, who had assumed the form of a man, met him on the way, but he also was quickly put to flight by Martin's piety.

His mission to his mother was successful, but although many others were converted by his example, his father remained a pagan. For a time Martin was persecuted by the Arians, and he was forced to subsist in exile by eating the roots of plants. On one occasion he lay near death from eating poisonous grass, but he warded off the effects by calling for God's help.

Martin, Sulpicius claims, was given the power to perform miracles. A catechumen who died without receiving baptism was restored to life by Martin's earnest prayers. Martin stretched himself at full length upon the dead limbs of the deceased, and perceiving by means of the Holy Spirit that power was present, he raised himself up and waited for two hours without misgivings, whereupon the dead man moved and opened his eyes, for he had been restored to life by the saint's faith.

On another occasion Martin restored to life a slave who had ended his life by hanging himself. Hardly any sick person came to him without at once being restored to health. When Martin kissed a leper, the man was instantly healed. The very threads of his garment wrought frequent miracles upon the sick; sections of his garments drove away diseases from the afflicted when the garments were tied around the fingers or neck of the afflicted. The daughter of a very holy man was cured of a fever when her skin was touched by a letter which Martin had written. The vision of the ailing was restored by Martin's touch, and he himself was healed of grievous wounds by the ministrations of an angel who applied healing ointment to the bruised members of his body.

By miraculous intervention Martin escaped falling trees, the knife of the assassin, and the fury of mobs. He was able to render a procession of men immobile in obedience to his commands. He could order flames of fire to consume idolatrous temples without doing harm to surrounding buildings, and he was so empowered as to be able to turn the fire back when it left its prescribed course. He razed pagan temples to their foundations and he reduced the altars and images of idols to dust, thereby delivering the people from their superstitions. Martin could command serpents to do his bidding, and in all such acts he displayed the piety proper to the distinguished office that he had come to hold as Bishop of Tours.

According to Sulpicius, Martin was in every way distinguished. He established a monastery where some eighty disciples followed his example, spending hours in prayer in their cells, while possessing all things in common, and enduring with humility all temptations and trials. The very angels spoke to Martin, and "As to the devil, Martin held him so visible and ever under the power of his eyes, that whether he kept himself in his proper form, or changed himself into different shapes of spiritual wickedness, he was perceived by Martin, under whatever guise he appeared." The Devil once rushed into Martin's cell with a great noise, holding in his hand the bloody horn of an ox. He sometimes appeared in the form of Minerva, Jupiter, or Mercury.

Martin was often assailed by crowds of demons, to whom Martin did not hesitate to preach. The ruses to which the Devil went in his temptations were truly great. The fiend once appeared surrounded by a purple light, clothed in a royal robe, with a crown of precious stones on his head, and gold shoes on his feet. His countenance was tranquil, so that no one would suspect who he was. Martin, while praying in his cell, was first dazed. The Devil pretended to be Christ, but Martin was not deceived and he detected the impostor, whereupon, "the devil vanished like smoke, and filled the cell with such a disgusting smell, that he left unmistakable evidences of his real character." In Sulpicius' words, "This event, as I have just related, took place in the way which I have stated, and my information regarding it was derived from the lips of Martin himself; therefore let no one regard it as fabulous."

Whether fabulous or not, Sulpicius' biography of the Gaulish Saint Martin (who died about 397, about twenty-three years before the death of his biographer) insures Martin a place in the company of saints whose lives make the Christian ideal both vivid and appealing.

THE CITY OF GOD

Author: Saint Augustine (354-430)
Type of work: Theology of history
First transcribed: c.413-426

Principal Ideas Advanced

Two cities, the city of God and the earthly city, now exist side by side and are inseparable from each other.

Those who believe in the true God may now enter into that heavenly city, al-

though such belief is no guarantee of any preferential treatment whatsoever during this life.

What characterizes each city, and each man within it, is the direction of love, whether it is toward the things of this world (the earthly city) or toward God (the heavenly city).

If any work deserves the title of a classic of Christian literature, it is most certainly Saint Augustine's *City of God.* Critical historians point to it as perhaps the first major philosophy of history, and its influence also spills over into literature, philosophy, and theology. Its size and its scope mark it as monumental, and its doctrines find their way into every sphere. It seeks no less a goal than to define God, man, and the world. To accomplish this goal Augustine chose the city as his metaphorical image because the city was in his day the center and model of culture and political life.

Augustine begins with his most famous distinction: the City of God has a temporal stage here below (journeying as a pilgrim among sinners) and an eternal abode (a blessed goal of perfect peace). Any earthly city is dominated by a passion for dominion, and from such a city the enemies of the City of God come. The unjust, however successful here, will not participate in the joys of the world to come, prepared by Divine Providence. The goods and evils of this life, on the other hand, are divided alike between the just and the unjust. Yet the good and bad who suffer are different even though they suffer the same trials. Though what they endure is the same, their virtues and vices are different. The tide of trouble tests, purifies, and improves the good, whereas it beats, crushes, and washes away the wicked.

Every man deserves some temporal affliction, no matter how good he has been, although the good will escape eternal punishment. The fact that the good often fail to speak out against evil for fear of the loss of some temporal advantage indicates that the good, as well as the bad, love and are attached to an earthly life. As God tested Job before, so the good must now stand adversity as a test of their mettle and of their love of God. Whatever good men lose in this life, it is always possible for such men to preserve their faith, their piety, and the treasures of the interior life. In the midst of adversity, the good man still has more than those who are evil.

Both good and bad men must sooner or later die. Neither has any basic advantage here. Death preceded by a good life is never evil; nothing makes death evil except what is to follow it. This earthly life is a school in which the servant of God is trained for life eternal. Refusing to be enslaved by temporal goods, he uses them as a pilgrim would. Yet as long as it is here, the City of God cannot be sure who belongs to it. Some who appear to be its members here will not be associated in the eternal felicity of the saints. Among even its notorious adversaries here on earth are men destined to be its friends, however little they now know it. On earth the earthly and the heavenly cities are linked and fused together, to be separated at the Last Judgment.

Despite these clear statements about the City of God in Book I, Augustine next turns to a task which diverts him for a considerable share of his work: challenging the view that it was the Christians who were responsible for the barbarian sack of Rome and the wars which desolated the world. Yet even in this practical and apologetic task, his earlier problem returns, since Augustine sees the issue as once again requiring him to justify God's ways to the world and to show how it is possible that good things come to the impious and the thankless while devastation falls upon both the good and the bad. Essentially what Augustine attempts to do is to show that the sack of Rome was due to internal reasons, corruptions which justly brought about this result.

Providence, of course, becomes one of Augustine's major themes. No matter what the apparent force of the evil and demonic powers, Augustine attempts to establish that God's ultimate providential plan can never be set aside. Whatever the apparent present destruction, absolutely nothing occurs outside God's ordaining power. And God's City offers more to those who join it than assurance of God's providential plan; it offers true remission of sins. In such a heavenly city, no longer delighting in immoralities, victory is truth, dignity is holiness, peace is happiness, life is eternity. Plunging into a fairly detailed analysis of important historical events, Augustine seeks to document his thesis beyond doubt, that events were actually not quite as Christianity's enemies conceived them and that the pagans actually worshiped false gods.

In reply to the question of the divine permission of oppression, Augustine replies that a good man, though a slave, is free; but a wicked man, though a king, is a slave. Happiness is actually a gift of God, and the only God men should worship is the one who can make them happy. God orders all things and knows all things before they come to pass. He whose foreknowledge cannot be deceived foreknows what He will choose to do. Some, in order to make men free, will try to give up God, but the fact is that our choices fall within the order of the causes which are known certainly by God and contained in His foreknowledge.

One who does not foreknow the whole of the future is most certainly not God, Augustine says in his most emphatic defense of divine determination. Yet, he adds, human will sometimes prevails—although the power which permits this is God's. How, in view of this strong defense of divine determination in all events, can anyone believe that the laws which govern the rise and fall of political societies would be exempt from the laws of God's providence? Thus the affairs of both the divine and the earthly cities are equally foreknown by God in his eternal plan. Yet the City of God is hated by the lovers of this world, because its ways differ from the ways of the world, and especially since the divine city is not subject to natural death.

The earthly city is given to both believers and unbelievers alike, but the joy of the Kingdom of Heaven God gives only to those who believe in Him; He rules and governs all things. Although His reasons may be hidden, they are never unjust. And it is impossible to reach God and the happiness of His Kingdom through the gods offered for worship by the state, since they are false gods. Since only belief in the true God will bring anyone to the City of God, Augustine gives detailed comparative arguments to document the unsatisfactory nature of the gods of the state. By way of contrast, he describes the qualities of the true God the Christians worship, inviting all to join in this worship and to enter the heavenly City of God while yet bound to the earthly city and its laws.

Books One through Seven are largely Church apologetics, defining the Church in relation to the world and justifying its presence here. When Augustine reaches Book Eight, he turns to philosophical and theological issues, first to the long-standing question of natural theology. Augustine wishes to reconcile and to make compatible the divine truth of Scripture with that of natural theology. Since God is Wisdom for Augustine, a true philosopher, or lover of Wisdom, will actually be a lover of God. Yet not all men who are called philosophers actually recognize their ultimate divine aim. Since theology means the study of the divine nature, genuine philosophers and theologians will find themselves converging on the same goal. From here Augustine goes on to a brief review of philosophy, particularly of Platonism, to justify his point.

The Platonists, Augustine discovers, have in their doctrine come closer to Christianity than has any other school. They posited an immaterial soul and an incorporeal God, premises Augustine takes as central to Christian thought. God's existence is simple and indivisible, and in the mind of man there is a superior form, immaterial and independent of sound, space, and time. Philosophy is a search for happiness, a search which can end only when a love of the good reaches fruition in God. Christians know that from the one, true, and infinitely good God they have a nature by which they are made in His image, a faith by which they know God and themselves, and grace whereby they reach beatitude in union with God.

Insofar as Platonists, or philosophers of any school, hold these truths concerning God, then they agree with the essentials of the Christian view. Augustine considers that his historical review and analysis, demonstrating the essential agreement of Platonism and Christianity, is sufficient to justify his choice of Platonic philosophy as the basis for his discussion of the problems of natural theology. The theories of gods and demons then common were legion, and Augustine uses his Platonism as a critical basis for demonstrating the inadequacy of such theories and for proving the existence of a single, good Deity. In the first ten books Augustine is concerned to refute the enemies of the City of God, but in Book Eleven he begins his discussion of the origin and destiny of the two cities, which, as he has said, are at present inextricably intermingled with each other.

For communication between God and the members of His city presently here, the mind of man is the means, being the most excellent part of man and having nothing superior to it except God himself. By the mind man comes closer to God than by any other means. In order to advance man toward truth, the divine Son put on humanity without putting off divinity, in order to serve as an even more effective mediator between man and God than man's mind alone could be. From here Augustine goes on to discuss the important questions of creation and time, issues of natural theology which must be settled in order to understand God's relation to both the heavenly and the earthly cities.

Everything, it turns out, revolves around the love of God. Since there is no other good which can make any rational or intellectual creature happy except God, man is made either miserable or happy by this relationship, and thus the cities are defined according to their orientation toward or away from God. God in creation arranged a hierarchy of beings so that, although some beings are higher on the scale than others, there is no being opposed to God. A defect can never be found in the highest good and a defect in any lesser being in the hierarchy cannot be present apart from some kind of good in that being. All natures are good simply because they exist, and each has its own measure of being, beauty, and peace. God having given each being its measure, is never to be blamed for any defect that offends us.

Sin can have no better name than pride, Augustine continues in his famous account of the nature of good and evil, and evil essentially means preferring what is less in the order of being rather than what is greater, turning away from God rather than toward Him. No efficient cause for evil can be found. An evil will is the efficient cause of a bad action, but there is no efficient cause of an evil will. The fault which produces evil begins when one falls away from the supreme Being and toward some being which is less than absolute. God can never be deficient in anything, while things made to be from nothing can be deficient.

The City of God has its origin partly in the body of angels, spiritually like God but lower in order, and partly from mortal men, created by the same God who created angels and who will one day unite the two groups. Following the Biblical account of Adam, Augustine sees the whole human race as taking its start from one man. And once again Augustine runs into the problem that perplexes him so often, the problem of time and its relation to eternity. He wanted to argue against those who hold that the world is eternal, and yet this meant giving an account of the creation of time by an eternal God.

Augustine confesses his inability to settle the problem of time with finality, but he adopts the now traditional view that what was to take place in its own time was already predestined and determined in God's eternity, and it is his co-eternal Word, the Second Person of the Trinity, who essentially serves as the instrument of creation. Augustine, then, begins with a doctrine of creation and inserts change into the eternal plan by the introduction of Jesus in His role of restorer of men and divine mediator. He creates the Christian view of the drama of history, but his announced central purpose is to dispose of the theory of inescapable and eternally repeated periodic cycles of time which cause identical occurrences in different times.

Augustine's aim, thus, is to give a newness to historical events, and yet he relates this newness to a providential order. Each historical event has never occurred before, and there are no unbreakable repetitious cycles in man's history. Augustine believes it possible to have occurrences which are both absolutely new and also part of an eternally ordered pattern of nature. It is quite possible, Augustine is sure, for God to create new beings, hitherto uncreated, and, in virtue of His ineffable foreknowledge, to do this without implying the least change in the divine will. In the first man God created He established the origin of the two cities or societies into which the human race is now divided.

Through sin man fell, that is, turned away from God; and since the direction of affection determines the society, the fall gave the City of Man its origin as a city composed of those whose interests are temporal and not divine. Because of his natural place near the top in the hierarchy of being, man has a tendency to seek his happiness through a knowledge of God, and because of the change brought about by the coming of Jesus Christ into the natural world, the natural direction of man's affections upward has once again been encouraged. In this life the two cities, defined by the direction of the love of the men who compose them, are intermingled and often indistinguishable; but those sometimes hidden men who compose the City of God shall eventually be lifted free and brought to their goal, happiness in the knowledge and love of God their creator.

SEVEN BOOKS OF HISTORY AGAINST THE PAGANS

Author: Paulus Orosius (c.385-?)
Type of work: Apologetics; philosophy of history
First transcribed: 417

Principal Ideas Advanced

Pagans who argue that the barbarian invasions are Rome's punishment for accepting Christianity ignore the fact that there was far more destruction and misery in pre-Christian times.

History abounds in calamities because it is the record of man's disobedience and punishment, alleviated only as God intervenes to bring men to repentance.

History is mainly told in terms of the Empires of Babylon and of Rome: Babylon, which ruled the world during the time of Israel, was permitted to perish; Rome, which was established to prepare for the coming of Christianity, has been preserved.

The barbarian invasions are, partly, Rome's punishment for persecuting Christianity, but may also be viewed as a step toward evangelizing the heathen nations.

Paulus Orosius was a young Spanish presbyter who, having escaped the hands of the barbarian invaders of Spain, visited Augustine in Africa and Jerome in Palestine. Augustine thought highly of Orosius' abilities and asked him to write a history of the world which would supplement Augustine's own work, the *City of God,* then only half completed. Orosius complied, and within scarcely more than a year he produced his *Seven Books of History Against the Pagans.* Nothing further is known of the author, but in an age which saw the destruction of many great works of the past, his *History* survived. A bull of Pope Gelasius (494) declared it "a most indispensable work," and helped make it the standard history book through a great part of the Middle Ages. It was translated into Anglo-Saxon by Alfred the Great (c.848-c.900).

Orosius' aim is clearly apologetic. The reader he has in mind is one who, in a world that is officially Christian, has refused to surrender his faith in the pagan gods, and who interprets the barbarian invasions as evidences of the gods' anger at the discontinuance of sacrifices. Orosius attempts to show that the history of the world is one long series of calamities, and that, compared with those which occurred in ancient times, the present disturbances are comparatively mild. The pagan gods, he maintains, never brought any relief from war and disaster, but since the coming of Christ, world conditions have been fairly tolerable because God in His providence was preparing the nations to receive the Gospel, and because as the Gospel spreads it inclines men's hearts to clemency and peace.

As evidence that there is one God who is the author of all things, Orosius appeals to natural understanding and to the teachings of philosophical sects. But, following Augustine, he maintains that "where reason fails, faith comes to the rescue; for unless we believe, we shall not understand." It is, therefore, the Biblical teaching concerning the creation of man, man's abuse of his freedom, and God's redemptive purpose that gives the clue for understanding human history. Sinful enterprise by itself can never stand; hence, men's grandiose schemes of empire and conquest are foredoomed. But God has not left men to their devices. With a view to bringing them to repentance, He has alternately chastened and blessed them. Such is the uniform experience of the past; and so, according to Orosius, it will continue until the end, except for an intensification of troubles in the last days when Christ comes to claim His Kingdom.

Orosius divides the history of the world into four epochs, corresponding to the Babylonian, Macedonian, Carthaginian, and Roman empires, but he does not find in this division any schema for understanding the human condition, as growing progressively better or progressively worse. For Orosius, the four world empires represent, rather, the four main geographical regions of the world. The East, North, and South each, in turn, tried to rule the world and failed; the West, says Orosius, is now having its turn, and if it also fails, no one should be surprised. The one thing that brightens the prospect is the fact that God has intervened in history with a view to winning men to reconciliation with Himself. But God redeems individuals, not empires, and the most that can be claimed is that, where redemption is effective, some curb will be imposed on sinful man's tendencies to destruction.

Although he recognizes four distinct regimes, Orosius argues that the Macedonian and the Carthaginian were less important than the other two. The main divisions of history are the Babylonian and the Roman world-empires. Orosius remarks that Rome freed herself from the Tarquin kings just at the time when Cyrus overthrew Babylon.

But between the time that Rome began to manage her own affairs and the time that she established her Empire, the Macedonians and the Carthaginians divided the world between them. Orosius proceeds to find certain correspondences between the history of Babylon and that of Rome, the most important being that the Babylonian empire began at the same time as God called Abraham to be the founder of the Israelitish nation, and that the Roman empire began at the same time as God sent his Son into the world to establish the Christian Church. The main difference (and in this, Orosius remarks, the people of Rome have cause to be glad) is that, whereas, in God's providence, Babylon must fall in order for Israel to rise, no such judgment was laid upon Rome. On the contrary, God fostered the rise of Rome through many centuries, and at last He conferred all power upon Caesar Augustus, so that universal peace might smooth the way for those who would proclaim the universal Gospel.

Within this historical framework, Orosius reviews the history of various nations, drawing upon the compendiums in use at the time. He makes no pretense at completeness. "I have," he says, "left out many details . . . and have abbreviated everything, since in no way could I have ever passed through so thick a forest of evils unless I had hastened my journey by frequent leaps." Quite frankly, he writes, he is looking for accounts of human misery. Other historians, he says, "were describing wars, whereas I for my part am more concerned with the miseries caused by wars," it being his design to show "in what way God has punished sinners, in what way He can punish them, and in what way He will punish them." Those Romans who complain that the barbarian invasions have interrupted their games and circuses ought, he says, to read the history of their own city and see what their forefathers suffered at the hands of Hannibal and, during the civil wars, at the hands of their own compatriots. He suggests that they have been so long freed from care as to regard the slightest anxiety as an intolerable burden. "They are the type of people," he says, "who consider those gentle admonitions by which we all from time to time are reproved, still more severe than the punishments exacted in other times about which they have only heard or read." Even the horrors which attended the destruction of Troy are for them merely pleasant stories to be recited and played.

When, in his seventh book, Orosius writes concerning Christian times, he attempts the awkward task of attaching rewards and punishments to those who favor and those who oppose the progress of the Church. Ten times, he says, the Romans persecuted the Christians, just as, in the time of Moses, the Pharaoh refused ten times to free Israel from its bondage; and, just as the Egyptians were smitten with ten plagues, so the Romans were punished after each persecution. In Orosius' view, the sufferings of his time are part of the punishment for the tenth (Maximian's) persecution; as that persecution was the most severe, so the punishment endures the longest. Orosius further maintains that those emperors since Constantine who defended the Church were rewarded and others were punished. The fate of Julian the Apostate, who perished miserably after trying to restore paganism, offers one example. But Orosius can also point to the Emperor Valens who, when the Goths asked that missionaries be sent to them, sent them teachers of the Arian persuasion. "Therefore," says Orosius, "by the just judgment of God Himself, Valens was burned alive by the very men who, through his action, will burn hereafter for their heresy." On the other hand, the Emperor Theodosius earned the blessing of Heaven. Hopelessly surrounded during his campaign in the Alps, he passed a whole night in prayer and on the following day was marvelously delivered in a battle which destroyed two of his antagonists at once, and brought order and tranquillity to the realm. "Thus Heaven gave judgment between the side that humbly placed its hope in God alone even without the aid of man and the side that arrogantly trusted in its own strength and in idols."

Orosius does not seem to have grasped the notion that Rome's domination of the world had come to an end. He does, however, have a just sense of the political engagements between Rome and the barbarians. In the past, he says, other nations have paid tribute to Rome in order to purchase peace; Rome is now paying tribute to the Goths for the same purpose. He adds that if anyone supposes that the Romans were more tolerable conquerors than the Goths, "his knowledge and understanding are quite at variance with the facts." Orosius also sees a connection between the barbarian invasions of the Roman territory and the evangelization of these peoples. "It would seem," he says, "that the mercy of God ought to be praised and glorified, in that so many nations would be receiving, even at the cost of our own weakening, a knowledge of the truth which they could never have had but for this opportunity."

One of the most remarkable qualities of Orosius' *History* is its catholicity of outlook. Orosius, a Spaniard, rejoiced that he was living in an age in which there was common fellowship between people of different nations. Driven from his own country by war, he found himself warmly welcomed in Africa and in the East. East, North, and South, he said, "all have the same law and nationality as I, since I come there as a Roman and a Christian to Christians and Romans." This, he says, could never have come about as long as polytheism prevailed. It is the work of "One God, Who established the unity of this realm in the days when He willed Himself to become known."

This catholicity of outlook makes Orosius a better historian than he would otherwise have been, enabling him to perceive the distortion which any kind of particularism introduces into men's judgments. The Romans, he points out, say that the world has fallen on evil times because the Goths have been victorious over them; but, in former times, when Rome was victorious, times seemed just as wretched to Carthage and Spain. Orosius concludes that people ought not to attach much importance to the measure of happiness which they momentarily enjoy, but ought to examine the way of life that they have chosen. In speaking of Orosius, Karl Löwith says, in *Meaning in History,* that only in the Swiss historian Jacob Burckhardt (1818-1897) do "we find a similar insight into the fallacy of our comparative judgments and into the correlation of action and suffering as the general pattern of all human history." Löwith adds that, whereas Burckhardt had the task of disabusing his generation of their optimistic impressions, the problem facing

Orosius was to dispel the pessimism of the ancient world, with its theories of cyclical decay, and to argue realistically for the comparative improvement which had taken place in Christian times.

Orosius' own hope, however, does not rest in merely historical prospects. He does not share even the millenarian hopes of Lactantius (d. c.320), but believes that in the last days persecutions will be revived. Just as the Egyptians, when they let Israel go, afterwards tried to drag them back into slavery and in consequence were drowned in the Red Sea, "so, alas," he says, "a persecution by the Gentiles at some future time awaits us while we are journeying in freedom, until we cross the Red Sea, that is, the fire of the judgment with our Lord Jesus Christ Himself as our leader and judge." For Orosius, redemption is transcendent to history, and eschatology points beyond time. This view, which neutralized the apocalyptic urgency of primitive Christianity, henceforth became the outlook of the Catholic Church.

THE ENCHIRIDION ON FAITH, HOPE, AND LOVE

Author: Saint Augustine (354-430)
Type of work: Theology
First transcribed: 421

Principal Ideas Advanced

Faith precedes reason, and the role of reason is that of understanding what is previously apprehended by faith.

Whatever is, insofar as it is, is good; being and good are convertible concepts; evil is a privation of the good and is dependent upon the good for its existence.

Original sin accounts for the introduction of evil into the life of man; this sin is defined as pride or self-elevation, and its consequences are ignorance and lust.

Salvation comes to man by the grace of God through faith; this grace is fully manifested in Jesus Christ, who unifies in Himself two natures, divine and human, in one person.

Man is born with a free will, but this free will is corrupted because of the Fall; and man's eternal salvation becomes effectual only through divine predestination.

Love constitutes the final definition of God and the crown of the Christian virtues.

The *Enchiridion* was written by Saint Augustine in response to a request by Laurentius to provide him with a handbook on Christian doctrine. Fulfilling this request, Augustine took as his framework the Apostles' Creed and the Lord's Prayer, and he concluded by showing that the principles of Christian living are to be found in faith, hope, and love. In the compass of these few pages some basic issues pertaining to faith and reason, the nature and origin of evil, salvation and grace, free will and predestination, are stated and discussed.

Augustine begins by clarifying his position on the relation between faith and reason and advances his theory of divine illuminism. In matters of knowledge of divine truth, faith precedes reason. The mind attains knowledge only because there is a prior illumination granted by God Himself. It is made clear to Laurentius that faith, which is itself a gift of God, must provide the starting point. This does not, however, entail a depreciation of reason as was proposed, for example, by Tertullian of Carthage some two hundred years earlier, when he maintained that divine truth is proportional to its rational absurdity. In the thought of Augustine reason plays an important role, and its role is that of clarifying and understanding that which is previously apprehended through faith. The program which he submits is one of faith seeking understanding.

The problem of good and evil, one of the central concerns in the thought of Augustine, is briefly sketched in this compendium of Christian beliefs. The good is defined as a natural harmony or order. The good thus defined is ontologically prior to evil, evil then being understood as the privation of an original good. In the background of Augustine's thought on this point is the Biblical doctrine of creation as well as the Platonic theory of being. Augustine's classical formula, *esse qua esse bonum est,* is at the same time an expression of the Biblical faith that God's creation is good and of the Platonic equivalence of being and value. It is on this issue in particular that the Augustinian synthesis of Jerusalem and Athens becomes apparent. Every being, insofar as it is a being, is good. All things that exist are good insofar as they have been made by a Creator who is Himself supremely good. However, insofar as existent things are not like their Creator in being supremely and immutably good, their good is subject to a diminution or privation. This privation is precisely what Augustine understands by evil. Thus, evil requires the good as the original reality of which it is a privation. Evil requires a host in which to dwell. So long as a being is in the process of corruption there must be in it some good of which it is being deprived. If perchance this being should be completely consumed by corruption, it would have neither good nor being. Every being, therefore, is good—infinitely good if it remains immune to corruption, finitely good if it is subject to corruption. In any case it remains a good. According to Augustine, there can be no evil where there is no good. The Augustinian relation of good and evil thus provides us with an exception to the logical rule that contrary attributes cannot be predicated of the same subject. Dark and light, black and white, bitter and sweet, beautiful and ugly are contraries which cannot exist at the same time in any one thing. This is clearly not the case with the contraries of good and evil. There is no difficulty involved, for example, in defining man as an evil good. He is good because he is a being; he is evil because part of this being has been corrupted. Evil is not an independent principle. It was thus that Augustine could refute the Manichean heresy (to which he was attracted during the early part of his career), which maintains that good and evil are independent cosmic principles that respectively account for the value and disvalue in human existence.

When we ask how it is that evil as the privation of the good makes its appearance in human existence, the answer must be original sin. This original sin has its locus in the Fall of Adam, in which all mankind shares. In his state of created goodness prior to the Fall Adam had the freedom to sin or not to sin. Attracted by the possibility of infinite knowledge, he transgressed his finite limits and affirmed for himself the knowledge and self-sufficiency which belong to God alone. Adam sought to elevate himself to the level of the Creator. This self-elevation, commonly called pride, is man's original sin, according to Augustine. The Fall of man comes about in that moment in which he seeks to negate his creatureliness and to affirm himself as God. Now the consequences of the Fall are for Augustine extensive in their implications. Ignorance of duty, concupiscence or lust, and the desire for what is hurtful follow in the wake of man's attempted self-elevation, and these in turn introduce error and suffering into the life of man. After the Fall man walks in darkness and loses his vision of the good. He neither knows the good nor is he able to do the good. At the same time, he is caught up in an incessant striving for power and for sensual gratification. The objects of power and sensuality when attained provide no ultimate satisfaction, and thus the soul of man remains turbulent and restless. His life becomes a frustrating cycle of exaltation and depression. His momentary pleasures and passing glory do not add up to happiness. They lead only to insatiable craving. Both the intellect and will of man suffer from this original corruption. This corruption is so pervasive that all efforts on the part of man to deliver himself from his state of perdition are futile. He cannot restore himself by any merit of good works. Before the Fall he possessed the freedom to sin or not to sin, but after the Fall this freedom is trammeled, and all his subsequent actions bear the taint of the original transgression. It is for this reason that man stands in the need of a Savior. God must come to man and effect that restoration which man cannot effect for himself. God extends salvation as a gift. Man is saved by the grace of God through faith.

By virtue of the Fall the creature is separated from the Creator. By virtue of divine grace the unhappy consequences of this separation are transfigured and man is restored. This theme of sin and grace is the pivotal point in Augustine's delineation of Christian doctrine. The emphasis here, as he repeatedly reminds Laurentius, is clearly Pauline. Both the Apostle Paul and Augustine have a horror of any suggestion of a doctrine of salvation by works. This was the central issue in Augustine's controversy with the Pelagians, in whose position he detected a facile deification of man, an attenuation of the reality of sin, and a consequent neglect of the need for divine grace. Augustine's theology of grace has its foundation in the message and person of Jesus Christ. Augustine's Christology, although never explicitly formulated, presents a view of Christ as the Son of God in whom two natures, human and divine, are united in one person. Just as each individual man unites in one person a body and a rational soul, so Christ in one person unites a divine nature, the Word or Logos, with a human nature. It is thus that Augustine's position becomes historically significant as one of the formative influences which shaped the Christological formula, *una persona, duae naturae,* which became normative at the Council of Chalcedon in 451. The saving work of Christ, in which the grace of God becomes effectual, proceeds from this unique event of a unified divine-human nature. Christ as Logos assumes a likeness of man's human, sinful condition without Himself committing any actual sin. He thus remains sinless, but at the same time He is able to wrest man from his state of perdition and to bring about his restoration. This grace, which becomes manifest in Jesus Christ, is both prevenient and following. It is clearly stated in the Scriptures, says Augustine, that the mercy of God "shall meet me" and that it "shall follow me" (Psalms 23:6). Grace comes to the unwilling to make them willing, and it follows the willing to sustain them in their continuing life of faith. Man does not seek God; God seeks man. In no sense is grace through faith a human attainment for Augustine. It is solely the gift of God.

It is within this context of sin and grace through faith that Augustine's teaching on free will and predestination must be understood. Although Augustine is concerned to safeguard the idea of human freedom, this freedom is a freedom which has not only clearly defined natural limitations but also a final limiting condition in the movement of divine grace. In the final analysis, the will owes its freedom to God. It is God who prepares the will for its initial reception of grace, and it is He who sustains it throughout the process of redemption. Man's freedom is incurably finite by nature, and it is fundamentally corrupted by the Fall. Indeed, after the Fall man's free will is so impoverished that he can do nothing without the prior action of the will of God.

As the thought of Augustine progresses, it becomes increasingly evident that predestination takes priority over freedom. This does not mean that freedom is ultimately denied in the Augustinian view, but it does mean that man's free will can operate only within the wider and ontologically prior context of a creating, governing, and redeeming will of God. To be sure, in the *Enchiridion,* as well as in the *City of God,* Augustine submits the distinction between God's foreknowledge and His foreordination, thus suggesting that God can foreknow the future state of His creatures without having foreordained it. But it remains incontestable, according to Augustine, that after the Fall the springs of free action are corrupted beyond the possibility of human restoration and all becomes the work of divine grace. From this proposition the doctrine of predestination follows as a necessary implication. God predestines for eternal salvation those whom He will. The unavoidable question then arises: What about those who suffer eternal damnation? Augustine argues that the will of God is omnipotent and is never defeated, and he also takes seriously the Biblical assertion that God "will have all men to be saved" (I Timothy 2:4). How, then, does one account for the eternal damnation of some? The apparent contradiction is resolved, argues Augustine, when we understand the Scriptural reference to mean that no man is saved unless God wills it. It does not mean that there is no man whose salvation He does not will; rather, it means that no man is saved apart from His will. And by "all men" we are to understand all varieties of mankind instead of all mankind as a corporate totality. God wills the salvation of kings and subjects, nobles and slaves, learned and unlearned, rich and poor, healthy and enfeebled. God wills the salvation of men from all positions and walks of life. But does he will the damnation of others? Apparently not. Augustine stops short of a doctrine of double predestination, later advanced by John Calvin, in which God predestines some to eternal life and others to eternal damnation. God does not predestine the damned. He leaves them to their own devices, and their fate is a consequence of justice. They receive their just desert. However, He does withhold grace from them, and why He visits grace on some and withholds it from others remains inscrutable to the finite and fractured intellect of man.

Augustine concludes his summary of Christian doctrine with a brief discussion on the centrality of love. Love provides both the final definition of the nature of God and the foundation for Christian ethics. Without love and its manifestation in faith, no important knowledge is possible, and no significant act can originate. Man responds to the creating and redeeming love of God through a resolute love of his neighbor. The motivating principle of Christian action is the love of God and the love of one's neighbor in God. From Christian love follow all the special duties and requirements which constitute the Christian life. Love provides the all-embracing directive for man's ethical existence.

THE COMMONITORY

Author: Vincent of Lérins (d. before 450)
Type of work: History of Christian doctrine
First transcribed: c.434

Principal Ideas Advanced

The basis of orthodoxy is Scripture and the tradition of the Church.

The test of orthodoxy when opinions differ is ecumenicity, antiquity, and consensus.

Progress in doctrine must not change the substance of Scripture and tradition.

The formation of orthodox beliefs about the Christian faith reached a high point of concentration in the fourth and fifth centuries. The *Commonitory* of Vincent of Lérins is one of the most significant treatises of that creed-making period when the Church was struggling to decide which among a diversity of opinions were right and orthodox and which were wrong and heretical. Councils debated the issues, especially the doctrines of the Trinity and Christology, and the fact that various councils, local and general, continued to struggle with points of doctrine is evidence enough that counciliar decisions were not always acceptable to large groups of Christians. It was a perplexing and attenuated condition.

The monk Vincent determined to record what he believed to be orthodox and to explain on what grounds beliefs should be so received. He tells us that he settled down to his task in a rural farmhouse outside his monastery and entitled his work, *Peregrinus' Treatise on behalf of the antiquity and ecumenicity of the Catholic Faith against the profane novelties of all heretics.* He nowhere mentions his own name in the treatise; but there is convincing evidence, which no one disputes, that Vincent of Lérins was the author, writing under the pseudonym of Peregrinus.

Vincent was certain that what is correct doctrine is based on Scripture, on "the authority of the divine law," but he realized Scripture is open to many interpretations. Everyone quoted Scripture in support of his opinions. Of course, the councils debated the various interpretations and decided by consensus what formulation should prevail. Could the matter be analyzed further? True, the Scripture rule was a fixed point, and a council decision was a historical fact of record, but the conciliar decisions were not arbitrary. Vincent believed that three elements were present: ecumenicity, antiquity, and consensus. He does not hold that these factors were formulated as principles by the orthodox party, but that they can be discerned by reflection. Nor does he hold that all are present to the same degree when the issues were being debated. All the opinions labeled heresy by the orthodox, however, fall foul of one or more of these tests. If not all accept a position in doctrine, then clearly the decision cannot be said to be universal, but it could be claimed to be the position of antiquity. Indeed Vincent curiously defines "catholic" or "ecumenical" as including "almost all universally." If the minority opinion claimed antiquity as, for example, in their support by Scripture, then the agreement or consensus of a universal council could be used against them.

This Vincentian Canon, as it is generally called, is applied to various deviant positions in the remainder of the treatise. The Donatists of North Africa were out of line with the imperial Church, and the Arians who at one time included "almost all the bishops of the Latin tongue" were out of line with the ancient faith.

Innovation is the dominant source of error and the confusion of good doctrine in the illustrations which Vincent uses. His own explicit aim was to avoid novelty in his exposition of the faith. The times in which he wrote were destructive of the old foundations of Roman civilization. The walls of the empire were crumbling; the internal life of great centers of the Roman tradition was decaying; monasteries were multiplying where men could find a haven from the confusing and demoralizing political scene. The great Christological controversies had evoked tremendous party spirit within the churches, and the Third General Council at Ephesus, 431, was just over when Vincent wrote in 434. Christendom was stirred by the conflict between the great sees epitomized by the battle between Cyril of Alexandria (376-444) and Nestorius (d.c. 451) at this council. Regional loyalties were strong, and the quest for truth was obscured and embittered by partisan power play. Vincent was a passionate traditionalist who saw nothing but a demonic tendency in innovation. He believed that the time called for conservatism and consolidation as opposed to experimentation and division. The decisions of the ecumenical councils had his vote, and he believed that all Christendom should rally around the most powerful group. Those who refused were spreading "poison"; they were "mad dogs," "pests," "diseased" and "would burn eternally with the devil."

He was not at a loss to explain why God had permitted the heretics to expound their doctrines and often to win considerable support. Plainly, God was testing His people when He allowed them to follow prominent teachers, to build up affection for them, and to form churches under their leadership. Nestorius, Photinus (early fourth century), Apollinaris (c.310-?) are singled out for discussion at length. They had all been involved in the protracted debates on the Person of Christ. It is the work of Origen (c.185-c.254), however, that Vincent deplores most deeply. "My opinion is," he wrote, "that although we are able to adduce many examples of this type of trial, there is almost no instance comparable to the trial brought on by Origen, in whom there were so many features so excellent, so unparalleled, so marvellous, that at first sight one would judge quite easily that credit should be given to all his pronouncements." That most erudite man, however, had been the father of many innovations, and the extent of his influence as a teacher of so many eminent Christians compounded the effect of his mischievous doctrines. Almost as bad as Origen among the Greeks was Tertullian (c.160-c.220) among the Latins. His learning, his literary style, his defense of the truth, were all most wonderful, but his later work was "more eloquent than faithful," Vincent writes, and he regarded Tertullian's views as deserving condemnation.

What may be said, however, about progress in doctrine? Creedal statements formulated by local and general councils were evidence of some sort of advance in belief. Vincent faces this question in section XXII of the *Commonitorium.* Of course, there must be progress, he argues, and it should be "as great as possible." But it must not be a change of doctrine. There is a great difference between altering the substance of the faith by introducing novelty, and making possible a growth of knowledge about the faith. The position, he suggests, is analogous to that of the development of reason in a person as he progresses from childhood to adulthood. The nature is the same, but latent possibilities are developed. In this way ample room can be allowed for clarification, definition, and strengthening of all authentic factors in the Christian religion. There can be new names but no new beliefs. All this progress, of course, must come by way of general consensus. What is new but heretical is sectional, local, and often individual.

The Church as a whole has to guard the deposit committed to its trust. This means guarding Scripture itself against misuse, for it is characteristic of the heretics that they fill their conversation, debates, and books with Scripture-proof texts, sprinkling their poisonous dishes, as it were, with "the perfume of the heavenly law." "We have not the slightest doubt," wrote Vincent, "that the devil is speaking through them." If the Devil uses the heretics, God uses the Church—not, of course, to initiate new doctrine, but to guarantee the correct understanding of the old.

An interesting question has been raised on this section in the *Commonitory* as to the relationship between some doctrines of Augustine of Hippo (354-430) and Vincent. The Pelagian controversy had caused Augustine to develop a belief in divine grace as absolute, being conferred without respect to human conditioning. This view is allied to a belief in a rigid predestinarian view of the operations of the divine will. Vincent, on the other hand, was unwilling to accept either the position of Pelagius or of Augustine and adopted a view which was later called Semi-Pelagian. He claims in section XXVI that it is heresy to teach that "there is a great and special and wholly personal grace of God, so that without any effort, without any zeal, without any industry, though they neither ask, nor seek, nor knock, those who belong to their number have a special arrangement with God. . . ." Augustine is not named, but it is probable that his position in this regard is being condemned by inference. Certainly Augustine would have disagreed with the place given by Vincent to human effort, and probably also with Vincent's reading of what was the content of antiquity in the evaluation of doctrine.

The *Commonitorium* as it has survived consists of one book and the summary of a second. What happened to the second book is unknown, and an ancient editor simply notes that "nothing more of it has survived than the last part, that is, only the summary given below." The summary indicates that the book contained a continuation of the same type of discussion given in the first book.

In the history of Christian doctrine the treatise plays an important part in the development of authority in relation to Scripture, tradition, and the Church. It omits all reference to an authority resting on Apostolic succession, and its criterion may be held to be more negative than positive in that it attempts to define what doctrines may be condemned rather than to single out those which may be developed.

THE DIALOGUES

Author: Theodoret of Cyrus (c.393-c.458)
Type of work: Christology
First transcribed: c.444

PRINCIPAL IDEAS ADVANCED

God the Word is immutable; He became incarnate by taking perfect human nature, not by being changed into flesh; and after the union, He remained unchanged, unmixed, impassible, while preserving unimpaired the nature He had taken.

Theodoret, the author of the *Dialogues,* was probably born in 393; he became a student of theology under Theodoret of Antioch, and in 423 he was consecrated as Bishop of Cyrus (Cyrrhus), where he served until his death. Theodoret was an able administrator and a prolific writer who played an important role in the controversies of his day. Besides the *Dialogues* he wrote numerous exegetical and theological works as well as an *Ecclesiastical History* which continued the work of Eusebius (c.260-c.399).

The *Dialogues,* Theodoret's principal Christological work, was written to vindicate Theodoret's orthodox views and to refute the Eutychian heresy. The latter position held that when Christ became man, He possessed a single nature and His body was not essentially like our own. Nestorius (d.c. 451) had defended the assumption that Christ had two natures. In reaction the Eutychians insisted that there was but one nature in Christ.

Theodoret points out that the orthodox doctrine of the Church insists that there are two natures in Christ, the divine and the human, and that there is no transfer of the attributes of one nature to the other. The natures are not mingled or confounded, but are united in a personal or hypostatic union, so that Christ is but one person. The divine and the human nature are thus inseparably united, not in such a manner as to form a third nature, which is neither human nor divine, but in a manner such that each retains its own properties unchanged, so that there is both a finite and an infinite intelligence, a finite and an infinite will. The properties of the one nature are not transferred to the other. Christ's humanity is not deified, and His deity is not reduced to His humanity. The union of the two natures is not a mere contact or indwelling, but a personal union which results in Christ's having two distinct natures and one person, so that He is at once both God and man.

The *Dialogues* consists of a series of discussions between Orthodoxos and Eranistes. The former represents Theodoret's understanding of the Apostolical decrees, whereas the latter is portrayed as the innovator of new doctrines.

The first part of the *Dialogues* seeks to show that the Godhead of the only-begotten Son is immutable; the second, that the union of the Godhead and the manhood of the Lord Christ is without confusion, and the third contends for the impassibility of Christ's divinity.

To attain the proper view of the nature of Christ, says Theodoret, it must first be recognized that Holy Scripture teaches that the Father, the only begotten-Son, and the Holy Spirit are one substance. What is predicated of the divine nature is common to the Son, to the Father, and to the Holy Ghost, but what is said of a particular hypostasis, a particular person of the Trinity, does not apply to the Holy Trinity. The term "God," for example, is common to the entire Trinity, but the name "Father" denotes the hypostasis to which it is proper. The names "Son," "Only Begotten," and "God the Word" do not denote the Holy Spirit or the Father, and the words "Holy Ghost" do not denote the Father or the Son but denote the hypostasis of the Spirit. Some terms are thus common to the Holy Trinity and some peculiar to each hypostasis. The term "immutable," however, is common to the Trinity as a whole, since it is not possible for a part of the substance to be mutable and a part immutable. The Father, the Son, and the Holy Ghost are immutable; thus, even though the Son became flesh, one cannot predicate mutation of His immutable nature. On the other hand, it is undeniable that when the Word was incarnate, it was not so simply in appearance; Jesus was not in reality God without flesh. The Son took upon Himself the seed of Abraham, and He wrought the salvation of mankind. The divine Word was made flesh, not by a mutation in His immutable nature, but by taking on a human nature. He who was born in Bethlehem was God; He was not God only, but also man; after the flesh He was an Israelite, a son of David, a man, and the eternal God.

The Holy Scriptures are the only source of true doctrine, Theodoret claims. The Scriptures clearly teach that the Son did not take an angelic nature, but the nature of a man. God was manifest in the flesh. The divine nature is not visible, but the flesh is visible. Through the visible the invisible was seen. When Jesus healed the sick, gave sight to the blind, and walked upon the sea, the almighty power of the Godhead was displayed. The Lord Christ had a body which He offered as a sacrifice, but His immutable nature did not undergo mutation into flesh. A body was prepared for Him by the power of the Holy Spirit, so that he was born of the Virgin Mary. In His humanity Jesus Christ is of the seed of David; in His deity, He is the immutable Son of God. As God and the Son of God, Jesus Christ was clad in the glory of the Father, and He shared the divine nature with Him. The one who in the beginning was with God and was God, the Creator of the world, took upon Himself the form of a servant, and He became God clad in human nature, so that He could accomplish the salvation of men. He was made in the likeness of man, and He acted and suffered as a man.

The divine Word is and was and will be immutable, but when He took man's nature, He became man, so that it is necessary to confess both natures, the divine and the human.

Two errors are to be avoided, Theodoret warns. The one confounds the hypostases, instead of recognizing three; such was the error of the Sabellians; the other error is to divide the substance and to introduce three substances instead of one; such was the error of the Arians.

Scripture teaches that there are three hypostases and only one substance. The man Jesus is the one Mediator between God and man; He is the Mediator because He does not exist as God alone. If Christ had not shared our nature, He could not have accomplished the work of redemption. Within Himself he unites distinct qualities, the Godhead and manhood. These two distinct natures are not to be confounded. In His divine nature He has neither beginning, nor end; He is eternal and co-eternal with the Father. Yet He is truly man. The Incarnation is real. Both qualities are proper: existence from the beginning, and generation from Abraham and David.

In Christ, says Theodoret, the two natures are not confounded, but unimpaired. Both His divine attributes and His human qualities are proclaimed in the Scriptures. When we speak of the two natures each must be carefully distinguished, so that we recognize that some attributes belong to the Godhead and some to the manhood. However, when we speak of the person, what is proper to the natures is to be applied to the person, and both sets of qualities, the divine and the human, are to be ascribed to the Savior. The same being is to be called both God and man, both the Son of Man and the Son of God, both David's Lord and David's son, both Abraham's creator and Abraham's seed. Each nature has its own properties, but the two natures are united in one person.

It is to be noted further, Theodoret concludes, that God the Word did not taste death or suffer. The divine nature is immutable and incapable of suffering. What is repugnant to the divine nature is impossible to it. Our Savior *as a man* underwent the passion; *as God* He remained incapable of suffering.

TOME

Author: Saint Leo I (c.400-461)
Type of work: Doctrinal epistle
First transcribed: 449

Principal Ideas Advanced

The Apostles' Creed and the Scriptures clearly attest to the fact that although Christ was truly human as well as truly divine, but He was one person.

As a result of being deceived by the Devil, mankind had incurred guilt and the loss of immortality.

By secret counsel, God devised the mystery of the Incarnation to ransom man from the power of the Devil.

Only one who is both God and man could pay man's debt and restore what he had lost.

The *Tome* of Leo I, "Leo the Great," is a long epistle, addressed by Leo, Bishop of Rome, to Flavian, Bishop of Constantinople. The letter contains Leo's theological opinions concerning the problem of the divine and human natures in the person of Christ. The occasion of the epistle was the controversy raised by the Abbot Eutyches (c.378-454), who had been condemned and excommunicated by a Synod at Constantinople on the charge of denying the humanity of Christ. Eutyches addressed a circular letter to all the Metropolitan Bishops, and thereby succeeded in winning the support of Dioscurus, Bishop of Alexandria, who, in turn, persuaded the Emperor to call a General Council at Ephesus, in 449. Leo, who did not attend the Council in person, sent three legates, bearing his *Tome*. But the Council, dominated by Dioscurus, refused the *Tome* a reading and declared Eutyches exonerated; indeed, it went so far as to excommunicate both Flavian and Leo. Matters were reversed only with the ascension to the throne of a new emperor, who summoned another Council, at Chalcedon, in 451. Here, Leo's *Tome* was received with general satisfaction, and it provided the substance of the formula which the Council adopted and which since that time has been regarded in the West as stating the orthodox doctrine concerning the Person of Christ. The Council of Chalcedon, besides annulling the proceedings of the Council at Ephesus, deposed Dioscurus, and raised the See of Constantinople to second place, after Rome, in order of precedence.

In his *Tome,* Leo censures Eutyches for indulging in speculation rather than applying his thoughts to Scripture, or even to the Apostles' Creed. The latter, says Leo, is decisive, inasmuch as it simultaneously declares that Jesus is the only Son of God and that He was "born of the Holy Ghost and of the Virgin Mary." As Son of God, He shares from eternity the power and glory of His Father, but as the Son of Mary, He had His beginning in time, and took upon Himself our passible nature, to make it his own. This birth in time, says Leo, took nothing away from nor added anything to His divine nature, but it added to our nature that by which alone mankind can conquer sin and death.

From the Apostles' Creed, Leo turns to the Scriptures. Eutyches had said that "the Word became flesh in such a way that Christ, born of the Virgin's womb, had the form of man but had not the reality of his mother's body." But the plain intention of Scripture, says Leo, citing Isaiah's words about the son of the virgin and Paul's declaration that Christ was the "seed of David according to the flesh," is that, although God "gave fruitfulness to the Virgin, the reality of His body was received from her." Thus, the flesh which the Word took was that same flesh into which God had breathed the rational spirit when he formed man in the Garden of Eden.

Leo knows that caution is needed, however, lest in reproving Eutyches's error he seem to support the opposite error of Nestorius (died c.451), who was condemned in 431 at the Synod of Ephesus. Nestorius had complained against a teaching very similar to that of Eutyches, and in his insistence on the separation of the divine and human natures in Christ, he had said that it was wrong to speak of Mary as "the Mother of God." His words were taken to mean that Christ was not properly God, but "a man, energized by the Logos of God."

In his *Tome,* therefore, while arguing for the genuine humanity of Christ and its distinctness from His divine nature, Leo specifically notes that "in the Lord Jesus Christ, God and man are one Person." Accordingly, it is permissible to say that Mary is "the Mother of God," and that "the only begotten Son of God was crucified and buried," even though Christ's birth and death occur only in His human nature and do not affect the divine.

Leo explains the necessity for the Incarnation as a means of ransoming man from the power of the Devil. Having himself fallen under divine sentence, Satan sought revenge against his vanquisher by using deception to corrupt man. But Satan failed to reckon with the immutability of God's purpose, which cannot be turned aside. By a secret counsel God devised a "hidden mystery" by means of which to restore man to immortality and endow him with those divine gifts of which Satan had deprived him. Following this divine stratagem, God would become man, to pay man's debt and bear man's punishment, yet He would do so without compromising His divine power or glory.

The marvelous paradoxes of the Gospel, says Leo, all follow from this mystery, as the lowliness of manhood finds in Christ a meetingplace with the loftiness of divinity. In His human nature, the Redeemer suffers; in His divine nature, He performs miracles. He that is laid in a manger is heralded by angels; He whom Herod strives to kill is adored by the Magi; He who submits to be baptized by John is saluted as the Son of God by a voice from Heaven; He who is grieved to tears for His dead friend, Lazarus, bids the same friend step forth from the tomb; He who hangs with pierced hands on the cross opens the gates of paradise to the dying thief. At all times, Christ is fully human as well as fully divine. Even after the Resurrection, when He appears inexplicably through closed doors and breathes upon His disciples the Holy Spirit, He partakes of bread and fish, and He urges those who doubt to touch the wounds of His passion, so that they may be convinced that He is no spirit but flesh and bone.

Leo charges that, in denying the true humanity of Christ, Eutyches has made void "the mystery whereby alone we are saved." Peter, when he confessed, "Thou art the Christ, the Son of the living God," affirmed that the selfsame person was both Son of God and Christ. Neither of these truths, says Leo, profits to salvation without the other. There is equal danger in believing either that Christ is only God or that He is only man. Eutyches, in affirming the former, has left man without salvation, since it is by the suffering which Christ endured in the flesh, and by the water and blood that flowed from His wounded side, that the Church lives and that mankind is cleansed of its sin.

The *Tome* of Leo is a polemic rather than a speculative work, intended to persuade its readers to favor Flavian's judgment condemning Eutyches and what came to be known as the Monophysite heresy. Leo, however, was a great statesman, and he rightly perceived the importance to the Church of arriving at a firm doctrinal position on so central a matter. In declaring that two natures, divine and human, are indissolubly united in Christ, yet in such a manner that divinity is not changed by Christ's passion, nor humanity absorbed by his divinity, Leo was only restating the position generally held in the West from the time of Tertullian. But his formulation of the crucial issues has classic strength and simplicity. Leo's declaration that two natures (*naturae*) were united without confusion in one person (*personam*) seems, indeed, to have provided the key terminology for the orthodox doctrine of the "hypostatical union." For, although Leo wrote in Latin, his distinction is obviously preserved in the Greek of the Chalcedonian Creed, which declares the Savior to be "one and the same Christ, Son, Lord, Only-begotten, in two natures (*physesin*), inconfusedly, immutably, indivisibly, inseparately; the distinction of natures being by no means taken away by the union, but rather the peculiarity of each nature being preserved and concurring in one person (*prosopon*) and one substance (*hypostasin*), not parted or separated into two persons, but one and the same Son and Only-begotten, divine Word, the Lord Jesus Christ."

Protestant scholars make a point of observing that Leo's treatise could not become the Rule of Faith for Christendom until it had been confirmed by a general Council, and that there is no suggestion at this date of the doctrine of papal infallibility, even on the part of so stanch an advocate of the Petrine supremacy as was Leo. It must be acknowledged, however, that Leo dissented from that action of the Council of Chalcedon which raised the See of Constantinople to seeming parity with that of Rome; and it is a glaring fact that, behind the theological controversies concerning the person of Christ, a momentous struggle for power was going on, in which the claims of Alexandria, Antioch, Constantinople, and Rome were being challenged. Leo, called by his successors, "The Great," did more than any of his predecessors to establish the dominance of Rome. But Leo was also a forceful preacher and an effective writer; he has been designated *doctor ecclesiae*. His sermons have supplied many lessons now found in the Roman breviary, and his *Tome* was read in medieval monasteries during the Advent season.

THE BAZAAR OF HERACLIDES

Author: Nestorius (died c.451)
Type of work: Christology
First transcribed: c.451

Principal Ideas Advanced

The Incarnation is the union of God and man, the nature (ousia) *of each being complete and remaining distinct from the other.*

The two natures are united in one prosopon, *so there is one Son, the Lord Jesus Christ.*

The prosopon *of the man Jesus and that of God are the same and they are both present in the one* prosopon *of Jesus Christ.*

Jesus Christ is born of the Virgin Mary, but God the Word is not born, and does not grow, suffer, or die.

Mary is not theotokos, *God-bearer.*

There are not two Sons, or two Christs.

The *Bazaar of Heraclides* is the exposition and defense in dialogue form of Nestorius's Christology. The English translation by G. R. Driver and Leonard Hodgson is made from the Syriac translation of about 535. It contains a detailed and repetitious statement of and argument for Nestorius's position, together with extended accounts of his treatment by the Council of Ephesus (431), of the turpitude of Cyril of Alexandria (d.444), and of the later persecution of Flavian (d.449), Bishop of Constantinople. Nestorius makes charges of violence and political maneuvering to put him in a false light at Ephesus. In his argument against Cyril he cites Scripture, the "three hundred and eighteen" of Nicaea, and many of the Fathers to give support for his own doctrine. He charges Cyril with deceitfulness, contradiction, hypocrisy, confusion of thought, and heresy. It is a heated polemic. Nestorius reveals not only a passionate earnestness but also logical acumen and constructive power. He, like others of his time, so far identified correct rational belief with Christian faith as to hold that doctrinal heresy meant damnation.

The charge against Nestorius was that he would not confess the Virgin Mary as "Mother of God," *theotokos* or God-bearer. Back of this phrase, in its acceptance or rejection, lies the whole problem of the Person of Christ. All agreed that there is One Lord Jesus Christ. All agreed also that Christ is God and man, human and divine. The critical issue was one *what?* and two *what?* This also involved the problem of *how* the two are united in the one. The trinitarian formula already approved employed two terms, *ousia* and *hypostasis:* God is three *hypostases* in one *ousia.* At first used as synonyms, *ousia* is now reserved for the essential nature of God, and *hypostasis* designates the three names for God in Christian faith; Father, Son, and Holy Spirit. Nestorius, however, usually assimilates *hypostasis* to *ousia,* although once or twice equating it with his own favorite term *prosopon.* For him the *ousia* or nature is the inalienable and incommunicable essence of God, and likewise of man. God is one *ousia,* man is another *ousia.* He rejects any teaching, such as that of Apollinarius (c.310-c.390), which replaces an element in human nature with one of the divine *ousia.*

How then are the two *ousiai* or natures united in the One Lord Jesus Christ? Nestorius uses the word *prosopon* to designate the One. He rejects "hypostatis" or natural union because this means to him two *ousiai* in one *ousia,* and this he scorns as irrational and impossible. It is this error with which he charges Cyril of Alexandria. To say, as Cyril did, that the eternal Word of God is the One Lord Jesus Christ means to Nestorius two things that are false and disastrous: (1) that the eternal Word who is God is "passible," that in His own nature He is born in time (Mary is *theotokos*) and grows and suffers and dies, and (2) that since the Son thus suffers as the divine *ousia,* the human *ousia* is wholly obliterated. Thus Christ is God but not man, and the whole claim to salvation in Christ is undermined.

Nestorius's own position is easily, and by him endlessly, stated. There are two *ousiai,* each complete, and the two are wholly distinct from each other. Each *ousia* has its nature and attributes which are inseparable from it. For the purposes of this doctrine, the most important difference between the natures is that one is passible and the other impassible. But each *ousia* also has a *prosopon.* The *prosopon* is not merely appearance or countenance. It is act, manifestation, role, and "dispensation." Granting, as he sometimes does, the distinction between *ousia* and *hypostasis,* Nestorius argued that each *ousia* has its own *hypostasis* and *prosopon.*

It is possible for each *ousia* to give its own *prosopon* to the other *ousia,* and to receive the other's *prosopon* in return. This is possible because the two *prosopa* are really identical. In Incarnation there is thus the one *prosopon* which is at once the *prosopon* of God and the *prosopon* of man. There are two *ousiai* or natures and one *prosopon*. This Nestorius calls the prosoponic union of God and man in the One Lord Jesus Christ.

The distinction between the impassible Deity and the passible humanity is preserved. Christ, who is the *prosopon* of God as well as of man, suffers in the flesh, the human *ousia.* He also is born in the flesh of Mary. He grows from childhood to manhood. Nestorius never tires of quoting Gregory of Nazianzus (329-389) as saying, "He who begins and gradually advances and is brought to fulness is not God, although on account of the manifestation which [took place] gradually, he is so called." But all this Christ does in His human nature. In His divine nature He does not suffer nor was He born of the Virgin Mary, for the Eternal Word cannot suffer and begin in time. A radical distinction is made between God the Word, which is the divine *ousia* solely, and Christ, or Lord, or Son, who is the union in one *prosopon* of the human and the divine *ousiai*. Nestorius does confess that Christ was born of Mary, but not that God the Word was born. He does say that from the conception by the Holy Spirit, the two *ousiai* were united in prosoponic union. He even grants that God the Word "passed through" the Virgin Mother, but not that He was born.

Nestorius repeatedly denies that he teaches "two Sons" or "two Christs." There is one Son, one Christ. And this one Son or Christ is God; He is also man, for He is made or composed of two *ousiai,* each of which is complete and distinct from the other. He will no more grant the two Sons than He will surrender the two natures. And each nature includes separately and distinctly all the attributes of the *ousia.* However, the human nature can and does take the divine *prosopon,* and the divine nature the human *prosopon.* Since the two *prosopa* are the same, this requires no change. It is exchange without change. The divine *ousia* has the divine *prosopon* by nature, and the human *prosopon* by union, as Nestorius repeatedly asserts.

The open question never adequately discussed by Nestorius is the nature of the *prosopon.* He does distinguish it from *schema,* or surface appearance. He also distinguishes it from will, which is an attribute of nature. It does not seem to have a merely functional meaning, although it clearly includes that. References to "dispensation" seem to involve the active role of God in history through the Incarnation. But there is no clear recognition of these questions or any attempt to answer them. Nestorius has a formula for which he finds support in Scripture, in the Creed, and in the Fathers. He even claims that Cyril himself says the same thing essentially, although Cyril also contradicts it. He felt that this formula was logically sound and of the greatest theological importance. Apparently his death came just after or perhaps before the end of the Council of Chalcedon which, although it repudiated Nestorius, to a large extent vindicated his argument; union of two natures in one *hypostasis* has more than a superficial resemblance to Nestorius's prosoponic union. The difference, and it is an important difference, lies in the fact that according to Chalcedon there is no human *hypostasis,* but only that of the Eternal Son; while with Nestorius there is a complete human nature, and the one *prosopon* of the union is as truly the human *prosopon* as it is the divine.

The open question with Chalcedon is that of the absent human *hypostasis,* and the question has been answered by the doctrine of impersonal humanity (*anhypostasia.*) The open question in Nestorius's thought is the manner of union of two *prosopa* which though the same belong equally to two numerically different and distinct *ousiai.* Nestorius never seemed to be aware of this theoretical problem, nor of the need to provide some theological or Scriptural basis for the affirmation that something in man is identical with a corresponding something in God. There is no suggestion, for example, that this might be the *imago dei.* The identity is simply affirmed.

THE DIVINE NAMES

Author: Dionysius, the Pseudo-Areopagite (fl. c.500)
Type of work: Philosophical theology
First transcribed: c.500

Principal Ideas Advanced

The names given to God cannot represent Him literally, for He is nameless; since the understanding and contemplation of God's actual nature is not accessible to any being, names for God must be used symbolically.

The Supreme Godhead is celebrated by every name while yet remaining nameless, although some names are applied properly to His unity and others only to His differentiated aspects.

The highest name is "Goodness," although the Trinity surpasses this name, as it does all names, since God is the nonexistent source of all existence.

The vast influence of Dionysius' masterpiece, on *The Divine Names,* is not understandable without some knowledge of its history. The author follows the practice of attributing his writing to a more famous personage, in this case to St. Paul's Athenian convert Dionysius the Areopagite. The actual author remains unknown, but the important point is that until the sixteenth century the Church accepted the writings as having been written by the early Dionysius. Thus, for centuries the theology of the Church reflected the views of an unknown author who initiated the greatest falsification in the history of Christian thought. Since the influence of Proclus seems present, the treatise is now dated as having been composed about the end of the fifth century. The author may have come from Syria, where speculative mysticism abounded, and he was widely read in the Eastern Church. Scotus Erigena's translation in the ninth century began a series of important commentaries in the West.

The Pseudo-Dionysius begins with the assumption that no proper concept of God can be formed or expressed in speech. Since the Godhead is beyond comprehension, every doctrine concerning God's nature must be derived from or be in harmony with Holy Scripture. The One, as Dionysius calls God, is beyond utterance and surpasses the reach of words; yet man must do his best to discourse about God. The ineffability of the One is due partly to the fact that the One is beyond existence; it is the *cause* of existence while itself not existing. This paradox results from the attempt to understand God by the use of names.

As a Christian theologian, Dionysius must meet the problem of the Trinity. It is clear, however, that Dionysius prefers unity to trinity as an ultimate concept, although he attributes a Trinitarian nature to his Godhead as a natural expression of its supernatural fecundity. It is generally agreed that the doctrine of God's fecundity is not one which became orthodox in Christianity, since the doctrine of the Trinity must remain as an inexplicable expression, an outpouring of a nature essentially beyond distinctions.

Symbolism is obviously highly important to a doctrine such as this, for no literal term or statement can in the nature of the case be wholly accurate. Since the Divine Being transcends all being, He obviously transcends all knowledge; He may be symbolized by terms but not grasped by them. On the one hand, we use the negative method and deny attributes as being inappropriate to God; on the other hand, we draw upon the whole of creation in an effort to characterize God properly. Like the Scriptural writers, Dionysius celebrates the One by every name while yet calling it nameless. Such a transcendent cause must both be nameless and, in some sense, the source of the meaning of all names.

The difficulty of these concepts, and the apparent contradiction often involved in their use, led Dionysius to label all such discussion of names (including this particular discussion) as esoteric. Those uninitiated into these matters should not become involved in the discussion of them, or else mockery and laughter will result. This brings to light the most difficult and also the most important characteristic of this subject; namely, that the study of the divine names requires new methods of thinking and the abandonment of conventional modes of logic. One must not despair when little progress is made or when the task appears to be impossible. The difficulty of the subject dictates that any outcome will be a compromise subject to objections, especially from those not used to such problems.

The first and perhaps most important distinction which Dionysius learns from his study of the names applied to the Divinity is that those names which are properly applied are applied not partially but to the whole, entire, full, and complete Godhead. Names not fully proper, then, can be detected when it becomes evident that they refer only to some special aspect, rather than to the Godhead fully and completely. Such partial application tends to split the Godhead, and the importance of maintaining unity indicates that any term which tends to apply only partially cannot really be a proper term for divinity. The aim is to exclude the confusion of all distinctions in the Deity.

Theology, then, has two methods: that of using names which fail to make distinctions and that of using names which reveal differences; properly understanding God means to keep the attributes which belong to each class separate. Undifferentiating names (for example, excellent, divine, knowing) belong to the whole Godhead and may be applied equally to any aspect of it; differentiating attributes (for instance, Father, Son, and Spirit) can neither be interchanged nor held in common. Undifferentiating attributes indicate the ineffable, hidden, unknowable Permanence, but differentiating attributes are emanations or manifestations. Undifferentiating attributes without any confusion are yet wholly commingled. Differentiating attributes indicate the passage of the Divine Unity into multiplicity. Divine things, even those revealed to us, are known only by such communications.

The ultimate nature of Divinity, what it possesses in its own original being, is beyond mind, beyond all being and knowledge. The originals of what the creature perceives as divine manifestations are only images, while the originals in the divine nature transcend and exceed the grasp of creatures. For instance, how Jesus was born in human form is beyond expression in language or grasp by the mind. That Jesus took man's substance is a mysterious truth which we have received, particularly mysterious in view of the fact that in spite of His assumption of the substance of man He maintained His full divine existence. The undifferentiated Godhead became differentiated without loss of unity.

Actually the Godhead is beyond even the distinction between unity and plurality, although it is the source of both and has unity as an undifferentiating name. In divine things the undifferentiated unities are always of more might than the differentiated attributes. Dionysius declares, furthermore, which name among the class of the undifferentiating names is most important, and it is not surprising that Dionysius should designate Goodness as the highest name. Dionysius notes here that it is increasingly difficult to gain knowledge about Divinity as one attempts to become more specific, but he continues in spite of this, arguing that such knowledge of Divinity as is possible must not be disregarded.

As one familiar with the Platonic tradition might expect, in beginning with the first and crucial attribute, Goodness, Dionysius uses the analogy of the sun. As the sun, through no choice of deliberation, but by the simple fact of its existence, sends forth its rays, so the Good sends forth the rays of its undivided goodness upon all things, according to the receptive powers of each. All things are endowed with soul and life, including even those things without soul or life. In beginning to speak thus more concretely about Divinity and its specific functions, Dionysius is forced into an appropriate negative method as he expresses characteristics in a transcendent manner by negative images.

Even the nonexistent shares in the Beautiful (Dionysius' second name) and the Good; for even what is nonexistent shares in the Beautiful and the Good, since by negation of all attributes nonexistence is ascribed superessentially to God. Here we see the beginning of the tradition which ascribes nonexistence to God as the most perfect way of preserving His perfection. All that has being comes from the Beautiful and the Good, including all those things which have no substantial being. Because of this, even "yearning" can be ascribed to God, since both yearning and its object have their pre-existent roots in the Beautiful and the Good.

In one sense, Divinity is the cause and producer and begetter of the thing signified, and yet, in another sense, it is the thing signified itself. There is but one simple Power which itself moves all things to be mingled in a unity, starting from the Good, going on to the lowest of the creatures, and returning through all the stages to the Good. But what about evil? The Good cannot produce things which are not good. Evil has less being than what is nonexistent and actually is further removed from the Good. Evil only destroys and debases; it is productive only by means of the action of the Good. If the Good were entirely removed, nothing would remain, neither the good nor the partially good nor the absolutely bad.

Actually both good and evil must have another origin or cause. Following Neoplatonic principles, Dionysius argues that no duality can be an origin; some unity must be the origin of all duality. Yet it is absurd to suppose that two entirely opposed things can owe their birth and their being to the same thing. This would mean that the origin was not unified, but divided, double, self-contradictory, and discordant. Such a situation in Divinity, for a Neoplatonist who treats unity as basic, is intolerable. Thus Dionysius' main problem is to give an account of evil and its origin such that evil becomes a part of and is not opposed to the Good.

Dionysius describes evil as a warping, a declension from right condition, a failure, a weakness or a loss of the power which would have preserved perfection. Evil things are so in a negative way, only in so far as they do not exist. In desiring evil one actually desires that which is nonexistent, the perfection which is absent. The only evil in anything lies in its inability to fulfill its natural functions. Since all things that have being are from the Good, matter must also come from the Good and in that sense cannot be viewed as evil. What is good comes directly from the one Universal Cause; evil comes from the many partial deficiencies. God knows evil only under the form of good. Evil is merely a weakness and deficiency of Good. Hence evil can have only an accidental cause and mode of existence. Evil exists nowhere simply as evil.

When Dionysius turns to the traditional term "being," he is forced to conclude that God is not existent in any ordinary sense, although in a simple and indefinable manner He embraces and anticipates within Himself all existent things. Just as all number pre-exists indivisibly in the number one, and this number contains all things in itself under the form of unity, so God is all things in that He is the cause of them all, and holds them together while He anticipates in Himself all beginnings and all fulfillments.

Hence, although all attributes, all the divine names Dionysius has discussed, can be affirmed of God, He is no one thing. He provides the limits of all things and yet He is a boundless infinitude, in a manner transcending all opposition between the finite and the infinite. Going out to all things, He remains in Himself. Not only is God so overflowing with wisdom that there is no limit to His understanding, but also He transcends all reason, intelligence, and wisdom. In seeking to understand the divine names, the human intellect is caused to transcend its intellectual nature. We are transported wholly out of ourselves and given unto God. Here is both the end of Dionysius' investigation of the names applicable to Divinity and the beginning of his mysticism.

ON THE HOLY TRINITY

Author: Anicius Manlius Severinus Boethius (c.480-c.524)
Type of work: Systematic theology
First transcribed: Before 524

Principal Ideas Advanced

The Christian belief in the unity of the Trinity is founded on the absence of difference and therefore of plurality in the Godhead.

Theology is that branch of speculative science which is abstract, dealing not with motion or matter but with that pure form which is Being itself and the source of all being; namely, the divine substance which is its own essence and which gives form and therefore being to everything.

Father, Son, and Holy Spirit are not identical, but there are not three Gods because predicates of relation affect neither the divine substance nor the divine unity.

The qualities attributed to God, such as justice, goodness, and greatness, are substantial or even supersubstantial because to be God is to be just or good or great, and these qualities may be ascribed to any one or to all the persons of the Trinity.

Boethius has been called by some the last Roman and the first scholastic and by some more a pagan philosopher than a Christian theologian. His theological tractates, of which the treatise *On the Holy Trinity* is representative, argue convincingly against his paganism but do not dispel the basically philosophical interests of the author. Boethius was a philosopher, and his self-appointed life work, although never finished, was the complete translation of Aristotle and Plato into Latin, together with commentaries that would reconcile their differences. His greatest contribution to the culture of the Middle Ages lay in the parts of this task which he did complete. It was he who established the Aristotelian philosophical terminology of medieval thought, the so-called *quinque voces* (five voices) of genus, species, difference, property, and accident. The importance of these terms is evident in his treatment of the Trinity.

Boethius lived in an age of change,

at the end of the classical world in fact, when the historical focus was shifting from the Mediterranean to western Europe and from the Romans and Greeks to the Germanic tribes. The Church had settled its central doctrinal problems at the great ecumenical councils or, in the West, by reference to the writings of Augustine (354-430), bishop of Hippo and the greatest of all Latin theologians. Theological creativity was on the wane, and an age of commentaries was commencing. Even Boethius acknowledges his indebtedness to Augustine in his essay *On the Holy Trinity*.

Boethius came from one of the eminent patrician houses of Rome. His father and father-in-law had served as consuls, and he himself was consul in 510 and saw his sons in this office in 522, although they were still minors. It must be remembered, however, that he lived under the kingdom of the Ostrogoths in Italy, who preserved the ancient Roman offices only as a semblance of legality and continuity. Boethius became a trusted adviser of Theodoric (c.455-526), the king of the Ostrogoths and an Arian. Politics, however, became his undoing; he was put in prison and executed by Theodoric for defending Albinus, an ex-consul, accused of treasonous relations with the Byzantine emperor. It was in prison that Boethius wrote his most famous work, *The Consolation of Philosophy*, which became one of the most widely read books of the Middle Ages. Because it contains nothing specifically Christian, the impression long prevailed that Boethius himself was not really a Christian. The short but lucid exposition *On the Holy Trinity*, together with his other theological treatises, provides evidence against that impression.

On the Holy Trinity consists of but six chapters and a preface on the difficulty of the subject. It is dedicated to Boethius' father-in-law, Quintus Aurelius Memmius Symmachus, an ex-consul and a Roman patrician. The first chapter states the belief of Christianity in the unity of the persons constituting the Trinity. Each person is God, but there are not three Gods. The cause of this union of the Trinity is the absence of difference. It was the Arians, Boethius claims, who argued for value distinctions within the Trinity and so converted it into a plurality. The author introduces a discussion of genus, species, and number as expressions of sameness and difference.

The second chapter continues the discussion of terms and method just begun. Boethius divides speculative science into three branches: physics, mathematics, and theology. The first deals with motion and is not abstract. The second deals with forms, not motion, and is also not abstract. Theology deals neither with motion nor matter and is abstract. Physics uses scientific concepts; mathematics, systematic ones; and theology, intellectual ones. Theology studies that form which is pure and not the image of any other form, which is Being and the source of being because everything owes its being to form and not simply to matter. The divine substance is form without matter; it is one, not the substate of anything.

The third chapter of *On the Holy Trinity* declares that there is only one divine essence without distinction according to accidents or substantial differences. To call the Father God and the Son God and the Holy Spirit

God does not create three Gods or a plurality, for this is a case of concrete rather than of abstract enumeration. To mention the sun three times does not produce three suns, and to call a sword also a blade and a brand does not make three swords. So it is with the three persons of the Trinity, among whom there is no difference. Still Father, Son, and Spirit are not identical although the same, and therefore number is involved.

Before clarifying the question of number, Boethius takes up in his fourth chapter the application of particular predicates or qualities to God. There are ten universally predicated categories: substance, quality, quantity, relation, place, time, condition, situation, activity, and passivity. Depending on their subject, they may denote substantial attributes or accidental ones, but when applied to God, they have a very different meaning. God is really a supersubstantial substance, and His qualities are substantial and not accidental. One sees this fact best with examples such as justice and greatness. To be God is to be just and to be great. To be a man is one thing, and to be a just man is another, not necessarily the same. Man may be great but not greatness itself. God, however, is identical with justness and greatness. In regard to the other categories, such as time and place, God is unique. God is everywhere, yet not in every place, because He does not occupy and is not contained by any place. He is eternal; He is in fact sempiternity or always present, always eternal. The categories of time and place as well as those of condition and activity are unlike those of substance, quality, and quantity because they are not substantial, but accidental. Hence, they are not simply applicable to God, who is not an ordinary subject; He is wholly substance.

The category of relation, however, has a special connection with the persons of the Trinity, and it is the topic of the fifth chapter of *On the Holy Trinity*. Because the category of relation has nothing to do with substance, predicates of relation, such as Father and Son, cannot alter or change their subject. In fact, the relation already belongs to or inheres in God's substance. There is no real difference in the subject, God, but only a difference of persons. There is no spatial separation in the Trinity and no essential or substantial differences.

In the final chapter, Boethius concludes that the divine substance preserves the unity and that the divine relations bring about the Trinity. He observes, moreover, that only terms of relation can be applied singly to each person of the Trinity because only these do not affect the substance of their subject. Thus, Boethius establishes the point expressed by the original title of his work: *The Trinity Is One God Not Three Gods.*

This treatise with its systematic explanation of the Trinity according to Aristotelian categories is representative of its age. It undertakes a task which each generation seems to find necessary, the task of comprehending the mysteries of faith and of giving them a rational exposition. Boethius continues this discussion in another essay directed to an unidentified John the Deacon. It is entitled *Whether Father, Son, and Holy Spirit May Be Substantially Predicated of the Divinity.* His conclusion is negative.

Each person of the Trinity is a substance, and the three are one substance. All predicates of substance such as justice, truth, goodness, omnipotence, and greatness must, of course, pertain to all three. Predicates such as Father, Son, and Spirit, which obviously pertain only to one person, are relative and not substantial, as the treatise *On the Holy Trinity* had already indicated. They are not predicated substantially of the divinity. But beyond this observation, Boethius affirms that even the Trinity is a relative predicate because it cannot be predicated substantially of each person.

These theological discussions of Boethius rest on dogmatic conclusions that were already established. The limits of discussion were already set. The degree of creativity possible to any writer on such topics was thus correspondingly restricted. In this respect Boethius could not be expected to produce something epochal. Still, his tractates are important to us as pointing the way into a new era of theology, the medieval and scholastic.

THE RULE OF ST. BENEDICT

Author: Saint Benedict of Nursia (c.480-c.547)
Type of work: Monastic rule
First transcribed: c.528

Principal Ideas Advanced

The communal life is essential for those who will undertake the way of perfection.

The discipline of the body is secondary to the discipline of the will through humility.

The worship of God is the main vocation of men, but manual labor and study are also important duties.

The Abbot is the vicar of Christ to his monks, and in submitting without murmur to his commands the monks work out their salvation.

The monastery is a congregation to which the monk attaches himself for life.

Christian monasticism, which originated in Egypt, was planted in Italy by Athanasius (293-373), whose *Life of St. Antony* stirred in many souls a resolve to undertake the life of abnegation. In the following century barbarian invasions provided additional incentive for men and women of all ages and rank to abandon civilian life either to join a religious community or to wander about begging hospitality. But, lacking leadership and adequate motivation, the movement rapidly became a scandal. Undisciplined individuals in ill-administered communities brought dishonor to God and ruin to their own lives because, as Benedict complains, they had no law, but called holy whatever suited their own will and fancy. Benedict himself, as a young man, undertook the hermit's life until his reputation for holiness led a nearby monastery to make him its ruler. His attempt to bring order to the monastic community was a failure, but, persuaded of the value of communal living, he went forth to organize several new communities in line with his ideals.

The *Rule of St. Benedict* is a full account of those principles and practices, derived from various sources, by which Benedict converted Western monasticism into a vigorous and wholesome institution, suited to play a historic role in preserving and propagating Christian civilization. His rule is to a considerable extent based on earlier rules of John Cassian (c.360-435) and St. Basil, as mediated to the West in the Latin version of Eastern monasticism.

Benedict considered the communal life essential for all who undertake the way of perfection. The life of a hermit, he writes, represents a higher attainment; yet it is not to be entered upon in the initial enthusiasm of conversion, but only after one has learned discipline by the help of others in a monastery. In principle, the rules which Benedict lays down for his monks constitute merely a beginning. They are the "least of rules" and have been "drawn up for beginners," he writes. When men have learned to live by them, they should desire to advance to higher degrees of perfection. In practice, however, as Benedict was astute enough to see, few monks will ever be able to dispense with these "instruments," and it is ordinarily assumed that those who enter the community are wedded to it until death.

According to Benedict, what man chiefly needs to achieve salvation is for his will to be humbled and tempered to obey the commands of Christ. Benedict speaks of monastic life in various terms: as a "school of the Lord's service" where men may overcome their habits of sloth and self-will; as a "workshop" where they are employed day and night with "instruments of the spiritual art," in order by the labor of obedience to return to Him from whom in disobedience they have departed; and as a training camp, where hearts and bodies may be drilled and accoutered to fight for Christ, the King. In contrast to oriental monasticism, which traces man's evil or ignorance to his body and hence views deliverance in terms of physical self-discipline and contemplation of reality, Benedict traces man's evil to pride and rebellion, and he views asceticism and contemplation merely as aids in the nurture of holy wills and affections.

Because Benedict does not regard materiality as the source of evil, he is more lenient than his Eastern counterparts in matters pertaining to the body. His monks are never deprived of food or sleep, and penance does not take the form of physical torture or privation. (An exception is that corporal punishment is recommended for boys.) In matters pertaining to the will, however, Benedict gives no quarter. Those who enter the monastery surrender everything to Christ, even the control of their own bodies; and this surrender means, in effect, that they yield absolutely to the will of the Abbot in all things. Such obedience is not acquired immediately, and satisfaction must be made for every fault. But the purpose of the satisfactions is to overcome pride and obstinacy, and punishment is designed accordingly. For example, an offender may be asked to prostrate himself at the door of the Oratory as the brethren pass in and out; or, for lighter offenses, he may have to take his meals apart from the brethren.

Taking as his text the Scriptural passage which says "Everyone that exalts himself shall be humbled, and he that humbles himself shall be exalted," Benedict charts the way of perfection in terms of twelve degrees of humility. They are: to keep in mind the fear of God and eternal punishments; to delight not in self-will but in Christ's service; for the love of God, to submit to one's superiors; to bear hardships without complaining; to confess one's evil thoughts and secret sins to the Abbot; to be content in the meanest circumstances; to think oneself the least worthy of men; to do nothing but what the rule and custom of the monastery direct; to maintain silence except when questioned; to refrain from laughter; to speak gently and soberly; and, at all times, to demonstrate humility by one's outward mien and conduct. By ascending these degrees of humility, beginning with fear of God, the monk will arrive "at that love of God which, when perfect, casts out fear." Then, his mind being conformed to Christ, the monk will no longer think of punishment or reward but, purged of vice and sin, he will rejoice in virtue and in love, and the Holy Spirit will dwell with him.

If this aspect of the *Rule of St. Benedict* seems unduly somber, let us remember the moral collapse which had accompanied the fall of Rome. Benedict's counsels were admirably suited for the rehabilitation of "tyrannical souls" (to use Plato's expression) which had overthrown all discipline and needed to be rebuilt from the ground up before they could be restored to the dignity of sons of God and workers in his Kingdom. Only to this extent is the *Rule of St. Benedict* somber, that it reprobates the base condition to which man has reduced himself. The condemnation does not extend to human nature or to creation generally. On the contrary, Benedict reaffirms the fundamental Hebraic conception of creation and man's place in it, and the major part of his program is what we may call a kind of occupational therapy, consisting of three parts: worship, labor, and study.

"The Divine Office," which Benedict also calls "The Work of God," is the major employment of the monks, in terms of importance, and consists in eight daily services of worship. Here, as for nearly all his rules, Benedict is able to cite Biblical authority, notably Psalm 118, as numbered in the Vulgate, where we read, "At midnight I arose to give praise to Thee," and again, "Seven times in the day I have given praise to Thee." The former text is the authority for what is called the Night Office; the latter for the seven day services: lauds, prime, tierce, sext, none, vespers, and complin. The *Rule* contains detailed instructions as to when these services are to be conducted, varying according to the seasons of the year, and what psalms, readings, and allelujahs shall be used. It further is explicit in requiring full and prompt attendance on the part of all the monks, and correct and intelligent performance of all parts of the service.

The services of worship, however, ordinarily require only five or six hours out of the day. Benedict provides for two work periods between services, one in the morning, one in the late afternoon. Another period, in the morning, is set aside for reading and study.

From sext until none (two-thirty or three p.m.), the monks are free to read or rest. The day ends with complin, after which complete silence is enjoined.

The monks regularly keep fast through the morning and have only noon and evening meals. On Wednesdays and Fridays, however, they fast until three o'clock. Their fare is simple but adequate. They each receive daily a pound loaf of bread, which is served with two cooked dishes and, when available, a fresh fruit or vegetable. A moderate amount of wine is allowed, but, except for the sick, no meat. A separate table, with special dishes, is provided for the Abbot, and guests are entertained there. The *Rule* provides detailed instructions concerning dress and sleeping quarters. No hardships are intended in any of these details, but at every turn the monk is reminded that he has no property which he can call his own, and no choice in what shall be appointed to him from the common possession.

No attempt is made toward achieving equality. On the contrary, it is a principle with Benedict that the Abbot must have in view the individual needs of each of his monks, both physical and spiritual, and it is part of the lesson of humility that other brethren should not murmur when, for example, the Abbot exempts an older monk from certain duties that are beyond his strength. An elaborate and self-contained establishment, such as the monastery was intended to be, requires a chain of authority and a distribution of responsibility. The Abbot must use great discretion in selecting the dean in charge of the divine office, the readers, the porters, and the cellarers. Furthermore, consideration must be given to whether a particular monk can assume special rank without being overcome with pride.

Within the provisions stipulated by the *Rule,* the Abbot exercises absolute control over his monastery. He is enjoined, whenever important matters come up, to assemble the monks and hear the opinions of old and young alike; but the decision is his alone. He is Christ's vicar, so far as his monks are concerned, and that is why they call him "Abbot," from the Aramaic word *Abba,* or Father. His actions must, of course, be answered for at the Judgment Day, and therefore he must avoid all favoritism and injustice, must govern by example as well as by the preached word, and must not hold back from such punishment as has to be imposed.

Benedict did not organize a monastic "order," in the medieval sense of that term, with many houses under a single administration. He thought of each monastery as an independent congregation, to which the monk attaches himself for life. The election of an abbot was left to the monks themselves, to be decided by a majority vote, although as a safeguard, lest a community fall upon evil ways, Benedict urged that the bishop of the diocese or abbots of nearby monasteries, or other Christians, take a hand in restoring discipline. His rule, although not original, and owing much to Eastern monasticism, provided the ground plan for Western monastic practices, and it has been a charter to which Western reformers have again and again had occasion to appeal.

PASTORAL CARE

Author: Saint Gregory I (c.540-604)
Type of work: Pastoral counseling
First transcribed: c.590

Principal Ideas Advanced

The office of pastor is a burden which most men are advised not to assume.

The care of souls is "the art of arts," and those who undertake it may do either great harm or great good.

Men's needs differ widely, and the pastor must have the skill to deal with each according to his particular circumstances.

While living in the spirit, the pastor must enter compassionately into the experience of those living in the flesh.

Historians are unstinting in their praise of Pope Gregory I, known to history as Gregory the Great. When he came to office, civil administration in Rome had completely broken down. Gregory raised armies, negotiated with barbarian invaders, and fed the populace; he also reformed certain abuses within the Church and promoted missionary activity. For these labors he was well prepared, having devoted all his life to Christian work and public service. Still, when by popular acclaim he was elected to be Bishop of Rome, he sought to avoid the office. This hesitancy on his part brought reproof from one of his fellow churchmen. In reply, Gregory composed the treatise *Liber regulae pastoralis* (Pastoral Rule), better known in English, since the time of Alfred the Great, as *Pastoral Care* from the phrase with which the book begins, "The burden of pastoral care. . . ."

The book deals with two main topics: first, the bearing of the office of pastor on the salvation of the incumbent; second, the bearing of the office of pastor on the salvation of those entrusted to his care. Gregory breaks the topic into a multitude of special exhortations, which resemble brief sermons or meditations on Biblical texts. Gregory, who belongs to the medieval rather than to the Hellenistic age, draws his material almost exclusively from the Scriptures. He did not make use of the classical authors in his writings, and although his Latin is celebrated for its simplicity and strength, he was not trained in the rhetorical tradition. Moreover, his work is only partly influenced by patristic learning. For the most part, in support of nearly every point he wants to make, Gregory uses a Scriptural citation. Some of these are direct applications of prophetic and apostolic sayings; others are pointed illustrations drawn from Biblical history; others, however, are oblique conclusions arrived at by the free use of allegory, as, for example, when he applies to the pastor the Mosaic directions against offering blemished animals as sacrifices.

Gregory demands that each one who entertains the thought of entering upon the office of pastor subject himself to profound self-examination. The responsibility which a physician takes upon himself, who holds in his hands the life and health of his patients, is a light one in comparison with that of the minister to men's souls. Gregory especially warns against undue eagerness to teach on the part of those who have a merely intellectual knowledge of salvation: "They hasten to teach what they have learned, not by practice, but by study." Those who are precipitant in undertaking the office of pastor are, he says, like a woman who gives birth before her time: ". . . they are filling not a home but a sepulchre."

The office of pastor is fraught with danger to those who minister as well as to those ministered to. Among the perils mentioned by Gregory is the tendency which a pastor has to neglect his own spiritual life when he is burdened with the cares of others. Any man who enters public life is subject to special temptations; a man who in private life knows quite well his limitations will, upon being exalted to office, invariably become conceited. The fact that his orders are executed promptly and that his subjects praise everything he does leads him astray. The danger is even greater in the case of the pastor. "The human mind," says Gregory, "is prone to pride even when not supported by power; how much more, then, does it exalt itself when it has that support!"

But, in spite of the dangers, there are those who ought to become pastors, who incur guilt if they refuse the office out of self-regard. There is a false humility, says Gregory, as well as a genuine humility. Vices frequently masquerade as virtues, and what appears to be humility may be sloth or even a kind of perverse pride. Those who hold back when they ought to serve do an injury to those persons who stand in need of their help.

Gregory acknowledges that some good men have desired the office of preaching while others no less worthy have been driven to it by compulsion. Isaiah, for example, volunteered: "Lo, here am I, send me." Jeremiah, on the other hand, was reluctant to go when commanded: "Ah, Lord God, behold, I cannot speak, for I am a child." Moses, says Gregory, admirably filled both parts, "who, though unwilling to accept the supreme rule of a great multitude, yet obeyed." But those who accept so great a responsibility must be clear in their hearts that it is not "the glory of that honor," which they seek, but "the ministry of a good work." When Paul said, "If a man desireth the office of bishop, he desireth a good work," he placed the emphasis where it belongs, says Gregory, who goes on to explain that in Paul's time the bishop would ordinarily be called upon to endure the tortures of martyrdom.

Gregory accepts the principle, common to the New Testament and to classic social thought, that men are unequal in ability and therefore in what is expected of them. The pastor, according to Gregory, must be spiritually superior to those who are committed to his care. He must live with his eye fixed on things spiritual, yet he must be compassionate toward those who are entangled with things carnal. Thus, Jacob saw the angels ascending and descending; thus, Moses frequently went in and out of the tabernacle. The pastor cannot sympathize with the trials of others without himself being assailed by temptations. Yet, if he trust in God and combine self-discipline with love for men, he need not fear for the health of his soul.

After these exhortations which bear upon the pastor's self-rule, Gregory turns to the practical problems which the pastor meets as he deals with different sorts of men. Gregory's considerable experience and keen intelligence brought him to the conviction that if the Christian teacher is to help instead of to harm those to whom he ministers he must be constantly alert to special demands of different kinds and classes of men. Gregory's method consists in giving directives by reference to opposites, such as poor and rich, joyful and sad, wise and dull, kindly and envious, slothful and hasty, quarrelsome and peaceable. There are forty of these combinations. Some of them represent differences in external conditions, health, or temperament; others represent differences of character and purpose. As far as possible, Gregory wishes to lay down rules. For example, the poor are to be offered consolation and encouragement; the rich, to be reminded of the dangers of pride. But Gregory is not unmindful of the fact that classificatory systems often break down in individual cases, and he recognizes that there is no single way of dealing with either poor or rich. Nathan wisely did not chide David, but very subtly led him to see the iniquity of his way.

The care of souls, according to Gregory, is "the art of arts," and it requires a special kind of practical skill. The pastor does not always need to be strictly candid with those whom he is trying to help, says Gregory. For example, when dealing with persons who are hardened to their faults, it may be necessary for the pastor to feign a despair that he does not actually feel. On the other hand, in order to make progress with the fainthearted, it is often wise to skirt their faults and to praise their virtues. Sometimes the pastor can best help the haughty by pretending that he needs them to help him, as when Moses won over his kinsman Hobab by asking him to be his guide.

Gregory is keenly aware of sins of the spirit, especially the faults of self-deception. Speaking of kindly-disposed persons, he points out that frequently their benevolence is merely that of spectators. He observes that abstemious persons are likely to be impatient and proud, and he admonishes that in order to be pleasing to God, the man who fasts must bestow on the poor what he subtracts from his own nourishment. Special dangers, he remarks, attend "those who prosper in their pursuit of temporal things." They come to respect the means to living and to lose sight of the things men live for, and thus they need to be reminded of the words of Solomon, "The prosperity of fools shall destroy them."

Gregory tried always to keep the affairs of man in the perspective of eternity. He viewed men's sins as affronts to God, and he trusted in God's pursuing grace to reconcile men to Himself. On the other hand, he stressed the need for men to respond to God's call, and the importance of human instruments in bringing men to repentance. If Protestants find his book lacking in any respect, it will probably be because Gregory thinks of sins in the particular ("We shed streams of water from our eyes when we weep for each sin separately, for the mind does not grieve for all sins equally at one and the same moment . . ."), rather than of sin as a condition of the heart. Thus he was inclined to look for "antidotes" to particular faults, and to prescribe penances. Still, the personal counselor, whatever his religious denomination, has much to learn from this wise and holy man.

THE LADDER OF DIVINE ASCENT

Author: Saint John Climacus (c.570-c.649)
Type of work: Monastic guide
First transcribed: c.640

Principal Ideas Advanced

Thirty steps representing the thirty unknown years in the life of Jesus reveal the progress necessary to attain spiritual perfection.

Beginning with the most important, renunciation of the world, one progresses through obedience toward repentance.

Silence is necessary, as is simplicity and solitude, for one who would achieve heaven on earth, a godlike dispassion, and perfection.

Although little is known except by conjecture about St. John Climacus, and in spite of the fact that no definitive text of his masterpiece exists, *The Ladder of Divine Ascent* or *Ladder of Paradise* has penetrated into numerous cultures and languages. In fact, it is not too much to say that it is one of the few definitive classics of the contemplative life, having provided inspiration for numerous monastic disciplines and still profoundly influencing many of those who seek religion through renunciation of the world. Much of the ground John Climacus covers is similar to that of a fifth century ascetical compilation known as the *Book of the Holy Men,* a collection of sayings attributed to the Desert Fathers. The idea of a ladder, with its thirty steps leading to spiritual perfection, may have been inspired by the Biblical account of Jacob's vision of the ladder.

Particularly in Orthodox monasteries, the influence of this work has been constant and decisive. Simeon the New Theologian, (949-1022) one of the outstanding figures in Byzantine monasticism, acknowledged his indebtedness to Climacus, and Climacus was of fundamental importance in the development of the Russian ascetical tradition. The purpose of the work was to guide the monks in their new life and, as traditional, was written in response to a request from a group of monks for a written guide, by one who himself claimed only to be a continual learner.

Following a long tradition, Climacus begins with a discussion of God, and he classifies people according to their relationships to God. God belongs to all free beings; to the faithful and unfaithful, the just and unjust, the pious and impious—just as the sun and the weather are for all. There are various ways of relating oneself to God, but the monk is one who loves as a mourning soul. Both asleep and awake he is unceasingly preoccupied with death. For him withdrawal from the world is voluntary hatred of vaunted material things and a denial of nature for the attainment of what is above nature. Since the monk's life is a contest, Climacus often compares the monk's state to that of the physical athlete. The monk must renounce all attachment to things, and a good foundation for his detachment is continence, fasting, and temperance.

The life of the solitary is a difficult one. In fact, it is so difficult that the most difficult problems of such a life are hidden from those outside of it, to whom it often appears easy. If others knew the difficulties of the monk's existence, few would renounce the world, since usually one renounces the world to escape difficulties. Very few men are ready to leave the world's advantages for what in fact are even greater difficulties. But a man troubled by his sins may eventually hate even his own flesh, and he may detach himself from the world and count it a disgrace to worry about anything that cannot help him in the hour of death. He who retains an attachment to anything visible, writes Climacus, is not yet detached from grief.

The monk renounces all business, all association with secular people and with parents; if he is victorious in these detachments, he receives rewards which the world cannot offer. If these rewards could be purchased in any other way, there would be no need for asceticism or solitude. Yet those who sail the spiritual seas know that the harbor of asceticism provides safety from worldly pressures, although it also exposes one to dangers of its own. Certain temptations are removed by removing oneself from the world, but new temptations come with the ascetic life.

Exile is the monk's state. Exile is separation from everything in order to keep the mind inseparable from God. Detachment is excellent, but exile is her mother. Exile involves running from places of sin as from the plague, and never looking back for fear of becoming useless. The family is left and the monk gains a new life—the remembrance of death. The solitary lives in a place which lacks opportunities for comfort and ambition, but provides the conditions for humility. Men who live in solitude are the warriors and athletes of Christ. The exile of the body and will must always precede obedience, the virtue which is most important to the monk's life.

Obedience, the absolute renunciation of one's own life, is clearly expressed in bodily actions and in the mortification of the limbs while the mind remains alive. Nor is obedience any less necessary at the end of the monk's life. Obedience is distrust of oneself, however good one may be, and perfect trust in one's superiors right up to the end of life. A man may question and examine before he enters on such a life, but once the arena has been entered, he must no longer judge his superiors. The temptation to judge his superiors is more difficult to resist than the natural temptations of the flesh.

Monastic discipline aims at the separation of body and spirit. If the monk learns to control his wandering mind in his distracted body, then amidst the actions and movements of his limbs he can practice mental quiet; in the midst of commotion he will be unmoved in soul. When he opposes discipline, when in conversation he tries to establish his own opinion, then he should recognize that he is sick with the Devil's disease, disobedience. From obedience comes humility, and from humility comes dispassion. It is not without peril for a monk to leave a group and attempt the solitary life on his own, since to do so is to be without the guidance of a spiritual superior, without the aid of the example of obedience.

Let the monastery be your tomb before the tomb, Climacus advises the monk. Constantly wrestle with your thought, and whenever it wanders, bring it back to you. Unbroken reflection is proper only to an angel, but the monk must strive to approximate it.

A servant of the Lord is the one who in body stands before men, writes Climacus, but who in mind knocks at Heaven's door with prayer. It is the Devil's prompting if anyone seeks to achieve any spiritual virtue prematurely. But keep at it, brother athletes, Climacus exhorts the monks; keep running fearlessly! The contemplative's steps lead to a new way of life, a life very much opposed to ordinary secular ways, a life with its own spiritual rewards and special difficulties.

The love of God sends a man into exile, and then obedience is born of self-condemnation. The thought of death is a constant aid to temperance, while solitude helps to establish chastity. Fasting quenches fleshly burning, and contrition wards off shameful thoughts. To win dependency, unceasing prayer is necessary, and to cure oneself of anger one must learn to love indignity. Detachment from the things of the senses will gradually lead to contemplation of spiritual things. Visible pride can be cured by grim condition, while quietness and solitude work against vanity. However, the only thing to do if one is with others is to seek dishonor. Only humility can destroy spiritual enemies.

Such are the items of advice John Climacus passes on to the monks as a guide for them in pursuing a spiritual life. The thirty steps leading to spiritual perfection for the solitary correspond in number to the thirty unknown years in the life of Jesus. Climacus points out that the solitary life is best pursued among a community of like-minded men, where authority can guide and a good community can excite mutual fervor among its members. Till the monk's very last breath, Climacus writes, the man who desires to attain the ultimate spiritual goal must never give up hope. Spiritual perception is a property of the soul itself, and through these thirty steps a dedicated man can be brought to perfect vision.

ECCLESIASTICAL HISTORY OF THE ENGLISH NATION

Author: Saint Bede ("The Venerable," c.673-735)
Type of work: Church history
First transcribed: 731

Principal Ideas Advanced

The defeat of the British peoples at the hands of the English invaders was a punishment for their sins.

When the British failed to preach the Christian gospel to the English nations, God sent missionaries from Ireland and from Rome.

Although the Irish missionaries were saintly men and zealous evangelists, they were mistaken in certain matters of worship and discipline.

The official recognition by the English of Roman ecclesiastical order has opened a new era of peace and godliness.

Bede, often called "the father of English history," was a priest and monk at the Benedictine monastery at Jarrow, which he entered as a student at the age of seven and from which he never had occasion to depart except for short visits to nearby churches and religious houses. Although Jarrow was a new monastery, its founder, Benedict Biscop (628-690), had brought back from Rome a good library and a chanter. Bede says, "I wholly applied myself to the study of Scripture, and amid the observance of monastic discipline, and the daily care of singing in the church, I always took delight in learning, teaching, and writing." A list of his writings includes, besides the *Ecclesiastical History*, numerous Biblical commentaries, lives of saints and churchmen, and treatises on the arts and sciences. The latter, in particular, were widely influential, not merely in England but also in France, prompting Continental scholars, such as Professor Étienne Gilson, to place Bede alongside Cassiodorus (c.485-c.580) as an important source of medieval learning.

In his *Ecclesiastical History of the English Nation,* Bede wrote with conscientious regard for the truth. His conception of history differs from that of the modern critical historian in that he was content merely to cite his sources, but he was aware of the importance of sources, and he tells us, in general terms, the authorities upon which his work rests. For information concerning the centuries prior to the coming of Augustine to Kent, he depended upon books written by others; for the critical years during which Roman Christianity was establishing itself on the island, he drew upon documents—such as the correspondence between Gregory I and Augustine—obtained for him from Canterbury and from Rome; for more recent developments, he made a point of consulting "men of good credit" from different provinces. "I humbly beseech the reader," he says, "that if he shall find anything set down other than truth in this that I have written, he will not impute it unto us, as the which have endeavoured with all sincerity to put in writing to the instruction of our after comers such things as we have gathered by common report, which is the true law of history."

Bede was English and his sympathies were wholeheartedly with the invaders who, beginning about 450, had gradually wrested the better part of the island from the hands of its native British inhabitants. The British, under Roman occupation, had accepted Christianity; and Bede quotes with appreciation the story of one of their martyrs, St. Alban, who was beheaded during the Diocletian persecution. But on the whole he regards them as a weak and indulgent people, unable to govern either their land or their passions once the Romans had withdrawn. The conquest, he says, was "God's just revenge of the wickedness of the people," like that which He executed on the Jews at the hands of the Chaldees.

Modern historians point out the comparative savagery of the English conquest of Britain and that, unlike the Gothic occupation of the Mediterranean provinces, it held no quarter for the vanquished. The Britons were either killed, driven back to remote portions of their island, or forced to emigrate across the sea, and a pagan and barbaric race took their place. As a result, the dispossessed had little opportunity, and no inclination, to impart to the newcomers any of the refinements of civilized life. More particularly, as Bede notes, "they never took care to preach the word of faith to the folk of the Saxons or English which inhabited the land along with them." But, says Bede, God's hand was with "his people which he foreknew to be saved," that is, the Anglo-Saxons; and in good season he "provided for the said folk much more worthy heralds of the truth, by whom they might be brought unto His faith."

This is the point at which Bede's story begins in earnest. The fact is, heralds came to the invaders from two directions. In the year 565, the Irish priest Columba founded a monastery at Iona, west Scotland, from which in succeeding generations Irish missionaries evangelized the northern portions of the Island; and in the year 596, the missionary Augustine (d.604), came from Rome, and established a church and monastery at Canterbury, in the south. Of the two "heralds of the truth," Bede's sympathies are all with those who came from Rome. Still, he tells with admiration the story of the rival missions.

One of the best known parts of Bede's *History* is the account ascribed by the author to "the tradition of our elders," of how Gregory the Great (c. 540-604), before he was made pope, saw in the slave market boys "of white skin and comely countenance and hair also of excellent beauty." Asking from whence they came, and being told they were called "Angles," he replied, "Well are they so called, for they have too an angel's face, and it is meet such men were inheritors with the angels in heaven." Gregory then asked the pope for permission to go as a missionary to this people; and, although he did not receive permission, when he became pope soon after, he sent Augustine to carry out the work.

Augustine arrived at Kent with a company of some forty persons, including interpreters. His arrival was smoothed by the fact that Ethelbert, the Kentish king, had married a Frankish princess who was a Christian and who had a chaplain with her. Augustine was courteously received, and at length he brought the king to embrace the Christian faith, who henceforth supported their mission with his possessions, although he "would force none to become Christian, . . . for he had learned from the masters and authors of his salvation that the service of Christ must be voluntary and not forced."

Bede records that Augustine tried to establish fellowship with the leaders of the British Christians, and he did succeed in meeting several of them in conference. Besides asking that they acknowledge him as the representative of the Universal Church, he required that they undertake three things: to change the date of celebrating Easter, to follow the Roman custom in baptism, and to join in preaching the Gospel to the English. When the Britons refused to acknowledge his authority, Augustine said that "if they would not have peace with brethren, they should have war with enemies." This threat was fulfilled, says Bede, when many monks and priests of the Britons were slaughtered by the pagan king Ethelfrith at Chester. Thus, "these heretical men learnt by the vengeance also of temporal death, that they had despised the counsels of eternal salvation offered to them."

The fortunes of Christianity were advanced by the marriage in 625 of Edwin, king of Northumbria, and the daughter of the Christian King Ethelbert. Among the influences contributing to Edwin's conversion was the counsel of the pagan priest Coifi, who avowed to him that there was no value whatsoever in the religion of his fathers and advised him to accept the new one "if you shall find after good examination that these things which be now newly preached to us be better and of more power." To this counsel the king's nobles agreed, one of whom compared man's life to the flight of a sparrow through a warm hall in the dead of winter. While it is in the hall, the sparrow does not feel the storm, but "after a very short space of fair weather that lasteth but for a moment, it soon passeth again from winter to winter and escapeth your sight." So, said the nobleman, is the brevity and uncertainty of our life on earth: "Wherefore if this new learning hath brought us any better surety, methink it is worthy to be followed." Coifi, the priest, then recommended that they curse and burn the temples and altars of their old religion, and that they all embrace the Gospel. The king agreed, and he and all his people were baptized.

About the time of Edwin's conversion, other Northumbrian princes, living in exile among the Irish, were also converted to Christianity. Oswald, Edwin's brother, was one of these. When he came to the throne of Northumbria, wars had caused the Christian party to take flight. The new king, therefore, turned to Ireland for reinforcements, and Aidan, a monk from Iona, was sent. Bede describes Aidan as "a man of marvellous meekness, godliness, and sobriety, and one that had the zeal of God, though not fully according to knowledge." He notes that Aidan had to preach to the Saxons by an interpreter, and that, on occasion "there was a gracious and pleasant sight seen, when the bishop . . . was preaching the Gospel, and the king himself was interpreter of the heavenly word to his aldermen and thanes." The Island of Lindisfarne was given to Aidan for the founding of a monastery, and during his time Christian missions flourished under the eager Irish brethren.

Irish Christianity had enjoyed two centuries of independence from Roman interference, during which several differences of practice had grown up. The main difference was that the Irish Church was administered by the abbots of large monasteries, whereas in Italy and France the Church was under bishops who acknowledged the authority of the pope. But overlying this important issue were minor differences, which loomed much larger in the eyes of the people. One of these had to do with the style of tonsure worn by the clergy and another with the date of the celebration of Easter. Inevitably, as more of the English embraced Christianity, and as the warring nations learned to live together in peace, the rival ecclesiastical parties came into conflict. The issue was formally joined by King Oswy of Northumberland, at Whitby, in 664. Bringing together representatives of the two groups, he proposed "that it behoved those who were united in serving God to keep one rule of living and . . . to search out what was the truer tradition." Colman spoke for the Irish, and Wilfrid for the Romans. Bede records their arguments at length. What decided King Oswy in favor of the Romans was Wilfrid's argument that Peter had received from Christ the keys of the Kingdom of Heaven. "I will not gainsay such a porter as this," Oswy said, "lest it may be, when I come to the doors of the kingdom of heaven, I find none to open unto me, having his displeasure who is proved to hold the keys thereof." His nobles consented, and "abandoning their former imperfect usage," says Bede, "hastened to change over to those things which they had learned to be better."

The Synod of Whitby opened the way for the Roman archbishop, Theodore (c.602-690), to carry through the work of standardizing the English Church. Arriving in England in 669, he toured the country, reorganized the monasteries after the Roman rule, and brought local bishops under his authority. A forceful leader, he not merely brought peace to the Church but also helped to unify the nations, so that, in Bede's words, "there was never since the English first came to Britain, any time more happy than at that present; when they both had most valiant and Christian kings and . . . the desires of all were wholly bent to the late joyful tidings of the kingdom of heaven." Theodore was himself a scholar, "fully learned in profane as well as in holy literature," and he did much to encourage learning by bringing books and scholars to England. "The proof whereof is," says Bede, "that even to this day some of their scholars yet living have as good knowledge of the Latin and Greek tongues as of their own in which they were born."

Such is the main story which Bede sets himself to tell. But Bede follows his sources into many curious byways, and he permits himself to interject matters of interest along the way. He quotes at length letters from popes and abbots designed to clarify doctrinal matters. Most of his written sources, where they deal with heroes of the faith, abound in tales of miracles; Bede records all of these. A book came into his hands which related the visit of Arculf, a bishop of France to the Holy Land. Bede condenses its description of Bethlehem, Jerusalem, and Hebron, and gives them a place in his book.

One passage, of great interest to students of English literature, is the account which Bede gives of the minstrel, Caedmon, who never having learned to play the harp or sing, dreamed that he was commanded to sing the praises of creation, and he discovered to his amazement that in his dream he had the gift of making verse. On rising, he remembered what he had sung in his sleep, and, mentioning it to the authorities, he was encouraged to take the monastic habit and to receive instruction in Christian teaching. Thereafter, says Bede, "whatsoever of the divine writings he learned by them that expounded them, he set it forth after a little time with poetical language, put together with very great sweetness and pricking of the heart, in his own, that is to say, the English tongue." Bede, who writes in Latin, makes no attempt to reproduce the poems, for, he says, "songs, be they never so well made, cannot be turned of one tongue into another, word for word, without loss to their grace and worthiness." But he testifies to the power which they had to turn men's lives toward God, and he adds that, though many of the English tried their hand at writing religious poems, none could match the cunning of Caedmon.

Bede was one of the favored generation which profited from the civil order and cultural enrichment which Archbishop Theodore introduced. The fact that he could live a full lifetime in peaceful pursuits only a century after the landing of Augustine on Kentish shores is by itself remarkable, not to mention the gentle humanity of his person, his love of poetry, and his knowledge of ancient authors. Bede was a celebrated teacher, whose students numbered in the hundreds. One of his disciples, Egbert (d.766), was later Archbishop of York, and founder of the celebrated cathedral school of York, where Alcuin (c.735-804), founder of the school of Paris, received his training.

The *Ecclesiastical History* by which Bede is chiefly known, besides being invaluable to historians, will probably continue to stand in the first rank of literary works because of its simple, unaffected style, and its sure handling of the picturesque and the dramatic. It was translated into Old English by Alfred the Great (849-899). The first modern translation was made by the learned Oxford scholar, Thomas Stapleton (1535-1598).

THE FOUNTAIN OF WISDOM

Author: Saint John of Damascus (c.675-c.749)
Type of work: Christian philosophy and theology
First transcribed: After 742

Principal Ideas Advanced

All knowledge of being can be treated under the five universals and ten categories of Aristotle, properly defined.

All heresies spring from four archetypes: Barbarism, Scythism, Hellenism, and Judaism.

An accurate exposition of the orthodox faith is grounded in the teaching of the Fathers, the Scriptures, and natural reason or philosophy.

Some books open up new periods in the history of thought, some bring periods to a close, and a few both end one period and begin another. The

Fountain of Wisdom falls in the last category. It marks the end of the patristic era and the beginning of Greek scholasticism. It is the summary of more than six hundred years of Christian theological development and the model for theological handbooks throughout the Middle Ages and, in some respects, down to the very present.

John of Damascus (Yanah ibn Mansur ibn Sargun) was the son of a Christian official in the court of the Caliph at Damascus. He himself became Logothete, or chief representative of the Christian community before the Caliph, until in about 715 he entered the monastery of St. Sabas near Jerusalem. It was under the protection of Islam that he wrote his attacks against the iconoclastic Byzantine Emperor Leo III, the Isaurian (717-740), and it was under his Arabian name of Mansur that he was anathematized by the iconoclastic council of 753. The iconclastic controversy, which lasted from 725 to 842, is reflected at many points in the *Fountain of Wisdom.*

The *Fountain of Wisdom* (*Fons scientiae*) is composed of three parts: the "Philosophical Chapters or Dialectica," "On Heresies in Epitome," and "An Exact Exposition of the Orthodox Faith." In no case does the Damascene claim originality. Indeed he disclaims it, and his use of sources is quite evident and sometimes clearly specified. The work was dedicated to a friend from the monastery, Cosmas (born c.700), who in 743 became Bishop of Maïuma (modern Gaza). Apparently Cosmas had asked John to write such a *summa theologica.* John's previous writings included a work on moral theology based on the fathers, the *Sacra parallela,* disputations with such heretical sects as the Manicheans, Nestorians, and Monophysites, and the *Life of Barlaam and Joasaph,* a Christianized version of the story of Buddha.

The first part or "Philosophical Chapters" of the *Fountain of Wisdom* was intended to present the best of Greek philosophy, but it consists mainly of the definition of terms. As such it is still valuable to the student of Greek theology. Foremost among the terms discussed are the Aristotelian universals: genus, species, difference, accident, and property. In providing definitions for these terms John was forced to treat also the questions of being, priority, division and subdivision, and definition and description. Then, after defining his terms and his method, he compared, contrasted, and related the terms to one another.

Having defined the universals, the Damascene then took up the categories: substance, quantity, relation, quality, time, place, position, state, action, and passion. In connection with these terms there is a useful discussion of such specifically theological concepts as hypostasis, enhypostaton, and anhypostaton, as well as, of course, hypostatic union. The last named term is of particular significance in understanding the dogma of the two natures and one person of Jesus Christ. Altogether the philosophical chapters are sixty-eight in number and are followed by an appendix on expressions used in the description of the natural world, such as "seasons" and "heavenly phenomena."

The sources for the philosophical chapters besides Aristotle's *Categories* include the *Introduction to the Categories of Aristotle* or *Isagoge* of Porphyry (c.232-303), a Neoplatonist philosopher, and the *Commentary on the Isagoge of Porphyry* by Ammonius Hermeae (fl. fifth century), a Greek philosopher and commentator on Aristotle. To these sources John of Damascus added a good deal of his own analysis of terms, especially of the theological ones.

The second part of the *Fountain of Wisdom* lists and describes more than one hundred different heresies. The Damascene believed that they all came originally from four parents or archetypes: Barbarism, Scythism, Hellenism, and Judaism. The first eighty chapters are taken verbatim from the *Panarion* of Epiphanius (c.315-403), a zealous defender of orthodoxy in his position as Bishop of Salamis. Unfortunately, only his summaries or table of contents are reproduced by John and not the excerpts from heretical writings, which are still of great value. To the last of these eighty heresies, the Massalians, there is added material from another, now unknown, writer, so that this chapter is now the principal source of information on that sect.

The next twenty chapters, 81-100, are from another unknown author, who perhaps had already borrowed the material from Epiphanius and thus provided almost the entire catalog of heresies in finished form to John of Damascus. In any case these twenty chapters deal with heresies from the time of Nestorius (died c.451) to that of the Greek emperor Heraclius (575-641). The discussion of the Monophysite heresy in Chapter 83 is one of the longest in the catalog and includes quotations from John Philoponus, the Grammarian (fl. sixth century), a Christian philosopher at Alexandria.

The final three chapters, 101-103, represent the direct contribution of John of Damascus. Here he attacks the Ishmaelites or Saracens on such grounds as the deficiency of the Koran and the worship of the famous Black Stone at Mecca. There is a short chapter against the Christianocategori (accusers of Christians) or Iconoclasts, and a chapter on the Aposchistae (makers of schism), apparently perfectionists who had separated themselves from the Catholic Church. This part of the work concludes with a doxology and a confession of faith.

Looked at as a whole, the heresies are grouped in roughly chronological order, although some, those of the Donatists, are out of place. There are groupings of Samaritan heresies, Jewish heresies, heresies of the Gnostic sects, of the Jewish-Christian sects, of Marcion and his followers, Christological heresies, and heresies against the discipline of the Church. Probably nowhere else could one find such a variety of heresies cataloged in such brief compass.

The third part of the *Fountain of Wisdom*, sub-titled "On the Orthodox Faith," is usually divided into four books. The first of these books discusses the Godhead in unity and trinity. The topic is, of course, one that occupied the attention of the Christian Church for well over three hundred years, until the definition of the Council of Nicaea (325) was reaffirmed by the Council of Constantinople in 381. John of Damascus was very respectful of the limitations of human reason in describing or defining the Godhead. He states that he will in no case exceed the teachings of the New Testament and the Church Fathers. His favorite Father, whom he cites most often in all four books, is Gregory of

Nazianzus (329-389), whose five sermons delivered in Constantinople in 380 and known as the *Theological Orations* have been a primary theological source for his successors. It is noteworthy that John nowhere cites any ante-Nicene Fathers. Apparently their orthodoxy could never be certain enough to satisfy him because they had no standard such as the Nicene Creed to which to conform. There is little place for proofs of the existence of God in the Damascene's theology. Only one proof is given. More important to John are the relationships between the three Persons, their unity and their distinctions. He is careful to note that some things are described or affirmed as if God had a body or a human nature. These expressions are all symbolical or figurative as are many of the names of God. In this connection the treatise on *Divine Names* by Dionysius the Pseudo-Areopagite (c.500), an anonymous Greek theologian, is a useful source.

The second book concentrates on the First Person of the Trinity, God the Creator. Beginning with the invisible creation, John maintains among other things that evil spirits foretell the future by guessing at events, while angels actually foresee them by the grace of God. Within the visible creation man is of the greatest interest. Some fifteen chapters are devoted to a description of man, his emotions and feelings, his senses and faculties, and his activity, be it voluntary or involuntary. This book concludes with the already venerable problems of providence and predestination. For his teaching on creation the Damascene turns especially to the Syrian theologian, Nemesius of Emesa (fl. c.390), who wrote *On the Nature of Man,* and to the Cappadocian theologian and bishop, Basil of Caesarea (c.330-379), who delivered a series of homilies on the six days of creation.

With the third book, "On the Orthodox Faith," John of Damascus moves into the realm of Christology where, as in the doctrine of the Trinity, only long years of debate had made dogma a reality. The problems here center around the Incarnation and the relationship of the two natures, divine and human, in the one person of Jesus Christ. Much of the presentation retains the polemic tones of the Nestorian, Monophysite, and Monothelite controversies of previous centuries. It is in discussing the two natures and one person that the categories of Greek philosophy as outlined in the first part of the *Fountain of Wisdom* are most prominent. Quantity, number, action, and difference all enter into the understanding of the Second Person of the Trinity in his Incarnation. John does not hesitate to divide Jesus' earthly activities between the two natures, but the real key to His person is the hypostatic union of God and man. This union can hardly be explained. The attempt to find suitable analogies, such as the red-hot knife which both burns and cuts always, falls short. Leontius of Byzantium (died 543), an anti-Monophysite theologian, and Maximus Confessor (c.580-662), who was one of the first to recognize the dangers of Monothelitism, are important as sources for this third book together with, as always, Gregory of Nazianzus.

The fourth and final book of this last part of the *Fountain of Wisdom* begins with Christology but moves shortly into a discussion of various aspects of faith and practice. There is a significant chapter on Mariology as well as on the veneration of saints and relics. John defends the cult of holy images almost as strongly as he does the Bible. He brings his book to a ringing conclusion with the doctrine of the bodily resurrection.

It was in his treatment of the somewhat miscellaneous and not then dogmatically defined theological topics of his book that the Damascene made greatest use of the Scriptures. The Fathers themselves had not said enough on these matters to be really helpful.

The *Fountain of Wisdom* is an impressive work for its very comprehensiveness. There had been others, such as Origen (c.185-c.254) with his *De Principiis* or Gregory of Nyssa (c.330-c.395) with his *Catechetical Discourses* or Theodoret (c.393-c.458) with his *Compendium of Divine Teachings,* who sought to propound the Christian faith in systematic form, and they may have served John of Damascus as models. They were, however, clearly overshadowed by John in the ability to synthesize and comprehend the many-sided teachings and traditions of the Church. All Greek theology up to his day, but no Western or Latin theology, was drawn upon for the *Fountain of Wisdom.* It is little wonder that this writing enjoyed considerable influence throughout the Middle Ages and was even translated into Latin in the twelfth century for the use of Western scholastic theologians.

SELECTED WRITINGS ON THE SPIRITUAL LIFE

Author: Saint Peter Damian (1007-1072)
Type of work: Ascetical theology
First transcribed: Eleventh century

Principal Ideas Advanced

Human learning, especially grammar and dialectic, is useless and even harmful, the only profitable studies for the spiritual man being the Holy Scriptures, commentaries, homilies, and martyrology, while logic is so far from being applicable to divine things that God is able to bring it about that an event which has occurred in the past has not occurred.

The monastic and preferably the eremitic way of life aiming at the peace of contemplation has three stages of ascetic ascent: the mortification of the flesh, in which fasting is fundamental while other modes of chastisement including flagellation may be employed; the discipline of the spirit, consisting in solitude, silence, and stability; and prayer, public and private, accompanied by tears.

Since reason has no legitimate function except as a handmaid to faith and since the life of nature is rejected unless swallowed up in grace, the state has no reality apart from the Church, temporal power being delegated to the emperor by the pope.

St. Peter Damian, born in Ravenna in or about January 1007, studied and taught in schools of northern Italy until in 1035 he entered the monastery of Fonte Avellana. Damian, himself a model of monastic rigor, was prominent as a leader of the reform movement in the eleventh century. His "Liber Gomorrhianus," dedicated to Pope Leo IX, frankly depicted the moral degradation of many of the clergy, while the "Liber Gratissimus" recommended a moderate solution to the problem of the validity of simoniacal orders. During the pontificate of Stephen IX (1057-58), Damian was elevated to the cardinal-bishopric of Ostia, probably as a result of the influence of Hildebrand.

Damian is known as an anti-dialectician, an opponent of worldly learning, particularly of grammar and philosophy. He writes in *The Book of "The Lord Be with You"*: "I spurn Plato, the searcher into the hidden things of nature, who set a measure to the movements of the planets, and calculated the courses of the stars; Pythagoras, who divided the round world into its regions with his mathematician's rod, means nothing to me; I renounce the much-thumbed books of Nichomachus, and Euclid too, round-shouldered from poring over his complex geometrical problems; the rhetoricians with their syllogisms and the cavillings of the sophists are useless in this matter. Let the gymnasts shiver in their nakedness for love of wisdom, and the peripatetics seek truth at the bottom of a well." Damian proceeds to scorn the inventions of crazy poets, the melodramatic adventures of pompous tragedians, the poisoned stream of scurrilities flowing from the noisy lips of comedians, the satirists' bitter banquets of insidious slander and the skilled speech and skilled argument of the orators. He desires instruction from the simplicity of Christ and asks to be taught "that of which the unskilled throng of dialecticians knows nothing."

In "On the Perfection of Monks," Damian angrily assails the monks "who follow the rabble of grammarians, who, forsaking spiritual studies, desire to learn all the follies of worldly skill, who, despising the rule of Benedict, love to apply themselves to the rules of Donatus." He compares such men with one who deserts the chaste spouse lying upon the bridal couch of faith to consort with the harlots of the stage. In his "De ordine eremitarum," Damian enumerates as volumes suitable for a monastic library the Old and New Testaments, a martyrology, sermons of the Fathers, allegorical commentaries on Holy Scripture by Gregory, Ambrose, Augustine, Jerome, Prosper, Bede, Remigius, Amalarius, Haimon, and Paschasius Radbertus. In the "De sancta simplicitate," human knowledge is rejected as harmful and useless. The serpent in Eden was the first grammarian, teaching Eve to decline "God" in the plural. The almighty God does not require grammar to draw men to Himself, since in the beginning of redemption, He did not send philosophers and orators, but simple men and fishermen. The jawbone of an ass by which Samson killed a thousand Philistines is interpreted allegorically to mean the tongues of humble and simple men, by whose preaching the humility of Christ is inculcated.

The opusculum "On Divine Omnipotence" uses philosophy against itself. In it Damian joins issue with St. Jerome, who had denied that God could make the past not to have occurred. God is shown to be able to do many things which He does not will, and His will is proved to be the cause of the existence of all things. Nothing can prevent Him from raising up a fallen virgin, either with respect to the plenitude of merits or to the integrity of the flesh. If it is objected that God is able to destroy Rome, but not to bring it to pass that Rome has never existed, the reply is made that the same reasoning would have to apply to the present and to the future as well as to the past. So far as the order of discourse is concerned, contingency is excluded from the present and the future as well as from the past. But such dialectical considerations have no application to God. Damian writes: "That which is from the argument of the dialecticians cannot easily be adapted to the mysteries of divine power; that which has been invented for the benefit of the syllogisms . . . let it not be obstinately introduced into divine law and let it not oppose the necessities of its inference to the divine power." Dialectic must remember that her position is that of a handmaid subservient to her mistress.

The spiritual writings of Damian inculcate the ideal of the contemplative life, and a severe course of ascetic exercises is recommended as the means to such a life. In the writing "On the Perfection of Monks" he declares that rest is the whole end of the monastic way of life and renunciation of the world. The images of divine illumination and spiritual marriage are employed to express the excellence of the contemplative state. Worldly knowledge is a hindrance rather than a help to this goal: "Who lights a lantern that he may see the sun, or candles that he may behold the glory of the stars?"

The ascetic life as an ascent towards contemplation has three stages: the mortification of the flesh, the discipline of the spirit, and prayer. The enjoyment of the end is not an automatic effect of the ascent of this ladder, but a gift freely given by God. The Augustinian note of dependence on the grace of God is stressed in Damian's "Sermon on the Holy Spirit and His Grace." Without the grace of the Holy Spirit no man, however hard he struggles and strives, can rise to good works or bring forth fruit pleasing to God. Our souls must then seek this Spirit without ceasing, if they are to receive the gift of grace.

Perfect mortification is achieved when the greedy gullet is kept in check, the wanton tongue compelled to be silent, the ears shut to scandalmongering, the eyes forbidden to look upon unlawful things, the hand bound for fear it should strike cruelly, the foot lest it should wander idly, and the heart withstood for fear it should envy the prosperity and happiness of another. Mortification is pursued not only as a means to contemplation but in imitation of Christ and as penitential suffering. In defense of flagellation, Damian writes: "I scourge both flesh and spirit because I know that I have offended in both flesh and spirit."

Severe rules for fasting are laid down. Bread, water, and salt are all that are needed in a perfect fast. The hermits at Fonte Avellana had a staple diet of bread and vegetables, while cheese, fish, and eggs were permitted. Meat was forbidden and wine used only in exceptional cases. Damian justifies these rigors of fasting as destroying the desires of our gullets and extinguishing the flames of lust. Yet he denies that he is condemning anything which God has made.

While fasting is fundamental in physical mortification, other forms of self-inflicted suffering are also to be employed. In the opusculum "De laude flagellorum," Damian defends the practice of flagellation, by appealing to the example of Christ and the Apostles. Since it is not likely that we will receive such treatment at the hands of others, if we are true disciples of Christ, we will inflict these chastisements on ourselves. Damian's influence led to the spread of the practice of flagellation. At length he found it necessary to dissuade some whose zeal led them to recite the whole Psalter once or more, scourging themselves throughout: "Wherefore . . . we have decreed that no one in the hermitage shall be compelled to use the discipline; and if holy zeal urges anyone to this he is permitted to scourge himself for the course of forty psalms, and no more, in any one day."

The second stage of the ascetic's progress, the discipline of the spirit, consists of solitude, silence, and stability. Solitude is best cultivated in the life of the hermit. Chapter Nineteen of *The Book of "The Lord be With You"* concerns the merits of the solitary life and contains an eloquent panegyric on the hermitage. While the monastic life is admitted to be good, the eremitic (hermitic) is to be preferred. The corrupt state of many of the monasteries of the day no doubt encouraged this preference for the solitary life. Damian regarded the monastery, even at its best, as a place of preparation for the desert.

Solitude is insufficient if unaccompanied by silence and stability. Silence is necessary because undisciplined tongues empty the soul of the strength of heavenly grace and weaken its healthful vigor. Unnecessary conversation leads to frivolous gossip and slander. Stability is no less important. Instability is a disease that deprives its victims of the benefits of the active and of the contemplative life. Restless pacing up and down within one's cell is itself a symptom of inner instability. Damian's journeys on papal business prevented him from fulfilling his own precepts in this matter.

The third stage of contemplation is prayer, both public and private. Prayer should be joined with tears of compunction. Tears that come from God bring assurance of the certain forgiveness of sins. Tears of spiritual joy bring with them the savor of divine contemplation. This water has its source in fire, for he who wishes to abound in these flowing streams must first kindle in his heart the fire of divine love.

Damian espoused a view of the relation between Church and state of one piece with his view of faith, reason, nature, and grace. For him the emperor derives his authority from the pope. The civil order has no reality apart from the spiritual, even as reason has no value apart from faith and nature no claims apart from grace.

MONOLOGION

Author: Saint Anselm of Canterbury (c.1033-1109)
Type of work: Scholastic theology
First transcribed: 1076

Principal Ideas Advanced

The existence of God may be demonstrated by rational proofs.

In its attempt to understand the nature of God, reason encounters certain rational antinomies, the chief of these being that God is at one and the same time a unity and also a trinity of Father, Son, and Holy Spirit.

Although God is ineffable, and all affirmations about Him are to be taken figuratively, man must believe in the triune God, for the human mind is made in order that it may believe in and love God.

The proofs show that God is that absolute good in whose goodness all relative goods participate; He is that self-subsisting being to whom all contingent beings owe their existence; and He is that single being in relation to whom all other beings are inferior.

Anselm of Canterbury was born at Aosta in northern Italy, most likely in the year 1033. In his middle twenties he left for France, where he traveled and where eventually he became a Benedictine monk after having studied under the famous Lanfranc at the monastery of Bec. For approximately thirty years he was an official of Bec, first as prior and later as abbot. He spent the last years of his life as primate of the English Church, having succeeded his old master Lanfranc in 1093 as Archbishop of Canterbury. These last years were stormy and unhappy ones for Anselm because of the widespread rejection in England of the claims of papal supremacy. He died in Canterbury in 1109.

Anselm ushered in the movement known as Scholasticism, which was to reach its zenith in the thirteenth century. Scholasticism took its name from its association with the monastic and cathedral schools of the eleventh and twelfth centuries—such schools as Bec, Laon, Chartres, and Notre Dame de Paris. Later, in the thirteenth and fourteenth centuries, some of these schools developed into such universities as Paris and Oxford, which became models for numerous later universities.

Anselm's work marks the transition from a tradition of heavy dependence upon the authority of the Scriptures and of the Fathers of the Church, in the direction of a much larger role for reason. He assumed that the traditional doctrines of the Church were the content of faith, and the act of faith itself was understood by him to be essentially a surrender of the will to the teachings of the Church. Still, reason is necessary for the explication and clarification of beliefs. Augustine's maxim *Credo ut intelligam* (I believe so that I may understand) was adopted by Anselm. The emphasis, however, was placed differently by the two men. Augustine was impressed by the necessity of believing before attempting to understand, whereas Anselm was impressed with the desirability of going beyond belief to understanding.

Anselm's decision to apply the methods of logic or "dialectics" to theological questions was not in itself novel, but his results reversed the predominantly heretical theological direction of other employers of the method. Berengar of Tours (c.999-1088), for instance, denied that the bread and wine were materially changed into the body and blood of Christ. The consecration of the elements adds to the elements—which remain bread and wine—the presence of the heavenly Christ, whose reality is wholly spiritual. Roscelin of Compiegne (Roscellinus, d. c.1125), afforded another example of the unorthodox possibilities of the dialectical theological method. He attacked the doctrine of the Trinity by declaring that either the Father, Son, and Holy Spirit are identical, or they are three separate Gods. As will be evident below, in the *Monologion* Anselm is attempting to show, in opposition to Roscelin, that reason supports the doctrine of the Trinity.

The *Monologion,* which was probably Anselm's first work, was written at Bec in 1076 in response to the urging of students who desired a wider audience for the thought of their mentor. In the *Monologion* (or Soliloquy), Anselm is concerned to demonstrate by rational proofs the existence of God, and other doctrines of Christianity which relate closely to the theistic affirmation. He employs three arguments for the existence of God.

The first argument begins with the premise that all men seek to enjoy those things which they consider good. When things are compared to one another, they are seen to be more or less good. There must, therefore, be an absolute good by which they are judged and in whose goodness they all participate. Since all good things possess their goodness through it and not through themselves, it alone is good through itself and is therefore the greatest good. That which is supremely good is also supremely great. There is, therefore, something which is the greatest and best of all things that are, and it is this "something" to which we give the name God.

The second proof runs as follows: Everything which exists has being either through something or through nothing. But from nothing, nothing comes. Everything, therefore, is through something. This something is either one or many. If the something is many, then all of the many are through a single thing, or each is through itself, or they are through each other. If all of the many are through a single thing, then all things owe their existence ultimately to that one thing. If each owes its existence to itself, then there must be a single power of existence which accounts for each thing, so that ultimately there is a single source of being. It would be absurd to hold that things owe their existence to one another, for that would mean that the same things are both the causes and the effects of one another. There is, therefore, a single thing to which all other things owe their being. This thing alone is not dependent upon something else for its being. All things that are good or great exist through this self-subsisting being. It is, therefore, supremely good and supremely great. Such a being is God.

The third argument is based upon the inequalities in the levels of being of the various kinds of reality. The horse has a higher nature than wood, and a man belongs to a higher level of being than a horse. It would be unreasonable to conclude, however, that there exists nothing whatsoever which has no superior, for such a conclusion implies an infinity of kinds of being. There is, therefore, some reality which is superior to all other realities.

That reality which is inferior to nothing is either one, or it consists of several essences, all of equal degree. But if there are several such realities they owe their equality to a single cause. This cause would be either the very essence of their natures or something external to their natures. If the cause is the essence of their natures, then they are essentially one. But if the cause of their superiority is something other than themselves, then they are inferior to the order of being represented by their cause. In any event, then, there can be no more than one being which is superior in excellence to all other beings. There is, therefore, a single being which is the greatest and best of all existing things. This supremely great and good being is through itself, and all other things are through it. This supreme being is through itself, not in the sense that it *makes* itself, but in the same way in which a light shines of itself. All other things are made by it.

Anselm's argument continues by affirming Augustine's teaching that all things in the created order were made of nothing. They pre-existed, not in the form of some shapeless material, but only in the mind of their Creator, just as an object of art pre-exists as a conception in the mind of the artist. And just as the artist's mental conception of a work of art can be reduced to words, so the creative activity of God is through a kind of inner speech. This inner speech of the supreme essence, by virtue of the fact that it is strictly within the Godhead, may be identified with the supreme essence itself.

Because the supreme being is better than any other nature, any quality which is absolutely better than its contradictory can be attributed to it. Thus the supreme being (or God) must be living, wise, powerful, true, just, blessed, and eternal. These attributes may also apply to human beings. The difference is that all God's attributes are essential to Him; God would not be God without these attributes. Man, however, receives these attributes from beyond himself. God, on the other hand, has not received them from an external source. We may not correctly say God *has* life, or justice, or eternity. Rather, he *is* life, justice, and eternity. His attributes and his essence are identical. God *is* justice as such, goodness as such, truth as such, being as such. Moreover, because of the unity of the divine essence, all of God's attributes constitute in reality but a single attribute.

Having powerfully stated the foregoing conception of God, Anselm then turns to an enumeration of the difficulties inherent in the conception. If God is eternal, then He must be simple, not subject to change or decomposition. But does not eternity also mean that God is distributed over infinite points of time? And does not divine omnipresence mean that God is distributed over all points of space? Still, to interpret God's simplicity as meaning that He is nowhere in time and space would be equivalent to denying his existence. Anselm proposes that the two extremes of God's simplicity (or eternity) and His omnipresence be reconciled by asserting that God is both omnipresent and eternal but not limited by time or space.

Another serious difficulty which Anselm acknowledges arises because there is nothing accidental or nonessential in God; in God there is no change. Every substance, however, has accidents or nonessential qualities. Hence God is not a substance. He is beyond all substance. At this point in his argument Anselm displays hesitation and apprehension, and he declares that although the term substance does not apply to God in the usual way, still, no better term can be applied to God, who not only most certainly exists, but is also the highest form of being.

The theological antinomies thus far described are minor compared to the most formidable and completely irresolvable antinomy of all: the doctrine of the Trinity of Father, Son, and Holy Ghost in the unity of the divine essence. The Word (or God as Son) is God insofar as He is thought or conceived by Himself. The Holy Spirit is the bond of love between God and the Word. The Holy Spirit is God's love for the Word and the Word's love for God, or God's love for Himself.

Having thus explicated the meaning of the Trinity, Anselm confesses, in seeming discouragement, that "the mystery of so sublime a subject transcends all the vision of the human intellect." He affirms, nevertheless, that the truth of the Trinity, although inexplicable, is supported by the balance of logical evidence. Still, the Supreme Essence in itself is ineffable, and all affirmations about it are to be understood figuratively, not literally. The surest approach to knowledge of God is to reflect upon that which most nearly resembles God; namely, the human mind. The more intently the rational mind attempts to know itself, the more surely will it ascend to knowledge of God. Human rationality is given in order that man may distinguish between good and evil and thus love the good and hate the evil. The mind is made in order that it may love the supreme good above all lower goods. But in order for the mind to be able to love God above all other goods it must strive for understanding of God. God is triune in nature, so that belief in the Trinity is necessary in order for one to be able to love God. Belief in God and love of God constitute a living faith which will be manifested by good works. The triune God alone ought to be worshiped in love and loved in worship, for He alone is the source of happiness and the refuge from adversity.

PROSLOGION

Author: Saint Anselm of Canterbury (c.1033-1109)
Type of work: Scholastic theology
First transcribed: c.1077-1078

Principal Ideas Advanced

Everyone must grant that God is to be understood as a being than whom no greater can be conceived.

A being than whom no greater can be conceived must be conceived of as existing in reality and not merely in thought, for that which is conceived of as having real existence is greater than that which is thought of as only a concept.

Because God cannot be thought not to be, He necessarily exists.

God is at one and the same time compassionate and passionless, just and merciful, sensible and incorporeal, omnipotent and unable to do wrong, unified in being and existing as the Trinity of Father, Son, and Holy Spirit.

The *Monologion*, Anselm's first writing designed to demonstrate the existence of God, was long, complicated, and uneven in the quality of its logic. Anselm was painfully aware of these deficiencies, and he resolved to formulate a brief, lucid, and irrefutable single argument for the existence of God as the supreme good. The product of this effort was the *Proslogion, or, Faith Seeking Understanding*, written about 1077-1078.

The alternative title to the book—*Faith Seeking Understanding*—indicates Anselm's conviction that although reason or "dialectic" is not the source of faith, faith seeks to go beyond belief to understanding. It would seem to follow, then, that the purpose of his argument is to nurture faith from its simple form as belief to its more mature form as understanding. But within the text of the *Proslogion* itself there are suggestions that the argument may also lead from nonbelief to belief in God. As we shall see below, Anselm's lack of clarity in defining the intention of his argument has opened the way for wide disagreement among his interpreters.

The first chapter of the book consists of an eloquent and moving prayer in which Anselm acknowledges that man "has lost the blessedness for which he was made, and has found the misery for which he was not made." He implores God for a restoration of the blessedness which comes with understanding, for "I desire in some measure to understand thy truth, which my heart believes and loves. For I do not seek to understand in order to believe, but I believe in order to understand."

The second chapter—consisting of but a single paragraph—contains Anselm's famous "ontological argument," one of the most discussed and disputed passages in the history of speculative thought. Anselm affirms not only that God exists, but also that God "is a being than which none greater can be thought." Even the Psalmist's fool, who said in his heart, "There is no God" Psalms 14:1; 53:1), knows what is meant by the expression "a being than which none greater can be thought." The fool understands immediately, too, that a "being than which none greater can be thought" exists at least in his understanding. If anyone continues to reflect upon the meaning of the foregoing definition of God, he will also understand that the being than which a greater cannot be conceived cannot exist merely as an idea. For if such a being actually exists only as an idea, it cannot be thought of as existing in reality, and yet that would be greater. In short, the very idea of a perfect being necessitates the actuality of such a being. One cannot understand what the term "God" means and think of God as not being. Since God cannot be thought not to be, He necessarily is.

Anselm's argument is based upon the presuppositions of Platonic realism, which pictured the relationship between thought and reality as such that whatever is necessitated in thought is also necessitated in actuality.

Before turning back to the historically significant part of the *Proslogion* which centers around the ontological argument, it should be indicated here that the bulk of this brief book consists of a discussion and defense of the seemingly contradictory attributes applied to God. Thus Anselm attempts to demonstrate that there are no contradictions in affirming that God is compassionate and passionless, just and merciful, sensible and incorporeal, omnipotent and incapable of doing wrong, eternal and in all places and all times, unified in being and existing as a Trinity of Father, Son, and Holy Spirit.

Anselm's ontological proof has never ceased to fascinate and challenge speculative minds, and few of the chief theological and philosophical minds of the Western world since the twelfth century have failed to respond in one fashion or another to the argument.

One of Anselm's worthiest adversaries was a contemporary Benedictine monk, Gaunilo, who lived and studied in the abbey of Marmoutier near Tours. In a brief and tightly argued treatise wittily entitled "In Behalf of the Fool," Gaunilo—while not denying God's existence—contends that Anselm's argument does not refute atheism. If it were true, writes Gaunilo, that God cannot be thought without His actual existence being understood, then no argument for God's existence would be necessary, for God's existence would be a proven fact as soon as one's understanding possessed the concept of God. And yet, he points out, Anselm distinguishes between having a thing in mind as an idea and the later idea of the actual existence of the thing.

The most frequently cited and most graphic part of Gaunilo's refutation centers around the case of the imaginary isle of bliss. Suppose, he argues, that someone should describe an island whose qualities far surpass the qualities of any other island, and then should conclude that such an island necessarily exists because it is perfect. Once one conceives of a perfect island, the island must exist in reality as well as in thought, else it would not be a perfect island. Such a conclusion, reasons Gaunilo, is no less absurd than the argument that God's existence is necessitated by the idea of God as perfect being.

How telling Gaunilo's blows are against Anselm's argument has been a matter of dispute for many centuries. It is fair, however, to point out that Gaunilo missed the main point of Anselm's argument, as Anselm himself indicates in his reply to Gaunilo's treatise. Only of God, replies Anselm, can it be concluded that it is impossible to conceive of His nonexistence. God alone is Being itself. Of God alone can it be said that to exist is part of His essence. Thus the nature of God's existence is sharply distinct from that of islands or any other kind of finite reality.

After Gaunilo's attack Anselm's ontological argument attracted hardly any notice until the thirteenth century. It enjoyed varying degrees of acceptance from such theologians as William of Auxerre (d.1231), William of Auvergne (c.1180-1249), Alexander of Hales (c.1170-1245), and St. Bonaventura (1221-1274). This mood of sympathy was broken by St. Thomas Aquinas (1225-1274), in whose thought there was a new emphasis upon the experience of the senses as the starting point for proofs of the existence of God. St. Thomas was to become the key thinker of the thirteenth century, and because of the continuing dominance of his thought in the Roman Catholic Church, his adverse verdict on Anselm's argument was enough to insure that the argument would not become central in Roman Catholic natural theology.

Thomas examines Anselm's argument in a number of places, including both of his chief works, *Summa contra gentiles* (I, 10-11) and *Summa theologica* (I, 2, i). In another source, *Quaestiones disputatae de veritate* (10, 12), he contends that there are three opinions regarding the question whether the idea of God is a first principle whose invalidity cannot even be thought. The first opinion is that belief in God does not rest upon such an idea, nor can God's existence be proved. God's existence can only be believed. The second opinion is that the mind does not know of itself that God exists, but His existence can be demonstrated from evidence external to the mind and known by the mind. The third opinion is that of Anselm and those who agree with him; namely, the opinion that the mind is persuaded of God's existence by the very idea of God.

Thomas rejects the first opinion as false, but he accepts each of the latter two as true in a certain sense. It is true only for one who has had direct knowledge of God that the idea of God requires the existence of God. Such experience, however, is extraordinary. The ordinary ways of knowing God both give indirect knowledge. One way is faith, and the other is rational demonstration of God as a necessary inference from particular facts known directly. For one whose experience is limited to these ordinary channels of knowledge it is not true that the existence of God is known to the mind from the idea of God.

The ontological argument of the French philosopher René Descartes (1596-1650) is significant both because he regarded it as a clarification of Anselm's argument and because Immanuel Kant (1724-1804) was responding to the Cartesian form of the argument when he formulated what is widely regarded as a cogent refutation of all forms of the ontological proof.

The clearest statement of Descartes' argument is found in his *Discourse on Method*. Descartes argues that if one has in mind the idea of a triangle, the idea implies the conclusion that the three angles of the triangle must equal two right angles. Still, there is nothing in this argument which necessitates the actual existence of a triangle. The idea of a perfect being, on the other hand, includes existence as intrinsic to the very idea, just as the idea of triangle necessitates the conclusion that the angles of the triangle are equal to two right angles.

The form of the Cartesian argument is very similar to that of Anselm's proof. The difference is that Descartes saw the proof as resting on purely rational grounds. Anselm, on the other hand, indicates through the devotional tone of the *Proslogion* that the logical exercise contained in the ontological proof was an expression of his Christian faith which was already assured of the existence and goodness of God.

In the *Critique of Pure Reason,* Immanuel Kant argues that the ontological proof is invalid. Using the Cartesian form of the proof, he says that the argument defines God as *ens realissimum,* the most real being, or the subject of all predicates which necessarily belong to absolute being. Kant rejects the traditional contention that existence is so related to God that God would not be God without existence. The conception of God is fundamentally the same whether God is conceived of as existing or not, just as a hundred dollars in one's imagination have the same fundamental predicates as a hundred dollars in one's wallet. Because existence is not a predicate which is intrinsic to absolute being, the ontological argument has no validity.

Although directed specifically against Descartes' version of the ontological proof, Kant's refutation has had the historical effect of widely discrediting all forms of the ontological proof, particularly in philosophical circles, notwithstanding such powerful philosophical defenders of the proof as Georg W. F. Hegel (1770-1831).

In recent years there has been a revival of interest in Anselm's argument, particularly in theological circles. This new interest has been generally attended by the claim that the so-called "proof" of Anselm is actually a form of theological affirmation rather than a philosophical argument. Thus, it has been contended that the *Proslogion* is an essay in mystical theology in which Anselm reduces to rational terms the import of his mystical vision of God. The Protestant Swiss theologian Karl Barth argues in much the same fashion by contending that the ontological argument was not a proof but rather an expression of a faith already held. Paul Tillich, the German-American Protestant theologian, contends that the ontological argument is valid as an analysis of the unconditional element which is necessarily present in all thought as the basis of the distinction between truth and falsity. Anselm's thought takes a wrong turn, however, says Tillich, in identifying this unconditional element with a "highest being." God is the Ground of Being rather than the highest being.

We have seen that historically the *Proslogion* has been interpreted sometimes primarily in terms of its element of *ratio* (reason) and has been judged by such interpreters as mainly of philosophical importance. Other theologians have been more impressed by the element of *fides* (faith) and thus view the work as essentially theological in significance. That the *Proslogion* has had such a history of interpretation points to the fact that in it the conjunction of *ratio* and *fides* remains ambiguous.

CUR DEUS HOMO

Author: Saint Anselm of Canterbury (c.1033-1109)
Type of work: Scholastic theology, soteriology
First transcribed: 1098

Principal Ideas Advanced

The necessity of the Incarnation can be proved by the use of reasoning alone, apart from any reference to a knowledge of Christ.

Man is a rational being whose purpose is to find happiness in fulfilling the will of God; man's sin is that disobedience wherein he witholds from God the honor that is due Him.

It would not be fitting for God to remit sins unless punishment is inflicted or satisfaction rendered, since this would introduce irregularity into God's Kingdom; but punishment would incur the ruin of man, and satisfaction cannot be rendered by one who already is under the obligation of total obedience.

Man must pay a debt to God, which only God is able to pay; therefore out of love for His creature and in congruity with His own nature, God wills to become man in order that the necessary satisfaction can be rendered.

The God-Man, who is the incarnate Son of God, offers up His sinless life to pay the debt of sinful mankind and to restore the Father's honor; since the Father cannot allow this deed to go unrewarded and yet the Son needs nothing, the reward accrues to the advantage of those for whom the Son died.

Anselm, Archbishop of Canterbury from 1093 to 1109, has been called the father of scholastic theology, since his systematic explication of the Christian faith and use of the dialectical method set a pattern for the great systems of theology that developed among the Schoolmen of the twelfth and thirteenth centuries. His *Why God Became Man (Cur deus homo)* is considered the classic presentation of the "Latin" doctrine of the atonement, and many scholars believe it is his greatest work. In it he set out to "prove" the rational necessity of Christ's incarnation and death, but although he thought the sheer reasonableness of his argument should be compelling for unbelievers, he insisted that the proof was not meant to establish faith but was rather to serve as an example of "faith seeking understanding."

In opposition to the "Greek" tendency to think of Christ's death as God's ransoming of mankind from the Devil, Anselm elaborated an understanding of the atonement within the context of the relationship between God and man. He sought to express the unfathomable depth of God's love and, at the same time, to suggest the horrendous character of man's sin. In his doctrine he introduces two ideas which have been very influential in the subsequent history of soteriology. The first is his theory of satisfaction, the source of which has been attributed to feudal custom and Germanic law, but is more likely to be found in the medieval church's practice of penance. The second is his notion of the absolute necessity of the atonement, and here we need to distinguish between that necessity which is grounded in the nature and will of God himself, and the rational necessity of Christ's incarnation and death; that is, the mode of salvation that Anselm intends to prove by the logic of reason, without appeal to what Christians believe about Christ.

Why God Became Man is written in the form of a dialogue or debate between Anselm and a friendly interlocutor named Boso, whose duty it is to raise and pursue the questions of faithful inquirers as well as unbelievers. The chief question to be answered is stated in this fashion: "For what reason or necessity did God become man and, as we believe and confess, by his death restore life to the world, when he could have done this through another person (angelic or human), or even by a sheer act of will?" Anselm divided the work in which he attempted to answer this many-faceted question into two parts. In the first he intended to answer the objections of unbelievers who deem the Christian faith to be contrary to reason, and to prove by necessary reasons alone the impossibility of any man's being saved without Christ. In the second he wished to show that man was created for the purpose of enjoying a blessed immortality, that it is necessary for this purpose to be achieved, but that the achievement depends upon God's becoming man and undergoing, as God-Man, all the things that Christians believe concerning Christ.

The first charge that unbelievers bring against Christians is that they dishonor God by affirming that he descended into the womb of a woman, was born, grew, and lived a genuine human life, dying on a cross between thieves. Anselm answers by pointing to the following parallelisms: as death came by the disobedience of man, so life is restored by the obedience of man; as sin had its beginning with a woman, so the Savior from sin ought to be born of a woman; and as the Devil conquered man by tempting him to eat of a tree, it is fitting for the Devil to be vanquished by man's bearing of suffering on a tree. Boso admits the beauty of this arrangement, but asserts that for unbelievers such talk sounds like pure phantasy. What they require are sound reasons why God either ought or could condescend to such things as Christians proclaim. Anselm retorts that surely it is reason enough when one considers that the human race, the creation so precious to God, was totally ruined; that it was not fitting for God's purpose for man to be thwarted; and that this purpose could not be achieved unless the Creator himself delivered the human race. When Boso asserts that it would be easier for man's mind to accept the notion of deliverance if it were accomplished by a being other than God, such as another Adam created completely new and sinless, Anselm explains that if man were saved from eternal death by any being other than God, he would then be adjudged the servant of that being rather than of God, and thus would not be restored to his original dignity.

Boso now poses another question often asked by unbelievers: Why is it that Christians speak of their salvation as a "redemption," since it is hard to imagine any bondage so captivating that God could not free man without going to the extreme of shedding His own blood? If Christians answer that

God redeems them both from sins and His wrath and from Hell and the power of the Devil in order to purchase back for them the Kingdom of Heaven, unbelievers merely inquire why God does not do all this by a simple command, or in some other way. If God cannot accomplish redemption by a simple command, is He omnipotent? If He could and yet chose to do it the hard way, is He wise? Does God come down from Heaven to defeat the Devil because the Devil has a just claim on man?

Confronted with this line of questioning, Anselm first makes clear that the Devil has no rights whatsoever vis-à-vis man. If it can be said that man suffers justly in his bondage to evil, then his punishment is a just judgment permitted by God in His incomprehensible wisdom, not a right given to the Devil. As for why God chose to redeem man in the way that He did, the sheer fact that this represents God's will, which is never irrational, should be sufficient reason. However, for the sake of those who contend that God's stooping to lowliness and suffering is contrary to reason, Anselm explains that in the Incarnation the divine nature of the God-Man undergoes no debasement, since divine nature is intrinsically impassible, that is, incapable of suffering. The Lord Jesus Christ is true God and true man, one person in two natures, and the humiliation refers to God's bearing the weakness of the human nature, which in turn is thereby exalted. Boso concedes the impassibility of the divine nature, but asks whether it is just for the Man whom God calls his "beloved Son" to be condemned for the sake of the guilty. Anselm replies that the idea that God the Father compelled this Man to suffer death is mistaken. It is rather the case that Christ voluntarily chose death in order to effect the salvation of sinful mankind. It is true that Christ was "obedient unto death," but this obedience is not demanded of Him by the Father, since this Man did not sin. Instead, it is an obedience by which the Son maintained justice congruent with the will of God, who was unwilling to restore the human race unless man performed a great act, equal to the Son's death. The Son, then, exercises the free obedience of a rational being, and the Father takes pleasure, not in the Son's suffering, but in His choice, which both honors the Father and effects salvation.

In his further exploration of the ground on which God forgives sins, Anselm points out that there would be no sin if angels and men rendered to God His due, which is the subjection of their every inclination to God's will. Sin is the withholding of the honor that man owes God, and, considering the contempt involved, it will not suffice merely to restore what is taken away. The restitution must be greater, corresponding to the magnitude of the dishonor, and this payment is the satisfaction that every sinner ought to make to God. It would be unseemly for God to remit sins without requiring satisfaction or punishment, since this would introduce disorder into His Kingdom, and the way of satisfaction is preferable to the ruination that would result from punishment. The difficulty is that no man is able to render satisfaction commensurate with his sin, since even his total obedience is only what every rational creature owes God already. The debt that man owes calls for the payment of something that is more than the whole world and all that is not God. Only God could pay such a debt, and yet the payment is required of man. Of necessity, then, salvation calls for the work of a God-Man.

For our sake and by grace God becomes man, and if we speak of a "necessity" here, we must understand that it is a necessity freely accepted in accordance with God's own changeless goodness, which desires to complete the purpose for which man was created; namely, the attainment of blessedness in the enjoyment of God. The God-Man is both perfect God and perfect man; the integrity of each nature is preserved, and yet the two natures meet in one person. The person of the Son of God takes into unity with Himself the manhood of the race of Adam, a man born of a virgin. Because man is meant to be immortal and suffers death only because of sin, this God-Man, who does no sin, is not obliged to die. On behalf of the race of Adam, however, He chooses to lay down His life in order to satisfy the debt that sinful man owes to God. This death of the God-Man in His human nature, freely undergone and yet with the divine wisdom and power that comes from the Incarnation itself, is an offering so precious that it far outweighs the sins of the whole world. An infinite dishonor is overcome by an infinite satisfaction. This self-giving of the Son to the Father merits a reward, and yet the Son needs nothing. Therefore, it is only just that the Father grant the Son His desire; namely, that His reward be assigned to those for whom he became man and for whose salvation He died.

Thus Anselm claimed to have shown by necessary reasons the necessity of the God-Man for the accomplishment of salvation, and his argument is said to corroborate the truth of the Old and New Testaments. The atonement is understood in a way that emphasizes God's mercy and, at the same time, maintains His justice.

THE STEPS OF HUMILITY

Author: Saint Bernard, Abbot of Clairvaux (1090-1153)
Type of work: Contemplative theology
First transcribed: 1129-1135

Principal Ideas Advanced

To learn the way to humility, one can first learn the twelve steps by which one moves from humility to pride; the order may then be reversed.

One moves from humility to pride by the following twelve steps: curiosity, frivolity, foolish mirth, boastfulness, singularity, conceit, audacity, excusing one's own sins, hypocritical confession, public defiance, assuming the freedom to sin, and habitually sinning.

One attains humility by ridding oneself of these vices.

Humility makes self-knowledge possible through reason; compassion makes knowledge of others possible through love; and contemplation makes knowledge of God possible through purity.

Thus, humility is necessary if one is to ascend to love and truth.

Saint Bernard states in the preface to *The Steps of Humility* that he is bold enough to write the work only because he has been urged to by others. To write from his own motives and to satisfy his own desires would be a violation of the virtue he intends to describe. Yet the first eight chapters do not concern the twelve steps to humility themselves, but the various steps toward truth. Thus, as is quite common in contemplative or mystical works, the treatise centers around a theory of knowledge. The work is neither purely ethical nor contemplative. Before the ethical and religious virtues can be discussed, an elaborate theory of knowledge must be developed. Humility is related to truth, Bernard writes, since humility is the way that leads to truth.

Knowledge of truth is the fruit of humility, for the achievement of humility clears the mind and makes unclouded vision possible. Truth is concealed from the proud and revealed to the humble. But what is humility as a virtue, and how does it prepare the way for truth?

Humility, Bernard tells us, is that which makes a man, thorough self-examination, contemptible in his own sight. (Once again the Socratic goal of self-knowledge as the means necessary to clear vision reappears, here connected with the ethical condition of self-contempt.) In self-contempt one understands oneself truly, thereby achieving the Socratic goal, but not in the Socratic way. Without humility, Bernard's contention is, no man can understand himself thoroughly, and without self-knowledge a grasp of truth is not possible. Thus, humility has its rewarding consequence.

The ascent to truth, it turns out, requires taking the twelve steps which lead to humility. (The number twelve is often important in Christian writings, perhaps because the number of Christ's disciples was twelve.) Humility, it is true, is bitter and purging, but it yields love, which is sweet and consoling, and contemplation, that solid and strengthening condition which so many mystics sought. Truth is to be found in three forms; in ourselves, in our neighbors, and in its own divine nature. Thus, we are instructed to seek truth first in ourselves and in our neighbors before attempting to see it in itself. Having attained self-knowledge, we can then purify our vision by brotherly love and thus prepare ourselves to enjoy the contemplation of truth in its own nature. Only if we develop compassion within ourselves for our brother can we hope to understand him, just as pure truth is seen only if the seeker after truth himself has a pure heart.

How is the mercy necessary for an understanding of our neighbor to be developed? Observe, we are told, what we are and that we are wretched indeed; thus we learn to be merciful; we cannot know mercy in any other way. No one can be merciful who is not himself meek. What is pride but love of one's own excellence, and what is humility except contempt for one's own excellence? Love of self deceives any man who judges himself, and thus humility is necessary to clear self-vision. Whoever wants to know truth must first rid himself of pride; after attaining humility he can then come to the first step of truth, self-knowledge.

The first step of self-knowledge leads to the second step of truth, for one learns about himself only by becoming contemptible in his own sight, a situation which makes him value mercy more than justice. When this happens, then one is ready to seek mercy from others, to learn the needs of others from having discovered one's own. From one's own miseries one learns to commiserate with others who are miserable, and thus to know them —which is the second step necessary to truth. We ascend the first of the three steps toward truth (self-knowledge) by the toil of humility. We climb to the second step (knowledge of others) by the emotion of compassion, and then on to the third (knowledge of God) by the ecstasy of contemplation.

Reason is what we use to examine ourselves, to achieve the first step of truth. Love is the means we use to sympathize with and to know others, and this entices us to the second level of truth. Purity lifts us to invisible heights, snatches us to the third and final stage of truth. Humility and love form a finally perfected soul, one in which neither the will resists reason nor reason dissembles truth. Bernard will climb the ladder of humility until, clinging to truth, he comes to the fields of love. Thus, humility is not really the ultimate virtue and goal but only the necessary means to achieving a vision of truth and a capacity for love. Yet the way that goes up also goes down, and the steps may be traveled in either direction, toward pride and a loss of ability to love, or toward humility, purity of vision, and depth of love.

Thus, an amazing and simple discovery is made. The way to humility, love, and truth is neither far off nor mysterious. Men have naturally and easily taken the twelve stages of the descent to pride. But the way down is also the way up. All that one who desires humility needs to do is to reverse the process by which he descended to pride; the twelfth step of pride is the first step toward humility. By ridding oneself of the vices which led to pride one can finally attain the state of humility. It is important, then, to understand how one descends to pride.

The first step toward pride is *curiosity*. It is through becoming curious that the humble man first begins to go astray. Neglecting the examination of himself, the man who is descending to pride begins to amuse himself by contemplating others; no longer interested in the self-examination by which he might make his faults known to himself, he turns his attention to what others are doing.

Curiosity, innocent in itself, leads to a fall from truth, because what one first observes out of mere curiosity, one may then go on to covet unlawfully and finally to aspire to possess for oneself. Furthermore, a soul made frivolous by its wandering eyes is no longer sobered by self-examination and is subject to extremes, first exalted to the pinnacle of pride, then plunged into the depths of envy.

The second step toward pride is *frivolity,* since the proud always seek what is cheerful and avoid what is gloomy. A proud person likes to make jokes and is easily and quickly moved to laughter. The third step of pride is *foolish mirth;* a person given to mirth thinks only of what pleases him, without regard to whether it is proper. Having descended thus far he can no longer restrain his laughter or conceal his foolishness.

The fourth step of pride is *boastfulness,* the habit of speaking constantly, not to edify anyone but to display one's learning. This base aim is not easily detected, but often a boastful person can be recognized by his volubility, by his using more words than he needs to convey his meaning. This fourth step is closely associated with the next, *singularity,* or egotism, the habit of calling attention to and dwelling upon oneself. *Conceit* is the next phase, the vice of believing all one says to be true, approving fully of one's own way while ignoring one's own motives. When praise is heard the conceited man ascribes it not to the ignorance or benevolence of the speaker, but to his own merits.

Will not the man who thinks himself superior to others be more forward than others? Probably, and the seventh step is logically that of *audacity*. The audacious man cannot confess his wrongs; he has come to think himself incapable of wrong and cannot tolerate his being thought so. To accompany audacity there is an eighth step, *excusing one's own sins.* Yet even worse than this is the ninth step, *hypocritical confession,* and this is an even worse state in which to be, since a false and proud confession is much more perilous than a willful and stubborn defense. Such a man is not at all like what he confesses himself to be; his interior is full of deceit. He condones his guilt by presumably confessing it; he conceals his guilt by presumably revealing it—thus, he compounds his sins.

As might be expected, pride eventually shows itself as *public defiance.* At this tenth step the individual becomes shameless and brazen, and the more he becomes so, the more he is driven on down to further defiance. What Bernard discovers now is that the first and early steps toward pride involved contempt of brethren, which then broke over into contempt for masters. This brings the sinner to the ultimate depths, to contempt for God. What began in secret, covered and appearing only in camouflaged forms, is now openly directed toward God Himself. The last restraint is gone, the last pretense fallen.

When even God is no longer feared we have reached the eleventh step, *assuming the freedom to sin.* Initially, fear of God held pride back; now the proud man is allured into satisfying his own desires, for he is made confident by a freedom that respects not even God. As lust awakens, reason is lulled to sleep and habit becomes binding. At the twelfth and final step toward complete pride he now allows himself to do whatever he pleases. He denies the existence of God, to whom he might be responsible. Astutely, Bernard observes that only the highest and the lowest fly without hindrance or exertion, the highest because they are so disciplined as to be above all law, the lowest because they recognize no external restraint. Truth makes the one secure; blindness is the security of the other. The fear of God is lost and contempt of God is incurred. *Habitual sinning* is the twelfth and last step of pride.

Bernard modestly claims to know more about the way going down than the way going up, and he did not think it proper and consistent with his goal of humility to attempt to describe the way upward toward humility. Yet if the way of descent in pride is carefully examined, the way upward to humility may be found as the reversal of that descent. In the descent he has described, Bernard hoped that his reader would find the steps leading to humility, and that, by ascending them, he might read them better within himself than in Bernard's book.

SOLILOQUY ON THE EARNEST MONEY OF THE SOUL

Author: Hugh of St. Victor (c.1096-1141)
Type of work: Mystical dialogue
First transcribed: Unknown; probably about 1133

Principal Ideas Advanced

A dialogue between a man and his soul reveals the gift which, when recognized, will direct the soul toward a true love of self, identical with a love of God.

True self-esteem is ultimately better for the soul than all the ephemeral objects to which it is presently attracted, since the soul is the object of divine love, and, in fact, God has already presented the pledge of His love (the earnest money given at the time of betrothal).

The nature of true self-esteem consists in seeking for the Supreme Good, to be achieved through self-examination and contemplation.

Although *The Earnest Money of the Soul* is not Hugh of St. Victor's chief work, nor his longest, in brief compass it presents an excellent sample of his famous mysticism, a mysticism thoroughly and rationally founded. This famous soliloquy on love attempts to reveal where true love is to be found and how it ought to arouse in the heart of the reader a desire for heavenly joys, which come through zeal in spiritual meditation. The work reveals Hugh's debt to Augustine and the Neoplatonic tradition.

Hugh begins by asking his soul what it loves above all things, and he declares that he knows already that love is the very life of the soul, and that without love the soul could not exist. Is it the beautiful things of the universe, Hugh asks, which the soul loves most? Most men's appetites are inflamed by beautiful things, and their number is infinite. The soul replies that it cannot love what it has not seen, and that it has been unable to find among visible things anything which ought to be loved above all else. His soul is in suspended animation; it cannot exist without love and yet it is not able to find a true object for its devotion among the visible things of beauty in this universe.

Man, the second person in the dialogue or soliloquy, now suggests to his soul that the reason it is unhappy is that, while attracted by a desire for temporal goods, the soul cannot find here a love of those things which are eternal. At least, however, from the soul's dissatisfaction with the temporal world's beauties, it has learned to direct love to a better object. The most important step has actually been made: through recognizing that it is not temporal beauties which the soul seeks, the soul has been prepared to be separated from all finite things willingly, if only a greater beauty can be found.

Yet, how, the soul asks, is it possible to love that which is not visible? And if temporal goods do not satisfy, and the invisible cannot be loved, then surely the soul is in a miserable state! No one can be happy without love, for unhappiness means not having what one esteems. To this Man replies that if he esteems the visible world, why not esteem himself instead, since as man he surpasses all visible beauties. The eye sees all but does not see itself.

Love, it is agreed, must have an object; it never permits itself to be solitary. Love ceases to exist if it does not pour forth the ardor of its affections, and yet the object of love must be upon something equal in station to itself. If a man recognizes first his own dignity, then he will not attach himself to things inferior, for fear of injuring his love. Thus, the soul learns that it must not, in fact cannot, seek a love that is either solitary or degrading, for should it do this its love will cease. The goal is now known: seek a love that will be yours alone and also one that is especially worthy.

Hugh compares love to fire. What is put upon it should burn with a pure flame, not with smoke or stench. What is put upon love is crucial to the person, since through love one is transformed into a being like the one to whom the lover is joined by affection. Since this is true, one must choose the object of his love carefully, knowing that it not only can, but necessarily will, change him in its process.

Then Man suggests to his soul a startling thesis: that the soul has a betrothed but does not know it. He is the most comely of all, but his face has not been seen. Could his face be seen, the soul would lose all doubts about its own fairness. For one so beautiful must have been attracted by an equal beauty, so that one can learn of his own soul's loveliness through discovering the beauty of the unseen one betrothed to the soul without its knowledge. How can such a loved one not be seen? Because he is absent. Thus, one is able to prostitute oneself to some shameful pleasure and never blush, scorning his wholly devoted love because it is unseen.

Next the soul is asked to consider the pledge money, proof of his devotion, which the unseen lover has given. If this could be seen, then perhaps by his very gift he could be recognized, known in his gift while yet remaining unseen. Learning this, perhaps the soul could see with what affection it ought to love him and with what zeal and diligence it ought to preserve itself unsullied for him. Now the problem is faced: What is the pledge money this unseen lover has given, how is it to be discerned and what does it tell the soul about its lover and itself?

To answer its question the soul is instructed: Look at the universe. Everything in it, the soul is told, serves the soul's needs. The pleasures and the needs are met by what nature provides. Nature is directed with one accord to the soul's service. Who does this? The gift is plain to see, but the giver is hidden. Each soul accepts the benefits bestowed, but few know their benefactor. When all of nature is taken as a gift to the soul, it indicates the greatness of the love of the giver—and the not inconsiderable worth of the receiving soul. By this gift of all of nature's benefits, two things are revealed: one who loves generously and one (the soul) worthy of being loved so greatly.

This being understood, the soul is free to love the benefits of nature, yet each one is seen in a new life, as a gift of promise, as earnest money of the betrothed, as the offering of a true friend. Nevertheless, the hardest part is still ahead, for it is easy to begin to prefer the gifts to the giver. Instead, the soul must constantly accept every gift nature has, but only as a token of an unseen lover. What is the rule? Honor him who gives, respect yourself, and honor his gifts for his sake. When the soul does this, its vision is changed and it sees every benefit of nature, everything it has received, as the pledge of a lover's devotion. Best of all, in such a love there is nothing which can cause sadness.

With all this, the soul still continues to question. The soul loves the giver now, but similar gifts are given to others. The soul loves the giver, yet the soul is not the giver's sole delight. How can a soul glory in such a privilege, if it is possessed in common not only with the brutes but with all living things?

Man replies to his soul's doubts: not all gifts are shared equally by everyone. Some gifts from the soul's betrothed are given in common with others, some are given as one of a special group, and some are given to the soul as the soul's alone. And here the soul wonders what would make it happy. Would it be happy if the world had been given to it alone, or is the problem not in the exclusiveness of the gift after all? Whether directly or indirectly, everything has been given to the soul and is at its disposal.

What about evil? Is the soul's gift diminished because in temporal goods both the good and the wicked participate in the same way? The Neoplatonic answer is given. The evil live for the sake of the good, not for their own sake, and they are permitted to live among the good in order to stimulate the lives of the good by their association. The lives of the wicked are a constant warning; the lives of the virtuous are the consolation of the soul. It would be good to delight in this love alone, but it is much more blessed to delight in it in the company of the many good men in this life, since a thing is known better through sharing. Such love, which is at once the love of all and the complete love of each is neither diminished by participation, nor exhausted by use, nor aged with time.

Is it possible to explain how this love can be present both in spirit and in reality to each of those whom he loves? Creation, the gift of life, comes to all and yet is fully present in each, and we do not have a mere colorless existence, but one which is beautiful and fair. We men have more of the glory of existence than do other creatures, since we have been raised to the level of the Creator's own likeness. When one considers all he has been given, beginning with existence itself, one must return His love. Instead, the soul often deserts its Lover and squanders its affections on others.

The most important argument, however, remains: Not only has existence been given as a gift by the soul's Lover, but also He has permitted Himself to be humbled in order to redeem man. This is the central Christian teaching. In creation He is exalted; in redemption He is brought low. He came down among men, took on their mortality, suffered His passion, conquered death, and restored mankind. Defiled by its own wickedness, the soul has by His grace been made beautiful again. What happens at this realization is the familiar phenomenon of conversion. The soul is indeed changed, turned now from its vague and uncertain infatuations, won over by the demonstration of so great a love; now it is turned toward its one true Love.

Immediately upon such a realization the soul's only question is how it can prepare itself by the use of the font of baptism, the basin of regeneration in which the soul may wash away the stain of past sins. Confession ends the dialogue, and the soul thanks God, whom the soul now recognizes as its true Lover, in virtue of all the gifts He has given in token of His affection. The soul has been given earnest money, actual demonstrations of God's undivided love, and because of these gifts the soul is now enabled to recognize its Spouse. From now on the soul will seek to keep itself untouched, undefiled and pure, without a stain, for Him. If once the soul was a harlot, vainly chasing pleasures in the world, now it has become a virgin. His love is bestowed on many, but it embraces each one individually. God's countenance cannot be seen, in answer to the soul's early question, but His presence can never be escaped. Now the soul takes God as its exemplar, desiring only to become more and more like Him. And if God loved the soul enough to demonstrate His affection when the soul was repulsive, how much more will He desire it when it has begun to be beautiful? Love Him only, pursue Him only, take Him only, and possess Him only.

KNOW THYSELF

Author: Peter Abelard (1079-1142)
Type of work: Christian ethics
First transcribed: Twelfth century

Principal Ideas Advanced

The human race shares in the punishment, but not in the guilt, of Adam's sin.

Certain weaknesses of the human mind make man prone to sin, but guilt is incurred solely in consenting to the suggestions of these weaknesses.

By reason, man is able to decide what is good; desire in itself is not sinful, but sin lies in the consent to desire.

God alone can correctly estimate the extent of a person's guilt; confession is not for the purpose of receiving absolution, nor is penance a sacrament.

Peter Abelard's *Know Thyself (Scito te ipsum)* was probably written a few years before the condemnation of some of his ideas in 1140 (or 1141) at the Council of Sens. In spite of the condemnation, Abelard's ethical views —which find expression in *Know Thyself*—had an important influence on medieval moral thought.

The divergence of Abelard's point of view from the theories then current provoked the opposition of William of St.-Thierry (c.1085-c.1148) and St. Bernard (1090-1153). Traditional Augustinian orthodoxy held that by the fall of Adam, mankind had been brought into a condition of sin and misery in which all men share the very guilt of Adam's first sin. Of himself, apart from divine grace, man is incapable of performing any good act. What is right and what is wrong is fixed by the eternal law of God. To sin is to fall away from what is good. Sin must be atoned for by penances so that the sinner may be restored to the life of grace.

For Augustine, sin had two causes. We sin because we do not know what we ought to do, or because we do what we know we ought not to do. The first is the sin of ignorance; the second is the sin of weakness. Sins are divided into two groups, grave (mortal) and light (venial), and appropriate penance is to be applied in each case.

Abelard's own view departed from the accepted view in several respects, the chief of which lay in his denial that mankind has contracted the guilt of Adam's first sin. Original sin refers solely to the punishment to which we are liable through the guilt of our first parent. Anyone may escape damnation by exercising his own will in good works. The human mind does have certain defects or qualities which dispose a man to good or bad actions. Defects of mind do not make man guilty, however, but only incline him to consent to what he ought not to do, or to leave undone what he ought to do. Such consent is sin, for it displays contempt of the Creator. To sin is to despise God; it is not to do for God what we believe we should do for him, or not to renounce what we think we should renounce on God's behalf.

Frequently we err, Abelard concedes, but we do so not because of an evil will. To consent wrongfully is to commit sin, but sometimes sin is committed without an evil will. Our weaknesses make us prone to sin, but they do not make us guilty; we are guilty only when we consent to the suggestions of our weaknesses. It is our task to master and to direct those defects which dispose our minds to evil. The Christian life is thus characterized by struggle, writes Abelard. We strive in a contest to obtain a victor's crown. Our opponent is our own evil will, over which we must triumph by subjugating it to the divine will.

God weighs our intention rather than the deed, Abelard declares. The deed itself adds nothing to our merit, no matter whether it proceeds from a good or an evil will. A man is not better or worse because of what he does. To give in to our desires is vicious, but we are not meant to be wholly without desire. It is not sinful to desire a woman, but it is sinful to consent to the desire. The good man conquers his desire, but he does not extinguish it; if he is not enticed into consent, he does not commit any sin.

We consent to what is sinful when we do not draw ourselves back from an evil deed, and are ready, if the opportunity is offered, to perform it. Anyone who has the intention to commit an evil deed is guilty before God as much as if he were caught in the act. Hence, the act of sinning does not add anything to guilt or to damnation before God; sin is not increased by the doing of an action. The soul is marred by nothing except what is of its own nature; namely, consent.

When certain acts which ought not to be done are committed under force or by ignorance, they are committed without any sin, Abelard writes. To consent to a covetous desire is, however, to be guilty of sin, though there be no sequel to this intention. A transgressor is, therefore, not one who does what is prohibited but one who consents to what is prohibited.

Whether a person actually gives money to the poor, or whether a sense of charity makes him ready to give alms, makes no difference to the merit of the intention. The opportunity may not be present although the will to be charitable is there. Actions which are right and actions which are wrong are done by good and bad alike; good men are separated from bad solely by their intention.

Abelard insists that it is the spirit of the action, the intention, and not the deed, which determines the virtue of the doer. The same action may be done from different motives: for justice by one person, for an evil reason by another. A diversity of intentions may cause the same act to be performed from different motives and hence to acquire different moral values.

Just as to wish is not the same as to fulfill a wish, writes Abelard, so to sin is not the same as to carry out a sin. In the first case, it is by the consent of the soul that we sin. In the second case, we fulfill in deed that to which we have previously consented. Frequently, we are led through three stages in the commission of sin: suggestion, delight, and consent. We are first led by the suggestion of something within us, and if we know already that such a deed is pleasant, our imagination is held in delight and we are thereby tempted in thought. At this point our desire ought to be repressed, says Abelard, and we ought to obey the command of God. If, however, we continue and give our consent to such delight, we are guilty of sin. By penitence we can here gain pardon, but we may in fact pass on and actually commit the sin.

Abelard insists that the spirit in which a thing is done rather than the action itself is what God considers. God weighs the guilt in our intention accurately. God sees where no man sees, and when he punishes sin he regards the will, not the work. It is because we consider only the deed, which we can see, and not the will, which we cannot see, that we frequently punish the innocent and acquit the guilty. God tries the heart and discerns our intentions.

According to Abelard, every sin is of the mind alone, for it is only in the mind that there can be contempt of God. Nevertheless, it is still possible to speak of spiritual sins, which proceed from the imperfection of the mind, and of carnal sins, which proceed from the weaknesses of the flesh.

By reason, a person is able to decide what is good, and he may consent to or refrain from the tendencies of his mind. It is from good intention that good action arises. An intention is good when it is right in itself; an action is good, not because it contains some good within it, but because it issues from a good intention. The same act, performed at different times by the same person may, because of the diversity of intention, be good on one occasion and bad on another.

An intention is good not simply because it seems good, writes Abelard, but because it is such as it is estimated to be; that is, because what it aims at is really pleasing to God. It is, however, not possible to say that the persecutors of Christ sinned in the sense that they had contempt for God, or consented to that which they ought not to have consented to. Since there is no sin except that against conscience, those who did not believe in Christ and who rejected the Christian faith because they believed it to be contrary to God, did not sin. The ignorance of those who crucified Christ freed them from the possibility of real guilt. Those who persecuted Christ may be said to have sinned in action only *(per operationem)*, but if they had acted contrary to their conscience and had permitted Christ to go free, they would have sinned in will and hence more grievously.

We need have little fear of God's holding us guilty of a fault when we do not violate our conscience, Abelard assures his readers; if we do not rightly know our evil deeds to be sinful, or if we do not really wish to do them, then such acts are not to be called sins.

It is, of course, possible to speak loosely and to call every unsuitable act, as well as infidelity, by the term "sin," even though no contempt of God appears. Properly speaking, however, sin is that which can never come about without personal guilt, and the latter cannot occur without intention. Infidelity, disbelief in the gospel, the rejection of Christ, and refusal of the sacraments involve exclusion from eternal life for those who are rationally full grown, even though such acts arise less from malice than as a result of ignorance.

The sinner may be reconciled to God by passing through three stages of penance: compunction, confession, and satisfaction. Penitence is grief of mind for what is done amiss. In some cases, Abelard writes, penitence arises from love of God for His kindness and is therefore fruitful; in other cases penitence is motivated by fear of some penalty. Where there is heartfelt contrition or true penitence, sin does not persist. The love of God which evokes our grief does not permit vice. We are immediately reconciled to God by our repentance, and we receive pardon for our former faults. Wherever there is true penitence, proceeding solely from the love of God, there is no sin, and no contempt of God remains. By inspiring penitence God renders the sinner worthy of divine forbearance. Hence, the sinner is not damned so long as he remains repentant.

Although the repentant sinner may by circumstances be prevented from coming to confession, he is in no danger of damnation if he dies with contrition on his lips. Ordinarily, however, the penitent confesses his sins to another person, as a sign of humility and true contrition and as a means of securing the prayers of others. The priest who hears the confession of the penitent is, however, unable to give absolution in a sacramental sense. A bishop may wish to increase or to diminish the punishment of a fault without moderation and discretion; he may wish to extend punishment indefinitely. In fact, however, Jesus' promise to the Apostles which gave them the power to remit sins was addressed to them alone, and not to all their successors indiscriminately. For unless the verdict of the bishops is in accordance with divine justice, writes Abelard, it is without validity.

In forgiving the penitent not every penalty is remitted by God. Many who sorrow for sin have died before they were able to offer penitent satisfaction. Such will give satisfaction in purgatory.

Confession is not always needed, however, says Abelard; it may be deferred or omitted altogether if the penitent feels that his confession would do more harm than good.

There are many priests without faith and discretion, Abelard claims. Confession to such men may be not merely useless but also dangerous, for such priests are not worthy of being heard in their petitions to God; they are ignorant of canon law and know no moderation in their prescription of penance. But although such priests are of no use to the penitent, the latter need not despair, provided repentance towards God has preceded confession and the receiving of penance. If less penance is imposed than the sin warrants, God will correct the error with punishment in purgatory. By fasting, prayer, and the denial of the flesh we can, however, escape such future punishment and give present satisfaction for sins.

In spite of the fact that much of Abelard's thought was condemned at the Council of Sens, his teaching exerted its influence upon medieval ethical theory, for it caused later theorists to lay stress upon the notion of motive *(intentio),* and it produced the practical test of deliberateness in judging the degree of guilt in mortal sin. However, the practical effect of Abelard's emphasis on intention was that the distinction between good and evil *acts* was obscured. Abelard's development of St. Augustine's suggestions concerning intention suffers from a lack of the sense of proportion which made Augustine's Christian ethics more immediately applicable to the problems of men.

POLICRATICUS

Author: John of Salisbury (c.1115-1180)
Type of work: Christian social philosophy
First transcribed: 1159

Principal Ideas Advanced

Instead of being surrounded by competent and industrious officials, the prince is surrounded by courtiers, who use philosophy to disguise the falsity of their position.

The true commonwealth is like a living body, with the clergy as its soul, the prince as its head, office-holders as its eyes, hands, and stomach, and the people as its feet.

The well-being of the whole depends upon each performing his proper function; in particular, the functions of the clergy and of the magistracy should be kept distinct.

The prince should be guided by the law of God, and he should respect the liberty of his people and seek their peace and prosperity.

The Plenitude of God's Goodness and Wisdom is mirrored in the just society.

The *Policraticus,* which was dedicated to Thomas à Becket (c.1117-1170), at that time chancellor to King Henry II, combines a satirical account of contemporary court life with a serious account of the nature of a Christian commonwealth. The author, although an Englishman by birth, studied for many years abroad, and is an admirable representative of the Christian humanism of the twelfth century renaissance. Personally acquainted with such diverse persons as Peter Abelard (1079-1142), Bernard of Clairvaux (1090-1153), and Pope Hadrian IV (c.1100-1159), he was, at the time when he wrote the *Policraticus,* secretary to Theobald, Archbishop of Canterbury.

The full title of the work is *Policraticus, sive de nugis curialium et de vestigiis philosophorum,* which means, literally, "Policraticus, or Concerning Follies of Courtiers and Remnants of Philosophers." While scholars disagree on the significance of the term "Policraticus," the obvious purpose of the work was to expose the evils to be found in the class of men which surrounded kings and bishops. Court life demeans those who enter upon it. To succeed as a courtier, one must combine the appearance of "philosophy and goodness" with all manner of folly and vice. But, says John, the courtier-philosopher is a monster, a kind of hermaphrodite, who "deforms womanly beauty with a harsh and bristly countenance, while he pollutes and defiles manhood with womanish weakness." He continues: "The court casts out philosophy utterly, and the true philosopher will in no wise participate in the follies of a court." John hurries to add that this need not be the situation, and that a wise ruler changes the complexion of his court. Nevertheless, he is quite explicit about court life in his day, both in England and in Rome. The pope, he says, is in an impossible position because of his court. He cannot administer justice if he accepts gifts; but he cannot achieve anything unless he offers gifts; and in order to have the means to offer gifts, he must accept them.

In the course of his book, John comments on numerous practices which, in his opinion, are hindrances to the welfare of the commonwealth. Among the targets of his wit are hunting, gambling, licentious music and drama, fortunetelling, and astrology. He complains, for example, that soldiers think only of "cutting a fine figure with clothes of brighter hue than others, and in so squeezing and twisting their linen or silken garments as to make them cleave as close to the body as a second skin." Interested in "the arts of pleasure" rather than in valor, they "would be more certain to capture the stronghold of Thaïs than that of Hannibal." Addressing himself expressly to Becket, he says, "I shall not forbid you to dress in raiment of gold, to dine daily in splendid state, . . . to do as is customary to do in these degenerate days, while remaining upright yourself, and to mock a world that mocks you with its allurements. For you are too great a man to be caught in its tentacles." But not many, he avers, are thus able to rise above temptation.

But John's commentary on the manners of his time is only one aspect of his work. Like Erasmus and Thomas More, who were to speak for Christian humanism in the sixteenth century, John of Salisbury has a well-articulated moral and political philosophy. John is an eclectic, who combines the skepticism of the Academics with the Ciceronian ideal of a just man, one completely formed in knowledge and virtue and able to express himself eloquently. He borrows, as suits his need, from Horace and Vergil, Lucian and Petronius. But underlying his whole philosophy is the Platonic and Augustinian conception of virtue as discipline and happiness as the harmonious subordination of the parts within the whole, according to the will of the Creator.

John's criticisms of ecclesiastical and political abuses presuppose his conception of a Christian commonwealth or republic in which the economic, civic, military, and ecclesiastical orders all work together to produce a society in which men and women can live justly and at peace with God and their fellows. Thus, at least from one point of view, politics should subserve morality and religion. From another point of view, morality and religion are the substance of a true polity; for, according to John, the well-being of the community is assured if each member performs the duty which God has assigned to him.

John elaborates his conception of the ideal state after the analogy of the human body, a figure widely used both by Christian and pagan authors. He says that, since the end of the commonwealth is the service of God, the soul of society is the priesthood. The head, which is responsible for governing the body, is the prince. The heart, "from which proceeds the initiation of good works and ill," is the Senate. The eyes, ears, and tongue are the governors and judges. The stomach and intestines are the fiscal officers. The hands are the soldiers and police. The feet are the artisans and husbandmen. In order for any part of the state to function well, all parts must work together harmoniously. The rulers must reverence God, must be informed, and must be trained for their particular tasks. They must remember that, being few in numbers, they exist for the advantage of the multitudes. The people, for their part, owe obedience and service to their superiors in return for protection and succor. John cites with appreciation Vergil's lines in the *Fourth Georgic,* concerning the political constitution of the hive of bees. He adds, "Then and then only will the health of the commonwealth be sound and flourishing when the higher members shield the lower, and the lower respond faithfully and fully in like measure to the just demands of their superiors, so that each and all are as it were members one of another by a sort of reciprocity, and each regards his own interest as best served by that which he knows to be most advantageous for the others."

John of Salisbury borrows his exposition of the body-politic from a treatise which he believes to have been written by Plutarch, called "The Instruction of Trajan," explaining that where the pagan author referred to "gods" he has substituted the singular "God." Thus, in all innocence, a medieval author and statesman conceives the Christian religion as taking the place of the ancient civil cultus, and the Church as performing a normal function in organized human society. The ancient Christian apologists, such as Tertullian (c.160-c.220), begged for a state without religious ties, within which Christians might enjoy the same civil rights as others. Augustine of Hippo (354-430), although he was thankful for a Christian emperor and was willing for the Church to receive material assistance from the state, nevertheless thought of the Church as belonging to a higher order than the state, and as seeking a different end. In John of Salisbury's view, however, Church and state are one body, and the priesthood and the magistracy are merely responsible for different functions of the common life. This view, of course, persisted after the breakup of the Middle Ages, into Protestant times, and by many people is not thought incompatible with the formal separation of Church and state. Washington Gladden (1836-1918), for example, advocating the "social gospel," argued that the human community is an organism, of which the Church is a normal part.

The supremacy of the priestly hierarchy over the prince is represented by John, as it had been previously by Bernard of Clairvaux, under the figure of the two swords. Like Bernard, John urges the Church to disengage itself from political matters, and, at the same time, he warns the state to quit interfering with the affairs of the Church. He maintains that both the material sword and the spiritual sword were given by Christ to the Church, and that the prince receives his power from the hand of the priest. But it is no part of John's claim to propose that the Church select the ruler or direct him in the administration of his duties. Rather, he maintains that the prince stands under the law of God, and must have sufficient learning to be able to discover for himself what that higher law demands. John argues that there are certain laws which have force among all nations; to see how these apply, the prince is advised to study the Code of Justinian. Other laws are inscribed in the Holy Scriptures, which the prince ought to read every day, particularly the book of Deuteronomy.

John holds that kings receive their offices from God, as part of God's general providence over mankind. He hesitates to say that they owe their position either to heredity or to popular election; for men sometimes come to the throne in devious ways, and piety demands that all kings be obeyed. Sometimes, he says, God imposes unjust and tyrannical kings upon a nation as a chastisement, in which case it behooves men to cry out to God for deliverance. God's law stands supreme, however; and if a tyrant commands men to do what is unlawful, they should refuse to obey him. In extreme cases, it is lawful to kill the tyrant. Here John puts in a word for "liberty," which, he says, is second only to virtue, "if indeed liberty can ever properly be severed from virtue." Liberty consists in "judging everything freely in accordance with one's individual judgment, and does not hesitate to reprove what it sees opposed to good morals." In order to have liberty, however, men must cultivate tolerance. "It is the part of a good and wise man to give a free reign to the liberty of others and to accept with patience the words of free speaking, whatever they may be."

Underlying John of Salisbury's conception of the state is something of the prejudice shared by Stoics and early Christians against all political authority. If men cultivated virtue, he says, reason and charity would so far prevail that princes and monarchs would not be necessary, or, at least, their rule would be no burden. John does not suppose that, in man's sinful condition, society can ever be rid of government. His desire is, however, that the prince will, above all men, be governed by moral considerations, will never seek his own interest above that of others, will embrace his subjects as brethren, and, when he has to correct them, will temper his strength with kindness. In short, John is committed to the ideal of a state founded on the goodwill of its rulers and the piety of its people, rather than on the distribution of power. It was this ideal which Niccolò Machiavelli (1469-1527) opposed in his book, *The Prince.*

John sees the ultimate duty of man in the light of the First and Great Commandment; namely, that God "is to be loved by all men alike and worshiped with all their heart, and all their soul, and all their strength." It is by love rather than by understanding that man draws near to God in this life, says John of Salisbury. For, the Divine Being can never be grasped by human intelligence so long as it is burdened with the body. But God can be loved, in two ways: directly, "by affection, which is a disposition of the mind," and indirectly, "by the display of works." Thus, according to John, the whole round of human activity may become a reflection of God's wisdom and goodness. Men have different characters and offices, with different virtues and obligations, but some portion of God's goodness is present in each of them. Just as the ray of the sun emits a red color when it falls on a carbuncle, and azure on a sapphire, so God's goodness appears in some men as prudence, in others as fortitude, and in others as temperance or justice. Only thus can the Divine Plenitude reveal itself to us here on earth: "But, in time to come, when through His grace we shall look upon Him face to face, and see Him as He is, then He will be all in all." Then also, says John, God shall be visible in the company of his elect "in such fulness of majesty that they shall lack nothing of any grace, and He alone shall be visible in them, and they shall be reckoned in His name, their true substance being preserved entire and without any changefulness of nature."

BENJAMIN MINOR

Author: Richard of St. Victor (died c. 1173)
Type of work: Mystical theology
First transcribed: c.1160

Principal Ideas Advanced

Man's highest good is the mystical contemplation of God.

Man's preparation for contemplation can be learned from the spiritual (allegorical) interpretation of the Biblical story of Jacob's family.

Man's preparation consists in progress in the virtues and the proper use of the senses, imagination, and reason.

The way to the higher knowledge of God is by way of self-knowledge, which can be gained only with the help of Christ, laborious effort, meditation, and prayer.

The highest form of contemplation lies beyond man's efforts and reason.

We know nothing about Richard's youth except that he was a native of Scotland and a very young man when he entered the abbey of St. Victor (near Paris), the most renowned of all the houses of the Canons Regular of St. Augustine. He served as prior from 1162 to 1173 and was greatly influenced by a previous prior, Hugh of St. Victor (c.1096-1141), whom he may have known personally. St. Victor sought to continue the early medieval tradition of monastic piety, with its emphasis on asceticism, contemplation, and the "Sacred Page." Unlike the Cistercian abbey of Clairvaux, however, it was open to every kind of learning, and it did not hesitate to employ the dialectic that was becoming increasingly characteristic of the learning of the schools.

Hugh and Richard mark an important turning point in the history of Christian mysticism. Mysticism in the West, where it was universally known as "contemplation" in the early Middle Ages, had been decisively shaped by Augustine of Hippo (354-430), John Cassian (c.360-435), and Gregory the Great (c.540-604). This Augustinian-Benedictine tradition remained essentially unchanged to the time of Bernard of Clairvaux (1090-1153). Mystics of this Western type experienced the reality and presence of God, and entered into union with God; they described their experiences; but they did not develop a "science" of contemplation. Both theology and contemplation remained inextricably linked to the Bible and to the experiences of devout men and women.

Hugh and Richard stood in this tradition, but they modified it considerably. It was through these two Victorines that the mysticism of Dionysius "the Pseudo-Areopagite" (apparently a Syrian monk writing around 500) entered the mainstream of Western spirituality. Its impact there, largely mediated by Hugh's commentary on Dionysius' *Celestial Hierarchy*, may be compared to that of the recovered Aristotelian corpus on Western thought. It promoted a growing systematization of mystical theology, and here Richard led the way. He described the soul's preparation for contemplation in *Benjamin minor*, contemplation itself in *Benjamin major*, and the fruits of contemplation in *Four Degrees of Passionate Charity*.

Richard's passion for unitive comprehensiveness and hierarchical constructions is clearly Dionysian. His most famous classification, the *sex gen-*

era contemplationis, occurs in the *Benjamin major*. Here he distinguishes (1) contemplation which is purely imaginative; (2) contemplation that is imaginative, but in a rational manner; (3) rational contemplation that speculates with the aid of the images of visible things; (4) purely rational (nonimaginative) contemplation; (5) suprarational contemplation; (6) seemingly contra-rational contemplation. This scheme is reflected in many medieval treatises on contemplation, including *The Mind's Road to God (Itinerarium mentis ad deum)* of St. Bonaventura (1221-1274).

Richard is distinctively Western in his psychological (experiential) interest. Man's ascent to contemplation is by the elevation of both heart and mind to God; in fact, it is the unification of man's "higher powers," (through concentration on the Supreme Unity) that facilitates (and is facilitated by) the mystical union with God. When later theologians argued over the relative priority of the will (love) and the intellect (knowledge) in the mystical ascent, neither side was completely justified in invoking Richard's authority in its own behalf. Where Richard is very clear is in his conviction, against that of Dionysius' first translator into Latin, John Scotus Erigena (c.815-c.877), that God can be known by created beings.

Benjamin minor is principally an allegory on the family of Jacob (Genesis 31:1-24; 35:16-20; Psalm 68:27). Jacob represents man as a rational spirit; Rachel, "the teaching of truth"; that is, reason producing "right counsel"; Leah, "the discipline of virtue"; that is, "ordered affections" producing "holy desires." Bilhah, Rachel's maidservant, stands for the imagination; Zilpah, Leah's maidservant, for sensation. The order in which these four women bear sons to Jacob represents the pattern of man's preparation for contemplation. First come the sons of Leah: the fear of the Lord (Reuben), sorrow for sin (Simeon), hope for forgiveness (Levi), and love of righteousness (Judah). Bilhah's son Dan represents a combination of the imagination with reason, while Naphtali represents the imagination in conjunction with the intelligence. Richard distinguishes here between reason and intelligence, assigning to the latter the capacity to transcend the corporeal world. Zilpah's son Gad represents abstinence; Asher represents patience. Leah's son Issachar represents the joy of inward sweetness; her son Zebulon, the hatred of sin; and her daughter Dinah, shame. Rachel's first-born son Joseph represents the supreme virtue of discretion. Rachel (reason) dies in giving birth to Benjamin (contemplation).

Richard sees a radical dichotomy between the worlds of body and spirit. Within the latter there is a triad of spirits, human, angelic, divine. To these correspond the traditional three heavens and three types of knowledge: faith, reason, contemplation. Man may (actively) ascend to the first two heavens; to the third heaven he must be (passively) carried. (See II Corinthians 12:3.) Richard likens true self-knowledge to a great mountain that towers over all the learning of this world, including Plato's and Aristotle's. He identifies it with the Mount of Transfiguration and asserts that we can ascend it only when truth itself, Jesus Christ, is our guide. The three disciples He chose represent work, meditation, and prayer, without which the ascent is also impossible.

He writes: "Would you see Christ transfigured? . . . Would you see and recognize Moses and Elias without any sign? Would you understand the law and prophecy without a teacher or commentator? Climb this mountain, learn to know yourself. Would you have the privacy of the Father's secrets? Climb this mountain, learn to know yourself."

The shining garments of Christ stand for a new type of teaching that is to be obtained only at the top of the mount of self-knowledge. They pertain to heavenly things, just as Christ's ordinary garments, that is, His ordinary teachings, pertain to earthly things. (See John 3:12.) At the top of this mountain, Christ can be believed only when He authenticates Himself by being met by Moses and Elias; that is, by the literal and spiritual sense of Scripture; for the Devil himself transfigures himself into an angel of light. Rachel dies and Benjamin is born when the Father's voice is heard; the disciples fall to the ground; senses, memory, and reason fail, and the soul is in ecstasy.

Richard is typical of the mainstream of medieval spirituality when he insists on ethical (ascetic) prerequisites for contemplation, the radical distinction of body and spirit, the subjective approach to God ("Know yourself"), and the possibility of a higher knowledge (Christ's shining garments). Richard does not indicate here whether he would keep this higher knowledge from the masses, or, with the Western homilectic tradition, utilize it for spiritual edification. In his emphasis on ecstasy Richard seems to follow Dionysius and to reverse the dominant tendency of Western spirituality, which had learned, beginning with St. Augustine, to recognize the reality while discounting the importance of ecstatic raptures. The earlier Middle Ages had not been greatly exercised over the possibility of mistaking the Devil for Christ, but this concern of Richard's was bequeathed to much of subsequent mysticism. His distinction between *speculatio,* in which man is active, and *contemplatio,* in which man is wholly passive, also proved to be very influential. It marks the beginning of a tendency to posit a radical discontinuity between ordinary spirituality ("acquired" contemplation) and mystical experience ("infused" contemplation). In requiring the corroboration of any "shewing" (*revelatio*) by both the historical and spiritual sense of Scripture, Richard shows himself a willing disciple of Hugh, who had insisted that the spiritual meaning of Scripture not be divorced from the historico-literal. While Richard wants to follow Hugh, it is plain that he (unlike his contemporary Andrew of St. Victor, who died in 1175) is no friend of the letter: "Therefore . . . let him show the authority of the Scripture, not only figuratively but also openly. It is a lovely and joyful spectacle when in the revelation of truth, clear reason presents itself at this point, and both the historical and the figurative reading concur in supporting that revelation. . . . Moses and Elias appear with the Lord on the mount, and they appear in majesty, not in the obscurity of the letter in the light of the spiritual understanding."

This Scriptural attestation is needed, however, only when the "showing" pertains to heavenly things: "If Christ teaches me about external things or about my own interior life, I accept him easily, as in those things which I can prove by my own experience."

In England, the *Benjamin minor* appears to have been the most popular of Richard's writings, and the unknown author of *The Cloud of Unknowing* (a fourteenth century mystical treatise) his most faithful disciple. On the Continent the *Benjamin major* was valued more highly, and its direct influence extends into the sixteenth century, when Catholic mystical theology was definitively formulated by the Spanish Carmelites Teresa of Avila (1515-1582) and John of the Cross (1542-1591).

TREATISE ON THE FOUR GOSPELS

Author: Joachim of Fiore (c.1132-1202)
Type of work: Eschatology; philosophy of history
First transcribed: 1202

Principal Ideas Advanced

To the enlightened understanding, the Bible foretells the end of the Church age in the year 1260.

The history of mankind unfolds in three stages: the first reveals God the Father; the second, God the Son; the third, God the Holy Spirit.

The clerical Church is limited to the age of the Son; the monastic orders are the true forerunners of the age of the Spirit.

Joachim, Abbot of Fiore (or Flora, or Flore), carried on the monastic revival which had previously been championed by Bernard of Clairvaux (c.1090-1153). Dante speaks of him in the *Paradiso* as "endowed with prophetic spirit," and he places him next to the great Franciscan, Bonaventura (1221-1274). But only within the last century have historical scholars begun to appreciate the scope of Joachim's influence, and, even more belatedly, to publish his long-neglected writings. The *Tractatus super quatuor evangelia,* which was published in Rome in 1930, is the first of several such works scheduled to be issued in modern critical editions. Some of Joachim's works were printed in the sixteenth century, but the *Tractatus,* which is a lengthy fragment left incomplete at Joachim's death, has been handed down only in manuscript copies.

All of Joachim's writings develop essentially the same body of ideas, a kind of apocalypticism which made bold to prophesy that history was about to enter upon a new paradisiacal age. Millenarian expectations had been repressed in the official teaching of the Church, largely through the influence of Augustine, who taught that the thousand-year reign of Christ spoken of in the book of Revelation was the age of the Church. But among diverse groups the idea remained popular that, just as on the seventh day God rested from creating the world, so, at the end of six thousand years of history, the human race would have rest. Joachim gave a new and powerful expression to these perennial hopes, by means of a system of interpretation which presumably enabled him to discover Biblical allusions to his own times.

Joachim's understanding of the Scriptures came to him as a sudden insight while he was studying the Revelation. "Suddenly," he says, "the eyes of my spirit were enlightened, and the fulfillment of this book and the harmony between the Old and the New Testaments was revealed to me." The hidden truth given him in this way was that, just as the Mosaic dispensation had been replaced by that of Christ, so the Christian dispensation must henceforth give way to the dispensation of the Holy Spirit. Using allegorical methods, traditional in the Roman Church, Joachim developed his views in three books: *The Harmony of the Old and New Testaments*, *An Exposition of the Apocalypse*, and *The Psaltery of Ten Strings*. In his *Treatise on the Four Gospels* he undertakes to carry out the same scheme on a more impressive scale. Joachim's use of the allegorical method does not impress historical scholars as original—except, as his editor Ernesto Buonaiuti says, "quantitatively." What mainly distinguishes Joachim's commentary from other allegorical works is that instead of finding doctrinal and moral teachings hidden beneath the historical meaning of the text, Joachim found prophecies.

Joachim had the same kind of problem which faces anyone who wishes to comment on the four Gospels synoptically. He found that the four Gospels form a single narrative covering Christ's life until the Galilean ministry; but, upon observing that the first three Gospels do not record the Jerusalem visits which are mentioned in the fourth Gospel, and that John, for his part, does not detail the Galilean work, he had to break up his commentary into different books. Of the three books completed, the first deals with the birth narratives, the baptism and temptation, and Jesus' early preaching, through the story of the wedding at Cana. The second book takes up the early Galilean ministry as recorded in the first three Gospels, printing the accounts, where they diverge, in parallel columns. The third book follows John's account of Jesus' ministry in Judea and Samaria, breaking off in the middle of John's fifth chapter, after the healing of the lame man at the pool of Bethesda. The omissions, transpositions, and other seeming discrepancies between the Gospels do not appear to have disturbed Joachim, nor does he go out of his way to harmonize them. He was convinced that the Gospels were not written according to men's wisdom, but were dictated by the Holy Spirit, who wishes through them to convey something more than the literal story of Christ's life on earth.

As is true of many present-day "students of prophecy," Joachim often finds his truth in out-of-the-way places. Matthew's account of the genealogy of Christ, which most readers skip, interests him because it enables him to set a date for the termination of the Church-age. Matthew mentions that there were fourteen generations from Abraham to David, fourteen generations from David to the Babylonian captivity, and fourteen generations from the Babylonian captivity until Christ. Added together, this gives the figure forty-two, which appears often in the Scriptures. For example, Elijah prayed that Israel should suffer drought for three and one-half years, that is, forty-two months; and the woman in Revelation is forced to dwell in the wilderness for 1260 days, or forty-two months. Now, the fact that both John the Baptist and Jesus began their ministries at the age of thirty suggests that, when the Holy Spirit says "generation," he means thirty years. All of this reminds Joachim that he is living in the fortieth generation after Christ's birth, and that only two generations remain before the dispensation of the Church reaches its end.

The fundamental framework of Joachim's system is presupposed in the *Treatise,* and it is supplied in the current edition in the form of footnote citations from his earlier works. Briefly, Joachim maintains that history is divided into three ages, corresponding to the three persons of the Holy Trinity. Each age has its forerunners and its leader (*Dux*). The first age, which was prepared by Adam and Abraham, began with Moses and "revealed God the Father in his glory"; the second, which was announced by David and Uzziah, began with John the Baptist, and "made known the Son to the Christian people"; the third, which numbered among its predecessors Paul, Antony, Benedict, and Bernard, will begin with the coming of "that Elijah" who is foretold in the closing verses of the Old Testament, and will "belong to the Holy Spirit, who, during this age, will be shown in his glory even as the Father was in the first, and the Son in the Second."

Once having discerned this scheme in Scripture, Joachim claims, the reader who possesses "spiritual understanding" is able to find it on almost every page of the four Gospels. For example, Elizabeth, the mother of John the Baptist, conceived a child after being barren for many years. The time of her barrenness stands for the first era, the age of the Mosaic law and the synagogue; the time during which she carried the future prophet in her womb stands for the second era, the age of Christ and the Church; the time when she was delivered of a son stands for the beginning of the third era, the advent of Elijah and the age of the Spirit. Joachim uses great freedom in interpreting his symbols. On one plane of interpretation, John is the herald of the Christian era; on another, he symbolizes the Elijah that is to come.

A further example of Joachim's exegesis is his interpretation of the wedding at Cana, when Jesus turned the water into wine. Those who read with only historical understanding are puzzled by the words, "On the third day." The third day of what? No connection is apparent. Those who read with spiritual understanding, however, recognize at once a reference to the third period of history, "in which the peace of God is given to the Church, so that it may contemplate him as King, and be united in marriage with him to whom it has been betrothed." In the narrative itself, the bridegroom stands for the ecclesiastical hierarchy; the bride, for Christian believers during the Church-age; the mother of Jesus, for the monastic orders within the Church; and Jesus, for the Holy Spirit, who shall abolish the sacrament of water-baptism and substitute for it baptism by the Spirit.

We have mentioned the fact that Joachim was trying, in his own day, to carry on the monastic revival which had begun with the founding of the Cistercian order about 1075, and had proceeded apace under Bernard. The movement represented a strong protest against the secularism of the Church, and had, in addition, many social and economic implications. Its advocates did not view it as a withdrawal from the world, but as entering upon a new and more promising way of life, in which feudal restraints and social inequalities were abolished. Joachim describes the monastic movement as preparing the way for the age of the Holy Spirit, in the same way as the Davidic monarchy and the Levitical priesthood prepared the way for the age of the Church. From Joachim's point of view, the Church, with its sacraments, its hierarchy, and its scholastic teaching, is a transitional moment between the dispensation of the Father and that of the Spirit. The institutional Church is still in bondage to the letter of the Law, and thus it beholds God darkly, as in a mirror. The monastic orders, however, represent a serious effort to enter into the spirit of Christ, and, dispensing with worldly compromises, to live according to the perfect will of God. Joachim does not deny the validity of the clergy or the sacraments, nor does he hold that the new age is already realized in monasticism. He maintains, however, that when the new Dux appears, he will set aside both the feudal and priestly orders, and establish an order in which the spiritual way now pursued by the monks will become the way of life for all men.

Besides writing and preaching, Joachim was active in monastic reform. His own ascetic principles were too severe for the monastery of Corazzo, in Calabria, of which he was the abbot, and he withdrew, with a few companions, to form a new abbey high in the mountains, under a rule which he himself drew up. From this abbey, known as St. John of Flore, other houses sprang up, and, in 1204, after Joachim's death, the "Order of Flore" was approved by Pope Innocent III. But Joachim's teaching spread rapidly outside his own order. There is ground for believing that he influenced Francis of Assisi (c.1182-1226), whose formal activity began about the year 1210; and it was among strict Franciscans, or Spirituals, that he found his most zealous disciples. One of these, a young teacher at the University of Paris named Gerard of Borgo San Donnino, wrote a book in 1254 called *The Eternal Gospel,* in which he pronounced that the age of the Holy Spirit would begin on schedule in 1260, and that the Franciscan Spirituals were the agents to bring it in. The controversy raised by this book resulted in disciplinary measures that dampened the Joachite movement within the Church; but the influence of the movement continued among fringe groups, such as the Fratricelli, and even in secular movements, such as that of the Roman revolutionary, Cola de Rienzo (c.1313-1354). Scholars argue that the optimistic, anarchistic, and egalitarian principles which were in this way disseminated throughout Europe have influenced social and political revolutions to this day. (See, for example, Karl Löwith, *Meaning in History,* 1949, Appendix I, "Modern Transfigurations of Joachism.")

Whether the Christian "hope" is this-worldly or other-worldly is still debated. (One needs but to recall discussions prompted by the meeting of the World Council of Churches at Evanston, in 1954.) Interestingly, apocalypticism, in this period of world wars, has come to be associated with an other-worldly eschatology. This was not true in the case of Joachim. Although he believed that divine manifestations would usher in the millennial age, he thought of it not as the termination of history, but as its fulfillment. The true successors of Joachim, therefore, are not those who set dates for history to end, but those who look for God's Kingdom to be realized here on earth.

According to the Augustinian world-view which governed the theology of the Middle Ages and continued to be the standard for the Reformation Churches, God stands outside His creation, and He intervenes only to save His handiwork from ruin; the contradiction between God's righteous demands and man's fallen conditions is accepted as normal and as not to be resolved except in eternity. Joachim of Fiore challenged these assumptions, and he thus prepared the way for the more modern view, which finds God progressively at work in nature and history.

Professor Löwith cites as an example of Joachim's influence the Enlightenment philosopher, Lessing, whose *Education of the Human Race,* 1780, profoundly influenced both French and German social and political thought. Lessing developed the idea of history as unfolding in three stages, stating that the Jewish and Christian dispensations must be superseded by a "new eternal gospel." Lessing believed that the new age would be introduced by reason and education; still, he maintained that it would come as a linear development out of the Judeo-Christian revelation. Referring to Joachim and his followers, he said, "Perhaps this doctrine of three world-ages was not at all an empty whim of these men; . . . they maintained the same economy of the same God, or, to let them speak my own language, the same plan for a common education of the human race. They only hastened it too much, believing that their contemporaries, who had just grown out of their childhood, could suddenly be made into adults, worthy of the third age, without proper preparation and enlightenment."

RETRACING THE ARTS TO THEOLOGY

Author: Saint Bonaventura (Giovanni di Fidanza, 1221-1274)
Type of work: Mystical theology
First transcribed: c.1250

Principal Ideas Advanced

The various forms of knowledge may be divided into four levels of illumination and then subdivided, according to distance from divine wisdom.

As each level and branch of knowledge is dissected, however, traces of divine similitude become evident, indicating that each has and discloses a divine origin.

Thus, each form of knowledge is directly relevant to and an assistance for theology, since, properly analyzed, all levels disclose a divine element and thus retrace their origin to God.

When it is placed beside Thomas Aquinas's *Summa theologica,* Bonaventura's *Retracing the Arts to Theology* may seem insignificant. Small it is, but unimportant it is not. In fact, what is so instructive about this little work is to see how much can be accomplished in so short a space. Moreover, like most of Bonaventura's works, this one is intricate in detail, encompassing a great deal in a short space and shaped into a very compressed form.

Now, in the twentieth century, it is interesting to see that Bonaventura opens his treatise with what afterwards became Kierkegaard's favorite Biblical passage, from the first chapter of James: *Every good and perfect gift is from above, coming down from the Father of Lights.* The metaphor of light is characteristic of those who, like Bonaventura, follow the Neoplatonic tradition. In fact, this Scriptural passage is central to Bonaventura's doctrine here, since it would not be possible to trace all of the arts to a theological source unless a divine light actually took various forms and appeared in many modes and levels. Divinity transcends normal natural modes, but it nevertheless is completely immanent, present behind and discernible through every order of nature.

Bonaventura begins with what is essentially a division of the sciences and the branches of philosophy, by distinguishing each as a form of light. First, there is an external light or the light of mechanical art, followed by a lower light of sense perception. Then there is the inner light or the light of philosophical knowledge. And finally there is the higher light or the light of grace and of Scripture. The lower light illumines artifacts, while the second reveals natural forms to us, and the third discloses intellectual truth. The fourth and last concerns saving grace, and this is the most crucial to man. Bonaventura, it is true, does not develop these analogies in detail. A sketch of related structures always seems to be sufficient for him.

The first (external) light, since it concerns artifacts, deals primarily with things exterior to man and intended to supply the needs of his body. As such it is servile and of a lower nature than philosophical knowledge. Since there are seven mechanical arts, this external light has seven subdivisions, and these taken together are sufficient for man's consolation, comfort, sorrow, or delight. Following this light, so important to man's basic needs, is the lower light of sense perception. This begins with a material object and needs the aid of corporeal light. In its turn, sense perception has five divisions, corresponding to the five senses. The sensitive life of the body actually partakes of the nature of light.

The investigation of intelligible truths is the third light, the light of philosophical knowledge. It is an inner light, since it inquires into inner and hidden causes, through inherent principles of learning and natural truth. Philosophy is, of course, subdivided into three divisions, rational, natural, and moral. Philosophy involves discerning the causes of being (in physics), grasping the principles of understanding (in logic), and learning the right way of living (in moral or practical philosophy). As a result, philosophy enlightens man as to the truth of life, the truth of knowledge, and the truth of doctrine. Physics, mathematics, and metaphysics are all combined in this general division, considering in turn generation and corruption, abstracted forms, and the ideal causes, leading back to one first principle, God.

Most important of all, of course, is the fourth light, illumining the mind for the understanding of saving truth. This is to be found in the light of Scripture. Such a light is properly called higher, since it leads to truths beyond reason and as such is not to be acquired by human research. It comes down from above, by inspiration from the Father of Lights. In a literal sense, this light is one, although in a mystical sense it has a threefold spiritual meaning; allegorical, moral, and anagogical. By these three means we are taught what to believe concerning Divinity, how to live, and, finally, how to be united with God. This divides men into doctors, preachers, and contemplatives.

There will, however, one day come a twilight, when all knowledge will be destroyed, followed by a day which knows no evening, the illumination of glory. All of the branches of knowledge are ordained as a means to a knowledge of Sacred Scripture. All illuminations of all knowledge are to be brought back, or traced to, the light of Sacred Scripture. As we discern this, we discern the Word begotten from all eternity as itself the medium of all perception. As the sense object is seen in perception by means of a similitude, so God has connected from all eternity a Similitude or Offspring. Through Him (Jesus) the minds of all who receive that similitude of the Father through faith are brought back to God.

Perhaps the best example of the similarity between divinity and sense perception can be seen in the delight one takes in sense perception, for in this we can see a similarity to the delight of the soul when it unites with God. In this way and in others, the Divine Wisdom actually lies hidden in sense perception, as in fact it does in all of the various forms of knowledge. As the artist produces a work according to a similitude in his mind, to take a further example, so the Invisible becomes visible and takes flesh in Christ. And most certainly, carrying the parallel further, the divine wisdom can also be found in philosophy, since the speaker begets words from mental concepts, following the same procedure of God in begetting the Eternal Word.

All natural philosophy, because it discloses primarily the various relations of proportion, duplicates the Word of God begotten and become incarnate. Since God is above, it is necessary that the apex of the mind itself be raised aloft, thus indicating in the process of philosophy the natural goal of the mind for union with God. What all of this analysis discloses most clearly, Bonaventura concludes, is how the wisdom of God lies hidden in all knowledge and in all nature. To discover divine knowledge hidden in the various forms of nature and levels of knowledge is the central meaning of retracing the arts to theology.

In this sense all divisions of knowledge are "handmaidens of theology," a phrase much objected to and much misunderstood. The divisions of knowledge "serve" theology by showing themselves to be, upon careful dissection, forms of divine light. Theology uses material and terms from every branch of knowledge precisely because every form of knowledge actually discloses, to an astute observer, its peculiar form of divine wisdom through the divine analogies to be discovered on every level. The way to illumination is wide, not narrow, since not one but every possible branch of knowledge is actually capable of leading a keen mind through itself to God Himself.

In everything perceived or known God lies hidden within: this is Bonaventura's amazing discovery and his central message to the reader. The fruit of every science is that through it faith may actually be strengthened, rather than diverted and diminished. It takes a discerning mind to discover this divine element present in every form of knowledge, but that it can be done makes every mode of knowledge an avenue to God and an aid to theology. For theology we need not go far afield from man's ordinary pursuit of knowledge but simply gain the discernment to discover how every level of knowledge may be traced directly to God.

The four lights described by Bonaventura form the basis of a complete theory of knowledge, a cosmology, and a metaphysics, and all four unite to form a theology. All the arts, all the branches of science, all the activities of men are accounted for here, and each becomes a step leading the mind further upward, toward its theological goal of divine union. God has left His traces in every facet of the natural world and in men themselves, and a careful mind may discover the divine light in all things and, retracing it to its divine origin, be led by the arts to theology. Each form and level remains distinct and independent, yet each serves to raise the mind farther on its way toward God.

This brief treatise by Bonaventura must be looked on as only a sketch. Bonaventura has compressed his whole system of philosophy and theology into one brief essay. In its simplicity, however, the account is in some ways more suggestive than a more elaborate and detailed discussion could ever hope to be. There is no question that Bonaventura belongs to the Platonic tradition, and writers of this persuasion have always suggested and sketched possible theories in a tentative fashion.

Viewed in this way, it is easier to understand why no evidence whatsoever is offered to support the theory. If illumination is a way to knowledge, the mind cannot be forced or coerced. A suggestion can be made, a hidden factor pointed out, and then the listening mind is free to discern or not to discern the qualities outlined for it. Thus, the theory serves as a verbal platform for consideration. The attempt is to raise the mind to new perception by means of the theory; in this case, the effort is to discern the divine presence implicit in every natural phenomenon and fundamental to every art and inquiry.

SUMMA CONTRA GENTILES

Author: Saint Thomas Aquinas (c.1225-1274)
Type of work: Christian apologetics
First transcribed: c.1258-1260

Principal Ideas Advanced

Theology has the two-fold task of expounding truth and refuting error.

The truth of the Christian doctrine of God, of creation, and of providence can be established by reason and probable arguments.

The truth of the doctrine of the Trinity, the Incarnation, and the atonement must be accepted by faith, but can be defended and explained by reason.

The highest good for man is the beatific vision, for attaining which both faith and reason are necessary.

According to tradition, the *Summa contra gentiles* was composed at the request of the Dominican order (of which Thomas was a member) with a view to the needs of its missionaries in Spain, where the influence of Islamic and Jewish philosophy was strong. But in Thomas's day the influence of such non-Christian thinkers as Maimonides (1135-1204), Avicenna (980-1037), and Averroës (1126-1198) was not limited to Spain, for European scholars generally were dependent on Moslem transmitters and interpreters for their knowledge of Greek science and philosophy. In the *Summa contra gentiles* Thomas, who was second to none in his mastery of Aristotle, brought Christian faith and pagan learning together, not as enemies, or even as strangers, but as natural counterparts and allies, although unequal.

Citing a text from *Proverbs* in which Wisdom declares, "My mouth shall meditate truth, and my lips shall hate impiety," Thomas explains that the truth which Wisdom seeks is that truth which is the origin of all truth, pertaining as it does to the first principles of all reality. It is the same truth which Aristotle made the subject of his *Metaphysics,* but it is also the same truth which was incarnate in the person of Jesus Christ. But, says Thomas, it belongs to one and the same science both to establish the truth containing its subject and to refute opposing errors. Hence, the two-fold task of theology.

That the *Summa contra gentiles* is intended primarily as a work in theology and not in philosophy, follows from the distinction which Aquinas makes between these two sciences. The task of philosophy, he says, is to know things according to their own natures; that of theology is to know things in their relationship to God. Furthermore, the procedure of philosophy is to begin with those things which are best known to man and then to proceed toward those things which are least known; that of theology, on the contrary, is to begin with that which, although least known to man, is inherently the most intelligible. In other words, philosophy starts with the knowledge we have of the creature and progresses toward knowledge of the

Creator, whereas theology starts with the knowledge of God, and considers creatures in the light of what we can know of Him.

A glance at the outline of the *Summa contra gentiles* is sufficient to show that it is primarily a theological work. There are four books. In view of the fact that the adversaries he had in mind were not Christian heretics, but Jews and Moslems who would not be convinced by an appeal to Scriptural authority, Thomas devoted the first three books to proving as much of the Christian faith as can be shown to be true by demonstration and probable argument. The fourth book expounds the truth of revelation, and covers those parts of the Christian faith which cannot be discovered by reason. In Books One to Three, as well as in Book Four, the argument begins with our knowledge of God and explains the world in relation to Him, first, as owing its existence to God, and second, as finding its fulfillment in God. Book One treats of God as He is in Himself; Book Two treats of the derivation of the creatures from God; Book Three treats of the creatures insofar as they are ordered toward God as their end. Book Four recapitulates the order, but on the plane of revealed knowledge: first, of the Trinity, then of the Incarnation, then of the sacraments, and finally of Heaven and Hell.

Many philosophical issues are raised in the course of the work, but they are subordinated to the theological plan. Ordinarily, they are introduced with a view either to showing that reason leads to the same conclusions as faith or to helping the mind comprehend what has been apprehended by faith. But occasionally the situation is reversed, and faith is able to further the interests of philosophy by correcting philosophy when it has gone astray and by answering questions which are philosophical in nature but which cannot be answered by reason alone. For example, the question whether the world is or is not eternal is a philosophical question to which reason cannot find the answer. Both Greek and Islamic philosophers made the mistake of inferring that it is eternal, but the Christian learns from Scripture that this answer is false. He could know it no other way than by revelation. But having received the true answer, the Christian perceives that the alleged arguments for the eternity of the world are not sound. Thus, the *Summa contra gentiles,* while mainly theological, is also a contribution toward Christian philosophy.

The reader, therefore, must be on guard against the popular notion that, for Thomas, whatever rests on reason is philosophy, and whatever rests on authority is theology. He must also disabuse himself of any notion that Thomas was more certain of the truths of reason than he was of the truths of revelation, and that he conceived it as the task of the theologian to justify revelation in terms of reason. Thomas had a moderately high opinion of man's reason, and he had an unlimited belief in the complete rationality of the universe. But these assumptions, particularly the last one, partake of the nature of religious faith, whether or not the faith confides in any authority. Actually, Aristotle and his Moslem interpreters held the same assumptions without connecting them with the God of revelation. Thomas took the further step of identifying the Intelligence which made the world with the God of the Bible. He concluded from this that reason and revelation cannot conflict, and that if reason seems to lead to conclusions contrary to those of revealed truth, some error is present in the use of reason. What private doubts Thomas may have entertained will never be known, but it seems probable that those are correct who say that, for Thomas, the question was not whether faith is compatible with what we know by reason, but whether reason is compatible with what we know by faith.

In this connection, the manner in which Thomas uses the proofs for the existence of God is instructive. We might have expected to find the Christian philosopher exerting himself at this point, bringing all his resources to bear upon the proof that God exists. The least he could do would be to distinguish between Aristotle's Unmoved Mover, who was supposed to determine the motions of the uncreated universe by the sheer force of its attraction for rational creatures, and the God of Moses, who gives existence to every creature and sustains it by His will and power. As a matter of fact, Thomas did nothing more than repeat, with careful analysis, the proofs which lay at hand in Aristotle and in the Arabian commentators. The explanation lies in the distinction Thomas makes between essence and existence and in his contention that only the existence of God is demonstrable. The proofs, then, as he understands them, tell us only that nature presupposes the existence of a being which is perfect in precisely those respects in which nature is imperfect. At this point, faith steps forward and joins hands with reason, saying, "This is the one we call God." Similarly, throughout Books One to Three, Thomas follows reason as far as it appears to him to lead; then, characteristically, he concludes each chapter with a Scriptural quotation or statement of faith from one of the doctors of the Church. In contrast, the procedure of Book Four is to cite the authorities at the beginning only afterwards and to adduce the reasons, to clarify meaning, and to answer objections.

Aquinas's theology, in this way, maintains a balance between faith and reason. The Platonic philosophy which the earlier Middle Ages took from Augustine saw no necessity to limit the claims of reason. Anselm (c.1033-1109), for example, who stood in that tradition, believed that reason can penetrate even the highest mysteries of faith, such as the necessity for the Incarnation and for the atonement. His celebrated ontological proof of the existence of God rested on the assumption that man's knowledge of God is implicit in the knowledge of the creature. But in the thirteenth century that tradition was challenged. That age saw great advances in many fields of knowledge, stimulated in large part by the recovery of Greek philosophical and scientific writings, with their Arabic commentaries and glosses. For the Church, the choice was either to resist the new learning or somehow to accommodate it. Inevitably, many saw no possibility other than open conflict. Some eagerly embraced the doctrine of the two-fold truth, which was connected with the name of Averroës; namely, that reason and revelation are irreconcilable, and that the latter, although necessary for the ignorant masses, has no value for the learned. Others, identifying Aristotelianism with pagan thought, took their stand firmly on faith and minimized the validity of reason. Thomas, together with his teacher Albertus Magnus (c.1200-1280), sought a middle ground. Both Thomas and Albertus Magnus affirmed that reason supports faith, but they claimed that the earlier tradition had been mistaken in supposing that reason can penetrate the mysteries of the divine being and of man's salvation. Thomas wrote voluminous commentaries on Aristotle's works nearly as rapidly as they were translated into Latin. Albertus was especially interested in the new sciences of nature. The Christian, these men maintained, had cause only for rejoicing at the new frontiers which had been opened to the Christian world, nor need faith suffer at any point. On the contrary, the more we know about the nature of things, they argued, the more we see the truth of God's revelation; and, in particular, the more exactly we understand the nature of man, including the limits of his understanding, the more clearly we see the inability of man's unaided reason to come to ultimate truth and to the blessedness which depends on possessing that truth.

Although Thomas departs from the traditional Augustinian position when he denies that the mysteries of the faith are fathomable by reason, he avoids going to the opposite extreme of maintaining that there is complete disparity between our reason and God's hidden essence. Following Aristotle, he maintains that human knowledge is dependent upon the senses; we arrive at intelligible truths only by abstraction from our sensible experience of the material world. For this reason, we cannot directly apprehend the divine essence. But indirectly, through what we know about nature, we can come to some knowledge of God. What we must remember is that there is a gradation of being and a dependence of the lower upon the higher, such that something of the perfection of the higher must be discernible in the lower. Thus, what we know about the world does not hold true of God exactly, but a certain proportionality between the creature and the Creator makes it possible for us to apply our intelligible notions to God indirectly, by way of analogy. In this way we can speak with some confidence of God's intellect, His will, His life, His love, His blessedness.

In Book One, where he discusses the nature of God, Thomas rarely clashes head-on with his infidel opponents. Important differences in principle are involved, but they are not the broad issues of popular controversy. These latter issues appear when, in Book Two, the discussion turns to the subject of creation, and Thomas, in defense of the Christian faith, is obliged to uphold the doctrine that God created the world out of nothing, that He created it freely, and that He created it at a particular point in time. The groundwork for Thomas's replies has, of course, been laid in Book One. Since, as he shows there, God alone is self-existent, the creature must depend entirely upon His will and power. Moreover, since there is nothing outside Himself for Him to consider, it follows that God's will is determined only by His knowledge of Himself and is therefore free. As to the world's having a beginning, there is, Thomas asserts, no conclusive evidence on either side, and hence the matter can be decided only on the basis of Scripture.

Another controversial issue between the Christians and the Moslems concerns the nature of the human soul and its relation to the body. Here Thomas takes issue with Plato, as well as with Averroës. Plato had maintained that the intellect is related to the body simply as mover. Averroës, who professed to follow Aristotle, maintained that there is one intellect which enlightens all men, but that it is united to no man's body. Thomas musters a great display of learning in favor of what he considers Aristotle's view; namely, that each man's intellect is his own, and that it is united to his body not accidentally, as mover, but essentially, as its entelechy or form.

Book Three is a consideration of the world, and especially of man, this time in relation to God as final cause. No vigorous polemics are found here, but numerous perennial topics are discussed, among them the nature of evil, man's felicity (whether it consists in willing or knowing), man's present incapacity for happiness, the problem of divine foreknowledge and the efficacy of second causes (including man's will), the laws of nature and the moral law, sin and its rewards, and the necessity for grace if man is to reach the end for which he was created. This part of the work corresponds to the *Purgatory* of Dante's *Divine Comedy*. It is a kind of *preparatio evangelica*. But Thomas was careful to state that none of the demonstrations of the first three books can be expected to convert men to Christianity. At best they show that in a world where there is so much evidence of divine wisdom and love, it is reasonable to ask whether God will not somewhere have raised man from his deeply unsatisfactory condition. Like Virgil in the *Purgatory,* Reason leads man up the mountain of human striving, but it cannot take him past the gates into Paradise.

Book Four is written from the perspective of one who stands beyond the gateway which divides reason and revelation. Reason is henceforth employed for the purpose of making revelation more comprehensible and of defending revealed truths against the attacks of pagans and heretics. Thomas explains that this book is written only for the consolation and edification of believers, not with a view to convincing unbelievers. On the contrary, he has a word of reproof for over-zealous protagonists who, by attempting to demonstrate things that are beyond reason, actually confirm men in their unbelief by leading them to suppose that Christians rest their faith on bad reasoning.

Thomas does not permit us to confuse reason and faith. Reason and faith are separate ways of knowing God, each disclosing something of Him that is not given by the other. Faith, of course, is the higher of the two, inasmuch as it enables man to lay hold of the means by which the soul is prepared for the perfect vision of God in the life to come—a vision which is another way of knowing God, distinct alike from faith and reason. But although faith is necessary to the beatific vision, it is not sufficient, except in conjunction with the other virtues. The recipient of grace is enabled to turn to God, but the turning must be his own, as well as the progress which he makes toward sanctification. To this end, reason is of the utmost importance—not merely the practical reason by which man is enabled to know God's law, but also the theoretical reason by which he contemplates God's truth. The latter is an incentive to godly living, because it moves the soul to admiration and reverence. But, in addition, it is its own reward, for contemplation of the divine is the highest good. According to Thomas, each being tends toward that which perfects it, and that which perfects human intellect is divine truth.

THE JOURNEY OF THE MIND TO GOD

Author: Saint Bonaventura (Giovanni di Fidanza, 1221-1274)
Type of work: Mystical theology
First transcribed: 1259

Principal Ideas Advanced

The soul of man can ascend to a mystical vision of God by passing through six stages in which it beholds God outside itself, through His traces and in His traces; within itself, by His image and in His image; and above itself, by contemplating God's essential traits and by reflecting on the Trinity.

By sense and imagination, reason and intellect, intelligence and the illumination of conscience, and by the aid of divine grace, the soul can at last pass over into God through the transports of contemplation.

The Journey of the Mind to God (*Itinerarium mentis ad Deum*) is the work of Saint Bonaventura, the Seraphic Doctor of the thirteenth century. Although the book is very short, it contains a system of Christian metaphysics, illustrates a philosophical method, and is representative of the Christian experience which culminates in a mystic vision of God.

The soul ascends to God by passing through a series of stages or steps. Since beatitude, the fruition of the highest good, is above us, it can be attained only if our hearts are elevated by a higher power. Divine help comes to those who seek it humbly in prayer.

The human mind has three aspects; the first, animality or sensuality, refers to the external body; the second, spirit, looks inward into itself; the third, mind, looks above itself. Since each of these aspects is twofold, there are six stages of the soul's powers, implanted in us by nature, by which we pass through the six stages of ascension into God. We mount from the depths to the heights, from the external to the internal, from the temporal to the eternal, through the powers of sense, imagination, reason, intellect, intelligence, and the illumination of conscience (synteresis).

Contemplation is unattainable without meditation, holy conversation, and devout prayer. Man was created for contemplation, but because of his sin he sits in the shadows and does not see the light of Heaven unless he is reformed by divine regenerating grace, imparted through Jesus Christ, the Word Incarnate. The first rung in the ladder by which we mount up to God is attained by reference to the whole sensible world, which as a mirror reflects the Creator's supreme power, wisdom, and benevolence.

The bodily senses serve the person who in contemplation sees things in themselves, in weight, number, and measure. From these traces of God's power one can rise to an understanding of the power, wisdom, and immense goodness of God as a living, understanding, spiritual, incorruptible, and immutable being. The senses enable the believer to consider the world in such a way that he discovers its origin, course, and terminus; they serve the rational inquirer by enabling him to discern the potential excellence of things.

The second stage of the ascent of the soul involves contemplation of God not only *through* sensible things but also *in* sensible things, to the degree that God is in them by essence, potency, and presence. God can be contemplated in all things which enter our minds through the bodily senses.

The doors of the five senses permit this world, the macrocosm, to enter the soul, the microcosm. Objects in the sensible world are shadows, echoes, and pictures—the traces and reflections of God. Sensible things are exemplifications set before our minds; through sensible things, which we see, we may be carried to the intelligibles, the divine ideas, which we do not see. The invisible things of God are signified by whatever inhabits the sensible world, because God is the origin, exemplar, and end of all created things; every effect is the sign of its cause, and the exemplification is the sign of its divine exemplar.

From the contemplation of God in and through his traces we have recourse in the third stage to the mirror of our mind, where the divine image shines. Here with the eye of reason, we become aware of a threefold power of the soul, the contemplation of which leads us to behold the image of the blessed Trinity.

The first power of the soul known to reason, that of memory, enables us to retain and to represent things present, past, and future, things corporeal and temporal, things simple and eternal. Since memory makes possible the retention of temporal things, it is the image of eternity whose indivisible present extends to all time. Memory is not formed solely from without by images (phantasms), but also from within by receiving simple forms from above and retaining them in itself. From its retention of the eternal principles and axioms of the sciences, memory has an undying light present to itself by which it remembers unchangeable truths. The operations of memory thus disclose that the soul itself is the image of God.

The second power of the soul known to reason is that of the intellect, which is concerned with the meanings of terms, with propositions, and with inferences. Since our intellect is conjoined with eternal truth, it knows with certainty under the guidance of the divine light.

The third power of the soul that reason knows is the operation of will found in deliberation, judgment, and desire. When we deliberate as to what is better, we can do so solely by reference to the best, so that the idea of the highest good is involved. Our deliberative faculty in judging involves an appeal to divine laws, and our desire for happiness is not fulfilled unless we attain the best and ultimate end.

The soul is thus so close to God that

memory leads in its operations to eternity; intelligence leads to truth; and the power of will leads to the highest goodness. Memory, intelligence, and will are consubstantial, coequal, and coeval. Thus, the mind, when it considers itself, rises through itself as through a mirror to the contemplation of God as the Father, Word, and Love; the Triune God; three persons coeternal, coequal, and consubstantial —one God.

The fourth level of contemplation of God as the First Principle is found within ourselves. By turning away from the sensible world, the mind can return to itself as to the image of God. It is, however, impossible for a fallen creature to enter into himself in order to delight in the Lord in Himself, unless he loves and has faith in the Mediator between God and man, Jesus Christ.

Since man is a fallen creature, the reflection of God in the image of the mind must be reformed, repaired by the gifts of grace, by the theological virtues of faith, hope, and love. By faith the soul recovers spiritual hearing and vision—hearing to receive the lessons of Christ, vision to behold the splendor of His light. The soul is illuminated by hope and perfected by love. The spirit is thus able, through its conformity, to mount upward to the heavenly Jerusalem.

By the reformation of the image through the theological virtues and through the delights of the spiritual senses, our soul is made hierarchical; that is, purged, perfected, and illuminated. God is then seen to be all in all through the contemplation of Him in the minds in which He dwells.

Man's mind, inhabited by the divine wisdom, is thus made the temple of the Holy Spirit, without whom no man can know the secrets of God.

God is contemplated not only outside us and within us, but also above us. He is seen outside us through His traces and inside us through His image. He is seen above us through His light.

There are two ways by which contemplation of the invisible and eternal things of God is possible. The first way provides the fifth stage in the soul's ascent; it involves contemplation of God's *essential attributes*. The divine unity is reflected in its primary name, which is *Being*. To contemplate the invisible traits of God insofar as they belong to the unity of His essence, the soul must concentrate on Being itself. When Being is contemplated with the illumination of eternal light, the mind understands that Being itself cannot be derivative. Lacking nonbeing, Being-itself has no beginning or end; it is eternal, most simple, most actual, most perfect, and one to the highest degree.

Since Being is most pure and absolute, that which is Being is simply first and last; Being, therefore, is the final cause and origin of all. Because Being is eternal and most present, it encompasses and penetrates all duration. Because it is most simple and greatest, Being is entirely within and entirely without all things; therefore, it resides in an intelligible sphere whose center is everywhere and whose circumference is nowhere. Because Being is most actual and immutable, it causes the universe to move. Because it is most perfect and immense, Being is within all, though it is not included in all; it is beyond all, but it is not excluded from all; it is above all, but it is not transported beyond all; it is below all, and yet it is not beneath all. Because Being is most highly one and all-inclusive, it is all in all, even though all things are many and it is only one. Being contains all power, all exemplary causality, and all communicability. It is omnipotent, omniscient, and all-good; from it and by it and in it are all things. To see this perfectly is to be blessed.

The second way the soul looks above itself to contemplate the invisible and eternal things of God, the sixth stage, is by reflection upon the most blessed Trinity, upon the properties of the persons of God. In the fifth stage of contemplation, Being is seen as the root and name of the vision of the essential traits of the Deity; in the sixth stage, it is the name *Good* which is the principal foundation of the contemplation of the divine emanations of the Trinity.

Since the Good is self-diffusive, the highest Good is the most self-diffusive. The greatest diffusion exists where it is actual, intrinsic, substantial, hypostatic, natural, voluntary, and perfect. In the highest Good there is a production which is actual and consubstantial, a hypostasis as noble as the producer. The Father, Son, and Holy Spirit constitute the greatest Good, the greatest diffusion. By contemplating the purity of goodness, the soul may see by the highest communicability of the Good that a Trinity of Father, Son, and Holy Spirit is necessary.

It is necessary that there be in the Trinity the greatest communicability and, therefore, the greatest consubstantiality, the greatest configurability, and the greatest coequality, coeternity, and cointimacy.

When we contemplate the Goodness that excells all goodness, the properties of the Trinity are manifest. We behold in wonder a plurality of hypostases, a unity in essence and in form, in dignity, in eternity, in existence and illimitability. For we wonder not only at the essential and personal traits of God in themselves, but on the sixth stage of our ascent we behold the miraculous union of God and man in the unity of Christ's person, the Eternal joined with temporal man. The most simple is here joined with the most composite. Communicability exists with individuality, consubstantiality with plurality, configurability with personality, coeternity with production, and cointimacy with mission—for the Son was sent by the Father, and the Holy Spirit by both.

The stages of the soul's ascent to God, as described by Bonaventura, reach their perfection on the sixth level when man comes to the point of beholding in the first and highest principle and the Mediator of God and men, Jesus Christ, those properties of which the likeness cannot in any wise be found in creatures and which exceed all the insight of the human intellect. Here the soul passes over into God through elevation. If this passage of the soul is perfect, all intellectual operations are abandoned, and the whole height of our affection is transferred and transformed into God in a mystical and secret manner, which no man knows unless he has received this mystic wisdom through the revealing power of the Holy Spirit.

SUMMA THEOLOGICA

Author: Saint Thomas Aquinas (c.1225-1274)
Type of work: Scholastic theology
First transcribed: c.1265-1274

Principal Ideas Advanced

Man's knowledge is mediated through the senses; whatever knowledge man has of divine things must be by inference from knowledge of material things.

God is the Supremely Real, who in knowing Himself knows all truth, and in willing Himself wills all good.

Such truths as are contained in the doctrines of the Trinity, the Incarnation, and the Resurrection must be known through revelation.

The world process is a double movement, flowing out from and returning to God, who is Himself unmoved.

Christianity is the complement of civilaztion, revelation an extension of reason, and grace the perfection of creation.

Thomas Aquinas's *Summa theologica* is a theological omnibus, written for the beginning student rather than for the accomplished scholar. It is a veritable "question box," in which unprofitable puzzlers take their place alongside the set questions of theological instruction. Because it is an introductory work, controversial matters are not pursued to the length they are in other of Thomas's writings. Nevertheless, partly because it was written after his various commentaries and earlier summas when Thomas was at the height of his powers, and partly because an intelligent "abridgment" of an increasingly unwieldy mass of theological material was overdue, the *Summa theologica* soon achieved authoritative standing. Modern readers will find many questions discussed which have ceased to be live issues since the thirteenth century, but they will also find classic discussions of such perennial questions as divine providence, human freedom and responsibility, and the moral law.

In the history of systematic theology, the *Summa theologica* would be a landmark if for no other reason than for the order it imposes on its material. Prior to its appearance, theological handbooks had followed the scheme of Peter Lombard's *Sententiarum libri quatuor* (c.1150), even when they were not directly commenting on that text. Thomas, for the first time, divides and orders the subject according to logical principles. Part One, theology proper, treats of the divine essence, of the Trinity, and of creation and providence. Part Two, moral theology, comprises two divisions, each as extensive as either of the other parts. The first (*prima secundae*) deals with the foundations of ethics; the second (*secunda secundae*) is an elaborate treatise on the virtues and the vices. Part Three, Christology, deals with the person and work of Christ, with the sacraments, and with the future life. The last part of the discussion of the sacraments and the whole of that on the future life was compiled after

Thomas's death by his disciples, and is known as the *Supplement.*

The outline of the *Summa theologica,* which is anticipated in the slightly earlier *Summa contra gentiles,* is an outgrowth of Thomas's efforts to give theology its rightful place among the sciences. The thirteenth century saw the rise of the first European universities, with separate faculties of law, medicine, arts, and philosophy. It is no mere chance that this departmentalization of knowledge coincided with Europe's rediscovery of Aristotle, who not only left masterful treatises on a wide variety of subjects, but also argued on principle that each subject requires to be treated in its own way. For example, Aristotle distinguished between the theoretical science of physics and the practical science of ethics; above both of these, he placed philosophy, which he also called theology. Thomas Aquinas, who accepted the new outlook and willingly appropriated Aristotle's conception of science, believed that theology needed to set its house in order. The boundaries between philosophy and theology needed to be more clearly drawn, with principles laid down which should govern the relations between reason and faith.

Having devoted many volumes to commenting on Aristotle's work, Thomas yielded to none in his technical mastery of the new philosophy. But *Summa theologica* is a theological work, and philosophy is here put at the service of Christian doctrine. An important instance is the use Thomas makes of Aristotle's theory of knowledge. According to the Augustinian view, which had prevailed in earlier scholasticism, man's intellect is able, by divine illumination, to possess immediate knowledge of supernatural reality. Not so, says Thomas, following Aristotle: man's knowledge, in this life, is always mediated through the senses, and whatever knowledge he has of divine things must be by inference from or by analogy with his knowledge of material things. It follows that what man can know about God by reason alone is strictly limited. He can know, as Aristotle showed, that there must exist a First Cause over nature, and he can know, by the "negative way" of abstracting from the imperfections of the creatures, something of the perfections of the Creator; but he cannot know anything of God's internal life, nor His purposes toward creation. Such truths as are contained in the doctrines of the Trinity, the Incarnation, and the Resurrection could not be known if God had not revealed them. Nevertheless, according to Thomas, once these truths have been revealed, reason can make them intelligible. Thomas considered himself a faithful Augustinian in all matters of essential Christian truth. The new task, as he saw it, was to preserve Augustinian theology by bringing it into its proper relation to the rest of human knowledge. For this purpose, it was necessary to subject Christian wisdom itself to the discipline of "the Philosopher" (as Thomas called Aristotle).

Thomas's devotion to Aristotle, however, did not affect his even more fundamental commitment to the Neoplatonic world view, transmitted to Western thought partly through Augustine, and partly by Islamic and Jewish philosophers, but most directly, as far as Thomas is concerned, through the writings of the sixth century Greek theologian who wrote under the name of Dionysius the Areopagite, who was in Thomas's day believed to be the convert of Paul mentioned in The Acts of the Apostles. Like the Neoplatonists (and Aristotle too, for that matter) Thomas saw everything as having its source and destiny in God. His theology is not the least anthropocentric, nor geocentric, nor even Christocentric. It is theocentric, in the fullest sense of the word. We are to study, says Thomas at the beginning of the *Summa,* God as he is in himself, God as the beginning of things, and God as the end toward which all things move. Christ is introduced as "the way to God." This, in Thomas's view, is the sum of theology.

Again, God, in Thomas's system, bears a much closer resemblance to the "Form of Forms" in Aristotle's philosophy, or to the One of Neoplatonism, than to the God of the Bible. God is the Supremely Real, who in knowing Himself knows all truth, and in willing Himself wills all good. In Aristotelian fashion, Thomas explains God's will as the natural inclination of God's intellect toward the Reality which it contemplates; and with Augustine he equates these principles with the three Persons of the Trinity.

In his doctrine of creation, Thomas modifies what, for the Neoplatonists, is essentially a necessitarian scheme, by insisting on the freedom of God's will. Nonetheless he explains creation much as the Neoplatonists did by urging that it was the perfection of God's goodness which made him want to increase the good by creating a counterpart to himself, a sort of "moving image of eternity" (as Plato put it), which will be as perfect as divine wisdom can devise. Called into being out of nothing, the created world will not have the simplicity and unity that belongs to the Creator; rather, its order will be that of an organism in which the whole is achieved by means of the differentiation of its parts. Accordingly, within creation there will be degrees of perfection and imperfection depending on the distance by which the creature is removed from the divine similitude. At the one extreme will be pure angelic intelligence; at the other, inert matter. Critically situated on the border between matter and intelligence is man, through whose composite being the whole world is in a manner represented.

It is essential to Thomas's conception of God that the creation involves no alteration or diminution of the divine Being, and that the eternal tranquillity of the divine life is not disturbed by the rebellion and sufferings, or by the redemption and glorification of man. In his terminology, the divine activity toward the world is a real relation as far as the creature is concerned, but ideal only (*secundum rationem tantum*) as far as God is concerned. Human history is the working out on the plane of man's existence of the world plan which God saw would bring the most good into being. That there must be sin and suffering, that men must endure the penalty of eternal damnation, that Christ must die in order that any might merit eternal blessedness—all these were included. How else could divine mercy and justice, wisdom and love be made fully known? Thomas does not hold back from the full Augustinian doctrine of predestination. God's foreknowledge and His election are presupposed in everything that takes place; specifically, it is by His decree that some receive grace and others are passed by.

Thomas's doctrine of grace is closely

connected with his Aristotelian view of human nature. According to this view, the perfection of any rational being comes only with the full knowledge of God; but man, because his knowledge is mediated through the senses, is not able by nature to behold God. Hence, when God created man, He supplemented man's natural powers with a supernatural gift of righteousness and holiness. Had our first parents continued to obey God, they need never have died but, after a time, would have been translated to eternal bliss. When they disobeyed, they lost the supernatural gift without which no true happiness is possible to man; but in addition, they brought upon themselves the stain of guilt, liability to punishment, and the corruption of their natures. This is the sad and guilty condition of the race which God visits with the gift of salvation. First, it is necessary that the sinner's will be rehabilitated by an infusion of grace into the soul, so that he may seek after God, abandon his evil ways, and receive the remission of his guilt. Faith is thus created in him, followed by the other virtues which then make it possible for him to pursue the way of salvation provided in Christ and made available through the instrumentality of the sacraments.

It is worth noting that Thomas considers God's grace and man's justification in the second part of the *Summa,* instead of after his discussion of the person and work of Christ, where the Reformers are accustomed to consider it. He treats of grace, together with law, as one of the principles or dispositions by which God in His providence leads mankind to beatitude, and he follows it with his treatise on the virtues: first, the theological virtues (faith, hope, and love); second, the cardinal virtues (prudence, justice, courage, and temperance). In this way, Thomas succeeds in emphasizing the relevance of grace to man's moral and civil life, but at the cost of making the work of Christ seem almost an afterthought. Luther's concern to link justification directly to the work of Christ arose out of a desire to avoid the latter consequence, although some might charge that he lost precisely the advantage that Thomas gains.

In his treatment of the person and work of Christ, Thomas follows the general path outlined by St. Anselm of Canterbury (c.1033-1109) in his book, *Cur Deus homo* (*Why God Became Man*); but, where Anselm had sought to demonstrate the necessity of God's Incarnation and passion, Thomas is content to show that the plan which God adopted is in accord with the divine nature and the way most suitable to our human situation. Prominent among the reasons he brings forward is that the infinite majesty of Christ's divine person and the sinlessness of His humanity makes His death especially appropriate as a recompense for our guilt. Other reasons emphasize the utility to man, limited as he is to sensible evidences, of having the Word of God made flesh for strengthening his faith and instructing him in virtue. Thomas is careful to explain that the coming of the Son and of the Holy Spirit into the world for man's salvation does not introduce mutability into the Eternal Godhead, since, like creation, Christ's presence is simply a manifestation in the world of divine wisdom and power. Thus, the union of a human nature to the person of the eternal Son does not alter the divine nature; but within the universe it makes every difference that the Son of Mary is effectively the Second Person of the Godhead. So with the Holy Spirit, who takes men's hearts for His temple: the power of God's Spirit works in a new way in the elect, restoring and enabling their wills; yet He does so without Himself undergoing any change.

In his doctrine of the sacraments Thomas stresses the point that the sacraments do not merely signify holy things; they are also instruments by which the benefits of Christ's passion are made effective in the lives of men for their sanctification unto eternal life. That divine grace should be ministered through corporeal signs is especially suitable because, as we have seen, man's thought and activity are by nature geared to sensible objects, but especially because, in his fallen condition, man is abnormally under the domination of material things. Thomas holds that the effective power of grace is contained in the sacraments themselves, if they are performed according to the intention of the Church; grace does not depend either upon the mind of the priest or upon the intention of the recipient, notably in the case of infant baptism; but mature persons of sound mind must will to receive the grace of Christ if the sacrament is to be effective in them.

Thomas's achievement is significant in that it effected synthesis of the Christian doctrine of salvation with a world view which owes its origins to non-Christian thinkers. The legitimacy of this kind of undertaking has been questioned repeatedly in the history of the Church. Is there any continuity between Christ and the world? Thomas, as we have seen, gives the affirmative answer. Christianity is continuous with creation; revelation is a supplement to reason; redemption is a moment in the universal drama; Christ is the center of world history; and the Church is not so much a challenge to civilization as its complement. Thomas is favorably disposed toward civilization wherever he finds it. The ancient Greeks and Romans, with no other resources at their disposal than those which make up man's natural endowment, rose to admirable heights. So did the Jews and the Arabs, with their partial and marred revelation. But, if non-Christians have achieved so much in science, art, law, and philosophy, how much more ought Christians to achieve under the economy of grace! There can, and should, be a Christian philosophy, a Christian art, a Christian morality, all built upon broadly human foundations, but corrected at some points and extended at others in virtue of the supernatural light of revelation.

SERMONS AND TREATISES

Author: Johannes Eckhart (c.1260-c.1327)
Type of work: Mystical theology
First transcribed: c.1300-1327

PRINCIPAL IDEAS ADVANCED

Union with God, interpreted at times as intimate communion of two selves, but more often as complete ontological fusion of being, is asserted as the highest goal of man's life.

The path to God, beginning with a movement from the external to the inner world, and ascending by degrees to its goal of union, is proclaimed.

The eternal birth, or birth of God, or God's Son in the soul, which is the goal of life, produces as by-products many good works as well as a new and altogether affirmative sense of human worth or dignity.

Despite the acknowledged significance of Meister Eckhart's writings, questions and disagreements hamper our study of him and his work. For this, Eckhart himself is in part responsible, for he regarded himself as a popular teacher and preacher rather than a writer. Thus, the *Treatises,* which include *Talks of Instruction, The Aristocrat,* and his *Defense,* appear to have been addressed to specific situations which have long since perished. His powerful and popular sermons may well have been delivered from notes rather than manuscript, thus raising unanswerable questions as to what he actually said and how much of the writing attributed to him is actually his.

A few facts concerning his life have been established. Johannes Eckhart was born at Hochheim near Gotha about 1260, the son of a steward in a noble's castle. As a youth he entered the Dominican Order and attended school at Cologne. He was made prior of his order at Erfurt, and then provincial vicar of his order in Thuringia. The *Talks of Instruction* appear to come from this early period. He seems also to have studied and preached at the College of Paris around the year 1300. Returning to Germany, he rose to higher posts in the Dominican Order. He was in Paris again from 1311 to 1314. Returning home, he gained a wide reputation as a popular preacher and teacher, first in Strasburg and then in Cologne. His sermons seem to come from this period of his life.

From 1321 to his death he was embroiled in charges of heresy. Popular mystical movements were spreading in Germany at this time, to the great distaste of Heinrich von Virneberg, archbishop of Cologne. In 1325 a charge of heresy was made against Eckhart, but he was formally cleared, perhaps because the investigator was also a Dominican. However, the archbishop, who was a Franciscan, persisted, and a second examination of his writings was made by two Franciscans who emerged with a formidable list of errors. Eckhart responded with his *Defense,* stating poignantly, "I am able to err, but I cannot be a heretic, since one has to do with the intellect and the other with the will." He was summoned to answer charges at the archbishop's court in Cologne early in 1327. Shortly afterward, an appeal to Rome was denied. He seems to have died soon thereafter. A papal bull of 1329 specifically refers to him as dead.

It is easy to classify Eckhart as a mystic, but less easy to give a precise and significant meaning to the term as here used. Indeed, the word *mysticism* is notorious for its elasticity of usage. The broadest reference is to religious or quasi-religious phenomena in which immediacy of knowledge is emphasized. The term *intuition* is often applied to such processes of immediate awareness or knowledge.

Other interpretations of mysticism add to this minimum definition one or more of the ideas which cluster about the term, such as the unity of man with God, experiences of ecstasy or rapture, the ascent of the soul to God, the absolute oneness of God, the idea of God as absolute or self-subsistent being, and the idea of emanation. These ideas also tend to group themselves in a historic tradition, which in the West includes such figures as Plato, Plotinus, Dionysius the Areopagite, and Scotus Erigena. Eckhart's writings show familiarity with many of these ideas, figures, and influences. It is also important to remind oneself that the whole ethos of medieval Christian thought and life was mystical in the primary sense noted above; Eckhart, like any man, was a child of his age.

Yet upon his influences Meister Eckhart placed the stamp of his own strong and intense personality and mind. His mysticism was the result of his own highly individual and deeply subjective religious life. Thus it is that as a result of Eckhart's influence, mysticism in the West has come to mean a form of inner individual experience that not only resists any logical or rational demonstration but also withstands or opposes it. Eckhart's mysticism was Eckhart's own intense, personal, and self-justifying religious vision.

It is for this reason that without seeming to renounce either one, Eckhart's mysticism moves beyond both traditional Christian religion and traditional Western philosophy. He used the terminology of traditional Christianity, and there is no reason to question his sincerity. Eckhart lived and died believing himself to be a loyal Catholic Christian. Yet upon closer inspection almost all the old traditional words received at his hands a new and altered meaning. Sometimes the altered meanings are not far from the old, but at other times, incompatibilities arise.

A similar point may be urged for Eckhart's relation to philosophic tradition. He frequently alluded to Plato and Aristotle, and he used what superficially appears to be a traditional terminology. Upon closer scrutiny, however, some or all of these terms are altered to serve as the vehicles of Eckhart's own unique intuition and message.

Whether one begins his journey into mystical theology by studying self or God does not matter, Eckhart tells us, for man and God are ultimately aspects of a single seamless unity.

It is important to point out that Eckhart nowhere taught a simple equation between deity and any actual or empirical human soul, or indeed between deity and all human souls or all being. For Eckhart there is, to be sure, from the beginning "a blood relationship" between man and God; we are His children, and it is our proper destiny to realize or fulfill this relation. In another metaphor, according to Eckhart's teaching, man rises by degrees to a relation sometimes characterized as intimate communion with God, but more often described as one in which all distinctions are left behind in the fullness of ontological union.

The beginning of this path to God

consists in coming to realize the clear and sharp difference between inner and outer world. Man must leave the world of things and creatures behind and enter the inner castle of the soul. He must, as Eckhart wrote, get beyond time and space. Just as inwardness is good, so conversely, concern with externalities or creatures is evil or sinful.

In many ways Eckhart's inwardness recalls that of Augustine and other previous mystics. Yet Eckhart lacks the guidance which Augustine received from Christian orthodoxy. Where Augustine in the inner recesses of his soul heard God speaking to him in Christian or Biblical tones, Eckhart found a darkness (or, paradoxically, he sometimes says a light) in which all distinctions are lost in total unity. So it is that Eckhart, along with many mystics before and since, identified God with this inward reality.

To achieve this inwardness man must have a pure heart, the complete absence of ulterior motivation. One must want God solely for God's sake, and not for any ulterior reason. The self or mind so conceived is asserted to be free. Indeed, by freedom of mind or self Eckhart meant precisely the capacity to shake oneself free of all attachment to finite things. Such a process is alternatively characterized as disinterestedness, as a losing of the self, and as a reducing of the self to nothingness. For Eckhart the virtue of humility, frequently recommended to his hearers, carried a similar meaning. Preaching from Biblical texts which command man to conform his will to the divine will, Meister Eckhart bade his hearers to lose themselves by getting beyond all finite things whatsoever. Perfection he defined not as perfect conformity to the will of God, but as emancipation from all finitude.

As a further step along this path, Eckhart called his followers to transcend the inner divisions or agents of the soul, thus realizing the soul's inner unity. The soul, he said quoting Aristotle, is "between one and two." By this course of introspection he sought to make it one. So it is that the mind or soul, emptied of detailed contents, achieves an inward autonomy which Eckhart never tired of calling the state of the spiritual aristocrat. It is a state of contemplative bliss beyond all motion and desire. In company with mystics of all times and places, Eckhart made it clear that this state must be directly experienced to be known. It grew directly out of his own experience, and the goal of the *Sermons* is to communicate it to his hearers. In this connection, it must be noted that there is in Eckhart not a trace of bizarre and aberrant emotionalism, which has been mysticism's frequent accompaniment.

The path of the soul to God has necessarily been intimated in this sketch of the soul's nature. While he spoke in detail of this path, or this relation, Eckhart had no unified or systematic formulation; he used, rather, a variety of metaphorical suggestions. His writings have at least one reference to six stages of ascent of the soul to God, by analogy with the growth of the human soul from infancy through childhood to a maturity in which he is at peace with himself and the world, and thence onward to a final and sixth stage in which he is transformed "in the divine eternal nature, having full perfection." He spoke analogously of three kinds of knowledge, sensual, intellectual, and aristocratic or mystical, in which "the soul communes with God face to face as he is." The intellect is described as that which in unity and vision sees "beyond the idea of God and truth until it reaches the *in principio*, the beginning of beginning, the origin or source of all goodness and truth."

By far the most frequent metaphor of Eckhart for the relation of the soul to God is that of birth—the eternal birth, the birth of God, or the Son in the soul. His exposition of the birth of the Son in the soul is an excellent illustration of Eckhart's interpretation of Biblical texts to fit his own meaning. In a Christmas sermon on the text, "Where is he that is born King of the Jews?" he asked where this birth takes place, and he responded that it takes place eternally in the essence or core of the soul. This process of eternal birth in the soul may be described as the emergence in the human mind of that awareness so greatly prized by mystics of all times and places, of unity with God. As already noted, this was sometimes interpreted by Eckhart as intimate communion, but more often, as complete ontological fusion.

To facilitate this consummation, the soul must be humble and passive to God. It must cultivate the ignorance which is beyond knowledge. It must cultivate forgetting, self-losing, and contemplating "the stillness."

Another recurring metaphor for the relation of God to man is Eckhart's repeated assertion that God pours His grace, indeed, that He pours Himself into the soul. In fact, Eckhart goes further, asserting that "God must give himself," that this pouring occurs necessarily. Such assertions make clear the similarity of Eckhart's thought to that of Plotinus, with its idea of emanation.

Like Plotinus and Plato, Eckhart uses the metaphor of light. He speaks of the sparks of God in the soul, of grace coming from God to man like the light emanating from the sun. The culminating mystical experience is also characterized as an experience of illumination and light. By these and other metaphors, Eckhart's sermons called man to the high destiny of unity with God. Repeating, but reformulating, a familiar Christian quotation, Eckhart asked, "Why did God become man? So that I might be born to be God. Yes—identically God."

Nowhere is Eckhart's ambivalent relation to the Christian tradition more apparent than in his view of the God who is the object of man's search. "God," said Meister Eckhart, "is being"—an assertion traditional enough in both Christianity and philosophy, but luxuriant in its variety of meaning. Had not Plato and Plotinus declared deity to be self-subsistent reality? Indeed, had not the Lord in Exodus replied to Moses' question regarding His name with the revealing words "I am that I am," and had not Aquinas just a generation before Eckhart brought these two meanings together in his great synthesis? So it was that Christianity asserted that God possesses in Himself the fullness and perfection of being which men as mortal creatures have only partially and unperfectly.

If it be asked how Eckhart's interpretation of absolute or supreme being departs from traditional interpretations, the answer lies in his view of the nature of Absolute Being and of the relation of this being to human or finite reality. The deity of Christianity is a personal God, while that of Meister Eckhart is an impersonal absolute unity which transcends all relations. As he specifically asserted in the title of one sermon, "Distinctions are lost in God." This distinctionless deity was apparently what Eckhart had in mind in his repeated distinction between God and Godhead. In other sermons he spoke of going beyond God to God, or beyond God to Unity. Truly, God is for Eckhart a fullness of being which surpasses our human comprehension. He, or rather It, is like a blinding or dazzling light in whose brightness all human distinctions are lost.

Eckhart's view of deity, while basically impersonal, is nonetheless affirmative in tone. As to its impersonality, in contrast to the view of man's conforming his will to God, Eckhart's view is one of impersonal contemplation of absolute reality. While there are some negative aspects of this vision, its dominant tone is affirmative. Eckhart spoke of God as darkness as well as light, sometimes of both as paradoxically juxtaposed. He repeatedly recommended humility and self-negation, and he charged his hearers to transcend the world of things. Yet on balance his vision is overwhelmingly affirmative in character. There is relatively little asceticism and no outright negation of the world's reality and significance. In style and temper Eckhart was more yea-saying than nay-saying. In contrast to the negative character of much mysticism, this affirmative temper of Eckhart's vision must be judged as, in part at least, the result of his own personality.

The practical fruits of Eckhart's view are similarly affirmative. While the goal of mystical unity is beyond all action, there are many clearly moral phases in this road to perfection. Eckhart is hostile only to those works which are prompted by ulterior motives or which beget self-righteousness. Indeed, it is justifiable to put aside contemplation in order to give food to a sick man. The spirit of Eckhart's thought is clearly one of respect for, and affirmation of, human personality.

In the case of the professional religious life, while he points out that no set of works is a sufficient or valid guarantee of perfection, he is actively hostile only to works of hypocrisy. The religious life is, again, part of the road to perfection. Here, as in the case of morality, one must keep the contemplative and active life in balance as one seeks the goal beyond. It was a bold new path that Eckhart blazed and walked. It was the result, as we have argued, of his own intense and individual subjectivity. Its impact was to be felt for centuries in the new emphasis on individualism and subjectivity. In this respect Eckhart is often spoken of as a precursor of modern times. His "God is Being" recurs from Spinoza to Hegel and Tillich. His mysticism of individual subjectivity has been a lure and a threat to religious thought ever since his time.

ORDINATIO: OXFORD COMMENTARY ON THE SENTENCES OF PETER LOMBARD

Author: Johannes Duns Scotus (c.1264-1308)
Type of work: Religious metaphysics
First transcribed: c.1302-1304

Principal Ideas Advanced

The human intellect can know God through natural reason, for knowledge of the infinite need not itself be infinite.

Since God is the first cause, the final end, and the supreme nature, He is infinite and He necessarily exists.

There is but one God, for no two Gods could both be infinitely knowing, infinitely good, and infinitely powerful.

The human intellect can know some certain truths without any special illumination.

The belief in a general resurrection of mankind cannot be demonstrated by reason; such a belief rests on faith alone.

Duns Scotus's *Ordinatio* is described by Allan Wolter, editor and translator of Scotus's *Philosophical Writings* (1962), as the subtle doctor's "most important work. . . ." The *Tract Concerning the First Principle* (*Tractatus de primo principio*), which is regarded by many scholars as Scotus's most effective statement of his natural theology, is said by Wolter to have been derived from the *Ordinatio*. The alternative title, *Oxford Commentary on the Sentences of Peter Lombard,* is perhaps the more familiar title. Wolter's edition is particularly interesting in that it contains both the original Latin and the translated passages, and it extracts from the monumental *Ordinatio* those questions concerning the nature and existence of God and the immortality of the human soul which are most likely to be of concern to Christian scholars who are interested in the development of Christian theology.

The *Ordinatio* is a final draft, checked by Scotus, of a report of Scotus's lectures at Oxford (c.1302-1304) in commentary on the *Sentences* of Peter Lombard (c.1100-1160). The work is devoted primarily to the exposition of Scotus's own views concerning the nature and existence of God.

Duns Scotus was a theologian in the Franciscan tradition; he was renowned for the extreme subtlety of his thought; hence, the descriptive name, "Doctor Subtilis." In his philosophical thinking Scotus drew heavily from the views of Aristotle and Augustine (354-430), and he placed himself in opposition to many of the ideas presented by Thomas Aquinas (1225-1274). Aquinas placed almost complete reliance on reason in his effort to know God, but Scotus argued that love and the will are more important than reason both in understanding God and in relating the soul to the divine. Scotus is important for his brilliant and early defense of the doctrine of the Immaculate Conception, the doctrine that Mary was without original sin. He is noted also for his view that God did not need to assume human form in order to save man after the Fall; according to Scotus, the Incarnation was not forced upon God, for God is eternally free.

Scotus describes metaphysics as "the transcending science," as that study which goes "beyond" (from *meta*) the "science of nature" (*physica*). Since questions concerning the existence and nature of God are questions which demand inquiry beyond the natural realm, the study of God (theology) is necessarily metaphysical. Of all the transcendental attributes or predicates, none is more fundamental or common than "being." Being is the "first object of the intellect," writes Scotus, because it has both primacy of commonness and primacy of virtuality; that is, everything either has being or belongs to that which has being.

Like Aquinas, Duns Scotus presented his theological findings in question and answer form. The present edition of the *Ordinatio* follows Scotus's discussion of metaphysics with the theologian's discussion of the question "*whether the intellect of man in this life is able to know God naturally.*" Scotus then presents arguments advanced by Aristotle to the effect that since God is not a sense object and since He is infinite, He cannot be known, and Scotus also refers to Gregory's opinion that the mind must contemplate only what is beneath God.

Introducing his argument in opposition to these claims, Scotus argues that since even negative conceptions (that is, conceptions as to what God is *not*) are meaningful only if they admit of rephrasing as positive ideas, a positive conception of God is possible if any conception is possible. The question to be considered is rephrased as follows: "Is it possible by natural means for man's intellect in the present life to have a simple concept in which concept God is grasped?"

After referring to the opinion of Henry of Ghent (d. 1293), Scotus presents his positive argument. In opposition to Henry's view that God cannot be known "through something incidental to Him," Scotus argues that any knowledge of God which is possible through consideration of some attribute must finally end with a "quidditative notion of God"; that is, with a notion of *what* it is that exhibits the attribute. In opposition to Henry's opinion that God is known in a general way only by analogy, Scotus maintains that God can also be conceived "in some concept univocal to Himself and to a creature."

Scotus then considers Henry's arguments in support of the conclusion that God can be known in a *most* general way, a *less* general way, and the *least* general way. These ideas are rejected, and Scotus argues that God is not known in His essence, that God can be known by concepts which apply to Him and not to creatures, and that God is known through intelligible species.

Returning to the claims made by Aristotle and Gregory, Scotus argues that the intellect can abstract from sense experience and in that way transcend such experience, that knowledge of the infinite need not itself be infinite, and (in opposition to Gregory) that knowledge of what is beneath God may be useful, not as a terminal object, but as suggesting some intelligible feature of the divine.

Scotus next considers the question, "Among beings does one exist which is actually infinite?" Various arguments are cited which have in common the claim that the supposition of an infinite being is either self-contradictory or incompatible with the existence of finite beings. Scotus's counter argument proceeds from a demonstration of the existence of such relative properties as primacy and causality to the conclusion that an infinite being exists since the relative properties in question can belong only to an infinite being.

The first of Scotus's conclusions in regard to the triple primacy of God is that "Among beings which can produce an effect one is simply first. . . ." Such a being cannot itself be caused, he then argues, but if such a being is not caused, it must exist "of itself." Three similar points are made in regard to the final cause, the ultimate end. Finally, the primacy of preeminence is established by the following three points: ". . . some eminent nature is simply first in perfection. . . ."; ". . . the supreme nature cannot be caused"; ". . . the supreme nature actually exists." God as the first cause, final end, and supreme nature possesses a triple primacy; such a being necessarily exists, concludes Scotus, because nothing incompatible with its existence can exist.

Scotus then argues from the relative properties of God to His absolute properties. If God is the first cause, the final end, and the supreme nature, He must be intelligent, endowed with will, and possessed of a knowledge of all things. A being capable of infinite causality, making reference to infinite knowledge, and unlimited in intelligence must be an infinite being. But it has already been established that a being which possesses triple primacy necessarily exists; therefore, God, as that being which has triple primacy and is infinite, necessarily exists.

Scotus then writes, *"I ask whether there is but one God?"* He considers a number of minor arguments advanced in support of the claim that there is more than one god, and he refers to the view that the unicity of God is to be accepted only on faith. In opposition to those who deny God's unicity (His status as the sole God), Scotus offers seven proofs, based on natural reason, of God's unicity. The proofs are based on the attribution to God of infinite intellect, infinite will, infinite goodness, infinite power, absolute infinity, necessity of existence, and omnipotence. A summary of Scotus's argument based on God's infinite intellect will indicate the subtlety of Scotus's thought: If there were two Gods, A and B, then A, as possessed of an infinite intellect, would know B perfectly. But if A does not know B's essence, A does not know B perfectly. And if A knows B's essence, the knowledge is posterior to B's essence; as posterior, A's knowledge could not be God's knowledge. Therefore, there cannot be two Gods.

Scotus asks whether the human intellect without "the special illumination of the uncreated Light" can know any "certain and unadulterated truth." Quotations from Augustine support the negative view, but Scotus argues for the positive answer by critical opposition to an opinion advanced by Henry of Ghent. Scotus claims that Henry's opinions lead to skepticism, and he rejects Henry's three points, which follow: (1) Infallible and certain knowledge cannot be abstracted from the mutable; (2) The soul, which is itself changeable, cannot be corrected by the mutable; (3) There is no way of distinguishing the true from what appears to be true. Scotus's corresponding rejoinders are as follows: (1) Not all sensible things are constantly in motion, and in any case it is possible to know immutable natures by contemplation of mutable things; (2) Although the soul is changeable in that it can move from error to truth, it need not, when in error, be corrected from the outside; the soul has the power of self-correction, particularly when it is dealing with logical matters; (3) Although the imagination may be unable, in dreams, to distinguish the true from what appears to be true, the intellect, which uses intellectual entities and not sense images, cannot suffer from this difficulty.

The question concerning the possibility of certain knowledge is answered in the affirmative by reference to the intelligible which reflects the divine intellect. Special illumination is not needed since the ideas themselves, as influenced by the divine intellect, provide assurance to the intellect of man.

The final question given in Wolter's selection from the *Ordinatio* is as follows: *"Can it be known by natural reason that there will be a general resurrection of mankind?"* Scotus, whose ability to generate rational arguments is clearly shown throughout the *Ordinatio,* reveals his intellectual honesty as he uses rational proofs in support of the conclusion that natural reason alone *cannot* support the belief in a general resurrection. He considers both *a priori* and *a posteriori* arguments for general resurrection, but he concludes that no proof is entirely satisfactory.

Scotus's discussion and rejection of *a priori* proofs begins with the Aristotelian point that the intellective soul is essential to man. It is then argued that the intellective soul is immortal, but although Scotus supposes that there is some reason for believing the soul to be immortal, he concludes that there is no way of demonstrating the truth of the immortality of the soul. Arguments advanced by Aristotle are carefully appraised, but Scotus finds them to be inadequate. The third proposition on which *a priori* proofs are built is the proposition that "the human soul will not remain outside the body forever." In criticizing this proposition, Scotus suggests that if the soul is immortal and immaterial, it is more likely that it remain outside the body than that it will rejoin the body.

Scotus notes that the desire for resurrection is a natural desire, but he does not agree with those philosophers who maintain that "A natural desire cannot be in vain" (Averroës, *Metaphysica*). He also considers the *a posteriori* argument that if virtue is to be rewarded, men must be resurrected; but he finds no natural reason for supposing that there is a ruler who works to achieve a balance of rewards and punishments. He gently suggests that "the good act is itself sufficient reward for anyone," and he quotes with approval Augustine's remark (in the *Confessions*) to the effect that inordinate desire brings its own punishment.

Scotus concludes that the belief in resurrection must be maintained by faith alone, and he refers to the view presented by Augustine (in *De trinitate*) that the belief in the immortality of the human soul is maintained not by reason but by Christ's injunction, "Do not be afraid of those who kill the body but cannot kill the soul."

Thanks is given to God for faith which "has made us most certain of those things which pertain to our end and to eternal life. . . ." With refreshing and elevating candor Scotus, the subtle doctor, concedes that there are divine truths which escape the natural reason of man. The faithful spirit of the Franciscan expresses itself in the midst of some of the most ingenious exercises of the intellect to be found in the writings of the medieval theologians.

DE MONARCHIA

Author: Dante Alighieri (1265-1321)
Type of work: Christian political philosophy
First transcribed: c.1313

Principal Ideas Advanced

The well-being of the world necessitates that mankind be ruled by a common government headed by a single Prince who is best able to actualize the whole capacity of the intellect, promote universal peace and freedom, establish justice, and rule mankind in a manner patterned after God's rule of the Universe.

The office of monarchy has rightfully been appropriated by the Roman people, for they are the most noble, were aided by miracles, were victorious over all contestants, and exercised jurisdiction over all humanity in pronouncing judgment upon Christ.

The Roman Monarch derives his power directly from God and not from the successor of Peter, the keeper of the keys of the Kingdom of Heaven.

Dante Alighieri, frequently referred to as the spokesman of the Middle Ages, exerted his influence upon the religious, philosophical, and political spheres of Western society. The emphasis of the *De monarchia* is political, but its effect upon subsequent questions of the relationship between the Church and state are indeed difficult to estimate.

The *De monarchia* is divided into three books. The first considers whether temporal monarchy is necessary for the well-being of the world; the second, whether the Romans rightfully appropriated the office of monarchy; and the third, whether the authority of the Roman monarch derives immediately from God or from some vicar of God.

In writing the *De monarchia* Dante was motivated by a love of truth and a love of his fellow-men, not by any cynical desire for personal power. By temporal monarchy, the Empire, Dante understood a single principality which extends over all peoples and has authority in all temporal matters. His work is an expression of his concern over the pretenses and failures of the

Papacy, and the book reflects the dying phases of the contest between the Roman Empire and the Papacy.

The purpose of the universal monarchy is not to promote the self-interest of the ruler, writes Dante, but to secure the well-being of those who are ruled. God makes nothing without a purpose, so that human society as a whole has an end, conformable to the proper function of the human race as a whole; namely, to actualize continually the entire capacity of the intellect, primarily in speculation, but secondarily in action. The human race can accomplish its work most freely and readily when it enjoys the calm and tranquillity of peace, for then the individual can grow perfect in wisdom and knowledge, and what modifies the individual affects humanity as a whole. The beatitude of humanity is best attained where universal peace prevails, for then the human race may fulfill its proper office.

The necessity of temporal monarchy, writes Dante, can be gainsaid by no force of reason or authority; on the contrary, it can be proven by the most powerful arguments. For when several things are ordained for one end, one must regulate or rule and the others submit to such regulation. The happiness of the individual depends upon the rule of the intellect over his other faculties, and the tranquillity of a city depends upon the direction and government of a king, but the well-being of the world requires a universal monarchy or Empire. Since the whole human race is ordered for one end, it is fitting that the leader be one, and that he be called Emperor or Monarch.

The order which is found in the parts of the human race should also be found in the human race as a whole. The individual, the family, the village, and the city are included in kingdoms, and the latter should be ordered to one Prince or Principality, to one Monarch or Monarchy.

With relation to certain parts, mankind is a whole, but with relation to a certain whole, mankind is a part; that is, in relation to particular kingdoms and nations, mankind is a whole, but in relation to the universe, mankind is a part. The several parts of humanity can correspond to the whole of humanity through the one principle only, that of submission to a single Prince. Humanity can correspond to the universe, or to its Prince, who is God, through one principle only, the submission to a single Monarch. Monarchy is necessary to the well-being of the world because the relation of kingdoms and nations to the Monarch should be patterned after the relation between humanity and God. Men are made in God's image, and God is one. God intends that everything should represent the divine likeness insofar as this is possible. Since God is a unity, writes Dante, the human race should dwell in unity, and this it does when it is subject to a single Prince, whose rule is, therefore, most in accordance with the divine intention and constitutes the best disposition of mankind. As the sons of Heaven, men ought to follow in the footprints of Heaven. The entire universe is controlled by a single mover, God; thus, the human race is best ordered when its movements are controlled by a single Prince.

A supreme judge is necessary to settle disputes, Dante adds. When strife is a possibility, there must be judgment, or imperfection could then exist without a perfecting agent. If a single Prince were not present, disputes between rulers would be interminable. The rule of the Prince is, however, not to be thought of as that of an arbitrary dictatorship. The world is ordered best when justice is pre-eminent in it. The Monarch is the person in whom justice dwells to the highest degree. The Monarch is to be free of avarice and to be filled with the love which, scorning all else, seeks God and the good of man. Love makes justice thrive. The Monarch is the universal cause of peace and well-being, and the good of men is to be loved by him above all others.

The human race is best ordered when it is most free, Dante claims; freedom is the greatest gift that God has given to men, and it is under a monarchy, not a democracy, oligarchy, or tyranny that man is most free. The aim of an upright government is liberty, that men may live for themselves, not for the sake of the ruler; the Monarch is the chief servant of all. His laws are not ordered for his own sake, but rather for the sake of the ruled. As the person best adapted for ruling, the Monarch is the best director of other man, for he is to possess the highest degree of judgment and justice and is, therefore, perfectly qualified, or especially well qualified, to rule.

What a single agent can do is better done by one than by many, Dante insists. Every superfluity is displeasing to God. Minor decisions concerning individual cities are not to issue from the Monarch directly, for the Monarch is to concern himself with general matters pertaining to all peoples, so that they may be guided to peace by a common government. That Monarchy is essential for the best disposition of mankind and for the well-being of the world is further evidenced by the fact that Christ Himself willed to be born in the fullness of time when Augustus was Monarch, during a period of unity.

The people of Rome have appropriated the office of Monarchy by right, Dante claims; since their rule is in accordance with the will of God, their rule is to be accepted. The rule of the Roman people, who have taken to themselves the office of Monarchy, is not by usurpation but by right, since the Romans are the noblest of men and thus deserve precedence before all others. The Roman Empire was aided by miracles, Dante points out, and thus it must have been favored by God. In subduing the world, the Roman people had the good of the state in view. Nature has set the Roman people apart in the world and has endowed them with the qualities suitable for universal sovereignty. God has decreed that the Empire belongs to the Romans, as is evident from their being victorious over all other contestants, whether nations or individuals. And, finally, the fact that Christ was born when He was, and that He died under Roman jurisdiction, offers conclusive evidence that the authority of the Roman Empire is just and extends over all humanity. For, if the Roman Empire did not exist by right, the sin of Adam was not punished, Christ did not suffer under a lawful judge, and His penalty was not punishment—consequences which are all obviously false.

The sole question that remains for Dante is to determine whether the authority of the Roman Monarch is derived from that of the Vicar of God, from the Church, or whether it proceeds directly from God. His answer is of consequence for subsequent developments in the relationship between Church and state.

The principle to be kept in mind in deciding this issue, writes Dante, is that God does not will what is counter to the intention of nature. The traditions of the Church, the papal decrees or Decretals, are unquestionably inferior to the Scriptures. Temporal power does not receive its existence, strength, or function from spiritual power. The latter does provide the grace which enables the temporal power to fulfill her function more perfectly. Since no vicar divine or human can be co-ordinate with the authority of God, the successor of Peter is in no way coequal with divine power, at least not in the operation of nature.

From the fact that Peter had the power to bind and to loose spiritual things, it does not follow that he has the power to bind and to loose the laws and decrees of the Empire, Dante claims. Those things that belong to the Church no one can rightly possess, unless granted them by the Church. However, the ruling temporal power does not belong to the Church. The Church has its own foundation, and the Empire has its own foundation. Christ is the foundation of the former, but human right is the foundation of the Empire. The Empire consists in the indivisibility of universal Monarchy; to apportion it would be to destroy it, and to destroy the Empire is contrary to human right. The Emperor cannot rightfully relinquish temporal jurisdiction.

Dante insists that imperial authority is not derived from ecclesiastical authority, although certain pontiffs, priests, and others, moved by their zeal for Mother Church, erroneously hold to the contrary. The Empire had power before the Church existed, and what was then nonexistent could not have been the source of the Empire's power.

The Church has received its power from God, not from nature. "The usurpation of a right does not make a right." The Church cannot give what it does not possess; what is contrary to the nature of anything cannot be a power of a thing, and the power to confer authority over the kingdom of our mortal life is contrary to the very nature of the Church. The nature of the latter is its informing principle, which is to be found in the life of Christ, comprised in His teaching and deeds. Christ disclaimed before Pilate any power of a ruling king when He said that His Kingdom was not of this world. As an exemplar of the Church, Christ had no temporal charge over His temporal kingdom.

Dante's answer, then, is that the authority of the Empire is directly derived from God who is the immediate source of its power. The Monarch of the world sustains an immediate relationship to God, the Prince of the Universe. For man alone occupies a middle place between the perishable and the imperishable, and as a mean shares the nature of the extremes. Man shares both natures and is ordained to two ends, the one perishable, the other imperishable. The first is concerned with temporal happiness; the second with life everlasting. Man attains his twofold end by diverse means: the one by moral and intellectual virtue; the other by faith, hope, and charity; the one by reason, the other by revelation. In accordance with his twofold end, man requires a twofold directive agent; the Supreme Pontiff to lead him to eternal life by means of revelation, and the Emperor to guide him to temporal happiness by means of philosophic instruction. The Monarch and the Pope are to rule independently under God.

The authority of the Monarch descends without mediation from God, the fountain of universal authority. Caesar ought to honor Peter, since human happiness is ordered to everlasting happiness, but the Monarch and the Pope have different spheres, and the Monarch has been set over the earthly sphere by God, who is alone the Ruler of all things spiritual and temporal.

THE DIVINE COMEDY

Author: Dante Alighieri (1265-1321)
Type of work: Allegorical poem
First transcribed: c.1320

Principal Ideas Advanced

Dante wakes to find himself in a dark wood, where he is confronted by a gay leopard, a savage lion, and a gaunt wolf.

Virgil becomes his guide through Hell; passing through Hell-Gate and the Vestibule (where the uncommitted spirits dwell), Virgil and Dante arrive at Limbo (where the unbaptized and the virtuous pagans wander forever), and then descend to witness the horrors of Hell: the circles of the Incontinent, the circles of the Violent, and the circles of the Deceitful.

In the frigid depths of Hell stands Satan beating his wings and, with his three mouths, devouring Judas, Brutus, and Cassius.

Reversing their direction at Satan's thigh bone (for they are then in the center of the earth), Virgil and Dante begin their ascent to the surface of the world.

Dante travels with Virgil to the top of Mount Purgatory; he then is accompanied by Beatrice through the heavenly spheres, and he finally comes into the presence of God.

Dante's title for his masterpiece was simply *Commedia,* a title chosen to indicate the triumph of God's love throughout the created universe. It was Boccaccio who, some forty years after Dante's death, spoke of the poem as "divine"—an epithet which has seemed so appropriate that it has become part of the title itself.

The poem is an allegory, as Dante himself explained to his patron, Can Grande della Scala. According to Dante, the poem has four levels: the literal, the allegorical, the moral, and the anagogical. Taken as a story, the *Divine Comedy* is an account of an imaginary pilgrimage which Dante made through Hell, up the mountain of Purgatory, and outward through the celestial spheres into the very presence of the Triune God. Taken as an allegory, it portrays the Christian's deliverance from sin and his ultimate beatitude. A scholar of encyclopedic range, the author describes his travels in terms of the best scientific learning of his day, and he enlivens his narrative with a wide range of historical and legendary personages. In effect, he has created a universal drama around the theme of man's Fall and redemption.

As the poem opens, Dante has lost his course and finds himself in a dark wood. The light of God quiets him, but his way is suddenly barred by a gay leopard, a savage lion, and a gaunt wolf (probably the symbols of incontinence, violence, and fraud). From his distress Dante is rescued by the poet Virgil, who explains that he has been sent, through the prayers of Dante's beloved Beatrice, to lead him to the gates of Paradise. Together they descend into the earth's interior, which is hollowed out like a great funnel outlined by concentric circles narrowing as they approach the earth's center. Sins of incontinence are punished in the upper circles, for such sins are regarded as less vicious than sins of violence and fraud. The uppermost circle is Limbo, where the unbaptized and the virtuous pagans reside; they experience no torment other than the sadness that attends a life without the hope of Christ. It is otherwise with the lustful, the gluttonous, the covetous, and the wrathful, who populate the next four circles; they have turned from the good to sell their souls for vanities, and thus they are condemned to be blown by the wind, to wallow in cold mud, and to roll great rocks—in various ways working out their futility and meanness. It is even worse, however, with those who, instead of merely mistaking the good, have turned with violence against it—whether in their own persons, or in the persons of their neighbors, or in the person of God: the murderers, suicides, blasphemers, and perverts. Lower still are those whose wickedness comes from abusing the highest human faculty, the understanding. These are the fraudulent and the malicious, a vast company ranging from seducers and flatterers to false friends and traitors. At the frozen bottom of Hell, visible only from his loins upward, is the monstrous figure of Satan. Dante and his guide have to climb past his shaggy figure in order to travel upwards through the other half of the earth's interior so that they may continue their journey to Purgatory.

As Dante imagines it, Purgatory is a mountain situated on an island in the watery hemisphere opposite to our own. The souls of believers do not ordinarily arrive there by traveling through Hell, but are conveyed across the sea by a heavenly boatman. Dante and Virgil see various groups which have not yet been allowed to pass through St. Peter's gate and to begin their progress up the mountain. They are persons who died in grace, but because of indolence, or neglect, failed in their lifetimes to prepare their souls for death. In fact, the gate is rarely opened, because entrance into Purgatory, as well as progress up the mountain, depends entirely upon the will of man, and perverse loves are hard to overcome.

Dante, upon entering the gate, has seven P's inscribed upon his brow—one for each of the cardinal sins (Latin: *peccata*): pride, envy, wrath, sloth, avarice, gluttony, and lust. The lower stages of the climb are the most difficult; but as he mounts, one after another of the P's is erased, and his feet move with less and less effort. The mountain is, essentially, a school in virtue. At each grade, the scholar is instructed by a series of sculptures which represent the virtue strived for and its opposite vice. For example, the proud are instructed by carvings representing the humble attitudes of the Virgin Mary, of King David, and of Emperor Trajan, and by a corresponding series representing the ruinous pride of Satan, of Saul, and of the general Holofernes. The proud themselves bear heavy stones to correct their postures; they beat themselves, and recite a version of the Lord's Prayer which magnifies the distance between God and His creatures.

Reaching the top of the mountain, Dante must bid farewell to Virgil, who, representing Reason, has brought him as far as he can come. He is welcomed to the Garden of Eden by a pageant of heavenly creatures symbolizing the Old and New Testaments and the theological virtues. There for the first time Dante beholds his beloved, Beatrice, who, as a symbol of Revelation, is to be his guide into the presence of God.

Dante's journey into Heaven begins without his being aware of it. As he and Beatrice mount with the speed of lightning, Beatrice explains to him that the native instinct of the soul draws it straightway to God as soon as every hindrance is removed. Their journey takes them through the ten spheres recognized by Ptolemaic astronomy, each of which represents a grade of spiritual achievement. The spheres this side of the sun's orbit represent respectively the blessedness of those weak in faith, in hope, and in love. The spheres of the sun and of those planets beyond it represent the blessedness of those who excelled in prudence, fortitude, justice, and temperance. Beatrice must explain to Dante that, although the absolute will of each of the Blessed is fixed towards its one true good, the conditioned will may deviate more or less. For example, the will of certain nuns was to keep their vows; but when they were forced to marry, they yielded rather than resist to death. So it happens that souls are unequal in glory, but without any being on this account discontent or desiring a higher place.

Dante visits each sphere in turn, passes through the sphere of the fixed stars, where he discourses with Peter, James, John, and Adam, and through the Primum Mobile, where dwell the angels and archangels. Dante comes at last to the Empyrean, the true Heaven of the Redeemed; and finally, in the company of St. Bernard, who replaces Beatrice as his guide, Dante is brought into the very presence of God and of Christ, where his sight undergoes alteration:

"O splendor of God through which I saw the lofty triumph of the true kingdom, give me power to tell *how* I saw it!

"There is a light up there which makes the Creator visible to that creature who, only in seeing Him, has its peace."

In the depth of the Eternal Light Dante beholds, first of all, the unitary scheme of all creation. Next, "three circles of three colors and of one dimension" appear to him, the second reflecting the first, and the third reflecting the other two. Finally, and most wonderfully of all, within the second circle there seems to be depicted "our image within itself and of its own color." The vision fades; the poet's powers fail:

"As one who in a dream sees clearly,
    and the feeling impressed remains
    afterward, although nothing else
    comes back to mind,

"So am I; for my vision disappears al-
    most wholly, and yet the sweet-
    ness caused by it is still distilled
    within my heart."

Even so bare an outline must suggest how closely Dante's allegory is interwoven with his narrative. This account cannot convey anything of the vividness of hue or richness of texture which Dante's masterly use of concrete images gives to the whole. Dante stands in the tradition of the Hebrew prophets. His vision of the Eternal does not detract from, but rather enhances his perception of things temporal. *The Inferno,* particularly, brings fresh, clear vision to bear upon the weakness, passion, and ignominy of men. We are shown the guilty in all their hatefulness, and are forbidden to sympathize with them as they languish in torment. At the same time, it is impossible for us to be indifferent to their ruin. Dante writes as one who cares.

Personal tragedies bear heavily upon him. For example, Ser Brunetto Latini (d.1294), whom he finds in the circle of the Sodomites, was once his teacher, a gentle and paternal man, who is still interested in Dante's literary progress. Their meeting is tender. Dante acknowledges his eternal gratitude to Brunetto and breathes the wish that he were yet among the living. But inevitably the older man, swept along by the fatality which attends his choice, must be off with his company in torment.

With even livelier interest, Dante follows the affairs of his native Florence, torn in civil strife and betrayed by Papal intrigue. From this center, his thought extends throughout the whole of Italy and of the Empire. He is vexed and saddened at the decay of the Church, and at the growing international anarchy, for which he can see only one remedy—that the Church shall restrict itself to matters spiritual and support the rights of the Emperor in the temporal domain. (See Dante's *De monarchia.*) So deep and abiding are Dante's convictions in these matters that he carries them to the very threshold of Eternity: there in the sphere of the Fixed Stars, Peter denounces the ruling pope, Boniface VIII, in terms which cause Beatrice to blush.

The close connection between the literal and allegorical aspects of the *Divine Comedy* is best understood if we think of the work as a stylized account of the author's own spiritual biography—a kind of confession. The interested reader should refer to Dante's earlier works, *The New Life* (c.1292), and *The Banquet* (c.1307), where he informs us of his youthful aspirations, of certain delinquencies into which he fell, and finally of his recovery through the study of philosophy. Following the conventions of courtly love, Dante makes his Beatrice the symbol of all that is good. Dying while in the bloom of youth, she left him desperate and adrift, until, as he is content to believe, she led him to philosophy in order to save him from perdition. The image of the Dark Woods and of the three beasts is transparently Dante's own condition when, in his middle years (the setting of the poem is 1300, when Dante would have been thirty-five years old), he set his face toward Heaven. Philosophy, in the person of Virgil, can do no more than bring him back to the angel whose gracious presence first lifted his thoughts toward things eternal. She reappears, therefore, as the symbol of revelation, by whom, when his soul has been freed from sin, he is to be led to his spiritual fruition. From the allegorical point of view, the punishments of Hell are a figurative account of the author's (and every Christian's) experience with temptation and sin, as the disciplines of Purgatory are quite explicitly an account of the measures by which the soul works out its salvation. Perhaps, in like manner, we are justified in concluding that the description of the beatific vision of Paradise is an expression of a mystical experience vouchsafed to Dante, comparable to that experienced by St. Paul, of which the Apostle said that he "beheld things not lawful to utter." In any case, the *Divine Comedy* deserves a place in the literature of mysticism, though it belongs to the class which Dean Inge (*Christian Mysticism,* 1899) calls "Nature-Mysticism," rather than to the speculative kind; that is to say, it realizes God in His creation and by means of natural symbolism instead of retreating from sense and imagination into the recesses of the soul.

The theological and philosophical framework of the *Divine Comedy* are adapted by Dante from Thomas Aquinas's great synthesis of Aristotle and Augustine. Thus, Dante cites Aristotle's *Ethics* and *Physics* as his authority for the divisions of Hell. But Thomas did more than make Aristotle an acceptable authority in the Church. It was he, more than any other, who committed Catholic theology to the distinction between the realms of nature and grace. According to Thomas, the realm of nature, including man, is intelligible to reason without the aid of revelation. Ethics and politics, therefore, do not require special revelation any more than astronomy or medicine. But because God has created in man a capacity for fellowship with himself, supernatural gifts are needed to bring him to perfection. Thus, according to Thomas, nature must be supplemented by grace, and reason by revelation. These are the theological assumptions underlying Dante's poem. Reason is sufficient to lead the soul to the very gates of Paradise, but, in order to find its way to the Empyrean and the objects of its love, it must have revelation as its guide. In like manner, a distinction should be observed between the offices of the Emperor and the Pope. Law and politics have not to borrow wisdom from the Church, to which is committed rather the ministry of supernatural grace.

Modern Protestants, while reading the *Divine Comedy,* cannot forget that they are reading a Catholic work: Thomas's distinction between nature and grace was repudiated by the Reformers, as well as, even more emphatically, the doctrine of Purgatory and of the intercession of the Saints. However, there is in the *Divine Comedy* a complete absence of crude supernaturalism, and no Protestant was ever more outspoken than Dante against the corruptions of the hierarchy. Standing at the threshold of the Italian renaissance, Dante represents the heights of Christian humanism, which, if it had been able to triumph within the Italian Church, might have preserved the unity of Western civilization by averting the Protestant revolt, on the one hand, and the rise of anti-Christian humanism on the other.

THE LITTLE FLOWERS OF SAINT FRANCIS

Author: Unknown
Type of work: Hagiography
First transcribed: In Italian, c. 1322 (probably earlier in Latin)

Principal Ideas Advanced

Saint Francis and his companions were holy men, practicing the Franciscan virtues of love of poverty, simplicity, humility, charity to the poor, compassion for all sufferers, and joyousness in the Lord—ideas which are illuminated and extolled in this tribute to the founder of the Franciscan Orders.

The Little Flowers of Saint Francis is a collection of anecdotes, mostly very brief, concerning Saint Francis and the first generation of Franciscans. It is not an academic biography of the saint or a history of the early years of the Order which he founded, for there is no historical truth in it. Yet it is unmistakably authentic. The truth it conveys is to be found, not in the events of its narrative, obviously legendary, but in the vivid and convincing impression it gives in its totality of the most Christ-like of saints.

The historical Francesco Bernardone, born in Assisi in 1181 or 1182, was the son of a prosperous merchant. His childhood was uneventful; his education was mediocre, even by twelfth century standards. He idled away his early youth in the company of the *jeunesse dorée* of Assisi, but though pleasure-loving and gay during those years, he was never dissolute, and he was always generous to the poor. When he was about twenty years old he suffered an illness which prevented him from carrying out his intention of becoming a soldier, and which was also the occasion for a change of heart. Thenceforward he led a devout and ascetic life, spending more and more time in solitary prayer, and devoting himself to service of the poor and sick, especially the lepers.

In 1209 he became convinced of his mission to preach, and he began to gather disciples; when their number had grown to twelve, he conducted them to Rome, where he succeeded in obtaining the verbal approval of Pope Innocent III for their way of life. Thus was founded the Order of Friars Minor. They were granted the use of the half-ruined Chapel of Saint Mary of the Angels, called the Portiuncula, on the plain below Assisi. They repaired the chapel and built for themselves shelters of branches; the little Portiuncula with its cluster of huts was to become the headquarters of the Order.

The aim of the friars was to live the

life of Christ as closely as possible, with no rule but the Gospels. In complete poverty and simplicity they went in pairs among the people, preaching, tending the sick, earning a bare subsistence by manual labor or, failing employment, begging their bread. They accepted only enough to satisfy their daily needs; they slept in barns or on the porches of churches; they owned nothing. The zealous preaching of the friars, their sincere humility, and their practical charity brought about a strong religious revival in Umbria. In 1212, Saint Clare, under the direction of Saint Francis, founded the Second Order, for nuns, the Order of Poor Clares.

The Franciscan Order grew with a rapidity which astonished even its founder. As recruits flocked in, many friaries were founded up and down Italy, then throughout Europe. Francis himself traveled to Dalmatia, France, Spain, Egypt, and Palestine. As the foundations multiplied and the number of friars grew to the thousands, the initial simplicity of life, guided by Francis's own counsel and example, had to give way to a more complex organization, similar to that of the other orders. During Francis's stay in Egypt and Palestine, from 1219 to 1220, there began internal struggles in the Order and divisions into parties; the dissensions were to become very grave after Francis's death. He hurried home when the news of the troubles in the Order reached him. At an extraordinary general chapter at the Portiuncula in 1221 he resigned as Minister General, giving as the reason for his resignation that the Order had grown beyond his powers of administration. In that same year he also composed his Rule and founded his Third Order, an order for laymen who wished to practice Franciscan virtues without entering the First Order.

In 1224, Francis underwent an experience which was for him the culmination of his many years of asceticism and contemplative prayer practiced in solitude, and which for his brothers in the Order marked him as a saint even before his death. He went up Mount Alverno with a few companions for forty days of fasting and prayer, terminating on September fourteenth, the Feast of the Holy Cross. On that day Francis had a vision of a Crucified Seraph flying toward him from the rising sun. The vision filled him with rapture, but when it ended he felt sharp pains in his hands, feet, and side; there on his own body he found the marks of the Passion of Christ. Though the stigmata became a constant torment to his body, he accepted them with spiritual joy; in spite of the suffering they caused him, and in spite of nearly total blindness, he continued to work at the revision of his Rule and other provisions for the welfare of his three Orders. He died in the Portiuncula on October 3, 1226. In 1228 he was canonized by Pope Gregory IX.

In the years immediately following the death of Saint Francis, the Friars Minor increased rapidly in numbers and spread all over the world; they entered the universities, where they challenged the supremacy of the Dominicans; they became prosperous and powerful. Meanwhile, the disagreements within the Order, becoming more acute, resulted in the formation of three parties: the Spirituals, who demanded literal observance of the Rule with a return to the way of life of Saint Francis and his first disciples; the party at the other extreme, composed of those who wished to abandon Franciscan poverty and simplicity of life; and the Moderates, who worked for a compromise. The quarrels of the three parties were not pacified until Pope Leo X, in 1517, divided the Franciscans into two branches, completely independent of each other: the Conventuals, allowed to own property as other Orders do; and the Observants, who observe the Rule closely in poverty and all other matters.

I Fioretti di Sancto Francesco is of anonymous authorship and uncertain date; what is evident is that it was written in the Italian of Tuscany of the fourteenth century. Scholars agree that its anecdotes were culled and translated from earlier Latin works. Its immediate source is the *Actus sancti Francisci et sociorum eius,* in turn compiled from earlier sources between 1322 and 1329. The *Fioretti* was compiled by several hands, perhaps in large part by Frate Ugolino di Monte santa Maria; it is possibly original in part. In spite of derivative subject matter and mixed authorship—circumstances usually unfavorable to high literary quality—the *Fioretti* is a minor literary masterpiece by virtue of its sincere simplicity and candor of tone, the winning naïveté of its narrative, its lively style, and the freshness and purity of its language, all of which qualities, except the last, come through translation unimpaired.

Chapters 1 to 38 retell the legends of Saint Francis and his companions; Chapters 39 to 53 recount anecdotes of the friars of the Province of the March of Ancona. Added to the *Fioretti* proper are "Five Considerations on the Stigmata," an account of how the stigmata were imprinted upon Saint Francis, and of their consequences for him and those who came to know about them in spite of his efforts at concealment. This account is followed by a report of the circumstances of the death of the Saint, and a rehearsal of the testimony to the authenticity of the stigmata. Some editions add also "The Lives of Brothers Ginepro and Egidio."

Consideration of the contents makes it clear that the *Fioretti* was composed by members of the Spiritual Party in the Order. The chapters concerning Saint Francis stress his love of poverty, his humility and simplicity, his devoted service to the poor, and his compassion for lepers, whom he tended with his own hands. The particular attention given the friars of the March of Ancona would follow naturally from the fact that the Spirituals were dominant in that Province. Furthermore, there is evidence of hostility—tempered by charity—toward the other parties. In Chapter 38, Saint Francis learns by divine revelation that Brother Elias (who became the head of the party of relaxation) is damned, but in answer to the earnest prayers of the Saint, the sentence of damnation is revoked. In Chapter 48, a friar has a dream in which he sees Brother Bonaventura (Saint Bonaventura, the most distinguished leader of the Moderates) attacking with claw-like nails brother John of Parma (one of the Spirituals); Saint Francis comes to the defense by cutting off the talons.

The chief interest of *The Little Flowers of Saint Francis* for modern readers lies in the inspired selection of anecdotes which show the Saint in his unique moral beauty of character. He is tender without sentimentality, gentle to all—even to his enemies—and strong beneath his gentleness. His humility and self-abnegation are the fruit of constant self-discipline; his love for his fellow men is practical, direct, and down-to-earth. He is always "joyful in the Lord, gay and pleasant," as his Rule enjoins.

The charming legend of his preaching to his "little sisters, the birds" is well known. Just as appealing is the story of the "simple, innocent, chaste" wild doves, captured and taken to market, whom Saint Francis rescues out of pity; in their gratitude they remain with him, domesticated and obedient. The episode of the taming of the Wolf of Gubbio illustrates the Saint's forbearance toward malefactors and also his practical good sense. He offers the Wolf a reasonable bargain: if "Brother Wolf" will stop attacking the townspeople they, for their part, will feed him daily. Saint Francis gives charity to robbers because sinners are reformed by kindness rather than by rebukes. The personality of the beloved Little Beggar of Assisi stands forth from these pages in all its spiritualized humanity.

DE CORPORE CHRISTI

Author: William of Ockham (c.1300-c.1349)
Type of work: Sacramental theology
First transcribed: c.1324

Principal Ideas Advanced

Truth concerning the sacrament of the altar must be apprehended by faith; that is, by acceptance of the teachings of the Bible and the Roman Church.

The Eucharistic dogma of the Church embraces the doctrines of the real presence, transubstantiation, and the integrity of the body of Christ in every particle of the consecrated element.

The common opinion that the accidents of the bread inhere after consecration in the "quantity" of the bread as in a substance is to be rejected.

William of Ockham's surname comes from his native village in Surrey, England. Many alleged details of his life and writings continue to be doubtful. We are able, however, with considerable assurance to divide his literary career into two great periods. The earlier of these two periods finds Ockham in Oxford. It begins with his commentaries on the four books of Peter Lombard's *Sentences,* and ends with his two treatises on the Eucharist, *De sacramento altaris* and *De corpore Christi.* Both treatises (which in printed editions have usually been treated as one work) were apparently written shortly before Ockham left for Avignon (probably in the late summer of 1324), where he had been called to defend himself at the court of Pope John XXII (1249-1334) against charges of heresy that had been made against him by a former chancellor of Oxford University, John Lutterell (died 1335).

The *De corpore Christi* constitutes

Ockham's answer to the hostile criticism that he knew had been aroused by certain statements concerning the Eucharist that he had made in his *Sentences* commentary. The answer is two-fold. In the prologue and the first seven chapters he spells out the Church's doctrine of the Eucharist, and he explicitly embraces it as his own. In the remaining chapters (VIII-XLI) he systematically develops his own contribution to the theological understanding of this doctrine, which consists primarily in a detailed philosophical discussion of the notion of quantity in relation to the ecclesiastical doctrine of transubstantiation.

The Eucharist is presented as a memorial of Christ's giving of Himself "on the altar of the cross," and as a daily mystical immolation of Christ in behalf of men, who err daily. Agreeing that it is improper to seek to investigate the "unspeakable loftiness" of this sacrament, Ockham professes his intention to limit his assertions to the positive doctrine of the Roman Church, and he explicitly submits his speculations (made "only for the sake of practice and of inquiring into the truth") to "the correction of all the skilled, orthodox Catholics who are interested." Noting that Pope Innocent IV (Pope, 1243-1254) had excused ignorance even of clearly revealed truth provided that it was accompanied by "implicit faith" in the teachings of the Church, Ockham pleads for similar consideration in the case of one inquiring into areas that are determined neither by Scripture nor by approved doctors.

The Eucharistic doctrine of the Church is presented under three heads: the "real presence" of the body of Christ in the sacrament, the transubstantiation of the bread into the body of Christ, and the integrity of the body of Christ in every particle of the sacrament.

Although the very body that was born of the Virgin, that suffered, died, rose again, and ascended into Heaven, that now is seated at the Father's right hand, and that will come again to judge the living and the dead, is contained under the species of bread, "it certainly is not seen by us with the bodily eye" (as Ockham was to be officially charged with teaching), but is mentally (*mente*) believed to be present by the faithful. The real presence is a truth that cannot be demonstrated by natural reason, but can be known only through faith. But it is clearly taught in Scripture and it is confirmed by "the eminent Doctors, the Holy Fathers, the most illustrious expositors of the divine scriptures" approved by the Roman Church; and Ockham presents several of their statements that have passed into the canon law of the Church.

The doctrine of transubstantiation is not to be found expressly in the Bible; "but this doctrine is believed to have been divinely revealed to the Holy Fathers, or to have been proved from passages of the Bible by a diligent and skillful examination." (This statement marks a modification of Ockham's earlier position that this dogma was not contained in Scripture, and rested solely on a post-Apostolic revelation received by the Church.) Three opinions are traditionally distinguished: (1) that the same substance which initially is bread becomes the flesh of Christ; (2) that the substance of the bread ceases to be, and the body of Christ begins to be, though the accidents (taste, color, weight, for instance) of the bread remain; (3) that the substance of the bread remains, together with the body of Christ, under the species of bread. Ockham says that the second opinion "seems to be the determination of the Roman Church" and its approved doctors. (Actually the more ancient and common opinion is the first, which was also held by Thomas Aquinas, c.1225-1274.) Aquinas held that the third opinion involves a contradiction, while John Duns Scotus (c.1264-1308) and Ockham deny this. Ockham had been attacked by Lutterell for stating that the third opinion would give rise to fewer intellectual difficulties than the second. Here he points out that this was only a hypothetical consideration, not intended to undermine the position of the Church. But he indirectly defends this speculation by saying that the position he shares with Scotus "seems to me more probable and more in accord with theology, because it rather exalts the omnipotence of God. . . ." Transubstantiation, properly speaking, produces only the body of Christ. But in a wider sense it might be said to include Christ's divinity, soul, blood, or corporal accidents, insofar as these are united with His body. (Elsewhere Ockham had labeled Christ's body the *terminus formalis* and the other facets of His personality the *termini per accidens.*)

That the whole body of Christ is present in the whole Host, and in every part of it equally, is proven by patristic authorities, by the consideration of the absolute power of God (which is said to be known frequently to supersede the natural order of things), and by such analogies as the "rational soul" (*anima intellectiva,* which is said to be equally in the whole body and in every part of it) and the presence of an angel (which is said to be a definitive presence in whatever place it happens to be, and in every part of that place).

The problem to which Ockham addresses himself is posed by the apparent conflict of the ecclesiastical dogma of transubstantiation with the Aristotelian science that was generally accepted in his time. According to this science, a thing consists of a substance (an essential nature) and accidents (accidental, or variable, properties) that inhere in the substance. According to the doctrine of transubstantiation, which was made an official dogma at the Fourth Lateran Council (1215), the substance of bread is changed into the body of Christ, while the accidents of the bread remain. The problem is: Wherein do these accidents inhere after consecration? It was universally agreed that they do not inhere in the body of Christ, for that would mean that the identical body of Christ might be moist in one place, dry in another, and mildewy in a third. The common opinion (shared by Thomas Aquinas, the *doctor communis*) was that the accidents now inhere in the "quantity" of the bread; and this "quantity" was defined as an absolute accident concretely (*realiter*) different from the other accidents, and from the substance. Ockham's argumentation is one sustained attack on this opinion.

Ockham describes quantity as extension, circumscriptive presence, involving a quantum, and, following John of Damascus (c.675-c.749, the great systematizer of Eastern Orthodoxy), as "having part separate from part." Quantity is not an absolute term, but a connotative term; that is, it stands, not for some entity "quality," but for some other entity, and indicates that that entity is a quantum. Ockham applies his famous principle of economy, often referred to as "Ockham's razor" (*"frustra fit per plura quod potest fieri per pauciora"*), to cut off "quantity" as a separate entity. Quantity, therefore, is not simply another accident; rather, it may be predicated of accidents. Quantity may also be predicated of substances; thus, the body of Christ is a quantum insofar as it has part separate from part; that is, the eye is not the foot, but separate from it. Now the absolute power of God is able to create causes without their natural effects, natural effects without their proper (secondary) causes, substances without accidents, and accidents that do not inhere in any substance. The absolute power of God is also able to cause to be present definitively (noncircumscriptively, nonquantitatively, not having part separate from part) a substance that is properly a quantum, and that without accidents; this is precisely how the body of Christ is present in the Eucharist as a result of transubstantiation. Now quantity may refer to the subject or to the predicate of a proposition. Subjectively (*a parte subiecti*), Christ's body may be a quantum, and present as such in the Eucharist (*quantitas corporis Christi est in sacramento altaris*). But predicatively (*a parte praedicati*), Christ's body is not quantitatively present in the Eucharist (*haec tamen est falsa, "substantia corporis Christi est in sacramento altaris quantitas"*).

The *De corpore Christi* may well be regarded as one of a long line of medieval attempts to implement the motto of Anselm of Canterbury (c.1033-1109): *Fides quaerens intellectum;* I believe in order to understand. Ockham's starting point is the authoritative doctrine of the Church. As a theologian (and this aspect of Ockham's work has not been accorded proper recognition in the traditional presentation of Ockham), he seeks to incorporate the implications of dogma in the logical framework of systematic thought. That is to say, he tries to enlarge the philosophical horizon by means of the data of revelation; to synthesize, as it were, the realms of nature and super-nature that were sharply distinguished in Thomism. This "synthesis" deprives man of the relative security of a universe functioning largely by means of natural law, which was only occasionally interrupted by miracles. Ockham's universe is moment by moment directly dependent upon the will of God, whose radical freedom poses an ultimate threat to man's existence. Ockham's doctrine of the Eucharist serves as a stark reminder of this wholly nonanalogical relationship between God and man. It magnifies the miraculous character of transubstantiation. For the conclusion of Ockham's argumentation about quantity is that the accidents do not inhere in "quantity," nor in anything else, but remain suspended, sustained only by the naked power of an omnipotent God.

A recent study (Erwin Iserloh, *Gnade und Eucharistie in der philosophischen Theologie des Wilhelm von Ockham,* 1956) has charged Ockham with giving a very limited and one-sided treatment to the Mass, and with divorcing the doctrine of the Eucharist from the experiential realm of personal participation. It may be said in Ockham's defense that he apparently understood his own work as a contribution on a particular point to a traditional Eucharistic doctrine which he accepted. At the same time, it must be conceded that there is little in Ockham's discussion of the Eucharistic mysticism that had transformed the Mass, during the high Middle Ages, from a mere cultic act into a personal religious experience. Ockham deals with certain authoritatively given data, and he approaches them, not from the perspective of his own Christian experience, but from the point of view of Aristotelian science. Ockham recognizes two religious authorities: the Bible and the Church. His whole Eucharistic theology in a sense grows out of the recognition of the Church's ability authoritatively to define dogma.

Ockham's views continued to arouse opposition. John Wycliffe (c.1329-1384) was not the only critic of Ockham. But Ockham's views were increasingly accepted, and when John Huss (c.1369-burned in 1415) was tried for heresy at the Council of Constance (1414-1418), his Ockhamist prosecutors Peter d'Ailly (1350-1420) and John Gerson (1363-1429) indicated that only the Ockhamist theory fully corresponded to the official dogma of the Church.

In the sixteenth century the Catholic position on transubstantiation seems to have been largely understood in Ockham's terms, both by the Protestant Reformers and by Catholic apologists. The authoritarian and logical approach, which seems to have largely dominated the Eucharistic theology of the period between Ockham and the Reformation, may have helped to prepare the way for the large-scale reaction against transubstantiation in the sixteenth century. At the same time, Luther (who was well acquainted with Ockham and with such Ockhamist writers as Peter d'Ailly and Gabriel Biel, c.1420-1495) found in them theoretical support for his doctrines of consubstantiation, the real presence, and the ubiquity of Christ's body.

Ockham's stay in Avignon lasted almost four years. A commission of six (including Lutterell) was appointed to try his case, and reported seven articles (out of fifty-one) explicitly heretical and thirty-seven false. Pope John XXII expressed his agreement with the report but never proceeded to a formal condemnation; nor did any succeeding pope. During this period at Avignon Ockham's fate became closely intertwined with that of Michael of Cesena (died 1342), general of the Franciscan Order, to which Ockham belonged. Cesena was in disfavor with the pope because of differences over "apostolic poverty," which the Franciscan general upheld and the pope condemned. Ockham became involved in the struggle, and in May, 1328, he fled with Cesena from Avignon. Both joined the forces of Emperor Louis the Bavarian (died 1347), whom John had excommunicated. Ockham spent the remainder of his life (1329-1349) in Munich, and he devoted this second period of his literary activity to political writing, treating the respective power of pope and emperor, the position of the pope in the Church, the heresies of Pope John, and other topics of this kind. When Pope Clement VI (1291-1352) laid down terms for the readmission of

Ockham and his party to the favor of the Church, no mention was made of any nonpolitical errors on Ockham's part. Whether Ockham accepted Clement's terms and died officially reconciled to the Church is not known.

THE ADORNMENT OF THE SPIRITUAL MARRIAGE

Author: John of Ruysbroeck (1293-1381)
Type of work: Mystical theology
First transcribed: c.1346

Principal Ideas Advanced

God's supreme command to man is the command to "see"; neglect of this command entails eternal perdition.

The purpose of man's life and labors is to meet Christ in love.

The life of God, Trinity in Unity, is an eternally simultaneous movement and rest; man can participate in this life on various levels.

Even at the highest level, where man rests in the Godhead, he is not purely passive, but active in contemplation and fruition.

Man is essentially united to God in that he exists ideally and vitally in God prior to his creation in time; this unity is the first cause, but not the efficient cause, of man's highest beatitude, which consists in his return to this unity through vision and love.

Grace, the moral code, and the authority of the Church and of the Bible are never transcended; they form the foundation of true spirituality.

John of Ruysbroeck takes his surname from his native village, located some three miles southwest of Brussels. At the age of eleven he left home and thereafter lived with his uncle, a canon of the collegiate church of SS. Michael and Gudule. After his own ordination he ministered at the same church for a quarter century. In 1343 he retired with his uncle and another canon to the nearby forest of Soignes, where they founded the priory of Groenendael and accepted the rule of the Augustinian canons. Ruysbroeck's saintliness and wisdom became known far and wide. Groenendael grew and became a center of spiritual life for the whole lower Rhine region. The great German preacher John Tauler (c.1300-1361) and the promoter of the *devotio moderna,* Geert de Groote (1340-1384), were among his friends that visited Groenendael. Of Ruysbroeck's eleven literary works, three were completed before his departure from Brussels, and several others, including *The Adornment of the Spiritual Marriage,* were probably begun there. The latter work was completed at some time prior to 1350. It is Ruysbroeck's most systematic work.

As Ruysbroeck stands at the head of the vernacular prose writers of the Low Countries, so he stands at the center of its spirituality. The spirituality of the Low Countries had imbibed the affective warmth of Bernard of Clairvaux (1090-1153). This warmth is clearly reflected in the writings of the two outstanding mystical writers before Ruysbroeck, the Cistercian Beatrice of Bethlehem (died 1268) and the Beguine Hadewijch of Antwerp (probably first half of the thirteenth century). Near the end of the fourteenth century the spirituality of the Low Countries divided into two streams, both of them greatly influenced by Ruysbroeck. The ascetic line was represented at Groenendael by John of Schoonhoven (died 1431) and is generally associated with the *devotio moderna,* the Brethren of the Common Life, and the canons regular of Windesheim. The more speculatively interested mystical line includes such men as John of Leeuwen (at Groenendael, died 1374); Denis (of Leeuwen, or of Rijkel) "the Carthusian" (1402-1471); the Franciscan Henry Herp (died 1477); and the Benedictine abbot Louis de Blois (1506-c.1566).

This indigenous spirituality was promoted by the *Rijmbijbel,* a vernacular version of the entire Bible in rime, and other translations of the poet Jacob of Maerlant (c.1235-1300).

A second major influence, more specifically formative for Ruysbroeck's mysticism, was the school of Meister Eckhart (c.1260-c.1327), which is sometimes identified with the movement known as the Friends of God, or more generally with German mysticism. It combined Plotinian, Augustinian, Dionysian, and Thomistic elements in a manner that did not always satisfy the guardians of orthodoxy. Heresy proceedings were brought against Eckhart himself, and in 1329 Pope John XXII condemned several of his theses. Eckhart's followers responded to this condemnation by avoiding the exceptionable phrases and generally emphasizing their doctrinal and moral orthodoxy.

A third potent influence in the spirituality of the Low Countries was the teaching generally associated with the Brothers and Sisters of the Free Spirit. This doctrine, variously described as antinomian, quietistic, or pantheistic, had made great inroads especially among the Beguines, and proved hard to eradicate. It derived largely from Amalric of Bena (died c.1204), a master in the University of Paris who was officially condemned in 1209, and Ortlieb of Strassburg (born c.1200); and more remotely from the Arab philosopher Averroës (1126-1198). Ruysbroeck is said to have carried on a campaign against this type of mysticism and its outstanding representative, one Bloemmardinne (Heilwige Blommaerts, died 1335), a woman of good birth and of outstanding reputation both for personal sanctity and miraculous powers, who had founded a *beguinage* in Brussels. Ruysbroeck was always careful to dissociate himself from this type of spirituality, and in his largely apologetic *Book of Supreme Truth* denounces its adherents rather vehemently. Throughout his writings, as in his life, Ruysbroeck displayed a deep concern for moral virtue, which he regarded as fundamental for all true spirituality. Ruysbroeck's efforts to prove himself orthodox were successful. He is the only major representative of the Eckhartian school whose writings have never been put on the Index, and in 1909 he was officially beatified.

Ruysbroeck bases his exposition on the four parts of the verse, "Behold, the Bridegroom cometh, go ye out to meet him" (Matthew 25:6). "Behold" indicates a divine command to see; men who "neglect this command and remain blind are all damned." The remark "the Bridegroom cometh" indicates the various times and manners of the coming of Christ, the Bridegroom; the bride is human nature. The injunction "go ye out" indicates the response that is required of men. The phrase "to meet him" indicates "the purpose of our labour and of all our life; that is to say, the loving meeting with our Bridegroom." Both the vision and the three-fold movement of divine coming, human response, and divine-human encounter take place at three different levels.

Book I is devoted to the "active life," which is the common life of virtue and religion that is necessary for salvation. Vision is here shown to depend on three factors: the light of divine grace, the voluntary conversion of the will, and the cleansing of the conscience through perfect contrition. The coming of the Bridegroom is said to be threefold: in the Incarnation, in a daily coming with graces and gifts (a special instance of which is Christ's coming in the sacraments), and at the Last Judgment. From the "loving observation" of the Bridegroom's coming, there arises in the human heart a yearning to follow Christ in His virtues; this going out takes place in charity and righteousness, which together lay the foundation of all the other virtues, humility. To meet Jesus, it is necessary with Zacchaeus (Luke 19:2-4) to climb the tree of faith, which "grows from above downwards, for its roots are in the Godhead," and whose twelve branches are the twelve articles of faith; to "come down quickly" (Luke 19:5) means "nothing else than a descent through desire and through love into the abyss of the Godhead, which no intelligence can reach in the created light. But where intelligence remains without" (here Ruysbroeck is quoting the mystical theologian Hugh of St. Victor, c.1097-1141), "desire and love go in."

The second level (Book II) is that of the "interior life," to which Ruysbroeck devotes some two-thirds of his treatise. Grace shines more brightly here; the conversion of the will encompasses also the unification of all of a man's powers, and the heart is cleansed from "all distracting images and attachments." Man is naturally sustained by three unities: the essential unity of his being, by which he exists, eternally one, in God; the active unity of his higher powers (memory, understanding, will) in the soul considered as spirit; and the vital unity of his bodily powers in the soul considered as the forming principle of the body. Now in the interior life Christ comes (1) in the unity of the bodily powers, as "driving and drawing" these powers toward Heaven, by heat and cold, weal and woe, hope and despair; (2) in the higher powers as strengthening, enlightening, and enriching the spirit in many ways, abundantly pouring Himself into man and demanding a response wholly transcending creaturely powers; (3) as "an inward stirring or touch in the unity of the spirit, wherein are the higher powers of the soul." Man's going out on this level includes beholding and glorifying God in the celestial hierarchies of His saints and angels; offering intercessory prayers for sinners and for souls in purgatory; instructing, reproving, serving, and praying for all good men; and peacefully possessing the unity of His spirit. The essential union of the human spirit with God, though "the first cause of all holiness and all blessedness," of itself "neither makes us holy nor blessed." Thus Ruysbroeck writes, "And so we have need of grace, which casts out sin, and prepares the way, and makes our whole life fruitful. And this is why Christ always comes into us through means, that is, through grace and multifarious gifts; and we too go out towards Him through means, that is, through virtues and diverse practices . . . for without the mediation of God's grace and a loving turning to Him in freedom, no creature shall ever be saved."

It is precisely in this respect the quietists are said to err: "Now mark this: when a man wishes to possess inward rest in idleness, without inward and desirous cleaving to God, then he is ready for all errors; for he is turned away from God, and inclined towards himself, in natural love, seeking and desiring consolation and sweetness and everything that pleases him . . . they believe themselves to be free, and to be united to God without means, and to be above all the customs of Holy Church, and above the commandments of God, and above the law, and above every work of virtue which can in any way be done. . . . They are empty of every virtue; and indeed so empty, that they will neither praise nor thank God. They have no knowledge and no love, no will, no prayer, no desire; for they believe that all that they could pray for, and desire, is already possessed of them. . . . And therefore they would be free, and obedient to none; neither pope, nor bishop, nor parson . . . sometimes . . . they are so cunning that one cannot vanquish them on the ground of reason. But through Holy Scripture and the teaching of Christ and our Faith, we may prove that they are deceived."

Ruysbroeck regards as similarly perverted the conviction of those who believe that "God works all their works" and that therefore they cannot sin.

The third level (Book III) is that of the "God-seeing life." Here the contemplative becomes the Light by which he sees. The eternal coming of the Bridegroom which he now experiences is the perpetual generation of Christ in the human spirit, which has now died to itself and entered the darkness of fruition. His going out is now in "contemplation and fruition, according to the way of God," for it is the will of God that men should return in a supernatural manner, through vision and love, to the eternally generated image in which they have their ideal being prior to their creation in time. The meeting at this highest level is a loving embrace, in the essential nudity and unity of the Godhead. "This is the dark silence in which all lovers lose themselves."

Attacks on Ruysbroeck's orthodoxy have always centered on Book III of *The Adornment of the Spiritual Marriage*. Henry of Langenstein (died 1397), formerly professor of theology at Paris and Vienna, and John Gerson (1363-1429), chancellor of the University of Paris and a mystical theologian of some stature, were the most prominent of his critics. In two letters (1399 and 1408) to the Carthusian Bartholomew Clantier, in a sermon preached at his university (1399), and in his treatise *De mystica theologia* (c.1402), Gerson seeks to connect certain teachings of Ruysbroeck with those of the condemned Amalric of Bena. Specifically, he objects to Ruysbroeck's conception of a super-essential union of man with God as the return of the rational creature to its primal archetype or exemplar in God, where the contemplative becomes the divine Light in which he sees God. Gerson was answered by John of Schoonhoven in two treatises, in which he explains that Ruysbroeck was not speaking of the union of identity (*per identitatem realis existentiae*) subsisting between the Father and the Son (John 10:30), nor of the moral union (*per consensum et conformitatem voluntatis*) common to all believers in the state of grace (Acts 4:32), but of that union in which the soul is melted by love and in a manner dies to itself (Galatians 2:20). Bernard of Clairvaux, Hugh of St. Victor, Gilbert of Holland (died 1172), and Thomas Gallus (died 1246) are the authorities he cites for this kind of union. The return of the rational creature to its ideal principle is also interpreted as a return by love, not by a reversal of the process of creation. With Bernard, the supposed author of the *Epistola ad fratres de Monte Dei* (actually William of St. Thierry, died 1149), he distinguishes between "being what God is" and "being God." That this distinction furnishes the key to the proper understanding of Ruysbroeck's conception of supreme beatitude is borne out by a statement in *The Book of Supreme Truth:* "This blessedness is essential to God, and superessential to all creatures; for no created essence can become one with God's essence and pass away from its own substance. For so the creature would become God, which is impossible; . . . yet all loving spirits are one fruition and one blessedness with God without distinction; for that beatific state, which is the fruition of God and of all his beloved, is so simple and onefold that therein neither Father, nor Son, nor Holy Ghost, is distinct according to the Persons, neither is any creature." The union is the one Christ prayed for: "That they all may be one; as thou, Father, art in me, and I in thee, that they also may be one in us . . ." (John 17:21).

THEOLOGIA GERMANICA

Author: Unknown. Attributed to an anonymous Teutonic Knight, sometimes known as "the Frankfurter"
Type of work: Mystical theology
First transcribed: c.1350

PRINCIPAL IDEAS ADVANCED

Since sin is nothing but disobedience or self-will, salvation, which is nothing but obedience or ceasing from self-will, must be wrought in the person who sins.

Freedom is self-surrender to God; self-assertion is the most miserable bondage; freedom from the law does not mean license.

To know and believe in Christ means to know and believe in the Christ-life; man's union with God is primarily a union with the will of God.

The *Theologia Germanica* was first published in 1516 by the German Reformer Martin Luther (1483-1546), who had come across it, without title or indication of authorship, and in incomplete form. Luther published two more editions in Wittenberg in 1518, and two further editions were published the same year in Augsburg and Leipzig; the treatise acquired its title, "German Theology" (sometimes written *Theologia Deutsch*), in that year. In all, some one hundred editions have been printed in Germany alone, and translations have been made into many languages.

The best manuscript, which dates from 1497, was discovered in Würzburg in the middle of the last century. It indicates that the author had been "a Teutonic Knight, a priest, and a warden in the house of the Teutonic Knights [an order founded in Jerusalem in 1118] in Frankfurt," who was also a Friend of God, and that he wrote against the Free Spirits. These Free Spirits may be defined as adherents of the more extreme branch of medieval mysticism, which pushed its understanding of God as immanent to the point of pantheism and antinomianism. The group seems to have flourished especially in the thirteenth century.

The Friends of God, a fourteenth century movement that flourished all along the Rhine and in Southern Germany, represents a conservative reaction against these excesses. Meister Eckhart (c.1260-1327), superior-general of the German Dominicans and a professor in Paris and Cologne, whose personality and writings form the foundation of the movement, and his greatest disciples, John Ruysbroeck (1293-1381), Henry Suso (c.1295-1366), and John Tauler (c.1300-1361), were all loyal churchmen. By disciplining their mystical experiences and speculations with Christian dogma and the common morality, they produced a literature which is regarded by many as the finest flowering of mysticism. German mysticism enriched and molded the German language; it largely determined German spirituality; it provided the foundations of German classical philosophy; and it cast a certain conservative hue over German social life.

The *Theologia Germanica,* written in the middle or second half of the fourteenth century, is generally regarded as the epitome of Eckhartian mysticism. Permeated by great moral earnestness, not to say rigorism, it sets forth simply and clearly the message of the Friends of God. It has not enjoyed much ecclesiastical approbation. Luther wrote in 1516 that he had never seen a more wholesome theology, but in his later years he came to repent his initial enthusiasm for the little book. The French Reformer John Calvin (1509-1564) categorically rejected it. Calvin's adversary Sebastian Castellio (1515-1563), the most prominent advocate of religious toleration in the sixteenth century, liked it well enough to translate it into Latin, as did the German rational-spiritualist Sebastian Franck (c.1499-c.1542). The book was placed on the Index by Roman Catholic authorities in 1621. It was revered by German and French Pietists. Forgotten by the Enlightenment, it has again found a goodly number of readers in the nineteenth and twentieth centuries.

According to the *Theologia Germanica,* God is the only substance and goodness. No created being has substance or goodness in itself, but only as it participates in God. Man can dispose himself for greater participation by renouncing whatever is not God, and the disposed man will get his reward. The renunciation of will, wisdom, love, desire, and knowledge means that God is acknowledged as the author of all these goods. To claim any of them for oneself is to touch God in His honor. Nothing is to be loved, nothing is to be the object of human satisfaction, but God. God may be considered in three ways: as Godhead, that is, as pure transcendence, without name, manifestation, knowledge, or will; as God, that is, as a being with personal distinctions, knowing, loving, and revealing Himself to Himself, not actively, but substantially; and as man, that is, as a being incarnate in Christ or in any man who has come to be a partaker of the divine nature, as pure love to all creatures, joined to a profound grief over their sins. God as man never resorts to force. The partakers of the divine nature are the poor in spirit, who are also the heirs of the Kingdom of Heaven.

Sin is defined as self-will, a turning from the unchangeable good to the changeable. Any willing "without God" is self-will. The Devil fell by claiming "for himself to be also somewhat." The message is clear: "For the more a man followeth after his own self-will, and self-will groweth in him, the farther off is he from God, the true Good, for nothing burneth in hell but self-will. Therefore it hath been said, 'Put off thine own will, and there will be no hell.'" Ownership derives from self-will; there is no ownership in Heaven. Sin does not exist substantially, in God; hence, the all-embracing love of God does not extend to sin.

Salvation is described in the *Theologia Germanica* in moral and psychological terms. The only cure for disobedience is obedience, and it must be effected in the one who disobeyed: "But how shall my fall be amended? It must be healed as Adam's fall was healed. . . . Mark this: man could not without God, and God should not without man. Wherefore God took human nature or manhood upon himself, and was made man, and man was made divine. . . . So also must my fall be healed. I cannot do the work without God, and God may not or will not do it without me; for if it shall be accomplished, in me, too, God must be made man. . . ." As Adam's obedience "fell and died" when he disobeyed God, so disobedience "fell and died" in Christ's perpetual obedience. The new birth that is necessary to enter the Kingdom of God (John 3:3,5) is nothing other than the birth of obedience. When Christ says that "No man cometh unto the Father but by me" (John 14:6), what is meant is that the only way to God is by following Christ's example; that is, by complete obedience. "No man can come unto me, except the Father which hath sent me draw him" (John 6:44) means that only as men catch a glimpse of the Eternal Goodness do their souls conceive "a longing to approach unto the Perfect

Goodness, and unite herself with the Father." This longing grows in proportion to the degree of completeness of the revelation.

The Frankfurter propounds a very characteristic view of freedom. God cannot exercise His will in Himself, since He is immutable; but He delights to exercise it in the creature: "Therefore the will is not given to be exerted by the creature, but only by God, who hath a right to work out His own will by means of the will which is in man, and yet is God's. And in whatever man or creature it should be purely and wholly thus, the will would not be exerted by the man but by God, and thus it would not be self-will, and the man would not will otherwise than as God willeth; for God himself would move the will and not man. . . . That which is free, none may call his own, and he who maketh it his own committeth a wrong. Now, in the whole realm of freedom, nothing is so free as the will, and he who maketh it his own . . . doth a grievous wrong. . . . But he who leaveth the will in its freedom, hath content, peace, rest and blessedness in time and in eternity. . . . Furthermore, mark ye that where the will enjoyeth its freedom, it hath its proper work, that is, willing. And where it chooseth whatever it will unhindered, it always chooseth in all things what is noblest and best. . . ."

Men enlightened by God live in the freedom of disinterested love, says the *Theologia Germanica;* they are motivated neither by "the fear of pain or hell" nor by "the hope of reward or heaven." There is a sense in which those who are "led by the Spirit of God" (Romans 8:14) are "not under the law but under grace" (Romans 6:14). They are free from the law in that the Christ-life is greater than the requirements of the law, and includes them.

The opposite view is the "false freedom" of the Free Spirits or Free-Thinkers. A preface included in the 1497 manuscript indicates that the *Theologia Germanica* "teaches . . . especially how and whereby the true and rightful Friends of God may be recognized and likewise the unrightful and false Free Spirits who are most harmful to Holy Church." The Free Spirits identify nature with God, while the *Theologia Germanica* identifies nature with the Devil; all things are to be loved only in One, the transcendent One in all things. Since "all deception beginneth in self-deception," the free spirits lack the sense of sin; they suppose that "it standeth quite well with them." Hence, they are guilty both of spiritual pride and high-mindedness and of a false, lawless freedom. They think themselves superior to "custom, order, measure, fitness, and the like" (which are, however, divinely ordained), and hence free to violate them. He who is poor in spirit, on the other hand, sees that these things are necessary, because "he cometh to see and understand aright, how that all men are bent upon themselves, and inclined to evil and sin, and that on this account it is needful and profitable that there be order, customs, law and precepts, to the end that the blindness and foolishness of men may be corrected, and that vice and wickedness may be kept under, and constrained to seemliness." Men naturally resemble the Evil Spirit more than they do God; for every man truly possessed with the Spirit of God, there are a hundred thousand or more possessed with the Evil Spirit.

Reason (perceiving, cognition) and will are the creature's highest gifts, and they cannot be separated. Faith (belief) precedes (experiential) knowledge. To know and understand Christ is to know and understand His life, and to believe in Christ is to think the Christ-life best of all. Love is defined as the practical pursuit of its object, by action conformable to the latter. Hence, when the *Theologia Germanica* claims that there is no true knowledge of God without love, what is meant is that the knowledge of God is practical. The true light and reason teach the soul to love only the perfect good, and for its own sake; love for the sake of a reward is an especially false kind of love.

Self-knowledge is praised as the highest art. But the real ideal of the *Theologica Germanica* is the Christ-life: to be to the Eternal Goodness what his own hand is to a man. Though the Christ-life be the most bitter of all, it is to be desired above all things; such a life cannot be attained by book-learning, but only by forsaking "this and that," the world of the many and the particular. Men endowed with considerable reason are in danger, in fact, of mistaking their own reason for the true light of God. The Christ-life is primarily a union of man with the will of God, and it requires submission to all things. Man's will must come to be wholly at one with God's, by a union which "standeth not in any man's powers"; the individual will must cease to be separate from God's, but it must not relinquish its distinct identity. This union with God's will becomes a permanent condition of the "inner man" and can be broken only by self-will. Such a view does not imply that a man should not be touched at all by "outward things." Perfection is not to be looked for at once: John Tauler says that some take leave of types and symbols too soon. Three stages in the ascent of will are recognized: purification, enlightenment, union. Time is portrayed as the "outer court" of eternity; Paradise is "all things that are"; Hell and Heaven may be experienced in this life; and it is possible (according to "St. Dyonysius") to "cast a glance into eternity" now. Christ was able to look with the right eye of his soul into eternity while looking upon the things of time with the left; but in other men the "left eye" must utterly cease to function if the "right eye" is to become operative. In expressing these views, the *Theologia Germanica* describes and fosters the Christian way to the sinless life.

THE DIALOGUE OF CATHERINE OF SIENA

Author: Saint Catherine of Siena (1347-1380)
Type of work: Devotional meditations; mysticism
First transcribed: 1370

Principal Ideas Advanced

Through proper self-knowledge the soul learns of its complete dependence on God.

True knowledge of God lies beyond human understanding and takes place in the mystical experience of the beatific vision.

Suffering is integral to the religious life, for it follows when the soul discerns its distance from God and it encourages the proper attitude of contrition.

God made of Christ a bridge by which fallen man may travel the road to Heaven.

The subtitle is uncommonly helpful for understanding *The Dialogue of St. Catherine:* "The Book of Divine Doctrine given in person by God the Father, speaking to the mind of the most glorious and holy virgin, Catherine of Siena, and written down as she dictated it in the vulgar tongue, she being the while entranced and actually hearing what God spoke in her." There are difficulties here for the modern reader to whom seraphic virgins, states of ecstasy, and mystical dialogues are unfamiliar, but once the reader learns something of the cultural milieu in which Catherine moved, it is possible to approach the work with some expectation of satisfactory understanding.

In Catherine's day the dominant religion was Roman Catholicism and the saintly or holy person was a familiar type in her society. Thought to be especially close to God, the saintly person was considered to be free from some aspects of fallen humanity; the prayers of such a person were considered especially efficacious, and the holy one was often accepted as a bearer of revelation, sometimes in the form of divine judgment against persons in high places as well as low.

Siena, an ancient walled city set on three hills in the mountainous north-central region of Italy, had suffered a disastrous loss of some eighty thousand of its population by plague the year after Catherine's birth in 1347. Catherine's twin sister died at birth, and only twelve of her twenty-four brothers and sisters reached maturity. She passed her childhood in the midst of her large family, all of whom lived in one small house. It is told that at the age of five she experienced levitation; at six she was vouchsafed a vision of Christ on His throne wearing papal vestments and papal crown; and at seven she dedicated her virginity to Christ. So grief-dispelling was her presence even as a child that she received the affectionate name of Euphrosyne. Becoming a member of the Dominican Third Order at sixteen, she spent three years in her house in religious seclusion and severe asceticism; subsequently she ministered to the sick and poor, and she sought the conversion of the rich. It is in keeping with her spirit of self-renunciation that Catherine prayed successfully for invisible stigmata; thus, she suffered the pain of Christ's wounds, but did not bear their marks.

Catherine's life was cast into a time of turbulence. The Church had fallen upon evil days in that the moral state of both the secular clergy and the papacy was generally acknowledged to be at a disgracefully low level. The pope himself had moved to Avignon, France, and his prestige was in serious decline. It was openly preached that the Roman Church was about to face a destructive end from which the devout should flee. Heretical movements were mounting. It was these conditions to which Catherine was destined to minister. The *Dialogue* with which we are here concerned, however, deals not with Catherine's political ideas, but rather with her fundamental religious convictions.

Catherine has been praised as having a permanent and foremost place among the guides of humanity. She dwells in her work on the sheer beauty of the soul in the state of grace as contrasted to the ugliness of sin. Throughout this extraordinary book it is not so much the teaching, which consists principally of the basic Roman Catholic creeds, but the remarkably sustained elevation of tone which is impressive.

The *Dialogue* is divided into four treatises of unequal length; the first, on divine providence, covers twenty-four pages; the second, on discretion, covers a hundred—as does the third, on prayer; the last, on obedience, runs to fifty-three pages.

The treatise on divine providence is introduced with an account of the soul rising in mystic ecstasy to ask God for help: first, for the self; second, for the reformation of the Holy Church; third, for men in general and particularly for the rebels against the Church; and, finally, in all things both worthy, general, and specific. Through proper self-knowledge the soul learns the humbling lesson that no one exists in and for himself, but only derivatively from the Eternal Truth or God. Proper self-knowledge dissipates narrow self-love and permits one to gain the knowledge of God which is beyond all human understanding. A natural accompaniment of this ineffable love of God is grief, for one soon becomes aware of one's own sin and of the sins of the world. Pain and suffering are to be borne in patience, for through the virtue of love, suffering leads to satisfaction and reward not only for one's self but for others also. It is not suffering, however, which is effective in the spiritual realm but the contrition which accompanies it.

God's grace is sometimes shown in His allowing men to know the world in order to see its instability. Indeed, Catherine reports God as saying that "the eye cannot see, nor the tongue relate, nor the heart think, how many are the roads and ways which I use, through love alone, to lead them back in grace, so that My truth may be fulfilled in them." Similarly, from the divine perspective the injustice practiced by the wicked man makes even more evident the justice of the man who bears injustice humbly and with undiminished faith. When a man receives injury from his neighbor, he proves his patience.

The treatise on discretion deals with that virtue of true knowledge which the soul should have both of itself and of God. Parables are given to show how love, humility, and discretion are united, how penance and similar works are merely means and are not of the essence of the soul, how God made of Christ a bridge by which fallen man could travel the road to Heaven, and how those that ignore the bridge are as trees of death whose fruits are sensuality, avarice, injustice, and error. Those thus damned are deprived of the vision of God; their conscience gnaws at them increasingly like a worm; they see the Devil; and they experience a fire which burns but does not consume since the soul, being spiritual, cannot be consumed as a material thing. In contrast, the blessed ones rejoice in God and experience the beatific vision.

In the treatise on prayer Catherine continues her presentation of the tenets of Roman Catholic orthodoxy, and she offers advice regarding what must be done in order for the full meaning of the tenets to be realized in the life of the individual. When the question is asked in the divine soliloquy about the way in which imperfection is lost and perfection acquired, the answer follows immediately: "By perseverance seasoned with the most holy faith." Even if vocal prayer is imperfect it should be practiced lest one fall into the worse state of idleness. Catherine speaks from the depths of personal experience of perseverance, and often her asceticism may be discerned. When, for example, God is discoursing on the glory of His charity and mercy, which are extended to the unjust as well as the just, He adds that He often gives "more to the sinner than to the righteous man, because the righteous man is able to endure privation, and I take from him the goods of the world that he may the more abundantly enjoy the goods of heaven." If there is in some an invincible ignorance, there must surely be in others an invincible faith, and Catherine's faith is such. When desolation, suffering, and persecution are interpreted as proofs of God's mercy and love and become causes for praise, it is clear that here is a faith forged in the crucible of personal experience and validated in the mystical union which lies beyond human understanding. It is to descriptions of the various phases of the mystic state that the remainder of this section is dedicated.

The final treatise on obedience makes explicit what has been implicit throughout: attainment of the state whereby one is able to receive the glorious divine vision depends upon one's unquestioning obedience. The perfectly obedient soul "passes by the assaults of the devils, mortifying and macerating his flesh, stripping it bare of all pleasures," for it clothes itself with the "labors of the order in a faith which despises nothing." The obedient soul remembers not "the injuries, pains, or blows inflicted upon her by his superior in the order, but calling him humbly, turns to him without anger, hatred, or rancour, but with meekness and benevolence." The pains of the present, after all, are scarcely comparable to the joys which will come to the obedient person later in Heaven. A recapitulation of the major themes brings the work to a close on an exalted note of mystical rapture.

Though Catherine will be remembered for her activities in the politico-ecclesiastical sphere, for her published prayers, and for her nearly four hundred letters which have been ranked as equal to the work of Petrarch for beauty and significance, it is her *Dialogue* which shows most clearly her claim to spiritual greatness.

THE REVELATIONS OF DIVINE LOVE

Author: Lady Julian [Juliana] of Norwich (c.1342-after 1413)
Type of work: Mystical theology
First transcribed: 1393

Principal Ideas Advanced

Although man sees some things as good and others as evil, God sees all things as good.

Christians must embrace the sufferings of Christ in order to receive the bliss of Heaven.

Man's sin and Fall is part of God's eternal purpose, and in the end men shall see why God ordained it.

God does not blame Christians for their sins, but pities them for their sufferings; yet more profound than His pity is His joy in the bliss which they shall have in Heaven.

In revealing these truths, Christ designs to teach Christians to rejoice in the great love which binds them to Him.

An early copyist prefaces the *Revelations of Divine Love* with the following statement: "Here is a vision shewn by the goodness of God to a devout woman whose name is Julian. She is a recluse at Norwich and is living yet in this year of our Lord 1413." We know little more than this concerning the name and circumstances of the author, who would have preferred to remain unknown, even as to the identity of her sex. On the other hand, Julian tells explicitly the date and the hours on which she received a series of visions, and she offers a great deal of information concerning her physical and mental condition during the visions. These details are germane to her purpose, because they attest the actuality of what Julian maintains was a true revelation which God gave to mankind through her. Julian believed in the truth of the Scriptures and the teachings of the Church, but she was convinced that out of His love for the elect and His desire to be known of them, God had revealed additional truths to her.

Julian relates that, as a young woman, she prayed for three things. The first was that she might have the knowledge of Christ's passion that was given to those who, like Mary Magdalene, were present at the Crucifixion. The second was that she might experience grievous sickness in her own body, so as to know all the temptations and sufferings of the dying, yet without bringing about the departure of her soul. The third was that she might receive "three wounds" in her life; namely, "the wound of true contrition, the wound of kind compassion, and the wound of earnest longing for God." She had asked that the sickness come when she was thirty years of age—and so it happened. For six days she hovered on the brink of death. On the seventh, she gradually lost all feeling in her body. When the priest held the crucifix before her, her sight began to fail and everything grew dark except the image of the cross. Then she thought of obtaining the "wounds" that she had previously desired, especially to know the suffering of Christ. Suddenly the revelations began. It was four o'clock on the morning of May 8, 1373 when the revelatory experiences began, and three in the afternoon when they ended.

During the fifteen revelations, Julian had no pain, but after they were ended, her sickness came over her again. When the priest spoke to her, she said that she had "raved during the day," and that the cross which he held before her seemed to bleed. The priest laughed at first, but was later convinced; Julian, feeling that she had betrayed God's revelation to her, was smitten with guilt. That night she dreamed that the Devil appeared to her; but, on waking, she thought of the truths which had been revealed to her and she was comforted. Then, on the following day, came the final vision, in which her soul appeared to her as a city, with Christ dwelling in its midst. "Know it now well," she heard Him say, "that it was no raving that thou sawest today. But take it and believe it and keep thee therein, and comfort thee therewith, and trust thereto; and thou shalt not be overcome." So the visions ended. But Julian continued over a period of twenty years to have "lightings and touchings" by means of which she saw further meanings in her visions. Thus, her book contains, besides vivid descriptions of her "shewings," long discussions of the truths which they were meant to convey.

Julian's description of her visions is complicated by the fact that she discerned three kinds of awareness present during each of "shewings": bodily sight, verbal understanding, and ghostly sight. By her bodily sight she beheld the crucifix that hung before her transformed into the likeness of the suffering Christ, His face soiled with blood and spittle, and contorted with pain. But while this vision continued, many things passed through her understanding concerning Christ's godhood and manhood, and concerning God's love for the world. At the same time, she had "a ghostly sight of his homely loving," that His love encloses us like a garment and that "he is to us everything that is good." Julian says that she cannot show the ghostly sight as fully as she would like, and must trust that God will help her readers to "receive it more ghostly and more sweetly than I can or may tell it."

The visions fall into four unequal groups. The first twelve have as their focus the passion of Christ, in which, as Julian considers it, is shown the height and depth of God's goodness, and the nothingness of the world outside His love and care. "I saw God in a point," she declares; "the sight, I say, was in my understanding, by which I saw that he is in all things." In this moment it was showed to her that, although man sees some deeds as good and others as evil, God sees that all is good, for "everything that is done is so in virtue of God's doing." Julian says the pain of these visions was such "the grumbling and frailty of the flesh" made her want to look away. She had, as she puts it, "an offer in my reason; it was said to me, as though by a friend: 'Look up to the heaven to his Father.'" But through faith she answered, "Nay, I cannot for Thou art my heaven." For, as she explains, she would rather have endured endless pain than enter Heaven other than by Him. Her devotion was soon rewarded. At the point when it seemed that Christ's life could endure no longer, His countenance changed. "This change in him changed me," she writes; "and I was as glad and merry as it is possible to be." Suddenly she understood that in our present life we are "on his cross, dying with him in our pains and our passion." When His countenance changes, this life is ended, and we are with Him in heaven.

The thirteenth revelation seemed to Julian the answer to a question which had long troubled her, for it had seemed to her that not pain but sin is the cause of all distress. "Thus in my folly, even before this time, I often wondered why the beginning of sin was not prevented by the great foreseeing wisdom of God; for then—or so it seemed to me—all would have been well." In this vision Jesus said, "Sin must needs be, but all shall be well. All shall be well; and all manner of thing shall be well." How this could be remained a secret, which prompted Julian to distinguish between those things which God wills to make known to us, and those which He hides in Himself. Nevertheless, she found "a mighty comfort" in the assurance that "in the last day" He would "make all well that is not well." Several consolations were given her in the meanwhile. One was that in all her visions of Christ she saw nothing of sin but only of pain. Another was the assurance that God sends suffering to His children, not because they have offended Him, but to prepare their souls for greater bliss.

One question which Julian wanted answered was never settled; namely, what happens to Satan and to men who die outside the faith of the Holy Church. While protesting that she is an orthodox believer, she finds it impossible to understand how "all manner of things should be well" if part of creation is damned. "But," she says, "I had no other answer to the difficulty in this shewing of our Lord's, except this: 'What is impossible to thee is not impossible to me; I shall save my word in all things—I shall make all things well!' "

The problem of sin has other aspects which troubled Julian. The most vexing, because of its practical importance, is the conflict which she presumed to exist between the teachings of the Church that sin deserves to be punished, and the disclosures of her revelations that God is love and that there is no wrath in Him. "If I take it thus, that we are not sinners or blameworthy," she writes, "then it seemeth as though I should err in failing to acknowledge the truth. But granted this truth—that we are sinners and blameworthy, good Lord, how may it then be that I cannot see this truth in thee, who are my God and my Maker?" The question seemed to her so basic and so important ("I need to know, as it seemeth to me, if I am to go on living here, for the knowing of good and evil"), that she cried with all her strength to God for help. In answer, God showed her a parable of a lord and a servant. The servant is shown as standing reverently before the lord, loving him and wishing to do his will; and the lord, returning the love, sends the servant to work in his field. The servant goes, but falls into a ravine and is hurt. Being able neither to rise nor to find any comfort, he forgets his master's love for him, and thinks only of his misfortune. Meanwhile, the lord, who knows what has befallen the servant, has two thoughts. The first is of great "ruth and pity" for the hurt that has come to his servant. This he shows on his countenance. His second thought, "more inward and ghostly," is of "joy and bliss" for the reward which he intends to bestow upon him. For the servant is not to blame for the condition into which he has fallen. As he lies in the ravine, he is "as lovable and as good inwardly as he was when he stood before his lord." Therefore, says the lord, because he has endured harm and evil for love of me, it is proper "to give him a gift that is better and more worshipful to him than his own wholeness should have been."

The interpretation of this parable was not given to Julian all at once. She took it at first as referring to Adam, the father of the race. Afterwards she saw that the "ruth and pity" which appeared outwardly was for the falling of the creaturely Adam, but that the "joy and bliss" which appeared to her ghostly sight was for the falling of His eternal Son. In this manner, Julian found an answer to her question. Looked at through the eyes of the flesh, while God does not blame us for our sin, nevertheless He appears to rue it and to pity our condition. Looked at through the eyes of the spirit, God does not even consider what we are at present but only what, in view of our love and faithfulness, we shall be; in this aspect, He does not view us as progeny of Adam but as members of the body of Christ.

In her efforts to expound the relationship of the spiritual elect to Christ (for Julian simply says that she received no revelation concerning the damned), the author elaborates the conception of the Motherhood of God, and particularly of Christ. "I beheld the working of all the blessed Trinity," she says; "in which beholding I saw and understood these three properties: the property of the Fatherhood, and the property of the Motherhood, and the property of the Lordship—in one God." God is our Father in that we have our being from Him, our Mother in His mercy toward us, our Lord in the grace with which He strengthens us. She goes on to explain, in line with her quasi-Platonic conceptions of man's constitution, that Christ is our Mother in a twofold sense: our higher, substantial part is grounded and rooted in Him, but so also is our lower, sensual part. It is in the lower part that man falls and suffers pain; this is the part of Christ that endures the anguish of the cross. In his higher part, man neither sins nor suffers pain; this is the part of Christ that is eternal, in union with whom the elect shall enjoy eternal bliss.

In the interval which preceded Julian's final revelation, her sickness had returned, she had in a manner been false to her vision ("I raved"), and she had been frightened by a nightmarish vision of the Devil. The final revelation was to her ghostly eye, showing her her own soul "so large as it were an endless world, and also as it were a blessed kingdom," in the midst of which sat Christ in His majesty, "comely of person, and tall of stature, the greatest bishop, most awful king, Lord of highest honor." It was then that the words were spoken which confirmed that her visions were "no raving," and encouraged her with the promise "thou shalt not be overcome." Here, she says, is the true comfort for Christians, not that they shall escape trouble and travail and distress, but that they shall not be vanquished. Sin, she goes on to say, will continue to vex the believer as long as he lives on earth; nor is anything more contrary to God than sin, which cuts us off from His blessed sight, and leaves us as dead for the time. But although we lose our vision of Him, He never loses sight of us. "In falling and in rising we are preciously kept in the same love. For," says Julian, "in the beholding of God we fall not, and in the beholding of ourselves we stand not. And both these be truth, as I see it. But the beholding of our Lord God is the higher truth."

This tension between the higher and the lower, which refuses, on account of the faith in the Incarnation, to deny the reality of pain and of sin while nevertheless affirming the transcendence of love and bliss, is characteristic of the best in Christian mysticism, or, more strictly, "apocalypticism." For Julian does not claim to be the possessor of any spiritual art by which she has access to divine life. On the contrary, she considers that the revelations granted to her were a ministration of Christ's love, who intends it as a favor not just to her but to her "even-Christians." "For," she explains, "I saw truly and understood in our Lord's meaning that he shewed it because he will have it known more than it is. In which knowing he will give us grace to love him and cleave to him. For he beheld his heavenly treasure with so great love on earth, that he willeth to give more light and solace in heavenly joy, in drawing our hearts from the sorrow and darkness which we are in."

THE CLOUD OF UNKNOWING

Author: Unknown
Type of work: Mystical theology
First transcribed: c.1375

Principal Ideas Advanced

Meditation on God's works of creation and redemption, although useful in early stages of the soul's preparation, must be covered in a cloud of forgetting before one can begin the mystical ascent.

The task of the mystic is to bring his understanding to a halt in a cloud of unknowing, and wait in that state for God to show Himself.

The soul that has achieved union with God becomes perfect in love and partakes in the work of redeeming fallen creation.

The *Cloud of Unknowing* is a psychologically penetrating essay of practical advice ostensibly addressed to a young monk who, having entered upon the life of an anchorite, wants to know how to achieve perfect union with God. Because the youth is without much learning, the author of the

Cloud of Unknowing undertakes to answer his question by replying in plain English. The author was a scholar, versed in the mystical writings of St. Augustine (354-430), Dionysius, the Pseudo-Areopagite (fl. c.500), and Richard of St. Victor (died c.1173). He ably transcended his learning, and he wrote from personal experience of the way he wanted to commend. Nothing is known about him other than what his writings disclose; namely, that he was a "clerk" in the Northeast Midlands of England in the second half of the fourteenth century.

The *Cloud of Unknowing* is in the tradition of the "negative theology" of Pseudo-Dionysius. Man's part in drawing near to God consists in emptying his mind of every thought. When he has brought his reason to a standstill, he must wait for God to disclose Himself. The experience of union is momentary and indescribable, but it is powerfully efficacious for man's redemption. We read: "This is the work of the soul that most pleaseth God. All saints and angels have joy of this work and hasten them to help it with all their might. All fiends be mad when thou dost thus, and try for to defeat it in all that they can. All men living on earth be wonderfully helped by this work, thou knowest not how. Yea, the souls in purgatory are eased of their pains by virtue of this work. Thou thyself art cleansed and made virtuous by no work so much."

The familiar distinction between the active and the contemplative life, symbolized by Martha and Mary in the Gospel narrative, is preserved in the theology of the *Cloud of Unknowing*. When Jesus said of the sister that sat at His feet, "Mary hath chosen the better part," he had reference, says the *Cloud of Unknowing,* to the higher part of the contemplative life. For the contemplative life starts where the active life ends, with meditation or mental prayer, in which the soul thinks of its sin, of Christ's mercies, of saintly men, or of the joys of Heaven; but meditation is useful only to bring the soul to that state of humility and obedience from which it can begin its ascent into the divine presence. The actual work of perfection requires that the mind rigorously empty itself of the very thoughts which are the staple of meditation. Every thought of God and of His creatures must be trampled down and covered with *"a cloud of forgetting."*

So far, the ascent is the work of man. By a travail that is hard and wearisome for the beginner but is lighter for those who have some practice, the soul must bring itself into "a darkness, and as it were a *cloud of unknowing,* thou knowest not what, saving that thou feelest in thy will a naked intent unto God." Beyond this, however, man's efforts are of no avail. Man can bring himself neither to see God by the light of understanding nor to feel Him by the sweetness of love. But if he keep himself in this darkness, smiting upon the cloud with "a sharp dart of longing love," it may be that God will favor him and perform his gracious work: "Then will he sometimes peradventure send out a beam of ghostly light, piercing this *cloud of unknowing* that is betwixt thee and him, and show thee some of his secrets, the which man may not and cannot speak. Then shalt thou feel thine affection inflamed with the fire of his love, far more than I can tell thee, or may or will at this time. For of that work that pertaineth only to God dare

I not take upon me to speak with my blabbering fleshly tongue."

The author has a carefully developed theology, basically orthodox, of which, however, only fragments are stated in the *Cloud of Unknowing*. One interesting feature of his system is his conception of time as made up of a finite number of instants, in each of which the heart experiences a "single striving." Man's responsibility is to love God perfectly in each fleeting moment: "Look not forwards and let the backwards be." In his fallen state, however, no man can do this. He can barely heed one instant in a hundred; and how can he make satisfaction for the times he has lost? For help, says the author, he must turn to Jesus, who, "by his Godhead is maker and giver of time," and "by his Manhood is the true heeder of time." Love, the author continues, knits man to Jesus and through Him to the blessed angels and all the saints, who, by "heeding of time" make satisfaction for the time which others have lost. "But," warns the author, "I cannot see who may truly claim fellowship thus with Jesu and his just Mother, his high angels and also with the saints, unless he be such a one as doth that in him is, with the help of grace, in heeding of time."

The fourteenth century witnessed the rise of numerous religious parties. The most outstanding example in England was that of the followers of Wycliffe (c.1329-1384), who are censured in the *Cloud of Unknowing* as being "fleshly living men of the world, which think the statutes of Holy Church over hard for them to amend their lives by," and who "burst up and blaspheme all the saints, sacraments, statutes, and ordinances of Holy Church." But the author is less concerned with these open heretics (as they seemed to him) than he is with pseudo-mystical practitioners within the Church who lead astray persons which were never suited to contemplation. "I tell thee," he says, "that the devil hath his contemplatives as God hath his." Such idle contemplatives are always yearning for "bodily showings," straining to turn their eyes inward, or to soar upwards into planetary spheres, failing, says the author, to comprehend the indifference of spirit to spatial distinctions, or that "nowhere bodily is everywhere ghostly." The *Cloud of Unknowing* contrasts the bizarre behavior of such false mystics with that of the true mystic, who, in virtue of the meekness and charity which he receives in union with God, becomes more "seemly" and "favorable" in the eyes of men than ever before.

Although it stands in the tradition which denies the possibility of knowing God through the reason, and demands that the soul forget every creature as well as every divine manifestation within creation in order to wait upon God, the *Cloud of Unknowing* is not in the least morbid or world-weary in temper. Admittedly, when one is in the *cloud of unknowing*, the feeling of his sin makes him loathe himself, but, according to the author, it never makes him desire "to un-be." "He liketh right well to be, and he giveth full heartily thanks unto God for the worthiness and the gift of his being, although he desire unceasingly for to lack the knowing and the feeling of his being." When, in perfect charity, he is "oned unto God," he does not lose his being: "For although it may be said in a manner that in this time God and thou be not two but one in spirit, nevertheless thou art beneath him . . . in nature." Moreover, that divine love which binds the soul to God comprehends every creature: "For charity meaneth nought else but love of God for himself above all creatures, and of man for God even as thyself." The proof thereof, writes the author, is that the Christian who has tasted of heavenly bliss no longer has preferences among men; he does not prefer kin above stranger, or friend above foe: "All men, he thinketh, be his friends, and none his foes."

THE FOLLOWING OF CHRIST

Author: Gerard [Geert de] Groote (Gerardus Magnus, 1340-1384)
Type of work: Devotional manual
First transcribed: c.1380

Principal Ideas Advanced

The main concern of a Christian life is to follow Jesus Christ and to deny the self.

The transitory world is a source of misery and must be renounced in favor of allegiance to the eternal world.

Constant self-examination is necessary to guard the soul from engagement with illusory pleasures and the temptations of the Devil.

Adversity and anxiety are the lot of man in this world and can be met and overcome only by those who follow the way of the Cross, for it is only through such humiliation that man receives eternal life.

Very few books on the devotional life have attained the eminence of *The Following of Christ* by Gerard Groote, the founder of a late medieval religious order commonly known as the Brethren of the Common Life. The book is the spiritual diary of this Netherlands spiritual leader. The work was written during various periods of Groote's life, and it covers a variety of topics. It is not unified in the formal sense as a planned treatise would be. The sections are separate in both time and subject matter so that the parts can be perused in any order agreeable to the reader without any loss of value. Such unity as the book possesses comes from the reflective devotional attitude of the author as he follows Christ according to his understanding of the significance of the Christian life.

While the volume is believed by many scholars to be correctly ascribed to Gerard Groote, the work has also been widely circulated under the title *The Imitation of Christ* and credited to Thomas à Kempis (c.1380-1471). What happened seems to have been that Thomas was assigned the task of editing the manuscript of the founder of his order and produced two editions, the first in 1427 and the second in 1441. In neither does he name the author, no doubt assuming his name to be known by those who would use the diary. But he closes the second edition with the historical note in Latin, "Finished and completed in the year of our Lord 1441 by the hand of brother Thomas van Kempen at Mount Saint Agnes near Zwolle." In this way his own name became associated with the book. Actually some of it was from the pen of the editor, for some liberties were taken with the manuscript both by way of arrangement of the contents and by additions to the text. In this enlarged form it was distributed widely even before the invention of printing, and since that time it has had phenomenal circulation and has been translated into many languages to the great benefit of all who value the development of the life of the spirit. [A separate account of the work as credited to Thomas à Kempis also appears in this volume.]

There are three distinct parts in the original version of Groote. Book One, under the title *De imitatione Christi,* was in the hands of many as an aid to monastic devotion shortly after the author's death in 1384. The twenty-five short chapters can be divided into three sections: the first, written by Groote as a layman; the second, after he entered the monastic life; and the third, a detached series of admonitions.

The concentration of thought is on the elevation of the mind in the light of the teaching of Christ on self-denial. It is this spirit of submissive obedience that matters in religion, far more than learning in the usual disciplines of education. The author himself was a man of great accomplishments as far as erudition was concerned and had been professor of philosophy and theology at Cologne. Hence, there is no encouragement given to ignorance as the parent of devotion. The question is rather that of assessment of the degrees of value to be placed on different kinds of knowledge. In the light of the fact that man's life is lived by the mercy and under the judgment of God, then all that makes the soul pleasing to its Divine Creator takes precedence over all that is merely pleasing to one's fellow man: "Right knowledge is not to be blamed; but a good conscience and a virtuous life are always to be preferred." Pursuit of this perspective leads to a drastic re-evaluation of the place of all temporal goods in life. Not only self-renunciation but restriction of association with other people and material things as an aid to interior discipline seems to be indicated. "It is a very great thing to live in obedience, to be under a superior and not to be one's own master," writes Groote. In this mood Gerard Groote entered the Carthusian monastery at Munnikhuizen on the Rhine.

The remaining eight chapters of Book One appear to be notes made while Groote was a novice. They place in high regard the life of seclusion and self-mortification. Contrasts with the world outside the monastery are frequent, and the many temptations to be avoided are the subject of the author's proverbial style of wisdom. Talkativeness, inquisitiveness, criticism of others, envy, and self-will are all snares to the devout by which he can lose his soul. Complete submissiveness to the community is difficult but obligatory: "You must learn to break your own will in many things, if you wish to live in peace and concord with others." This is the opposite of an ideal of aggressive self-assertion in the competitive world of commerce where the financial profit and loss account is the criterion of success or failure. The attention in monastic devotion is on the self, but not in its aggrandizement. It is self-abnegation in the belief that all the transitory world is vanity and vexation of spirit, and all that matters is the cultivation of contemplation on the eternal.

This fundamental point of view comes out clearly in the admonitions which end Book One. The great company of martyrs "hated their lives in this world, that they might keep them into life eternal." Groote weaves this theme in and out of his reflections; he sees the history of the Church as a story of toil and struggle against clever devices of evil to embroil the virtuous man in temporal affairs. Every moment must be made subject to the needs of others, and regular self-scrutiny is encouraged lest some wickedness penetrate the citadel of the soul. "Prepare yourself as a man to fight against the wickedness of the devil," he counsels. "Bridle your immoderateness and you will easily conquer every inclination of the flesh." Every person is to suit the discipline of the soul to his own needs and opportunities. Since men have different problems to overcome, flexibility must be permitted and even encouraged in all spiritual exercises.

The medieval theme of contempt of the world is never missing from these chapters, and the negative emphasis on what a virtuous man will not do is the subject of sentence after sentence. "It is truly a great misery to live here on earth," Groote writes; or again, "For to eat, to drink, to watch, to sleep, to rest, to labor and to satisfy all the needs of nature is truly a great misery, unhappiness and affliction to a devout man, who would fain be released and freed from all sin." Clearly, unless such an attitude is balanced by a compensating joy and satisfaction in obedience to Christ, Groote points out, it can be morbid and destructive of Christian regard for others outside the monastery who do not have the leisure to pursue intensive periods of self-examination and must attend to the business of mundane commerce. It could also be taken as a denial of the wisdom of the Creator in providing the world for man's habitation. At times Gerard Groote himself appears to lose this balance and to be too contemptuous of the temporal order.

Book Two opens with a quotation from the Gospels, "The Kingdom of God is within you," and this is understood as a reference to the interior life of each individual. "Learn to despise exterior things," the author admonishes, "and to apply yourself to interior things"; thereafter absorption in the affairs of earth are condemned in particular after particular. The heart that desires peace must follow Christ in suffering, misunderstanding, adversity, and humiliation: "Had you but once penetrated deep into the heart of the sweet Jesus and tasted only a little of his burning love, you would not be anxious about your own weal or woe; but you would rather rejoice when humiliation comes upon you, for the love of Jesus makes a man despise himself." True strength is inner strength; true security is found only in unqualified humility and obedience; true joy will come when the Cross is changed to a crown in the final consummation of union with Christ.

In the second part of Book Two the author composes a dialogue between Christ and the devout Christian and further develops the theme of disengagement from the world through indifference to the things which concern many other men. Interpreters of this section have seen in it an occasional reference to Groote's own trials when he became a preacher in the diocese of Utrecht, after he was advised not to complete his monastic vows. His public utterances on the love and goodness of God, and his caustic denunciation of the morals of the clergy, brought crowds to listen. The bishop, however, was not happy about the outspoken preacher and in 1383 stopped his troublemaking by withdrawing his license. Protests went unheeded, and an appeal was finally made to Rome for redress of the wrong, but no answer came before Gerard Groote's death in 1384.

It was during the period of his fame as a preacher of what is called the "Modern Devotion," that some others of like mind gathered round him, and the community of the Brethren of the Common Life was founded, through which educational work was done all over Europe.

The Following of Christ concludes with a series of admonitions in preparation for holy communion. It was in this section that Thomas made considerable changes, perhaps not always for the better, and it is here that the Roman Catholic allegiance of the author is most prominently expressed. Much of this Third Book would be impossible as a guide to devotion for those influenced by the Reformation. The fervency, sincerity, and humility of Groote are deeply impressive, however, and in this all Christian people can be at one when confronted with the claims of discipleship.

TRIALOGUS

Author: John Wycliffe (c.1329-1384)
Type of work: Polemical theology
First transcribed: 1382

Principal Ideas Advanced

God, man, and the universe are intelligible and necessary.

The Bible contains all truth and is the sole authority in religious matters.

Moral virtue and man's acceptation in God's sight are one and the same, and depend upon grace.

The wealth of the clergy and the mendicancy of the friars are contrary to the teaching of Scripture.

Transubstantiation and the "treasury of merit" are heretical conceptions.

Generally speaking, John Wycliffe (or Wyclif) was known to his contemporaries as a peerless scholastic, to the fifteenth century as an archheretic, and to the Protestant reformers as the *doctor evangelicus.* The

Enlightenment appreciated Wycliffe's anticlericalism; the nineteenth century hailed him as the "morning star of the Reformation," and the twentieth century has reacted by portraying him as a much less admirable figure. The definitive study of Wycliffe's thought, as contained in his very extensive writings, remains yet to be made.

The *Trialogus* was completed after Wycliffe's censure by the Blackfriars Council of 1382 and before his first apoplectic stroke later on in the same year, which left him an invalid. It represents his final convictions, and comprehends both his essential philosophic positions and his main reformatory concerns. The work consists of four books, and is written in the form of a "trialogue" among the champion of truth, Alithia; its adversary, Pseustis; and the judicious Phronesis, who represents Wycliffe's own point of view.

Book I (*"De Deo"*) deals with the nature and attributes of God and with the ideas in the mind of God. It includes a discussion of the Trinity, which Wycliffe proceeds to prove by natural reason. Just as we reason from the perception of motion to the First Mover, he writes, so we can reason from the perception of the trinal nature of the soul (*memoria, ratio, voluntas*) to the trinal nature of the Deity that created it. For Augustine (354-430) does not regard this trinity of powers in the soul as three powers that inhere accidentally in it but as three distinct entities (*tres res*), any one of which is essentially the soul, just as any one of the three divine Persons is essentially God. But if God's self-intellection is a personal reality, His intellection of extrinsic objects is not a personal reality, but a necessary truth; namely, the intelligibility of objects, which logically precedes their producibility; otherwise God would be able to produce an object which He did not understand, and thus to act unwisely (*non sapienter*). But how, then, could God create man wise (*homo . . . sapiens*)? Hence, Augustine rightly asserts that it is impossible to make a wise man apart from these exemplary ideas. These truths are formally distinct from each other and from God, but essentially they are God. For the "subtle evangelist" says that "whatever was made was life in him" (a common medieval reading of John 1:3,4: *"quod factum est in ipso vita erat"*); namely, in Him who said, "I am the way, the truth, and the life" (John 14:6). Ignorance of this metaphysic and of these eternal truths or ideas is wholly due to ignorance of the language arts (*artium sermocinalium*); namely, grammar and rhetoric; while, more generally, an erroneous understanding of Holy Scripture (which, according to Augustine, contains whatever truth there is) is due to ignorance of grammar and logic.

Book II (*"De mundo"*) deals with the unity and necessity of the world, time and eternity, primary matter, psychology, the theory of knowledge, the doctrine of angels, predestination, and astronomy. Of special interest is Wycliffe's rational proof of the immortality of the soul, since this doctrine was not given the status of dogma in the Roman Church until 1517, when it was affirmed by the Fifth Lateran Council.

Book III (*"De virtutibus peccatisque et de salvatore"*) in some respects seems to move in the direction of Reformation thought. Wycliffe's conception of faith, however, is wholly traditional. He defines faith as the "supernatural and habitual apprehension of truths to be believed." He recognizes that "faith" sometimes refers to the act of believing, the habit (*habitus*) from which the act proceeds, or the truth that is believed; and he distinguishes between unformed faith (*fides informis*) and faith that is formed by love (*fides caritate formata*). Love is the supreme virtue, the wedding garment without which no one shall be admitted to the celestial wedding of Christ and His Church. The love of God is understood as the love of His law, and all sin is attributed to ingratitude, but also to unbelief, for as long as a man is mindful of God he does not sin. All sin is to be avoided; if God Himself commanded a man to sin, it were better to disobey God than to sin. Nevertheless, "through the infinite compassion of God, the fall of man . . . has been made to subserve the introduction of a greater amount of good than would have resulted from his continuance" in the state of innocence. Man is incapable of moral virtue as long as God's grace is absent, and since the meritoriousness of a man's work depends on divine acceptance of it, a man cannot know his moral status apart from a special revelation. Nevertheless, "the grace of predestination, or final perseverance, cannot fall away from any one." There is only one mortal sin: final impenitence. God alone can punish or remit sin; hence, "prelates in granting indulgences, commonly blaspheme the wisdom of God." Men ought to be mindful of the commandments of the Lord, rather than of "the bulls of the pope, and the pretensions of the religious orders," writes Wycliffe. To disdain the authority of Scripture is equivalent to disbelief in Christ. The veneration that is accorded to the saints ought to be given to Christ.

It is especially in Book IV (*"De signis"*) that we encounter Wycliffe the reformer. He attacks the avarice of the clergy, the lethargy of the laity, and the noxiousness of the friars, all in the process of subjecting the reigning sacramental theory and practice to a searching critique.

Just as the Old Testament assigned no source of revenue beyond the tithe to the priests and Levites, so Christ and the Apostles taught by precept and example that the clergy should be content with the provision of its bare needs. By turning their back upon the institution of Christ, the clergy has accumulated tremendous wealth. Temporal lords (to whom Christ showed six distinct favors in His lifetime) by endowing the Church have begotten Antichrist. From the time of Constantine, the secular power has been diminished by the usurpations of the papacy. To restore to the secular lords their full power would mean the end of wars, greater freedom for the preaching of the Gospel, and an increase in the number of those who "wing their way to heaven." Wycliffe suggests that a gradual recovery by the Crown of the wealth of the Church should not be difficult, since title to the large benefices passes to the Crown upon the death of the incumbent, until the installation of his successor.

Wycliffe is no less opposed to begging friars than to rich priests. By begging, the friars deprive the needy and violate the law of nature, the commandment of God, who said, "There shall be no needy man nor beggar among you" (Deuteronomy 15:4, Vulgate), and the counsel of Solomon, who said, "Give me neither poverty nor riches." The friars' main defense, that Christ Himself practiced mendicancy, is answered by the allegation that Christ was not asking as a beggar for what was another's, but as a lord for what was His own. But mendicancy is only one of the faults of the friars. They also, writes Wycliffe, "have fallen into a radical heresy, for they pretend expressly in . . . letters, that the individuals to whom they grant them, shall be made partakers of merits from themselves after death." In thus making merchandise of their pretended merits, the friars even go beyond the popes, for the latter insist on contrition as prerequisite for the validity of an indulgence, while the friars do not. "Yet we know that God cannot remove the guilt of the sinner unless he be truly contrite." The whole notion of a "treasury of merits," Wycliffe insists, is "rude blasphemy."

The Friars make a simoniacal use of the office of preaching, Wycliffe continues, for they abuse their privilege of hearing confessions, neglect the evangelical law of brotherly admonition, and teach Eucharistic heresies. While they pose as Christ's poor ones, the friars, Wycliffe calculates, cost England 60,000 marks annually for the support of some four thousand of them. These "false brethren" err in subjecting themselves to some rule other than the rule of Christ, and in teaching men to rely on their pretended merits rather than on "the graciousness of Christ."

Wycliffe discusses each of the seven sacraments recognized by the Roman Church and expresses his dissatisfaction with the way they are understood and administered. For him, "Christ, in his own person, is a sensible sign, and as it seems to me, the sacrament of sacraments." In the sacrament of matrimony, the essential thing is that there be genuine (not merely verbal) consent, an actual being-joined-together by the Lord. The sacrament of holy orders no longer follows the New Testament pattern, which identifies the office of bishop and presbyter, and recognizes deacons only as a second order. Wycliffe reinterprets the sacrament of penance so as to make contrition (its essential element) a feeling that is perfected by oral utterance to God alone ("confession") and private confession to a priest ("satisfaction"). Auricular confession, said to be the invention of Pope Innocent III (1160-1216), should be made optional, as not essential to salvation. Modern bishops cannot claim Peter's authority to bind and loose, since they resemble Peter neither in spiritual power (to work miracles) nor in lowliness and holiness of life. Confirmation and extreme unction lack a proper scriptural foundation, he claims, and together with baptism and all the rest they are encumbered with unauthorized ceremonies.

The most detailed discussion is devoted to the sacrament of the Eucharist. For a thousand years, Wycliffe says, until Satan was loosed (see Revelation 20:1-8), Rome was in agreement with the "ancient doctrine" that the bread, which Jesus said was His body, truly is and remains bread. Wycliffe writes: "Mice . . . have an innate knowledge of the fact, that the substance of bread is retained, as at first; but these unbelievers, who deny this ancient doctrine, have no such knowledge. . . . What, I ask, could move our Lord Jesus Christ, thus to take away the power of judgment from his worshippers? In no way doth it redound to their good, nor can it be established by reason or Scripture, that it is necessary for men to be so deceived; for bread and wine, retaining their old form, would be a fitter representation of the body and blood of Christ, than an accident without a subject. . . ." "Quantity," being itself an accident, cannot serve as the subject. Nor can accidents exist *per se*. "And so Antichrist, in this heresy, overturns grammar, logic, and natural science; and, what is more lamentable, destroys the meaning of the Gospel. . . . The reason why men fall into this heresy, is that they disbelieve the Gospel, and embrace in preference the papal laws and apocryphal sayings. . . ."

When the sacramental bread is said to be the body of Christ, Wycliffe continues, this is to be taken as a figure of speech. For "the body of Christ . . . remains above in the skies, stable and unmoved, so that it has a spiritual existence in the host, but not of the dimensions, nor according to the other accidents appertaining thereunto in heaven. Hence it seems to me that the body of Christ, and so Christ in his humanity, may extend spiritually to every part of the world."

The body of Christ is then present "corporeally, substantially, and essentially" only in the (improper) sense in which the fullness of the Godhead is said to be dwelling in Christ bodily (Colossians 2:9). The sacrament is consummated "whenever Christ operateth with a man"; hence, a duly ordained priest is not absolutely necessary for the consecretion of the element, nor does his proper intention necessarily assure effectuality.

Wycliffe seems to represent the "intellectualistic" approach to theology that is usually associated with Christian Platonism and, in Latin theology, with Saint Augustine. Wycliffe's doctrine of the ideas represents this understanding of being as ultimately necessary and intelligible. His doctrine of God, man, sin, and salvation clearly reflects an awareness of the reality of the chain of causation which seems to be the peculiar characteristic of one strain of late-medieval Augustinianism. His great predecessor here was Thomas Bradwardine (c.1290-1349), who died as Archbishop of Canterbury. Both Bradwardine and Wycliffe represent a "conservative" reaction against the developing Ockhamism of their time. While Wycliffe and William of Ockham (c.1300-c.1349) agreed in their opposition to papal pretensions and to certain common scholastic views (for instance, that "quantity" is the subject of the accidents of the Eucharistic bread), their theological orientation was fundamentally different. Wycliffe recognized but one source of authority, the Bible, and would subject all ecclesiastical practices and pronouncements to the rule of Scripture; he identified moral virtue and merit in the sight of God, making both absolutely dependent upon the presence of infused grace; and he saw as one the totality of what God can (or could) do and what God in fact does do (or rather, has done from all eternity).

The boldness with which Wycliffe pressed the claims of Scripture and reason upon the ecclesiastical establishment, especially in his denial of transubstantiation, eventually cost him the support of politically powerful men. One by one, his followers within the University of Oxford were induced to recant. The Lollards, who drew their inspiration from Wycliffe, failed to maintain the high Augustinian theology of their master. Wycliffe found an apt disciple in John Huss (c.1369-1415) in Bohemia, and was condemned together with Huss by the Council of Constance in 1415. Some historians have seen in the English Reformation the realization of Wycliffe's ideals. Others have noted a certain theological kinship to John Calvin (1509-1564). Still others consider him the pioneer of English Nonconformity.

ON ECCLESIASTICAL UNITY

Author: John Gerson (1363-1429)
Type of work: Polemical theology
First transcribed: 1409

Principal Ideas Advanced

As the Church is essentially one in Christ, it has the right to promote its outward unity and to procure for itself an undoubted vicar of Christ.

Equity (divine and natural law) is to override positive law; the interests of the Church are to override all other interests.

The Church (represented by a general council) is superior to all its members (including the pope), for that which cannot err is superior to that which can err.

John Gerson was born December 14, 1363, as Jean Charlier in the French village of Gerson, near Rheims, the son of devout, poor peasants. He rose to become one of the best known and respected men of his time, and one of the most important figures in the later Middle Ages. Educated at the University of Paris, he earned his doctorate in theology and in 1395 succeeded his former teacher Peter d'Ailly (1350-1420) as chancellor of the university. He still occupied this position at the time of the Council of Constance (1414-1418), where he represented the university, the archdiocese of Sens, and the kingdom of France. One of the leading figures at this council, he must share the responsibility for the death of John Huss (born c.1369) and Jerome of Prague (born c.1370), who were burned as heretics in 1415 and 1416, respectively. The accession to power in France of the faction of the duke of Burgundy, which had been repeatedly censured by Gerson for the assassination of the duke of Orleans, prompted the chancellor to go into exile in Germany and Austria. In 1419 he found refuge in a Celestine monastery in Lyons, where he died in 1429.

Gerson was one of the most noted preachers of his time, whose spiritual fervor, reminiscent of Bernard of Clairvaux (1090-1153), found expression in a moving eloquence that was widely admired. A leading theologian of the nominalist (Ockhamist) school, he was at the same time a pillar of ecclesiastical orthodoxy. A moralist and counselor of the Christian conscience, he became known as the *doctor consolatorius*. As an educational reformer, he sought to infuse the warmth of Christian mysticism, particularly as it had been developed by the school of Saint Victor, into the scholastic curriculum. He is best known, however, as a leader of the conciliar movement, and as one of its important theorists.

Conciliarism, in brief, was the theory that the Church as a whole is superior to any and all of its members, including the pope, and that it exercises this authority through representative general councils. Late-medieval conciliarism had its roots in certain canonistic traditions, which were first gathered into a system by the Dominican John of Paris, who died in 1306. Marsiglio of Padua (c.1275-1342) and William of Ockham (c.1330-c.1349) were noted conciliarists, but their interest centered more in the Church as the collectivity of the faithful than in the general council as representing it. The outbreak of the Great Schism in 1378 gave considerable impetus to the spread and elaboration of conciliarism. Two German professors at the University of Paris, Conrad of Gelnhausen and Henry of Langenstein, wrote important conciliarist treatises during the early period of the schism, urging the calling of a general council in order that it might be determined who was the legitimate pope. In the 1390's two new approaches were proposed. One was to withhold recognition from both claimants until all reasonable doubts could be dispersed. This approach was intermittently adopted by the kingdom of France, Church and state collaborating in a manner that was to become the characteristic of Gallicanism. The other approach was to seek to persuade both pontiffs to abdicate. This approach, known as the *via cessionis*, was supported by the University of Paris and its chancellor, Gerson. It led directly to the Council of Pisa, which was called by cardinals of both obediences for the express purpose of ending the schism. The council opened its sessions on March 25, 1409. On June 5 both reigning popes were deposed, and the council proceeded to elect a new pope, Peter of Candia, who assumed the name Alexander V (reigned 1409-1410). Neither Benedict XIII (reigned 1394-1417) nor Gregory XII (reigned 1406-1415), however, surrendered their claims to the papal office, so that there were then three popes. Conciliarism had actively asserted itself; it did not triumph until the Council of Constance obtained the abdication of Gregory XII and effectually deposed Benedict XIII and John XXIII (antipope: 1410-1415), the successor of Alexander V. Its triumph was short-lived, however, as the new pope, Martin V (reigned 1417-1431), and his successor Eugenius IV (reigned 1431-1447) exerted every effort to undermine the supremacy of the general council over the papacy, which had been solemnly affirmed in the decree *Sacrosancta* of 1415. The victory of the papacy in this struggle may be dated from 1439, when Eugenius, having succeeded in "translating" the Council of Basle first to Ferrara and then to Florence, obtained the consent of the leaders of the Greek Church to reunion and the proclamation of his own supremacy.

Gerson's treatise *De unitate ecclesiastica* was composed immediately after the chancellor had addressed the English delegation on its way to the Council of Pisa (January 20, 1409). It reflects the stage of conciliarist thought at this point of time, and purports to answer certain objections urged against the *via cessionis*. It is concise, and arranged into twelve propositions.

In Proposition I Gerson strikes a note that is now considered to be the keynote of late-medieval conciliarism: the interdependence of unity and reform in the Church. Gerson connects them by asserting that "the unity of the Church has been hampered by the sins of her sons; the remedy is their reform." It is evident, however, that Gerson here uses the term "reform" in a sense different from that of more radical conciliarists, such as Dietrich of Niem (c.1340-1418), who had specific constitutional and administrative reforms in mind. Gerson appears to think of reform in the traditional individualistic sense of a spiritual and moral rebirth, a turning from sin and a returning to Christ. While all conciliarists after the outbreak of the Great Schism sought both the unity and the reform of the Church, it seems appropriate to make a distinction among them. The "moderate" conciliarists, men like the cardinals Peter d'Ailly and Francis Zabarella (1335-1417), were not basically anti-papal at all; their main concern was the ending of the schism, and for that reason they looked upon the council as primarily an emergency measure for the restoration of the virtually absolute papal monarchy. The "radical" conciliarists, such as Dietrich of Niem and Matthew of Cracow (died 1410), recognized in the Roman curia the primary source of ecclesiastical corruption and decline, and were therefore more interested in reform than in the restoration of a single papal headship. At this time Gerson still belonged to the "moderates."

In Proposition II Gerson affirms that the essential unity of the Church always remains in Christ, the head of the Church, in whom all are one. But as divine and natural law enable any corporate body to procure its outward union, so the mystical body of Christ, the Church, has the right, through a general council, to procure for itself an undoubted vicar of its true head. Such a vicar is not really essential to the unity of the Church, for from time to time the Church is left without one, as at the death of a pope. Legal principles, therefore, are to be cast aside in favor of the theological principle of expediency, which requires the sacrifice of the interests of both contestants to the interests of the Church as a whole (Proposition III). Both contestants owe all that they are to the Church; hence they should be ready to offer their all, even their own lives, for her well-being. To surrender the primacy is not to abandon the flock, but to unite it (Proposition IV).

According to Gerson, the general council is not bound by all the provisions of positive law, but can proceed on the principle of equity. The application of this principle *doctrinaliter* belongs above all to those learned in theology, and only in a secondary way to those skilled in canon and civil law (Proposition V). If the two contestants refuse to abdicate, they should be condemned, and a new pope chosen, provided that the entire council approves the choice of two-thirds of the cardinals, or the greater and wiser part of them (Proposition VI). The alleged rights of both contestants are vitiated by their contrariety to natural and divine law (Proposition VIII). The Church should go back to the state it occupied before the outbreak of the schism; papal pronouncements made since then should be held in abeyance. If both contestants submit their abdication to the council, they are to be assured of sufficient security and rank (Proposition IX).

In Proposition X Gerson asserts that to affirm that one has completely fulfilled his duty in seeking the unity of the Church is rather to remain obstinate in one's error. Though he refuses to anticipate a conciliar decision as to whether this is actually the case now, he does not hesitate to say that circumstances may arise in which it would be permissible to withhold obedience from a duly elected pope, to coerce him even to the point of imprisoning him, or to maintain neutrality. For the pope is subject to the whole Church as one capable of error is subject to what can never err. Gerson here seems to maintain the infallibility of general councils. Conciliarism generally opposed the infallibility of the Church to the fallibility of the pope, but some leading theorists like William of Ockham, Conrad of Gelnhausen, and Peter d'Ailly distinguished the Church from its representative body, the general council, and attributed infallibility only to the former. Gerson does not seem to make the distinction.

When Gerson asserts that the conciliar program expresses only the common obligation of all Christians (Proposition VII), he reflects the general tendency of the later Middle Ages to emphasize the role of the laity in Church affairs. The Fourth Council of the Lateran (1215) had set the pattern for the councils of the later Middle Ages in aiming at the representation of the whole Church: the general council was no longer exclusively an assembly of bishops, but it included lower clergy and laymen. Ockham had insisted on the widest possible representation of laymen—even women—and had laid down the pregnant principle that all in authority have the right and duty to participate in the process of legislating for the Church. Peter d'Ailly advocated this Ockhamist position at Constance because of the abnormal situation, and asked that titular bishops be excluded from the suffrage, while doctors of theology and of civil and canon law be admitted on the ground that they exercise authority over their pupils. Gerson specifically commends King Charles VI of France (reigned 1380-1422) for concerning himself with the affairs of the Universal Church, as indicated by his open letter *Pax ecclesiastica* (1408), in which he threatened once again to withdraw obedience from Benedict XIII.

In Proposition XI Gerson asserts that it is not necessary to determine absolutely which of the contenders is the true pope. Those who are in doubt may do conditional penance. Just as a legitimate pope would be sinning in failing to promote the unity of the Church, so his opponents may be pardoned if they were always prepared to obey the Church and the truth that was known to them. In this proposition we catch a glimpse of that concern for the conscience which earned Gerson the title *doctor consolatorius*. We also see a principle enunciated which, though not originated by the late-medieval nominalists, was greatly developed and extended by them: the principle of implicit faith. Earlier it had been held that laymen (including the ignorant lower clergy, according to Pope Innocent IV) were not required to know Christian doctrine beyond a very few fundamentals, provided they affirmed that they believed implicitly whatever the Church believed. Heretical beliefs were held by Innocent IV to be harmless in laymen, so long as they were not aware that their beliefs differed from those of the Church. From the time of Ockham on, professions of implicit faith became common even among theologians.

If it seems unlikely that a new pope will be universally accepted, Gerson concludes, then the cardinals should make some other provision. They might, for instance, adopt the proposal of the Council of France (probably the Fifth French National Council of 1408) that there be no election if either of the present claimants should die. The cardinals assembled at Pisa notoriously failed to heed this warning, and consequently simply added a third claimant of the papal throne.

One can trace fluctuations in Gerson's conciliarism. Noteworthy is an initial burst of enthusiasm, expressed in several sermons of 1391 and 1392, and in the theses he defended in connection with his obtaining of the master's degree, in 1392. At that time Gerson did not hesitate to violate the royal injunction against public discussions of reunion, and perhaps even advocated its repeal in the presence of the king. When the university voted in favor of the "subtraction" of obedience from the Avignon pope (1395), it was over the opposition of the chancellor. Gerson saw in such a move an attack upon the traditional constitution of the Church that would at the same time aggravate the divisions in the ranks of the faithful. The "subtraction" was nevertheless made effective throughout France in 1398. Gerson continued his opposition, writing in defense of Benedict XIII, and in 1403 witnessed the restoration of obedience to the Avignon pope. Thereafter his attitude towards the papacy hardened, and by November, 1406, he was affirming the propriety, despite provisions of canon law to the contrary, of general councils not presided over by the pope or a papal legate. From the election of the supposedly conciliatory (Roman) Pope Gregory XII (November, 1406) to the latter's abandonment of the policy of reconciliation by the creation of new cardinals (May, 1408), Gerson was again counseling moderation. Then followed the period dominated by the prospect of the Council of Pisa, and from then on Gerson's conciliarism becomes increasingly radical. His sermon *Ambulate dum lucem habetis* (1415) may have saved the Council of Constance after the precipitate flight of (the Conciliar) Pope John XXIII. His treatise *De potestate ecclesiastica,* read at Constance on February 6, 1417, is one of the most comprehensive expressions of the conciliarist theory of ecclesiastical authority. Gerson envisaged a permanent subordination of the papacy to the general council, in the spirit of the decree *Frequens* adopted at Constance in the same year.

Conciliarism may be interpreted as an intermediate stage between the internationalism of the medieval Church and the ecclesiastical nationalism that was to emerge more strongly in the fifteenth and sixteenth centuries. Whereas in the earlier stage the control of religion had been mainly in the hands of the ecclesiastical hierarchy, and in the later stage came to be increasingly in the hands of the state, for a brief period the leadership of the Western Church was assumed by the universities, above all by Paris. From the beginning of the Great Schism until well into the sixteenth century, the University of Paris was the head and heart of the conciliar movement. Even after its defeat by the papacy, conciliarism survived as a potent influence in many universities, notably Paris, Vienna, Erfurt, Cracow, and Cologne.

Gerson seems to have been aware of a certain connection between Conciliarism and higher learning, between the university and the general council. This connection apparently revolves around the concept of equity, which dominates his *De unitate ecclesiastica.* As the ordinary hierarchical order of the Church is superseded by the authority of the Church as a whole, exercised through a general council, so the ordinary canonical laws are superseded by the principle that underlies all laws, the principle of equity. In Proposition V Gerson finely distinguishes between the determinative and the doctrinal application of equity. The former, a quasi-judicial function, belongs to the council. The latter, a teaching function, belongs primarily to scholars learned in theology, and secondarily to those skilled in canon and civil law. In the sermon *Vivat rex* (1405) Gerson specifically defended the right of the university, as the "Mistress of Truth," to proclaim the truth and to uphold the faith. In the sermon *Pax hominibus* (1409) Gerson stressed the cosmopolitan character of the university and deduced from it a duty to seek universal peace and unity.

TREATISE ON THE CHURCH

Author: John Huss (c.1369-1415)
Type of work: Church theory
First transcribed: 1413

PRINCIPAL IDEAS ADVANCED

The pope and the cardinals do not constitute the Church; the true Church is made up of the body of the predestinate in Heaven, on earth, and in purgatory.

Christ, not the pope, is the head of the Church; since the pope can err, he is to be obeyed solely when his teachings and life conform to those of Christ and the Apostles.

The spiritual power to retain and to remit sins is given to the Church, but neither pope nor priest can absolve except when absolution has first been given by God.

John Huss, the author of the *Treatise on the Church,* was burned as a heretic, on July 6, 1415, for the views written in the *Treatise.* The work is Huss's defense of views he acquired from John Wycliffe (c.1329-1384), from whom Huss draws heavily, particularly in the early chapters. The book was written in answer to a document signed by eight doctors belonging to the theological faculty of the University of Prague. The document called for the absolute submission to the commands of the pope and other ecclesiastical superiors. The work of John Huss, like that of Wycliffe, is protestant in opposition to the accredited ecclesiastical system of Rome. It is a work of first importance among works on the Church, and it was to be a forceful influence a century later during the troubled time of the Reformation.

The Church, as Huss conceives it, is one throughout the world. The bond of its unity is predestinating grace. The Holy Catholic Church is the totality of the predestinate, present, past, and future. The Church universal is one, but it is divided into the Church *militant,* the predestinate now waging war against the flesh, the world, and the Devil; the Church *dormient,* the number of the predestinate suffering in purgatory; and the Church *triumphant,* the blessed at rest in Heaven, who kept up Christ's warfare against Satan and have finally triumphed.

The visible Church is a mixed body made up of predestinate and reprobate. Christ alone is the head of the universal Church. The universal Church is not constituted by the pope and the cardinals, nor is the Church limited to that body over which the apostolic see has jurisdiction. The Roman Church is a part of the Church militant, and as long as the pope and his college follow Christ, it is in dignity its chief part, but no partial church can be the Holy Catholic Church. It is noteworthy that the Roman Church was in the past properly called a company of Christ's faithful, living under the obedience of the Roman bishop, just as the Antiochian Church was called the company of Christ's faithful, under the bishop of Antioch.

The visible Church is not inerrant, Huss claims, and the pope and his college of cardinals may be soiled with wickedness and sin. Unless the lives of the prelates are in accordance with the teachings of Christ, their authority is not binding. The foundation of the Church is the faith upon which the Church is built, not a faith in popes, but a faith in the Rock, Jesus Christ.

A Christian must believe explicitly and implicitly all the truth that is in Scripture, not the sayings of the saints which are apart from Scripture; nor should he believe papal bulls, except insofar as they are founded on Scripture. God cannot deceive or be deceived; the pope may deceive and be deceived.

Huss writes firmly that Christ, not the Roman pontiff, is the head of the Church. When, in Matthew, Christ says: "On this rock I will build my church," the term "rock" does not refer to Peter, nor to the Papacy, but to Christ himself. Christ alone is the chief foundation of the Church. Peter never was, nor did he claim to be, the head of the Holy Catholic Church. Christ appointed Peter as Captain and Shepherd because of the pre-eminence of virtues which fitted Peter to rule the Church. Peter excelled in faith, humility, and love. The person who is called to be Peter's vicar and who shares the faith and virtues that Peter had is his true vicar, but if he walks in opposite paths, then he is the legate of Antichrist and is at variance with Peter and Jesus Christ.

With respect to the power-authority of Christ, given to His vicars, as expressed in the words, "I will give unto thee the keys of the kingdom of heaven," the power to bind and to loose sins, "and whatsoever thou shalt bind on earth, shall be bound in heaven, and whatsoever thou shalt loose on earth shall be loosed in heaven," Huss notes that such power is spiritual. It is, however, not given to a person, but to the whole Church militant. The vicar of Christ is not able to absolve or to bind, to forgive sins or to retain them, unless God has given remission previously. The ignorant believe that the priest first binds and looses men, and then God follows, but God's act of binding or loosing is absolutely first. The power of remitting sins and retaining them is, therefore, simply a declaratory power. The priest can absolve from sin only when such absolution has previously been granted by God. (Huss declared himself opposed to the practice of granting indulgences.)

Every vicar of Christ may in fact err even in those things which concern the faith. God alone knows infallibly whose sins may be remitted, and God alone cannot be moved by a wrong motive in binding or loosening. The vicar that refuses to impart absolution to one truly penitent cannot truly refuse absolution to one whom God has already absolved.

No one is saved unless he is meritoriously subject to Jesus Christ, and it is the latter who is the true and sole Roman Pontiff, for He is the head of the universal Church and of every particular church. The pope at Rome is not the head of the Church or even necessarily the vicar of Christ. On occasion the Roman bishop has been unlettered, a heretic and antichrist; that is, a pope living contrary to Christ. The pope may be the vicar of Christ and may be so to his profit, if he is a faithful minister predestinated unto the glory of the head, Jesus Christ.

The accepted notion that the pope is the head of the Church and that the college of cardinals is the existing body of the Church, is rejected by Huss because that notion is not known by the bodily senses, discovered by infallible intelligence made known through revelation, or laid down in sacred Scripture.

It is not necessary for salvation for Christians to believe that anyone is the head of any church whatsoever unless the evangelical life and works of the claimant plainly establish him as Christ's vicar.

It is, moreover, erroneous to hold that the college of cardinals is the body of the Church, for the college by itself does not include all the predestinate, the true Body of Christ. Christ is the head of the Church and each of the predestinate is a member.

No one truly occupies the place of Christ or of Peter, unless he follows Him in his life, nor does any person otherwise receive procuratorial power. The vicarial office demands the conformity of life and authority to the power of Him who appoints. When a pope is humble, when he pastures the sheep on the Word of God, when he is meek, patient, chaste, and solicitous in the service of the Church, then he is the vicar of Christ, so far as the outward senses can determine. If he lives otherwise, however, the pope is the vicar of Antichrist. No pope is the manifest and true successor of Peter if the pope lives at variance with the principles of Peter. Nor are the cardinals the manifest and true successors of the college of Christ's other apostles, if they do not live as did the Apostles and keep the commandments of Jesus Christ.

The government of the Church need not be carried on by the pope and the cardinals. God is able, without assistance, to rule His Church. In fact, for three hundred years the Church was so ruled. In those early centuries, the office of the apostles consisted solely in good living, in teaching, in baptizing, and in healing; the regimen of the apostles was free of pomp and luxury. God is in fact able to bring His Church back to its pristine state by taking away the government from the pope and the cardinals and giving it to others.

The prelate who is proud, who lives in luxury and greed, who does not feed the sheep, but oppresses them and scatters them, is neither to be followed nor obeyed. The standard of ecclesiastical judgments is the law of God.

According to Huss, the Scriptures are the norm of our behavior; they are, however, to be explained solely as the Holy Spirit requires, not according to human fancy. The opinion of no man, including that of the pope, is to be held if it plainly contains falsehood or error, as it surely does when it contradicts the Scriptures. Obedience should be rendered to the pope and the cardinals only as long as they teach the truth according to the law of God.

A man cannot be morally virtuous if he does not obey God, but when obedience is rendered to man, rather than to God, then it is evil obedience, so that everyone obeying evilly is disobedient to God. He who commands ought only to command things in agreement to the law, and the person who obeys ought never to act contrary to the will of God.

The faithful disciple of Christ ought to consider how a command emanates from the pope, whether it is the express command of Christ's law or of any Apostle. If the command of the pope is the command of Christ, the believer ought to obey humbly and reverently. However, if the believer knows that what the pope commands is at variance with the teachings of Christ or is detrimental to the good of the Church, then the believer ought to resist it lest he become a partner in crime.

When a superior of the visible Church commands that preaching be restricted to cathedrals, parochial, or cloistral churches, and that chapel services cease, such a command is contrary to that of Christ, and it is not to be obeyed. The believer can appeal to the true head of the Church, to Jesus Christ. For He is superior to any pope in deciding a case; He cannot err, nor deny justice, nor can He condemn where there is no demerit.

If the pope puts aside the law and a devout profession of the Gospel, and gives heed to human tradition—if he abandons the manner of life followed by Christ, and becomes secular in his interest, then to rebel against such an erring pope is to obey Christ the Lord.

Work that is commanded by a pope or other prelate for which there is no reason or utility to the Church of Christ ought not to be performed. We ought to realize by faith that God never commands us to do anything which is neither meritorious nor profitable to salvation. No one should obey man in anything, Huss insists, even the least thing, if it is opposed to the divine commands. As we must obey what is lawful, so we must resist our superiors when they walk contrary to the commands of Christ. Inferiors and laics ought to examine and to judge intelligently the commands of superiors, for no human decree is valid or to be observed unless it can be seen to exemplify a divine commandment of Christ.

The believer who disobeys in a state of grace without committing mortal sin need have no fear of the excommunication of man. For no judge can excommunicate a man unless the man himself has already excommunicated himself by his offenses. Only those who depart from the Lord's commandments are truly excommunicated. Whoever excommunicates another falsely for temporal gain is himself in danger of true excommunication. The true believer need not fear excommunication, suspension, nor interdict; he need fear only that he become unfaithful to the teachings of Jesus Christ.

THE IMITATION OF CHRIST

Author: Thomas à Kempis (c.1380-1471)
Type of work: Counsels on spiritual life
First transcribed: c.1418

Principal Ideas Advanced

The aim of the true Christian should be to imitate, insofar as it is possible, the model given to him in the person and in the life of Christ.

To achieve this aim means to discover the spiritual, the inner life, to turn completely away from the affairs of the world and our own outwardly directed desires.

Humility, contrition, self-discipline, and a willingness to submit to spiritual authorities, are all necessary if one is to achieve the goal of the imitation of Christ's life, reconcilation with God, and spiritual peace.

The unspoken assumption of Thomas à Kempis's *Imitation of Christ* is that the Christian is expected to attempt to follow the life of Christ. Christ's life ought to be of first consideration for all who desire enlightenment and freedom from spiritual blindness. Whoever wants to understand the words of Christ must, if he desires success, strive to make his whole life conform to that of Jesus. Discoursing learnedly on the Trinity is beside the point, if one lacks humility, Thomas asserts; for a true Christian it is better to feel contrition than to be able to define it.

The model life is the contemplative one. Its aim is to despise the world and to draw near daily to the Kingdom of Heaven, to withdraw one's heart from the love of visible things, and to direct one's affections to things invisible. Of what use is knowledge without the fear of God? A man who is humble pleases God more than does an intellectual who charts the courses of the stars but neglects his own soul. On the other hand, a man who truly knows himself realizes his own worthlessness and does not take pleasure in the praises of men. An inordinate desire for knowledge, Thomas advises us, should be restrained, for such desire leads to anxiety and deception. There are many things which matter little whether they are understood or not. In fact, it really is not wise to busy oneself with anything except what furthers salvation.

Unless one's life is more holy than the average, Thomas advises, the more complete and excellent one's knowledge the more severe will be God's judgment. A genuine understanding and a humble approval of oneself is, actually, the best and most valuable of all lessons. No one has a harder goal or a fiercer struggle than the man who strives to conquer himself. At best, knowledge will contain an element of obscurity, just as all perfection in life is accompanied by some imperfection; and a humble knowledge of oneself is a safer road to God than a long study of the sciences. However, it is not learning itself that is to blame, for in itself it is worth while, but a sincere conscience and a holy life are always preferable.

On the Day of Last Judgment one will not have to account for what one has read but for what he has done, Thomas continues. If one chooses to be great rather than humble, he will simply perish in his own conceit. As far as action is concerned, the problem is that evil told about someone is believed more easily than if the report were good, and the problem in the self is that a man who is not perfectly dead to self is easily tempted and overcome even in small matters. True peace of heart comes only from resisting the passions, not from yielding to them, and whoever puts his trust in men or in any creature, Thomas warns us, is being very foolish.

To want to go to other places and constantly to desire change is what unsettles many. These desires represent opinions, Thomas asserts, and if God is to dwell among us, sometimes our own opinions must be sacrificed for the sake of peace. Public gatherings lead to a discussion of worldly affairs, and this is a hindrance since, even with the best intentions, it quickly corrupts and ensnares us in vanity. Any outward consolation, such as these discussions, may be an obstacle to inner and divine consolation. How can anyone be at peace as long as he meddles in affairs other than his own? If only we can become completely dead to self and be free from inner conflict, then we can savor spiritual things and come to deserve an experience of heavenly contemplation. Even the outward observances of religion, if relied upon, deter genuine devotion.

The happiest fact of all, however, is that the man who could root out one fault each year would soon become perfect. Even trouble speeds us on our way toward this goal, since it compels a man to search his own heart. If only men could place such complete trust in God, Thomas exclaims, that they would no longer need the comfort of men, that would be ideal. Temptations, although troublesome, are to be preferred to too smooth a life, since through temptations we are humbled, cleansed, and instructed and thus brought to depend more on God. Since we are born with an inclination toward evil, temptation comes from our own nature and will be with us as long as we live. Yet the beginning of all evil temptation is an unstable mind and a lack of proper trust in God.

Disciplining ourselves in various ways, says Thomas, is the only way that we can hope to live in peace and harmony with others. Yet discipline is not limited to the rigors or form of the monastic life. Only the transformation of our way of life and a complete mortification of the passions can make us truly religious followers of the Christian way of life. Solitude and silence help. Whoever wants to live an inward and spiritual life must withdraw from the crowd. No man can live in the public eye without risking the loss of his soul. In silence and quietness a devout soul can make progress. Too much freedom is a detriment. Discipline the senses and examine yourself strictly, Thomas advises, since the more strict the self-examination the more cause for sorrow.

No happiness will be found until men turn to God. Since everyone, including king and pope, has trouble and anxiety, his lot is the happiest who is able to suffer for the love of God. The inner life is greatly hindered by the body, but that difficulty is simply something man must put up with in this life. What can be done is to discipline the body with penance, in order to enjoy a sure hope of salvation. Keep yourself a stranger, Thomas urges, and be a pilgrim on earth. It is better to learn to endure a little now, in order to avoid more grievous trouble, and he who really loves God will not fear death or punishment or judgment or Hell. Nevertheless, the fear of Hell can act as a restraint against sin, even if the love of God does not. The stricter we are with ourselves, the greater will be our spiritual progress.

After having given these counsels in the spiritual life, Thomas à Kempis turns to consider the inner life. Here is the most important area for concentration, since all true glory and beauty, he is sure, are really to be found within the soul. The inner man never becomes wholly immersed in outward affairs, and so it is easier for such a man to understand himself. If the inner life is rightly ordered, a man is not troubled by the strange and perverse ways of others. All good things turn to the advantage of the inner man, since a discontented or restless man is tormented by suspicions. Simplicity and purity are the most important qualities to develop in the inner life, since simplicity reaches out after God while purity is able to discover and to enjoy Him. Any man who turns wholly toward God loses his sloth and becomes transformed into a new creature.

To become interior and devout is our goal, Thomas avers, but this cannot be reached until each man refrains from criticism of others and pays attention to his own faults. This is what we all must do if we really desire true peace and union with God. Set everything else aside and attend to yourself, Thomas urges. Yet not even the self is our ultimate aim or value, since the soul that loves God will come to regard all things other than God as worthless. True and lasting glory involves nothing of worldly glory. And neither external praise nor blame disturbs a man who has achieved great tranquillity of heart. Everything else must be surrendered for the sake of the love of Jesus. But if any man should forget and turn aside to worldly things, he will soon cause

Jesus to leave him and he will lose His grace.

Pride is to be avoided and contrition desired, and any consolation or contemplation which leads to either ought to be avoided. Seeking comfort is a sign of self-interest, and any self-centered man is really mercenary. Pure love of Jesus is free from all self-interest and self-love. Yet the problem is, and Thomas à Kempis freely recognizes it, that man is not by nature inclined to chasten the body and to bring it into subjection. A life of contrition is in a sense a dying life, since certain natural instincts are starved. The discipline of self cannot really be achieved by man's own strength without divine assistance. Yet there is no better way than contrition, no way more comfortable, to achieve salvation.

Turning to the means to achieve inward consolation, Thomas à Kempis advises us never to think ourselves to be anything because of our own good deeds, but instead to remember our sins with deep sorrow. Leave the examination of God alone and consider rather how much good we have left undone, Thomas advises. Love is our greatest asset and guide in achieving inward consolation, since it is born of God and is free and unrestrained. Humility is also necessary here, and in fact is much more necessary and desirable than a great store of learning coupled with vain complacency. Self-interest as a motive is often hidden, and as long as it exists, even in a secret form, it will be nothing but a hindrance and a burden.

Obedience is a key quality here too. Any man who is unwilling to submit freely and willingly to his superior shows that his lower nature is not yet under his control. It is hard, Thomas à Kempis agrees, to subject oneself to the spiritual authorities of the temporal Church for God's sake, and yet it is absolutely necessary to achieve grace. Since what is impossible by nature can be made possible by grace, obedience is an issue of no little import. And the man who hangs on to life and self-assertiveness gets little for his reward, since life is subject to so many sorrows and calamities. The sacrifices necessary to achieve inward consolation are well worth it.

Our mind should seek to rest in God above all things, remembering God's blessings. Four things will bring us peace: possessing less rather than more, regarding ourselves as lower than others, praying to have God's will fulfilled through our acts, and always doing the will of others rather than our own will. Curiosity brings only evils, whereas a mind free from such desires is excellent above all else. Self-love only hinders our search for God and trouble actually helps us find Him. There is no loss at all involved if we forsake creatures in order to find the Creator. God is fully gracious to those who love Him.

A surrender of the self, in the way Thomas à Kempis describes, will bring us freedom of heart, he is sure. No longer will a man thus free be overanxious. If man has no personal goodness of which to boast, then his peace does not depend upon himself or upon any man, but upon God alone. Distractions can be avoided, distractions of outer things which would take away inward consolation. Man's trust should be entirely in God, in times of peace and in times of trouble as well. Grace cannot be granted to the worldly minded, but through the imitation of Christ, by following His way of suffering and self-denial, all men can turn their minds from the worldly toward the inner life, and place their hopes and trust in God alone.

OF LEARNED IGNORANCE

Author: Nicholas of Cusa (Nicolaus Cryfts or Krypffs, c.1401-1464)
Type of work: Mystical theology
First transcribed: 1440

Principal Ideas Advanced

Since from God there is an outflow of all things, the question arises as to how the creation returns to unity with its Creator.

In God there is a reconciliation of contraries, but such a situation places God beyond rational grasp, so that knowledge of this fact is a learned ignorance.

The basis of the understanding of God is usually mathematical, for it is by reference to quantities that one can grasp the various features of God as constituting both the maximum and the minimum in such a manner that reason is necessarily transcended.

Since number includes all things that are capable of comparison, Nicholas of Cusa (Nicolas Cusanus) argues in *Of Learned Ignorance* that number is a fitting framework for discussion. Yet the subject he proposes to discuss is the most difficult of all: the divine nature; here the best efforts yield only ignorance. It is nevertheless beneficial, Nicholas's thesis runs, to understand why we are necessarily ignorant about the divine. The better a man knows his own ignorance, the greater his learning will be. If we are to deal with ignorance as our greatest learning, then we will have to determine the precise meaning of the "maximum" or "greatest." If the term "maximum" means that nothing greater can exist, then being and the maximum are identical. Furthermore if all things are united with the maximum because it is the maximum, then the minimum also coincides with the maximum, since nothing can be placed in opposition to the maximum.

The maximum is Nicholas's name for God, and the study of Him is above reason; to the minimum Nicholas gives the name Jesus. In the discussion of these ultimate concepts and in the attempt to reconcile their apparent opposition, one must take all terms symbolically rather than literally, since the foundation for learned ignorance is the truth that the absolute is beyond our grasp and can only be indicated. A finite intellect cannot by means of comparsion reach the absolute truth of things; the intellect can never grasp any truth with such precision that the truth could not be comprehended with infinitely greater precision. All we know of truth, then, is that the absolute truth is beyond our final reach. Ontological truth is unobtainable in its entirety. The better we learn this lesson of ignorance, writes Nicholas, the closer we draw to truth itself.

The simple absolute maximum is greater than our powers of comprehension, and nothing in existence can be greater than it. On the other hand, the minimum is that which cannot be less than it is. But neither can the maximum be less than it is. Thus, Nicholas argues, it is evident that the minimum is identical wtih the maximum. The maximum quantity is infinitely great, while the minimum is infinitely small. Therefore, the minimum is as much a superlative as the maximum. Furthermore, distinctions exist only for things susceptible of "more" and "less"; and, since distinctions cannot exist in the absolute maximum, the maximum is above any form of affirmation or negation. Being without distinction, the absolute maximum is all things while yet being none of them. The absolute is at once the maximum and minimum of being.

The basis for learned ignorance is that there is no difference between the two affirmations (1) that God is light and (2) since God is light at its highest, He is light at its lowest. This paradox is beyond our understanding, which is fundamentally unable by any rational process to reconcile contradictories. Nicholas claims that the discovery of God's paradoxical nature forces us to admit our ultimate ignorance, not because we know nothing, but because what we do discover about the divine nature we are unable to reconcile rationally. Yet an absolute maximum is intelligible, able to be named. It remains ineffable, beyond our comprehension, only because the intelligible attributes we learn are rationally irreconcilable. Number is still our best aid here, for Nicholas does not leave understanding at this point of ignorance, which is the beginning, not the end of learning. For number too, it is one and the same thing to call a number infinite and to say that it is the minimum.

Unity is a minimum, Nicholas continues, a simple minimum that coincides with the maximum. Unity cannot, therefore, be a number, although it is the principle of all number. Considering number led Nicholas to the conclusion that absolute unity (following the Neoplatonists) is a most fitting attribute of God; but the divine unity is of a special kind, concerning which intellectual difficulties arise. God's unity is such that He is actually all that is possible. God, consequently, is infinite unity. Number, since it is a being of reason, owes its existence to our power of comparing and distinguishing. The reality of number is limited to the reality it has in the mind. Therefore, number could not exist if it did not necessarily proceed from unity. Number and unity and God are thus linked in a necessary and yet ultimately baffling way—baffling not because we cannot discern these basic relationships but because we cannot fully reconcile that which we so clearly discern.

Nonbeing and minimum being are identical with the maximum, since nothing can stand in opposition to it. All that can be said or thought, Nicholas concludes, can be exhausted by the following propositions: it is, or it is not; it is, and it is not; it neither is nor is it not. Here the problem is posed at its extreme. Nicholas feels obligated to assert every possible form of being and nonbeing as applied to the maximum in order to preserve its ultimate status as the maximum. Yet doing this leads to assertions which seem not reconcilable. The name "maximum" must mean that being in this highest, although indescribable, way is predicated of it more than of any being that can be described. The problem is that the ultimate description requires so many statements that God remains indescribable.

Nicholas then proposes unity, equality, and connection as a trinity which is at once a unity. Such a three-in-one is required in order that from unity, eternality, and equality, we shall be able to see how diversity, inequality, and changeableness arise. Strangely enough, such a concept of unity is not itself a simple notion. We have a connection of unity only when we grasp that each thing is a unity, that unity itself is all things and that, as a consequence, each thing within unity is also all things. There is, then, only one correct way of understanding the Supreme Unity and that is as a trinity. Unity at its highest and most perfect understanding necessarily presupposes these co-relationships: intelligent being, intelligible object, and act of understanding. Thus, the correct concept of unity must be as a three-in-one. Unity, in fact, is a trinity, for nondivision, distinction, and connection all have their origin in unity and constitute its essential meaning.

The mathematical parallel has led to new ways of reasoning about God, which in this context do not seem out of order. New modes are valid and possible, which in no way correspond to the simple, natural order. In this setting, a new mode of reasoning does not seem out of order. The examples which number provides, when number is correctly interpreted, lead to a new truth and understanding. Following this path, the reader experiences a wondrous delight and advances in the new way of learned ignorance. Reasoning about God requires learning new forms, modes of reasoning which deny normal ways of thought. The grasp of these new ways which bypass simple understanding enables one to realize in what respect learning is necessarily a learned ignorance, a learning incapable of final statement or full reconciliation with pedestrian norms.

Symbolism, of course, is necessary in such a novel situation. No image can reproduce divine nature accurately enough to rule out another image more faithful and precise. Mathematics furnishes some good examples of precise imagery, and in fact mathematical symbolism is necessary where things divine are concerned. Symbols are a necessary approach to things divine, and mathematical signs supply a certain indestructible certitude. From here Nicholas goes on to explore certain mathematical relationships between the finite and the infinite, and particularly the way in which the potentialities of the finite are actualized in the infinite. Mathematical examples assist one in rising to the intelligible order, and then what is impossible in the material order is seen as not only possible but as absolutely necessary in the divine order.

An infinite line is the infinite actualization of all that is potential in a finite line; this mathematical analogy indicates to us the way in which the maximum is the infinite actualization of all that is simply and absolutely possible. Mathematical symbols and analogies help one to see what otherwise could not be seen easily or directly; in the maximum, absolute possibility itself and infinite actual existence are perfectly identified. No intelligence comprehends God and yet, through the knowledge gained by such mathematical comparisons and considerations, He is known. Intelligence can be learned in this respect; it is ignorant only in that it discovers its own final inability ever to comprehend God. Sciences are inadequate to comprehend His nature, and in this respect wisdom finally is ignorance and pretentious language is meaningless.

God can be approached by removing all that has participated being, but the difficulty is that when one does this there seems to be nothing left. Once one mentally removes all that has participated being, such an entity is hard to grasp, and yet exactly what seems nothing to the intellect is the incomprehensible maximum. God actually encompasses all things, even contradictories, just as a circle encompasses all that exists and all that does not exist. The circle is a crucial theological figure, Nicholas argues, and he claims that all theology is circular and lies within a circle. Even the terms of the attributes are truly convertible. Infinity seems to make attributes equal and to embrace contradictories.

Nicholas, of course, is quite partial to the method of negative theology. Such a method is absolutely indispensable, he argues, since without it no thinker could reach high enough or be able to reach to God as ineffable. In theology negative propositions are true, and affirmative ones are inadequate. Of the negative ones, those are more true which eliminate greater imperfections from the infinitely perfect. Through negative theology we are in a position to see that absolute truth exists, though we are still unable to comprehend it. Degrees cannot be admitted in the infinite; absolute equality is predicable of God alone.

God is the opposite of nothing, Nicholas asserts, with being as an intermediary. Thus, it becomes clear that Nicholas's method of "learned ignorance" actually yields some quite explicit statements about God, even though He is beyond comprehension. The creature comes from God, yet it cannot add anything to Him who is the maximum. The plurality of things is due to the fact that God is nothing. The universe for Nicholas is only a restricted form of maximum; the universe is infinity contracted to the relatively infinite. Absolute unity admits no plurality, whereas the unity of the universe does. In the universe identity consists in diversity, just as unity consists in plurality. Universe means universality; that is, a unity of distinct things. The entire universe was brought into being by a simple emanation of the restricted maximum from the absolute maximum.

Apart from God every being is limited, and there is no potency, form, or act which is not God. Only in their finite state is it true that the forms of things are distinct. In the absolute the forms are not many and distinct but one. One infinite exemplar is all that is needed and one alone suffices. Our ignorance that is learning has shown that in God identity is diversity. Nicholas incorporates the doctrine of the Trinity and of the Holy Spirit in extraordinarily abstract discourse, and in his third and last book he interprets the person of Jesus in abstract and dialectical categories. Nicholas believes fully that God is not comprehensible, and yet out of his considerations as to why this is true he nevertheless develops a complete theology, and he thereby wrests learning from his ignorance.

THE SCALE OF PERFECTION

Author: Walter Hilton (d. 1396)
Type of work: Devotional guidebook
First published: 1494

Principal Ideas Advanced

The achievement of a mature and deeply satisfying Christian experience requires serious effort and self-discipline.

The scale or ladder to the heights of authentic Christian love and devotion is one which must be climbed one step at a time.

The ascent to Christian fulfillment involves both God's grace and man's deliberate and often arduous effort.

Whether one practices an active or a contemplative Christian life, he must avoid emotional extremes; he must demonstrate a love of truth, and he must pay attention to the practical demands of life.

In the practice of the devotional life, one must turn not to Rome or to Jerusalem, but to his own inner soul.

The Scale of Perfection is the chief work of Walter Hilton, who occupied a central position in the small group of English mediaeval mystics which included Richard Rolle (c.1295-1349), Julian of Norwich (c.1342-after 1413), and the anonymous author of the *Cloud of Unknowing*. Hilton, about whom little is known, was an Augustinian canon of the Thurgarton Priory, near Southwell in Nottinghamshire. In *The Scale of Perfection* Hilton produced a devotional guidebook which reflects the varied demands made on him as an official of a religious order composed of men who devoted themselves not only to meditation but also to land and property management. His book circulated in numerous manuscripts for over a century before it was printed in 1494. No less a student of English mysticism than Evelyn Underhill observed that probably no other work of its kind has so wide and enduring an influence.

Intent upon maintaining unswerving orthodoxy at a time when Lollard and Wycliffe followers were being combated, Hilton relies most heavily upon the Bible, especially the Psalms and St. Paul, and upon St. Augustine (354-430), St. Bernard (1090-1153), St. Bonaventura (1221-1274), and Richard of St. Victor (d.c.1173). The influence on Hilton of the mystical theology of Dionysius the Pseudo-Areopagite (fifth century), with its stress on the paradoxes of mystical experience, is also easily discerned. Hilton, however, makes no attempt to impress his readers with erudition or to pose as an exceptionally pious man. Nor does he claim for himself the heights of mystical rapture. He observes that while his subject is the contemplative life he does not himself "have it in feeling and in working as I have it in saying." Hilton demonstrates a greater concern for truth and for common sense practicalities than for the bizarre and the emotional: "It sufficeth to me for to live in truth principally, and not in feeling."

The Scale of Perfection is not a storehouse of esoteric wisdom for initiated souls, but "a way-book for the soul traveling in spirit to Jerusalem." In his book Hilton checks the natural desire of the ardent beginner for special experiences and consolations, warns against the religious formalism which stresses religious practices as the end and not as the means to the devotional life, and expresses a common sense attitude in respect of physical austerities: "Rather use best meat and most costly if it less hinder the keeping of the heart than to take only bread and water, if that hinder him more." It is not surprising that Hilton has been praised for his sanctified common sense.

The *Scale* (or ladder) presents the difficulties on the road to that perfect flowering of the interior life of love and prayer to which in a greater or lesser degree every authentic Christian is called. The image of the ladder, a very common one in mystical writings, is used. Man must take one step at a time on the way, the gradual ascent doubly conditioned by God's grace and man's deliberate and arduous striving. As Evelyn Underhill observes in her discerning introduction to the 1923 edition of Hilton's masterpiece, the underlying theological structure is the concept of man's soul, which is not only the image of God, but also a reflection of sin, which has impressed upon the mortal soul another pattern or "dark image." The goal of the spiritual life is the restoration of the soul to its proper status by a remaking or reformation which will obliterate the false or dark image.

The book is addressed generally to those who crave the deeper consciousness of reality and feel the impulse to a more complete consecration. It is written in particular to a recluse in her cell, who is dedicated to the life of prayer. Hilton prepares the reader for a deep analysis of motive, for the gradual awareness of the self-deceiving tendency to rationalization within the spiritual life. What helps man most to God, says Hilton, is attending to God and not to the self. Man needs to concentrate his whole will and feeling on this goal, the attending to God, as the true goal of the spiritual quest.

There are two manners of life, Hilton declares, the active and the contemplative. The active consists in love and charity exercised exteriorly by good or "corporal" works. The contemplative is reflected in perfect love and charity. Within the contemplative there are three sections on the scale of perfection. On the lower section one knows God, yet it is the knowing of God as one knows water, unsavory and cold, before the miracle of wine, when cold reason is changed into spiritual light and burning love by the gift of the Holy Ghost. The next section on the scale of perfection is affection, the knowing of God by feeling. The rung of affection may be brief, "a little tasting of the sweetness of the love of

God," or prolonged on a higher level through spiritual exercise. The highest section is reached when one both knows and feels the knowing and perfect love of God. A man begins the contemplative life on earth, but full perfection, beyond the highest level of knowing and feeling, is reserved for Heaven. No living man can have the height of the contemplative state continually and habitually.

The knowing of God by man comes not by the sound of ear, sweetness of mouth, nor through any bodily sensation, writes Hilton. The knowing and feeling extends beyond the physical so that man may know and feel what is the length of the endless being of God, the breadth of the wonderful charity and goodness of God, the height of His almighty majesty, and the bottomless depths of His wisdom. The contemplative life demands that man conform his soul to God. Three means are known that can bring a soul to contemplation: the reading of holy Scripture and good books, spiritual meditation, and diligent prayer with devotion. One needs to have humility, firm faith, resolute will and purpose to seek after God. Right humility requires man to put out of his heart all imprudent looking into other men's actions. It drives one wholly to behold oneself as if there were nothing other than God and the self. A trivial sin in oneself is considered more grievous than a mortal sin in another, if a man possesses right humility within himself.

The necessity of prayer within the contemplative life is constant. Prayer is not the cause for which God has given grace, but it is a way or means by which grace freely given comes into the soul. When man awakes out of his sleep, he should whisper the prayer of the spirit, not of the body, a prayer free from all fleshly thoughts and affections. Prayer is an ascending of the desire of the heart to God by withdrawing it from all earthly thoughts. There are various prayers: the vocal prayer of the individual, the prayers of the Church, the vocal prayer which comes from the affection of the heart, the prayer which is only in the heart, a prayer without speech which brings great rest and quietness of soul and body. Prayer is not voice or reason, but it is in the great stillness of voice and softness of heart. In order to rid prayers of vain thoughts, man must mentally make and frame between himself and God a full purpose and intention to serve God with all the powers of his soul by his present prayer. He must *begin* and *do* as well as he can.

There are no specific rules for spiritual meditation, Hilton warns. However, a period of deep sinful awareness is necessary for everyone, followed by a meditation on Christ's humility in His humanity. This meditation brings about the union of spiritual insight with devout affection, the opening of the spiritual eye to the humanity of Christ, *the fleshly love of God.* Temptations are not to lead men away from spiritual meditation, but to encourage the development of a more complete trust in God. The temptation which comes from God develops within man the full willingness to suffer and abide in His will.

Man should know the measure of his spiritual gift. Hilton compares the man who seeks spiritual knowledge to the hound that runs after the hare and grows very weary when he sees only other hounds. When the hound sees the hare (for himself) he will not spare himself until he has caught it.

So it is for man when he sees his own soul, when at last he glimpses the prize rather than the many souls around him. Man must enter into himself, know his own soul (the fairness and foulness of it) and its powers. From this insight comes the desire for spiritual work in order to recover again that dignity and nobleness which one has lost.

Nothing else but the name of Jesus is spiritual health for spiritual illness, declares Hilton. The three powers of the soul: memory, will, and understanding, call into man the remembrance, the sight, and love of the most blessed uncreated Trinity which is God. Man in the contemplative life seeks his lost image. This is done by speaking the name Jesus, which is all goodness, endless wisdom, love and sweetness, joy, glory, everlasting bliss, God, Lord, and salvation. One is to desire Jesus with such devotion that one's thought is set upon nothing else. Such a contemplative person feels no stirring of vain-glory, or self-love, or any evil affection. Then he observes by what manner of prayer, meditation, or exercise of devotion he has found the greatest and purest desire for Him and the most feeling of Him. Then he is to use this kind of prayer, meditation, spiritual exercise on the scale (ladder) to perfection. One ought never to cease from the spiritual desiring and loving of Jesus while he lives, Hilton declares.

The contemplative life is to seek, and to seek is to suffer. One must not turn to Rome or to Jerusalem, but one must turn within. Jesus seeks to find His image reformed within man; otherwise, He is a stranger. Steps to the conforming of the image within to the image of Jesus are (1) to cease for a time all physical work, (2) to detach one's thought from all the bodily senses, (3) to seek one's soul, the dark and ill-favored image, and (4) to think about the soul's image. The soul is the nought within; it is the darkness of conscience and a lacking of the love of God and light, the nothingness which *is* emptiness, darkness, and heaviness.

When a man comes home each night to a disorderly home and a chiding wife, he finds no comfort within; so the soul finds no comfort in itself, but only the disorder of spiritual blindness and the great chiding of guilty or fleshly thoughts. Thus, the soul, like the man, grows weary and retreats. However, advises Hilton, this is the moment when the soul must stay and suffer the pain of its discomfort. The soul must abide therein, face the darkness, and hate and loathe it, for within this darkness is spiritual peace which one will not find with all one's seeking unless one passes through the nought and experiences spiritual travail. The nought is the image of a false, inordinate love of oneself, from which spring the seven deadly sins: pride, envy, anger, sloth, covetousness, gluttony, and lechery. In order to defeat these sins, man must face the nought within himself.

Out of this encounter comes humility, the knowing of oneself and the ability to separate the sin from the sinner. True humility hates sin and truly loves the sinner. A man can hate sin only when he has faced the truth within himself. He is humble who truly knows himself as he is, for humility is truth. The humble man loves himself and his neighbor only in God or for God: "Leave thy prayer for thy neighbor, take time and find God in his need, listen and feed his speech in its need."

The scale of perfection is the journey to Jerusalem: "I would fain be at Jerusalem." Enemies appear along the journey attempting to destroy the desire for the love of Jesus. Some cry that the right confession has not been made and that there is further need to ransack the soul. Yet the task has already been done. Hold on the way and think only on Jerusalem, Hilton writes. Others will say that man is not worthy of God's love, yet it is because of unworthiness that one seeks God's love. Dangers of sickness, madness, fancies, melancholy, poverty or bodily mishap, and of secret temptations and illusions will come, making the one desire for the love of Jesus seem futile. Then attacks of men will come, attempting to make the traveler hateful and angry. Later, enemies will try flattery—but think only on Jerusalem, Hilton advises, and maintain this sole desire (love of Jesus) through prayer and spiritual exercises. One is not to tie himself to habitual devotions which never alter in their pattern. Meditation is a means and not an end.

The soul moves through faith, the gracious imagination or spiritual knowledge of God, to feeling, the faith and imagination of Jesus in His manhood, and finally to the spiritual feeling of the Godhead in unity with humanity. One knows God in two ways: first in imagination and then in understanding. The latter is the beginning of contemplation proper. Understanding is the gate to Love uncreated (God). Through it one sees that the Father makes the soul, the Son redeems it, and the Holy Ghost justifies it. One cannot love God by sheer might. It is a great folly, Hilton declares, for a man of his own head or willfulness to press or strain himself too much in spiritual matters: "And then is the soul more suffering than doing, and that is pure love." The opening of the spiritual eye, however, requires both the grace of the Holy Ghost and the will of human effort. The opening of the spiritual eye brings purity of spirit, spiritual rest, inward stillness, peace of conscience, elevation of thought, loneliness of soul, a lively feeling of grace, and a meekness of heart.

Advice is given by Hilton to the practical man who is engaged in the "mixed life," being neither purely active nor solely contemplative. He is to exercise and use the desire for God: (1) by rising in the night after sleep to pray, (2) by calling out good thoughts and meditations wherein he feels the greatest ease and pleasure, (3) by thinking of his own sins and then of the sins of all Christian brethren (one may make of another man's sins a precious ointment to heal one's own sin *if* one thinks with compassion and deep sorrow), (4) by thinking of the humanity of Christ, His birth, passion, and works, and (5) by thinking of the virtues and the Saints, the holiness of the Lord, the blessed Lady, the power, wisdom, goodness, mercy of God, and the real miseries of this life. Again, advice is given to use discretion in devotions, to take them moderately. No man suddenly becomes supreme or perfect in grace.

ENCHIRIDION MILITIS CHRISTIANI

Author: Desiderius Erasmus (c.1466-1536)
Type of work: Christian ethics
First published: 1503

Principal Ideas Advanced

The true Christian life is a warfare against the evils of ignorance, ignoble desire, and weakness of purpose; the battle is waged not so much between men as within man himself.

The greatest defense against evil is faith in and imitation of Christ, reinforced by prayer and enhanced by knowledge of Scripture and other sources of ancient wisdom.

In order to achieve the victory of eternal life over eternal torment a Christian should march along level ground, not climbing to unreal heights of complete protection by divine grace or sinking into a pit of despair because the battle seems overwhelming.

The highest expression of religious devotion is found not in the formalities of ritual, in the vain and subtle disputations of Scholastic theologians, in the veneration of saints and relics, or in the opinions of the crowd, but in the practice of virtue motivated by inward piety; the highest pleasure is the happiness derived from a pure conscience.

Desiderius Erasmus was a man of diverse talents and contrasting moods, who, perhaps more than any other prominent individual of his era, reflected in his personality and his writings the tensions of the Western world during the early sixteenth century.

Hans Holbein (1497-1543), German painter, captured the serious and gentle mood of Erasmus in an unpretentious portrait displayed in one of the small rooms at the Louvre. In this portrait Erasmus is seen with pen in hand and manuscript before him, his face revealing a deep and placid concentration intent on a serious task before him: an attitude characterizing the emotional tone and ideas expressed in his *Enchiridion militis Christiani* (*Manual of the Christian Soldier*).

Another glance at a different mood of Erasmus might reveal a cynical sneer reminiscent of the satire in *The Praise of Folly* or a whimsical smile depicting the light humor found here and there in various stories collected in the *Colloquies*. Although there is righteous indignation and typical Erasmian sarcasm expressed in the *Enchiridion*, its overtones are generally sober, and its ideas are presented in a straightforward manner.

Erasmus's life was devoted to scholarship and religious reform. In the *Enchiridion* this Renaissance scholar projects those tenets of Christian Humanism which exalt ancient literature and ask for a return to the simple piety of early Christianity, untarnished by centuries of ritualistic and linguistic corruption. He uses the framework of the *Enchiridion* to support one of his chief concerns: an enlightened, reformed, theologically purified Church.

Erasmus focuses on the individual as a means to this restoration, and his *Enchiridion* provides guidelines for the life worthy of the name "Christian."

Erasmus suggests, therefore, that the ideal of an enlightened, reformed, theologically purified Church worthy of its head (Christ) will be achieved only if each member of the body (Christians collectively) becomes enlightened, reformed, and enabled to understand theology at its source (the Scriptures).

Pacifist though he was, Erasmus uses the analogy of warfare for this treatise. The Christian life is a warfare against the forces of evil, especially the evil tendencies within the individual. "*Enchiridion*" means both "dagger" and "manual," and the author employs the term in both senses.

Erasmus maintains that each Christian is a soldier who must arm himself with a "dagger" and carry it at all times to ward off the forces which prevent him from leading a life of virtue. The "dagger" is fashioned of rules of conduct which will aid his offensive and defensive positions. These rules also comprise his "manual."

The *Enchiridion* contains thirteen chapters, with Chapter 8 enumerating twenty-two such rules or "weapons." In the opening chapters Erasmus chides Christians who are lukewarm in the struggle against the vices which engulf man. Citing the battle-scarred Job of Hebrew tradition, Erasmus reminds his readers that all life is beset by turmoil for the righteous as well as the wicked. It is a man's soul which is at stake in the warfare, and the struggle involves not only man's integrity, but also his eternal life.

Erasmus uses the term "soul" in different ways. He speaks of the "soul-body" or "spirit-flesh" divisions often used in Pauline description of man's battle with himself and the world, and in other instances he uses a three-fold division of "spirit-body-soul," acknowledging the thought of Origen (c.185-c.254), head of the Catechetical School at Alexandria. Using the latter three categories, Erasmus makes the soul an interacting agent between the other two: "The spirit renders us gods; the flesh, animals; the soul makes us men."

Erasmus was appalled at the lack of concern on the part of some Christians who did not behave as if they were fighting under a banner of Christ at all. He describes them as men who become greatly concerned if they break an arm or have a fever but do not seem to understand the gravity of a sick soul (here "soul" means higher faculties producing sympathy, virtue, intelligent decision): "You see your brother suffering indignities, yet your mind is not in the least moved. . . . Why at this point does your soul feel nothing? Surely because it is dead. Wherefore dead? Because God, its life, is not present. Where God is, there is love."

"Know thyself," Erasmus says, as others before him said. A man can never contend successfully with the evil around him until he understands and can conquer himself.

In his discussion of self-knowledge and self-mastery, Erasmus dips into Platonic and Stoic philosophy for several analogies likening individual man with a political state. Reason, the "king," must govern all "lower classes," the base passions, such as envy, lechery, lust. The "nobles" are affections such as piety, love, and mercy, which help the "king" rule a harmonious "state."

If the Christian is to rule himself, he must guard against three main enemies: (1) blindness, which leads to ignorance, (2) the flesh (ignoble desire), which incites his base passions against his reason, and (3) infirmity, which causes him to waver in the path of virtue.

If a person is ignorant, he pursues the worst instead of the best. In order to clear his vision he must investigate what should be shunned. If a person knows what is best, he still faces the onslaught of harmful desire, which renders his reason ineffective. In order to overcome this desire, he should hate evil thoughts and love good ones. Even if he knows what is best and loves good thoughts, his infirmity may cause him to stumble, especially if virtue eludes him and he is caught in a snare of boredom or temptation.

What is the best defense against evil? Faith in Christ. Erasmus means an active faith involving conduct, even martyrdom if necessary. A Christ-like man is one who follows the teachings of Christ: "Set before you Christ as the only goal of your whole life, to whom alone you dedicate all zeal, all efforts, all leisure and business. Indeed, think of Christ not as an empty word, but as nothing else than love, simplicity, patience, purity—in short, whatsoever he has taught."

If Christ is to be more than an empty word, the Christian soldier must fortify his defenses by an *understanding* of Christ, and in order to gain that understanding, he must turn first of all to the Scriptures. But the Christian also must seek other avenues of enlightenment to help him understand the Scriptures. For those avenues he should turn to those most prepared to speak authoritatively on Scripture, especially to those who are concerned with the spiritual meaning and not merely the letter: Paul (d. c.65), the Apostle; and the Church Fathers, especially Origen (c.185-c.254); Ambrose (c.339-397), Bishop of Milan; Jerome (c.342-420), translator of the Vulgate Bible; and Augustine (c. 354-430), Bishop of Hippo, who are in a better position to speak authoritatively than are modern theologians who follow such men as John Duns Scotus (c.1264-1308), Scholastic theologian. Such men as Duns Scotus, Erasmus contends, often speak *about* the Scriptures without having undertaken a careful study *of* them.

Erasmus would have the student trace his quest for understanding still further by directing him to the Greeks and Romans and other extra-Biblical sources which provide examples of virtue worthy of imitation: "Nor ought you to despise pagan authors, for they too are often good moral teachers."

The revelation of divine wisdom neither begins nor ends with Christ, but reaches its perfection there. For philosophical guidance Erasmus especially recommends the Platonists, "for the reason that in very many of their opinions and in their way of speaking they approach as closely as possible the prophetic and gospel pattern."

The Scriptures, the commentators, and the classical writings are best understood in their original languages, Erasmus claimed, thus advancing another Humanistic idea. Erasmus did not write for the common man, and the unsophisticated soldier (John, the German, who may or may not be fictional) to whom Erasmus dedicates the *Enchiridion* would have found many of the classical references difficult to appreciate.

Knowledge is not always sufficient protection against evil. Knowledge must often be fortified with prayer, for "pure prayer . . . is a citadel inaccessible to the enemy." The two are necessary complements, for knowledge helps one pray intelligently, and prayer helps subdue passions which knowledge can not always conquer unaided.

Man may be the highest of creatures "for whose sake alone God fashioned this wonderful machine of the world," says Erasmus, but he reminds man, lest he be overelated, that whatever has made him beautiful, great, or famous, is a gift from God, but whatever has made him sordid is his own doing. The Christian soldier should therefore beware of being haughty after victory, for the underlying credit belongs to God in the struggle against the Devil (the vices which plague man).

Erasmus warns the soldier that the consequences of following the Devil cannot be compared with the consequences of following God. The former path brings eternal death (which is not the fire of Hell, in Erasmus's view, but everlasting mental torment), and the latter path brings immortal life.

Erasmus cautions that sudden death for one who is a slave to the Devil could result in an eternal death. The soldier, however, should not give up the fight because of its rigors and the possibility of defeat; moreover, he should not put down his weapons in utter dependence on the protection of God. Salvation is a co-operative effort.

Erasmus had a firm belief in free will, and his views of the nature of man and his destiny were semi-Pelagian; that is, he believed that man is capable of exercising free will to choose the good, which aids his own salvation, although he is dependent upon God's gift in the atonement by Christ to erase the taint of original sin.

Indeed, it is a man's ability to choose the good over the evil which determines his skill as a Christian soldier. Erasmus acknowledges the difficulty of living in society, with all the mundane pressures and conflicts which are presented by demands of family, friends, enemies, in addition to the human desires for recognition, comfort, and pleasure; nevertheless, Erasmus asks, "What is this that the miserable call pleasure?", and declares that "the true and only pleasure is the joy of a pure conscience. The most elegant banquets *are* enjoyed in the study of the Holy Scriptures. The most pleasing songs are the psalms of the Holy Spirit. The most joyous fellowship is the communion of saints. The highest delights are in the enjoyment of truth. Only purify your eyes, your ears, your palate, and Christ will become sweet to you."

The Christian must withdraw from the demands of the world and his own mundane drives and live "in Christ." By this thesis Erasmus does not mean that it is necessary for the Christian to live *away* from society or mystically to withdraw himself while in the *midst* of society ("monasticism is not godliness, but a kind of life, either useful or useless to anyone depending on one's habit of body and of temperament"), but it is necessary for him to live subject to the standards of Christ and not to the standards of the world: "If you are in the world, you are not in Christ." Erasmus does not mean by this statement the geographical world, for he characterizes the world as false ambition, evil desire, harmful delights;

that is, as whatever is detrimental to a virtuous life.

Erasmus would say to anyone seeking praise that he should seek God's praise, not the praise of men, which is fickle, because men may retract whatever honor they have bestowed. Honor comes only from true virtue, Erasmus maintains, and honor granted by men is perilous and tentative: "Think how blessed is the tranquility of a modest and private life, removed from all clamor of pride. On the other hand how thorny, how full of care, perils, pains, is the life of the powerful! . . . How complete the crash from the heights!"

A Christian, therefore, should not be influenced by the opinions of the crowd. Christ is the archetype of opinion and behavior, and Erasmus suggests that it is far better to imitate Christ's behavior than it is to revere His image; it is better to practice the virtues of the saints than to visit their shrines or touch their relics; it is far better for a Christian to reconcile himself to a brother he has injured or to one who has injured him than merely to recite platitudes about Christian love.

Do not retaliate an injury, says Erasmus, for this increases the pain; sometimes by leniency the injury can be cured, and a former enemy then becomes a friend.

This sentiment of reconciliation exemplifies one of the gentle and serious moods of Erasmus, "Prince of the Humanists," who was to find himself several years after writing the *Enchiridion* involved in the midst of religious controversy which made many of his former friends enemies as he tried to work for reform within a unified Church when the breach became "irreparable."

Many of the sentiments expressed in the *Enchiridion* may have been influenced by the training Erasmus received under the Brethren of the Common Life during his early school days at Deventer. He respected the sincere piety of the Brethren, although he deplored their lack of enthusiasm for classical learning.

Another source of inspiration may very well have been a man whom Erasmus admired a great deal, Jehan Vitrier (c.1454-?), Prior of the Franciscan monastery at St. Omer, where he composed at least a portion of the original manuscript.

The *Enchiridion* was written in 1501 and first published at Antwerp in 1503 among a collection of other works entitled *Lucubratiunculae* (which could be translated "little works composed at night"). Later editions were entitled *Lucubrationes* (which could be translated "studies by lamplight"). The *Enchiridion* appeared in at least seven more Latin editions after the original, the last one being issued in 1540, and it was translated into English, French, German, Dutch, Czech, and Spanish.

At first the *Enchiridion* was not very popular, but later, especially after the translations appeared, it enjoyed greater popularity for a number of years, and then its fame diminished.

THE PRAISE OF FOLLY

Author: Desiderius Erasmus (c.1466-1536)
Type of work: Christian satire
First published: 1511

Principal Ideas Advanced

Not wisdom but folly dominates the life of man.

Folly leads both to self-deception and to the deception of others.

There are different forms and degrees of folly, from the amiable self-deception which makes life livable and pleasant, to the hypocrisy that covers the greatest evils.

The folly of Christian faith and devotion is the true wisdom.

Erasmus says that he wrote *The Praise of Folly* (*Moriae encomium*) in seven days while a guest in the home of his friend Sir Thomas More (1478-1535). It was published two years later in Paris and was at once received with acclaim even by many who were the obvious victims of his satire, including Pope Julian II. Translation into many languages soon followed. The first English translation was made in 1549 by Sir Thomas Chaloner. The one most commonly used today is from the pen of John Wilson and appeared in 1668. Quotations herein are from that translation.

The Praise of Folly is the most famous work of what was known as "Fool Literature" which had its distinguished beginning in Sebastian Brant's *Narrenschiff*, published in 1494. Such writing represents the license and indulgence once granted to the "Court Fool," now transferred to the higher levels of culture. With Erasmus it is the rational mind of the humanist and scholar at work exposing the hypocrisies and ridiculing the pretensions of men in all walks of life, including even the most honored and powerful of men. But Erasmus wrote with such a light touch, and "folly" is so frankly commended in his book by the Goddess of Folly herself, that a sophisticated society could take his criticism in good part and enjoy laughing at itself. In any case there is no hint that anyone is expected to do anything about the reign of the Goddess of Folly other than to laugh with her at the role of folly in the affairs of men.

The Goddess, who appears as the speaker throughout, starts with an account of her place among the gods, and with references to the more ribald side of their lives. Even the highest of the gods must lay aside their dignity to beget their children, she says. All are indebted to her, indeed, for being born! She is the giver of the pleasures of life. Youth is valued because it has not yet learned wisdom, and old age is blessed by a return to childishness. The gods that are most popular are Bacchus, Pan, Venus, and Flora, all of whom bring pleasures and gaiety into the lives of men. Folly has the advantage over wisdom in that wisdom comes from reason, while folly is the fruit of passion. And the joy of life is derived not from reason, but from passion, not from wisdom but from folly.

Wisdom is limited to the head; passion has its domain in all the rest of the body. In all the enjoyments of life—sex, feasting, delight in children, friendship, and matrimony—we indulge in foolish praise and flattery. Folly sweetens all human relations. Even a wise man must flatter himself; self-love is a necessity.

Taking war as "the very root and matter of all famed enterprises," in spite of the fact that everybody loses more than he gains by it, Folly shows how inept and useless the philosopher is. For war is "manag'd by Parasites, Pandars, Thieves, Cut-Throats, Plowmen, Sots, Spendthrifts and such other dregs of mankind, not Philosophers." The wise man has no place in public affairs or in the life of cities. Politicians use flattery and deceit to control the people. It is tyrants who are deified, so the man of wisdom and prudence is useless. On the other hand, folly leads men to attempt great things and to achieve them. Men, like actors, play roles in life; they are inwardly quite the opposite of what they appear to be. Life is a comedy in which we all change our roles at will; we could not get along otherwise.

The prudent man would make himself odious if he were to point out the miseries and hypocrisies of men. The Stoic is cold and unfeeling, having no passion (folly); he cannot properly take the part of a ruler; he is a failure as a husband, and impossible as a guest. It is better to be a "middle fool."

There are so many ills in life, says the Goddess of Folly, that wisdom would lead men to suicide. But by the help of folly everyone eagerly seeks life, and delights in it, even the old and infirm. Philosophers say that all these miseries are good because they are part of man's condition, but the philosophers are mistaken. Science is of the Devil, and the imposition of laws and the rules of grammar on man is an evil thing. The happiest ones are those who follow nature (folly). Among all the professions those who come nearest doing this are the physicians and the politicians. It is best to live like the flies and the birds; that is, according to nature.

The Goddess quotes Homer and Pythagoras on the misery of man, who by seeking wisdom tries to go beyond what nature has made him. Fools are the happiest, the Goddess declares. It is said that princes will not listen to wise men because wise men speak the truth. "And yet this is found by experience among my Fools," the Goddess says, "that not only Truths but even open reproaches are heard with pleasure; so that the same thing which, if it came from a wise man's mouth might prove a Capital Crime, spoken by a Fool is receiv'd with delight."

The Goddess takes her cue from the logicians and makes a distinction between two kinds of madness, "the one that which the vengeful furies send privily from Hell, as often as they let loose their Snakes, and put into men's breasts either the desire of War, or an insatiate thirst after Gold, or some dishonest Love, or Parricide, or Incest, or Sacrilege, or the like Plagues, or when they terrifie some guilty soul with the Conscience of his Crimes; the other, but nothing like this, that which comes from me, and is of all things the most desirable; which happens as oft as some pleasing dotage not onely clears the mind of its troublesome cares, but renders it more jocund."

Among those who follow folly's better way the Goddess mentions hunters with their ridiculous ritual of dismembering a buck, gamblers with their passion for dice, and fortunetellers and others who use magic charms and prayers to secure success or to avoid certain evils. Some saints "are good for one thing, others for another. And some there are that are good for more things than one; but chiefly, the Virgin Mother, to whom the common people do in a manner attribute more than to the Son." This is all from folly; "whereas if some scurvy Wise fellow should step up, and speak things as they are, as, To live well is the way to die well; the best way to get quit of sin is to add to the money thou giv'st, the Hatred of sin, Tears, Watchings, Prayers, Fastings, and amendment of life: Such or such a Saint will favor thee, if thou imitatist his life;—these, I say, and the like, should this Wise man chat to the people, from what happiness into how great troubles would he draw 'em?"

Men make claims to nobility and diligently trace out their ancestry; each nation and city prides itself on its greatness. But any serious attempt to get back of these opinions destroys the joy of life, says Folly. Happiness comes through thinking things beautiful and costly even though they are neither. The Goddess Folly removes cares. There is no formal worship of her, but all do her service.

So much for the common folk. Erasmus now turns to the "Wise men." He writes with feeling on this theme. He lists the pedantry, the contentiousness of grammarians, poets, rhetoricians and writers of books, and he points to their mutual praises, and to their attacks upon one another. Even the learned indulge in some of this. He pays his biting respects to the advocates, to the philosophers with their speculations about natural phenomena, and to the divines with their fine distinctions and the subtleties of their theology: "As, whether there was any instant of time in the generation of the Second Person; whether there be more than one Filiation in Christ; whether it be a possible proposition that God the Father hates the Son; or whether it was possible that Christ could have taken upon Him the likeness of a Woman, or of the Devil, or of an Ass, or of a Stone, or of a Gourd; and then how that Gourd should have preach't, wrought miracles, or been hung on the Cross . . . ."

The arraignment of the professional divines is followed by a pertinent reference to the Apostles and to the simple and genuine account they give of faith and love, of the Eucharist and baptism, of worship and the meaning of spirit, and of grace. Erasmus declares, through his Goddess, that they confuted the heathen not by syllogisms, but by their good lives and miracles. Some of the divines see their folly, but most of them are happy in it and pursue their fine definitions and their judgments upon things heretical or questionable as though the whole of the faith rested upon their doings.

The monks and those who profess their religiosity come in next for similar treatment: "most false in both Titles, when both a great part of 'em are farthest from Religion, and no men swarm thicker in all places than themselves." They are all absorbed in the small matters of their dress, their names, the details of their rites and prayers, the distinctions between themselves, and between themselves and others. "In a word," says Folly, " 'tis their only care that none of 'em come near one another in their manner of living, nor do they endeavor how they may be like Christ, but how they may differ among themselves." The sermons of these religious men are derided for both matter and method. Use of far-fetched analogies, proving of doctrines by analysis of words or finding a theological meaning in the first letters of a formula, and other devious and meaningless performances are held up to ridicule. These men add to their strange logic the arts of rhetoric in equally dubious fashion, and they exaggerate the modulations of voice which they have learned from teachers of elocution. The parting comment of the Goddess on these people shows that even Folly cannot be proud of their performance: "But I willingly give over these Stage-players, that are such ingrateful dissemblers of the courtesies I have done 'em, and such impudent pretenders to Religion which they ha'nt."

Princes and "Court-Lords" are subjected to severe treatment by the Goddess. If a prince took to heart the great responsibilities that rest upon him, and if he realized that his character and conduct affect so much the lives of all men, he would be overwhelmed by his duties and would henceforth live a life of rigorous discipline. But, as a matter of fact, the prince leaves all these cares to the gods and devotes himself to the hunt and to all kinds of frivolous and costly formalisms. The "Court-Lords" are interested only in their pleasures and fine clothes, in their feasting and entertainments, and in rivalries for the favors of the prince.

Cardinals and bishops are much the same, declares Folly. Instead of living the lives of devout men and giving themselves to the care of the faithful, they are busy with the increase of their own wealth and dignity. Popes would do well to imitate their Master, to live simple lives, and to give themselves wholly to the care of their flock. But actually they are absorbed in the glories of their office and in their titles and ceremonies. They are always given to war, Folly insists; "Nor are they destitute of their learned flatterers that call that palpable Madness Zeal, Piety, and Valor, having found out a new way by which a man may kill his brother without the least breach of that Charity which, by the command of Christ, one Christian owes another." The real care of the people is passed on by the popes to the bishops, by the bishops to the parsons, by the parsons to the vicars, by the vicars to the mendicants, who finally give it over to the monks.

The Goddess now returns to her argument that folly is better than wisdom, and she quotes classical writers to prove it, while providing examples from life. The last part of the satire moves into the realm of Scripture. Here another distinction is made implicitly in the nature of folly. The book begins, as will be remembered, with Folly's quoting the pagan gods and citing their conduct as support for a kind of folly that releases gods and men from the ordinary decencies and moralities, and frees them to indulge their natural desires. But now a new meaning of folly is gained from the Christian faith. For example, St. Paul's words are quoted: "God hath chosen the foolish things of this world," and "It pleased God by foolishness to save the world." Even the authority of Christ is invoked: ". . . Christ gives Him thanks that he had conceal'd the

Mystery of Salvation from the wise, but revealed it to babes and sucklings, that is to say, Fools." Christ is called the Lamb of God, and His disciples are His "sheep, than which creature there is not any thing more foolish. . . . And Christ himself, that he might better relieve this Folly, being the wisdome of the Father, yet in some manner became a fool, when taking upon him the nature of man, he was found in shape as a man; as in like manner he was made Sin, that he might heal sinners." "To speak briefly," Folly declares, "all Christian Religion seems to have a kind of allyance with folly."

The treatise closes with an account of the "madness" of the spiritually minded few who seek in this life the experience of things eternal. These fools have found the true wisdom, and are indifferent to the worldly satisfactions and enjoyments that most men seek. They have a foretaste of future happiness. Here Erasmus, in his proper person, exclaims "But I forget myself and run beyond my bounds."

AN OPEN LETTER TO THE CHRISTIAN NOBILITY OF THE GERMAN NATION

Author: Martin Luther (1483-1546)
Type of work: Polemical theology
First published: 1520

Principal Ideas Advanced

The Romanists have surrounded the doctrine of papal supremacy with three "walls" of supporting arguments by which they frustrate all attempts to reform the Church through the temporal powers, the Bible, or a council.

The Romanists contend that the "spiritual estate" is superior to all temporal authority, that the pope alone has the authority to interpret the Bible, and that only the pope may call a council.

In the Christian Church baptism confers upon all members the same basic status and responsibilities, so that the right to interpret the Scriptures and to call reforming councils belongs to all Christian believers.

The Christian princes and noblemen of Germany must take the initiative in wresting German political and religious life out of corrupt papal control, and in reforming German religious practices and institutions.

Luther's *Open Letter,* or *Address,* appeared in German under the title *An den christlichen Adel deutscher Nation von des christlichen Standes Besserung.* It was the first of the three so-called "Reformation treatises" of 1520, all of which Luther wrote in response to his conviction that his break with the medieval Church was irreconcilable and that he had the duty of assuming the leadership of the mammoth task of reforming Christendom.

Luther's opposition to the medieval Church increased steadily after his initial dramatic act of nailing to the doors of the Church of All Saints in Wittenberg his famous ninety-five theses on October 31, 1517. His protest against the abusive sale of indulgences was to assume minor importance in comparison with his questions about other features of the Church. Between October of 1518 and June of 1519, Luther investigated with intense scrutiny the evidences for the claim of absolute papal authority, a claim which he himself firmly upheld when he first raised questions about indulgences.

Papal claims to absolute authority were based largely upon a collection of documents now known as the Pseudo-Isidorian or False Decretals. The collection dates from the middle of the ninth century and purports to be the work of a certain Isidore Mercator. The Decretals included decisions of popes and councils from the first century through Gregory II in the eighth century. They had been regarded as authentic for over six and a half centuries. Luther discovered, to his indignation and amazement, that many of the documents were forgeries. Both disturbed and relieved by his discovery, he was forced to come to a quick conclusion on the question of papal authority when he was challenged to debate the subject with John Eck, a theologian who taught at the University of Leipzig.

Eck was a clever and brilliant debater, and he accomplished his purpose of leading Luther into declaring himself in agreement with certain heretical views which the Church had definitely condemned. Specifically, Luther was led to acknowledge agreement with certain views of the Bohemian reformer John Huss (c.1369-1415), who had been condemned and sentenced to death in 1415 by the Council of Constance. Eck was able, at the end of the debate, to point to Luther as a heretic who not only rejected the pope's authority but who also seemed to reserve to himself the right to agree or disagree with councils of the Church.

After an initial melancholy reaction to the Leipzig debate, Luther's spirits quickly rallied, and he faced up to the deep division of outlook which separated him from the supporters of the papal claims. In the three treatises of 1520 Luther undertook to make clear to himself and to the public the ground on which he stood.

The *Open Letter* is closely related to a tract which was published on June 26, 1520, bearing the title *The Papacy at Rome: A Reply to the Celebrated Romanist at Leipzig*. The concluding paragraph of the tract contains in germinal form the argument of the *Open Letter*, which was composed in June but which did not appear in print until the middle of August. While Luther was at work on the *Open Letter* the bull of excommunication which formally banished him from the Church was signed by Pope Leo X.

In the *Open Letter* Luther writes as a German who is outraged at the exploitation of the German people by the greedy and luxury-loving pope and the enormous entourage which made up his splendid court. Luther had come to the conclusion that the only hope for lifting the burden of Roman oppression off Germany and restoring the life of the Church to Biblical foundations was through the initiative of the newly elected emperor, Charles V, and the German princes and nobility who ruled the relatively autonomous German provinces. The *Open Letter* was a challenge to these men to assume the initiative in reforming the Church.

The Romanists, or defenders of papal supremacy, have frustrated all attempts to reform the Church, claims Luther, by erecting "three walls" around themselves. When under pressure from civil or temporal powers, they argue that the spiritual power is superior to the temporal. When they are confronted with Scriptural evidences that the Church has fallen into corruption, they respond with the argument that the pope alone has the right to interpret the meaning of the Bible. When threatened by a council, they reply that only the pope may call a council. Luther assaults the three walls one by one.

The distinction which the Romanists make between the "spiritual estate" (consisting of pope, bishops, priests, and monks) and the "temporal estate" (consisting of princes, lords, artisans, and farmers) is completely false, says Luther. All Christians belong to the same estate and have the same basic status in the Church. A cobbler who is a baptized Christian believer is no less a member of the spiritual estate than a bishop. Ordination does not confer upon priests any special graces but simply designates them as set apart to do a particular kind of work in the fellowship of Christians. If a pope or bishop or priest fails to do his task properly, he is as deserving of public censure and civil punishment as is a dishonest or incompetent cobbler or tailor. Baptism ordains every Christian to responsibility for the Word of God and for the well-being of the Church. Baptism, then, is the warrant which grants to the Christian princes and nobility the right and the obligation to reform the life of the Church.

The second wall, writes Luther, is even less substantial than the first. He points to the irony of the claim of the papists that the pope alone is authorized and competent to interpret the Scriptures even though many of the popes had been ignorant of the Bible and had contradicted it grossly in the conduct of their lives. Luther further argues that canon law contained many heretical and unchristian ordinances which reveal ignorance or disregard of the Bible. Luther ironically suggests that, since the Romanists claim that the Holy Spirit never leaves them, the Bible is really not needed and might as well be burned.

The right and ability to interpret the Scriptures belongs to those who possess the true faith and are imbued with the spirit and mind of Christ. Every Christian has the duty to understand and defend the faith and to rebuke all errors, no matter by whom they are committed.

The third wall falls of itself, claims Luther, once the other two are leveled. Just as all Christians have the duty to judge papal behavior by Scriptural standards, just as much so is it the right of all Christians to use councils as a method of insuring the spiritual health of the Church.

Luther points out—and historical evidence supports him—that the Council of Nicaea (325) was called by the Emperor Constantine I and not by the bishop of Rome, and that later emperors likewise called councils. On the basis of the priesthood of all Christian believers, he contends, it is the duty of those who are in a position to do so to call a free council to deal with the papacy and its manifold abuses.

The critics of the papacy should not be deterred by any threats or by excommunication, for God does not give to the pope the power to excommunicate those who are doing their Christian duty.

Having made his case for the legitimacy of the initiative of the German princes and nobles in calling a reforming council, Luther goes on to enumerate in great detail the abuses with which such a council should deal. His bill of indictment is a vivid account of conditions in the German Church and of the economic, political, and social consequences and implications relating to those conditions.

The center of corruption in the Church, affirms Luther, is the pope, with his insatiable appetite for opulence and splendor. Surrounding the pope are the cardinals, who appear to be fully employed in collecting and enjoying the revenues from the richest convents, benefices, and endowments in Europe. The papal court is enormous, including three thousand secretaries and numerous other functionaries, all of whom are waiting eagerly for more German benefices to fall open, even though they have no intention of performing the ecclesiastical duties theoretically connected with the benefices. More German money goes annually to the papal court than to the German emperor.

Rome systematically robs Germany through the system of *annates*, whereby the holder of a benefice must turn over to the pope one half of the first year's income. The system of *annates* was set up about a century before, supposedly as a way of financing a war against the Turks, but the money has never been used for that purpose.

Some of the most shameless methods of raising money, Luther goes on, are those connected with the granting of ecclesiastical exemptions from the requirements of ecclesiastical and moral laws. For appropriate sums monks are permitted to leave the cloistered life, priests may gain permission to marry, and bastards are declared legitimate.

Luther's list of corrective measures is long and specific. He calls for the German princes and noblemen to take command over the system of Church revenues and to abolish entirely the *annates*. He also calls for complete jurisdiction of civil authorities over all temporal matters, with the pope's authority limited to the affairs of the Church. Then, striking an unusually forceful blow at papal power, he demands a German national church, with its own ecclesiastical council as the final court of appeal.

Turning to a long list of less radical proposals, Luther continues his assault upon the corrupt practices and institutions of medieval Christendom. Pilgrimages should be discouraged because they are inducements to immorality and shirking of work. The large number of mendicant orders should be reduced so as to cut down on the number of vagrant monks. All convents and nunneries should be thoroughly inspected, and nuns who wish to return to the world should be permitted to do so. Holy days—which have become numerous—have become occasions of debauchery and drunkenness. Sunday alone should be observed as a special religious day. Endowed masses should be forbidden. Canon law should be abolished, partly because the pope himself disregards it and perverts its meaning, and partly because the Bible is a sufficient guide for the Christian life.

Turning from reforms relating directly to the Church, Luther next directs his attention to economic and social questions. He deplores the luxury and ostentation in dress of the richer classes of Germany. Garments made of wool and flax and other common materials are suitable for everyone. The Germans are foolish to let their money flow out to foreign lands for luxury items of food and dress when Germany is bountifully supplied with the necessities of life. In general, Luther was suspiciously opposed to the economic trends which betokened the end of the old feudal agrarian economy and heralded a new economy based upon money and trade. Thus he speaks out against the great trading companies which reaped enormous profits by securing monopolies in the staple articles of commerce.

Of all the works which make up the enormous corpus of literature which came from Luther's pen, none had such an instantaneous and dramatic effect as did his *Open Letter*. He appealed to German national pride, and his religious proposals were such that their adoption would clearly strengthen the hands of the German civil rulers at the expense of the pope. The emperor Charles V decided to stand by the papacy, but enough of the German princes responded to Luther's appeals that his movement gained sufficient political protection to guarantee its wide success in Germany. Although it would be a mistake to interpret the Protestant movement as fundamentally political in significance, it is nonetheless true that it both aided and benefited from the tide of nationalism which was rising in Europe in the sixteenth century. The *Open Letter* exemplifies the spirit of both movements, for Luther was writing both as a proud German and as a man motivated by deep religious convictions.

THE BABYLONIAN CAPTIVITY OF THE CHURCH

Author: Martin Luther (1483-1546)
Type of work: Polemical theology
First published: 1520

Principal Ideas Advanced

The elaborate system of sacraments by which the Roman Church enslaves its members cannot be justified by reference to the Bible.

A true sacrament must have been instituted by Christ, must include a promise of a specific spiritual benefit or grace, must include an outer sign or symbolic act, and requires faith on the part of the recipient.

Only baptism and the Lord's Supper qualify as true Christian sacraments.

The Roman Church has corrupted the Lord's Supper by withholding the cup from the laity, by the doctrine of transubstantiation, and by teaching that the Mass is a sacrifice which man offers to God.

It is a spiritually beneficial practice for one to confess his sins to a Christian brother and to receive comforting assurance of divine forgiveness, but the Roman sacrament of penance places the emphasis upon the penitent's contrition and works of satisfaction rather than upon God's forgiveness.

Confirmation, marriage, and ordination may be regarded as Church rites, but they are not sacraments.

In the conclusion of his *Open Letter to the Christian Nobility* Luther wrote: "Ah well, I know another little song about Rome and about them. If their ears itch for it I will sing them that song too, and pitch the notes to the top of the scale." His *Babylonian Captivity of the Church*, published on October 6, 1520, is the "little song" which Luther had in mind.

The *Babylonian Captivity* contrasts with the political tone of the *Open Letter*. Whereas the *Open Letter* assaults the theoretical foundations of the vast temporal power of the papacy, the *Babylonian Captivity* strikes at the sacramental system, the theological and religious heart of Roman Christianity. In attacking the sacramental system and theology of Rome, Luther also set forth his own sacramental theology. The *Babylonian Captivity* sums up and expands upon conclusions which Luther had reached in shorter earlier writings on the sacraments. It stands as the most influential of his theological writings.

In the preface to the *Babylonian Captivity* Luther expresses a spirit of truculence and self assurance which indicates the depth of his breach with Rome and his firm intention to reform the Church. He expresses regret at his previous caution in dealing with the subjects of indulgences and the papacy. He suggests that the booksellers burn his writings on these two subjects. He is now ready to affirm categorically that indulgences are nothing but deceitful tricks and that the papacy represents nothing more than the greed of the Roman bishop.

Luther opens his assault on the Roman sacramental system by denying that there are seven sacraments. He vacillates somewhat on the question of how many sacraments he accepts, suggesting initially that there are three (baptism, penance, and the "bread" or Lord's Supper). He also affirms that in the strictly Scriptural sense there is only one sacrament—Christ—who is available to man under the three sacramental signs of baptism, penance, and the Lord's Supper. His final conclusion, however, reached after careful examination of each of the Roman sacraments, is that "there are strictly speaking, but two sacraments in the Church of God—baptism and bread. . . ." It was this last view which Luther continued to espouse and which almost all Protestant bodies adopted.

Luther's criteria for determining the validity of a sacrament are as follows: A sacrament must, first of all, have been instituted by Christ himself. Second, a sacrament must include a promise of a specific spiritual benefit of grace. Third, a sacrament must include a sign or symbolic act. Fourth, a sacrament requires faith on the part of the recipient, faith here being understood as grateful acceptance of the promise of God which is symbolized and conveyed by the sacrament.

The most extensive section of the

Babylonian Captivity consists of Luther's examination of the Eucharist or Lord's Supper, on which subject he had already published, in 1519, his *Treatise on the Blessed Sacrament.* Through their perverse interpretation of the Eucharist, contends Luther, the papists hold in captivity and subjection the members of the Church. The first perversion is the refusal to permit the laity to drink the consecrated wine as well as to eat the bread, which refusal suggests that only the priests may partake of the entire sacrament. Luther refers to the Biblical passages which describe the Last Supper (Matthew 26, Mark 14, and Luke 22) and concludes that anyone who receives the Lord's Supper is entitled to both the bread and the wine. He cites the writings of Cyprian (c.200-258), Bishop of Carthage, as evidence that the laity in the early Church received both elements.

The second papist perversion of the Lord's Supper is the doctrine of transubstantiation as the form of stating the miracle of the real presence of Christ in the elements of bread and wine. Transubstantiation is the doctrine that the accidents, or qualities, of bread and wine which are evident to the senses (such as color, taste, odor) remain, but the substance or essence which can only be thought but not sensed is miraculously changed into the body and blood of Christ. Luther describes this doctrine as an invasion of Christian theology by Aristotelian philosophy, and he urges an interpretation of the Eucharistic miracle based upon the Christian doctrine of the Incarnation. Human nature does not have to be transubstantiated in order for it to be the dwelling place of the Godhead, and neither do bread and wine have to be transubstantiated in order for them to bear the real physical presence of Christ. Thus the Eucharistic bread and wine remain bread and wine in every way.

A third error which has crept into the Roman understanding of the Lord's Supper, Luther contends, is that the Mass—of which the Lord's Supper is the center—is regarded as a good work and sacrifice. In actuality, says Luther, the Mass is the promise or testament which Christ left behind at His death. It is the promise of the remission of sins. Man's appropriate response to this promise is faith, or trust in the promise. To make it clear that the Mass is the medium through which the Church communicates Christ's promise of the remission of sins, the priest at Mass should speak out loudly and clearly, and in the language of his hearers rather than in some strange liturgical tongue. The Mass is not a gift or sacrifice which the priest offers up to God; it is, rather, God's gift of his Son for the remission of man's sins.

Baptism, contends Luther, has remained essentially uncorrupted. Its basic meaning is its communication of the divine promise of salvation. This promise is complete in baptism, and does not have to be ratified or reinforced through good works or holy vows. To assume that baptism must be supplemented is to show one's lack of faith in God's promise as expressed by baptism. The application of water to the body is the outer sign of one's acceptance of the promise of God. Baptism signifies death and resurrection, the dying of the old life of faithlessness and the rising of the newly justified man. The newly regenerated man is secure in God's promise of redemption and thus is free from all threats and terrors from human sources, and free, too, from anxiety about the elaborate requirements which the papists have falsely identified with Christian responsibility.

Baptism is the basis of the equality of all Christians. The functions of priests and monks "differ no whit in the sight of God from the works of the rustic toiling in the field or the woman going about her household tasks, but . . . all works are measured before Him by faith alone. . . ."

Having emphasized the importance of faith in the heart of the recipient of a sacrament, Luther recognizes that he must face the queries of those who ask if infant baptism is of no effect since the infant is incapable of faith. Falling back upon a position stated by Thomas Aquinas (1225-1274) and going back to St. Augustine (354-430), Luther contends that the faith of those who present the infant and witness his baptism is capable of effecting changes in the infant.

It is in order at this point to recognize that Luther adhered to a realistic view of the Lord's Supper and baptism. That is, he regarded those sacraments as being genuine vehicles of divine grace which effected objective changes in the lives of the recipients.

Luther accuses the papists of having completely abolished the proper understanding of the sacrament of penance. Instead of assuring the guilty consciences of men of the forgiveness of Christ, the Church tyrannizes its faithful by constantly reminding them of its own power to forgive or damn.

The Roman Church's division of penance into contrition, confession, and satisfaction introduces further perversion. By teaching that contrition precedes faith in the promise of divine forgiveness, they make forgiveness a reward for human merit rather than a free gift of divine grace. Thus the Church encourages men to trust, not in God's mercy, but in their own contrition.

The man-centered character of penance is further emphasized in the importance attached to satisfaction. Tortured consciences are driven to pilgrimages, fasts, vigils, and scourgings. The fact that the Church gives absolution or forgiveness prior to satisfaction helps to keep the emphasis on satisfaction. If absolution came after satisfaction, as it properly should, then one could expect Christians to devote more attention to faith and the living of an amended life.

Although he eventually comes out with a list of sacraments which omits penance, Luther strongly endorses private confession because it is morally and spiritually salutary. Confession does not, however, have to be to a priest. It is fit to confess one's sins to any Christian brother, for the lips of any Christian may speak the message of comfort and reassurance which constitutes the faith of the Church.

Confirmation is not a sacrament, contends Luther, but it derives historically from the practice of laying on of hands, as when Christ blessed young children, and the Apostles imparted the Holy Spirit, ordained elders, and blessed the sick. Despite its indirect New Testament antecedents, confirmation is not a sacrament, for it contains no word of divine promise to which faith may respond.

Luther rules out marriage as a sacrament because, like confirmation, it contains no word of divine promise. Marriage is a universal human institution which preceded Christianity, so that there are no grounds for arguing that it is a special means by which the grace of Christ comes to man.

Quickly dispensing with the sacramental question relating to marriage, Luther goes on at length to discuss various social and personal questions related to marriage, and in these passages he reveals a great depth of experience as a counsellor. He castigates the elaborate regulations of the Roman Church which defined eligibility for marriage, particularly those rules specifying "hindrances." Can anyone justify, Luther insists, a rule which forbids any relative of a deceased husband, even to the fourth degree, from marrying the widow of the dead man?

Luther's permissiveness in regard to marital matters takes such a radical form in the *Babylonian Captivity* that many editions of the book leave out those sections. Impotence of the husband is a just reason for annulment of a marriage, contends Luther, and yet to seek such an annulment through the legal processes might bring painful embarrassment. In such a case it is permissible for the wife, with the husband's consent, to bear children by another man and to convey the public impression that the children belong to her legal husband. If the husband should refuse his wife such permission, says Luther, "rather than allow the woman to burn or to commit adultery, I should counsel her to contract a marriage with another and flee to distant parts unknown." Luther is to be understood here, not as an advocate of sexual license, but as one struggling with desperately acute human problems which he knew about through concrete instances.

The sacrament of ordination, says Luther, is an invention of the pope, not of Christ. It receives no mention in the New Testament. In a sense, baptism is ordination, for "as many of us as have been baptised are all priests without distinctions. . . ." Ordination, in the more narrow meaning, is "nothing else than a certain rite of choosing preachers in the Church." As far as the Scriptures are concerned, one who performs for a while the tasks of the ministry may then become again a layman, since he is a minister by virtue of the tasks which he performs and not by virtue of ordination.

Luther traces the sacrament of extreme unction to the practice reported in James 5:14f. of anointing the sick with oil. Still, Christ did not institute the practice, and nowhere in the Bible does one read of any rite which fits the description of extreme unction. The intent of the rite described by James, and by other Biblical writers, was clearly to restore the health of those who were ill, not to prepare a dying man for death.

We end up, then, says Luther, with only two sacraments—baptism and the Lord's Supper—which meet all the requisite criteria.

Luther ends the *Babylonian Captivity* by an oblique mention of his own excommunication, which had been signed in Rome several months earlier but which had yet to be published in Germany. He humorously refers to the *Babylonian Captivity* as "a portion of the recantation I shall make," and promises that his pen will shortly produce other "recantations."

A TREATISE ON CHRISTIAN LIBERTY

Author: Martin Luther (1483-1546)
Type of work: Soteriology
First published: 1520

Principal Ideas Advanced

Through faith (trust) in God as revealed in Jesus Christ the soul of the Christian achieves complete freedom from all adversities which may affect the body.

The gift of divine justification makes the Christian free of any necessity of making himself worthy through ceremonial, legal, and moral works.

One who regards his own works and merits as necessary for his salvation thereby shows his distrust of the absolute sufficiency of the mercy and goodness of God as manifested in Jesus Christ.

Although completely free from any necessity to do anything for his own salvation, the Christian will subject himself to whatever discipline is required in order to express his faith in God and his concern for his fellow men.

The justified Christian will love his neighbor without any thought or hope of reciprocation, just as the Christian himself is the beneficiary of the free and unconditional love of God.

The man of faith will not interpret his liberty as license to disregard all ceremonies and routines, but he will despise only that ceremonialism which expresses a lack of faith in God.

Published in both German and Latin in November of 1520, Luther's *Treatise on Christian Liberty* was the last of his three "Reformation treatises" of 1520. Absent from *Christian Liberty* is the polemical tone of the *Open Letter to the Christian Nobility* and the *Babylonian Captivity of the Church*. The book is deeply devotional and contemplative and exhibits the more strictly religious aspects of the many-sided personality of Luther.

Luther concluded the *Babylonian Captivity* with the promise of *Christian Liberty*, but the immediate occasion of the fulfillment of the promise was his agreement to make a conciliatory gesture toward Pope Leo X. The agreement was the fruit of the arduous labors of Karl von Miltitz, a German diplomat who represented Pope Leo.

Miltitz was sent to Germany originally to bring Luther to Rome, but he became convinced that the only hope of ending the dispute between Luther and the papacy was by handling the matter in Germany. At Miltitz's suggestion Luther and Leo X had written conciliatory letters to one another in March of 1519, but neither letter reached its destination. Luther's debate with John Eck in Leipzig (June, 1519) seemed to end all hope of a settlement, but Miltitz persisted in his peacemaking efforts, even after a papal bull of excommunication was on its way to Luther in the summer of 1520.

Late in August of 1520 Miltitz attended at Eisleben a meeting of monks of Luther's order, the Augustinians, and urged them to try to persuade Luther to write the pope a letter assuring the pope that his attacks had not been directed against the pontiff personally. Luther agreed to this plan, even though he had no confidence that any positive results would come of it.

In October Luther had yet to write his letter to Leo, when Miltitz arranged a meeting with the former. Luther again promised to compose and send a letter, accompanied by his written version of the dispute which had been raging then for almost three years. The historical account of the dispute—in very brief scope—was included in the letter, and the accompanying treatise was *Christian Liberty*. Whether Leo actually ever received Luther's letter and the accompanying treatise is not known.

Luther's tone in the letter is respectful, but there is nothing in it to indicate an attitude of submission or contrition. Although he denounces the Roman curia, he is careful to exempt Leo X from the charges which he levels at the curia. He pictures Leo X as an essentially good and innocent man surrounded by a corrupt and conniving court, as one who "sittest as a lamb in the midst of wolves, like Daniel in the midst of lions, and, with Ezekiel . . . dwellest among scorpions." He ends the letter with a reference to *Christian Liberty* as a sample of the kind of study in which he "would prefer to be more profitably engaged, as I could be if your godless flatterers would permit me, and had hitherto permitted me." It is difficult to believe that Leo X, who was a man of humanist outlook, would have been other than contemptuous of Luther's letter and indifferent to *Christian Liberty*.

The subject of *Christian Liberty* is the paradoxical relationship between liberty and bondage in Christian experience. Luther states this relationship in two propositions: "A Christian man is a perfectly free lord of all, subject to none. A Christian man is a perfectly dutiful servant of all, subject to all." The first part of the treatise is an exposition of the first proposition, and the second part expands upon the second proposition.

The freedom of the Christian man is an inner liberty which belongs to man's soul, not to his body. No kind of misfortune which affects the body can harm the soul, and the soul receives no benefit from any adornment or chastisement of the body.

The liberty and health of the soul depend upon one thing alone, the Word of God which is contained in Jesus Christ. The soul which possesses the Word of God is rich and needs nothing else for its well-being, for this possession confers liberty, wisdom, peace, righteousness, and joy. Without the Word of God the soul is smitten.

The Word of God may be appropriated only by faith. No amount or quality of works will bring the reward of the Word of God. One cannot trust (have faith) in both his own works and in the Word of God. (By "works" Luther has in mind, it is clear, primarily the elaborate set of requirements spelled out in the sacramental system and the canon law of the Roman Church.) Faith alone justifies man.

In a slightly mystical passage very likely inspired by Johann Tauler (c.1300-1361), Luther describes the union of the soul with Christ as analogous to the union of husband and wife in marriage. The soul and Christ claim one another, so that the man of faith may claim for his own all that belongs to Christ, and Christ claims for Himself all that belongs to the man of faith. Christ's victory over sin, death, and Hell now belongs to the Christian. Christ the Bridegroom, rich in all spiritual graces, bestows all that He has upon the poor wicked soul who is joined with Him in faith.

Just as Christ is King, so every Christian is king, lord over all circumstances, completely secure against all harm to his soul. Just as Christ is priest, so every Christian is a priest, bearing Christ to his brothers, praying for them, and ministering to their needs. Some Christians ought to be set aside for full time public ministry to their brothers, but these ministers are not fundamentally distinct from their lay brethren. There is no justification for any Christians' lording it over their brethren.

Turning to the Christian's responsibility for proclaiming the Gospel, Luther insists that it is not enough to recount the acts and sayings of Christ. The point of preaching is to move men to faith in Him, "that He may not only be Christ, but be Christ for thee and for me, and that what is said of Him and what His Name denotes may be effectual in us."

Turning from the inner man or soul, whose freedom is secured through faith in Christ, Luther turns next to the outward man. In this section of his treatise Luther expounds the meaning of the second basic proposition of his work: "A Christian man is a perfectly dutiful servant of all, subject to all."

Faith is completely sufficient for the nurture and well-being of the inner man, the soul. But in his earthly existence man is also a body, and he is set in the midst of other men. Thus the Christian may not take his ease in the life of faith. He must subject his body to the discipline necessary to make it conform with and express the faith of the inward man. The outward man lusts for the world and for its own advantage, so that the soul must seek to keep the body in check. The works involved in these efforts are not, it is important to note, attempts to justify oneself, efforts to gain salvation. They are the products of a justification already given by God and not the means to the achievement of justification. "Good works do not make a good man, but a good man does good works. . . ." Faith alone makes a man good, and only unbelief makes him evil.

Good works are expressive not only of faith in God, but also of love for the neighbor. Just as Christ did not live for Himself alone, so the Christian, as long as he is in the body, lives for other men. Thus he disciplines his body that it may be a more effective instrument of his love for his fellow men. The life of faith, then, produces acts of service to the neighbor, performed not in order to save one's soul, but out of joyous gratitude that one's salvation is already assured through Christ. Nor does the Christian do good to his neighbor in order to enjoy the gratitude or reciprocating deeds of his neighbor. Just as God bestows his blessings upon men without considering their deserts, so the Christian, too, gives himself unconditionally in service to his fellow men. Just as God gives himself freely to man in Christ, so the Christian is to be a Christ to his neighbor.

St. Paul, who taught a similar doctrine of Christian liberty, and whose writings deeply influenced Luther, quickly discovered (I Corinthians: 5, 6) that libertinism is likely to emerge as a perverted understanding of Christian liberty. Luther warns against such a misunderstanding of his doctrine. Some, he says, will want to show that they are Christians and free men by despising the traditional ceremonies and traditions of the Church. The Christian, however, shows his faith by avoiding both libertinism and fastidious ceremonialism. He will oppose anyone who misinterprets liberty as providing opportunities for contempt towards tradition rather than for service for one's neighbors. And he will also oppose the ceremonialist who, in his trust of ceremonies, has neither faith in God nor concern for his neighbor. But one must be patient and kind to the ignorant and timid multitudes who are held captive by the ceremonial requirements of the Church. Ceremonies are indispensable to the life of worship. But, like all works, they must be expressive of faith in God rather than objects of faith. Thus ceremonies are not to be despised, but uncritical trust in them is to be despised.

Christian Liberty contains the classic expression of the theme of justification by faith, a theme often identified as the heart of Luther's theology and as his basic religious insight. What, precisely, is intended by the phrase "justification by faith"? "Justification" is righteousness or goodness. Luther understood righteousness as a condition of the will, an attitude. He was at pains to avoid identifying righteousness with external works or behavior. The moral and religious quality of the will, he believed, depends upon the object and the strength of its trust and allegiance. The truly righteous (justified) man has trust (faith) in the goodness of God rather than in his own capacity for goodness. The goodness of God as manifested in Jesus Christ is absolutely sufficient for man's salvation. Christian faith, then, is a trustful acceptance of God's gift of Himself in Jesus Christ. It is the acceptance of one's own forgiveness. To try to merit this gift by performing righteous deeds is to exhibit a lack of confidence in the goodness of God.

To state that justification by faith is Luther's revolutionary insight can be misleading inasmuch as both "justification" and "faith" are processes within man. Luther's concern was to correct what he regarded to be the basic fault of medieval Christianity, its man-centered character. Justification he understood as God's work through Christ, and he taught that faith, man's appropriation of the divine gift, depends completely upon the divine initiative. Thus faith is possible only because of grace, and faith is, indeed, a gift of grace.

The basic theme of Luther in *Christian Liberty* was not new but was, rather, a powerful restatement of a theme prominent in the thought of St. Paul and St. Augustine. In one crucial respect Luther's thought in the *Christian Liberty* has closer affinity with that of St. Paul than with St. Augustine's ideas. Like Paul, Luther emphasizes faith as the proper response of man to God, and love as the proper response of the Christian to his neighbor, whereas Augustine had emphasized love (*caritas*) of man for God as well as for neighbor. Luther's affinity with Paul underscores the radically theocentric and Christocentric character of the thought of both men. Each was reluctant to affirm that man was capable of loving God as God loves man, and each pictures the Christian as the channel which conveys divine love to other humans.

In the *Open Letter* and the *Babylonian Captivity* Luther had tried to indicate the anthropocentric character of medieval piety. *Christian Liberty* is designed to pilot the Church back to a theocentric-Christocentric base for its life.

LOCI COMMUNES RERUM THEOLOGICARUM

Author: Philipp Melanchthon (1497-1560)
Type of work: Systematic theology
First published: 1521

Principal Ideas Advanced

Self-love is original sin, a native propensity within man that taints all his so-called good deeds, so that all men are truly sinners—as the evidence from the study of the mind and from Scripture abundantly shows.

Sin pertains to man's inner being, to his heart, his emotions, and it is impossible for man to obey the two commands to love God and neighbor, for self-love tyrannically dictates man's actions.

Man stands condemned, knowing that he must keep the law but unable to do so until the grace of God brings forgiveness of sins and turns his heart from himself to God and neighbor.

Man remains a sinner, even after receiving grace, for he does not cease to be a human being, but he is consoled in knowing that his sin is not imputed to him; and the knowledge of a God who forgives and cares for him temporally and eternally makes him relatively less selfish in his actions.

Man cannot make himself righteous; meritorious works are a pretense and a delusion.

The *Loci communes* of Philipp Melanchthon was the first systematic statement of Protestant theology. It appeared in April, 1521, antedating John Calvin's *Institutes* by fifteen years. Melanchthon sought to draw a system of doctrine solely from the Scriptures, a goal which in his day was radically new in theological science. In doing so, he disparaged the commentaries of the scholastic theologians as "silly, insipid, and impious," for they were rooted in the thought of men rather than in the Word of God; and he heaped scorn on ancient philosophers, particularly Aristotle, for "egotistic" principles of morality, doubt, and criticism, which bar the way to Christ and render truth elusive. The Bible, and especially Paul's letter to the Romans, provides man with the truth about his nature and destiny, Melanchthon believed.

Melanchthon joined the faculty of

the University of Wittenberg in 1518, and under the influence of Martin Luther developed a love of Scripture that made all other writings seem inferior. He wanted even his own book to be only a guide to and in no way a substitute for the Bible. From Scripture he drew his three principal topics of sin, law, and grace, and under these he subsumed free will, vows, love, hope, baptism, penitence, confession, customs, and government. He sought to arrange and relate the ideas in Scripture so that they could be easily understood. This practice gave his work a freshness in contrast to arid scholastic disputations and a practicality in view of the Protestant emphasis on the Bible as final authority, but it prevented him from using the tools of philosophy to explore his ideas. Melanchthon sensed this limitation and in subsequent editions he deliberately curtailed or omitted many of his tirades against philosophy.

Under his first topic, "Sin," Melanchthon held that man cannot of his own free will perform works that will merit justification before God. The Bible teaches that all men are sinners and that a bad tree bears bad fruit; good works born of man's free will are impossible for his will is already bound. Scripture, Melanchthon argued, teaches that all things happen by necessity or according to divine predestination, and hence there can be no freedom of the human will. Melanchthon's language was unfortunate at this point, for he meant that man because of his sinfulness cannot do meritorious works, not that he has no power to choose. In later editions and writings he emphatically rejected determinism.

A study of the mind also shows that man's reasoning faculty is controlled by the will or emotions, Melanchthon declared, for one cannot choose to love or not to love, to hate or not to hate. Emotions must overcome emotions, for reason lacks the power to do so; since sin is rooted in the heart, in the inner emotions of man, man is not free to do good works and thus to merit the grace of God.

In the heart of man, Melanchthon wrote, as the Bible and the study of the mind both witness, sits original sin, a native propensity, an inborn impulse, an energy, a self-centeredness that vitiates all altrusim. Self-love turns all concern for others or for God into an oblique or direct love of self, so that the two basic commandments, to love God and love neighbor, are shattered. As long as this self-love is uncurbed, man can produce only shadows of virtues. "All men according to their natural powers are truly sinners and do always sin," Melanchthon claimed. To say that man's "good" works merit righteousness is but to deceive and to deepen man's spiritual blindness, for every attempt to merit righteousness is motivated by a love of self. Holy works, pilgrimages, veneration of relics, vigils, and fasts become self-love in disguise.

Law, both natural and divine, Melanchthon declared, was given to man that he might be aware of his sinfulness. In addition to the natural laws of self-preservation and reproduction which man shares with animals, man possesses a law of conscience which tells him that he ought to love God, ought to refrain from injuring his fellow man, and ought to share all things. This is the natural law, or light, that is implanted in every man, a law inscribed on the soul of each man, to rule and shape character, although it is often barely apprehensible.

By the sharing of all things Melanchthon did not mean communism, for he believed that the best way to share and to serve was for each man to possess and manage a portion of the common property, and that the established ways of buying, selling, and contracting were the best practical means for achieving this. These imperatives in natural law have their parallels in Scriptural commands to love God, love neighbor, and love by serving.

But self-love in man's heart makes it impossible for man to keep the law except in an external manner, for he loves God in order to gain merit for himself; he injures others thinking he can promote himself; and he uses his share of the common property for his own rather than for the public good.

The divine law demands obedience which man cannot render. From this circumstance man knows he is condemned, lost, helpless. At this point, Melanchthon maintained, the Gospel consoles man by revealing God's benevolence and willingness to forgive sins, and by imparting the gift of the Holy Spirit to man's heart to turn it from love of self to love of God and neighbor. Man does not totally escape his natural propensities, however; they remain as long as he is in this world, but man's feeling of gratitude and joy for the revelation of divine benevolence makes praise to God and service to man rather than self-concern the center of motivation.

Even so, this feeling of gratitude is not man's doing; it is the product of faith, beholding the divine mercy promised in Christ. "Faith is the constant assent to every word of God; a thing that cannot be done except the Holy Spirit of God renews and illuminates our hearts," Melanchthon wrote. In the state of faith man knows that he cannot merit righteousness by keeping the law, but he keeps the law and does good works and praises God out of joy and gratitude for the mercy that God has revealed.

Melanchthon then applied these ideas to various questions that had arisen. Since the Gospel bestows salvation gratuitously, without regard to our "meritorious works," is man free to do as he pleases? No, because the Spirit that reveals this to man is the Spirit of love in which all law is summarized. Man keeps the law because the will of God is the law, and the Holy Spirit is but the living will of God active in man. Christian liberty means that the Christian keeps the law but keeps it spontaneously from the heart—in fact, that he would do what the law enjoins even if there were no law. The law is not abrogated; it is fulfilled on a different level of motivation; man cannot dispense with the demands of law, for he is never fully possessed by the Spirit, and the flesh in this life is never fully crucified. Man needs constantly through the law to be made aware of sin and to hear the consolation of the Gospel. Melanchthon indicated in this a process of sanctification after justification.

The sacraments are signs; they do not justify. They do not merit righteousness. The sacramental signs of baptism and the Lord's Supper have been divinely given as tokens of God's grace. There is no Scriptural basis for any others. Baptism signifies a passing through death unto life, the submersion of the old man and the awakening of the new; faith alone justifies. The Lord's Supper is a sign to confirm our wavering consciences and to certify to us the Gospel and the remission of sins.

In keeping with Romans 13, Melanchthon accepted magistrates as stewards who carry the sword and guard civil peace, their power deriving from God. If a magistrate's commands are contrary to the word of God, they are not to be obeyed; but otherwise they are to be obeyed, even when that which is ordered is tyrannical, for love demands that tyranny be suffered if it cannot be changed without public disturbance and sedition. Melanchthon applied the same rule to ecclesiastical magistrates saying that they are not to be heard when they command something contrary to Scripture, and they are not to be obeyed if they command something outside of Scripture so as to bind consciences, as in the case of celibacy and forbidden meats, even though these commands themselves are not evil. Christian love enjoins one to suffer if necessary to avoid offense and injury, but in the presence of Pharisees demanding observances one may violate human traditions to show that it is no sin to do so; thereby one asserts the liberty of Christians that results from justification by faith.

Again and again Melanchthon lashed out at those who without grace feign good works and pretend that they are meriting God's love, calling them howling Pharisees, whitewashed sepulchres, Roman tyrants, sophists, and theologasters. Melanchthon believed that justification was the work of God through faith; he could not delegate any portion of justification to man's merit.

Martin Luther (1483-1546) praised the *Loci communes* saying it should be placed in the Canon. Johann Eck (1486-1543), Roman Catholic theologian, answered its unorthodoxy in 1525 with *Enchiridion locorum communium adversus Lutheranos,* and Johannes Cochlaeus (1479-1552), Catholic theologian, branded it as "heretical, abominable, and putrid."

For a hundred years it was used as a textbook in dogmatics in Lutheran seminaries, and it was made required reading at Cambridge University in England. Two of Melanchthon's students, Victorinus Strigel (1524-1569) and Martin Chemnitz (1522-1586), wrote commentaries on it.

The *Loci* went through many editions. Georg Strobel, Church historian, traced it through three basic periods. In the first period, 1521-1525, eighteen Latin editions appeared. In the second period, 1525-1535, numerous Latin editions came from the press, showing by their changes that Melanchthon was actively enlarging, amending and revising. In the third period, 1535 on, still more Latin versions appeared with changes, especially in 1540. The earliest German translations were done by Georg Spalatin, the first one appearing in 1522; from 1526 to 1536 Justus Jonas was the chief translator, and in the third period, Melanchthon undertook the task.

The various editions contained significant changes. Melanchthon depended heavily on the writings of Paul, particularly on Romans. In his emphasis on justification by faith he made statements about free will which seemed to lean toward determinism: "The Spirit teaches that all things happen necessarily according to predestination." In later editions Melanchthon clearly rejected determinism as something that would lead to fatalism. In subsequent editions, Melanchthon changed many such sentences and phrases so as to emphasize man's ethical responsibility, changes which later involved him in controversies over synergism, controversies concerning exactly how much man does or does not do in the process of salvation. Melanchthon maintained that man at least accepts or rejects the mercy of God, although such is not even a possibility without the Word and the Spirit first drawing and inviting man. Melanchthon also altered the vicious remarks about philosophy which he made in his zeal to combat work-righteousness. He later saw the usefulness of philosophy in developing ethics and maintaining the common welfare.

Three hundred years after it was first published, Philip Schaff, Church historian, aptly described the *Loci* as marking an "epoch in the history of theology." The influence of this masterful work continues to be felt in modern theology.

THE BONDAGE OF THE WILL

Author: Martin Luther (1483-1546)
Type of work: Polemical theology
First published: 1525

Principal Ideas Advanced

Erasmus is in error in holding that man is endowed with a power to change the desires of his will in matters that pertain to salvation.

Free will is a term which applies solely to God, for apart from the spirit of God man is unable to do what is good.

Arguments based upon Biblical injunctions to choose between life and death fail to support the notion of free will, since they simply tell man what he ought to do; they in no way imply that man has the ability, apart from God's grace, to do what he ought.

Other arguments seek to support free will by distorting clear passages of Scripture by allegorical interpretations, thereby ignoring the fact that the doctrine of free will ultimately denies the omnipotence and foreknowledge of God.

The Bondage of the Will is Martin Luther's answer to Erasmus's *Diatribe on Free Will* (1524). Luther begins by recognizing no authority other than the Scriptures. The Church can decree nothing that the latter do not contain. The Scriptures are neither obscure nor ambiguous, and yet the Spirit of God is necessary before they can be understood and believed.

Luther accuses Erasmus of inconsistently holding that our will is both active and passive in the acquisition of eternal salvation. Erasmus held that it is irreligious and idle speculation to seek to determine the role of the will in matters pertaining to salvation. Luther, on the contrary, argues that it is both possible and important to discover the role of "free will" and its relation to the grace of God. The question of free will is a wholesome part of Christian doctrine, Luther insists. To know what free will is, it is necessary to know what the human will does and how God's will is related to the human will.

Luther's basic thesis is *"that God foreknows nothing by contingency, but that He foresees, purposes, and does all things according to His immutable, eternal, and infallible will."*

What we do may appear to be contingent, writes Luther, but in reality, with respect to the will of God, what we do is done necessarily. The term "necessarily" does not properly connote compulsion, but the necessity of immutability. The will, whether divine or human, does not act by compulsion but by willingness and desire. Our corrupt will is of itself, apart from divine grace, unable to do good. Man's salvation is beyond any power that he has; it depends solely upon the will of God. Before the Spirit of God works in us we do nothing to gain our salvation. The evil that a man does apart from the Spirit of God is done not against his will, as by violence, but spontaneously and with a desire for doing evil.

The "free will" that Luther denies is the alleged freedom that a man has to do what is good, in the sense of meriting salvation. Man is not free to change the bent of his desires; he cannot change a corrupt will, which loves that which is evil, into a will that desires and loves that which is good. Such a change is effected solely by the Spirit of God. When the latter is at work in a man, his will is changed, so that without compulsion it desires and craves what is good.

The term "free will" in its fullest sense is applicable to God alone, Luther writes, for God alone does what He will on earth and in Heaven. Man may be said to exercise free will in the use of his goods and possessions, if it be remembered that his acts are overruled by the freedom of God; but in matters related to his salvation, man has no free will, for he is in bondage and slavery either to the will of God or to the will of Satan.

Luther seeks to establish the validity of his own position, first by refuting the arguments advanced in support of free will, second, by meeting objections to his own arguments, and third, by contending for the grace of God against free will.

In support of free will Erasmus contends that the human will is able to apply itself to, or to reject, things which lead to eternal salvation. The human will is thus thought to possess a power or faculty to choose or to refuse the words and works of God that lead to salvation; that is, to choose or refuse the Gospel and the law. Luther, on the contrary, maintains that Erasmus's position ascribes to the will what is beyond its capacity and comprehension. Apart from the Holy Spirit no man knows, believes in, or desires eternal salvation. To endow the will with the power to work salvation is to ascribe divinity to it, for the power of God alone can will not to sin and to embrace the law and the Gospel. Free will is and remains a divine term because it signifies a divine power.

Once the will has lost its liberty, it is compulsively bound to the service of sin and cannot will any good; the term free will then becomes an empty term;

that is, it fails to designate any actual faculty of man.

Advocates of free will may seek to base their view on such a passage of Scripture as Ecclesiasticus 15:15-18, in which it is written that God made man from the beginning and left him to his own counsels, enjoining him to keep His commandments, and presenting him with a choice between life and death.

Such a passage in no way suggests free will, writes Luther, for it militates against free will, in that it subjects man to the precepts and will of God. Such a passage in no wise asserts free will, he claims, since it does not teach that man has the power to keep the commandments of God.

Nowhere in the Scriptures is man told that he is able to keep the commandments; he is rather constantly reminded of his impotency. Such expressions in Scripture as, "If thou wilt," ". . . if thou hear," ". . . if thou do," do not state what man can do, but what he ought to do.

To the objection that man is mocked if he is told to choose when in fact there is but one course of action open to him, Luther replies that such injunctions are given so that a man might better see his own impotency. The words of the law do not assert the power of the will, but they teach man what he ought to do and they make man aware of his own sin. Such words as "choose," "keep," and "do" in the Scriptures convey the precept to be kept; they do not describe any power of man.

Imperatives in Scripture prove nothing concerning human ability, Luther claims, for imperatives simply enjoin what ought to be done and what ought not to be done. To interpret them otherwise would be to assert that free will can do all things without grace.

It is a part of man's blindness and misery that he believes himself to be free, when in fact the words of the law show us only what we ought to do but cannot. What ought to be is not the same as what has been; what is exacted is not the same as what has been performed; and what is required is not the same as what has been rendered.

The Biblical expression "I desire not the death of a sinner" offers divine mercy to the world. Such mercy is received by those who are touched by the law and know their sin. That some are touched by the law and others unaffected is wholly attributable to the secret will of God.

It is, therefore, necessary to distinguish between God preached and God hidden, between God's Word and God Himself. God wills many things that are unknown to us. What and why God wills is unknown. When we speak of God preached, writes Luther, we can say that God desires that man should be saved, but it is hidden from us why God does not change every human will. The secret will of God belongs to God's incomprehensible nature.

With the coming of Christ into the world, writes Luther, grace was offered; if man will believe, he is given the opportunity of becoming a child of God, and yet the believer is led to such faith, not by free will, but by the Spirit of God, for all things take place from His immutable will.

To seek to evade the force of the arguments against free will, it is necessary, Luther claims, to interpret the teaching of Scripture allegorically. To call God into question is to demand that God cease to be God. For God is that being for whose will there is no cause or reason to be assigned in terms of which God's acts can be judged. There is no rule or standard outside God. Nothing is superior or equal to God's will; the divine will is itself the rule of all things. God's will would no longer be the will of God if it acted by any rule or standard, or from any cause or reason outside God. What God wills is right not because He is bound by some standard or rule, but simply because He wills it.

Moreover, Luther continues, we could not believe the promises of God unless what He promises takes place of necessity. What God foreknows must take place of necessity, or God would otherwise be deceived in what He foreknows. The free will of man is thus incompatible with the prescience and omnipotence of God. To grant God's foreknowledge and omnipotence is to grant that whatever we do is done by His omnipotence. What we do we do, not because of free will, but because God brings about whatsoever comes to pass according to the counsel of His infallible will.

In the case of Judas's betrayal of Christ, for example, Judas willingly betrayed Him, without any compulsion or force, but this willingness on the part of Judas was foreknown by God and immutably decreed to take place.

The necessity of which Luther speaks is not a necessity of force with respect to the act, but a necessity of mutability in reference to the time. The question is not whether Judas was willing or unwilling to become a traitor, but whether or not God infallibly predetermined by His decree that at a certain time Judas should will to betray Christ. Judas did not have it in his power to will not to become a traitor. To deny this is to render the immutable foreknowledge of God mutable.

Before man is regenerated into the new creation of the Kingdom of the Spirit, man does nothing and tries to do nothing to become a part of that Kingdom. It is the Spirit alone that regenerates and causes men to persevere as members of His Kingdom.

By the law man gains a knowledge of sin, Luther writes; man is cast down and afflicted, not to be delivered by the law or by himself, but only by the redeeming love of Christ. Free will does not move a man to the righteousness of God, for God alone can draw a sinner unto Himself. God alone can justify a sinner, and this He does freely, not because the sinner has any merit of his own. God's grace comes by the purpose of God, by divine election and not by any endeavor of our own.

If salvation were dependent upon man, instead of upon the grace of God, no one would be saved, and all would perish together. If we believe, however, that Christ redeemed us by His blood, we must also believe that the whole man was lost. Because of original sin, nothing is left in man devoid of the Spirit; apart from God, man cannot turn to what is good, but must turn towards evil. It is to God alone that the judgment of righteousness belongs; the potter has power over the clay.

Luther's *Bondage of the Will*, as an extreme but consistent answer to Erasmus's faith in the freedom of the human will, is an important contribution to the Augustinian tradition within Protestant thought.

ON THE ERRORS OF THE TRINITY

Author: Michael Servetus (1511-1553)
Type of work: Systematic theology
First published: 1531

Principal Ideas Advanced

The orthodox doctrine of the Trinity, that there are three persons in one substance in the Godhead, leads to tritheism and is to be rejected in favor of the Scriptural doctrine that there is one God who manages Himself in different dispositions or dispensations.

Christ is the Son of God, equal with the Father in power rather than in essence; God the Father is alone God in nature.

The Holy Spirit is not a third person of a triune God, but is rather an activity or disposition of God, a divine impulse that works in us.

The doctrine of the Trinity has led to sophistical quibbling; the doctrine arises out of Greek philosophy rather than out of the Scriptures, and it is largely responsible for the alienation of the Jews and the Mohammedans.

Michael Servetus, Spanish scholar, scientist, and physician, influenced the religious thought of the Reformation by the publication of *De trinitatis erroribus libri septem* (1531), and his *Dialogorum de trinitate libri duo* (1532). His last work, *Christianismi restitutio* (1553), for which he was condemned, was at once so utterly destroyed that its historical influence was negligible.

Both the Reformers—Calvin in particular—and the Roman Catholics condemned the views of Servetus and approved of his execution at the stake on October 27, 1553. In 1553, Servetus's views served as the fountainhead of subsequent anti-trinitarian tendencies which culminated in Unitarianism.

Servetus's *Dialogues on the Trinity*, published a year after his *On the Errors of the Trinity*, differs from the earlier work in tone, but the *Dialogues* does not disavow the position taken in the *Errors*. The latter intended to point out the errors in the traditional doctrine of the Trinity and to reformulate Biblical doctrine in a manner more compatible with reason and piety.

The *Errors* is divided into seven books. The work shows evidence of a carefully considered plan, and yet it is frequently repetitious and crude. The substance of Servetus's argument is set forth in Book One; the remaining six books take up certain aspects in more detail and with considerable repetition.

Servetus admits that Jesus is the Son of God and that He is God, but he does not admit the orthodox view of the Trinity. The orthodox doctrine of the Trinity, embodied in the Nicene, Constantinopolitan, and Athanasian creeds, insists that the terms Father, Son, and Spirit are not expressive of relations within a single person, but are personal designations. The word *hypostasis*, "person" in English, is used to indicate that the Father, Son, and

Spirit express necessary and eternal relations in the Godhead. The three persons are a trinity in unity. The persons are not to be confounded, nor is the substance to be divided. The three persons of the Trinity are one substance, equal in glory, majesty, and power.

Servetus also speaks of Christ as equal with God, but he claims that Christ's equality is in power, not in nature or essence. Jesus, according to Servetus, was not a hypostasis, but an actual son. The first point to be made is that Jesus Christ is a man. The discussion of the Trinity should not begin with the Word, but with the man, Jesus Christ. Many texts of Scripture and the early writers of the Church clearly attest that Christ was a man, and His miracles clearly show that Jesus was the Christ.

The second point, according to Servetus, is that Christ is the Son of God; the almighty power of the Word of God overshadowed Mary, so that Jesus is the real Son of God by nature, not an hypostasis. God is called the Father of Jesus Christ, just as earthly fathers are the fathers of their own sons. He is the Son of God by nature; others are sons by adoption. The sense in which Christ is the Son of God is higher than the sense in which men become sons of God through faith in Christ.

The third point, continues Servetus, is that the Scriptures clearly prove that Christ is God. He is man according to the flesh, but in the spirit He is divinity. The notion that the human nature shares its properties with God, the *communicatio idiomatum,* is a sophistical quibble. God has in fact shared the fullness of His deity with a man and has given Christ a name above every name. God was in Him in singular measure; the real Christ is complete in divinity. God does not share any of man's imperfections, but He shares His full deity with Christ. Christ is God in appearance, not in nature, but by grace. It was given to Him to be God by way of privilege. The Father alone is God by nature. The expressions "God and Christ," "Christ and God," indicate that Christ is a being distinct from God. The Father alone is the invisible God. God and Christ are distinct beings, and yet the word "God" can be used in a sense in which it can be said that Christ is very God. Before all time Christ was in the Spirit of God. The equality which Christ had while He existed in the form of God, He had by reason of the authority or power that God gave Him. His equality is an equality of power. The Old Testament use of the word "Elohim" for beings less than the supreme God serves as an indication of the nature of the deity of Christ. As the Word of God, Christ came down from Heaven; He is not a second God, but He was made equal to God in power.

Christ is not one in nature with the Godhead. God does not consist of two beings in one nature. To admit a metaphysical equality is not the intention of Paul when he says in Philippians 2:6 that Christ, being in the form of God, thought it not robbery to be equal with God. If Christ were the second person of the Godhead by nature, how could he be said to have the appearance of deity? Christ existed in the likeness of God, was equal to God in power, not in nature or essence; since He bore the humble form of a man, it was not robbery for him to be on an equality with God. He did not neglect the work that His Father had appointed Him to accomplish, nor did

He seize a kingly tyranny over the world.

The notion of three beings in one nature is the work of philosophical imagination, Servetus insists. The Holy Spirit regarded as a third separate being leads to a practical tritheism, and even if the unity of God is insisted upon, such a plurality of gods is no better than atheism.

The Scriptures know of no such nonsense. "For by Holy Spirit it means now God himself, now an angel, now the spirit of a man, a sort of instinct or divine inspiration of the mind, a mental impulse, or a breath. . . ."

In Book Two of his *Dialogues on the Trinity,* Servetus retraced the statement that the Holy Spirit is an angel. The Holy Spirit can be said to be created, only in the sense that God created a new *disposition* in Himself. The Scriptures mention the existence of God the Father, and of the Son, but the Holy Spirit is mentioned not as a separate being, but as an activity of God, as an in-breathing or in-working of God's power.

God disposes or manages Himself in three different ways, writes Servetus. The Father is the whole substance; it is from Him that three wonderful dispositions or aspects shine forth; the Father, the Son, and the Holy Spirit are not three by virtue of any distinction of being in God, but simply through a disposition or dispensation of God in various forms of deity.

The traditional orthodox view of the Trinity is a delusion, Servetus insists; a trinity in one being cannot be imagined; the notion of three beings is a pure phantasm, and what cannot be understood ought not to be received. Nothing can be in the mind which is not in the senses first. Since no one has ever had a sensation of three beings constituting a single nature, to conceive of a multiplication of beings without conceiving of a multiplication of essences or natures is impossible. The orthodox doctrine of the Trinity cannot be proven from Scripture or established by logic. The Scriptures clearly teach but one God, and one Christ, His Son. The admission of three persons is the admission of three entities, of three substances—in effect, a plurality of Gods.

According to Servetus, the doctrine of the Trinity has given rise to countless ridiculous subtleties which are wholly foreign to the Mohammedans, though Mohammed holds Christ and the Apostles in the highest honor. It has prevented the Jews from believing that Christ is the Messiah promised in their law. The doctrine of the Trinity is due to the introduction of Greek philosophy into the doctrine of the Church, whereas the latter should be founded on the belief that Jesus Christ is the Son of God.

Christ is the Word of God, a disposition or dispensation in God by which He has revealed His will to us. The Word God uttered at the creation of the world is the Christ who became flesh and is the Son of God, descended from Heaven. Christ is God's voice become flesh. The world was created by the Word, not by a being. In Christ there is the whole nature and essence of God. Christ is in the Father, just as the voice is in the one that speaks; the Father and Christ are one, just as the ray and the sun are one light.

Before creation, the Word existed and was begotten when first God uttered it; afterwards it was incarnate in Jesus, God's Son. The titles ascribed to Christ ascribe high praise to Him, but they do not mean that He was an abstract being. He is rather the wisdom of God that came forth from God. The Word was a disposition, an aspect, of God at the beginning of the world; the Word was never the Son. God is above all distinctions of time, so that God and the Word existed causally before the world. The Word is a disposition of God above all distinctions of time; it is not the Son. To believe that Jesus is the Christ is the very essence of Christianity; it is the belief which ensures our salvation.

The Scriptures never pay attention to natures, says Servetus, but only to appearances and dispositions. The differences between the persons, or dispositions, are to be judged in the manner of their appearing. God is manifested in three different persons or dispositions. In Christ the real image of God is manifest. When the Word became flesh in Christ, it ceased to exist. Since Christ has ascended to God, Christ is as really in God as the Word was with God before. The Word is in no way identical with the Son. The Word prepared the way so that the glory of Christ could be manifest. Christ is the very image of the substance of God, but the substance of God has nothing to do with the divine nature. The substance of the Father is the Father's way of subsisting. The essence of God is mingled with the angels, for God is the essence of all things, and all things are in Him. Christ is the disposition of God which wrought everything in the world. In Himself God is incomprehensible; He is known solely through Christ, by faith and not by philosophical speculation.

Servetus's views represent a radical departure from Christian orthodoxy; their positive contribution to the Reformation is that they provoked a violent negative reaction, which necessitated that the Reformers unequivocally affirm their belief in the basic Christian doctrine of the Trinity, as confessed by the Holy Catholic Church.

A DIALOGUE OF COMFORT AGAINST TRIBULATION

Author: Saint Thomas More (1478-1535)
Type of work: Spiritual direction
First transcribed: 1534-1535

Principal Ideas Advanced

Tribulation is part of the just man's life; the only basis for comfort is faith in God's promise to reward the believer in Heaven.

Much of the anguish of tribulation is in the mind.

Suffering is medicinal; bearing it patiently, the Christian makes payment for his sins, and even lays up a store of merit.

Pagan philosophers have many helpful things to say for our consolation, but lack the one thing needful; namely, the hope of reward in Heaven.

Sir Thomas More, whom Henry VIII had raised to the position of Chancellor of the realm on account of his liberal outlook, fell from the royal favor when he opposed Henry's resolve to divorce Catherine. Afterwards, having been imprisoned in the Tower for refusing to swear the Act of Supremacy, he was executed on the charge of treason. He wrote *A Dialogue of Comfort Against Tribulation* during his imprisonment; his intention was to console his family.

Unlike the celebrated *Utopia* (1516), which was written in Latin, the *Dialogue of Comfort Against Tribulation* was written in colloquial English. The author amuses himself by representing the work as having been written in Latin by a Hungarian, and as having found its way into English as a translation from the French. The *Dialogue* purports to be a series of conversations between an elderly Hungarian gentleman, Anthony, and his young nephew, Vincent, at a time when Hungary is about to be invaded by the Turks. Anthony, a man of learning and broad experience, having twice been a prisoner in Turkey, is near death. The thought of his dying at the time of the Turkish peril is a special trial to his children and friends, because it has become their custom to lean on him for advice and comfort. At Vincent's request, therefore, Anthony undertakes to call to mind such things as he has read and thought which may be of use to his family in laying up "a store of comfort" in their hearts "as a treacle against the poison of all desperate dread that might rise on occasion of sore tribulation."

The patriarchal tone of the work reflects the actual situation between More and his family, who, as is shown in Holbein's painting "The Household of Sir Thomas More," lived surrounded by his children and grandchildren. That was during the happier days of which Erasmus wrote, "In More's house you would see that Plato's Academy was revived again, only, whereas in the Academy the discussions turned upon geometry and the power of numbers, the house at Chelsea is a veritable school of Christian religion." In prison, appointed to martyrdom, his modest wealth confiscated by England's Grand Turk, Sir Thomas was able to do little for his loved ones except point their thoughts to God. "For," as Anthony says to Vincent, "God is and must be your comfort, and not I. And He is a sure comforter, that (as He said unto His disciples) never leaveth His servants in case of comfortless orphans: not even when He departed from His disciples by death, but both as He promised, sent them a comforter, the Holy Spirit of his Father and Himself, and made them also sure, that to the world's end He would ever dwell with them Himself."

The comfort to which More directs his reader is uncompromisingly Christian. Tribulation, he argues, is a normal part of the just man's life, and loss of property and bodily injury are not great disasters. Those who think that such difficulties are important are governed by imagination rather than by exact understanding. In reality, every man is a prisoner under sentence of death, with no certain hold on this world's good, and with no security from bodily harm. Such being man's condition, his only comfort is in God, who, by his Word, has promised to reward men in heaven. The root and origin of all comfort, therefore, is the faith that the Scriptures are God's Word. Those who truly believe will be able "to command a great mountain of tribulation to void from the place where it stood in our heart," but those of little faith "shall be scant able to remove a little hillock."

More understands very well the mental anguish into which men are often plunged by adversity. There are, he says, those who refuse any kind of comfort. He describes the vacant-eyed dullness of persons who are so overwhelmed with their sorrow that they lie in deathly lethargy, refusing to think of anything, and thereby gradually lose all memory and understanding. Another sort respond with frenzied impatience and are so poisoned and antagonized by their loss that one hardly dare speak to them. Both kinds, says More, are guilty of mortal sin: the former of sloth, the latter of anger. When, in contrast, the believer finds that he is able to seek and find consolation in God, he receives a fresh impression of that divine favor which Christ has visited upon us, and he finds comfort in the mere fact that he is able to desire comfort.

More deals at length with delusions and morbid obsessions, especially with those which come to a man in the night. When cut off from normal human intercourse, as a prisoner is likely to be, man loses his perspective, and he easily falls prey to fears and scruples which at other times he would not entertain. The temptation to despair and to self-destruction is particularly to be reckoned with, and suicide often appears to the distempered mind to be a religious duty. In such an hour, says Thomas, besides calling upon God for help, one must resist the call of death by the use of reason; the prisoner must tell himself "that a great part of this temptation is in effect but the fear of his own fancy." The devils, he says, are not themselves able to throw us down, even though, like people calling to a man when he is walking across a high bridge, they may arouse destructive fears in one who would otherwise walk safely.

More stresses the fact that tribulation is usually more mental than physical. This is especially the case with that form of tribulation which is common to every righteous man, and never far from him; namely, temptation. Trouble is more difficult to bear when it is avoidable than when it is unavoidable; religious persecution is troublesome to conscience because such persecution is usually avoidable. The Turkish peril, concerning which Anthony speaks in the *Dialogue,* was of this kind. So was More's own tribulation. He was, his biographer tells us, soundly rated by his wife for obstinately lying in prison when he had only to yield to Parliament and be restored. More's reply was, "Don't you think, Mistress Alice, that this place is as near to heaven as Chelsea?" To her petulant reply, he answered, "Suppose I were to go back to my house in Chelsea, how long do you think we would live to enjoy it?" "Possibly twenty years," she said. "Twenty years!" said he; "Why, if you had said a thousand years it would have been something, and yet he would be a very bad merchant that would put himself in danger to lose eternity for a thousand years; how much the rather, as we are not sure of it for one day."

More's counsel to those who are threatened with loss or harm for the sake of the Gospel is to make themselves familiar with what they must face and "to appoint with God's help in their own mind before hand, what thing they intend to do if the very worst fall." Most of the terrors which cause men to flee are imaginary, and if such terrors be pondered and weighed by the reason, they are not as fearful as they seem at first.

It was no part of More's plan, however, to deny the actuality of affliction and pain. On the contrary, he takes as one of his main sources of comfort the medieval doctrine that merit is acquired by suffering. Through God's grace, he says, every tribulation is "either medicinal or more than medicinal." Tribulation is "medicinal" when we suffer for our sins; the more we suffer in this life, the less we have to suffer in purgatory. Tribulation is "more than medicinal" if it has no connection with our sin but is sent to prove a man's patience and to increase his merit. More permits Vincent to raise the Protestant objections against penance and purgatory, and, generally, against the whole doctrine of merit. In reply, Anthony says that he can see no very deep difference between the Lutherans and the Catholics on the matter of faith and works. "Like as we grant them that no good work is ought worth to heavenward without faith, . . . so this one thing or twain do they grant us again, that men are bound to work good works if they have time and power, and that who so worketh in true faith most, shall be most rewarded." But he says that great damage is done by preachers who emphasize faith so strongly that people are encouraged to neglect the obligations which Christ lays upon His disciples, especially the duty to fast. As to purgatory, it would be a consolation to Anthony were he able to believe that the Protestants are right, but he declares that he dare not go against the received interpretation of the Scriptures from the days of the Apostles down to the present time.

Because Sir Thomas stands at the threshold of the English renaissance, it may be surprising to find him so deeply committed to the traditional Christian viewpoint. One might have thought, from reading *Utopia,* that he was ready to embrace a kind of minimal faith, composed of the best elements in paganism. But that work seems to have been more a satire on the times than an expression of his positive convictions. The *Dialogue* is, nevertheless, an unmistakably Renaissance work. The very fact that Christianity is something to be discussed and reasoned about instead of merely taken on authority is itself enough to put the work in a new category, and the dialogue form shows More's enthusiasm for the classical revival. The author also shares the new interest in fables and folk tales, and he brightens the tone of what might otherwise be a somber work with several humorous tales which could have appeared in Chaucer or Erasmus.

More's familiarity with pagan philosophy is abundantly evident. But his considered judgment is that the natural reasons which pagan philosophy adduces are not able to give sufficient comfort of themselves, because they neglect the special point which is not only the chief comfort but is also that without which all other comforts fail; namely, "the referring the final end of their comforts unto God." "We shall therefore," he says, "neither fully receive these philosophers' reasons in this matter, nor yet utterly refuse them: but using them in such order as shall beseem them, the principal and the effectual medicines against these diseases of tribulation shall we fetch from that high, great, and excellent Physician, without whom we could never be healed of our very deadly disease." Thus, with all its echoes of Seneca and Plato, particularly of the *Phaedo* (the dialogue in which Socrates bids farewell to his friends), the true original of More's *Dialogue* is found in St. John's Gospel, chapters fourteen to seventeen, in which Jesus takes His departure from His disciples and promises never to leave them comfortless.

THE INSTITUTES OF THE CHRISTIAN RELIGION

Author: John Calvin (1509-1564)
Type of work: Systematic theology
First published: 1536, 1539, 1559

Principal Ideas Advanced

The knowledge of God and the knowledge of man are inseparable, for knowledge of man's imperfection leads to knowledge of God's perfection, and knowledge of God's perfection is prerequisite to self-knowledge.

The redemption of lost humanity is to be sought in Christ alone, without whom the knowledge of God as creator is useless.

The moral law promulgates the rule of God's righteousness.

Faith is the origin of repentance; justification is obtained exclusively by the righteousness of Christ.

God's eternal decree alone has determined the eternal destiny of every person.

Baptism testifies to man's purgation; the Lord's Supper testifies, by analogy, to man's redemption.

John Calvin's *The Institutes of the Christian Religion* was published in 1536, but it did not receive its final form until 1559. Calvin's *Institutes* was the first attempt to systematize the theology of the Reformed churches of the Reformation; it is still unsurpassed as a theological treatise.

The two main topics of Calvin's treatise, the knowledge of God and the knowledge of man, are inseparable topics, for—Calvin insists—no one can survey himself without realizing that his own existence is a subsistence in God. Knowledge of man's ignorance, unhappiness, depravity, and corruption leads to the perception that in the Lord alone and in His perfection can true wisdom and happiness be found. Yet, on the other hand, Calvin writes, true self-knowledge must be preceded by the contemplation of the perfect nature of God.

In Calvin's opinion, it is not sufficient simply to have the notion that there is such a being as God. God requires us to know that we owe everything to Him, that He is the source of all good, that we are subject to His authority, and that we must love and obey Him.

The knowledge that God requires of us is not to be sought in man alone. Such knowledge is natural to man, since man has an innate sense of deity, but man needs a source of truth which will direct him to the Creator of the world, and he finds it in the Scriptures, which are self-authenticated, carrying with them their own evidence of authority. The believer's conviction that the Scriptures are the Word of God is produced not by the testimony of the Church, nor by rational proofs, but by the inward witness of the Holy Spirit.

What is taught in the Scriptures concerning the nature of God is sufficient to overthrow all idolatrous beliefs and practices, Calvin claims, for the Scriptures teach that there is one God, one divine essence, in which there is a trinity of persons. Each person is a subsistence in the divine essence, related to the others, yet distinct from them by reason of an incommunicable property.

The *Institutes* places considerable emphasis on the absolute sovereignty of God. God is described as an omnipotent creator, a governor by providence who allows no event to occur which is not an expression of His divine will. The Calvinistic claim that it is only through the grace of God, working on the souls of those whom He has predestined to be redeemed, that any men are saved, is a further expression of the conviction that God, by His divine will, directs everything that happens in nature and in the course of human affairs. God wills those acts by which men express their freedom and are responsible: such a view may be paradoxical, but it is consistently Calvinistic.

Calvin asserts that the Scriptures acquaint us with ourselves by informing us of the original state at our creation, and of our state after Adam's Fall. Created in the image of God, man's soul was endowed with a mind capable of distinguishing the good from the evil and of discovering by the light of reason what ought to be pursued or avoided. In his primitive state of perfection, man possessed reason, understanding, and the necessary prudence and judgment to regulate his earthly life and to attain eternal happiness with God. He also possessed a free will, upon which his choice depended, so that, if he had chosen, "he might have obtained eternal life."

Calvin writes that since the sin of Adam we have fallen from our original state of integrity and that to know ourselves we must be aware of our present state of misery. Adam's sin of disobedience obliterated the divine image and resulted in the loss of wisdom, strength, sanctity, truth, and righteousness, not only for himself, but for his posterity, so that his every descendant is born with the contagion of sin and is defiled and polluted with innate depravity. The entire human race is involved in Adam's guilt and corruption and is, therefore, justly condemned in the sight of God.

In his present fallen condition man is despoiled of freedom of will and is subjected to the miserable slavery of sin. Man is now destitute of all rectitude, Calvin writes, for man has of himself no power for the pursuit of righteousness. Apart from the special grace that is bestowed only upon the elect in regeneration, man cannot perform good works. His natural gifts have been corrupted and his supernatural gifts have been taken away. Man's reason is incapable of attaining spiritual wisdom; that is, he cannot know God; nor can he know God's favor towards men, a favor on which salvation depends; nor does man know the way by which he ought to regulate his life according to God's law. Nevertheless the common grace of God sometimes restrains sin in the unregenerate, who are often "invested and adorned by God with excellent talents." (Here Calvin refers, as Dante did, to those who might be called "virtuous pagans.")

The human will is by nature so entirely vitiated and depraved that everything it produces is evil, Calvin claims. When destitute of grace, men are in slavery to the corruption of their own evil desires and are not moved toward what is spiritually good. The will, rather, is subject to the dominion of sin and is in bondage. Whatever good men enjoy is from God, and whatever evil they suffer is from themselves. Everything that is the product of man's corrupt nature deserves condemnation, for having been corrupted by the Fall, man now sins voluntarily, not reluctantly, not under external constraint or compulsion, but with the strongest propensity of his own disposition. Such necessity in no way precludes voluntary bondage to sin; all men are under voluntary servitude.

The sole remedy for such bondage, Calvin suggests, is to be found in divine grace. It alone can correct the depravity of man's nature. It is God who begins the good work in men, by bending their hearts towards righteousness, and by confirming them to perseverance. The will is then created anew, converted from evil tendencies to good. Whatever is good in the will is the work of grace alone, a work performed only by God; man's salvation is entirely gratuitous. God's grace is not bestowed upon all men, writes Calvin, but solely upon the elect, not on the basis of any merit, lest any should boast. The direction of the human will towards what is good is from the very first dependent upon the will of God, and the perseverance, the subsequent constancy of the elect, is likewise due to that selfsame grace, so that all ability that a convicted sinner has is derived from grace alone.

The entire human race perished in the person of Adam until God appeared as the Redeemer in the person of His only begotten Son. The redemption of lost humanity is to be sought in Christ alone, without whom the knowledge of God as creator is useless. Knowledge of God, without knowledge of the Mediator, Jesus Christ, does not afford salvation. Christ responds to the faithful of all ages, including the faithful during the Old Testament times. The Law was in fact given to encourage the people of Israel during the period of hope for salvation by the Messiah.

The Law, writes Calvin, is like a mirror in which man beholds his impotence and his iniquity, and the consequences of both. The moral law remains in full force for the faithful, for it promulgates the rule of God's righteousness and makes men attentive to His will, by enjoining them to obedience.

In Old Testament times the Law tended to excite in the faithful an expectation of the Christ that was to come; yet it is only in the Gospel that Christ is clearly revealed. The saints of the Old Testament were, however, partakers of the same inheritance, and they hoped for the same salvation through the grace of the one Mediator, Jesus Christ. For Christ was the pledge of the Old Covenant as well as of the New.

According to Calvin, the Old Testament differs from the New Testament, in spite of this basic unity. For in Old Testament times man's celestial inheritance was exhibited under the figures of terrestrial blessing; the Old Testament was promulgated without the efficacy of the Spirit; it was a covenant not of liberty but of bondage; it denoted the Law, rather than the Gospel, and it dealt with a single nation, rather than with the nations of the earth.

The fullness of man's redemption was accomplished by Christ becoming man in order to fulfill the office of Mediator. Jesus the Christ is truly God and truly man, asserts Calvin. Christ assumed a real humanity; and invested with flesh, the Son of God became also the Son of man, not by a confusion of substance, but by a unity of person. The divine and the human natures constitute the one person of the Mediator; each nature retains its own properties, and yet together they constitute a single Christ, who as redeemer fulfills a threefold office, that of prophet, priest, and king. As a prophet, He reveals the will of God for our salvation, by His word and spirit; as a priest, He offered himself, once and for all, as a sacrifice to satisfy divine justice, and by continually interceding for us, He reconciles us to God; and as a king, He rules and defends us, subdues us to Himself, and conquers our mutual enemies.

As our redeemer, by His death, resurrection, and ascension to Heaven, Christ has procured our salvation. He alone merits the grace of God.

How then is the grace of Christ received? Our enjoyment of Christ and of all His benefits, Calvin answers, depends upon the secret and special operation of the Holy Spirit, who works faith in us, and unites us to Christ, illuminates our minds, and renews our wills.

It is by faith, Calvin writes, that we who are the adopted sons of God enter into the possession of the Heavenly Kingdom. For faith consists in a knowledge of Christ, not in reverence for the Church; it is a knowledge of the benevolence of God towards us. The knowledge of faith exceeds that of the understanding; it is an acknowledgment, a persuasion of the veracity of God; it consists more in certainty than in comprehension. It places the goodness of God beyond all doubt and uncertainty, for we apprehend that salvation and everlasting life is obtained. Faith grafts us into the body of Christ.

Faith is the origin of repentance, for the latter can arise only when a man knows himself to be of God, and does turn from sin and seek new obedience. Repentance is properly followed by confession of sin to God alone. There is no need of confession to a man, nor of further satisfaction or indulgences for the remission of sin. Believers ought to present themselves as living sacrifices, and be transformed, and take up the cross, always remembering that it is by faith alone that they are justified. The justification of the sinner is an act of God whereby God esteems him as a righteous person and remits his sins through the imputation of the righteousness of Christ; however, this in no way implies that justification is not accompanied by good works. Justification is obtained exclusively by the righteousness of Christ.

Man is never saved by his own righteousness, writes Calvin, but if he is regenerated by the Spirit of God, he will devote himself to true holiness. The entire life of the Christian should be an exercise in piety, for the Christian is called to become holy. The Christian is at liberty with respect to the yoke of the law, but he yields voluntarily to the will of God, without necessarily being under obligation with respect to things which are in themselves indifferent.

The principal exercise of faith is to be found in prayer, for nothing is revealed to us that is to be expected from God, for which we are not commanded to pray. To pray properly, the heart and mind should be suitably composed, free of all external cares; we should pray for no more than God permits. Our petitions should reflect a real sense of our indigence; they should be offered without distrust, and without any sense of our own merits, while at the same time the petitioner recognizes that it is Christ alone, not the saints, who is able to intercede for him at the throne of Grace.

Salvation is not offered to all, but only to some, Calvin writes; for some are predestined to salvation, others to destruction. God gives to some what He refuses to others. God's eternal decree has determined the destiny of every person; some are foreordained to eternal life and others to eternal damnation, without any consideration of merit, solely upon the basis of His gratuitous mercy. The voice of the Gospel is addressed to all men, but the gift of faith is bestowed only upon a few.

The validity of election does not depend upon human consent, Calvin insists. The elect are effectually called to salvation, and the reprobate are appointed to be instruments of God's wrath; being devoid of the Spirit they can do nothing except what deserves His curse.

To maintain the preaching of the Gospel, God has deposited His treasure with the Church. He has given His authority to His pastors and teachers to promote the unity of the faith, and He has instituted two sacraments to nourish and support the faith.

The Church is universal or catholic in that it includes all the elect of God, the dead as well as the living, the Church invisible, as well as the Church visible. The latter is to be found wherever we find the word preached purely and the sacraments administered as Christ instituted them.

The government of the Church is ordained by God. To edify the Church, its ministers must themselves study and proclaim the Word of God as it is contained in the Scriptures. The Church has no authority, however, to make laws which bind the consciences of men in those respects in which they have been set at liberty by Christ.

The Church has no power of the sword, no authority to punish or coerce; its jurisdiction is spiritual, and to this end it must maintain discipline, consisting of private and public admonitions, and in extreme cases, of excommunication.

The Christian faith is supported by the preaching of the Word and by the sacraments, the latter being an outward sign by which the Lord seals the promises of His good will in our consciences and gives us support in our weaknesses.

Two sacraments and two only present us with a clear exhibition of

Christ: baptism, which testifies to our purgation and ablution; and the Lord's Supper, which testifies to our redemption.

As a sign of initiation, baptism admits us into the Church. Baptism is proposed to us by the Lord as a token of our purification; it shows our mortification in Christ and our new life in Him, and it testifies that we are so united to Him as to be partakers of all His benefits. Baptism of infants assures them of God's pardon, although no man will be saved by baptism alone, for God must first have elected to save the soul and thereby have endowed it with the faith which makes baptism efficacious.

In the Lord's Supper the bread and wine represent the nourishment that we actually receive from the body and blood of Christ. The sacrament provides us with the assurance that the body of the Lord was once offered as a sacrifice for us, and His blood was once shed for us, for our salvation. The corporeal objects themselves undergo no metaphysical change, but they conduct us by analogy to the realm of the spiritual. When bread is presented as a symbol of the body, we are led to the comparison, that as bread nourishes the physical body, the life of the soul is sustained by the body of Christ; likewise as wine nourishes and refreshes the physical body, so the advantages of the remission of sin are conferred on us by the blood of Christ.

The elements of the Sacred Supper are signs of the working of Christ's spirit; their efficacy is not a function of man's power. According to Calvin, Christ "pours his life into us . . . not by putting before us a vain or empty sign, but offering there the efficacy of his Spirit, by which he fulfils his promise." Only those who are faithful to Him enjoy the fruits of His Spirit, but the Spirit is what gives the sacrament its efficacy. There is also the suggestion that the elements signify not only Christ's Spirit, but also His body: "If it is true that the visible sign is offered to us to attest the granting of the invisible reality, then, on receiving the symbol of the body, we may be confident that the body itself is no less given to us. . . ."

Calvin's *Institutes* is more than a standard work of theology. It provided the confessional foundation for the Reformed (in distinction from the Lutheran) branch of Protestantism, including English and American Puritanism. Its influence has, therefore, penetrated the cultures of many of the Western nations.

A SHORT AND CLEAR EXPOSITION OF THE CHRISTIAN FAITH

Author: Ulrich Zwingli (1484-1531)
Type of work: Reformed theology
First published: 1536

PRINCIPAL IDEAS ADVANCED

The faith of the Zurich Reformation has been falsely accused of departing from the ancient Christian truth.

Sacraments are signs and symbols of holy things and are to be reverenced only because they commemorate what has already happened; sacraments cannot remit sins or confer blessings.

The Lord's Supper witnesses to the birth and passion of Christ to both believers and nonbelievers; the body of Christ is eaten only spiritually.

Included within the visible Church are the elect and non-elect; the elect are also members of the invisible Church.

Ulrich Zwingli, a leader of the Reformation in German Switzerland, inaugurated a new phase of the Protestant movement when, in 1519, he began his duties at the Cathedral in Zurich. On that New Year's Day he announced that he would discard the traditional practice of expounding on the appointed Scriptural texts and begin his preaching with the first chapter of Matthew and proceed through the New Testament. The new pastor was departing from the old ways. The essay *A Short and Clear Exposition of the Christian Faith* was designed as a summary statement of his work; it was written in 1531 at the end of his career.

Zwingli was born in 1484, in the village of Wildhaus in Switzerland. His education was received at the Universities of Basle, Berne, and Vienna, where he came under the influence of the humanists. His study of classical philosophy, of Greek and Roman history, and of the mode of thought and expression he learned from Erasmus (c.1466-1536) carried through his life's work. He studied Erasmus's Greek edition of the New Testament with such diligence that he was able to recite the body of Pauline literature by memory.

The Swiss and German Reformation movements had common bonds. Though Zwingli did not attribute his own work to that of the German Reformer, he did say that Luther gave him the courage to preach what he learned from Paul. The sole authority of Scripture, the denial of celibacy, the reduction of the number of sacraments, the centrality of the doctrine of justification by faith, and the rejection of medieval ecclesiastical organization were ties which united these two early leaders of the Protestant Reformation. But there were differences. Zwingli was turned to the Reformation by study and reflection; he did not undergo the same struggle of soul that Luther had experienced in his early days. And Zwingli's Swiss patriotism led him along paths which were foreign even to Luther's loyalty to Germany, for Zwingli was engaged in political activities and looked for the establishment of the Kingdom of God on earth, which would be visible in the "elect" at Zurich. Zwingli was willing to take up arms to defend the Church, and unlike Luther he did not regard the use of force as a prerogative only of civil rulers.

Above all else, it was Zwingli's use of the Bible which gave the distinctive character to the Zurich form of the Reformation. In Zwingli's opinion, current practices of the Church, such as celibacy, fasting, and the veneration of images, had no Biblical foundation and therefore could not be binding. In carrying out the "restoration of primitive Christianity" Zwingli was led to abolish the Mass and curtail other practices; the reform in Zurich was clearly more puritanic in nature than that stemming from Luther.

Zwingli's reform was vigorous. Other towns followed his lead and with the increasing evidence of support for him the lines of separation with Catholic dominated regions became sharp. Armed conflict ensued.

At Marburg in 1529, the Lutherans and Zwinglians sought to find ways to unite their respective groups. The central and continuing point of conflict of these two branches of Protestantism concerned the Lord's Supper. Luther insisted on the real physical presence of Christ in the sacrament, and he could not tolerate Zwingli's assertion of only the spiritual presence. No union of the groups was effected. Zwingli returned to Zurich to deal alone with the political and military circumstances which his reform had produced. In the Battle of Kappell (1531) he was killed while carrying the chaplain's banner.

A Short and Clear Exposition of the Christian Faith was published by Heinrich Bullinger (1504-1575) in 1536, some five years after Zwingli's death. The essay was designed to state the Zurich Reformer's position on theological, social, and political matters to Francis I. The division between the two major branches of the Reformation over the Lord's Supper had already occurred, and Zwingli found himself in an increasingly hostile environment. He hoped to win Francis and even the entire French country to the Reformed faith. The essay itself dealt with the essential points of controversy and did not intend to be a complete resumé of the faith; it offered a summary of Zwingli's position on a number of topics with which he dealt at more length elsewhere.

A humanistic thread runs throughout his essay. It was characteristic of Zwingli to use Scripture as the basis for any doctrines which were specifically Christian, though he was not unwilling to derive added support for such doctrines from non-Christian literature; he argued from reason and the testimony of speculative philosophers when he dealt with issues which were common to philosophy and theology. In his outline of his position on the doctrine of God, he cast his discussion more in philosophical than Biblical terms. When he dealt with the theme of Church and state, examples from Greek and Roman history were corroborated by Biblical references. When he discussed eternal life, he was mindful of the interests of Francis I, a well known patron of the Renaissance. In the life to come the faithful will commune not only with Abraham, Moses, Isaiah, David, Peter, and Paul, but also with Theseus, Socrates, Aristides, Antigonus, Numa, Camillus, and the Catos and Scipios. This assertion of the final salvation of some of the "heathen" marked a clear separation of Zwingli from other phases of the Protestant Reformation and offered evidence of the type of reform characteristic of those so greatly influenced by the humanists. Zwingli wrote, ". . . there has not lived a single good man, there has not been a single pious heart or believing soul from the beginning of the world to the end, which you will not see there in the presence of God."

Zwingli is most noted in the history of Christian thought for his position on the Lord's Supper. In this essay he summarized his earlier tract entitled, "On the Lord's Supper" (1526). He defined a sacrament as a sign and symbol of holy things. In the Lord's Supper the body and blood of Christ are eaten spiritually, not naturally and literally. According to Zwingli, "the papist teaching that the body of Christ is eaten in the same form and with the same properties and nature as when he was born and suffered and died is not only presumptuous and foolish but impious and blasphemous." The discussion of the papist doctrine had been central in the debates of the time, and Zwingli took pains to point out to Francis that his position was not heretical: ". . . we never taught a single word that we have not taken from Holy Scripture or the Fathers." The risen body of Christ is at the right hand of God, Zwingli argued; Christ's body cannot be in more than one place (as the papists and Luther, Zwingli argued, had suggested); therefore, Christ's body cannot be present at the Lord's Supper. The humanity of Christ or the body of Christ is not eternal and is not omnipresent, Zwingli added. With numerous Biblical references, Zwingli asserted that ". . . as regards a natural, essential, and localized presence the humanity is not here, for it has left the world. Hence the body of Christ is not eaten by us naturally or literally, much less quantitatively, but sacramentally and spiritually." If the body of Christ is literally present, then the Christians are open to the charge of cannibalism. But in the New Testament we learn that "Ministering women used to honour the body of the Lord by washing and anointing it, not by feeding upon it."

Another distinctive aspect of Zwingli's doctrine of the Lord's Supper centered around his understanding of the sacrament as offering "historical faith." He wrote, "All celebrations, monuments and statues give historical faith, that is, they remind us of some event, refreshing the memory like the feast of the passover amongst the Hebrews or the remission of debts at Athens. . . ." The celebration of the sacrament is of benefit even to the unbelievers. "For whether they receive it or not, it testifies to all that which is of the power of the sacrament, the fact that Christ suffered. But only to the faithful and pious does it testify that he suffered for us." The Lord's Supper does not give faith; faith is presupposed. Those who take the sacrament without faith do not participate sacramentally. If one does partake as a public act without faith, then the judgment which will rest upon that individual will be more severe than that passed on the impious unbeliever.

In summary, Zwingli wrote, "Therefore whether we like it or not, we are forced to concede that the words: 'This is my body,' cannot be taken naturally or literally, but have to be construed symbolically, sacramentally, metaphorically or as a metonymy, thus: 'This is my body,' that is, 'This is the sacrament of my body,' or, 'This is my sacramental or mystical body,' that is, the sacramental and representative symbol of the body which I really assumed and yielded over to death."

On one other major point Zwingli sought to clear up what had been charged against him. The Protestant reformers had frequently been accused of minimizing "good works." In writing to Francis, Zwingli likened the discussion of faith and works to the duties of subjects to kings: "Supposing someone has performed a great service for your majesty, but not sincerely. Do you not say at once that you owe no debt of gratitude to the one who performed it because he did not do it from the heart? . . . The same norm and standard applies in relation to good works. The source of works must be faith." Some of the more extreme forms of the Reformation were tending to an antinomian position, and Zwingli took care to dissociate himself from that movement. To him, the intent of the "work" is primary; faith comes first, and works issue from that. The works in themselves have no bearing on one's relation to God; man is justified by faith.

The tenor of the essay is defensive and apologetic. Zwingli was attempting to state his understanding of the Christian faith in terms which were compatible with the beliefs of Francis, though there is no evidence that he was at all successful. The essay serves as an excellent, though brief, summary of Zwingli's position on the central issues of the Swiss Reformation.

FOUNDATION OF CHRISTIAN DOCTRINE

Author: Menno Simons (1496-1561)
Type of work: Apologetics; Church order
First published: 1539

Principal Ideas Advanced

Christians must not merely believe that God forgives sins; they must be converted from their worldly living.

Baptism does not regenerate a man, but it is a sign that he has been converted from the world and lives according to the will of God.

The Lord's Supper is not a sacrament, but a memorial of Christ's death, and a loving fellowship; it is a rite to to be partaken of only by those who live godly lives.

By strict discipline, the Church is to be kept pure from all false doctrine and practice, and those who do not live godly lives are to be excluded from its fellowship.

The followers of Christ, being peaceable and nonviolent, will aways be the victims of the world, which follows Antichrist.

Magistrates ought to obey Christ and further His righteousness, but without resorting to tyranny and unnecessary force.

Before he became a leading Anabaptist, Menno Simons was a Catholic priest, with a superior education which included knowledge of the Church Fathers, both Greek and Latin. Shortly after his ordination, in 1524, he began to be troubled by the kind of doubts Protestants were raising against the sacrifice of the Mass, and he started to restudy the Scriptures. His enlightenment, according to his own testimony, was gradual; and he began to be recognized by some as an evangelical preacher while still within the Catholic Church. Even after he had been persuaded of the Anabaptist position, which may have been as early as 1531, he did not break with the Church. Instead, he opposed the excesses of the more radical Anabaptist sects, such as the followers of John of Leiden, against whom he wrote a booklet in 1535. Later that year, however, the horrors perpetrated against Anabaptists in his native Friesland became such a personal burden that he resolved to renounce the Catholic Church publicly (January 30, 1536).

After a brief retirement, Menno Simons joined the moderate Anabaptist group which had been founded in Zurich in 1525 and had followers in Netherlands, and he was ordained an elder in 1537. In constant personal danger, he preached and organized churches in Holland, Northwest Germany, and Holstein, writing extensively on the controversies which rent the church at that time. His *Foundation of Christian Doctrine* (first published in the dialect of the Baltic coastal regions), which was written with a view to exhibiting the Biblical foundations of the Dutch Anabaptist Brethren, later called the Mennonites (the followers of Menno), was his most widely read and influential work.

The fundamental idea set forth in the *Foundation* is the need for followers of Christ to live holy lives. In enforcing this demand, Menno and the Brethren believed that they were merely continuing the true Church of Christ and His Apostles. "Ours is no new doctrine," says Menno; "It is the old doctrine which was preached and practiced in the church for more than 1,500 years, the doctrine by which the church was begotten, is being begotten, and will be begotten to the end." Christ came calling men to repent of their sins, to cast themselves upon the promises of God, and to turn from the ways of the world. Menno Simons made it clear that those who follow Christ will have to sacrifice possessions and loved ones, and bear grievous afflictions from wicked men and from the Antichrist. But most of those who call themselves the representatives of Christ, Menno argues, whether they be Catholic, Lutheran, Zwinglian, or members of Corrupt Sects (Menno's designation for the radical Anabaptist groups), have never repented of their sins or turned their backs on the world. Of the Protestant preachers of justification by faith alone, he writes, "They preach nothing but the grace, the favor, the mercy, and the love of God before their covetous, proud, showy, impure, drunken, and impenitent church, little realizing that the whole Scriptures testify that such folk cannot inherit the kingdom of God."

Menno's insistence upon adult baptism is closely connected with his conviction that those who confess Christ must repent and be converted. The practice of infant baptism has, he says, no justification in the Scriptures, and is contrary to the command of the Gospel, "Go ye into all the world, and preach the gospel to every creature; he that believeth and is baptized shall be saved, but he that believeth not, shall be damned." Menno considers the usual arguments for infant baptism, such as the one based on Paul's comparison of baptism and circumcision. Paul, says Menno, is referring not to the circumcision of the flesh but to the circumcision of the spirit; hence there is no argument here for the baptism of infants, but the very opposite. For the Mennonites, the washing with water does not confer regeneration, but symbolizes the change that takes place in the hearts of believers when they confess Christ and declare their obedience to Him. Menno writes, "For the testimony of Jesus they are prepared to forsake their homes, possessions, lands, and lives, and to suffer hunger, affliction, oppression, persecution, the cross and death for the same; yes, they desire to bury the flesh with its lusts and arise with Christ to newness of life. . . . Therefore we are buried with him in baptism into death; that like as Christ was raised up from the dead by the glory of the Father, even so we also should walk in newness of life." Menno does not deny that the grace of Christ saves infants, but he insists that they are saved without being regenerated. For regeneration to take place, there must be a hearing of the Word, then a sincere believing; afterwards, Christ is put on and the Holy Spirit is given. It is of some interest that during the time of Menno, Anabaptists did not practice immersion, but affusion. Menno speaks of baptism as "a handful of water."

Similar concern is manifested by Menno concerning the Lord's Supper. The Catholic teaching that Christ is sacrificed anew upon the altar, and that whenever the priest pronounces the words of consecration over the bread and wine, the Lord, "willing or unwilling . . . must descend and land on their idolatrous hands," Menno could only regard as an abomination, an invention of Antichrist, analogous to Aaron's golden calf. There is no hint of such a thing in Scripture, he says, not even of the teaching that the Holy Supper is a sacrament endowed with power to forgive sins. On the contrary, Christ ordained it to be a memorial of His atoning death, a fellowship of love among the redeemed. Only those who eat and drink inwardly, by faith, are true partakers of the feast; and those who come to the table with impenitent hearts eat and drink damnation to themselves. Menno laid great stress upon what is now called "close communion," and in the interests of a pure Church he enforced a rigid ban or excommunication against backsliders, except when they gave evidence of repentance. He also stressed the necessity for true believers to shun all contact with those who preach Romish doctrine, since these not only do not have the truth but are in the service of Antichrist.

Menno's general theological position is not very different from that of Luther and the other Reformers. He takes his stand flatly on "the whole Scriptures, both the Old and New Testament," which he commonly refers to as the Word of God. Through the Scriptures, and through the Word Incarnate, God has called men to repentance and salvation, says Menno; those who do not obey it will not be able to stand before the judgment seat, while those who humbly seek God's will therein have an infallible rule for this life and that to come. While he would not give the creeds or councils any authority independent of Christ and the Scriptures. Menno nevertheless agreed with "the twelve articles" (that is, the Apostles' Creed), and with the ancient symbols which set forth the doctrines concerning the Trinity and the person of Christ.

What chiefly distinguishes the doctrine of the Mennonites and other Anabaptist groups from the Reformation churches is an emphasis upon blamelessness of conduct which would seem to some Lutherans and Calvinists a kind of legalism. Menno affirmed, with the Reformers, the doctrine of original sin, the necessity of Christ's death as an atonement, and the need for men to be regenerated by the power of the Spirit. He further agreed that Christians cannot, in this life, achieve perfection, because of the weakness and sinfulness of the flesh. But he gave more emphasis than the Reformers to the ethical standards of the Gospel, particularly to those passages which insist that in order to follow Christ men must take a stand against the powers of this world.

Closely connected with the demand for purity of life is Menno's doctrine concerning the Church. None of the leaders of the Reformation had abandoned the Catholic idea of the Church as an objective, supernatural institution by means of which divine grace is made available to men, irrespective of the subjective intention of its ministers. Such discipline as they enforced was meant to keep the Church true to the principles of its institution. In contrast to this notion of an "inclusive" Church, the Mennonites reaffirmed the principle of an "exclusive" Church, gathered out from the midst of the world and set apart to holiness. Menno was aware of the distinction between the Church "visible" and the Church "invisible." He believed that the same frailties which keep the individual from achieving perfection make it impossible to have a Church in which there are no hypocrites. Nonetheless, says Menno, every effort must be made to keep the visible Church "irreproachable in life before the world, so far as man, who is able to judge only that which is visible, can see."

The relation between the Church and the world must, in Menno's view, always be one of more or less open hostility. The forces of Christ and of Antichrist are at war, and shall be until the end of the world. Moreover, as Christ must suffer at the hands of His enemies, so those who are His disciples must expect to suffer. Persons who love houses and lands and the approbation of men more than they love Christ are not His disciples. No compromise, therefore, may be made with the powers of this world in the interests of security and worldly well-being. The Gospel, moreover, forbids the Christians ever to use force. In opposition to the "corrupt sects," notably the Münsterites, who appealed to the example of the Old Testament and sought to establish the Kingdom of Heaven by the sword, Menno emphasizes the difference between the Old Covenant and the New, and he insists that the Gospel demands nonresistance. "Iron and metal spears and swords we leave to those who, alas, regard human blood and swine's blood about alike," he says.

Menno and his followers were, in fact, the victims of cruel and persistent persecution, and part of the practical aim of the *Foundation of Christian Doctrine* was to enter a plea for toleration. Like Tertullian in his *Apology*, Menno tries to clear away popular misapprehensions concerning the beliefs and practices of the Brethren. They are, he insists, not causing any harm to anybody; they are quiet, law-abiding citizens, fully aware of their obligation to obey the civil authority in all matters which do not contradict the commands of the Word, and willing to suffer evil rather than to perform it. If they have to lay down their lives, they will do so; but they cannot do so without protesting that injustice is being done, and reminding the authorities that they are fighting against God. Menno fails, however, to arrive at a clear conception of the "secular" state, uncommitted with respect to the principles of any religion. Because the state owes its authority to God, he conceives that it is obliged to enforce Christian morality and to prevent the propagation of false religion. "This," he says, "is the task to which you are called: namely to chastise and punish, in the true fear of God with fairness and Christian discretion, manifest criminals, such as thieves, murderers, Sodomites, adulterers, seducers, sorcerers, the violent, highwaymen, robbers, etc. . . . also to restrain by reasonable means, that is without tyranny and bloodshed, manifest deceivers who so miserably lead poor helpless souls by hundreds of thousands into destruction. . . . Whether the deceivers are priests, monks, preachers, baptized or unbaptized, it is your task to restrain them so that they may no longer retract from the power of the almighty majesty of God . . . nor introduce such ridiculous abuses and idolatry under semblance of truth as has been done until now." In this way, he says, without force or bloodshed, and in all love, rulers and magistrates "may enlarge, help, and protect the kingdom of God."

Menno writes with the fervor, and with much of the flavor, of a Biblical prophet. His thought and expression are saturated with the language and imagery of the Scriptures. He is strong in his denunciation of sin and hypocrisy in all classes, but he is without rancor or impatience. He expresses the confidence that, having made the great renunciation, he is on Christ's side; he declares himself filled with the same joy and peace that is manifest in the writings of the Apostles, with whom he hopes for the imminent return of Christ and the end of the world's woes.

THE NECESSITY OF REFORMING THE CHURCH

Author: John Calvin (1509-1564)
Type of work: Protestant polemics (polemical theology)
First published: 1544

Principal Ideas Advanced

Christianity consists primarily of the knowledge of the proper worship of God and of the source of salvation.

Sacraments and Church government are of secondary importance; their function is to preserve the aforesaid knowledge.

The religious establishment prevailing in Europe prior to the Reformation was marked by the extinction of the aforesaid knowledge, and by the corruption of the sacraments and of Church government.

Protestants have not separated from the Church; they have restored it.

The prevailing abuses and divisions cannot wait to be settled by a general council; secular authorities must restore the unity of the Church by bringing the religion of their territories into conformity with the aforesaid knowledge, which finds its locus in Christ.

From the time of the first publication of his *Institutes of the Christian Religion* in 1536, John Calvin was recognized as an authoritative and effective spokesman for the Protestant Reformation. Always laboring for harmony and a common front on the part of the churches of the Magisterial Reformation, he frequently noted the debt owed by these churches to the pioneering work of Luther, though his own views proved to be more congenial to the non-Lutheran or Reformed churches.

It was Calvin's intention to advance the Reformation by supporting the views of Luther and by establishing continuity with the Church Fathers. There are many instances of his skillful use of passages from Gregory, Augustine, Cyprian, and other Fathers of the Church; and there are many avowals of his concern to advance the ideas of Luther.

The Necessity of Reforming the Church is a "supplicatory remonstrance" presented to the Emperor Charles V (reigned 1519-1555) and the estates of the Empire assembled at the Fourth Diet of Spires, in 1544. Calvin wrote it at the instance of Martin Bucer (1491-1551), the Strasbourg reformer. The work is at once an apology for what had been accomplished by the Reformation up to this point, and a challenge to the emperor, the princes, and the free cities to preserve and extend these accomplishments. This appeal to the secular power to reform religion differentiates the Magisterial Reformation from the Radical Reformation, which tended for the most part to discountenance such "interference," and from the reform-minded Catholics, who tended to look to a general council or to existing ecclesiastical institutions to effect the work of reform. Calvin's coolness to the idea of a general council reflects a second stage in the evolution of Protestant thought on this subject. The enthusiasm for a council, which had been expressed by Luther and others, had been dampened by years of delay and by the political complexion which the conception of a council had assumed, as well as by second thoughts on the likelihood of a general council being guided solely by the Holy Spirit and the authority of Scripture.

Basic to Calvin's argument is his definition of Christianity as the knowledge of the proper worship of God, together with the knowledge of the source of salvation. Sacraments and Church government are given a secondary place, as being not ends in themselves, but means for the preservation of this two-fold knowledge. Calvin contends that this two-fold knowledge was lost amidst the corruption of the sacraments and government of the pre-Reformation Church.

Calvin defines proper worship as being basically the recognition of God as "the only source of all virtue, justice, holiness, wisdom, truth, power, goodness, mercy, life, and salvation; in accordance with this, to ascribe and render to Him the glory of all that is good, to seek all things in Him alone, and in every want have recourse to Him alone." Worship includes prayer, praise, thanksgiving, adoration, and obedience, all directed solely to God himself. God abominates, says Calvin, all impure worship, such as prayer and adoration directed to the saints, ceremonialism, or "will-worship," which proceeds from man's fertile imagination rather than from the will of God.

Calvin claims that the Reformation has rebuked idolatry (which includes for him the veneration of saints, images, and relics), and has inculcated a spiritual worship. Will-worship (see Colossians 2:23) has been curbed: extra-Scriptural practices have been abolished, while divinely-ordained rites (such as baptism) have been given a spiritual meaning. Prayer has been reformed: the saints have been displaced by Christ as man's intercessor; the uncertainty that pervaded late-medieval piety has been replaced by confidence; an unknown tongue (Latin) has given way to the vernacular.

Calvin argues that the proper knowledge of the source of salvation involves three steps: (1) the sense of individual wretchedness, (2) the knowledge of Christ's mediatorial work, and (3) the personal assurance of salvation in Christ. He sees such knowledge obscured by the scholastic interpretation of original sin as "little more than excess of bodily appetite and lust," an interpretation which neglects "blindness and vanity of intellect . . . and . . . inward depravity of soul." The knowledge is obscured also by the attribution to men of an imaginary free-will, and by the teaching that men are justified by faith plus works, a view which deprives men of the certain assurance of the divine favor, and hence of all true confidence.

The Reformation is credited with restoring the true knowledge of salvation. It has recovered the conviction that man cannot save himself. His free will consists only in spontaneity, not in ability to do the right in his own strength. Such a doctrine of the will, says Calvin, inculcates in men true humility and true gratitude. Good works are accorded due praise, but Calvin affirms as Protestant convictions the beliefs that man's acceptance before God does not depend on good works but solely on the gratuitous divine mercy, that there are no works of supererogation, and that men's good works are acceptable to God only in Christ.

The "pollution" of the sacraments in the pre-Reformation Church is said to consist in the addition of five spurious sacraments to the two instituted by Christ, and in the corruption, both in form and meaning, of these two. Calvin insists on the distinction between "mysteries instituted by Christ" and pertaining to eternal life, and human ceremonies, no matter how wholesome in themselves. With respect to the two genuine sacraments, he insists that the elements be always accompanied by the word, that is, by an intelligible explanation, so that men's hearts and minds might be directed to Christ. Transubstantiation is rejected as contrary to the words of Christ and as "abhorrent to the very nature of a sacrament," which requires a visible symbol of the spiritual truth signified, not "some empty phantom that mocks the eye." The elevation and adoration of the consecrated bread are likewise rejected as unscriptural corruptions. The sacrifice of the Mass has been replaced by a genuine communion, where both clergy and laity partake of both the bread and the cup. The use of the vernacular makes the service understandable to all.

With respect to Church government, Calvin alleges that the pastoral office had fallen into dissuetude and that the episcopal succession had been interrupted long ago. In the true Church all rulers are teachers, but the pre-Reformation clergy was notorious for its failure, even its inability, to teach. There can be no episcopal succession, says Calvin, where there are no canonical elections; the pre-Reformation Church was notorious for its indifference towards the life and doctrine of its candidates; the people were deprived of their rightful voice in episcopal elections; the rights of the clergy were usurped by the bishops, and the rights of the episcopate by the pope. The Roman "episcopate" stands condemned not only by its failure to preserve the truth of God, but also by its enmity to that divine truth.

Calvin lays it down as a Reformation principle that civil laws ought to be carefully obeyed, but that God is the only legislator for the conscience. Human traditions were odious to the Reformers on two main grounds: some, impossible of being fulfilled, led men to hypocrisy and despair; others "made the commandments of God of none effect." The Reformation consequently abolished such "human traditions" as abstinence from meat on Fridays, clerical celibacy, and compulsory auricular confession.

Calvin proceeds to deal with some eight basic charges made against the Reformation by its opponents. To the charge that the Reformers have disturbed the peace of the Church, Calvin replies that this charge has always been brought against men of God. But when the prophet Elijah was thus charged, he replied that not he, but the sins of Ahab and his house were the real troublers of Israel (I Kings 18:18). Christ Himself was a stone of stumbling and a rock of offense to His countrymen (Romans 9:31-33).

To the charge of undue rigor Calvin replied by admitting that in the life of the Church there have always been some blemishes which it is necessary to overlook. But the abuses prevalent in the papal church of the sixteenth century were too serious to be overlooked. The idolatrous veneration accorded to images and saints, the people being deprived of religious services in their own tongue, the honor of man's salvation being divided between Christ and the sinner, the selling of sacraments and other rites, the keeping of the cup from the laity in the Lord's Supper (contrary to the explicit command of the Lord), the fancied transmutation of bread into the body of Christ, the loss of a teaching ministry and of liberty of conscience—tolerance extended to such abuses as these would be criminal indifference, Calvin writes, an insult to Christ and a neglect of the Church's fatal wound.

When it is said that the time is not auspicious, or that the condition of the Church is so desperate as to make attempts at reformation mere futile gestures that aggravate the pain, Calvin replies that "the restoration of the Church is the work of God, and no more depends on the hopes and opinions of men, than the resurrection of the dead, or any other miracle of that description. Here, therefore, we are not to wait for facility of action, either from the will of men, or the temper of the times, but must rush forward through the midst of despair. . . . What the success will be it is not ours to inquire."

Were the results of the Reformers' efforts all bad, Calvin claims, what they did would still remain the work of God. But the results have not been bad. Idolatry, superstition, and error have been curbed. Many pious persons testify that through the teachings of the Reformers they have for the first time found peace of heart and mind. Men of vicious lives have been converted. Taken all in all, Calvin boasts, the adherents of the Reformation exceed the best of the Papists in "innocence, integrity, and true holiness."

Calvin ridicules the charge that the Protestants lack discipline. He compares the clerical discipline of Rome, which allows children twelve years old to be made archbishops, which tolerates nonresidence and pluralism and every kind of personal defect, with the teaching ministry of the Reformation churches. For the laity, there is no discipline in the Roman Church as long as its authority is unreservedly acknowledged; in many of the Reformation churches, on the other hand, excommunication is used as an effectual check on the religion and morals of the people.

When it is said that Protestant lords have expropriated the wealth of the Church, Calvin professes himself unwilling to defend all that has been done along this line. Yet he calls attention to the fact that what was called the wealth of the Church was largely used to feed an idle clergy that either labored to no purpose or else perpetrated sacrilege. In a better age, he notes, poverty was deemed the glory of the clergy. While the revenues appropriated by Protestant princes are used in part for secular purposes, the remainder is used to support "true ministers, who feed their flocks with the doctrine of salvation." In many cases monasteries have been supplanted by hospitals or schools.

To the "last and principal charge" of schism Calvin replies by distinguishing the name of "church" from the reality, and accusing the papal party of making a specious use of the name. The Prophets of the Old Testament and the Apostles of the New, he avers, also had trouble with the "church" of their day. While they did not forsake the divinely approved worship of this pretended church, yet they did not share in any idolatry. Protestants likewise have not forsaken the true Church, but have rather returned to it. Since the Church is essentially above all the body of Christ, Calvin insists that care be taken not to separate the body from its head. The body denies the head when it refuses to acknowledge sound doctrine; that is, the Gospel. For since, according to Ephesians 2:20, the Church is built upon the foundation of the Apostles and Prophets, a well-ordered Church is uniformly distinguished by two marks: the preaching of sound doctrine and the pure administration of the sacraments. Moreover, the true Church is one that "from incorruptible seed, begets children for immortality, and, when begotten, nourishes them with spiritual food (that seed and food being the word of God) and which, by its ministry, preserves entire the truth which God deposited in its bosom." The unity of the Church, therefore, which Calvin asserts to be held in sacred esteem by the adherents of the Reformation, is a unity that is based on union with Christ, and attested by a common consent to "sound doctrine."

Pastors are mere ministers and witnesses of the truth of God, and hence to make the unity of the church dependent upon obedience to them, rather than upon the truth which they are to proclaim, is to substitute the means for the end. To make the unity of the Church dependent upon submission of the pope is unreasonable: "I deny that See to be Apostolical, wherein nought is seen but a shocking apostasy—I deny him to be the vicar of Christ, who, in furiously persecuting the gospel, demonstrates by his conduct that he is Antichrist—I deny him to be the successor of Peter, who is doing his utmost to demolish every edifice that Peter built—I deny him to be the head of the Church, who by his tyranny lacerates and dismembers the Church, after dissevering her from Christ, her true and only Head."

Calvin writes that he is not averse to the reformation of the Church by means of a general council. But since the various nations of Christendom are too busily engaged in making war, or in other secular pursuits, and since the pope is doing all he can to prevent the meeting of a general council, this approach to reformation is not a promising one. Since, moreover, Calvin continues, a council approved by Rome would turn out to be a council controlled by Rome, and since the evils rampant in the Church threaten at any moment to bring about the "breaking up of the whole Church," which, according to Calvin, would be "the most miserable thing of all," it is up to the German princes to reform religion in their lands, before it is forever too late. Calvin notes that heresies like Donatism and Pelagianism were dealt with by provincial synods. Though the bishops should be taking the lead in working for reformation, Calvin writes, their failure to do so does not discharge the princes from their obligation, which derives from their possessing the means to effect it.

A DISPUTATION OF THE SACRAMENT OF THE EUCHARIST

Author: Peter Martyr Vermigli (1500-1562)
Type of work: Sacramental theology
First published: 1549

Principal Ideas Advanced

In the sacrament of the Lord's Supper the substance of the bread and wine is not altered.

The body and blood of Christ are spiritually present and are joined sacramentally to the bread and wine; they are received by faith, hence only by believers.

The life of Peter Martyr Vermigli has recently been aptly characterized as that of an ecumenical reformer. (J. C. McLelland, *The Visible Words of God; An Exposition of the Sacramental Theology of Peter Martyr Vermigli*, Edinburgh and London, 1957.) Certainly Peter Martyr's labors in behalf of the Reformation knew no national boundaries. Born in Italy, probably in Florence, he enjoyed at least the beginnings of a classical education before entering the Order of Augustinian Hermits. He continued his studies in the monastery and was able to attend lectures at the University of Padua, then a famous center of Aristotelian studies, where he obtained the doctorate in divinity. A successful preacher and administrator, he found time to teach himself Greek and Hebrew in order to further his study of the Bible. During a three-year stay at Naples he came under the influence of the "Evangelical Catholic" Juan de Valdez (c.1500-1541) and subsequently distinguished himself as a vigorous monastic reformer. In 1541 he became prior in Lucca. His educational and disciplinary reforms led to the establishment of a Reformed congregation which survived for several years. It was at Lucca that he first administered the communion in an evangelical manner. He was forced by impending persecution to flee the city in 1542.

He was warmly welcomed in Zurich, in Basle, and in Strassburg, where he succeeded Wolfgang Capito (1478-1541) as professor of theology. Here he won the lifelong friendship of the reformer Martin Bucer (1491-1551), who encouraged him to deepen his knowledge of the Church Fathers. While generally in theological agreement with Bucer, Martyr deplored the latter's tendency to use ambiguous language in order to obscure differences among Protestants concerning the Lord's Supper.

In 1547 King Henry VIII of England (reigned 1509-1547) died, and though initially it was resolved to make no major changes in religion during the new king's minority, certain steps were taken to advance the cause of the Reformation in England. One of the most important of these steps was the invitation extended almost immediately to Peter Martyr to become Regius Professor of Divinity at Oxford. He was soon recognized as the chief instrument of Archbishop Thomas Cranmer (1489-1556) in making the Anglican Church truly Protestant.

The accession of Mary the Catholic to the English throne (1553), forced Martyr to return to Strassburg. Here he continued for three years as professor of theology, but under heavy pressure from the Lutheran party, who finally procured an order from the senate ordering him to avoid certain issues and to "restrain his zeal" on others. Rather than submit to the curtailment of his academic freedom, Martyr accepted a call to become professor of Hebrew in Zurich.

During this last period of his life, Martyr was invited to take part in the Colloquy of Poissy (1561), held before the Queen-Regent of France (Catherine de Medici, 1519-1589), like himself a native Italian. He was instrumental in rallying support for his disciple and successor in Strassburg, Jerome Zanchius (1516-1590, another Italian), who was under heavy attack from the Lutherans.

Of all Martyr's "ecumenical" labors, his work in England appears to have been most fruitful. The University of

Oxford had not taken kindly to Protestantism, and Martyr often seemed to be fighting a lonely battle, in which he was mainly sustained by the support of Archbishop Cranmer and the young King Edward VI (1537-1553). The opposition seized upon Martyr's exposition of I Corinthians 10:16,17. Martyr was challenged to a disputation about the nature of Christ's presence in Holy Communion, and though his challenger fled the country, the traditional point of view was defended by three scholars of the University. The commission in charge of the debate, headed by the king's tutor, Richard Cox (c.1500-1581, chancellor of the University and later Bishop of Ely) did not render a formal decision, though Cox in his closing remarks highly commended Martyr. The disputation took place on May 29, 30, 31 and June 1, 1549. Martyr had the proceedings printed the same year, and an English translation was published soon afterwards.

In his opening statement Martyr defends disputations in general on the ground that they do not necessarily lead to strife and discord, and that Christ and the Apostles did not hesitate to enter into disputations. He notes that the common people are greatly addicted to the traditional view of the Lord's Supper, which he is combatting with his three theses:

"1. In the sacrament of the Eucharist, there is no transubstantiation of the bread and wine, into the bodie and bloud of Christ.

"2. The bodie and bloud of Christ is not carnallie and corporallie in the bread and wine; nor, as others speake, vnder the shewes of bread and wine.

"3. The bodie and bloud of Christ is sacramentallie conionied to the bread and wine."

He calls attention to the fact that, in deference to the usage of Scripture, he has used the terms "carnallie" and "corporallie" rather than their scholastic equivalents "substantiallie" and "reallie." He defines the sacramental conjunction as "a most effectual signification" that must be clearly distinguished from a "mere" signification, which he associates with the Anabaptists, the Marcionites, the Valentinians, and the Manichees.

The opening statement of his first opponent, Dr. Tresham (a canon of Christchurch), invokes against Martyr's theses the authority of the Gospels and of St. Paul, the consent of the whole world and perpetual usage, the "great authoritie of our holie mother the church" expressed in its decrees against men like Berengar of Tours (c.999-1088) and John Wycliffe (c.1329-1384, Oxford scholar and reformer), the testimony of "the right catholic fathers" properly interpreted, and the official pronouncements of the government of the present king.

The disputation of the first day revolved around certain arguments from the Bible and the Church Fathers that can be summarized in three points. (1) Martyr argues from the fact that Scripture nowhere teaches a change of substance, but rather refers to the bread as bread even after its consecration, to the conclusion that the substance of the bread remains. He supports this conclusion by citations from Origen (c. 185-c.254, head of the Catechetical School in Alexandria), Epiphanius of Salamis (c.315-403, Metropolitan of Cyprus), John Chrysostom (c.347-407, patriarch of Constantinople), Augustine of Hippo (354-430, greatest of the

Latin fathers), Cyril of Alexandria (died 444, widely regarded as the best writer on Christology in the Eastern Church), Pope Gelasius I (reigned 492-496), and Pope Gregory I (reigned 590-604). His opponent replies that transubstantiation is implied in Jesus' words, "This is my body," and that the Scripture passages cited by Martyr must be interpreted figuratively. (2) Martyr invokes the authority of Cyprian (died 258, Bishop of Carthage) and of Theodoret (c.393-c.458, Bishop of Cyrrhus), who used the analogy of the two natures in Christ to illustrate the co-existence of true bread with the true body of Christ in the Eucharist; Irenaeus (c. 130-c.200, Bishop of Lyons) is cited as using the analogy of men's bodies, which without change of substance, were changed into immortal bodies through partaking of the Communion. (3) From the fact that Christ's (literal) body was created, Martyr argues to its restriction to one locality at any one point of time; namely, since the Ascension, to Heaven.

During the course of the second day's disputation, Martyr spelled out his doctrine of analogy, which is regarded as central, not only for his eucharistic theology, but for his theology as a whole: "In all sacraments there ought to be an analogie or proportion observed and kept betweene the sacrament and the matter of the sacrament. . . . Seeing therefore the Eucharist hath for the matter of the sacrament both the bodie of Christ, and the mysticall bodie; ye which by transubstantiation take awaie the bread and wine, ouerthrowe the analogie, which consisteth therein; that even as we be naturallie nourished by bread and wine, so by the bodie and bloud of Christ, we are nourished spirituallie, both in the outward and inward man. And as concerning the mysticall bodie, therein dooth the similitude stand; that even as bread and wine consist of much gathering and pressing togither, that is to saie, of manie graines of corne, and manie grapes; so the mysticall bodie standeth of manie members, which growe vp togiether in one."

Martyr calls attention to the fact that a sacrament is, by definition, a sign. Augustine, Tertullian (c.160-c.220, earliest of the great Latin Fathers) and Jerome (c.342-420, author of the authoritative Latin version of the Bible) are cited as teaching a figurative interpretation of the saying, "This is my body."

On the third day, Martyr defined his position with respect to the problem of authority in religion. He acknowledges the inward authority of the Holy Spirit and the outward authority of Holy Scripture. The Church Fathers do not possess an independent authority of their own: "Trulie I will not contemne the fathers, naie rather I will attribute much to them, when they speake according to the scriptures. . . . [Yet since] I see that manie are addicted vnto them superstitiouslie, which perpetuallie crie out; The fathers, the fathers, and doo thinke them to be euermore against vs, I thought it good to shew such men, that they make most of all for vs." His attitude towards Church councils is similar.

Martyr proceeds to show that in the sacrament there are two kinds of eating, proper and metaphorical, and two kinds of nourishment, natural and spiritual. He approvingly cites Irenaeus to the effect that by the second kind of eating, that is, by embracing the body and blood of Christ in faith, men's minds are "filled with the spirit and with grace; secondlie, our bodie is renewed, that it may from daie to daie become a fit instrument for the spirit, and so made more capable of the blessed resurrection." It is no "feined flesh" that is received, but the true body of Christ. Nor is the sacrament absolutely indispensable: ". . . for both with the signes and without the signs, while we consider in our minds Christ crucified for vs, and his bloud shed for vs, and doo so beleeue, we are truelie made partakers of him: but yet the signes being ioined therewithall, which the holie Ghost vseth as instruments, for the better printing of faith in our minds, we are verie much holpen. For we be verie slacke vnto diuine things, and therefore we haue need of outward sacraments."

On the fourth day Martyr summarized his arguments. In support of the first of his three theses he notes that (1) Augustine said that we are made partakers of Christ's body and blood in baptism, yet there is no transubstantiation there; (2) Paul said: "Ye are the body of Christ" (I Corinthians 12:27), and there is no transubstantiation here, though upon reflection Christ will be found to be more intimately joined to His people than to the sacramental bread; (3) transubstantiation by analogy supports the Marcionites, who attributed only the appearance of a human body to Christ; (4) transubstantiation involves a miracle wholly unknown to the Fathers; namely, the preservation of accidents apart from their proper substance; (5-7) if transubstantiation were a fact, then Christ ate Himself when he partook of the Last Supper, and many other absurdities follow that require a multitude of miracles in order to be explained. In support of his second and third theses Martyr points out that (1) there is no advantage to be derived from a Christ hidden in the signs that is not abundantly vouchsafed by Christ in Heaven; (2) Jesus Himself "confuted the carnall eating of his bodie" in dealing with the Capernaites (John 6:22-65); (3) Augustine called the sacraments visible words, and Jerome agreed with him that we eat the flesh of the Lord by means of the word; (4) men are cleansed in Christ's blood every time they turn to him in faith and repentance; (5) Scripture knows only two comings of Christ, not a third in the sacraments; (6) the definition of a sacrament as a visible signs of an invisible grace agrees far better with "signification" than with transubstantiation; (7) truths of Scripture should be interpreted in a simple way that will be conducive to faith and that will not necessitate a multiplication of absurdities and "miracles." Since eating the body of Christ is an act of faith, it is evident that unbelievers do not receive the body and blood of Christ in the sacrament.

Martyr was to publish several more works dealing with the nature of Christ's presence in the Lord's Supper, notably the eight-hundred-page *Defensio . . . adversus Gardinerum* (1559). John Calvin (1509-1564), the mastermind of Reformed Protestantism, regarded his work on the subject as definitive. It should be noted, however, that Martyr's position is actually closer to that of Ulrich Zwingli (1484-1531), the Reformer of German-speaking Switzerland, and closest to that of Thomas Cranmer. Martyr and Cranmer share with Zwingli the denial of a substantial presence of Christ in the sacrament. They also share with him

—and with the Catholic tradition before the late-medieval ascendancy of the view that the Mass is a literal sacrifice, propitiatory for the living and the dead—the understanding that the Lord's Supper is above all a eucharist, a sacrifice of praise. Martyr expresses it thus: "The substance of our sacrifice is, a giving of thanks for the bodie of Christ given vpon the crosse. And by reason of this giving of thanks, faith and confession, the fathers said, that the bodie of Christ is offered in the supper."

Cranmer beautifully elaborates his conception in his rendering of the prayer *Supplices* in the First Book of Common Prayer, which was introduced in the English churches some eight days after the conclusion of Martyr's Disputation. The prayer supplicates God "to accept our sacrifice of Prayse and thanks-geuinge . . . and here wee offre vnto the (O Lord) oure self, oure souls, and bodyes, to be a reasonable, holy and liuelie sacrifice vnto thee."

When Cranmer wrote *A Defense of the True and Catholic Doctrine of the Sacrament* in 1550, the doctrine he defended was essentially the same as Peter Martyr's.

THE DECADES

Author: Johann Heinrich Bullinger (1504-1575)
Type of work: Sermons on Reformed doctrine
First published: 1549-1551

Principal Ideas Advanced

The Holy Scriptures of the Old and New Testaments are the sole rule of faith and practice, from which we learn what we are to believe concerning God, and what God requires of us.

From the Scriptures we learn the content of true faith: that God is our creator, sustainer, and the redeemer of fallen humanity by means of the sacrificial death of His Son, Christ Jesus.

By faith in Christ, without works, we are freely justified, pardoned, and forgiven of our sins, and are made righteous so that the fruits of righteousness, good works, are then brought forth.

The Church of Rome is not the true Church; the latter is inwardly constituted by true believers and is visibly found wherever the Word of God is faithfully preached and the sacraments of baptism and the Lord's Supper are properly administered.

Johann Heinrich Bullinger was born in 1504 in a small town near Zurich and was educated at the University of Cologne, from which he received a Master's degree in 1522. Bullinger was intimately acquainted with Ulrich Zwingli (1484-1531), and he was very much influenced by the latter's view of the Eucharist. In 1531 Bullinger was appointed to the pulpit of the Cathedral of Zurich to fill the vacancy left by the death of Zwingli. Bullinger occupied this important post until his death in 1575. His publications were voluminous and frequent; his pastoral, ecclesiastical, and civil activities were many, and his home was ever open to befriend refugees from countries ravaged by religious persecution. His moderation and sincerity were eminently conspicuous during his long unsuccessful efforts to effect a reconciliation between the Lutherans and the Church of Zurich on the question of the sacraments. He did manage to reach an agreement with John Calvin (1509-1564) and Guillaume Farel (1489-1565) on the Lord's Supper, thereby uniting the churches of Zurich and Geneva on the issue.

The *Decades* consists of five groups of ten sermons, published in English in four volumes. The first and second decades were published in Latin in 1549, the third and fourth in 1550, and the fifth in 1551. There have been three editions of the English translation of the *Decades;* namely, in 1577, 1584, and 1587. The sermons were widely read, and they exerted considerable influence outside Switzerland, especially in the Church of England, during the reign of Queen Elizabeth, where the sermons were required reading for those studying to be preachers.

The fifty sermons of the *Decades* cover the whole range of Reformed doctrine and practice. They are marked by a strict adherence to the Scriptures of the Old and New Testaments, by doctrinal content, by clarity, and by Reformation piety. They successfully combine doctrinal exposition with devotional meditation, controversy with charity, predestination with responsibility, and the law with grace.

Bullinger shared with the Reformers the conviction that the Scriptures and the Scriptures alone constitute the sole infallible authority in all matters pertaining to faith and practice. Several sermons are devoted to this theme. According to Bullinger, every doctrine of the Christian faith, every rule as to how to live rightly, well, and holily, and all true and heavenly wisdom are to be derived from the testimonies and determinate judgments of the Word of God, and from no ecclesiastical body.

The *verbum Dei,* the Word of God, signifies the very speech of God and the disclosure of God's will; it was first uttered by Christ, the Prophets and Apostles, and then registered in writings which are rightly called holy and divine. The Word of God declares truly that God is just, good, pure, immortal, and eternal, so that what He has declared in His word is also to be received as true, just, without deceit, without guile or error, and as holy, pure, good, immortal, and everlasting.

Since God alone is truth, Bullinger writes, and since the Word of God is truth, it is God who is the beginning and cause of His Word. From the beginning of the world, God revealed Himself to the world by speaking to men in a voice easily understood by men. He spoke to Adam, to Abraham, to Moses, and to the Prophets.

Bullinger tells how holy men of old taught their children what God had revealed: that of His natural goodness, He desired men to know the truth and to be like God Himself, holy, happy, and blessed. For this reason, in the beginning God created man in His image, so that man, too, could be good, holy, immortal, and the blessed partaker of God's good gifts. Man did not remain in this happy condition, for because of the influence of the Devil, and his own disobedience, man fell into sin, death, and misery, thereby changing his image into that of the Devil.

Because of His infinite mercy, God did not leave man in the state of sin and misery into which he had fallen, but He began anew the work of salvation, by which man is restored and set free from the bondage of sin and is once again made like unto God. To accomplish this work of redemption, Bullinger writes, God appointed the Incarnate Word, and by this taking of flesh, He united man to God. Finally, by dying in the flesh, God Himself cleansed, sanctified, and delivered mankind. By giving man His Holy Spirit, God made him once again similar in nature to Himself; that is, absolutely blessed and immortal. There remains, moreover, a great day of judgment, in which, though all men are gathered together, yet the righteous alone will receive the reward of Heaven, whereas the wicked will be consigned to eternal perdition.

God is the God of all men and of every nation, Bullinger claims. God has revealed His Word so that all men can come to a knowledge of the truth and the benefit of salvation. God has revealed Himself to men in order that they may know of Him and be saved; by faith in Christ, men might know who He is, and by what means salvation is possible.

Every point of true godliness is taught us in the Holy Scriptures, Bullinger insists. Nothing more is needed, neither the traditions of men, nor the inventions of deceivers.

Bullinger states that it is erroneous to believe that the Scriptures are so dark that they cannot be read by laymen, and he claims it is equally false to affirm that men have no need of exposition. It is God's will that His Word be understood. The difficulties that the Scriptures contain can be overcome by study, diligence, faith, and by skillful and proper means of interpretation. The Scriptures are difficult only to the unlearned and the malicious, not to the zealous and the godly reader. To the later they are plain and most assuredly certain.

A holy exposition of Scripture is, however, most profitable to the godly, Bullinger writes. The Scriptures are not to be corrupted by foreign expositions, nor by introducing human fantasies. They must never be expounded in a way that is contrary to the articles of Christian belief, nor must their exposition be repugnant to the love of God and our neighbor. The Scriptures are to be expounded with zealous heart, after earnest prayer, in a manner that takes note of the occasion upon which something is spoken, and of what precedes, what follows, and of when it was spoken; and of what order, to whom, and by whom it was uttered.

Bullinger agreed with the other Reformers, with Luther, Calvin, and Ulrich Zwingli (1484-1531) that the Scriptures cannot be properly interpreted in a manner that denies the true faith. For, with them, Bullinger held that it is by faith alone that a sinner is justified. To the mind, faith is a most evident seeing; to the heart a most certain perceiving of things invisible and eternal. Faith is a steadfast assuredness of conscience, which embraces Christ as He is offered in the Gospel; faith is a gift of God, poured from Heaven into man, by which he is taught with an indubitable persuasion to lean wholly on God and His Word. The latter contains God's promise of eternal life and of all good things in Christ; it contains all things that are to be believed.

The beginning and cause of faith is God Himself, who inspires faith in our hearts by his Holy Spirit, writes Bullinger. To implant faith, God uses ordinary means; namely, the preaching of His Word. By sending His Holy Spirit into our hearts and minds, God causes us to believe what we have learned to believe from the teaching of His word. True faith is not an irrational acceptance of everything possible; it is ruled and bound to the Word of God; it bends toward God and leans on His Word alone. The object and foundation of true faith is God and His Word alone. The Word holds that God in Christ promises life and every good thing through Him. True faith is ignorant of all division, Bullinger insists; it is the true knowledge that maketh us wise. To have faith is to believe that all the words of God are true, and that God has a good will towards all mankind, not only in general but towards the individual believer. Thus, each Christian believer believes that the soul is immortal, that our bodies rise again, that the faithful will be saved, and that unbelievers will perish.

Faith makes us happy and alive, Bullinger asserts; it joins us to God, and it justifies without works. To justify is to acquit from judgment and to lift the sentence of condemnation. To justify is to remit offenses, to cleanse, to sanctify, and to give life everlasting. Justification is the absolution and remission of sins; it is the washing away and forgiveness of sins, the deliverance from condemnation. Justification means to be adopted by God as His sons. Before the judgment seat of God, when our condemnation was to be pronounced, Christ took our sins upon Himself, and by His sacrifice on the cross, He purged us of our iniquities, so that upon Him God laid our fault and punishment. The pain and offence of our sin have been taken away by Christ; with His stripes, we are healed. The pain, punishment, and correction were laid upon our Lord. Whoever believes in the only-begotten Son of God partakes of His righteousness, is justified by Him, absolved from sin, and made heir of everlasting life.

Bullinger describes faith as a gift of God's grace, containing within it the promise of righteousness. Our own merits and works have no place in justification. Our works are never perfect, but our salvation is assured by God's free gift. It does not follow from the fact that the faithful are justified by faith without works, that faith is utterly destitute of good works, for wherever there is faith there are good works. After the faithful are justified and made righteous, they bring forth the works of righteousness. True faith is in fact the very wellspring and root of all virtues. From it springs peace of conscience, patience, hope, and charity, the fulfilling of the law, which contains the very sum of good works.

The content of true faith is summarized in the Apostle's Creed, Bullinger writes; the works that it produces are summarized in the love of God and the sincere love of one's neighbor, in the keeping of the moral law as found in the Ten Commandments.

The believer who unfeignedly turns to God in an act of repentance and who humbly acknowledges his sins in true confession to God is forgiven by Him, who alone is to be adored and worshiped.

Christ alone is the intercessor and advocate with the Father; the saints are not to invoked, nor does the Church stand between God and man. The Church, says Bullinger, is the whole company of the faithful, those who are triumphantly in Heaven, and those who are militantly on earth; it is not identical with its visible institutional form. The true Church, the invisible Church, is made up of true believers, and is free of heretics and hypocrites.

According to Bullinger, the visible Church of God on earth has two special and principal marks, the sincere preaching of the word of God, and the lawful use of the sacraments of Christ, of which there are two, baptism and the Lord's Supper. The upstart Church of Rome is not the Church, Bullinger insists, for the Church of Rome has departed from the true Church, and thus no longer bears its marks.

A DEFENSE OF THE TRUE AND CATHOLIC DOCTRINE OF THE SACRAMENT

Author: Thomas Cranmer (1489-1556)
Type of work: Reformation theology
First published: 1550

Principal Ideas Advanced

The Lord's Supper is a sacrament to be observed in the Christian Church in accordance with the teaching of the New Testament.

The Roman doctrine of transubstantiation is a perversion of the Apostolic and patristic tradition.

Christ is truly present in the Lord's Supper spiritually and wholly but not substantially or corporeally.

Repentance and faith on the part of the communicant are necessary to effective reception of the elements.

Because the Mass is so prominent and central in Roman Catholic religious observances, it was inevitable that all who supported the Reformation movement found themselves involved in a discussion of its revision. The title of Thomas Cranmer's first book devoted to the subject suggests the context in which he worked: *Defense of the True and Catholic Doctrine of the Sacrament of the Body and Blood of Christ.* Cranmer's treatise did not propose to set forth a position that was new in Reformation writing, but to clarify his own position as Archbishop of Canterbury and to support the main lines of criticism of the Roman position. The work established Cranmer's reputation as a competent theologian, despite bitter criticism by rival thinkers.

The plan of the book is simple and

straightforward. It is divided into five parts dealing in succession with the true observance of the Eucharist, the central error of the doctrine of transubstantiation, the nature of the presence of Christ in the bread and wine, the reception of the elements, and the nature of the sacrifice involved.

All the Reformers made much of Scriptural exegesis in order to demonstrate how far removed from Apostolic teaching the history of doctrine had travelled, and the Archbishop made ample use of previous studies. He was widely read and did not allow his administrative duties to rob him of his theological research interests. His industry therein is manifest. Especially to be marked is his competency in the use of patristic literature. It might not be too much to say that he set an example and tone which influenced Anglican scholars thereafter. To be able to demonstrate that Roman doctrine had departed from the teaching of the Church Fathers as well as from Scripture was a telling device of debate when tradition counted heavily in settling points of dispute. Another line of defense involved the use of arguments of reason, by which Cranmer hoped to expose the contradictions and absurdities of the doctrine being examined. "The papistical doctrine," Cranmer averred, "is against all our outward senses." The point, of course, is not that all the tenets of religion must be validated by sentient experience, for Cranmer acknowledged freely that faith claimed matters to be true which were unseen. What was in question was the sheer incredulity with which reason confronted the claims made for Eucharistical transsubstantiation, the miraculous change of bread and wine to the body and blood of Christ. The substance of the elements of the sacrament was changed, it was said, while the accidents, or characteristics, remained the same. The explanation rested on Aristotelian metaphysics. The separation of substance and accidents was a metaphysical divorce, which Cranmer believed to be utterly irrational, as indefensible as it was unnecessary for a true doctrine of the Lord's Supper. Thus, he writes: "And although all the accidents, both of the bread and the wine, remain still, yet, say they, the same accidents be in no manner of thing, but hang alone in the air, without anything to stay them upon." Cranmer could not accept change which did not involve change of the accidents or sentient qualities.

It was Cranmer's contention that the real presence of Christ was in the elements, but the body of Christ was not present substantially. He was far from supporting a theory of bare signs or mere symbols. The body of Christ is in Heaven, he contended, and it will return only at the last day. The real presence is not to be equated with the historical presence in the incarnate life of Jesus before His crucifixion.

It was absurd to Cranmer that the body of Christ should be said to be masticated and torn by human teeth like a piece of corporal flesh in a cannibal feast. On this he animadverts at length in his answer to a criticism by the Bishop of Winchester, Stephen Gardiner (c.1490-1555). Cranmer claims for his own opinions that they hold "that Christ is present in His sacraments, as they teach also that He is present in His word, when He worketh mightily in the hearts of the hearers." The body of Christ is truly present but sacramentally, not organically, and not in such a manner that the body of Christ is really two, one in Heaven and the other on the altars of the churches.

It would be saying too much to claim that Cranmer is always intelligible in these distinctions on which he wrote at great length in his treatises on the Eucharist. However, his point that the historical Incarnation is to be distinguished carefully and clearly from the sacramental presence is one which Cranmer affirms most persuasively.

The real presence is in the sacrament whether discerned by the recipient or not, Cranmer contends. When the elements of the sacrament are taken by the faithful, they are efficacious in spiritual benefits; when they are taken by an unworthy person, they are figurative only and do not convey grace. A helpful analogy is suggested by consideration of the fact that during His earthly ministry God was present in the person of His Son, but was not always recognized and received as such. Faith is necessary to discern the truth. The spiritual state of the recipient is a necessary factor in the action, and this subjective condition must be accorded full significance together with the objective divinely promised deed and action. Worship is not to be directed to the bread: "All that love and believe in Christ Himself, let them not think that Christ is corporally in the bread, but let them lift up their hearts unto heaven and worship Him sitting there at the right hand of His Father." The tendency is thus always to keep close to the common thrust of Reformed doctrine that the Christ who comes in the sacraments is the same Christ who comes in the preaching of the Word; and though the media are different and demand explanations appropriate to the three media of pulpit, table, and baptistry, it is the same Lord who is effectively communicating Himself in all three in accordance with the conditions of faith: "This spiritual presence of Christ is to the man who putteth his whole hope and trust of his redemption and salvation in that only sacrifice which Christ made upon the cross."

What is effected by a worthy participation in the Eucharist? It is undoubtedly a remembrance of the ultimate sacrifice on the cross, and the Archbishop insists on this over and over again. There is recollection and gratitude for a finished work by which men may be saved from their sins.

Christ is not only remembered, however, but also spiritually received as the faithful recipient shares in communion; God works in the heart of the recipient in all things necessary to his salvation. This is expressed in the idea of eternal life which is to be regarded both as a future realization of the purpose of God for His people, and also as a present gift which is bestowed in time and will be consummated beyond death. The presence of Christ and His very life are in the believer rather than on a table or altar in material substances.

Thus, Cranmer argues, the Eucharistical communion produces ethical effects in character and conduct. There is, as it were, an offering which the faithful give to God as a response to the offering which God has provided for them. Any thought that a man can accept the Holy Spirit without manifesting the fruits of the Spirit is a grave error. "Wherefore," writes Cranmer, "whose heart soever this holy sacrament, communion and supper of Christ will not kindle with love to his neighbors and cause him to put out of his heart all envy, hatred and malice and to grave in the same all amity, friendship and concord, he deceiveth himself, if he think that he hath the Spirit of Christ dwelling within him." In this way faith and works are united in sustained obedience, and the life of Christ is continued in the life of each believer. Participation in the sacrament is itself an act of obedience which sustains and depends on that which initiates it. The analogy is pressed that just as eating and drinking ordinary food nourishes and strengthens the physical body, so sharing in the Lord's Supper nourishes and strengthens the soul for the fight against evil.

Further, the bonds of union which unite Christians in the Church are strengthened. Cranmer follows St. Paul closely in teaching that participation in this sacrament is not just an individual matter. The unity of the Body of Christ is involved, and the faithful "so be joined unto Christ; and also together among themselves, that they do make but one mystical body of Christ, as St. Paul saith: 'We be one bread and one body, as many as be partakers of one bread and one cup.'" Thus, the love of Christ for His Church becomes the love which ought to be experienced within His Church. By viewing the dramatic action of the communion service, the hearts of all are inspired to sacrificial concern for the benefit of the community.

All this is said at length and enforced with repetition. Yet the polemical context is always so pressing that Cranmer has to meet the counter arguments of the Roman protagonists; consequently, a great deal of space is allotted to negative arguments. The use of negative arguments is characteristic of almost all the ponderous theological treatises of Cranmer's time, and the practice makes many passages very complex and not always free from ambiguity. Weighty scholarship was marshaled by both sides to support the older and the newer causes. Cranmer's contribution to the momentous struggle added greatly to the Reformed cause and was offered at a time when matters were at a critical stage in England. It is not the novelty of his views, but the correlation of them with the main doctrines of the Reformed party at a level of impressive learning that makes his work on the Lord's Supper one of the great treatises in the history of theology in England.

THE MAGDEBURG CENTURIES

Author: Matthias Flacius (1520-1575) [and others]
Type of work: Church history
First published: 1559-1574

Principal Ideas Advanced

[*A landmark in the history of ecclesiastical historiography, this thirteen-volume work surveys the history of the Christian Church from the first to the end of the thirteenth century, devoting a volume to each century (hence the name "Centuries") and following the same order of topics in the treatment of each century. A product of the second generation of the Reformation, its purpose was apologetic and polemical: a defense of Protestantism and an attack on Roman Catholicism.]*

The Church suffered a gradual deterioration after the Apostolic age, especially in the Middle Ages.

The Protestant Reformation restored the Church to its pristine purity.

A proper estimate of the *Magdeburg Centuries* requires that this work be seen in its historical context. The historians of the Middle Ages were chroniclers who for the most part recorded local history based on hearsay and often embroidered with legends. The humanists of the Renaissance introduced a critical use of sources and challenged the correctness of some prevailing opinions about the past. Following in their footsteps, the Protestant Reformers discovered in history a useful weapon to combat their opponents. Neither humanists nor Reformers, however, attempted anything more than an occasional foray into one or another corner of the past. It remained for the generation following the Reformation to attempt a bold and systematic interpretation of the whole sweep of the Church's history.

The man who was responsible for the first major undertaking of this kind since Eusebius of Caesarea (c.260-c.340) had written his great *Ecclesiastical History* twelve centuries before was Matthias Flacius. A native of Istria, in the present Yugoslavia, Flacius was diverted from the study of Catholic theology by an uncle who directed his attention to the reform proposals of Martin Luther (1483-1546). In 1541 Flacius went to Wittenberg, where under Luther's influence he finally reached settled religious convictions and adhered to them steadfastly, and even stubbornly, the rest of his life. For several years he taught in the University in Wittenberg, but when he became involved in a bitter controversy with Luther's colleague and successor, Philip Melanchthon (1497-1560), he found it expedient to move to Magdeburg. Later he was made professor of the New Testament in Jena, but there, too, he became embroiled in quarrels and spent his last years wandering about from Frankfurt to Strasbourg and to Basel.

It was during his stay in Magdeburg that Flacius developed his ambitious project of a history of the Church. "I am contemplating a great undertaking," he wrote to a friend in 1553, "an undertaking which is indeed beyond my strength but which, if carried out, could be of extraordinary benefit to the church. . . . I desire that a history of the church be written in which may be described, chronologically and systematically, how the true church and its religion gradually deteriorated from its original purity and simplicity in the time of the apostles. . . . The history should also describe how from time to time the church has also been restored by some truly godly men, how the light of truth now shone more brightly and now was more or less obscured by the growing darkness of godlessness, until finally in our own time, when truth appeared to be almost completely annihilated, through the boundless blessing of God true religion has been restored in its purity once again." In these words we have a good description not only of the early plan but also of the actual execution of the work.

The first thing Flacius did was to gather about himself a number of collaborators. A "society" was organized, headed by five "inspectors." Besides Flacius, these included Ebeling Allemann, a consul; Martin Copus, a physician; and John Wigand and Mathew Judex, clergymen, all living in Magdeburg. Through correspondence and the dispatching of emissaries, source materials were then gathered. "Traces of the church's history should be sought in the oldest documents," Flacius suggested. "The true history should be drawn out of the very depths of the sources and brought to light." The most diligent of the collectors of source materials was Marcus Wagner. He searched the libraries of Denmark, Scotland, Austria, and various parts of Germany. Books and manuscripts were bought, parts of others were laboriously copied, and everything was shipped to Magdeburg. There, under the direction of the inspectors, seven students were hired to copy excerpts from the assembled books and manuscripts. These were then arranged by century and divided according to predetermined topics. In all of this, Wigand reported, Flacius was "the captain and chief pilot."

The materials for each century were arranged in the same order according to sixteen topics, which became chapters in the published work. The first was a brief preview of a century, "that the reader may know what he ought to look for." The second described the extent of the Church, and its geographical expansion or retraction in a given century. The third recorded the persecutions suffered or the peace enjoyed. Major emphasis was given to the fourth chapter, headed "The Teaching of the Church." Here the findings were arranged according to a recurring pattern: teachings about the Scriptures, God, creation, angels, man and the Fall, original and actual sin, law, Gospel, predestination, justification, faith, good works, prayer, baptism, confession and absolution, the Lord's Supper, church, ministry, miracles, Antichrist, human traditions, marriage, magistracy, death, the end of the world, the Last Judgment, Heaven and Hell, and Purgatory. This long chapter is followed by the fifth, which treats the heresies of a given century. The sixth describes the rites and ceremonies employed by the Church and adds a section on the "customs of Christians." The seventh deals with the organization of the Church, the eighth with schisms, and the ninth with councils convened during a given century. The three succeeding chapters provide some account of the lives of prominent bishops, heretics, and martyrs. The thirteenth chapter describes miracles reported to have occurred. The fourteenth describes the location and condition of the Jews, and this is followed by a chapter given to an account of other religions. The final chapter reports the political changes that have taken place in the Roman Empire.

The first three volumes, which surveyed the first three centuries of the Church's history in the fashion indicated, were published in quarto by John Opirinus in Basel in the year 1559. They bore the title *Ecclesiastica historia . . . secundum singulas centurias . . . congesta per aliquot stu-*

diosos et pios viros in urbe Magdeburgica; that is, "Ecclesiastical History, century by century, compiled by a number of learned and godly men in the city of Magdeburg." The fourth volume appeared from the same press in 1560, the fifth and sixth in 1562, the seventh and eighth in 1564, the ninth in 1565, the tenth and eleventh in 1567, the twelfth in 1569, and the thirteenth in 1574. Three additional volumes, covering the fourteenth to sixteenth centuries, were in preparation but were not completed when, one after another, the leaders of the project died, and accordingly these volumes were never published.

The most obvious weakness of this history is its mechanical plan. The arrangement of the materials by centuries is arbitrary and does not do justice to movements in the life of the Church which were not confined so neatly within the span of a century. Apart from the centurial plan, the treatment of topics within each volume as separate and unrelated units contributes to the impression of artificiality. Persecutions are reported in the third chapter, but martyrs are not dealt with until the twelfth. Heresies are treated in the fifth chapter, but heretics not until the eleventh. Much more serious is the fact that, although the greatest emphasis is placed on the doctrines and the proclamation of the Church, what is said about teachings and beliefs is not related at all to how Christians lived and worshiped. The disjunction of the chapters is such that the reader is confronted with a lifeless mass of data and does not receive an organic impression of the Church as a living organism. Moreover, the rigidity with which the order of topics is pursued in volume after volume made it impossible to organize materials around men and movements that give a particular age its distinctive character.

The diligence in assembling sources at a time when great libraries and bibliographical tools were not yet available has already been mentioned. The compilers also gave evidence of a critical use of these sources. It was relatively easy to demonstrate that certain teachings and practices which were widely believed to have originated with the Apostles were actually of much later origin. It required more acumen to show that some canons and decrees of the early Middle Ages were forgeries. The objectivity of such historical criticism becomes suspect, however, when it is observed how uncritical the centuriators were in accepting as genuine the spurious epistle of Pontius Pilate to Emperor Tiberius. One can hardly avoid the conclusion that the underlying apologetic and polemical purposes of the history influenced its writers to be credulous when they were defending their own positions and critical when they were attacking the positions of their opponents. A case in point is the difference in the treatment of ancient and medieval miracles.

Despite such serious shortcomings in the *Magdeburg Centuries,* this work was a notable achievement. It was distinguished from all preceding works in the field of Church history by the comprehensiveness of its treatment, by the clarity of its organization, and by the extraordinary richness of its detail. It was reprinted and widely used. In the eighteenth century several attempts were made to revise and complete the work, but none of these was carried to a conclusion. Perhaps the best evidence of the greatness of Flacius' achievement was the fact that this "pestilential work," as it was called, was imitated by Roman Catholic opponents. Casare Baronius (1538-1607) undertook to demonstrate that the Church during the Middle Ages represented a continuation and not a deterioration of the Apostolic Church. This he attempted by gathering an equally prodigious amount of information and arranging it in a rigidly chronological fashion, year by year. The fruits of his labors were published in the twelve volumes of his *Annales ecclesiastici* (Rome, 1588-1607), which traced the history of the Church to the end of the twelfth century.

THE LIFE OF ST. TERESA OF ÁVILA

Author: Saint Teresa of Ávila (Teresa de Cepeda y Ahumada, 1515-1582)
Type of work: Spiritual autobiography
First published: 1562

Principal Ideas Advanced

True devotion consists in complete resignation of the self to God, who will work the good through those who obey Him.

The pillar of devotion is mental prayer, of which the first degree entails great human effort, although in subsequent degrees supernatural grace is chiefly effective.

The Christian ought to obey the Church even when it is wrong, confident that God will overrule its errors.

When St. Teresa wrote her *Life,* she still had twenty years to live. Her celebrated autobiography, therefore, gives no indication of the busy career as organizer and administrator upon which she was shortly to enter. Hitherto she had been preoccupied with her interior life, with supernatural visitations, and with mental prayer. The *Life,* accordingly, is devoted largely to these matters. Yet it is not a devotional manual or a treatise on mystical theology, but an animated personal narrative. Its bulk attests the vigor which the author brought to everything she did, just as its content betokens her lively sensibility and keen intelligence. Teresa wrote her *Life* on the instruction of one of her spiritual advisors, and the book was ostensibly for the use of priests and nuns. Her language is racy and idiomatic, and her story unfolds in an easy and informal manner.

If Teresa devotes comparatively little attention to the external events of her life, this is because up to the time when she founded her first monastery, there were not many events to relate. She laments the passing of childhood innocence, and the "wicked" life into which she fell at an early age. She finds little cause to complain of her parents, except that her mother read "tales of chivalry," and allowed these to fall into the hands of her children; but one of her cousins, with whom she liked to play, is severely censored for leading her into vain and frivolous practices. As she tells it, her fear of a bad reputation kept her from mortal sin, and she would have nothing to do with boys. But, because she was an active and self-willed girl, she seemed to herself always to be doing something wrong, especially considering her firm conviction that we must despise the world and strive for the joys of Heaven.

Teresa had her first taste of convent life when, on the death of her mother, she was placed in an Augustinian monastery as a boarder. Though she found life in the convent pleasant, she could not decide to give up the world entirely. This resolution was taken after she had returned to live with relatives, when, through the influence of religious books and the congenial example of a friend, she decided to enter the Carmelite monastery in Ávila. Because her father would not give his consent to her becoming a nun, she prevailed upon one of her brothers to take her to the convent; but, notified by the nuns of his daughter's action, the father came and "offered up his Isaac on Mount Carmel."

A serious illness, which overtook Teresa when she was in her early twenties, brought her to the threshold of death and left her with a paralysis from which she was three years in recovering. Earlier, Teresa had prayed that she might experience sickness in order to learn patience, and at first she bore her affliction with joy; but later, thinking how much better she could serve God in health, she prayed to be made whole. That, she says, was a mistake. We ought "to resign ourselves absolutely to the disposition of our Lord, who knows best what is for our good."

Teresa has little that is specific to tell us concerning her next fifteen years. These years cannot have been uneventful; but, as Teresa looks back over them, they seem to have been a time of lukewarmness and compromise, mainly due to her neglect of prayer: "I could wish I had permission to say how often at this time I failed in my duty to God, because I was not leaning on the strong pillar of prayer. I passed nearly twenty years on this stormy sea, falling and rising, but rising to no good purpose, seeing that I went and fell again."

When she was forty years old, a change took place which she regards as her true conversion. A picture of the wounded Christ and a copy of St. Augustine's *Confessions* were instrumental in bringing her to a new pitch of devotion. Kneeling before the picture, she felt as never before her inability to do anything of herself, and she was finally able to place her complete confidence in God. "It seems to me that I said to Him that I would not rise up till He granted my petition. I do certainly believe that this was of great service to me, because I have grown better ever since." The trouble had been that, from the time that she recovered from her illness, she had been trying to "reconcile God and the world." Now "the grounds of the warfare" were changed; having accepted "the vanity of the world," and having resigned herself to serving God in everything, she found a joy that she had not known since the time of her illness.

As Teresa entered upon her new commitment, she became increasingly dissatisfied with the lax discipline of the Carmelite order. When it came to her attention that the original rule had been much stricter, she determined to set up her own monastery and to govern it according to the original rule. Her efforts met with determined opposition from the city of Ávila and from numerous groups within the Church. The Father Provincial of her order, after first granting her permission, bowed to pressures and told her to abandon her plans. There were those, however, who encouraged her to go ahead, and by proceeding secretly, she was able to present the Provincial with a *fait accompli.* She had some struggles with Satan, who ventured to suggest that she had failed in her obedience; but she fended off the temptation by promising before the Holy Sacrament not to enter the house without the Provincial's permission. This he granted, after rebuking her (mistakenly, as she avers) for being motivated by the desire for fame.

In her struggles to found her monastery, Teresa was partly sustained by visions and voices, which, from her fortieth year, came to her with increasing frequency. Once, when she was having difficulty paying the workmen, St. Joseph, who was her particular saint and for whom her monastery was to be named, appeared to her, assuring her that God would provide the means. Another time, Mary and Joseph appeared together with a garment which they draped about her as a sign that she was cleansed from her sins, after which they promised that her desires to build the monastery would be realized. Another time it was the saintly hermit, Peter of Alcantara, then deceased, who appeared for the purpose of advising Teresa in the matter of an endowment which she had under consideration.

Of her "voices" or "locutions," Teresa says: "[They] are so frequent that I cannot count them; many of them are reproaches, and He sends them when I fall into imperfections. They are enough to destroy a soul. They correct me, however; for His Majesty gives both counsel and relief." Teresa explains that, although not heard with the bodily ear, these voices are perfectly distinct, and impossible to shut out or ignore; furthermore, she believes, there can be no possibility of confusing the voice of God with that of evil spirits or with suggestions of one's own mind. "The words formed by the understanding effect nothing," she says; "but, when our Lord speaks, it is at once word and work; and though the words may not be meant to stir up our devotion, but are rather words of reproof, they dispose a soul at once, strengthen it, make it tender, give it light, console and calm it."

Teresa's ecstasies, transports, and raptures occasioned much discussion in her own time. Her early advisors inclined to say that her experiences were of Satanic origin, and she suffered great anxiety until she found more understanding confessors. The *Life* abounds in careful descriptions of these mystical experiences, since part of Father Ibañez's purpose in having her write the *Life* was to put these experiences on record.

Of more value, however, to the student of religion is Teresa's lengthy discourse on mental prayer. Speaking without reference to the standard theological works on the subject, and recounting only what she had learned by experience, Teresa distinguishes four degrees of prayer. These, she says, may be compared to four ways of watering a garden. The first degree of prayer requires great effort on man's part and is like drawing water from a well bucket by bucket. Beginners in prayer must practice meditation, self-examination, and humiliation; and, despite the great labor involved, the rewards seem small. At the second degree, which Teresa compares to the introduction of an irrigation pump, supernatural aids are given. Some of man's other faculties begin to co-operate and to assist the will, and the spiritual satisfactions are great. The third state of prayer is like a running brook, in that the inspiration is provided by God's Spirit, and nothing remains to man's faculties save to direct its flow. Finally comes the prayer of union, in which the soul is freely watered as by a gentle shower of rain, at the cost of no human effort. The secret of progress in mental prayer, says Teresa, in words which were given to her by the Lord, is: "[The soul] undoes itself utterly, My daughter, in order that it may give itself more and more to Me: it is not itself that lives, it is I." Teresa was of the opinion that numerous devout persons who practice faithfully the first stage of prayer are permitted to experience the second stage, but that comparatively few attain to the third and fourth stages. The fourth stage, the prayer of unity, is not (we are reminded) the same as ecstasy or rapture.

A faithful daughter of the Counter Reformation, Teresa accepted on principle the absolute authority of the Catholic Church. To many mystics the institutional framework of religion has been an intolerable constraint, and there have been devout Catholics who felt little or no need for the sacraments. Not so, Teresa, for whom devotion to God required that one first do violence to the self. But obedience had a curious twist in the case of Teresa. Fully aware that Churchmen are fallible, she obeyed them as a matter of principle, but was, meanwhile, confident that God would shortly overrule human folly. Thus, when the Father Provincial called her to account for having secretly built her monastery, she saw herself in the role of Christ before the Sanhedrin: "I prayed and implored our Lord to help me, and my father St. Joseph to bring me back to his house. I offered up to him all I was to suffer, rejoicing greatly that I had the opportunity of suffering for his honour and of doing him service. I went persuaded that I should be put in prison at once; but this would have been a great comfort. . . . When [the Provincial] came, I was summoned to judgment, rejoicing greatly at seeing that I had something to suffer for our Lord. . . . I thought of Christ receiving sentence, and I saw how this of mine would be less than nothing."

As a matter of fact, Teresa was the founder of one of those distinctive orders that find their place in the Roman Catholic Church. With the able assistance of the zealous young monk who came to be known as St. John of the Cross (1542-1591), she established the Reformed or Discalced ("barefoot") order of Carmelites, and she promulgated a new type of mystical devotion which has not always been well-received within the Church. In many respects, the quietism of Miguel Molinos (1640-1697), who was imprisoned by the Inquisition for teaching that God visits men's souls by direct illumination without the aid of Gospel or sacrament, was a development of Teresa's teaching; and the Discalced Carmelites in France were particularly sympathetic to quietist teachings. (See, for example, Brother Lawrence [Nicolas Herman, c.1605-1691], *The Practice of the Presence of God.*)

DE REGNO CHRISTI

Author: Martin Bucer (1491-1551)
Type of work: Church doctrine; systematic theology
First published: 1577

Principal Ideas Advanced

The Church is the Kingdom of Christ, in which a covenant relationship with God has been established.

The doctrine of predestination means an election to salvation; salvation is dependent upon the eternal counsel of God, and for that reason man may be absolutely certain about salvation.

Special ministers are appointed by God to be responsible for doctrine and discipline within the Church; the elect allow themselves to be governed and guided by these ministers, who also teach, confining themselves strictly to the Holy Scriptures.

The marks of the true Church are the Scriptural character of its doctrine, the proper administration of the sacraments, its discipline, and its care of the poor.

The Kingdom of Christ is to be established in England by a reorganization of the political, social, and religious institutions within the country, so that the law of God will become the moral ideal for all.

In 1549, Martin Bucer, the Reformer of Strassburg, was invited to come to England by the Archbishop of Canterbury, Thomas Cranmer (1489-1556). It had been determined by Cranmer that Bucer would become Regius Professor of Theology at the University of Cambridge. While in England, Bucer wrote a book entitled *De regno Christi* (*Of the Kingdom of Christ*, written 1550; published in the *Scripta anglicana,* 1577). Bucer presented his book to King Edward VI, the reigning monarch of England at that time.

De regno Christi is Bucer's mature theological work, and it is the closest to a systematic theology of any of his works. In *De regno Christi,* Bucer was concerned to apply the doctrines of the Reformed Protestant Church to the political order. The fundamental ideas of the Reformation—concerning sin, grace, justification, and sanctification—were reproduced basically in harmony with the position of Martin Luther (1483-1546) and Philipp Melanchthon (1497-1560).

Bucer's work is a theologian's attempt to draw out the practical implications of theological ideas. Chapters on education, relief of the poor, marriage and divorce, business and the trades, judges, prisoners and penalties present in detail Christian suggestions for the conduct of practical affairs. The book is more an essay in social reform than it is a standard work of Reformed theology. Bucer concerns himself with the Church and its relationship to the state, and with the problem of how the Christian faith could be best exhibited to and practiced in the secular world.

For Bucer, theology was Biblically-oriented, and he believed that the

Christian faith was relevant to every aspect of man's life. Church organization and Church discipline were, he believed, essential ingredients of the Christian Gospel, and could be employed to make religion more meaningful to man.

In *De regno Christi* Bucer defined the nature of the Kingdom of Christ as "an administration and attainment of the eternal salvation of the elect of God, by which he himself, our Lord and King of heaven, by his doctrine and discipline administered through special ministers appointed for that purpose . . . gathers his elect to himself and incorporates them in himself and his church, and in it so governs them that, purged more fully from their sins, they may live well and blessedly." Bucer emphasized, therefore, the moral character of the Kingdom. The Gospel was to be the source of moral power. Love is the norm for the Kingdom. When love is established among men, then Christ rules. Morality was also conceived to be law. The Old Testament and the New Testament are not to be distinguished as Martin Luther had done in terms of Law and Gospel, said Bucer. Rather, the will of God, which is given in the whole Bible, is to be realized in all of the activities of life and to include the whole social and cultural life of man. The Kingdom comes only when the commandments of God and the truth of the Bible have permeated all life.

The Kingdom, however, consists also of the elect; that is, of those whom God has chosen for participation in the Kingdom. But election is realized only by the incorporation of the Christian into the Church of Christ. The Church is the "Kingdom of Christ" in which a new covenant with God has been established.

Bucer's idea of predestination is related closely to his concept of *Spirit*. Christ, who grants election by His Spirit, has by this act constituted the Church. The elect are those who have received the Spirit and are enabled to believe the Word and to live a virtuous life based upon the Holy Scriptures. The Kingdom of Christ is, therefore, Christ's lordship over those whom He has elected. It is they who make up the Christian Church. The Church is, furthermore, an institution or organization with offices and a polity, which permit the elect to form a community. The elect can gather about the Church; they can hear the Word and be obedient to the Word in their lives. Christ rules the Church through the ministers, which are his instruments for Church order. The elect, Bucer said, allow themselves to be guided and directed by the "ministry," which is "regularly constituted." This community is a community of love, whose membership is dependent upon ethical obedience to the commandments of God and Christ.

Throughout Bucer's discussion of the Kingdom of Christ, there is an emphasis upon its moral character, as well as upon the moral demands upon the individual which make him part of the Kingdom. In addition, Bucer emphasized Church discipline. Christ's "order" is superior to all human institutions, and for that reason, obedience to His word and commandments contribute to the shaping of human life. The word of Christ must be obeyed as a law.

Bucer never set up a sharp contrast between the Kingdom of Christ and the secular order. The political order has a spiritual task, he insisted. The ruler or the magistrate must be responsible to the community to provide the best life for its citizens. He must promote the highest ideals of morality, peace, and concord. But because Bucer asserted that the highest kind of morality is founded upon religion, it is the duty of the magistrate to establish the true religion in his country. The temporal order must be so constructed that the moral power of the Kingdom can influence the lives of every subject within it. Bucer asserted that although the secular government had to contribute to the creation of the Kingdom, the true magistrate is the Christian magistrate—all others are tyrants. The magistrate who is a Christian, and who serves the state, must not use religion for the maintenance of peace (as the tyrants do), but must propagate the Christian Gospel so that the Kingdom might be established. In this way, a Christian magistrate or ruler can serve the Church in a *direct* way. The Christian state is therefore that political structure which attempts to place all life under the law of the Bible.

Bucer called the Christian state the "commonwealth"; that is, that human community in which the welfare of the people is guaranteed by the Christian consciousness of the government. But the Christian state is also that state which has best utilized the political structures available, with the result that peace is a reality within that state.

Bucer did not believe that there should be a distinction between the state and the Kingdom. Legislation is based upon the precepts of Christ and the Decalogue, which Bucer equated with the law of God. Bucer did not believe that the existence of such a state might weaken the traditional forms of the Christian faith. According to Bucer, the sovereign in a kingdom (in England for example) is obliged, by virtue of his divinely appointed office, to promote a reformation of the Church. Bucer thereby provided the first distinctively Protestant theory of the supremacy of the British monarchs in matters involving the Church.

Bucer's plan to reorganize the Church in England presupposed that all of the social, cultural, and political life of England must be reconstituted according to the law of God. It was the responsibility of the state, however, to insure the welfare of its citizens. To do so involved the establishment of universities and schools, the regulation of begging, usury, and class differentiation. Bucer also believed that it was the task of the state to regulate marriage and divorce laws.

The type of Church structure and polity which is designated by the term Reformed ("Calvinistic") is in essence based upon the ideas of Martin Bucer. It was John Calvin, the Reformer of Geneva, who carried out Bucer's ideas and made them normative for the Reformed Church in Europe.

The Reformation had taken place in Strassburg sometime in the early 1520's. A group of highly educated and respected preachers had been converted from Roman Catholicism to the newly-expressed Lutheran Protestant faith. Bucer was the leader of this group within the Strassburg church community. The city council in Strassburg had encouraged the acceptance of evangelical practices in the parishes of the city, and the council permitted preachers to be elected by the separate parishes within the city. A reorganization of the Church took place soon after, which included the concept of Church property, the role of education within the churches, the nature of welfare programs, as well as a moral code ("Sittenmandat") and other policies to revitalize the Reformation church of Strassburg. The city council subsequently ordered the appointment of church wardens to help supervise the care of souls in the parishes. The wardens were elected by the city council and had as their task "the supervision of ministers," and the building of a vigorous Christian congregation in the city. Later the wardens received the right to determine true doctrine and to encourage discipline and regulate morality. In 1539, Bucer, recognizing the ineffectiveness of the office of church warden, insisted that the Church be constructed along the lines of the New Testament. There were to be four classes of officers: preachers, elders, teachers, and deacons. (It is easy to see the similarity between this and Calvin's "Ordonnances ecclesiastiques.") The elders, with the preachers, were to be responsible for the moral and religious discipline of the Church members, and were empowered to admonish and even excommunicate if necessary.

Bucer's order for the administration of the Church was based upon the belief that the government was responsible for the temporal and eternal welfare of its subjects. The government had to regulate religion; it was to be the guardian of a temporal order which supervised and ordered man's duties toward God. The true religion was to be established, and all idolatry destroyed. A moral atmosphere was also to be created which would be compatible with the true religion. The Church and its various functions, however, had to be respected, because it alone could determine the nature of preaching, the administration of the sacraments, and other spiritual acts within the Church.

Bucer's plan for the Church of England was based upon his Strassburg experiences. He wanted to create a "Christian commonwealth," in which Christ would be the King, governing through His Word. Christ's vicars, Bucer wrote, are the preachers who administer the Word and the teachers who interpret the Word. The sociopolitical order must be subject to the Word of God. Since under the Word of God, the civil government maintains order within the society, it may use the power of law and the sword. The Church also exists under the Word of God, and thus the Word of God becomes the authority for the related spheres of Church and state.

Although Bucer was not completely successful in establishing his Church orders in Strassburg, and although he was unable to transform the Church of England in any direct way, his program for the Kingdom of Christ has influenced entire generations of Christians in their considerations of the nature of Church polity and of the relationship of Church and state.

A TREATISE OF REFORMATION WITHOUT TARRYING FOR ANY

Author: Robert Browne (c.1550-1633)
Type of work: Separatist polemics (polemical theology)
First published: 1582

Principal Ideas Advanced

The respective spheres of Church and state must be sharply distinguished.

The Church is a voluntarily gathered congregation, united by covenant, and characterized by the personal holiness (righteousness) of its members.

The work of reformation must be carried forward without delay, until the suppression of all wickedness in the Church is accomplished.

The chief means of reformation is the power of preachers to excommunicate Church members that persist in wickedness.

The chief significance of this treatise is that it marks the point at which a strain in the Reformed tradition breaks away from this tradition and assumes an identity of its own. Brownism is the outgrowth of Elizabethan (Calvinistic) Nonconformity, which stands at the opposite extreme within the Reformed tradition from the "Erastianism" that underlay the Anglican establishment, and that was explicitly espoused by John Whitgift, Archbishop of Canterbury from 1583 to his death in 1604. The Archbishop regarded Church and state as simply two aspects of the one body politic, to be governed by the Crown in Parliament. The Puritans or Nonconformists strove for a Church that would be free from state control, while using the state to enforce the "godly discipline" that its exponents drew from the pages of Sacred Writ. Robert Browne virtually asserted the mutual independence of Church and state. While he did not hesitate to ascribe to the state an unlimited sovereignty in civil matters, he wholly denied its competence to interfere with the proper functioning of the Church, which he described as the inward and spiritual rule of Christ over His people by means of the Word, with such outward organization as this spiritual rule will give rise to.

Robert Browne was born of a family that had long been prominent in Rutlandshire. The date of his birth lies between 1550 and 1556. He was educated at Corpus Christi College, Cambridge, then considered a breeding ground of Nonconformity. Obtaining his bachelor's degree in 1572, he taught school for a while, but he was subsequently dismissed for his extreme religious views. After serving as a private tutor and preaching on the side, disdaining episcopal authorization, he settled in Norwich (1580) where he gathered, together with Robert Harrison (died c.1585), an assembly that may be regarded as the first Independent or Congregational church in England. The constitutional basis of this church was the covenant that was signed by all the members in 1581. Persecution that included the arrest of Browne and members of his church induced the two leaders and a group of their followers to take refuge in the Low Counties. In 1581 they settled in Middelburg, Zeeland, then a center of English commerce with the continent.

Here Browne published three treatises (1582) that were often bound together, and that constitute the bulk of his literary output. The longest of these, *A Booke which sheweth the life and manners of all true Christians; Also the pointes and partes of all divinitie, that is of the revealed will and worde of God, are declared by their severall Definitions, and Divisions in order as followeth,* is a systematic exposition of Browne's theology. The title is representative of the content: while "all divinitie" is discussed, Browne's main interest is in Christian life and conduct. Of central importance is his definition of the Church: "The Church planted or gathered, is a companie or number of Christians or beleeuers, which by a willing couenant made with their God, are vnder the gouernment of god and Christ, and kepe his lawes in one holie communion: because Christ hath redeemed them vnto holiness & happiness for euer, from which they were fallen by the sinne of Adam. The Church gouernment, is the Lordshipp of Christ in the communion of his offices: whereby his people obey to his will, and haue mutual vse of their graces and callings, to further their godliness and welfare."

A Treatise upon the 23. of Mathewe . . . is incomplete, and has often been omitted in published editions. Here Browne reprobates the use of (Aristotelian) logic and rhetoric in the exposition of the Bible, and sets forth his conception of proper Bible study, illustrating it by means of the exposition of verse one of Matthew 23. The text breaks off shortly after the point at which he had commenced to do the same thing for verses two and three. His approach is to expound the meaning of the verse and any difficulties that may be contained in it, to show the relation of the verse to the whole body of divinity, and to reveal whatever difficulties that may arise in connection with it; then to make the application, which includes proofs, rebukes, and exhortations. It is in this passage that he denies both that the Church of England is a true Church, and that those who refuse to separate from the fellowship of the former can in fact belong to the latter. He denounces the bishops as Romish beasts, and describes the alleged calling of Anglican clergy as illusory, because of the treatment they accord Christ and those who would restore Him to His rightful place in the Church. Sacraments administered within the Anglican establishment are said to be no more valid than those of the Church of Rome.

A Treatise of reformation without tarrying for anie, and of the wickednesse of those Preachers which will not reforme till the Magistrate commaunde or compell them is the best-known of the three treatises. It might be argued that it represents a more consistent application of the principles advanced by the French reformer John Calvin (1509-1564) in *The Necessity of Reforming the Church,* written some thirty-eight years earlier. Both Calvin and Browne affirm that Jerusalem is to "be built again . . . even in troublous times" (Dan. 9:25); Browne goes further and explains that this is true even though it is the magistrate that is causing the trouble, and that reformation must not tarry "for anie." Both Calvin and Browne were charged with subverting the authority of princes and alienating men from the Church; both reply that their opponents are "the men which trouble Israel," because they are rebelling against the rule of God (I Kings 18:18). Where Calvin had argued that certain great and fatal abuses had required the immediate reformation of religion, Browne argues that Protestantism is guilty of tolerating and practicing wickedness, and that *any* wickedness in the church is inconsistent with the Church's character as "the house of the living God, the pillar and ground of truth" (I Timothy 3:15). Browne was thus advocating the very rigorism that Calvin had disowned. It might be argued, however, that Browne's position was at least approximated by the later practice, if not the earlier theory, of Calvinist Geneva. ". . . there is nothing which the Lorde will not breake," wrote Browne, "if it be against his glorie, neither anie wickednes which the gouernement of his Churche is not able to put downe." As at Geneva, the chief weapon of Church government is to be excommunication. The name of God is said to be polluted by the presence of wicked persons at the communion table. The righteousness of God's people is interpreted to the effect that no open wickedness is to be allowed to continue among them: offenders are to be admonished and reclaimed, or, if this proves impossible, to be separated from the Church. "Therefore doth Paule call that parte of church gouernment, which is to separate the vngodlie, the power of our Lorde Iesus Christ." He adds, "For thereby are the Kings bounde in chaines, and the Nobles with fetters of yron, that they may execute vppon them, the iudgement that is written, Such honor bee to all his Saintes" (Psalm 149:8,9). While the emphasis seems to lie on personal imperfections, institutional faults are to be remedied as well: the observance of Christmas, Easter, Whitsuntide, and other such "traditions," which Browne says were "receyued from Baal," are to be abolished.

Browne is emphatic in distinguishing between spiritual and civil government, and he counts upon New Testament texts for proof. Where Christ says that His Kingdom is not of this world (John 18:36), the fact is that bishops and magistrates rule over the Anglican establishment, which is therefore a part of the world. According to I Corinthians 12, Christ's spiritual Kingdom has a certain hierarchical structure all its own: ". . . first Apostles, secondlie Prophetes, thirdlie, teachers, &c. Also helpers and spiritual guides." All these are understood as charismatic gifts, to be recognized and utilized by the churches. The present leaders of the Church of England are called blind guides, builders who reject the Kingdom and Spirit of God, to whom Christ is a stumbling-block. Refusing to see the spiritual implications of Christ's parable of the leaven (Matthew 13:33), they want Christ's Kingdom set up "with observation" (Luke 17:20); that is, by order of Parliament or the decrees of the bishops; until then they are unwilling to do anything, and continue to wear the yoke of Antichrist. Despising the true honor that comes from God alone (Job 5:44), they insist on honors bestowed by men, such as "The right Honorable my Lorde. &c. who is my very good Lord and Maister." Christ says that His Kingdom is within men (Luke 17:21), and Browne understands this above all in a moral sense: "Goe to therefore, and the outwarde power and ciuil forcings, let us leaue to the Magistrates . . . but let the Church rule in spirtuall wise, and not in worldlie maner: by a liuelie lawe preached, and not by a ciuill lawe written: by holinesse in inwarde and outwarde obedience, and not in straightnesse of the outwarde onelie."

Adopting the traditional image of the two swords, Browne accuses the clergy of having failed to use the sword that belongs to them, namely excommunication, and having borrowed the sword of the civil magistrate to inflict all sorts of nonspiritual penalties. As a result, the clergy is said to be despised by the people.

The proper task of the civil magistrate is "to rule the common wealth in all outwarde Iustice, to maintaine the right, welfare, and honor thereof, with outward power, bodily punishment, & ciuil forcing of men." Browne relies upon this affirmation of the legitimacy of the magistrate to answer the charge of Anabaptism hurled against him. When it is said that Moses, the kings of Judah, or the leaders of the postexilic community in Jerusalem had not only a civil but also a spiritual authority, Browne replies that as spiritual guides they prefigured and foreshadowed the Kingdom of Christ, which since His coming in the flesh is no longer exercised in shadow and type, but directly and properly; moreover, there are certain functions with respect to the Church which pertain to English magistrates as much as to Old Testament kings. Both are to protect the rights of the Church, as much as those of any other member of the commonwealth; both are to supply the temporal necessities of the Church; both may enforce Church laws on Church members; and both may command reformation. The last-named function, which is Browne's main concern, he attributes to the magistrate as a right, rather than a duty. Basically, reformation is the responsibility of the Church, and it is the preachers' shame that they wait for the magistrate to compel them to do their proper duty. Since when, asks Browne, is it the sheep's place to force the shepherd to do his job? Browne's criterion for distinguishing Christian from non-Christian magistrates is whether the magistrate supports or opposes the churches' proper functioning. A government that forcibly removes and imprisons divinely called preachers, whose call has been approved and ratified by the Church, thereby demonstrates its non-Christian character. While the civil government is charged with providing the temporal necessities of the Church, the Church is not ultimately dependent on this support. Browne notes that historically the Church has flourished most when the state was openly hostile. The state as such is exempt from Church control. But the magistrate as an individual is as much subject to pastoral care and discipline as any other Christian. A Christian magistrate will willingly submit to Church discipline; and with non-Christian magistrates the Church has nothing to do.

Browne flatly rejects the common theological distinction between ordinary and extraordinary callings. Lawful pastors and preachers of the present day, he asserts, are no more subject to state control than were the Apostles and Prophets. In fact, all ministers of the New Covenant surpass in dignity John the Baptist, who in turn outranked all that came before him

(Luke 7:28). Yet Scripture attributes to the prophet Jeremiah power over the nations, to pull up and root out, to build and to plant (Jeremiah 1:10). So the government of the Church is included in the pastor's calling. This conception of the role of the pastor marks a further departure from mainline Calvinism, which insisted on placing Church government in the hands of a representative body that included, in addition to ministers, a number of lay elders.

For Browne the covenant is of central importance, but he is not a covenant theologian, either of the Continental or of the English school. The covenant idea functions for him in much the same way it functioned for the continental Anabaptists; namely, as the foundation of Church polity. It implies three principles: the outward autonomy of the individual congregations, the voluntary principle with respect to Church membership, and visible holiness as the specific characteristic of the visible Church. So Browne calls attention to the fact that Israel's covenant with its death penalties did not take effect until it had been voluntarily embraced (Exodus 19:3-8). He denies that covenant blessings can be inherited, thus striking at the heart of covenant theology; each generation, he affirms, must enter into covenant with God by a free choice of its own. Hence a Christian is defined as one who "is redeemed by Christ vnto holines & happines for euer & professeth the same by submitting him self to his lawes and gouernmēt." "The Lordes kingdome is not by force . . . ," Browne writes, "for it is the conscience and not the power of man that will drive vs to seeke the Lordes kingdome. . . ."; for "the Lordes people is of the willing sorte." He uses the verse that "the kingdom of God suffereth violence, and the violent take it by force" (Matthew 11:12) to prove that it requires effort to attain the Kingdom, a persistent pressing on, and that the worthy, who do so persistently press on, must not tarry for the unworthy. The constitutive element of the Church is therefore the holiness of its members, and the toleration of any open wickedness means a denial of the very nature of the Church. Christian morality, however, goes beyond the avoiding of what is unlawful to the doing of that which is most expedient. Browne recognizes a measure of human autonomy in ethics when he assigns the determination of what is most expedient to the individual.

Shortly after the publication of Browne's three treatises trouble arose in his church which led to his removal from the pastorate and the disintegration of his congregation. The majority, led by Robert Harrison, joined the regular English church in Middelburg, which was then pastored by the Puritan Thomas Cartwright (1535-1603). Others accompanied Browne to Scotland, apparently after he had composed *A Trve and Short Declaration, Both of the Gathering and Ioyning together of Certaine Persons: and also of the Lamentable Breach and Division which fell amongst them,* late in 1583, and *An answer to Master Cartwright His Letter for Ioyning with the English Churches,* which seems to have been published in 1584. When he continued to expound his separatist convictions and denied the jurisdiction of the Scottish Kirk over him, he was briefly jailed, early in 1584. Returning to England, he was imprisoned at the instance of the bishop of London for giving expression to his views, and was later excommunicated by the bishop of Peterborough for failing to answer to a charge of unauthorized preaching. This excommunication, which threatened him with perpetual imprisonment under the writ *De excommunicato capiendo,* may have been instrumental in procuring his formal (and humiliating) submission to the Church of England, which took place in 1586. He now procured a teaching position, which he held until 1591, when, through the good offices of his kinsman Lord Burghley (1520-1598; the leading member of Queen Elizabeth's Privy Council), he was made rector of Achurch-with-Thorpe, a small Northamptonshire village. He apparently retained this position until his death in 1633. It was openly said during his lifetime that though outwardly conforming, he retained his convictions concerning the nature and polity of the Church. It also appears that he was afflicted with a form of intermittently violent insanity that led to his final imprisonment (in Northampton Gaol, for assaulting a policeman) that lasted from 1631 until his death.

Though Robert Browne outwardly renounced his views, the term "Brownist" came to be applied to every form and degree of separatism. In 1618, *An Arrow against the Separation of the Brownists* distinguished three groups: the followers of Francis Johnson (1562-1618), who separated from the Church of England because of its alleged corruptions without denying that both it and the Church of Rome are true Churches; the followers of John Robinson (c.1575-1625; pastor of the Pilgrim Fathers), who denied that the Church of England was a true Church but allowed religious fellowship with the godly within it; and the followers of Henry Ainsworth (1571-c.1622), who renounced all religious fellowship with the Church of England and all its members. While the Puritans that settled the Massachusetts Bay and the Connecticut Valley insisted that they were not separatists or Brownists, their views were not far removed from those of Browne, and Browne is commonly regarded as the father of Congregationalism. The Independents, who flourished under Oliver Cromwell (1599-1658, creator of the New Model Army; Lord Protector of England, 1653-1658), substantially reflected in their theory and practice the views of Browne.

Congregationalism has been described by the German theologian and sociologist Ernst Troeltsch (1865-1923) as the unhappy marriage of Calvinism with the sect type. The unhappiness of this marriage apparently prompted many of its children to turn to a purer form of sectarianism. John Smyth (c.1554-1612) was only the most prominent of many separatists who ceased to be Calvinists and became General Baptists. But we should also note a second marriage between Calvinism and sectarianism, from which issued the Particular (Regular) Baptists, who shared with Browne his Calvinistic theology, his congregational polity, his recognition of the civil authority of magistrates, and his denial of the validity of any baptism that is not administered on the authority of a "gathered" Church. Finally, we should see in Browne a pioneer of two principles that have decisively influenced the religious history of (English-speaking) America: the voluntary principle with respect to Church membership, which he championed unequivocally, and the principle of separation of Church and state, which he espoused with remarkably few reservations.

THE DARK NIGHT OF THE SOUL

Author: Saint John of the Cross (1542-1591)
Type of work: Manual for mystical contemplation
First transcribed: c.1587

Principal Ideas Advanced

The goal of man's soul is ascent toward union with God, and in order to attain this goal the soul must pass through several dark nights.

The dark night of the senses is first, in which all attachment to the outer world is cut off and the direction of the self is turned completely inward.

The self cut off from sense is not peaceful but must pass through a spiritual dark night, since the soul must be emptied of all content, made completely arid, if it hopes for union with God.

Since its origin in the turmoil of John's stormy life and final imprisonment, *The Dark Night of the Soul* has been a classic and a manual for contemplative mysticism. Born in a fertile but decadent Spain as the result of an attempt at monastic reform, this single work has had extraordinary influence on all who seek to understand and to follow the spiritual and mystical way in the religious life. Furthermore, its highly structured form offers in its own way a complete theology.

The ascent to Mount Carmel is the theme, and in the ascent the soul will experience several dark nights in preparing itself for union with God. Instruction is necessary so that the soul may learn to free itself from all that is temporal. Yet even this is not enough, since the spiritual itself can be a burden. Complete nakedness and freedom is the goal, since only a spirit thus free of both temporal and spiritual impediments can hope for union with God.

Darkness actually provides security and protection for the soul, John writes; consequently, darkness properly entered into is not to be feared but is to be sought as the soul's ally. The suspension of the senses produces bliss, although not before the soul has gone through the preliminary torment that darkness and absence first produce. Not to see is also to remain unseen, so that sensual and spiritual darkness protects as much as it also seems to destroy. Advance in such a spiritual life requires careful instruction and advice.

Such doctrine, of course, seems difficult if not impossible or contradictory to those not used to such devious routes. Without any question, to follow John's advice means to go against the natural order, or at least to reverse it, but the advice is, nevertheless, not without its own logic or its own explanation. The nature of the dark night can be made intelligible, although its grasp requires some subtlety and some progression on its path. Darkness is the means to achieve divine light; what appears its opposite is actually the means thereto. Perfect union with God requires the emptying, the transformation of the self.

Human knowledge itself cannot reveal these mystical trails or lessen the darkness through which the soul must pass, since the darkness is the inevitable result of the very attempt to transcend human reason and to prepare the soul for a higher level. Ordinary experience is not sufficient to give an accurate description of the soul's journey. Only the person himself who travels the dark road can have an inner awareness of it, and even he cannot express it adequately in words. Words describe the approach and the stages of preparation, but they are not adequate to the state itself.

Not everyone will allow himself to be led in this manner; thus, few can hope to come to understand this way. In fact most souls impede God's activity by resistance and imprudent behavior; they refuse to surrender themselves to God. The self must be surrendered first before the way can be understood, and few are willing to do that. Even souls who venture to allow themselves to be led spiritually will at first believe themselves to be completely lost, since God leads them along a lofty path of dark contemplation and spiritual aridity.

Such a soul is filled with darkness, misery, and affliction, so that the difficult task for the spiritual counselor is to develop the sensitivity to distinguish this low state of the normal soul, a state brought on by spiritual advance, from the lost and directionless state of the abnormal soul. Those who begin the development of a spiritual life expecting immediate rewards are in for disappointment, since their first progress will have all the outer appearance of a loss, and to the undiscerning their condition will seem no different from the morbid condition of one abandoned by God. Inexperienced counselors, such as Job's, will jump at the conclusion that such a soul must harbor evil, and they will fail to discern the first stage of spiritual progress.

Spiritual progress has as its first fruits the knowledge of one's own misery, and this is perhaps the greatest affliction a soul can feel. In the first night of contemplation, God gives the soul this light of self-knowledge, but it is a terribly revealing light, the first effect of which is to plunge the soul into a lower condition. Increased sin also causes a similar affliction, so by what signs can a spiritual advance which is genuinely purgative be distinguished from the anguish of increased burden? An apparent loss may precede an actual deepening, but on the other hand some think themselves to be advancing spiritually when actually their spirituality amounts to nothing.

The road is not smooth or even upward in an advance toward God, but instead it is filled with dark night and with apparent immediate losses. Such a night is caused by purgation, by emptying present content, and the first such cleansing involves the sensual part of the soul, leading to the first dark night of sense and desire. The second dark night involves the spiritual part of the soul. These first two nights involve the active part of the soul, but after them comes passive or infused contemplation, when the soul has ceased its activity and is subjected to God.

The purgation of the sensual part of the soul is experienced at the start of contemplation, but the night of the spiritual life comes only to persons more advanced in the spiritual life, when God has begun to raise them toward a state of union with Him. The first dark night is caused by the soul's emptying and purging itself of all sense appetites regarding the external things of the world. Step by step a soul frees itself from all desire for the things of the world which it possesses, and such a denial and loss is like night to all of man's senses.

Such a road must be traveled by faith, since its way is as dark to the understanding as it has now become to the senses. God at this point is also like a dark night to a soul in this state of emptying itself of desire for the sense world. The last part of such a night, however, is like the end of night or the early dawn, close to the light of day or close to the divine light. Absence and purging bring darkness as a necessary testing stage. Faith is required since reason cannot guide here, but the transition to light by means of elimination and darkness is necessary.

Deprived of the pleasure which the desire for things makes possible, the soul enters its own dark night. Because of desire, natural man is nourished and fed by whatever his powers and faculties take pleasure in. Emptying itself of all things, the soul that has denied and cast away and silenced pleasure and desire remains as in the darkness of night. Of course, this denial is especially depressing because it is a denial not only of physical delights but also of internal pleasures.

What possesse and harm the soul are not the things of the world but rather the will and desire for them. What enters into the soul is not the thing but the desire for it, so that the elimination of desire is by far the most important goal. The affections which a soul has for creatures is pure darkness in the eyes of God. He who loves a creature becomes as low or lower than the creature. The soul that loves anything other than God renders itself incapable of transformation and thus incapable of pure divine union.

A man who has desires is a slave to them, and thus freedom cannot dwell in a heart that is subject to desires. The elimination of desires brings temporary darkness and even torment, but it also brings genuine freedom to a soul so detached. The love of God and the affection for creatures are contraries. One will does not have room both for a love of creatures and a love of God; one or the other must be eliminated if spiritual purity is to be achieved. Desires make the soul dark and blind, although advance brings a form of temporary blindness too. Even the least desire tarnishes the soul and makes it impure. If one is to enter into divine union, all desire and attachment living in the soul must die.

These things the soul can actively do for itself, but once having passed through the night of sense and desire, the spiritual night begins, and here the soul's activity begins to cease, for it has made itself passive before God by its sensual purity and spiritual rigor. The four natural passions of joy, hope, fear, and grief must be silenced and tranquilized, and in its silence the spiritual soul finds quietude and rest.

Nothing now wearies the upward flight of the soul, and nothing oppresses it when it is cast down. To achieve this state, the soul must be set on fire by a longing for the things of the spirit.

The dark nights of the spirit, faith, hope, and love, are for the soul nights of great promise. The soul seeks a "secret ladder," the steps of which are hidden both to sense and understanding, so that with respect to the natural light of reason the soul is left in darkness. The soul goes forth in darkness, passing beyond all the limits of nature and reason, in order to ascend by the divine ladder of faith, which leads to and penetrates the innermost being of God. Faith as a marvelous means to God is comparable to midnight before the dawn. The brilliance of the light of faith finally overwhelms and eclipses the light of the understanding. Supernatural being, communicated by love and grace, overcomes the dark night of the soul.

HISTORY OF THE REFORMATION IN SCOTLAND

Author: John Knox (c.1505-1572)
Type of work: Reformation Church history
First published: 1587 (complete edition: 1644)

Principal Ideas Advanced

The reformation of religion in Scotland was a rebellion not against lawful authority, but against the unjust and un-Christian use of authority by Church and state.

The persecution of its critics by fire and sword is evidence that the Roman Catholic Church was an instrument of Satan for the suppression of the true Evangel of Jesus Christ in Scotland, and continuance of the rule of this form of religion should be prohibited.

The preservation of the proceedings and documents of the Scottish Reformers would vindicate the justice of their cause and assist in the establishment of an authentic Apostolic Church.

The History of the Reformation of Religion within the Realm of Scotland by the Scottish Reformer John Knox is a combination of a collection of historic documents, a vindication of a party cause, a nationalist broadside, a virulent Anti-Romanist treatise, and an autobiographical diary. It is certainly one of the most exciting books in all the vast literature of the Reformation. There is a rough, unfinished feeling about it as if a polished literary style would have been unsuited to the stormy events narrated. The author was passionately devoted to the cause he advocated, and he was himself the chief Reformer in the movement whose history he reports. If some books of religious history can be classed as objective, Knox's *History* is not one of them. Every page of it is written with a bias that is unconcealed and uncompromising. His pen is a weapon, his ink is undiluted, and his inspiration is the belief that he was fighting a battle for God and the Gospel.

So far as is known no attempt was made to publish the works in Knox's lifetime, though the Second Book seems to have been prepared for publication should events have taken a turn such that a vindication of the Protestant cause would have been necessary. Much of the narrative was written while the events being recorded were actually happening and, hence, it reflects the mood of the changing fortunes of the Protestant party. The reader feels that he is actually on the scene, feeling the tensions of the moment, and watching the gyrations of the nobles and Reformers as they watched the gyrations of one another.

The personal correspondence of the Scottish Reformer shows that he was capable of great tenderness and concern for domestic matters, but when he was confronting the public affairs of religion in Scotland, he was aflame with holy fire and the indignation of an Elijah facing the priests of Baal. He knew what was at stake in success or failure. On the continent of Europe and in England he had been on familiar terms with many of the leaders of the Reformed cause, and he had seen at first hand the immensity of the struggle to initiate, and then to sustain, freedom from the Roman Church. No one could accuse Knox of illusions about the price that had to be paid.

His own introduction to the gravity of the issues left an indelible mark on his outlook. In the *History* he tells of his first involvement when attending upon George Wishart in Lothian, near Edinburgh. Wishart was apprehended as a preacher of reform in 1546, and he was burned alive at St. Andrews at the instigation of, and in the presence of, Cardinal Beaton. This was John Knox's first lesson in the realities of the Roman version of ecclesiastical power, and one lesson was enough. Thereafter he spoke of "bloody wolves," "bloody butchers," "monsters and hypocrites," "sergeants of Sathan," and "that Roman Antichrist." Knox was an implacable foe of what he regarded as the knavery, lechery, cupidity, and inhumanity of the Roman Catholics. He objected also to the theological errors of the idolotry of the Mass and the commercializing of the Evangel. His fiery language, black and white categorizing, scorn of trimmers, surging invective, outrageous innuendoes, all tumble together in a tempest of eloquence: "I am called, Madam, to ane publict functioun within the Kirk of God, and am appointed by God to rebuk the synnes and vices of all." Thus spoke John Knox about himself to his Queen.

This vivid chronicle of Scottish affairs consists of five books, the first four certainly written by Knox, and the fifth by an unknown person. The Laing manuscript is generally conceded to be that which Knox himself supervised in transcription, and it was published by David Laing in his definitive edition "The Works of John Knox," in 1846-1848. The first edition by Vautrollier, 1586-1587, was suppressed; and the second by David Buchanan, 1644, included the fifth book. The writing is full of vernacular phrases, involving both Scottish and English usage, and it finds parallels for everything in Biblical antecedents, especially in the accounts of the kings and prophets of Israel. An excellent version with modernized spelling, edited by William Croft Dickinson, appeared in 1949.

What is now Book Two was the first part of the *History* to be written, and only as the work proceeded and opportunity permitted was the rest added. About the middle of Book Two, a reference to October, 1559, establishes the date of composition of that part. In September, 1560, Thomas Randolph, Scottish agent for Queen Elizabeth of England, wrote to Sir William Cecil, the English Secretary of State, that he had spoken to John Knox about his *History,* of which at that date one book had been written. In the year immediately following, Book Three was added, and Book One was undertaken in 1566 as an introduction and background. Book Four followed later in the same year. There are clear evidences that revisions were being made right up to the Reformer's death in November, 1572. His secretary, Richard Bannatyne, reported to Parliament that he had "certain scrolls, papers, and minutes" of things done after 1564 which needed to be put in "form and order," and it is possible that some of this material was used for Book Five. Within the work as a whole there is some overlapping of accounts, and subsequent editors have sifted out errors which the author's own revision did not catch.

If the *History* is taken in its final form, the narrative opens with an account of the first martyrs for reform at the beginning of the fifteenth century, "after that horrible and universal defecteuon from the trewth which hes cume by meanes of that Romane Antichrist," and it closes with the arrival of the Reformer in Scotland in May, 1559, to take up again the rapidly advancing cause. The cumulative effect of persecution on those who were disgusted with the rapacity and morals of the clergy is emphasized. Of the burning of Patrick Hamilton, for example, it was said that, "the reik of Maister Patrick Hammyltoun hes infected as many as it blew upoun." The French alliance became critical with the marriage in 1558 of the young Queen Mary (1542-1587) to the Dauphin Francis, for it tied Scotland to the strong Roman Catholic dynasty in France, and the repercussions of this in the relations with England were momentous, especially when Mary became Queen Consort of France. Her mother, Mary of Guise (1515-1560), was Regent in Scotland, and she had to depend increasingly on the resident French forces. The fact that Frenchmen were appointed to offices of state exasperated many of the Scottish nobility. Thus, self-interest stimulated recruitment to the reform cause.

In Scotland the Reformation was not a revolt of priests, but a revolt of sections of the people and the civil leaders. It was both a reformation and a revolution. The Scottish nobility had always been a rough and turbulent lot with longstanding family feuds to settle, a state of affairs that Knox did not fail to describe and evaluate caustically. No one needed to counsel him on the mixed motives of the men around him. The acceptance by the Scottish Parliament of the Confession of Faith (in August 1650) but vacillation concerning the *Book of Discipline* (1560) indicates the obtuseness of party men who condemned the papacy but would not finance adequately the Protestant ministry.

Many of the abuses to which the Scottish reform platform called attention were paralleled in other lands—abuses such as the rapacity of the Church, the centralization of power in the prelates, and the ineffectiveness of self-reform. It was a combination of local factors, however, rather than a single item, that produced the explosion; for example, the brutal repression of criticism, circulation of information about successful reform elsewhere, the French involvement, the duplicity of the Queen and her mother, and the zeal of Knox himself.

The Second Book is as much a repository of documents as it is an apologetic for the Protestant Lords of the Congregation, as the important alliance of anti-French noblemen was called. Clearly religion, politics, economics, and family rivalries all played a part in the Scottish Reformation. Knox highlights the irritation caused by the presence of the French, for he considered that the document might have to be utilized in influencing opinion at the Court of England. Every effort was made to show that amid all the alarms and skirmishes of this period, peaceable and legal means of action were pressed to settle matters. The Lords were not rebels, anti-royalists, or a brawling fringe group, but men with a just cause desirous of stable government and friendship with England.

Sufficient strength was gathered to depose the Queen Regent, but the reinforcement of the French troops reduced the Reform party to despondency. Appeal was made to England for more open assistance, and the Second Book ends with a prayer which catches the mood of that hour: "Look upoun us, O Lorde, in the multitude of thy mercyes for we ar brought evin to the deape of the dongeoun."

The Regent's famous taunt comes at the beginning of Book Three, "Whair is now Johne Knox his God? My God is now stronger than his, yea even in Fyff," Fife being the shire in which the Lords had been strong. Her "blasphemous rayling" was short-lived. An English army entered Scotland to reinforce the faltering Protestant nobility, the Treaty of Leith was negotiated, the French were removed, and the Parliament of Scotland accepted the Confession of Faith in 1560. Even at the moment of triumph, however, there was disappointment. The *First Book of Discipline,* designed to order the Scottish Church and to provide for a Reformed ministry, was subscribed to by representatives of the Great Council of Scotland, and they promised to enforce its provisions. They defaulted. So Knox incorporates the book in full, but says that he does it "to the end that the posteriteis to come may juge. . . ." Having ousted the avaricious prelates, he was faced with the avariciousness of a "corrupt generatioun."

The young and beautiful Queen Mary, a widow two years after her marriage to Francis, arrived from France in August, 1561, on a day that was overcast and unseasonably "dolorous," which many of the godly read as an ominous portent. Mass was celebrated in Holyrood Abbey and the fears of the Protestants multiplied. Knox, in an interview with his Queen, used courteous but plain words, and said that he would be "also weall content to lyve under your Grace as Paull was to lyve under Nero." Princes who murdered the godly should be opposed, he argued; and he wrote,

"Thair blynd zeall is no thing but a verray mad phrenesie; and thair foir, to tack the sweard frome thame, to bynd thair handis, and to cast thame selfis in preasone, till that thei be brought to a more sober mynd, is no disobedience against princes, but just obedience, becaus that it aggreith with the will of God." There was no court flattery in such sentiments.

The Queen had her own type of answer, and the struggle for power intensified. Knox was arraigned for treason, but he defended himself boldly and successfully. The attack came next at the General Assembly itself in a long and powerful offensive on Knox's opinions on the respective rights of the Queen, the people, and the Assembly on political and religious obedience, and again the skill of the Reformer frustrated the Queen's spokesmen.

The style of the Fifth Book lacks the sparkle and pungency of the other four. It covers events from 1564 to the renunciation of the Crown by the Queen in favor of her infant son James, and the appointment of a Regency again. Her second marriage, in 1565, to Henry Stuart, Lord Darnley, was a mistake; and her third, in 1567, to the Earl of Bothwell was disastrous. In the end Knox was still minister at Greyfriars Kirk in Edinburgh; the Queen abdicated in 1567, and she was committed as a prisoner to Lochleven Castle.

There is drama in Knox's story of the Scottish Reformation. Great ideas took possession of the minds of men and forced the pace of history. If God predestines events as Calvinism taught and as John Knox believed, it was a predestination which inspired rather than discouraged those who were influenced by it. Reform of the medieval Church called for tremendous courage, for the idea of toleration on both sides was unthinkable. Entrenched power had to be challenged not only in theory, but also by the willingness to live dangerously. The Old Testament was of greater assistance than the New Testament at least as an armory of precedents for sixteenth century polemics.

The intertwining of the economic and the spiritual, the greed of the worldlings and the patriotism of the nationalists, the unchastity of the religious office holders and the domestic principles of the pious, make assignment of motives a difficult exercise. But the moral force within the reform movement can easily be discerned. The Reformers may have been superstitious, ignorant, and cantankerous, but they knew that the clergy had taken vows which they were supposed to keep. When the clergy were corrupt and rapacious, even the most dull-witted could see a need for change. The Reforming party exploited this loose living in appeals for support and for the denunciation of all the existing ecclesiastical regime. If the morals of the Roman Antichrist were low, the Reformers argued, the value of Roman theology and of the Roman claims to authority could be no better.

No doubt the Reformers were intolerant and fanatic at times, but they were willing to seek open debate that all the world might examine the justness of their cause. The *History* of John Knox was just such an enterprise. It attempts to preserve the documents which would vindicate the conduct of his party against misrepresentation and to record both the acts of the Scottish Reformers and the abuses of political and religious power which provoked their rebellion.

A TREATISE OF EXCOMMUNICATION

Author: Thomas Erastus (1524-1583)
Type of work: Ecclesiology
First published: 1589

Principal Ideas Advanced

The visible Church must be sharply distinguished from the invisible Church.

The visible Church is a community based on a common faith, from which no one professing that faith should be excluded.

Christian princes and magistrates have the right and duty of governing the Church in their dominions, and to deal with violations of the moral code.

Thomas Erastus was born Thomas Lieber or Lüber in Baden, Switzerland, in 1524. He grew up in the Reformed (Zwinglian) faith. His baccalaureate was acquired in Basel, and his doctorate in medicine in Bologna.

In 1557 he began to teach at the University of Heidelberg, and in 1559 (and again in 1573) served as rector of the university. He not only lectured on medicine, but also was widely known and esteemed as a skillful physician, and as an opponent of the anti-traditionalist Theophrastus Paracelsus (1493-1541). In 1560 he assisted the Reformed theologian Peter Boquinus (died 1582) in his debate against the Lutheran theologian Johann Stoessel (1524-1576) and gained the respect of Frederick III, Elector Palatine from 1559 to 1576, who embraced the Reformed faith after this Heidelberg debate. Erastus served on the Church council of the Palatinate until 1564, and in every way exerted himself to advance the Reformed religion. Though the bulk of the population remained Lutheran, the policy of the Palatinate after 1566 was increasingly oriented towards the various Reformed bodies of Western Europe, which looked largely to Geneva for leadership. As a result, the partisans of Geneva, led by the theologian Caspar Olevianus (1536-1587; co-author of the Heidelberg Catechism of 1563), became increasingly insistent in their demand for a system of presbyteries that would include lay elders and that would exercise Church discipline, including the power of excommunication; that is, depriving Church members of the privilege of participating in the Lord's Supper. When one of the Genevan party, the English exile George Withers, proposed the thesis (in 1568) that a well-ordered Church includes a presbytery that shares with the ministers the exercise of Church discipline and that is able to excommunicate even princes, there were riots, and Erastus felt himself constrained to write in opposition to the excommunicators. He formulated his views in 103 theses, which he sent to a number of divines outside the Palatinate. His views were to some extent endorsed by the theologians of German-speaking Switzerland, notably by Henry Bullinger (1504-1575) of Zurich and Johannes Haller (1523-1575) of Berne. The opposite point of view was most ably presented by Theodore Beza (1519-1605), since 1564 the leading minister in Geneva, and echoed by the three Heidelberg theologians whose views had been solicited by the elector. Before the end of 1569 Erastus had compressed his views into seventy-five theses, to which he appended his *Confirmatio thesium* (a five-book reply to Beza and a one-book reply to the Heidelberg theologians). The whole work was printed in 1589, probably in London and with the encouragement of Archbishop John Whitgift (c.1530-1604).

The Latin title of the seventy-five theses succinctly indicates the author's frame of reference: *Explicatio gravissimae questionis, utrum excommunicatio quatenus religionem intelligentes et amplexantes a sacramentorum usu propter admissum facinus arcet, mandato nitatur divino, an excognita sit ab hominibus.*

Erastus states that from the beginning of the "Excommunicating Frenzy" (about 1566) he looked upon it as a basically wrong approach, even though he himself at that time held excommunication to be Scriptural. With only about one-thirteenth of the population sympathetic to Reformed doctrine, he felt that a positive approach was essential. The "saving truths" should be propagated so as to bring people into the fellowship of the Church, rather than to expel them. His fundamental charge against excommunication, as indicated by the Latin title, is that it is an invention of men, which he dates from the end of the second century. He professes to admire the zeal and good intentions of those who originated the practice, but notes that excommunication greatly augmented the Church's hold upon men and states, and the growth of superstition.

Erastus argues from the sacraments of the Old Testament Church, which, with Calvin, he holds to be "altogether the same" with respect to the things signified as those of the New Testament Church. Christ himself did not bar Judas (who left before the Last Supper of his own accord, if at all) or the other disciples, even though they had just striven amongst themselves as to who should be the greatest. Erastus elaborately examines the opponents' prooftexts in Matthew 18:15-17, I Corinthians 5:3,11, and I Timothy 5:29. In the case of the first of these passages he concludes that Jesus is teaching the Jews to submit minor differences to the tribunal of their own nation; namely, the Sanhedrin. In the second passage, Paul is speaking of "cutting off" an offender, not from participation in the sacraments, but from life itself and from the suspension of private familiarities, such as eating together. In the third, public rebuke, is mentioned but not excommunication.

Actually the sacraments are not to be construed as means of penalizing men for their wrongdoings, but rather as inducements to true conversion: "The end and designes of this Institution of the Lords Supper, are, that we may commemorate in the most solemn manner the Death of our Lord: That we may pay our Homage in a publick Recognition and Thankfulness, for the

Deliverance he hath purchased for us: That we may remind our selves, and by our presence bear testimony to others, that we have no other Food of Life, but a Crucified Saviour; no other Drink, but his Bloud poured out for us; That we may declare our selves as well penitent for our past course of Life, as that we have enter'd upon thoughts and resolutions of a better; and that we embrace the Christian Doctrine, are the members of Christ, belong unto his Church, in which we desire piously and religiously both to live and to die. . . . He that by the aid and impulse of the Holy Spirit hath the thoughts of his heart right at the time of his receiving, the Scripture turns him not away; but God only knows whether and how long he will hold on to his good purposes and resolutions. 'Tis our duty to hope always the best of all men, however we may sometimes be mistaken: nay, we ought to address our hearty prayers to God, that he would vouchsafe to strengthen and confirm both us and them in all true Religion and Virtue. But still the sinner is to be told of his faults, is to be reprehended, admonished, and advised, that he may so try himself that (as the Apostle cautions) he eat and drink not Damnation to himself."

Of fundamental importance for Erastus's conception of the proper relationship of Church and state is the distinction between the invisible and the visible Church. These two bodies are not mutually inclusive; hence, what unites men to one does not necessarily unite them to the other. Erastus says: ". . . we are made Members of Christ . . . by that Faith alone which worketh by Charity: and 'tis by Infidelity onely that we fall from this Consortship. And therefore no body can give us admission into this Society, or shut the doors upon us, but he that can impart to us a lively Faith, and again withdraw it at his pleasure."

Membership in the Church is based on profession of this faith, approbation of the same doctrine, and use of the same sacraments. Since "the whole World are to be invited, and by all the Allurements and Arts of men, won and brought into" participation in the first two of these marks, it is most unreasonable that they should be deprived of the third. Moral failings do not debar men from the fellowship of the Church. The extent of Christ's external kingdom should be no narrower now than the boundaries set unto the Jews, among whom all the circumcised were admitted to the privileges of the Temple, while wrongdoers were punished by civil punishments.

Erastus asserts that the office of the lay (nonteaching) elder is not Scriptural, since in New Testament times the elders and bishops were one and the same. The nearest approach to it is Paul's suggestion that the Church institute a tribunal to determine causes between its members. (I Corinthians 6:1-6). Erastus admits the legitimacy of such an institution as long as the Church is "under a Profane Government (as in the Dominions of Turks and Papists)," and he assigns to it the task of admonishing disorderly ministers and profligate members. But such a function becomes obsolete as soon as the civil magistrate becomes Christian, pious, and orthodox: " 'Tis a most pernicious Error, and big with dangerous consequence, that so many think no better of a Christian Magistracy, than of an Heathen one, whose power is to be allowed of no farther than meer Temporals." The Calvinistic presbyteries are superfluous, since Christian rulers have the right not only to order the religion of their dominions but also to deal with every manner of vice. The position of Christian rulers today is analogous to that of the rulers of the Jewish state under the Old Testament. However, "'twas lawful for the High Priests under the Old Testament, to meddle with the arts of Government and Secular affairs, as they were the Types of Christ our King and High Priest: but under the Gospel 'tis another case, IT SHALL NOT BE SO WITH YOU, says Christ."

Erastus quotes Wolfgang Musculus (1484-1563) to the effect that nature does not allow two absolute and independent governments over the same people without one being subordinate to the other.

Wolfgang Musculus, professor of Greek and Theology in Berne, was the most consistent and thorough exponent of the view that would make the Church a department of the state, the view generally known as Erastianism. The Magisterial Reformation (Lutheran, Reformed, Anglican) depended everywhere on the civil government (the magistrate) for its success; where it triumphed, it was perhaps inevitable that state Churches should develop that were with various degrees of completeness subject to the control of the state.

German-speaking Switzerland apparently had no doubt that the authority of the magistrate extended permanently to the control of the religious life of the community; Ulrich Zwingli (1484-1531), Henry Bullinger, and Rudolf Gualter (1519-1586), who succeeded one another as head minister in Zurich, all shared the basic convictions of Musculus and Erastus, which found their ideal in the Christian state. When John Whitgift (from 1583, Archbishop of Canterbury), sought for a theoretical justification of the Anglican state Church, he found it in this German-Swiss tradition. His Calvinistic opposition, the Puritans, meanwhile contended for the kind of ecclesiastical autonomy and discipline that had been won in Geneva after a long and bitter struggle. The Calvinist and Zwinglian views of Church polity had collided in Lausanne in the 1540's and 1550's, and their contest in the Palatinate was but a renewal of this struggle. Only after the Palatinate had reverted to Lutheranism at the death of Frederick III (1576) and all the Reformed professors had been expelled from the University of Heidelberg (Erastus was professor in Basel the last three years of his life), did the two Reformed factions coalesce.

When Theodore Beza published his *Tractatus pius et moderatus de vera Excommunicatione, et christiano Presbyterio, Erasti manuscriptis thesibus oppositus* in 1590, it was in this more irenic atmosphere. While he upholds the Genevan Church polity as the ideal towards which all churches should strive, he recognizes that polity may legitimately vary with local conditions. He asserts that the whole controversy would have been unnecessary if Erastus had all along maintained his final position that he is not concerned to retain those in the Church who do not profess the pure Christian doctrine. But for Beza such a profession is nullified by blasphemy, immorality, or unbelief; for there can be no salvation without sanctification. Excommunication serves to safeguard the glory of God as well as the safety of the individual, lest he eat and drink to his own condemnation. The visible Church is not only a confessional community (as for Erastus) but also a divinely instituted school of salvation and of the Christian life (analogous to Erastus's Christian state, but on a higher level). It approaches far closer to the invisible Church than Erastus had thought proper. Beza does not question the political (civil) sovereignty of the state in this treatise, but he distinguishes, as Erastus had refused to distinguish, between the person and the office of the magistrate: as a person, even the highest magistrate is subject to the discipline (and excommunication) of the Church.

TREATISE ON THE LAWS OF ECCLESIASTICAL POLITY

Author: Richard Hooker (c.1554-1600)
Type of work: Anglican apology
First published: Books I-IV, 1594; Book V, 1597; Books VI-VIII, 1648-1662

Principal Ideas Advanced

Christian society is taught both by the natural light of reason and by the supernatural light of Scripture.

The Presbyterians are mistaken in supposing that Scripture, which contains the whole truth necessary for salvation, also gives detailed instructions for the government of Christian society.

Since the ceremonies and discipline of the Church of England serve the cause of Christianity, they ought not be exchanged for those of Geneva.

Hooker's *Ecclesiastical Polity* is commonly regarded as laying the foundations of Anglican theology, providing, as it does, a well-reasoned case for the existence of a national Church, a Church faithful to the essential principles of the Reformation, subject to the decrees of the Crown, and guided by a decent respect for tradition. The work was composed in response to the criticisms of the Elizabethan settlement which were launched against it by Presbyterians, such as Thomas Cartwright (1535-1603). Hooker divided his subject into eight books, of which only the first five were published during his lifetime. The books beyond the first five are sometimes omitted in modern editions, but they are particularly interesting as sources of Hooker's ideas on the doctrine of the episcopacy and on the relation of Church and state.

Hooker stood in the line of renaissance humanism which drew alike from Christian and pagan sources. His account of the moral and civil law is especially indebted to Aristotle, but he owes his views of the relation between nature and grace, reason and revelation, and civil society and the Church to Thomas Aquinas. On these classic grounds he stood to do battle with the strict partisans of the Protestant Reformation, who, although not without classical learning, strove on principle to purge the Church of its non-Hebraic accretions and maintained that for the Christian the only rule of faith and practice is to be found in the Old and New Testaments.

The Puritans with whom Hooker had to contend (not to be confused with the later Puritans, who were often Independents and Congregationalists) were Presbyterians who took the Churches of Geneva and Scotland as their models. The zeal and singleness of mind with which the Presbyterians pressed their cause was an expression of that severe piety which finds its center in submission to the irresistible decrees of a Sovereign God who leaves nothing to the agency of man. As God justifies His elect by the death and resurrection of His Son and sanctifies them by the power of His Spirit, so He instructs and governs them by the Scriptures, preached and applied by those whom He has called to be His ministers. Since the Scriptures, being perfect, tell us everything that God wills us to do, either expressly or by legitimate inference, anything done without Scriptural warrant is presumptuous and sinful. Chief among the principles which the Scriptures lay down are: government by ministers, lay-elders, and deacons; a simple order of worship consisting of psalms, prayers, offerings, and the preaching of the Word; the observance of weekly Sabbaths but not of holy days; and the authority of the Church, through its ministry, to discipline the ungodly and to command the civil power. Besides these matters of Church polity, however, the Scriptures also give a complete regimen for men in their daily life. Such, at least, was the Presbyterian teaching which challenged the existing order of the Church of England and to which Hooker attempted to reply. His book, which is a polemic from beginning to end, owes its bulk to the detail with which he treats a multitude of particular charges made against the practice of the English Church by a number of Presbyterian writers.

Hooker acknowledged the genius of Calvin and praised his achievements in the city of Geneva, but the Calvinist dogma that Scriptural principles provide an exclusive and sufficient rule of life was, he maintained, as dangerous as the claims which the Anabaptists made for their visions and revelations. For to pretend that the whole rule of life is contained in the Scriptures is to subvert the foundations of governments, families, and corporations, which have never been based on Scriptural injunctions but on universal principles of human nature which manifest themselves in custom and through reason. Even to use the Scriptures wisely, says Hooker, presupposes reason and discretion in man.

Whereas jealousy for the sovereignty of the Creator's will led the Puritans to deprecate any excellence that might be claimed for the creature, reverence for the Creator's wisdom led Hooker to affirm the universal goodness of God's handiwork. He maintains that God's will is simply His affirmation of His own eternal law, and that nothing takes place within the created world except by the law of nature which the Creator has laid down. Like Aristotle, Hooker represents the world in teleological terms by describing each creature as having a natural end toward which it strives. Man's nature, no less than that of other creatures, is governed by wholesome dispositions, which lead him to form societies and to invent useful arts. Moreover, man has been endowed with reason, by means of which he is able to apprehend the laws which govern his estate, as is witnessed by morality, civil justice, and the "law of the nations" (*ius gentium*). According to Hooker, we are just as much bound to acknowledge God's law when it is disclosed in nature as we are bound to acknowledge it when it is revealed in the Scriptures.

The necessity for the Scriptures, says Hooker, arises when the natural must be supplemented by the supernatural. The light of nature would, Hooker believes, have been sufficient for man's spiritual as well as for his physical wants had he remained faithful to the duty taught by reason. The good to which his soul aspires is that union with God which is the natural perfection of the intellect. Because of his disobedience, however, man has lost that good, and nature provides no way of recovering it or of escaping the punishment which follows from violating the law. Thus, in His wisdom, God has seen fit to provide a supernatural way, by the incarnation and death of His Son, and it is this new way, together with the duties it imposes, that the Scriptures declare. Admittedly, the Scriptures also comment on our natural condition and present an excellent summary of the moral law. But the primary purpose for which the Bible was given is to provide that supernatural light which teaches the way of salvation; the Scriptures are perfect only in that they omit nothing necessary for man to reach salvation. Thus, the Romanists are in error when they maintain that the Scriptures must be supplemented by tradition. But the Puritans are also in error whenever, by their devious exegesis, they undertake to draw from the Scriptures all sorts of instructions which God never intended.

Having thus laid down the respective functions of reason and revelation, Hooker was in a position to formulate his principles of ecclesiastical polity. He makes a distinction which the Presbyterians were unwilling to allow; namely, a distinction between matters of faith and matters of polity. Since the former, says Hooker, have to do with truth, they are the same for all times and places, but the latter have to do with virtue, and hence they vary according to circumstances. It is reasonable, therefore, to believe that the Scriptures contain all that is needful to faith but do not lay down rules for the worship and government of the Churches. The facts are, says Hooker, that at no time has the Church been governed by Scriptural rules (even Calvin's Geneva kept the use of wafer cakes in communion and the custom of godparents at baptism, neither of which is warranted by the Scriptures), nor are the Puritans able to extract that "complete, particular, immutable form of church polity" which they affirm the Scriptures contain. But it is not surprising that immutable laws are not provided by God, for He has given man both reason and discretion, and He requires man to use these natural endowments as far as they avail.

Hooker's position, therefore, with respect to worship and discipline, was that the Church should follow local usage insofar as it serves the goal of salvation. The development of English common law is, he says, an example of the way in which customs grow up and come to have the force of law. When the need arises, particular customs should be changed; but for remedying defects it is not necessary or in the least desirable to pull down the whole social fabric. Similarly, according to Hooker, the visible Church (for matters of polity do not apply to the mystical Body of Christ, which is the invisible Church) is composed of social groups, united in their declaration of the common faith but divided by differences in race, language, custom, location, and civil allegiance. The common end of all churches is to bring men into more perfect fellowship with God through Christ. But how this is to be done may vary from place to place. Feasts and fasts, vestments and ceremonies, tithes and endowments need not be uniform so long as they perform useful functions in the life of the Church.

The Calvinists had arguments besides those based on the Scriptures. As uncompromising champions of pure Christianity against what they considered the anti-Christianity of Rome, they urged that, as a matter of strategy, the Reformed churches in all countries should follow the order of Geneva so as to present a strong and united front against the enemy, and furthermore, that because the danger of apostasy to Rome was an ever-present reality, true Christians should make every effort to avoid any practice which might seem to unite them with Rome. Against these proposals, Hooker defended the English way, which he described as the practice of avoiding sharp breaks with the past and of doing all things in moderation. Writing while the French Catholics and Protestants were engaged in civil war, Hooker was able to maintain that English gradualism is better suited than French radicalism to gain the end which both desired.

In the matter of Church government, Hooker argued for the retention of the episcopacy as against government by presbytery, and he was not inclined to admit that the Genevan and Scottish Churches had any right to their innovation. He denied that the Scriptures give any warrant for the Presbyterian practice of ordaining lay elders, and he maintained that bishops are the successors of the Apostles. An important part of his plea concerned the power of ordination, which he maintained was the prerogative of bishops, although apparently he left room for exceptions.

The most far-reaching difference between the positions advocated by Hooker and by the Presbyterians had to do with the relationship between the Church and the state. Neither party favored the separation of Church and state; the question was simply whether the Church was to be subject to the civil power, or vice versa. The Presbyterians maintained a position similar in some respects to that of Rome. They denied that the magistracy has any say in the government of the Church, but they alleged that the magistracy is under the rule of the Scriptures, which none but the ministry of the Church is authorized to interpret. Hooker, for his part, defended the Elizabethan settlement, according to which Parliament advised the monarch on matters civil, while the hierarchy advised it on matters ecclesiastical, with the government vested in the Crown.

Hooker's calm and moderate plea had little influence in his own day or in the strife-torn years to come. But with the restoration of the episcopacy after the civil wars, his work quickly came into eminence, chiefly as a platform for the Latitudinarian party. In addition, his excellent discussion of natural and civil law, of the role of reason in determining justice, of government by consent of the governed, and of the advantages of gradual change over sudden revolution, was to exercise permanent influence on English political thought.

TRUE CHRISTIANITY

Author: Johann Arndt (1555-1621)
Type of work: Christian ethics
First published: 1606

Principal Ideas Advanced

The purpose of the Holy Scriptures is to restore human nature from the Fall.

To love Christ is to copy Christ's most holy life, to transcribe in one's own life the humility, meekness, and patience of Christ; it is to turn from sin and self-love, in true inward repentance and faith, thereby inheriting the promises of grace and the joy of life eternal.

Johann Arndt, the author of *True Christianity,* was a forerunner of Pietism. Against the orthodoxy of his day Arndt stressed the necessity of an inner experience with God. He had little interest in theological controversy and external formality in religion. Instead, Arndt sought to inspire an inner sense or feeling which corresponds to the performance of external duties. The whole intention and design of his book is to explain how Adam is to die and how Christ is to live in us.

According to Arndt, Christianity consists of a true, lively, and practical faith, which brings forth unfeigned godliness and the proper fruits of righteousness. To be a Christian is not only to believe in Christ, but also to live in Him as He again lives in us.

Conformity to the image of God, according to which man was created, consists in the conformity of man's soul, of his mind and spirit, of his powers and faculties, to the Divine Being and His attributes, virtues, and properties, to the extent that such can be imaged in a creature.

Man ought to understand, Arndt emphasizes, that as the image bearer man is united to God in a union which is the soul's chief tranquillity, its only true rest, from which flow peace, joy, and eternal happiness.

The disobedience of man to God in the Fall of Adam divested man of perfect righteousness and stripped him of the divine image, so that man became spiritually dead, inwardly like the Devil, altogether earthly, and given to self-love and self-will.

Arndt claims that man's fallen nature

is restored in Christ by a new birth, a work of the Holy Spirit, by which a child of damnation and wrath is transformed into a child of salvation and grace. The sinner is made righteous through faith, the Word, and the sacraments. The powers of his soul are enlightened, renewed, and sanctified. Every Christian undergoes a twofold birth; the one is after the flesh, but the other after the spirit; the first is natural, while the second is supernatural, spiritual, holy, and blessed. By the second birth a new being is formed, a new man is begotten and produced, a new creature is born in whom the image of God is again manifest.

True repentance, writes Arndt, is wrought in the soul by the Holy Spirit. Man acknowledges his transgressions and he concedes that God's wrath is justified; he is truly sorry for the evil that he has done, and by faith he now perceives the grace of God in Jesus Christ, and thereby he obtains remission of his sins.

The carnal pleasures are mortified, self-love and pride are crucified, when a man becomes a true Christian. The Christian does not simply cease committing great and outward sins, but he also looks inward and searches the inmost recesses of the mind and heart in order finally to convert himself from self-love to divine love, from worldly lusts to a spiritual life, from a participation in sensual pleasures to an enjoyment of the virtues of Christ, by walking in His steps and believing in His word.

The true Christian tames and mortifies his own will and permits himself to be led by the will of God. The true inward penitent offers a contrite heart as the best and most acceptable sacrifice to God. His heart is heavy with earnest sorrow for having offended a good and gracious God. He is full of fear and trepidation, and yet he is sustained by a lively faith.

True Christian faith, according to Arndt's conception, is a solid trust, a certain and firm persuasion of the grace of God promised to us in Christ. By faith the remission of sins is freely conferred upon us, not for any merits of our own, but for Christ's alone. The forgiveness of our sins is our justification, which is eternal before God, for it is neither of men nor of angels, but it takes place because of the obedience of the Son of God Himself, by His most perfect ransom and precious merits. The good work of Christ is appropriated by us, and applied to us, so that neither the imperfections of our life nor any of our sins now condemn us, for they are covered by the veil of grace.

Where true faith is, there Christ is with all His righteousness and holiness, with all His merits, justification, adoption, and inheritance of life eternal. The habitation of Christ within the heart of the believer is a quickening principle, a vital force, an effectual transformation. Faith transplants the believer into Christ and gives Christ freely to him. The heart is made clean, the soul is sanctified, the seed of God is sown in man, so that the heart is purged of earthly thirsts and easily soars heavenward.

The Kingdom of God now dwells in the heart of the believer and the very law of God is inscribed upon the human heart. No man can lay claim to Christ and His merits without true repentance. Those who cleave to their sins do not profit by Christ.

The formal Christian has the form

of godliness but denies its power. To profess to believe in Christ and then to lead an un-Christian life is not Christian but anti-Christian. Such mockery is blasphemy; such deception is a new crucifixion of Christ. Where the *life* of Christ is not, Arndt insists, Christ is not. Many make a great noise for religion, but their lives are filled with greed and covetousness, with pomp and pride, insincerity, and fraud. To such lives the life of Christ is by its nature opposed. The life of the Christian is nothing else but the most pure and sincere love of God and of men. It issues forth in courtesy, in meekness, patience, mercy, veracity, purity, and simplicity; in contempt of the world and its honors; in refusal of wealth and pleasures; in the denial of ourselves, and in the bearing of the cross continually, with all manner of affliction, for the sake of Christ; and in daily study and thirst after the Kingdom of God, as motivated by a desire to fulfill the divine will in all things.

True Christians are few in number, Arndt declares; God alone knows where and who they are; but whoever they are, Christ both is and will be with them. Anyone who does not imitate the life of Christ has not yet seriously repented and is not to be reputed a true child of God. For the sake of Christ, the Christian must be willing to die to all his sins, to his own self, and to the world.

Man ought to love nothing other than God, and it is impossible to love God unless a person is sincerely displeased with all his sins. Self-love corrupts true judgment, expels virtue, and blinds the understanding.

Contempt of ourselves is the first step to obtaining acceptance with God, Arndt writes. To find grace and mercy, a Christian ought to declare himself unworthy in his own judgment, and he ought to trust only in the heavenly grace of Jesus Christ.

Not the Christian name, but a Christian life is the mark of the true Christian, a life of love and humility, unspotted by sin, and marked by perfect righteousness.

Arndt concludes by insisting that Christ alone is the medicine of the soul, the source of honor, the fount of good works, and a remedy against all calumnies. Christ crucified is ever before us as a book of life, from which we may learn the sacred wisdom of God. The crucified Christ presents us with the deplorable sight of our sins, and He enables us to recover from the Fall by leading us to a sight of the most gracious will, providence, and fatherly care of God.

THE DECLARATION OF SENTIMENTS

Author: Jacobus Arminius (1560-1609)
Type of work: Theology
First published: 1608

Principal Ideas Advanced

The view of predestination which holds that God has decreed to save particular persons and to condemn others without any consideration of their own free decisions is not contained in the writings of Scripture, nor is it compatible with the justice, wisdom, and goodness of God, nor with the nature of man, created in the image of God.

God has rather decreed to appoint His Son as the redeemer of mankind so that those who repent and persevere will be saved.

God's decree to save and to damn particular persons has its foundation in His foreknowledge, so that He elects those whom He knows will believe and He condemns those whom He knows will reject the grace offered to them.

Jacobus Arminius was born in the Netherlands in 1560. From 1603 until his death in 1609 he served the University of Leyden as a Professor of Divinity. His theological views are distinctive for a particular theory of predestination which bears his name. Most significant among his collected works, translated from the Latin in three volumes, are his *Apology against Thirty-One Defamatory Articles* (1609) and his *Declaration of Sentiments* (1608). In both these works Arminius attempts to vindicate himself against attacks that had been made by those who opposed his views on predestination and accused him of attempting to introduce innovations into theology.

The system of doctrine defended by Arminius has exerted considerable influence and has been the source of much controversy. It was formally condemned by the Synod of Dort which convened from November of 1618 to May 1619, since the supporters of Arminius presented a Remonstrance against the decisions of the Synod of Dort, they were at first known as Remonstrants, but in subsequent years they were designated as Arminians.

In his *Declaration of Sentiments* Arminius rejects the views of predestination that were held in his day. It was believed that God had precisely and absolutely decreed to save certain men by His grace or mercy, and to condemn others by His justice. God had, moreover, made such a decree without any consideration of righteousness or sin, obedience or disobedience, on the part of any one class of men.

In order to execute His decree, it was further held, God determined to create Adam, and all men in him, in a state of original righteousness; besides which God then ordained them to commit sin, that they might become guilty of eternal condemnation and be deprived of original righteousness.

God had, moreover, according to the conventional view of predestination, positively willed to save certain persons, and to that end He had decreed them not only to salvation but also to the means of salvation. God had decreed to conduct and to bring such persons to faith in Christ Jesus and to perseverance in that faith. God would lead such persons to these results by a grace that is irresistible, so that it would not be possible for those He has elected to do anything other than believe, persevere in faith, and be saved.

By His absolute will God had foreordained some people to perdition and had decreed to deny to them that grace which is necessary and sufficient for salvation. Since He would not in reality confer grace upon them, they would be placed neither in a condition of possible salvation nor in any capacity for believing or for being saved.

Some theologians of Arminius's day presented a more modified view than the conventional one just described. They refused to lay down the Creation or the Fall as a mediate cause foreordained by God for the execution of the preceding degree of predestination. Others did not allow any part of election and reprobation to begin until after the Fall of man.

No matter how this doctrine of predestination was modified, Arminius found it unacceptable in its currently accepted formulations. Arminius argues that such a doctrine is no part of the foundations of Christianity. Christianity is founded on the decree of God by which Christ is appointed to be the Savior and Head of those who will be made heirs of salvation. The doctrine of predestination does not comprise within it the whole or any part of the Gospel, Arminius insists. The Gospel consists partly of an injunction to repent and believe, and partly of a promise to bestow forgiveness of sins, the grace of the Spirit, and eternal life. The doctrine of predestination does not even tell us what kind of men God has predestined; such a doctrine embraces a mystery known only to God, a mystery as to which persons are to be saved and how many. It is a doctrine that is not necessary to salvation, either as an object of knowledge, belief, hope, or performance.

Arminius continues by pointing out that the doctrine of predestination was never admitted, decreed, or approved in any council, either general or particular, for the first six hundred years after Christ. Moreover, none of those doctors of the Church who held orthodox views for the first six hundred years after Christ ever propounded or approved this doctrine. It does not even agree with the harmony of the confession published in the name of the Reformed and Protestant Churches at Geneva, and it is doubtful whether it agrees with the Belgic Confession and the Heidelberg Catechism.

When strictly maintained, Arminius argues, the doctrine of predestination is repugnant to God's wisdom because it represents Him as decreeing something for an end which is not good; namely, eternal perdition. The doctrine is repugnant to the justice of God because it affirms that God has absolutely willed to save certain individuals and has decreed their salvation without having any regard for their righteousness or obedience. It is opposed to His justice because it affirms that God wishes to subject His creatures to misery, although He does not consider the creature to be a sinner. The doctrine is repugnant to the goodness of God, a goodness which is a disposition in God to communicate His own goodness insofar as His justice considers it to be proper. The doctrine of predestination ascribes to God the act of willing the greatest evil to his creatures; and it claims that from all eternity He preordained that evil for them, even before He determined to bestow any good upon them.

Such a doctrine, Arminius writes, is contrary to the nature of man, for man was created after the divine image, which consists of the knowledge of God and holiness; thus, man was qualified, empowered, and placed under obligation to love, worship, and serve

God. The doctrine is inconsistent with the freedom of man's will, in which, and with which, man was created; furthermore, the doctrine is prejudicial to man's inclinations and to his capacity for the eternal fruition of salvation in that the majority of men are thought to be prevented from salvation not in consequence of any preceding sin, but solely because of predestination.

The strict view of predestination is diametrically opposed to the act of creation, Arminius continues. To intend the eternal perdition of a creature is not to communicate a good, but a preparation for the greatest evil. Reprobation is an act of hatred, an act which derives its origin from hatred, whereas creation is the communication of good; creation is a perfect act of God, by which He manifests His wisdom, goodness, and omnipotence, and creation is therefore not subordinate to any other preceding act of God.

The doctrine of predestination is at open hostility with the nature of eternal life and eternal death. The former is described as a crown of righteousness and the latter as the wages of sin, so that neither the one nor the other is determined by decree apart from any consideration of sin and obedience.

The doctrine is also inconsistent with the nature and properties of sin, Arminius argues. If a person is under the unavoidable necessity of sinning because of the divine decree, sin could not be called disobedience and rebellion, nor could it be the cause which moves the divine will to reprobate.

Predestination is likewise repugnant to the nature of divine grace, Arminius claims, for predestination interferes with free will, and makes grace irresistible. The doctrine is injurious to the glory of God for, according to the doctrine, God is the author of sin, so that in fact God moves to sin by an act that is unavoidable. Moreover, the doctrine is highly dishonorable to Jesus Christ, since it excludes Christ from that decree of predestination which predestinates the end, and it does not make Christ the foundation of election.

Such a doctrine is also hurtful to the salvation of men; it discourages solicitude about being converted from sin unto God; it extinguishes zeal for prayer and good works. It takes away the fear and trembling with which we are commanded to work out our own salvation, and it produces a despair. It inverts the order of the Gospel and is in open hostility to its ministry, and it very easily renders pastors negligent. It subverts the very foundation of religion by undermining a love for justice and hatred of sin.

In contradistinction to the generally accepted opinion, Arminius held that with respect to the salvation of sinful man, the first absolute decree of God was to appoint His son, Jesus Christ, as Mediator and Savior, who by His own death might destroy sin, and by His obedience might obtain the lost salvation and communicate it by His own virtue.

The first decree was followed by a second decree in which God decreed to receive into favor those who repent and believe, and, in Christ, for His sake and through Him, to effect the salvation of such penitents and believers as persevered to the end, but to damn as aliens from Christ and to leave in sin, and under wrath, all unbelievers and impenitent persons.

In a third divine decree God decreed to administer in an efficacious and in a sufficient manner the means which are necessary for faith and repentance; and He decreed to have such administration instituted according to divine wisdom and justice.

In a fourth decree God decreed to save and to damn certain particular persons. This decree had its foundation, however, in the foreknowledge of God. From all eternity God knows those individuals who will, through His prevenient grace, believe, and who through his subsequent grace will persevere, and He also knows those who will not believe and will not persevere.

Such a view of predestination is the sum and substance of the Gospel, Arminius writes. This doctrine is not subject to any of the preceding criticisms. For in His providence, God both wills and performs good acts, whereas He only freely permits those which are evil. In his primitive condition, after creation, man was enabled to perform the truly good, with the assistance of divine grace. In his fallen state, man, of and by himself, is incapable of thinking, willing, or doing what is really good. He must first be regenerated and renewed by the Holy Spirit, and even then he is in constant need of divine grace. To the latter is to be ascribed the commencement, the continuance, and the consummation of all good. For grace is a gratuitous affection by which God looks kindly towards a sinner and gives His Son so that whoever believes in Him inherits eternal life and is justified in the eyes of God. Grace is an infusion, into the human understanding, will, and affections, of the gifts of the Holy Spirit, of faith, hope, and charity, without which man is unable to do anything good. Grace is the perpetual assistance which enables the regenerate man actually to will what is good; it enables God and man to will and to work together, so that man may do the good that He wills. The grace imparted by the Holy Spirit is sufficient to enable men to repent, and to believe and keep the commandments of God.

INTRODUCTION TO THE DEVOUT LIFE

Author: Saint Francis of Sales (1567-1622)
Type of work: Spiritual counsel
First published: 1609

Principal Ideas Advanced

The religious life is not a special vocation for a few Christians, but a possibility and so a duty for all.

It is not achieved without ordered discipline, which makes possible a steady progression away from sin and towards virtue.

Each stage of the devout life has its own basic requirements, and we are shown how we can practice the disciplines of meditation and prayer.

The *Introduction to the Devout Life* was the outcome of prolonged experience as a director of souls. As Provost of Geneva, Francis of Sales had offered counsel to men and women in search of spiritual guidance, and he had written a large number of letters dealing with specific problems or perplexities. He had accumulated a good deal of material, and the incentive to set it in due order came from his association with Mme. de Charmoisy, an earnest and able woman married to a relative of his, who placed herself under St. Francis's direction. For her, St. Francis composed a series of letters of instruction, and he then rearranged and rewrote the material and published it as the *Introduction to the Devout Life*. St. Francis was perfectly aware that his work represented a breach with tradition. He was a bishop (though, since Geneva was his see, he was nonresident), and it had always been assumed that bishops would be concerned with practical affairs. But it seemed to him eminently appropriate that a chief shepherd should guide and direct men's souls. Moreover, it had previously been taken for granted that a spiritual director would chiefly be preoccupied with the needs of those who, having isolated themselves, could give their whole attention to such matters. "Those who have treated of devotion," he wrote, "have almost all had in mind the instruction of persons very much withdrawn from the society of the world, or at all events they have taught a kind of devotion which leads to this complete withdrawal. My intention is to instruct those who live in towns, in households, at the court, and who, by reason of their circumstances, are obliged to lead an ordinary life in outward show." It had been generally assumed that such people, involved as they were in secular activities, could not be expected to give any serious thought to devotion. But St. Francis would not concede this point; he writes that "a vigorous and constant soul can live in the world without receiving any worldly taint." He concedes that it will not be an easy task; those who undertake it will need help, and St. Francis proposes to provide it. He states that he has no illusions about the difficulties which are involved in living a disciplined religious life in secular surroundings, and he expresses his hope that his little book will encourage those who have hitherto assumed that the undertaking is impractical.

The *Introduction to the Devout Life* was planned with great care, and St. Francis himself points out to the reader the general pattern which this guide book of the spiritual life will follow. He assumes that anyone who embarks upon a course of devotion must have responded to holy impulses, but at first these may represent no more than an intermittent desire to be better than in the past. These vague promptings must therefore be confirmed and consolidated, and to this end St. Francis lays down a course of simple meditations. Initially, of course, he defines devotion (which "is no other thing than a true love of God"), he describes its nature and its excellence, and he demonstrates its relevance to all kinds of life. There is no single pattern of holiness, he claims. The monk pursues one path, the bishop another; in spite of their different activities both strive after the same end. In the same way the married person, the soldier, the courtier, the lawyer may exercise a genuine religious vocation in a diversity of ways, but all aim at true devotion. And here St. Francis observes that most of the patriarchs and holy men of scripture were engaged in callings which took them into the world and kept them there. But good will requires guidance, and a spiritual director is consequently necessary.

St. Francis was aware that discipline is an inseparable part of devotion and that discipline springs from the simple fact that our lives stand in need of cleansing and reform. We must admit our involvement in mortal sin and turn from it. We must learn not only to restrain the evil act but also to rebuke the evil impulse. But this can be achieved only if we train ourselves to control our appetites and desires. At this point the shrewd and practical wisdom which marks the *Introduction* begins to emerge. In order to help us to root "sin and the principal affections to sin" from our hearts, St. Francis sets out a series of meditations, one for each day, to be used in a prescribed order.

The subject of the first meditation is creation; we then turn to the end for which we were created, the benefits which God bestows upon us, the nature of sin, the significance of death, the inevitability of judgment, the pains of Hell, and the joys of Heaven. The last two meditations deal with the decisive choices which the believer makes: the way he "elects" Heaven and selects the devout life.

The series of meditations follows a clear sequence, and each one is developed according to a simple pattern. The believer first prepares himself for meditation; he consciously places himself in the presence of God and asks for guidance and inspiration. Next he ponders, one by one, the chief "considerations," by which St. Francis means the essential facts which determine our posture and position with regard to the subject under study. This kind of serious reflection naturally awakens emotional responses ("affections") and prompts some kind of moral decision ("resolution"). In this section, St. Francis sets forth as many as half a dozen points which ought to be embraced by our widening reflection. As the meditation draws to a conclusion, the neophyte is instructed to include at least three steps: thanksgiving for God's mercies as these are suggested by the subject under consideration; oblation, in which he offers himself to God; petition, which invokes God's aid in bringing to good effect the affections and resolutions awakened by the meditation. Finally, the believer pauses to consider in retrospect what has engaged his mind and soul, and to "gather a little nosegay of devotion from the considerations which he has made, in order to inhale its perfume throughout the day."

At this point, St. Francis's method appears with special clarity. His system is devised to meet the needs of ordinary people. It does not make unrealistic demands upon time, but sets forth step by step a means by which any earnest seeker can discipline his life. The wisdom of St. Francis's approach is based on a profound understanding of the human mind. He is aware of the difficulties involved; he asks enough to be demanding, but not so much as to be discouraging. Renouncing the old life means that we forsake not evil in general, but those forms of it to which we happen to be inclined. So he offers directions for turning away from venial sins, from "affection to useless and dangerous things," and from evil inclinations.

The purpose of the *Introduction* is primarily positive, and St. Francis therefore turns to the constructive disciplines which lift the soul to God. Prayer, of course, is of supreme importance, but many people fail in this discipline because they are uninstructed. "Above all," says St. Francis, "I recommend to you prayer of the mind and heart, and especially that which has for its subject the life and passion of our Lord; for by beholding him often in meditation, your whole soul will be filled with him; you will learn his disposition, and you will form your actions after the model of his." But St. Francis is too wise to believe that people will learn how to pray by being exhorted to do so. Therefore he sets forth a system of meditation. The first step is to master the art of placing oneself in the presence of God, and here St. Francis enumerates four ways by which one can learn to do so. One should begin with "a lively and attentive apprehension of the omnipresence of God"; then one realizes that the God who is everywhere is, in a special way, in the heart of the worshiper; the third stage is to realize the particular concern which the Savior feels for all His people; the fourth is to use the imagination to visualize Christ in His concrete acts of mercy and love, so that by dwelling in His presence one can dwell in the presence of God. But this is by no means the whole essence of preparation for prayer. One should also specifically invoke God's aid and ponder the mystery of His grace. Finally, one turns to "affections" and "consideration" and recapitulation.

The devout life is one in which the virtues of Christian discipleship are increasingly manifested, writes Francis. But even the devout man needs counsel. Consequently St. Francis considers one by one the various virtues which ought to appear more consistently in the devout lives. He begins with patience, and then he proceeds to humility, both as an outward aspect and as inward disposition. He shows how humility helps us to come to terms with our own nature, and with what wisdom it must be exercised, lest we gain a reputation for hypocrisy. He points out the need of gentleness in our dealings with others and the inescapable demand that we learn to control our anger. By the same token, we should treat ourselves with similar restraint, "never fretting at ourselves or at our imperfections." It is one thing to have a firm and dispassionate dislike of our faults; it is another to nag ourselves about them. In discharging our daily tasks we must always be diligent and careful, never anxious or worried. Chastity must be preserved but need not be equated with celibacy: St. Francis holds virginity in high esteem but has wise counsel for married people, and he insists on the honorableness of the marriage bed. He dwells on the importance of poverty of spirit—which need not be incompatible with the possession of wealth. He is concerned that the true nature of friendship be appreciated. There are vain friendships and evil ones, but when properly understood friendship is one of God's good gifts, and it should be cherished in the spirit of gratitude. St. Francis has wise words on company; he explains how to use it and when to withdraw from it. He examines clothes and the standards by which we judge them; speech, and the standards to which it should conform; games and recreations, and the ways of determining their moral value. Some forms of recreation are permissible but dangerous, and here we need to exercise great care. In addition we must learn to be faithful both on great occasions and on small ones, and in all things we must manifest a just and reasonable spirit.

It is never a simple matter to live a life marked by such virtues. The Christian will always encounter temptations; he must be prepared to meet them. St. Francis advises everyone to learn a proper measure of indifference to the comments of the children of this world. We shall find that we are constantly in need of courage. St. Francis was not concerned merely to emphasize the fact of temptation; he wanted to help the Christian to understand its nature and overcome its power. He distinguishes between small temptations and great ones, and he shows how each type is to be mastered.

What St. Francis envisages is a regular course of discipline, renewed year by year, by means of which the Christian can steadily grow in grace. To achieve spiritual growth involves careful examination of ourselves and of our progress: How do we stand toward God? Have we advanced in understanding and mastery of ourselves? Do our relationships with others adequately reflect our spiritual concerns?

Then, with the care which characterizes all his work, St. Francis turns to the enumeration of "considerations" which will promote our advance. We must dwell on the serious importance of the soul and the high excellence of the virtues. We must dwell on the example of the saints, and we must meditate deeply on the love which Christ bears us. We must lose ourselves in the contemplation of the eternal love of God for us. Then we must make sure that all these thoughts and emotions issue regularly in such conduct as both reflect and confirm them.

Anyone who reads the *Introduction to the Devout Life* will have no difficulty in understanding its great and continuing influence. It provides the foundation for one of the recognized systems of spiritual direction in the Roman Church. In all Christian bodies, thousands have found, and still find, that this book of religious counsel is sane, wise, deeply perceptive, and unfailingly helpful.

THE TRUTH OF THE CHRISTIAN RELIGION

Author: Hugo Grotius (1583-1645)
Type of work: Apologetics
First published: 1622

Principal Ideas Advanced

That the Christian religion is more reasonable and more worthy of acceptance than any other religion is evident from the authority and trustworthiness of its sacred books, from the superiority of its precepts and doctrines, and from the inferior teachings of paganism, Judaism, and Islam.

The truth of the Christian religion is as certain as the truth of reason, as the evidence of the senses, and as other truths based upon the testimony of trustworthy witnesses.

The Truth of the Christian Religion, written by Hugo Grotius in 1622, seeks to demonstrate that Christianity is true by examining the evidence in its support, and by comparing Christianity with pagan religion, Judaism, and Mohammedanism.

The work is divided into six books. Book One seeks to demonstrate that there is but one all-perfect God who is the cause of all things and the Governor of the universe. Book Two offers arguments in support of the thesis that Christianity is true and that it excels all other religions. Book Three deals with the authority of the Old and New Testaments, and Books Four, Five, and Six, respectively, compare Christianity with paganism, Judaism, and Mohammedanism to demonstrate that Christianity alone is the true religion, the religion which man must embrace if he is to attain happiness after this life.

Religion is not foolish or empty, Grotius writes, since the existence of God is proven by the rational necessity of a first cause and by the universal assent of every nation. By our senses we observe that some things have a beginning and cannot be the cause of their own existence, for if they were self-caused, they would have been before they were, which is impossible. Such contingent things must then have derived their existence from something else; namely, from God, a cause which never had a beginning but exists necessarily. What exists necessarily cannot be a species of beings and must therefore be a single being, to which all perfection belongs in an infinite degree; therefore, God is a living infinite God, eternal, omnipotent, omniscient, and completely good.

When it is said that God is the cause of all things that have a real existence, writes Grotius, we do not mean that God is the cause of evil actions, for man and some other intelligences superior to man were created by God with a liberty of acting, and liberty is not itself evil although it may be the cause of what is evil.

That the world is governed by the providence of God is evident from the fact that men and animals provide for their young, which perfection, as it is a part of goodness, ought not to be excluded from God. An all-wise, omnipotent being cannot but know, direct, and govern everything which is done, for He seeks always to promote the good of the whole.

God is concerned with the deeds of men, Grotius assures the reader. Since in this life the wicked often go unpunished while the righteous suffer, we can expect judgment after this life, an expectation confirmed by the traditions of almost all civilized people, which is in no way repugnant to reason, but is rather supported by a natural desire of immortality and by a sense of impending judgment.

That the Christian religion is most true and certain is evident from certain matters of fact and from the nature of its doctrine. That there was such a person as Jesus, that He died an ignominious death and yet was worshiped after His death by wise men, is generally acknowledged, not only by Christians, but also by Jewish and pagan sources.

That Jesus was worshiped after His death by wise men is explicable solely on the assumption that they found that the reports concerning His miracles and resurrection were true and founded upon the sufficient testimony of credible witnesses.

There is no reason, Grotius insists, to assume that the belief in the Resurrection of Jesus is false, for the belief does not involve the contradiction of affirming that the same person was alive and dead at the same time; it asserts, rather, that a dead man was restored to life by the power of the One who first gave life to man. By raising Christ from the dead, God the Father put his seal of approval upon the work of his Son and confirmed the truth of His doctrine.

Not only is the Christian religion based upon historical facts, Grotius argues, but its very doctrines are inherently superior to all others. The worship that it prescribes, the rewards that it offers, the precepts it enjoins, and the method by which it is to be propagated are in keeping with man's moral nature and with a conception of an all-wise, all-good, and all-powerful God; Christianity is therefore more excellent, more perfect, and more worthy of devotion than any other religion.

The reward promised by Christ to His disciples goes beyond earthly pleasures, writes Grotius. The end of man is another life after this, in which there is no death, pain, or sorrow, but only the highest joy, not only in the soul, but in the resurrected body. Man will behold God; all things will be glorified.

The Christian religion excels all other religions in the exceeding purity and holiness of its precepts, both in the worship of God, and in other particulars. Christian worship is free of cruelty, of human sacrifice and lewdness. It teaches men to worship God with a pure mind and through the performance of right acts. The chief part of religion consists in a steadfast faith, sincere obedience, trust in God's promises, and in a true love both of God and of one's neighbor, not in a servile obedience prompted by fear of punishment. Christian service is a joyful service, which is enjoined upon the believer, who prays not for riches and honor, but only for such things as are for the glory of God, for whatever leads to eternity, for the pardon of past sins, and for the inspiration of the Holy Spirit.

The Christian religion further excels all others in the manner in which it was delivered and propagated. The divine nature of its teacher is apparent from the testimony of Jesus' disciples, who described Him as being without sin. What He commanded others to do, He did himself; He was faithful to God throughout his life; He was a lover of mankind, even of His persecutors. He was seen after His return to life, and He was taken up into Heaven, where He obtained the highest power; He was himself possessed with the glory that He promised. His doctrines spread with remarkable success, in spite of persecution and without the use of force, so that their very success ought to be regarded as greater than any miracle.

To understand fully the Christian religion, Grotius avers, it is necessary to go to the books that contain it. The books of the New Testament were written by those whose names they bear. The authors knew about the matters of which they wrote, and since they had no desire to lie, what they said must be true, since falsity proceeds either from hypocrisy or ignorance. God has in fact given remarkable testimony to the sincerity of the authors of the New Testament by working miracles through them.

The writings of the New Testament

contain nothing that is impossible nor disagreeable to reason. The books are free of inconsistencies, and what they declare is further confirmed by the books of the Old Testament and by the records of the Jewish religion.

Present-day Judaism, while superior to paganism, has only a part and the beginning of the truth, writes Grotius. The Jews are the offspring of holy men; they were often visited by the prophets of God. The Messiah was born of them, and they were the first teachers of Christianity.

The Jews ought not to look upon Christians as their enemies, Grotius declares; rather they ought to accept the miracles of Christ as sufficiently attested and as based upon the same kind of evidence which persuades the Jews of the miracles done by Moses and Elisha.

The authority of a doctrine cannot be more effectually recommended to man by God than by the working of miracles. The miracles of Christ ought, therefore, to be taken as signs of the truth of what Jesus taught. He urged the worship of the true God and taught men to reverence the writings of Moses. Jesus himself observed the Law of Moses when on earth; no part of the ancient Law was subsequently abolished, except whatever precepts had no intrinsic goodness in them.

Jesus ought to be accepted by the Jews as their own Messiah, says Grotius; He fulfills the extraordinary promise of the Messiah which is found in the books of the Old Testament itself. That He was of the seed of David, that He was born of a virgin, healed the sick, was the instructor of all nations, and suffered and died—all these truths were foretold by the prophets.

The further superiority of Christianity to paganism and Mohammedanism is readily seen, Grotius contends. Reason alone is sufficient to show that there is but one God, the cause of all things. It is foolish to pay homage to many deities and spirits, some of which are evil. To worship departed men, stars, gross matter, brute creatures, and things lacking real existence is most disagreeable to right reason.

The wisest heathens shared many of the principal beliefs of the Christian religion; for instance, that religion does not consist of ceremonies but is in the heart, that the soul is immortal, and that the divine nature can be joined to the human. What is found as disorganized belief among the pagans is unified by the Christian religion, and what is difficult to believe in Christianity is matched in paganism by things far more incredible.

A confrontation of Christianity and Mohammedanism shows that the latter is directly opposed to Christianity, writes Grotius. Mohammedanism is calculated for bloodshed; it delights much in ceremonies, and it encourages belief while refusing critical examination.

Mohammed and his followers admit that Jesus, Moses, and the disciples were sent by God, and yet many things in the Koran contradict their teachings. For example, the Apostles teach that Jesus died on the cross, rose again from the dead, and was seen by many persons; Mohammed says that Jesus was secretly taken into Heaven before the Crucifixion, and that what was fixed to the cross was only an effigy of Him.

To assert that the Koran is uncorrupted and that the writings of Moses and of the disciples of Jesus are corrupted overlooks the fact that copies of the Gospels in many languages were disseminated throughout the world and have been preserved by many sects.

A further comparison of Christianity and Islam discloses the superiority of the former, continues Grotius. Mohammed says that Jesus was the promised Messiah, born without a human father; that He healed the sick and restored the dead to life; and that He was taken up into Heaven. Mohammed says that he himself was sent with arms, not miracles; and the body of Mohammed rests in the grave. Christianity was propagated by miracles and by the blood of the martyrs; the teachers of Islam did not endure any grievous troubles, nor do they undergo death for their faith. Mohammedanism spread by the sword; its precepts are also inferior in that divorce is permitted, revenge is enjoined, and needless rituals and prohibitions are reintroduced.

Grotius concludes his apology by arguing that Christians can safely put their trust in the God, who made all things, and they may be fully persuaded that He takes care of man; and furthermore, Christians can have faith in Jesus, since there is no other Savior. The holy doctrine of Christ is to be preserved as a valuable treasure, and the Scriptures are to be read by Christians prepared to obey God; through being faithful, they will inherit a future happiness.

THE WAY TO CHRIST

Author: Jakob Boehme (1575-1624)
Type of work: Mystical theology
First published: 1623-1682

Principal Ideas Advanced

Deity exhibits a threefold nature as Father, Son, and Holy Spirit; the first being Abyss, or Ungrund, *which is beyond all the determinate realities of nature and creation, and which also exhibits opposing aspects of love and wrath; the second, or Son, being the wisdom and love which redeems man as well as the rest of creation; the third being the vitality in nature and creation.*

Man, who is a creation or objectivation of God, has a twofold nature, one which aspires to communion with God, and the other which persists in the arrogant self-centeredness which is the source of evil.

Nature, or creation, also shows a twofold aspect, being in itself alienation from God and hence a lower and evil realm, yet being in relation to Deity the sacramental realm in which God is manifested.

The writings and life of Jakob Boehme may both be regarded as the expression of the mystical exaltation which was literally the defining characteristic of this remarkable man. The claim he made for one of his writings, that "not Art but the Holy Spirit wrote this," might well be extended to include all his numerous writings, and as far as the facts can now be made out, his life as well. The great illumination in which, as Boehme put it, "the Gate was opened to me" occurred in 1600 at the age of twenty-four, and the impact of this experience may be seen in the whole subsequent course of his life. Yet it is also important to note that from childhood onward a kind of direct religious perception of great clarity and intensity was a quality of all Boehme's life and experience.

He lived his entire life, except for a few months of enforced exile, in his native town of Goerlitz in Germany. His parents were farmers, but apparently because of delicate health he was apprenticed to the cobbler's trade. In 1599 he married a butcher's daughter. Of this happy union were born four sons and probably two daughters.

Following the illumination of 1600, Boehme began to write down his experiences. However, his first book *Aurora* did not appear until 1612. It aroused the violent opposition of the Lutheran pastor, Gregorius Richter, who secured from the local government a prohibition of any further writing by the inspired shoemaker. Boehme respected this ban until 1618, when he began again to write and publish his mystical reflections, which seemed to Richter dangerous heresies.

The Three Principles appeared in 1619, *The Three-fold Life of Man, Answers to the Forty Questions of the Soul, The Six Great Points,* and other books in 1620, and *Signatura rerum* in 1621. Yet the bulk of Boehme's writing was published posthumously. The present volumes, *The Way to Christ,* was actually not originally written as a single book, but as a series of tracts on the common theme of redemption in Christ. They were written between 1622 and 1624, and at least two of them were unfinished at the author's death in 1624. In that year a friend published three of them, *Of True Repentance, Of True Resignation,* and the *Supersensual Life* under the title *The Way to Christ.* A second edition, which followed four years later, added two more tracts, and by the 1682 edition of Boehme's works the number had grown to eight. The first English translation was made in 1644. The most recent English translation by John Stoudt in 1947 includes seven tracts, omitting *On The Four Complexions* because of its antiquated psychology.

Pastor Richter continued to attack Boehme, who responded with a dignified defense of *The Way to Christ.* Opposition led to a few months of exile in Dresden and other cities in 1624, where the greatness of his thought was acknowledged and acclaimed. He returned home to Goerlitz later the same year, where he died on November 20.

Boehme's influence on subsequent religious and philosophic thought has been strong and varied. The year of his death was also the year of George Fox's birth, symbolizing Boehme's influence on Fox and the Quakers. An equally great impact may be seen on the Anglican, William Law. Romantic philosophers and literary men in Germany, England, and America show an influence of which Hegel, Schelling, and Emerson are only three illustrations.

Boehme's viewpoint has been characterized as Christian Gnosticism and theosophy. Yet these terms are accurately descriptive only if they are taken in a strictly etymological sense, designating a kind of knowledge which occurs as a direct aspect of religious experience and which illuminates the mysteries of God and the world. Boehme's writings everywhere assume that there is such a knowledge and that he is in possession of at least some aspects of it.

Other identifiable influences on Boehme's mind range from the Bible, which he knew thoroughly and quoted perceptively, through the tradition of western mysticism to the alchemy of Paracelsus. This last influence affected his vocabulary more than it did the content of his message.

Boehme's writing is remarkably objective in character. It is about God and the world, rather than himself. Yet, between the lines there is a clear and persistent symbolic reference to the human self and its relation to ultimate reality. Also, Boehme's writing is a product of the tragic time of war and upheaval in which he lived. The fascination shown in his writings for evil, conflict, and tragedy must be regarded as a response to his age.

One must not neglect to add that Boehme is a powerful religious genius expressing through his writings his own unique vision. In this respect, he has been characterized as the last great Western mystic.

His system of thought is obscure, complex, and not everywhere consistent. Also, the importance of the system in relation to specific individual insights varies widely from document to document. The most basic category of the system is the threefold nature of Deity as Father, Son, and Holy Spirit, with the Father generally characterized as the *Ungrund* or Abyss. The Abyss is literally no-thing, for it is beyond the realm of nature and creatureliness where things exist. He (or It) is conceived voluntaristically, and exhibits two wills, respectively good and evil, love and wrath, light and darkness. The concept of Deity or Godhead as Abyss may be regarded as the result of Boehme's attempt to find onto-logical foundation for his radical view of human freedom. It is a freedom pregnant with all the possibilities of evil, conflict, and tragedy.

In contrast to the Father, the Son is all light and wisdom, and to Him the enlightened soul clings in faith and salvation. The Son is the redeemer from all the world's tragic evil. Boehme's conception of the Virgin Sophia is in effect a mystical feminine rendering of the Logos. The third person of the Trinity is an expression of the indwelling vitalities which guide the course of the world upward to God. The world of nature and creature is an objectification, or as Boehme put it, an exhalation or emanation of deity.

Boehme's interpretation of mysticism emphasizes voluntarism and freedom in both God and man. Like God, man has two wills, one an aspiration toward God, and the other an arrogant self-centeredness, which is the fruitful and characteristic source of evil in human life. The radical and irreducible freedom of man is, according to Boehme, to be redeemed or saved in Christ. Hence, the importance of *The Way to Christ* in the author's whole work and system of thought.

Of the seven treatises which comprise *The Way to Christ,* all but one are essentially religious in nature, and that one, entitled *Of Divine Contemplation,* while basically philosophical, is by no means irrelevant to religion.

The other six can be characterized as working documents emerging from the author's full and rich religious life. Taken as a group, these essays constitute a kind of last testament from the author.

The first of the tracts, entitled *Of True Repentance,* was written in 1622 and 1623, and its purpose is accurately characterized in the title. The essay alternates between exposition of the theme and prayers and confessions which exemplify the process of repentance. There is also dialogue with the reader, who is assumed to be a fellow traveler on the road to repentance. There are also instructions for resistance of temptation. The quality of religious life here expressed is intense, clear, and profoundly Christian.

The treatise contains an extended dialogue between the soul and the Virgin Sophia. The latter has been likened to the world-soul of Hegel or Goethe, yet, as previously indicated, a kind of mystical feminine interpretation of the Logos seems a more appropriate and adequate characterization. Boehme uses a wealth of erotic imagery, already current in the tradition of mysticism, to characterize the religious life and its unique quality of immediate knowledge. "The Gates of the Paradisiacal Rose-garden are only understood by those children of Christ who have experienced it," he writes, or again he asserts of repentance, "The Person who wants to reach divine contemplation and speak with God within himself must follow this Process and then he will reach it."

The second tract, *Of True Resignation,* deals with the resignation of the creaturely and natural self to God. Resignation means not impersonal or stoical acquiescence, or Oriental obliteration of selfhood, but rather a conforming of the human will to God. It is the want of this conformity which is the source of evil in all its manifold aspects. In this respect, the treatise might be characterized as an inquiry into the origin and conquest of evil.

The discussion begins with a distinction between the arrogant vanity of the creature taken in himself and the achievement of a will in harmony with God. This leads to a distinction between the God-centered reason, which is Eternal Light, and the man-centered reason, which boasts its egocentric viewpoint.

The process of resignation by which the latter is changed into the former is no mere acquiescence or negation of selfhood, but a dynamic transformation of the human will. "There is no other way to God than through a new mind which turns away from evil and enters into repentance for past sins, departing from iniquity, willing it no more but enveloping its will in Christ's Death. . . ."

Both man's faith and God's grace are paradoxically related in the process of repentance. The whole process, moreover, is essentially inward. Externalities of religion are in themselves completely futile. Boehme never tires of saying that the realities of religion achieve authenticity only in proportion to their inwardness.

Of Regeneration, or, Of the New Birth, written in 1622, continues many of the lines of thought of the first two tracts. Regeneration is held to consist of replacing the old and evil will of Adam with the new will of Christ in a man's life. The old and evil will is characterized as it emerges in Adam and is reproduced in his descendants. Its taproot is a self-centered and evil imagination, and its outcome is a replacement of the divine light and vitality by fleshly vanity, darkness, and evil imagination.

Boehme speculates concerning the nature of the Fall of Adam, concluding that it took place not with the eating of the fatal apple, but in Adam's sleep, during which it is asserted that "he died to the angelical world . . . and . . . departed from the eternal image which was of God's generation." During this same sleep Eve was taken from Adam's rib. Upon awakening, both man and woman began their fallen life of evil and external imagination.

The fourth treatise, *Of the Supersensual Life, A Dialogue Between a Scholar and His Master,* was also written in 1622. The Disciple opens the conversation by asking how he may come to the "supersensual life" in which he sees God and hears him speak. The Master replies that to do this he must "leap" into the realm beyond natural and creaturely reality. Asked if it is far, the Master replies, "It is within you."

The conversation then concerns the ways in which this change is to be effected. The Master says first that one must be silent as God was before creation. The Disciple asks how he can achieve this state without "destroying Nature." The Master's answer is that a detachment of the self from the world of things is a first step.

The conversation turns to the radical paradox involved in loving and hating the self. The Master argues for a hatred for the creaturely self of arrogance and self-will, and yet he affirms the self with which man seeks God. Asked where love dwells in man, the Master replies in a similar spirit, that love dwells "in that place in man where he is not." Such love burns out the "I-ness"; that is, the egotism in natural and creaturely man.

The Disciple shifts the conversation again by asking where the soul goes after death. The Master's successive responses add up to the conclusion that Heaven and Hell are not to be regarded as locations, but as actualization of the relations of God's love and wrath to man. The Master continues to reflect upon the theme of Judgment Day, arguing that in that day the strife, tension, and tragedy of history will be surmounted by God's love.

The fifth tract, dated 1624, is entitled *A Dialogue between an Enlightened and Unenlightened Soul.* The conversation begins between the troubled and unenlightened soul and the Devil, and continues between the unenlightened or troubled soul and an enlightened soul. To the modern reader it is reminiscent of the allegorical conversations of John Bunyan of a generation after Boehme.

To the Devil, the soul asserts her inherent nobility, and the Devil replies with an elaboration of the Biblical temptation "to be a real Lord of heaven and earth." Once she has succumbed to temptation, evil proliferates in the troubled soul in the forms of arrogance, avarice, envy, and wrath.

In this sorry condition, the troubled soul meets Jesus Christ, who counsels repentance. However, the Devil is on hand to prevent this course and to counsel worldliness. At this point, an enlightened soul becomes the troubled soul's advisor and guide. She suggests surrender, and explains the upward path to salvation. As a consequence "the Distressed Soul now began her walk under Christ's patient guidance.

. . . Thus did she come again to true rest and become a child of God."

The sixth tract, *Of Divine Contemplation,* was written in 1622 and was unfinished at the author's death. It is essentially a philosophic meditation on the basic themes of Boehme's thought, on God, good, and evil, man's mind and will, and the realm of nature. We begin with human reason which acknowledges its limits, yet knows that it has originated from the supernatural ground of God's essence. Indeed, the suffering, conflicting wills of nature and creation likewise presuppose a divine will. Conversely, out of the strife and anguish of creation come the faith and peace of God.

Human life and, indeed, all of creation are regarded as objectivations of the divine will. Yet beyond all will and willing is that which is without will and is eternally one; namely, the Abyss or *Ungrund.* The beginning of all substance is the Logos; and the world is to be regarded as emanated Logos, "disposed into individualities." The unique designation of each thing is known as its signature. Such, in brief and summary statement, is Boehme's vision of God and God's creation.

The final tract of the volume, *Of Divine Prayer,* was written in the last year of its author's life; the essay is unfinished. The philosophical reflections of the previous treatise are here turned to religious practice in a discussion of the nature and art of prayer. As in the first treatise, the method alternates between exposition of the theme and practical illustrations of it.

Real prayer, the author assures us at the outset, is inward in nature. It is a disposition of the human heart, rather than a form of words. This disposition is a distinctive attitude of dependence on God; it is the essential function of prayer to realize or fulfill this dependence.

Prayer is not similar to an address to any worldly king, for the good reason that before God man has no rights whatsoever, yet from God man receives in abundance, as did the prodigal son from his father.

The greater part of this treatise is not argument or exposition, but confessions, acts of repentance, and prayers for varied occasions of human life. Of such prayers related to the other themes of the book man's way to Christ consists. In summary, *The Way to Christ* may be said to consist of expositions of some of the many aspects of this path, together with Boehme's own travel diary along the way.

DEVOTIONS UPON EMERGENT OCCASIONS

Author: John Donne (c.1573-1631)
Type of work: Devotional essays
First published: 1624

Principal Ideas Advanced

Sudden illness reminds man of his frailty and by removing customary distractions may bring man closer to life's essentials.

Physical illness affords man an insight into the sickness of the soul which is sin.

Each man is a world possessing both temporal (physical) and eternal (spiritual) qualities.

Each man's origin is the same: God.

No man is able to escape involvement in the life of all men.

Few who say "No man is an island" are aware of their indebtedness to Dean John Donne and his *Devotions upon Emergent Occasions*. Few who have read Ernest Hemingway's *For Whom the Bell Tolls* connect the title with the musings of a bed-ridden Anglican prelate of the sixteenth century. So profound and eloquent are Donne's meditations on life, illness, and death that it is not surprising to find them receiving the tribute of passing into the common speech and being mined as a source of titles for contemporary literary works.

The form of the *Devotions* is unusual in that each of the twenty-three portions into which the book is divided represents a stage of the author's illness and recovery. In clinical detail every sympton of both physical and mental condition is described. Though the occasion of the *Devotions* was an actual serious illness, the presence of Donne's characteristic stylistic devices suggests that the completed work is the result of careful composition after his recovery.

The work abounds with wit, extended similes and allusions, erudition in widely varying fields, and paradox, all infused with a passionate sincerity.

The work begins with a description of the first stages of Donne's illness. "Variable, and therefore miserable condition of man; this minute I was well, and am ill, this minute. I am surpriz'd with a sodaine change, and alteration to worse, and can impute it to no cause, nor call it by any name." There is no doubt as to the reality of his attack, for by Section Three he is bedridden and by Section Four the doctor is summoned. Section Five is entitled "The Physitian Comes" and Six, "The Physitian Is Afraid." In Sections Eight through Twelve the doctor consults with others and takes various measures to test the disease. However, the treatment is not successful as the title of Section Thirteen reveals: "The sickness declares the infection and malignity thereof by spots." The crisis comes and in Sections Sixteen through Eighteen are found the patient's famous meditations on death, passages written as the bells in an adjoining church toll. By Section Nineteen Donne has passed the crisis, for "At last, the Physitians, after a long and stormie voyage, see land; they have so good signes of the concoction of the disease, as that they may safely proceed to purge." The remaining sections deal with the treatment offered by the doctors, and the work ends with a warning against "the fearefull danger of relapsing."

A curious framework for devotional meditations is this with its discourses on the relative importance of the heart, brain, and liver, and reference to such quaint medical practice as the applying of pigeons to Donne's feet in order to draw the "vapors" from his head. How is it that such a volume of quaint and curious lore should prove so enduring? The answer lies in the fact that Donne used this most private and yet most universal of experiences, illness, as the point of departure for his far-ranging contemplative excursions. The pigeon-purging may be cited as an illustration of his method.

On the theory that "vapors" caused the illness, Donne's doctors applied pigeons at his feet to draw the vapors from his head. Donne takes the occasion of this purging to muse upon his responsibility for the vapors: "What have I done, either to breed or to breath these vapors?" Though he is told it is his melancholy, Donne holds that it is rather his study and his calling which has caused him this suffering: "I have done nothing wilfully, perversely toward it, yet must suffer in it, die by it."

Not long content to remain at the factual level Donne employs this personal problem as an analogy for the ills of the state: "These vapors in us, which wee consider here pestilent, and infectious fumes, are in a State infectious rumors, detracting and dishonourable Calumnies, Libels. The Heart in that body is the King; and the Braine, his Councell; and the whole Magistracie, that ties all together, is the Sinewes, which proceed from thence; and the life of all is Honour, and just respect, and due reverence; and therefore, when these vapors, these venimous rumors, are directed against these Noble parts, the whole body suffers."

Donne finds religious significance in this pigeon-purging. God has provided this remedy in nature as a "type" or symbol to man that by the visitation of the Holy Spirit the vapors of sin shall descend and be trod under foot. One is reminded of the descent of the dove at the baptism of Jesus. Donne exhorts his readers to join him in drawing down the vapors of pride, wit, and self-will to the simplicity of the sacraments and obedience to the word of God.

Though there is much to admire in the *Devotions,* most readers find it too introspective, too erudite and esoteric, too metaphysical. Other manuals of devotion such as *The Imitation of Christ* by Thomas à Kempis (c.1380-1471), *The Scale of Perfection* by Walter Hilton (d.1396), *Private Devotions* by Lancelot Andrewes (1555-1626), or the essays *Holy Living* and *Holy Dying* by Jeremy Taylor (1613-1667), are less difficult in content and more direct in style. For one unfamiliar with Donne's work it is difficult to believe that the *Devotions* is a natural reflection of the author's religious sentiments. Yet when the *Devotions* is put next to Donne's other works, it is apparent that it is a characteristic expression. Displays of wit and learning abound throughout the whole of Donne's work from his early love poetry through his sermons and prayers.

Whatever the obstacles of Donne's style it is certain that the three sections (Sixteen to Eighteen) dealing with the tolling bell have earned for this work a secure niche in the history of English letters and the literature of Christian devotion. The passages are best appreciated when read aloud, for then the force of the argument and the felicity of the speech are most apparent. Donne hears the bells of the church adjoining his house toll for the funeral of a neighbor: "Here the Bells can scarse solemnise the funerall of any person, but that I knew him, or knew that he was my neighbor; we dwelt in houses neere to one another before, but now hee is gone into that house, into which I must follow him."

Donne reflects that this may well have been himself whose death is being noted. "Why might not I have been that man, that is carried to his grave now?" The balm of death as an end of suffering causes Donne to remark: "God hath kept the power of death in his owne hands, lest any man should bribe death. If man knew the game of death, the ease of death, he would solicite, he would provoke death to assist him, by any hand, which he might use."

With the further tolling of the bell Donne is moved to think of the Church universal and of the brotherhood of humanity: "All mankinde is of one Author, and is one volume; when one Man dies, one Chapter is not torne out of the booke, but translated into a better language; and every Chapter must be so translated; God emploies several translators; some peeces are translated by age, some by sicknesses, some by warre, some by justice; but God's hand is in every translation; and his hand shall binde up all our scattered leaves againe, for that Librarie where every booke shall lie open to one another. . . ."

There is perhaps no finer section in the *Devotions* for observing Donne's most characteristic style and content. Having used the metaphor of the Author and His book to speak of the universal Church and of man's eternal destiny, Donne develops his metaphor of the bell: "No man is an Iland, intire of it selfe; every man is a peece of the Continent, a part of the maine; if a Clod bee washed away by the Sea, Europe is the lesse, as well as if a Promontories were, as well as if a Mannor of thy friends or of thine owne were; any mans death diminishes me, because I am involved in Mankinde; And therefore never send to know for whom the bell tolls: It tolls for thee."

In these passages are found the reasons for the *Devotions'* becoming a classic of literature and devotion. Here are themes of perennial and universal interest treated with consummate artistry. For the reader not sharing Donne's religious faith the *Devotions* has the appeal of dealing with situations no human being avoids: illness, mortality, and musings over the meanings and mysteries of life. Any reader is able to appreciate these themes and to be moved by the manner of their presentation, a manner which, with unforgettable literary effectiveness, portrays passionate human concern.

From the beginning, however, the *Devotions* has held an audience which sees in it strong Christian teaching. Though the validity of the *Devotions* is as much dependent on Donne the man as on Donne the Dean, the two were one, and the work deserves a reading on the theological level. To read it solely as introspective literature is to misread it, for the literary devices were used to add power and vividness to basic theological positions.

In these passages cited above, for example, the rhetoric should not be allowed to obscure the central theological affirmation: "I am involved in mankinde." No wavering here, no romantic isolation, no psychic narcissism, but instead a coherent statement supported by logical reasons which have the compelling power of an exact science. Through the medium of enforced isolation and suffering Donne learned the paradoxical truths of the Gospel: one finds by losing, one is never less alone than when alone. The nearly mortal illness becomes a symbol of the human condition not only in its frailty and sinful inperfection but in its need to realize the meaning of suffering in the providence of God. By losing all the customary securities and by being withdrawn from the usual distractions, Donne could concentrate upon the fundamental matter of his relationship to God. As his illness may be taken for the sinful state of man, so the recovery may be seen as the redemption, and the relapse as the falling back into sin. The tenth expostulation, for example, made against the serpent in Eden, follows a discussion of the body's sickness as symbolizing the sickness of the soul.

The reader who is familiar with Donne's other works is best able to appreciate the place of death in the *Devotions*. Donne was a child of his age in his preoccupation with death, but in the *Devotions* he views it in a less bizarre manner than he does elsewhere. He is neither hysterical nor unconcerned, nor does he long excessively for it. He sees it as part of God's providential plan to bring an end to man's sinning. He prays: "Let this prayer therefore, O my God, be as my last gasp, my expiring, my dying in thee; That if this bee the hour of my transmigration I may die the death of a sinner, drowned in my sins, in the blood of thy sonne. And if I live longer, yet I may now die the death of the righteous, die to sinne, which death is a resurrection to a new life. Thou killest and thou givest life."

As he had recovered from his illness, so would his soul recover to rise at the last to return to its source in God. Aware though he was of the sickness of sin, Donne never so identified human finitude with sin as to forget his Christian affirmation of his divine origin and of his being a joint heir with Christ. Even if he were merely dust and ashes, Donne observes, he could still speak unto the Lord since the Lord is Creator even of dust and ashes. But Donne insisted that he was nothing less than the breath of God, and thus it was right that he should breathe the pious expostulations of the *Devotions*. No contemporary reader can fail to benefit from the testimonies of this man whose physical and spiritual suffering forged his art and his humanity into one matchless instrument for the service of God.

OF CONSCIENCE, ITS POWER AND CASES

Author: William Ames (1576-1633)
Type of work: Puritan ethics and casuistry
First published: 1630

Principal Ideas Advanced

Conscience is the judgment of the practical intellect, by which a conclusion is drawn from the moral law as to one's state before God or to the moral character of one's actions.

Casuistry, or the study of cases of conscience, is a necessary discipline because of the liability of conscience to error and doubts.

The virtues as formulated in classical philosophical ethics can properly be evaluated only by reference to the divinely revealed moral law and the evangelical doctrine of redemption and grace.

The moral law summarized in the Decalogue is substantially the same as the natural law which provides the synteresis or major premise of the syllogism of conscience.

William Ames, a son of Puritan parents, studied at Christ's College, Cambridge, under William Perkins (1558-1602). In 1610, he left England and became a preacher in the Hague. In Holland, he defended Calvinism against the Remonstrants and served as a secretary at the Synod of Dort in 1618. From 1622 to 1632 he was Professor at Franeker. His most influential writings were his *Medulla theologiae* or *Marrow of Theology* (1627), in which, under the influence of Petrus Ramus (1515-1572), he develops theology as a practical science, and his *De conscientia eius iure et casibus,* in which he follows his teacher Perkins in developing a doctrine of conscience with detailed investigation of difficult cases.

Ames defines conscience as man's judgment of himself, according to his subjection to God's judgment. Conscience as a judgment belongs not to the will or emotions, but to the intellect. Although the will may incite the understanding to moral judgment and although emotional states are its consequence, conscience itself, according to the etymology of the word and its usage in Scripture, is a practical judgment of the understanding. Ames differs from his teacher, William Perkins, who represented conscience as a faculty of the soul. Conscience is the very act of moral judgment, by the power of the understanding, and it flows from a certain habit of the soul. In this view, Ames is in agreement with Thomas Aquinas, as opposed to Scotus, Bonaventura, and Durandus, who defined conscience as a habit of the soul.

The judgment of conscience in such acts as accusing, excusing, or comforting is discursive and may be formulated in a practical syllogism. "The Major of that Syllogisme, wherein the whole judgement of conscience is laid open, treateth alwaies of the Law, the Minor of the fact and state; and the conclusion of the relation that ariseth from our fact or state, by reason of that Law; which is either guilt or spirituall Joy." Conscience is thus a "Law," a "Witness," and a "Judge" in relation to the major premise, minor premise, and conclusion respectively (Romans 2:14,15; Revelation 20:12; I John 5:10).

The major premise is given by the synteresis or repository of law; the minor is called syneidesis, and the conclusion, the *krísis* or judgment itself. "Synteresis is properly an intellectuall habit, whereby we give our consent to the principles of morall action. It differeth not therefore from the Law of nature which is naturally written in the hearts of all men: but in respect onely."

Synteresis can never be completely extinguished or lost in its principle. No man is so depraved as to be completely without a conscience. In its widest sense synteresis includes all consequences following from the principles of natural law and all practical truths accepted by faith in divine revelation. An enlightened conscience receives the precepts of Scripture in addition to the natural law and its consequences. The adequate and full rule of conscience is thus the revealed will of God. Although men are bound in conscience to observe properly instituted human laws, human laws qua human are not binding.

In discussing problems relating to erroneous, doubtful, and scrupulous consciences, Ames proceeds from a division of human actions into good, bad, and indifferent. Conscience can make an indifferent action to be either good or bad and a good action to be evil, but not an evil action to be good. The erroneous conscience binds, in that to act against its judgment is sinful, even when it judges something unlawful to be lawful. The necessity of sinning that arises in this case is due to the error of conscience, not to the nature of the law. Nothing may be done of which the conscience is in doubt. In doubtful cases the safest alternative should be chosen. Action against irrational scruples of conscience, however, is recommended.

In considering the minor premise of the syllogism of conscience, Ames raises the question of how it is possible for a man to do anything against a dictate of conscience which precedes or accompanies his action. Ames replies by denying the intellectualist doctrine that the will is determined by the last practical judgment of the understanding. Although a man cannot will what he does not know, a simple apprehension of an object, without any practical judgment, may suffice to elicit an act of will. The understanding propounds what is good to the will "with a kind of indifferency of judgement, as not having any necessary connexion with the universal good." Though the will is determined by the understanding as to the specification or kind of thing to be willed, yet it enjoys a liberty of exercise in which it moves itself, the understanding, and the other faculties. This doctrine of the primacy of the will distinguishes Ames's account of man's moral nature from the view of the primacy of the intellect commonly adopted by Reformed theologians.

From the conclusion of the practical syllogism follows either an excusing and approval or accusation and condemnation, together with suitable affections of joy or sorrow. Men do not always draw the logical conclusion even when the premises are admitted. A conscience that judges rightly is said to be honestly good; one which excuses and comforts to be peaceably good. Ever since man's Fall, the conscience can be both honestly and peaceably good only by the sprinkling of the blood of Christ and by the sanctification of the Spirit. Among the corollaries derived by Ames from the thirty-eight positions summarizing Book I of the treatise are the following: "The greatest violation of conscience is the greatest sin. The greatest anguish of conscience is the greatest punishment. . . . The interpretation of the Scriptures, or a judgement to discerne Gods will for a man's selfe, in his own conscience, belongs to every man."

Book II opens with a definition of a case of conscience as "a practical question, concerning which, the conscience may make a doubt." Cases are matters of doubt to be resolved by argument and include all questions in which, the general doctrine of faith and obedience being supposed, inquiry is made into a man's duty on particular occasions. Cases of conscience are divided into two classes, those concerning a man's state before God and those concerning actions performed in that state. Puritan casuistry characteristically treats inquiry into the state of the soul as the fundamental occupation of conscience. Assurance of salvation is held to be attainable, though with difficulty, in this life. Consequently, a man must examine himself as to his being in a state of sin or of grace. This question can be resolved by examination of one's behavior, outward and inward, by the attitude of the heart toward God's law, by a reflex act of the mind, and by a certain spiritual feeling. The remainder of Book II discusses cases relating to the state of man, under such headings as the state of sin, postponement of conversion, preparation for conversion, effectual calling, temptations against faith, adoption, sanctification, the conflict between flesh and spirit, progress in sanctification, the first-fruits of glorification in the feeling of God's love, temptations, and conscience of sin. The book closes with a series of selected propositions from *De tentationibus,* a work by William of Auvergne (c.1180-1249), Bishop of Paris.

The last three books of the *De conscientia* concern cases relating to moral duties. In these books Ames achieves an impressive synthesis of Biblical moral teaching and Aristotelian ethical theory. The Aristotelian framework provides a skeleton which is clothed with the living body of Scriptual precepts. Book III discusses basic ethical principles, including the cardinal virtues, while the two remaining books examine cases arising from the implications of the Decalogue.

Ames begins with a consideration of obedience in general, since the duty which God requires of man consists in obedience to His revealed will. Obedience requires knowledge, with which is associated the fear of God. Humility, uprightness, and zeal are dealt with in relation to obedience; peace of conscience is considered as a consequence of obedience. A discussion of virtue follows, in which the Aristotelian analysis of virtue as a habit is illustrated and supported by an abundance of Biblical texts. Virtue is not set in antithesis to pleasure, but pleasure and joy flowing from the exercises of virtue are observed to be signs that a virtue has been acquired. The particular virtues are then analyzed, first prudence or spiritual wisdom, with which watchfulness is associated, then fortitude, in connection with which assurance, perserverance, and patience are examined, and finally temperance; a chapter on drunkenness follows. For each virtue, Ames inquires as to its nature and the motives and means for acquiring it.

After the virtues, good works are discussed as well as the adiaphora (indifferent things), voluntary action, and sins of heart, speech, and behavior. Good works must not only be in conformity with the law of God as to their matter, but also be performed from the right motives and directed to the glory of God. The conscience of sinful men is not a sufficient or infallible rule, but only a rule subordinated to the Word of God. Ames adopts the probabilioristic position in casuistry and advises the choice of the safer side in doubtful cases; that is, the side in which there is no danger of sinning. On the question of choosing between two sins, Ames holds that, in the case of apparent conflict of duties, the greater duty absolves a person from the performance of the lesser. Choosing the lesser of two evils refers to physical rather than moral evil. But if a person supposes he must commit one of two sins, conscience can pass no judgment in favor of either, although the person who commits the lesser sin, sins less.

Voluntary action is analyzed in Scholastic Aristotelian fashion. Actions are rendered involuntary by violence, chance, and such ignorance as is the cause of the action. Ignorance of the law does not excuse, and willful ignorance is itself sin and increases the guilt of sins that result from it.

Book V, Chapter I, contains an important discussion of the nature and types of law. After considering four paradigm cases of the use of "jus," Ames distinguishes natural and positive law. Natural law consists of practical principles known by nature and of the consequences derived from those principles. Positive divine law is added to natural law by special revelations. Natural law is the same as the eternal law, but positive law is not thus designated. The case of Abraham's being commanded to slay his son is no suspension of the natural law, but only a change of the matter with which the law is conversant. Only man as a rational being is properly subject to natural law. Yet all things have a natural inclination to their end. Man possesses some such inclinations in common with animals. A striking appeal is made to texts (Isaiah I:3, Jeremiah 8:7, 2 Timothy 3:3, Jude 10) accentuating the unnaturalness of sin by reference to the behavior of brute beasts. The *jus gentium* embraces both natural and positive law and something intermediate, so far as it derives from common agreement and custom. The commands of the natural law are inadequately formulated as "to live honestly, not to injure anyone, and to give every one his own." This is in part tautological and in part ambiguous. The Golden Rule is both natural and divine law, but it may not be applied indiscriminately. Civil law must be based on the natural law, either as a conclusion from general principles or as the determination and application of a general rule. Civil law makes not good men, but good citizens. The moral law of the Decalogue is identical with the natural law, except for the determination of the seventh day in the Fourth Commandment. The necessity for republication of the natural law in the Ten Commandments stems from the depravity of nature which entails blindness of reason, perversity of will, and disturbance of emotions. The human heart retains but a remnant of the law, which, like an old painting, must be restored with a new brush. Right practical reason is found pure and entire nowhere except in God's written Law.

RELIGIO MEDICI

Author: Sir Thomas Browne (1605-1682)
Type of work: Personal religious commentary
First published: 1642 (pirated); 1643 (authorized)

Principal Ideas Advanced

The world of faith and the world of science are marvelously intertwined, and the one should never be divorced from the other.

Reason and belief are complementary, but the pervasive atmosphere of man's religious quest should be one of mystery and wonder.

The manifold marvels of the world delight those who see in them God's handiwork, and they deliver men from arbitrary dogmatism.

Religio medici, a justly celebrated work of private musings on religious truths, was written by Sir Thomas Browne, probably in 1635. It circulated in manuscript for some years, and after surreptitious editions had appeared in 1642, Browne himself published it in 1643. The author was thus a comparatively young man, but he writes with a whimsical detachment that would seem appropriate in a person twice his age. He writes as a doctor, and he admits that medical men have a poor reputation for religious zeal; but he also writes as a Christian, and his faith is no conventional pattern of belief. Others may owe their religion to baptism and education; Browne is a Christian because, having studied the matter with care and reflected on it at length, he finds himself "obliged by the principles of grace and the laws of mine own reason, to embrace no other name but this."

At the very outset Browne insists that zeal is compatible with charity. He considers that he stands in the tradition of the Reformation, but he dislikes divisive labels. He accepts discipline in his personal life, but sees no reason why it should issue in a surly temper. "My common conversation I do acknowledge austere," he writes, "my behavior full of rigor, sometimes not without morosity; yet at my devotion I love to use the civility of my knee, my hat, and hand, with all those outward sensible motions which may express or promote my invisible devotion."

Browne expresses a regard for forms of religious observance when such forms are helpful and not superstitious, and he is able to respond to the devotional forms of those from whom he differs: "I could never hear the Ave-Mary Bell without an elevation, or think it a sufficient warrant, because they erred in one circumstance, for me to err in all, that is, in silence and dumb contempt." So he describes an attitude at once strict with himself and charitable towards others, combining exacting standards of moral behavior with a tolerance of ceremonial forms. This freedom from the fury of contemporary religious invective is one of the most striking features of Browne's work. He does not accept a position because some authority has propounded it, nor reject it because some one reputed to be an opponent has supported it. When Scripture does not answer his questions, he does not borrow the rules of his religion either from Geneva or from Rome.

The strong appeal of *Religio medici* lies partly in the spirit which pervades it, partly in the material with which it deals. Browne takes a subject of fundamental importance. He deals with man's relation to his God and to the world about him, and he deals with both aspects of his subject with candor, originality, and great imaginative power. Throughout his work he maintains a delicate balance between two kinds of reality and two types of knowledge. He is concerned with faith and science, with God and the world of phenomena, with the knowledge that comes only because God reveals it and with the truth which we grasp only because we search for it. His approach is at times akin to that of Sir Francis Bacon (1561-1626), but he presses forward with the examination of God and his works with greater zeal than his famous predecessor ever did. It is an open question as to the extent to which *Religio medici* can be regarded as an expression of the scientific ferment of the age. It is Browne's aim to keep his sources in just equipoise. He will neither ignore the distinctive sources of truth which God's Word provides nor will he shut his eyes to the evidence of nature: "Thus there are two books from which I collect my divinity; besides that written one of God, another of his servant Nature, that universal and public manuscript, that lies expans'd unto the eyes of all. . . ." He is troubled that Christians so often "disdain to suck divinity from the flowers of Nature." But Browne does not intend to make the opposite mistake, and become so engrossed in the examination of Nature that he forgets God. He will so study all phenomena that he will be able to detect the wise purpose that has fashioned them, and he will recognize in all things created the functional beauty of means perfectly adapted to ends. "And thus," he says, "I call the effects of Nature the works of God, whose hand and instrument she only is." Or, as he more succinctly expresses it, "Nature is the art of God."

Browne therefore refuses to subscribe to the sharp distinction between natural and revealed religion. His delight in the "general beauty in the works of God" delivers him from the narrowness which characterizes many of his contemporaries, but his respect for Scripture saves him from the perils of a vague natural pantheism. And above all, he is constantly overawed by the majesty of the central theme of all religious speculation. In one of his most telling phrases he urges his readers to "think magnificently about God," and no words could more accurately convey the distinctive quality of his book.

It would be a mistake to regard *Religio medici* as a serious contribution to the study of either science or religion, or even of the relations of the one to the other. There is the evidence of much delight in the world which science studies, but few explicit references either to the tasks or achievements of science. There is constant consideration of religious subjects, but little attempt to work out anything approaching a system of divinity. Browne allows great scope to revelation. He also insists on the place of reason and the role which it should play in the religious life. "The world," he says, "was made to be inhabited by beasts, but studied and contemplated by man: 'tis the debt of our reason we owe unto God, and the homage we pay for not being beasts."

Browne's emphasis on man's rationality is carefully balanced by an awareness of the limits of the utmost that man can know. He admits that there are truths which "serve as luminaries in the abyss of knowledge," but he is also aware that everything runs out into mystery. There is an obscurity too deep for our reason, and thus, he says, "I teach my haggard and unreclaimed reason to stoop unto the lure of faith." Browne affirms the proper role of reason and yet insists on its due subordination. It is this attitude which explains the contemplative quality of his book. He observes the visible phenomena of the world about him, but he also ponders unseen and unfathomable truths. He reflects on the wisdom and eternity of God and finds that the one renews and the other confounds his understanding. He knows that God is wise in all things, "wonderful in what we conceive, but far more wonderful in what we comprehend not."

Nor is a due and proper balance merely the formal pattern of Browne's thought. Man's life is composed of many parts. Reason often clashes with faith, and emotion often disturbs reason. We are exposed to the perils of something that approximates to an inner civil war, "for there is in our soul a kind of triumvirate, or triple government of three competitors, which distracts the peace of this our commonwealth." "Sturdy doubts and boisterous objections" attack the serenity of man's spirit, and are artfully employed by our ancient enemy, the tempter, to work us ill. So Browne introduces his vivid picture of playing at chess with the Devil, who yields a pawn in order to gain a queen, "and whilst I labored to raise the structure of my reason, he strived to undermine the edifice of my faith."

Browne does not minimize the problems of belief. He is well aware of the difficulties in the sacred narratives and of the incongruities in the Biblical text. He can construct a comprehensive catalogue of doubts and can cite all the problems latent in the miracles. He is a believer, but without the arrogance of dogmatism, and he is constantly reminded that the citadel of faith is built on the edge of the abyss of doubt. He will believe, but he will "never betray the liberty of my reason"; he is willing to question, but he refuses to become obsessed with doubts. Browne is thus concerned with both faith and reason, and their relation constituted the central problem of his age. But it can hardly be claimed that Browne made a serious contribution to its philosophical solution. It may be questioned whether he even recognized the central issue in the problem. His mind makes sorties into this complicated jungle and lights up its obscurities, but it never demarcates the boundaries of the problem. To change the figure of speech, his subtle intelligence plays like summer lightning over the landscape of man's terrestrial life, but it never strikes with electrifying power to the center of man's problems.

There is a mystical bent to Browne's writings, but he can hardly be regarded as a genuine mystic. He is aware of the mysterious dimensions of life, but he does not intend to lose himself in them. The true mystic can hardly retain the slightly quizzical quality which marks Browne's outlook. Nor can the mystic survey life with the somewhat detached objectivity which Browne maintains. But perhaps the fundamental reason why he never loses himself in a cloud is that his religious faith coalesces with a strong ethical seriousness. Here, again, we can observe an unusual combination of qualities. Browne is mystical, yet concerned with the problems of daily life; he is metaphysical, but intensely moral; he contemplates eternity, but he has no intention of escaping from the responsibilities of time. He delights in beauty but he does not "feed on rainbows." He dwells in a rarefied atmosphere, but it is not "too thin for breathing."

A book like *Religio medici* draws on many sources, but depends on none of them. It reflects Stoic influence and shows traces of Scholasticism. Browne's mind has been shaped by science and by contacts with men of varying backgrounds. His greatest obligation is to Platonism, which inculcated the charitable outlook, the broad and generous tolerance which pervades his book. The wide variety of his intellectual interests is clear to even the most casual reader; one is aware that a keen and well-instructed mind has ranged widely over the field of human thought and knowledge; it has brought home much curious lore, although the author communicates it in almost random fashion.

This explains the immediate appeal of *Religio medici* to its contemporaries. The seventeenth century was an age of shifting cross currents, and Browne touched its interests at many points. He made only an amateur's contribution to the central problems of authority and faith, but he placed these great issues in a new perspective. He proved that it is possible to be earnest about these important matters without descending to foul-mouthed and bad-tempered dogmatism. He gave his age what it badly needed: a fresh expression of an individual man's belief. He showed that man is a true microcosm and that the visible world is a reflection of the invisible world. He showed that a subject of fundamental importance could be treated with entire candor by an author of imaginative power, originality, and good will. But the book would not have retained its unique place as a literary and religious classic unless it possessed qualities which appeal perennially to men. The engaging character of its author inevitably attracts all save the most doctrinaire minds. His curiosity, his charity towards others, his humility about himself, and his sense of the mystery and wonder of life make him a rare and delightful companion. His wit flickers over the most solemn subjects, yet his basic seriousness and sincerity are never in doubt. And he clothes his thought in a form peculiarly appealing and appropriate. He has an inexhaustible gift for epigram. His turns of expression are as arresting as they are quaint. He can be colloquial and magniloquent by turns. He can awaken the emotions and give poetic form to universal human feelings. He can bring the beauty and power of the spiritual world within the reach of the ordinary person. The somber magnificence, lit by flashes of quaint wit, give to *Religio medici* a quality which it shares with few other books. It lives because it speaks to something undying in the heart of man.

THE BLOODY TENENT OF PERSECUTION

Author: Roger Williams (c.1603-1683)
Type of work: Christian social philosophy
First published: 1644

Principal Ideas Advanced

It is the prerogative of God alone to punish those who reject Christianity.

In the realm of civil affairs Christians are to associate on a basis of equality with all men, whatever their religious convictions.

Old Testament references to instances in which the rulers of Israel punished idolaters provide no warrant for the later civil rulers to suppress false religious beliefs, for the teachings of Christ regarding the treatment of non-Christians have superseded the teachings of the Old Testament.

Roger Williams, author of *The Bloody Tenent of Persecution,* was born into a shopkeeper's family in London, probably in 1603. His education at Charterhouse and at Pembroke Hall, Cambridge University, was made possible by the generous support of Sir Edward Coke.

While still in England, Williams became aligned with the Puritans, a religio-political party which regarded the Church of England as inadequately purified of Roman Catholic features of belief and ceremony. He adopted the views of the radical or "Separatist" Puritans, who advocated separation from the Church of England rather than internal reform efforts.

Williams sailed for New England in December of 1630 and arrived in Boston on February 5, 1631. He rejected the ministerial call of the church in Boston because of that church's refusal to separate from the Church of England. An offer from the church at Salem was withdrawn after Governor John Winthrop expressed disapproval. Williams then left for the colony at Plymouth, which was avowedly separatist. Here he lived for two years, making his living by farming, but also occasionally preaching in the Plymouth church. He became increasingly unhappy because of the nonseparatist implication of the behavior of Plymouth church members who attended Church of England services during visits in England. Finally, in 1633, he left Plymouth and returned to Salem, where he was fondly remembered. There he became an unofficial assistant to the pastor.

At Salem, Williams enlisted enthusiastic support for his separatist views, but his religious and political teachings alarmed the rulers of the colony. He insisted that the rightful owners of the land inhabited by the colonists were the Indians, and that the royal charter provided no valid claim. He declared that an oath constituted a religious affirmation and that, therefore, magistrates had no right to require oaths of unregenerate persons. He claimed, further, that the civil authorities had no right to enforce the first four commandments, which define religious duties, and that the magistrates' responsibility was limited to enforcing those commandments the violation of which resulted in social disorder.

The civil and ecclesiastical leaders of Massachusetts were spurred to a determined effort to silence Williams when, in the spring of 1635, the church at Salem chose Williams to succeed their deceased minister, Samuel Skelton. At the July meeting of the General Court of Massachusetts Bay, Williams was asked to appear and explain his views. Fellow ministers who appeared as witnesses testified that Williams should be removed because of his heretical views, but they were powerless to interfere with the affairs of an independent Congregational church. The General Court, however, was in a position of greater power. Salem was petitioning the General Court for land in Marblehead Neck, and the General Court refused to act on the petition unless the Salem church dismissed Williams. Williams himself broke the deadlock when he insisted that his church break with all other Congregational churches in Massachusetts because of their violation of the principle of local congregational autonomy in calling for government aid in suppressing his unpopular views. In effect he was asking his parishioners to declare that their church alone was the true church, and this the majority of them were unwilling to do.

In October of 1635 the General Court again required Williams to appear, and he was charged with denying the authority of the magistrates in religious matters and with spreading seditious ideas through letters. Williams adamantly defended his acts, and he was sentenced to banishment. Initially he was allowed six weeks in which to leave the colony, but he was later granted permission to remain until the next spring.

Forbidden to preach publicly, he continued to present his views in meetings at his home. Williams received word in January, 1636, that the exasperated colonial authorities planned to deport him immediately to England. He fled to the wilderness south of Massachusetts, where he was helped through the winter by Indians. In the summer of 1636 he founded the village of Providence, which grew rapidly because of the influx of refugees from Massachusetts. In 1644 he secured from Parliament a charter which designated Providence and several other settlements as the colony of Rhode Island.

It was during his stay in London in 1643-44 that Williams wrote and had published his *The Bloody Tenent of Persecution.* His stay in England was a feverishly busy one which saw the publication of several works, including his brilliant anthropological study of New England Indians entitled *A Key into the Language of America,* a book which immediately established his reputation and fame.

Although written in great and obvious haste, *The Bloody Tenent of Persecution* contained thoughts which Williams had been formulating for eight years. The book was designed to refute the philosophy of Church-state relations which the civil and religious authorities of Massachusetts had decided upon, as well as to state Williams's own views. The special target of the book was the Reverend John Cotton (1584-1652), acknowledged dean of the Massachusetts clergy and one of the chief figures in the prosecution of Williams. The first half of *The Bloody Tenent of Persecution* replies directly to Cotton's criticisms of a tract written in Newgate prison by an Anabaptist. The second half attempts to rebut a document entitled *A Model of Church and Civil Power* which the associated ministers of Massachusetts Bay had sent to the people of Salem in the autumn of 1635 in an attempt to show them the errors of Williams's teachings. Williams mistakenly attributed the document largely to the hand of Cotton, who had nothing to do with its writing. Still, Williams correctly interpreted Cotton's thinking on the question of Church-state relations, and Cotton felt compelled to defend his views. In 1647 he published a book bearing a typical seventeenth century polemical title, *The Bloody Tenent Washed, and Made White in the Blood of the Lambe.* In 1652 Williams issued a rejoinder entitled *The Bloody Tenent Yet More Bloody by Mr. Cotton's Endeavour to Wash it White in the Blood of the Lambe.*

The confusing and disorganized quality of *The Bloody Tenent of Persecution* is remedied to a certain extent by twelve lucid one-sentence statements by which Williams opens the book. Most of the statements are basic propositions which are developed and defended in the book, while others are simple descriptions of the contents of the book. Following the list of twelve statements is an address to Parliament in which he urges that body—at that time largely Presbyterian—not to use its powers to enforce or proscribe religious belief. After the appeal to Parliament comes a statement addressed "to every courteous reader." In some of the most eloquent prose of the book, Williams points out the inconsistency of a political policy which permits citizens to read the Bible but which does not allow them to interpret the Bible in any fashion other than that approved by the state.

Williams next moves into the first of the two main parts of his book, the first part being directed against Cotton's answer to the tract mentioned above. Cotton—arguing in the fashion of a scholastic logician—acknowledges the wrongness of persecuting any conscience that is "rightly informed," and he also maintains that it is wrong to punish an erroneous conscience until after one or two admonitions. If, however, the sinner continues in his error, then he may be punished, for once he has been instructed he no longer sins out of obedience to conscience, but against his conscience. In the case of minor matters, those in error may be tolerated if they exhibit a spirit of Christian meekness and love. If, however, one professes even minor error in an arrogant and boisterous spirit so that he disturbs the civil peace, then he is to be punished according to the seriousness of the disturbance.

The question which is most natural to a modern mind is, How could Cotton so confidently set himself up as the judge of right and wrong conscience? Williams, on the other hand, saw the issue—as did Cotton—as a matter of correct interpretation of the Scriptures. He agreed with Cotton that the passages concerning the wheat and the tares (Matthew 13:24-30, 37-43) are crucial for understanding how heretics and non-Christians should be treated by ecclesiastical and civil authorities. In the parable of the wheat and the tares the master instructs his servants to leave the tares alone in order not to damage the wheat. In response to his disciples' request for an explanation of the parable, Jesus states that the tares will be destroyed by fire at the Final Judgment.

Cotton interpreted the tares as Church members, outwardly holy, who at heart were not Christians. Because churches and ministers cannot be certain who the real Christians are, they must not presume to rid the Church of hypocrites. Both the civil and Church authorities, however, are able to recognize those who openly deny or pervert the faith of the Church and lead others into heresy or schism, and both the state and the Church have the right to admonish and suppress such persons.

Williams's reply to Cotton takes the form of a dialogue between "Peace" and "Truth," both of whom serve as the author's protagonists. The dialogue develops a lengthy and involved exegesis of the Biblical passages concerning the wheat and the tares. Williams declares that the tares refer neither to hypocrites within the Church nor to disturbers of the civil peace. Jesus clearly had in mind "anti-Christian idolaters," those who reject Christianity. Jews, Moslems, and persons of other non-Christian persuasions and of no religious persuasion at all will eventually be judged and punished of God. It is not, however, the function of the Christian Church or of civil governments to suppress non-Christians. Indeed, in the realm of civil affairs, it is proper for Christians and non-Christians to deal with one another freely and to enjoy the same rights. The virtues which make for civil order and harmony have no special relationship to Christianity or any other religion. Just and stable civil societies may exist quite independently of Christian influence. The skills which are necessary for governing men are to be compared with the specialized skills of a physician, a musician, or a ship's pilot. None of these skills has any necessary relationship to the religious faith of the practitioner, and religious profession should not be a test of office for the magistrate any more than for a ship's pilot.

Within the setting of civil society, Williams's argument goes on, a church has the same nature and status as a medical society or a business corporation. A religious society has its own functions, which are distinctly separate and different from those of a civil society. Civil harmony and order are the responsibility of the state and not of the Church. Christians have a duty as Christians to protect the purity and integrity of their churches, but they have no warrant whatsoever for ridding civil society of Jews, Moslems, pagans, and others who do not properly belong in the Church. Such persons are clearly qualified for full membership in civil society.

John Cotton and other New England ministers were able to cite in favor of the Church-state arrangement in Massachusetts numerous Old Testament accounts of cases in which religious and civil leaders co-operated in violently suppressing idolaters. Williams acknowledges that ancient Israel did engage in such practices. He argues, however, that ancient Jewish society existed by a special covenantal arrangement with God, an arrangement which has existed with no other people, which has been superseded by Christ, and which, therefore, has no authority as a model for Christians.

By its very nature, Williams affirms, Christianity tolerates opposition and rejection, and it seeks to persuade only through peaceful means. By its very nature it cannot be communicated through coercive means. Furthermore, attempts to suppress religious error usually result in more fanatical devotion to the erroneous views.

Williams makes it clear that he is no religious indifferentist. Toleration of religious error is to be distinguished from approval. Evil is to be tolerated for the sake of greater good, both the greater good of civil harmony and that of the promotion of Christianity through appropriate means. Because Christianity is the true religion, the civil magistrate owes it his approbation and the submission of his own will. To non-Christian religions the magistrate owes permission but not approbation. In his official capacity, however, he owes equal protection both to the worshipers of Christ and to those who reject Christ.

The civil and ecclesiastical rulers of Massachusetts, Williams charges, have confused the "garden" which is the Church with the "wilderness" which is the world. By compelling outward conformity with the ways of Christ, they have produced a confused mixture of the Church and the world, so that the Church contains the unregenerate as well as the regenerate. Such a national church conforms to the Old Testament, but it has no warrant in the teachings or example of Christ. Christ appointed no civil authorities to promote and defend His Church.

The fame of Williams and of his greatest book rests largely upon the support which they provide for the doctrine of separation of Church and state. *The Bloody Tenent of Persecution* articulates a clear theory of both Church and state, but it is important to note that Williams's insistence upon separation was motivated chiefly by his concern for the purity and integrity of the Church as a community of regenerate men. He was not motivated —as have been many thinkers since the eighteenth century—by the belief that the state, if left free to act on the basis of reason instead of religious dogmas, can continually improve the quality of human existence.

THE KEYS OF THE KINGDOM OF HEAVEN

Author: John Cotton (1584-1652)
Type of work: Church polity
First published: 1644

Principal Ideas Advanced

The Keys of the Kingdom are the key of knowledge and the key of order; the latter may be considered to be two keys representing the powers of Church order: liberty, which belongs to the brethren; and authority, which belongs to the elders.

The recipients of the Keys are individual churches and not presbyteries or bishops.

Although independent of each other, churches ought to be associated for their mutual benefits into synods.

The Church's power does not extend to temporal affairs.

John Cotton, who for twenty years was vicar of St. Botolph's Church, Boston, Lincolnshire, fled England to avoid being arrested for his refusal to kneel at the sacrament and was involved, shortly after coming to Massachusetts, in Anne Hutchinson's (c.1591-1643) revolt against the New England clergy. He and John Winthrop (1588-1649) opposed the antinomian beliefs of Anne Hutchinson. When Mrs. Hutchinson was condemned in 1637 by the General Court, Cotton devoted his full effort to the preservation of peace and order in the New England churches. In the *Keys of the Kingdom,* and in other works of like character, Cotton set forth what was, in effect, the official teaching of the New England churches on the subject of Church polity. Two English divines, Thomas Goodwin (1600-1680) and Philip Nye (1596-1672), both members of the Westminster Assembly, contributed a joint introduction and saw the work through the press. Testifying to the virtual identity between "the Congregational way" in New England and in the mother country, they praise the author for having described a middle-way between Brownism (see Robert Browne, c.1550-1633) and Presbyterianism. The error of the former, they say, lies in drowning the votes of the elders in the popular majority, and that of the latter in swallowing up the interests of the people in the jurisdiction of the presbytery; whereas, the wisdom of Cotton's plan lies in the balancing of powers and privileges so that, while action is not impeded, the danger of tyranny is removed.

Cotton derived the title of his book from the words of Christ to Peter, in Matthew 16:19: "To thee will I give the keys of the Kingdom of Heaven; and whatsoever thou shalt bind on earth, shall be bound in Heaven; and whatsoever thou shalt loose on earth, shall be loosed in Heaven." Cotton distinguishes two sorts of keys. The first is the key of *knowledge,* which, he says, belongs to all Christians alike, because every man is responsible for knowing the Scriptures and believing on Christ for his justification. To exercise the key, Cotton says, it is not necessary for a person to be a member of a church, although normally it is expected that he will. In the present work, Cotton is not primarily concerned with this first key, but with the second, that of *order.* This key is "the power whereby every member of the Church walketh orderly himself, according to his place in the Church, and helpeth his brethren, to walk orderly also."

Properly speaking, there are, according to Cotton, two keys of order. The first is that of power, or interest, or, as it is called in the Scriptures, *liberty.* This power belongs to the people. It includes the right to choose their own officers, to send out missionaries, to refuse membership to undesirable persons, to join with their officers in excommunicating offenders from the sacraments, and to enter into communion with other churches. When the congregation has serious cause to complain against its officers, it may appeal to a synod representing the several churches; and, if they get no satisfaction, they can withdraw their support.

The second key of order is that of *authority*. It is vested in officers (elders and deacons) chosen by the people. These have the right to preach, to teach and to exhort, to call the church together, to examine candidates for membership, to ordain officers upon their being selected by the congregation, to inform the people of the law in cases of disciplinary action, to pronounce sentence after the people have determined the matter of guilt, and to withdraw the ordinances from the people in cases where the whole congregation is stubbornly at fault.

Cotton was careful to base his teaching upon the Scriptures, and he appeals frequently to the practice of the churches in the Acts of the Apostles. Another passage often referred to is Matthew 18:18, in which it is reported that, concerning the brother taken in a fault, Christ commanded that, if he proved obdurate, he should be brought before the Church. It was to the Church that Christ said, "Whatsoever ye shall bind on earth shall be bound in Heaven; and whatsoever ye shall loose on earth shall be loosed in Heaven." Cotton regards this passage as giving the true sense of Christ's words to Peter when he gave him the Keys of the Kingdom. Following Augustine, Cotton says, "Peter received the keys in the name of the Church."

Besides Scripture, however, Cotton had before him the example of English civil law. In a well-ordered Commonwealth, he says, there is a "right and due establishment and balancing of the *liberties* or *privileges* of the people (which in a true sense, may be called a *power*) and the *authority* of the Magistrate." In like manner, he continues, the safety of the Church lies in "the right and due settling and ordering of the holy *power* of the *privileges* and *liberties* of the Brethren, and the ministerial *authority* of the Elders." The English practice of trial by jury affords a close parallel to the way in which Cotton conceives people and officers conjointly exercising discipline. The verdict of a jury is, Cotton says, an exercise of popular liberty, whereas the judge's sentence is an act of authority. Each has a power of judgment, but the powers are different, and neither is effective without the other.

After having distinguished the different keys, Cotton raises the question as to who is the "first subject of the power of the keys." Cotton's answer, fundamental to the whole principle of independency, is that the "particular Church or Congregation" is the "first subject of all Church offices, with all their spiritual gifts and power." He finds no suggestion in the New Testament of a national church, or any hierarchy or church court, such as there was among the Jews. The Apostles, he says, were ministers plenipotentary, empowered to establish churches, and, where no church was, to exercise the power otherwise vested in a church. But the New Testament gives no indication that this exceptional office was intended to be permanent. On the contrary, as churches were established in various parts of the world, they became the residual seat of power, and the keeper of the two keys of Church order. Thus, "the Brethren of a particular Church or a Congregation, are the first subjects of Church Liberty . . . ; the Elders of a particular Church, are the first subjects of

Church Authority"; and "both the Elders and Brethren, walking and joining together in truth and peace, are the first subjects of all Church Power, needful to be exercised in their own body."

In the course of proving these propositions, mainly through interpreting Scriptural texts, Cotton establishes the chief points of Congregational, as distinguished from Episcopal and Presbyterian, Church polity. Each congregation is equal in authority to every other; their elders or overseers likewise have equal power; and it rests with the individual congregation, not with a bishop or presbytery, to certify the calling of a minister and, with the local elders, to ordain him.

Cotton holds back, however, from the most extreme form of independency. While he sees the dangers of any kind of union to the independency of particular churches, he is also aware of the constant tendency of churches to degenerate and to fall into apostasy. He finds it one of the duties, therefore, of particular churches to consult and consent together on weighty matters, and to assume mutual care for one another; and the Scriptures are his authority (for example, the Conference at Jerusalem, Acts 15) for holding that "a Synod of Churches, or of their messengers" has immediate power from Christ, the head of the Church, to undertake disciplinary measures where particular churches fall into grievous error. The need for such a higher authority is imperative in cases where a congregation is rent by factions. Christ, says Cotton, gives authority to a church only when it is "agreeing together in the name of Christ" (Matt. 18:19). Where there is disagreement, the Church loses its power, rendering it necessary for the synod to take action. Scripture indicates, however, that synods should exercise their power with great restraint, so as not to diminish the liberty and authority of the particular congregation; thus, the Jerusalem Conference resolved not to lay upon the churches "other *burthen,* but those necessary things."

One further question was of major importance to the New England churches, as it was also to the churches of England. This was the question of the relation between the Church and the Commonwealth. It seemed clear to Cotton that, since the Kingdom of Heaven does not include the "world," but only the Church, and, in the world to come, Eternal Life, there is no warrant for inferring, with the Papists and with some Presbyterians, that Christ gives the Church power to bind and loose in temporal affairs. Inasmuch as it derives its power from Christ, the Church must insist that, within its own province, it is independent of the secular power; at the same time, it must recognize that Christ has given to the magistrate the power of the sword, and that, in matters which concern civil peace, the Church must obey its earthly rulers.

Many, if not most, Churchmen in our day would agree with the following of Cotton's opinions in the matter of Church and state: namely, that the Church should submit to hold property under the laws of the state; that it should support the state with public prayers in times of national calamity; and that, when persecuted, it should refrain from resorting to force in its own defense.

But one opinion which John Cotton shared with his brethren and with most Churchmen of his day, both in

Europe and in America, was the one to which Roger Williams (c.1604-1683) took exception; namely, that the establishment of pure religion is a concern of civil peace. To support this view, Cotton has to turn to the Old Testament, where it is often pointed out that Israel's misfortunes were due to the nation's having forsaken the worship of Jehovah. A Christian Commonwealth, Cotton concludes, must take whatever action is necessary, "partly by commanding, and stirring up the Churches, and Ministers thereof to go about it in their spiritual way; partly also by civil punishments upon the wilful opposers, and disturbers of the same," in order to see that religion is kept true to the word of God. Cotton draws the line, however, at forcing men to enter into full religious communion. Here, he insists, the prerogatives of the Church to receive and exclude people from membership are at stake. To employ civil power at this point would be "not a *Reformation,* but a *Deformation* of the Church."

Cotton's influence on both ecclesiastical and civil affairs was equal to that of any New England minister of his time. His contemporary, William Hubbard, wrote: "Whatever he delivered in the pulpit was soon put into an order of court, if of a civil, or set up as a practice in the church, if of an ecclesiastical concernment." Cotton has sometimes been called an opponent of democracy, because, when treating of the classical alternatives of democracy, aristocracy, and monarchy, he stated that democracy is not countenanced by Scripture. But if we understand by democracy a workable arrangement in which the powers of the people are balanced against the powers of government, Cotton was a democrat, and he may be considered to have been one of the architects of the American system.

LEX REX

Author: Samuel Rutherford (c.1600-1661)
Type of work: Theology; political philosophy
First published: 1644

Principal Ideas Advanced

Nature has endowed every man, and hence every community of men, with the right of self preservation, and this right can never be surrendered to any civil power.

All power of government is from God mediated through the people or their representatives, and the purpose of the will of God in this regard is the good of men.

The relationship between a ruler and his subjects is based on their consent so that in the event of a ruler becoming a tyrant and acting to the destruction of the people or their liberties, they may resist lawfully, as a community, by reverting to the law of nature which was given by God for their protection.

By an extension of the natural law of self preservation, nations may lawfully assist other nations that are subject to tyranny.

When *Lex rex, a Dispute for the Just Prerogative of King and People* appeared in 1644 it was an immediate sensation. Members of the Westminster Assembly of Divines were said to be excited about its devastating attack on the absolute power of kings, and Samuel Rutherford, one of the Scottish Commissioners to the Assembly, was the object of high praise for his grasp of one of the most thorny issues of the times. Seventeen years later, in 1661, the Restoration of Charles II to the throne of the Three Kingdoms reversed the political climate and *Lex rex* was solemnly burned at Edinburgh and St. Andrews by order of the Scottish Parliament. Its author would most surely have been executed had not his death intervened.

Lex rex (The Law and the Prince) is a treatise on constitutional law as it related to the royal authority. The Stuart Kings James I and Charles I had asserted absolutism as a divine right of kings; they claimed to be above positive law and to be responsible directly to God for their discharge of the royal function. The claim was supported in an extreme form by John Maxwell, sometime Bishop of Ross, in a book entitled *Sacro-sancta regum majestas or The Sacred Prerogative of Christian Kings,* and *Lex rex* was written by Samuel Rutherford, Professor of Divinity at St. Andrews, as a rejoinder.

The book was written as a series of questions and answers, the questions being about such debated issues as whether government is warranted by the law of nature, and whether a kingdom may lawfully be purchased by the sole title of conquest.

The answer to the question as to whether government is warranted by a divine law makes a distinction which pervades the whole discussion. Government in general is from God; hence, support of it is an act of piety. On the other hand, a particular form of government, such as a monarchy, aristocracy, or democracy, is a human institution for the good of man; that is, there is a clear distinction warranted by the light of nature as well as by the Scriptures between the principle of government and the person designated to govern.

Again, another basic opinion is offered on the question as to whether government rests on a state of nature. Certainly it is natural for man to live in societies, but the mode of society he prefers is quite a different matter. There is nothing in the nature of things that determines one man to be a king and another to be a subject. "All men be born equally free," Rutherford writes. Magistrates are appointed in accordance with a natural desire for orderly social life as a secondary stage in the idea of what is natural, having its most obvious expression in family life where a father governs his household.

If government is in the form of a monarchy, it is not because monarchy is the immediate appointment of God, for other forms could also have divine approbation. Mediately, however, a monarchy may be from God as He guides His people to choose a form of magistracy. Actually the power of government is in the people, for every man has the right to preserve himself from violence; and consequently the people appoint as many officers for government as their safety and peace warrant. "No man cometh out of the womb with a diadem on his head, or a sceptre in his hand," Rutherford writes; but the people may put these symbols there as they delegate this or that person by divine guidance to be their prince, as Saul was chosen by the free suffrages of the people and anointed by Samuel, the prophet. The arguments of John Maxwell in support of God's immediate choice of a king independent of the people are so much rubbish, Rutherford claims; and in the course of his book he pursues his adversary relentlessly down a labyrinth of polemical alleys, flays him with Scripture and pagan tome, scorns his argumentative powers with virulent counterattack, and demonstrates that, "this Plagiarus hath not one line in his book which is not stolen." This "unchurched Prelate," Rutherford argues, referring to Maxwell, either proves too little, or too much, or nothing at all, and does not even do justice to the authors from whom he steals his material.

The king and lower magistrates hold their offices under God, it is contended in *Lex rex,* not only in the sense that they are chosen by God through the parliament of the people, but also because God endows them with gifts of government. Physically the king is "but a mortal man" with the same passive capacity as all other men. As Solomon asked for divine assistance for his royal task, so do all other rulers require grace for the discharge of their function. The authority of government in a prince is superior to that enjoyed by other men, but it is a matter of degree. Parents, employers, and magistrates all have authority by God in some measure. If "the necessity and temper of a commonwealth" require a monarchical government, then the king is the supreme civil authority, but he is only one among many other ranks of authority all of whom are responsible to God for the governmental gifts with which they have been endowed by divine favor. They are not appointees of the king so much as appointees of the people acting in concert, and they may discharge their functions independently of the royal power. Samuel Rutherford is emphatic on this point that all civil authorities are not delegates of the king but expressions of the natural and divine power resident in the citizens; that if there is a divine right of kings, there is also a divine right attached to all ranks of magistracy and a divine right of the people as a whole. He says, "The constitution is so voluntary, as it hath below it the law of nature for its general foundation, and above it, the supervenient institution of God, ordaining that there should be such magistrates, both kings and other judges, because without such, all human societies should be dissolved."

In Question IX a critical turn in the exposition is raised by the query, "Whether or no sovereignity is so from the people, that it remaineth in them in some part, so as they may, in case of necessity, resume it." It is certainly not true that any individual can take upon himself the right to remove a tyrant, for the power of government originates in the citizens as a whole, or their representatives. "The subject of royal power, we affirm, the first and ultimate, and native subject of all power, is the community," Rutherford insists. Should tyranny develop, this same community can act to redress the wrong. God never gave any magistrate the power to perpetrate wickedness, but only to promote the good. The tyrant is a servant of Satan, and it is the obligation of godly men to resist the works of the Devil. Not all the power of the people is vested in a parliament, and not all the power of a parliament is vested in the king. No arbitrary power is given to either parliament or king, "nor is there any arbitrary power in the people, or in any mortal man." Clearly the community retains the right to reform in cases of flagrant abuse of power, though they "are to suffer much before they resume their power."

It matters not whether a king inherits his throne by birth or achieves it by war, all government is conditional, as is abundantly illustrated in the Old Testament which Samuel Rutherford accepts as a final criterion for every phase of human activity. When Rutherford appeals to the law of nature he never doubts that it concurs with Scripture, for God who speaks through both cannot be thought to contradict Himself. In Question XVIII, "What is the law of the king, and his power?" Rutherford dips into Biblical exegesis in a tremendous display of learning to demonstrate from an awesome array of authorities in divinity that the prophet Samuel did not sanctify tyranny or teach that the only resort of a people was to pray and suffer patiently. A similar exhaustive treatment is given in a crucial passage in the New Testament in Question XXXIII, "Whether or no the place, Rom. XIII, I, proves that in no case is it lawful to resist the king." Because the passage speaks of "the powers that are ordained of God" and not of kings only, Rutherford claims that it tells more against "the cavaliers' unlawful wars against the parliament and estates of two kingdoms."

The practical question of the justification of a defensive war against Charles I was uppermost in the mind of the author, and especially the Scottish involvement with the English parliamentary forces. Not only had the general questions of Church and state been raised acutely for the whole Protestant cause by the Counter-Reformation, but the fact of civil war in Britain was in urgent need of theological and constitutional defense. Samuel Rutherford had been deeply involved in the struggle in Scotland to re-establish Presbyterian church government after the imposition of episcopacy under Archbishop William Laud (1573-1645). The tremendous effort which was necessary was successfully concluded in 1638, and *Lex rex* echoed many of the arguments which had been used for the Scottish "Second Reformation." This local concern appears in Question XXXVII, "Whether or no it be lawful that the Estates of Scotland help their oppressed brethren, the Parliament and Protestants of England, against Papists and Prelates now in arms against them, and killing them, and endeavouring the establishment of Popery, though the King of Scotland should inhibit them." Examples of assistance to the distressed are educed from Scripture; Scottish help for European Protestants is cited, and the help that England gave to the Reformation in Scotland is recalled. God is not pleased with "lip-love" to one's neighbor. We are our brother's keeper; we must bear one another's burdens, and the law of gratitude demands action. Not least, a victory of the Papists and Prelates in England would expose Scotland to the same fate: "We should but sleep to be killed in our nest, if we did not arise and fight for King, church, country, and brethren." Rutherford is careful to show that he is not fighting the King as such, but defending him against his true enemies who have turned him against his own good.

A discussion of the merits of monarchy follows, a question which the author faces unwillingly. "It is a dark way," he says. Unlimited monarchy is clearly bad. There must be restraints against the possible subversion of all laws, liberties, and religion at the hands of a wicked prince. No doubt there are good points in all forms of civil order, and as good a case as any can be made out for a monarchy. Samuel Rutherford declares himself undecided, for he recognizes that all human structures are open to sin, and a monarch is no nearer wisdom than other magistrates. Perhaps the convenience of a monarchy is its best support. If the king fails in his duty and covenant with the people, and if he will not suffer correction, then he may be dethroned by God, through the instrument of the people. The right of self preservation is natural and cannot ever be surrendered; and when a king becomes a tyrant and destroys his subjects, they are released from their fiduciary bond, and they may oppose and depose him. *Salus populi, suprema lex:* the safety of the people is the supreme law.

Lex rex in its title preserves the priority which ought to prevail. The king is not above the law, for he is obliged to administer the laws enacted by parliament. In Question XLIII Samuel Rutherford asserts the state of the matter in the history and laws of Scotland, and in the confessions of faith of the Protestant churches. By the coronation oath King Charles I swore that he would maintain the true religion and rule according to the will of God and the laws of the land, and in this way he accepted limitations on his royal power, and the primacy of law as the foundation of responsible government.

This great work of Rutherford had been preceded in Scotland by the celebrated treatise *De jure regni apud Scotos* of George Buchanan (1506-1582), a scholar and humanist of international fame and tutor to James VI of Scotland, to whom Buchanan dedicated his book in 1579. James VI became James I of the united kingdoms of Scotland and England, and his son, Charles I, was the monarch about whom Rutherford was concerned. John Knox (c.1505-1572) in his *History of the Reformation in Scotland* had faced the same issue with Mary, Queen of Scots, the grandmother of Charles I. The core of the solution to the constitutional question is the same in these three works by Scotsmen; namely, that monarchs are responsible to God and the people and cannot place themselves above the public good. The authority of a king is relative to his use of it. "I desire," wrote Buchanan, "that the people from whom he derived his power, should have the liberty of prescribing its bounds; and I require that he should exercise over the people only those rights which he has received from their hands." In the light of these sentiments it is not surprising that Buchanan's book met with the same fate as that of Rutherford's and was banned in Scotland.

DE RELIGIONE LAICI

Author: Edward Herbert, First Lord of Cherbury (1583-1648)
Type of work: Theology
First published: 1645

Principal Ideas Advanced

All religions rest their claims partly on reason and partly on faith.

What they rest on reason is common to all religions and consists in five catholic truths.

The beliefs which rest on faith are of two kinds: those concerning the past, and those concerning the future.

Faith concerning things past has partly to do with historical beliefs, which are profitable insofar as they support the catholic truths, and partly with mystifications, which are useful only to enhance the authority of priests.

Faith concerning things future is more directly authenticated in the human breast, and such faith gives hope for a blessed immortality.

Part of Lord Herbert's interest in religion undoubtedly arose from the desire to find a practical foundation for toleration and peace. As English ambassador to France under James I, he was well acquainted with the extent of religious dissension in his time: Europe was embroiled in the Thirty Years' War; Holland was torn with the Arminian controversy; France was restless under the Edict of Nantes, and England was on the verge of revolution. Religion, Herbert said, ought to lay upon men an obligation to peace; hence, when one beheld the clergy almost everywhere inciting to animosity and strife, there was reason to inquire whether they had not mixed vain and pernicious matters with the truth. In *De religione laici,* Herbert provides the layman with an apparatus for discriminating true from false belief, and for bringing the clergy to book.

But Herbert's interests in religion went deeper. Living at a time when the New Learning was regarded by many as a means of extending man's domination over nature, Herbert was more impressed with the prospects which it opened for the development of man's inner life. In this respect, his essay on lay religion is no mere political tract, but a sermon designed to point men on the way to their perfection.

Herbert's underlying philosophy is set forth in *De veritate* (1624), where, as the title suggests, his purpose was to examine truth, and to distinguish knowledge from "revelation, probability, possibility, and error." The essay describes man as a microcosm, endowed with inner forms of apprehension which naturally conform with all objects of the universe. Native instincts give man true images of the natural world, and provide him with "common notions" by means of which to understand them. By an inner sense, he has infallible knowledge of fundamental truths of metaphysics and morals. Error comes in on the discursive level, so that man has need of a method which will enable him to ask the right questions in the right circumstances. A major purpose of *De veritate* was to provide that method. In distinction from knowledge, which has its foundation in man's natural faculties, "revelation" depends on the authority of him who proclaims it. Insofar as revelation makes claims respecting the past, it must be judged, like all history and tradition, in terms of probability; insofar as it makes claims respecting the future, it appeals to a special faculty of the soul which yearns for the eternal and infinite.

In *De religione laici,* Herbert does little more than apply these principles to the problems of religious knowledge. All religions, he says, have at their foundation certain "common notions," which answer to natural instincts in man, and therefore are true: "namely, 1. That there is some supreme divinity. 2. That this divinity ought to be worshiped. 3. That virtue joined with piety is the best method of divine worship. 4. That we should return to our right selves from sins. 5. That reward or punishment is bestowed after this life is finished." These articles, which Herbert calls "our catholic truths," do not depend at all on a particular faith or religious tradition, having been "acknowledged as true throughout the world, by every age." They are, in his opinion, not merely the foundation of positive religion, but are by themselves sufficient for piety and virtue. Thus, every religion has its basis in reason.

Every teaching beyond these catholic truths pertains to faith; and, as we have seen, faith must be distinguished, according as it is directed toward the past or toward the future. Faith in the future, says Herbert, "proceeds from the highest faculty of the soul," being the root of all piety and devotion. "For by the light of this Faith we gaze upon God, with its tongue we speak to Him, with its hand we lay hold upon Him; in no other way are we inspired, exalted, preserved." Presumably there would be little quarrel between faith and reason, or between different religious traditions, if people were more zealous in this branch of faith. Unfortunately, religious teachers lay most of their stress upon the other kind of faith, directed toward the past. This kind of faith, which corresponds to no natural faculty, depends upon the reports and testimonies of men, and is more or less probable according to circumstances. "Mankind is given complete liberty regarding Faith about the past, and regarding doctrines proceeding from such Faith," Herbert writes.

For Herbert, the Christian religion possesses no special prerogatives over the other religions of mankind; God is not tied to any time or place. Yet, because Herbert was writing for Europeans, he applied his criteria particularly to the Jewish Scriptures, and asks, "What in the Sacred Scriptures may be called the pure and undisputed word of God?" It is certain, he says, that not everything in the Bible has equal authority, because included in it are the words of "villains, women, beasts, nay of the devil himself." First, we find there "our catholic truths, which as the undoubted pronouncements of God, transcribed in the conscience, are to be set apart and preserved," while the rest is brought under investigation. Second, we find a great deal of Hebrew history, and "no small heap of miracles published among them." These stories were told, according to Herbert, with the obvious purpose of applying and enforcing the catholic truths. How many of the stories a man believes, after considering the likelihood of each one's claim to be true, and whether a particular story does indeed promote piety and morality as it was intended to do, is for each man to decide. Third, there is a mass of esoteric material, "special covenants, secret and allegorical allusions, nay even some expressions too concise, or incoherent, and difficult to understand." Here, in the special covenants, Herbert finds the origins of most of the special claims which divide the churches. On grounds cited later by Rousseau's Savoyard priest, that a man must be impossibly erudite to determine the merits of alternate interpretations, and that God does not make exact scholarship a requirement for salvation, Herbert argues that this part of Scripture can be ignored by the layman; it is, he claims, the special preserve of priestly orders and serves as a means of mystifying the people and enhancing the authority of the priests.

Herbert admits that, in urging men to stick to the catholic truths, he is taking something away from religion, but, he says, he is taking nothing away from virtue and piety. As an instance, he takes the teachings of the Church respecting the remission of sin. Our reason tells us that God will forgive a man if he repent of his sin, but only on the condition that he mend his ways. The priests, however, drawing from the third class of Scriptural matter, hedge forgiveness about with all sorts of provisions and special dispensations, and so make repentance either too light or too heavy, in either case defeating the purpose of Universal Providence. Granted that by these means "the herd may sometimes be impelled to a juster pattern of life," they are rendered no more virtuous at heart, nor are they spared the implacable judgment to come.

Herbert does not deny the value of a priestly group. Unlike the later freethinkers, who, as Steele said, without the word "priestcraft" would be struck dumb, he grants the need of men set apart as teachers of the young, as preachers of virtue, as public intercessors, and as ministers of charity and mercy. We are reminded that Herbert had a celebrated example of the virtuous priest in his own brother, the poet, George Herbert (1593-1633).

Priests of virtuous and exemplary life, Edward Herbert says, ought to be revered because they "check the headlong license of the common people, they call attention to the means of eternal salvation engraved on the conscience, they introduce penitence, they make known God the Rewarder, they improve all things, finally, in the direction of moral excellence." In this way, faith and tradition fortify reason, without taking anything away from it.

The lay believer, whom the author has in view, is designated throughout the treatise as "the Wayfarer," a term which means something more than "pilgrim," in view of Herbert's cabalistic and Neoplatonic affinities. Herbert describes each man as passing through four "lives": in the parental seed, in the womb, in this world, and in the world to come. He points out that, as each of these lives changes into its successor, something gross and rudimentary is left behind, and that the new life is by contrast more full and satisfying. This process, says Herbert, establishes a probability in favor of a blessed immortality. But in these matters, dealing with the higher kind of faith, we are not left with mere probable inference. Among the faculties of our mind, we are told in *De veritate,* is one which longs for "eternal and infinite objects"; not to be confused with the ordinary faculties by which we calculate the future, it is "a divine intellectual faculty" and "a supernatural sense which proceeds directly from God." By means of it man comprehends the infinity of worlds, both large and small, the transcendence of God, who "fills, informs, and encompasses the infinite itself in the vastness of His unity"; by it he further knows the sublimity of his own being, and that it can attain to all these things. For, "since the faculty of sight reaches to the sun and even to the stars, while the understanding and the will refer to the infinite and eternal, is it to be supposed that in spite of our aspirations we do not reach and grasp them?" Once we have cast off the limitations of the flesh, we shall find "that the secrets of all things are revealed, and that nothing exists in the infinite which we may not hope to attain."

Lord Herbert is sometimes called "the father of Deism" because his five catholic truths became a sort of *credo* in anti-clerical circles. But popular Deism owes more to Newton and Locke than to Herbert, whom Locke was at special pains to refute. It is more correct to think of him as a link in the long history of English Platonism and as having as his successors Lord Shaftesbury, Coleridge, and the Cambridge Platonists.

THE FOUNDATIONS OF FREEDOM

Author: John Lilburne (c.1614-1657) and associates
Type of work: Puritan political philosophy
First published: 1648

Principal Ideas Advanced

The people of a nation should decide who should receive the power of government.

Government must serve the interests of the people and its power is limited by the natural liberties of man.

Of all freedoms, that of conscience in matters of religion is first in importance.

All men are to be equal before the law with no special privileges or exemptions by reason of birth or function.

The importance of documents is not measured by their length. *The Foundations of Freedom: or An Agreement of the People* is a mere pamphlet in size, but it is a concentrated precipitation of ideas that had been germinating in England ever since Magna Carta (June 15, 1215), the eminent curb on the arbitrary power of government. The Second Agreement, as the 1648 pamphlet is usually called, was the product of a committee of sixteen appointed by the groups most involved in planning political strategy; namely, the Parliament, the Army, the Independents, and the Levellers. It had been preceded by tremendous activity by the Levellers, as the associates of Lilburne were nicknamed, who were determined to oppose the tyrannical use of power by any party in England. The position of the country at the time when the Second Agreement was drawn up was unsettled to the point of being dangerously explosive. The council of Army officers had decided to be rid of King Charles, and Parliament had just been purged of its Presbyterian strength. The Independents were in power, especially in the Army. The time had come, the Levellers believed, when decisive action should be taken to reform the constitutional basis of government by an assembly elected by the "well affected" of the people on a broadly distributed franchise.

Briefly, the proposal was to dissolve the existing Parliament speedily and elect a Commons of three hundred to be called the Representative. All citizens twenty-one years of age and over, except those of the servant class or who had declared themselves to be disaffected by support of the King, or who were opposed to the Agreement, were to be included in the electorate. The Representative would hold office for periods of seven years. Careful arrangements were laid down for the electoral process to insure the absence of corruption.

In anticipation of the successful completion of the election, the Levellers specified the powers of the new national assembly in a document of nine articles; namely, *The Foundations of Freedom*. The document deals with such matters as conscription, recrimination, equal privileges, interference with lawful process, preservation of common rights, emergency measures, corruption, and the subordination of the Army to the decisions of the Representative. Above all, and placed first, freedom of conscience in religious matters is to be firmly upheld. The Representative is not "to compel by penalties or otherwise, any person to any thing in or about matters of Faith, Religion, or God's Worship, or to restrain any person from the professing of his Faith, or exercise of Religion according to his conscience, in any house or place (except such as are or shall be set apart for the publick Worship)." The actual arrangements for the general settlement of religion is left to the discretion of the Representative so long as it does not involve compulsion or the promotion of Popery.

Thereafter the most clamant grievances calling for redress are listed, all of them being flagrant abuses which the Levellers had been speaking about for some time. No one should be compelled to witness against himself or be left in custody without trial for longer than three months, and at the trial all communications were to be in English. Business is not to be restrained, public levies are to be equitable, debtors are not to be imprisoned, life and limb are to be respected, tithes for the support of the clergy are to be abolished, interest on loans is not to exceed six per cent per annum, and in general flagrant injustices are to be rectified.

The whole document is an extraordinary example of the flowering of democratic ideas, and it anticipated much that was later enacted in the modern British Commonwealth, the United States, and in other areas where representative democracy has been established.

Lilburne recorded in *Legal Fundamental Liberties* that the points of greatest sensitivity were the items on freedom of conscience and the right of the Representative to punish where no law covered the case. Army men were in favor of some restriction on liberty of conscience, and in this they were not alone in the land. For years the Presbyterian party had spoken of this liberty as a hydraheaded monster. It was argued that since religion covered a large territory, to permit man to define the limits of liberty would be inviting anarchy. On the other side there were many who were just as strongly convinced that coercion in religious affairs was indefensible. The pulpit and the members of the congregation should both be free to speak their minds as they believed God was leading them. Such a doctrine was advocated in the Baptist meetings which Lilburne and some of his associates attended. These men had suffered scorn and privation at the hands of state religion, and they were in no mood to permit power of persecution to have legal status in their blueprint for a better world. Freedom to dissent and to be protected in their sustentation of it was a fundamental freedom. As diligent students of the Bible, they had come to know their status in the Kingdom of God as the priesthood of all believers, and they were not prepared to settle for a second-class citizen status in the Kingdom of England. The rank and file of the Army were also now a vocal group, and they supported religious liberty as the key to all other liberties.

Lilburne and his friends had expected that the Agreement of the People would be submitted to the people forthwith, first to the regiments and then to the districts. Their chagrin was bitter when the document was submitted instead to a council of officers, who proceeded to open up the Agreement for revision and then to produce their own version. Lilburne's opinion on these proceedings was caustic. The officers were "a pack of dissembling juggling knaves," full of deceit and looking to their own interests. He published his copy of the Agreement, agreed to by a majority of the committee of sixteen, under the title *Foundations of Freedom,* with a prefatory epistle commending it. Thus this notable expression of democratic ideas was made available to great numbers who were eager for a constitutional settlement and demanded it along these lines.

Despite the frustration of seeing a revised form of the Agreement submitted by the council of officers to the Purged Parliament but allowed to lie there without action, it was a high moment in Leveller religious and political aspirations. John Lilburne had succeeded as a result of his stormy career in and out of prison in identifying some of the major ills of England and in obtaining agreement on some remedies by a composite committee of responsible persons. Since the electorate was not to be confined to property owners, the governing assembly would be genuinely a people's Representative. The law's vexatious delays, under which he had long suffered, would be mitigated, and the clergy whom he despised would be shorn of their legalized plunder, called "tithes."

It might have been expected that some reference would be made to Kingship and the House of Lords. There matters apparently were left open, the principal point being that whoever governed was to exercise power in the interests of the people. This was in accordance both with the ancient maxim that the safety of the people is the supreme law, and also with the main thrust of Biblical example. Saul was made King of Israel by the popular acclamation of the people, as the pamphleteers stated again and again. In the Independent Churches the common man demanded a voice in the church meeting as a saint of God, able to read the Word of God as well as any parson, major general, or noble. Here in the church meeting democratic ideas were nurtured and freedom was translated from theory to actuality, and ideas fostered here were applied to larger issues.

Lilburne was in many ways vain and inclined to quarrelsomeness, but he knew the minds of the common people, and he had an immense following, as was obvious when he was suffering imprisonment from time to time. The Levellers knew how to organize petitions and could obtain many thousands of signatures in a few days. Their main leader never lost a chance to exploit his misfortunes by telling all (with running commentary) in a pamphlet. He was so well versed in the law and in expressing himself that, although *The Foundations of Freedom* is said to have been drawn up by "several well-affected Persons," it can be safely assumed that John Lilburne had a considerable part in framing it, and, in any case, was so identified with its ideology and publication that it may well be ascribed to him.

The "Principle which we profess," he wrote in the preface, is "To do unto you, as we would all men should do unto us," and this Gospel precept he believed was the rule of equity. In signing it "Thy truehearted Countryman," he was expressing his sense of identity with all the "well affected," as well as his belief that authority in government rests finally with the people at large, and that its aim is to promote and preserve their liberties.

PRECES PRIVATAE

Author: Lancelot Andrewes (1555-1626)
Type of work: Devotional manual
First published: 1648

Principal Ideas Advanced

God is revealed both in nature and in history.

Each day of the week offers distinctive reasons for the prayerful worship of God.

Although penitence involves confession, it also expresses the hope of reconciliation with God.

Thanks should be given to God for the wonders of His creation and for the particular blessings which men enjoy.

Master of Pembroke College, Bishop of Chichester, of Ely, and of Winchester, chaplain to Elizabeth I, to James I, and to Charles I, Lancelot Andrewes was one of the great public figures in the history of the English Church. He was, at the same time, a profoundly contemplative person who spent hours each day in meditation and prayer, drawing upon a wide range of devotional materials, which he gradually composed into a personal prayer book.

Andrewes's manuscript copy of his book seems to have been lost, but copies had been made, for one of them was presented by Andrewes to William Laud (1573-1645), later Archbishop of Canterbury. The original was a polyglot work, mostly in Latin, but with portions in Greek and in Hebrew. As early as 1630 printed versions in English began to appear. The task of correcting, translating, and editing the work has engaged scholars through the years, culminating in an excellent critical edition by F.E. Brightman in 1903.

Preces privatae, sometimes anglicized to *Private Devotions,* is remarkable in that, although nearly every sentence in it is drawn from some other author—either from the Scriptures or from some earlier devotional work—Andrewes has built the materials into an edifice of his own, like a chapel constructed of stones brought together from many places. What sets it apart from numerous other devotional works which affect the language of tradition is that Andrewes has mined not so much felicitous expressions as determinate thoughts. Moreover, he rarely takes from any one passage more than the two or three lines which are needed in terms of the architecture of the whole. Hence, if one is interested in a collection of the well-known prayers of the Church, he must look elsewhere.

We have spoken in terms of a chapel, for, although Andrewes was a bishop, the *Preces* was composed to meet the needs not of the Church but of the individual believer. But, even as in chapels there are differences of style, so there is diversity in works of devotion. Some are boldly irregular, with obscure crypts and lofty vaults, pierced by shafts of colored light; others are orderly, well-lighted, and carefully appointed. Andrewes's work is of the latter sort. Patiently detailed and logically divided, it offers an interesting parallel to the scientific works of Francis Bacon, who likewise combined zeal for classification with a feeling for the importance of real things. Not in flights of ecstasy but in steady, controlled awareness of all that is taking place both within the soul and outside in the world, Andrewes finds man's highest fulfillment. The devotional life, as Andrewes describes it, is a systematic endeavor to lift the mind out of infantile slumber into the full waking consciousness of responsible manhood. Like others of his time, Andrewes was aware of man's inner conflicts, and he devoted many pages to acts of penitence; but he never lost sight of the great procession of creation, of God's revelation in nature and in secular history, as well as in Scripture, so that he regarded confession and penitence as but parts of a complete regimen, which take their place alongside acts of praise, thanksgiving, and intercession.

In the struggles which were threatening to rend the Established Church at that time, Andrewes followed Richard Hooker (c.1554-1600), who tried to preserve the Church's Catholic heritage against the attacks of the Presbyterians. Andrewes's disagreement with the Low Church party in England hinged on the celebrated Puritan principle, according to which Scripture is held to be the sole rule of faith and practice. The Puritans did, indeed, develop a rich and profound devotional life based exclusively upon Biblical passages, but by their rule they were prevented from offering to God prayers which originated outside the sacred canon. Andrewes follows the principle elaborated by Hooker; namely, that God's revelation is as wide as the creation, and that the guidance of the Holy Spirit is present in the teaching and liturgy of the Church, no less than in the pages of Holy Writ. Puritans would, therefore, object to many passages in the *Preces*, which are drawn from the Apocrypha, from the Church Fathers, from medieval *Horae* and *Breviaries*, and even from the prayerbooks of Jewish synagogues. Still, they could hardly quarrel with the main conception of the work, which is guided entirely by Biblical conceptions, notably God's revelation of Himself in the works of creation, in the divine names, and in redemptive history. These themes interweave and reinforce one another in ways which reveal profound feeling for Biblical typology.

Andrewes's prayers fall into two broad categories: those appointed to special times, and those framed according to special subjects. The first third of the book is devoted to prayers for the morning and the evening. The series of seven morning prayers, one for each day of the week, is especially noteworthy because of the sensitive use made of Biblical symbols and types. Thus, on Sunday, Andrewes commemorates the creation of light, the resurrection of Christ, and the sending of the Holy Spirit; on Monday, the creation of the firmament, the giving of the Law, and the prayers of Job and of the Canaanitish women; so, on through until Saturday, when he commemorates the Sabbath, the burial of Christ, the cessation of sins, and the souls of the departed.

Of the remaining portion of the *Preces* the largest section is devoted to prayers of penitence. Several complete penitential prayers are given, expressing contrition, confessing sins, pleading for mercy, purposing amendment, petitioning for help, and drawing assurance. The language, drawn chiefly from Scripture, is explicit and firm. The emotional power is largely latent, lying not in the expressions themselves but in the associations which they call forth from a mind thoroughly acquainted with the Scriptures. A reference to "Magdalene at the feast, Peter in the hall, the robber on the rood," is characteristic. On the same page, we read of those who forsook "angel's food" for "leeks and garlick," and "the Father's table" for "swine's husks." This is followed by an allusion to the Galatian Christians: "Woe is me, woe is me insensate! Who did bewitch me in this sort to play the fool?" Then comes a further reflection on the parable of the Prodigal Son: "O if Thou but vouchsafe to receive me, my mind is wholly to return: for then it was better with me than now it is." Such is the texture of nearly the whole book. The feelings it calls forth are of the kind which the believer consciously shares with the whole of Christ's Church.

But, with Andrewes, penitence is not so much an affair of feeling as it is one of reason. His confession is a full indictment of himself by the Law, by God's mercy, by comparison with other creatures and less fortunate men, and it is as detailed and specific as the Devil himself could have drawn up. But his plea for mercy is no less carefully argued. The divine nature, the divine names, a multitude of promises, redemptive acts, and parables are used to overthrow any fear or scruple which might prevent the soul from approaching God. Here is a faith that knows its kinship to reason, yet manages to avoid the excesses of legalism and dogmatism.

Andrewes's prayers of thanksgiving are chiefly notable for their comprehensive attention to detail. A typical prayer begins with a meditation on the seven days of creation, surveys the general station of man, then enlarges upon the atoning work of Christ, to praise Him "for all the good things He did, the evil things He suffered, from the cratch to the cross," for His triumph over death, and for the gift of the Holy Spirit. There is hardly an event in the Gospel narrative that is not worked into this lengthy meditation, as the mind is led from the nativity through the stages of Christ's earthly ministry, to His rejection, condemnation, torture, and crucifixion. To the story of Christ's passion, beginning with the hour of His arrest and ending with the release of His spirit upon the cross, Andrewes devotes more than one hundred items. The cumulative power of this long narrative is then effectively discharged by means of a prayer from the Sarum *Horae* (Paris, 1514), based on the ritual for anointing the various members of the body in Extreme Unction, which mentions the sacred head, hands, side, and feet of the Savior and concludes, "And I, Lord, am wounded in soul: behold the multitude, the length, the breadth, the depth of my wounds, from the crown of the head to the sole of the feet, and by thine heal mine."

A different kind of thanksgiving, of which Andrewes includes several examples, tells the particular blessings which God has bestowed upon the worshiper, including the nation, the city, the church into which he was baptized, the schools which he has attended, the parishes and dioceses which he has served, his family, friends, and neighbors. Sometimes he mentions these in general expressions, drawn from tradition; but at other times he anatomizes his life in circumstantial language, as in the following: "Glory be to Thee, o Lord, for that I am, I am alive, I am rational; for nurture, preservation, governance; for education, citizenship, devotion, religion; . . . for my parents honest and good, teachers, benefactors ever to be remembered, colleagues likeminded, hearers attentive, friends sincere, retainers faithful. . . ; for all these and all things else which we wot of, which we wot not of, open and privy, . . . I confess to Thee and will confess, I bless Thee and will bless, I give thanks to Thee and will give thanks, all the days of my life."

The work also contains prayers of intercession both general and special, and prayers for special occasions, such as before attending Holy Mysteries, and before going on a journey. Because the work was never intended for publication, but only for Andrewes's own use, it is freighted with allusions to the stirring times in which the author lived. The prayers are formally interesting in that they reflect, in both phraseology and thought, the influence of the liturgies of the ancient Greek Church; they are personally moving in that they express a constant humility. But if the reader is always conscious of the author, he is more vividly aware of the continuing consciousness of Christendom. The work will always be cherished by Christians who value their connection with the Church invisible as well as visible, triumphant as well as militant.

THE RULE AND EXERCISE OF HOLY LIVING AND HOLY DYING

Author: Jeremy Taylor (1613-1667)
Type of work: Spiritual direction
First published: 1650, 1651

Principal Ideas Advanced

The benefits of Heaven are reserved for those who have lived and died in a holy manner.

Holy living consists in remembering our heavenly calling while practicing our calling on earth, and in living sober, just, and godly lives.

Holy dying is an art to which each man must accustom himself before he loses his strength; there is no salvation for the deathbed penitent.

In order to prepare himself for his heavenly destiny, man must overcome the attractions of the present life; sickness, as a kind of penance and mortification of the flesh, is to be accounted a blessing.

A clergyman who sided with the royalist cause, Jeremy Taylor spent the years of the Puritan ascendancy in Wales, as chaplain to Richard, Earl of Carbery, to whom the present work is dedicated. In the preface to *The Rule and Exercise of Holy Living,* Taylor refers to the scattered condition of the Church during those Puritan years; many Christians were deprived of the Church's ministrations and, thus, individual Christians were left to find their own salvation.

Taylor's book is designed to trace

the "narrow way to heaven" in a straightforward way, without controversy and speculation. "I have told what men ought to do, and by what means they may be assisted; and in most cases I have also told them why; and yet with as much quickness as I could think necessary to establish a rule, and not to engage in homily or discourse."

The Rule and Exercise of Holy Dying was originally published as a separate work. It was begun during the last illness of Lady Carbery and was composed especially to help her. She died, however, before the work was completed. "She knew how to live rarely well," writes Taylor, "and she desired to know how to die; and God taught her by an experiment." Together, the two books constitute a detailed handbook for Christian living, together with suitable prayers for every occasion.

Taylor stood in the High Church tradition, for he was a protégé of Archbishop Laud. In opposition to the Puritan principle, that the Scriptures alone provide the rules of faith and practice, Taylor took the broad view of Christian origins, and he depended on instruction from extra-Biblical as well as Biblical sources. Although he was as ready as the Puritans to use Scriptural examples of his rules, he was just as likely to draw illustrations from one of the Fathers or from some Greek historian. For example, charity is enjoined on the recommendation of St. Jerome, who wrote, "I do not remember to have read that ever any charitable person died an evil death," and of Cyrus the Persian, who said on his deathbed, "I have been a lover of mankind, and a friend, and merciful; and now I expect to communicate in that great kindness which he shows that is the great God and Father of man and mercies."

Taylor also repudiated the Protestant teaching of justification by faith alone, and he argued that the covenant of grace, no less than the covenant of nature, lays a strict obligation on man. "Either you must renounce your religion," he says, "or submit to the impositions of God and thy portion of sufferings." He explains that, whereas in the Old Testament, pardon of sins consisted in no more than the removing of the punishment, in the Gospel it includes turning a man from his iniquities. Pardon of sins, he says, is sanctification; a man is not forgiven unless he forgives; he is not saved unless he live a holy life. Stories of deathbed repentance were particularly odious to Taylor. "Our religion," he says, "hath made a covenant of sufferings, and the great business of our lives is sufferings." Thus, it is incredible that God will "take a deathbed sigh or groan, and a few unprofitable tears and promises, in exchange for all our duty." The main complaint Taylor makes against the Roman Church is concerning its teaching that Extreme Unction will save a soul from Hell.

Following in the way that Richard Hooker (c.1554-1600) marked out for the Church of England, Taylor seeks to identify Christianity, at least in its moral aspects, with "the law of nature and great reason." Christianity has regard for all the fundamental necessities of life, underwrites all its natural relations, and leads to the consummation which God intended when he created man. Taylor finds the divisions of man's duty in the words of Paul, that we should live "soberly, righteously, and godly in this present world." The first of these, says Taylor, comprises our duties to ourselves, including temperance, chastity, modesty, and contentment; the second, our duty to our fellows, including obedience to superiors, responsibility to inferiors, fulfillment of contracts, and restitution of wrongs committed; the third, our duty to God, including both internal and external actions of religion.

Of special interest, in view of the political upheavals of the times, is Taylor's account of obedience to superiors. As his own loyalty to the royal family would suggest, he upholds the absolute right of kings over subjects. Other obligations, he says, rest on contract, but obedience to superiors, whether parents or the king, derives from the command of God. Obedience, he explains, is a complex virtue, including nearly all others—humility, self-denial, charity to God and to others, and victory over unruly passion. For this reason, rebellion is "the most unnatural and damned impiety," worse even than idolatry. That men should count it otherwise betokens, in Taylor's view, a fundamental perversion of the order of creation, the same kind of unreasonableness which led Satan and his hosts to revolt against their King. But even the devils preserve their appointed ranks and obey their superiors in rebellion. Heedless of all order, and deluded by the vain promises of ambition and greed, men hope to better their worldly estate by a crime which will damn them for eternity.

The contrast between this world and eternity is fundamental to Taylor's piety. Although he recognizes that a man's trade or profession is a calling, and that in some sense we serve God in performing honestly the work of this world, he nevertheless maintains that our proper service to God lies in acts of devotion which prepare the soul for Heaven. He urges us to take the utmost care of our time, to employ every possible moment in prayers, reading, meditating, and performing works of charity, "ever remembering so to work in our calling, as not to neglect the work of our high calling." He says that what we sow in minutes and spare parts of our time will bring us eternal rewards, for "God rewards our minutes with long and eternal happiness; and the greater portion of our time we give to God, the more we treasure up for ourselves."

Reasoning in this way, Taylor is led to take an extreme stand against all those things which tend to bind our affections to this world. He warns against "balls and revellings," "garish and wanton dresses," "banquets and perfumes," "feasts and liberty," and "the company of women that are singers." To humble the flesh he recommends exercises similar to those developed by Buddhists and Jains. We are to reflect on the uncleannesses which the body sends out from "its several sinks," one of the foulest of which is situated in the middle of the face. If this is not enough to wean us from the flesh, we may visit hospitals and charnel houses in order to acquaint ourselves with the body in its various stages of decay. He relates the story of a young hermit who, having failed by prayer and fasting to overcome his passion for a young lady, and hearing that she had died, secretly visited her vault and wiped the moisture from her decaying carcass with his mantle. Henceforth, when temptation returned, all he had to do to overcome it was to wrap his face in the mantle.

From these precepts, it will be seen how exactly Taylor agrees with the claim that "to live is Christ, and to die is gain." Holy living is, in his opinion, but a preparation for holy dying; since the latter is the gate of Heaven, sickness and old age are not to be considered as enemies but as friends. The sick man, in Taylor's view, is nearer to Heaven than the healthy man, because Heaven consists in the absence of sinful affections; in sickness the soul begins to untie "the strings of vanity that made her upper garment cleave to the world and sit uneasy." While the flesh sits uneasy, the spirit "feels itself at ease, freed from the petulant solicitations of those passions which in health" never abate. Even the groans of the sick man are so many penances by which the soul is prepared for Heaven.

Taylor was writing during troubled times, and he may on that account have been inclined to exaggerate the suffering of human life. "As our life is very short," he writes, "so it is very miserable. . . . God, in pity to mankind, lest his burden should be insupportable, and his nature an intolerable load, hath reduced our state of misery to an abbreviature." These words were written during the time that Hobbes, from a different philosophical perspective, was commenting on the shortness and incommodiousness of life. Unlike Hobbes, Taylor found a redeeming feature in man's suffering, arguing with the Stoics that there is no evil except in relation to men's desires, and that desires can be controlled. It is part of the discipline that God has set before us, says Taylor, that we should bear pain joyfully. Few outside the Roman communion have written with greater enthusiasm for the suffering of martyrs. "God could not choose but be pleased with the delicate accents of martyrs," he writes, "when in their tortures they cried out nothing but 'Holy Jesus,' and 'Blessed be God.' " Moreover, he ventures, "if we had seen St. Polycarp burning to death, or St. Lawrence roasted upon his gridiron, or St. Ignatius exposed to lions, or St. Sebastian pierced with arrows . . . we should have been in love with flames, and have thought the gridiron fairer than the ribs of a marital bed; and we should have chosen to converse with those beasts, rather than those men that brought those beasts forth. . . ."

Perhaps Taylor's enthusiasm for the martyrs is excessive, yet there is no question that, from the literary point of view, Taylor is one of the great artists of seventeenth century prose, with scarcely an equal in his love for a beautiful expression and a recondite reference. Nevertheless, if all worldly things are vanity, why should Lucan and Petronius be spared? One can use them to moralize with, but Taylor goes beyond this, as when, in a peroration on our duty toward departed loved ones, he tells Petronius's story of the young widow of Ephesus who, after vowing to die in her husband's sepulchre, was wooed by a guard there, and afterward, when her new husband needed an extra corpse, contributed the body of her first. All of this Taylor recounts in full detail, merely to emphasize the impropriety of immoderate grief.

Tolstoy, when the distaste for life drove him to condemn the world, did not spare his art. Was Taylor less perspicacious? Or, profoundly touched with the sadness of man's condition, was he employing his muse to help make men's grief more tolerable? More likely, he reasoned that in cultivating the art of rhetoric he was doing no more than exercise the calling which was laid upon him, and, as it were, sweetening the medicine that it was his duty as a physician of souls to minister. Among the prayers of intercession which he frames is one for the clergy: "Remember them that minister about holy things; let them be clothed with righteousness, and sing with joyfulness. Amen."

THE SAINTS' EVERLASTING REST

Author: Richard Baxter (1615-1691)
Type of work: Devotional meditations
First published: 1650

Principal Ideas Advanced

In God's loving purpose a final rest is designed for His children, and their highest felicity consists in attaining this rest.

The achievement of this goal requires on our part serious examination of our present position and earnest consideration of the character of that rest which awaits us.

The goal also presupposes constant discipline of various kinds and at different levels, in order that our present lives may qualify us for our future state and prepare us to enjoy it.

The Saints' Everlasting Rest was one of Richard Baxter's earliest works; it has always been his most famous one. When he wrote it, Baxter had already laid down the lines along which his lifework would proceed. He had demonstrated his remarkable gifts as a preacher and pastor, and the first phase of his notable ministry at Kidderminster was behind him. He had refused the chaplaincy of Oliver Cromwell's regiment of horse, but had served in a similar capacity with Colonel Whalley, and had been deeply shocked at the ferment of heretical ideas at work in the parliamentary army. Then serious illness overtook him. He found a refuge in the home of Lady Rouse, but he was convinced that his days were numbered and that his end was near. It was in this mood that he conceived his book, and it is the background of this anticipation of death which gives his work its distinctive quality. Baxter always wrote with the urgency of a man persuaded that his life was trembling on the brink of eternity, with little time in which to fulfill his mission.

His point of departure is a text of Scripture: "There remaineth therefore a rest to the people of God" (Heb. 4:9). Even in the natural life of man there is nothing so welcome to us as rest; "it is not our comfort only, but our stability." For the Christian, rest has a more intense significance; "it is the perfect, endless enjoyment of God by the perfected saints." This is the believer's final destiny, but it is a state open only to those who choose God "for their end and happiness." The goal must be clearly envisioned and resolutely pursued. We must also realize our present need, and acknowledge our basic dependence upon God. "When once we begin to trust our stock of habitual grace and to depend upon our own understanding or resolution, for duty and holy walking, we are then in a dangerous, declining state." The next step, Baxter writes, is to have "an inward principle of spiritual life." God does not treat us as inanimate objects; there must be that within us which can respond to His promptings. We can make no progress, however, unless we propose to enter by the proper gate, and "Christ is the door, the only way to this rest."

So far Baxter has been preoccupied with prolegomena. Can we define this rest more closely? It means, in the first place, that we no longer need to rely upon the means of grace which sustain us in our present state. The heavenly rest also means a perfect freedom from all evils. It involves, Baxter writes, "the highest degree of the saints' personal perfection, both of body and soul." But the core "and principal part of this rest is our nearest enjoyment of God, the chief good." This in turn presupposes the complete and wholly satisfying exercise of all our powers in the enjoyment of God. We progressively discover the true significance of that much-neglected duty, praise, and through the praise of God we unify our whole being. Knowledge finds its proper content and takes its rightful place. Love proves to be a profoundly personal yet a completely mutual relationship, and we see how remote is our true rest until we realize that God always loves us with a constancy to which our love of Him responds with ever-increasing completeness. We discover that mutual joy is the outcome of mutual love, and Baxter seems fully launched on his exploration of the inner meaning of the heavenly rest when he checks himself; such confident penetration of ultimate mysteries must be the result of man's spiritual pride, and Baxter returns to matters where Scriptural evidence promises a more assured knowledge.

It is clear that certain climactic experiences will be the prelude to the everlasting rest. Christ will appear; the general resurrection will take place; the Last Judgment will separate the saints from the sinners, and the saints will be crowned. Then all will discover the excellencies of the rest laid up for those who will receive it. They will see that it is a purchased possession, yet a free gift; it belongs to saints and angels, yet it derives its joys immediately from God himself. From this we may confidently assume that it will also be seasonable, because it will come to those wearied with the trials and burdens of an evil world. It will be suitable, in that it will be perfectly adapted to the new nature of the glorified saints. It will be perfect, since sin and suffering will have no place in the experience of the saints. And it will be everlasting.

So great a privilege is reserved for those for whom it is specifically designed. It will belong to the people of God, to those who have been chosen in God's good providence before time began. They are elect. They have been given to Christ. They have been born again. They know their own unworthiness, and they try to disguise neither the helplessness of the creature nor the all-sufficiency of Christ. Their will is consequently changed; they consciously enter into a new covenant with Christ, and they persevere in the spiritual duties which they have undertaken. The privileges of the saints are set in sharper contrast by comparing them with those who will forfeit this rest. The unregenerate will lose the personal perfections of the saints. They will have "no comfortable relation to God, nor communion with him." They can expect no part in the profound joys which belong to those who respond to God, know His nature, see His face, and experience His love. They will also forfeit the blessed society of angels and glorified saints. But all their losses will be heightened because the dimness of their understanding will be cleared away, and with fuller knowledge and clearer consciences they will know the measure of their failure. This means that those who lose the saints' rest forfeit all the enjoyments of time (their delusory interest in God and Christ, their hopes, their false peace of conscience, their secular joys, their sensual delights), but they also suffer all the torments of Hell.

Such serious considerations should surely compel the believer to give the most earnest heed to the rest of the saints. It is not surprising that the worldly and the profane neglect the matter; it is beyond measure strange that the godly do so. Magistrates, ministers, and ordinary persons are equally remiss in this regard, and to disturb those who are so foolishly secure, Baxter addresses a series of "awakening questions" alike to the upright and to the sinners. Perhaps this kind of discipline will break through the security of the complacent, and acquaint them with the terrors to which they will be subject while their title to the saints' rest remains in question. Self-examination can lead to certainty on this matter. That is why unregenerate natures, worldly companions, and Satan himself combine to discourage us. And since assurance does not come quickly, it is easy to grow discouraged and forbear the effort. Since it is dangerous to be wrong on this matter, it is necessary to make the effort, and Baxter lays down simple rules to govern our self-examination. Lest we be deluded, we must ask ourselves two simple but vital questions: (1) Do we make God our chief good? (2) Do we heartily accept Christ as our Lord and Savior?

The people of God ought to excite others to seek this rest. It is obvious and unfortunate that they fail to do so. This necessary task would begin in pitying the misery of men's souls. It would proceed through an appropriate course of education to the provision of suitable "public ordinances." Men properly qualified by learning and eloquence have a particular duty to urge others to seek this rest; so have those acquainted with sinners, those who have wealth or influence, and physicians who attend the dying.

No reasonable man will expect that the saints' everlasting rest will be available on earth. Our present afflictions are too great, even though they may stimulate us to hasten toward our true goal. We are too likely to rely on our comforts and cling to them. To do so is to court disaster, because those who seek the creature rather than the Creator inevitably invite trouble. But if we cannot enjoy heavenly rest on earth, at least we can plan for it. We can train ourselves to contemplate the joys of Heaven, and this will both encourage a proper disposition and evidence a Christian frame of mind. Thus, we shall avoid the obstacles to the kind of life which entitles us to enjoy the saints' rest. We shall not live in any known sin. We shall not let our outlook be circumscribed by worldly horizons. We shall not be lured into sharing the company of the ungodly. Specious theories will not beguile us in religion, and we shall avoid a proud and slothful spirit. In addition we shall practise the duties which promote this kind of life. We shall keep our minds on Heaven, because we realize that where our treasure is our hearts will rightly be at home, and we shall make every possible effort to know our true interest in this kind of disciplined yet otherworldly attitude. We must train ourselves to talk often and seriously about the abundant life. In every task we undertake we should strive to raise our hearts to the plane on which such life becomes possible. This will require an alert vigilance to detect and improve all possibilities and events. We should develop the neglected habit of praise. We should dwell often on the thoughts of God's infinite love. We should be sensitive to the promptings of the Holy Spirit. And this exalted conception of the devotional life rests ultimately on a simple and elementary duty: we must not neglect our bodily health. Baxter writes, "Thy body is a useful servant if thou give it its due, and no more than its due."

A disciplined religious life does not unfold automatically, and Baxter devotes much space to detailed instructions regarding the time and place suitable for "heavenly contemplation," as well as the temper most appropriate to it. Meditation and prayer should not be at the mercy of impulse or desire. There should be stated, suitable, and frequent times set aside for it each day. The Lord's Day offers exceptional opportunities, and we should not neglect the incitements of affliction, or disappointment, or bereavement. The place where we engage in this discipline of prayer should be suitably private and quiet, lest interruptions distract or noise disturb us. There is a frame of mind which conduces to meditation. Our minds must be free from secular preoccupation. Godly thoughts have little chance when they are constantly being jostled by worldly interests. This means that we must embark on this discipline "with the greatest solemnity of heart and mind. There is no trifling in holy things." So we should begin with a proper sense of the greatness of this undertaking, and of the profound seriousness of the issues at stake.

"Heavenly contemplation" is supported by what Baxter calls "consideration," which he defines as "the great instrument by which this heavenly work is carried on." It "opens the door between the head and the heart." It provides the standards which guide the affections, and it maintains a due sense of proportion in every phase of our life. It gives reason its due place and maintains it in proper vitality. But in keeping the proper balance between the various elements of our personal life, we must allow the emotions to play their appropriate role. The emotions cannot be left to chance excitement; they must be trained and exercised. Baxter therefore examines the contribution to the full life made by love, desire, hope, courage or boldness, and joy. These emotions must be given due and deliberate exercise. The order in which they should be practiced does not have to be always the same. All of them need not be "exercised" on all occasions, and the interrelations between them may vary from time to time. But they can be gathered up and given full scope in two important disciplines: soliloquy and prayer.

It is difficult, as Baxter admits, to maintain the spiritual glow at full intensity. He knew the limitation of abstract reasoning, so he allows a place to "sensible objects," provided they are cautiously used. Since the heart is always treacherous, we shall do well to ponder its reluctance to take its duty seriously, its disposition to waste its opportunities through trifling, its habit of wandering from the point, and its eagerness to cut short its spiritual exercises. We need to be continually on our guard.

And so, in conclusion, Baxter gives an example of what he means by "heavenly contemplation." In a mood of sustained exultation he passes from meditation on the saints' rest to a long prayer that we may all so consider our final destiny that we shall not forfeit the rest "which remaineth to the people of God." But it is possible for the preacher to be cast away, and his final word is a plea for the author himself: "O suffer not the soul of thy most unworthy servant to be a stranger to those joys which he describes to others . . . that so these lines may not witness against me; but proceeding from the heart of the writer, may be effectual, through thy grace, upon the heart of the reader, and so be the savior of life to both! Amen."

A PRIEST TO THE TEMPLE

Author: George Herbert (1593-1633)
Type of work: Pastoral theology
First published: 1652

Principal Ideas Advanced

The pastor is Christ's deputy in the task of bringing men back to obedience toward God.

With the teaching of Scripture and of the Church the pastor mingles knowledge of the human heart and of worldly circumstances.

His preaching is characterized by holiness rather than by eloquence.

Visiting among the people, he is "in God's stead," admonishing, rewarding, and blessing the flock.

He must know law and medicine in order to be all things to his people.

George Herbert left a promising career as a scholar, poet, and courtier to take holy orders. His book of religious verse, *The Temple* (1633), shows the attraction which wealth, beauty, honor, and conviviality held for him, and with what effort he persuaded himself of their vanity. *A Priest to the Temple,* alternately entitled *The Country Parson, his Character, and Rule of Holy Life,* is a prose work, composed while he was rector of the rural parish of Bemerton. Because Herbert lived only three years longer after his ordination, the book is not so much the wisdom of a seasoned clergyman as it is the ideal with which an exceptionally perceptive and devout man entered the vocation. But coming at a time in history when the Church of England was engaged in defining its position, Herbert's model priest proved a helpful guide for others besides the author, and played an important role in molding the Anglican priesthood.

The book comprises thirty-seven short chapters, bearing such titles as "The Parson's Knowledge," "The Parson in His House," and "The Parson in Circuit." The parson whom we meet in these chapters considers himself to be Christ's deputy in the task of "reducing Man to Obedience to God," and he shares both the dignity and authority, and the patience and mortification of his Lord. Appointed to labor among poor and hard-working people, the pastor lives a simple, abstemious life, avoiding any luxury which will add to the burden of those he serves, and endeavoring by his example to inculcate in them the virtues of sobriety, cleanliness, and honesty. Wherever he goes, he is Christ's minister, admonishing, catechizing, and blessing the people. He is ordinarily sad, from thinking on the Cross of Christ and on the sins of the world, and from observing daily the spectacle of ungodliness and misery; yet, because he knows that perpetual severity is hard to bear and that a good disposition is a help to virtuous living, he occasionally condescends to human frailty, and mingles some mirth in his conversation. He is distinguishable from his Puritan counterpart by his peaceableness, his willingness to bear with his people in their love for old customs, his freedom from the extremes of scrupulosity, and his pride in God's house and the quality of its appointments.

Without making his parson a bookish man, Herbert gives primary importance to the parson's knowledge of Scripture, of Christian doctrine, and of practical affairs. It is presupposed that he has received a good schooling, has read the Fathers and the Schoolmen, and is capable of understanding commentaries on the Scriptures. But study needs to be supplemented by prayer and self-discipline, and Herbert says that the parson's library is his holy life. Herbert suggests that each parson should, in his early years, compose his own book of Divinity, using the Church Catechism as a basis; for, he says, although the world is full of such books, "every mans own is fittest, readyest, and most savory to him." Such a book will become a storehouse of material for sermons, when "diversly clothed, illustrated, and inlarged," and will help make the pastor a good catechist, which is part of his responsibility.

Herbert exalts the office of preaching. His parson regards the pulpit as "his joy and his throne." He chooses texts that are devotional rather than controversial, "moving and ravishing texts, whereof the Scriptures are full"; and he interprets these in their whole and obvious meaning, instead of crumbling them into parts as many expositors are wont to do. He will use every art to bring the Scripture's meaning home to his hearers, including specific allusions to local affairs with which the people are familiar, and he will illustrate his meaning in terms of ordinary experience gleaned from "tillage and pastorage." But his sermon never will become an exhibition of wit, learning, and eloquence, or lose the character of holiness.

Herbert never speaks of Sunday as the Sabbath, but, as the day set apart for public worship, Sunday is considered to be the most important day of the week for the rural pastor. As soon as the pastor awakes on that morning, he falls to work, like a market-man on market day, beginning with prayers for himself and for the people, that nothing will take place which is unworthy of the majesty of those offices which he is about to perform. When the hour comes, he goes, with his family attending him, to the Church, where he reads the divine service twice, preaches in the morning, and catechizes in the afternoon. He spends the rest of the day visiting the sick, reconciling neighbors that are at variance, and personally admonishing those whom his sermons do not reach. In the evening, he entertains some of his neighbors, taking occasion to discourse on things both profitable and pleasant, both as concerns the Church and the state. Having performed these things, he permits himself the thought that he has "in some measure, according to poor and fraile man, discharged the publick duties of the Congregation"; and he closes the day, as he began it, with prayer that the Almighty may accept his imperfect service and improve upon it.

On weekday afternoons, the country parson is found "in circuit" among his people. "When he comes to any house, first he blesseth it, and then as hee finds the persons of the house imployed, so he formes his discourse." Always he "is in Gods stead to his Parish," commending and censuring what he finds. If anything is well spoken, he enlarges it; if ill said, he corrects it. "This is called keeping Gods watch." The parson does not lack boldness to speak the word of admonition to the rich when he finds them idle, ill-employed, or over-indulgent, it being in his mind how many things want doing in the land, and how important it is that every man find his vocation. But the parson by preference visits the humbler of his flock, finding no person or care beneath his attention. "Wherfore neither disdaineth he to enter into the poorest Cottage, though he even creep into it, and though it smell never so lothsomly. For both God is there also, and those for whom God dyed: and so much the rather doth he so, as his accesse to the poor is more comfortable, then to the rich; and in regard of himselfe, it is more humiliation."

Charity to the poor is one of the parson's chief obligations. "The Countrey Parson," Herbert says, "is full of Charity; it is his predominant element." He is openhanded with his own small competence, even where it is a question of not "providing a stock for his children," for he assures himself that he better provides for them by lending his money to God than by putting it in the bank. But his concern extends beyond the satisfaction of men's material wants. He tries to teach men that every creature has his good things only from God, that God rewards men's labors, and that He especially remembers the compassionate. Herbert distinguishes between the charity of the pastor and that of lay people. Christians are to give to the poor as unto Christ, but when the priest gives, this is more on the order of God ministering his gifts to men. Therefore, the priest properly requires of those who receive of him that they say their prayers, the creed, and the commandments, and if they are perfect in these he rewards them, even as in all his charities he gives most to those who live best. "So is his charity in effect a Sermon."

Even though the country parson takes his spiritual duties seriously, he is not one to suppose that his responsibility ends with the cure of souls. On the contrary, he "desires to be all to his Parish, and not onely a Pastour, but a Lawyer also, and a Phisician." When controversies arise, he will try them, as judge, in the presence of three or four able members of the parish, and, after consulting with them, will hand down judgment. As judge, he will always hew to exact justice, down to the value of a pin, but afterwards, as pastor, he may admonish for charity. Sometimes, if the case be difficult, he will recommend that it be carried to the courts, in which case he will try to prevail on the contesting parties to go to law as brethren and not as enemies. Similarly, when sickness arises, he or his wife, or if neither has any skill, "a young practicioner" whom the parson keeps in his house for the benefit of his parish, will ever be at hand to help. The study of anatomy and medicine, particularly of herbs, will be throughout his life a pleasant diversion from his theological studies, and a great service to the people.

Living close to the people, it is important that the country parson be married. Herbert considers virginity a higher state than that of matrimony, but circumstances being what they are, the unmarried priest must exercise excessive precautions against scandal; hence, it is ordinarily better to be married, but to a woman who completely shares the parson's aims, and who, by her skill and sympathy, will make his a model household, and will be able to assist in the ministry to the sick and the poor. Both his children and the household servants will be brought up in an exemplary fashion, so that when they go forth, each will carry the ministry into his ranks. For, "as in the house of those that are skill'd in Musick, all are Musicians; so in the house of a Preacher, all are preachers."

Herbert's Christianity has three main articles: that man fell from God by disobedience, that Christ is the means of calling men back to God, and that the priesthood has the task of carrying on Christ's work of reconciliation. Repentance and new obedience are the aims which he has always in view, but he is not disposed, with his brother Edward (see *De religione laici*, 1645), to minimize the efficacy of such institutions as the sacraments and the priestly benediction. In the presence of the mystery of holy communion, says George Herbert, the priest himself is thrown into confusion, and prays, "Lord, thou knowest what thou didst, when thou appointedst it to be done thus; therefore doe thou fulfill what thou didst appoint; for thou art not only the feast, but the way to it." With the reformers, he wishes to remove from religion all that is superstitious, and all that is tawdry and degrading, but without taking anything away from the holiness and reverence with which these things are performed. But some reformers, in their efforts to avoid idolatry, have, he complains, gone to the opposite extreme of "coldness and Atheism." Herbert's picture of the rural church, decently appointed, but in nothing extravagant, is a pleasant alternative to the starkness of the Puritan chapels, as well as to the luxury of the Catholic cathedrals, and has become the model for Anglican church builders, much as his parson has become a model for the Anglican clergy.

DIDACTICA MAGNA

Author: Johannes Amos Comenius (1592-1670)
Type of work: Philosophy of Christian education
First published: 1657

Principal Ideas Advanced

Man's life on earth is merely a preparation for his life in Heaven.

Education is essential if man is to live profitably on earth.

The child should be educated in knowledge, virtue, and piety, for these virtues correspond to the three parts of the soul.

Didactic is the art of education, and, like other arts, its successful practice consists in imitating the order of nature.

All children should receive the same education until the age of twelve, and this teaching, which should be conducted in the vernacular, should comprehend the principles of science, art, and humane learning, as well as morality and religion.

Johannes Amos Comenius (Komensky) was a bishop of the Church of the Bohemian Brethren, who, partly because of the Thirty Years' War, lived much of his life as an exile in Poland, England, Sweden, Germany, Hungary, and Holland. His success as a teacher, and his industry in preparing graded materials for young pupils, led both the English and the Swedish governments to consult him in connection with their programs of educational reform. The *Didactica magna* was written in Bohemian between 1628 and 1632, but was first published in a Latin version at Amsterdam in 1657.

Comenius believed that he was merely implementing two suggestions made by Martin Luther in 1525, who asked, first, that there be schools founded in every town and village for the instruction of all children "in useful knowledge, in morality, and in religion," and, second, that some better method of instruction be evolved so that, instead of resisting learning, children might be drawn to it. Comenius brought to his task the enthusiasm of an age which is remembered for the work of Francis Bacon (1561-1626), and René Descartes (1596-1650).

In spite of the wars that had left

him homeless, Comenius believed that a new day was dawning in Europe. Scientific advances and mechanical inventions suggested to him that great benefits would accrue to morality and religion if men were to bring to the cultivation of human nature the same diligence and acumen which they had applied to understanding and mastering the physical environment.

Comenius is a reminder, however, that the harbingers of the New Learning did not completely break their ties with the Platonized Christianity which underlies so much of Western culture. He believed that the visible world was created to be a nursery for man, and that it would endure no longer than was necessary for the number of the elect to be filled up. He writes that man's life occurs in "the mother's womb, the earth, and the heaven." As the first place of life is preparatory to the second, so the second is preparatory to the third, and the third will abide forever.

Education, as Comenius describes it, is but the preparatory part of man's life on earth. Unlike other infants, the human child must be taught if it is to realize its full potentialities. There is one, and only one, way to do this efficiently: specialists must take the children in hand and fashion them into men and women, or, more specifically, into Christian men and women. Because of the limited number of years which God has allotted to man on earth, it is of utmost importance that the education be completed by the time the person reaches physical maturity.

The scope of man's education, says Comenius, corresponds to the tripartite nature of the soul. Man's intellect is given him for the purpose of knowledge; his will for the purpose of choosing between what is advantageous and what is harmful; his memory for the retention of all things hitherto learned and for reminding him of his dependence upon and his duty toward God. "From this it follows," Comenius writes, "that man is naturally required to be: (1) acquainted with all things; (2) endowed with power over all things and over himself; (3) to refer himself and all things to God, the source of all." Man's chief end, says Comenius, is to serve God, His creatures and ourselves, and to enjoy the happiness that comes from knowing, using, and loving these three rightly. Both as respects serving and enjoying, "Learning, Virtue, and Piety" are essential prerequisites. All else (health, strength, beauty, riches, honor, friendship, good-fortune, long life) are "but extrinsic ornaments of life," like the case of a watch or the trappings of a horse. "It follows, therefore, that we advance toward our ultimate end in proportion as we pursue Learning, Virtue, and Piety in this world."

Comenius recognizes no limits to the scope of human knowledge. He accepts the view that man is a microcosm, in which the whole universe is inwardly comprehended. All knowledge is present to man, just as a plant or tree is present in the seed. He cites Pythagoras as saying that, because man naturally possesses all knowledge, a boy of seven, if properly questioned, should be able to answer correctly all questions of philosophy; and, except that he believes that the mind ripens more slowly than Pythagoras suggests, Comenius agrees. In another place, however, he cites Aristotle's teaching that the mind is "a blank tablet on which nothing was written, but on which all things may be engraved." That there may be a conflict between thinking of the mind as a seed and as a blank tablet does not seem to have occurred to him.

Comenius admits that "exact or deep knowledge" of all the arts and sciences is more than any man can acquire in a whole lifetime, much less during his formative years; nevertheless, since the child of God is destined to know all things, his education should be universal in scope. That is to say, he should learn the principles, causes, and uses of all the important things in the world; for he must never, in his journey through life, encounter anything so strange to him that he cannot form a true judgment concerning it and turn it to its proper use.

To this end, a systematic organization of education is necessary. Everywhere, in nature as well as in art, says Comenius, order is "the soul of affairs." He cites as examples the solar system, insect societies, the human body, military organizations, and machines. Seemingly impossible undertakings are brought to completion by "the all-ruling force of order; that is to say, the force derived from arranging all the parts concerned according to their number, size, and importance, and in such a manner that each one shall perform its own proper function as well as work harmoniously with and assist the other parts whose action is necessary to produce the desired result." If the goal of educating all children in all knowledge seems a formidable one, says Comenius, that is because we have not hitherto acquired the educational art.

"Didactic," says Comenius, "signifies the art of teaching." He calls his work the "Great Didactic" because it comprises "the whole art of teaching all things to all men, and indeed of teaching them with certainty, so that the result cannot fail to follow." The business of any art is to eliminate chance by means of circumspection. By studying nature and learning its way, the artist or craftsman is able to bring things to pass with the same infallible certainty which characterizes the course of nature itself. Hitherto teachers have possessed no art, comparable to that of the engineer or the horticulturalist, which would enable them to say, "In so many years I will bring this youth to such and such a point; I will educate him in such and such a way." But Comenius expresses confidence that his method will supply the lack.

Comenius's universal claims for his method rest upon his avowedly *a priori* method. Unlike educationists who depend merely upon experience, he sought out the principles upon which education must be based. His method consists in finding suitable analogies in nature and in the crafts. For example, a bird chooses the springtime to multiply its species; similarly, a gardener, to set out his plants; so, "the education of men should be commenced in the springtime of life." Again, before the bird lays an egg, it prepares a nest; a gardener, before he begins to set plants, has the soil, the tools, and the tender slips all in readiness; so, the teacher must first prepare maps, phrase books, diagrams, and models, and must observe the right order in presenting subject matter.

Although Comenius sometimes writes as if the mind develops organically, all that he means to suggest is that the texture of the brain is at some times better suited to receive impressions than at others. For the most part, he uses purely mechanical models. The mechanism of a clock interests him, and it suggests a model for understanding everything in creation. Not merely man's bodily movements, but those of his soul also, may be understood in terms of "the weights" of desire which incline it this way and that, with reason serving as an "escapement" which makes is possible to blend the active and passive elements. More pertinent to the educational art is the parallel with printing. Comenius invents the term "didachography" after the analogy of "typography," and he develops at length the concept of impressing knowledge on the mind by uniform symbols ("class-books"), ink ("the voice of the teacher"), and pressure ("the school-discipline, which keep the pupils up to their work and compels them to learn"). "Our discovery of didachography," says Comenius, "facilitates the multiplication of learned men in precisely the same way that the discovery of printing facilitated the multiplication of books," enabling us for the first time to expect the fulfillment of the divine prediction, "The earth shall be full of the knowledge of God, as the waters cover the sea."

Comenius's *a priori* principles led him to numerous practical innovations, which cause twentieth century educationists to place his name along with those of Johann Pestalozzi (1746-1827) and Friedrich Froebel (1782-1852) as one of the founders of modern pedagogy. One of his contributions is the insistence on the use of visual aids. The mind, he says, is like a mirror: ". . . in order that the mirror may duly receive the images of the objects, it is necessary that these latter be solid and visible, and be also placed before the eyes." Mere verbal presentations are like clouds, and make an unsatisfactory impression. For example, a skeleton and models of the nerves and viscera should be used in teaching anatomy; and pictures should be used in teaching the vocabulary of foreign languages. Another application of his principles was the rule that no materials should be permitted to enter the mind of a learner which would prevent his receiving images without confusion. Scholars should have books, written specifically for them, which contain nothing except the matter that the educator wishes to impress upon their minds. Further, instruction should be carefully graded, so that the child will have time to master simple materials before more complicated ones are introduced. This, in turn, demands lesson plans and schedules. The school year should contain the same number of days each year, so that each class may complete its allotted task, and all the students will enter the next grade together. "This," he adds, "is an exact analogy of the method used in printing when all the copies of the first page are printed first, then those of the second page, and so on."

Comenius's principles also suggested to him numerous reforms in connection with school curricula. For one thing, his insistence on universal knowledge led him to place natural science and the crafts alongside the seven liberal arts. Further, his theory of child development led him to argue for what he calls a "vernacular school," for all children ages six to twelve. A "Latin school" for students thirteen to nineteen would, according to his plan, prepare pre-professional students for the university.

One of Comenius's objections to the schools of his time was the result of their neglect of morals and piety. In his *Didactica* he seeks to remedy this. He urges that sciences, arts, and languages be taught as "purely subordinate subjects," so that the child will understand that "all that does not relate to God and the future life is nothing but vanity." Thus, the Holy Scriptures must "rank before all other books." Children, he reminds us, are "plants of Paradise." The schools have the responsibility for seeing that the students develop into "steadfast and noble-minded" men and women. Or, to change the figure somewhat, children are soft and malleable substances which can take any shape, and the schools are "forging places of humanity," in which virtuous and godly men are fashioned.

The reforms suggested by Comenius follow *a priori* from his principles. However, in spite of urging that "this art of instilling true virtue and piety may be elaborated on a definite system and introduced into schools," Comenius has almost nothing to say about how this can be done. His chief recommendation is that the teaching of pagan authors should be eliminated. There is nothing of value in them, he says, that cannot be found in Hebrew and Christian writers, and there is much that is vicious and false, which could only corrupt the image which Christian education is trying to impress on the young.

OLIVER CROMWELL'S LETTERS AND SPEECHES

Author: Oliver Cromwell (1599-1658)
Type of work: Letters and speeches
First published: 1845

Principal Ideas Advanced

God is at work in the affairs of nations and individuals, and it behooves all men of serious outlook to walk in humble obedience to God's will.

It is easier to recognize God's guidance in dramatic events or in personal experiences than in the more complicated developments of political life.

The complexities of public life lay upon the righteous the duty to work together in fulfilling God's purposes.

Oliver Cromwell's letters and speeches are documents which give personal quality to the narrative of a remarkable career. Cromwell was a writer only in the most incidental sense. Primarily he was a man of action, and he bestrode the middle years of the seventeenth century as the supreme example of the Puritan soldier and statesman. To an extent seldom true of great men, fame was thrust upon him by circumstances. Until the outbreak of the first civil war of the Puritan Revolution, he was a relatively obscure figure: a country gentleman of modest means and a silent back-bencher in the House of Commons. He had had no training in the arts of war; he became a remarkably successful soldier, and the German Imperial General Staff used to cite him as one of the most notable examples of a great cavalry leader. When the Long Parliament assembled, no one would have guessed that among all its members Cromwell was the one destined to attain supreme political power.

In Cromwell's *Letters and Speeches* we catch glimpses, fleeting and none too frequent, of this amazing development. The earliest letters show us an active member of parliament organizing the military concerns of his party in the area which he represented. The need was urgent; the requisite steps were obvious, and Cromwell writes with directness and vigor concerning issues both complex and confused. His commands are clear and explicit, and we can see the resources of the eastern counties being mobilized to serve the parliamentary cause. What is even more important, we can already detect the distinctive attitudes which made Cromwell a great military leader. He realized that the quality of an army depends on the character of its men. He approved the zeal shown by the leaders at Huntingdon in raising a company of foot, but he wanted to see it changed into a troop of horse, "which indeed will by God's blessing, far more advantage the cause than two or three companies of foot; especially if your men be honest, godly men, which by all means I desire." "I beseech you," he writes on another occasion, "be careful what captains of horse you choose, what men be mounted: a few honest men are better than numbers. . . . If you choose godly honest men to be captains of horse, honest men will follow them. . . . I had rather have a plain russet-coated captain that knows what he fights for, and loves what he knows, than that which you call 'a gentleman' and is nothing else. I honor a *gentleman* that is so indeed!" His sense of the importance of the cause, together with his sympathy with the men who supported it, explains the invincible morale of the force which Cromwell raised and led. This made the Ironsides one of the most famous regiments in history.

Many of his letters directly concern military developments. Immediately after the battle of Marston Moor (1644), he sent a beautiful message of sympathy to Colonel Valentine, whose son had been killed. The letter begins with a vivid account of the encounter, of how his wing had charged and scattered Prince Rupert's horse troops and then the enemy foot soldiers: "God made them as stubble to our swords. . . . Give glory, all the glory, to God." He refers movingly to his friend's loss, but adds, "let this public mercy to the Church of God make you to forget your private sorrow." After the battle of Naseby (1645) the same note recurs. "Sir," writes Cromwell to the Speaker of the House, "this is none other but the hand of God; and to him alone belongs the glory, wherein none are to share with him." But he realized that divine mercies are mediated through human agents, in this case the honest men who had served parliament faithfully, and who must not be discouraged. "He that ventures his life for the liberty of his country, I wish he trust God for the liberty of his conscience and you for the liberty he fights for."

It is at this point that one of Cromwell's great concerns begins to emerge clearly from the *Letters*. Distinctions of religious affiliation are often magnified; among soldiers fighting for a great cause, they become irrelevant. In a long dispatch after the storming of Bristol, he concluded with a strong plea for toleration: "Presbyterians, Independents, all have here the same spirit of faith and prayer; the same presence and answer; they agree here, have no names of difference: pity it is it should be otherwise anywhere! All that believe have the real unity, which is most glorious; because inward and spiritual, in the Body and the Head. . . . And for brethren in things of the mind we look for no compulsion, but that of light and reason."

Though there is no doubt of the graphic quality of Cromwell's military dispatches (after all there is no source for the first and second civil wars to compare with his letters), the center of interest gradually shifts to other matters. There was the uneasy and increasingly disturbing political maneuvers which culminated in the second civil war and which slowly brought Cromwell to the reluctant conclusion that the duplicity of King Charles I ("that man of blood") made it impossible to trust him any further. There was the turmoil in the army, culminating in the Putney debates. There was trouble with the Presbyterian faction in Parliament; there were the earliest attempts to fashion a new constitution by which the country could be governed. By sheer necessity, Cromwell was pushed by events and by the vacuum at the head of affairs into the position of supreme power as Lord Protector (1653). His aims were clear, but it was far from obvious how they could be achieved. Here, too, the *Letters and Speeches* reveal the increasingly acute dilemmas which Cromwell faced. The problems of the Church were in themselves difficult to deal with. How could the ministry be maintained? Were tithes an intolerable affront to the freedom of religious worship (as some of the sects claimed) or were they, under existing circumstances, the only possible way of supporting the Church? Was toleration synonymous with confusion?—or was it a sincere and promising attempt to translate man's religious freedom into feasible social forms? It is true that certain groups, like the Anglicans and Roman Catholics, suffered a measure of persecution, but Cromwell claimed that such repression was prompted by political, not by religious, motives; these people suffered, not for their convictions but because they engaged in subversive activities. In his attitude to the Jews, Cromwell was more open-minded than most of his contemporaries. But the task of giving effect to a policy of toleration was always difficult, and Cromwell found himself beset with problems. As time passed, the extremer elements among the Puritan sects were increasingly hostile; they were more vocal in their abuse, more ready to engage in plots.

The urgent, indeed the insoluble, problem of the Protectorate was that of devising a system of government which could preserve order and maintain public confidence. This is the difficulty with which Cromwell's speeches are increasingly preoccupied. His dilemma was that he believed in ruling with the people's consent, but he was unable to secure it. The disconcerting but inescapable fact was that his rule rested on force. He was the head of the state because he was the commander of the army. Military rule is expensive and unpopular, and the experiment of maintaining order by the major-generals did nothing to commend the Protectorate to the people. Cromwell tried more than once, and by more than one method, to secure a parliament that would prove co-operative. But even when its members were chosen by a method designed to guarantee similarity of outlook and aim, the result was the same. In his first speech to the first parliament of the Protectorate, he could refer to a dayspring of divine prophecy and hope, and urge the members to struggle toward it. He could even speak of resigning his authority into their hands, but before long he was sternly reminding them that he was responsible for order and could not allow them to tamper with the foundations of government. The problems created by parties form a constant refrain in his addresses, and he complained bitterly on the spirit of faction which jeopardized the achievements of the Protectorate. That these achievements were both genuine and considerable, he left them in no doubt. The reform of the law, the settling of the Church, the maintenance of peace at home, the establishment of respect abroad—these formed a notable record, yet all the time those who should have co-operated with him were intent on fomenting trouble. Cromwell was well aware that France and Spain held his power in wholesome awe, and he wrote to Cardinal Mazarin with an authority which English rulers had not recently been able to assume. He could intervene with effect on behalf of Continental Protestants, but he could not get English Puritans to agree among themselves or to unite in his support.

This problem of unity became increasingly urgent, and among other things it explains the episode which occupies so much space in the latter part of the *Letters and Speeches:* the offer of the crown to Cromwell (1656). This might have re-established a pattern of authority with which Englishmen were familiar, and the majority of the nation might have settled down under a new dynasty. But in the army the suggestion caused deep concern, and Cromwell finally rejected it because it further jeopardized the precarious unity upon which his regime rested.

The *Letters and Speeches* are a source of primary importance for the history of the English civil wars, the Commonwealth, and the Protectorate. Here we see events through the eyes of one of the chief participants in them, a man, moreover, who had an amazing gift for direct and vivid narrative. We can share in the turmoil of battle and we can appreciate the mounting perplexities which made government so difficult. As we close the work we can appreciate how fortunate Cromwell was in the hour of his death. We realize how insoluble were the difficulties besetting "the rule of the saints" and how inevitable therefore was the restoration of Charles II. But the great value of the work does not relate to political developments. This is a Christian classic because it is a clear and moving revelation of the character of one of the greatest of the Puritans. We do not see, of course, the whole of Cromwell's very complex nature. From other sources we know that when faced with a difficult problem he often suffered agonies of indecision, but when he acted, he did so with swift and irresistible force. We can sense a little of the former quality in some of the political letters and speeches from the later years of his life. We can see the decisive vigor clearly enough in the early letters describing his activities during the initial stages of the first civil war. When he felt that he was fighting the Lord's battles his characteristic qualities appear most clearly. Then his sense of God's presence and his submission to God's will find humble expression. Events become the stage on which the divine purpose is being accomplished, and it is his high privilege to be a fellow laborer in this great task. This is what makes his battle dispatches among the great documents of militant Puritanism.

But there is a less public side to Cromwell's religious life. He can write to friends and relatives with a directness which makes his Christian convictions both clear and contagious. He can write, too, with a simplicity largely free from the dogmatism which sometimes defaces the expressions of Puritan beliefs. And he can deal wisely with the spiritual perplexities of others. His letter on the spirit of fear and the spirit of love is still one of the most perceptive statements on an important theme. Fear, he says, is the natural result "of a bondage spirit," and is the antithesis of love: "The voice of fear is: If I had done this; if I had avoided that, how well it had been with me! . . . Love argueth in this wise: What a Christ have I; what a Father in and through him! What a name hath my Father: merciful, gracious, long-suffering, abundant in goodness and truth; forgiving iniquity, transgression and sin. What a nature hath my Father: he is LOVE;—free in it, unchangeable, infinite! . . . This commends the love of God: it's Christ's dying for men without strength, for men whilst sinners, whilst enemies. And shall we seek for the root of our comforts within us,—what God hath done, what he is to us in Christ is the root of our comfort: in this is stability, in us is weakness. Acts of obedience are not perfect, and therefore yield not perfect grace. Faith, as an act, yields it not; but 'only' as it carries us into him, who is our perfect rest and peace; in whom we are accounted of, and received by the Father,—even as Christ himself. This is our high calling. Rest we here, and here only."

DUCTOR DUBITANTIUM

Author: Jeremy Taylor (1613-1667)
Type of work: Moral theology
First published: 1660

Principal Ideas Advanced

Conscience is man's rational capacity for knowing the laws by which God governs him for his own perfection.

All law is of divine origin; the teachings of Christ perfect the law which is present to man's natural understanding.

Human law derives its authority from God, and thus it is to be obeyed as a matter of conscience.

Jeremy Taylor completed his *Ductor dubitantium* in time to dedicate it to the new king, Charles II, upon the restoration of the Stuart dynasty to the throne of England. The dedication was appropriate to the occasion. Better than Thomas Hobbes (1588-1679), who had been Charles's tutor, Taylor expresses the principles to which the Stuarts gave their allegiance. In Taylor's view, the king, like Moses, descends from God to the people with the two tables of the law (religious and civil) in his hand. Under no law himself except that of God, the king is governed solely by "the arguments . . . of conscience." A book on conscience, therefore, seemed particularly apt to both king and people.

The artificiality of the title (for the work was written in English and bears the subtitle, *The Rule of Conscience in all her General Measures*) prepares the reader for a work of erudition. Taylor does not draw his examples from his own time, nor does he venture to set forth rules based on his own pastoral experience. Rules and cases alike are taken from classic literature, from the Church Fathers, from civil and canon law, and from Spanish and Italian books of casuistry. Even his method of subordinating cases to rules he borrows from antiquity. "I took my pattern," he says, "from Tribonianus the lawyer, who out of the laws of the old Romans collected some choice rules which give answer to very many cases that happen."

Ductor dubitantium, which comprises the last two volumes of Taylor's collected works, is divided into four books of unequal length. The first book is a discussion of conscience in its various modes (true and false, confident and doubtful, probable and certain). The second is an exposition of divine law, drawn chiefly from the New Testament. The third book, by far the longest, is an exposition of human law, with special reference to civil law, ecclesiastical law, and the law of fathers of families. The fourth book, which is comparatively brief, is a discussion of the questions of free agency and of human happiness. It is characteristic of Taylor that he finds Aristotle's doctrine of the four causes underlying his divisions. Conscience, he says, is the formal cause of good and evil; the laws of God and man are their material cause; and man's freedom and his happiness, respectively, are their efficient and final causes. Taylor describes his book as "a general instrument of moral theology," and, while he hopes that it will be useful to laymen who are learned and wise enough to "guide themselves in all their proportions of conscience," he warns that in difficult cases men ought to consult a priest. It is mainly for such pastors of souls that the work is intended.

Taylor maintains that conscience belongs to the rational part of man. He is careful to distinguish conscience from both the natural tendencies which man shares with the lower animals, and the kind of practical intelligence which we call prudence. Conscience is the part of man's reason by which he judges according to law. Taylor explains that God governs nature by providence and rational beings by commands. Strictly speaking, there is no law in nature; law is superadded. Similarly, conscience is not a natural faculty, but a gift. But law and conscience are needed to perfect man's nature, and one of the indications of the rightness of conscience is whether it accords with our natural tendencies.

There are two kinds of judgment included under the name of "conscience." The first (designated in Greek by the word *synteresis*) is the knowledge which men have of moral axioms; the second (designated by the word *syneidesis*) is the capacity which they have for recognizing the moral character of particular acts. For example, in the affair of Bathsheba, David might reason: "Whatsoever is injurious ought not to be done; but to commit adultery is injurious; therefore it ought not to be done." This, says Taylor, is the first act of conscience, by means of which the mind is supplied with principles of action. The second act of conscience applies the conclusion of this syllogism to the particular case. Thus: "Adultery ought not to be done; this action I am about to do is adultery; therefore it ought not to be done."

Because conscience is the part of man's reason which informs him of God's commands, he is always bound to obey it. But numerous questions about the fallibility and certainty of conscience now arise. In general, Taylor's confidence in man's reason, both moral and speculative, is strong and constant. There are, of course, matters that are beyond our ken, in which case ignorance is unavoidable, but a great deal of ignorance can be overcome and is therefore inexcusable. Taylor holds that a man ought to obey his conscience even when it is in error, for though he sins in obeying an erroneous conscience, he sins even more in defying it.

A conscience is not erroneous unless it carries the conviction of being right. More frequent is the doubtful conscience, which needs to be instructed, usually not in principles but in their application. Here the art of casuistry comes into play, and Taylor accommodates the reader with rules for balancing various types of probability and for tempering justice with charity. Taylor avoids the excesses to which some casuists have gone, but he does not take the easy course of omitting knotty problems. Thus, in discussing whether it is lawful to bribe a corrupt judge to make him do justice, Taylor argues that, although bribery is an ill-sounding word, to give money is itself an indifferent thing; and that, if a judge is ready to receive money on any terms, giving him money to do a good act is not necessarily to commit a fault.

While the formal correctness of an act depends upon whether one follows his conscience, its material correctness depends upon its conformity to law. Therefore, the most profitable way of leading the doubtful conscience is to instruct it concerning the various kinds of law.

All law, according to Taylor, has divine origin; because God is preeminently a rational being, all law is naturally intelligible to man. From the first commands that a child can learn to the highest rules of ascetic religion, God's law is one continuous whole. Christianity is neither more nor less than the moral law of nature in its final perfection. It "binds no more upon us than God did by the very reason of our nature." In the Old Testament, God modified these laws according to man's weakness, as when, by Moses, He permitted polygamy, although monogamy is the rule of nature; similarly, He instituted religious ceremonies, such as circumcision, which go beyond the requirements of natural piety. But when Christ came, these pedagogical devices were swept aside, and God's law was exhibited in its simplicity and perfection. Even the worship demanded by Christ is, according to Taylor, purely spiritual: "The whole design of the laws of Jesus Christ is to be perfective of the spirit, and His religion is a spiritual service; that is, permanent and unalterable, virtuous and useful, natural and holy, not relative to time and place, or any material circumstances, nor integrated by corporal services."

Taylor distinguishes, however, just as the Roman Church has always done, between precepts and counsels; that is to say, between those words of Christ (chiefly prohibitions) which bind the Christian absolutely, and those which, though they point the way to perfection, must be understood as being relative to the individual's strength and stature, and which, therefore, bind in varying degrees. Speaking of the Sermon on the Mount, Taylor writes that it is a great mistake to suppose that everything spoken there is a law; many parts of it are "progressions and degrees of Christian duty." On the other hand, Taylor is careful to note that these counsels of perfection are not optional. God, he says, follows the course of our natures, and although in the early stages of our walk He accepts our minimal duties, he expects us to pass on towards perfection.

Turning to laws which have their origin in human commands, Taylor reiterates the principle that all law derives its authority from God. The authority of the parent over his child, like that of the prince over his people, and of the bishop over his flock, derives from the divine institution, and is enforced and authenticated to man's reason by the teaching of Scripture. Numerous questions of conscience arise from the conflict between human laws and divine, and Taylor freely admits that there are cases in which a man is bound to follow his conscience in disobedience of the commands of men. In their legitimate spheres, however, authorities ought to be revered. Thus, children ought never to marry contrary to their parents' command; parishioners ought never to hold conventicles against their bishop's order; and citizens ought never to assemble or organize themselves in defiance of the king's command.

These principles, of course, particularly those which bear upon the authority of the bishop and of the prince, were all being tested in Taylor's time, as well as the further question concerning the prince's authority over the Church. Taylor takes his stand on the side of the prince wherever possible. He holds that Parliament acted treasonably in raising arms against the Crown, and thus Parliament deserved to be punished accordingly; that Presbyterians and Independents were guilty of disobeying the Apostolic order of bishops; and that Papists and Presbyterians alike subverted the divine institution in maintaining that the Church has any political authority over the prince. The prince, according to Taylor, is under the law of God, so that when he does wrong it is possible to reason with him, but it is never permissible to censure him in public. Moreover, a mere citizen may find it difficult to understand the justice of the king's cause, because public morality stands on a different footing from that of private morality.

Taylor is an interesting example of the new rationalistic tendencies at work within seventeenth century English theology. He holds uncompromisingly to the Scriptures and to the creeds, but at the same time he argues that revelation is perfectly intelligible to human reason. Traditional theology has often distinguished between human reason and divine, and it has maintained that while there is a proportionality between the two, divine reason is often incompatible with human reason. Taylor denies that this is true. To allege that God tells us something and means something different from what we can understand Him to mean would be, he says, to charge God with hypocrisy.

In addition to maintaining that Christianity is inherently reasonable, Taylor also maintains that, by accumulating probable arguments, one can demonstrate the truth of all its teachings. "Since," he says, "there is . . . nothing to be said for any other religion, and so very much for Christianity, every one of whose pretences can be proved as well as the things themselves do require, and as all the world expects such things should be proved; it follows that the holy Jesus is the Son of God, that His religion is commanded by God, and is that way by which He will be worshipped and honored. . . . He that puts his soul upon this cannot perish; neither can he be reproved who hath so much reason and argument for his religion." Perhaps it is not overventuresome to find here the seeds of those lay developments in religious thought later exemplified in John Locke's *The Reasonableness of Christianity* (1695), and in John Toland's *Christianity not Mysterious* (1696).

A CHRISTIAN DIRECTORY

Author: Richard Baxter (1615-1691)
Type of work: Pastoral theology
First published: 1665

Principal Ideas Advanced

Because the only good in this life is that which tends to man's eternal happiness, man ought to employ his time and energies with a view always to God's glory and his soul's salvation.

Nothing which is contrary to God's law is ultimately good; hence, it is never permissible to disobey God's comandments in order to advance what we believe is good.

God has set some men in authority over others; civil magistrates and religious authorities have their power from God and not from those over whom they rule.

It is the duty of all men in this troubled world to forbear one another and to seek peace.

Richard Baxter wrote *A Christian Directory* when, because of his nonconformism, he was no longer permitted to preach. The work, which fills five large volumes, is devoted mainly to "practical cases of conscience, and the reducing of theoretical knowledge into serious Christian practice." It was, he maintained, a necessary labor because the Romanists were still far ahead of Protestants in this department of theology, even after the good beginning made by Jeremy Taylor in his *Ductor dubitantium* (1660).

The contents of *A Christian Directory* are propounded as rules or directions rather than as questions and answers, so as to enable the reader to resolve his own particular cases. Beginning with directions for the conversion of sinners and the strengthening of weak Christians, Baxter sets forth seventeen "Grand Directions," in which the essential obligations of the baptismal covenant are explained under the heads of the believer's duties to the three Persons of the Trinity. The particular directions which make up the rest of the work are distributed under four heads: Christian ethics (or private duties); Christian economics (or family duties); Christian ecclesiastics (or Church duties); and Christian politics (or duties to our rulers and neighbors).

A theological moderate in his day, Baxter was too much of a rationalist to please the Calvinists, and too much of a Biblicist to please the Arminians. Baxter took it for granted that the Scriptures are the Word of God, and he agreed with the Puritans generally that the Bible contains "whatever it is necessary that man believe, think, or do, in all ages and places of the world." But he maintained that, in order to be effective, the Scriptures must be addressed to men's reason. The Devil, he said, keeps his hold on men by silencing reason and causing it to slumber; but the Scriptures in their very nature excite reason, and effective preaching consists in showing men that sin is unreasonable. Baxter's constant plea for tolerance in matters of religion was based upon his confidence in the power of reason to overcome enmity and sloth.

When Baxter speaks of reason, he seems ordinarily to have had in mind the prudential judgment which distinguishes man from animals and by means of which man conducts his worldly business. All that man needs to do is to extend the scope of his understanding until it includes his immortal destiny, and he will quickly see the need for reconciliation to God and the truth of those matters revealed in Holy Scripture.

In Baxter's view, the things of this world are little more than "dreams and shadows, and valuable only as they serve us in the way of heaven." Our present life and circumstances are given us on trial, in order that we may prepare ourselves for the life that is to come after. An eternity, either of happiness or misery, awaits every man. Whence it follows that the only good in this life is that which tends toward our eternal happiness;

whatever distracts us from that goal is evil.

The sobriety with which Baxter and most Puritans faced life is implicit in their acceptance of the rational scheme of things. Man dare not stop until he has rationalized every move that he makes. Here, for instance, is the basis for the Puritan's characteristic attitude toward sports and toward sensuous pleasure. Recreation in itself is lawful and even, for some men, a duty; it serves to exhilarate the spirits and to exercise the natural parts so as to fit the body and mind for better serving God. Similarly, the satisfaction of our fleshly appetites is in itself good; God desires to give man greater pleasure, not less, and he approves the delights of the senses as long as they are kept subordinate to heavenly delights. But all our activities must be kept under the government of reason: "Take nothing and do nothing merely because the sense or appetite would have it; but because you have reason so to do."

The most characteristic manifestation of Baxter's attempt to rationalize the whole of human life is his attitude toward the use of time: "Time being man's opportunity for all those works for which he liveth, and which his Creator doth expect from him, and on which his endless life dependeth: the redeeming or well improving of it, must needs be of most high importance to him." Not merely are we accountable for not wasting a minute; we are held for putting every minute to the best possible use. Here the good is enemy of the best. Sleep beyond what is necessary for health, inefficient work habits, and leisurely habits of dressing and dining are all "thieves of time" and hence to be avoided. One can waste time in the performance of devotional exercises; busy persons are advised to have a child or a servant read to them a chapter from the Bible while they are dressing or at table. Everyone must, of course, have some time during the day for private prayer and meditation, but those fitted for an active life cannot lawfully take as much time for these matters as the aged and the weak. Indeed, the contemplative life, so much lauded by the Romanists, is reserved by Baxter for those who are disqualified from active labor.

So far, it has been possible to set forth Baxter's thought in terms of consequential ethics. The Christian religion appears as a higher kind of prudence: "That only is good in this life, which tendeth to the happiness of our endless life; and that is evil indeed in this life, that tendeth to our endless hurt." But man cannot know in detail the conditions of true happiness; hence, for direction in life one must obey the laws which God has revealed to man in nature and in the Scriptures. Baxter's thought here assumes the characteristics of formalistic ethics.

The clearest examples of Baxter's ethical method are cases connected with telling the truth. Baxter discusses typical moral dilemmas in which a person is given the alternative of either permitting obvious evil to take place or telling a lie: "Is it not contrary to the light of nature, to suffer . . . a parent, a king, myself, my country, rather to be destroyed, than to save them by a harmless lie?" "No," answers Baxter. In the first place, we can never be certain that our falsehood will accomplish the end we hope for. In the second place, there are lawful means enough to save lives when saving lives is what is best. The rule, therefore, is "Obey God, and trust him with your lives, and he can save them without a lie, if it is best: and if it be not, it should not be desired." Baxter gives a comparable answer to the question whether it is lawful to steal bread in order to save one's life. He admits that the common good takes precedence over private good, and that property rights may be violated if the public interest is at stake; but to take another man's property for one's private benefit, even though it be to preserve one's life, is forbidden.

The basis for Baxter's social philosophy is provided by strong determination always to obey the law of God, and not by any attempt on his part to estimate the consequences of man's actions. To oppress one's fellow man is wrong, according to Baxter, because he who keeps men so destitute that they die of sickness is a murderer; and murder is always wrong. Slavery is not wrong in every circumstance, there being different kinds of slavery; but catching Negroes by piracy in order to sell them is thievery of the worst sort; moreover, it is a heinous sin to buy such a slave, except for the purpose of setting him free. All killing in war is murder if the war be unjustly waged. The professional soldier is worse than a thief, because thieves kill only an occasional individual, but soldiers murder thousands at one time. Whether a man ought ever to bear arms is a more difficult question. Baxter, who served as a chaplain with the Parliamentary armies during the Civil War, finds it almost impossible to determine whether particular wars are just or unjust. A wise man, he avers, may prefer to be "abused as a neuter" than to risk being guilty of the blood of an unjust war.

The reader must not infer from the abridged form in which we have cited Baxter's directions that he had a few simple rules by means of which every moral problem may be resolved. On the contrary, as the length of his *Directory* attests, Baxter was fully aware that circumstances alter cases, and that each case must finally be decided on its individual merits. Thus, while he held that outright lying is never permitted, he was willing to grant that there are times when intentional deception is a duty, for instance in the case of a physician or a statesman, "for," says Baxter, "all dissimulation is not evil, though lying be." In order to deal with the wide variety of instances which present themselves, the author frequently turns aside from the practice of setting out directions, and poses typical questions. For example, in connection with his directions concerning the relations of husbands and wives, he takes up eighteen questions dealing with the problem of separation and divorce. To the question, "Who be they that may or may not marry again when they are parted?" Baxter's reply is that a person released on the grounds of the other's adultery may remarry, but not any person released on any other ground. Still, he says, one must consider the possibility of reconciliation; and how necessary it is to the well-being of the innocent party to marry again. In the last analysis, the best he can say is that there is no absolute prohibition against the innocent party's remarrying.

The difficulty which we often face in discovering our duty must not mislead us into supposing that one opinion concerning it is as good as another; "The 'esse' is before the 'scire,'" Baxter writes; "the thing is first true or false before I judge it to be so." Whenever we are in doubt we must keep distinct "the being of a duty," and "the knowledge of a duty."

Baxter declares that one of the most dangerous errors of his time is the view that a man is bound to do everything that his conscience tells him is the will of God. No man, says Baxter, has the duty to obey his conscience when it is in error. One must avoid sin by avoiding error. "God hath appointed means for the cure of blindness and error as well as other sins; else the world were in a miserable case."

Baxter introduces a third major principle of obligation, besides those of prudence and obedience to law; namely, that of authority. According to Baxter, God, who is Lord of all the world, has delegated power to men in their various social relations. Thus, He has given the husband authority over the wife, and parents authority over children. In like manner, He has ordained that rulers shall have power over nations, and that the ministry shall lead the Church. Some part, therefore, of every man's duty consists in obedience to those over him.

In discussing the issue of political sovereignty, Baxter takes a position somewhere between those who argue for the divine right of kings and those who argue for the sovereignty of the people. In Baxter's opinion, the people determine, by their explicit or implicit consent, whether they shall be governed by a king, or by an aristocracy, or by elected representatives; but in choosing who shall govern them, they do not bestow power on the government, any more than a woman bestows authority on the husband she chooses, or the soldier on the commander under whom he enlists: "Rulers therefore are God's officers, placed under him in his kingdom, as he is the universal, absolute sovereign of the world; and they receive their power from God, who is the only original of power." The power which individuals have over their own lives is of a different kind from civil or political power; the latter is brought into being by God's act and not by resignation of His natural power to an artificial head.

Baxter's theory of Church government is similar to his theory of politics, except for his contention that in the Scriptures God specifies how churches are to be governed in spiritual matters; namely, by elders or presbyters set apart and ordained for this purpose. Baxter argues that the word "church" ought to be applied only to particular assemblies of believers, just as the word "school" is applied to particular assemblies of scholars. There are many schools in England, as there are many churches; but it would be absurd to speak of the School of England. So, there can be no national church. But, says Baxter, the temporal affairs of the churches must fall under the civil power; the magistrate or king, and not the presbytery, has authority over "the temple, the pulpit, the tithes, &c."

It must be remembered that Baxter wrote on these matters during one of the great formative periods of Western political and ecclesiastical history, and that he personally had much at stake. At the time of the Restoration, he was offered a bishopric by Charles II, but he refused; and when the Act of Uniformity was imposed shortly thereafter, he chose to cast his lot with the persecuted ministers. Meanwhile, Quakers, Anabaptists, Independents, Presbyterians, Jesuits, Erastians, Arminians, high and low Anglicans, and numerous other parties were bitterly contending for positions of power. In Baxter's writings, on the other hand, there is almost complete absence of a spirit of contention. From time to time he raises his voice against the exclusivist claims of a religious party, notably the Romanists; but mainly he was interested in restoring unity. He declares that he accepts the Puritan principle, according to which the Scriptures are the only rule of worship and government, but he points out that the Scriptures are silent on a great many matters, and insists that what is not forbidden is lawful. He says, paraphrasing the Cambridge philosopher, Henry More (1614-1687), "It would do much more good in the world, if all parties were forwarder to find out and commend what is good in the doctrine and worship of all that differ from them. This would win them to hearken to reforming advice, and would keep up the credit of the common truths and duties of religion in the world, when the envious snarling at all that others do, both tend to bring the world to atheism, and banish all reverence of religion, together with Christian charity from the earth."

Although Baxter's voice of reason and moderation was little heeded in his time, his writings exercised great influence on the development of nonconformist thought in subsequent generations. Unfortunately, his intellectualism and legalism are easier for men to emulate than the high religious spirit with which his own thinking was always imbued.

GRACE ABOUNDING TO THE CHIEF OF SINNERS

Author: John Bunyan (1628-1688)
Type of work: Spiritual autobiography
First published: 1666

Principal Ideas Advanced

The memory of past mercies helps support the Christian in his time of trial.

There is no salvation in mere adherence to Church ritual nor in attempting to fulfill the works of the law.

Only those are saved who receive the "new birth," and whose sins are removed by the blood of Christ.

Trials and temptations alternate with joy and peace while the Christian is in this world, compelling him to rely absolutely on Christ for his full deliverance.

Grace Abounding to the Chief of Sinners records John Bunyan's inner struggles from his childhood through the first term of his imprisonment. It is the closest thing to an autobiography of any of his numerous books, but those who turn to it in hopes of finding a circumstantial account of the author's life are disappointed. The book is a spiritual exercise, in many ways comparable to the *Confessions* of St. Augustine. Bunyan set down the record of his own fears and deliverances in order to assist the members of his congregation during the time he was prevented from ministering among them. He hoped that when they read it they would realize what God had done for each of them; for, says Bunyan, the remembrance of God's help in time past is a great support to the Christian in his temptation.

Bunyan tells but little of his boyhood. His parents, although of low social standing, made the effort necessary to have him taught reading and writing, but we infer that they were not especially devout. As a child, however, John Bunyan was tormented with thoughts of his soul's damnation. He writes, at the age of nine or ten, "in the midst of my many sports and childish vanities, amidst my vain companions, I was often much cast down and afflicted in my mind therewith, yet could I not let go my sins." These fears abated with the passing years, and Bunyan became "the very ringleader of all the youth that kept [him] company, into all manner of vice and ungodliness." But, though he avoided religion, and took pleasure in reviling it, his heart trembled whenever he saw a religious man doing anything wicked.

It was only after he had served his term in the Parliamentary army and was married to a young woman of Christian upbringing, that Bunyan began to read Christian books and to attend church services. The outward forms of religion took great hold upon him. He admired the liturgy, the vestments, and the choir, and he was quite carried away with "a spirit of superstition," as he later came to view it. He attended church two times a day and recited and sang with the others; but he did not alter his way of life. Once, after the parson had preached against Sabbath sports, he was playing a game of cat when he seemed to hear a voice from Heaven saying, "Wilt thou leave thy sins and go to heaven, or have thy sins and go to hell?" He paused in the midst of his play long enough to reckon that he was damned already for former sins; then, in a kind of despair, he returned to his game.

During this time, however, he overcame his habit of swearing. He had been reproached for his profane language by a shopkeeper who was herself no model of virtue. A secret shame made him wish that he might be a child again and that his father might teach him to speak more decently, for the habit of swearing was too strong, he thought, for him ever to give it up. Yet, from that day on, to his great astonishment, he did not swear any more, and he found that he spoke better and more pleasantly than before.

An acquaintance grew up between Bunyan and a man who talked much about the Bible; and, liking the talk, Bunyan began reading the Scriptures for himself, especially the historical parts, for he could make nothing out of the epistles of Paul. The result was a complete conversion in his outward manner of life. He gave up dancing, Sabbath games, and even his great passion, bell-ringing, to undertake a life of rigid self-denial. The Bible seemed to him a book of rules which he had to follow if he were to gain Heaven, but, as he then understood it, if now and then he should break one of the rules, all he had to do was to repent and to promise that he would do better next time. He went on in this way for a year or more. Giving up his pleasures cost him many a struggle, but he was wonderfully satisfied in his own eyes, and he thought that he "pleased God as well as any man in England."

Working one day at his trade in Bedford, he heard three or four women sitting at a door in the sun, talking in the manner of nonconformists about things that had not hitherto entered his hearing. Bunyan, who "was now a brisk talker also in matters of religion," readily entered the discussion, but he could not understand at first what the women meant by "a new birth," and "their miserable state by nature," and how it was that "God had visited their souls with his love in the Lord Jesus." Much affected, he went not long after to consult Mr. Gifford, their pastor. "In a dream or vision," he says, "I saw [these people at Bedford] as if they were set on the sunny side of some high mountain, there refreshing themselves with the pleasant beams of the sun, while I was shivering and shrinking in the cold, afflicted with frost, snow, and dark clouds." A wall surrounded the mountain, and Bunyan saw himself testing it, trying to find a gap through which he might pass, and finally succeeding in squeezing through and sitting down with them in the sun. The mountain, Bunyan explains, signifies the Church; the sun, God's merciful face; the wall, the Word which separates the Christian and the world; and the gap in the wall, Jesus Christ.

Henceforth Bunyan read the Scriptures more zealously than before, but, having passed through formalism and legalism, he found experimental religion to contain new and greater vexations. In the first place, everything now seemed to hang on the validity of God's Word, particularly on His promises. How could one be sure that the Scriptures were not fables? How could one know that Christ is God's Son? "Everyone," he writes, "doth think his own religion rightest, both Jews and Moors and Pagans! and how if all our faith, and Christ, and Scriptures, should be but a think-so too?" But there was always the further question whether, supposing the Scriptures are true, he in particular were one of God's elect. Mostly it was the latter doubt that troubled Bunyan. His sense of God's presence and of Christ's mediation was too vivid for him long to be troubled by atheism. But, knowing the contradictions of his own heart, he was unable to go for any length of time without uncovering some evidence which, in the light of God's Word, seemed to number him among the reprobate. So persistent and so encompassing was this fear, that Bunyan devotes approximately a third of *Grace Abounding* to narrating the struggles to which it gave rise.

Bunyan had been permitted to experience many of the joys and consolations to which his evangelical friends testified. For instance, there was the time he was traveling into the country, thinking about the wickedness of his heart, when the Scriptural passage came to his mind which declares that God has "made peace through the blood of his cross." "I was made to see," he says, "that God and my soul were friends by this blood; yea, I saw that the justice of God and my sinful soul could embrace and kiss each other through this blood. This was a good day to me; I hope I shall not forget it."

Reading the Bible, he found ever deeper meanings disclosing themselves: "Oh! now, how was my soul led from truth to truth by God! even from the birth and cradle of the Son of God to his ascension and second coming from heaven to judge the world." It seemed to him that Christ spoke to him through the pages of the Gospel and made them talk with him and comfort him. He was sure that his soul cleaved to Christ, and that his love for Christ was "as hot as fire."

At this moment of pride, Satan disclosed to him a secret resentment against Christ, and a temptation to sell Him in exchange for the good things of this life: "Sometimes it would run through my thoughts, not so little as a hundred times together, Sell him, sell him, sell him!" The temptation stayed with Bunyan for days and weeks. Moreover, a fear constantly haunted him that would sometime weaken and yield to the temptation. Then, one morning, while he was lying on his bed and answering the tempter, "No, no, not for thousands, thousands, thousands," he was aware that there passed through his heart the thought, "Let him go, if he will!" With this, the struggle ended. "Down fell I, as a bird that is shot from the top of a tree, into great guilt, and fearful despair." The Scriptural verses which speak of Esau selling his birthright and finding no place of repentance stood in judgment over him. He was sure he had committed the unpardonable sin and that he would be numbered with those who, having been enlightened and then having fallen away, find it impossible to renew their repentance. Now all those passages which speak of the fullness of Christ's grace were so many coals of fire heaped on his head. For, this one who so loved sinners as to wash them from their sins in His own blood was the very one of whom Bunyan had said, "Let him go if he will." God could forgive David and Peter, and even the wicked Manasseh, great as their sins were; but, Bunyan believed, their sins were not the same as his: "This one consideration would always kill my heart, my sin was point-blank against my Saviour."

After months of gloom, brightened with only occasional streaks of hope as one or another Scriptural passage gave brief encouragement of forgiveness, Bunyan at last found assurance in the account of those "cities of refuge" which Joshua ordained as sanctuaries for persons found guilty of manslaughter. Bunyan noted that willful murderers were not given refuge, but only those who had not lain in wait to shed blood and had not hated the slain man; and this seemed to fit his case: "I hated him not aforetime; no, I prayed unto him, was tender of sinning against him; yea, and against this wicked temptation I had strove for a twelvemonth before; yea, and also when it did pass through my heart, it did in spite of my teeth; wherefore I thought I had a right to enter this city, and the elders, which are the apostles, were not to deliver me up." Bunyan was encouraged to reread the various Scriptures which had previously condemned him. Considering them carefully, and weighing "their scope and tendency," he was able to discriminate between his sin and that for which God casts men away.

Bunyan now enjoyed sufficient consolation to seek admission into the fellowship of Mr. Gifford's congregation, and after two or three years he was marked by some of its leading members as one suited to be a preacher. It appeared, upon trial, that he had unusual gifts for proclaiming the Gospel; and within a short time hundreds were coming to hear him preach. Then, after about five years, he was arrested by the Crown in its drive for religious uniformity. Presumably he could have remained at liberty if he had given bond to stop preaching; but, unable to do this, he chose to go to prison.

Bunyan goes on to show that, despite his preaching, during the whole time he was never without temptations. After the first few times he took communion with Mr. Gifford's congregation, he experienced a temptation to blaspheme the ordinance, and he was forced to pray to God to keep him from cursing those who received the cup. Another time, when overcome with sickness, his sense of guilt made him afraid of death, until he remembered the Scriptural passage which says, we are "justified by his grace, through the redemption that is in Christ Jesus." Another time, when "a great cloud of darkness" hid from him the face of Christ, he was seized by the expression, "I must go to Jesus." "At this," he says, "my former darkness and atheism fled away, and the blessed things of heaven were set within my view." He asked his wife if there were a Scriptural passage which says, "I must go to Jesus," but she could not tell. Then, like a bolt, it came to him: "Ye are come unto mount Sion, . . . and to Jesus the mediator of the new covenant, and to the blood of sprinkling, that speaketh better things than of Abel."

Bunyan notes, in the conclusion of his book, that his fears and consolations seemed to alternate in a remarkable way. "I have wondered much at this one thing," he writes, "that though God doth visit my soul with never so blessed a discovery of himself, yet I have found again, that such hours have attended me afterwards, that I have been in my spirit so filled with darkness, that I could not so much as once conceive what that God and that comfort was with which I have been refreshed." In short, there is no end to the Christian warfare. The abominations of the human heart are with us always, compelling us daily to trust in Jesus to help us and carry us "through this world."

Grace Abounding is written in the simple and unadorned language of one who is making a confession to God. Bunyan lays a kind of restraint on himself, noting, in his Preface, "I could have enlarged much in this my discourse. . . . I could also have stepped into a style much higher than this in which I have here discoursed, and could have adorned all things more than here I have seemed to do, but I dare not. God did not play in convincing of me, the devil did not play in tempting of me . . . ; wherefore I may not play in my relating of them, but be plain and simple, and lay down the thing as it was." The result is, nonetheless, a great work of art, quite as affecting in its way as *The Pilgrim's Progress,* in which Bunyan did permit himself the enlargement which seemed out of place here.

PARADISE LOST

Author: John Milton (1608-1674)
Type of work: Religious epic poem
First published: 1667

Principal Ideas Advanced

Satan conspired with other fallen angels to corrupt Adam and Eve through temptation.

God realized that man would fall, but He granted man His grace, for man's fall was to be through temptation by evil; and He decided to send His Son to answer death with sacrificial death and thus to achieve man's salvation.

In the guise of a serpent Satan led Eve to eat the fruit of the Tree of Knowledge, and Adam shared her disobedience; hence, Adam and Eve were banished from Eden, but not before hearing how the Son of God would become a man and would give His life for all men.

Paradise Lost is generally conceded to be one of the greatest poems in the English language; and there is no religious epic in English which measures up to Milton's masterpiece. Dante's *Divine Comedy* rivals it as poetry, and in the opinion of many critics Dante's poem exceeds Milton's in poetic virtue; but the *Comedy* is an Italian work, and hence comparison is to some extent not possible.

To say that *Paradise Lost* is a great poem means that persons who know poetry and who judge it, and who have been accepted by most educated men as qualified to judge, have been more strongly drawn to Milton's poem than to most other poems in the language. There is no question but that the principal appeal of the poem resides in its poetic quality: the quality of the imagery, and the quality of the work as a composition in which sound and rhythm contribute sentiment and color to meaning. But it is interesting to consider to what extent the Christian idea accounts for much of the poem's power; a new dimension of understanding is achieved once one considers Milton's work as a serious response to the problem of evil, as something other than a sentimental attempt to "justify the ways of God to men."

Poetry does religion a service in that it contributes drama and feeling to events, mythical or historical, on which the injunctions of religion rest. But religion does poetry a service in that it provides literature with a subject matter that appeals to man's deepest feelings. When a religion which has moved men for centuries inspires a poet whose use of poetic form is masterful enough to justify his taking that religion as his subject, the result can be a creative phenomenon which is itself capable of surviving the centuries. So it is with Dante's *Divine Comedy* and Milton's *Paradise Lost*.

If Milton had by temperament and the ordinary adventures of life been drawn into the sectarian task of apologizing for some particular version of the Christian faith, his work would surely have been affected; *Paradise*

Lost, as an attempt to cast the struggle between good and evil into imagery of universal significance, could not have been written. But Milton disliked the emphasis on ritual in the English Church, and he resisted his father's efforts to lead him to the ministry. His interest in reforming the corrupt clergy led him to ally himself with the Presbyterians, with whom he later became dissatisfied; and his love of freedom led him to be critical of Parliamentary censorship of the press (*Areopagitica,* 1644). He supported those who regarded Charles I as a threat to the freedom of the English people, and his *Tenure of Kings and Magistrates* (1649) presented an argument in favor of executing tyrants. He was appointed, in 1649, Latin Secretary to Oliver Cromwell, and his active defense of the Commonwealth government, as in his *First Defense of the English People,* led to his blindness two years later. The Restoration (1660) forced him into hiding, but he soon found that the new government was willing to allow him to continue his poetic labors.

Thus, it was as a champion of religious integrity and of human freedom that Milton came to the task of putting into poetic form the great story of man's Fall. In considering how Adam and Eve were led to taste the forbidden fruit, Milton was able to draw upon his experience of corruption in both Church and state. The resultant poetic myth has a frightening relevance to the life of any man, and the tragedy of man's Fall is relieved only by the creative intervention of Christ (whose regenerative effect is portrayed and praised in Milton's minor poem, *Paradise Regained,* which was completed in 1667).

The story of *Paradise Lost* is the familiar Genesis drama, together with embellishments suggested by Milton's imagination at work on other Biblical material and (probably) on such other literary works as Phineas Fletcher's *Locustoe* (1627) (or its English version, *The Apollyonists*); Giambattista Andreini's sacred drama, *L'Adamo* (1614); and Joost van den Vondel's *Lucifer* (1654).

Milton begins his poem by stating its subject:

> Of Man's first disobedience, and the fruit
> Of that forbidden tree whose mortal taste
> Brought death into the World, and all our woe,
> With loss of Eden, till one greater Man
> Restore us, and regain the blissful Seat,
> Sing, Heavenly Muse. . . .

He asks the Muse to illumine "what in me is dark . . . / That, to the highth of this great argument,/ I may assert Eternal Providence,/ And justify the ways of God to men."

The usual problem for a religious man is the problem of justifying his ways to God. But philosophers and theologians, and other persons who find themselves challenging the grounds of their religious convictions, are faced with a unique and disturbing problem: the problem of justifying the ways of God to man. The problem arises because of the presence of evil in the world. If God is the creator of all being, then He is the author of death and suffering; and how is this consequence to be made compatible with the idea of God as an omniscient, omnipotent, benevolent Father?

It is clear from the outset of *Paradise Lost* that Milton has no quarrel with God. He asks, not for a divine explanation, but for insight concerning the cause of the fall of man: "Say first . . . what cause/ Moved our grand Parents, in that happy state,/ Favoured of Heaven so highly, to fall off/ From their Creator, and transgress his will. . . ." Man was created as an innocent being; there was nothing in his nature which of its own account could lead to transgression. So Milton must have reasoned, for he asks his question about the cause of the Fall so as to suggest that the cause could not have been *in* man, but from the outside. Thus, he asks, "Who first seduced them to that foul revolt?" The answer is immediately forthcoming: "The infernal Serpent . . . ," Satan, the "Arch-Enemy," who because of pride rebelled against God and then, in league with the fallen angels, conspired to attack God through corrupting His creation, man.

The religious use of Satan as the image of evil is ineffective if Satan is conceived to be the entire cause of moral evil. If Satan is the author of evil, God is powerless to hold Satan in check; and if anyone is to blame for the Fall of man, it must be Satan, not man. Milton's problem, then, is the problem which an initial consideration of the problem of evil provokes: the problem of using the image of evil, Satan, in such a manner as not to diminish the glory of God or to minimize the responsibility of man.

It is unlikely that any resolution of the latter problem can be entirely satisfactory to the mind of man. If Adam and Eve were innocent; if prior to the seductive blandishments of the Serpent, they had known only the good; if no experience provided them with evidence by which to recognize evil at work, how then can they be held accountable for succumbing to temptation? The answer must be that God created man with the freedom to choose, and He demanded obedience; man was expected to obey not because he had reasons, but because there was a sufficient cause of moral obedience; namely, the injunction from God Himself. But to accept God as the sufficient ground of obedience must be an act of faith; it could not, at least with Adam and Eve, have been a commitment justified by experience of good and evil. And although faith in God is superior to any other faith, it could not have been known to be superior (and, in any case, once the dependence on God is known to be a superior kind of dependence, it is no longer faith; such knowledge rests on experience).

Perhaps, then, there is no way of intellectually solving the problem in regards to Adam and Eve. But if Adam and Eve are taken, not as first parents, but as images of human beings faced with the choice between good and evil; if the story of their Fall is taken not as a case in support of moral recrimination, but as an argument for obedience to God; and if the hope of Paradise regained is shown to be justified through faith in Christ, the "greater Man" who can "restore us," then the tale of Paradise lost becomes an effective expression of that Christian commitment by which the problem of evil is not so much solved as settled. The answer, then, is like Christ's answer to the Grand Inquisitor (in Dostoevski's *The Brothers Karama-*

zov); His kiss was not an argument or a proof; it was an act of wholehearted acceptance of the other.

Milton's poem tells how Satan, after debating the matter with the fallen angels, decides to fly to the world, there to attempt the perversion of man (Books I and II). God observes Satan's journey to earth, and He tells His Son that Satan will succeed in the effort to corrupt Adam and Eve (Book III). Milton then describes God as asking the question which Satan's temptation of man suggests: If man falls, whose fault is it? God's answer—and it is an answer to which the poet must give priority—is that the Fall will be no one's fault but man's. Speaking of man, God says wrathfully, "Whose fault?/ Whose but his own? Ingrate, he had of me/ All he could have; I made him just and right,/ Sufficient to have stood, though free to fall." God justifies His gift of freedom to man by declaring that obedience through necessity would be morally worthless; such obedience would give no pleasure to God. "They themselves decreed/ Their own revolt, not I," God declares, and thus He frees Himself from the possible accusation that He is to blame for man's Fall. However, man is to find grace, God decides, because man's Fall is to be brought about by temptation wrought by the angels whose fall, unlike man's, was "Self-tempted, self-depraved. . . ." The Son of God welcomes His Father's words; it would be inconsistent with the divine nature if man were to be denied grace after a fall brought about by Satan's fraud as well as by man's folly. Christ then offers to become mortal and to pay "death for death," in order that neither man nor Justice will die eternally.

Milton's resolution of the problem of evil, then, is the central Christian resolution. Man was created a free moral agent; if he errs, he, not the evil to which he succumbs, is to blame. But evil is whatever tempts man, and if man were in no way tempted, it is unlikely that he would fall. Thus, God's grace is not inappropriately granted, although it is freely given. Christ's sacrifice will be genuine, for He will suffer and die as a man; but His sacrifice will be regenerative, for the Resurrection will show that the divine is more powerful than evil: ". . . I shall rise victorious . . . Death his death's wound shall then receive, and stoop/ Inglorious, of his mortal sting disarmed. . . ."

In sending Raphael to tell Adam of Satan's rebellion and of Satan's plot against their innocent state, God provides Adam and Eve with the knowledge they need to choose good in preference to evil (Books V-VIII). Thus, Milton universalized the Adam myth; Adam becomes as every man in that he knows of evil and of the seductive power of temptation. The Biblical Adam enjoyed no such advance warning. Eve, also, has ample warning, for she overhears the angel's advice to Adam; furthermore, on the morning of the temptation, Adam pleads with her not to leave his side. But she declares herself strong enough to resist evil (Book IX).

When Satan in the guise of the Serpent succeeds in persuading Eve to taste the fruit of the Tree of Knowledge, he wins because of Eve's pride and over-confidence (Book IX). As Milton portrays her, Eve is no ignorant child of nature; she is woman warned; consequently, she is everywoman, just as Adam is everyman.

Christ is sent to judge the sinners (Book X). In sending the divine Son, "Man's Friend, his Mediator," God shows the mercy which, prior to man's Fall, He had decided upon. The God of Genesis is a wrathful God, intemperate in His judgment; but the God of *Paradise Lost* judges man in His person as Christ. Thus, man has no recourse; he cannot blame God for man's disobedience, nor can he accuse God of intolerance. Man's only hope of salvation, then, is through Christ. Michael is portrayed both as the angel who is to lead Adam and Eve from Paradise and as the bearer of the news that man is to have Christ as Savior (Books XI and XII).

What Milton accomplished in *Paradise Lost* is the transformation of the Biblical account of man's Fall into a Christian myth, a promise of salvation through Christ. In casting this new story into some of the clearest and most moving poetry in the English language Milton performed an artist's service to his God.

PENSÉES

Author: Blaise Pascal (1623-1662)
Type of work: Reflections on the Christian religion
First published: 1670

Principal Ideas Advanced

Man must learn to reflect upon himself and seek to understand himself in relation to the rest of nature; the Socratic dictum, "Know thyself," becomes the guiding principle of philosophical and religious inquiry.

The human condition is characterized by a peculiar ambivalence of misery and grandeur; on the one hand, man experiences a disproportion within himself and in his relation to nature; on the other hand, he is the highest of all creatures and sovereign over the world of nature.

Man's rational knowledge suffers significant and far-reaching limitations; the heart plays a more important role than does reason in disclosing both the human condition and the reality of God.

The existence of God is not settled by metaphysical demonstrations of the rational intellect; the issue is settled through a concrete existential decision in which man must wager either for the existence of God or against it.

The fundamentals of the Christian religion are its belief in the corruption of human nature and its doctrine of redemption through Jesus Christ.

Pascal's *Pensées* (*Thoughts*) consists of fragmentary notes and aphorisms which he had intended to use in the writing of an "Apology for the Christian Religion." Ill health and an untimely death precluded the realization of this project. In the effort to preserve Pascal's acute insights into human life and his suggestive observations about God and religion, the Port-Royalists compiled and edited the fragmentary notes of the projected "Apology" eight years after Pascal's death. It is in the form of this revision that the notes have come down to us today.

Like the Athenian Socrates, Pascal teaches that the task of the existing individual is to know or understand himself. "One must know oneself. If this does not serve to discover truth, it at least serves as a rule of life, and there is nothing better." Pascal does not disparage man's efforts to gain knowledge of the vast expanses of the universe, but he suggests that before entering upon such a quest man would do well to reflect seriously upon himself and to see what proportion or disproportion there exists between himself and nature. In pursuing this basic question of self-knowledge Pascal formulates some penetrating insights into the life of man. His *Pensées* is to be understood not as an attempt at a formulation of a systematic philosophy or theology but rather as an attempt at an elucidation of the human condition in its manifold concreteness.

When man once reflects upon himself, he finds that his condition is characterized by a pervading ambivalence and ambiguity. In comparison with the Infinite, he is nothing; in comparison with the nothing out of which he has been made, he is the crown of creation. On the one hand, he is incurably limited in power and wisdom; on the other hand, he is but a little lower than the angels. He is capable of the lowest, but also capable of the highest. He bears the stamp of finitude, but he also carries with him the image of the Infinite. This is the essential ambiguity or paradox which characterizes the human condition. "What a chimera then is man! What a novelty! What a monster, what a chaos, what a contradiction, what a prodigy! Judge of all things, imbecile worm of the earth; depositary of truth, a sink of uncertainty and error; the pride and refuse of the universe!" Man stands at the crossroads between the finite and the Infinite; in him flesh and spirit meet. There is both a misery and a grandeur which qualifies the existence of man.

Man's ineradicable finitude imposes some clearly defined limits on the reach and range of human reason. Man as a "thinking reed" exhibits the power of reason, but he does so only under the conditions of a limited and fractured existence. Man remains incapable of certain knowledge; his highest rational principles are never immune to doubt. "Our reason is always deceived by fickle shadows; nothing can fix the finite between the two Infinites, which both enclose and fly from it." There is an inescapable uncertainty or existential doubt which is part of the human condition.

It is necessary to distinguish this existential doubt of which Pascal speaks from the calculated, methodological doubt of Descartes. The doubt of Descartes was a provisional doubt, to be used as a technique for arriving at indubitable propositions and to be suspended the moment that such propositions are made known. Pascalian doubt is neither calculated nor provisional. It is part of the finitude of man, indicating an element of insecurity and risk in every existential truth. Such a doubt can never be overcome or even assessed through the exercise of man's rational faculty. This does not mean that reason must thus be displaced. It does mean, however, that knowledge involves more than simply the response of the mind and that in dealing with those truths which concern man most deeply "the heart has its reasons, which reason does not know."

The threat of emptiness and meaninglessness is another determinant of the human condition. Man seeks to find satisfaction and meaning for his life in the pursuit of various finite and temporal goods, but his endeavors fail to provide an ultimate satisfaction or a final meaning. In the section entitled, "The Misery of Man Without God," Pascal examines the threat of emptiness in connection with the phenomenon of diversion. Man seeks various diversions and distractions so as to fill the emptiness or void of his existence; this is why men love bustle, noise, and amusements. But this frantic pursuit of various activities and amusements fails to provide satisfaction. It only diverts man's thoughts from himself. Indeed, the pursuit is undertaken for the purpose of escaping from himself, for man lacks the courage to face the weariness, emptiness, and despair which threaten his existence. Men will spend entire days chasing hares which they would not have accepted prior to the chase. They are not interested in the object of the chase, but only in the chase itself, which diverts their thoughts from themselves and screens them from the existential negativities of their condition. It is for this reason that solitary confinement is the most horrible of all punishments. All avenues for diversion are cut off and the self must contend with itself in its solitude. Man lives and moves in emptiness, engaged in an abortive search for satisfaction through diverting activities, refusing to accept his finitude and the conditions of his estranged existence.

It is this description of the human condition as it is characterized by its various negativities that drives Pascal to his wager for the existence of God. The wager thus becomes a matter of existential concern. In no sense is the wager for Pascal an objective, disinterested, calculated undertaking, the outcome of which remains a matter of indifference. It has to do with a possible answer, or lack of such, to the ultimate issues of life. If God does not exist, the human condition is threatened with final despair. The wager thus confronts man with an existential choice qualified by ultimate concern. The wager is formulated in terms of a forced option which presents an inescapable decision. Either God exists or He does not. Shall one decide for His existence or against it? There is no rule of certainty to govern one's decision. It remains a matter of risk. Man is thus confronted with an inescapable decision in the presence of an inescapable uncertainty. In the face of this inescapable uncertainty he wagers. If he believes in God, and if God does exist, he gains everything; if he believes, and God does not exist, he suffers only a finite loss. On the other hand, if he disbelieves, and God exists, he loses everything; and if he disbelieves, and God does not exist, he reaps only a finite gain. The odds thus favor belief in God's existence. If one believes, there is an infinity to gain and only a finite truth to lose; if one disbelieves, there is an infinity to lose and only a finite truth to gain.

It is evident that the truth of God's existence cannot be determined through the use of pure reason. Pascal breaks with the whole tradition of natural or philosophical theology. "The metaphysical proofs of God are so remote from the reasoning of men, and so complicated, that they make little impression; and if they should be of service to some, it would be only during the moment that they see such demonstration; but an hour afterwards they fear they have been mistaken." The philosophical proofs, in the last analysis, are rejected by Pascal on two counts: they lack certainty and they remain irrelevant to religious experience.

Thus, the God of the philosophers is displaced by the God of Abraham, Isaac, and Jacob, and by the God who revealed Himself decisively in Jesus Christ. Pascal had written the fragmentary notes compiled in the *Pensées* in preparation for an apology for the Christian religion. This intention is evident throughout. Only the Christian religion has provided man with an adequate picture of the distortions and corruptions present in man's nature, and with a teaching of deliverance from this condition through redemption by Jesus Christ. As a committed adherent to this religion, Pascal in his theological reflections remains consistently and emphatically Christocentric. "Not only do we know God by Jesus Christ alone, but we know ourselves only by Jesus Christ. We know life and death only through Jesus Christ. Apart from Jesus Christ we do not know what is our life, nor our death, nor God, nor ourselves."

DISCOURSE CONCERNING THE HOLY SPIRIT

Author: John Owen (1616-1683)
Type of work: Puritan theology
First published: 1674

Principal Ideas Advanced

The doctrine of the Holy Spirit is clearly grounded in Scripture.

The Spirit was active at the first creation, has been revealed in power in the old and new dispensations, and is responsible for the new creation.

The work of the Spirit is seen in raising the believer to new life and in maintaining him in progressive holiness.

What a former generation knew as "Owen on the Holy Spirit," but which is the *Discourse Concerning the Holy Spirit,* is a massive and composite work in five sections, representing one of the major theological contributions of one of the greatest of the later English Puritan writers. Owen was chiefly, but by no means exclusively, a theologian. The first stage of his Oxford career was cut short by William Laud (1573-1645), who objected to Owen's Puritan views, but these views were responsible for Owen's rapid rise under the protection of Oliver Cromwell (1599-1658). As dean of Christ

Church and vice-chancellor of Oxford, Owen played an important role on a stage far wider than the university. His administrative experience gave him practical wisdom, which was combined with both evangelical fervor and Christian charity. When the restoration of Charles II drove him into nonconformity he was already a learned scholar, a famous theologian, and a prominent public figure. During the remaining two decades of his life he poured out a stream of major works, most of which arose out of the controversies of the period.

Many of Owen's books dealt with the central doctrines of Christianity. His works on the Spirit are neither abler nor more extensive than his works on the atonement and the Trinity, but they deal with a subject which had been consistently neglected. The doctrine of the Holy Spirit had never received the dogmatic development accorded to the other central affirmations of the faith, and Owen's work is important not only because of the quality of his thought, but also because it examines with great thoroughness a topic which has usually been accorded the most perfunctory treatment.

The first of Owen's five works on the Holy Spirit is *A Discourse Concerning the Holy Spirit,* itself a book of 650 quarto pages. It was followed by *The Reason of Faith* (1677), *The Causes, Ways and Means of Understanding the Mind of God* (1678), *The Work of the Holy Spirit in Prayer* (1682) and *On the Work of the Holy Spirit as a Comforter* (1693, posthumously). These, it is obvious, cumulatively represent a sustained preoccupation with the doctrine of the Holy Spirit to which there are few (if any) parallels in the history of theology. Owen treats his subject with the expansiveness, even prolixity, which a seventeenth century theologian felt free to claim and in which his contemporaries were willing to indulge him, but even a modern reader senses at once that we have here the work of a great man exploring a great subject.

In the first book of the *Pneumatologia* (the foundation work among the five) Owen deals with the preliminary topics which a thorough examination of the subject presupposes. The Scriptures speak of spiritual gifts and promise them. This in itself, Owen writes, would make the Spirit an important subject of study—particularly when one considers the central place which the Spirit occupies in the Bible. But when misguided enthusiasts invest their fantasies with the Spirit's authority, and when men glorying in their own intelligence presume to slight its significance, the task of examining Scriptural teaching on the subject assumes more than passing importance. Men can be guided by false spirits as well as by the divine Spirit, but we have been given a rule by which to test them (I John 4: 1-3).

The next step is to consider the names and titles by which the Bible speaks of the Spirit, for if there is confusion at the beginning we can hardly hope for clarity as we proceed. We must also be aware of the nature of the reality with which we are dealing, and Owen is concerned at the outset to establish the personal character of the Spirit. He argues that the nature of God is the foundation of all religion, and what this nature is we know because of divine revelation. God has revealed Himself as Three in One, and from this we can see that the Spirit is not an impersonal cosmic energy, but a manifestation, an activity of the Godhead itself. The very language of Scripture is conclusive proof that the Spirit is personal; the properties assigned to it (to *Him*) presuppose a personal subsistence. This divine personal Spirit is active now and has been active from the very beginning. Creation was accomplished through His instrumentality, and Owen carefully examines the distinctive role of the Spirit therein. The whole Godhead, of course, was involved in creation, and the Spirit's special task was to perfect what the Father created. So Owen examines what the Spirit did in spreading out the heavens and marshaling their hosts, in fashioning the earth and making the creatures who inhabit it, and, most significantly of all, in creating man. The same Spirit who creates preserves all things, both natural and moral. But there are mysteries here which cannot be easily probed nor lightly disregarded. In relation to God's will, the Spirit is described as given or sent in relation to His own will. He is spoken of as proceeding or coming.

The strongly Biblical foundation of Owen's theology is seen in the way he deals with the activity of the Spirit as this is described in both the Old and New Testaments. Under the old dispensation he finds that the way was prepared for the new, and he examines the significance of prophecy, inspiration, miracles, and the special gifts which can be directly attributed to the Spirit. In every area, the natural faculties of men's minds were heightened, whether the area involved was political, moral, intellectual, or physical. The importance of the Spirit in the new dispensation which was inaugurated in the New Testament can be seen in the fact that the full outpouring of the Spirit is the great promise concerning the new creation. The ministry of the Gospel rests on this promise, a promise which extends to all believers. Each person is commanded to pray for the Spirit. On the eve of His departure Christ solemnly promised to send His Spirit. He even specified the ends which the gift of the Spirit would serve, and He made clear that the new creation (to be completed by the Spirit) would be the principal means by which God's glory would be made known. The Head of this new creation is Christ, and we can see the significance of the Spirit if we observe the way in which the presence and power of the Spirit are made manifest in Christ.

At this point Owen embarks on a careful discussion, worked out in considerable detail and in strict loyalty to trinitarian presuppositions, of the part played by the Spirit in the Incarnation of the Word. It is clear that the Holy Spirit is the immediate efficient cause of all divine operations. It is of the Spirit that Scripture speaks in connection with the conception of Jesus. It is the Spirit which accomplishes the sanctification of His human nature. He anoints the Savior with power and gifts; the Spirit guides, conducts, and supports Christ throughout His ministry. The Spirit is responsible for miraculous works, but He also endows Christ with the spiritual graces of love, zeal, submission, faith, and truth. The Spirit sustains Christ in the final ordeal of His crucifixion and death, and in the triumph of His resurrection. And since the ascension of Christ the Spirit bears witness to Christ and brings to mind the truth as it is in Him. In all this, the implications for a doctrine of the Godhead are carefully noted, The faith proclaims one God, not three, and in every activity of the Godhead all three persons are involved.

Owen deals with great sophistication with the most complex and subtle theological truths. But he does not forget that the New Creation concerns men and women. In particular, it concerns them as they are members of the Church, for the Church is built upon the foundation of the promise of the Spirit, and the erection of the Church is likewise committed to the Spirit. The Spirit performs the work of Christ in those who are the members of Christ's Body, and thus the Spirit is the author of all grace.

Owen, it is clear, is a careful and Biblical theologian, but he is competent to proceed further and construct an elaborate superstructure on the Spiritual foundations. A great deal of the interest and value of his principal book on the Spirit lies in his exposition of the stages of the New Creation. The focal points of an elaborate discussion of the new life in the believer are regeneration and sanctification. The presuppositions of the new life are provided in the Gospel, especially in the Incarnation and the atonement. But man is dead in trespasses and sins. Regeneration declares that what has been dead can be made alive. The Good News has been proclaimed; it must be appropriated, and the distinguishing mark of Owen's work is the close connection he establishes between the Holy Spirit and the reawakening of the soul that is sunk in sin. A new creature is formed, with a new nature and capable of a new life. This is not a magical transformation. It has the most profound moral significance, and it requires, on man's part, a specific response. Man must be converted; he must turn from his sin. His mind, his affections, his conscience must be touched. But a man cannot simply decide to abandon his sins by his own wisdom and in his own strength. Hence, Owen carefully studies the state of corruption into which man has been plunged by his sin. The mind has been deprived of saving light, and it is overwhelmed by a darkness which is both objective and subjective. So the natural man lives in a state which is described as spiritual death.

Owen's careful study of nature and sin is the necessary prelude to a consideration of the work of the Spirit in regeneration. There is no possibility of new life for people living and dying in a state of sin. The vicious circle must be broken; deliverance is by God's grace alone, and the agent of God in this new act of creation is the Holy Spirit. This is all much less remote from modern experience than the twentieth century reader might suppose. The analysis of man's plight is conducted with great psychological insight, and it is significant that the argument is enforced by an appeal to the experience of that profound psychologist, St. Augustine.

The new life will be a holy life, and it will be progressively so. Owen therefore studies with equal care the power of the Spirit in sanctifying the believer. This subject also presupposes a study of sin, not now as a past state of bondage and death but as a present and dangerous alternative to holiness. The filth of sin must be purged away; it can be purged away by the blood of Christ. Then the task of strengthening the believer begins.

Sanctification is a progressive advance that is open only to the believer whose life is filled and transformed by the Spirit. Here the positive work of sanctification comes under careful scrutiny.

The value and importance of Owen's work on the Spirit is considerable. Historically this is one of the most faithful and complete reflections of the Puritan mind. The main lines of Calvinist thought are clearly present. God, His presence, His power, His continuing activity are the presuppositions of the work. The great doctrines of Reformed theology appear one by one. In particular, Owen shows with some care how election is the cause of and a motive for holiness. It is clear, also, that the best type of Puritan theology was never abstract or theoretical. The argument is constantly related to practical issues, and the great theological doctrines are applied to the immediate necessities of man's situation. Even more important is the fact that Owen provides perhaps the only Protestant study, on a major scale, of one of the neglected doctrines of Christian theology. In recent years there have been numerous signs of a revival of interest in the theological implications of the Spirit. So far most of the books which reflect this renascence have been small in scale and many of them have been slight in significance. Owen may sometimes be diffuse, but he is always massively learned and soundly Biblical. His argument is developed in great detail, and both in aim and in effect his work is impressively constructive.

TREATISE CONCERNING THE SEARCH AFTER TRUTH

Author: Nicholas Malebranche (1638-1715)
Type of work: Philosophical theology
First published: 1674

Principal Ideas Advanced

God is the sole cause of events in nature and of corresponding perceptions in the human mind.

The laws which God has prescribed are so disposed that events and perceptions exist in perfect parallel, activity in nature being the occasion, but not the cause, of activity in the mind.

By the senses we learn to preserve the body, but the senses often deceive us; the highest truth is to be found in the immediate awareness of God and in the apprehension of the ideas in the divine mind.

The *Treatise Concerning the Search After Truth* is the principal work of Nicholas Malebranche, a French priest trained at the Sorbonne and a member of the Oratory. Malebranche was profoundly influenced by the philosophy of René Descartes (1596-1650) and of Descartes' disciple, Arnold Geulincx (1624-1699); the philosophy which emerged is known as occasionalism.

Malebranche posits a parallelism between events in nature and events in the mind, a parallelism due to the activity of God. Malebranche inherited Descartes's dualism between extension and thought. Extension and thought were considered by Malebranche to be too dissimilar to interact; each, then, must act according to its own law, without affecting the other. God has so regulated matters that when the will acts there is movement in the body and when there is an injury to the body pain occurs. The physical event is the "occasion" of the mental event, without being its cause.

The human mind, says Malebranche, is situated between God, its Creator, and material beings; it is intimately related to God and is thus exalted above all things, while because of its connection with the body, it is prone to misery and error. The relation of our minds to our bodies is not one of absolute necessity, but our mind's relation to God is absolutely indispensable, natural, and necessary.

The nature of all things is regulated by the will of God, Malebranche claims; the human soul is so united to God that it receives from the eternal truth, which presides over the understanding, a knowledge of its duty. To the degree that the mind increases its union with God, it grows more luminous, and when unaffected by its union with the body, and solely attentive to the pure ideas of the mind, while listening to God, the mind cannot possibly fall into error, for God does not deceive those who interrogate Him.

Knowledge is acquired through the attention of the mind, not by sensations and passions, writes Malebranche. The opposition that the body makes to the mind should be withstood; sensible things are not to be made the object of our attention, and the reports of the senses are to be subjected to disbelief.

Malebranche claims that the truth of all things must be pronounced by the mind, according to its internal light, without listening to the confused and false verdict of the senses and imagination. Our senses, he writes, are given to us solely for the preservation of our body, and it is because of them that we fall into error. The senses are most exact in telling us of the relations which our body has to bodies around us, but they are incapable of instructing us concerning the nature of bodies. The senses are never to be raised above the understanding. We ought never to give our entire consent to anything that is not entirely evident. To doubt the senses out of prudence and caution, because of wisdom and penetration of mind, is the mark of the true philosopher. The moving force of bodies is nothing but the action of God, for bodies have no force to move themselves; their moving force is the will of God, which is always efficacious.

God by His efficacious will performs whatever is performed by the motion of bodies and the wills of minds. Creatures have no efficacious action themselves; God's power is communicated to them by means of natural laws which God established on their account.

Man wills and determines himself, says Malebranche, only to the extent that God causes him to will; man alone sins, but sin, error, and concupiscence are nothing; in themselves man's volitions are impotent; God works all notwithstanding them, for man's volitions produce nothing.

God is to be seen in all things, writes Malebranche; we ought to be sensible of His power and force in all natural effects. No power, force, or efficacy is to be attributed to secondary or natural causes. In everything it is God that works all; nothing resists Him, because He can do whatever He wills.

According to Malebranche, "God by the first of Natural Laws positively Wills and consequently causes the Collision of Bodies; and afterwards employs this Collision as an Occasion of establishing the Second Natural Law; which regulates the communication of motions; . . . thus the actual Collision is the Natural, or Occasional, Cause of the Actual Communication of Motions; . . . these two Natural Laws . . . are sufficient to produce such a world as we see. . . ."

To attain truth, says Malebranche, the philosopher must realize that the thoughts of the soul which depend upon the body concern only the body and thus are either obscure or false. In any case, such thoughts can serve only to unite us to sensible goods and to what procures them. It is not only necessary to rid ourselves of the delusions of sense, Malebranche warns, but also we must guard against the deception caused by the vision of our imagination and the impressions that other men's imagination exercise upon our mind. Truth is obtained by the admission of the clear ideas which the mind, or pure understanding, receives through its necessary union with the divine Logos.

The limitation of the mind is a source of error, Malebranche points out, for the mind cannot grasp anything of an infinite nature. Human reason cannot comprehend such mysteries as the Trinity. Since the principles of the Christian faith are not known to reason, reason must submit to faith in the Scriptures.

Our minds are dependent upon God for all their thoughts, writes Malebranche. God has in Himself the ideas of all the beings He has created, and since God is united by His presence with our souls, in that He is the place of spirits, as space is the place of bodies, the mind can see the ideas in God which represent created beings. The mind can see all the works of God in God. We can see only what God desires us to see. Our sufficiency is of God, not of ourselves. God is the light that enlightens every man. Men are entirely impotent without God. Unless we know God in some way, we know nothing at all. When we see material and sensible things, we do not have sensations of them in God, but they proceed from God, who acts upon us. When we perceive something sensible two factors appear: pure idea and sensation. Sensations are modifications in our soul caused within us by God. Pure ideas, which are joined to sensations, are in God, and we know them only because God discloses them to us. The idea in God is joined to the sensation in us by God; thus, when objects are present, we believe them to be so, and we have the proper sentiments and passions with relation to them.

The senses and imagination are confined to sensible things, Malebranche writes, but the pure intellect, our understanding or reason, enables us to have pure ideas and to see truths in God and to learn eternal laws.

The dependence of our minds upon the will of God enables us to perceive all things through the presence of God, who comprehends everything in the simplicity of His essence. God makes our souls to feel pain and pleasure and all other sensations by the union He has instituted between our souls and bodies. By means of the union between the will of man and the representation of the ideas included in the divine essence, God enables our souls to know whatever they know; this union is caused by the will of God; He alone can enlighten us.

According to Malebranche, "God is the intelligible world, or the place of Spirits, as the material world is the place of bodies. That is, from His Power they receive all their modifications; that 'tis in His Wisdom they discover all their Idea's; and 'tis by His love they are influenced with all their regulated motions: And because His Power and His Love are nothing but Himself; let us believe with St. Paul, that He is not far from every one of us, and that in Him we live and move, and have our Being."

There are four ways by which the mind knows things, writes Malebranche. The first is the manner by which the mind knows God. God alone penetrates the mind and discloses Himself to it, by enlightening the mind from His own substance. We see God with an immediate and direct vision. Although the knowledge that we have of God in this life is imperfect and confused, God is intelligible by Himself immediately.

The second way of knowing things is the way by which we know bodies; that is, by their ideas, by reference to something different from themselves. Bodies together with their properties are seen in that divine being which contains them in an intelligible manner; they are seen in God, and thus they are seen in the most perfect manner. Whatever is lacking in our knowledge of extension, its figures and motions, is attributable to the defectiveness of our minds, not to the defectiveness of the divine ideas.

The third way that the mind knows is the way by which it knows the soul; that is, by means of internal sensation, or conscience. The soul is known not by reference to the idea of the soul, nor is it seen in God; the soul is known, although imperfectly, by conscience, by reference to what one feels within. The *existence* of the soul is more clearly apprehended than is the existence of the body, but the *nature* of the soul is less well known than is the nature of the body.

The fourth way by which the mind knows is the way by which it knows the souls of other men and of pure intelligences; that is, by conjecture. By conjecture we know that the souls of other men are of the same species as our own. We presume that what we feel in ourselves is felt by others, and that God influences other spirits just as He influences our own.

The mind of man is limited, Malebranche claims; it is by nature subject to error. Even the least things have infinite relations which are beyond the scope of a finite mind.

Just as bodies move in the material world, so spirits move toward God in the spiritual world. By faith, writes Malebranche, we know that the order of nature has been inverted by sin, and we realize that our inclinations are disordered, so that instead of seeking

God, we seek our ultimate end in ourselves. But we are properly inclined only when we are inclined to the good in general, only when we love our neighbors as well as ourselves.

The cause of our adhesion to sensible things is sin, says Malebranche, for sin has estranged us from God, and thus we are now made dependent on our bodies. Since the Fall of Adam God is withdrawn from us, and we know Him as our good only by the grace of Jesus Christ. God alone is our true good, and whatever is real in the motions of the mind is the work of God, although He is not the author of our sin, or of our concupiscence. Actual grace is necessary before we can act rightly. The mind of man is preserved by God so that it can know and love Him. Whatever God wills is proper solely because He wills it, and He is just.

One of the most deplorable consequences of original sin, writes Malebranche, is that we no longer see God in all things and love Him in His works. The mind wanders and forgets God, who enlightens the mind. In a sense, the mind wills and determines itself, insofar as God causes it to will, for otherwise there would be no future reward and punishment; but inasmuch as God is the cause, man is inclined to will the good.

God acts in the simplest way and always with order, Malebranche concludes. God is an infinitely perfect being, whose knowledge and wisdom are without limits, so that every means by which He wishes to execute His designs are known to Him. The salvation of man is accomplished by repentance, self-denial and obedience, through Christ Jesus and His grace.

AN APOLOGY FOR THE TRUE CHRISTIAN DIVINITY

Author: Robert Barclay (1648-1690)
Type of work: Apologetics
First published: 1676 (Latin); 1678 (English)

Principal Ideas Advanced

The Christian faith is a living and vital experience, not a formal pattern of scholastic ideas, yet it can be presented as an ordered system without sacrificing its reality.

Man's true felicity is to know God, and this knowledge can be appropriated only by those who are enlightened by the Spirit; but this Spirit is clearly related to Scripture and to the work accomplished by Jesus Christ, who brings us into a new and living relationship with God.

Christian witness must be translated into appropriate forms of life if it is to affect those about us.

In his *An Apology for the True Christian Divinity* Robert Barclay provides, as the subtitle of his work announces, "an explanation and vindication of the Principles and Doctrines of the People Called Quakers." It was one of the earliest formal statements of the position of the Society of Friends, and in many ways it remains the most important and impressive of Quaker manifestoes. It stands in its own right, however, as one of the major theological works of an age much given to theological writing. Barclay's Scottish background may explain a degree of formal theological structure not common in Quaker works, and it also accounts for occasional traces of Calvinism not wholly congenial to his coreligionists.

Barclay opens his work with a characteristically Quaker address to King Charles II: "As it is inconsistant with the truth I bear, so it is far from me to use this epistle as an engine to flatter thee . . . ," but he takes occasion to repeat the story of Quaker sufferings and to reaffirm their innocence. He reminds the king of the degree to which his own career reflects the marvels of divine providence, and he submits that this should surely teach the king not only a humble awareness of the precariousness of human dignities but also a keen awareness of "how hateful the oppressor is both to God and man." At the forefront of his work, Barclay places a noble plea for liberty of conscience.

To explain his method, Barclay adds a greeting "unto the friendly reader" and a letter "to the clergy . . . unto whose hands these [theological theses] may come." He has no intention, he says, of relying on scholastic subtleties; the "simple, naked truth" which God has given men for their guidance has been overlaid by "school-divinity" which "brings [us] not a whit nearer to God, neither makes any man less wicked or more righteous than he was."

The main body of the *Apology* consists of fifteen propositions. Barclay gives them initially in condensed form and then expounds each of them in detail. He begins with the true foundation of knowledge. The height of all happiness is to know God, and therefore "the true and right understanding of this foundation and ground of knowledge is that which is most necessary to be known and believed in the first place." This knowledge can come only in an appropriate and appointed way, and Barclay's second proposition defines immediate revelation. The testimony of the Spirit "is that alone by which the true knowledge of God hath been, is, and can be only revealed," and it is by the agency of the Spirit that He has disclosed himself. Because there is an inner and essential consistency in the truth, the witness of the Spirit can never contradict the outward testimony either of the Scriptures or of right and sound reason, but this does not imply that the testimony of the Spirit can in any way be subjected to any external standard. The inward illumination of divine revelation "is that which is evident and clear of itself, forcing, by its own evidence and clearness, the well-disposed understanding to assent, irresistibly moving the same thereunto."

Barclay's next step is to consider Scripture and to examine its relation to direct revelation. The Bible contains the record of the revelations of the Spirit of God to the saints, and these are preserved for us in the form of history, prophecy, and "a full and ample account of the chief principles of the doctrine of Christ." Yet the Scriptures are a secondary, not a primary source, "because they are only a declaration of the fountain and not the fountain itself, therefore they are not to be esteemed the principal ground of all truth and knowledge, nor yet the adequate primary rule of faith and manners." The Scriptures are always subordinate to the Spirit. By the Spirit we know that the Scriptures testify to the truth; by the Spirit we, like the inspired authors, are led into all truth. "Therefore according to the Scriptures, the Spirit is the first and principal leader." The necessity of the truth so revealed is emphasized by the natural state of the men to whom it is disclosed. We are the posterity of Adam, which "is fallen, degenerated and dead, deprived of the sensation or feeling of this inward testimony or seed of God, and is subject unto the power, nature and seed of the serpent." The subtle influence of our fallen condition pervades our whole being; we can know nothing aright, and all our thoughts about God and about spiritual things are unprofitable. Here the Socinians and Pelagians, who exalt a natural light, are clearly wrong, but so are those who believe that the seed of iniquity is imputed to infants before they actually join themselves to it by transgression.

The fifth and sixth propositions concern the universal redemption which has been wrought on behalf of man by Jesus Christ. Barclay introduces the subject with a catena of Scriptural texts, all of which emphasize God's mercy toward the sinner and the all-embracing scope of the salvation which He has wrought in Christ. "The saving and spiritual light" thus shed abroad is no less universal than "the seed of sin" which it counteracts. What is necessary is that men improve "the first and common grace," and where this happens it is easy to believe that those who stand outside the pale of formal grace may be saved. Some of the old philosophers and all who happen to live where the Gospel has not been preached are not beyond hope, provided they do not resist that grace which in a measure is granted to all. "This certain doctrine then being received (*to wit*) that there is an evangelical and saving light and grace in all, the universality of the love and mercy of God towards mankind (both in the death of his beloved Son, the Lord Jesus Christ, and in the manifestation of the light in the heart) is established and confirmed against all the objections of such as deny it." So the benefits of Christ's death are not restricted to those who have "the distinct outward knowledge of his death and sufferings"; those who are excluded from this knowledge "by some inevitable accident" may also be made partakers in the mystery of His death. If they allow "his seed and light" to work in their hearts they are brought into fellowship with the Father and the Son; by the indwelling power of the Spirit they are turned from the evil to the good; they learn to do to others as they would be done by, and by thus obeying the inclusive injunction of Christ they manifest their obedience to His will. The error of those who have taught universal redemption has usually lain, says Barclay, in making salvation dependent on outward knowledge of the truth as it is in Christ, but salvation actually comes through "that divine and evangelical principle of light and life, wherewith Christ hath enlightened every man that comes into the world."

The results of universal redemption now demand attention, and in the seventh proposition Barclay considers justification. The result of receiving the light is "an holy, pure, spiritual birth" within us, and it is manifested in holiness, righteousness, purity "and all these other blessed fruits which are acceptable to God." What Barclay means by a holy birth is clear: it is Jesus Christ formed within us and working His works in us. As we are sanctified, so we are justified in the sight of God. But the new relationship with God is in no way due to our initiative nor is it the result of anything we do; it is the work of Christ, "who is both the gift and the giver, and the cause producing the effects in us." When this new relationship becomes a reality, the "body of death and sin" is crucified and removed. Our hearts are united and subjected to the truth; they no longer respond to the suggestions of evil but are free from actual sinning and transgressing of the law of God. In this sense we can be described as perfect, but perfection allows for growth, and if we cease to attend on the Lord we shall discover to our cost that we are never beyond the reach of sin.

Perserverance is the subject of the ninth proposition. Barclay claims that the gift of the inward grace of God is sufficient to enable us to work out our salvation, but if we resist God's gift, we become subject to condemnation. When grace has been at work in a life to cleanse and renew that life and to lead it toward fuller perfection, it is still possible to fall from grace and to make a shipwreck of faith. Nevertheless, it is also possible to attain such an increase and stability in the truth that we need no longer fear total apostasy.

Barclay now turns to questions which touch the distinctive Quaker witness concerning the life of the Christian community. His tenth proposition deals with the ministry. Every true minister is ordained, prepared, and supplied by the gift or light of God. By the leading and moving of the Spirit a minister should be guided to work where, when, how, and among whom it is right to work. The person who is inwardly illuminated by God ought to preach, whether or not he has received human training or authorization, while those who lack the Heaven-imparted gift, even when admirably qualified, may be no better than deceivers. Those who have been taught and inspired by God will share freely what they have received, and they will not look for reward or treat their vocation as a source of profit. Related to the ministry is worship (the subject-matter of the eleventh proposition). "All true and acceptable worship of God is offered in the inward and immediate moving and drawing of his own Spirit, which is neither limited to places, times, or persons." Worship as devised by men and prescribed as to form is "abominable idolatry in the sight of God," and men of sensitive spirit will separate from all such travesties.

In the twelfth and thirteenth propositions Barclay sets forth the Quaker position on sacraments. The New Testament speaks of "one baptism," but it points to "a pure and spiritual thing, to wit, the baptism of the spirit and fire, by which we are buried with him, that being washed and purged from our sins, we may 'walk in newness of life.'" He dismisses the baptism of infants as "mere human tradition," lacking Scriptural warrant. In the same way, the communion of the body and blood of Christ is inward and spiritual. It is a participation in His life by which our inward nature is daily nourished by His indwelling presence. Barclay concedes that Christ's disciples for a time kept up the outward observance of the rite, but this was a temporary concession to the weakness of new believers. As in the case of other signs, like washing one another's feet, it was but the shadow of better things, and it ceased among those who had obtained the substance of spiritual understanding.

In the fourteenth proposition Barclay limits the power civil magistrates can claim in matters which are purely religious. The Quakers never denied the authority of civil power in the government of this world, but they hotly denied the right of the magistrate to interfere in questions beyond his competence. God had reserved to Himself power and dominion over conscience, and He alone can rightly govern and instruct it. It is therefore a transgression of God's prerogatives to force the conscience of any man; to do so by killing, fining, banishing, or imprisoning, especially on the ground of mere differences in worship or belief, is the sure evidence of "the spirit of Cain the murderer." No man, of course, can invoke conscience in order to prejudice his neighbor in life or estate, or to veil conduct prejudicial to society. An appeal to conscience cannot be the refuge of hypocrites or scoundrels.

In his final proposition Barclay comes to outward forms of social behavior. The pattern of man's life will be governed by his true purposes, and since the chief end of all religion is to redeem man from the spirit and vain conversation of this world and to lead him to inward communion with God, it follows that all the vain customs and habits of the world will be rejected by those who come to the true fear of God. "Hat honour" and all other forms of social obsequiousness, together with "all the foolish and superstitious formalities" involved, must be repudiated. So must "unprofitable plays, frivolous recreations, sportings and gamings," which waste precious time and divert man's attention from its proper objects. The man of sensitive spirit will forsake these things "as knowing they are contrary to the will of him who redeems his children from the love of this world and its lusts and leads them in the ways of truth and holiness, in which they take delight to walk."

So Barclay reaches his conclusion. The system he has outlined is described by him as being clear, consistent, and Scriptural. He states that the Quakers may be few in numbers and humble in social status, but they can justly claim to enjoy God's blessing and to know His presence. And in characteristic seventeenth century fashion, the book ends with an ejaculation of praise and an outpouring of prayer.

THE PILGRIM'S PROGRESS

Author: John Bunyan (1628-1688)
Type of work: Religious allegory
First published: Part I, 1678; Part II, 1684

PRINCIPAL IDEAS ADVANCED

Christian, a lonely pilgrim, makes his way from the City of Destruction to the Celestial City.

He encounters various obstacles—including the Slough of Despond, the Hill of Difficulty, the giant Despair, and a treacherous river—but he is aided by Evangelist, three Shining Ones, Discretion, Prudence, Piety, Charity, Hopeful, and others.

Christian's wife, Christiana, also makes the journey to the Celestial City; she and her sons are assisted by Mercy, Mr. Greatheart, Mr. Honest, Mr. Valiant-for-truth, Mr. Steadfast, and others.

Christian's adventures are an image of the lonely experience of conversion; Christiana's pilgrimage shows that the courageous journey of the exceptional person (her husband) makes the way easier for others.

In a versified "Apology for his Book," John Bunyan, the English preacher and author, tells how his celebrated allegory, *The Pilgrim's Progress,* came into being. While he was engaged in writing a more conventional work on Christian living, Bunyan found that the analogy of the pilgrim kept creeping into his work, and the references to the pilgrim grew to such proportions that, as a workmanly writer, Bunyan was obliged to excise them. For his own satisfaction, however, he set down the allegory on separate pages, where he could give reign to his imagination without fearing men's reproaches for the novelty of it. When, after many doubts, he decided to publish the first part, the work won immediate popularity. Its influence was so great that another writer ventured (as happened with Cervantes' *Don Quixote*) to publish a second part. Bunyan himself, therefore, returned to the theme and issued his own sequel, thus completing the work as we know it. In the closing paragraph of Part II, Bunyan tentatively promises a third installment, which, however, he never wrote.

Part I recounts the pilgrimage of Christian, a lonely soul, who made his way, not without encouragement and instruction, but mainly by his own sincerity and valor, to the Celestial City. Misunderstood by his family, scorned and persecuted by his neighbors, he fled from his native place, The City of Destruction, with a burden on his back and a book in his hand. He had no directions to follow except the word of Evangelist, who told him to make for the Wicket Gate, but even this he could not see. For illumination he had only an uncertain light. Before he reached the Gate, Christian fell into the Slough of Despond, and afterwards was waylaid by Mr. Worldly-Wiseman, who would have him turn aside to the comfortable village of Morality. But Evangelist found the pilgrim and again showed him the Wicket Gate, through which Christian entered, and came up a hill to the Cross, where his burden fell off his back. Three Shining Ones then clothed him with new raiment, set a mark on his forehead, and gave him a roll with a seal upon it—his safe-conduct to the Celestial City. After climbing the Hill of Difficulty, Christian fell asleep and dropped his roll, which he must later come back for. He found fellowship and encouragement at the Palace Beautiful in the presence of the damsels Discretion, Prudence, Piety, and Charity. But he still had to fight Apollyon in the Valley of Humiliation, and he barely escaped martyrdom (which befell his companion Faithful) at Vanity Fair. Once, when the way was rough, he climbed a stile in order to walk in By-path Meadow, only to lose his way and find himself at Doubting Castle, where he fell prey to the giant Despair. After languishing in a dungeon, Christian remembered the key of Promise and made his escape. He was now nearing the Delectable Mountains, from which he could see his journey's goal. But there remained the river which all must cross; in passing through it Christian was nearly drowned by the remembrance of his sins, but he was sustained by the hand of his companion Hopeful, with whom at last he entered the Celestial City.

Part II relates how Christian's wife and sons, moved by his death, undertook the journey upon which they had refused to accompany him. They were accompanied by a young woman named Mercy, and from time to time as they progressed along the route, others joined them: Mr. Greatheart, who was commissioned to be their conductor, Mr. Honest, Mr. Valiant-for-truth, Mr. Steadfast, as well as Mr. Feeble-mind, Mr. Ready-to-halt (who traveled on crutches), Mr. Despondency, and the latter's daughter, Mrs. Much-afraid. They covered the same ground as did Christian, yet their experiences were not the same. It is notable that Christiana and her companions bore no burdens: at the place of the Cross, where Christian was delivered of his burden, they only paused to reflect on the meaning of Christ's death. The enemies which Christian had fought, and others besides, were ably subdued by Greatheart. The town of Vanity still kept its Fair, but a Christian community also flourished in its midst, and there were other signs that the witness of Christian and Faithful had not been without effect. There, as elsewhere on the journey, they stayed awhile to refresh themself in Christian homes. The sons grew to manhood, married, and took their places of responsibility alongside Greatheart, who, thus reinforced, drew up plans to assault Doubting Castle and liberate any who were imprisoned there (notably, Mr. Despondency and Mrs. Much-afraid). Thus, they all came to Beulah Land, in the Delectable Mountains, and settled with other pilgrims to await their particular calls to cross the river. When the call came to Christiana, she had time to bless her children, to encourage her companions, and to bequeath her few belongings to the poor. She entered the river calmly with the words, "I come, Lord, to be with thee, and bless thee," and, though her children wept, Mr. Greatheart and Mr. Valiant played upon the cymbal and harp for joy.

The lonely adventure of Christian in Part I reflects Bunyan's personal experience of conversion, his long imprisonment under Charles II (which was voluntary, in the sense that by abjuring his calling he could probably have been set free), and the mingled passions engendered by a Calvinistic conviction, which knows that things are not what they seem and which is nevertheless unable to penetrate to what they are. The journey is, however, that of an exceptional person. As a pastor and spiritual counselor, Bunyan came to understand that salvation is not restricted to those who serve God directly. As path-breakers and heroes, the pastors make it possible for others less doughty to follow after. These lives, being less exposed, may even realize a kind of perfection denied to the former, as Solomon in some ways surpassed his father David. Even those of little faith (Mr. Feeble-mind, Mr. Ready-to-halt, and the others) complete the journey when they are fortunate enough to fall in with the company of more resolute believers. Not so, however, for those of bad faith (Mr. Worldly Wiseman, Mr. Formalist, Mr. Talkative, Mr. By-ends) who, presumably, have all experienced convictions of sin and have feared for their state, but "understand not that such convictions tend to their good; and therefore they do desperately seek to stifle them, and presumptuously continue to flatter themselves in the way of their own hearts."

The conception of life as a pilgrimage had been exploited by other writers prior to the time of Bunyan. So had the method which dramatizes spiritual struggles in terms of the hazards of nature and the malice of men. Bunyan's originality appears in the power and conviction which the allegory takes in his hands. Fanciful pictures from medieval tales of chivalry and poetical symbols from the Holy Scriptures combine with realistic descriptions and characterizations from English village and country life to form a story which not merely demands credence for itself but tends to give the lie to our everyday way of viewing things.

The Pilgrim's Progress is a mirror of the spiritual awakening known as Puritanism. John Bunyan was not one of the originators of that movement, for he was active late in the seventeenth century; rather, his work was a faithful expression of the transformation which the Reformed teaching worked in the lives of ordinary people. Countless details in the work reflect the warmth and sincerity of the spirit of these men and women, which was grave and serious, but not in the least wanting in vigor or cheer. Bunyan's love of good food, his enthusiasm for music, his appreciation of feminine grace and masculine courage, and above all his delight in the company of family and friends help the reader to form a true picture of what Puritanism was in its prime. But the value of the work does not lie in these details. While he was a thorough Puritan, the author's genius enabled him, like every great artist, to transcend the time and the locale in which he wrote, and to present the character of the Puritan Englishman in its universal aspects. In contemporary terms, *The Pilgrim's Progress* tells how a man, with a circle of his fellows, is lifted out of the mass where nobody really exists, and, by way of hard decisions and fast commitments, wins the dignity of a name—*Christian.*

THE TRUE INTELLECTUAL SYSTEM OF THE UNIVERSE

Author: Ralph Cudworth (1617-1688)
Type of work: Apologetics
First published: 1678

Principal Ideas Advanced

The physical system of the world, made intelligible by the science of mechanics, needs to be integrated into a more comprehensive intellectual system, which includes life and mind.

There is universal and public truth, directly discernible to human reason.

The existence of God, demonstrable by pure reason, is also necessary to the understanding of movement and order in nature.

Besides the mechanical causes in nature, a plastic or purposive cause is at work in nature.

The soul, being the effective agent in the life of the body, is also, in man, a compendium of the Divine Mind.

Religious and moral knowledge, as well as scientific, are based on natural truth, inherent in reasonable beings; Christian revelation was necessary to retrieve men from error and re-establish them in the right way.

Ralph Cudworth was a fellow and master at Cambridge University and, with his friend Henry More (1614-1687), a leader in the philosophical group known as the Cambridge Platonists. *The True Intellectual System of the Universe* is a massive fragment. Its three volumes comprise only Book One of the original project, which was to have consisted of three books: the first directed against atheism; the second, against the teaching that God's will is sovereign over truth and justice; the third, against fatalism and predestination. It is clear that Cudworth's first concern lay in vindicating the eternity of moral principles, and man's freedom and responsibility, but he went into such detail in his argument against atheism that he failed to achieve his initial goal. From the point of view of the modern reader, this is unfortunate. We would readily have seen Book One shortened by two-thirds, in order to have the rest of the argument, for Cudworth is worth reading when he is expounding his own philosophy, but he is wearisome and unprofitable when he turns to the history of philosophy to buttress his position.

In entitling his work *The True Intellectual System of the Universe,* Cudworth intended to show that what he was doing in the sphere of man's moral and religious concerns was analogous to what his contemporaries among the natural philosophers were doing when they sought to describe the true *physical system* of the universe. A thorough-going rationalist, Cudworth was not satisfied with a philosophy which, though it makes the corporeal world intelligible, leaves morality and religion in a state of confusion. He was alarmed by atheistic philosophers, like Thomas Hobbes, who too hastily affirmed that the physical system is all there is, but he was hardly less disturbed by theistic philosophers of nominalist turn, often abetted by religious authoritarians, who, although they continued to affirm belief in God and moral principles, contended that these exceed the powers of understanding. *The True Intellectual System* seeks to avoid both these conclusions, and, without taking anything away from the science of mechanics, to integrate the physical system into a more universal system in which the noncorporeal parts of the universe are also included.

Cudworth's confidence in the possibility of such a system depends upon the old distinction between knowledge and opinion, a distinction which had been effectively revived in the seventeenth century by Galileo and Descartes. The truth or falsity of all universal and abstract propositions, he maintains, is directly evident to man's mind. "In these intelligible ideas of the mind, whatsoever is clearly perceived to be, is; or which is all one, is true. Every clear and distinct perception is an entity or truth, as that, which is repugnant to conception is a non-entity or falsehood." Sense experience, by contrast, is a private thing, relative to the one who possesses it. It was one of the great achievements of the new physics, says Cudworth, to show that colors, tastes, and odors, which we naturally and habitually attribute to the physical world, are actually fancies and passions in us, and that the only qualities which really belong to matter are extension, magnitude, figure, position, motion, and rest. These latter qualities, being abstract and universal, are clearly and directly perceived by every rational being, and constitute "a public, catholic, and universal truth." In Cudworth's opinion, Descartes had forsaken solid ground in maintaining that our certainty with respect to self-evident truth rests on the veracity of our Maker, rather than on the necessity which the mind discovers in its ideas. He particularly complains against the thought, allowed by Descartes, that the sum of four and four might have been other than eight, if God had willed it so. These irrationalist elements were to reappear in the Christian apologetics of the Common Sense school, but Cudworth rigorously opposed them, insisting that the real is inherently rational, and that it is the prerogative of spiritual beings to apprehend the real.

It is part of Cudworth's polemic against the atheists to argue that all men naturally have the idea of one omnipotent and omniscient God, upon whose Providence the world depends. This part of his demonstration is, as he says, philological, rather than philosophical, being a kind of natural history of religion, based on Greek and Latin sources. The pagans were polytheistic, but, Cudworth maintains, this did not prevent them from having knowledge of the Supreme Numen, or universal God. The ancients believed in both minor deities and in a supreme god, and they distinguished between them; their fault consisted in making offerings to natural deities of worship which should have been reserved as offerings for the true God. In spite of numerous errors, Cudworth maintains, pagan theologians arrived at a remarkably clear apprehension of God, even approximating the idea of three eternal substances within the unity of the Divine Being. Atheism, on the other hand, nowhere represents the natural belief of men, and philosophers such as Democritus, who deny the existence of God, show thereby that they possess the idea of that which they deny.

Cudworth's favorite proof for the existence of God is the celebrated ontological argument, which holds that the idea of a perfect being includes the idea of His existence. While Cudworth rejects the argument in the form in which Descartes stated it, he accepts that modification of it best known through the writings of Leibniz. As Cudworth frames it, the proof requires two steps. Because the idea of a being whose essence includes, among all other perfections, necessary existence, is not inconceivable, it follows that such a being is at least possible. But of a necessary being, it further follows that if it is possible for it to be then it *must* be, because "if it might have been, though it be not, then would it not be a necessary existent Being." Hence, Cudworth concludes: "God is either impossible to have been, or else he is. For if God were possible, and yet be not, then is he not a necessary but a contingent Being, which is contrary to the hypothesis."

The ontological proof, says Cudworth, is as valid as any proof in geometry; nevertheless, he concedes, it may not convince the generality of men, because the capacity of the recipient must be taken into account. He therefore offers, as a further proof, the kind of argument found in Locke's *Essay on Human Understanding* (1690), which rests on the assumption that there must be as great power in a cause as there is in its effect. It is agreed, says Cudworth, between theists and atheists that "something or other did exist from all eternity, without beginning." The only question between them is whether this being is to be thought of as "a perfect Being and God, or the most imperfect of all things whatsoever, inanimate and senseless matter." To the unprejudiced mind it is perfectly evident "that lesser perfections may naturally descend from greater," but "utterly impossible, that greater perfections, and higher degrees of being, should rise and ascend out of lesser and lower." He concludes: "Wherefore it is certain, that in the universe things did not thus ascend and mount, or climb up from lower perfection to higher; but, on the contrary descend and slide down from higher to lower: so that the first original of all things was not the most imperfect, but the most perfect Being."

It is this principle, that the less perfect can only be understood in the light of the more perfect, which provides the basis for Cudworth's "intellectual system of the universe." As we have seen, he welcomed the mechanist, or, as he called it (disregarding the differences between Empedocles and Democritus, and between Descartes and Gassendi), the "atomist" theory of the corporeal world. Much better than the Aristotelian doctrine of occult qualities, the atomist theory "renders the corporeal world intelligible to us; since mechanism is a thing that we can clearly understand, and we cannot clearly and distinctly conceive any thing in bodies else." But, by making a clear distinction between mental and physical qualities, the atomists not merely enable us to form a clear idea of the material world, but also demonstrate that the material world is not intelligible in material terms alone. Since matter is nothing but "extended bulk," there must be, in addition to matter, some incorporeal substance to account for order and movement in the world, as well as for life and thought. The atomist theory, therefore, far from requiring atheism, is properly a help toward establishing theism, and this, Cudworth maintains, following the line of argument of the French Catholic Epicurean, Pierre Gassendi (1592-1655), was evident to the discoverers of the theory; namely, the Eleatic and Pythagorean philosophers. They were led to atomism, as a means of understanding the corporeal world, by the principle *ex nihilo nihil,* but they were consistent enough to see that, by the same principle, there must be something besides atoms to account for their motion and arrangement. The atheistic atomists, Democritus in ancient and Hobbes in modern times, were motivated by moral rather than by intellectual considerations. Without God, their systems are unintelligible, but their desire to escape from moral responsibility is so strong that they are content with an imperfect system.

Just as the atomist theory is compatible with belief in God, so is it compatible with human freedom; but for this to be so, says Cudworth, some amendment must be made in the Cartesian world-view. A difficulty arises from the fact that when Descartes rejected the Aristotelian doctrine of essential causes, he also rejected "all final and intending causality." It follows that, in order to account for law and order in the world, Descartes had either to leave the whole natural order of things to mechanical causation, or to fall back on the constant and immediate intervention of God Himself. But when he took the alternative of assuming a natural order, he acknowledged, in effect, that there is no purpose in nature, and that what seems purposive is merely the result of chance. This is contrary to reason, as well as destructive of freedom and morality. Hence, Descartes sometimes leaned to the other alternative, by explaining the order of the world in terms of God's immediate activity. But this alternative is no less deleterious to morality than the former, besides the fact that an assumption of God's intervention cannot explain the slow, sometimes bungling manner in which nature achieves its purpose. It is reasonable, therefore, says Cudworth, to infer that between the Divinity and the mechanical and fortuitous nature, there is an artisan nature, "subservient to deity, as the manuary opificer, and drudging executioner thereof." This world-fashioning "plastic nature," as More and Cudworth call it, is recognizably the World-Soul of Neoplatonic philosophy. It is an incorporeal substance, because endowed with life and mind, but it acts in a somnambulant fashion, without choice and discretion, and has a Higher Providence presiding over it.

The souls of men and animals, says Cudworth, are immaterial, but their life is bound up closely with matter. Descartes was wrong in identifying the soul with consciousness or thought, and, in consequence, he failed to understand the soul's role in presiding over the life of the body, not only in men but also in animals. Souls, says Cudworth, are formed by plastic nature, but they are independent agents. Although their activity does not require local motion, it is not without any spatial connection, "having not only such an essential inside, bathos, or profundity in it, wherein it acteth and thinketh within itself, but also a certain amplitude of active power ad extra, or a sphere of activity upon body." Like Lord Herbert of Cherbury (1583-1648), Cudworth describes minds as microcosms, each one recapitulating within itself the essential structure of the world. As God continually comprehends in his archetypal intellect the sum total of all that ever is or could be, so the mind of man, being a kind of "ectypal model or derivative compendium," virtually and potentially contains within itself the totality of all forms, which are unfolded and displayed "as occasion serves and outward objects invite."

In a separate essay, entitled *Concerning Eternal and Immutable Morality,* intended as part of the *magnum opus,* but first published in 1731, Cudworth develops his thesis that moral good and evil are discerned by the mind in the same way as are other essential truths. The argument is directed mainly against those who, like Hobbes, maintain that justice is based merely on convention. Cudworth seeks to show that moral qualities exist "by the necessity of their own nature," and are knowable by us through our intellectual powers. But the essay is directed also against certain philosophers and theologians who, while acknowledging that morality transcends the will of man, base it on the arbitrary will of God. Concerned always to assert the rationality and intelligibility of things, Cudworth insists that the will and power of God, although they command the existence of all created things, cannot cause things to be anything other than whatever the necessity of their natures demands. It is not by command that an act is just or unjust; all that laws do is to stipulate that an act must be performed, on pain of punishment. Cudworth's inquiry takes him to the highest reaches of metaphysics. "There is," he says, "in the scale of being a nature of goodness superior to wisdom, which therefore measures and determines the wisdom of God, as his wisdom measures and determines his will." Some innovators, he complains, have limited the idea of God, making it consist of nothing but will and power. They had better follow the wisdom of Plotinus and of the Jewish cabalists, who expressed the divine nature in the mystical representation of an infinite circle, whose inmost center is simple goodness, whose inner area is wisdom, and whose circumference is will or activity.

While Cudworth writes as a Christian, his attitude toward Biblical and ecclesiastical authority is latitudinarian. In *The True Intellectual System* there is very little reference to revealed religion, the most explicit statement being a sketch, never developed, in the outline to Chapter Four. Somewhat in the manner used by Locke in *The Reasonableness of Christianity* (1695), Cudworth suggests that because men failed to make proper use of their natural reason, and fell into superstition and idolatry, God, out of compassion, "designed himself to reform the religion of the pagan world, by introducing another religion of his own framing instead of it." There is nothing absurd, he says, in the supposition of the Divine Glory indwelling the pure soul and body of the Messiah; indeed, Christ's death and resurrection have vindicated the divine plan, since paganism has, through their means, been effectively destroyed. Moreover, Cudworth finds the Christian doctrine of the Trinity, although a mystery, better in accord with the demands of reason than the Platonist doctrine, for, whereas the latter tried to maintain that the three hypostases or persons are numerically one (*monoousios*), the Nicene Fathers maintained no more than that the three persons are essentially the same (*homoousios*). This claim left Cudworth vulnerable to the charge by orthodox churchmen that he was a Tritheist.

The True Intellectual System enjoyed considerable popularity well into the eighteenth century, mainly outside theological circles. It was translated into Latin and subjected to a learned commentary by the German scholar J. L. Mosheim, in 1733. That it is no longer extensively studied is due largely to its excessive and uncritical use of historical materials. We can still appreciate seventeenth century Christian philosophy, but not the historiography of that time.

DISCOURSES UPON THE EXISTENCE AND ATTRIBUTES OF GOD

Author: Stephen Charnock (1628-1680)
Type of work: Puritan theology
First published: 1682

PRINCIPAL IDEAS ADVANCED

The existence of God is known by all men and can be demonstrated by rational argument.

Eternity, immutability, omnipresence, omniscience, infinite wisdom, and omnipotence are incommunicable attributes of God.

These attributes, together with such moral attributes as holiness, goodness, and patience, and the prerogative of sovereign dominion over all creatures, are manifested in God's works of creation, providence, and redemption.

After ministering in Southwark for a time, Stephen Charnock became a fellow of New College, and later Senior Proctor at Oxford (1649-1656). He went to Dublin as chaplain to the Governor, and in 1675 he accepted a call to Crosby Square, where he remained as one of the ministers ejected under the Restoration.

The *Discourses upon the Existence and Attributes of God*, published posthumously, is a classic of Reformed natural theology. Charnock draws heavily on the work of Thomas Aquinas and other Scholastics, while he works within the framework of Biblical revelation. His interest is practical as well as speculative. A discourse on practical atheism follows that on the existence of God, and the discourse of God as a spirit leads to a discussion of spiritual worship. Each of the discourses (including those on the attributes of eternity, immutability, omnipresence, knowledge, wisdom, power, holiness, goodness, dominion, and patience) begins with the exposition of a text of Scripture and ends with "uses" or applications to Christian experience and practice.

After expounding the words of Psalm 14, "The fool hath said in his heart, There is no God," Charnock argues that the folly of atheism is revealed by the light of reason, as stated in Romans 1:19-20 and other passages of Scripture. The first rational argument he advances for the existence of God is that of the *consensus gentium:* There has been a universal, constant and uninterrupted, natural and innate agreement in the notion of a God and practice of religion. This consent could not be by mere tradition, nor by political contrivance, nor the effect of fear.

The second reason Charnock gives for believing in God is the cosmological proof, which Charnock considers to be not merely a probable, but a demonstrative truth. The objects and persons of the world declare the existence of a God in their production, harmony, preservation, and purposes. No creature can make itself, nor can any creature make the world. It follows that there is a first cause of things, which we call God. The harmony of the world's parts, contrary qualities linked together and one thing subservient to another, declare the being and wisdom of God.

The third reason is from the nature and constitution of man the microcosm. The whole model of the body is grounded upon reason, each member having its exact proportion, distinct office, and regular motion, while the soul is the greatest glory of this lower world, in the vastness of its capacity, the quickness of its motions, its union with the body and, above all, in the witness of conscience to the moral law and the judgment of God, together with the vastness of the desires in man and his real dissatisfaction in everything below himself.

The fourth and last reason is drawn from extraordinary occurrences in the world, including extraordinary judgments, miracles, and fulfilled prophecies.

Among the "uses" may be mentioned the pernicious consequences of atheism for nations and for individuals, including the atheist himself, the wisdom of being firmly settled in the truth of God's existence, and the folly, once the existence of God is admitted, of not worshiping Him and thinking often of Him.

The eternity of God is discussed by Charnock on the basis of Psalm 90:2. Eternity is a negative attribute, excluding beginning, end, and succession. There is no succession in the knowledge of God or in His decrees. God is His own eternity, and all His perfections are eternal. Scripture accommodates itself to human weakness in using the language of time to describe the divine eternity. God's eternity is evident in the name "I AM" (Exodus 3:14). God has life in Himself. Eternity is implied by God's immutability, infinite perfection, omnipotence, and original causality. Eternity is an incommunicable attribute, proper to God alone. Even if a creature existed from all eternity by the will of God, its eternal existence would in the nature of things be merely contingent, not necessary.

The immutability of God, expressed in Psalm 102:26-27, concerns His being and perfections. God is unchangeable in His essence. Otherwise He would not truly be, or be perfectly blessed. God's knowledge is immutable. Otherwise He would not be omniscient or a fit object of trust to any rational creature. God knows not by species, but by His own nature and by one intuitive act. Since His knowledge and will are the cause of all things, the distinction between past and future does not affect the knowledge which God has. The manner of God's knowledge is incomprehensible to a finite creature, even to one in Heaven. God is also unchangeable in will and purpose. The will of God is God willing. God's will and understanding concur in everything. There can be no reason for change in the will of God, neither lack of foresight, nor natural instability, nor want of strength. Things willed by God are not immutable as is the divine will itself.

Charnock argues also that the immutability of God's will is consistent with its liberty. God is also unchangeable as to place, because he has ubiquity. Immutability is implied by God's perfection, simplicity, eternity, infinity, and omnipotence, as well as by the order and government of the world. Furthermore, immutability is an incommunicable attribute; no creature can be unchangeable in its nature. There was no change in God when He created the world, Charnock writes, for there was no new will or power in Him, nor a new relation acquired by Him. Nor was there any change in the divine nature of Christ when He assumed human nature: "The glory of his divinity was not extinguished nor diminished, though it was obscured and darkened under the veil of our infirmities." Repentance and other affections are ascribed to God anthropomorphically, but they cannot involve any change in God. Nor does a change of laws by God imply any change in God.

God is omnipresent; that is, He is essentially everywhere present in Heaven and earth. Bodies are circumscribed in their places; angels and spirits are present at one point only at one time, while God alone fills all places, yet so as not to be contained in them. Our knowledge of God, Charnock argues, is by way of negation; omnipresence is a denial of limitation of place. There is also an influential omnipresence of God, universal with all creatures. God is essentially present in all places, with all creatures, without any mixture, without any division or multiplication of Himself, not by extension or diffusion, but totally in every part of the world as well as beyond the world. Omnipresence is also an incommunicable attribute; the human nature even of the exalted Christ is not omnipresent.

Psalm 147:5 is the text for Charnock's discourse on God's knowledge. God has an infinite knowledge and understanding. All nations acknowledge the knowledge as well as the existence of God. God has a knowledge of vision, by which he knows Himself and all real things, past, present, and future, as well as a knowledge of simple understanding, the object of which is all things possible though not willed by Him. The knowledge of things possible is only speculative in God, while the knowledge of things decreed is practical as terminating in the act of creation. There is a knowledge of approbation as well as apprehension in God. God alone knows Himself comprehensively and by His own essence. Thus, God transcends all creatures, and His understanding is truly infinite.

God knows all creatures, Charnock argues, all their actions and thoughts, as well as all their evils and sins. He knows all future things. What is now past was once future. God has predicted future events; God knows His own will and therefore must know all the future. If He did not know all future things, He would be mutable in His knowledge. God foreknows all creatures, certainly and eternally, incommunicably and incomprehensibly. God knows all future contingencies, all chance events and free choices. What is accidental with respect to the creature is not so for God. If God did not foreknow the free choices of men, he could not govern the world. He foreknows free acts, whether good, indifferent, or sinful. But God's foreknowledge does not deprive the human will of freedom. No man is compelled in any of his voluntary actions. God's foreknowledge does not add to the sequence of human actions, but only beholds them as present, as arising from their proper causes. God foreknows events because they will come to pass; but events are not made to be future by God's knowledge of them. God foreknows not only our actions, but also the manner of those actions as free. God's foreknowledge and human freedom are alike certain, even though the human understanding cannot fully reconcile them.

The mode of God's knowledge is incomprehensible to us. He knows by His own essence, by one act of intuition, not discursively or successively as we do. He knows all things independently, distinctly, infallibly, immutably, and perpetually; that is, in act.

The wisdom of God is distinct from knowledge. Wisdom consists in acting for a right end, in observing all circumstances for action, in willing and acting according to a right judgment of things. Knowledge has its seat in the speculative understanding, wisdom in the practical.

Charnock describes the Son of God as the essential and personal wisdom of God. The wisdom of God is identical with the divine essence. Wisdom is the property of God alone, as Pythagoras admitted in preferring to be called a lover of wisdom rather than wise. God alone is wise necessarily, originally, perfectly, universally, perpetually, incomprehensibly, and infallibly. The wisdom of God is taught by Scripture and is abundantly evident in the government of the world. As the fountain of all wisdom in the creatures, God is Himself infinitely wise.

Charnock's discourse on the power of God follows an exposition of the twenty-sixth chapter of Job. The power of God is not to be understood in terms of His authority and dominion, but by reference to His strength to act. Absolute power is that by which God is able to do all things possible; ordinate power is that by which He does what He has ordained to do. Absolute power does not respect things repugnant to the nature of God. God's ordinate power is free and belongs to His will. "The power of God," Charnock writes, "is that ability or strength whereby he can bring to pass whatsoever he please, whatsoever his infinite wisdom can direct, and whatsoever the infinite purity of his will can resolve."

With Aquinas, Charnock would rather say that some things are impossible than say that God cannot do them. Some things are impossible by their own nature; for example, contradictions. Some are impossible because of the nature of God or His glorious perfections. Thus, it is impossible for God to be ignorant or lie. Other things are impossible as a consequence of the determined will of God. Reasons advanced by Charnock for accepting the doctrine of divine omnipotence are: (1) the power that is in creatures, (2) the infinite perfection of God, (3) the simplicity of God, and (4) the miracles that have been in the world. The power of God appears in creation, government and, most admirably, in redemption.

The moral character of God is examined in Charnock's remaining discourses on the attributes of holiness, goodness, dominion, and patience. The same method of exposition exemplified in the preceding discourses on the incommunicable attributes is followed. The discourse on the dominion of God stresses the prerogative of sovereignty. Sovereignty or dominion is not bare power, Charnock asserts, but the "right of making what he pleases, of possessing what he made, of disposing of what he doth possess." The notion of sovereignty is inseparable from the notion of a God. This dominion is independent and absolute, yet not tyrannical, and managed by the rules of wisdom, righteousness, and goodness. Divine sovereignty extends over all creatures and is eternal in its foundation and duration, though exercised only from the creation. The first act of sovereignty is making laws, which is essential to God. As proprietor and lord of His creatures, God manifests His dominion in choosing some persons for eternal life and in bestowing grace where He pleases, disposing the means of grace to some, not to all. The dominion of God is manifested further in His government of men and nations and, finally, in the work of redemption in Christ.

Charnock concludes the discourse on God's dominion with an exhortation to humility, praise and thankfulness, promotion of the honor of this sovereign, fear and reverence, prayer and trust, obedience and patience. The discourses on the attributes are appropriately followed by one on the divine providence. Consideration of these sublime and profound themes may elicit the expression of admiration and adoration in the words of Romans 11:33, "O the depth of the riches both of the wisdom and knowledge of God! How unsearchable are his judgments, and his ways past finding out!"

THE PRACTICE OF THE PRESENCE OF GOD

Author: Brother Lawrence (Nicholas Herman, c.1605-1691)
Type of work: Devotional manual
First published: 1692, 1694 (Present collection, 1703)

Principal Ideas Advanced

Instead of approaching God in the way prescribed in books, it is sufficient to place oneself directly in God's presence and surrender all one's acts to His direction.

God can be served as well in the kitchen or on the battlefield as in the Church while receiving the Sacrament.

The service of God is primarily an affair of the will and not of the understanding.

God is to be served for His own sake only, and not for the benefits which His service brings.

The Practice of the Presence of God is a memoir on the life and thought of a lay monk known as Brother Lawrence (Nicolas Herman). The book has lately enjoyed great popularity with Protestants. Brother Lawrence wrote but little and destroyed most of what he wrote because it seemed inadequate. But Abbé Joseph de Beaufort, the superior of the Parisian monastery where Lawrence lived, gathered up a few letters and some fragments of meditations, and he supplemented these with notes from conversations and with his own recollections, to present the picture of a truly unforgettable character.

In his youth, Brother Lawrence had been a soldier; then, after being wounded in battle, he became a gentleman's valet. In the monastery he served for fifteen years in the kitchen until, because of his lameness, he was put to work as a cobbler. What makes his manual one of the most highly esteemed devotional works is the true simplicity of its authority.

When he was asked in his old age by what method he had arrived at his constant sense of God's nearness to him, Lawrence usually said that his method was to throw away all methods. "Having found in several books different methods for going to God and various practices of the spiritual life, I thought that this would serve rather to trouble my soul than to make easy for me what I aspired to and sought after, which was nothing else than a means of belonging wholly to God. This made me resolve to give all for all." Chiefly, Lawrence emphasized the necessity of simply believing that God is present in all His creatures, that He is wise, merciful, and all-sufficient. When he first began his practice, he used to arrange his work so that he had time to pray between duties. Then he accustomed himself to speak to God while he was working. In the end, he ceased to observe separate times of prayer, except those enforced on him by the discipline of the community. "It was a great mistake," he said, "to believe that the time of prayer should be different from the other, for we are as much obligated to be united to God by action, at the time of action, as by prayer in its time."

Lawrence admits that, at first, he had difficulty in setting aside distracting thoughts and fixing his mind on God. But in time, the practice of talking with God became habitual, and the sense of God's presence rarely left him. "I possess God as tranquilly in the bustle of my kitchen—where sometimes several people are asking me different things at one time—as if I were on my knees before the Blessed Sacrament. My faith sometimes even becomes so enlightened that I think I have lost it; it seems to me that the curtain of obscurity is drawn, that the endless, cloudless day of the other life is beginning to dawn."

One of the most popular passages in the book is that in which Lawrence tells how he relies on God to help him when he has a particularly difficult or unpleasant chore to perform. One must, he says, speak to God very frankly, saying, "My God, I would not be able to do that, if Thou didst not help me." Then God gives him strength. Trips outside the monastery to purchase supplies were a chore; he felt he had no head for business; furthermore, he was lame. But "he simply told God that it was his affair, after which he found that everything turned out nicely." Although he had an aversion for kitchen work, he gained considerable skill during the fifteen years that he was occupied there. He said, "I turn my little omelette in the pan for the love of God; when it is finished, if I have nothing to do, I prostrate myself on the ground and adore my God, Who gave me the grace to make it, after which I arise, more content than a king. When I cannot do anything else, it is enough for me to have lifted a straw from the earth for the love of God."

Brother Lawrence's first sense of God's goodness and love came to him when he was eighteen. One winter day, while he was looking at a tree stripped of its leaves and thinking that in the spring it would have flowers and foliage, "he received a profound impression of the providence and power of God, which was never effaced from his soul." For many years however, he did suffer from a sense of his sinfulness and from fear lest he should be rejected by God. All of a sudden, a change took place: "My soul, which until then was always troubled, felt a profound interior peace, as if it were in its center and place of repose." After that time, his fears never returned. He merely placed his sins before God and trusted for mercy. Sometimes it seemed to him that God took him by the hand and paraded with him before the heavenly court, "to show off the miserable one whom it pleased Him to honor."

Lawrence drew a sharp distinction between the understanding and the will, discounting the former. "In the way of God," he said, "thoughts count for little, love does everything." He disparaged the practice of meditating on great subjects, such as sin and death, Heaven and Hell, and he recommended instead that men concentrate on "doing little things for the love of God." Thoughts, he said, spoil everything; that is where evil begins. His advice was to reject every thought that enters the mind insofar as it is not relevant to the task one has in hand. Even so, one ought not let his mind run ahead of what he is doing. When the time comes for action, one sees in God "as in a clear mirror" all that is necessary to do for the present.

In the ordinary round of duty, Lawrence paid no attention to what his hands were doing, nor could he afterwards remember what he had done, his mind being entirely fixed on God, thanking Him and "making an infinity of other acts." On those occasions when his occupation diverted him from thinking of God, "there came to him some remembrance which took possession of his soul, giving him some most engrossing idea of God." At such times, he was frequently so exalted that he was moved to dance and sing for joy. Losing himself in God, he achieved a remarkable indifference to things affecting his own welfare. His superior says that no jealousies, fears, or disappointments seemed to touch him; yet it was not as if he were withdrawn from what transpired around him. He took an interest in the welfare of all in the monastery and was charitable toward the unfortunate who came to the gate seeking alms. He possessed "great common sense," and, although he was not fond of declaring his thoughts, when obliged by his superiors to declare his thoughts on some question, "his answers were so clear and to the point that they needed no comment." Eventually, his reputation extended outside the monastery, and people turned to him as a spiritual director.

It is important to recall that Brother Lawrence lived at the time during which quietism was making its appearance among French Catholics, and that the monastery in which he lived belongs to the "discalced" (barefoot) branch of the Carmelite order, which owed its foundation to the sixteenth century Spanish mystics, St. Teresa (1515-1582) and St. John of the Cross (1542-1591), who gave quietism its initial impulse. How far Brother Lawrence himself was influenced by the movement is uncertain; but the Abbé, in holding him up as an exemplar, was clearly supporting the cause that sent Mme. Guyon (1648-1717) to the Bastille. Like the quietists, Brother Lawrence sought to love God without any consideration of his own advantage. Says Abbé de Beaufort, "Far from loving God in return for His benefits, he had so disinterested a charity that he would have loved God even though there had been no punishment to avoid nor any reward to attain, and desiring only the good and glory of God and forming his Heaven of the accomplishment of his holy Will." The surges of joy which Lawrence experienced were not ungratefully received; still, he warned against the danger of cherishing the gift for its own sake and neglecting to raise one's thoughts to the Giver. In his opinion, raptures and ecstasies are found only in devotees who fall into that error.

Students of world-religions may find in the way of Brother Lawrence an analogy to the "yoga of selfless action" represented in the *Bhagavad Gita.* Like Krishna in that work, Lawrence is able to advise a soldier that, far from destroying the courage of men at arms, the presence of God fortifies them even on the most dangerous occasions: "A brief remembrance of God, an interior act of adoration, even while one may be running with sword in hand, are prayers which, however short they are, are nevertheless pleasing to God."

THE JOURNAL OF GEORGE FOX

Author: George Fox (1624-1691)
Type of work: Spiritual autobiography
First published: 1694

Principal Ideas Advanced

The power of the Lord is over all His works, and manifests itself in the affairs of men.

In the experience of one of His servants, therefore, we see how this power operates: how it leads him in his quest, satisfies him with a growing understanding of the truth, and sustains him in all trials and adversities.

The Lord, who "had a great people to be gathered," drew them together into the Society of Friends.

The Journal of George Fox is one of the most remarkable religious works in the English language. For its directness, simplicity, vividness, and spiritual power it has few equals. And yet it is a book which it is not easy to classify. Strictly speaking it is not a journal at all, since it does not profess to be a day-by-day account of a man's experience. It is a fragment of autobiography, composed in mid-career, and never completed. Fox was a prolific author, but he preferred to use an amanuensis rather than to write himself. About 1675 he dictated to his son-in-law, Thomas Lower, an account of his life till that date. What approximates most closely to a journal is the section describing his travels in the West Indies and on the American continent. After Fox's death, the task of editing his autobiographical remains was committed to Thomas Ellwood, and it was in Ellwood's edition that the world knew this work until early in the twentieth century. Ellwood took his task seriously, perhaps too seriously. He tamed somewhat the vigor of Fox's unconventional style. At appropriate points he inserted letters or manifestoes which Fox had written, and he provided a narrative to carry the story beyond the point at which Fox's own account ceased. He also secured from William Penn a prefatory tribute to Fox, and this remains one of our most illuminating pictures of this remarkable man.

Fox briefly indicates his relatively humble origin, and he describes his earnest attitude as a child. His relatives thought such seriousness must be the mark of a future minister, but his father apprenticed him to a shoe maker. When he was about nineteen, he passed through an intense and prolonged spiritual crisis. The suggestion that he join his companions at the public house in drinking healths aroused scruples in his mind, and he withdrew—immediately from the company of his associates, gradually from that of his friends and relations. For some time he traveled "up and down as a stranger in the earth, which way the Lord inclined my heart," and he attributes his wanderings to the fact that he was "afraid both of professor and profane, lest, being a tender young man," he should be injured by associating with either.

Gradually the pattern of Fox's mature convictions began to take shape. He says that the true believers were those who had been born of God and had passed from death unto life; he realized that to go to Oxford or Cambridge was in itself no sufficient preparation for the ministry. He discovered that in Christ there was an answer to his doubts and temptations, and that the secret of spiritual victory lay in Christ's presence and power. "Christ, who had enlightened me, gave me his light to believe in," Fox writes; "he gave me hope, which he himself revealed in me; and he gave me his spirit and grace, which I found sufficient in the deeps and in weakness."

Fox's new insight made him impatient of the old ways, and his convictions combined with his nature to make him uncompromising in denouncing them. So began the long series of interruptions of public worship, rebukes to blind preachers, challenges to existing patterns both in church order and social convention. His methods awakened resentment; this often showed itself in violent forms. The upshot of disturbing one church service was a rush of angry parishioners, who swept him into the church yard and severely beat him. In describing such episodes Fox is amazingly detailed and circumstantial. As the blows rained about his head, he noted the expressions on the faces of his assailants and the precise inflections of the words they used.

The vividness with which many of these incidents are recounted carries us back into the midst of seventeenth century life. Nowhere else do we get so photographic, yet so living a picture of the words and actions of those who make up that elusive body, the populace of a bygone age. In the midst of this vibrant setting we have this strangely vital man. It is easy to sympathize with his antagonists. Often Fox seems deliberately, even wantonly, provocative. He seems to assert a doctrinaire witness in a particularly offensive manner. He seems to provoke the violence in submitting to which he finds his superior virtue vindicated. To concede this is merely to admit that not all readers find Fox a consistently attractive figure. The rebukes which he administered to others might indicate unyielding honesty, but they give the impression of self-consciously superior virtue. The letters which he wrote from prison were not calculated to conciliate the officers of the law, and when face to face with his critics Fox was no less blunt in denouncing the shortcomings of others and insisting on his own rectitude.

But even those who disliked him were compelled to admire his courage and his integrity. He feared the face of no man. When driven from a town by brutal mobs he often returned at once, ready to face again the worst that they could do. A threatening group hemming him round or a man with a drawn sword caused him no dismay. This courage was unquestionably one element in the strange ascendency which he established over others. Violent crowds became quiet, hostile men "became loving," and Fox could pass on to continue among others this revolutionary work which he was everywhere initiating.

Related to Fox's courage was his integrity. People recognized his sincerity and responded to it. After his imprisonment in Scarborough Castle, the soldiers bore generous tribute to his quality. "He is as stiff as a tree and as pure as a bell, for we could never stir him." It was sincerity, reinforced by unfailing courage, which compelled others to give heed to his witness. But it was not simply the testimony of a brave and honest man which gained their reluctant admiration. The story of Fox's life bears constant witness to his ability to win the loyalty and adhesion of men and women of education and social prominence. Margaret Fell (later his wife), Thomas Ellwood, Isaac Penington, and William Penn all testify to his capacity to touch people of the upper as well as the lower strata of society. The explanation lies in the amazing spiritual vitality to which *The Journal* bears witness. "The power of the Lord" is a phrase constantly on

Fox's lips. To this he always attributed the hold he established over groups and individuals. "And the truth of the Lord came over him so that he grew loving." The vigor of a rugged personality might explain the way he sometimes overbore opposition; it cannot account for the degree to which he won over those whom he silenced.

Though Fox frequently conciliated his antagonists, the victory was often slow in coming, and in the meantime he had abundant experience of the suffering which religious nonconformity could cause. The narrative is punctuated with accounts of trials and imprisonments. We see how hard it was, in the face of strong prejudice, to secure even the rights which the law guaranteed to a prisoner. Fox always insisted on what he regarded as his due rights; he did not hesitate to argue with his judges, to call them to task, or to denounce them. Such conduct increased the likelihood that he would be committed to prison, and so we have detailed descriptions of the interiors of a large number of seventeenth century jails. We see the ordinary discomforts to which prisoners were usually condemned: cold in winter, heat in summer, insanitary conditions, vexations from the jailer and from fellow inmates, as well as the problems of securing food and drink in the casually organized prisons of the day. Sometimes Fox found himself consigned to a dungeon; in Doomsdale in Launceston he stood in excrement over his boot tops and was almost always stifled by the stench. Accounts of such hardships are an inseparable part of almost all early Quaker journals; the comments explain why mortality was so high among prisoners and why the Friends made such persistent efforts to secure the release of their companions. As a picture of judicial methods and penal conditions in the seventeenth century, the *Journal* is both a historical source of great importance and a human document of intensely moving interest.

As the *Journal* progresses we witness the emergence of the Society of Friends. Fox was an organizer of some capacity, and he provided the Quakers with a structure which saved them from the fate which most of the small sects of the seventeenth century suffered. This, in its full development, lies beyond the period with which the *Journal* deals. But we can also observe something of greater interest than the fashioning of an institutional structure; we can trace the development of the distinctive witness of the Society of Friends. Perhaps most important of all is the insistence on the inwardness and vitality of religion. This explains the protest against forms, ceremonies, observances, and sacred buildings. But this was the negative aspect of an important positive truth. It is not enough to quote Christ and His Apostles; the decisive question is, "What canst thou say?" Men must learn to listen to the Spirit of Christ speaking in their hearts. If we would only pause to hear Christ's voice, we could live in the power of His endless life, we are told. The "inner light" is another way of expressing the same truth. It is important to notice that this inward and personal illumination of the believer was, for Fox, related in the most intimate way with the figure of Jesus of Nazareth. This association gave concreteness and character to his interpretation of the Spirit.

Less vital but more immediately observable were certain other aspects of

Quaker belief. The pattern of silent worship begins to emerge, though Fox was on occasion a vehement preacher and was much given to forceful and vocal prayer. The *Journal* abounds in incidents which illustrate Fox's refusal to remove his hat when customary social usage demanded this gesture; indeed, the problem of "hat honor" figures prominently in the accounts of the legal proceedings in which Fox was so frequently involved. So, too, does his refusal to swear. Since taking an oath had an important preliminary role in a prisoner's testimony, it was always possible, if other methods failed, to sentence Fox to prison for contempt of court. "Plain speech" also had legal as well as social implications. Fox believed that the distinction between "thou" and "you" in personal address rested on hypocritical obsequiousness, and that evangelical simplicity required us to address all alike as "thou." But when applied to magistrates and judges, this had disconcerting results.

In Fox's *Journal* the repudiation of violence is clearly present. When a fellow prisoner at Scarborough threatened to fight him, Fox walked up to him with his hands in his pockets, and pointed out "what a shame it was for him to challenge a man whose principle he knew was not to strike." In London, when a rough soldier threatened to kill all Quakers, Fox went to him and offered to submit to his violence, "and the truth came so over him that he grew loving."

What principally emerges from the *Journal* is a vivid picture of a remarkable man. The book is noteworthy for its originality, sincerity, and power because these are precisely the qualities which mark the man himself. The graphic directness of the work shows us the age and its people, but above all the *Journal* makes us aware of Fox. He was, as William Penn said, "an original, being no man's copy." Penn's preface forms an excellent epitome, since it is the tribute of one great religious leader to another. Fox, Penn tells us, "was a man that God endued with a clear and wonderful depth, a discerner of others' spirits, and very much a master of his own." So he was able to open the truth to others, and bring them under its constraint. His "exemplary sobriety, humility, gravity, punctuality, charity and circumspect care in the government of church affairs" made those whom he gathered about him a society able to maintain itself in the world and to bear an increasingly effective witness. "Never heed," said Fox on the eve of his death; "the Lord's power is over all weakness and death; the Seed reigns, blessed be the Lord." This admirably epitomized the testimony of his life. It explains the abiding influence of his most remarkable book, the *Journal*. And it justifies the "short epitaph" with which Penn closes his tribute: "Many sons have done virtuously in this day, but dear George Fox thou excellest them all."

THE REASONABLENESS OF CHRISTIANITY

Author: John Locke (1632-1704)
Type of work: Philosophical theology
First published: 1695

Principal Ideas Advanced

Although theological systems are often unreasonable, there is nothing unreasonable in Christianity as taught in Scripture.

Adam's sin deprived all men of eternal life, but this was restored to all men through Christ.

Through the covenant of grace, God has offered to forgive any man's sins on condition that he believe in Christ.

The universal failure of mankind to profit from natural reason and natural religion in matters of correct belief and conduct, and the comparative improvement which Christianity brings in this respect, suggest that Christianity is indeed a divine revelation.

In his *An Essay Concerning Human Understanding* (1690), John Locke distinguishes between what we can know, and what we merely judge, believe, or opine. In the strict sense, we can know only that which is intuitively evident, or that which is logically demonstrable from evident truths. All else is belief, no matter how high the probability in its favor. Our knowledge of any event in the external world is never more than a highly probable belief. Such beliefs are called *reasonable,* not in the sense of being logically demonstrable, but in the sense that they are not logically contradictory, and that probable reasons can be adduced which persuade us to give them our assent. The same principle, according to Locke, applies to the claims of revealed religion. In *The Reasonableness of Christianity* Locke does not attempt to demonstrate that the claims of Christianity are evident to reason, but that there is nothing incredible or improbable in them, and that they can be supported by good arguments.

Theologians have done their cause more harm than good, says Locke, by refusing to let the words of Scripture speak in a plain sense. The story that the Bible tells is simple, intelligible, and quite in harmony with reason. Consider, to begin with, the account of Adam's disobedience and Fall. The Scriptures say quite plainly that what befell Adam and his posterity was the loss of immortality and blessedness. This account is reasonable. Adam had no claim on eternal life, nor did his descendants, nor does the Bible say that death, which is natural to all finite creatures, is the punishment for sin; nothing at all is said about eternal damnation, which the theologians read into the word "death," but only that Adam and his posterity should cease to enjoy the benefits of life. One may reasonably complain about the justice of the doctrine, alleged by the theologians, that God punishes Adam's posterity for a fault that was Adam's alone, but there is no reason to complain about what Scripture teaches. Furthermore, Scripture teaches that just as in Adam all die, so in Christ shall all be made alive. Thus, through Christ, God freely bestows on all men that immortality which Adam lost for us, which is another way of saying that Christ nullifies the effects of Adam's indiscretion; Christ acts for all men, believers and unbelievers alike, and places every man that comes into the world in the same independent position in which Adam stood, with the difference that, if a man sins, he cannot lose his immortality, but must endure the consequences of his sin throughout eternity.

Locke borrows, with some modification, the Puritan concepts of the alternative covenants of works and of grace. By the covenant of works, a covenant which God made with mankind, every man has the option of undertaking to fulfill the righteousness of the eternal moral law, to be rewarded if he succeeds, but to be punished if he fails. But because God knew that few could expect to enter the Kingdom of glory on such terms, He devised a covenant of grace, according to which a man need only assent to the proposition that Jesus is the divinely appointed Messiah and undertake to live the best life of which he is capable, in order to enjoy the full benefits of divine favor.

Such, according to Locke, is the beautiful clarity of the Scriptural teaching. Numerous passages from the words of Christ and of the Apostles show the necessity of believing that Jesus is the Messiah. His miracles and the manner in which He fulfills the Old Testament prophecies, together with the holiness of His life and the purity of His doctrine, combine to bring to men's hearts the conviction that this one was indeed the Son of God. But the Scriptures are equally forceful on the other point; namely, that no one shall be numbered among the blessed with Christ who has not also repented of his wickedness and made an effort to live a good life. He need not be perfect, as the covenant of works requires, but he must have made a sincere attempt. For, according to Locke, nothing could be more unreasonable than that God, being just, should receive men into His favor without requiring that they amend their lives.

The question arises, what judgment awaits those who, through no fault of their own, have never learned of the covenant of grace? Locke points out that we do not know what God's wisdom affords to these persons. To men of Israel, before Christ's time, the way of grace was opened in terms of the Promise, which they were asked to believe, and the Mosaic law. Why not suppose that to every nation and clime God has proved Himself equally gracious, and opened conditions well within every man's capacity, which, if he conforms to them, will open to him a blessed eternity? Part of God's eternal law is that a man should forgive not merely his friends but his enemies if they repent and show amendment. Would not God, therefore, as the Author of this law, and as One who is merciful, "forgive his frail offspring, if they acknowledged their faults, disapproved the iniquity of their transgressions, begged his pardon, and resolved in earnest for the future to conform their action to this rule, which they owned to be just and right?" The hope of reconciliation and atonement is, Locke believed, part of "the light of nature," the "candle of the Lord," the "spark of the divine nature and knowledge in man," and is certainly not excluded by anything in the Gospel.

But if God's mercy is thus widely extended, what reason is there to believe that God sent His Son into the world, and that He made it a requirement of salvation that men believe in Him? Locke attempts to show that Christianity has proved its worth in practical terms, thus vindicating those who claim that Christianity is the work of God. Generally speaking, Locke's argument is that, outside the pale of Christianity, natural religion and natural reason have failed. Locke, it will be remembered, maintained (in *An Essay Concerning Human Understanding*) that the existence of God, as the Author and Legislator of our world, is demonstrable to reason in the strict sense. So, he maintained, are the principles of morals. These have a certainty of the highest order for those persons who are capable of following a rational demonstration. But nowhere has philosophy succeeded in impressing these truths effectively on the lives of men in the way that the preaching of Christ has done.

The power of the Gospel, Locke maintains, stems almost exclusively from the impression which Jesus' holy and miraculous person makes upon those who hear the Gospel story; for the masses of mankind, this is as it must be. "The greatest part cannot know, and therefore they must believe. And I ask, whether one coming from heaven in the power of God, in full and clear evidence and demonstration of miracles, giving plain and direct rules of morality and obedience, be not likelier to enlighten the bulk of mankind, and set them right in their duties, and bring them to do them, than by reasoning with them from general notions and principles of human reason?" Nor is this way of teaching suited only to the humbler sort. "The most elevated understandings cannot but submit to the authority of this doctrine as divine; which coming from the mouths of a company of illiterate men, hath not only the attestation of miracles, but reason to confirm it, since they delivered no precepts, but such, as though reason of itself had not clearly made out, yet it could not but assent to when thus discovered, and think itself indebted for the discovery." Locke warns us against the kind of arrogance which might lead educated persons to overlook their own debt to Christianity and suppose that by their reasons alone they could have arrived at the rational systems of belief that they now entertain. They are, he says, like one traveling along a highway who applauds the strength of his legs for the rapid progress which he is able to make, little thinking how much he owes to those who drained the swamps, bridged the streams, and cleared the woods, in order to build the road which he walks on.

As we have seen, Locke does not deny the idea of the miracle. In fact, he accepts, as part of the story of Christ, His birth of a virgin, and His resurrection from the grave. He does, however, give little time to the systems of the theologians, paying no respect at all to their theories of the Trinity, the Incarnation, and the atonement. By limiting his account of Christianity to simple belief in and obedience to Christ, he is able to maintain a link between faith and reason, not merely for the vulgar, but for the learned as well.

CHRISTIANITY NOT MYSTERIOUS

Author: John Toland (1670-1722)
Type of work: Deistic theology
First published: 1696

Principal Ideas Advanced

There is nothing mysterious or incomprehensible in Christianity.
True religion must be reasonable and intelligible.
Reason is the judge of what is regarded as revelation.
No event can be called miraculous which is contrary to reason.
Though the clergy may seek to hide the message of Christianity behind the veil of revelation, man can penetrate to the inherently reasonable nature of the New Testament.

John Toland's *Christianity Not Mysterious: or, A Treatise Shewing that there is nothing in the Gospel Contrary to Reason, Nor Above it: And that no Christian Doctrine can be properly call'd a Mystery,* first published in 1696, marked the beginning of the deistic controversy. Though the essay was condemned by many within the Church and was ordered to be burned by the parliament of Ireland, it is not noted for the strength of its message, its style, or the reputation of its author.

The context in which the book appeared accounts in large part for the furor caused by its publication. A decade earlier the Act of Toleration (1689) had been issued by William and Mary; this Act, which offered toleration to the dissenters within the Church of England, enlarged the bounds of permissible theological discussion. The deist movement began at this time, though many of its major ideas were anticipated by the earlier Cambridge Platonists and Latitudinarians. The deists were concerned with a reasoned and reasonable Christianity, stripped of doctrinal accretions, devoid of reliance on miracles and supernatural intervention in natural events, and freed of the weight of institutional and clerical control. Though it was not as extreme as subsequent expressions of deistic thought, *Christianity Not Mysterious* served as an opening wedge for later deistic writings. The major intent of Toland's essay, an intent which, in turn, reflected the dominant interest of eighteenth century English deism, was to examine the relation of the content of Christian faith to the form in which it is expressed.

Toland had three main aims in view: to show (1) that true religion "must necessarily be reasonable and intelligible", (2) "that these requisite Conditions are found in Christianity . . ." and, (3) "that the Christian Religion . . . was divinely revealed from Heaven."

Behind the work of Toland and his successors stood the commanding figure of John Locke (1632-1704). Though Toland did not make any direct reference to this British philosopher, the relation between them was clear. Locke's *The Reasonableness of Christianity* (1695) touched on the interests of the later deistic movement; namely, the simplicity of Christianity, the stress upon the ethical assertions of the Gospels, the nondogmatic character of Christian faith, and its inherently reasonable nature. Locke's *Essay Concerning Human Understanding* (1690) proved to be more influential on deism than did his excursion into theology. Locke defined reason as natural revelation; we can call nothing revelation which is in conflict with reason. Knowledge involves a relation, agreement or disagreement, between ideas. That which is "mysterious" or incomprehensible is by definition beyond all understanding and, therefore, is as foreign to faith as to knowledge.

It was a reasonable, nonmysterious Christianity which Toland sought to promulgate. He wrote that since "*Reason* is the only Foundation of all Certitude," reason is to be used as a judge of revelation. "Again, since nothing reveal'd, whether as to its *Manner* or *Existence,* is more exempted from its [reason's] Disquisitions, than the ordinary Phenomena of Nature, . . . we . . . maintain . . . that *there is nothing in the Gospel contrary to Reason, nor above it; and that no Christian Doctrine can be properly call'd a Mystery.*" God does not demand that man believe what is improbable; probability is not knowledge and, Toland wrote, ". . . I banish all *Hypotheses* from my *Philosophy. . . .*" Toland and other deist writers viewed reason as a separate and, if properly used, infallible faculty of the human mind. This insistence on reason as the sole judge of truth was characteristic of English religious thought in the first half of the eighteenth century.

The role of revelation was thus circumscribed by this view of reason. Revelation served as a "means of information," though what is revealed must not conflict with reason and possibility. God could not disclose that which was unintelligible or impossible. Toland's intent was not to disparage revelation, as did later deist writers, but to recast the significance of revelation and to provide the ground for the transfer of the function of revelation to that of reason. Reason is, therefore, of more importance than revelation in the same way in which "a *Greek Grammar* is superior to the *New Testament. . . .*"

A prime cause of his thorough attack on traditional methodology stemmed from his notable distrust of the organized Church and its clergy. Throughout history, he wrote, the clergy has been unwilling to unravel the doctrines of Christianity; instead, they have made "the most trifling things in the World *mysterious,* that we might constantly depend upon them for the Explication." The result has been obscurantism. Those who held to the dictum of Tertullian (c.160-c.220), "I believe because it is absurd," were scathingly attacked by Toland. He wrote that "many affirm, that tho the Doctrines of the latter [Gospel] cannot in themselves be contradictory to the Principles of the former [Reason], as proceeding both from God; yet, that according to our Conceptions of them, *they may seem directly to clash:* And that tho we cannot reconcile them by reason of our corrupt and limited Understandings; yet that from the Authority of *Divine Revelation,* we are bound to believe and acquiesce in them; or, as the *Fathers* taught 'em to speak, *to adore what we cannot comprehend."* In Toland's judgment, this "refuge" protected the mysteries but caused such confusion that it was no longer possible to determine what is essential to the Gospel. If, Toland claims, we affirm that the Christian believes on the ground of revelation and not of reason, then "I know not what we can deny that is told us in the Name of the Lord." There is no reason to hide behind the cloak of revelation when examination would show that there is nothing in the New Testament that is contrary to or above reason. The fact is, Toland insisted, *"no Christian Doctrine can be properly call'd a Mystery."*

The accompanying change in attitude toward the authority of Scripture became explicit in *Christianity Not Mysterious.* Though Toland assumed the centrality of the New Testament writings for Christianity, he insisted that evidence of its "divine" character depended on reason. There is no "different Rule to be follow'd in the Interpretation of *Scripture* from what is common to all other Books." He continually appealed to the meaning behind the New Testament words, though his statement of the intent of the New Testament writers reflects all too frequently the perspective of the eighteenth century English enlightened man. The validity of the miracles recorded in Scripture received his attention and, here again, he insisted that a miracle must be inherently intelligible and possible; no event can be called miraculous which is contrary to reason. "The *miraculous* Action therefore must be some thing in itself intelligible and possible, tho the manner of doing it be extraordinary."

Thus, there is nothing in Christianity which is fundamentally mysterious or unknowable. In those New Testament passages which refer to the "mystery" of the Gospel, the term mystery is used to mean *"things naturally very intelligible, but so cover'd by figurative Words or Rites, that Reason could not discover them without special Revelation. . . ."* But what is unclear to the Jews and the pagans has now been made clear; the "Vail is actually taken away . . ." and "the Doctrines so reveal'd cannot now be properly call'd *Mysteries."* There is nothing inconceivable in the New Testament. All ideas must exist in our consciousness; that which is inconceivable could not be. When Christ spoke in parable what He said was not incomprehensible, but it appeared mysterious only for those for whom the truth was not unfolded. Faith does not imply assent to that which is above reason.

Toland could not subscribe to the thesis that because of sin man's reasoning power was corrupted. This position is essential to the theology of John Calvin, who argued that though man was originally able to determine the nature, will, and providential concern of God by means of his insight into the created world and by use of his God-given capacities, this endowment had been lost in the Fall. This view Toland could not accept. *"For, not willing to own their Ignorance and Miscarriages (which proceed from Passion, Sloth, or Inconsideration) they would remove all the Blame from their Will, and charge it upon a natural Impotency not in their Power to cure.*" According to this view, Toland argued, man has become no more than an animal or machine, or at best, one who seeks to escape the responsibilities of using his reason. In contrast, the center of man's potential lies in his capacity to fathom the nature and will of God and in his freedom to exercise this ability. "But 'tis the Perfection of our Reason and Liberty that makes us deserve Rewards and Punishments. We are persuaded that *all our thoughts* are entirely free, we can expend the Force of Words, compare Ideas, distinguish clear from obscure Conceptions, suspend our Judgments about Uncertainties, and yield only to Evidence."

The deist movement had little lasting effect, though it did serve to open the questions of the authority of the Scriptures and the relation of natural and revealed theology. It is striking how little interest Toland and other deists had in the person of Jesus of Nazareth. Their interest was primarily in an intellectual defense of Christianity, though the product they defended had little relevance for the man in the pew. The amazing lack of historical perspective shared by most of the deists meant that their interpretation of Christianity reflected much more the concerns and interests of eighteenth century England than it did the intent of the New Testament writers themselves. Their critique of traditional theological affirmations, however, served to shape a new Christian perspective which has had significant consequences.

MAGNALIA CHRISTI AMERICANA

Author: Cotton Mather (1663-1728)
Type of work: Ecclesiastical history
First published: 1702

Principal Ideas Advanced

The rising generation of New England is in danger of neglecting its heritage and needs to be brought back to the principles and practices of its founders.

New England owes its foundation to divine favor, but Satan has manifestly worked for its destruction.

The memory of New England's great men should be held up for imitation; the doctrines and regulations of her synods should be taught and defended; supernatural influences, both divine and Satanic, should not be ignored.

Cotton Mather's *Magnalia Christi Americana,* subtitled "The Ecclesiastical History of New England from its first Planting, in the year 1620, unto the year of our Lord 1698," is not a consecutive narrative, but a collection of essays, memorials, and addresses intended to call a wayward generation back to the principles and practices upon which the colony was founded. In the opinion of this third-generation New Englander, whose forebearers on both sides were prominent Puritan ministers, God's eye had selected the location and His hand had prospered the building of this wilderness Jerusalem. Quite predictably, God's great enemy, Satan, had used every means within his power to overthrow it. The title, which may be translated "The Wonders of Christ in America," attests to the divine favors which the Plantation had enjoyed from its beginning; but in the course of the book the author also gives many examples of the "cunning and malice of Satan" as he endeavored to undo God's work.

Apparently Cotton Mather was not the only person who was concerned for the future of the colony. As early as 1679 a series of divine chastisements in the form of fires, crop failures, shipwrecks, epidemics, and Indian wars prompted the General Court of Massachusetts to call a synod of churchmen to discuss two questions: "What are the provoking evils of New England?" and "What is to be done, that so those evils may be reformed?" The synod found that the Ten Commandments were being disobeyed to an alarming degree, and it called for a renewal of the covenant throughout the churches. Pastors preached on the subject, and a special catechism was drawn up so that the people "might *echo* back, upon fit questions, those things which were needful to be *known* and to be *done,* relating to the reformation of the land." But these efforts to "recover the dying 'power of godliness'" failed, and apostasies increased. "The *old spirit* of New-England," says Mather, "hath been sensibly going out of the world, as the *old saints* in which it was have gone; and instead thereof the *spirit of the world,* with a lamentable neglect of *strict piety,* has crept in upon the rising generation." Not merely apostasies increased, but troubles also, so that, in 1689, the General Council again took notice of the situation, and solemnly declared that the colony was "in eminent danger of perishing, if a speedy *reformation* of our *provoking evils* prevent it not."

Cotton Mather and, even more importantly, his father, Increase Mather (1639-1723), exerted great influence upon public events of the time. Cotton Mather shows no false modesty in his work, but sometimes he neglects to mention a detail, such as the fact that it was on petition of his father and other ministers that the General Court was prompted to call the reforming synod of 1679. Moreover, it is only by reading between the lines that one can detect the emergence of a new, liberal sentiment, which contested the conservativism of the Mathers. For example, no mention is made of so prominent a figure as Solomon Stoddard (1634-1729), the grandfather of Jonathan Edwards and his predecessor in the pulpit at Northampton, who, in opposition to the Mathers, favored admitting to communion persons not members of the Congregational churches if they exhibited "a good conversation and a competent knowledge."

One of the things which the reforming synod felt that it could do was to reaffirm its adherence to the doctrinal standards which had been adopted by the New England Churches in 1649. Mather devotes the fifth book of the *Magnalia* to reprinting and commenting upon the Savoy Declaration, which is the Congregationalist version of the Westminster Confession of 1647; the New England Platform of Church Discipline, of 1649; and other "acts and monuments" by which successive synods attempted to reinforce the principles of the "scriptural reformation" to which Puritanism was dedicated. The seriousness and competence with which Mather's generation set themselves to the task of reviving their churches by certifying the orthodoxy of their teachings and the legitimacy of their government gives food for reflection, especially in view of the subsequent history of Christianity in New England.

Book Five is a hub around which the rest of the *Magnalia* turns. The four preceding books are given over to praising New England's great men; the two following, to reporting instances of God's goodness and of Satan's malice toward the colonies.

The books devoted by Mather to the founding of New England and to the lives of her magistrates, her ministers, and the graduates of Harvard College are a disappointment to the modern reader. Mather, who had a prodigious knowledge of ancient language and literature, affects to find parallels between the New England worthies and the heroes of Israel, Greece, and Rome. Thus, introducing John Winthrop, Governor of Massachusetts, Mather writes: "Let Greece boast her patient Lycurgus, the lawgiver, by whom diligence, temperance, fortitude and wit were made the fashions of a therefore long-lasting and renowned commonwealth; let Rome tell of her devout Numa, the lawgiver, by whom the most famous commonwealth saw peace triumphing over extinguished war and cruel plunders; and murders giving place to the more mollifying exercises of his religion. Our New-England shall tell and boast of her *Winthrop*, a lawgiver as patient as Lycurgus, but not admitting any of his criminal disorders; as devout as Numa, but not liable to any of *his* heathenish madnesses; a governour in whom the excellencies of Christianity made a most improving addition unto the virtues, wherein even without *those* he would have made a *parallel* for the great men of Greece, or of Rome, which the pen of a Plutarch has eternized."

Most of Mather's biographical notices are brief, rarely exceeding six or seven pages, except for those devoted to Boston's four greatest divines. His biography of Sir William Phips (1651-1695) is, however, sixty-five pages in length and contains hints, at least, of the vigor and romance that surrounded this colonial patriot. Indeed, the *Magnalia* is an important source for the life of Sir William, whom Mather knew personally and served briefly as secretary. Mather's account tells of Phips's remarkable rise from shepherd lad to shipbuilder, and of Phips's adventures in connection with recovering Spanish gold and laying siege to Quebec. But, perhaps because the matter was sufficiently well-known to his readers, Mather becomes almost unintelligible when he recounts the civil upheaval which resulted in the overthrow of Governor Andros and the appointment of Phips, in 1691, to take his place. Here Cotton Mather was in a unique position to record an important historical development, since his father was the colonial representative in London who won the concessions from the new monarch. But his account, though full of charges and vindications, is so short on facts as not even to mention Governor Andros by name. Phips was a highly controversial personage, with the deportment of a typical seventeenth century sea captain. But by Mather's report he was a model of discretion, "a person of so sweet a temper, that they who were most intimately acquainted with him, would commonly pronounce him, 'The best conditioned gentleman in the world!' "

Because it was during Phip's brief administration that the witch-mania arose in Salem, Mather discusses that issue in his biography of Phips as well as in the later section devoted to supernatural manifestations. Mather believed in demon-possession and witchcraft, and had no doubts respecting its occurrence in New England. His writings and sermons on the subject were in great part responsible for exciting the persecutions. It is true that he and his father urged caution when a commission was appointed to bring the witches to trial, and they argued that demons could impersonate innocent people and so deceive honest witnesses; but these warnings were little heeded until the affair reached such dimensions that common sense demanded that a halt be called. "The last courts," Mather says, "that sate upon this *thorny business,* finding that it was impossible to penetrate into the whole meaning of the things that had happened, and that so many *unsearchable cheats* were interwoven into the *conclusion* of a mysterious business, which perhaps had not crept thereinto at the *beginning* of it, they *cleared* the accused as fast as they *tried* them; and within a little while the afflicted were most of them delivered out of their troubles also; and the land had peace restored unto it, by the 'God of peace, treading Satan under foot.' "

Mather commends the judges for consulting precedents and learned writers on the subject of witches, and he testifies to their "conscientious endeavor to do the thing that was right." But he also defends the governor for reversing the former accusations when it became clear that "there was a going too far in this affair." Among the reasons that Mather gives for halting the trials and acquitting those already condemned was that when the numbers kept growing and many of blameless life were included, it began to appear that Satan was using the trials as a means of dividing the colony against itself. It also struck Mather that, of the nineteen that were executed, all denied the crime to their deaths, in spite of the fact that some were intelligent and pious persons; this was in marked contrast to the usual behavior of Puritans convicted of crime, who, as Mather reveals in other parts of his work, were zealous in confessing their sins as they went to the scaffold. In the end, he concluded that the affair at Salem "proceeded from some mistaken principles." But he continued to affirm the existence of witchcraft and demonic possession, and he gathered from the trials new material for refuting those modern Sadducees who deny the existence of supernatural beings. Anyone who wishes to read how Goody F. and her daughter rode their broomsticks to witch meetings can find it all in the chapter entitled "Thaumatographia Pneumatica, Relating the Wonders of the Invisible World in Preternatural Occurrences."

Probably the most interesting part

of the *Magnalia* is Book Six, devoted to "Illustrious Discoveries and Demonstrations of the Divine Providence in Remarkable Mercies and Judgments of Many Particular Persons." It is to the alertness of the President and Fellows of Harvard College that we owe this record, for they sent a proposal to the clergy of New England recommending that the churches collect for the benefit of posterity instances of "all *unusual accidents,* in the heaven, or earth, or water; all wonderful *deliverances* of the distressed; *mercies* to the godly; *judgments* on the wicked; and more glorious fulfillment of either the *promises* or the *threatenings* in the Scriptures of truth; with *apparitions, possessions, inchantments,* and all extraordinary things wherein the existence and agency of the *invisible world* is more sensibly demonstrated." Because Increase Mather was the President of Harvard, and Cotton Mather the most energetic of its fellows, the various narrations that were in this way collected have found their repository in the *Magnalia.* In this book the author lays aside his declamatory manner, and he proves himself a master of description and narration. His circumstantial stories of shipwrecks and pirates, of Indian raids, adulteries, and murders must have contributed greatly to the popularity of the *Magnalia* in his own day.

Mather concludes his *Magnalia* with an account of "disturbances given to the Churches of New-England," an account otherwise entitled "A Book of the Wars of the Lord." Here, after speaking briefly of the difficulties ministers had in collecting their salaries, and of scandals occasioned by "high professors of religion" falling into open sin, he chiefly deals with heretical teachings. Particular notice is given of Roger Williams (c.1603-1683), as advocating rigid separatism; of Anne Hutchinson (c.1600-1643) as a leader of antinomianism; and of Quaker and Anabaptist groups which tried to get a foothold. It is amusing to hear Cotton Mather call Williams *quixotic,* and embarrassing to hear him charge Anne Hutchinson with lying and tale-bearing, while he himself passes on the report that she, when great with child, gave birth not to anything human but to thirty monsters. He has no patience with Quakers, whom he calls lunatics, and he argues that the colonies have good cause to guard against these "dangerous villains"; still, he seems to be of the opinion that a minor punishment might be sufficient for discouraging them—perhaps shaving their heads. Toward the Anabaptists he is less severe. He can understand their scruples concerning infant baptism, but he considers that their separate societies are dangerous because they permit uneducated persons to preach; and he finds them intolerant when they deny that the Congregational churches, since they baptize infants, are truly churches.

Mather was aware that the temper of the times had changed. People had become critical of the persecution of religion and had come to accept the necessity for a degree of forbearance. Nor did Mather wish to fall behind enlightened opinion in these matters. Quoting from one of his own sermons, he writes: "A man has a *right* unto his life, his estate, his liberty, and his family, although he should not come up unto these and those blessed institutions of our Lord. When a man sins in his political capacity, let *political* societies animadvert upon him; but when he sins only in a religious capacity, societies more purely *religious* are fittest then to deal with him." Taken in context, this is no ringing declaration for religious freedom. Magistrates are told that it is their duty to "punish all the vices which disturb the good order and repose of human society," and that "to live without any *worship* of God, or to *blaspheme* and *revile* his blessed name, is to be chastised as abominably criminal." But at least those who are recognizably Christians ought to be tolerated, even though they dissent from the New England way. "Nor," declaims Mather, "would I desire myself to suffer persecution upon a clearer cause than that of testifying against our persecution of other Christians that are not of my own opinion."

The general assent with which these remarks were received by representative leaders in the province encouraged Mather to prophesy that, as long as this temper prevailed in the people of New England, "sectaries will never be able to make any great impressions upon them." He concludes: "Well, the enemy of the New-English churches is hitherto disappointed: *hac non successit, alia aggrediatur via*—he has not been successful in this region; let him try another."

THE SCRIPTURE-DOCTRINE OF THE TRINITY

Author: Samuel Clarke (1675-1729)
Type of work: Theology
First published: 1712

Principal Ideas Advanced

The New Testament is the sole source for theological statements concerning the person of Christ and His relation to God the Father.

Traditional dogmatic definitions of the doctrine of the Trinity lead in the direction of Sabellianism or Tritheism.

In the New Testament the Son is regarded as subordinate to the Father.

The Word of God is derived from the Father, though the precise relation of the Word of God (the Son) to the Father cannot be explained by human reason.

Samuel Clarke's *The Scripture-Doctrine of the Trinity,* published in 1712, marked the beginning of the Arian controversy in English religious thought. Though the essay has not been regarded as an unusually perceptive or imaginative theological treatise, it is noted as one of the major works of eighteenth century English liberalism.

The term "Arianism" stems from the controversy of the fourth century when the Christian Church was in the process of defining its position on the relation of Jesus Christ to God the Father. Arius, a presbyter in the Church of Alexandria, was accused of heresy by his bishop for asserting that the Son of God was brought into being by the Father, that He was not co-eternal with the Father, and that "there was a time when he was not." Under the Emperor Constantine, a council was called to deal with the Arian position, and at Nicaea in 325 Arius and his followers were declared heretical and the first Nicene Creed was formulated.

Eighteenth century Arianism had different interests from those of its fourth century progenitors, but the label continued to be used. Whereas the earlier controversy revolved more centrally around metaphysical questions, Clarke and his fellow critics of the traditional trinitarian formula centered their attention on an examination of Scripture with the aim in view to show that nowhere can one find Biblical justification for the doctrine. For this reason, English Arianism had closer ties to the Socinian movement than to fourth century Arianism.

The seventeenth century English Socinians, related to the sixteenth century Polish group, adopted an essentially unitarian position. They viewed Christ as a creature, and they interpreted His entire mission as that of a prophet calling men to live the righteous and ethical life. Though they discarded the traditional affirmations of original sin and predestination, together with the satisfaction theory of the atonement, and centered their attention on the ethical commands of Christ, they accepted in a most orthodox fashion the Biblical accounts of the miracles and other narratives relating to Jesus of Nazareth. The dogmatic definitions of the Church concerning the person of Christ were viewed as perversions of the simple New Testament gospel. In the 1690's a number of Socinian tracts appeared in England. These were immediately attacked by the more orthodox theologians, though with no great success. By the beginning of the eighteenth century the orthodox churchmen equated the Socinian and the developing Arian positions. Many felt that Arianism would become Socinianism and thus that it must be rooted out; the doctrine of the Trinity had become one of the most debated theological issues of the church.

The Scripture-Doctrine of the Trinity was published in the midst of this discussion. It sought to focus the issue on one central question: What does the Bible say? Clarke's contribution to the entire debate involved an analysis of Biblical texts, rather than, as had been the case in fourth century Arianism, a critique of philosophical ambiguities. He sought to dissociate his own view from that of the Socinians. Though the orthodox defenders of the trinitarian formula took up the charge of the Socinians, that the doctrine was irrational, and sought to defend it on rational grounds, Clarke focused the issue on an analysis of the New Testament. In his other works, however, Clarke did not shun the task of indicating the rational basis of Christianity, of formulating rational grounds for the existence of God, and of arguing that no article of the Christian religion is contrary to reason; but this effort was not the central task in his essay on the Trinity.

Thus Clarke's work had two major objectives: (1) to dissociate his position from that of the Socinians and (2) to show that the traditional doctrine of the Trinity led to the greater heresies of Sabellianism and tritheism. It is indicative of Clarke's effort that he himself disclaimed the label Arian, though not with conspicuous success. Consistent with the dominant concern of this period in English religious thought, he sought a return to primitive Christianity and a re-evaluation of the use of the traditional Nicene and Athanasian creeds.

His method of approach is stated in the first words of his book: "As, in Matters of *Speculation and Philosophical Inquiry,* the only Judge of what is right or wrong, is *Reason and Experience;* so in Matters either of *humane Testimony* or *divine Revelation,* the only certain Rule of Truth is the *Testimony* or *the Revelation itself.*" In clearing up disputed theological points, the tradition of the Church serves as a helpful guide, but it can by no means be the only authority; Scripture alone is the true guide. In addition, and not unlike John Toland (1670-1722), the deist of the previous century, Clarke argued that Scripture must not conflict with reason; the disciple of Christ is not obliged to believe that which is contrary to his reason. But his central point was that ". . . the *Books of Scripture* are to Us Now not only *the Rule,* but the *Whole* and *the Only Rule of Truth* in matters of Religion." His task, therefore, was clear, and the three parts of his essay deal with the following topics: (1) an examination of Biblical texts which make direct or indirect reference to the doctrine of the Trinity, (2) a statement of the theological propositions concerning the trinitarian doctrine which the Scriptures allow, (3) an attempt to reconcile the liturgies of the Church of England with his understanding of the Biblical text. There can be no doubt that throughout Clarke's treatise his effort is to remain a loyal churchman and to rescue from obscurity the Biblical doctrines concerning Jesus Christ. The foundation of the Christian religion, he wrote, is "The *Supremacy of God the Father* over all, and our *Reconciliation and Subjection* to him as such our *Supreme Governour;* the *Redemption* purchased by *the Son;* and the *Sanctification* worked in us by the *Holy Spirit*. . . ." The confusion of this simple truth has resulted in "*Tritheism, Sabellianism, Arianism,* and *Socinianism*" which have ". . . to the great disparagement of Christianity, puzzled the plain and practical Doctrine of Scripture, with endless speculative Disputes. . . ."

In Part I of the essay, Clarke examined every New Testament text, 1,251 in all, which related to the question. He did not attempt an elaborate analysis of the passages he cited, but sought only to list them under relevant categories. The following are samples of the headings he used: "*The Passages of the New Testament, wherein He is stiled the One or Only God,*" with seventeen Scriptural references; "*The Passages wherein He is stiled God absolutely, by way of Eminence and Supremacy,*" with 319 Scriptural references; *The Passages wherein it is declared, that All* Prayers and Praises *ought* primarily *to be offered* to Him, and that every thing *ought to be directed* ultimately to His Honour and Glory," with ninety Scriptural references. In this manner Clarke dealt with all passages refering to God the Father, the Son of God, and the Holy Spirit. His comments on the passage in the Gospel of John, "In the beginning was the Word, and the Word was with God, and the Word was God," reveal his own position. For Clarke, the phrase, "and the Word was God," had three possible interpretations: "The *first is;* that the Word was *That same*

Person, whom he was *with. . . .*" But this interpretation, Clarke argued, leads to the heresy of Sabellianism. A second possible interpretation is that ". . . the Word was Another *Self-existent, Underived, Independent Person, co-ordinate to Him with whom he was. . . .*" This view, however, is a polytheistic denial of the unity of God. The only possible interpretation of the passage, therefore, is that ". . . the Word is a Person, *deriving* from the Father (with whom he existed before the World was), both his Being itself, and incomprehensible Power and Knowledge, and other *divine* Attributes and Authority, in a Manner not revealed, and which humane Wisdom ought not to presume to be able to explain: And This is the Interpretation of the Learnedest and most Antient Writers in the Primitive Church." This analysis, however, avoided the theological problem; it actually served to cloud rather than clear the issue. There are striking resemblances between Clarke's position and that held by the men who dominated Christological discussion after the Council of Nicaea; they also feared that the phrase, "of the same substance," which the Nicene Creed used when dealing with the relation of the Son to the Father, led to Sabellianism, and yet they did not want to commend the Arian position. This was also Clarke's dilemma, but he solved it by an ambiguous statement; his interpretation of the passage, "and the Word was God," could itself be interpreted in an Arian fashion, though its lack of theological precision could allow for an interpretation which was not dissimilar from that made by the later defenders of the Nicene decision.

The second part of his essay reflected much more clearly a position in accord with Arianism, though again, theological clarity is frequently lacking. He sought to maintain the supremacy of God the Father, while avoiding a clearly Arian position. For example, he wrote: "The Scripture, in declaring the *Sons Derivation* from the Father, never makes mention of any Limitation of *Time;* but always supposes and affirms him to have existed with the Father *from the Beginning,* and *before All Worlds.*" The statement has an Arian ring to it, but it is not a precise statement. It is this consistent ambiguity in Clarke's thought which made it so easy to characterize him as an Arian, especially when he did not accept with ease the traditional doctrinal statements and when any criticism of the doctrine of the Trinity called immediately to mind the recent Socinian debates. Seldom did he make a statement so clearly Arian as this: "The *Son,* whatever his metaphysical Essence or Substance be, and whatever divine Greatness and Dignity is ascribed to him in Scripture; yet in This He is evidently *Subordinate to the Father,* that He *derives* his *Being* and Attributes from the *Father,* the *Father* nothing from *Him.*"

In the concluding section of the volume Clarke sought to show how his interpretation of the doctrine of the Trinity could be compatible with Anglican liturgical forms. To be sure, Clarke did not consider himself at variance with the true understanding of the formularies of the Church.

In summary, *The Scripture-Doctrine of the Trinity* was an effort of a theologian in the period of developing English rationalism to defend the doctrine of the Trinity on Biblical grounds, while avoiding the extremes of Sabellianism (as exemplified to Clarke in the Athanasian Creed) and Socinianism. The work, however, served more to illustrate the dominant interests of the period—namely, the reliance on Scripture and the avoidance of philosophical terminology in theological formulation, and the accompanying dependence on reasonableness—than it did to offer a consistent or original interpretation of the doctrine of the Trinity.

A SERIOUS CALL TO A DEVOUT AND HOLY LIFE

Author: William Law (1686-1761)
Type of work: Devotional philosophy; devotional guide
First published: 1728

Principal Ideas Advanced

Devotion consists not merely in prayers but in a life devoted to God.

Religion and philosophy agree that a devout life is the only prudent life both now and hereafter.

The rules of religion apply to all the actions of one's life.

Our active life should be devoted to useful occupations and to works of charity and mercy.

Our contemplative life should be disciplined by a daily regimen of prayer and meditation.

William Law, a clergyman of the Church of England and (until he refused to take the oath abjuring the Stuarts) a fellow of Cambridge University, believed that although the official religion was continuing to call men to a devout and holy life, its call was neither seriously meant nor seriously taken. The forms of prayer poured contempt upon life in this world and avowed affection only for things of Heaven, but neither people nor priests really attempted to govern their lives according to these professions. A growing number favored abandoning the prayers in favor of a frank secularism. Law favored keeping the prayers and bringing men's lives back under the rule of devotion.

Devotion, according to Law, does not consist merely in prayers. Prayer is an important part of devotion, but devotion is nothing less than "a life given, or devoted, to God." In his view, Christianity prescribes rules governing all the ordinary actions of life; and if one does not make it his daily study to govern his conduct by these rules, he may as well give up saying his prayers. The Christian is called upon to lay everything upon the altar; his time, his wealth, his abilities are no longer his; and whatever he does (what he eats, how he dresses, where he spends his leisure, how much he charges for his wares) must be governed by the rules of religion.

But William Law was living in the

"age of reason" and of "enlightenment." In his opinion the demands of religion are no different from those of reason. He was not interested in the doctrinal controversies which had rocked the Church for nearly two centuries. In his opinion, Christian orthodoxy agrees in essential points with true philosophy, as represented by Socrates, Epictetus, and Marcus Aurelius. It is a kind of ethical eudaemonism, a higher prudence, which rightly estimates the vanity and bitterness of earthly striving and knows the peace and fruition that comes with ordering one's life according to righteousness. Law never doubts that our earthly life is merely a preparation for an eternal life to follow, so that those who neglect to improve their opportunities stand convicted as fools. But he does not rest his case on an afterlife; even here and now, he maintains, a life regulated by the rules of religion is sweeter and more joyous than a life which is governed by the spirit of the age. Piety, according to Law, should be based on the eternal laws of nature.

Law regards every individual as called to devote his life to God. There is, he maintains, no other way of salvation. He sets aside the view that Christ's death is a substitutionary atonement for the sins of men; he argues instead that Christ is our representative, whose death makes our sacrifices acceptable to God. "And we are to suffer, to be crucified, to die and rise with Christ; or else His Crucifixion, Death, and Resurrection will profit us nothing." Law accepts the Catholic distinction between "two orders" of obedience. Some, he admits, are called to serve God in the married state while carrying on the common business of the world, and others are called to retire from the world and to live in virginity and poverty in order to carry out more fully the requirements of God's love. But he finds in this distinction no excuse for laxity. It is, according to Law, quite possible to serve God perfectly whatever our circumstances. If our lives lack the luster which adorned the piety of the early confessors, there is no need to look for the cause in differences of circumstances or of ability. The only cause for anyone's failure to live Christianly is that he "never thoroughly intended it."

A Serious Call consists of two main parts. The first half is an attempt to set a pattern for serving God in the external affairs of life. The second half is a guide to prayer and to the interior life.

Whether because his own experience was limited, or because he had in view the circumstances of his likely reader, the author addressed his practical suggestions almost entirely to middle class people of comfortable station. His remarks to tradesmen are limited to the brief suggestion that it is agreeable to the will of God for them to sell such things as are useful in life at a "reasonable" profit and that it is wrong to make it the end of commerce to enrich themselves. He has much more to say about how the men, and particularly their wives, should spend the wealth and leisure which comes to them. Their great temptation, Law says, lies in "the indiscreet use of such things as are lawful to be used." There is nothing unlawful in eating and drinking, in buying houses and lands, in taking one's ease with pleasant company, but there is great danger in the "vain and imprudent use" of these things, which, although not so immediately destructive as gross sins, are none the less inimical to piety and fatal to man's true end. Holy living is an art which consists in "the right and prudent management" of things lawful in themselves. Mastery in the art is gained through following the strict rules laid down by religion.

In Law's opinion, persons of leisure and of some estate are the ones referred to in the Gospel parable as having received five talents. They are not permitted to squander their time, their health, and their fortune, but must employ these in improving their own souls and in assisting others to improve themselves. In Law's opinion we do this, as far as our active life is concerned, when we impose upon ourselves a voluntary poverty and employ our time and our goods for the relief of the poor and the unfortunate. In brief, charitable activity should be the main employment of those who do not have to earn their own bread. As God bestows His largesse upon the deserving and the undeserving without discriminating between them, so His servants should give to any who appear to be in need, without inquiring too minutely into their circumstances. Law, however, does value the principle of helping others to help themselves, and he praises the discretion of a godly woman who helped set up tradesmen in business, paid the rent of working men while they were sick, made good the loss of a horse or a cow to a poor family, and reared three children whom she took from the home of profligate parents. He especially enjoins tenderness and friendliness toward old people and toward the sick and the maimed.

Law's directions for the nurture of the inner life take the form of a daily order for prayer. One should set apart a place to which he may retire six times a day in order to recover his spiritual presence and to present himself before God. He should begin by chanting a psalm. Law is very particular about this. Singing, he says, is a generic talent. Its value in devotions is that it awakens the soul, calls it to its proper duty, and addresses it toward Heaven. Following this exercise, Law recommends the use of formal prayers, chiefly for the power which their exalted language has to make us sensible of the Divine Nature. But when our hearts are stirred sufficiently to frame their own praises and petitions, traditional forms should be laid aside.

According to Law, we best employ these devotional hours when we form the habit of taking up the same subject every day at the same time. He suggests the following plan. On rising (and it will be early, for religion is no friend of sleep or of sloth), our first acts should be to praise and thank God and to offer up body and soul to His service and glory. At nine o'clock, we should pray for humility. At noon, our theme should be love, and we should take upon ourselves the burden of intercession for all God's creatures. At three o'clock we should seek resignation and conformity to God's will. At six o'clock, we should confess our sins, reviewing all our actions for the day and acknowledging our shortcomings. There remains only the preparation of the soul for sleep, when the most proper subject is death. Approximately half of *A Serious Call* is taken up with this schedule of prayer and with the author's meditations upon the themes suggested.

A remarkable feature of the book is

the series of character sketches, seemingly drawn from life. Cognatus is a clergyman, orthodox and meticulous with the liturgy, but also a diligent observer of the markets, a man esteemed by his parishioners most of all for his advice on the time for selling wheat. Calidus is a great merchant who does business from dawn till late at night, when he dines heartily at the tavern; his prayers are short ejaculations, but he never misses saying them in stormy weather because he always has something or other at sea. Flavia is a maiden woman with a small income, which she expends mostly on dress, and by judicious management outdoes many ladies of greater fortune; she thinks that those who play cards on Sunday are atheists, but as soon as she comes from church she will tell you all the cards she held at the last night's party. Miranda, her sister, on the other hand, is the pious woman whose exemplary works of charity were mentioned above. These are but samples from an impressive gallery of eighteenth century types; these character sketches help to make *A Serious Call* something of a literary as well as a religious classic. Samuel Johnson said that it was the finest work of its kind in any language, and he testified to the influence it had exerted on his own life. "I took up Law's *Serious Call to A Devout and Holy Life,*" he said, "expecting to find it a dull book (as such books generally are) and perhaps to laugh at it. But I found Law quite an overmatch for me."

CHRISTIANITY AS OLD AS THE CREATION

Author: Matthew Tindal (1655-1733)
Type of work: Deistic theology
First published: 1730

Principal Ideas Advanced

Because the nature of God is unchangeable, it can be inferred that God will treat all men at all times in the same way by supplying them all with the same sufficient means of recognizing and discharging their duties.

The religion of nature is the standard of judgment of what is acceptable in revelation, for the latter can add nothing to the perfection of the former.

Whether externally or internally revealed, true religion is constant in both doctrine and precept.

The Gospel is a republication of the religion of nature.

Christianity as Old as the Creation is the best known work of Matthew Tindal, Fellow of All Soul's College, Oxford. First published in 1730, it marks the culmination of deism. The work is a skillful collection of the arguments upon which the deists relied. Its express purpose is to distinguish between religion and superstition. Like such predecessors as John Toland (1670-1722) and Anthony Collins (1676-1729), Matthew Tindal espoused a religion which, it was claimed, any man at any time was capable of discovering by reason.

God has provided men with the means of knowing what He requires of them, writes Tindal. Natural religion, the religion man can discover, differs from revealed religion only in the manner of its being communicated. Natural religion is the *internal* revelation of God, whereas revealed religion is the *external* revelation of the same God. Since God is Himself unchangeable, infinitely wise and infinitely good, natural and revealed religion can differ in nothing as far as their content is concerned.

From the very beginning God has given men a rule or law for their conduct, the observance of which renders them acceptable to Himself. What originates with a perfect, all-wise God must itself be perfect. An absolutely perfect religion cannot be altered, nor increased nor decreased. Man's original religion is as immutable as God, its author. Revelation, therefore, can add nothing to a religion that is absolutely perfect, universal, and immutable.

Not only has God given mankind a law, Tindal continues, but also He has given sufficient means for making men capable of knowing what His infinite goodness would have them know. God was always willing that every man should come to the knowledge of true religion, and since the Christian religion is the only true and absolutely perfect religion, it was designed for all mankind from the beginning. The name "Christianity" is of more recent origin, but the Christian religion itself has existed from the beginning; it is as old and extensive as human nature; it is in fact the law of creation, implanted in us by God Himself. God from the beginning has given all men sufficient means to know, believe, profess, and practice Christianity.

The means by which the whole race of mankind is able to discover what God would have them know are those faculties which distinguish man from the animals. Reason enables man to discover whether there is a God who is concerned with human affairs and who has given certain laws for human conduct.

God will judge men because they are rational, writes Tindal; the judgment will be exactly proportional to the use that men make of their reason. If the proper use of reason could not justify man before God, it would be vain to use reason at all. Our human condition would indeed be miserable if men were held to be criminal whether they used reason or not. If God would have everyone know His will at all times and has given no means other than reason, then the use of reason must be the means by which God would have us know what to profess and to practice. God has made us rational creatures. It is our reason that tells us that it is the will of God that we act up to the dignity of our natures and it is also reason that tells us when we do so. What God requires us to believe and practice must itself be a reasonable service, and whether what is offered to us as such is really reasonable must itself be judged by reason. Reason is the judge of what is reasonable. Nothing should be admitted into Christianity except what our reason tells us is worthy of having God for its author.

God requires nothing of men but

what is founded on the nature of things and on the immutable relations which things have to one another. Whenever men sincerely try to discover the will of God, they become aware of a law of nature, or reason, a law which is common or natural to all rational creatures. This law, like God Himself, is absolutely perfect, eternal, and unchangeable. The Gospel never intended to add or to detract from it. The purpose of the Gospel was to free men from their own superstition. True Christianity is, therefore, not a religion of yesterday, but it is the religion which God dictated at the beginning, and which He continues to dictate to all men.

The Gospel has been disclosed by Jesus, the person who was sent by God. By living what He taught, Jesus has set us a noble example, and just as He was highly exalted for so doing, we too may expect a suitable reward if we do our best to follow the divine precepts, which are the same whether revealed in the Gospel or discovered by reason.

Mankind was always under a law, even before the external revelation of the Scriptures was given, Tindal asserts. God has given the animals sufficient means to act in their own preservation. He certainly does not have less kindness for the immortal souls created in His image. God has given to men the light of understanding by which they can discover what makes for the good of their souls. Man is capable of perceiving eternal truths and of knowing what will contribute to his temporal and eternal happiness.

The Gospel is not a new religion but a "republication" of the religion of nature, Tindal claims. Natural religion is able to demonstrate with certainty that there is an absolutely perfect Being, the source of all other beings and of their perfections. That such a being exists is as certain as our own existence. It is, moreover, equally demonstrable that no creature can add to or detract from the happiness of a being who is infinitely happy in Himself. God did not create His creatures for His own good, but He created them for their own good. To imagine otherwise is to suppose that God was not perfectly happy before the Creation, and that His creatures could add or detract from His happiness by the observance or nonobservance of certain rules.

Since God is infinitely happy, all wise, and all good, nothing can be included in the divine law unless it promotes the common interest and happiness of His rational creatures; and, conversely, whatever does benefit His rational creatures must be included in the divine law.

God cannot require anything of us unless it contributes to our happiness, and He can forbid only that which leads to our suffering. His laws can lead only to our good, and His infinite power can bring to pass only what he designs for our good. Thus, concludes Tindal, to sin against such a being is to act against ourselves, against our reasonable natures.

Our reason is not limited to a demonstration of the existence of God and of the nature of the divine perfections. We can also demonstrate the nature of the duties God requires of us, both in relation to Himself and in relation to ourselves and to one another.

By recognizing that God has endowed us with such a nature that we desire our own good, and by realizing that God could not require anything that would do us harm, we know that we should act in relation to ourselves in such a way that our natural appetites will become regulated so as to achieve the exercise of reason, the health of the body, and the pleasure of the senses.

Our duty with respect to our fellow man is readily ascertainable if it be remembered that God is the common parent of all mankind, and that the whole human species is under the divine protection, so that God will punish anyone who injures anyone else. It is a person's duty to deal with others as he would have them deal with him in like circumstances. God has so constituted men that they are able to assist one another in the concerns of life. Infinite goodness has sown the seeds of pity in the human heart; God Himself has implanted in man, His image bearer, a love for His species, a desire to perform acts of benevolence.

Man's duty is always the same, since inconstancy cannot belong to the infinitely wise and powerful being. God is free of all partiality. His laws extend to all times and places. Since religion consists in the practice of those duties that result from man's relation to God, religion is as constant as God.

From the beginning of the world until the end, our duty to God and man is unalterable, Tindal emphasizes. Duty is always plain and clear; it is never changed in whole, or in part; hence, no person, if he comes from God, can teach any religion other than natural religion, or give us any precepts other than those which natural religion suggests. True religion is thus a constant disposition of our minds to do all the good we can; and by so doing we render ourselves acceptable to God in answering the end of His creation.

Human actions are guided by man's innate desire for happiness, a desire that is fulfilled by the perfection of man's nature, by living up to the dictates of right reason.

The religion of nature is absolutely perfect Tindal asserts; revelation can neither add to nor take from its perfection. In fact, the truth of revelation itself is to be judged by revelation's agreement with natural religion. All particular precepts that fail to contribute to the honor of God or to the good of man fail to carry any obligation.

The failure to make reason the judge concerning the nature of God and the duties He requires of us has given rise to all sorts of superstitions, bigotry, and intolerance. The abandonment of reason has debased God by clothing Him in our own infirmities; it has resulted in the practice of placing man's individual conscience in the hands of corrupt men, in the hands of priests and clerics. True religion, Tindal insists, consists in imitating the perfections of God; nothing arbitrary is contained in a religion that comes from God. To insist upon obeying human ordinances as necessary to pleasing God is to suppose that some men who obey the law of nature may yet suffer eternal punishment for not obeying certain other laws. It is erroneous to hold that God requires in the Gospels what the law of nature does not. It is superstitious to represent God as a most cruel being who damns men to eternity for mistaken opinions and who condemns men for sins which reason cannot oppose.

To magnify revelation is to weaken the force of reason and nature, Tindal claims; to venerate revelation is to strike at all natural order, for there cannot be two conflicting standards of divine government. Fortunately, most men are, by reason, able to distinguish between religion and superstition and thus to extricate themselves from a reliance upon revelation.

The thesis defended by Tindal and other deists, namely, that a man can at any time discover his duties by exercising reason, and that there is a natural religion as old as the creation, was later to collapse under the criticism of philosophers such as David Hume (1711-1776), who argued that the religion of primitive man consists of a medley of crude superstitions.

The optimism of deism with respect to the rationality implicit in human nature and the subjection of revelation to the tests of reason exerted and continues to exert its influence upon liberal forms of Protestantism.

THE ANALOGY OF RELIGION

Author: Joseph Butler (1692-1752)
Type of work: Apologetics
First published: 1736

Principal Ideas Advanced

By analogy the course and constitution of nature can be shown to support the religious doctrines that man is to live in a future state, rewarded or punished for his present virtuous or vicious acts; that our present life is a probation; and that because of human apostasy a new dispensation is necessary.

The new dispensation of providence has been revealed by God, proven by miracles, and carried on by the Mediator, Jesus Christ.

Objections to religion can equally be alleged against the course of nature itself; they are inconclusive, and the weight of the evidence is on the side of religion.

The *Analogy of Religion, Natural and Revealed, to the Course and Constitution of Nature* is a masterpiece of Christian argument by Joseph Butler, who at the time of his death in 1752 was the Bishop of Durham in the Church of England. Butler's *Analogy* attempts to dispose of objections against Christianity and to reveal the evidence for it. The existence of God as an intelligent author of nature and a natural governor of the world was not at issue in the eighteenth century. There was, however, an ever-increasing conviction that Christianity was a fit subject for ridicule. The *Analogy* seeks to prove that there is strong evidence for the truth of Christianity, and that Christianity cannot be shown to be false.

The work is divided into two parts; the first deals with natural religion; the second, with revealed religion. The argument of the entire work is an application of analogical reasoning to religion. The teachings of religion are observed to correspond to the known constitution and course of nature, so that objections to the former amount to an attack on the latter.

Degrees of likeness between things or events yield probable evidence, which, in contrast to demonstrative evidence, admits of degrees, and produces a presumption, an opinion, or a full conviction. To an infinite intelligence, Butler claims, no possible object of knowledge is merely probable, but for finite creatures "probability is the very guide of life."

If we presuppose the existence of an author of nature, Butler argues, the analogy between the system of revelation and the known course of nature makes it probable that they have the same author, and to the extent that the teachings of religion are shown to be like the course of nature, such analogies will either amount to a practical proof of their truth or will serve to answer objections against them.

The objection to the doctrine that mankind has been appointed to live in a future state is answered by showing that there is no reason to hold that death destroys living agents, or even suspends their powers of reflection. It is probably true that we shall live on in a future state in which every one will be rewarded and punished. In our present life we are governed in such a manner that one course of action is followed by the reward of pleasure, and another by the punishment of pain. There is nothing incredible in supposing that the future will be like the past, and that an infinite being is a righteous governor, who will punish and reward men in exact proportion to their virtues or vices.

The principles and beginnings of a moral government are discernible in nature, so that the final judgment of man in terms of distributive justice differs only in degree, not in kind, from what we now experience. There is a strong presumption that our present life is a probation for a future state.

We are under God's moral government, Butler insists, and we must give an account of our actions, both in our natural and our moral capacity. That we are now in a state of trial is attributable to our own nature, our inordinately excited passions, and the circumstances of our environment. The state of trial taught by religion is rendered credible because of its likeness to our present danger of losing temporal happiness. No more is required of men than they are able to do. Their success and happiness or their failure and misery depends upon their own diligence or negligence.

Butler contends that the general analogy of providence enables us to apprehend the danger of yielding to temptations and of losing a future good to satisfy an inferior interest. It may not be possible for us to understand the reasons why we have been placed on trial, but the end is our improvement in virtue and piety, so that we may enjoy a future state of happiness. The state of trial is analogous to our childhood education as preparation for our mature years. The present world is a state of moral discipline for another; it is a state of discipline for moral improvement, for what we become is the effect of what we do.

Butler grants that a fatalist might allege that a moral plan is impossible, but if the principle of universal necessity is reconcilable with the order of nature, it is also compatible with religion.

The teachings of religion are sufficiently credible to encourage men to live a life of virtue and piety. Butler concedes that God's scheme for the moral government of the world is not perfectly comprehended, but we are in no way competent to pass judgment concerning the course of providence. If we were not ignorant, if we could comprehend the whole plan of God, Butler argues, then what appear to be irregularities would be found to be consistent with and a part of justice and goodness.

The light of nature in nowise minimizes the importance of Christianity and the necessity of revelation, Butler insists. That revelation is not useless is shown by the condition of men in the heathen world, by man's skepticism in matters of importance, and by the general ignorance and inattention of men. Even if it were possible for man to reason out the whole system of natural religion, there is no probability that he would, and he would still need to be reminded of it. The very best of men are in need of supernatural instruction.

To minimize the importance of the Christian revelation is to forget that it has been given by God and that in addition to restating the truths of natural religion with increased light, attested to by the authority of miracles and prophecy, revelation also contains a record of what is not discoverable by reason; namely, a disclosure of the particular dispensation of God's providence in achieving man's salvation through the Son and the Holy Spirit.

The disclosure of God's special dealings with men places us under the moral obligation to render worship to the Son, our Mediator, and to the Holy Spirit, our Sanctifier. Such duties cannot be neglected with impunity.

Christianity is credible, Butler claims. There is no presumption against revelation in general on the ground that it is not discovered by reason or experience, since many things in the natural and moral system of the world are also beyond our natural faculties. There is, moreover, no reason to hold that everything that is unknown must be like what is known, although the scheme of Christianity is not unlike the scheme of nature. Nor is there a presumption against the miraculous character of revelation. The power exercised to make a world at the beginning, before there was a course of nature, could be further extended to make a revelation, and even after nature received its appointed course, there is no presumption against the occasional occurrence of miraculous interpositions.

There are, as a matter of fact, Butler insists, no valid objections against the Christian revelation. Objections raised against Christianity are based on the false supposition that we already possess knowledge as to what God's revealed dispensation ought to be, a knowledge that we do not possess even with respect to the natural governance of the world.

The situation with regard to revelation is analogous to that of natural information. We have no *a priori* knowledge of what God will permit us to know, or of the means to be used, or of the degree of evidence we can achieve.

The real issue is not whether the Christian revelation is what we might have expected God to reveal, but whether or not it truly is revelation. Moreover, Butler argues, it is invalid to object to the Scriptures because of their alleged obscurity and ambiguity, unless the Scriptures themselves promise that they are free of such faults. The authority of Scripture can be overturned, if, and only if, it can be shown that there is absolutely no proof of the miracles originally wrought to attest its authority, that there is nothing miraculous in its success, and that it contains no prophecy of events that human wisdom could not foresee.

Serious objections to Christianity are not forthcoming, Butler writes. If objections are to be made they must be made against the evidence for Christianity. For the analogy of nature makes it highly credible that if a revelation is to be made, it must contain many things different from what might be expected. Christianity is a scheme that is beyond our comprehension; it is not to be judged by reason. We do not have sufficient knowledge to protest against its wisdom, goodness, or justice.

The presence of a divine Mediator between God and man is, moreover, in accordance with the analogy of nature, Butler argues. Our life and its blessings are due to others. Prior to revelation, however, we have no means of knowing whether a mediator was necessary, or how the work of redemption was to be accomplished.

That the evidence of religion is considered doubtful is in no way inconsistent with the analogy of nature, Butler claims, for there is also much uncertainty concerning our temporal interests. Nor is the fact that Christianity is not universally revealed either an argument against its justice or inconsistent with its wisdom and goodness.

There is positive evidence for Christianity, Butler argues. The two most direct and fundamental proofs of Christianity are the miracles and the prophecies recorded in the Scriptures.

With respect to miracles it is to be observed that they are recorded in books which, until proved to the contrary, are to be regarded as genuine history. From its inception, Christianity was accepted upon the basis of miracles, and thus it differs from all other religions. Its success constitutes evidence of the actuality of the miracles recorded, for unless they were fully convinced of the truth of miracles, the Apostles and their contemporaries would not have undergone the suffering and martyrdom provoked by their belief in miracles.

Human testimony is a natural ground of assent, and even when marked by enthusiasm, such testimony is not overthrown unless there is either incredibility in the things attested or conflicting testimony. The evidence of testimony can be destroyed either by a proof or a probability that the witnesses are incompetent to judge the facts to which they bear witness, or that they are under some indirect pressure in giving evidence. Neither case is likely in Christianity. Because of the importance of their Christian beliefs, Christians would not want to be deceived themselves, nor would they wish to deceive others.

With respect to prophecy, Butler observes that the obscurity of a part of a prophecy in nowise destroys the proof of foreknowledge of the parts that are understood. The fact that a long series of prophecies is applicable to certain events constitutes proof that the events were intended to be known.

Collateral evidence may also be adduced from the character of the Christian revelation, from its content, and from facts relating to it. It is, however, easier to attack Christianity than to defend it, Butler concedes, for it is easier to assault a single point than to accumulate the whole mass of evidence in its defense. However, when the positive evidence for Christianity is considered in mass, and the objections against it are carefully considered, as well as the practical consequences of its denial, then if complete satisfaction as to its truth is not given, the most extreme skepticism cannot reach further than a middle position between complete satisfaction of the truth of Christianity and complete satisfaction of its falsity. If the proper evidence for Christianity is presented and considered, the skeptic cannot avoid the serious apprehension that Christianity might be true, although he may still doubt whether it be so. "If this be a just account of things," Butler writes, "and yet men go on to vilify or disregard Christianity, which is to talk and act as if they had a demonstration of its falsehood; there is no reason to think they would alter their behavior to any purpose, though there were a demonstration of its truth."

Butler's *Analogy of Religion* is significant as an attempt to stem the tide of deism and skepticism with respect to the reasonableness of the Christian faith. Its argument exerted considerable influence upon orthodox Christians, and the work commanded and continues to command the respect and attention of both its defenders and its opponents.

THE JOURNALS OF GEORGE WHITEFIELD

Author: George Whitefield (1714-1770)
Type of work: Spiritual autobiography
First published: 1738, 1740, 1747

Principal Ideas Advanced

Jesus Christ is the one Mediator between God and man; each man must achieve a new birth through Christ.

Success in converting men to the love of God is the effect of God's free grace.

God bestows His saving grace on only a certain number of men; the rest of mankind will suffer eternal death, the wages of sin.

The *Journals* of George Whitefield originally appeared as individual publications. They constitute the spiritual autobiography of a man who has been called the prince of preachers. Whitefield was born in 1714 in Gloucester, England. He confesses that as a child he hated instruction and was much given to lying, filthy talking, foolish jesting, and Sabbath breaking. Such actions later served to convince him that he was conceived and born in sin, that by nature nothing good dwelt within him, and that had he had not been restrained by the free grace of God, he would have been banished from His divine presence forever.

Whitefield attributed his early sense

of calling to the free grace of God, for although corruption worked strongly in his soul and produced early and bitter fruits, the very early influence of the blessed Spirit upon his heart satisfied him that God's love for him was everlasting, and that he had been separated from his mother's womb to be a preacher of the Gospel.

With considerable financial difficulty he managed, at seventeen years of age, to enter Pembroke College of Oxford University, where he resisted the worldly temptations of student life, and he began the practice of praying and singing psalms several times each day.

At Oxford he came into contact with the despised Methodists, and under the influence of his never-to-be-forgotten friend, Charles Wesley (1707-1788), Whitefield came to know that true religion was union of the soul with God and Christ. He now knew for the first time that to be a Christian he had to become a new creature, and that God had begun a good work in his soul, for he had experienced the new birth.

Whitefield now began to receive instruction in the faith from Charles Wesley. From the Methodists he learned to live like a good soldier of Jesus Christ and to live by rule so that not a single moment of his time would be wasted. Everything that he now did was done to the glory of God. No means were left unused which Whitefield thought would lead him nearer to Jesus Christ. Acts of charity were performed each day. Whitefield visited the sick and prisoners, and he read to the poor. The course of his studies was entirely changed. Whereas before he had been occupied in studying soulless sciences and superficial books, he now resolved to read only such as entered into the heart of religion and which led him directly into an experimental knowledge of Jesus Christ.

Whitefield now passed through a period of trials and temptations, during which he incurred the contempt of his fellow students, provoked the displeasure of the Master of the College, and suffered periods of illness. It was during a period of absence from the University that Whitefield's soul was enlightened by God in the knowledge of his free grace, and in the necessity of being justified in his sight by faith only. After extensive soul-searching Whitefield was ordained at Gloucester in 1736, and his formal ministry began. He finished his degree of Bachelor of Arts at Oxford, and then he continued his work of distributing money and books among the poor prisoners. His early attempts at preaching were marked by increasing popularity. The congregations were very large, and the doctrine of the new birth and justification by faith in Jesus Christ which he preached made its way like lightning into the hearers' consciences.

The publication of his sermon *On the Nature and Necessity of our Regeneration or New Birth in Christ Jesus* marked the beginning of a spiritual revival or awakening at London, Bristol, Gloucester, and Gloucestershire. Whitefield's preaching began to attract considerable attention. He generally preached nine times a week to thousands. On Sunday mornings, long before day, the streets were filled with people going to church. The people gave liberally, but Whitefield preached gratis, and the money collected went to charity.

As Whitefield's popularity increased,

opposition also increased. Many of the clergy grew angry, and complaints were made that the churches were so crowded that there was no room for the parishioners. Whitefield was accused of being a spiritual pickpocket who used charm to get the people's money. A few clergymen would not let him preach in their pulpits. His practices of keeping company with the dissenters was criticized, but his sermons were called for everywhere. He was offered large sums of money if he would stay in England, but he was determined to go to Georgia, for which he set sail in December of 1737, at the age of twenty-three.

The account of his voyage to America at the end of 1737 was sent back to England in the early summer of 1738. Although it was designed for the edification of his personal friends, it was published without the author's consent and became known as Whitefield's *First Journal*. A slightly revised edition was then published and went through four editions in 1738. The *First Journal* enjoyed such a marked success that Whitefield published six more journals detailing his life down to March, 1741.

During his second voyage to America in 1739, Whitefield wrote the story of his early life prior to his ordination in 1735, which he published in 1740 with the title *A Short Account*. It was on his third voyage to America in 1744 that he wrote *A Further Account* (published in 1747), which covered the period following his ordination until the time of his *First Journal*. His works were republished in a revised form in 1756. *An Unpublished Journal* covering Whitefield's second tour in New England between August 1744 and the spring of 1745 was recently discovered in the Library of Princeton Theological Seminary and was first published in the December, 1938, number of *Church History*.

Whitefield lost no opportunity to care for the souls of men. Even aboard ship on his voyages to and from America he continued to preach, to read prayers, and to visit the sick. Whenever he could he held private conversations concerning our fall in Adam, and the necessity of our new birth in Christ Jesus. He catechised whoever would listen.

Whitefield continued his evangelical ministry in the New World. He continued to preach that Jesus Christ is the one Mediator between God and man, and he proclaimed unhesitatingly the judgment to come.

Upon his return to England after his first stay in America, Whitefield was warmly received. Crowds continued to flock by the thousands to hear his message that we are justified by an act of faith in Jesus Christ, without any regard to past, present, or future works. He reports that God enabled him to speak upon the doctrine of the new birth.

In all his success Whitefield remained humble, filled with love, peace, and joy in the Holy Spirit, attributing all success to the free grace in Christ Jesus, which Whitefield freely offered to all sinners who would lay hold of Christ by faith. Many who heard were touched to the quick and felt what was spoken, uttering hearty and loud amens. Many conversions were wrought. In February of 1739, because he was refused the use of a church, Whitefield began to preach outdoors to tens of thousands, in spite of official opposition on the part of the officials of the Church of England. In spite of slanderous remarks to the effect that he was mad and that he had said he was the Holy Ghost, Whitefield found his way into the hearts of the people; he preached with a passionate power that brought souls home to Christ. At no time did he desire separation from the Established Church. He saw no reason to leave the Established Church, no matter how badly he was treated by corrupt members and ministers. He judged the state of the Church, not from the practice of its members, but by its primitive and public constitutions; and as long as the articles of the Church of England were agreeable to Scripture, Whitefield purposed to preach them without bigotry or party zeal.

Thus, in spite of all opposition and threats, Whitefield continued to preach throughout the length and breadth of England, as well as throughout the colonies of the New World. In Georgia he established an orphanage for children, and he utilized the funds he raised from his ever-growing audiences to maintain it.

His dependence upon the Spirit of God for his message, and the effect that he had upon his audience can be seen from an entry made in his *Seventh Journal,* on November 2, 1740, concerning his preaching in New York: "Preached in the morning with some freedom, but was dejected before the evening sermon, and when I came into the pulpit, I could have chosen to be silent rather than speak. After I had begun, however, the Spirit of the Lord gave me freedom, and at length came down like a mighty rushing wind, and carried all before it. Immediately, the whole congregation was alarmed. Crying, weeping, and wailing were to be heard in every corner; men's hearts failing them for fear, and many were to be seen falling into the arms of their friends. My soul was carried out till I could scarce speak anywhere. A sense of God's goodness overwhelmed me. A little boy was much concerned, on the pulpit stairs. One of my friends asked him why he cried. 'Who can help it?' he said, 'Mr. Whitefield's words cut me to the heart.' After I came home, I threw myself upon the bed and in awful silence admired the infinite freeness, sovereignty, and condescension of the love of God."

Whitefield was interested in theological issues. He regarded his converts as remarkable proofs of the doctrine of God's eternal election and everlasting love. For if believers are to do God justice, they will acknowledge that God first chose them. If God has chosen the believer, it must be from all eternity, without regard to anything foreseen in them. It is God's electing grace that assures that Christ did not die in vain and that sinners will in fact be saved.

Although Whitefield's preaching emphasized faith and repentance, he was motivated by the Calvinistic doctrine of election and predestination. His theology included the doctrine of a free and electing grace. Whitefield did not hesitate to disagree strongly in a letter to John Wesley in answer to the latter's sermon entitled *Free Grace.* Whitefield rebuked Wesley's doctrine of universal redemption and his attack on the doctrine of predestination. Against Wesley, Whitefield firmly held that God intends to bestow His saving grace, through Jesus Christ, only to a certain number, and that the rest of mankind will suffer eternal death, which is the proper wages of sin.

The doctrine of election in no way

dampened Whitefield's enthusiasm for evangelistic preaching; he believed that the God who appointed salvation for a certain number also appointed the preaching of the Word to bring them to it. The Gospel was designed by God to be the power of God unto the eternal salvation of the elect, but since no one knows who are the elect and who are the reprobate, the ministers of the Word must preach to everyone. The doctrine of election in no way tended to destroy Whitefield's desire for the salvation of sinners, for as a true lover of the Lord Jesus Christ, he continued to preach until the day before his death in 1770.

THE JOURNAL OF JOHN WESLEY

Author: John Wesley (1703-1791)
Type of work: Spiritual autobiography
First published: 1739 and following, seriatim

Principal Ideas Advanced

The command to live holy lives needs to be accompanied by a free proclamation of Christ's atoning work and of the witness of the Holy Spirit in the hearts of believers.

The work of God in the lives of men is often accompanied by emotional upheavals, but the evidence that it is God's work lies only in the moral changes it produces in men's lives.

Christians ought to gather in small societies for their mutual improvement, and these societies ought to be organized in a common undertaking.

The educational, economic, and social needs of men are a worthy concern of these societies.

John Wesley began keeping a diary during his student days at Oxford upon reading in Jeremy Taylor's *The Rule and Exercise of Holy Living and Holy Dying* (1650-1651) that a Christian ought to keep systematic account of how he employs every hour of his time. About 1739, when Methodism was beginning to be a controversial issue, Wesley published the parts of the diary which he considered most material to his cause, together with "such little reflections" as came to his mind. Throughout his life he continued this practice, recording his thoughts daily, and later publishing excerpts. Over his long life, twenty-one installments were made available to an eager and growing body of followers. Wesley kept his diaries in a private cipher, transcribing only the parts he thought would enhance the cause of evangelical revival. In 1909, Nehemiah Curnock unraveled Wesley's code and, drawing upon previously unpublished materials, produced the standard modern edition of the *Journal*.

John Wesley came from a remarkable family. In an age when piety was greatly in decline, his father, Samuel

Wesley (1662-1735), and his mother, Susannah, daughter of a famous nonconformist clergyman, kept alive the best traditions of the English Church. At John's request, his mother set down in writing the rules which she used in bringing up her family. The letter in which she recounts these principles is one of the most interesting parts of the *Journal*. Strict by modern standards, Susannah was nevertheless sympathetic and, above all, understanding. Her principle was to conquer the child's will early. "As self-will is the root of all sin and misery," she wrote, "so whatever cherishes this in children insures their after-wretchedness and irreligion; whatever checks and mortifies it promotes their future happiness and piety." She taught her children their prayers and catechism as soon as they could speak, and she taught them to read at the age of five, using the Bible as a textbook. For six hours a day for a quarter of the year, her house was turned into a school. In addition, she set aside a regular time every night of the week to talk to one of her children in private. Observing that children sometimes lie in order to avoid being punished, she made it a rule that whoever, when charged with a fault of which he was guilty, confessed and promised to amend, would be spared punishment; and consequently she commended and frequently rewarded children when they were obedient, especially in matters which went against their inclinations. Distinguishing between intention and performance, she argued that when a child did something wrong, if the intention were to obey, the will to do well should be accepted with kind words and the child tenderly directed how to do better in the future.

But if, in this way, Samuel and Susannah Wesley laid the foundation for Methodism, it must not be supposed that when the young John Wesley went out into the world he was already a saint. He had devout qualities, but, as a fellow at Oxford, he was an enthusiastic sportsman and far from immune to the charms of young women. After his ordination, in 1726, John acted for more than a year as his father's curate, at Epworth, finding time to attend village fairs and dances with his sisters, to shoot plover, and to read plays. Twice he was in love, but he was too poor to think of marriage.

It was one of his young lady acquaintances who directed Wesley's attention to the writings of Thomas à Kempis and of Jeremy Taylor, which, together with William Law's *A Treatise of Christian Perfection* (1726) and *A Serious Call to a Devout and Holy Life* (1728), intensified his interest in religion. His younger brother, Charles (1707-1788), who had come up to Oxford while John was away, had begun to meet with two friends; they met to help one another with their studies and with their spiritual life. John, on his return, was welcomed into the group and soon became its leader. Besides meeting three or four times a week, the members made it a practice to visit the prison regularly and to distribute alms to needy families. Such a display of piety seemed excessive, not merely to students but also to university officials, and there was some talk that "the censors were going to blow up The Godly Club," or, as they were sometimes called, "The Methodists."

Wesley's understanding of Christianity at this period of his life centered on the ideal of Christian perfection. In a sermon before the University, January, 1733, entitled "The Circumcision of the Heart," he stressed the need for "that habitual disposition of the soul, which in the sacred writings is termed holiness, and which directly implies the being cleansed from sin; from all filthiness both of flesh and spirit; and, by consequence, the being endued with those virtues which were in Christ Jesus." This concern for perfection and holiness, which was so characteristic of high church Anglican theology in the previous century, was the main motive in Wesley's life when he visited America in 1735, where he ministered for two years, chiefly in Savannah, Georgia. His purpose in going to America had been to convert the Indians; but his high-church practices were too rigorous even for the colonists; and he fled from Georgia in order to avoid prosecution at the hands of influential persons whom he had offended.

The story of Wesley's acquaintance with the Moravian Brethren during the crossing of the Atlantic is well known. The joyful confidence which these simple people possessed in time of storm convinced Wesley that his was but "a fair summer religion." "I went to America," he says, "to convert the Indians; but O! who shall convert me? who, what is he that will deliver me from this evil heart of unbelief?" (January, 1738.) Commenting later on his experience, he says that he had trusted too much to his own works and his own righteousness and not enough in the free mercy of God. The Moravian Brethren tried to show him "a more excellent way," but he was "too learned and too wise to understand." (May, 1738.) This was his condition when, a few months after his return to England, he attended a religious meeting on Aldersgate Street, where he heard one of the Moravian Brethren reading Luther's preface to the Epistle to the Romans. "About a quarter before nine," he writes, "while he was describing the change which God works in the heart through faith in Christ, I felt myself strangely warmed. I felt I did trust in Christ, Christ alone, for salvation; and an assurance was given me that He had taken away my sins, even mine, and saved me from the law of sin and death." (May, 1738). Wesley confesses that, when he returned home, he was still buffeted by temptation and doubt, but, he says, there was this difference that, whereas before, the temptations often got the better of him, now help came from Heaven and he was always conqueror.

The witness within his heart to the forgiveness of his sins greatly strengthened Wesley's preaching. After a visit to the Moravian churches in Germany, he entered upon a busy but undistinguished ministry in London and vicinity. A society which he had formed the previous year now numbered thirty-two persons. Besides meeting with them, he visited jails and workhouses and preached in different churches to growing congregations. That the churches, one after another, refused him their pulpits did not prevent his keeping a busy round of appointments. Still, it was only when, on the urging of George Whitefield (1714-1770), whose ministry closely paralleled his own, Wesley so far broke with formality as to consent to preach in the open, that great numbers were enrolled in his following. From then on, Wesley could well say,

"I look upon all the world as my parish."

Although not the dramatic orator that Whitefield was, Wesley nevertheless proved an impressive speaker. Because of the force of his argument and his burning conviction, many hearers carried away the impression that Wesley was speaking to them personally. Frequently, various individuals shed tears, fell into fits, and cried out hysterically. Such emotional displays, which his rivals deplored under the name of "enthusiasm," Wesley defended. He explained that it was not the external signs that he rejoiced in but in the changed lives which resulted. He said to his critics, "You deny that God does now work these effects; at least, that He works them in this manner. I affirm both, because I have . . . seen (as far as a thing of this kind can be seen) very many persons changed in a moment from the spirit of fear, horror, despair, to the spirit of love, joy, and peace; and from sinful desire, till then reigning over them, to a pure desire of doing the will of God." (May, 1739.)

But it was Wesley's mastery of organization, rather than his effectiveness as a preacher, that contributed most to the success of his revival. Preaching in the open was unorthodox, but forming religious societies was very much in the approved Anglican tradition. Wherever Wesley preached, he organized groups. Classes of twelve were formed, each under a leader who was responsible for assembling the others for weekly class meetings, for taking their offerings (typically a penny a week), and for reporting to Wesley which ones were in good standing. Wesley visited each class once a quarter and on each visit gave a ticket "under his own hand" to each member whose "seriousness and good conversation" was reported to him. The class leaders became a kind of lay ministry who were assembled in district conferences once a year.

It was Wesley's intention that, so far as feasible, the members of his "connexion" would continue to be members of their respective parishes and receive sacraments from the local clergy. The arrangement worked hardships in many instances, and because there were only a handful of priests in his organization, Wesley was pressed to have some of his lay preachers ordained. At first he availed himself of the services of an accommodating bishop of the Greek Orthodox Church to lay hands on his candidates for ordination. Afterwards, however, arguing that he was as much a bishop as any man in England, he performed the ordination himself—so far had he moved from his early High-Church principles. Nevertheless, to the end of his days he resisted those in his societies who wanted to separate from the Anglican Church. To one group he said (January, 1787), "If you are resolved, you may have your service in church-hours; but remember, from that time, you will see my face no more." This altered their purpose, and "from that hour I have heard no more of separating from the Church."

From the time he began to preach the gospel of free forgiveness, Wesley ran into opposition from within the Church. When he took to field-preaching, he incited the fury of all sorts. Magistrates tried to arrest him and his preachers and impress them into the militia, on the grounds of vagrancy. Landowners threatened to drive him from their towns. Mobs of ordinary people sought to break up the meetings, not infrequently under the impression that Wesley was a Roman Catholic and that he was working in the interests of the Pretender to the Crown. Wesley showed great courage and adroitness in dealing with these mobs, and he often succeeded in winning the leaders to his side.

It was given to Wesley to outlive most of his enemies and to see his work everywhere bearing fruit. Even those who did not approve of his gospel could scarcely object to the changes which they saw in the lives of men. Wesley records a letter which he wrote to *The Chronicle* (January, 1761) on the changes he had lately found in Newgate prison. The place was clean. Men were provided with tools and materials so that they might work. "By the blessing of God on these regulations the prison now has a new face: nothing offends either the eye or ear; and the whole has the appearance of a quiet, serious family." Similar changes were found in textile factories. In Epworth, Wesley reports, there were four of these, employing large numbers of workers. Some of the workers attended prayer meeting, and finding themselves dissatisfied with the immoral conditions that prevailed at their work, they urged their fellows to make the factories models of propriety. In May, 1782, Wesley visited three of these factories and "found religion had taken deep root in them. No trifling word was heard among [the workers], and they watch over each other in love."

The social products of Methodism were by no means accidental. Far ahead of his time, Wesley took a direct interest in the education and economic condition of his converts. He established schools, opened dispensaries, and organized loan funds. One of his most effective innovations was the publication of a wide range of books and pamphlets at low cost, partly for children in the schools, but also for the general public. It has been remarked that no man in the eighteenth century did so much to create in the English people a taste for good reading.

Another innovation was less effective. Convinced that electricity has healing properties, he procured apparatus which he made available to any who desired treatment. The patients became so numerous that he had to set up three different centers. "Hundreds, and perhaps thousands," he says, "received unspeakable good, . . . so that when I hear any talk of the danger of being electrified (especially if they are medical men who talk so), I cannot but impute it to great want either of sense or honesty." (November, 1757.)

As a student, Wesley had exhibited a strong classical taste, and throughout his life he read widely in both ancient and modern authors. He personally composed Latin and French grammars, wrote short histories of Rome and of England, and made selections from Milton and Isaac Watts for use in Methodist schools. Of Handel's *Messiah,* he writes: "In many parts, especially several of the choruses, it exceeded my expectation." (August, 1759.) He was, of course, inclined to judge the products of human culture from the standpoint of eternity; if he was willing to commend the play "Adelphi" by Terence as "an entertainment not unworthy of a Christian," (December, 1768), he was equally ready to censure the misanthropy of Rousseau and "his brother-infidel, Voltaire." (February, 1770.) Taken by friends to visit the British Museum when he was seventy-seven, Wesley remarked on the wide range such a place afforded one's curiosity, but added that he could not resist reckoning what account man would have to give to the Judge of the quick and dead for the time and money expended in collecting all these things. (December, 1780.)

The work which Wesley originated made great demands upon him. He was constantly moving, preaching fifteen sermons a week and traveling from five to eight thousand miles a year, over all parts of the British Isles. When he married he said, "I cannot understand how a Methodist preacher can answer it to God to preach one sermon or travel one day less in a married than in a single state." (March, 1751.)

Because of Wesley's itinerate life, the *Journal* is an excellent travelogue. Wesley was a keen observer of nature and places, and the excitement which his presence everywhere caused was a source of countless anecdotes. Occasionally, a comment suggests that Wesley might have liked to settle down, as, when in his seventy-ninth year, he admired the pleasant garden and shady walk of a certain Miss Harvey. "How gladly could I repose awhile here!" he writes. "But repose is not for me in this world." (July, 1782.) The next summer he did take a little vacation—a trip to the Netherlands, where he was welcomed as a dignitary and saw many things of interest.

"I am now an old man," he writes near the close of his *Journal,* "decayed from head to foot. My eyes are dim; my right hand shakes much; my mouth is hot and dry every morning; I have a lingering fever almost every day; my motion is weak and slow. However, blessed be God, I do not slack my labour: I can preach and write still." (January, 1790.)

That Wesley could write, and that he kept his powers to the end, his *Journal* is witness. The man "whose eloquence and logical acuteness," Macaulay said, "might have made him eminent in literature, whose genius for government was not inferior to that of Richelieu," left, in his *Journal,* a monument which is, in its own way, a world classic.

SEASONABLE THOUGHTS ON THE STATE OF RELIGION IN NEW ENGLAND

Author: Charles Chauncy (1705-1787)
Type of work: Criticism of revival movements
First published: 1743

Principal Ideas Advanced

The Great Awakening has caused disruption in the order of the churches of New England.

Antinomianism and revivalism tend to develop similar theological concerns. The itinerant clergy intrude upon settled congregations; by their unwarranted accusations against the pastors of churches they have denied the true fruits of the new birth of regenerated Christians.

True conversion involves a transformation of the mind as well as the heart, though primary attention in the "awakenings" has been given to the affections.

In the fourth and fifth decades of the eighteenth century the churches along the Atlantic coastline were in the midst of the First Great Awakening, the revival of religion which affected practically all American church life. Two names stand out as contemporary interpreters of that period: Jonathan Edwards (1703-1758) and Charles Chauncy (1705-1787). Edwards, the famed pastor of the church in Northampton, Massachusetts, and renowned Calvinistic theologian, had been a prime figure in promoting the revivals. Assisted by George Whitefield (1714-1770), Gilbert Tennent (1703-1764), and others, Edwards, through vivid theological imagery and tireless labor, sought to awaken sinners to their true condition. In 1736 he published an essay entitled *A Faithful Narrative of the Surprising Work of God in the Conversion of Many Hundred Souls in Northampton*, which received wide attention in the New England churches. Only seven years earlier Edwards had received the mantle of leadership for a large segment of Congregationalism from his grandfather, Solomon Stoddard (1643-1729). A mere five years earlier Edwards had visited Boston to deliver his first lecture before the clergy of that area. An unassuming member of his audience was Charles Chauncy, then assistant to Thomas Foxcroft (1696-1769) in the Congregational Church of Boston.

Charles Chauncy, a graduate of Harvard in 1721 and great grandson of his namesake and second President of Harvard, was to serve the Boston Church for sixty years. His name was brought to the attention of the New England churches when he published his own interpretation of the revivals under the title *Seasonable Thoughts on the State of Religion in New England.*

The immediate effect of the revivals was divisive, in both political and theological matters. In the coastal and inland regions, churches divided over the issues raised by the "awakening." Edwards and Chauncy represented two developing parties in New England church life. Edwards, a graduate of Yale, spoke for an increasingly larger group within western Massachusetts and Connecticut Congregationalism; from him stems the New Divinity or consistent Calvinist theological tradition which was carried on by such men as Samuel Hopkins (1721-1803) and Joseph Bellamy (1719-1790). Chauncy, reflecting the more liberal interests of the eastern Massachusetts churches, gradually made more evident his dissent from the more severe aspects of Calvinism. Though his sympathy for the developing Arminian theology was not clear by the early 1740's, he later became one of the key spokesmen for the movement. When the revival began neither Edwards nor Chauncy was conscious of being anything other than a loyal defender of the Calvinistic tradition, but it was not long until the dispute over the revivals had turned into protracted theological warfare.

After the second wave of the revival (1741-1742), Chauncy became publicly concerned about its excesses. A main cause for his developing disenchantment were the visits of itinerant clergy to the Boston area. George Whitefield, Gilbert Tennent, and James Davenport had stopped to preach in the vicinity. At the same time, Edwards, in Northampton, was concerned lest the churches of New England fail to give the revivals their full support, and in 1741 he published *The Distinguishing Marks of a Work of the Spirit of God.* This essay, while critical of some of the excesses of the revivals, sought to encourage the clergy of New England to promote the revival movement. Chauncy felt that the essay needed an answer; the conflict had now been brought to the printed page.

The publication of Chauncy's *Seasonable Thoughts* made clear his dissent from the practices and underlying theology of the revivals. By drawing out the more severe aspects of seventeenth century New England antinomianism, he attempted to make the implications of the awakenings evident to all his readers. The threat, posed by the revivals, to the order of the New England churches had become evident to him in conversations with other pastors. "Few, perhaps, have taken more Pains to inform themselves than I have done. I have been a Circle of more than three hundred Miles, and had, by this Means, an Opportunity of going thro' a great Number of Towns in this, and the neighbouring Government of Connecticut, and of having personal Conversation with most of the Ministers, and many other Gentlemen, in the Country, and of setting a Correspondence with several of them, with a particular View to know, as nearly as might be, the Truth of Things, upon better Evidence than that of meer Hear-Say." He was now convinced: "There never was a Time, in this Land, wherein there was such flocking after some *particular Ministers,* and *glorying* in them, as though they were Gods rather than *Men;* never a Time, wherein *Men's Professions* and *Affections* rose higher; never a Time, wherein *Conversions, numerous* Conversions were so much boasted of: Would to God, there was no Reason to suspect the Truth of any one of them!" He observed that ". . . there may be a very *specious Shew* where there is not the Substance of Religion. . . ."

Edwards and the other supporters of the Awakening had declared the new vigor in the churches to be evidence of God's work in this land of "steady habits." It was this claim that Chauncy wanted to examine. Unlike the revivalists, Chauncy insisted that man could not ordinarily be converted without considerable preparation; the mind as well as the heart needed transformation for a true conversion. The public evidences of a "new birth" are no sure sign of an inward change; it is too easy, Chauncy argued, for a man to deceive himself and to be mistaken about his true state. Though it is not possible for one man to peer into the heart and mind of another to discover if the "change" has been a work of God, there are certain evidences which, if they continue, give strong support for the claim of regeneration. These signs are: love to God and love to neighbor, joy, peace, long-suffering, gentleness, goodness, meekness, and temperance. But, unfortunately, it is frequently the case that these new gifts are lacking in those who have been converted by the revivalists. In their place appear physical disturbances, untempered criticism, and unjustified accusations. "Moreover," Chauncy writes, "the Way in which these Terrors spread themselves is a Circumstance, that does not much favour their *divine Origin*. They seem to be suddenly propagated, from one to another, as in a great Fright Consternation they often begin with a single Person, a *Child*, or *Woman*, or *Lad*, whose *Shrieks* set others a *Shrieking*. . . . And where this has been the Case, there is no great Difficulty in finding out the Cause: Tis far more reasonable to look for it in Nature, than in Grace."

Chauncy attributed much of the excess of the revivals to the itinerant preachers; he describes the preachers as "the true Cause of most of the Disorders." Whitefield, Tennent, and Davenport were not successful diplomats; they entered the "Lord's vineyard" with enthusiasm, not with trepidation. As a result they did not shun attacks on settled clergy or refrain from accusing them of being unconverted and, therefore, unworthy pastors. The Boston area had received visits from these traveling parsons and the eastern Massachusetts churches did not relish their outspoken ways. Chauncy's concern was clear. "I complain not of People's hearing Ministers that are not their own, as they may occasionally happen among them; Nay, I object not against *one* Minister's coming among the People of *another*, on Purpose, that they might have the Benefit of his Gifts and Labours; provided there be a mutual Agreement between *All* the Parties concern'd, and the Case such as may properly call for such an Expedient: But for Ministers to make a Business of going out of their own, into other *Men's* Parishes, unask'd; or, at the Desire of only some disaffected People; And this, in known Opposition to the *settled* Pastors: it's contrary to all *Reason*, as well as *Scripture*, and subversive of all Order in the *Churches;* Especially, when they carry the Matter so far as to *creep into private Houses*, when they can't any longer force themselves into the *Pulpits*. . . ." "Scripture," "reason," and "order": these words recur throughout Chauncy's essay. The New Testament does not encourage the kind of preaching the revivalists offer; reason demands a critical attitude, not merely an emotional response; and the order of the churches must be preserved, or chaos will result. Itineracy can lead only to the disruption of the Church and its Gospel.

Chauncy's *Seasonable Thoughts* was not a theological essay, but it was the first full-length critique of the Great Awakening. Unlike Edwards, Chauncy could analyze the revivals without becoming involved in theological speculation; Edwards could never extricate himself from theological reflection. In addition, Edwards could excuse the excesses of the revivals by arguing that these were but accompanying and secondary features of a "work of God," but Chauncy saw the repeated displays of emotionalism and extravagance as inevitable and undesirable components of the "awakenings." This, in short, was Chauncy's point: "There is the Religion of the Understanding and Judgment, and Will, as well as of the Affections; and if little Account is made of the former, while great Stress is laid upon the latter, it can't be but People should run into Disorders." This advocate of stability, order, and reasonableness was to become one of the leaders of more liberal Arminian theology later in the century and he continued to be a thorn in the side of the consistent Calvinism of Edwards and his successors.

A TREATISE CONCERNING RELIGIOUS AFFECTIONS

Author: Jonathan Edwards (1703-1758)
Type of work: Christian ethics
First published: 1746

Principal Ideas Advanced

True religion consists in great part of holy affections.

The affections are vigorous inclinations toward something, or away from something; love, desire, hope, and gratitude are of the former sort; while hatred, fear, anger, and grief are of the latter.

The true religious affections differ from the false affections in the following twelve respects: they are spiritual; they are grounded in the excellence of divine things considered in themselves; they are founded on the moral excellency of divine things; they arise from the mind's enlightenment by divine things; they are attended with a spiritual conviction of the certainty of divine things; they are attended with evangelical humiliation; they are attended with a change of nature in the soul; they promote the spirit of love which was in Christ; they are attended with a Christian tenderness of spirit; they exhibit a beautiful symmetry and proportion; they increase the appetite for spiritual attainments; and they lead to the practice of a Christian life.

Jonathan Edwards' *Treatise Concerning Religious Affections* is a careful attempt to resolve a question of critical pertinence during the Great Awakening of 1740-1743: How is the genuine piety of the true believer to be distinguished from the spurious piety of the emotionally affected convert? How is true religion to be distinguished from false? Edwards put the question in the following manner: "What is the nature of true religion? and wherein do lie the distinguishing notes of that virtue and holiness, that is acceptable in the sight of God."

The thesis is presented almost immediately: "True religion, in great part, consists in holy affections." Edwards claims that this idea is supported by a passage from I Peter 1:8: "Whom having not seen, ye love: in whom, though now ye see him not, yet believing, ye rejoice with joy unspeakable, and full of glory." The words of the Apostle suggest that Christians under persecution were sustained by "a supernatural principle of love to something *unseen;* they loved Jesus Christ. . . ." Furthermore, although the persecuted Christians experienced great suffering, they knew a great spiritual joy. Love and joy—these are holy affections by which true faith can be known. But the problem was to discover signs by which the true religious affections could be distinguished from the false. Not all love and joy are of the gracious and spiritual sort; if it is by reference to the affections that true religion is to be understood, there must be ways of distinguishing the true, holy affections from the false.

But before Edwards could undertake the task of distinguishing the signs of true religious affections, he had to clarify the notion of the affections. He defines the affections as "the more vigorous and sensible exercises of the inclination and will of the soul." The faculty of the soul by which it perceives and speculates, a faculty which Edwards calls the understanding, must be distinguished, he argues, from that other faculty by which the soul is inclined or disinclined, by which it likes or dislikes, is pleased or displeased. The latter faculty, he writes, "is sometimes called the *inclination:* and, as it has respect to the actions that are determined and governed by it, is called the *will:* and the *mind,* with regard to the exercises of this faculty, is often called the *heart.*"

Edwards is careful to point out that what are ordinarily called the affections do not differ essentially from the will; the will is the soul's faculty of inclination, and the affections—such as love and hatred—are distinguishable from the inclinations of the soul which we would call acts of will, only by the greater vigor and liveliness of the affections.

If true religion consists in "vigorous and lively actings of the inclination and will of the soul, or the fervent exercises of the heart," and if by the affections one means precisely the more vigorous and lively of the soul's inclinations, then it follows—so Edwards insists—that true religion consists, in great part, of the affections.

One would be misreading Edwards if one supposed that what Edwards here proposes is that true religion be distinguished from false religion by reference to sentiments, feelings, or emotions. Edwards' criterion is not subjective, for he has defined the affections as inclinations; his definition is pragmatic. It is by the quality of the whole response of the human being to the divine—by the vigorous inclination toward the divine—that the true believer is to be distinguished.

Among the affections which are signs of true religion are the following: godly fear; hope in God; love of God, Christ, and mankind; the hatred of sin, holy joy; religious sorrow, mourning, and "brokenness of heart"; gratitude, compassion, mercy, and zeal. Edwards cites passages from Scripture which lend support to his claims in regard to the particular religious affections.

Of all the affections, Edwards writes, love is the chief religious affection, the "fountain of all other affections." Christ, "the perfect example of true religion and virtue," was the greatest instance of the exercise of the holy affections; and love received its most transforming expression through Him.

Having at some length argued in support of his thesis, Edwards draws some inferences from the proposition that true religion consists in great part of the holy affections. He asserts that those are in error who would abandon the affections as being insubstantial. If true religion lies in the holy affections, then the effort must be made to move those affections; that is, to affect the hearts of men.

Having devoted Part One of his book to the nature of the religious affections and to their importance, Edwards in Part Two reviews twelve presumed signs of the true affections, and the author argues that the presumed signs are not signs at all. One cannot conclude, for example, from the height of affections—that is, from their pitch and intensity—that they are true religious affections; nor can one suppose that when affections are raised to a high degree, they are not true religious affections. Nor can the fact that some affections have a great effect on the body be taken as a sign one way or the other, that those affections are holy. Nor can the tendency of some affections to make men "fervent and abundant" in talking about religious matters be taken as a sign of the spirituality of the affections (nor can it be taken as a sign that the affections are not holy). Nor is the fact that sometimes the affections arise through no effort on the part of the persons who have them, a sign of their being, or not being, true religious affections. Other features of affections which are not significant one way or the other are the following: their being occasioned by Scriptural passages, their giving the appearance of love, their being of great number and of many kinds, their following awakenings of conscience, their disposing persons to spend a great deal of time in external religious duties, their leading persons to praise and glorify God with their mouths, their giving the conviction that the divine is being experienced, and their enabling a person to be affecting and pleasing to the truly godly.

Before going on to present the distinguishing signs of truly holy affections, Edwards warns the reader that there are no rules by which one man can with *certainty* distinguish the true followers of religion from the false; nor can any saint know of his saintly condition with certainty, particularly if he has fallen into "a dead, carnal and unchristian frame." Nor can it be hoped that knowledge of the signs of true religion will lead hypocrites to reform themselves. The rules are nevertheless useful, especially for those who are themselves truly holy, provided that the rules, or signs, are not taken as sufficient in themselves, but as matters to be considered in the context of the Christian experience.

Edwards devotes the remainder of his book to a careful and detailed exposition of twelve signs of true religious affections. He regards extended discussion of the signs as necessary because language is not flexible enough to permit him to make himself clear unless he makes the effort to explore the depth of meaning involved in each summary remark about the signs. Early in the book Edwards remarks: "It must be confessed, that language is here somewhat imperfect, and the meaning of words in a considerable measure loose and unfixed, and not precisely limited by custom, which governs the use of language." To appreciate the true character of Edwards' ideas, then, one must go to the book itself.

The true religious affections "arise from those influences and operations on the heart, which are *spiritual, supernatural* and *divine.*" The first sign, then, is *spirituality,* by which Edwards means, not an aspect of the soul as distinguished from the body, but the state of one in whom the Spirit of God dwells; such a one is directly under the influence of the divine supernatural.

The second sign of true religious affections is that they are directed toward the *excellence* of divine things, not out of self-love, but as moved by the glory of the divine considered for its own sake.

The true religious affections are founded, in particular, on the *moral* excellence of divine things. In presenting this third sign of true affections, Edwards emphasizes the power of *holiness.* Although true religious affections are aroused by the excellence of the divine, it is worthy of special mention that they are provoked by the holiness, the moral virtue, of the divine.

The fourth sign of true affections is that they arise from the mind's *understanding* of divine things; enlightenment stirs the affections.

The spiritual *conviction* of those who enjoy truly gracious affections can be taken as a fifth sign of the true affections; those who are truly religious have no doubts about the truth of the Gospel.

Evangelical humiliation is the sixth sign of the gracious affections. By evangelical humiliation Edwards means the sense of insufficiency that a Christian has when he considers how ineffective he would be without God's help, and how unlikely it is that he will be worthy of that help.

The seventh sign of the true religious affections is that they lead to a *change of nature;* the truly religious person is so affected by the divine that he is transformed.

The truly gracious affections *promote the spirit of love,* meekness, mercy, and forgiveness, which Christ possessed. The presence of such a spirit is the eighth sign of the true affections.

The ninth sign is *softness of heart,* the Christian tenderness of spirit. Unlike those who have false affections, true believers do not seek the exaltation of themselves; those with a true love of the divine are not bold or forward.

Those who possess truly gracious affections exhibit *symmetry and proportion* in their affections; the saints "have the whole image of Christ upon them. . . ."

The eleventh sign discussed by Edwards is the *increase of spiritual appetite* which accompanies the true religious affections.

Finally, Edwards presents, as a twelfth sign, the tendency of the true affections to promote *Christian practice.* Since by the affections Edwards meant the inclinations of the soul, and since the inclinations can be understood only by reference to practice, it is inevitable that the true affections "have their exercise and fruit in Christian practice."

Most writers on religious subjects are aware of the difference between the mere profession of belief and the true practice of it, but few writers have, like Edwards, made that difference clear. Edwards' final sign is, in effect, a general sign of the true religious affections. If one wishes to distinguish between the true and the false believer, one has only to see the difference that is made in the lives of those whose inclinations are toward the divine. For Edwards, as for William James, a true religious belief is neither an idle idea nor a passing sentiment; it is an active commitment to the ideal and the divine, and it shows itself in practice. The *Treatise Concerning Religious Affections* is a sensitive appraisal of the difference that true religious affections make in the life of the Christian.

THE DIARY OF DAVID BRAINERD

Author: David Brainerd (1718-1747)
Type of work: Spiritual autobiography
First published: 1749

Principal Ideas Advanced

Men must live in such a way that God alone is exalted.

Salvation is through faith in the righteousness of Christ; but before anyone can believe, he must be emptied of all pride and self-righteousness.

Christians ought to pray and work for the conversion of all nations, and to hope for the reign of Christ throughout the world.

David Brainerd is usually remembered in Church history as one of the early Colonial missionaries to the Indians. His enduring importance, however, is rather owing to his *Diary,* which was widely read in evangelical circles both in England and in America during the century following his death. This essentially private record of a soul struggling to be at one with God was partially edited by Brainerd in the closing weeks of his life and was published with additional materials by Jonathan Edwards (1703-1758) as *The Life and Diary of David Brainerd.* Neither Brainerd nor Edwards believed in perfectionism, and there is no attempt in the published any more than in the private work to represent the author as without faults. "But," says Edwards in the Preface, "notwithstanding all these imperfections, I am persuaded, every pious and judicious reader will acknowledge that what is here set before him is indeed a remarkable instance of true and eminent Christian piety in heart and practice, tending greatly to confirm the reality of vital religion, and the power of godliness, that it is most worthy of imitation, and in many ways calculated to promote the spiritual benefit of the careful observer."

David Brainerd was born in Connecticut and reached manhood during the New England Awakening, the religious revival of 1740-1743. A serious youth from a Christian home, he accepted without question the Calvinistic doctrine of God's sovereignty and of the efficacy of Christ's death for the salvation of the elect. His difficulty came when, in line with the new revivalist emphasis, he tried to achieve a personal experience of salvation. Examination of his life merely convinced him that he was among the damned; and the demand of evangelical preaching that he trust only in Christ in order to be saved seemed an impossibility. Frequently, he says, he rebelled against God: "I could not bear that it should be wholly at God's pleasure, to save or damn me, just as He would." But, reflecting on his rebellion, he was more than ever convinced that he belonged to those who deserve to be condemned.

For over a year he spent much of his time in prayer and fasting, spending whole days "in almost incessant cries to God for mercy, that He would open my eyes to see the evil of sin and the way of life by Jesus Christ." Gradually he came to understand that all his religious strivings were centered in himself and that he had no profound regard for God. These thoughts oppressed him, until, one Sabbath evening while "walking in a dark, thick grove," he seemed to have a sense of "unspeakable glory" in his soul. There was, he says, no vision or image, "but it was a new inward apprehension or view that I had of God, such as I had never had before. . . . I never had seen before anything comparable to it for excellency and beauty; it was widely different from all the conceptions that ever I had of God, or things divine. . . . My soul was so captivated and delighted with the excellency, loveliness, greatness, and other perfections of God, that I was even swallowed up in Him. At least to that degree that I had no thought at first, about my own salvation, and scarce reflected there was such a creature as I." In this way, he was brought to exalt God alone, and to subordinate his own life "to aim at His honor and glory, as King of the universe." In addition to perceiving the sovereignty of God, he had a new sense of the wisdom and grandeur of "the way of salvation" which God had ordained, and he became amazed that "all the world did not see and comply with this way of salvation, entirely by the righteousness of Christ."

The sense of God's presence, which remained with Brainerd unbroken for several days, was to return to him frequently through the remainder of his life, in spite of grievous periods of distress and darkness. If Brainerd had been a Roman Catholic, he would no doubt have withdrawn from the world, which, from this time forward, appeared to him always as a distraction, tending to draw his thoughts away from God. But, being a Puritan, he decided to attend Yale College and to prepare himself for the ministry, in spite of his premonitions that his studies and associations would prevent him from leading a life of strict devotion.

The faculty at Yale was unsympathetic with the Great Awakening; and when, during Brainerd's second year, a spirit of revival was felt among Yale students, occasion was found for expelling Brainerd from the College. Two books, parts of the *Diary,* which were written immediately following this trying experience, were destroyed by the author shortly before his death; but the matter is rehearsed at two times subsequently, when evangelical ministers tried to get the college to reverse its decision. With wonderful humility, Brainerd used the event to teach himself meekness and love toward men, and to wean himself away from attachment to worldly honor and approbation.

After his expulsion, Brainerd read theology with various ministers, an experience which may well have been more satisfying than attending Yale would have been. In the course of his devotions, he began to intercede "for poor souls and for the enlargement of Christ's kingdom in the world," and he felt that he ought himself to undertake something for the salvation of "the heathen."

In 1743, he was engaged by the Scottish Society for the Propagation of Christian Knowledge to carry on missionary work, first among the Stockbridge Indians in New England, and later among the Delaware Indians in Pennsylvania and New Jersey. The work at first gave little encouragement, at least for one who sought to bring the experience of vital religion to others. Remarkably, however, Brainerd's preaching produced among the Indians, who had never heard the Gospel before, all the manifestations which characterized the revival of religion in the churches. In the course of a few months, Brainerd brought his new converts to an understanding of Christian doctrine and to an acceptance of Christian obedience which, he testifies, equaled that of awakened Christians anywhere.

The *Diary* tells very little about Brainerd's missionary achievements, being almost entirely a record of his own spiritual pilgrimage; but, at the request of the Scottish Society which employed him, he also kept a *Journal*, in which he related the circumstances of his labors at greater length. Brainerd did not write in order to entertain, and the *Journal*, strictly a report of the progress of Christ's mission, is unadorned with geographical or ethnographical details. An exception is a detailed account of a sacrifice and dance which he came upon at the Indian town of Juneauta, on the Susquehanna: "I sat at a small distance, not more than thirty feet from them (though undiscovered), with my Bible in my hand, resolving, if possible, to spoil their sport, and prevent their receiving any answers from the infernal world, and there viewed the whole scene." Another is his report of a meeting with an Indian priest, who was something of a reformer among his own people. The priest received him with great courtesy, and told him his own experience. "It was manifest," writes Brainerd, "he had a set of religious notions that he had looked into for himself, and not taken for granted upon bare tradition; and he relished or disrelished whatever was spoken of a religious nature, according as it either agreed or disagreed with his standard." Indians looked upon the Indian priest as a fanatic, but Brainerd remarks, "there was something in his temper and disposition that looked more like true religion than anything I ever observed amongst other heathens."

For the most part, the *Journal* is an account of Brainerd's work at Crossweeksung, in New Jersey, and of the difficulties and discouragements he met with at other points where he regularly preached. The encouraging work at Crossweeksung began with a handful of women and children, who "like the woman of Samaria," traveled several miles to bring their friends together to hear him. In two weeks' time, some fifty persons were brought together; they listened twice a day as Brainerd taught them. When he had to leave, they urged him to come again. One woman said "she wished God would change her heart"; another that "she wanted to find Christ"; a chieftain "wept bitterly with concern for his soul." A month later, when Brainerd returned, "a surprising concern soon became apparent among them." All their conversation seemed to turn on religious matters. In the evening, they would not eat their food until they sent for him to ask a blessing on it. When he preached, there was scarcely one in ten that did not weep and cry out for his sins.

Brainerd made it a point to present to them only "the love and compassion of God in sending His Son to suffer for the sins of men," and thus he said nothing of the wrath of God upon unbelievers. But many of his hearers had the same kind of scruples as he had experienced, and, though invited to come and partake of God's love, were distressed "because they felt themselves unable to come." About a week after his return to Crossweeksung, while he was preaching, "the power of God seemed to descend upon the assembly 'like a mighty rushing wind.'" There was a universal crying out for mercy, those who had previously obtained relief were greatly comforted, and were able to help distressed friends. Many remained for hours, insensible of the time, praying for salvation. "This was indeed a surprising day," writes Brainerd, "and seemed enough to convince an atheist of the truth, importance and power of God's Word."

Like Jonathan Edwards and John Wesley, when they were faced with emotional upheavals caused by their preaching, Brainerd was careful to distinguish between experiences which "appeared solid, rational, and scriptural," and "visionary scenes, imaginary terrors, and all manner of mental disorders and delusions." He relates the story of an Indian woman who went into a trance, and cried out for Christ to take her. "I am very sensible," he says, "there may be great joys arising even to an ecstacy where there is still no substantial evidence of their being well grounded. But in the present case there seemed to be no evidence wanting in order to prove this joy to be divine, either in regard of its *preparatives, attendants,* or *consequents.*"

Brainerd first entered upon his Indian work in the spring of 1743. He was forced to leave it in the fall of 1746 because of tuberculosis, which had plagued him since his student days. When he left Crossweeksung, it was clear that death was not far off. He was advised to travel when he was able, as a means of prolonging life; but much of the next twelve months he spent in bed, attended by loving friends. He died in Northampton, Mass., at the home of Jonathan Edwards in October, 1747, at the age of twenty-nine.

In the closing months of his life, Brainerd had the opportunity, long denied him, of fellowship with other ministers. He expressed himself at this time much concerned about the counterfeits of true religion, particularly the rise of a kind of sectarian piety which offered salvation by faith without stressing the necessity for godly living. Against these "antinomians," he maintained that "humiliation, self-emptiness, or full conviction of a person's being utterly undone in himself" is essential to a "saving faith," and "that persons being never effectually to die in themselves are never truly united to Christ, and so perish." Another concern which he emphasized was the "future prosperity of Zion," and the necessity for ministers to devote themselves steadfastly to the task of advancing the Kingdom of Christ throughout the world. It seemed to him that the people of Scotland, who sponsored his mission, were more zealous in this matter than those in New England.

The violence of Brainerd's illness sometimes disturbed his reason toward the end, but between attacks of fever he enjoyed great serenity. "I think my mind never penetrated with so much ease and freedom into divine things," he writes after one spell of sickness; "I never felt so capable of demonstrating the truth of many important doctrines of the gospel as now. And as I saw clearly the truth of those great doctrines, which are justly styled the doctrines of grace; so I saw with no less clearness, that the *essence of religion* consisted in the soul's *conformity to God,* and acting above all selfish views, for *His glory,* longing to be *for Him,* to live to *Him,* and please and honor Him in all things. And this from a clear view of His infinite excellency and worthiness in Himself to be loved, adored, worshiped, and served by all intelligent creatures."

FREEDOM OF THE WILL

Author: Jonathan Edwards (1703-1758)
Type of work: Philosophical theology
First published: 1754

PRINCIPAL IDEAS ADVANCED

The act of volition is determined by the strongest motive which comes to the mind.

Man, being totally depraved, is under a moral necessity of sinning, though he has the natural ability not to sin; that is, there is no physical impediment or external force preventing him from willing the good.

The Arminian notion of liberty as involving self-determination, indifference, and contingency is neither logically defensible nor theologically accurate; the freedom of self determination is inconsistent with moral responsibility.

Man's salvation does not depend on any action of man but is entirely within the control of divine initiative and determination.

In 1754, Jonathan Edwards published *A Careful and strict Enquiry into the modern prevailing Notions of the Freedom of Will, Which is supposed to be essential to Moral Agency, Vertue and Vice, Reward and Punishment, Praise and Blame.* This essay has served to establish Edwards as America's greatest philosopher-theologian and one of the most incisive minds in Christian history. In the two hundred years since its publication over twenty editions have appeared in America and England.

The *Freedom of the Will,* or the *Inquiry,* as Edwards called it, was written during the winter months of 1753 while Edwards was pastor of the small Indian mission church in Stockbridge, Massachusetts. In 1750 he had been dismissed from the pastorate of the Congregational Church in Northampton, Massachusetts, where he had served since 1727. Though the cause for his separation from that church cannot be traced to one source, his strong and persistent defense of Calvinism was a primary factor. In the seven-year period, 1751-1757, during which he served the Stockbridge mission, he was able to complete several of his major treatises: *A Dissertation on the Nature of True Virtue, The Great Christian Doctrine of Original Sin Defended,* and the *Inquiry into the Freedom of Will.* His departure from Stockbridge in 1758 to assume the Presidency of the College of New Jersey (Princeton) and his illness and death in March of that year put an end to a distinguished theological career.

During Edwards' lifetime, the Arminian movement gained support in England and America. Jacob Arminius (1560-1609), a Dutch Reformed theologian, had sought to overcome the harsher aspects of seventeenth century scholastic Calvinism. The issues he raised were dealt with by the Synod of Dort (1619) which reasserted stringent Calvinism: total depravity, unconditional election, limited atonement, irresistible grace, and perseverance of the saints. The Arminians, who were condemned by the Synod, were in conflict with the doctrine of irresistible grace and stressed the view that the decrees of God are conditional upon man's acceptance. In the eighteenth and nineteenth centuries, the Arminians placed more emphasis on human responsibility and agency; less attention was given to divine initiative and decree. The center of Arminian thought in Edwards' time was England, and his treatise was prompted by the writings of men such as Daniel Whitby (1638-1726), John Taylor (1694-1761), and Isaac Watts (1674-1748).

The theological issue with which the *Inquiry* dealt is simple to state but difficult to solve. If God foreknows human volition, is man's will free? If man's will is self-determined, is God sovereign? Are freedom and necessity exclusive terms? In dealing with this general problem, Edwards divided his essay into two major divisions: 1) the definition and clarification of terms; 2) an analysis of the Arminian position.

The will is determined by the "strongest motive." By motive Edwards meant "the whole of that which moves, excites or invites the mind to volition, whether that be one thing singly, or many things conjunctly. . . . And when I speak of the *strongest motive,* I have respect to the strength of the whole that operates to induce to a particular act of volition, whether that be the strength of one thing alone, or of many together." Every effect has a cause; every act of volition will be the result of the choice of the "greatest apparent good" or "strongest motive." There is a necessary relation between an act of the will and its cause. But this "necessity" may be of two kinds. "Moral necessity" is the "necessity of connection and consequence" which arises from moral causes; "natural necessity" is the "necessity of connection and consequence" which arises from natural causes. Moral necessity is as absolute as natural necessity. For there to be freedom of will, man must have natural ability to will; that is, there must not be any physical impediment or natural defect or extrinsic factor which prevents him from doing as he wills. But man may be morally unable to will other than he does and yet his will is free. Edwards defined "moral inability" as a "want of inclination" or "want of sufficient motives in view" to produce the act of volition. Thus, freedom and liberty meant the "power, opportunity or advantage, that any one has, to do as he pleases." When this discussion is tied to the doctrine of total depravity, the implications of this view become clear. Man, because of original sin, is morally unable to will the good; yet he has no physical impediment standing in the way. Man is free, but free only to sin. To put it in another way, man is free to do what he wills, but not to do what he does not will. Because man is inherently depraved, he does not will to do the good.

In Part II of the essay, Edwards turned to the problem of whether there can be any freedom of the will as the Arminians spoke of it. According to Edwards, the Arminian idea of liberty involved three points: 1) self-determination of the will; that is, the will is not dependent on any cause outside itself; 2) indifference; that is, previous to the act of volition the mind is in a state of equilibrium; 3) contingency; that is, the will is governed by no necessity. Edwards dealt with each of these assertions.

If the will is self-determined, which means that it has its actions under its control, every volition must arise from a previous volition. As the train of choices is carried back, Edwards argued, we must come to the first volition in the whole series. If that first volition be self-determined, then it is not really the first volition, for a previous volition must have determined it. Yet, if that first volition is not determined by a preceding act of the will, the will is not self-determined. If the first act of the will is not free, in the Arminian sense of freedom, then none of the following acts are free. Thus, it follows that the will cannot be self-determined.

The argument that the act of volition is the result of the mind's state of indifference was equally inconsistent to Edwards, for this view implies that the mind prefers a choice, but has no preference. The "grand argument . . . that among several things the Will actually chooses one before another, at the same time that it is perfectly indifferent . . . is the very same thing as to say, the mind has a preference, at the same time that it has no preference." Edwards' assumption that every effect has a cause, that every act of volition is the result of the "strongest motive," would not allow this Arminian position. In a similar vein he dealt with the idea of liberty as consisting in contingency. Either an act of the will has a cause or it does not. If it does, it is not contingent, but necessary; that is, dependent on its cause. If it does not have a cause, which Edwards would allow only for the argument, then the will operates contingently without any determining cause. Under such circumstances, however, the will would not be active but passive; it would will by accident. Such willing would be mere capriciousness, not liberty or freedom, and consequently the freedom of indifference cannot allow for moral responsibility.

Underlying the Arminians' position was their difficulty with Calvinistic theology in relation to human responsibility. If man's will is not self-determined, they argued, then man is not deserving of praise or blame for his actions. Edwards agreed that if the "necessity" under which man wills is a *natural* necessity, then an act of volition cannot be described as praiseworthy or blameworthy. But if the act is done under "moral necessity," then the agent is subject to judgment. Man cannot will except as causally determined; hence, the only question is one concerning the nature of the cause. Since man is unable without the saving grace of Christ to do anything good and acceptable in God's sight, he is under a *moral* necessity to sin, the conditions of which have been determined and foreknown by God. "Providence infers some kind of necessity of all events, such a necessity as implies an infallible, previous fixedness of the futurity of the event. . . ."

Edwards did not intend to suggest that God commits sin, but that He is the "disposer of events" in such a way that sin will inevitably follow, though for holy ends. God's foreknowledge of events does not limit man's freedom. Critics then charged Edwards with making God into the cause of sin and, therefore, denying human responsibility. But, as Edwards argued, since all free actions are necessary actions, since no free act is undetermined, God's determination of events does not preclude human freedom. Man is free, even though he sins, because the "strongest motive" which determines his mind is a sinful motive; nevertheless, it is man's will that is responsible, not God's will. Man is responsible for his actions even though they are committed under a moral necessity of sinning. Freedom consists in the absence of any external compulsion, not in the absence of all causes whatsoever. Thus, in attempting to reconcile God's sovereignty with human freedom, Edwards calls attention to the fact that man chooses in accordance with his inclination; that is, as determined by the "strongest motive." Man is free, even though his nature puts him under a moral necessity to sin; that is, man is free, and in the exercise of his freedom he wills to sin.

Edwards' position illustrates the dilemma of a Calvinist who was both a revivalist and a predestinarian. God has determined that some will be damned, others saved. How is it possible to call men to repentance and also to assert God's predetermined election of some and damnation of others? The only solution that Edwards offered was to insist that although the "means of grace," that is, Church communion, participation in the sacraments, hearing and reading the Word, do not determine a man's ultimate destiny, unless one attends to the "means of grace," evidence is given of a lost condition. Edwards always presupposed that God's choice of some and damnation of others was in no way affected by man's action, except that those who participated in the Church gave stronger evidence of their saved state. The work of redemption is entirely God's action. True faith does not depend on man's "free" will, but on the sovereign Will of God; conversion is not the result of man's self-determination, but of God's impressing the soul with holy affections; the perseverance of the saints is due not to human action, but to God's saving and sustaining grace. Man's salvation is not dependent on his contingent, self-determined will, but is "absolutely fixed in God's decree. . . ." Reason and Scripture attest to this fact, Edwards claims.

The *Inquiry* prompted immediate discussion, though few who challenged Edwards were his equals. By far the best reply was that of James Dana, *An Examination of the Late Reverend President Edwards's 'Enquiry on Freedom of Will'*, published in 1770.

Throughout the remainder of the eighteenth century the essay of Edwards received attention from its defenders and opponents. The *Inquiry into the Freedom of Will* is a key document in the total theological work of Jonathan Edwards.

THE GREAT CHRISTIAN DOCTRINE OF ORIGINAL SIN DEFENDED

Author: Jonathan Edwards (1703-1758)
Type of work: Theology
First published: 1758

Principal Ideas Advanced

The doctrine of original sin is a cornerstone of the Christian Gospel.

Unless man were totally depraved, there would be no need for the redemptive work of Christ or the Scriptural requirement for a change of heart for entrance into the Kingdom of God.

To explain sin by asserting that it is the result of bad example or the misuse of freedom is to neglect its basic cause.

The universality of sin is evidence for the inherent depravity of human nature.

Any transgression of God's law deserves eternal punishment, and no good act can remove the damage to God's moral government.

Jonathan Edwards' *The Great Christian Doctrine of Original Sin Defended; Evidences of Its Truth Produced, and Arguments to the Contrary Answered* was published shortly after his death in 1758. Though the subject had long been a primary concern of Edwards, he had to wait until the later years of his life, during the time of his missionary work at Stockbridge, Massachusetts, to complete the treatise. The essay was directed against Arminian theology and was specifically prompted by the work of the English theologian, John Taylor, who published *The Scripture-Doctrine of Original Sin* in 1740.

The Arminian movement began in reaction to the severe and legalistic flavor of scholastic Calvinism and its stringent assertions of total depravity, unconditional election, and irresistible grace. Jacob Arminius (1560-1609) and his followers regarded themselves as Calvinists, but were concerned to uphold the moral responsibility of man for his actions and the necessary response of man to God's redeeming work. In the eighteenth century Arminian theologians openly attacked such key Calvinistic assertions as the doctrine of the total depravity of man and the imputation of Adam's sin. They emphasized man's ability to comply with the demands of the Gospel. By the third decade of the eighteenth century Arminianism in England had become orthodoxy, not heresy.

In his essay, John Taylor argued that Scripture does not teach the imputation of Adam's sin to his descendants. Our nature is not to blame for our sin. Sin is the choice to do wrong, though nothing within man's nature compels such action. The denial of original sin, the emphasis on moral responsibility as in itself incompatible with a doctrine of total depravity, the denial of the doctrine of election, the stress on moral living, the rejection of creed or confession as being determinative of theological formulation—these were the interests of Taylor and the Arminian movement of the eighteenth century. Jonathan Edwards was the only theologian of the time to give Taylor's essay a thoroughgoing critique; others tried, but most, like Isaac Watts, found themselves embarrassed by the answers a strict Calvinist should give.

Edwards' *Doctrine of Original Sin Defended* is a different kind of work from his *Inquiry into the Freedom of Will,* though these two are complementary and integrally related. In the *Inquiry* Edwards argued from certain given premises and proceeded through logical analysis and semantic clarification to reduce the Arminian position to confusion. The later work, *Doctrine of Original Sin Defended,* attempted to refute the Arminians on the basis of common evidence. Edwards insisted that his opponents were simply not facing up to the hard facts of life and that their explanations for the existence of human wrongdoing were highly superficial and grossly misleading. No Arminian would deny that man is sinner, but the Arminians differed with the Calvinists concerning the nature and extent of sin.

In his analysis, Edwards' first appeal was to the "evidences of original sin from facts and events, as founded by observation and experience. . . ." The very fact that there is an acknowledged tendency to sin in man, as is witnessed to in history and present experience, displays the "propensity" of man's nature. It is irrelevant to speak of "the innocent and kind actions, even of criminals themselves . . . and of the prevailing innocence, good nature, industry, felicity, and cheerfulness of the greater part of mankind." To argue that men are able to do some good is the same as "to pronounce that road a good road to go to such a place, the greater part of which is plain and safe, though some parts of it are dangerous, and certainly fatal to them that travel in it. . . ." Good cannot balance out evil. Any transgression of God's law, of whatever degree, deserves eternal punishment; no good act can erase sin.

Taylor and other Arminians attempted to explain the existence of sin. One of these arguments was similar to that expressed by the fifth century monk, Pelagius (c. 360-c.420); namely, that man sins because of bad examples of his predecessors. This argument, to Edwards, "is accounting for the thing by the thing itself." It does not explain the "bad example." That "bad examples" are general all over the world and "have been so from the beginning, is only an instance, or rather a description of that corruption of the world which is to be accounted for." Some argued that sin is a misuse of freedom. The Arminians had continually insisted that if men are to be morally responsible for their action, the sins they commit must be the result of free choices. In reply Edwards asks the question: "If their wills are in the first place as free to good as evil, what is it to be ascribed to, that the world of mankind, consisting of so many millions, in so many successive generations, without consultation, all agree to exercise their freedom in favor of evil?" His own answer was that the general and continuing disobedience of man is evidence for the fact that the cause of sin is "fixed, and that the fixed cause is *internal,* in man's nature. . . ."

There were three main arguments used by Arminian theologians against the doctrine of total depravity. Taylor, for example, insisted that if man is totally depraved, then he is under a necessity of sinning; a necessary sin is not a sin. Edwards dealt with this charge in his *Inquiry into the Freedom of Will,* in which he made the celebrated distinction between moral and natural necessity, insisting that moral necessity in no way cancels accountability, though natural necessity does.

The Arminians also argued that if men come into existence in a state of corruption, God must be the author of sin. Edwards offered another explanation. In creating man, God implanted within him two kinds of principles. One was of an inferior nature, the natural principle, which the "Scriptures sometimes call *flesh.*" In addition, the superior principle, that is, the image of God, was also present. As long as these two principles operated within Adam's nature, he lived in communion with God. When he sinned, however, the superior principle left him and Adam was "in a state of darkness, woeful corruption and ruin; nothing but flesh without spirit." Adam's sin, therefore, was due to the violation of his own inferior nature and not to any creating act of God.

A third Arminian challenge to the doctrine of total depravity rested on a rejection of the imputation of Adam's sin to his descendants. Taylor regarded this imputation as unjust, because no man should be held responsible for another man's wrongdoing. There are two traditional interpretations of the doctrine of imputation. One, traducianism, asserted that Adam's sin was transmitted through human genes; parents pass on guilt to their children. Another interpretation, the federal theory, spoke of Adam as the representative of mankind; when he sinned, his guilt was imputed to his descendants because Adam was chosen to stand in their place. Jonathan Edwards offered another interpretation. He answered Taylor by saying that God has always treated Adam as being one with his posterity. "The *first existing* of a corrupt disposition in their hearts is not to be looked upon as sin belonging to them, *distinct* from their participation of Adam's first sin: it is as it were the *extended pollution* of that sin, through the whole tree, by virtue of the constituted *union* of the branches with the root. . . ." Man's involvement in Adam's first sin is the result of a personal identity between Adam and his descendants. "And therefore the sin of the apostasy is not theirs [Adam's descendants'], merely because God *imputes* it to them; but it is *truly* and *properly* theirs, and on that ground, God *imputes* it to them." Edwards was denying the traditional ways of defending the imputation of Adam's sin to mankind and asserting that men sin because of their "constituted oneness" with Adam, a oneness which is dependent upon God's continual creation of each individual through time as one with Adam.

In discussing the centrality of the doctrine of original sin in the scheme of the Christian Gospel, Edwards also considered corollary issues. He devoted an entire section of his treatise to the relation of this doctrine to the work of Christ. "The representations of the redemption by Christ, everywhere in Scripture, lead us to suppose, that *all* whom he came to redeem, are *sinners;* that his salvation, as to the term *from which* (or the evil to be redeemed from) in *all* is *sin,* and the deserved *punishment* of sin." If men were not totally and inherently sinners, the work of Christ would be unnecessary and meaningless. Scripture also insists that a "change of heart" is necessary for entrance into the Kingdom of God. If men were not totally and inherently sinful, there would be no need to undergo such a "change of heart." The whole scheme of the Christian Gospel rests upon the doctrine of original sin.

Edwards' essay provoked lengthy and involved debate. Some Calvinists were unhappy with Edwards' metaphysical excursions, especially in relation to his discussion of imputation. The Arminians were not convinced by his argument, for they were still bothered by the problem of moral responsibility; neither the *Inquiry into the Freedom of Will* nor the *Doctrine of Original Sin Defended* solved this issue for them. Edwards' treatise, however, served to keep the doctrine of original sin in the forefront of New England theological debate for the remainder of the eighteenth century.

THE CREED OF A SAVOYARD PRIEST

Author: Jean Jacques Rousseau (1712-1778)
Type of work: Philosophy of natural religion
First published: 1762

Principal Ideas Advanced

Although man's intellect cannot fathom these matters, his heart witnesses to the existence of God, to the freedom of the will, and to a life beyond the grave.

Positive religions are inferior to the natural religion of the heart; men ought, however, to worship God according to the usage of the country of their birth.

The Christian Gospel, in spite of many absurdities, speaks faithfully to men's hearts.

When, in *Émile,* Rousseau comes to the question how his young man is to be taught religion, he tells of the encouragement which he himself received as a youth from a kindly but unorthodox priest whom he chanced to meet during his wanderings in northern Italy. *The Creed of a Savoyard Priest* is Rousseau's reconstruction of remarks privately made to him when the priest judged that his pupil was ready to consider fundamental religious ideas. The ideas expressed are those of Rousseau's own maturity. How far the anonymous Savoyard is responsible for introducing them to Rousseau is difficult to determine.

Writing in France at the height of the Enlightenment, Rousseau takes the ground of natural theology. Reason and the testimony of the heart are pitted against revelation and authority. Rousseau objects that alleged revelations are always remote in time and place, so that their claim to be authentic is properly an object of historical scholarship, not a requirement for holy living. The testimony of the heart, on the other hand, is immediate and universal. Montaigne to the contrary notwithstanding, man's heart everywhere inclines him to revere the Author of Nature, and to obey the law which is inscribed in conscience.

Rousseau protested against the extreme forms which rationalism had taken in his time. Like contemporary pietists, who found more reality in the "religion of the heart" than in the dogmas of the churches, he found feeling to be a surer guide than the arguments of the philosophers. "In vain," he makes his priest declare, "do you argue this point with me; I feel it, and it is this feeling which speaks to me more forcibly than the reason which disputes it." And again, "If all the philosophers in the world should prove that I am wrong, and you feel that I am right, that is all I ask." We must note, however, that the feeling (*sensibilité*) of which Rousseau speaks is less an emotion than a kind of moral insight comparable to what English philosophers such as Lord Shaftesbury (1671-1713) referred to as "moral sense." Rousseau's complaint is directed against strict materialists like Julien Offray de La Mettrie (1709-1751), who tried to reason out the nature of the world and man on the basis of certain axioms concerning matter and motion. It is against their "absurdities" that the native witness of the heart speaks out.

The vicar's beliefs may fairly be described as a variety of deism. Beginning with reflections upon his own nature, he arrives at three fundamental principles of belief. The first is that, just as in man there is an active principle or will which is the origin of our spontaneous motions, so in the world at large we may reason back from one cause to another until we come to a spontaneous, voluntary action. "I believe, therefore, that there is a will which sets the universe in motion and gives life to nature," says the vicar. The second article of his creed arises out of the uniformity and harmony of nature, which is so far from the chaos which would have resulted if the world were simply the result of chance. These considerations point him to an intelligent, thinking being. "If matter in motion points me to a will, matter in motion according to fixed laws points me to an intelligence; that is the second article of my creed," claims the vicar. The third principle has to do not with God but with man's place in the order of things. Reflecting upon the disparity within man's breast between the part of him which raises him to truth, justice, and benevolence, and that part which draws him downward and enslaves him to matter, the vicar concludes that man's soul belongs to another realm than the body: "Man is therefore free to act, and as such he is animated by an immaterial substance; that is the third article of my creed."

From these three principles, says the vicar, the remainder of his system can be deduced. He is particularly concerned to deal with the problem of evil, which, as in Rousseau's earlier *Essay on Inequality* (1754), is explained as arising out of human progress. Essentially, the solution offered by the vicar is the Stoic solution: "There is no evil but the evil you do or the evil you suffer, and both come from yourself." Evil arises only out of disorder, but there can be no disorder in the physical world. Hence, evil "exists only in the minds of those who experience it; and this feeling is not the gift of nature, but the work of man himself." He admits that God has an obligation to His creatures; namely, to perform all that His act of creating them implied. But man can have no complaint on this score, because "God's justice consists in demanding from each of us an account of that which he has given us." To question whether God was wise and benevolent in not preventing us from doing wrong is to murmur against Him "because he has made man of so excellent a nature, that he has endowed his actions with that morality by which they are ennobled, that he has made virtue man's birthright." Happiness, according to the vicar, does not reside in the absence of pain or struggle, but in the sense of achievement which comes from being a co-creator with God. God has limited man's power, the vicar points out, so that man's misuse of freedom cannot upset the general order; thus limited, man's capacity for choosing his own way is his greatest dignity.

God's providence is further vindicated in the assurance of a life beyond the grave. "Had I no other proof of the immaterial nature of the soul," says the vicar, "the triumph of the wicked and the oppression of the righteous in this world would be enough to convince me." But, as we have seen, there are other evidences that the soul does not die, and these arguments suggest not only that the righteous will be happy, but that the wicked too will repent once they have been freed from the deceit and grossness of their bodily senses. God has no need for vengeance, says the priest. Such Hell as there is "is here in the breast of the wicked." When men have ceased to be bad, they can never be miserable. If, contrary to these speculations, there is eternal punishment, we must submit our feeble reason to divine justice, but if the remorse of the wicked comes to an end, so that the same peace shall be the lot of all mankind, then we shall be grateful. "Is not the wicked my brother?" asks the vicar; "How often have I been tempted to be like him? Let him be delivered from his misery and freed from the spirit of hatred that accompanied it; let him be as happy as I myself; his happiness, far from arousing my jealousy, will only increase my own."

In eighteenth century Europe, as the priest points out, there are three major faiths: the Jews have one revelation, the Christians two, the Turks three. Because it is impossible to decide between them, each man is wise to follow the faith in which he was brought up. He can do this without subscribing to all its dogmas and without hating or persecuting adherents of other faiths. Moreover, he should do it, both for his own and for his neighbor's well-being, for, according to Rousseau, "irreligion, and the argumentative philosophic spirit generally . . . assaults life and enfeebles it, degrades the soul, concentrates all the passions in the basest self-interest, in the meanness of the human self; thus it saps unnoticed the very foundations of all society."

In line with these principles, the Savoyard priest advised the youthful Rousseau to return to the Church of Geneva, which is commended by the vicar for its purity of life. As for himself, brought up in the Roman Church, he could imagine no higher privilege than serving as a priest in a humble mountain parish, mixing works of charity with reverent worship, and teaching men the sublime truths of the Gospel.

The vicar testifies that the Gospel speaks with the voice of the heart itself, so simply and convincingly that one might well ask whether it is not of divine, rather than human, origin. He finds the portrait of Christ quite without parallel in human history, and, contrary to the vogue of eighteenth century deism, he refuses to place Socrates on the same level with Christ. However, the Gospel contains inconsistencies and other features repugnant to reason, which make one wary of accepting it as divine. Let a man, therefore, suspend judgment "in the sight of the Divine Being who alone knows the truth," and respect in silence what he can neither leave aside nor comprehend. Such "skepticism," continues the vicar, need not be painful, because it does not extend to matters of practice. It is not to be confused with the destructive skepticism of the dogmatic philosophers who, claiming that they alone are enlightened, overthrow all that men revere, rob the afflicted of their consolation, remove the bridle from men's passions, and abolish the very distinction between virtue and vice. "Truth, they say, can never do a man harm. I think so too," says the vicar; "and to my mind that is strong evidence that what they teach is not true."

A PLAIN ACCOUNT OF CHRISTIAN PERFECTION

Author: John Wesley (1703-1791)
Type of work: Theology of holiness
First published: 1766

Principal Ideas Advanced

Christian perfection is attained when perfect love of God and neighbor rules a person's heart and words and actions.

Christian perfection is a gift of God's grace that may be experienced in earthly life, occurring sometime after justification and before death and being wrought by faith.

Christan perfection is both instantaneous and gradual; the process of sanctification (cleansing from sin) that begins with justification (forgiveness of sin) may culminate in an instant in entire sanctification (perfect holiness).

Christian perfection is not necessarily permanent, for it may be lost and recovered; it may also be improved, and growth in grace is expected after entire sanctification and, indeed, throughout eternity.

Christian perfection is not absolute, for God alone is absolutely perfect; nor should it be called sinless, unless the term "sin" is limited to denote a voluntary transgression of a known divine law.

John Wesley, a priest of the Church of England from 1728 until his death in 1791, was the leading spirit of the Evangelical Revival in Great Britain during the eighteenth century. Together with his brother Charles (1707-1788) and George Whitefield (1714-1770), a forceful preacher who leaned toward a Calvinist theological position, Wesley organized the "societies" and "bands" within the Anglican communion that subsequently were called "Methodist," a term initially meant to be derisive. One of the cardinal emphases of the Methodist movement was personal holiness, and Wesley explicated and defended this doctrine in his *A Plain Account of Christian Perfection.*

Theological emphases are rarely understood apart from their historical context, and this is true of John Wesley's call for Christians to lead a holy life. In a time when deism offered an absentee God and rationalism a shallow moralism, there arose an alarming lack of spiritual vitality and discipline in the Church of England, which seemed more intent upon political affiliation than the regeneration of the individual and social life of the people. The laboring classes were becoming more and more estranged from the established Church, and public morality and responsibility had reached a low ebb. Religious figures sensitive to the problems of the age began to express concern, but it was the Wesleys and their co-workers who both focused and fanned the protesting spirit and kindled a revival that swept through the British Isles and then to America. The heart of the message proclaimed and sung by these eighteenth century evangelists was "salvation through Jesus Christ," and the response demanded was "faith working through love."

In *A Plain Account of Christian Perfection,* which he published in 1766 at the age of 63, John Wesley looks back upon forty years of teaching this most controversial of all Methodist doctrines. His purpose, he declares, is "to give a plain and distinct account of the steps by which I was led, during a course of many years, to embrace the doctrine of Christian perfection." He believes he owes this to "the serious part of mankind"; namely, those who desire to know all the truth as it is in Jesus. For Wesley, "all the truth" included not only justification by faith, but also the holy life of love.

Already in 1725, when only 23 years old, Wesley had resolved to dedicate his whole life to God, since he was convinced that there was no middle way between serving God and serving the Devil. At that time he was greatly impressed by the emphasis on purity of intention in *Rules and Exercises of Holy Living and Holy Dying,* devotional writings by Anglican Bishop Jeremy Taylor (1613-1667). During the following two years he was further affected by the stress on the inward religion of the heart in *Imitation of*

Christ, the medieval ascetical writing attributed to Thomas à Kempis (c.1380-1471), and by the spiritual writings of William Law (1686-1761), whose *On Christian Perfection* and *A Serious Call to a Devout and Holy Life* convinced Wesley that it was impossible to be "half a Christian."

Wesley asserts that in 1729 he began not merely to read but also to study the Bible as the one and only standard of truth and model of pure religion, which he defined as "a uniform following of Christ, an entire inward and outward conformity to our Master." In his renowned sermon on "The Circumcision of the Heart," which he preached in St. Mary's Church at Oxford University on January 1, 1733, Wesley struck the note that characterized his understanding of perfection; namely, that *love* is the perfect good, the sum of the perfect law. He exhorted his hearers with these words: "Let the spirit return to God that gave it, with the whole train of its affections. Other sacrifices from us He would not: but the living sacrifice of the heart hath He chosen. Let it be continually offered up to God, through Christ, in flames of holy love."

This understanding of Christian perfection as perfect love, and of perfect holiness as the habitual disposition of soul that implies being cleansed from sin and from all filthiness of flesh and spirit and being endued with those virtues that were in Christ Jesus, remained unchanged throughout Wesley's missionary service in Georgia, his inspiring encounter with the German Moravians, and his famous heart-warming experience during the reading of Luther's *Introduction to Romans* at Aldersgate Street Chapel on May 24, 1738. These experiences undoubtedly deepened his understanding of faith and the need for individual conversion, but the essence of Christian perfection remained the same throughout the remainder of his life. A perfect Christian is one who loves the Lord with all his heart and soul and mind and strength, and Wesley intended that a Methodist be no less than this.

The Methodist doctrine of perfection, celebrated especially in the various volumes of hymns and sacred poems published by John and Charles Wesley, drew sharp criticism from opponents who argued that there is no perfection on earth and that the mere notion of perfection not only attacked the Reformation principle of justification by faith, but also dishonored Christ by implying that some Christians could reach a stage in life in which they no longer needed a Savior. Wesley expresses surprise that the doctrine should be so misunderstood, since he and his brother had always held to justification by faith and had ascribed the whole of salvation to the mere grace of God. The point the Wesleys wanted to emphasize is that Christ not only justifies the sinner, but also renews him in the image of God, in righteousness and true holiness. The gift of salvation entails both the forgiveness of sin and the cleansing from sin, the latter being the work of the Holy Spirit, who dwells in the heart of the man of faith and sets him free.

Wesley takes care to specify the nature of Christian freedom. Perfection does not imply freedom from ignorance or mistake or temptation or any of the numerous infirmities connected with flesh and blood. Nor does perfection imply freedom from doing good or from attending all the ordinances of

God, such as participating in the Lord's Supper, searching the Scriptures, fasting, and praying. The freedom of "perfect Christian" is a freedom not to commit sin (knowingly) and a freedom from evil thought and evil tempers. The perfect Christian is both outwardly and inwardly devoted to God, and he has the mind of Christ, so that all his thoughts, words, and actions are governed by pure love. Wesley conceded that one filled with pure love might make a mistake that would occasion a transgression of God's perfect law and thus require Christ's atonement, but it was his opinion that such an error is not properly called a "sin."

Every Christian, including those who live without sin, needs Christ as Mediator. All are dependent upon Christ, just as branches are dependent upon their root. The free gift of grace is not simply from Christ, but also *in* Him, and all blessings depend on His continual intercession. Furthermore, even the best of men need Christ to atone for their involuntary transgressions of the divine law, those omissions, shortcomings, mistakes, and defects of various kinds that are inseparable from mortal existence. Since Wesley defines sin as "a voluntary transgression of a known law," he does not consider involuntary transgressions to be sins in the proper sense. Because of the ambiguity of the phrase, however, he prefers never to speak of "sinless perfection." He also makes it clear that Christian perfection is not absolute, since absolute perfection belongs to God alone; Christian perfection is capable of being lost and recovered and improved, since one never stops "growing in grace."

In regard to the question when perfection is attained in life, Wesley contends that it happens instantaneously, being wrought by faith in a moment, and this generally just before death. Nevertheless, it should be striven after and expected *every moment,* and it often occurs years before death. The Christian life begins with justification, when man's sin is forgiven, and continues from this point of new birth with a process of sanctification which involves the gradual removal of all inward sin. Perfection is reached in the instant that all sin is removed and man is entirely sanctified. For this reason it can be conceived as both gradual and instantaneous.

Wesley was convinced that few attain perfection in this life, because there are few who really seek it. Although he emphasized that it was a gift received by faith, he also stressed that faith is not given by God unless it is diligently sought in the way He has ordained; namely, through vigorous obedience, vigilant watchfulness, daily self-denial and cross-bearing, regular prayer and fasting, and close attendance upon all the ordinances of God. Wesley saw little use of speaking about perfection to anyone who was not striving after it, for the doctrine would inevitably be misunderstood.

To the question how one can know that he has attained perfect love, Wesley answered that there is no infallible proof. No one is in a position to judge another, although "reasonable proof" would certainly include clear evidence of exemplary behavior for some time before the supposed change, the rendering of a distinct account of the time and manner wherein the change was wrought, and an indication that all subsequent words and actions were holy and blameless. An individual might judge himself to have attained perfection if he has experienced the gradual mortification of sin and the renewal to a full life of love, but to this must be added an indispensable element: the inner testimony of the Holy Spirit.

Although Wesley was deeply impressed by the witness of personal experience and by the visible fruits of the Spirit, he was opposed to "enthusiasts" who made a vain show of perfection, and who fancied that they could no longer be tempted or feel pain, or that they had special gifts of prophecy and of discerning the spirits. Such enthusiasm, asserted Wesley, is the daughter of pride, and it leads quite naturally to antinomianism. Rather than having purity of intention, the mind that was in Christ, and the love of God and neighbor, enthusiasts distort Scripture, disesteem reason, expect the end without the means, misunderstand growing in grace, and fail to consider that love is the highest gift of all.

In spite of its terminological and theological difficulties, the doctrine of Christian perfection was filled with profound meaning by John Wesley, who believed in the promise and power of the Spirit to effect a "real, inward change" in the believer, and who took seriously the injunction of Christ: "Therefore ye shall be perfect, as your Father who is in heaven is perfect." (Matthew 5:48.)

THE JOURNAL OF JOHN WOOLMAN

Author: John Woolman (1720-1772)
Type of work: Religious autobiography
First published: 1774

Principal Ideas Advanced

The person who truly loves God loves Him in all His manifestations in the visible world; that is, in all living beings, animals as well as men.

All men, if they patiently listen for the inner divine voice, will hear it clearly and certainly.

The individual should live according to the light of his conscience no matter what his neighbors or the world in general may think of his actions.

John Woolman was born in 1720 into a large Quaker family in Northampton, Burlington County, in West Jersey, about twenty miles east of Philadelphia. His first twenty-one years were spent on his father's farm, after which he became an assistant in a general store in nearby Mount Holly. He learned the trade of tailoring from his master and later established his own business. He married in 1749 and was the father of one child. He was a schoolmaster for a period of time and published a primer. Active among the Friends, he often undertook extensive journeys—often uncomfortable and sometimes dangerous—to visit Friends' meetings in the American colonies. He died while in England.

These are the externals of the life of

Woolman but they tell us little of the power and lasting influence of the man. It is the inner development of John Woolman, as revealed in his *Journal*, that indicates the profound relevance for our time of this simple, unpretentious man. Woolman began his *Journal* when he was thirty-six. Due to the fact that he was well-read from early childhood, the *Journal*, as well as his other works, is written in a felicitous and often moving style.

Although Woolman is careful to note details of his life and especially of his travels, these act merely as a framework for the development of his spiritual life. The *Journal* more than anything else is a diary of the development of an amazingly sensitive conscience. But Woolman could not rest with the cultivation of the inner life. Like Friends before and since, he was impelled by conscience to witness publicly to his convictions. At times this attitude marked him as curiously individualistic and eccentric.

Woolman begins the *Journal* with an account of his religious growth. From early childhood he was intensely serious. "Before I was seven Years old I began to be acquainted with the Operations of divine Love. Through the Care of my Parents, I was taught to read nearly as soon as I was capable of it; and, as I went from School one seventh Day, I remember, while my Companions went to play by the Way, I went forward out of Sight, and, sitting down, I read the 22d Chapter of the *Revelations:* 'He shewed me a pure River of Water of Life, clear as Chrystal, proceeding out of the Throne of God and of the Lamb, *etc.*' and, in reading it, my Mind was drawn to seek after that pure Habitation, which, I then believed, God had prepared for his Servants. The Place where I sat, and the Sweetness that attended my Mind, remain fresh in my Memory."

It is to be expected that a child who so early became aware of the demands of the religious life was to suffer many temptations and backslidings. Looking back, Woolman makes much of his involvement with "wanton" company, but, like Augustine, he was writing many years after the event and from a puritanical viewpoint and thus no doubt exaggerates the seriousness of his offenses. In time he put such "snares" behind him and by attending regularly the Friends' Meetings and by reading the Scriptures "and other good Books" so developed in piety and devotion that he was recognized by his fellow Friends as worthy of recognition as a minister. (Among the Friends, of course, ministerial status did not involve clerical duties.)

Woolman's developing sensitivity was not restricted to his fellow man; he "was early convinced in Mind" that the person who truly learns to love God and to "exercise true Justice and Goodness" loves Him "in all his Manifestations in the visible World." For a person to say he loves God and at the same time to act cruelly toward "the least Creature, is a Contradiction in itself." Throughout his *Journal* Woolman expresses the most poignant concern for the sufferings of animals.

Woolman chose to learn the trade of tailoring because he was convinced that it was the kind of occupation that would leave his mind free to ponder religious problems. He admitted, however, that there were times when he found it difficult to repress the feeling that he should aspire to a more exalted station in life. But Woolman's tailoring did not shelter him from problems of conscience. Indeed, so successful did his business become that he found it necessary to discontinue these profitable sources of income in order to preserve his peace of mind.

It was his literacy, relatively rare then, that caused Woolman's greatest problems and, it can be said, made it possible for him to struggle with the greatest evil of his day. Because of his facility with the pen he was often called upon to write bills of sale, wills, and other legal documents. This inevitably put him in the position of being the instrument by which human beings were exchanged as chattel. The problem of slavery, from the day he was first called upon to write a bill of sale to the day of his death, was to be Woolman's major concern. His first bill of sale of a Negro was his last; he wrote it only because the sale was to an elderly member of the Society of Friends. Woolman, uneasy in conscience, executed the instrument although protesting that he believed ownership of slaves inconsistent with Christianity. "This in some Degree abated my Uneasiness; yet, as often as I reflected seriously upon it, I thought I should have been clearer, if I had desired to have been excused from it, as a Thing against my Conscience. . . ." Woolman never hesitated again. From that day forth, whenever the occasion arose, he spoke his conscience to those making the request of him and, so earnest was his concern that many consciences were quickened thereby. Woolman, instead of being the instrument of evil, became an instrument of manumission.

John Woolman's campaign against slavery was not limited to his business life, however. Increasingly he agitated within Friends' circles against the evil. He spoke in countless meetings throughout the colonies and published several tracts. He is often given credit for the major effort against slavery among the Friends, an effort which resulted in abolition of slaveholding in that body by the eve of the Revolution.

If Woolman's effort in behalf of abolition was his most dramatic accomplishment, it was by no means his only concern. His *Journal* is the record of the development of a multitude of religious and social concerns. Woolman had to witness against snares to the soul wherever he found them and no matter how much personal discomfort resulted. For example, he found it necessary for conscience's sake to give up the use of sugar because it was the product of slave labor. His self-consciousness must have been intense when he gave up the use of dye in his clothing because dye, too, was produced by slave labor and was responsible for the concealment of all manner of uncleanliness. Probably his most poignant protest was his refusal to accept space in the cabin of the ship that took him to England toward the close of his life. Such ornate comfort was more than his conscience would allow. So he holed up in the steerage where in cramped, stifling conditions his heart went out to the mariners who lived such a terrible life and who, as Woolman lamented, were subject to all manner of strong temptation.

His compulsion to witness inevitably clashed with practices sanctified by society. When he was requested to billet a soldier in his home in 1758 during the French and Indian War, Woolman was hard-pressed. He could not condone violence. But because he could not refuse hospitality to a fellow being, he chose the course of passive obedience and allowed the billeting. But when after the man was gone his military superior attempted to recompense Woolman for his room and board, Woolman refused to accept the money. Later, fearing that his motive had been misunderstood and that he was considered a benefactor of the army, he sought out the officer to make it clear to him that he had acted from conscience.

A humorous example of his didactic ways is seen in an incident involving a juggler who was to appear at a local "Publick-house" in Mount Holly. The showman created such a favorable impression the first evening he presented his act that his show was held over for another performance. Hearing of it, Woolman "felt an Exercise on that Account: So I went to the Publick-house in the Evening, and told the Man of the House that I had an Inclination to spend a Part of the Evening there; with which he signified that he was content. Then, sitting down by the Door, I spake to the People as they came together, concerning this Shew; and, more coming and sitting down with us, the Seats of the Door were mostly filled; and I had Conversation with them in the Fear of the Lord, and laboured to convince them that, thus assembling to see those Tricks of Slights of Hand, and bestowing their Money to support Men, who, in that Capacity, were of no Use in the World, was contrary to the Nature of the *Christian* Religion.

"There was one of the Company, who, for a Time, endeavoured, by Arguments, to shew the Reasonableness of their Proceedings herein; but, after considering some Texts of Scripture, and calmly debating the Matter, he gave up the Point. So, having spent about an Hour amongst them, and feeling my Mind easy, I departed."

It is part of the greatness of Woolman that so few of his concerns put him in the class of the moral zealot. This is due to the fact that he never allowed the demands of his conscience to blind him to the inevitableness of differences of opinion among men. His convictions did not transform him into a fanatic. Woolman believed that all men, if they tried, could "get down to the Rock, the sure Foundation, and there hearken to that divine Voice which gives a clear and certain Sound . . . ," but he knew that all life involves effort and that not all men can be expected to hear the voice at the same time. Woolman in following his conscience could condemn sin, but his gentle heart always went out to the sinner. Because John Woolman never forgot our common humanity his *Journal* remains a living testament to a great man and a continuing challenge to mankind.

DIALOGUES CONCERNING NATURAL RELIGION

Author: David Hume (1711-1776)
Type of work: Philosophical theology
First published: 1779

Principal Ideas Advanced

The arguments of natural theology which seek to establish the nature or existence of God by a priori *arguments or by analogies drawn from sense experience are invalid.*

Inferences based upon observed characteristics of the world do not justify the claim that there is a spiritual world beyond the material world, for the latter may contain within itself its own principle of order.

A priori *arguments are equally futile, for whatever is a matter of fact can be conceived as not existing; existence is never demonstrable as necessary.*

The sole conclusion that can be reached by natural theology is that the cause of the world probably bears some remote resemblance to human intelligence.

Theologians and philosophers have sought to reach conclusions concerning the existence and nature of God without appealing to revelation. David Hume's *Dialogues Concerning Natural Religion* subjects all such efforts to a critical analysis. The existence of God is not called into question. Any effort, however, to discover God's nature, either by rational argument or by inferences drawn from sense experience, is subjected to severe criticism.

The choice of the dialogue form makes it difficult to ascertain David Hume's own position with certainty. The three principal characters in the dialogue, Demea, Cleanthes, and Philo, respectively represent the orthodox rationalist, the theist, and the skeptic.

That Philo's principles are closer to the truth than those of Demea, and that those of Cleanthes are even nearer to the truth than those of Philo, is the conclusion of Pamphillus, the narrator of the dialogue. Whether David Hume chose Philo or Cleanthes to be the winner of the argument is of historical interest; the subsequent importance and significance of the dialogue largely rests upon the fact that many have since declared Philo to be the victor.

The Dialogues Concerning Natural Religion, together with Immanuel Kant's *Critique of Pure Reason* (1781), led some to abandon natural theology altogether and others to seek to reformulate their arguments. Among those who abandon natural theology, some seek to get rid of God entirely, while others regard Humean skepticism as an ally which enables them to appeal unabashedly to revelation. No matter which course is followed, it is in any case evident that no serious student of philosophical theology can neglect David Hume's *Dialogues.*

Demea and Philo agree verbally in their opposition to Cleanthes' attempts to draw inferences about the nature of God from the nature of the world. Philo and Cleanthes agree in their opposition to Demea's *a priori* argument to establish the infinity and unity of the Deity. The main debate takes place between Philo and Cleanthes. It reaches its culmination in Part XI when Philo abandons his cavils against arguments from design and draws attention to the presence of natural and moral evil within the world.

Demea, the representative of orthodox rationalism, is opposed by Cleanthes and supported by Philo in his insistence upon the incomprehensibility of the divine nature. Demea's distrust of arguments based upon experience and probability does not stem from skepticism but from the conviction that it is impious to pry into the nature and essence of God. To reach conclusions which represent the Deity as similar to the human mind and understanding is to make ourselves the model of the whole universe. We cannot legitimately make inferences from ourselves to God. Human modes of thinking, ideas, and sentiments do not resemble anything true of the Deity. By reading a human author, a reader enters into the author's mind, but the order of the world, the book of nature, contains an inexplicable riddle. God's ways are not man's ways. Human reason is changing, whereas the incomprehensible nature of God is immutable and simple. There is no acquisition, diminution, change, or succession in God. To argue *a posteriori* from the world to God is to forget that a finite effect can never prove an infinite cause.

The infinity of the divine attributes and the unity of the Supreme Being can be demonstrated with absolute certainty, Demea insists, by the following *a priori* argument. Granted that everything has a cause and that nothing can be the cause of itself, either there is an infinite succession of causes and effects or there is an ultimate cause that is necessarily existent. The first disjunct is false. Therefore, there is an ultimate and necessarily existent cause.

Why, Demea asks, is it false to suppose that there can be an infinite succession of causes and effects? Because each effect within the infinite chain of cause and effects exists by reason of the immediately preceding cause. The chain, itself, however, requires a cause or reason as much as does any individual member of the series. For why did this particular succession of causes exist from eternity, and not some other series, or no series at all? Why is there something and not nothing? Why did this particular possibility become actual and not some other? If there is no necessarily existent being, every supposition is equally possible. The consequent of this conditional is, however, false, for there is just this particular possibility that has been actualized. To deny the consequent of a conditional is to deny the antecedent. There is, therefore, a necessarily existent Being who carries the reason of His existence in Himself, and who cannot without contradiction be supposed not to exist.

Cleanthes attacks Demea's *a priori* argument as ill-grounded and of little consequence to piety and religion. A cause implies a priority in time and a beginning of existence. What exists from eternity has no beginning and, therefore, cannot have a cause. The material universe could have some unknown qualities which make it a noncontingent and necessarily existent being, except that the expression "necessary existence" has no meaning. For, if God is thought of as an existent being, that is, if His existence is taken to be a matter of fact, then His existence is not demonstrable. For, if "God exists," is demonstrable, "God does not exist" implies a contradiction, since nothing is demonstrable unless a contradiction is implied by its contrary. However, if we can clearly conceive of God as existing, we can also conceive of Him as not existing, since whatever we can conceive of as existent can also be thought of as nonexistent. Consequently, since God can, without contradiction, be conceived of as not existing, the proposition that God exists is not demonstrable. No matter of fact is ever logically demonstrable or necessary.

Cleanthes' attack on Demea is not prompted by skepticism. Complete skepticism makes survival impossible and is belied by the skeptic's reliance upon the maxims of science, ethics, and prudence in his daily conduct. Cleanthes admits that God possesses many powers and attributes which are incomprehensible, but unless our ideas are true as far as they go, then the name "God" lacks meaning. Demea's pious utterances are in fact more dangerous than Philo's skepticism. For, Philo's skepticism, like Descartes', is methodological, as he himself admits in Part XII when he states: "A purpose, an intention, a design strikes everywhere the most careless, the most stupid thinker; and no man can be so hardened in absurd systems as at all times to reject it. . . ." Demea's insistence that there is no analogy between the human mind and the divine mind, between the nature of the world and the nature of God, is virtually identical with an atheism which asserts that a first cause is unknown and unintelligible. A totally simple and immutable mind is no mind at all. It makes no sense to use the word "God" unless something is known about His nature. Such knowledge is attainable. The nature of God can be inferred from the nature of the world. The similarity of the world to a giant machine composed of an infinite number of little machines indicates the adaptation of means to ends throughout nature, and such adaptation, analogous to human design, permits the ascription of intelligence, thought, and wisdom to the Deity. A rational cause is needed to account for the works of nature.

Philo's attack on Cleanthes originates in a methodological skepticism which presupposes the insufficiency of human reason to attain theoretical certainty with regard to the first principles of any system. His doubts do not arise on the practical level, for in the final section of the *Dialogue,* Part XII, Philo acknowledges that he is deeply religious and, in spite of his argument against design, he concedes that "no man can be so hardened in absurd systems as at all times to reject it. . . ." He permits natural theology to conclude that "the cause or causes of order in the universe probably bear some remote analogy to human intelligence . . . ," although such a conclusion does not provide the basis for any inferences that affect human life.

Philo does not object to Cleanthes' appeal to experience, but he insists that our ideas cannot go beyond experience. We may call the original cause of the universe God, but the attributes of the divine being are incomprehensible, since there is no reason to hold that the perfections of the Deity bear any analogy to the perfections of human creatures. We have no experience of the whole of the world, nor do we experience the origin of worlds. To suppose that the material world requires a mental cause is to forget that the mental world would itself require a cause. If the material world is dependent upon an ideal world, why not trace that ideal world to another, and so on *ad infinitum?* If it is possible to stop at all, why not stop at the very beginning, with the material world? "By supposing it to contain the principle of its order within itself, we really assert it to be God. . . ."

Moreover, even if we ascribe the material world to a mind like the human mind, Philo continues, there is still no reason to ascribe perfection or unity to the deity. The world may be the product of trial and error, or the work of many finite gods who came into being and are themselves corporeal.

Since there is an absence of data for the formulation of any system of cosmology, and there are no rules to follow, the world can be regarded as an animal with a deity for its soul. The world may contain its own eternal principle of order, attended by continual upheavals and changes. Philo then suggests that the origin of the world may be attributed to vegetation or to generation, rather than to reason and design; its resemblance to a plant or animal is greater than its likeness to a machine.

The present order of the world need not be explained in terms of design. For by supposing a finite number of particles, capable of finite transpositions, and given an infinite duration, every possible order or position must be tried an infinite number of times.

At the end of Part X, Philo admits that such objections to intelligence and design are forced, based upon dodges, subterfuges, cavils and sophisms. His more serious arguments seek to show that the existence of a cause, bearing some similarity to human intelligence, does not warrant the ascription of moral attributes to the Deity. The issue is not whether misery is fleeting and momentary, nor whether it is outweighed by happiness, but why there is misery at all.

The present situation in which man finds himself might be compatible with the antecedent conviction that the world is the effect of a finite deity, but the world provides no basis for the inference that there is a supreme, benevolent, powerful intelligence.

Philo argues that the presence of pain, the uniform course of events, the frugality with which creatures are endowed with powers and faculties, and the inaccurate workmanship of the machine of nature preclude the inference that the Deity has moral attributes, although if we already had *a priori* knowledge of the moral qualities of the Deity, the circumstances of the world could be harmonized with them. From the phenomena of the world, it appears that the original source of all things is morally indifferent.

It is absurd to think that the Deity has human passions and is concerned with our vices and follies, Philo continues. A rational religion can be beneficial to a society, but the religion of the masses often ends in superstition and is detrimental. Remote promises and threats of future rewards and punishments are not as effective in promoting a stable social order as is man's natural inclination to honesty and benevolence.

David Hume's *Dialogues* is important to Christian thought, for many Christians have since heeded Philo's concluding words and have made philosophical skepticism "the first and most essential step towards being a sound, believing Christian. . . ."

THE JOURNALS OF HENRY MELCHIOR MÜHLENBERG

Author: Henry Melchior Mühlenberg (1711-1787)
Type of work: Diaries of a clergyman
First published: 1942-1958 (written: 1742-1787)

PRINCIPAL IDEAS ADVANCED

The German-speaking colonists of the Lutheran faith shared with many of their English-speaking neighbors of other persuasions a common understanding and practice of Christianity which was derived from similar roots in European Pietism.

It was a common practice in the eighteenth century for religiously inclined persons to keep diaries. Whatever other purposes may have moved them to do so, it was usually one of their aims to practice the kind of self-scrutiny which was a characteristic spiritual discipline of the time. Another aim was to preserve for the edification of others a record of a religious pilgrimage through life. Some journals of this sort which have come down to us have become religious classics. Among them, to mention only a few by way of illustration, are the journals of John Wesley (1703-1791) and George Whitefield (1714-1770), leaders respectively in the Methodist movement in England and the Great Awakening in America; David Brainerd (1718-1747), missionary to the American Indians; and John Woolman (1720-1772), Quaker opponent of slavery, war, and intemperance.

A contemporary of all these was Henry Melchior Mühlenberg. In response to repeated pleas from Lutheran colonists in southeastern Pennsylvania, he was sent to America from his native Germany in 1742. On his arrival in Philadelphia he revitalized existing congregations there and in nearby settlements. When he became aware of Lutheran colonists elsewhere, he made missionary tours into other parts of Pennsylvania, into New Jersey, New York, Delaware, Maryland, South Carolina, and Georgia. He entered into correspondence with still others, notably in Virginia and Nova Scotia, whom he was not able to visit. Wherever he went he revived the religious interest of German settlers and helped them to strengthen existing congregations or establish new ones. He secured additional ministers from Germany and contributed to the training of a native Lutheran ministry in America. He drafted congregational constitutions and was the leader in the formation in 1748 of the "Ministerium of North America," the first permanent Lutheran synodical organization on the Western continent. For forty-five years, until the time of his death, he was the recognized leader of his church and became known as "the patriarch of the Lutheran Church in America."

Like many of his contemporaries, Mühlenberg regularly jotted down entries in a diary. He did so not only as a spiritual exercise and for the sake of supplying others with edifying reading, but also in order to keep a record of his activities and make it easier to report on these to his ecclesiastical superiors in Europe. When he had leisure he expanded his original jottings into fuller accounts of his experiences, often pointing a moral, analysing situations and personalities, and adding bits of wry humor. Laboriously made copies of such journals were often sent to Germany to supplement more formal reports. A few excerpts from these were published in the so-called Halle Reports (*Hallesche Nachrichten*), a series of seventeen pamphlets printed in Halle, Saxony, between 1750 and 1787 under the general title "Reports of the United German Evangelical [Lutheran] Congregations in North America, Especially in Pennsylvania" and intended as missionary propaganda to awaken interest in and solicit funds for the expanding Church enterprise on the other side of the Atlantic ocean.

Very few portions of the journals were published in this way during Mühlenberg's life. Manuscript copies of the unpublished diaries were preserved in European archives and by his descendants in America (one of his sons was Peter, 1746-1807, a general during the American Revolution, and another was Frederick, 1750-1801, first speaker in the Congress of the United States). So they remained until, in connection with the 200th anniversary of the arrival in America of Henry Melchior Mühlenberg, the extant manuscripts were collated, edited, translated into English, furnished with notes, and published in three stout volumes between 1942 and 1958. Prefaced by a later account of his early life, the journals proper begin with January, 1742, when Mühlenberg was making preparations for his voyage to America, and conclude with a brief entry made on September 29, 1787, when he baptized a child. Eight days later he died. There are few gaps to interrupt the daily record of forty-five years of intensive activity in what Mühlenberg often called "the wilderness" of colonial America.

As one would expect, the *Journals* constitutes the major source for our knowledge of the man who wrote them. Mühlenberg emerges as a sharp-eyed observer of men and events, although he tended to interpret things through the rather jaundiced eyes of a Pietist. He was a man of action, with a gift for administration. The situation in which he found himself demanded that a multitude of things be done, that divergent opinions and personalities be reconciled, that methods of the Old World be adapted to the needs of the New World. For the most part he measured up to the requirements of the task imposed on him. Yet he was a man of sensitive mold who often shrank before the necessity of making hard decisions.

Of even greater importance is the light which his journals throw on the life and manners of the people among whom Mühlenberg moved. He showed great interest in the illnesses which afflicted them and the medicines which were available. He recorded the changing prices of food, clothing, and other necessities of life. He observed the work of men and women in town and country, and with rather less sympathy noted their recreation and play. He discussed the slavery of Negroes, the servitude of white redemptioners, and the condition of American Indians. He commented on schools and courts, marriage and family life, modes of travel and the movements of people.

The relation of Church and state was of immediate concern to Mühlenberg, and since he lived through the years of the American Revolution it was inevitable that he should often reflect on it. In fact, he lived in an area which became one of the major theaters of military operations. At the beginning of hostilities he moved from Philadelphia into the country, but he soon found himself between the American encampment at Valley Forge and the British troops who were occupying Philadelphia. He witnessed the movements of soldiers, heard the rumble of cannons, ministered to the wants of fleeing refugees, and deplored the destruction caused by what he called "an unnatural war." His sympathies were especially engaged because his son Peter substituted a military uniform for a clerical gown and his son Frederick abandoned the ministry to enter politics, but the father steered a precarious course of political neutrality between the contending parties.

Useful as are all these contributions to our knowledge of the war, colonial life and manners, and Mühlenberg himself, the chief value of the *Journals* lies in its contributions to Church history. The German and Dutch Reformed, Presbyterians, Anglicans, Quakers, Moravians, Methodists, Mennonites, and others appear again and again on the pages of the *Journals,* but most of the attention is naturally devoted to Lutherans, whether of Dutch, Swedish, Finnish, or German provenance. Here we have firsthand accounts of how Lutherans built their churches, secured their ministers, conducted public worship, established schools, developed social concerns, and grew in numbers and strength.

The journals show to what an extent colonial Lutherans shared in the spirit which was characteristic of the Great Awakening of the eighteenth century. Not only do George Whitefield, Gilbert Tennent (1703-1764), and other representatives of the Awakening move in and out of the diary entries, but similar emphases on conversion experiences and on legalistic patterns of Christian conduct are seen to have informed the life of Lutheran colonists. This is not surprising when it is remembered that most of the Lutherans carried over with them from Europe an understanding and a practice of the Christian faith which had been shaped by Pietism. Moreover, most of the ministers were men who, like Mühlenberg himself, had been nurtured in Pietism and had been sent to America and continued to be supported through those institutions which the leader of German Pietism, August Hermann Francke (1663-1727), had founded in Halle, Saxony.

Although the *Journals* of Henry Melchoir Mühlenberg remained relatively unknown until the middle of the twentieth century, when they were for the first time published in their entirety, they deserve a place alongside the journals of such other religious leaders of the eighteenth century as Wesley and Whitefield, Brainerd and Woolman.

SONGS OF INNOCENCE AND OF EXPERIENCE

Author: William Blake (1757-1827)
Type of work: Religious poetry
First published: 1789 (*Innocence*); 1794 (*Experience*)

Principal Ideas Advanced

The child looks upon God as a loving father; nature is benign although it is challenging.

To the child, Jesus is the Lamb, which the child loves.

But experience shows the world to be corrupted; death, jealousy, fear, and ugliness destroy the child's naïve image of reality.

Behind the horror of man's acts there is a constant Mystery.

William Blake's two small collections of poems of childhood, collected into a single book, *The Songs of Innocence and of Experience,* contain some of the most haunting expressions in literature of the reality innocence cannot anticipate and of the Mystery experience cannot know. Who has read "The Lamb" ("Little Lamb, who made thee?/ Dost thou know who made thee?/") without thereby learning forever the forgotten experience of sensing the divine presence with the open eyes of innocence? And who has read "The Tiger" ("Tiger! Tiger! burning bright/ In the forests of the night. . . .") without learning through fear the awful power of the divine Creator? Blake's genius combined the images of Lamb and Tiger into a paradoxical pair, innocence and experience united by Mystery. Neither innocence nor experience provides a full view of reality, Blake appears to claim; neither is complete without the other; he who loves the Lamb has yet to know the Tiger; he who trembles before the Tiger is in fearful danger of forgetting the Lamb.

The songs of innocence are happy songs, as Blake explains in an introductory verse. What musicians and singers have celebrated through music, the poet now celebrates through poetry. And to bring the mind to a clear perception of the nature which is the smiling face of God, Blake adopts the pastoral convention: "And I made a rural pen,/ And I stain'd the water clear,/ And I wrote my happy songs/ Every child may joy to hear."

"The Echoing Green" tells of the carefree play of children and of the rising of the sun. The old folk watch and remember the days when they, too, played on the green. Finally, the sun descends; the children return to the laps of their mothers, and it is the end of play on the echoing green.

Such a poem, which in its directness and simplicity expresses the joyful quality of the child's existence, suggests the dimension beyond the child's understanding; old age and death are witnesses as the children play; the joy of the children finds its echo in the sober recollections of the old folk as the sun descends.

"The Shepherd" is a song which, without any direct allusion to the divine presence, sketches in eight effortless lines the image of divine care;

while the shepherd watches, the lamb and the ewe are "in peace,/ For they know when their shepherd is nigh."

The poem "Infant Joy" tells us that the name of an infant should be Joy, for the infant's life is one of smiles and songs. But what is the song of innocence when the child is black? Sadly, it is a song of experience and of trust in God. In "The Little Black Boy" Blake achieves his most poignant image. The black child knows that he is different: "White as an angel is the English child,/But I am black, as if bereav'd of light. . . ." But there is no bitterness in the child's mind, for his mother explains that man must learn to bear the beams of God's love; black bodies are evidence of the power and all-pervasive presence of that love. The promise is that when God calls, the black boy will move out from the cloud and rejoice, like a lamb, around the golden tent of God. And then the black boy speaks, out of innocence and love, and declares that when he and the English boy are free from their clouds, "I'll shade him from the heat, till he can bear/ To lean in joy upon our Father's knee;/ And then I'll stand and stroke his silver hair,/ And be like him, and he will then love me."

"Laughing Song" is an expression of unconditional joy. The woods, the stream, the air, the hills, the meadows, the grasshopper, and all the girls with their "sweet round mouths" sing, "Ha, Ha, He!" The song of "Spring," which follows, is a song of welcome to the year, and once again the joy of childhood makes itself felt in all its delightful innocence.

As one continues to read of laughing and playing children, and as one contemplates their dreaming innocence (as in "Cradle Song"), one realizes that the wonder and novelty of childhood is in its distance from the adult world. The mother sings, the nurse calls to the children that the sun is descending. We all see the smile of the Maker on the face of the dreaming child, but we know that He wept for man, and we know, too, that the mother weeps while she prays that her child's dreams be happy dreams. Moments of experience intrude upon innocence, for innocence cannot be innocence except through the eyes of the mother, the nurse, and Old John, who sits beside the green and laughs at the children.

The promise of suffering, a doleful promise which puts into sharp relief the joy of the children, is a promise fulfilled in the lives of the children who are chimney sweepers. The poem "The Chimney Sweeper" begins with the lines, "When my mother died I was very young, /And my father sold me while yet my tongue/ Could scarcely cry ''weep! 'weep! 'weep! 'weep!' /So your chimneys I sweep, and in soot I sleep." In a dream of death the child joins with thousands of sweepers freed from their coffins by an angel with a bright key, and the sweeps are told that God will be their Father and that they will know joy. Tom, the sweep, rises in the dark of morning and goes forth with his brushes; he is warmed by the hope for a better life than the one he knows.

With the changing note introduced by the poem "The Chimney Sweeper," the songs begin to warn of suffering and of the coming of the night, but the promise of God's compassion still brightens the songs of innocence. Though the little boy is lost, God will find him; though man sorrows, God feels his sorrow and weeps for him.

The poems in the *Songs of Experience,* however, give unqualified expression to human despair and cynicism. Delightful as the songs of innocence are, they cannot be convincing except as expressions of innocence, for the child is ignorant of life, and he plays and laughs without knowledge of the onset of darkness. With such knowledge comes bitterness; in these poems the earth is pictured as filled with stony dread and as covered with locks of gray despair. Jealousy, selfishness, and fear spoil the quality of existence. The nurse's song is now one of depression, and she calls to the children to come home, for their time is wasted in play. Man is like a fly who at any moment can be brushed away by some blind hand. Nor does the Church provide an answer: the Chapel is locked, and "Thou shalt not" is written over the door. Priests with black gowns bind "with briars my joys and desires." A little vagabond cries out that the Church is cold but that were it an ale-house, he could be "healthy and pleasant and warm. . . ." The "invisible worm" with "dark secret love" destroys the rose. Now children are seen in poverty and tears; when the child sinks on its mother's breast, it is out of profound weariness after long struggle.

In the poem "London," Blake shows the dreadful limit of man's disillusionment. Every face shows marks of weakness and of woe; cries of men and infants reveal "mind-forg'd manacles"; the cries of the chimney sweep appall the "black'ning church" and the sigh of the soldier "Runs in blood down palace walls." Finally, the curse of the youthful harlot "Blasts the new-born infant's tear,/ And blights with plagues the marriage hearse."

Nothing in the *Songs of Experience* suggests an escape from the knowledge of man's corrupting power. In his innocence the child knows God as Father; if sorrow comes, the shepherd will shelter the lamb. But experience shows that man corrupts everything, including the joys of childhood; man destroys the Church, the state, the city, and the quality of his own existence, through his fears and vices. Man corrupts even Mystery so that the tree of mystery casts a "dismal shade" and "bears the fruit of Deceit."

How, then, can Blake have hoped for a positive statement? The *Songs of Experience* are songs of unconditional despair and cynicism. God is pictured as making a Heaven out of man's misery, and priests are shown as destroying everything joyful and lovely in the life of man.

But if one supposes that the *Songs of Innocence* presents the spirit of God's love, as that spirit is confirmed in a state of innocence, although the child's view of life is false, one may also suppose that the *Songs of Experience* shows the spirit of God's love as that spirit is corrupted through experience, although the mature view of life is true. Experience corrupts the natural and divine world the child knows. Since even the conception of God becomes a human abstraction, it is not surprising that the adult is often resentful and blasphemous toward God. The way out of paradox, then, cannot be through pure innocence or through pure experience, for innocence is naïve and experience is corrupt; paradox is resolved only when the spirit of innocence throws a divine light on the corrupting power of man. Through reading these contrasting books one understands the profound sense in which the child, for all his innocence, is right in his sentiment, while the man, for all his experience, is mistaken in his.

RELIGION WITHIN THE LIMITS OF REASON ALONE

Author: Immanuel Kant (1724-1804)
Type of work: Moral theology
First published: 1793

Principal Ideas Advanced

Religion is founded on moral concepts, particularly upon that of man as a free agent.

The central problem of religion is the opposition of good and evil; since an essentially good moral disposition can yet perform evil acts, explanation of man's possibility for self-restoration is required.

God is the moral Lawgiver and Judge, Jesus is the divinely given moral example of a perfect moral will, and natural religion is a moral ideal founded entirely on pure practical reason.

Morality, Kant tells us in *Religion Within the Limits of Reason Alone,* is based upon the idea of man as a free agent, and religion at its core is founded upon moral concepts. As a free agent man binds himself to unconditioned laws through the use of his reason, and without this moral activity religion would not be possible. Although guilt and reward depend upon the idea of man as free, it is not necessary to add to morality the idea of a Being over man, in order that man might be provided with a ground for duty other than the moral law. Morality itself does not require religious sanction. When it is a question of duty, morality is perfectly capable of ignoring all ends.

By virtue of practical reason, then, morality is self-sufficient. Yet it is still quite possible that morality is related to such an end as religion proposes, although that end does not arise out of morality itself. If we take the idea of a highest good in the world, then we must postulate a most holy and omnipotent Being who alone could unite the two elements of this highest good; namely, duty and happiness. Thus, the idea of a highest Being arises out of morality although morality is not its basis. Morality ineluctably leads to religion, to the idea of a powerful moral Lawgiver whose will can and ought to be man's final end. In religion the holiness of moral law becomes the ultimate cause.

Human power is not sufficient to bring about happiness in the world proportionate to man's worthiness to be happy. Thus, an omnipotent moral being must be postulated as ruler of the world, under whose care this balance will finally occur. However, despite the fact that religion surpasses

morality, it cannot or ought not to declare war on reason, since religion will not be able to hold out against reason in the long run. The philosopher as a teacher of pure reason must confine himself to its narrower sphere. Revelation and Biblical theology remain unavailable to him, although he can examine revelation in the light of moral concepts. Mysteries concerning the divine nature must first be transformed into moral concepts if they are to become comprehensible to everyone.

The central problem of religion for Kant, since he approaches it from the perspective of morality, is that of the opposition of good and evil. How shall we account for the principle of radical evil in human nature, and how can the fact of evil be reconciled with the good and with morality? Kant works within the Biblical framework in claiming that the world began in a good state and that evil was introduced into it. We live, then, not in an original state but in a later and altered condition. By nature man's soul should be born healthy and free from evil. But could it be that man as a species is born neither good nor bad? We call a man evil only because the actions he performs are contrary to law. The "nature of man," then, is only the subjective ground of the exercise of his freedom.

The source of evil can only be in a rule made by the will for the use of its freedom. There is in man an ultimate ground for the adoption of either good or evil maxims, and the ultimate ground for the adoption of either maxim must itself lie in free choice, although such a fact cannot be revealed in experience. Good or evil is innate in man only in this sense, that the ground for the use of freedom is present in man at birth. However, man must decide; he must exercise this freedom. His disposition with respect to the moral law can never be indifferent, never neither good nor evil. In fact the will must always be something specific, always either good or evil.

"Propensity" means the subjective ground of the possibility of an inclination. A propensity towards evil must then consist in the subjective ground of the possibility of the deviation of maxims from the moral law. In this capacity for evil, Kant distinguishes three distinct degrees: frailty of human nature, impurity of the human heart, and wickedness or corruption of the human heart. This latter is a propensity of the will to accept maxims which neglect the incentives springing from the moral law and to favor other incentives which are not moral. Wickedness reverses the ethical order of priority among the incentives of a free will. On the other hand, the spirit of the moral law is that the law is sufficient in itself as an incentive; although it is still true that propensity to evil can inhere only in the moral capacity of the will, without such a capacity neither the moral law nor evil would be possible.

"Man is evil" means that he is conscious of the moral law but has nevertheless provided by his maxims for occasional deviations therefrom. Yet the ground of evil cannot be placed either in man's sensuous nature or in a corruption of his morally legislative reason. Because it concerns a relation to the will which is free, it must be apprehended *a priori* through the concept of evil, so far as evil is possible under the laws of freedom. Even the most wicked man does not repudiate the moral law in the manner of a rebel.

The distinction between the good man and the one who is evil is not due to a difference in the incentives for their maxims. The distinction depends, rather, upon subordination; that is, upon whether it is the moral law or self-love that is given priority. Evil is a matter of priority of incentive, not the absence of any incentive that is present in the good man. Man is evil only when he reverses the moral order of the incentive (the moral law first, self-love second). Evil is radical only in the sense that it tends to corrupt the ground of all maxims.

In order to make evil morally intelligible, it must always be connected with a continued state of free will. No matter how evil a man has been up to the moment of an impending free act, it is still his duty to better himself, and such a situation is intelligible only if it always remains within his power to do so. However, the rational origin of the perversion of our will, its making lower incentives supreme among its maxims, always remains inscrutable to us. There is then no conceivable ground from which the propensity to moral evil could originally have come. Its factual presence is undeniable but its origin is a mystery. Nevertheless, rationality is not thwarted, since there always remains hope for a return to the good from which man has strayed. Despite a corrupted heart the evil man still possesses a good will.

Man is created for good, Kant is convinced, and the original predisposition in man is good. Consequently, man himself must have made himself into whatever he has become morally, whether good or evil. An injunction to become better men resounds continually in our souls, and hence it must be within our power. We have never lost our greatest incentive, respect for the moral law. Hence the restoration of man to a good state requires nothing but the establishment of the purity of the moral law as the supreme ground of all our maxims. Original goodness is merely the holiness of maxims, doing one's duty for duty's sake. Man's moral growth, then, begins in transforming his cast of mind and in the grounding of a character, not in the improvement of his actual practice. When the moral law commands that we *ought* to be better men, Kant is convinced that it follows inevitably that we must *be able* to be better men.

There is present in us an active cause of evil to be combated, although natural inclinations considered in themselves are good. The cause of evil cannot be sought in the inclinations but only in that which determines the will as a free will, and it is our duty to oppose evil, to elevate ourselves to the ideal of moral perfection. Kant declares that Jesus is to be regarded as the divinely given moral example. Through His teachings, His conduct, and His sufferings we have as perfect an example of what it means to be a man well-pleasing to God as one can expect to find in external experience, since the archetype is really to be found in our own reason and not outside it.

Was Jesus divine? Kant answers this continually crucial theological problem by saying that He may be regarded as superhuman to the degree that His unchanging purity of will was innate and not achieved. Since all transgression on His part was utterly impossible, He must be set radically apart from mortal men. Divinity consists of the unalterableness of a holy moral will, render-

ing such a being immune to temptations. This is the ideal of the Son of God which is set up before us as our model. Thus, the good in us, when it appears in the guise of an action, is always inadequate to a holy law. Action itself is always defective in man, since motives other than pure will are always and necessarily involved.

Having once seen such a good and pure disposition, we acquire confidence in its permanence and stability. Yet the judge within a man, when he considers his own past and his future destiny, pronounces a severe verdict upon himself. He sees the model of the holy will, but he also sees his necessary distance from it. There exists no salvation for man except the sincerest adoption of genuinely moral principles into his disposition, yet how shall this be accomplished? Moral religion consists, then, in the heart's disposition to fulfill all human duties as divine commands. For this purpose miracles are superfluous. True religion, which once may have used miracles as expedients, can now maintain itself on purely rational grounds.

Nothing is more certain to Kant than that, if anything flatly contradicts morality, it cannot be of God. Anything holy must be moral and an object of reason. The idea of a moral Governor of the world is something presented by our practical reason. Thus, the universally true religious belief conformable to this requirement of practical reason is belief in God as holy Legislator, benevolent Ruler, and righteous Judge. The highest goal of moral perfection in finite creatures is love of the law; the equivalent in religion of this idea would be an article of faith, "God is love." Religion is the recognition of all duties as divine commands.

Natural religion, as morality, is a pure practical idea of reason. Here then is a complete religion, one which can be presented to all men comprehensively and convincingly through their own reason. The one true religion is nothing but laws, those principles whose unconditioned necessity we become aware of, and which we recognize as revealed not empirically but through pure reason. True enlightenment involves conceiving the service of God as being, first and foremost, a free and hence a moral service. Whatever good man is able to do through his own efforts (under freedom, without supernatural assistance) can be related to *nature* as distinct from *grace*. At least we know the laws of freedom, the moral laws, whereas we cannot know anything at all about supernatural aid. Thus, natural religion was for Kant religion within the limits of reason alone.

SYSTEM OF DOCTRINES

Author: Samuel Hopkins (1721-1803)
Type of work: Systematic theology
First published: 1793

Principal Ideas Advanced

God as the Sovereign Creator and Ruler of the world has determined all things that come to pass, including physical and moral evil as necessary means to the greatest good of the whole.

Sin is selfishness or self-love, while virtue is identified with disinterested benevolence or love of being in general, entailing a willingness to give up one's private interest and happiness for the greater good of the whole.

Original sin, consisting in exercises or acts and therefore indistinguishable from actual sin, involves man in no inability to obey the law of God except his inclination to disobey, thus leaving him without excuse for his sin or for his opposition to the Gospel.

Samuel Hopkins's *System of Doctrines* is the first comprehensive treatise of New England or New School Theology developed on the foundation of the speculative views propounded by Jonathan Edwards (1703-1758) in his treatises on the will, on virtue, and on God's design in creation. As a student, Hopkins had spent over eight months in the Edwards home, and in later life he maintained a close relation to his teacher as well as to Joseph Bellamy (1719-1790) and Stephen West (1736-1819). His life as a pastor in Great Barrington, Massachusetts, and later in Newport, Rhode Island, exemplified the principles of self-sacrificing love he inculcated. His emphasis on the role of reason in theology aroused the admiration of William Ellery Channing (1780-1842). Hopkins's progressive outlook is expressed in his Preface to the *System:* "And there is no reason to doubt, that light will so increase in the church, and men will be raised up, who will make such advances in opening the Scripture . . . that what is now done and written will be so far superseded, as to appear imperfect and inconsiderable, compared with that superior light with which the church will then be blessed."

Many of the theological loci are handled in the style of traditional Calvinist dogmatics. The innovations of Hopkinsianism are largely developments of themes derived from the work of Jonathan Edwards, principally the identification of virtue with disinterested benevolence. While Channing's impression "that President Edwards was a great deal indebted to Dr. Hopkins for his later views of religion" (Letter of February 14, 1840) is not supported by evidence, Hopkins himself claimed to have improved upon Edwards in more definitively stating the opposition of holiness to self-love.

The entire moral character of God is viewed by Hopkins as comprehended in love or benevolence. This benevolence has the highest good of being in general for its object. Benevolent love involves love of complacence, or delight in goodness. Divine love is perfectly disinterested, in opposition to all self-love or selfishness. Impartial benevolence requires God to be the chief and supreme object of His love and to make Himself the chief end of creation. To regard God as an almighty tool existing only for His creatures is to inculcate a wholly selfish religion. Infinite benevolence seeks and promotes the greatest good of the whole and is consequently the enemy of all who oppose this good. Thus the wrath of God against sin proceeds from love, and infinite benevolence requires the due punishment of the offender. The absolute, uncontrollable sovereignty of God may also be identified with omnipotent love, doing whatever it pleases, infinitely above any control or obligation to any other being. The sovereignty of God is not arbitrary but is exercised in infinite wisdom according to the dictates of moral perfection.

The distinctive Hopkinsian doctrine of the decrees of God is a rigorous deduction from the above conception of divine sovereignty. Hopkins quotes the Westminster Shorter Catechism: "The decrees of God are his eternal purpose, according to the counsel of his own will, whereby for his own glory he hath foreordained whatsoever comes to pass." The glory of God is understood as involving the greatest possible good or happiness of creatures as an expression of the greatest possible exercise and exhibition of His goodness. Only in our imperfect and partial conceptions are the glory of God and the good of the creature two distinct things. Every detail of the universe has been predetermined for the attainment of this end.

The foreordination of all events is held to be consistent with the liberty and moral agency of creatures. Flight from foreordination to foreknowledge does not make the assertion of freedom easier, for foreknowledge supposes the future to be fixed, and if not by God's decree, then by blind fate. Even if foreordination and freedom cannot be reconciled by us, we ought to accept both on the testimony of Scripture as well as of reason. Hopkins does not stop here with many theologians, but in the Edwardian tradition proposes a rational solution of the antinomy. The only internal liberty of which we are conscious consists in our voluntary exercises, in choosing and willing. Freedom of will therefore consists in the exercise of volition and not in the absence of determining events. No other freedom is conceivable, and this freedom is established by the divine decree making the determinate choice of the will certain.

The crucial problem in relation to the divine decrees is the problem of evil. Here the clarity and consistency of the Hopkinsian solution is unequaled in the torturous history of this thorny problem. Hopkins boldly asserts that God is the cause of both natural and moral evil. After dismissing inconsistent positions, Hopkins observes that "it is abundantly evident and demonstrably certain from reason assisted by divine revelation, that all the sin and sufferings which have taken place or ever will, are necessary for the greatest good of the universe, and to answer the wisest and best ends, and therefore must be included in the best, most wise and perfect plan." There are things that appear evil when considered as being in isolation, but there is no absolute evil in the universe. The argument follows a Leibnizian pattern to the extent of claiming that no two possible worlds can be indifferent in the divine mind, since there must be a sufficient reason for the choice of the one rather than the other. Scripture also plainly teaches that all moral evil is designed by God to answer a good end and to contribute to the greatest good.

Moral evil cannot be the origin or cause of itself. Consequently to assert that God is the cause of moral evil is not to deny His infinite holiness. To hold that the origin or cause of sin must be sinful is to render the problem of the origin of moral evil insoluble. To ascribe sin to a negative cause is unsatisfactory, for a negative cause is really no cause. To say that sin is merely a negative thing is an evasion. If sin has no positive existence, then there is no sin. That people find the divine causality of sin shocking is no indication of its falsity. Common sense and emotion are not to be followed when their dictates are contrary to those of sound reason and the plain declarations of divine revelation.

The immediate exertion of divine power is the proper efficient cause of every event. The preservation of creatures in existence is really continued creation, and the fixed law and course of nature is nothing but the divine will operating in a certain steady fixed manner. Events contrary to this order are called miracles.

Some points related to the doctrine of original sin represent innovations destined to exercise a far-reaching influence in New England theology. Although Hopkins teaches that Adam as the natural and confederating head of the human race involved his posterity in his disobedience and the resulting curse, he explains that he does not mean that sin takes place in the posterity of Adam in consequence of his sin or that they are constituted sinners by his disobedience. The offense of Adam is not imputed to the innocent, but by a divine constitution there is a certain connection between Adam's first sin and his posterity's sinfulness. The distinction between original and actual sin is denied. All sin is actual, and original sin or total moral depravity consists in exercise or act as much as any sin can do. This view appears to be a consequence of the Hopkinsian theory of the will, and it was further developed in the "exercise theory" of Dr. Nathanael Emmons (1745-1840). Human responsibility for sin is stressed by the distinction between natural and moral inability. Man's inability to obey the law of God is entirely a function of his inclination to disobey. Man's natural ability is intact, but his moral disability is total and criminal.

Sin consists in exercises directly opposed to disinterested benevolence. Sin is self-love, the exclusive regard for one's own interest. Every degree of self-love is intrinsically evil. Where there is no selfishness there is no sin. Disinterested benevolence does imply a proper regard for self, but the benevolent person seeks his happiness not as his own, but as included in the interest of the whole.

The redemption of man by Jesus Christ is the greatest instance of the exercise of the benevolence of God. The atonement provided by God the Son through His suffering the punishment of sin in place of sinners is sufficient atonement for the sins of the whole world and provides the basis for a universal offer of salvation to sinners. But since mankind is totally depraved, none to whom the offer of salvation is made would comply with it, were it not for a special work of the Holy Spirit renewing the hearts of men.

Regeneration as the work of the divine Spirit is distinguished from conversion, its effect consisting in the exercises of the regenerate. Regeneration is instantaneous, and man is wholly passive in it. The subject of regeneration is the heart or will, not the intellect. Enlightenment of the mind is no part of regeneration, nor is the word of God a means to the change of heart. Light and truth belong to active conversion, not to regeneration.

All truly Christian exercises consist in disinterested affection, the willingness to give up any lesser good for the greater. The benevolent person is disposed to relinquish his own interest and happiness for the greatest good of the whole. The *System* does not explicitly teach that a man should be willing to be damned for the glory of God but in *A Dialogue between a Calvinist and a Semi-Calvinist,* the doctrine of disinterested submission to the will of God is expounded and defended.

In the preaching of the Gospel, Hopkins insisted on the duty of immediate repentance. All activities of the unregenerate could only be expressions of total depravity and therefore could not be the performance of any duty. Sincere striving is therefore an effect of regeneration, while unregenerate striving only adds to the sinner's guilt.

Appended to the *System* is a *Treatise on the Millennium.* The dedication to the people who shall live in the days of the millennium expresses the author's enthusiasm for this favorite theme. Hopkins cherished the hope that the number of the saved during the millennium would be so great that the total number of the redeemed would far exceed that of the damned. The harsh features of his system are thus softened if not absorbed by the spirit of benevolence that suffuses the whole.

EARLY THEOLOGICAL WRITINGS

Author: Georg Wilhelm Friedrich Hegel (1770-1831)
Type of work: Theology
First published: 1907

Principal Ideas Advanced

The positive elements of Jesus' teaching were made the basis of historical Christianity to the exclusion of the rational elements.

Catholicism and State Protestantism have made Christianity an enemy of free rationality by appealing to force and by the dogmatic character of their teaching.

The religion of Jesus overcomes the alienation which abstract thought produces.

Christ's teaching, that God is love, reconciles nature and morality.

Faith, not reason, is the highest stage of man's development.

Hegel's essays on Christianity, which antedate their author's emergence as a philosophical luminary, were never prepared by him for publication. Presumably Hegel came to regard them, as historians in our time are likely to do, as merely preliminary studies, in which he had not yet found the system which made him famous. Particularly interesting is the movement of Hegel's thought in the interval between *The Positivity of the Christian Religion* (1795-6) and *The Spirit of Christianity* (1798-9), during which interval he passed from the atmosphere of the Enlightenment to that of Romanticism. The work entitled *Early Theological Writings* is not a unified book, but a collection of essays and fragments.

Hegel's interest in theological problems was deeply personal. While he was a student at the theological seminary in Tübingen, he was torn between loyalty to Christianity and to the philosophical ideals of the Age. In many respects, Greek classicism was more appealing to him than the Hebraism of the gospels, and both seemed superior to the ecclesiasticism of Catholicism and State Protestantism. In *The Positivity of the Christian Religion,* Hegel reviews the history of Christianity in an effort to distinguish between what belongs to the teachings of Jesus and what was added by his successors.

By a "positive" religion, Hegel means one which is based upon authority, attested by miracles, and accepted on faith. It is at the opposite pole from philosophy, which is based on truths of nature and reason. The Hebrews, according to Hegel, had no conception of reason and no interest in truth; their religion was purely of the positive variety. Jesus, because He was a Jew ministering to Jews, was forced to clothe His teaching in a positive garb. On this account, He spoke much of His own credentials as a divine teacher, and He catered to his hearer's demand for miracles. But the truth which He sought to impart was that which is given to every man by his moral sense; thus, Jesus used positive religion merely as a means for bringing His teaching home to the hearts of men.

The effect of Jesus' method was to broaden the minds of His disciples. The narrow, nationalistic outlook of Judaism was broken down and replaced by one as comprehensive as reason itself, and a legalistic concern with the externals of conduct gave place to an appreciation of virtuous motives. Thus far, reason received its due. But because Jesus rested His teachings on an appeal to historical faith, His disciples never learned the independent use of reason, and they conceived that their task was simply to preserve and to transmit the teaching which they had heard.

Hegel contrasts the pupils of Socrates and those of Christ, to the disadvantage of the latter. The friends of Socrates, says Hegel, were attracted to him because of his virtue and his philosophy, instead of accepting the latter on the authority of his person. Thus, when they founded schools of their own, they did so in their own right, considering that they were at liberty to teach the truth as they understood it. Because they were concerned mainly with the spread of virtue and truth, they bore no hostility toward members of other schools, or toward devotees of popular religions, except insofar as others strayed from the path of righteousness. It was, indeed, their deepest conviction that every man has a right to his own convictions and his own will.

By contrast, the disciples of Jesus were imbued with a spirit of partisanship and sect which required them to contest any departure by members of their group from the supposed teachings of the Master and to regard as enemies members of the popular religions and of philosophical schools. Because they accepted their doctrine on the authority of God, the disciples could not but regard any defection from it as sinful and disobedient, and therefore as deserving of punishment. Thus, in the hands of Jesus' first disciples, Christianity abandoned the rational element of His teaching and became purely and simply a positive religion, which it has continued to be to this day.

Hegel recounts bitterly the conquest of Christianity over the State, as a result of which, in Protestant as well as in Catholic countries, infidelity or heresy became a civil offense. He further complains against the injustice done to men's minds when as children they are trained in a dogmatic tradition. By filling their minds with imaginary fears and hopes, instead of teaching them to use their understanding, the Church enslaves them as truly as when it resorts to civil measures. The morality that follows from such a faith, even when formally correct, can never be motivated by that love of goodness which Jesus intended, but will always be calculated toward self-interest.

Except for echoes of Kant's categorical imperative, *The Positivity of the Christian Religion* hardly goes beyond Rousseau's *Creed of the Savoyard Priest* (1762), or, for that matter, Herbert of Cherbury's *De religione laici* (1645). Hegel's subsequent essay, *The Spirit of Christianity,* belongs instead to the age of Schelling and Schleiermacher. Hegel seems to have gone through a period of self-estrangement, in the course of which he came under the influence of the Romantic revolt and emerged as a Christian mystic. Such, at least, is the interpretation of Richard Kroner, the biographer of these years. In his latter phase, instead of viewing Christianity in terms of Kant's ethical teachings, Hegel argues that reason and morality are transcended in what Kroner calls "the Pantheism of Love." The unity of nature now appears to him violated by the demands of the moral law, and he turns to religion to find the means of bringing them together in a higher unity. (The essentials of Hegel's later dialectic appear here.)

In *The Spirit of Christianity,* as in the earlier work, Hegel shows his bias toward the Greeks, who, as he represents them, lived in sympathetic unity with nature, loving life, and calling the world their own. The Hebrews, on the contrary, are described as having been dominated by abstract reason, somewhat in the manner of Immanuel Kant. Unable to love the world, the Hebrews sought salvation by condemning it and by pledging their allegiance to the idea of unity, to an object of thought. In this way, says Hegel, the Jews introduced into history that radical alienation which sets righteousness against beauty, duty against inclination, and the universal against the individual. Viewed against their Jewish background, the significance of the Gospels lies in their proclamation of the reconciling power of divine love.

Hegel maintains that the ethical teaching of Jesus was not based on reason, as he earlier supposed. On the contrary, Jesus shows that the law must serve man; He has no hesitancy in overstepping it on the slightest provocation; and He is more hopeful for spontaneous sinners than He is for legalistic moralists. In the Sermon on the Mount, He shows the insufficiency of law by pointing to the love which transcends it; not in the universality of laws such as those opposing murder, but in the spirit which reconciles a man with his brother, does man find deliverance. In the Parables of the Kingdom, Jesus shows the beauty and freedom that is possible for man once he puts away the bondage of law and lives in loving confidence toward the world and toward his fellowman.

But Hegel is now less interested in Jesus' exhortations than in what He has to say about reconciliation and forgiveness. Any law brings condemnation to men's hearts, which even punishment cannot remove. Only a love which is higher than law is able to bring wholeness to the guilty soul. Such is the love which Jesus proclaims, the universal love of God, no longer merely an object of thought, but the true Author of all life and being. Jesus' own consciousness of divine sonship, combined with His sense of oneness with man, is the perfect expression of Unity. He sought to impart this communion to His disciples through the symbolism of the Last Supper; but the effect was only to set Himself between His followers and the divine love; moreover, the fellowship and love which His disciples were able to find with each other through Him was an exclusive one, which left them unreconciled with the rest of the world. The true religion of Jesus, therefore, is not the religion of the churches. In His God "*all* beings are united; in him there are no members, as members, of a community."

In *The Spirit of Christianity* Hegel makes religion the final goal of human development, in opposition to the stand which he took later, for example in *The Phenomenology of Spirit* (1807), in which he places philosophy higher than religion. In this connection, the *Fragment of a System* (1800) is interesting, supporting, as it does, the stand taken in *The Spirit of Christianity*. In the *Fragment,* Hegel develops a philosophy of organism, finding in "life" the reconciliation of unity and diversity. "Reflection," on the other hand, is radically divisive, since whatever proposition is propounded, another must be excluded by it. In order, therefore, for man to find unity, he must transcend reflection and take his stand in "a reality beyond all reflection." This movement Hegel calls religion; by its means, "finite life rises to infinite life," and, thus, "The culmination of faith, the return to the Godhead whence man is born, closes the circle of man's development."

ON RELIGION: SPEECHES TO ITS CULTURED DESPISERS

Author: Friedrich Schleiermacher (1768-1834)
Type of work: Philosophy of religion; apologetics
First published: 1799

Principal Ideas Advanced

Modern culture's alienation from religion stems from failure to see beyond the latter's corrupt outer form, whereas the inner essence of religion is actually the center of all that is humanly normal and highest.

Independently given in man's nature and experience, and essentially different from knowing and doing, religion can be neither established nor supplanted by science, philosophy, morality, or art; nor does it threaten their autonomous activity.

Within the life of the spirit, religion's locus is the union of feeling and intuition; its "object"—which cannot literally be conceived as an object—is the Universe, the Ground and Unity of all that is.

As essentially concrete and historical, religion mediates between the Ultimate and the finite in its universal corruption; thus Christianity, centering upon this mediation, or redemption, embodies in the purest and highest way the principle of religion itself.

As Schleiermacher is the "father of modern theology," so *On Religion* is in many ways its primary manifesto. Nurtured in Moravian piety, the author had also entered avidly into the mind and spirit of the time. With Immanuel Kant (1724-1804), of whom he was critical, Baruch Spinoza (1632-1677), and J. G. Herder (1744-1803), as main philosophical sources, Schleiermacher wrote under the immediate stimulus of the Romantic circle in Berlin, where he had come as a hospital chaplain in 1796. *On Religion,* which appeared anonymously, was his first work, but it caught the attention of German intellectual leaders and quickly established Schleiermacher's significance. While the impress of Romanticism is deep, the import of the book far transcends that particular movement, the more so through Schleiermacher's repeated revisions (1806, 1811, 1821) and appended explanations, following the discontinuation of his Romantic associations. As professor of theology at Berlin, as original contributor to philosophy, pedagogy, and philology, as moving preacher and ecclesiastical statesman, Schleiermacher became one of the shaping forces of his age. Yet no later work, not even his monumental *The Christian Faith,* has eclipsed the inspiration and thrust with which *On Religion* launches a program of mediation between thoroughgoing openness to modernity and steadfast loyalty to the Christian substance.

Though not oral deliverances, the five parts of the book are appropriately called "speeches" because of their rhetorical, declarative style. Upon a groundplan of solid argumentation, Schleiermacher seeks to persuade and to encourage empathy and identification. The first speech, the "defense," establishes the apologetic premise that the author understands and shares the values of his audience. He too is committed to that free and higher life of the spirit for which modern culture stands. But also partaking by special affinity in the reality of religion, he is fitted for the necessary task of mediation. The complaints of the "cultured despisers" of religion are largely justified—indeed they have a prophetic function—as directed against the outward representations of religion in the present day. Thus, in fact, the "despisers" are allies of what religion truly is, just as it, in turn, is the ultimate stay of all that is enduring in their vision of beauty, truth, and good. But to grasp this, the "despisers" must go beyond the distortions to the incorruptible inner essence of religion.

Hence, the second speech, longest and with the fifth the most important, is devoted to the "nature of religion." Schleiermacher attempts to vindicate his subject by appeal to its foundational origins. He seeks the origins not in history but in human nature itself. Contrary to common opinion, religion is neither a knowing nor a doing, nor is it a combination of the two. It is an abuse of religion to defend it as a prop for some other spiritual or cultural function. Science, metaphysics, art, and morality have their autonomous scope, in which religion, rightly understood, has neither the right nor the need to interfere. For religion has its own distinct domain in man's being. "True science is complete vision; true practice is culture and art self-produced; true religion is sense and taste for the Infinite." As the awareness of the Infinite in the finite and of the Eternal in the temporal, religion can neither be based upon nor threatened by knowledge or action. "If man is not one with the Eternal in the unity of intuition and feeling which is immediate, he remains, in the unity of consciousness which is derived, forever apart."

The first edition gave more prominence to intuition (*Anschauung*), the later ones to feeling (*Gefühl*). But the view is consistently maintained that religion's locus is that primary, nonobjectifiable moment or dimension of consciousness wherein feeling and intuition are as yet undifferentiated. "It fills no time and fashions nothing palpable. It is the holy wedlock of the Universe with the incarnated Reason. . . . It is immediate, raised above all error and misunderstanding. You lie directly on the bosom of the infinite world." But since religion is the consciousness of our immediate relationship to the Ultimate (the Universe, the All), it does not simply stand apart from knowing and doing. Without obtruding into cultural functions, it nevertheless comprises their integrating fulcrum, the ground from which they spontaneously arise and in which they cohere.

Schleiermacher goes on to explain that the traditional doctrinal content of religion need not be the stumbling block that rigid, rationalistic interpretation can make of it. Doctrines are not to be estimated as science or metaphysics, but as expressions of religious intuition and feeling. Some venerable notions have been accused of opposing natural law. But miracle, for instance, "is simply the religious name for event" when the event is seen as the operation of the Eternal. And revelation, another belabored idea, should be regarded as any truly original insight into man's relation to the Infinite. Nor can the essential interests of religion be identified with the theistic concept of God as a being distinct from the world, or with the theory of life after death. Religious feeling may employ such concepts, but in immediate certitude it precedes them and does not rest upon their correctness.

With this statement of its general nature, Schleiermacher turns in the third speech to the "cultivation of religion." He stresses the spontaneous and intuitive character of religious receptivity. "Instruction in religion, meaning that piety itself is teachable, is absurd and unmeaning." Merely imitative religion is a contradiction in terms. There is discipleship, but never by coercion. Everything depends upon awakening the seed that lies in each soul, for an individual's religion must be his own most sincere possession. Schleiermacher finds the contemporary state of religious cultivation deplorable, a condition which he traces to utilitarian preoccupation with the finite. There prevails a moralistic rationalism which no longer envisages the Infinite, and this is reinforced by the antithetical supernaturalism which puts the Infinite outside and apart from the finite. Against both, Schleiermacher welcomes as a sign of hope those tendencies of his audience which drive beyond self-sufficiency to the ground and limits of life. The strengthening of religious consciousness is greatly expedited by the free play of the imagination and the creative art embodied in the advance elements of modern culture.

The fourth speech takes up "association in religion, or church and priesthood." Schleiermacher proceeds from a distinction between the true Church, which is the natural and wholesome fellowship of the really pious, and the ecclesiastical institution, which "is very far from being a society of religious men." In the true Church there is no distinction of priest and layman, no intolerant separatism, and no demand for conformity to external authority. Individuality and free association are equally encouraged. Institutionalism does not exist, and no competing concerns detract from the all-pervading centrality of religion itself. However, if this were the entire Church, none but saints could belong. The actual ecclesiastical institution, for all its faults, mediates between the ideal Church and the world. Its educative purpose makes compromises unavoidable, although these should be held constantly under the corrective of the ideal. Schleiermacher takes particularly to task confessional exclusivism, religious professionalism, and the intermingling of Church and state. He calls for increasing openness and communion among the ecclesiastical bodies, for the overcoming of clericalism, and for the liberation of the purely religious from debilitating alliances with other interests.

The subject of the fifth speech is "the religions." The interpretation of *On Religion* as a whole turns upon the relation which this last part bears to the foregoing, especially to the second speech. For if the latter were taken as a full exposition of its essence, religion would appear as only an ideal generality, without decisive connection with any historical religion. But in the concluding speech Schleiermacher makes emphatically clear that he conceives the essence of religion to embrace the concrete historicity and particularity of the religions. Their plurality is not to be compared with the plurality of churches. For each authentically individual religion consists in a unique intuition of the Ultimate. Instead of being segregated behind ecclesiastical walls, differences of intuition should be allowed to work upon, enrich, and define each other. Lack of appreciation for other religions has no basis in religion itself. For the more adequately one apprehends the Infinite, the more humility and openness one will have for the unlimited range of its manifestations. Schleiermacher sharply repudiates the project of "natural religion," partly because it would reduce the living variety of religion to a series of abstractions, and partly because it proposes to remove religion from its historical bases to a supposedly more secure footing in reason. But "resistance to the positive and arbitrary is resistance to the definite and real. If a definite religion may not begin with an original fact, it cannot begin at all. There must be a common ground for selecting some one religious element and placing it at the centre, and this ground can only be a fact."

Thus the reality of religion is given in the concrete variety of the positive religions. But since these religions arise in time, they are subject to decay and death. Schleiermacher describes Judaism, which concentrates on the idea of divine reward and punishment, as "long since dead." How, then, does it stand with Christianity, which finally emerges as the real burden of Schleiermacher's apology? Is Christianity simply one among the other historical religions, each mediating in its limited and transient way between the Infinite and the finite? No, for it is "just the intuition of the universal resistance of finite things to the Whole, and of the way the Deity treats this resistance. Christianity sees how He reconciles the hostility to Himself, and sets bounds to the ever increasing alienation by scattering points here and there over the whole that are at once finite and infinite, human and divine." Christianity is the principle of religion itself. "It manipulates religion as matter for religion." Because of the corruption infecting all actual religiousness, including its own churchly existence, Christianity wages perpetual warfare in behalf of the ideal. Under the weight of the world's selfishness and the attendant evil, the dominant Christian tone is holy sadness. But the Christian spirit never comes to rest in simply an emotional state. On the basis of the life of Christ, it is always seeking the reconciliation and reunion of the finite with the Infinite, of every creature with God. Jesus never claimed to be the only mediator; indeed, He calls his disciples to be sharers and instruments of his purpose. And "nothing is more unchristian than to seek uniformity in religion." Nevertheless, as the Bible's authority is established not through dogma but through experienced power, so Christ proves Himself to all who are grasped by His "whole efficacy" as the One "who has become historically the center of all mediation."

Thus Schleiermacher, through a critical analysis of religion's integral role in human existence, reaches his climax and conclusion in the presentation of the redemption centered in Jesus Christ as the criterion and fulfillment of religion. Religion's ideal essence, considered in the second speech, is balanced by the concrete, historical specifics of the fifth speech. The tension between these two components—the general nature and need of religion, and the particularity of historically given revelation—has been a principal dynamic of modern theological development. The greatness of Schleiermacher's youthful masterpiece consists in the way in which it both determines and anticipates so much of that development.

NATURAL THEOLOGY

Author: William Paley (1743-1805)
Type of work: Apologetics; philosophy of religion
First published: 1802

Principal Ideas Advanced

The existence of a cosmic Designer can be demonstrated to be highly probable on the basis of empirical evidence drawn from nature.

Empirical evidence, further, can support the conclusion that this Designer possesses the characteristics of the Christian God.

Natural Theology was the crowning achievement of William Paley, Archdeacon of Carlisle, England, but while it remains the work for which this eighteenth century thinker is principally remembered, Paley's interests and achievements ranged widely within the fields of philosophy and theology. Son of the headmaster at Giggleswick School, Paley showed excellence in his early studies and later at Cambridge, where soon after his graduation in 1763 he gained a considerable reputation for his brilliant lectures on moral philosophy. Together with the English philosopher Jeremy Bentham (1748-1832), Paley is credited with laying the foundations of the ethics of utilitarianism.

After leaving Cambridge for an ecclesiastical "living" at the time of his marriage in 1776, Paley engaged himself in writing and in supporting various liberal movements for reform. His highly successful book in ethical theory, *The Principles of Moral and Political Philosophy* (1785), was adopted as a standard text at Cambridge, exerting an inevitable influence on developments in British moral philosophy. Translating his ethical theories into practice, Paley was active in the movement to abolish slavery in Britain; because of his abolitionist efforts (and his liberal political sympathies) his ecclesiastical advancement was blocked by more conservative persons in positions of authority. Far from conservative, Paley threw himself into an unsuccessful campaign for the reform and simplification of the Thirty-Nine Articles of the Anglican Church and thus dashed any lingering hope for advancement beyond his position of Archdeacon.

Other books followed, now in the field of theological apologetics to which Paley turned with energy and lucidity. *Horae Paulinae* (1790) and his *View of the Evidences of Christianity* (1794) led up to his master work in apologetics, *Natural Theology*, published only three years before his death.

The significance of *Natural Theology* was not in its originality—others had been saying similar things for years before Paley's book appeared—but, rather, in the consistency of its method and the thoroughness of its argument. Thanks to these qualities, *Natural Theology* remains the definitive statement of the classical teleological argument. His theistic proof is essentially an empirical argument, and in Paley is found a consistent empiricist whose approach and method were perfectly suited to his subject matter.

The senses, for Paley, are our sole trustworthy avenues to knowledge of the reality surrounding us; the inferences of natural knowledge should always be grounded in experience; finally, all beliefs so established—including those of theology—are to be judged as more or less probable hypotheses rather than as necessary truths or indubitable demonstrations. By amassing empirical evidence in support of a given hypothesis, however, a belief may be shown to be overwhelmingly probable; under such circumstances, disbelief must be condemned as arbitrary and irrational.

Paley provided his readers with a vast store of the best scientific data available to him, the overwhelming effect of which was to show—as conclusively as empirical methodology allows or requires—the irrational absurdity of atheism. Never before or since *Natural Theology* has empirical fact been served up in such indefatigable abundance and variety to support belief in God.

Paley's argument divides naturally into two parts; the first part is devoted to proving the existence of a Designer of the experienced world, while the second part is dedicated to deriving empirically the theistic characteristics of this Designer.

The proof for the existence of a cosmic Designer begins with an analysis of the criteria used in everyday experience to determine whether or not something is the product of design. Paley contrasts, in what is probably his best known single example, the characteristics of a stone with those of a watch. The watch, unlike the stone, requires explanation in terms of purpose or design because the former is found to be composed (1) of parts (springs, cogs, and so on) nicely fashioned to work together in the joint accomplishment, (2) of an end result (steady movement of a pointer around a visible face) which the parts alone or in different combination would have been incapable of bringing about, and (3) of some identifiable useful product (marking the hours of the day). Experience teaches us that when these characteristics are present they are due to intelligent design; that is, to the action of a designer.

Such design-implying characteristics are abundantly present in nature as well as in human artifacts. No one would doubt that the telescope, composed of parts fitted together to accomplish a valuable effect beyond the powers of any of the parts taken separately, must be explained in terms of design; no more, then, can one doubt that the eye, which manifests even more ingenious utilization of individually impotent parts for the sake of a valuable total result—vision—than does the finest telescope, must have been designed. The empirical criteria justifying one's inference that the existence of the eye is best accounted for as the product of an intelligent Designer are abundantly present. Only stubborn prejudice could lead one to refuse to draw the sole conclusion sanctioned by repeated experience.

Philosophic objections aimed at justifying such prejudice, Paley contends, are all without weight. Shall we appeal to mere chance as accounting for the complex facts of natural design? Such an appeal is no more than the willful clutching of an ungrounded and vastly improbable hypothesis in irrational preference to the one hypothesis for which widespread experiential precedent has been established. Shall we look to "natural law" or to some "principle of order" as an alternative explanation of the facts? Such an attempted escape is literally unintelligible, Paley maintains, since "natural laws" and "principles" are only *descriptions* of nature's working; to suppose them to be *agents* is to make a serious logical blunder leading to conceptual confusion and to the fallacy of treating an abstraction as though it were a concrete thing. Can the hypothesis of a Designer be evaded by postulating an infinite regress of undesigned causes to account for the present facts? Such a route, Paley insists, is indeed an evasion, since no question is adequately answered by appeal to the intrinsic absurdity of a literally infinite sequence of causes. Somewhere the sequence as a whole must be rooted in a sufficient cause, and the marks of design, as we have seen, require this sufficient cause to be no less than an intelligent Designer. No more impressive to Paley are objections arising from our own incapacity as finite designers to produce—or to observe directly the cosmic Designer at work in producing—the natural objects which have the marks of design. One need not himself be able to produce every contrivance that is recognized (and admired) as the product of intelligence; nor need one actually observe the production of every artifact or type of artifact in order to be justifiably confident of its status as falling within the class of intelligent contrivances.

Although Paley goes on to present other examples of natural contrivances, each serving to support the same conclusion, he acknowledges that each piece of evidence taken alone is sufficient to prove his point. But the weight of his argument, he holds, is cumulative; its total effect should be to sweep away completely any hesitation in acknowledging the existence of a Designer.

A contrivance need not, indeed, work perfectly—or even very well—to be recognized as a contrivance. Unless its status as a product of design were first granted, it would be logically inappropriate to accuse it of "working well" or "working badly" at all. Natural contrivances, therefore, Paley points out, would not even need to be so skillfully wrought as is the eye, to support conclusively the hypothesis that a cosmic Designer exists.

The eye, like other products of the cosmic Designer, is, however, clearly a masterpiece of organization. From such considerations we may learn not only of the existence of the Designer (with whom we have until now been exclusively concerned) but also of His characteristics. We recognize, on reflection, that personal pronouns are fully appropriate with respect to Him, since the characteristics of any designer must be those—intelligence, consciousness of purpose, volitional powers—which constitute the very meaning of "personal" within our experience.

What kind of person is this Designer? He is beyond all finite measure *powerful,* it is clear, since the forces of the natural order that He has designed exceed our comprehension; thus, He is *omnipotent.* He is beyond all finite measure *knowing,* since His intelligence manifested in the observable universe passes beyond our limits of conception; thus, He is *omniscient.* He is *everywhere active,* as is indicated by the uniformity of nature as far as our farthest observations can extend; thus, He is *omnipresent.* He has *been from "the beginning"* of created time, since the contriver must precede His contrivance; thus, He is *eternal.* As the producer of the world, He is *not dependent* on His product for His own existence; thus, we can empirically understand Him to be *self-existent.* The Designer is found, therefore, on empirical grounds, to be powerful, omnipotent, omniscient, omnipresent, eternal, and self-existent; who is such a Designer if not God?

God's existence has thus been proved, Paley concludes, but unless the world's apparent evil due to suffering can be explained on this hypothesis, such a proof is no more than a mockery. But the presence of evil is explainable. Pain is itself useful to living organisms which, without sharp warning to deter them, might easily destroy themselves in countless ways. Suffering is never inflicted for its own sake; if God had desired pointless suffering, how much more effectively He could have made us miserable! Teeth are for eating, not for aching. What is more, pleasure is added to the world to an extent entirely beyond that necessary for the mere maintenance of biological functions. Benevolence, not its opposite, can best account for the facts. Despite the sufferings of the world, God's goodness is secure; into His everlasting arms we may put our trust for help with difficulties yet unsolved.

Unsolved difficulties in Paley's position there may indeed be, but these seem to have had little effect in discouraging the immediate and widespread popularity of *Natural Theology,* whose influence in Britain and America for the half-century after its publication was immense. Required reading in many colleges, universities, and schools of theology in the early decades of the nineteenth century, *Natural Theology* helped to mold popular theological thinking to a marked extent. Even today sermons, and occasional articles in mass circulation media, may be found to reflect the arguments presented in this classic source. Gradually, however, Paley's argument lost favor in the latter half of the nineteenth century and in the twentieth century, largely because of the growing philosophical influence of David Hume (1711-1776) and Immanuel Kant (1724-1804), whose criticisms of Paley's line of reasoning actually antedated the publication of *Natural Theology,* but also because of the triumph of the evolutionary concept of natural selection, a nonpurposive explanation of the facts on which Paley based his case.

The teleological argument itself, nevertheless, has not so easily been disposed of. Even Immanuel Kant, one of the argument's most effective critics, expressed his respect for the motives which led Paley to appeal to the hypothesis of cosmic intelligence, and numerous modern, post-evolutionary versions of the classical argument from design have continued to appear.

Opposed to the whole enterprise, of course, are those theological movements, prominent in the present century, which have neither place nor patience for the argument from design or for rational apologetics in general. From such a theological perspective Paley and his modern counterparts are engaged in an illegitimate quest after knowledge in the place of faith, understanding in the place of mystery, and investigation in the place of revelation. Paley might well have understood this objection, since he clearly recognized the difference between natural and revealed theology, accepted both, and firmly rejected any attempt to substitute one for the other, but he would have been unhappy to have been forced to choose between his head and his heart, as though they were somehow ultimately incompatible. Paley's attempt was to show that reason and faith can co-operate, neither violating the other but, rather, each offering support to the other. That attempt has fallen into considerable—though not universal—disfavor in the mid-twentieth century; it remains for the future to determine whether theologians generally will once again find merit in Paley's ideal.

THE PHENOMENOLOGY OF SPIRIT

Author: Georg Wilhelm Friedrich Hegel (1770-1831)
Type of work: Philosophy of religion
First published: 1807

Principal Ideas Advanced

Phenomenology as a philosophical method involves the presentation of successive forms of consciousness in their claim to truth, the criticism of the internal incoherence of each shape, the transition to new configurations which presuppose the previous experience of consciousness, and the objective of a self-contained, coherent, and comprehensive synthesis.

Religion appears in a preliminary way within the phenomenological dialectic as the state of the unhappy consciousness at the level of the individual self-consciousness and as the struggle of enlightenment with superstition at the level of the self-alienation of spirit in culture.

Religion as a phenomenological moment proper appears toward the end of the phenomenological process as the conscious manifestation of Absolute Spirit in various forms.

Religion as the form of Absolute Spirit in its totality culminates in revealed religion, in Absolute Spirit aware of its identity with Absolute Being.

Even though Hegel's early intellectual development was theological rather than philosophical, his posture toward the Christian religion was ever that of critic rather than that of apologist. His passion for the naturalness of pagan Greek religion forced into relief the repressive aspects of Christian religion. Hence the question: How was the teaching of Jesus transformed into the positivity of the Christian religion? In this formulation Hegel pictured the teaching of Jesus as essentially autonomous, its claim to authority resting solely upon its intrinsic moral rationality. Through the work of the early believers, Christianity was transformed into a positive religion, a heteronomous religion, depending for its authority upon the arbitrary concept of divine will and upon the repressive functions of the Church conceived as a state.

Further probing of this problem led Hegel to an expansion and revision of the terms of his problem. The idea of a heteronomous religion was projected as the spirit of Judaism. The teaching of Jesus was regarded as emphasizing the transcendence of love, whereby the individual might be reconciled to his fate. The teaching of Jesus was constrasted with the Kantian idea of an autonomous moral law, a hopeless ideal because it reflected the tension between "ought" and "is" and thereby rendered impossible any genuine reconciliation with fate. The ideal of love as a religious self-consciousness found its ultimate expression in reconciliation with death and in the consequent outpouring of the Spirit. Thereby the Christian community was stamped as a universal religion of love. Yet within the life of the Church tensions remained between the ethics of obligation and the ethics of virtue, between acceptance and hatred of the natural world, between the concept of the Church as community and as state. The existence of these tensions meant that religious reconciliation in principle had not become reconciliation in fact and that the Christian religion has not been reconciled with its destiny in the world.

Hegel abandoned theology when he became convinced that the self-contradictions within Christianity could not be surmounted within the theological context. Yet Hegel abandoned theology for philosophy only when he was able to formulate a philosophical method which transcended the abstractness and lifelessness of the philosophy he found current. Hegel's thought became explicitly philosophical when he was able to give philosophical expression to his theological experience, when he found a philosophical method thoroughly imbued with religious insight.

In the *Phänomenologie des Geistes* Hegel presents this method. Phenomenology for Hegel means the logic of the experience of consciousness. The subject of phenomenology, consciousness, is neither the natural consciousness of unreflective experience nor the pure rational ego of universal science, but the tension between the two. Various forms of the natural consciousness each in turn present themselves as claims to absolute truth, yet in the process of presentation, each experiences its own onesidedness and hence its death as a claim to absolute truth. The experience of consciousness is at once the experience of the negation of every form of the natural consciousness and the subsuming of each annihilated form in the depth of succeeding forms of consciousness. Each moment of the natural consciousness is crucified in its claim to truth, yet through this death finds its resurrection in the new context of the developed scientific consciousness.

The intelligibility of the phenomenological process also depends upon the object of the development. The dialectical presentation of the various forms of consciousness is also the logical unfolding of the self-manifestation of spirit. Only because the Absolute is already secretly at work in the development of consciousness is consciousness enabled to sustain the burden of its complex experience. Seen from this perspective, phenomenology is the *parousia* of the Absolute. Each moment of the experience of consciousness is not simply an experience of an object but is also a particular form of relation between subject and object. Hence, the lack of coincidence between subject and object which immediately appears as a lack of correspondence is really a lack of coherence. This lack of coherence, which the full manifestation of spirit demands, drives consciousness to the next necessary attempt to formulate a relation between subject and object in which the lack of coherence in the previous moment is overcome. The object in the succeeding moment is not the object as it appeared in the previous moment, but rather the totality of the previous experience of the object. In this sense, the phenomenological process may be said to be a dialectical series of transfigurations of consciousness.

Phenomenology presupposes that consciousness is capable of experiencing an object in its essence, though in an alienated form. An object has an essence in itself apart from its relation to consciousness; at the same time it has an essence for itself and for others. The effective realization of the object takes place when these aspects of its essence can be reconciled and the object can appear in and for itself. Phenomenology also presupposes that consciousness is in principle capable of experiencing all essences. Consciousness is potentially infinite and universal and thereby that mode in which Absolute Spirit can fully manifest itself. The correlation of the essential experiences of consciousness within consciousness means that the necessary process of phenomenology aims at the full manifestation of Absolute Spirit as concrete universal. The process is toward universality inasmuch as the moments of natural consciousness are negated in favor of broadening contexts. The process is toward concreteness because each new form of manifestation of spirit presupposes the results of what has already transpired. The end of phenomenology comes when consciousness is no longer compelled to go beyond itself, when the Absolute realizes itself fully in consciousness.

A profoundly critical moment in the phenomenological dialectic is the state of the unhappy consciousness. This moment arises in connection with the struggle of the individual self-consciousness to attain certainty of itself. Prior to this moment is the duality of master and slave, forms of self-consciousness which exhibit the character of independence and dependence apart from awareness of the implicit dependence of both upon the objective mediation of labor. From this, stoic and skeptical forms of self-consciousness emerge as shapes in which the self, conscious of the implicit dependence upon objective reality in the self-understanding of master and slave, seeks to establish an independence of self-consciousness from the world. Stoicism is the abstract form of self-consciousness which thinks itself universal and free, while skepticism is aware of itself as a particular self-consciousness indifferent to the being of the world. Yet stoicism cannot overcome the fact that it is a particular self-consciousness, and skepticism cannot overcome its positive existence in the world.

The unhappy consciousness is constituted by the unification of the stoic and skeptical forms of consciousness within a single consciousness. The unhappy consciousness recognizes both changeless and changeable elements in itself without being able to reconcile them. These elements are internally present in a way such that the triumph of one over the other means the annihilation of the self. The first, immediate, level of the unhappy consciousness is devotion toward the changeless as transcendent. In this form the changeless is inapproachable; it is transcendent and unrealizable because it remains a mere hope. A second form of the unhappy consciousness is the attempt to reconcile the changeless and the changeable through sacrifice and good works. This is a reconciliation which fails genuinely to reconcile, for the individual consciousness is not resigned in its work, but is conscious of its work as the particular effect of its own will; thereby the changeless appears in the work only in a correspondingly arbitrary way. Only in the third form of the unhappy consciousness, when the consciousness despairs ever of achieving reconciliation with itself and abandons its claim to self-certainty, does reconciliation occur. Mediation appears, but not as the act of the self-consciousness seeking its own certainty. Mediation is understood to come from beyond the self. The self experiences a sense of being lifted up out of its irreconcilable contrition and established at one with the kingdom of reason.

Another moment in the phenomenological process bearing upon religion is the struggle of enlightenment and belief. This moment arises in relation to the appearance of spirit, self-alienated in culture. Spirit here appears as a form of culture, as "belief," as thought in its universal unreflective immediacy. Belief is a cultural reflection which looks upon a supersensible Absolute as the object of devotion.

Antithetical to belief is "pure insight," spirit in its universal negativity. Pure insight is a spiritual shape characterized by the idealization of pure reason, understood to be self-justifying by its very rationality. These two manifestations of spirit as cultural forms exhibit different relations to the world. Belief is devoted to a supersensible reality, in terms of which this world is valued as vain and empty. Yet this world is necessary for belief because it is the place where belief is found and where service of the Absolute is practiced. Pure insight is present in the world, but it is not present in complete actuality. Pure insight exists as the pure intention to rationality, as the call to resolve the contradictions of the actual world by rational judgment.

Self-alienation of spirit in culture appears in its most radical form in the struggle between these two spiritual configurations. This struggle begins as a contest between the content of belief and the method of insight. In the course of this struggle belief, as naïve unreflective consciousness, is transformed into superstition because it is defended by deception and despotism and because its claims are falsified by enlightenment. Enlightenment is a kind of infection too widespread by the time of discovery to be overcome.

This struggle between belief and insight seems to issue in the victory of enlightenment, for enlightenment ends the possibility of unreflective consciousness. Enlightenment attacks in belief what it finds to be superstitious, and it questions the historical evidences of religious faith. Ironically, what enlightenment attacks is not what belief intends, and the historical evidences are not the grounds of religious faith. Enlightenment is victorious insofar as belief proceeds to defend itself by appealing to rational proof and historical evidences. By such action belief loses its immediacy and its genuine unreflective rationality.

The victory of enlightenment, however, does not overcome the self-alienation of spirit in culture. Enlightenment in vindicating its claim has failed to acknowledge its own abstractness. It has not recognized its own essential nature as a universal negativity depending for its rationality upon the superstition it discovers in its opponent. This essentially negative character of enlightenment manifests itself in the course of establishing pure insight in culture. The pure intention of rationality is transformed into the terror of absolute freedom.

Religion as a phenomenological moment proper occurs only when the spirit is fully conscious of itself as Absolute. Thus, religion is not merely a form of the individual self-consciousness or a form of culture. Religion is the self-consciousness of Absolute Spirit lending its form to individual and to culture alike. Religion as a phenomenological moment presupposes the entire preceding dialectic and is constituted by the grasping of this process according to the special nuances of the forms of religion and the penetration of these configurations into the totality of experience.

Natural religion is religion in which Absolute Spirit presents itself in the form of an immediate awareness of itself as an alienated other. The diversity of shapes in natural religion gives rise to a religious self-consciousness whereby Absolute Spirit appears as the embodiment of the spirit of the free community. This is religion in the form of art, a religion in which Absolute Spirit is conscious of itself as self-creating and free. Religion in the form of art finds its highest expression not in visual or plastic form, but in the medium of language, in which the divine expresses its self-consciousness. From the cultic language of hymn and oracle, religion as art develops forms of embodiment in the epic, tragedy, and comedy. In these latter forms religion expresses itself as spiritual action, mediated to the community through drama. In the epic, the world of the gods is connected with the world of men through the hero. In tragedy the world of the gods becomes a context of fate, and the connection of the world of the gods with the world of men is tragically divided between the powerless wisdom of the chorus and the ironic action of the hero. The world of tragedy, sundered by the fateful self-contradictions of conscious action, is a world from which the religious consciousness recoils in pity and terror. Yet the tragic moment has done its work, so that the self-understanding of religion in the form of art passes into the shape of comedy. The figures within the comic drama are consciously identified with the fate to which they are bound. It is their individuality, not their destiny, which constitutes their mask. In comedy, religion as the embodiment of the free ethical consciousness abandons itself as a mere vanity of individuality disguising the conscious identity of self with universal fate.

Only then can revealed religion become manifest. Revealed religion presupposes the abandonment of religion in the form of certainty of self and discovery of self in reconciliation with fate. The former process now appears as a yearning after revealed religion, wherein the Absolute Being manifests itself as Absolute Spirit in its self-consciousness. In this incarnation, the self-consciousness of Absolute Spirit is discovered and known to be identical with Absolute Being. In revealed religion, self-consciousness as spirit is disclosed to be at home with its object, Absolute Being.

Nevertheless, revealed religion is Absolute Spirit in the immediate universality of its self-certainty. The present moment of revelation is transformed into a past whereby the Absolute Spirit is known as a continuously resurrected Spirit. This shows that the mediating process is incomplete even though revealed religion has found expression. Revealed religion in its immediacy knows Absolute Spirit in the mode of imaginative idea or as pictorial thought. For Absolute Being to realize itself fully and for Absolute Spirit to manifest itself fully, revealed religion must be converted into conceptual thought and translated into absolute knowledge. Only then is the form of knowledge coincident with the truth known. Only then does Absolute Spirit know itself in its phenomenological fullness, as the "intellectually comprehended organization . . . of the ways in which knowledge appears." This moment of the self-knowledge of Absolute Spirit, Hegel writes, is the conclusion of phenomenology and the beginning of the systematic articulation of philosophical truth.

UNITARIAN CHRISTIANITY

Author: William Ellery Channing (1780-1842)
Type of work: Theology
First published: 1819

Principal Ideas Advanced

The Bible must be interpreted in the light of its cultural setting, the laws of nature, reason, and critical analysis.

The unity of God cannot be reconciled with the doctrine of the Trinity.

The unity of Christ cannot be reconciled with the doctrine of two natures in one person.

The moral perfection of God is incompatible with the doctrines of election, the innate moral depravity of man, and eternal damnation.

The work of Christ (atonement) was to prompt in man a love for God and Christ and benevolence to one's fellow men.

William Ellery Channing's essay *Unitarian Christianity* was published in 1819, the same year it was delivered as a sermon at the ordination of Jared Sparks in Baltimore, Maryland. It is a concise credo of early American Unitarianism.

Channing was born in Newport, Rhode Island, on April 7, 1780. In American theology, the age was dominated by conflicting interests. On the one hand, Calvinism, reinvigorated and reinterpreted by Jonathan Edwards (1703-1758), reigned supreme, though challenges to its structure were then being heard. Jonathan Edwards had restated traditional Calvinistic theology in clear and unmistakable language. The topics of divine election, predestination, and original sin received new definition from his incisive mind, and these issues were brought once again to the forefront of New England theological debate. His successors, Samuel Hopkins (1721-1803), Joseph Bellamy (1719-1790), and Jonathan Edwards the Younger (1745-1801), developed the school of thought which became known as the New Divinity theology. A second group, commonly called the Old Calvinist party, sought to soften the logically coherent and severe Calvinism of Jonathan Edwards and his followers, and continued the liberalizing of Calvinistic theology which had begun with the Half Way Covenant (1662) and which found expression in the work of Solomon Stoddard (1643-1729), pastor of the Congregational Church in Northampton, Massachusetts. The Arminian theologians, led by Charles Chauncy (1705-1787) and Jonathan Mayhew (1720-1766), were openly critical of Edwardsean thought; they emphasized the benevolence of God, His parental character, and the role of reason in theology. Out of the Arminian tradition and in opposition to the New Divinity and Old Calvinist parties grew Unitarianism.

William Ellery Channing received his early religious education under Samuel Hopkins, the New Divinity minister of the Congregational Church in Newport, Rhode Island. His formal education was received at Harvard, where he graduated in 1798. After serving for two years as a tutor to a family in Richmond, Virginia, he returned, in 1800, to Newport to study with Hopkins. In 1801 he entered Harvard Divinity School and in 1803 was ordained as a Congregational minister at the Federal Street Church in Boston, Massachusetts.

During these early years of his life, Enlightenment thought came to have its impact on American theology. Deism achieved vocal and prominent supporters; rational theology found open and avid proponents. The Boston area became the center of Arminianism in America and the seedbed for "liberal" theology. In 1805 the Unitarians won control of Harvard when Henry Ware (1764-1845) was elected to the Hollis Professorship of Divinity.

When, in 1819, William Ellery Channing was asked to deliver the ordination sermon for Jared Sparks at Baltimore, Maryland, he prepared the sermon, "Unitarian Christianity," which became the first clear statement of American Unitarianism. The essay prompted a protracted and involved debate in New England circles and engaged the attention of churchmen in the other parts of the country. Within a month after its delivery, the sermon was printed in Baltimore, with a second edition following shortly; within a year further editions were published in Boston.

Channing's essay was concerned with two general problems. First, he sought to establish the principles by which Scripture should be interpreted. Second, he sketched the doctrines which Scripture, properly interpreted, enunciates.

While displaying the interests of Enlightenment thought, the essay was not as deviationist as is often thought. Channing's position rested on firm Biblical grounds: "Whatever doctrines seem to us to be clearly taught in the Scriptures, we receive without reserve or exception." Channing did insist, however, that reason must be used in the interpretation of the Bible, for, like other liberal spokesmen, he was certain that no Scriptural doctrines could be in conflict with reason. A comparison of Channing's work with that of the English Arian, Samuel Clarke (1675-1729), who published *The Scripture-Doctrine of the Trinity* in 1712, shows clear similarities at this point. Clarke, a leading figure in the Arian movement of the eighteenth century, was widely read by the American Unitarians. The insistence that Biblical faith teaches nothing contrary to reason was a characteristic affirmation of Channing and his followers.

Unlike Samuel Clarke, who analyzed some 1,250 verses of Scripture to ascertain the meaning of obscure phrases and who assumed that the Biblical record was its own interpreter, Channing insisted that since the Bible is a product of a particular culture, it needs interpretation and historical criticism. "We reason about the Bible precisely as civilians do about the constitution under which we live. . . ." Channing was among the first in America to appreciate the work of the German Biblical critics. Language, cultural setting, Jewish history, and philology are indispensable tools for an understanding of Scripture.

On this basis, then, Channing laid out the doctrines derived from the study of the Bible. The largest bulk of the second part of the sermon dealt with the doctrine of the Trinity and the nature of Christ. "The proposition, that there is one God, seems to us exceedingly plain." In Channing's opinion, this simple truth has been obscured by discussions of the distinctions between being and person. The trinitarian formula presented three divine beings, having "different consciousness, different wills, and different perceptions, performing different acts, and sustaining different relations. . . ." To Channing this was "irrational and unscriptural," for the Bible is very clear in distinguishing Jesus from God the Father. "We challenge our opponents to adduce one passage in the New Testament, where the word God means three persons, where it is not limited to one person, and where, unless turned from its usual sense by the connexion, it does not mean the Father." His overriding concern was to uphold the unity of God; for him there were no reasonable or Scriptural grounds for asserting that there are three persons in the Godhead. Channing was clearly separating himself from the trinitarian position formulated at the Council of Nicaea in 325.

On the same grounds he rejected the Formula of Chalcedon (451), which declared as orthodox dogma the doctrine that in Christ there are "two natures, without confusion, without change, without division, without separation. . . ." Here again, Channing asked for "some plain, direct passage, where Christ is said to be composed of two minds infinitely different, yet constituting one person." He could find none.

The argument of the "trinitarians" that unless Christ were God, of the very nature of God, no atonement could occur, Channing found intolerable. Anselm of Canterbury, the medieval theologian, in his treatise, *Cur Deus homo* (*Why God Became Man*), had developed the theme that man's rebellion or sin against an infinite God deserves infinite satisfaction which man is incapable of offering. Therefore, only one who is of the very nature of God could offer this recompense; namely, Jesus Christ. This "satisfaction theory of the atonement" received further statement from John Calvin. Channing rejected this view as an "imposition on common minds, and very derogatory to God's justice. . . ." Instead he spoke of Jesus as having been sent by the Father "to effect a moral, or spiritual deliverance of mankind; that is, to rescue men from sin and its consequences, and to bring them to a state of everlasting purity and happiness."

This affirmation of the unity of God, the subordination of Christ to God the Father, and the moral rather than substitutionary work of Christ reflected a view of the nature of God which Channing held. God is like a parent, a benevolent father, who seeks to restore his children to a life of obedience, knowledge, and love of the Creator. "We believe that God is infinitely good, kind, benevolent, in the proper sense of these words; good in disposition, as well as in act; good, not to a few, but to all; good to every individual, as well as to the general system."

Because he knew personally of the results of theological disputation and was aware of its painful expressions in Christian history, Channing made a plea for tolerance and charity. "We can hardly conceive of a plainer obligation on beings of our frail and fallible nature . . . than to abstain from condemning men of apparent conscientiousness and sincerity, who are chargeable with no crime but that of differing from us in the interpretation of the Scriptures, and differing, too, on topics of great and acknowledged obscurity." His admonition to the ordinand Jared Sparks summed up his view of the ministry and his understanding of the nature of the Gospel: "Be careful, lest the desire of defending what you seem truth, and of repelling reproach and misrepresentation, turn you aside from your great business, which is to fix in men's minds a living conviction of the obligation, sublimity, and happiness of Christian virtue."

In later writings Channing developed the topics which were only lightly touched on in his essay on Unitarian Christianity. The central issue of debate between the growing Unitarian movement and its opponents was over the nature of man. In the essays entitled, "The Moral Argument Against Calvinism," "Likeness to God," and "Honor Due All Men," Channing contributed to the discussion. His "Unitarian Christianity" stands out not as an *Institutes of the Christian Religion* but as a clear statement of the Unitarian position in contrast to the heritage of Calvinism and as a catalyst for later debates.

THE JOURNAL OF FRANCIS ASBURY

Author: Francis Asbury (1745-1816)
Type of work: Spiritual autobiography
First published: 1821

Principal Ideas Advanced

The Christian must not rest content with the grace by which God forgives sin; he must strive also for the grace by which he may live a holy life.

Method and discipline are necessary not merely for the achievement of personal holiness, but also for the public communication of the Christian life.

The presence of God's Spirit in the preacher and in the hearer is essential to the saving and sanctifying of souls.

The apostolic bishop, by traveling throughout the Church, helps give unity to the Body of Christ.

Sent to the American Colonies in 1771 by the conference of Methodist societies of Great Britain, Francis Asbury kept a *Journal,* as did most of his confreres. As the years went by and American Methodism passed through the inevitable strains of rapid growth, Asbury, who meanwhile had become the mainstay of the movement, began to publish his *Journal*. Extracts were printed in *The Arminian Magazine,* a Methodist periodical which he helped found in 1788. The complete *Journal* was published in three volumes in 1821 and, together with his *Letters,* has been republished (1958) in a carefully edited and annotated edition.

Asbury reflected on the requirements of a good journal. On reading the first volume of John Wesley's *Journal,* in the year 1795, he wrote: "I am now convinced of the great difficulty of journalizing. Mr. Wesley was, doubtless, a man of very general knowledge, learning, and reading, to which we may add a lively wit and humour; yet, I think I see too much credulity, long, flat narrations, and coarse letters taken from others, in his Journal: but when I come to his own thoughts, they are lively, sentimental, interesting, and instructing. The Journal of a minister of the Gospel should be theological: only it will be well to wink at many things we see and hear, since men's feelings grow more and more refined." Although much of the work of editing his own *Journal* was left to others, Asbury reviewed the transcribed material, and noted: "I have buried in shades all that will be proper to forget, in which I personally am concerned; if truth and I have been wronged, we have both witnessed one day of triumph."

From this record, Asbury emerges as a truly apostolic figure in whom love of God and concern for men's souls are constantly pushing upon the limits of human endurance. The Gospel which Asbury labored to proclaim had a dreadful urgency about it, demanding that men renounce this world and hope for consolation in the world to come. The Christian ought not merely to trust in the grace by which God, through Christ, pardons men's sins; he ought also, by all means, to claim the second grace, that of sanctification, by means of which the power of sin in a man's life is overthrown and he is enabled to live from hour to hour and moment to moment in the knowledge of God's will and the joy of God's presence. It may be that persons who do not have the grace of sanctification will not be saved—one can only hope to meet them in Heaven; but those who persevere in sanctification need have no fear of death, but may even desire it, knowing that it releases them from the sorrows and pains of this life and gives them entrance to the unclouded joys of God's presence.

Methodism, as is well-known, originated in the effort to systematize the life of holiness. John Wesley followed William Law, who, in *A Serious Call to a Devout and Holy Life* (1728), showed the higher prudence involved in applying to private prayer and philanthropy the method of keeping accounts and observing schedules, but Wesley took the further step of applying the new techniques of organization and management to the task of communicating the godly life to others. At the age of eighteen, Francis Asbury became a preacher in the Wesleyan movement; he was twenty-six when he answered the call from colonial America. The remainder of his life he spent in "methodizing" frontiersmen; that is to say, in not merely preaching to them and praying for them, but also organizing them so that the work of God's grace might not be lost through worldliness or sloth.

Asbury's own life is an example of strenuous discipline, worthy of a place in the accounts of the great saints and missionaries of Christendom. Under the most harassing conditions, since he lived on the road (as far as there were roads) and slept wherever he could spread his blanket, Asbury observed a careful regimen of prayer and study. Schooled only through his thirteenth year, he made himself a learned man by spending every available hour in reading and writing. Chronically ill, he rode five or six thousand miles a year, accepting only his expenses and a trifling salary, which he dispensed in charity. That his life was burdensome, he never conceals, but his eminently sound mind never lost its sense of proportion or gave way to despair. "My soul at times is in heaviness through manifold temptations," he wrote in South Carolina in January, 1796; "I felt an impression on my mind when at prayer that I felt too much, and might fret myself because of evil doers; I resolve, through grace, to be more resigned to the Lord, and less distressed, lest I should lightly sin against God or myself in unnecessarily injuring my health." A few days later he wrote: "Friday, 5, I spent in reading and writing, and observed it as a day of fasting and prayer. I felt myself under dejection of spirit. Ah! what a dreary world is this! my mind is under solemn impressions—the result of my reflections on God and souls. I will endeavour not to distress myself above measure. If sinners are lost, I cannot save them, neither shall I be damned for them. I was happy last evening with the poor slaves in brother Wells's kitchen, whilst our white brother held a sacramental love feast in the front parlour upstairs. I must be poor: this is the will of God concerning me."

The spiritual foes which Asbury felt he had chiefly to contend with were formalism and antinomianism. Formalism had, in his opinion, destroyed the usefulness of the Episcopal and Puritan churches, especially in the older centers, such as Philadelphia and Boston. No good, he maintained, could come from "reading prophets" and "systematical preachers." By contrast, the Methodist preacher depended upon God to grant a certain "warmth" to his speech, and "melt" the hearts of his hearers. Frequent meetings of small, local societies and annual camp meetings attended by thousands helped keep the spirit aflame. The other danger lay in antinomianism, which was the term Asbury used for the teaching that man is saved by Christ's death alone. Asbury claimed that the overemphasis upon justification by faith, together with the Calvinistic doctrine of the perseverance of the elect, led to neglect of evangelical obedience. Methodist preachers, on the contrary, did not hesitate to proclaim that following Christ requires giving up worldliness, sin, and folly, and living in accordance with one's heavenly calling.

Asbury himself lived under extreme austerity, quite as if he had taken monastic vows. (In addition to the hardships incidental to his labors, he regularly kept Friday as a day of fasting.) But he made no attempt to impose any formal regimen on his followers, or even on preachers. The concept of worldly, as over against godly, behavior was, however, clear both to him and to his hearers. Methodists were expected to shun alike the vain, frivolous life of fashionable urbanity, and the boisterous freedom of the frontier tavern. The Methodist social-consciousness showed itself early in Asbury's uncompromising stand against slavery. Because of his insistence, Negroes regularly attended services together with white people. On one occasion, when the Negroes were forced to stand outside a half-filled chapel, Asbury declared his intention never to preach in that place again.

It was Asbury, more than any other, who introduced the episcopal form of government into Methodism. When, after the War of Independence, Wesley recommended that the American societies separate from the Protestant Episcopal Church, he appointed Francis Asbury and Thomas Coke (1747-1814) to be superintendents, but Asbury and Coke, appealing to the New Testament use of the word "episcopos," decided to adopt the title "bishop." Asbury made it a point to study the government of the early Church. He concluded that the essential characteristic of apostolic bishops was that they traveled and by this means welded the separate churches together into the unity of the Body of Christ. This describes quite accurately the work of Paul and Barnabas, and equally describes the function performed by Wesley in England and Asbury in America. Asbury maintained that a sedentary bishop, no matter whose hands have been laid on his head, is no bishop at all, since the Church of Christ is not an organization ruled over by officials but a living body which draws its life from Christ's presence in it. The so-called Episcopal and Presbyterian churches, Asbury said, are really so many separate congregations, since neither Presbytery nor Episcopacy does anything to provide effective communication between isolated churches.

For all his zeal and singleness of purpose, Asbury was not a narrow denominationalist. Before the Methodist societies withdrew from the Anglican communion, he was faithful in attending its ordinances, and he stood on friendly terms with many of its clergymen. At all times he was cordial with ministers and laymen of other churches insofar as a common love of Christ and obedience to the Gospel provided a basis for spiritual fellowship. Sensitive to the dangers of sectarianism, he was, however, convinced that it is necessary for those responsible for governing the Church to take a firm stand against heresy and hypocrisy, and he maintained that such action is not schismatic. "Schism," he said, "is the dividing real Christians from each other, and breaking the unity of the Spirit." For Christians to separate themselves from nominal believers or to exclude these from their fellowship is not schism.

Asbury's *Journal* is an important document, not merely for Church historians, but for anyone interested in American history. Few men can have possessed a wider and more intimate knowledge of the early American terrain and its people than this man, who, for forty of the most interesting years in the nation's history, moved each year from New England to Georgia, and as far west as there were settlements. As an Englishman who refused to bear arms against the Motherland, Asbury was suspect during the early years of the Revolution, but his refusal to abandon his societies gradually earned him the respect of the young nation. Asbury admired Washington, whom he once had the honor to meet, and he was frequently a guest in the homes of governors and other important citizens. But he seems to have had little interest in political developments. At one place he writes, "I visit, dine, and ride out every day; but it is very hard work for me to eat, drink, talk, and do nothing. As I am not a man of the world, the most of the conversation about it is irksome to me." This does not mean that Asbury was an impractical man; rather, it reflects the fact that he was fully occupied with the task of running a kingdom within a kingdom; his time was spent in thinking of the needs of hundreds of societies, stationing preachers, meeting annual conferences, raising money, founding colleges, and organizing publication societies. The testimony of his practicality is that when Asbury came to America there were perhaps a thousand Methodists. When he died, there were two hundred thousand.

THE CHRISTIAN FAITH

Author: Friedrich Schleiermacher (1768-1834)
Type of work: Systematic theology
First published: 1821-1822

Principal Ideas Advanced

Systematic theology is a description of the religious self-consciousness, characterized by a feeling of absolute dependence, which presupposes the existence of God.

In the Christian faith this self-consciousness is determined by the antithesis of sin and grace, with redemption being achieved through the perfect God-consciousness of Jesus Christ.

Just as the divine was in Jesus Christ, so a common divine Spirit animates the Church, through which God-consciousness is constantly increasing its influence in the world.

Friedrich Schleiermacher's *The Christian Faith,* it is generally agreed, has a significance for Protestant systematic theology or dogmatics comparable to John Calvin's *The Institutes of the Christian Religion,* and marks the beginning of the modern era in systematic theology. The book was written in 1821 while Schleiermacher, already well known for his *On Religion: Speeches to Its Cultured Despisers* (1799), was professor of theology at the University of Berlin. While Schleiermacher's system has never won general acceptance, Protestant theologians throughout the nineteenth century, and thus far in this century, have felt it necessary to understand the approach to theology set forth in *The Christian Faith.*

According to Schleiermacher, dogmatics as a theological discipline is based on our understanding of the Christian Church. The religious self-consciousness, which Schleiermacher defines as a feeling of absolute dependence, necessarily leads to the formation of a fellowship or communion. There are several possible forms of such communions (fetishism, polytheism, monotheism), which represent different stages of human development. Monotheistic religions, which represent the highest level of development, may be either active and ethical in nature (Judaism and Christianity), or passive and resigned (Islam). Christianity as a type of ethical monotheism is distinguished from other types in that everything in Christianity is related to the redemption accomplished by Jesus of Nazareth. Christian doctrines are accordingly descriptions of the Christian religious affections, and it is the task of dogmatic theology to systematize the doctrine prevalent in the Church at a given time.

In the selection of dogmatic material care must be taken to guard against a number of natural Christian heresies. Jesus Christ must not be interpreted as having been so much different from man that He is unable to redeem man, but also He must not be understood as having been so much like man that He Himself needs redemption. Man, on the other hand, must not be regarded as being so bad that he cannot be redeemed, nor must he be considered to be able to redeem himself and to need no redeemer. Schleiermacher furthermore feels that it is necessary to distinguish between Roman Catholic and Protestant understandings of the Christian faith. Both Roman Catholicism and Protestantism agree that Christian piety arises only in the Christian fellowship, but Roman Catholicism, according to Schleiermacher, makes our relationship to Jesus Christ depend on our relationship to the Church, whereas Protestantism makes our relationship to the Church depend on our relationship to Jesus Christ.

In the formation of Schleiermacher's dogmatic system, its Protestant character is assured by appealing to the Protestant confessions, which in turn appeal to the New Testament Scriptures. (Schleiermacher did not feel that the Old Testament is determinative for an understanding of the Christian faith.) Though the content of the Scriptures must be expressed, Biblical vocabulary need not be used. Rather the dialectical character of the language used and the systematic arrangement of the material presented give dogmatics its essential scientific form. Central to the system is the antithesis between man's inability to inform all moments of life with the feeling of absolute dependence, and the increasing ability to do this communicated to man by Jesus Christ. It is necessary therefore to set forth the doctrines which this antithesis presupposes, as well as those doctrines which this antithesis determines. The basic form of dogmatic proposition is a description of the human self-consciousness as characterized by the feeling of absolute dependence. From this basic form, however, other forms may be derived, propositions which describe the constitution of the world and propositions which describe divine attributes, since the world and God are the correlates to which the Christian self-consciousness points. These three forms of propositions, accordingly, appear throughout the system.

In the first part of the system Schleiermacher discusses the religious self-consciousness which is always both presupposed by and contained in every Christian religious affection. God is known through the feeling of absolute dependence (which for Christian faith is also a relationship to Jesus Christ). Recognition of this feeling of absolute dependence, which must be intuited, takes the place of proofs for the existence of God. In the feeling of absolute dependence, however, we are also aware that we are involved in the natural order, that we are parts of the world. The relationship in the religious self-consciousness between God and the world must therefore be examined.

Traditionally a distinction has been made between the creation and the preservation of the world; but, according to Schleiermacher, as far as the feeling of absolute dependence is concerned, creation and preservation are indistinguishable. Nothing can be excluded from origination by God. The divine creative activity, which conditions all change, must itself be conceived nontemporally, and thus as being fundamentally different from all human activity. Divine preservation coincides with the interdependence of nature. Thus the concept of miracle, as implying events which do not represent natural causation, is not required. Divine activity is recognized in both good and evil, though in evil only as it is related to good as one of its conditions. No distinction need be made between influences that issue from the mechanisms of nature and those which issue from free causality; both are equally ordained by God.

Schleiermacher, in discussing the divine attributes which may be derived from this understanding of the relationship between God and the world, points out that these attributes must be closely related to the feeling of absolute dependence, and that they are to be understood primarily in terms of causality. The absolute divine causality must, however, be distinguished from the causality of the natural order, at the same time that it is equated with this causality in its comprehensiveness.

The four attributes which Schleiermacher discusses in this connection are the eternity, the omnipresence, the omnipotence, and the omniscience of God. The eternity of God suggests not unlimited time, but something fundamentally different from time. Eternity implies changelessness, but since there is eternal omnipotence, God is also active. God's omnipresence affirms his spaceless causality, whereby space itself is conditioned. God is omnipotent in the sense that all nature is dependent upon divine causality, which as eternal and omnipresent differs from finite causality at the same time that the divine causality is completely presented in the totality of finite being. Since God's knowledge is identical with His almighty will, the possible as distinct from the real cannot be an object of the divine knowledge. Hence, God's omniscience means that God knows all that is; and all that God knows, is. Schleiermacher argues that divine foreknowledge does not exclude freedom, since we can have foreknowledge of what is at the same time our own free activity.

The universality of the feeling of absolute dependence presupposes an original nontemporal perfection of both man and the world. The world, which has not changed in any fundamental sense since its creation, can be known (the ideal aspect of its original perfection) and used (the real aspect of its original perfection). Man's original perfection consists in the fact that, in fellowship with other men, both in knowing and doing, he is capable of God-consciousness. No attempt is made, however, to define the condition of the first man. The original perfection of man is to be seen in Christ rather than in Adam.

The second part of Schleiermacher's system explicates the religious self-consciousness as it is determined by the antithesis of sin and grace, and it is divided into two sections dealing with our consciousness of sin and our consciousness of grace.

Sin, according to Schleiermacher, is a hindrance of the power of the spirit by man's sensuous nature. Given man's original perfection, sin arises as there is unequal development of will and insight. Though man is incapable of the good apart from redemption, he is capable of responding in some sense to grace, and he can thereby achieve civil righteousness. Original sin is individual and corporate. There is original sinfulness as well as original perfection. The actual sin of each generation is the originating original sin for the next generation, and original sin issues in actual sin. The sins of the redeemed, however, according to Schleiermacher, are always diminishing, nor do they obstruct the spiritual life, whereas the sins of the unredeemed are habitual and contagious, and they vitiate the God-consciousness. Yet even among the unredeemed there is a faint shadow of the good.

Without sin nothing in the world could properly be regarded as evil, but sin being given, there is both natural and social evil. Social evil and sin are directly related, though natural evil and sin are related only indirectly. Sin and evil are equally related only when one views the total community, although this equivalence may not be evident in the case of the individual.

Since sin is related to redemption, in that the merely gradual and imperfect unfolding of the power of God-consciousness is one of the necessary conditions of the human stage of existence, God may in this sense be said to be the author of sin. God's holiness, however, is that divine causality through which conscience in all corporate life is conjoined with the need for redemption. God's justice means that evil and sin are connected, but only so as to deter sin.

Schleiermacher next discusses the second aspect of the antithesis of sin and grace, as he describes the consciousness of grace. Man approaches blessedness through the influence of a divinely effected corporate life working in opposition to the corporate life of sin. In the Christian fellowship redemption is effected through the communication of the supernatural sinless perfection of Christ, but human receptivity is such that this perfection can also become natural. In the fellowship with God achieved through Jesus Christ His perfection is active while the believer is passive. The divine in Christ was the perfection of His God-consciousness, which developed gradually, but in such a way that there were no conflicts with His sense nature. In the union of the divine and the human in Christ the divine was active and the human passive, but in the state of union the activity was common to both.

Christ's redemptive activity consists of the fact that He brings believers into the power of His God-consciousness, and He may thus be understood in terms of the three offices of prophet, priest, and king. Christ as a prophet taught the original revelation of God in Himself, explaining both His calling of communicating eternal life in the Kingdom of God, and His unique relationship with the Father. With this teaching prophecy came to an end, since no more perfect understanding of man's relation to God is possible than that which is found in the teaching of Christ. Christ's priestly office includes His perfect fulfillment of the law and His atoning death, by which we are animated to fulfill the divine will. Through His suffering punishment is abolished, for in fellowship with Him evil is no longer felt as punishment. His death occurred as He persisted in His redemptive activity, and we are also called to share His suffering and so to persist in our vocation. Christ now represents us before the Father to establish our fellowship with the Father and to support our prayers. Christ's kingly office consists in the fact that everything that the Christian fellowship needs for its well-being continually proceeds from Him. Since this is a Kingdom of grace, Christianity is not a political religion or a theocracy. Christ exerts a purely spiritual lordship, and therefore separation of Church and state is entirely appropriate.

Those assumed into living fellowship with Jesus Christ are regenerated and sanctified. Regeneration involves conversion, whereby man repents and believes, and justification, whereby man is forgiven and adopted by God. In sanctification the natural powers of the regenerate are put at the disposal of Christ, producing a life akin to His in perfection and blessedness. Since the sins of the regenerate are always being combated, they carry forgiveness with them and have no power to annul the grace of regeneration. No new sin enters and the truly regenerate cannot fall away from grace. Good works are the natural effects of faith, though the regenerate do not trust in them.

In discussing the constitution of the world in relation to redemption, Schleiermacher sets forth his doctrine of the Church and the means of grace. The Church originates as regenerate individuals come together to form a system of mutual interaction and co-operation. It appears that God has not willed that all those living at any one time should be uniformly taken into the Kingdom of Christ. Schleiermacher believes, however, that all are ultimately foreordained to blessedness. Predestination occurs through the divine government of the world. The elect are chosen, as Christ was chosen, to further the work of redemption; this explains why some are chosen prior to others.

The common spirit which animates the believers in the Church to co-operation and reciprocal influence is in the Christian fellowship what the divine was in Christ. It differs in that the union that is formed between the divine and the human in the Church is not a person-forming union.

The Church in its relation to the world retains its self-identity through the essential and invariable features of the Holy Scriptures and the ministry of the Word, which is the witness of Christ, and through the ordinances of baptism and the Lord's Supper, which form and maintain the fellowship.

The authority of the Scriptures is based on faith in Christ. The Scriptures are the first in a series of presentations of the Christian faith, and the norm for all succeeding generations. While originality continues in the Church, everything must be in harmony with the original Scriptures. The ministry of the Word is performed by the spontaneously active members of the Church for those primarily receptive, and there is to be both a public ministry as well as a more informal and occasional ministry of the Word. Through baptism the individual is received into the Church, and due to the promise of Christ baptism is a channel of justifying activity. Ordinarily the Word should be known to the baptized person so that baptism and regeneration can coincide. Yet parents may prefer infant baptism with the understanding that it be supplemented with confirmation. In the Lord's Supper the spiritual life of Christians is strengthened as, according to the institution of Christ, His body and blood are administered to them. Schleiermacher claims that a new statement interpreting the connection between the body and blood of Christ and the elements of bread and wine is needed, a statement which will avoid both the extreme of affirming such a connection independent of the act of participation, as well as the extreme of denying any connection whatever between the elements and spiritual participation in Christ. The power of the keys is the power of the Church to decide what belongs to the Christian life and to deal with individuals in accord with such decisions. This power resides in the whole congregation. Its legislation must remain subject to constant review. Excommunication is allowed, but it must be only temporary. Prayer in the name of Christ has no other object than the divine good pleasure. Thus Christian prayers either express resignation or thankfulness. The inward state giving rise to such prayer is one of the conditions for the emergence of the result.

Since the world exercises influence on the Church, there is an antithesis between the visible and the invisible Church. The visible Church is divided and fallible, while the invisible Church, which is the active element in the visible Church, is undivided and infallible. Schleiermacher believes that the impulse leading to division will gradually weaken, though he grants that some divisions are effected by the Holy Spirit. There should not, however, be complete suspension of fellowship between different parts of the visible Church, since the visible Church thus separates itself from the unity of the invisible Church. The visible Church is fallible in that no definition of doctrine can be regarded as eternally valid. Error, however, is removed in the Church by the corrective power of truth (the Scriptures are the freest from error), which never ceases to work in it.

The consummation of the Church, which implies that no other religion remains as an organized fellowship, due to the continuing power of sin in succeeding generations, will not be reached in time. Yet it remains as an ideal to be achieved ultimately through the kingly power of Christ. The Christian conception of life after death is derived from faith in Christ. Since Christ was capable of survival, all of the human race must be capable of it too, though we are unable to imagine the form this future life will take. Schleiermacher does recognize some tension between attempts to affirm the consummation of the Church and to maintain at the same time continuity in the personal survival of the individual. He attaches greater certainty to the concept of the consummation of the Church, though he prefers to affirm also the universal restoration of all souls.

The divine attributes which relate to redemption are love and wisdom. Love is the only attribute which is simply equated with God. We sense divine love directly in redemption, from which the God-consciousness grows. Hence it represents to us the essence of God. Where almighty love is, there also absolute wisdom must be. Through the divine wisdom the world, as the scene of redemption, is also the absolute revelation of God, and the world is therefore good.

Schleiermacher concludes his system with a discussion of the doctrine of the Trinity, a doctrine he regards not as an immediate utterance of the Christian self-consciousness, but as a combination of several such utterances. The doctrine of the Trinity attempts to assert a union of the divine essence with human nature in Christ and in the Church. There are difficulties, however, in simultaneously affirming unity and distinctions in the Trinity. Schleiermacher observes that no fresh treatment was given this doctrine at the Reformation, and he suggests that further doctrinal development at this point is needed.

AIDS TO REFLECTION

Author: Samuel Taylor Coleridge (1772-1834)
Type of work: Moral and spiritual aphorisms
First published: 1825

Principal Ideas Advanced

Reflection or self-knowledge is the means by which man realizes his spiritual end.

Religious prudence, morality, and spiritual religion are stages of man's spiritual development.

Because of sin, man needs divine grace in order to realize his highest potentialities.

Christian theology may be purged of speculative error by using the moral sense as a touchstone for what is true.

Confirmation of the truth of Christianity is found in the way it answers to the deepest needs of man's spirit.

Aids to Reflection, Coleridge tells us, is a didactic work, written especially for "the studious Young" as they complete their formal education, but also for "as many in all classes as wish for aid in disciplining their minds to habits of reflection." Coleridge was convinced that in order to realize his potentialities as a spiritual being, a man must cultivate the habit of self-examination or reflection. The book consists of a series of aphorisms taken from leading English churchmen; to the aphorisms Coleridge adds his criticisms and comments. In this way he hoped not merely to develop in the purposeful reader a skill in and habit of reading critically, but, more fundamentally, to awaken the innate faculties of the reader's spirit so that he would learn to appropriate inwardly and by natural affinity truths which for others are matters of rote.

Coleridge's interest in religion and in metaphysics dates from his early years. While he was a student at Cambridge, he became an enthusiastic disciple of the mechanistic psychologist, David Hartley (1705-1757), and preached in Unitarian chapels. Later, he embraced a more Platonic type of philosophy and became an appreciative member of the Church of England. *Aids to Reflection* is a mature work, in which the author affirms the inadequacy of morality without religion and maintains that those who rightly understand the exigencies of their own inner development will perceive that the central affirmations of Christianity are true. Revelation is, thus, something beyond reason, but not unreasonable.

Against the materialistic philosophy which his age inherited from the eighteenth century, Coleridge raised anew the protest that man is not merely an object of nature. As a creature of flesh and blood, he is intelligible in physical categories; but as will, spirit, personality, he is incommensurate with material things, and, in a perfectly intelligible sense, "supernatural." According to Coleridge, this view of man is the meaning of the Scriptures when they say that man is made in God's image and that man's most important undertaking is to seek to recover that image. In this undertaking, man is a responsible agent. He must make it his business to achieve salvation; nevertheless, anyone who tries to attain salvation and makes any progress in the endeavor must admit that man does not labor alone; indeed, he can achieve nothing unless God is also actively involved in the same undertaking.

According to Coleridge, three kinds of undertaking are necessary if man is to achieve his end. The first is religious prudence, by means of which a man removes himself from temptation's path and generally endeavors to take advantage of all circumstances which will further his design. The second is morality, which, according to Coleridge, is not to be confused with prudence, because morality is concerned not with means and ends, but with obedience to law. Obedience comes much nearer than prudence to man's proper goal; namely, conforming his will to the perfect will of God. The man who undertakes to be moral cannot rest content with his current achievements but must constantly be pressing on; therefore, morality, in its higher reaches, becomes religious. On this plane, however, man is forced to recognize the limitations of his own efforts and his need for a Divine Redeemer. Thus, for its perfection, morality requires spiritual religion, Christianity, through which the soul of sinful man is born anew and enabled to overcome its hindrances.

These three aspects of man's moral quest—prudence, morality, and religion—provide the three divisions of Coleridge's book and the basis on which he selected his aphorisms. Since some of the aphorisms are immediately helpful, they are left by the editor to speak for themselves. Others are of the sort that are apt to raise questions in men's minds and may even turn them away from Christianity. These call forth Coleridge's criticisms, not always sympathetic, although, on the whole, Coleridge has excerpted only from writers with whom he can agree: Jeremy Taylor (1613-1667), Henry More (1614-1687), and, more often than either of these, the Scottish archbishop, Robert Leighton (1611-1684).

Coleridge's eminently moral approach to Christianity finds expression in a certain impatience with purely speculative theology. The God of the philosophers, he says, answers to a purely intellectual need. Reason requires us to think in terms of unity, substance, attributes, and causes; and theologians who have a philosophical bias tend to mistake these ideas (*entia rationalia*) for real objects (*entia realia*), and to confuse them with the Living God who is the "supreme Object of our Faith, Love, Fear and Adoration." Many of the difficulties which people find in the doctrines of the theologians stem from this source; for example, the teaching that God's sovereign power leaves no freedom to the creature. But, says Coleridge, whenever a doctrine runs counter to conscience or to the interests of morality, it is to be rejected. He even raises the question whether it is legitimate to proceed by rational inference from one genuinely religious notion to another. Thus, the experience of redemption is firm ground for the notion that Christ is divine, but no basis for inferences concerning the internal life of the Godhead, of which we have no comparable revelation. "Grant, that in thus *realizing* the Notion I am warranted by Revelation, the Law of Conscience, and the interests and necessities of my Moral Being! Yet by what authority, by what inducement, am I entitled to attach the same reality to a second Notion, a Notion drawn from a Notion? It is evident, that if I have the same

Right, it must be on the same grounds. Revelation must have assured it, my Conscience required it—or in some way or other I must have an *interest* in this belief. It must *concern* me, as a moral and responsible Being."

Coleridge limits himself, therefore, to discussing those doctrines of the Church which are directly related to man's moral and spiritual endeavor, and mainly to three: the doctrine of election and reprobation, the doctrine of original sin, and the doctrine of vicarious atonement.

In discussing election, Coleridge stresses the difference between persons and things. The extreme Calvinists, such as Jonathan Edwards (1703-1758), err, he says, through failing to recognize the distinction between nature and spirit. Their notions of predestination all rest on the fallacy of supposing that the same kind of necessity governs spirits as governs physical objects. Still, there is no reason to go over to the opposite position and deny altogether the efficacy of God's will in the lives of men, and Coleridge favors the moderate Calvinism of Archbishop Leighton over the Arminianism which generally characterized post-Restoration Anglican thought.

Coleridge agrees with Jeremy Taylor that original sin is an indubitable fact in human experience, but he takes issue with Taylor's contention that Adam's descendants have their sinful natures as a punishment for their first father's offense. Man sins, according to Coleridge, when he acts on some private maxim which is opposed to the universal law of right reason in the conscience. The sin originates in each man; otherwise, it would be no act of the will and no sin. But, since sin is common to all, it must have a common ground. "And this evil Ground we call Original Sin. It is a *Mystery,* that is, a Fact, which we see, but we cannot explain." Moral feeling, on the other hand, is adamant against the view that the descendants of Adam are guilty because of some supposed participation in Adam's act.

The mystery of redemption or atonement, says Coleridge, is central to Christianity, as the doctrines of election and original sin (which are known to most high religions) are not. But he holds that traditional theology has often interpreted the role of Christ's death in ways that give offense to reason and the moral sense, especially in teaching that Christ made satisfaction for our sins. This view, Coleridge says, is unscriptural, resting on a misunderstanding of the metaphorical nature of Paul's writings. If, instead, we follow the words of Christ Himself, as recorded by John, we see that the redemptive act is a regeneration or rebirth, which accords entirely with our moral need and with our spiritual experience of redemption in Christ.

For Coleridge, the moral faculties in man not merely provide the best guide for understanding Christianity, but in addition constitute the only adequate certification of its truth. Instead of arguing about the moral sense, the only practical course is to try it. In the posthumous work called *Confessions of an Inquiring Spirit* (1840), Coleridge says, "The truth revealed through Christ has its evidence in itself, and the proof of its divine authority in its fitness to our nature and needs;—the clearness and cogency of this proof being proportioned to the degree of self-knowledge in each individual hearer." Those who maintain the necessity of founding Christian faith on a belief in the infallibility of Scriptures are, he says, setting an obstacle in the way of many a person. Told that everything in the Bible is God's word, they will reject the entirety, but encouraged to read it in a free manner, bringing to it the same degree of reverence that they willingly accord to the writings of any wise man, they will find much in it "coincident with [their] pre-established convictions," and they will henceforth recognize what they have read as "the recorded workings of the Word and the Spirit in the minds, lives, and hearts of spiritual men."

Coleridge is aware that this appeal to inward conviction is likely to be confused with the kind of popular religious teaching known as "enthusiasm," and he insists on observing a distinction. Those who trust in visionary experiences and who talk confidently about "feeling" the presence of God's Spirit make the mistake of confusing the natural with the supernatural. The properties of things and the affections of our bodies belong to a different order from Spirit, which is commensurate rather with conscience and reason. Coleridge quotes the pagan philosopher Seneca (c. 3 B.C.-A.D. 65) to show that there is long-standing authority for identifying Spirit with reason. "A Holy Spirit abides within us," says Seneca, "the observer of our evil, the guardian of our good. Just as He has been drawn by us, so He himself draws us. No one is a good man without God."

The distinction between the realms of nature and Spirit corresponds closely to Kant's distinction between *phenomena* and *noumena*, as Coleridge readily acknowledges. Phenomenal knowledge, which the English Platonists called "discursive reason," and which Kant called "understanding," has sense experience as its basis and reason as its organizing principle. Here necessity manifests itself according to the law of causality, and human freedom in terms of the hypothetical imperative, or prudence. Our knowledge of the noumenal world, properly called reason, transcends the realm of sense, and lays hold directly on eternal truth. Speculative reason discloses the necessities of logic, and practical reason the categorical imperatives of conscience and the moral law. These distinctions are, according to Coleridge, among the most important aids to reflection, particularly as they enable us to avoid dealing with religious matters in sensible terms. They also help us toward an understanding of the nature of salvation. Speaking of *practical* reason, Coleridge says, "Whenever by self-subjection to this universal Light, the Will of the Individual, the *particular* Will, has become a Will of Reason, the man is regenerate: and Reason is then the *Spirit* of the regenerated man, whereby the Person is capable of a quickening intercommunion with the Divine Spirit. And herein consists the mystery of Redemption, that this has been rendered possible for us."

Aids to Reflection was the most popular of Coleridge's prose works, enjoying a wide public in both Great Britain and the United States. Its appearance in an American version greatly influenced the transcendentalist movement in New England.

ON THE ADAPTATION OF EXTERNAL NATURE TO THE MORAL AND INTELLECTUAL CONSTITUTION OF MAN

Author: Thomas Chalmers (1780-1847)
Type of work: Natural theology
First published: 1833

PRINCIPAL IDEAS ADVANCED

If by external nature the whole order of human society, as well as the physical world, is understood, the adaptations of external nature to the mind of man are prolific of evidence for the wisdom and moral attributes of a deity.

General considerations as to the supremacy of conscience, the pleasure of virtue and the pain of vice, and the law of habit lead to particular conclusions concerning adaptations, including those found in the civil, political, and economic structure of human society.

Evidence for the immortality of the human soul as well as for the attributes of God can be derived from a study of nature and society.

Thomas Chalmers, Professor of Divinity in the University of Edinburgh, destined to play a leading role in the disruption of the Church of Scotland and the foundation of the Free Church, was the author of the first of the Bridgewater Treatises *On the Power, Wisdom and Goodness of God as Manifested in the Creation.* Subsequent treatises in this series included John Kidd's *On the Adaptation of External Nature to the Physical Condition of Man,* William Whewell's *On Astronomy and General Physics,* Charles Bell's *The Hand: Its Mechanism and Vital Endowments as Evincing Design,* Peter Mark Roget's *On Animal and Vegetable Physiology,* William Buckland's *On Geology and Mineralogy,* William Kirby's *On the History, Habits and Instincts of Animals,* and William Prout's *On Chemistry, Meteorology, and the Function of Digestion.*

Chalmers devotes an introductory chapter to general and preliminary observations. The concept of external nature is to be understood in a wide sense as comprehending "not merely all that is external to mind, but all that is external to the individual possessor of a human mind." Relations between mind and mind, as well as between mind and matter, are to be viewed as attesting a wise and beneficent contrivance.

The argument for the wisdom and goodness of God is drawn chiefly from "the obvious adaptation wherewith creation teems, throughout all its borders, of means to a beneficial end." The evidence for design increases with the number of independent circumstances that concur for the production of a useful result. Anatomy thus provides more intense evidence for a God than does astronomy.

The laws of matter are to be distinguished from the dispositions of matter. Atheists tend to reason exclusively on the laws, and to overlook the dispositions of matter, Chalmers claims. The argument for theism rests on the dispositions of matter more than on its laws. Matter is "distributed into such parts as to ensure a right direction and a beneficial application for its powers," he writes. In performances of human art, matter does not receive laws or properties, but is arranged into parts by the workmanship of the designer. Without involving ourselves in the metaphysical obscurity surrounding the origination of matter, says Chalmers, we can "discern, in the mere arrangements of matter, the most obvious and decisive signatures of the artist hand which has been employed on it."

Mental phenomena lack the complexity possessed by bodily organs. In consciousness we are aware only of simple antecedents followed by simple consequents. Whether the mind is regarded as a complex of faculties or as a simple substance passing into different states, there is the same strength of evidence for a God. Although the argument derived from these materials is not as strong as that from the collocations of matter, mind does "furnish a peculiar argument of its own, which, though not grounded on mathematical data, and not derived from a lengthened and logical process of reasoning, is of a highly effective and practical character notwithstanding." The phenomena of mind present immediate evidence that they are the effect not of blind, unconscious matter but of an intelligence. The phenomena of mind inform us distinctly of the attributes of God, Chalmers states, while the phenomena of matter tell us more decisively of the existence of God.

The study not of the mind itself, but of the adaptation of external nature to its constitution, allows ample room for the evidence of collocation. The great object of philosophy, in which Chalmers obviously includes the natural sciences, is to ascertain the ultimate principles into which all natural phenomena may be resolved. Secondary laws may be shown by further analysis to be derived from primitive or elementary laws. Evidence of divine goodness based on such a secondary law as that of the tides is independent of the discovery of the primary law, gravitation, into which it is resolvable. Secondary laws "attest the multitude of useful parts in nature; and the skill, guided by benevolence which has been put forth in the distribution of them." This principle applies to mental as well as to material phenomena.

Part One of Chalmer's book considers the adaptation of external nature to man's moral constitution and opens with a chapter on the supremacy of conscience. The subject discussed is not ethical principles as such but man's moral nature, the fact that man has a conscience which tells him that moral law is binding. Conscience is sovereign *de jure*, though not *de facto*. It has the right to command, even though inferior principles of our nature rebel. The distinctive function of conscience is the regulation of all the other powers and passions of humanity. Chalmers acknowledges his agreement with Bishop Butler (1692-1752), whose sermons he speaks of as "the most precious repository of sound ethical principles extant in any language."

In the phenomena of conscience, Chalmers writes, nature offers her strongest argument for the moral character of God. In spite of aberrations in man's present constitution, the voice of conscience bears undying testimony to the supremacy of rectitude and provides the strongest argument that "in spite of all partial and temporary derangements, Supreme Power and Supreme Goodness are at one." The theology of conscience is both more widely diffused and of more practical influence than the theology of academic demonstration. The rapid inference from the law of the heart to the lawgiver appears like intuition. Yet it is an inference rather than an innate idea or instinctive sense of the divine. Though often greatly obscured, this testimony has never been wholly obliterated in any country or at any period of human history.

Conscience follows up her mandates with an obvious discipline of rewards and punishments, Chalmers claims; present satisfaction and remorse are tokens of future judgment.

The laws of conscience comprise all the virtues inscribed by God on the human heart and provide an argument for the moral character of God, in that they must have been transcribed from the prior tablet of His own nature.

The diversity of moral judgments among men does not nullify this argument, continues Chalmers, for diversity can be accounted for by the distorting effect of passion and interest. Disagreement in moral judgments is compatible with basic agreement as to moral principles. Differences in understanding account for differences in moral judgment. When conscience is rightly informed, she speaks the same lessons in all countries. Chalmers concludes: "In proportion as the understandings of men become more enlightened, do their consciences become more accordant with each other."

The theological inference is drawn not from the physical origin of conscience, but from the fact of its uniformity. Scientific discussion of the derivation of conscience from simpler or anterior principles in the human constitution does not affect the validity of the argument. Nor is the inference destroyed by the actual prevalence of vice in the world. Wherever there is vice there is occasion for the most impressive exercise of conscience in the remorse, terror, and bitter dissatisfaction experienced in the hearts of the wicked.

A second general argument from the moral constitution of man is based on the inherent pleasure of the virtuous affections and the misery of the vicious affections. Distinct from the pleasure attendant on the sense of the rightness of an act, there is a pleasure in the very sensation of virtue, and likewise a pain in moral evil itself, distinct from the pain inflicted by conscience. It is a proof both of a benevolent and righteous God that He should so have framed our mental economy that right and wholesome morality is palatable to the taste of the inner man and moral evil is essentially and inherently bitter.

Chalmers calls attention to Bishop Butler's distinction between pleasure taken as the final object of our desire and that pleasure which is inseparable from gratification of any desire whatsoever. This distinction strikes at the root of the selfish system of morals. The disinterested exercise of an affection brings satisfaction to the extent that the object of the affection and not the pleasure is in view.

While there is a certain pleasure in the indulgence even of evil affections, the pleasure of an affection such as anger consists largely in the removal of a pain, the emotion itself being an exceedingly painful one. A good affection has also a peculiar tendency to immortalize its objects, while an evil one destroys them. This tendency suggests the final triumph of virtue, at least in the sense that virtue alone is capable of a blissful immortality. The union of virtue and happiness is a contingent appointment of the Deity, at once the evidence and the effect of the goodness that is in His own nature.

The power and operation of habit provides material for a third general argument. Chalmers rejects the associationist theory of habit propounded by Thomas Brown (1778-1820), but points out that the argument from the power of habit is independent on any philosophical theory. It is a fact that the man who enters on a career of vice enters on a career of headlong degeneracy. The law of habit, enlisted on the side of righteousness, strengthens our resistance to vice and facilitates the most arduous performances of virtue. The acts of virtue ripen into habits, resulting in the formation of virtuous character. Death intercepts the view of the ultimate result of this process, from which it remains possible to draw a strong argument for immortality. On the side of the outcome of vice, the forebodings of guilty fear as to future punishment are even more striking than expectations of reward by the virtuous.

External nature may be viewed as adapted to the moral constitution of man with reference to the supremacy of conscience, the inherent pleasures and pains of virtue and vice, and the law and operation of habit. The exercise of conscience is capable of resuscitation even in the most abandoned criminals. Reciprocal influences between mind and mind in society multiply the pleasures of virtue and the sufferings of vice. Finally, the law of habit provides a ground for moral education and thus encourages the expectation of a permanent as well as a universal reign of virtue in the world.

Special and subordinate adaptations of external nature to man's moral constitution are found in the mechanism of the mind by which affections such as resentment and shame serve for the maintenance of peace and decency in the life of society. Detailed attention is given to affections toward family and property that conduce to the civil and political well-being of society as well as to those conducing to the economic well-being of society. The advantages of the natural order are stressed by Chalmers, particularly in connection with the origin and rights of property, and he also delineates the disadvantages of deviations from this order by human legislation. Even the Malthusian doctrine of population is found to exhibit a pure case of adaptation to the external nature of the world by the moral nature of man.

The prevalence of truth in the world subserves the general good. The sustenance of the virtue of honesty on the soil of selfishness speaks emphatically for the wisdom and goodness of God. Man is not a utilitarian either in his propensities or his principles, but his inclinations have been so adapted to the external world that great utility results from God-given constitution. "Virtue is not right because it is useful," writes Chalmers, "but God hath made it useful because it is right."

From the capacities of the world for making a virtuous species happy, conclusions are derived which bear on the character of God and the immortality of man. The problem of evil cannot be adequately resolved by a sentimentalist theism that conceives of God as exclusively determined by benevolence. The connection of suffering with sin manifests the righteousness of God. The original design of the Creator can be read in the normal tendency of things, as distinguished from the tendencies exhibited by a deranged system. Not only the inequalities of the present system, but also the adaptation of desires to corresponding objects in nature may provide intimations of immortality.

The adaptation of external nature to the intellectual constitution of man is discussed briefly in the concluding part of the work, which ends with an illuminating analysis of the defects and uses of natural theology.

THE CHRISTIAN SYSTEM

Author: Alexander Campbell (1788-1866)
Type of work: Biblical doctrine and practice
First published: 1839

Principal Ideas Advanced

The unity of the Christian Church should be promoted on the foundation of those beliefs and practices contained in the Bible only.

A Christian is to be defined not by creeds, but by personal faith in Jesus as the true Messiah, and by obedience to Him as lawgiver and King.

Christian baptism is the means of regeneration to those who so believe and is not to be administered to any others.

Dissatisfaction with the divided state of Christendom has been a matter of great concern to many thoughtful Christians, and the name of Alexander Campbell is prominent among them. Campbell's *The Christian System in reference to the Union of Christians and Restoration of Primitive Christianity as plead by the Current Reformation* had as its inspiration the hope that it would contribute to harmony among Christian communions. The Christian Church, Disciples of Christ, or Campbellite movement, as it was variously called, was the product of a movement of reform in the interest of unity with which Thomas Campbell (1763-1854) and his son, Alexander, were closely identified. The theme in Alexander Campbell's words was, "How may schisms cease and all Christians unite, harmonize and cooperate in one great community, as at the beginning?"

There was no hope of harmony, Campbell argued, in debating controversial points of systematic theology. By the title, *The Christian System,* Alexander Campbell did not mean to suggest that he was offering another system of theology. In his opinion theology had done great mischief in the Church, and he wanted no more of it. There was to be no highway to unity through syncretism.

Since the only book held in common by all Christians was the Bible, on it alone, Campbell asserted, could unity be advocated with any hope of success.

It was this article of faith which the author believed to be the distinguishing feature of his work. "Not until within the present generation," he wrote, "did any sect or party in Christendom unite and build upon the Bible alone." What he was advocating was a restoration movement with the primitive Church as the ideal and the Bible as the only textbook.

Campbell, of course, realized that other Christian groups accepted the Bible as a foundation for their faith. Indeed, in his opinion, the mystery was why the Bible should be accepted as central and yet "should work no happier results than the strifes, divisions and retaliatory excommunications of of rival Protestant sects." It could not be supposed that the Bible itself could be part of the cause of diversity. The fault, then, must lie in the churches, and in particular, in their failure to act upon the Scriptures. Lip service to the Bible was substituted for obedience. Campbell confesses in the Preface that it had taken him over twenty years' labor to discard his own misreadings of Scripture, and he identifies *The Christian System* as the result of his rigorous re-examination. He reduces the "capital principles" of Christianity to the form, *"Faith in Jesus as the true Messiah and obedience to him as Lawgiver and King, the ONLY TEST of Christian character, and the ONLY BOND of Christian union, communion and cooperation, irrespective of all creeds, opinions, commandments and traditions of men."*

From this vantage point the author proceeds to discuss the multiphasic interests, both theoretical and practical, of a Christian institution. He is careful to deny that what he had written is authoritative for the churches; "We speak for ourselves only," he writes, and he claims truth for his views only as they agree with *"the Bible, the whole Bible, and nothing but the Bible."*

In the first chapter the systematic nature of the universe is asserted; the second chapter is given to the Bible. Large claims are made for the Bible's contents; "There is not a spiriual idea in the whole human race that is not drawn from the Bible." To ascertain the true significance of these spiritual facts all the tools of exegesis should be employed, Campbell writes; the student must approach the Bible in humility, for without a teachable spirit even the interpreter's skill may prove faulty.

Other facets of belief are then reviewed by Campbell in a plain style of writing so as to avoid the technical language of the creeds. The result is a disputatious section on the spirit of God, a section which critics from classic trinitarian traditions found unsatisfactory. The Chalcedonian definition of the Godhead, together with Christology, is dismissed as theology that is unbiblical. Also, in Campbell's doctrine of man, contrary to some theology, ample room is given to the conditional nature of salvation. Man makes his own election or choice, Campbell claims; his view is a change from the ideas of Augustine and Calvin, ideas which influenced popular Christian beliefs during the period when Campbell wrote.

In his discussion of the facts of the atonement, Campbell reveals a point of some interest in his support of the explanation of the Dutch scholar, Hugo Grotius (1583-1645), as against that of the medieval theologian, Anselm (c.1033-1109), by refusing to think of sin in terms of a debt which has to be paid, and preferring to describe it as a crime which may be pardoned by the Moral Governor. According to Campbell, the divine pardon or forgiveness is accompanied by reconciliation and deliverance, and the whole wonderful act of grace was arranged before the foundation of the world. The literal way in which Campbell accepts Scripture is illustrated when Campbell claims "that Jesus, himself, intimates that the whole affair of man's redemption, even to the preparation of the eternal abodes of righteous, was arranged ere time was born."

Over against this literalism, there is a great deal of discussion of the relative significance of other Scriptural allusions. Campbell writes: "Thus the *death of Christ* is forced on our attention by the law, by the prophets and by the necessity of the case, enlightened Reason being in the chair, as the only real, true and proper sin-atoning offering." Enlightened reason functions as an evaluating agency in the clarification of truth and would thus appear to qualify the claim that doctrine can be determined by the Bible only. And, again, on the same issue Campbell is insistent on the personal presence of Christ with His people, and it is this personal identification that is the core of the idea of salvation. Faith is not simply belief in "any doctrine, testimony or truth, abstractly, but belief *in* Christ; trust or confidence in him as a person, not a thing." This conception of faith is, no doubt, true; but it is a different and additional factor in the position which emphasizes the Bible. In a similar manner, it might be said that Campbell's strong objections to the traditional statements of Christian doctrine lose some of their force when he proceeds to write a large book of orderly doctrinal exposition. The principle of attending to the Bible only, if taken at its face value, would seem to make a volume of interpretation superfluous. It may well be that the author was forced to operate on a broader base than his initial principle permits, although his practice is not inconsistent with the thesis that the Bible is an indispensable and authentic measure for the determination of doctrine.

For Alexander Campbell the principal effect of his emphasis on the Bible alone was his rejection of the traditional doctrine and practice of infant baptism. It can best be stated in his own words: "Infant baptism and infant sprinkling, with all infantile imbecility, immediately expired in our minds, as soon as the *Bible alone* was made the only measure and standard of faith and duty. This foundation of the Pedobaptist temple being instantly destroyed, the whole edifice leaning upon it became a heap of ruins . . . the piles of rubbish that remained was immense." What replaced the former key concept was a doctrine of baptism which also separated Campbell from the Baptists. At first he was received among them, but separation came when he insisted that baptism to the repentant believer was the means of receiving absolution from sin. Campbell often expounded his views at length, for the point was one of great importance for anyone passionately interested in Christian unity. The significance of baptism had been a cardinal matter in disunity. Therefore, Campbell carefully guards himself from any notion that he believed immersion as such brought about the experience of regeneration. The physical action had to be associated with repentance, faith, restitution and all the personal and spiritual conditions stated in the New Testament as necessary to salvation. Nor was he willing to commit himself to the position that without baptism no one could be saved. His contention was that the New Testament connected baptism with all the blessings of salvation so openly and explicitly that he was compelled on the basis of his Bible principle to preach it in that form.

The "Breaking of the Loaf," as the author called the Lord's Supper, commemorates the crucifixion of Jesus Christ and ought to be a weekly institution because the Apostolic Church observed it every time they met for a stated worship service. If the Resurrection is marked each week by the observance of the first day, then it is incongruous not to mark the death of Jesus just as frequently. This breaking of the loaf was, in fact, the primary purpose of Apostolic gatherings on the first day of the week. Presiding officers in the churches should normally be in charge of this service in the interest of good order. Every Christian as a messenger of the Gospel has a right to preach, baptize, and officiate at the breaking of bread, but this right should not be asserted when the ordained officers are present.

In matters of discipline, Campbell contended a congregation should act through its elders to examine the charges and proceed appropriately. If repentance is not apparent, then the offender may, with justification, be excluded from the community. Wherever possible, investigation and all handling of the unfortunate situation should be done privately.

Campbell suggests that where the Bible does not offer an explicit guide on matters related to the ordering of congregational life, expediency should be followed in the interest of good order. On these concessions and forbearance will be expected, and the minority will acquiesce in the decision of the majority, with the law of love the guide of both.

This is the kind of Christian institution that Alexander Campbell believed could be justified by the Bible principle, and on the basis of it he believed that all Christians could find truth, unity, and love.

LECTURES ON REVIVALS OF RELIGION

Author: Charles Grandison Finney (1792-1875)
Type of work: Practical theology
First published: 1835

Principal Ideas Advanced

Revivals are necessary to keep Christians awake and to provide the proper conditions for bringing sinners to repentance.

Revivals can be promoted by man's efforts, through prayer and through the art of persuading men; revivals are hindered by the worldliness of Christians.

Insofar as men can be brought to obey God, economic and social difficulties will disappear.

Compelled by ill-health to pause in his career as a revival-preacher, Charles G. Finney delivered his celebrated *Lectures on Revivals in Religion* from the pulpit of the Chatham Street Presbyterian Church, New York City, on Friday evenings during the winter of 1834-5. The lectures were given extemporaneously, but were taken down and published in the *New York Evangelist,* a weekly periodical which Finney had been instrumental in founding. They appeared as a book in May, 1835.

Finney had been a schoolteacher and lawyer's clerk before he was converted at the age of twenty-nine. After studying theology privately with a Presbyterian minister in Western New York State, he was ordained under the Plan of Union worked out in 1801 between the Presbyterian and Congregational Churches. Revivals, of course, were not unknown in Calvinist denominations, but the meetings conducted by Jonathan Edwards (1703-1758) and George Whitefield (1714-1770) differed in important respects from revivals conducted by Methodist and Baptist frontier preachers. With Finney, many of those differences disappeared. Finney modified the Calvinistic theology until it was scarcely distinguishable from Arminianism, in order to make room for human agency in the salvation of souls. He also permitted and encouraged certain emotional responses, such as "groaning in the Spirit," which were familiar to frontier revivals but were not approved by the more conservative preachers. These innovations, together with the steady success of his meetings, first in frontier towns, but later in the cities as well, brought Finney under censure from leading Congregational and Presbyterian churchmen. His *Lectures on Revivals in Religion* is his reply to his detractors. The lectures present a more or less systematic exposition of his own grassroots theology and a vigorous criticism of the staid, tradition-bound religion of the older churches.

Finney maintains that saving souls is the most important work in the world, and that it is a work in which every Christian must be actively engaged. Although he interprets religion broadly as including all the ordinary duties of life, and warns against supposing that piety is limited to private devotions and church work, he nevertheless insists that the only reason God leaves men and women in the world after they have been converted is to help in the work of converting others. It is all very simple and logical. The world is in a state of sin and rebellion against God. Every one who dies in his sin is destined to eternal punishment. God does not want any to perish. He sent Christ to make atonement for all men, and He is willing to give them new hearts by His Spirit. But the task of converting sinners to Christ remains with the Church. Since, for every opportunity missed, a soul is plunged into Hell, the lives of Christians ought to be lived at fever pitch, like those of a rescue party during a disaster. But the temptations of the flesh cause Christians to relax their efforts and to lose their sense of urgency. That is the reason revivals are necessary—to keep Christians awake to their own mission, and also to arouse sinners to their danger.

Calvinists, according to Finney, are used to excusing themselves from responsibility for the salvation of their fellow men, on the ground that nothing but the grace of God can convert the hearts of sinners. Thus, they customarily wait for revivals as a farmer waits for rain. Finney openly rejects this teaching. While not denying that God's Spirit is essential for a man's conversion, he maintains that human agents are also necessary. His teaching is that revivals are "to be *prompted*, by the use of means designed and adapted specially to that object." He cites the example of a minister who believed that since revivals come at five-year intervals, there is nothing man can do to hurry them. It happened that, about a year after a revival, this minister began to grieve in his soul at the number in his congregation who were still unconverted, and he set his pencil to work calculating the probabilities as to how many would die and go to Hell before another revival was due. The following Sunday he took the figures with him to his pulpit, not expecting any revival but merely to share his grief with his people. The effect, however, was to awaken more than forty adult heads of families to the peril of their souls, and a great revival took place. Another time, a young convert was responsible for showing her Calvinist minister his error. She came to him with her Bible, pointing to the passage in which God promises to send his Spirit when men ask him in faith. The minister tried to show her that such promises are always qualified by an "if it be thy will." She went away uncomprehending, but left such an impression on the minister's mind that he searched the Scriptures and saw that no such condition is attached. He told his church what he had found, and a revival ensued.

Among the means of promoting revivals, first in importance is prayer. By prayer, Finney does not mean simply the offering up of desires to God, but rather a persistent wrestling with God until He is moved to act. Speaking from the text, "What things soever ye desire when ye pray, believe that ye receive them, and ye shall have them," Finney points out that the Scriptures are filled with promises which bind God to do the things which believers desire of him. It is up to Christians to claim these promises, but they can do this only by pouring out their souls in an agony of desire and resolution. Finney gives the example of a Christian who was daily oppressed with the burden of souls, until his body weakened of his great effort, and he died, "a prevailing prince in prayer." The dedicated man had prayed systematically, keeping a map of the world before him. Finney says, "I have known him pray as if he would do violence to heaven, and then seen the blessing come as plainly in answer to his prayer, as if it was revealed, so that no person would doubt it, any more than if God had spoken from heaven."

Finney explains that prayer does not change God's mind, but that it produces changes in men which render it consistent for God to do what he could not consistently do otherwise. In any case, men must prevail with God in order to obtain his blessing. This is so certainly true that, when a revival occurs, one can be sure that somewhere someone has been praying for that particular church to be revived.

The other means of promoting revivals have to do with influencing the minds of men. This requires knowledge and skill. Finney remarks that men are at great pains to learn what is necessary for them to know in order to conduct their wordly business; how much more should they study how to promote the conversion of sinners, seeing this is the main business of every Christian! In two addresses on the text, "He that winneth souls is wise," Finney points out that wisdom consists in "the selection of the most appropriate means for the accomplishment of an end." He then undertakes to set forth the means for accomplishing the "infinitely desirable end, the salvation of souls." In particular, he calls attention to the need for ministers to understand "the philosophy of the human mind." Truth, according to Finney, does not automatically turn men to righteousness. It must be used cunningly, with a view to the emotions that it can be made to arouse. "Truth, when brought to bear upon the mind, is in itself calculated to produce corresponding feelings. The minister must know what feelings he wishes to produce, and how to bring such truth to bear as is calculated to produce these feelings." He must know how to use the truth in order to stir believers to a revival pitch, and he must know how to confront sinners with the truth in such a manner that they will be convicted of their sin and converted to righteousness. "A wise minister will be successful," Finney maintains. Learning does not guaranty a minister success, neither does piety. The work of winning souls is like any other craft. If a man "understands his Bible, and understands human nature, and knows how to bring the truth to bear, and how to guide and manage minds, and to lead them away from sin and lead them to God," there is no reason for him to fail.

If piety itself is not sufficient to produce a revival, the lack of piety is nevertheless enough to prevent one. Finney compiles a long list of sins of omission and commission. In order to promote a revival, Christians must go over their lives in a systematic fashion, enumerating their shortcomings. The fact of recalling them will generate an agony of remorse and lead to prayer and renewed effort. Among the sins to which Finney calls attention are such general ones as ingratitude, pride, want of love for God, and unconcern for one's neighbor. But he is also specific. "Resistance to the Temperance Reformation," he says, "will put a stop to revivals in a church." Similarly, "revivals are hindered when ministers and churches take wrong ground in regard to any question involving human rights," notably slaveholding.

Finney further maintains that Christians must resist all forms of worldliness, especially parties and dances, extravagance in dress and in style of living, and the use of such luxuries as coffee, tea, and tobacco. Such practices, he says, are sinful chiefly in diverting the Christian from his main enterprise; they constitute a misappropriation of divine gifts, as well as being a temptation toward more grievous sins.

Finney views the Christian life in simple terms. He maintains that there is no such thing as a conflict in a man's duties toward God, and he concludes that Christians ought to strive for nothing short of complete perfection. He argues that honest business practices are more profitable than dishonest ones and will gradually prevail over dishonest ones, especially in a Christian country such as the United States. He reasons in the same way concerning politics, maintaining that Christians ought to vote for honest men, and not to pay attention to party issues. We have observed that Finney opposed a Christian's holding slaves, but he was not an ardent abolitionist, urging rather that "the only hope of the country, the church, the oppressor, and the slave was in *wide spread* revivals." In opposition to millenarian groups, he maintained that the Kingdom of God will be established in the world by evangelical means before the return of Christ.

The influence of Finney upon American Protestantism is apparent, at least in a general way. His disregard for the older theological traditions, his contempt for clerical pretensions, his Biblical fundamentalism, his confidence in the power of religion to solve all the world's problems, and his dogmatic notions concerning what constitutes a godly life were widely reflected in the piety of middle-class Christians in the new churches which sprang up across the nation. No doubt many of these characteristics would have appeared without Finney, as frontier democracy became a molding force in the churches, but the personal influence of Finney, which was equalled in the nineteenth century only by that of his younger contemporary, Dwight L. Moody (1837-1899), was no doubt a decisive factor. The influence of Finney's intense activism is especially interesting to contemplate. After Finney's time, partly under the influence of Horace Bushnell (1802-1876), many churches reacted against revivalism and turned their energies in the direction of social reform. Those, on the other hand, which continued to emphasize revivals became increasingly indifferent to the wider applications of Christian teaching. Both parties, however, liberals and fundamentalists as we call them today, retained Finney's dynamism, together with something of his penchant for simplistic solutions.

THE LIFE OF JESUS CRITICALLY EXAMINED

Author: David Friedrich Strauss (1808-1874)
Type of work: New Testament criticism and theology
First published: 1835-1836 (in two volumes)

Principal Ideas Advanced

Rigorous critical understanding of the Bible requires that supernaturalism and rationalism give way to the mythical approach, which views the Biblical stories not as the efforts of eyewitnesses to record facts, but as fictitious representations of religious ideas; here for the first time the mythical approach is to be applied comprehensively to the accounts of Jesus in the four Gospels.

That an account is mythical and not factual is determinable in two principal ways: negatively, through conflict with the modern conception of the world, as in the representation of divine and demonic beings intruding miraculously in the causal process; positively, through agreement with pre-existing ideas or tendencies at work in the religious community which has produced the account in question.

The mythical representations of the life of Jesus in the Gospels are derived mainly from Jewish Messianic expectations; the precise influence of Jesus' actual personality and history, which undeniably worked upon these expectations in some measure, is now irrecoverable.

However, radical historical criticism does not threaten faith, since the latter's immediate security lies not in past facts but in ideal truths, which truths, are, in fact, better upheld by the mythical than by the orthodox or any alternative approach.

In the relationship between Christianity and modern knowledge, no factor has been more critical than the higher criticism of the Bible; and in the development of criticism no single work has played a larger role than *The Life of Jesus Critically Examined.* Educated at Tübingen and Berlin, David Friedrich Strauss, the twenty-seven-year-old author, had been deeply influenced by the historical theologian Ferdinand Christian Baur (1792-1860) and the philosopher Georg Wilhelm Friedrich Hegel (1770-1831). He had studied closely the development of recent theological thought, including both technical Biblical research and such new systematic construction as that of Friedrich Schleiermacher (1768-1834). From this preparation came a work which combined brilliant historical competency with incisive discussion of theological issues. The book's radical conclusions brought furious reaction, which ruined Strauss's academic career. As a celebrated man of letters, he moved in later life further and further from orthodoxy, until, finally, in *The Old Faith and the New* (1872), his abandonment of the Christian perspective became explicit. The English translation, by the novelist George Eliot (1819-1880), of *The Life of Jesus Critically Examined* is from the fourth German edition of 1840, in which Strauss restored and elaborated the positions advanced originally, after having temporarily modified them under the storm of his critics.

At the beginning of the nineteenth century, Biblical interpretation was dominated by an antithesis between two main approaches. According to *orthodox supernaturalism,* the Scriptures contained a literal history correct in details, including the accounts of the miracles. For *rationalism,* on the other hand, the face value of stories out of keeping with natural law was used as a point of departure for the interpreter to offer his own plausible explanation of the original happening. For instance, the story of Adam's fall in Genesis might rest upon the actual eating of a poisonous fruit, or the descent of the dove at Jesus' baptism upon a tame bird fluttering about fortuitously. In this way the Biblical history was drastically revised, but it was still conceived as literal history. Meanwhile, another approach had been gaining currency. During the eighteenth century the *mythical theory* had been employed by some to discredit Christianity. But by the time Strauss wrote, there was a considerable volume of positive Christian interpretation using the concept of myth in the treatment of such elements of the Bible as the creation narratives and even, among advanced scholars, the stories of Jesus' miraculous birth. Eclecticism was becoming the rule, in which some matters were regarded mythically, some explained rationalistically, and others—especially where Jesus Himself was concerned—accepted as truly supernatural history.

In Strauss's judgment such eclectic procedure is an unacceptable compromise, with dogmatic presuppositions covertly circumscribing scientific rigor. The new undertaking he proposes is a thoroughly objective and consistent testing of the Gospels by the mythical theory. Without denying an underlying factual component, he "applies the notion of mythus to the entire history of the life of Jesus; recognizes mythi or mythical embellishments in every portion, and ranges under the category of mythus not merely the miraculous occurrences during the infancy of Jesus, but those also of his public life; not merely miracles operated on Jesus, but those wrought by him."

Myth is the creation, from and for a believing community, "of a fact out of an idea," the use of a "historical semblance merely as the shell . . . a religious conception." Strauss distinguishes *pure* from *historical* myth, the latter having a groundwork of individual fact—which has, however, been sublimated into interpretive representation. From both types of myth he further differentiates *legend,* also factually based but so garbled by long oral transmission as to defy precise assessment of the historical kernel. These, along with *editorial redaction,* are the categories of analysis used by Strauss in his minute dissection of the Gospels. His scheme requires the hypothesis of a considerable period of preliminary transmission, prior to the crystallization of the documents in their present form. Thus it collided with the still prevailing tradition of the eyewitness authenticity of the Gospels, which, were the mythical theory valid, must apparently be understood as forgeries. Apart from the intolerable offense that faith would feel in this thought, it seemed also historically incredible that such forgeries could have been accepted by the primitive Church. Strauss neutralizes these obstacles by arguing that the eyewitness character of the Gospels is in fact indemonstrable, the evidence pointing to a relatively late traditionary origin. On the other hand, knowledge of how the myth-forming process works in the developing self-portrayal of a religious community, together with knowledge of ancient notions of literary authenticity, precludes imputation of deliberate fraud to the Scriptural authors and editors. There were, moreover, the two primary factors of the Jewish Messianic expectations and the actuality of Jesus. Hence the Gospel myths, as such, did not have to evolve *after* Jesus' appearance. They already existed ready-made and had only to be transferred and adapted to Him. The Gospel stories were shaped by evangelists who hoped to show the fulfillment of the Messianic prophecies in the Old Testament.

How identify myth? Strauss proposes to use both negative and positive criteria. In the first place, we are sure that nothing can truly have happened which "is irreconcilable with the known and universal laws which govern the course of events." This categorically eliminates the miraculous, for philosophy and science teach us that the "absolute cause never disturbs the chain of secondary causes by single, arbitrary acts of interposition." Similarly, whatever is contrary to general and habitual human behavior, as remembering the long speeches presumably quoted in the Fourth Gospel, or whatever is psychologically or morally implausible, as the Sanhedrin bribing the watchmen at the tomb—all such matter is decidedly suspect. Furthermore, a historical account must be consistent with itself and with other accounts. Positively, myth is indicated by a poetical form, but more especially by a congruency in substance with ideas prevailing within the circle from which a narrative proceeds. For example, the tendency of the Jews to represent their great men as the children of parents who had long been childless renders doubtful such a story as that of John the Baptist's birth. However, all such considerations grow stronger *in concurrence.* Strauss is cautious of putting too much weight upon any one strand of evidence. In any event, he argues, the boundary between the mythical and the historical, in records such as our Gospels, "will ever remain fluctuating and insusceptible of precise attainment." One could hardly expect better than this of the first comprehensive application of the mythical theory to the life of Jesus.

In his actual handling of the Gospel materials, Strauss is ruthlessly critical but not undiscriminating. He painstakingly adduces and ponders the evidence. His criteria indicate that myth-forming faith has been at work everywhere. But even if there are no remaining islands of pure, untouched fact, Strauss often detects an influence of the original Jesus in and through the myth. The problem, for instance, of Jesus' formal education is conditioned by the undoubted fact of His unique genius. That there is likewise an historical core underneath the mythicized narratives of the baptism by John, the teachings, and the ministry in general, Strauss is far from denying. In treating the details, he often feels the trace of history most strongly in the Synoptics.

Nearly three hundred pages are devoted to the climactic narratives of passion and the Resurrection. On his presuppositions Strauss must acquiesce in the dilemma of the modern "cultivated intellect . . . : either Jesus was not really dead, or he did not really rise again." Despite mythical embellishments, of the death there is a "precise and internally consistent attestation" —something altogether lacking with respect to the Resurrection. Whence, then, the Easter faith, with its power to revivify the shattered band of disciples? Strauss conjectures that it arose first in Galilee, where Peter and the others had fled to avoid persecution. Over weeks and months the mythical imagination found the means of resolving the apparent contradiction of Messianic hope. According to the Scriptures, it was necessary that the Messiah should die, and just as certain that He should rise again. Visionary enthusiasm, which proved transferable to Paul and others, did the rest. By the time the Resurrection claim got back to Jerusalem, it was too late to test it by the facts.

So much, then, for the question of the Gospel history as such. Strauss acknowledges that he may appear to have annihilated the heart of Christian belief; but, he insists, this is not in fact the case. Hence he sets out, in a concluding dissertation, "to re-establish dogmatically what has been destroyed critically." He reviews the orthodox Christological dogma, which the modern mind can no longer literally accept. Against it arose rationalism's picture of Jesus as a distinguished man, intellectually inoffensive but religiously empty. Schleiermacher's Christology was a noble effort, but its eclecticism could fully satisfy neither faith nor science. More promising had been the symbolical interpretation of Christ suggested by the philosopher Immanuel Kant (1724-1804). Yet Kant's symbol had remained merely ideal—representing the moral law rather than the reality of redemption. A really adequate standpoint at last emerges, however, in the speculative Christology inspired by the philosophy of G. W. F. Hegel. According to Hegel, religious ideas are symbolic expressions of philosophical truth—not merely of the ideal, as with Kant, but of the real. This insight supplies the basis for affirming the supreme truth of the whole complex of Christian symbols and dogmas; thus faith can be satisfied. But so also is the critical intellect appeased; for the symbols are true mythically, poetically, pictorially—and not literally.

In the symbol of the Incarnation, the speculative Christology perceives the truth that Absolute Spirit becomes finite and concrete over against itself. Strauss writes that the "man of Divine essence . . . is the power that subdues nature, a worker of miracles; but as God in a human manifestation, he is dependent on nature, subject to its necessities and sufferings. . . ." The abasement of God extends even to death, to the "lowest depths of the finite." But the Resurrection symbolizes the eternal return of God to God; and as the divine has come down to man, so man's spirit shares in the divine eternity. Thus the estrangement of the finite from the infinite is overcome in reconciliation and reunion. There is, however, a disagreement among those who profess to follow Hegel, as to how, or rather as to *where,* the idea of reconciliation has been realized and manifested. Some would maintain that the realization has occurred in the individual man Jesus. Strauss rejects this as an abortive effort, still at odds with science. For him, the proper subject of the Christ myth is not an individual but the human race as a whole. "Humanity is the union of the two natures . . . ," Strauss writes; "By faith in this Christ, especially in his death and resurrection, man is justified before God; that is, by the kindling within him of the idea of Humanity, the individual man participates in the divinely human life of the species."

Thus would Strauss retrieve, for the philosophically minded, the religious substance which his criticism had seemed to destroy. His book revealed unmistakably to the Christian world how formidable and relentless a challenge lay in objective historical research. It also stated, clearly and concisely, one of the alternatives according to which Christian faith might attempt to reconceive and thus honestly to understand itself in a scientific world. Strauss has been much attacked, but as a catalyst of modern Christian reflection he has had few equals.

THE DIVINITY SCHOOL ADDRESS

Author: Ralph Waldo Emerson (1803-1882)
Type of work: Religious epistemology
First published: 1838

Principal Ideas Advanced

The natural world exhibits a rational order, and man's ability to understand, use, and enjoy the world indicates a fundamental kinship between the human mind and the natural world.

There is a rational, fixed cosmic order of moral law which man recognizes intuitively.

The rational structure of the natural world and of moral experience indicates that the world is the product of a single benevolent cosmic mind and will.

Religion is the apprehension of the reign of divine law in the world of nature and in human experience.

The Christian Church has attempted to make a demigod of Jesus Christ, whereas His own intention was not to call attention to Himself but to stimulate men to discover God within their own souls.

Emerson's *An Address,* commonly referred to as the "divinity school address," is to be understood against the background of the emergence in America of Unitarianism and of the radical outgrowth of Unitarianism known as transcendentalism.

By the middle of the eighteenth century the hold of Calvinistic theology on New England Congregationalism was loosening. To prosperous business and professional men as well as to some clergymen such doctrines as double predestination and total depravity did not seem compatible with human dignity or divine justice. Gradually there developed—particularly in eastern Massachusetts—a faction of liberal clergymen who emphasized human freedom and moral responsibility, and who raised questions about the trinitarian conception of God. The friction between liberal and orthodox clergymen became intense in 1805 with the election of a liberal, Henry Ware, to the Hollis professorship of divinity at Harvard University.

The evolution of the liberal faction into a denomination separate from Congregationalism was greatly accelerated in 1819 as the result of a sermon preached by William Ellery Channing (1780-1842), minister of the Federal Street Church in Boston. Entitled "Unitarian Christianity," the sermon was preached in Baltimore at the ordination of a Unitarian minister, Jared Sparks. In the sermon Channing exalted reason as the final religious authority. Employing the test of reason, he rejected the Trinity, Christ's twofold nature, and the sacrificial atonement. Channing's sermon became the platform of the Unitarian movement, and by 1825 over a hundred churches had organized themselves into a new denomination, the American Unitarian Fellowship.

Transcendentalism was a protest on the part of a few highly articulate and productive writers against the excessive and essentially negative rationalism of the more orthodox form of Unitarianism. The transcendentalists were romantics who believed that religious experience consists not so much of rational belief in propositions as of a direct, intuitive apprehension of God which engages the emotions and moral sensibilities as well as the intellect.

The transcendentalists, who constituted a small school of thinkers rather than a denominational movement, borrowed freely from Platonic philosophy and Oriental religions and philosophies. They also acknowledged indebtedness to the eminent German philosopher Immanuel Kant (1724-1804), who taught that knowledge contains elements contributed by the structure of the mind, as well as elements from sense experience. Kant confined knowledge to mathematics and the natural sciences, contending that religious and moral truths belong to a different category of experience from that of knowledge.

The transcendentalists became interested in Kant and other German philosophers through the British writers Thomas Carlyle (1795-1881) and Samuel Taylor Coleridge (1772-1834). Both these men had great influence upon the transcendentalists. Coleridge was a chief source of the distinction between reason and understanding, so important in Emerson's thought. Reason is man's intuitive faculty; it simply perceives; it does not deduce or prove. The understanding, on the other hand, compares, struggles, and argues. Man's moral, religious, and esthetic experiences are based upon reason, whereas understanding is involved in man's more mundane practical activities. The reason apprehends those realities which transcend the sense: God, the soul, duty, and beauty.

Emerson's intellectual odyssey into transcendentalism began with his experiences as a Congregational minister. Ordained in 1829, he became pastor of the Second Church in Boston. He resigned from the pastorate after three years because of his inability to accept the Lord's Supper as an obligatory and regular part of Christian worship. His departure from the pastorate was amiable, and he continued to supply pulpits for several years after his resignation in 1832. Increasingly, however, he grew weary and impatient with the trivial and joyless quality of church services. Journal entries in 1837 and 1838 reveal a growing desire on his part to deliver a public manifesto to the American clergy in which he would point out the disparity between their pathetic performance and their magnificent calling. His opportunity came in the spring of 1838 in the form of an invitation from the senior class of the Divinity School at Harvard. On Sunday evening, July 15, 1838, he delivered his address to the Harvard theological students and an audience containing many clergymen of the Boston area. The address was published later in the same year.

The *Address* begins with a rhapsodic celebration of the glories of nature in midsummer. Turning from vivid descriptions of the beauties of the world, Emerson comments upon the significance of man's capacity to subdue the powers and enjoy the beauties of nature. There is a rational order in nature as evidenced by the kinship between the human mind and the natural world.

Just as there is a rational order in the behavior of the universe, so, too, he argued, there is a rational, fixed cosmic order of moral law to which man conforms in his virtue. Man intuitively recognizes the divine laws of morality. Even when he violates moral principles he does so with the remorseful recognition that he was made for virtue and that vice is a violation of his nature. Virtuous behavior is always ennobling, whereas mean deeds immediately diminish one's moral stature.

The rational structure of the natural world and of moral experience indicates, Emerson claimed, that the world is not the product of blind forces, but of a single cosmic mind and will. Every event is the product of that mind. God is not only the source of rational order; He is also benevolent and just. God is the positive, dynamic force of goodness in the world. Evil is nothing positive, but is the absence of good, just as cold is the absence of heat.

Emerson goes on to describe religion as essentially the apprehension of the reign of divine law in the world of nature and human experience. Religion is man's apprehension of the world as the expression of divine rationality and benevolence. To the religious man all reality becomes resplendent in its exhibition of benevolence and rational order. Religious sentiment is deifying to man, because it leads him to seek his own fulfillment in virtue. Worship makes man illimitable by lifting him out of his self-centeredness and by making him aware of the "deeps of Reason."

Religious and moral insight can come only through the intuitions of one's own reason. The intuitions of reason cannot be taught, Emerson insisted; they can only be experienced. The truth which another person announces can be accepted only if one finds the same truth in oneself. When a nation or society neglects its own primary experience of reality and depends upon the experience of other peoples or other ages, cultural degradation sets in and there is a loss of vitality in the Church, the state, art, letters, and life generally.

Upon the basis of the conception of religion enunciated above, Emerson proceeds next to a criticism of Christianity in its historical development. He pays tribute to Jesus Christ as a religious genius who was acutely aware of the divine dimension in all reality and experience. "Alone in all history he estimated the greatness of man. One man was true to what is in you and me. He saw that God incarnates himself in man, and evermore goes forth anew to take possession of his World." Jesus was divine because he became the medium of God's activity. But Jesus' intention was to point to himself only by way of indicating the possibilities open to all men, not in order to claim special status for himself. The Church, however, has misinterpreted the significance of Jesus by trying to convert his intuitions of reason into conclusions of the understanding. The Church has surrounded Jesus with titles and claims which kill sympathy for him. The Church has made of Jesus a demigod who demands our submission rather than a friend who desires our joyous fulfillment. Whereas the Church has been preoccupied with the unique qualities of Jesus, it was Jesus' own intention to stimulate men to discover about themselves what he discovered about himself; namely, that God dwells within the soul.

Not only has the Church misinterpreted Jesus. It has also misrepresented revelation as over and done with, a thing of the past, as though God once lived but is now dead. Turning more directly to the young prospective preachers before him, Emerson challenges them to preach their own souls. The impotence of organized religion is due to the failure of preachers to proclaim the truths which grasp them personally. A sermon is inevitably dead when the preacher abandons the intuitions of his own reason for books which tell about the faith of other people of other ages.

It is the function of the preacher, Emerson proceeds, to "convert life into truth." In his sermons the true preacher "deals out to the people his life—life passed through the fire of thought." The preacher must make his hearers aware that God *is,* not *was,* and that God speaks still. The wisdom which one finds in his own immediate experience is to be preferred to all the secondhand wisdom which the world has to offer. The preacher who models his thought upon that of St. Paul, or George Fox, or Swedenborg, or any other man—no matter how saintly or wise—is doomed to mediocrity. Emerson admonishes his clerical hearers to bards of the Holy Ghost so that they may "acquaint men at first hand with Deity." When you encounter your parishioners, he advises them, let them see in you a divine man; let your presence elicit their "timid aspirations" and their "trampled instincts."

The magnitude of the controversy which followed Emerson's address to the divinity students may be indicated by the fact that he was not invited to speak again at Harvard until 1865, twenty-seven years later. Some denounced him as an atheist, and from some quarters there came the suggestion that he deserved no better than Abner Kneeland, who was currently serving a jail sentence for blasphemy. Emerson himself had no taste for argument, but he quietly went ahead with plans to publish the address. The most determined attack against him came from the eminent Harvard Unitarian theologian, Andrews Norton. An address which Norton gave to Harvard divinity alumni was published under the title *A Discourse on the Latest Form of Infidelity*. Norton's reaction to Emerson's address was typical of the shock and anger of the more orthodox Unitarians. The orthodox Unitarians defended themselves as genuine Christians, and they were acutely aware that if they did not denounce Emerson, then they would be extremely vulnerable to the Congregational charge that the abandonment of the trinitarian conception of God leads to a dissolution of the whole structure of orthodox Christian belief.

It is not difficult to understand why the *Address* shocked Congregationalists and Unitarians alike. It humanizes Jesus and deifies man. It pictures God as a benevolent force, immanent in the processes of nature and history, and it omits any mention of God as a transcendent judge of man's sinfulness. Evil is defined simply as absence of good rather than as a dynamic force such as Satan. There is no suggestion of the retention of the concept of original sin. Christ is essentially the revealer of man's possibilities rather than a special manifestation of God. The Bible is a secondhand source of religious truth and thus is secondary in authority to the intuitions of reason.

Despite all of the clerical opposition which the *Address* aroused, it is now clear in retrospect that its theological ebullience and optimism constituted a special expression of the heady confidence characteristic of America in the era in which Emerson wrote. The romanticism and optimism were closely akin to that of the various forms of Protestant Evangelicalism which provided the primary religious expression on the American frontiers in the pre-Civil War decades of the nineteenth century. Both the transcendentalists and the evangelicals insisted upon a warm, firsthand experience of God, an experience which engaged the emotions as well as the mind. Both movements emphasized virtue and philanthropy. Both movements looked hopefully to the redemptive possibilities of the future. Apart from the more sophisticated thought forms of transcendentalism, the main difference between the two movements was the absence from transcendentalism of any emphasis upon tragedy, suffering, or sacrifice as necessary to religious fulfillment.

THE KINGDOM OF CHRIST

Author: Frederick Denison Maurice (1805-1872)
Type of work: Theological ethics
First published: 1838

Principal Ideas Advanced

Jesus Christ has actually established a universal, spiritual society, His Kingdom, of which every man is a member, whether he recognizes Christ as his head or not, and of which the ordinances of the Church are signs.

Men in every society have longed in different ways for the head or representative of all mankind; the Bible identifies this head as Jesus Christ, promised by the Old Testament and manifested in the New.

Even when religious principles outlive the particular religious bodies through which they have been expressed, those principles are of enduring value to the Catholic or Universal Church.

Since the nation and the Church are mutually correcting and supporting in their divinely appointed functions, nationality does not hinder, but furthers, the Church's universality.

It is nothing extraordinary for a theologian to stress the sovereignty of Christ. Frederick D. Maurice, however, was remarkable for the consistency with which he allowed the actuality of Christ's Kingdom to dominate other elements in his thought and for the robust way in which he was prepared to act on the basis of this central conviction. *The Kingdom of Christ* is one of the earliest and most important statements of Maurice's steadfast insistence that God's love for all mankind be announced to men and take shape in their economic, social, political, and religious life.

Maurice was born into the household of a Unitarian minister. He attended Oxford, where his attention was drawn especially to Plato, who was greatly to influence Maurice's thought. He had an intellectual affinity and a warm personal admiration for the English poet-philosopher, Samuel Taylor Coleridge (1772-1834), although he never met or personally heard him. Rebaptized in 1831, Maurice was ordained in the Anglican communion in 1834. He was appointed (1840) Professor of English Literature and History at Kings College, and later (1846) he gained the chair of Divinity there. Following the publication of his *Theological Essays* (1853), he was dismissed. Maurice and the social reformer Charles Kingsley (1819-1875) issued *Politics for the People* (1848) and fostered Christian Socialism to meet the challenge of Chartism. As an educator he was of great importance, founding Queen's College (1847), the first of its kind for women, and serving as Principal at the Working Man's College (1854). From 1866 to his death he was Professor of Moral Philosophy at Cambridge.

When a controversy arose among the English Quakers, Maurice wrote to urge an acquaintance not to abandon Friends' principles but to consider whether Quakerism as a system based on those principles could possibly be an adequate witness to the Gospel. *The Kingdom of Christ* (1838, with a new, expanded edition appearing in 1842) is the refashioning of a series of twelve such letters to a Quaker. Happily, the finished work preserves much of the tone of friendly concern, discussion, and admonition of its original form. Its generally unsystematic character is compensated for by the quality of its dialogue.

The several positions discussed are more than foils for the author's own argument: each party occupies, according to Maurice, a position necessary to the health and integrity of the Catholic Church (universal, not Roman). Throughout the book, Maurice is conversing with the Friends, "pure Protestantism," Unitarianism, contemporary philosophical thought, and the Roman Catholic Church. The first part of the book is devoted to a historical and critical examination of the "principles" of each of the first four of these groups and the "systems" fathered by those principles; the Roman Catholics receive special attention in the second part. Maurice seeks to demonstrate that each religious body as a system has proved to be inadequate, not because it has followed mistaken principles but because it has not been sufficiently true to its principles.

Maurice examines the "traces of a spiritual constitution" in the early ages of the world and finds that the clearest indications of such a moral constitution for mankind is that men exist in families and in nations. With help from Scripture to interpret the signs of this spiritual constitution, he finds that the faith of Abraham, "the beginner of the church on earth," was "that there is a God *related* to men and made known to men through their human relations." This truth was exhibited in the covenant with the family and then in the covenant with the nation. The family and nation depended, however, on a third relationship, a universal one. There are two possible forms for a universal society: one which destroys the family and national principles, the other which expands them. The first is what is called the World in Scripture; the second, what is called the Church. The principles of the world are the natural tendencies and inclinations of men; such tendencies exist in the heart of every family and nation and threaten to become predominant. "When they become predominant," Maurice writes, "there ceases to be any recognition of men as related to a Being above them, any recognition of them as possessing a common humanity." The Church, as the special witness to these facts which men tend to deny, must never lose its distinctness and universality.

The subject of the New Testament is the Son of David and Son of Abraham who comes preaching the Gospel of the Kingdom; Jesus is affirmed by the Evangelists to be the King. This Son of God and King of Israel certainly died, actually rose with His body, appeared to those who knew Him, and spoke and ate with them. This for the Evangelists ". . . is the accomplishment of the union between heaven and earth; it is no longer a word, it is a fact." Maurice describes the person and work of Christ mainly in the terms suggested by the fifth chapter of Romans, the Christ-Adam relation. He says that by Christ's obedience unto death He, as the second Adam, brought mercy to mankind in place of what was brought by the first Adam. Christ is the Lord and head of every man whether each man recognizes it and acknowledges Christ or not; for Christ's coming, humility, obedience and resurrection have in fact changed man's moral situation. The creeds accurately describe who Christ is and the character of His work. All men have witnessed to Him insofar as they have needed and have sought the perfect man, a Prince, divine humanity. Christ is "the Man," the representative of all mankind. Man's constitution is that he is created in Christ. By His incarnation, death, and resurrection Christ revealed and established a spiritual and universal Kingdom of which all men are members, whether or not they acknowledge him.

The "signs" of this universal and spiritual society are baptism, the creeds, forms of worship, the Eucharist, the ministry, and the Scriptures.

The universal Church baptizes a child because the child has a human form and countenance which Christ bore, and because in renouncing the evil society which is opposed to humanity adults do not abandon their children to that society. Baptism is the token of the redeemed covenant family, ". . . the sign of admission into a Spiritual and Universal Kingdom, grounded upon our Lord's incarnation and ultimately resting on the name of the Father, the Son, and the Holy Spirit. . . ."

If by baptism we are acknowledged as spiritual creatures united to the supreme spiritual Being, by the creed, as an act of allegiance, we claim our spiritual position; we assert our union with that Being. When Maurice defends the creeds against various assailants, he does so on the grounds that they are declarations of "belief in a name, and not in notions." In fact, there is no road into "mere notionality" as certain and direct "as that of rejecting all common and united forms of utterance."

Prayer presupposes that a restoration has already taken place, since the very idea of "a Church which is not built upon the confession of a restored humanity is a contradiction in terms." Maurice writes: "The very essence of their prayers is this: a cry that those sins which they feel in themselves, under which they are groaning, which they have committed, may not be, as they have been, their masters, and the masters of the universe." The act which is most fit for man, most thoroughly joyful, is that of thanking and blessing God.

Given the necessity and validity of the Lord's Supper, Maurice declares that he must protect the Eucharist from misinterpretation by both the Protestants and the Romans. The Protestants, he says, continually lose sight of the finished sacrifice of Christ in their anxiety to assert the importance of human faith; and the Romans constantly try through a violent effort of recollection, assisted by visible images and presentations, to bring back the very event of our Lord's crucifixion. Maurice accepts the term "recollection" because there is nothing in it which is not applicable to "a Living Actual Presence. What I plead for is the duty of recollecting that presence in the Eucharist, *because it is there.*"

The ministry has a crucial, even decisive, function. "Upon the character of this agency must depend the whole character of the Kingdom itself," Maurice claims. The Gospels present Christ as training His disciples for an *office;* He breathed on His disciples after the resurrection, and He bestowed on them the gift of the Holy Ghost. The disciples understood that the powers thereby confirmed belonged to them officially and not personally. The "officers" were to bring before men the fact that all men are subject to an invisible and universal Ruler; the task of the disciples was to exhibit Him to men in that character and in those offices which He came to perform: they were to look upon themselves in no light other than as ministers. As Christ was the great absolver, so the priest truly absolves and does not merely preach forgiveness of sins.

The episcopate contains the various functions committed by our Lord to His immediate disciples. The bishops have all the needful power for performing these functions. The episcopal succession is rightly maintained "expressly as a witness of the permanent constitution of the Church, and therefore of the continued abiding of Christ in it, and of each Bishop in each age being his servant and the receiver of gifts and power directly from Him. . . ." Maurice makes a distinction, over against the Roman Church, between a "representative" and a "vicarial" doctrine of the ministry. Once ministers are made vicarial, the scheme of "Popedom," alien to the New Testament, is initiated.

The Scriptures not only interpret to us the signs of the universal and spiritual Kingdom, but are themselves such a sign. They become intelligible when seen as a unified witness to a permanent Kingdom. Their credit should not be sustained by the miracles they record, nor by the consistency of the facts they register, nor by their ideal truth. Although Maurice finds "monstrous and heretical" the idea that the Bible was dictated, he concedes a verbal inspiration in the sense that inspired thoughts find for themselves a suitable clothing in words.

The universal Church, far from being against national churches, vindicates their necessity. Catholicity, existing in different lands in national churches, corrects and teaches the nations, and it benefits from the nations it instructs. The universal Church witnesses against the dangers of nationalism in religion, and national churches hinder the universal Church from becoming despotic.

The principle of an eye for an eye and a tooth for a tooth lies at the heart of a state and explains what a state is. Vengeance must be somewhere, Maurice writes, "and the State is that which teaches each man that there is a Lord [to whom vengeance belongs] . . . whose authority he is bound to acknowledge and upon whose authority every act of private vengeance is an infringement." The office of the state is to restrain the acts of self-will; the office of the Church to bring out by loving methods the free-will of which the self-will is a base counterfeit. The office of the State is to punish the overt, foolish acts which proceed from private judgment and which disturb the commonwealth; the office of the Church is to teach men how to rise above those private judgments and to attain that manly judgment which is one of the most important qualifications of a good citizen.

Maurice's thought and action engendered lively discussion among his contemporaries. Some of them, like Kingsley, John Stuart Mill (1806-1873) the social philosopher, and Alfred Lord Tennyson (1809-1892), the poet, were avid in their praise. Others were perplexed by Maurice's method of thinking, put off by his Christian socialism, or worried by his universalism. In any case, his manner of attributing actuality and objectivity to God's redemptive actions, his Christocentricity, his dialectical mode of thought and expression, and his declaration of freedom for Biblical criticism, have given Maurice a hearing beyond his own century, country, and denomination.

HISTORY OF THE DEVELOPMENT OF THE DOCTRINE OF THE PERSON OF CHRIST

Author: Isaac August Dorner (1809-1884)
Type of work: History of doctrine
First published: 1839

PRINCIPAL IDEAS ADVANCED

The history of the Christian Church is marked by the attempt to develop the doctrine of the person of Christ in a manner faithful to the teaching of Scripture, in which due recognition is given to the twofold nature, the divine and the human, united in one person.

There has been a tendency throughout the course of the history of the Church to deny one or the other element, or to mix them improperly.

The fullness of the Christian life can be attained solely when the conception of the nature of Christ is freed from distortions and is made to embody the insights developed throughout the course of centuries.

Isaac August Dorner's *History of the Development of the Doctrine of the Person of Christ* is a comprehensive and an exhaustive critical study of the original sources pertaining to the Christological problem. The work is divided into two main divisions; the first part is published in two volumes; the second, in three volumes. The first part of the book covers the history of Christian doctrine up to 381, by which time the essential elements in the human and divine person of Christ had been recognized. The second part deals with the development of the doctrine of Christ from 381 until 1800.

Dorner begins by claiming that although the idea of a union between God and man is found in some degree in almost every religion, the manner in which Christianity asserts the idea of the God-man is entirely unique. The universal and perpetual belief of the Christian Church is that the unity of the divine and the human has appeared in a personal and unique mode in Jesus of Nazareth.

Christianity gives expression to what is sought in other religions, and it embraces many truths which they contain, but the idea of the God-man, so peculiarly characteristic of Christianity, did not arise outside Christianity, but wholly from within. The idea of the God-man is original and essential to Christianity, Dorner writes; it is found nowhere else, and where it is lacking, Christianity has vanished.

Dorner insists that all genuine historical investigation leads to the conclusion that the cause of the Christian idea of the God-man is to be ascribed to Jesus' own consciousness of Himself, and His own self-disclosure to others. From the very beginning of its existence the Church accepted this basic Christian truth in its totality, although not in its fully developed form. The Church could not immediately give a precise theological definition of the contents of its fully developed faith, a faith that was already complete in all its parts. Consequently, the Church limited itself to such declarations as the immediate occasion required, declarations which were to some extent incomplete and therefore unsatisfactory to a later age, when the Church was called upon to repudiate unchristian positions and to assert the Christian truth in opposition to them. In subsequent ages the Church never sought to assert anything new; she merely had to maintain and freely utter that which she had always borne within herself.

The history of dogma, as Dorner conceives it, is concerned not with the doctrinal declaration of Christ and His Apostles, but with the faith that is developed into Church doctrine. Its task is to show how the objective testimony concerning Christ, given once and for all in Scripture, is disclosed to the consciousness of the Church under the guidance of the Holy Spirit.

It is to be noted, however, that the Pauline and Johannine form of doctrine, although of decisive and directing influence upon subsequent developments, does not differ essentially from that of the synoptic age of Christology. Within the canon of the New Testament there is no writing that does not presuppose the essential divinity of the Son, who stands in an ontological relation to the Father, and who, together with the Father and the Holy Spirit, constitutes the Holy Triad.

New Testament Christianity does not appear in precisely constructed dogmas, Dorner points out, but rather in the form of Christ's witness of Himself in word and deed, and of the faith of the Apostles testifying concerning Him, to which witness is added that of the Holy Spirit, to establish faith in those who have accepted it.

After Christianity had been established in human hearts, it became necessary to understand more exactly and conceptually what had been disclosed by the Holy Spirit through the Apostles. The attacks on Christianity largely contributed to the consolidation and conceptualization of Christian doctrines. The latter are, however, not merely a human product, for the knowledge of the Church also partakes of the divine Spirit.

Within the first period of Christological development, until 380, the ideas concerning the essential elements of the person of Christ were established. The unity of the Godhead and the manhood of Christ was presupposed. The true human body of Christ, its actual existence, its functions and natural affections, and the fact of His birth, death and resurrection, were subjects of the common conviction of the Christian world. With respect to Christ's deity, the divine in Christ was everywhere recognized, and the Christian community knew itself to be eternally reconciled and united with God in Christ. The problem, however, Dorner explains, was to understand the nature of Christ's human soul and to determine how the divine in Christ is related to the divine of the Father. The further task that was to be accomplished was to gain an understanding of the Trinity.

The Church successfully combatted opponents both of Christ's deity and of His humanity. Ebionism entirely put aside the view of the divinity of Christ and asserted that the truths of the Church held only for His humanity; Docetism, on the other hand, proposed to find the deeper meaning of Christianity by stressing the higher aspect, Christ's deity, at the expense of His humanity.

The Church maintained its witness both for the true Godhead and the true manhood of Christ. The two fundamental Christological heresies were defeated by the formulation of the doctrine of the Logos who became perfect man.

At the Council of Nicaea in 325, Dorner notes, the Church confessed the eternal hypostasis of the Son and His essential equality with the Father. It rejected the notion of hypostasis without deity, as taught by Arianism, a refined form of Ebionism, and it rejected the notion of a deity without a particular hypostasis, as taught by Sabellianism, a refined form of Docetism.

The Nicene Creed unconditionally claimed deity for the Son; it left unexamined, however, the questions of the precise nature of the hypostasis, the mode of its generation, and the basis of the Trinity in the Christian idea of God, and thereby it left room for the further doctrinal struggles of the Council of Constantinople in 381, and the Council of Chalcedon in 451.

The Church still needed to understand the living unity of the two aspects of the personality of Christ. Each period in the history of the Church was called upon to give its conception of this unity. The Church never wearied in its struggle against the tendency to detract from or to deny the individuality and reality of either the divine or the human nature. Some represented the divine nature as transformed into the human; others represented the human nature as transformed into the divine. Still others represented the one nature as tempered and modified by the other, so that the result was a mixture of both factors.

A second tendency that needed to be rejected, Dorner reports, was the view that regarded the two natures as mutually exclusive contrarieties, each of which possessed distinctive characteristics. Some suggested that the divine and human natures are one to the extent that the latter is the temple of the former. Others regarded the union as mechanical and appealed to the mere power of God as being able to conjoin and to form into one whole two natures which differ in essence and have no internal connection. Still others regarded the union as relative; they maintained that the Logos, who is present in all things, stood in a distinctive relation to the man Jesus, so that Jesus was honored by God with the rank of Sonship, a title which by nature belongs to the Logos. Others regarded the union as moral, consisting mainly in the sympathy with the divine which was experienced by the man Jesus.

The Church was to affirm that in Christ there is to be recognized a duality of the divine and human, and yet the two infinitely and essentially different natures which constitute this duality are united in one person.

The Council of Chalcedon, held in 451, repudiated those who tried to destroy the mystery of the divine economy by introducing a duality of sons. It rejected the notion that the Godhead is capable of suffering, and it refused to say that the two natures were intermixed, or that the form assumed by the Logos was other than human, nor would it listen to those that claimed that previous to the union there were two natures, but afterwards only one. Instead it insisted that Jesus Christ was perfect in deity and perfect in humanity, with a body and a reasonable soul, of the same substance with the Father with respect to His Godhead, and of the same substance as ourselves with respect to His humanity, except that He was without sin. The peculiarity of the two natures was not abolished by their union, but remained unmixed, and undivided, combined, however, into a single person and one hypostasis, one and the same Son and only begotten, who is both God and man.

From the year 381 until the Reformation, Dorner writes, there was an increasing tendency to lay undue stress upon the divine aspect of the person of Christ. From 451 until the Council of Frankfurt in 794, the doctrine of the two natures formulated at Chalcedon received its logical completion. In the Middle Ages, from the ninth century to the Reformation, the dyophysite foundation of the Symbol of Chalcedon commenced to decay, and instead of Christology the Church occupied the central position, which led to the substitution of the saints, and the sacrifice of the Mass for the human aspect of Christ.

The magical character attached to the doctrine of grace in the Middle Ages had discernible consequences in Christology, Dorner claims. The human aspect became the garment of the divine; incarnation became theophany, and nihilianism (the idea that Christ, as human, was nothing) was substituted for the proper idea of a God-manhood.

The Scholastics sought to show that it was not necessary for God to become man, and substitutes for Christology made their appearance. The human nature of Christ was treated as impersonal, and the personality of man, under Pelagian influence, was emphasized. Some theologians, like Thomas Aquinas, remained true to tradition, but returned to simpler mystical views of the person of Christ and lost interest in the rational development of Christology. Others again took up the position of Adoptianism, the view that Christ was the adopted Son, not the true Son. The result was a decay into skepticism and a blind subjection to the authority of the Church. Among the mystics the continuity of the process of development of Christology was maintained, but they too failed to advance beyond the impersonality of Christ's humanity, although they did regard the latter as the perfection of human nature.

It remained the task of the Reformation to formulate the real equiponderance of the two aspects of the person of Christ. In its doctrine of the *Communicatio idiomatum,* the Lutheran Church was not satisfied with the mere unity of the ego, and it did not allow the human aspect to be absorbed in the divine hypostasis. It declared instead that the main problem is to understand the union of the two natures, and it put forth much effort to effect a solution. For Luther the union is regarded principally as a union of natures, the result of which is the union of the person. The whole Son, in whom dwelt the whole deity, assumed humanity. Everything human was thus appropriated by the divine nature, and the humanity of Christ received for its own that which belongs to the divine nature. Christ became man so that through him the man Jesus might become God.

The Reformed churches did not represent a new view of the doctrine of the person of Christ; they occupied the ground of the Council of Chalcedon and defended it against sects of every kind. With the Lutherans, they renounced Ebionism and Nestorianism, as well as the Doceticism of the Christology of Roman Catholicism. However, the Reformed churches did maintain that although the Word was united with a human person, He filled the world from the beginning.

Unfortunately, Dorner writes, the views of the Lutherans and the Reformed Churches did not prevent the rise of Socianianism and the subsequent decay of Christology into a one-sided subjectivity that finally resulted in the destruction of Christology by the subjective philosophy and defective Christology of men like Friedrich Schleiermacher (1768-1834).

It is to be hoped, however, Dorner concludes, that the evangelical Church may again be successful in reaching an agreement that fully embodies the Church doctrine concerning the person and the work of Christ. Dorner himself later worked out an elaborate Christology in Hegelian terms, in his *System of Christian Doctrine,* published posthumously in 1885.

THE ESSENCE OF CHRISTIANITY

Author: Ludwig Feuerbach (1804-1872)
Type of work: Philosophical theology
First published: 1841

Principal Ideas Advanced

Religion is the progressive attainment and deepening of self-knowledge; Christianity is a historically unique expression of this self-knowledge.

The study of God is at the same time the study of man; therefore, theology is reduced to anthropology, and anthropology is exalted to theology.

The basis of thought is matter, and the being of man cannot be understood independently of his biological existence.

God is the infinite universal essence of humanity, distinguished from the particular finite individual consciousness, which is always an inadequate representation of the species.

The essential significance of the doctrines of Christ, the Trinity, Revelation, and the Sacraments resides in their contribution to man's understanding of himself in his natural existence.

Ludwig Feuerbach's masterpiece, *The Essence of Christianity,* fell upon the official Christendom of the early nineteenth century like a bombshell. Its impact was felt by philosophers and theologians alike. It made explicit the anti-Hegelian presuppositions of Feuerbach's thought and provided a foundational reinterpretation of Christian doctrine. The anti-Hegelianism which is expressed is determined by a pervading existential attitude similar to that of Søren Kierkegaard (1813-1855), the Danish thinker who was attacking Hegel in Denmark at the same time. It was Feuerbach who cautioned his reader against wishing to be a philosopher to the neglect of being a man, and who urged him to think by existence rather than through abstraction. This existential attitude became the basis for his critique of orthodox academic theology.

Feuerbach found academic theology to be arid and sterile, and he sought to restate the essence of Christianity in such a way that it would become relevant for man's concrete, physical existence. He proposed a Christian realism, intended to illumine the being of man as he lives and moves in the marketplace. His concern was to make religion relevant and real, and to achieve this end he found it necessary to naturalize religion and to humanize God.

In the thinking of Feuerbach, religion is a process of enlightenment in which man progressively attains self-consciousness. This insight betrays Feuerbach's debt to his former teacher, Hegel, whom he later attacked. Viewed from one perspective Feuerbach is an anti-Hegelian; viewed from another perspective he is a neo-Hegelian. He is anti-Hegelian in his existential attitude as well as in his rejection of the dialectic of spirit as the ground of reality. For Feuerbach nature itself governs spirit, and matter becomes the basis of thought. Spirit is made dependent upon nature and the Hegelian dialectic is set upon its head in a way which reminds one of the anti-Hegelian protest of Marx. But both Feuerbach and Marx made use of the categories and basic insights of their chief opponent. Feuerbach's definition of religion as the progressive attainment of self-knowledge is clearly informed by the Hegelian definition of history as the progressive self-actualization of freedom working out that which it is potentially. Thus the anti-Hegelian protest of Feuerbach, when it comes full circle, leads to a neo-Hegelian naturalistic theology.

In such a theology the reality of God and the reality of man are convertible. Theology is understood in terms of anthropology, but this reductivism, argues the author, should not be taken in a negativistic sense. To make God relevant to our concrete, immediate existence, to make Him real, we must make Him human. However, in doing so, at the same time, we make man divine. Thus the reduction of theology to anthropology leads to an elevation of anthropology to theology.

To equate the divine nature with the human nature is not, however, to identify every human being as a god. The equation of God and humanity has to do with the essential humanity from which the individual representative is always in some sense alienated. The distinction between the divine and the human is simply indicative of the distinction between human nature in general, or the species, and the particular individual who is a member of this species. In no sense does Feuerbach speak of God as the particular individual. God is the universal essence of humanity. "*Man has his highest being, his God, in himself;* not in himself as an individual, but in his essential nature, his species. No individual is an adequate representation of his species, but only the human individual is conscious of the distinction between the species and the individual; in the sense of this distinction lies the root of religion. The yearning of man after something above himself is nothing else than the longing after the perfect type of his nature, the yearning to be free from himself, i.e., from the limits and defects of his individuality," writes Feuerbach. God, understood as essential humanity, involves both a descriptive universal and a prescriptive ideal. God is the species, and as such He is the universal in terms of which every member of the class is able to understand itself as a member and thus to achieve self-consciousness. But this species which defines the particular is at the same time an archetype or an ideal. It is prescriptive as well as descriptive. God is the harmonium of human perfection. He is the ideal of humanity, and thus He is the ground of self awareness and the principle of self-actualization.

Having understood God as essential humanity one can then proceed to describe the nature of God in terms of His distinctive attributes. Feuerbach accepts the classical attributes which are found in the literature of the tradition. Love, justice, and personality, for example, can legitimately be attributed to God. Indeed, all the attributes which describe human nature can be applied to God insofar as God is nothing else than human nature freed from its individual limitations. All the attributes of the human nature *ipso facto* become attributes of the divine nature. Insofar as these attributes are purified by being freed from the limits of any particular individual, it must properly be said that God is not *a* being who loves, but He is love itself; He is not *a* being who exercises justice, He is justice itself; He is not *a* person but personality itself.

Feuerbach thus devotes himself to an analysis of the "essence of Christianity," and he finds in Christianity a historically unique expression of that knowledge of self which characterizes religion more generally. He is looking for the key to the riddle of the Christian religion, and he purports to extricate its true meaning from the accumulated mass of contradictions and delusions. The pivotal doctrine of Christianity is the doctrine of Christ, a doctrine which teaches that God is incarnate in the particularity of human existence. It is thus that Christ provides the final answer to the problem of the relation of the universal and the particular, the ideal of humanity, the real man. "The most unequivocal expression, the characteristic symbol of this immediate identity of the species and individuality in Christianity is Christ, the real God of the Christians," Feuerbach writes; "Christ is the ideal of humanity become existent, the compendium of all moral and divine perfections to the exclusion of all that is negative; pure, heavenly, sinless man, the typical man, the Adam Kadmon; not regarded as the totality of the species, of mankind, but immediately as one individual, one person." Christ takes up in Himself the divine essential humanity and a particular historical existence and thus becomes a powerful symbol of deified humanity. Christ is the symbol of the consciousness of the species and the unique instance of particularized divine perfections. To say with the Apostle Paul that we are all one with Christ thus means that we have ascended to the love of the species or essential humanity. Every one who is able to make this movement is a Christian; in a sense, he becomes Christ Himself. Every man must strive to become his own Christ.

In the history of Christianity, trinitarian and Christological considerations became interrelated. In distilling the essence of Christianity Feuerbach seeks to unravel the mystery of the Trinity, and to make the doctrine of the Trinity, like the doctrine of Christ, relevant for man's understanding of himself in his natural existence. The Trinity is a symbol for man's consciousness of himself in his totality. It indicates the inseparability and interrelation of distinct qualities and powers in the human psyche. The traditional images of the triadic structure of mind, will, and love illuminate this basic point. God as essential humanity is mind expressed as self-consciousness. But mind exhibits a three-fold structure in that mind is at the same time the subject of self-consciousness, the object of self-consciousness, and the relation of knowing itself as object. A similar triadic structure becomes apparent in the examination of will and love. A God who does not know His own being and does not will His own acts is a God without consciousness, who is thus reduced to an absurdity. The Trinity is the divine self-consciousness expressing itself in both diversity and identity.

Revelation indicates the movement whereby the particular existing man has disclosed to him the nature of his essential humanity. Every revelation is simply the revelation of the species to its member. In revelation man's universal being and possible perfections are disclosed to him, and we see once more that theology can be explained through anthropology. "That which comes from God to man," Feuerbach writes, "comes to man only from *man in God,* that is, only from the ideal nature of man to the phenomenal man, from the species to the individual. . . . And so in revelation man goes out of himself, in order, by a circuitous path, to return to himself! Here we have a striking confirmation of the position that the secret of theology is nothing else than anthropology—the knowledge of God nothing else than a knowledge of man!"

Remaining consistent with his thesis that the essence of Christianity can be explained through anthropological categories, Feuerbach interprets the sacraments of baptism and the Eucharist in terms of their natural significance. Baptism is understood as a celebration of the physical healing power of water and of nature. Water is the purest of all liquids and thus it provides us with the most appropriate symbol for the divinity of nature. Because of this natural quality and significance, water is consecrated as the vehicle of the Holy Spirit. The Eucharist also testifies to the creative powers of nature. The significance of the bread and the wine resides in their natural efficacy. In no sense do the elements contain a mystical manifestation of supernatural grace. There is operative neither the transubstantiation nor the consubstantiation of supernatural theology. What is given in the sacrament is the *sensuous* bread and the *sensuous* wine, elements which symbolize the creative forces of nature by dint of which our physical existence is nourished and maintained. Thus the relevance of the sacraments for man's concrete existence is set forth, and Christianity is once again seen in the context of its anthropological intent.

THE TRANSIENT AND PERMANENT IN CHRISTIANITY

Author: Theodore Parker (1810-1860)
Type of work: Transcendentalist sermon
First published: 1841

Principal Ideas Advanced

The doctrines and forms in which Christianity is expressed in every age are transient.

The core of Christianity, which is equivalent to natural religion, is the permanent element.

The truths in the teachings of Jesus are attested not by his personal authority nor by the Scriptures but by intuition.

Theodore Parker's *The Transient and Permanent in Christianity,* delivered at the ordination of Charles Chauncy Shackford as minister of the

Hawes Place Church in Boston, May 19, 1841, established Parker as a leading proponent of transcendentalist views in American religion. This sermon reveals Parker's debt not only to Ralph Waldo Emerson, whose *Divinity School Address* at Harvard in 1838 had precipitated the transcendentalist controversy within the Unitarian movement, but also to the German proponents of higher criticism of the Bible.

Although the sermon appears to have created little stir among Parker's fellow Unitarians present for the occasion, several orthodox ministers in attendance published a summary of what they considered the more objectionable parts and demanded to know whether the Unitarians accepted or rejected such blasphemous sentiments. In the ensuing debate Parker reestablished the right of independent thought and speech in the Unitarian churches.

Parker begins his sermon with a tribute to the teachings of Jesus which, he says, have come down through the centuries despite the fact that Jesus did not write them down or found an institution to preserve them. Jesus entrusted them to the air in complete confidence that his words were for eternity. They have been translated into every tongue and have been the inspiration of countless men and women at all levels of society for eighteen centuries. The words of countless great men, though preserved in metal and stone and preserved by institutions, have died out; great kingdoms have risen and fallen; but the pure religion of Jesus has inspired a whole new civilization and the words of Jesus are as alive today as when he spoke them.

The pure religion taught by Jesus is fixed and certain, Parker claimed, and it grows more influential as men grow more wise. But this cannot be said of what men call Christianity. The Christianity preached, taught, and accepted by the people has taken on different forms in every place and time. Just as the forms which Christianity has assumed in past ages have changed and passed away, so will the forms it now assumes become outmoded. "Transient things form a great part of what is commonly taught as religion. An undue place has often been assigned to forms and doctrines, while too little stress has been laid on the divine life of the soul, love to God and love to man." Forms, no matter how beautiful or how useful, says Parker, are only the "accidents" of Christianity, not its "substance." The rationalizing Unitarians, for instance, have retained only two rites of the Christian church and these in very attenuated form. But it is possible that a future age may revive old forms or, indeed, invent new ones to suit its needs.

The doctrines of Christianity, says Parker, are just as changeable as its forms. Just as there is a "true system of nature," no matter how interpretations of nature may differ according to the power of observation of the individual, so there is "but one religion which is absolutely true," although man's understanding and interpretation of it continually changes. The doctrines of Christianity change from age to age and what is called heresy at one time is accepted as orthodox and infallible in another. At one time Arius is in the ascendant, at another Athanasius; some men are burned at the stake for affirming what other men are burned for denying.

Parker asserts in his sermon that inherited theological doctrines have come more from Judaism, heathenism, and philosophy than from "the principle and sentiment of Christianity." The doctrine of the Trinity, for example, is derived from philosophy rather than from religion and is so subtle that it cannot even be expressed.

Theological forms and doctrines are transient, here today, gone tomorrow. Only slowly and gradually is mankind by patient observation and reasoning working out a true view of nature, on the one hand, and of philosophy and theology on the other. Meanwhile, says Parker—making a point at the heart of transcendentalism— "the great truths of morality and religion, the deep sentiment of love to man and love to God, are perceived intuitively, and by instinct, as it were. . . ."

The transitoriness of doctrines can be illustrated by the way the Old and New Testaments have been treated over the centuries. There was a time when men were burned for holding to a scientific principle which conflicted with some part of the Old Testament. The Old Testament was considered to be miraculously inspired—infallible. Men were expected to believe that the legends of the Old Testament were literally true, that God spoke in human words, violated His own laws, and displayed all manner of fickleness. "Even now he is deemed an infidel, if not by implication an atheist, whose reverence for the Most High forbids him to believe that God commanded Abraham to sacrifice his son, a thought at which the flesh creeps with horror; to believe it solely on the authority of an oriental story, written down nobody knows when or by whom, or for what purpose; which may be a poem, but cannot be the record of a fact, unless God is the author of confusion and a lie."

The Old Testament has not always been held in idolatry, says Parker. Jesus and Paul did not hold it so, and later Christian teachers have differed widely in their interpretations of the content of those books. Modern criticism, indeed, is revealing that the Old Testament books are often made up of materials from different authors and times and that the authors, as pious as many of them were, often were mistaken in their claims and predictions.

Further displaying his knowledge of developments in higher criticism, Parker points out that in much the same way the New Testament has been held to be the work of infallible writers. This has been true despite the fact that there are obvious differences between, for example, the Gospels of Luke and John, and that Paul and Peter are revealed as having had serious disagreements. Furthermore, the New Testament contains "accounts which shock the moral sense and revolt the reason, and tend to place Jesus in the same series with Hercules, and Apollonius of Tyana. . . ." Yet these books of the New Testament which were brought together by "caprice or accident" are insisted on as "the infallible word of God, the only certain rule of religious faith and practice." But, Parker points out, the Bible provides no foundation for this attitude; the authors of the various books reveal themselves as quite fallible men. In truth, attitudes toward the Bible continually change.

Another illustration given by Parker of the "transitoriness of doctrines" has to do with interpretations of the nature and authority of Christ. Some regard Christ as the infinite God; some believe him to be a combination of God and man; others look on him as a man like ourselves who sets an example of what we may be. Despite the existence of various interpretations, it is said that the truth of Christianity rests on the personal authority of Christ. But Parker does not see why a religious truth should rest on the authority of him who utters it any more than a scientific truth should depend on the person who establishes it. The truths of Christianity do not depend on the personal authority of Jesus any more than "the axioms of geometry rest on the personal authority of Euclid and Archimedes. The authority of Jesus, as of all teachers, one would naturally think, must rest on the truth of his words, and not their truth on his authority."

But these questions concerning the origin and form of the Bible and the nature and authority of Christ are not religious questions, says Parker, but theological. They are accidentals, having nothing to do with the truth of Christianity. For Parker, the truth of Christianity, which he, in effect, identified with absolute, natural religion, does not depend on Jesus. Parker is willing to go so far as to state that if Jesus had taught at Athens rather than at Jerusalem, if he had performed no miracles, if he had never been thought to be anything but human, if the Old Testament had perished at his birth, Christianity still would be true. Parker points out that the present views regarding the Bible are changing under the impact of higher criticism. But this does not matter really, for this is a question which concerns theology rather than Christianity. The truth of Christianity is not dependent on the Bible nor on the personal authority of Jesus. Jesus was, says Parker echoing Emerson, the "organ through which the infinite spoke."

Next Parker carries his argument to its logical extreme. He says that if it could be shown (but he does not believe it can be) that Jesus never lived —that the Gospels are fabrications— none of the truth of Christianity would be lost. Much of the beauty and character of the Christian religion would be lost, certainly, but not the truth. Again stressing the intuitive path to religious knowledge, Parker says that Christianity is "true, like the axioms of geometry, because it is true, and is to be tried by the oracle God places in the breast. If it rest on the personal authority of Jesus alone, then there is no certainty of its truth if he were mistaken in the smallest matter, as some Christians have thought he was in predicting his second coming."

The Bible, according to Parker, is held in idolatry. It is treated as a fetish. But he believes the time will come when bibliolatry will give way before the recognition of what the Bible really is. Then its "puerile conceptions of God" will be seen as fictions and its beauty and depth of true piety will be appreciated. In poetic terms, Parker pays tribute to the Bible and its contributions to the lives of men through the ages.

The time also will come, he says, when error will be swept away and Christ will be seen for what he really is. "Then we shall see and love the divine life that he lived." Then men will see him as a brother, a son of God as they are sons of God. But if we mistakenly make a god of him, as did the early Christians, his significance for the life of man disappears. "His virtue has no merit, his love no feeling, his cross no burden, his agony no pain. His death is an illusion, his resurrection but a show."

Doctrines and forms, then, are transient. Opinions change in every age so that men of one age cannot truly appreciate the faith or the discords of another. "The contest about transubstantiation, and the immaculate purity of the Hebrew and Greek texts of the scriptures, was waged with a bitterness unequalled in these days. The Protestant smiles at one, the Catholic at the other, and men of sense wonder at both." Indeed, the time will come when our doctrines will be smiled at and our present theological controversies abhorred.

But while these great changes take place true Christianity—by which Parker means "absolute, pure religion" —remains the same from generation to generation. Its purpose is to unite men with God as Christ was united to Him in a life of obedience and goodness. But Parker is careful to add that it is a state of perfect freedom. Conformity is not demanded of men. Men should think uprightly but not necessarily alike. Unlike certain Christian groups, true Christianity does not insist on conformity but respects "individual genius and character."

Real Christianity, says Parker, encourages us to outgrow forms and systems of doctrines so that we can approach closer to truth; it makes us realize that the Bible is servant, not master; it makes us appreciate holy words of men of old, but it also makes us realize, more importantly, that God speaks to us through conscience, reason, and faith; it makes us realize that Jesus was a man whose sonship was won by faithful obedience to God and who by his teachings and the beauty of his dife helps us through life to within the gates of Heaven; it encourages us to create the Kingdom of God on earth in preparation for our entrance to the Kingdom on high.

Old forms, reiterates Parker, give way to new to keep up with changing times and each new form will capture some of the truth, but not the whole. There are always some who do not see the permanent element in religion and cling to transient things while suspecting and denouncing those who would do away with theological error. As always, so now, there is a clash between those who see through the transient forms to the permanent and those who do not. "The question puts itself to each man, 'Will you cling to what is perishing, or embrace what is eternal?' This question each must answer for himself."

CONCLUDING UNSCIENTIFIC POSTSCRIPT

Author: Søren Kierkegaard (1813-1855)
Type of work: Existential philosophy of religion
First published: 1846

Principal Ideas Advanced

Christianity proposes to base eternal salvation upon the temporal event of God's having become man, but this event lies outside the scope of historiography and every other kind of objective knowledge.

The absolute paradox of the God-man can be appropriated only in the passionate subjective inwardness of faith, which has the character of an infinite leap.

Since subjectivity is the truth and the purpose of individual existence, the highest accentuation of subjectivity answers and fulfills existence.

General religiousness, or the religion of immanence, develops existential pathos through resignation, suffering, and guilt; but, presupposing this pathos, Christian faith maximally accentuates subjective existence through relationship to the historical God-man.

Concluding Unscientific Postscript is the principal philosophical work of a thinker often named as the founder of existentialism. He could with equal accuracy be described as the greatest modern philosopher of *faith*—specifically of the Christian faith in the God-man, Jesus Christ. Kierkegaard was born and spent his life in Copenhagen where, though he never entered the ministry, he finished the course of theological study in 1840. Through wide reading he responded avidly to an immense range of aesthetic and intellectual stimuli, but in philosophy his leading ideas were especially conditioned by a preoccupation with and reaction against the system of G. W. F. Hegel (1770-1831). An exceedingly prolific writer, Kierkegaard brought forth much of his earlier authorship, up through the *Postscript,* under pseudonyms representing different stances within his own turmoil and development. The style is eminently personal. Seeking at all cost not to become a "paragraph in the system" (of Hegel), he aims through irony, humor, and "indirect communication" to evoke subjectivity, to touch the reader's real existence. Severely critical of inauthentic tendencies which he discerned in the established Church, Kierkegaard was driven in the years just preceding his early death to the so-called *Attack upon Christendom.* This series of polemical articles registers the tragic denouement of one of the most passionate spirits in all literature. Kierkegaard collided violently with the modern age—and with all inauthenticity. But his collision was in the name and for the sake of Christ.

The *Postscript* received its title from the fact that it appeared as a sequel to a book about one-sixth its size which had been published two years previously (in 1844). In the earlier work, *Philosophical Fragments,* "the problem posed and formulated . . . , but without pretense of solving it, was as follows: *Is an historical point of departure possible for an eternal consciousness; . . . is it possible to base an eternal happiness upon historical knowledge?*" Writing under the pseudonym Johannes Climacus, Kierkegaard had undertaken to analyze the problem purely as a dialectician and not as a believing Christian. In fact, the *Fragments* is an outcome of the attitude of treating the problem simply in itself, without regard for the "historical costume" of Christianity—although it had been acknowledged that "Christianity is the only historical phenomenon which in spite of the historical, nay, precisely by means of it, has offered itself to the individual as a point of departure for his eternal consciousness. . . ." Against this backdrop the *Postscript* comes forward, in part, as the supplying of the historical costume, this being conceived as an inquiry into the "objective problem" of Christianity. But, Kierkegaard insists, the real difficulty lies in the individual's relationship to Christianity. Thus the bulk of the *Postscript* is devoted, not simply to the costume, but to a new dialectical assault on the *subjective* problem: "How may I, Johannes Climacus, participate in the happiness promised by Christianity?"

In the last quarter of the eighteenth century the problematic nature of the historical element in Christian faith had been expressed in the dictum of the German philosopher G. E. Lessing (1729-81): "Accidental historical truths can never become the proof of necessary truths of reason." Lessing had maintained that the historical nature of the object of faith created an "ugly wide ditch," requiring a "leap" of which he was incapable. In a crucial respect the subsequent movements of theological construction had all sought to resolve, or to avoid, the problem thus posed. Hegelianism in particular, in its theological aspects, circumvented Lessing's problem by representing the historical, in its conceptually essential meaning, as a necessary truth of reason, or, in other words, as logically deducible. Thus to a thinking man, to whom mere faith would not suffice, no leap would be required after all. The essence of Christian truth, distilled from a mythical literalism, could be objectively demonstrated.

To Kierkegaard this approach seemed both comically and tragically wrongheaded. That men under the spell of an all-encompassing objectivity, forgetting the predicament of their individual sin and guilt, could propose to resolve the problems of life in pure theory, is comical, he comments. But it is also tragic, for the serious business of living is "the task of becoming subjective." Lessing had been right, Kierkegaard writes; the historical cannot become the proof for the necessary and eternal. A "leap" is precisely what is required. God alone can grant the condition for the leap. The subjective appropriation of the condition, or, what comes to the same thing, the leap itself, is *faith*. The Hegelians talk of going beyond mere faith. But has faith become so easy for everyone? Kierkegaard asks. Is it the elementary, childlike stage of truth, beyond which a mature speculative reason can now move? On the contrary, from the human point of view faith is infinitely difficult. It presents an insuperable obstacle to the understanding, whose role is not to go beyond faith, but to discern and hold fast the obstacle which serves as the occasion of faith.

Kierkegaard is at pains to clarify that he means specifically the Christian faith in the historical God-man. Such an object of faith presents what is really a double obstacle to the understanding. In the first instance, the historical aspect posits a breach which no objective research can span, since research at best yields only approximate results; whereas, for an infinite concern an approximation is still infinitely deficient. In the second instance, the affirmation that the Eternal has entered time is rationally absurd, the "absolute paradox." But this is precisely what differentiates Christian faith in relation to immanental religiousness, or "religiousness A," as Kierkegaard calls it. For "religiousness A" God is, as it were, everywhere in general, but nowhere in particular. Now this kind of God-consciousness, producing the pathos of resignation, suffering, and guilt (wherein the individual knows of God, but cannot relate decisively to God), is a necessary preamble to the Christian faith. But the peculiar nature of the Christian object of faith, the historical God-man, introduces a new level, the "paradoxically dialectic," or "religiousness B." Here, with the thought of an eternally decisive relationship to an indemonstrable and logically absurd event in time, it becomes meaningful to speak of faith. "For the absurd is the object of faith, and the only object that can be believed." That is to say, any other object would in some measure be accessible to objective *knowledge*. But, Kierkegaard writes, "without risk there is no faith, and the greater the risk the greater the faith. . . ." Not only of historiography, but of all empirical and speculative proofs, it must be said that "results are only rubbish. . . ."

By thus embracing Lessing's dilemma, Kierkegaard achieves a position from which some of modern Christianity's most troublesome difficulties can be constructively met. In the first place, as the *Philosophical Fragments* had spelled out, the problem of contemporaneity with the Christ event is resolved by shifting attention from the concrete *whatness* to the paradoxical *thatness* of the event. The original disciples were existentially no closer to the paradoxical object of faith than we are. For the Incarnation as such can neither be seen nor comprehended; and, as it demands of us an infinite leap, so it demanded no less of those who walked with Jesus in the flesh. By the same token, the *radical demand for faith* eclipses any difference, not only between the first century and the nineteenth, but between all sorts and conditions of men. The erudite and clever man has no advantage over the simple, since faith lays an unconditional and immeasurable claim upon all alike. This means, too, that the possibly debilitating effect of modern historical skepticism upon faith is forestalled. What historiography could or could not recover is no longer relevant, since the fulcrum of faith is not Jesus as an object of research but the witness to the Christ as the "absolute paradox" with respect to which all matters of concrete detail are incommensurable. In the decision of faith the *historicity* of Christ is posited. Kierkegaard's view hinges upon this. But no empirical, objective data can influence the decision one way or the other. Thus freed from hampering distractions, the issue of faith can assume again its full depth and seriousness. This, really, is Kierkegaard's leading motive: to restore to faith its authentic gravity. Made to appear irrelevant and contemptible by purveyors of intellectual progress, Christian faith (strictly *as* faith) was being left to recede into the backwaters of modern culture. Kierkegaard will bring it forward again—*as* faith, not as something "beyond" faith—as still the highest and most inexhaustible possibility that can confront an existing individual.

Hence the *Postscript* is a treatise in Christian apologetics, but the kind of apology it develops is inverse and dialectical. Instead of assembling objective proofs of Christian doctrine, it seeks to expose, indirectly and evocatively, the *congruency* between faith in Christ and human existence. It is in this enterprise that Kierkegaard becomes the author of the existential philosophy. The evolvement of his argument has two dimensions. On the one hand, *negatively,* he seeks to show that, contrary to Hegelian idealism, the rational is not the real; essence is not identical with existence. Real existence is a matter of radical individuality in anxiety, suffering, and despair; and philosophy, if it is not to become comical, must reckon with these categories. Ethics subsumes the individual under the universal, and immanental religiousness seeks God in the universal. But ethics and all forms of immanence founder decisively on the problem of *guilt.* Thus the individual is driven, by the dialectic of existence itself, to the alternative of guilty despair *or* the leap of faith which establishes a relationship to God in time (the God-man). This is the one dimension of the argument. On the other hand, *positively,* Kierkegaard sets forth a world view in which the development of maximal passionate inwardness is regarded as the aim and fulfillment of life in time. Again in opposition to Hegelianism, stress falls upon the individual subject in his responsible *freedom.* Inwardness is heightened by the existential pathos which culminates in guilt. But the highest conceivable accentuation of subjective inwardness is occasioned by faith in the absolute paradox, by a decisive personal relationship to God's act in time. This commitment of faith is not something accomplished and thereafter simply possessed. It requires the constant engagement of one's whole existence; and it strains one's powers to their uttermost—including, be it noted, the powers of the understanding. Kierkegaard will not allow Christ to be had "in an aesthetical hodgepodge, just as though Christianity were wholesome fodder for simpletons because it cannot be thought, and as though the characteristic that it cannot be thought were not precisely the hardest to hold onto . . . especially for clever pates."

Now since *"an objective uncertainty held fast in an appropriation-process of the most passionate inwardness is the truth,* the highest truth attainable for an *existing* individual," Christian faith provides eminently the conditions of truth. Such faith not only redeems from guilt; it fulfills the purpose of creation. But this congruency is not one that can be objectively exhibited; it too requires, and is posited by, the act of decision which faith is. Faith is quite consistent with itself, in that it remains empty until it is subjectively appropriated.

There is much, especially by way of personal reference on Kierkegaard's part, that cannot even be mentioned in a brief account of the *Postscript.* The inimitable style and method of approach cannot be conveyed at second hand. The book stands as one of the great instances of all time of faith seeking understanding and *vice versa*—and of the interplay between faith and understanding. No source has been more determinative for the contemporary Protestant understanding of the relations between faith and reason, with the possible exception of Immanuel Kant (1724-1804). Kant, too, was a philosopher of faith, for whom reason exhibited the essential human function of faith. By comparison with Kant, Kierkegaard's faith stands out as paradoxical, and as specifically the faith in the historical Incarnation.

CHRISTIAN DISCOURSES

Author: Søren Kierkegaard (1813-1855)
Type of work: Homilies
First published: 1848

Principal Ideas Advanced

Because of his ability to take thought for the morrow, man is tormented by anxiety.

Through affliction, he learns the hopelessness of finding joy in temporality, and he may learn to rejoice in the hope of eternity.

Merely nominal Christians fall under the condemnation of even those passages of Scripture in which they are accustomed to take comfort.

Only those who have personally committed themselves to Christ share in the hope of the Gospel.

Alongside his widely-known pseudonymous works, Søren Kierkegaard published in his own name an impressive list of religious books, which he called "edifying discourses." *Christian Discourses* stands in this series. Because he was never ordained, although he had received theological training, Kierkegaard scrupulously refrained from calling his writings "sermons"; and, only toward the end of his life, as his personal faith became more firmly established, did he venture to designate them "Christian."

Christian Discourses is a large volume, comprising four parts which might have been published as separate books, inasmuch as each part was conceived separately and developed along distinctive lines. It was a sound insight, however, which led Kierkegaard to bring them under one cover; for, like the movements of a symphony, the parts offset and complement one another.

The first set of discourses, entitled "The Anxieties of the Heathen," is based on the well-known text from the Sermon on the Mount, in which Jesus exhorts His followers not to give thought to food and clothing, to their standing among men, or to the uncertainties of the future, "for after all these things do the heathen seek." Presumably, says Kierkegaard, one could determine what the anxieties of the heathen are by journeying to pagan lands. Another way would be to journey to a Christian land ("But what am I saying?" interposes the author;

"we are in fact living in a Christian land!") and note what anxieties are absent there. But the Gospel uses neither of these ways. Instead it points to the birds of the air and the lilies of the field, which are neither heathen nor Christian, and lets them answer the question. These creatures, although they have needs comparable to those of the heathen, do not have the anxieties of the heathen. Poor by any man's standards, they do not know the anxiety of poverty as the heathen do. On the other hand, because they do not pray for their daily bread, and hence do not know that God is their Father, they are not rich in the way Christians are. Birds are merely carefree.

Kierkegaard explains that it is *thought* which makes the difference. The birds take no thought, and therefore they do not know anxiety. The heathen supposes that taking thought is the way to overcome poverty, and thus he is burdened with the care of poverty. The Christian also takes thought, but not as the heathen do; his care is to relearn the ignorance of the birds and flowers, and so be freed from care. "For it requires no art to be ignorant," writes Kierkegaard, "but to *become* ignorant, and by becoming so, to be ignorant, that is the art. To this extent the Christian is different from the bird, for the bird *is* ignorant, but the Christian becomes ignorant."

Poverty, Kierkegaard points out, is not the real root of the heathen's anxiety. Man likes to think that his concern is the straightforward one of obtaining subsistence for himself and his family; but actually his chosen role of breadwinner is a means to bolstering up his ego, of vindicating his importance, and of making a place for himself in the eyes of others. Meanwhile, he has no thoughts of God, and, in effect, he denies that he is God's creature.

So it is with all the anxieties of the heathen. The rich heathen is anxious in his abundance, and the man of rank is anxious in his pride. Unable to live for today, as the Christian does, he torments himself about tomorrow. "Tomorrow I shall perhaps hunger, even if I did not today; tomorrow a thief will perhaps steal my riches, or slander my honor, corruption my beauty, the envy of fate my good fortune—tomorrow, tomorrow!" The thought would drive him to madness if he did not find ways of busying himself in order not to think at all. At heart convinced that all the higher things of life are vanity, he manages to go on living, but in a dispirited fashion, having lost not merely God but his own self as well.

In the second set of discourses, Kierkegaard turns from the anxieties of the unbeliever to the joys of the believer. Taking as his text the saying of Paul: "We glory in tribulations also . . . ," he entitles this part of his discourses, "Joyful Notes in the Strife of Suffering." His theme is the contrast between man's temporality and God's eternity. The hope of youth, Kierkegaard says, lies in temporally finding the temporal; for example, the love of one's beloved. Suffering bereaves the youth of this hope as a storm strips the blossoms from a cherry tree. But suffering may be the occasion for a new hope to stir within the human breast, the hope of eternity: "O thou sufferer, whatsoever thou hast lost, thou hast lost only something temporal, it is impossible to *lose* anything else; and whatsoever thou hast lost, there is something to be gained, the eternal, which thou dost gain eternally."

Following the Apostle, Kierkegaard grounds the hope of eternity in God's fathomless love. Were it not, says Kierkegaard, for the love of God, man in his freedom would never exist. Were God merely omnipotent, man would be nothing, for omnipotence would crush him. "But God who creates out of nothing, who almightily takes from nothing and says, 'Be,' lovingly adjoins, 'Be something even in apposition to me.' Marvellous love, even His omnipotence is under the sway of love!" Hence, that "misfortune is good fortune" which tears our affection from this world and fixes it on God.

The third group of discourses is entitled "Thoughts which Wound from Behind—for Edification." From Kierkegaard's *Journal,* we learn that this was the first part of *Christian Discourses* to take shape in his mind. It has no unifying theme, but each discourse is based on some Scriptural passage with which Christians have come to feel comfortable, and gives the passage an uncomfortable application.

The Scripture says, for example, "Now is our salvation nearer than when we became believers." "When," Kierkegaard asks, "didst thou become a believer? . . . Test thyself therefore by means of this saying. It is a blessed comfort to dare to know that one's salvation is nearer than when one became a believer—but surely it is true that one must be certain one has become a believer. This saying therefore may serve to comfort, but also it may as it were come upon one from behind."

Again, the Scripture says, "The resurrection of the dead is at hand, of the just and of the unjust." People are eager for any kind of information about immortality, and thus they ask whether there really is a life beyond the grave, whether it is personal, whether people will recognize one another, and whether one will remember only his happy moments. Men regard these as serious questions. But what about the little matter of the just and the unjust? "Immortality is not a life indefinitely prolonged," says Kierkegaard; "but immortality is the eternal separation between the just and the unjust." The Scripture, Kierkegaard says, is as reassuring as it can possibly be to those who desire immortality: "Thou art immortal, whether thou wilt or no." One cannot ask for greater assurance—unless this "whether thou wilt or no" should prove disquieting!

The first three parts of *Christian Discourses* abound in flashes of that irony for which Kierkegaard is famous. An important aspect of Kierkegaard's mission, as he understood it, was to protest against the pseudo-Christianity of official Christendom. The fourth part, however, entitled "Discourses at the Communion on Fridays," is in an entirely different tone. Kierkegaard remarked, in his *Journal,* that the contrast between the third and fourth parts of *Christian Discourses* "is as sharp as possible and as searching: the one is like a commemoration of the Cleansing of the Temple—and then the quiet and most heartfelt of all acts of worship: a communion on Fridays."

The addresses of this group (two of which were delivered by Kierkegaard before a sprinkling of worshipers in the Cathedral on Fridays, with the noises of commerce dimly audible in the background) are faithful to the purpose of a communion meditation, and direct the hearers' thoughts to Christ memorialized on the altar. Of the two which he delivered, one is an application of the text, "Come unto Me"; the other, of the text, "My sheep hear my voice, and I know them, and they follow me." All the addresses emphasize the strictly personal character of the relation between the believer and Christ. Like the sun, Christ shines on all men; but, unlike the sun, Christ makes a distinction among those on whom He shines. Not all men are known of Christ, nor do all who come to the altar receive Him. "For physically," says Kierkegaard, "one can point to the altar and say, 'Behold, there it is,' but, spiritually understood, the altar is *there* only if thou art known by Him."

Those who have studied the life of Kierkegaard remember that Holy Week, 1849, marked a crisis in this author's spiritual development, and that after that time he felt himself free to speak more directly about Christianity than he had before. *Christian Discourses* barely antedates this last of Kierkegaard's conversions ("metamorphoses," he called them), but in a sense also anticipates it.

CHRISTIAN DOGMATICS

Author: Hans Lassen Martensen (1808-1884)
Type of work: Dogmatic theology
First published: 1849

Principal Ideas Advanced

Dogmatic theology is an integral part of the Christian Church; a confessing Church cannot exist without doctrines and dogmas.

Dogma is a "truth of faith," and it receives its authority from the revelation of God witnessed to in the Holy Scriptures.

The essence of the Christian faith is Jesus Christ, who is the founder of the Christian religion as well as the redeemer of the human race.

The miracle of the Incarnation influences man by creating a new spirit within him, but at the same time the Incarnation is a cosmic event, affecting the entire history of the universe.

The Apostolic Church contained Christianity in its genuine and authentic form; by means of a reliable tradition this has been transmitted intact to the contemporary Church.

Hans Lassen Martensen was professor of theology at the University of Copenhagen, Denmark, as well as Bishop of the Danish State (Lutheran) Church. He was able, more than any of his contemporaries, to relate the dominant German theology in Europe to the theology of his native Denmark. His work *Christian Dogmatics* (which had as its subtitle in the British edition, *A Compendium of the Doctrines of Christianity*), published first in 1849, was considered to be the normative expression for Christian theology and for "true Christianity" in nineteenth century Denmark.

Martensen looked upon theology as an integral part of the life of the Church. The theological task of the Church is to present, in a systematic way, the truths of the Christian faith. Martensen writes in the Introduction to *Christian Dogmatics,* "Dogmatic theology treats of the doctrines of the Christian faith held by the community of believers, in other words, by the Church. A confessing and witnessing Church cannot be conceived to exist without a definite sum of doctrines or *dogmas.* A dogma is not a *doxa,* not a subjective, human opinion, not an indefinite, vague notion; nor is it a mere truth of reason, whose universal validity can be made clear with mathematical or logical certainty: it is a truth of *faith,* derived from the authority of the word and revelation of God;—a positive truth, therefore, positive not merely by virtue of the positiveness with which it is laid down, but also by virtue of the authority with which it is sealed. Dogmatics is the science which presents and proves the Christian doctrines, regarded as forming a connected system."

The dogmatic theologian attempts to attain an intelligent faith, but always from within the Christian Church. This task, however, is never inseparable from a personal experience of Christian truth. Dogmatics begins not with doubt or speculation, but with the fullness and certainty of the Christian faith. Martensen wrote that "Dogmatics serves, therefore, not to rescue faith in the time of its exigency, but to glorify it. . . ."

Hans Lassen Martensen was dependent philosophically upon Georg Wilhelm Friedrich Hegel (1770-1831), the great German idealist. In Hegel's system, everything in history is considered to be necessary and significant. Nothing can be considered accidental or indifferent. The Idea, the Absolute, unfolds itself in history according to its own laws, with the result that, according to Hegel, every event in the "dialectical" development of history is free. Nothing external can intervene and disrupt the basic laws of historical development. Within Hegel's philosophical system, it is quite clear that revelation yields no truth which cannot be attained by speculative thought. Religion, for Hegel, represents an imperfect *representational* form of knowledge, whereas speculative thought (speculative idealism) represents a higher, perfect, *conceptual* form. Revelation, therefore, is considered to be a necessary historical event, a consequence of the self-unfolding of the Absolute in a particular time and place. It brings, however, no new truth with itself. For Hegel, there is *no* inherent contradiction between reason and revelation. The highest form of religion, Christianity, and the highest form of philosophy, speculative idealism, have really the same content. They vary solely in terms of the different forms they assume.

On the basis of this position, a number of Hegel's followers, David F. Strauss (1808-1874) (author of *The Life of Jesus*) and Ludwig Feuerbach (1804-1872) (author of *The Essence of Christianity*) among them, drew the obvious conclusions and maintained a skeptical attitude toward New Testament miracles and revelation. Martensen, who was Hegelianism's foremost representative in Denmark, was aware that within Hegel's system there could be no contradiction between reason and revelation, between the philosophy of idealism and the Christian faith. Martensen believed, however, that he could "go further" than Hegel by reconciling Hegel's philosophy with the orthodox New Testament faith.

The Christian faith, for Martensen, is only one aspect of the comprehensive world-view of the Christian. Reason, as well as imagination, is the organ of religious perception. No religion, therefore, and the Christian faith in particular, could succeed as a historical religion without developing a comprehensive and ideal view of the universe, "an imaginative view by which the invisible is blended with the visible," as Martensen writes.

Revelation is defined, therefore, as God's communication of Himself to His creatures. This revelation is direct and unambiguous because it is related to the spirit within man. In this way, the revelation is apprehended by a free, conscious, historical being. Revelation and history, therefore, are never to be separated. Martensen writes, "If we may, in truth, speak of a sacred, divine revelation, then there must be a history within history, there must be within profane history a *sacred history,* in which God reveals Himself as God; a history in which is revealed the sacred design of the world as such, in which the word of God so encases itself in the word of man that the latter becomes the pure organ for the former, and in which the acts of God are so involved in the acts of men that the latter become a perfectly transparent medium through which the former may be seen." Sacred history is seen to be the history of election, a deliberate selection of a people within profane history. First Israel is elected, and then Christ, who is the fulfillment of election.

The essence of Christianity, for Martensen, is Christ Himself. Christ is not only the historic founder of the Christian religion, but also the redeemer of the human race. The Incarnation is the fundamental miracle of Christianity, but also of world history. His presence in history is miraculous not simply because Christ is a moral and religious genius, but rather because Christ initiates a cosmic change in the universe. Christ begins a new development in the conscious life of man. The human race in its entirety receives a new spirit because of the revelation of Christ. Martensen emphasized, however, that the Incarnation which introduces this new spirit to man is the same event which created the Christian Church.

Furthermore, the Christian faith does not disturb the forces and powers resident in nature. Rather, the revelation of Christ and the Kingdom of Christ "pronounces the last potency of the work of creation." The new creation in Christ does not destroy nature, but anticipates a new nature. A new system of laws appears, a system which exhibits the harmony of the laws of nature and freedom. The present creation, Martensen insisted, which shows an "unappeased strife" between spirit and nature, is but a transitional period. According to Martensen, ". . . the point of unity between the natural and the supernatural lies in the teleological design of nature to subserve the kingdom of God, and its consequent *susceptibility* to, its *capacity of being moulded* by, the supernatural, creative activity. Nature does not contradict the notion of a creation; and it is in miracles that the dependence of nature on a free Creator becomes perfectly evident."

Christian dogmatics must be Biblical as well as confessional. The Bible itself, Martensen maintained, points to a *confessing* Church. In Martensen's lengthy discussion of the difference between Protestantism (the Evangelical Church) and Roman Catholicism, it is in the interpretation of the Holy Scriptures that the major point of controversy can be found. The Protestant looks at the Church and claims (as does the Roman Catholic) that the Spirit of the Lord is within the Church and is leading it to truth. But the perfect union of the Spirit and man, which is called Inspiration, and which constitutes the essence of the apostolate (that is, which assures the truth of the Christian Church), is assigned by the Protestant to the beginning of the Church. The Roman Catholic, on the other hand, holds to a living apostolate in the Church which perpetuates itself throughout all time. The Protestant admits the relative merit of tradition, but he insists, says Martensen, that the Holy Scriptures of the New Testament are the "only perfect, authentic and absolutely canonical expression of the original fulness of the apostolic spirit."

For this reason, the Apostolic Church contained Christianity in its genuine form. But Martensen believed that this authentic original form of the Christian faith had been transmitted to the present generation by means of a reliable tradition. The Reformers, particularly Luther, Martensen believed, saw this fact very clearly. The only perfect, trustworthy form of Apostolic tradition is found in the Holy Scriptures. But the tradition is transmitted in an authentic way only when it is controlled by the Holy Scriptures. Tradition is adequate only when it can be criticized on the basis of the Holy Scriptures. It is for this reason that the Lutheran Reformation was a Reformation which reasserted the primacy and authority of the Holy Scriptures for the Church.

The Lutheran Reformers took a positive attitude toward dogma and adopted the ecumenical "symbols," the Apostolic, Nicaean, and the Athanasian creeds, as the purest expression of the dogmatic tradition. Scripture and dogmatic tradition were *not* separated by the Reformers, but were simply put in their proper relation to each other. The formal principle of the Protestant Evangelical tradition is, therefore, the Holy Scriptures, in their indissoluble connection with the confessing Church. The external canon of Christianity, that which fixes something as normative or authoritative, whether Scripture or the Church itself, points directly to the internal canon, the regenerated Christian mind. It is here, in the Christian mind, that the Spirit of God witnesses with the spirit of man. Martensen maintained that "Only to that mind in which Christianity, in which the spirit of the Scriptures and of the church, is present as an inner principle of life, do the Scriptures and tradition unfold their contents; without this internal canon they remain unintelligible."

For Martensen, the Christian is governed by two principles, the subjective and the objective, the personal and the historical. Luther's consciousness of the "freedom of the Christian man" was the confidence that faith possessed the Spirit which leads to truth, as well as the conviction that the revelation of God in Christ was extended within the Christian Church.

Martensen's *Christian Dogmatics* is therefore based upon the Holy Scriptures, and it represents an attempt to construct a Biblically-oriented foundation for the Christian faith. The doctrines of the Church which Martensen dealt with and criticized were all related to their Biblical origins. The ecumenical symbols of the Christian Church were employed as well, in order, as Martensen said, "to hold to that type of sound doctrine which is therein contained." In this way, Martensen was convinced that he was preserving an association with the Apostolic Church. He believed, too, that the creeds of the Lutheran Church, in particular the Augsburg Confession, could be employed in order to provide "sound doctrine" for the contemporary Church.

Søren Kierkegaard (1813-1855), the existentialist philosopher-theologian, was extremely critical of Martensen (and Hegel) because he felt that there was an absolute contrast between philosophical idealism (Greek, Platonic, Hegelian) and New Testament Christianity. He interpreted revelation as the moment in which the divine comes into the human; that is, when the Eternal and the temporal meet. Revelation takes on the characteristics of something unanticipated and is thereby necessarily paradoxical. The only possible response to the revelation of God in Christ is one of faith, a "condition" which is given by God himself. Christianity is, for Søren Kierkegaard, the truth of revelation, which is given at a particular time (the moment of revelation) and in a particular form (the Incarnation). This revelation is *incompatible* with the dialectic method of speculative idealism. Idealism and Christianity are absolutely irreconcilable, Kierkegaard asserted. Reason cannot understand the revelation of God in Christ. Thought, Kierkegaard insisted, meets the unthinkable, the miraculous, the *Miracle*. The event of God in Christ transcends all of the categories of human reason and understanding.

Kierkegaard looked upon the idealism of Hegel as asserting that human beings possess the truth of salvation, that they are in immediate relationship to God, against which Christianity asserted that human beings do not possess saving truth. This is a contradiction which can never be reconciled, and Kierkegaard criticized Martensen for believing that he could create a synthesis of idealism and Christianity.

GOD IN CHRIST

Author: Horace Bushnell (1802-1876)
Type of work: Liberal theology
First published: 1849

Principal Ideas Advanced

Language is by nature symbolic and imprecise and must be used in a non-literal fashion.

The doctrine of the Trinity is not a description of God's ultimate being, but only of the modes of God's revelation to man.

The atoning work of Christ is not a "satisfaction" made to God, but a concrete expression of God's forgiving love.

A revival of religion can occur only when doctrinal differences are minimized and when tolerance and charity are shown in theological disputes.

Horace Bushnell lived the major portion of his life in New England and served for twenty-six years as pastor of the North Church (Congregational) in Hartford, Connecticut. Because of his formal education at Yale (Class of 1827) and his vocation as a minister, he was thoroughly acquainted with the theological issues of the day. He stood at the juncture of American theology when Calvinism had lost its great spokesmen, and the defenders of Unitarianism and transcendentalism occupied the center of the stage. His early training under Nathaniel William Taylor (1786-1858), Professor of Divinity at Yale College, made him conscious of the need to mediate between Calvinism and the increasingly popular "liberal" theology.

In 1848, fifteen years after he had accepted the pastorate of the North Church, Bushnell was invited to speak at the major centers of theological education in New England: Harvard, Yale, and Andover. The titles of the addresses he gave in 1848 and which are included in *God in Christ* are, "Concio Ad Clerum: A Discourse on the Divinity of Christ" (Yale), "A Discourse on the Atonement" (Harvard), and "A Discourse on Dogma and Spirit; or the True Reviving of Religion" (Andover). To supplement these three essays, Bushnell prepared, in 1849, a "Preliminary Dissertation on the Nature of Language, as Related to Thought and Spirit," which he included as the prefatory treatise in the collection of his essays. The four discourses make possible an appreciation of the distinctive contribution of this New England theologian to American theology; his later work was an elaboration of the theories developed in this one volume.

The nature of theological language was a central problem for Bushnell. The churches had become accustomed to tedious and arid theological controversy; the religious vocabulary of the past was no longer useful. He sought an understanding of language which would discourage literalism and irrelevance.

The theme of the essay was the proposition that infinite ideas cannot be contained in finite words. Language is more "an instrument of suggestion, than of "absolute conveyance for thought, since it acts suggestively, through symbols held up in the words, which symbols and words are never exact measures of any truth. . . ." Precise theological formulations are impossible; words are only symbolic. "Words of thought or spirit are not only inexact in their significance, never measuring the truth or giving its precise equivalent, but they always affirm something which is false, or contrary to the truth intended." To be sure, "language . . . has a literal character in regard to physical objects. . . . But, when we come to religion and mental science, our terms are only analogies, signs, shadows, so to speak, of the formless mysteries above us and within us." The theologian must freely use adjectives to give as full a picture of a word as possible; he must "multiply words and figures . . . to present the subject on opposites sides or many sides." In Bushnell's view, therefore, the interpretation of Scripture has more to do with poetry than with doctrine or dialectics. All forms of Christian doctrine, including creeds and catechisms, express the limited points of view and historical contexts of their authors and must, therefore, be open to change and re-examination; they must be seen as proximate statements, never as the full truth. Yet Bushnell did not sympathize with the Unitarian rejection of historical creeds; he argued that all available perspectives on theological mysteries contribute to our understanding.

In the address delivered at Yale, "The Divinity of Christ," Bushnell applied his understanding of the nature of language to the doctrine of the Trinity. What he came out with was satisfactory neither to the Unitarians nor to the orthodox Calvinists. Bushnell argued that the traditional statement that there are three persons in the Godhead is meaningless if taken in a metaphysical sense; belief in a real and metaphysical Trinity of persons in the divine nature produces only confusion in thought. He preferred to speak of God as one and to say that in Him there is a "strict personal unity" of mind, heart, will, and consciousness. But with this as the starting point, how can we speak of Jesus as God? The answer is that although the doctrine of the Trinity is not a description of God's ultimate being, it is a description of the modes of God's self-disclosure. Words will not permit a description of the being of God; language is here unfaithful and always incomplete. But as God makes Himself known through revelation, we do find evidence of the Trinity, of the modes of His self-disclosure. Man could not have knowledge of God as He is, unless God chose to disclose Himself through finite form: "He must let forth His nature in sounds, colors, forms, works, definite objects and signs." This does not mean, however, that man will comprehend God as He is, for to know God fully would be to know only a "larger man than ourselves, and set this larger man in the place of Absolute Being." But since God does have the capacity for self-expression, a power to represent Himself in finite form, man can know Him in part. He makes himself known to us as Father, as Son, and as Spirit.

We have in Bushnell's thought what may be called an "instrumental Trinity"; the doctrine of the Trinity is a useful doctrine only when seen as the way in which God reveals Himself, not as a description of His absolute nature. Bushnell's arguments was as much opposed to what he considered to be the "tritheism" of the traditional formulations as it was to the superficiality of Unitarianism.

There is in Bushnell's essay a kind of agnosticism. His discussion of the issues confronting the Council of Chalcedon (451) where the doctrine of the two natures, divine and human, united in one person (Christ) was enunciated, avoids the essential problem. As he said, to investigate "the mystery of the person of Jesus, when it is given us only to communicate God and His love, is in fact to puzzle ourselves with the vehicle, and rob ourselves of the grace it brings." But his reason for not further exploring the nature of Christ was simply that language is not adaptable to such an investigation. Bushnell did not deny the Chalcedonian decision, or affirm it, but rather he asserted that Jesus "stands before us in simple unity, one person, the divine-human, representing the qualities of his double parentage as the Son of God, and the son of Mary." This was as far as he was willing to go.

At Harvard he turned to a discussion of the work of Christ, the doctrine of the atonement. The medieval theologian St. Anselm (c.1033-1109) had enunciated what is commonly called the "satisfaction theory of the atonement." To Anselm, God needed to be satisfied for the sin man has committed; the slate cannot be wiped clean without recompense and this is the work of Christ. Christ, being God and man, is the only one who can offer satisfaction. To Bushnell, this transfer of guilt and punishment from the condemned to the innocent is unjust and cruel. The theory of the seventeenth century jurist, Hugo Grotius (1583-1645), commonly called the "governmental theory of the atonement," presented equal difficulties. Grotius argued that without punishment for sin, which Christ has taken upon Himself, divine government of the universe would crumble; chaos would reign. But this theory, which dominated New England theology during the period of Calvinist domination, was equally unsatisfactory to Bushnell, because it did not take into consideration the individual sinner. If man does not undergo a change himself, if he does not suffer through the pain of separation from God which is the result of sin, then the result is the "worst conceivable form of licentiousness." These theories did not express Bushnell's understanding of the justification of man by God. "Justification is that which will give confidence, again, to guilty minds; that which will assure the base and humiliated soul of the world, chase away the demons of wrath and despair it has evoked, and help it to return to God in courage, whispering still to itself—soul be of good cheer, thy sins are forgiven thee." The atonement by Christ was seen, therefore, as "interrupting the flow of justice by delivering men, or assisting them to deliver themselves from the penal consequences of transgression; . . . a confidence equally repugnant to justice, that God will freely accept, embrace, and even justify the transgressor who forsakes his sin." The purpose of the atonement was to make men penitent and eager for forgiveness, and to emphasize the "integrity" and "sanctity" of God's law. Christ accomplished these ends through His teaching, His obedience, and His sacrifice.

At Andover Bushnell turned his attention to the controversies engaging the New England churches. He made an impassioned plea for tolerance and charity among the theological disputants. While not denying the need for creative theological work, he regretted that the passion of discussion had led to a hardening of lines between parties and to division within the churches. Bushnell was convinced that it was dogmatism which had brought division. If the New England churches had embodied "the simple love of God under some such badge, for example, as the Apostle's Creed, it is very probable to me that the causes of the division would never have existed." Instead, disputes concerning the Trinity, the atonement, the nature of man, and the means of regeneration, abounded. Bushnell called for a revival of religion, but he insisted that this could take place only "through . . . an esthetic elevation in the sensibilities of our souls, which only the closest possible union of the life to God can produce."

Bushnell the transcendentalist came into focus at Andover. The Hartford pastor was actually minimizing the severe and obvious theological conflicts of his day. He himself must have known that although the Apostle's Creed could be subscribed to by all, Unitarian and Orthodox alike, its common acceptance would serve no purpose other than to discourage controversy. The warmth of Bushnell's own religious sensitivity, however, showed through in appealing style.

The publication of *God in Christ* precipitated further theological controversy. Charges of heresy were brought against Bushnell. Though he was supported by his own church, he was from this point on regarded with suspicion by the orthodox. Though later writings tended to bring him more in line with his inherited Calvinism, this volume marks Bushnell as the father of liberal theology in America.

TRAINING IN CHRISTIANITY

Author: Søren Kierkegaard (1813-1855)
Type of work: Existential exegetical reflections
First published: 1850

Principal Ideas Advanced

Christ is a contemporary reality present to every believer; existential contemporaneity rather than objective historical knowledge of His personality constitutes His essential significance for the Christian.

Christ disclosed in his contemporaneity is the God-man, who, in relation to the human understanding, appears as the Paradox and the Offense; as the Offense Christ appears in two forms: in His collision with the established order and in His claim to be God.

Christianity is not a doctrine; truth is a mode of being rather than a set of propositions and definitions; in the truth of Christianity the Teacher is more important than the teaching.

Christianity receives its genuine expression in the Church militant rather than in the Church triumphant; the task of the Christian is to be a follower of Christ rather than simply an admirer.

With the publication of his book *Training in Christianity,* Søren Kierkegaard openly launched his protest against the established Church. This protest reached its culmination in the publication of the *Attack upon Christendom* four years later, in 1854. In the former the author's protest was subtle and subdued; in the latter the protest became violent and envenomed. Although intermittently polemical in nature, *Training in Christianity* has for its central task a positive formulation of what it means to be a Christian in Christendom. Christendom, according to the author, has unwittingly done away with Christianity. The essential task thus becomes that of reintroducing Christianity into Christendom.

What does it mean to be a Christian? This is the lead question which directs the discussion of the author's work. Various answers are presented in which various themes are elaborated, but the theme of contemporaneity is central. To exist as a Christian is to exist contemporaneously with Christ. The Christian is he who acknowledges Christ as a present reality, as the object of his faith and as the pattern and paradigm for his ethical decisions. It is the existential rather than historical significance of Christ that provides the touchstone for the Christian. "For in relation to the absolute there is only one tense: the present. For him who is not contemporary with the absolute —for him it has no existence. And as Christ is the absolute, it is easy to see that with respect to Him there is only one situation: that of contemporaneousness. The five, the seven, the fifteen, the eighteen hundred years are neither here nor there; they do not change Him, neither do they in any wise reveal who He was, for who He is is revealed only to faith." Christ as an item of objective historical knowledge becomes a matter of indifference for the believer. He is not someone of whom we learn through a study of history. He is a living reality, seen through the eyes of faith, contemporaneous with each generation. His reality is such that it transcends both time and place.

This Christ of Christianity, disclosed in his contemporaneity, is the God-man, the Absolute Paradox, the Offense. It is for this reason that the understanding must come to a standstill in His presence. From the standpoint of human reason Christ as the God-man is not only a paradox but also an offense for reason and society alike. This offense takes two forms. In one of its forms it indicates a collision with the established order. Here the contradiction appears within society and can be elucidated through the use of social categories. The first form of the offense has to do not with the God-man as such, but with Christ as teacher who insists on inwardness and consequently rejects the empty externalism of the established order. At the time of His decisive revelation in Jesus of Nazareth this offense was disclosed in His attacks on the Scribes and the Pharisees, who at that time represented the established order. But this offense is not bound to a particular time and place; it constitutes a permanent and continuing revolt against God. Wherever a claim for the complete commensurability between the externals of society and the inward life of man is set forth, Christ appears as the offense who collides with this externalization and secularization.

The second form of the offense is

more decisive. Kierkegaard speaks of it as the *essential* offense. This has to do with the fact that Jesus, as an individual man, speaks and acts as though He were God. Furthermore, the offense is heightened in that Jesus is of the lowest class, subjected to humiliation, a lowly man, born of a despised maiden, son of a carpenter, friend of the poor and afflicted, the most impotent of men and, nevertheless, one who declares Himself to be God! Not only does He declare Himself to be God, but He invites all those who labor and are heavy-laden to come hither so that he might give them rest! He who himself is in need of help offers to help others, and asks even to help those who despise Him. It is here that the offense becomes explicit and occasions denial and rejection. It was this which led Peter to deny Christ. That a man should fall into humiliation, affliction, and ultimately into the power of his enemies is human; but that the one who declares Himself to be God should do so is an occasion for denial. The essential offense thus places the individual squarely before the God-man, tests his faith, and calls him to decision.

Clearly the penetration to the existential significance of Christ as the God-man and the Offense is not a matter of demonstrations and proofs. It is, says Kierkegaard, as though Christ were to say: "By way of proofs no man cometh unto me." Christ becomes the God-man in the act of existential faith, an act which must be repeated throughout the life of every individual and in every generation. Every generation has to begin anew with Christ. Faith is a repeatable existential possibility and is lost in the moment that it is transformed into a set of propositions or doctrines. Christianity is not a doctrine. The truth of Christianity indicates a mode of being or manner of existence rather than a sum of propositional assertions and definitions. "Christianity understood, the truth consists not in knowing the truth but in being the truth." Truth, existentially apprehended, is a way of life, patterned after Christ as the paradigm in the situation of contemporaneity. The God-man is the unity of God and a concrete individual in a concrete situation which has significance for every other concrete situation. The most fantastic distortion of all, according to the author, is to transform the concrete contemporaneity of Christ into a speculative unity of God and man *sub specie aeterni* (as did those who came under the spell of Hegel). There is no contradiction in the idea of the speculative unity of God and man in general, but there is a contradiction between being God and being a particular, concrete man.

The truth of Christianity is embodied in the life of the Teacher, as this life unites in itself the lowly existence of a humiliated and suffering man and the quality of eternity. It is thus that the Teacher is more important than the teaching. The teaching is already an abstraction from the truth of his existence. The error of Christendom, says Kierkegaard, is that it has done away with the Teacher, and only the teaching remains. Insofar as Christ as the Teacher *is* the truth of Christianity, all direct communication is rendered impossible. The truth of a teaching can be directly communicated, but the communication of the truth of the Teacher, or the truth of an Incarnate Existence as it is actually lived, requires indirect means. This is why

Christ lived and taught *incognito,* and revealed himself only to those who made the movement of faith and sought to follow his life of perfect obedience. But this faith and obedience of the follower was soon replaced by belief, and the next stage was to comprehend this belief as a doctrine. It was to this end that the help of philosophy, and more specifically Hegelianism, was solicited. Beliefs and doctrines cast in philosophical form are "reasonable" and directly communicable. But the truth of Christianity is precisely the Paradox and the Offense which is neither rationally intelligible nor directly communicable. It requires the inward transformation and appropriation which constitutes the peculiar quality of existential faith.

This existential faith and obedience constitutes the marrow of the Church militant, which according to the author must be clearly distinguished from the Church triumphant. The Church triumphant is the Church of established Christendom. It views Christianity simply as an extension of world-history, marking a higher stage in the development of the human race. Christianity becomes an intramundane process; the Church and the world become synonymous. In the Church triumphant it is easy to be a Christian for there is no essential difference between the Christian and the non-Christian. The offense of Christianity is transformed into a gentle doctrine of consolations which are there just in case man some time during his life finds need of them. In the Church triumphant the essence of Christianity is dissolved. The offense is secularized, human sin is attenuated, religious commitment is confused with social commitment, and faith is externalized. In one of his more polemical and ironical passages the author writes: "Everyone is baptized as an infant; later, but while he is still a child, he is confirmed—presumably in order that as early as possible everything may be arranged about that sort of passport which is so necessary if one is to get through the world without receiving a reproof from the magistrate. And of everyone who as an infant was baptized, as a boy or a girl was confirmed, it is certain that he is a Christian—by consulting the parish register one can ascertain this." In short, the Church triumphant has reduced the Christianity of Christ to cultural Christianity. It is against this cultural Christianity that the Church militant must wage a continuing war. It is only in the Church militant that one can become a Christian, properly speaking. The Church militant accentuates the offense and teaches that love of God is hatred of the world.

Corresponding with the distinction between the Church militant and the Church triumphtant is the distinction between the "admirer" and the "follower." The admirer looks at Christ from a distance and sings praises of His noble qualities—at least on Sunday morning. The follower also admires Christ, but above all he seeks to resemble Him. He strives *to be* what he admires; he discerns that the object of his admiration makes a claim upon him. To be an admirer is easy; indeed it pays well. To be a follower is difficult. It entails resolute commitment and suffering, both of which receive their most intensive expression in the life of Him who is to be followed.

THE WORKS OF LYMAN BEECHER

Author: Lyman Beecher (1775-1863)
Type of work: Evangelical theology
First published: 1852 (Volumes I and II); 1853 (Volume III)

Principal Ideas Advanced

Calvinism rightly understood teaches the moral government of God over free, accountable subjects, who, although possessing the natural power of contrary choice, universally manifest a moral inability to live a holy life because of the bias to sin inherited from Adam.

Since men invariably, though voluntarily, sin in every act from the moment they become responsible moral agents, they are utterly dependent for their salvation upon the regenerating work of the Holy Spirit.

The democratic institutions of America depend upon belief in God and upon obedience to Him in accordance with the teachings of the Bible; therefore, atheism and its political consequences must be resisted.

America is a land especially blessed of God and the scene of considerable moral and social progress, but the times call for a revival of evangelical religion and a reform of morals which will eliminate the evils of national life, such as intemperance and dueling.

The Works of Lyman Beecher provides excellent insight into the issues, interests, and controversies which marked the life of an eminent American preacher and revivalist during the first half of the nineteenth century. A man of great eloquence and power in the pulpit, Beecher also became embroiled in the theological disputes which divided the Calvinistic divines of his time. Beecher began his ministry as a Congregational pastor and served in Litchfield, Connecticut, and Boston, Massachusetts, before entering the Presbyterian Church and assuming the presidency of Lane Theological Seminary in Cincinnati, Ohio, a post which he held from 1832 to 1851. As a pastor he acquired a reputation as a passionate crusader against such evils as intemperance and dueling, and in Boston he was one of the fiercest enemies of Unitarianism. His move to the West involved him almost immediately in a heresy trial in which he was accused of betraying the tenets of the Westminster Confession of Faith. The collection of Beecher's sermons and essays considered here, although not complete, brings together some of the most important writings of his career and reveals not only the workings of his own versatile mind but also something of the spirit of the age.

Calvinistic theologians of Lyman Beecher's day were engaged in heated controversy regarding the doctrines of original sin and human depravity. The federal theology of the Westminster Confession (1643-1648), which the Puritans brought to New England, taught that the entire human race was involved in Adam's Fall, both by direct participation and by legal representation, so that all men share his guilt and come into the world with a wholly corrupt nature. Jonathan Edwards (1703-1758), the initiator of a tradition which is commonly known as "the New England theology," set forth his own version of original sin in which he reaffirmed the unity of Adam with his posterity and defended the theory of inherited guilt and depravity. The successors of Edwards gradually moved in an Arminian direction in the interests of securing a better defense of human freedom and responsibility. Beecher was one of those in this tradition who contributed to the modification of the older Calvinistic and Edwardian views.

In particular, Beecher was associated with the views of "the New Haven theology," whose chief spokesman was Nathaniel William Taylor (1786-1858) of Yale Divinity School. Although claiming to be loyal to the essentials of the Edwardian view, Taylor actually moved a considerable distance from it in that he repudiated the imputation of Adam's sin to his progeny and denied that men come into the world with a nature that is already, in the strict sense, corrupt. The heart of his position was that all sin is personal and voluntary. However, men are born with a nature so deteriorated that all, without exception, will sin as soon as they attain the power of moral agency, unless or until grace intervenes. While sin is certain, it is not necessary, since men have the natural ability of contrary choice and lack only moral inclination. In short, Taylor's view was that original sin consists, not of the sharing of Adam's guilt or of his corrupt nature, but only of hereditary and perverted powers which manifest themselves at the dawn of moral consciousness in voluntary disobedience. These views, while paradoxical in nature, provided a theology well suited for revivalistic purposes, and they enabled Taylor to defend more easily the moral government of God. Beecher agreed substantially with Taylor on these points and insisted that to do so was to be true to the real intent of the Calvinistic system.

While a majority of the Congregational theologians adopted the moderate Calvinism of Taylor, the Presbyterians were more evenly divided between the Old School men, who preferred the sterner views of human guilt and corruption, and the New School men, who found "the New Haven theology" agreeable. It was this conflict among Presbyterians which occasioned Beecher's heresy trial. Although Beecher was accepted into the Presbytery of Cincinnati upon his arrival to take up his duties at Lane Theological Seminary, the Old School moderator, Joshua L. Wilson, preferred charges against him, including among other things the charge that Beecher's concepts of man's native ability, human depravity, and the effectual calling of the Holy Spirit were heterodox. The trial began in June of 1835 and ended with Beecher's acquittal, since a majority of the judges held New School opinions. The two sermons which were entered as evidence against him ("Dependence and Free Agency" and "On the Native Character of Man"), a detailed record of the trial, and his lengthy defense (as published later in a revised form under the title, *Views of Theology*) are contained in Volume III of Beecher's *Works*. In his sermons Beecher's position is clear enough, and his basic agreement with Taylor is beyond question. However, in his defense before the Presbytery he used every semantic device and every subtlety of thought possible in an attempt to harmonize his theology with the Westminster Confession. The unwary reader can easily be led astray as Beecher maneuvers to make Old School language teach New School doctrines.

A great deal of Beecher's effort was devoted to establishing the distinction between natural ability and moral inability in Adam's descendants. In referring to natural ability Beecher meant to suggest that man, before and after the Fall, had all of the requisite capacities and faculties, such as reason, conscience, and will, to enable him to function as a free agent with the power of contrary choice. Beecher argues that only if man has such ability can God justly hold him responsible for his sinfulness in the moral government of the world. This means that men, even in their fallen state, can render obedience unto God in the sense that they can be loyal, for they sin, not by an inexorable necessity, but by voluntary choice. Moreover, in any given case of wrong choice the sinner could have and ought to have chosen otherwise than he did. However, while men since Adam's defection have the natural ability to live a life of holiness, they are characterized by a moral inability to do so. Moral inability is the lack of inclination in a free agent because of a contrary choice. In the fallen state all men come into the world with a nature so perverted that the will manifests a general and abiding decision against God which issues only in wrongdoing until the Holy Spirit acts to regenerate the sinner. In the strict sense, however, the children of Adam are not born guilty or with a nature that is already corrupt. Men are held accountable only for the sin which proceeds from their own voluntary decision. Original sin, then, consists of the inheritance from Adam of a constitutional bias which, with unfailing certainty, becomes the inevitable occasion, though not the necessary cause, of sin and nothing but sin from the first moment that a person attains the power of moral choice. Thus, men are wholly dependent on the regenerating work of the Holy Spirit for salvation.

Volume I of Beecher's *Works* is dedicated to the working men of America and contains a series of lectures on "Political Atheism" and on intemperance. In the former Beecher is concerned not only with theoretical disbelief in God but also with the anarchistic, socialistic, and egalitarian social philosophy which he associated with it. Asserting that governments are necessary to restrain the evil propensities of men, Beecher defends private property and inequality of condition in society and argues for the necessity of a strong rule of law undergirded by a morally alert citizenry. He further maintains that the free institutions of America are dependent on belief in the Deity, warning that chaos, violence, and tyranny are the inevitable concomitants of atheism. Beecher does not identify his foes very clearly, but he does refer to the existence of certain anarchistic and atheistic societies in this country, to some revolutionary groups in Germany, and to the radicals of the French revolution who attempted to establish a new atheistic religion based on the worship of the goddess Reason. Running through this whole discussion is a sense that the present age is marked by great social and moral progress and that America has been divinely chosen to usher in a new era of human well being in the world.

In his rebuttal of atheism Beecher attempts to demonstrate the rationality, morality, and political relevance of the Bible. He presents the cosmological and theological arguments for the existence of God, maintains the necessity of a special divine revelation, argues for the inspiration of the Bible on the basis of prophecy and miracles, defends the morality and political philosophy of the Old Testament, insists that God's government of the world is moral, and urges that Jesus is the best friend the working man has.

The six lectures on intemperance in Volume I and the eight sermons in Volume II indicate some of the practical concerns of Beecher. After outlining the nature, causes, signs, and evils of excessive drinking, he urges a strictly enforced national prohibition of the manufacture and sale of ardent spirits. Beecher also condemns dueling and contends that if the people will withhold their votes from all political candidates who support it, the way can be opened for its abolition. An ordination sermon delivered in Massachusetts compares the "Evangelical System" (Calvinism) with the "Liberal System" (Unitarianism), arguing that the former is the faith once delivered to the saints and that the latter, as a system, tends toward laxity of morals. Something of the subtlety of Beecher's homiletical logic becomes apparent in the conclusion he draws from the Biblical premise that the righteous love the truth. Since the wicked portion of the populace uniformly detest Calvinistic tenets and the most pious people of the land are agreeable to them, he maintains that this is evidence of the correctness of the "Evangelical System." While he is careful not to pronounce Unitarians as a body to be immoral, he does hint that those who are loose in their morality, as evidenced by their attendance at plays, dances, and masquerades, are more likely to be in the Unitarian than the Calvinistic camp. Following the sermon, there is a long defense of it which Beecher made in response to a Unitarian reviewer who maintained that Beecher's ideas were too Arminian in tendency to qualify as real Calvinism and that he had vilified the Unitarians by casting aspersions upon their morality. The sermon and the response cover one hundred and seventy pages.

Two sermons, "The Government of God Desirable," and "The Bible a Code of Laws," deal with the moral government of God, which is a basic theme of Beecher's theology. He contends that God's blessedness and man's eternal salvation are dependent upon the sovereignty of God over all things. By divine moral government Beecher means the rule of God over free, accountable human subjects on the basis of revealed laws maintained by appropriate rewards and punishment. In the remaining sermons Beecher asserts the necessity and practicality of a reformation in morals, defines the duties of local churches, specifies ways of combating the evil designs of Satan, and offers a plan for rebuilding some of the weak or abandoned churches of Connecticut.

ATTACK ON CHRISTENDOM

Author: Søren Kierkegaard (1813-1855)
Type of work: Criticism of secularized Christianity
First published: 1854-1855

Principal Ideas Advanced

The official established religion of Denmark is an utter contradiction of the Christianity of the New Testament; this contradiction results from the wealth and status enjoyed by the official state Church and its spokesmen.

Christendom is so dull, stupid, and lacking in both understanding and vigor that it cannot even answer attacks made on it.

The Christianity of the New Testament demands a radical break with the world.

Christianity is essentially an individual affair, both in its true expressions and in its protests against abuses.

The *Attack on Christendom* is a collection of materials written by the Danish philosopher-theologian Søren Kierkegaard in the last two years of his life. The first group of articles consists of twenty-one items published in the years 1854 and 1855 in a political journal entitled *The Fatherland,* followed by a short essay independently published on May 16, 1855, in Copenhagen, entitled "The Midnight Cry." The second set of materials consists of ten editions of a little paper entitled *The Instant,* published between May and October of 1855. The first nine of these bear the imprint: Copenhagen, Published by C. A. Reitzel's Estate and Heirs, Bianco Luno's Press. The last edition bears no imprint and is presumed to have been finished by its author just prior to his journey to the hospital with a fatal illness on October 2, 1955, and to have been released posthumously. The material was collected after Kierkegaard's death and given the title it now bears. Since it represents its author's sharp and sustained criticism of conditions in the Danish Church during his lifetime, it has been judged by some commentators to be more in the nature of a popular diatribe than a serious theological work.

The first six of the twenty-one items from *The Fatherland* were written as Kierkegaard's reactions to a funeral eulogy preached by Professor Hans Lassen Martensen (1808-1884) for the deceased Danish Bishop Jakob Mynster (1775-1854). Mynster died on January 30, and Martensen delivered his tribute on the fifth Sunday after Epiphany (February 5, 1854) extolling Bishop Mynster as a "witness to the truth." Kierkegaard immediately penned his first attack upon Martensen but did not release it until December of that year, when Martensen was appointed to the chair left vacant by Mynster's death. Kierkegaard objected vigorously in this and the succeeding articles to the possibility that an official and comfortable ecclesiastic in the Church of Denmark could be a witness to the truth of Christianity as portrayed in the New Testament. The Christianity of the New Testament seemed to Kierkegaard to demand a breach with the world, while official clergy enjoyed the comforts of their dependence upon the world. Priests and deacons who are not in danger can hardly be considered witnesses to the truth. The fact that Martensen was appointed to the bishopric left vacant by the death of Mynster means that Kierkegaard's strictures were aimed at him as well.

The attack was prompted by, but not confined to, the Mynster-Martensen incident. The remaining fifteen articles from *The Fatherland* extended the attack to conditions in the whole established state Church. It was Kierkegaard's single thesis that the type of Christianity set forth in the New Testament simply did not exist in the Denmark of his day. It was Kierkegaard's purpose to prompt the honesty required to admit this fact. Kierkegaard suggested that honesty is required to see poverty as the fundamental requirement of New Testament Christianity. Anyone can know, he suggested, what New Testament Christianity requires, except priests who benefit financially from the fraudulent substitute they perpetuate in its name. The honesty of shoplifters and usurers, who admit selfish purposes, is to be preferred to the pretense of the clergy which uses pious platitudes to cloak its betrayal of the Gospel.

Kierkegaard told his readers that they should not feel guilty about absenting themselves from ecclesiastical functions. But he did not seek to organize a mass protest and his objection remains an essentially individual one. He invited others to make their own individual protests, but he had no interest in starting a rebellion.

In places Kierkegaard seems to be satisfied by the fact that he was not directly embroiled in the behavior he castigates. At other places he expresses guilt for his part in the total condition of Christianity in his day. He admits his melancholy for his involvement and his own need of punishment, yet he insists that nothing could be gained by punishing him with excommunication since his membership in the Church was of no importance. He briefly considers the consequences of joining the Roman Catholic Church, but he finds it no better than official Protestantism. His entire approach remains an intensely individualist insistence that the New Testament demands poverty, risk, and suffering on the part of Christians. Moreover, he flatly argues that grace cannot be a substitute for lack of rigor in the Christian life.

The material in the second part of the collection is entitled *The Instant.* The significance of the title lies in Kierkegaard's understanding of the existential meaning of the present moment. The writing is not detached, for it partakes of the polemical present. Kierkegaard expresses a dislike of the present even though he is called upon to live in this conflict. He bids farewell to detachment with a flourish of sorrow.

The existential meaning of the present also signifies the decisive character of the attack Kierkegaard was making on the Christian institutions and behavior of his contemporaries. He turns the premise to suggest that the real attack on Christianity in his day was being made by the priests who were urging men to take Christianity lightly. He admonishes the Danish people to "Take an emetic!" in order to get rid of the false kind of Christianity to which they had been introduced by the thousand functionaires, or official clergymen.

When Kierkegaard becomes the object of counterattack he interprets the outbursts as proof that he was correct in his criticism. The New Testament predicts that men who defend the Gospel will suffer persecution, and Kierkegaard comforts himself by the implications in his own case. He renews his criticism of state Christianity with its temporal comforts and promise of easily earned eternal blessedness. Kierkegaard doubts that any further gain for true Christianity can be made until the state religion has been swept away. He ridicules the idea that the state, a human and temporal institution, can use the official cult as a protection for the divine. He blames the idea of a state church for the fact that the gate to Christianity has been made wide and deceptive. The idea of establishment is "ridiculous" and the name "God" is transformed from a symbol of awe and majesty into mere "twaddle."

"Thanks be to you, ye Government Clerks," he writes, "ye Counselors of Chancery, Counselors of Justice, Counselors of State, and Privy Counselors, thanks for the enormous amount of scribbling ye have had to do to arrange for His Majesty's subjects all and sundry in a cheap and comfortable way the attainment of eternal blessedness; thanks be to you, ye clerical counselors; truly ye have not done it for naught, for ye have your percentage; yet after all it is no more than reasonable that ye should be thanked."

Kierkegaard takes the words from Matthew 23:29-33 and Luke 11:47ff., in which Christ castigates the scribes and Pharisees for supposing that if they had lived in the days of their fathers they would not have shed the innocent blood of the prophets, and Kierkegaard turns the words upon the Danish clergy of the nineteenth century. He suggests that the priests should keep silent rather than kill or criticize the prophets of the present times. He implies that if Christ were to come again He would heap upon the Danish clergy the same bitter criticism He gave the scribes and Pharisees in his day. The priests are especially guilty for they have perverted the image of Christ by picturing the Christian life in terms of comfort and money.

Kierkegaard treats the idea of the state and the idea of Christianity in antithetical terms. Although the strength of the state is directly proportional to numbers in population, Christianity is vital with an inverse relation to numbers and its strength is dependent upon the intensity of devotion found in the few. "One single true Christian is enough to justify the assertion that Christianity exists." Because the state and Christianity stand in sharp juxtaposition the state should get out of the religious domain. It should no longer support priests or underwrite theological education. This opposition of Kierkegaard to a state religion should not be confused with more recent theories of separation, for Kierkegaard's view is based upon a radical individualism and a distrust of the state's influence on religion rather than upon a judgment that separation of the two realms is best for the general life of both.

Kierkegaard's bitterness toward the official clergy appears in such a variety of forms that only by reading the book will the reader sense the depth of the antagonism. Any state supported functionary in religion will spoil what he teaches. The private practice of religious preaching might mean that most practitioners would starve. The clergy do well to ask the public to include them in its prayers, for they most certainly need them. But despite the variety of form which Kierkegaard's criticism takes, it retains a common and even repetitious theme.

A true Christian, Kierkegaard holds, is more rare than a genius, yet the evangelists of Danish Christendom win thousands of converts in a short time. Whereas Christ won a dozen followers in three years, the popular evangelists of the nineteenth century "win" as many as three thousand in an hour! The author blasts the Sunday orators who make a popular success of preaching poverty. These "silken and velvet orators" create tears and put them in a bottle. It is this dangerous and even dishonest destruction of Christianity undertaken in pretense of its support that elicits Kierkegaard's most profound disgust. "Persecution, maltreatment, bloodshedding," he writes, "has by no means done such injury, no, it has been inestimably beneficial in comparison with the radical damage done by official Christianity, which is designed to serve human indolence, mediocrity, by making men believe that indolence, mediocrity and enjoyment of life is Christianity. Do away with official Christianity, let persecution come—that very instant Christianity again exists."

Kierkegaard's bitter criticisms called attention to grave faults, but he has been accused of excess and of lacking the spirit of love found in the New Testament. In his memoirs, Bishop Martensen made a reply to Kierkegaard, but the issues at stake between the two men, especially the issue concerning the individual's place in relation to the Church as the community which bears Christ's name, have not been resolved to this day.

THE NATURE OF THE ATONEMENT

Author: John McLeod Campbell (1800-1872)
Type of work: Soteriology
First published: 1856

Principal Ideas Advanced

Explanations of the work of Christ on behalf of men in terms of punishment by God and satisfaction of His justice are unacceptable to an enlightened conscience.

A moral and spiritual approach must be substituted for a legal approach, and this is supported by the witness of Christ in the Gospels.

Christ the Son offers to God the Father a perfect confession of, and repentance for, human sin; and the Father who delights in mercy accepts this repentance, and men are forgiven and share in eternal life.

The thesis which John McLeod Campbell incorporated into his volume on *The Nature of the Atonement* had cost him his ministerial status in the Church of Scotland. He stood at the bar of the General Assembly in 1831 and heard himself deposed as a heretic, by an almost unanimous vote, for holding and teaching views unacceptable to the Church about the significance of the work of Christ. His pastoral work as a minister was beyond reproach, and in personal character he was held in high regard by all. But he came to believe by the study of Scripture and reflection upon religious experience that the love of God was universal and not limited to the elect, and that filial, not legal, perspectives were best suited to explain God's relationship to men.

In 1856 he published his book *The Nature of the Atonement and its Relation to Remission of Sins and Eternal Life*. It was often republished and is regarded by some authorities as the most significant work on the subject by a British writer of the nineteenth century. He lived to receive an honorary doctorate from the University of Glasgow, a testimonial to his worth from many of the most noted people in Scotland, and to know that his views were being accepted by an increasing number of churchmen.

The purpose of the book is to isolate from among the many aspects of the atonement the one which had most significantly engaged his attention, namely, what the atonement of Christ was in itself, rather than the extent of its influence or the sum of its achievements, although he fully recognized that these are all intertwined. Previous expositions, he believed, did not satisfy the enlightened conscience of the age, nor did they do justice to the teaching of the New Testament. He makes much of this appeal to what he calls "internal evidence"; that is, the way in which the moral consciousness will respond affirmatively to the truth when truth is presented to it. This self-evident principle of validity constitutes the authority to which the Scriptures themselves appeal, the fact that the divine revelation of truth arouses an answering witness in the spirit of man. In this experience is the strongest evidence for the truth of the Christian faith.

Any serious man reflecting on himself in the light of the Gospel will discover that his self-consciousness confronts him with his personal involvement in guilt and with the kind of life he would hope to attain. These may be called the retrospective and prospective witnesses of conscience. The sense of sin is more than the superficial awareness of imperfection. It is the deeply disturbing realization that we do not love God and neighbor as we ought and that we need a remedy. What we long for is a new life principle within us, the eternal life of the Gospels, not primarily in future terms, but as a present experience of the life of God in the soul. This twofold testimony of self-awareness is the necessary preparation for understanding what the atonement is about.

The Christian message itself makes demands on us, and John McLeod Campbell points out that the first of these is that we recognize the truth that God delights in forgiving men their sins and guilt. This is a fundamental recognition which must precede atonement itself. God does not require to be appeased, propitiated, or changed in His attitude to man as if

He delighted in damnation. It is His desire to bridge the gap between the retrospective and the prospective witnesses of self-consciousness.

If this be so, then why should there be any need to proceed with a work of atonement? Could not God of His clemency simply pronounce general forgiveness and thereby end the estrangement? Why the necessity for atonement?

Such questions are serious issues and any answer must not ignore the fact of divine mercy. Indeed it is just the fact that we are dealing with infinite love and not just infinite power that is the key to the difficulty. Love is never cheap, but costly in sacrifice; it is willing to forgive sin, but it cannot ignore the power and reality of sin. The internal evidence of our spirit responds affirmatively only to a love that is really aware of what sin is, a love that does not bestow its favors promiscuously and gratuitously. Hence the necessity of a manifestation of love in depth, and this Christ reveals. The nature of the atonement, then, will be consistent with the nature of God as manifest in Christ, and it is at this point that previous explanations have been unsatisfactory. Campbell willingly concedes that all due weight must be given to the place of the holiness of God, the wrath of God, and the realities of law and justice in salvation, but they have been used in a misleading and erroneous way by theologians. Instead of being contributions to hope they have been construed as barriers. God is a Savior because He is holy and just, not despite His righteousness.

When he examined Martin Luther's commentary on the Epistle to the Galatians, McLeod Campbell gave his assent to the Reformer's expositions on redemption, grace, justification by faith, and especially on the personal appropriation of Christ as the indispensable core of the salvation. He found little, however, to enlighten him about the precise nature of the reconciling deed of Christ. Luther seems to assert the identification of Christ with man's curse and death, and His unity with eternal righteousness, leaving the two aspects of Christ's nature in apparent opposition and contradiction. The Savior bears the sin of the world, but it is not clear how this redemptive task was possible. That Christ became a sinner, as Luther's terms literally taken would imply, could not be true.

On the other hand, the prevailing Calvinism did not satisfy the enlightened conscience to which Campbell continually appeals. What he calls the earlier form, that of Jonathan Edwards (1703-1758), the New England divine, was deficient on two counts: (1) it restricted the atonement to the elect, those chosen by God from among mankind to receive salvation, and (2) it conferred on the elect a legal standing as if law and not love were the center of the Gospel. In its prevailing forms in the nineteenth century theologians had struggled to modify the details of the earlier Calvinist scholasticism, but they kept the same kind of language. Instead of describing divine justice as giving every man his due, the Calvinists spoke of God as a Moral Governor who demands only such punishment as will vindicate the principle of moral law; or they argued that Christ died for all men, but only the elect would be touched by sovereign grace to respond; or they held the view that the divinity of Christ gave infinite value to suffering of short duration, in place of the older view which understood divinity as making Christ capable of infinite suffering. Campbell is sympathetic to the motives which prompted such revisions and to the admission that the older theories had elements in them repugnant to a mature conscience. He believed, however, that this patching of the old garment was useless. Justice rather than love was still central, and punishment as a method of understanding the death of Christ still prevailed. "As long as Christ's sufferings are held to be *penal,*" he writes, "which, even when the old form of words is most departed from, is the expression still used, I cannot see what difference it makes." He gladly acknowledges that the practical piety and pastoral care of many were better than their theories would suggest, but the nature of the atonement expounded needed a radical shift at its foundation from a legal to a filial base, from God as Judge to God as Father. This he proceeds to make by restructuring the atonement around the belief that men are erring sons to whom God the Father offers restoration through the work of His incarnate Son.

The atonement, it is argued, is to be understood in its own light; that is, in the light of the significance of the persons involved as grouped in family realities. The key is in the words of the fortieth Psalm and attributed to Jesus, "Lo, I come to do Thy will, O God," which is the very essence of sonship. When Christ suffered for sin, it was the suffering of infinite love in the face of human ingratitude, and not a primitive unloading of divine revenge and wrath from inexorable divine justice. The atonement has two aspects: (1) that involved in Christ's "dealing with men on the part of God," and (2) that involved in "His dealing with God on behalf of men."

The first, or retrospective aspect, as Campbell calls it, covers the Son's witness to, and vindication of, the love of the Father, so that He could say, "He that hath seen me hath seen the Father." This love must not be confused with an amiable tolerance of sin. Sin is condemned in perfect accordance with the idea of the wrath of God against it, and its enormity is confessed to the Father by the Son on behalf of all sons. In a memorable sentence Campbell asserts this key position, "This confession, as to its own nature, must have been *a perfect Amen in humanity to the judgment of God on the sin of man.*" In a striking metaphor he holds that by this perfect response and repentence Christ "absorbs" the judgment of God and satisfies the claim of divine justice. At one time Jonathan Edwards had opined that justice demanded either "an equivalent punishment or an equivalent sorrow and repentance," but he had dismissed the latter alternative as inoperable. What Campbell does is to take it and demonstrate its validity. "We feel," he writes, "that such a repentance as we are supposing would, in such a case, be the true and proper satisfaction to offended justice."

The second, or prospective, aspect of this moral and spiritual interpretation of the atonement deals with what God desires men to become. The Father delights in answering the intercession of the Son by granting men remission of sins and eternal life. This remission is not a legal title, an imputed righteousness, but a spiritual state, an active sonship, bestowed here and now. Our own nature while in sin had this capacity of sonship, and we vaguely knew our need. It is Christ who reveals this "hidden capacity for good that is in man" by demonstrating it in His own life. We reproduce what Christ did on our behalf when we share His confidence in the Father's love, and walk as obedient sons. Campbell writes, "We get near to God just as the measure in which in the spirit of Christ we thus livingly adopt His confession of our sins—in this measure and no further."

When this understanding of the atonement became clear and convincing to Campbell, he confesses, it was like the appearance of light in a dark place and a relief to his spirit. His conscience responded to it eagerly, and it had the practical merit, he believed, of making the pastoral task of the ministry perspicuous and effective for human need. The very significance of the Christian Faith was transformed; unity and simplicity in perspective was substituted for a jungle of legal arguments that seemed to remove theology from the witness of the Gospels. This understanding was not clarity in the sense of removing all mystery from the ways of God to man, but it removed unnecessary and erroneous mystification arising out of the dominance of a conception of God as power and arbitrary will. It assumed a prior commitment to Christian faith, and it attempted to hold firmly to a natural sequence of explanations originating in the nature of God as Father, whose desire is to bestow eternal sonship on those who had rebelled against Him.

The Incarnation was the self-disclosure of the love of God, initiating a life which grew in a unity of obedience, a life which was truly a life of faith involving "the conception of a progressive development of the eternal life in our Lord's human consciousness." Even in the darkest moment of the Crucifixion, in "the cry of dereliction," this faith did not fail. Campbell protests with vigor against any idea of a staged performance, a planned legal transaction, an elaborate fiction of imputed guilt, a concentration on commerical balance sheet theories, in connection with the life of Christ. He believes that it is a commendable feature of his own explanation that it sees the nature of the atonement as one with the nature of the Christian life of obedient sonship, and that the relationship between the divine Father and the perfect Son provides a sufficient, consistent, and morally satisfying context within which justification and sanctification can be realized. The necessity of the atonement must be explained in terms of self-sacrificing love. To defend it in legal and punitive terms is to invoke "moral repulsiveness and intellectual contradiction." This appeal to self-evidencing light is the ultimate authority on which Campbell rests his case, a basis which he believes is the same as that by which Christ Himself commended His teaching. "If we consider the record of His personal ministry," he writes, "we shall see Him ever taking His hearers to a light already given in the Spirit, and in every man; to which light it is that He appeals in claiming to be received."

Attempts have been made to trace the antecedents of this position of Campbell, but such attempts have met with only debatable success. There are so many discussions on the work of Christ throughout theological literature that it would be surprising if none of the ideas of this Scottish theologian were present anywhere else. For example, there was a work by a fellow Scot, Thomas Erskine of Linthalen (1788-1870), called *The Brazen Serpent* (1831), which was probably known to Campbell, for the two men were friends; and it advanced some of the ideas of the moral repentance theory. Campbell does not mention this book, but he sees his own roots in independent study of the Bible and in reaction to Luther and some Calvinist divines. The truth of the matter probably is that serious questioning of traditional positions was being done by many Presbyterians who were separated from the Church of Scotland, men such as Edward Irving (1792-1834) and Thomas Carlyle (1795-1881), with whom Campbell was acquainted.

What is true beyond dispute is that *The Nature of the Atonement* was the first book on the subject by a competent thinker to work out in a careful and systematic way the particular thesis he defends. Campbell believed he was opening up new ground. Where he is conscious of borrowing he acknowledges it, and he clearly defines his departure from prevailing views. Others have attempted to improve on his exposition, and all subsequent writers have had to reckon with his pioneer labors.

CHRISTIAN NURTURE

Author: Horace Bushnell (1802-1876)
Type of work: Philosophy of Christian education
First published: 1860 (*Views of Christian Nurture*, 1846)

Principal Ideas Advanced

Children are amoral, not depraved, and they stand in need of Christian nurture.

The Christian atmosphere of the home and the religious and moral life of the parents are the formative influences on the Christian nurture of children.

The Church is a school for Christian nurture, and it is similar to a large family displaying the love of God to its members and to the world.

Through gradual Christian nurture the power and reach of the Kingdom of God on earth will be increased.

In 1846 the Massachusetts Sunday School Society published Horace Bushnell's *Views of Christian Nurture*, which, in a later and more widely read revised edition, was entitled *Christian Nurture*. Though the book has often been associated primarily with the field of religious education, it is in addition a theological essay.

Bushnell was born in Litchfield, Connecticut, educated at Yale College and the Theological School of Yale, and was at the time of the publication of *Views of Christian Nurture* pastor of the North Church (Congregational) in Hartford, Connecticut. When the 1860 edition of *Christian Nurture* was printed he had retired from his pastorate and was devoting his time to writing and traveling.

His attention had been directed to the subject of revivals and growth in Christian life ever since his arrival at Hartford in 1833. Bushnell was never a successful revivalist. The North Church in Hartford did not enjoy the fruits of periodic "awakenings," as did the First Congregational Church in the same town. During the early years of his Hartford ministry, Bushnell sought to encourage new declarations of faith, but he was notably unsuccessful; though, in 1834, forty-one new members joined his church, only four made a profession of faith in 1835 and only twelve in 1836. In that day a minister's success was measured by the number of conversions he brought about.

The battles over revivals had a long history in New England. During the First Great Awakening (1734-1735; 1740-1741) the Congregationalists split into Old Lights and New Lights, the opponents and defenders of the revivals respectively. Jonathan Edwards (1703-1758) was a key figure in these discussions and a supporter of the revivals; the Arminian theologian, Charles Chauncy (1705-1787), led the Old Light party. The issue remained alive for the next century. The advocates of revivalistic measures insisted that regeneration and conversion are the work of God and that such changes are not dependent on human effort. From the pulpit the New Light parishioners heard of their sinful, helpless plight; they were told that men are lost until God regenerates their souls and thereby encourages them to confess publicly their new "state." The Old Lights were less confident of the lasting effect of sudden conversions and thus minimized or resisted the call of the revivalist preacher. The theological basis of the Old Light position was Arminian: the opponents of revivalism believed in man's ability to determine himself. The conflict between the Old and New Light positions arose again during the Second Great Awakening at the end of the eighteenth century and dominated much of the theological discussion of the early decades of the nineteenth century. The New England churches, therefore, had been involved in these debates for a considerable period of time before Bushnell undertook an examination of the basic theological conflicts underlying the difference of opinion.

Until the time of Horace Bushnell, surprisingly little attention had been given in New England theology to the religious education of children. The young had been treated as adults; conversion was said to be their only hope. But during the 1830's and 1840's, partly as a result of the growth of the Sunday School movement, attention turned to the child, and theology had to be accommodated to the abilities of youthful apprehension. Theological reconstruction had to take place; the nature of religious experience had to be redefined. It was too much to expect children to experience divine separation, wrath, and judgment.

In this context Bushnell began to write and speak on the subject of Christian nurture. As he had been taught by Nathaniel William Taylor (1786-1858), Professor of Divinity at Yale College, Bushnell believed that the child was amoral, not depraved.

With proper Christian nurture no child need be forever lost and condemned.

The center for the development of the child's religious life is the home. The mother and father were, for Bushnell, the "natural and moral image" of God; the love of the mother for her child reveals the character of the love of Christ for all men. The impressions the child receives from his parents determines his religious development. Bushnell insisted that "a child is really not born till he emerges from the infantile state, and never before that time can he be said to receive a separate and properly individual nature." What happens to the child during this period of development shapes his attitudes and life.

Bushnell stressed the requirements laid upon parents to create the family atmosphere conducive to the proper nurture of children. Discipline of the parents is as essential as discipline of the children. He admonished parents to show that "religion is a first thing with you. And . . . not in words and talk, but visibly first in your love—that which fixes your aims, feeds your enjoyments, sanctifies your pleasures, supports your trials, satisfies your wants, contents your ambition, beautifies and blesses your character." Such is the nature of Christian education.

The child does not need to undergo a sudden conversion, but rather "the child is to grow up a Christian, and never know himself as being otherwise." The "organic unity of the family" is the natural organ for creating the Christian life and serves as the instrument for Christian or non-Christian ends. The relationships, opinions, prejudices, motives, and spirit of the home create the "atmosphere which passes into all and pervades all, as naturally as the air they breathe."

The Hartford pastor offered specific advice to parents on the conduct of family life. Good table manners, personal neatness, proper dress, avoidance of self-indulgence, observance of the Sabbath, punctuality, are all given mention. In the second half of his essay entitled "The Mode," Bushnell wrote a guide book for families desiring the Christian nurture of their children and of the adults themselves.

The role of the Church in this process did not escape his attention. In his own words, "The Church of God is a school, and the members are disciples, or learners." The Church is seen as a large family, seeking to manifest the love and spirit of Christ to the world. Baptism of infants and children is essential and once baptized they should be treated as members. It had been customary for ministers to regard baptized children as unregenerate, to stir them to a conversion experience. But Bushnell argued that children who have been baptized have been received into the covenant of the church; they deserve Christian nurture. "For there is a nuture of grace, as well as a grace of conversion; that for childhood, as this for the age of maturity, and one as sure and genuine as the other." The Christian expectation is that the child will develop in the faith and claim for himself the covenant into which he has been entered by his parents. In criticism of the practices of many New England churches, Bushnell argued that baptized children should be enrolled as Church members, subject to Church discipline, and that "when they come forward to acknowledge their baptism, and assume the covenant in their own choice, they ought not to be received as converts from the world, as if they were heathens coming into the fold, but there should be a distinction preserved, such as makes due account of their previous qualified membership; a *form of assumption* tendered in place of a *confession*. . . ."

An aim of Christian nurture was to broaden the power and reach of the Kingdom of God on earth. Though there is the Gospel command to convert the world, there is also the mode of increasing "Christian population." The Church needs to rediscover "that conversion over to the church is not the only way of increase; that God ordains a law of population in it as truly as he does in an earthly kingdom, or colony, and by this increase from within, quite as much as by conversion from without, designs to give it, finally, the complete dominion promised." Thus, the child growing up in a Christian family creates an influence which draws others into the circle, which, in turn, ever widens in scope and increases in number. This force generated by Christian nurture will be "mighty enough to overlive, and finally to completely people the world." The Church would have a converting power on the outer world, while within its life children and adults would grow in the Christian graces. Here Bushnell was reverting to the older Puritan ideal of a society redeemed by the Church.

Christian Nurture met with strong opposition. Bushnell was challenged by members of his own Ministerial Association; Presbyterian and Episcopalian critics took note of the book and, though approving many of its criticisms of the necessity for conversion experience, argued that the Hartford pastor had minimized the role of special divine grace in regeneration and had concentrated too much on attempting to attract the lukewarm and "natural" man. It took the passing of another generation to see the import of this volume for American theology. Though the essay received notoriety in its own day, it became almost a handbook for religious educators in the early twentieth century.

THE LIFE OF JESUS

Author: Ernest Renan (1823-1892)
Type of work: Biography of Jesus
First published: 1863

Principal Ideas Advanced

The four Gospels are legendary biographies and therefore must be critically evaluated and imaginatively interpreted in order to sift the authentic material from pious embellishments.

Jesus, a person of infinite charm and conscious of a unique intimacy with God, began his ministry proclaiming a pleasing theology of love.

A rebuff from the Jewish leadership in Jerusalem was followed by an increas-

ing apocalyptic emphasis, a radical alienation from the world, and a final martyrdom.

Jesus stands at the summit of the human race, the embodiment of mankind's purest idealism, and the perfecter of the world's absolute religion.

Publication of *The Life of Jesus* by Joseph Ernest Renan was one of the most important events in the nineteenth century attempt to write the biography of Jesus. No book in the long series of lives of Jesus was more widely discussed or the subject of as much controversy as this one, not even the *Life of Jesus* (1835) by David Friedrich Strauss (1808-1874), whose mythological and Hegelian interpretation of Jesus had acutely raised many of the issues that were to be in the forefront for many decades. Renan's rejection of the miraculous and his emphasis upon the legendary elements in the Gospel story gained him an immediate notoriety among orthodox Christians, but the long range significance of his book rests on other grounds. Not only was it the first work of its kind for the Catholic world and a charming literary achievement, but, more importantly, it also brought the problem of the life of Jesus to the attention of the entire educated world of his day. Running to ten editions during the first year after its publication, it was one of the most famous books of the century.

Generally speaking, the attempt to write a life of Jesus has gone through two periods, the pre-critical and the critical. The pre-critical period ran on into the eighteenth century and included the orthodox writings, which presupposed the Christian dogmas about Christ and accepted all four Gospels in their entirety as reliable authorities, and the rationalistic writings of the Enlightenment period, which presented a life of Jesus free from all miraculous and dogmatic considerations. The first produced the Christ of the creeds, and the second produced an idea of Jesus as an enlightened modern man and a teacher of ethics. The critical period can be conveniently said to begin with the work of Hermann Samuel Reimarus (1694-1768). The historians in this tradition based their work on a careful study of the sources and sought ostensibly to present objective accounts of the life and ministry of Jesus. The German scholars were in the forefront of the nineteenth century critical quest of the historical Jesus and have continued to take the lead in introducing new phases of this area of research. The twentieth century has given birth to a widespread conviction in New Testament circles that the prodigious attempt to write a biography of Jesus has been a monumental failure and that the whole Christological problem must be put in a quite different context due to the recognition that the Gospels are not sources of biographical data but testimonies of faith in Jesus as the Christ. Renan's *Life of Jesus* was an important stage in the development of the nineteenth century phase of the critical quest of the real Jesus of history.

A Frenchman by birth, Renan originally set out to become a Catholic priest, but a reading of the critical theology of the German scholars raised a serious doubt in his mind as to the truth of Christianity. He acquired a reputation as a man of letters and as an authority on the Semitic languages and Oriental archeology, and this reputation gained for him a commission from the French government in 1860 to make a research expedition into Syria. Here Renan wrote his famous work. He reports that under the inspiration of the actual sites of Jesus' ministry, the Gospels became alive, enabling him to see on the pages of a "fifth Gospel" a real and admirable human figure. Published in 1863, *The Life of Jesus* was the first in a series of volumes by Renan dealing with the origin and history of the early Church, but none of his subsequent works attracted extraordinary attention. The world remembers Renan only for his life of Jesus.

Two decisive issues in Renan's presentation of Jesus are his attitude toward miracles and his assessment of the Gospel sources. Renan does not rule out miracles as absolute impossibilities, but he does assert that no miracle has ever been satisfactorily shown to be authentic. Since none of the wonders reported by the New Testament took place under scientific conditions, they may be conveniently dismissed and viewed as the natural product of the mind of the age at work idealizing one of its greatest heroes.

In the light of the questions raised by the publication of Strauss' *Life of Jesus,* it became evident that anyone who desired to write a biography of Jesus had to come to some conclusions regarding the nature of the Gospel sources and the manner of their literary composition. Renan was familiar with the most advanced positions taken by the German scholars, and he devoted a considerable part of his first chapter to a discussion of his views regarding the nature and composition of the four Gospels. He regarded all the Gospels as legendary biographies; that is, as works containing a core of factual material embellished with a considerable amount of pious fiction. The original documents underlying the Synoptic Gospels are discourses about Jesus brought together by Matthew and a collection of narratives prepared by Mark from the preaching of Peter. These documents, mixed with other sources and connected in some way with each other, form respectively the present Gospels of Matthew and Mark. Luke is a later work of less historical value compiled from second-hand sources, including no doubt the sayings of Matthew and the narratives of Mark. The Fourth Gospel presents a distinct case. The long discourses are not genuine, but some of the narratives and settings have the sure ring of authenticity.

The Gospel materials, then, according to Renan, must be critically evaluated and interpreted by the biographer. What is called for is an imaginative and sympathetic grasp of the personality of Jesus in its fullest dimensions so that the data provided by the Gospels can be harmoniously combined to form an organic whole.

Jesus was born, according to Renan, in Nazareth of Joseph and Mary and was taught the Hebrew language and religion in the local synagogue school. Knowing little about the political realities of his time, Jesus absorbed the eager hopes of Israel for a blissful future and saw in the splendors of the natural beauty around him a transparent symbol of an ideal order of existence. After the death of Joseph, Jesus continued for a while to work as a carpenter, but soon, under the inspiration of an extraordinary consciousness of God, he set out to call men to the practice of the pure religion of the heart, a religion which consists of intimacy with and imitation of the beneficent Father in heaven. Renan describes Jesus as an amiable carpenter, filled with an infinite sweetness and charm, wandering happily about Galilee and teaching a delightful theology of love and the brotherhood of man.

Attracted by the reputation of John the Baptist, Jesus and his intimates journeyed to the wilderness of Judea to receive baptism and to join for a while the followers of John. The encounter with this stern, pessimistic preacher tended to make the gentle idealist deviate from his path, but after the arrest of the Baptist, Jesus returned to Galilee and to his own message, now more conscious of his own originality and better informed in the ways of preaching and mass leadership. The idea of an imminent revolution which would establish the Kingdom of God on earth became more prominent in his message. As Renan describes the early ministry, much vagueness accompanied Jesus' thought of the coming new order, but it was conceived as a spiritual transformation to be brought about largely by the conversion of the poor and the outcast, although apocalyptic ideas of divine intervention hovered around the dark edges of his thinking. Jesus regarded himself as the Son of Man, who, as prophesied by Daniel, would be the herald and heir of the new Kingdom; he allowed the people to adore him as the Messiah and the Son of David.

Gathering about himself an inner circle of disciples, Jesus moved about the territory in and about Capernaum and the Sea of Galilee preaching a pleasing message of love and light in the presence of a natural environment which inspired only noble thoughts. He rode through throngs of admirers on a gentle mule, and he taught the poor of the bliss that was to be theirs. With his followers Jesus enjoyed the simple joys of life. What Renan presents at this stage is a sentimental pastoral idyl in which fair maidens, laughing children, and carefree fishermen surround Jesus and are daily intoxicated by the elevated joy which vibrates through them under the spell of the charming prophet, the azure sky, the peaceful pastures, the delicate flowers, and the shimmering sea.

The spell of this idyl was broken by a visit to austere, fanatical Jerusalem with its proud priests and formal religion. Jesus found there little sympathy and much coldness. Revolting against the legalistic, sacrificial worship of the Jews, he returned to his native Galilee by way of Samaria with a new revolutionary fervor and an intensified apocalyptic note in his preaching. The sweet theology of love was complicated by predictions of a stormy end to history and the inauguration of a new age amid fiery clouds and stern judgment. The scene grew progressively darker as Jesus became so attached to his transcendent expectation that he was alienated from the realities and cares of the world, and a strange desire for martyrdom took possession of him. During this same time he was forced against his will by popular pressure to become a miracle worker. Legend soon added greater supernatural deeds to his actual healings, and perhaps the family of Mary and Martha actually co-operated to help make possible the miracle of the raising of their brother Lazarus. Jesus was never fully absorbed in his apocalyptic expectations, however, for at the very height of his preoccupation with them he was establishing the foundations for a continuing Church. He taught the disciples secretly and instituted among them, long before the last week in Jerusalem, the breaking of bread and the drinking of wine in a fellowship meal.

After some eighteen months Jesus returned again to Jerusalem to spend the last half year of his life. Public success had given increase to the opposition and unbelief that had existed from the beginning in some quarters. The opposition was led in Jerusalem by the Pharisees and the defenders of the established religious order, which was radically threatened by the pure religion of the heart advocated by Jesus. The drama hastened to its end amid controversy, intrigue, personal struggle, betrayal, and the continuing adoration of Jesus by the faithful. The religious leaders condemned Jesus for corrupting the religion of Moses and they convinced Pilate of his disloyalty to the state. After his crucifixion and burial, rumors began to fly that Jesus had risen.

Renan offers no certain explanation of how belief in the Resurrection arose, but he thinks that in some way it must have been connected with the imaginative mind of Mary Magdalene, from whom Jesus had cast out seven demons.

In Renan's view the greatness of Jesus is to be seen in the fact that he introduced a new spirit into the world. His purity of heart, his perfect idealism, his vision of a world filled only with love and tenderness, and his conception of a worship concerned only with the intimacy of the human spirit with God, enshrine the best that mankind has ever conceived. Jesus gave the world a religion free from fixed dogmas and hindering rituals, the essence of which is the communion of a pure heart with a loving God whose presence fills the world. He stands at the summit of the human race as the greatest triumph of the human struggle for nobility. Whatever the future brings, Renan is sure that "Jesus will not be surpassed. His worship will constantly renew its youth, the tale of his life will cause ceaseless tears, his sufferings will soften the best hearts; all the ages will proclaim that, among the sons of men, there is none born who is greater than Jesus."

APOLOGIA PRO VITA SUA

Author: John Henry Cardinal Newman (1801-1890)
Type of work: Autobiography and Christian apologetics
First published: 1864

Principal Ideas Advanced

God is manifested through nature and history; He is especially present in the sacraments and in His Body, the Church.

The Protestant emphasis upon the subjective experience of God has led to the neglect of objective truth, and has resulted in schism.

The Anglican Via Media, *though an attempt to recover the holiness, apostolicity, and catholicity of Christ's Church, is mistaken because the Establishment is schismatic in origin.*

The only bulwark against rationalism, skepticism, and atheism is the Church of Rome.

In the apology which he delivered before the Athenian assembly, Socrates said that he had to answer, besides the charges expressly brought against him by Anytus, a host of false accusations which had been circulating for many years. Newman's case was much the same. The ostensible purpose of the *Apologia pro vita sua* was to refute a pamphlet written against him by the clergyman and novelist, Charles Kingsley (1819-1875). But Newman recognized that there was no point in simply dealing with the particular arguments Kingsley had brought against him. It was a "bias of the court," he claimed, "that prepossession against me, which takes it for granted that, when my reasoning is convincing it is only ingenious, and that when my statements are unanswerable, there is always something put out of sight or hidden in my sleeve." For three decades Newman had been advocating religious beliefs which, to the majority of Englishmen, were more Romish than Protestant. When, at the age of forty-four, he joined the Catholic Church, the bitterness knew no bounds. There were many who could say, "I told you so!" There were others who charged that all those years Newman had been a Jesuit, secretly assigned to the task of winning converts from within the Anglican Church. The *Apologia* is mainly an attempt to persuade people of the genuineness of his profession by recounting the history of his opinions. The book is, in effect, a spiritual autobiography. Only in the introductory and concluding chapters is attention paid to Kingsley's pamphlet.

A precocious youth, imaginative, and carefully schooled, Newman was converted to the religious life in the autumn of 1816, about the time of his entrance to Trinity College, Oxford. Among the books which he read at this time were William Law's *Serious Call to a Devout and Holy Life* (1728), which impressed him with the unmitigated warfare between the Kingdom of God and the Kingdom of Darkness, and Thomas Newton's *Dissertation on the Prophecies* (1758), which convinced him that the Pope was Antichrist. It was also at that time he discerned "that it was the will of God that [he] should lead a single life." Thus far the influences on his life had been primarily Protestant and Puritan; only after he was made a fellow of Oriel College, in 1821, where John Keble (1792-1866) and Edward Pusey (1800-1882) were also fellows, did he become concerned with the task of recovering for the Establishment the marks of the true Church (holiness, apostolicity, and catholicity) which led to the Oxford Movement.

Among the factors that entered into Newman's thinking at the beginning of his public life were the following: a strong anti-Erastian sentiment "against the profanation of Christ's

Kingdom, by that *double usurpation,* the interference of the Church in temporals, of the State in spirituals," an appreciation of the sacramental system, "that is, the doctrine that the material phenomena are both the types and the instruments of real things unseen," and a mystical sense, deriving from the Alexandrian philosophies of Clement and Origin, of the divine presence "hidden behind the visible things . . . whose robe and ornaments those objects were."

So spiritual an interpretation of Christianity might have disposed a man to retire to some rural chapel and let the world take its course. The fact that Newman could never bring himself to hide his light and that he spent his long lifetime clashing with the earthly-minded, first in the Anglican and later in the Roman communions, helps account for the difficulties which his behavior constantly raised. No one perceived more clearly than did Newman himself the paradox of an unworldly soul cast in a worldly role. After quoting a letter which he had written in 1837, where he entertains the notion that John Bull is in fact one of the "angels, principalities, and powers" of which apocalyptic writers were accustomed to speak, he comments: "I am aware that what I have been saying will, with many men, be doing credit to my imagination at the expense of my judgment —'Hippoclides doesn't care;' I am not setting myself up as a pattern of good sense or of anything else: I am but vindicating myself from the charge of dishonesty." The paradox appears in the very fact that, instead of pouring out his life story to God in the form of a *confessio,* as many have done, he was moved to write an *apologia.*

Here, in fact, seems to be the key to Newman's spiritual development, that, as opposed to Protestant individualism and subjectivism, which tended to make religion purely an affair of man's inner life, Newman recovered a sense of the objective and social character of divine revelation, as manifest in history, particularly in the sacraments, the dogmas, and the discipline of the Church. Against the maxim, "The Bible and the Bible only is the religion of Protestants," he came to hold that "the sacred text was never intended to teach doctrine, but only to prove it, and that if we would learn doctrine, we must have recourse to the formularies of the Church," and gave up subscribing to the Bible Society. As to the doctrine of justification by faith, he maintained that, although in Luther's mind it was a paradox, in Melanchthon's it was a truism with which no one, either in the Anglican or the Roman Church, would disagree. The principle of "private judgment" seemed to him the essence of impiety, leading to rationalism, liberalism, skepticism, and atheism.

During the years of his association with the Oxford Movement, Newman was mainly concerned with recovering what he and his associates believed was the essential teaching of the Anglican Church, which they viewed as a *via media* between Protestantism and Romanism. His contention was that Protestants are heretical, particularly in their teachings concerning the Church and the sacraments, and have cut themselves off from the Apostolic succession. But for many years Newman also contended, with scarcely less emphasis, that the Roman Church was corrupt and idolatrous in its veneration of saints and particularly in its subservience to the pope. The Anglican Church, at least in its seventeenth century form, had preserved both apostolicity and holiness. Admittedly, in the eighteenth century, it had been influenced by Protestantism and by rationalism, and it had lent itself to national and imperial aims. But, in the eyes of Newman and his associates, these elements were alien elements which had to be expurgated so that the true dogma and liturgy might be restored, and the independence of the Church from civil policy recovered. Such was the tenor of innumerable articles, sermons, and scholarly works which appeared in the 1830's.

A series of pamphlets called *Tracts for the Times,* to which Newman was a leading contributor, was the main source of controversy. In 1841, Tract 90 of the series, which sought to demonstrate that the Thirty-Nine Articles, the official Anglican statement of belief, could be interpreted as teaching Catholic doctrine, created such a stir that Newman's bishop prevailed on him to conclude the series.

By this time, however, Newman had begun to have second thoughts. For one thing, he was no longer certain that the Roman Church was reprobate, and he had set about working for a reunion between the Churches of England and Rome. Again, he had come to ask whether the Anglican Church were not in schism, the same as the Calvinistic and Lutheran groups. He believed that it could truly claim apostolicity and even holiness (at least with as much right as Rome), but he was not satisfied that it could claim catholicity. Finally, the opposition which the Oxford Movement had encountered from the Anglican hierarchy and from the great majority of the denomination gradually brought him to the conclusion that there was no ground for hoping that the Establishment would ever again possess the marks of the true Church.

Having arrived privately at these conclusions, Newman was understandably embarrassed by his public position. Many of his younger associates, driven by the logic of their position, were going over to the Roman Church—a move which, for some months, Newman opposed on the grounds that it was an undue exercise of "private judgment" and that Anglicans ought to submit to their own Church discipline and pray for the day when the Churches would be one. For himself, Newman proposed to resign his important position as vicar of St. Mary's Church, Oxford, and retire to a lay standing within the Anglican communion. In fact, he did move in this direction, in 1843; but in 1845 he professed faith in the Roman belief, and he resigned all his connections at Oxford. A year later, in Rome, he was ordained a priest of the Roman Catholic Church, and, after some years, returned to England and to the kind of animosity which called forth the *Apologia.*

As Newman viewed the controversy twenty years later, he and his friends had been engaged in a last-ditch stand against "liberalism," whether religious or political. He knew and feared the inroads which higher criticism and post-Kantian idealism were making into the Church. But he was no less alarmed at the prospect of a Parliament dominated by economic interests and a hierarchy dominated by Whig appointees. "Against the anti-dogmatic principle I had thrown my whole mind," he writes; "I was one of those who had kept it at bay in Oxford for so many years; and thus my very retirement was its triumph. The men who had driven me from Oxford were distinctly the Liberals; it was they who had opened the attack upon Tract 90, and it was they who would gain a second benefit, if I went on to retire from the Anglican Church." This is one of the few places Newman expresses any regret. He had an impressive following in Oxford, which, however, would not follow him from Anglicanism to Romanism, "but would at once leave Anglicanism and me for the Liberal camp." To this disillusioned following, Newman felt that he owed an apology, a reasoned defense, even though it involved admitting that when he had argued for the Anglican Church as the *via media,* he had not read the Church Fathers critically enough.

No doubt many who were attracted to the Catholic revival in Newman's time were influenced by romantic sentiments and the desire to escape from the prospects of a bourgeois civilization into an imaginary past. But this was not the case with Newman. Perhaps it is more illuminating to think of him as a successor to Edmund Burke (1729-1797). Newman very much disliked being called a "conservative," a term which does not apply very well to Burke, either; but in an age which made a fetish of freethinking and individuality of belief, both Newman and Burke stressed the need for roots, and the importance to the individual of respect for the past and of obedience to authority. Intellectually, too, Newman belongs to the same tradition as Burke, along with Bishop Joseph Butler (1692-1752), a tradition which opposed to a facile rationalism a system of reasoning based on probability. Newman writes: "I say, that I believed in a God on a ground of probability, that I believed in Christianity on a probability, and that I believed in Catholicism on a probability, and that all three were about the same kind of probability, a cumulative, a transcendent probability, but still probability; inasmuch as He who made us, has so willed that in mathematics indeed we arrive at certitude by rigid demonstration, but in religious inquiry we arrive at certitude by accumulated probabilities—inasmuch as He who has willed that we should so act, cooperates with us in our acting, and thereby bestows on us a certitude which rises higher than the logical force of our conclusions."

ECCE HOMO

Author: Sir John Robert Seeley (1834-1895)
Type of work: Biography of Jesus
First published: 1865

Principal Ideas Advanced

The life and work of Jesus are plainly understandable if viewed without theological presuppositions.

Jesus proposed to revive theocracy (the rule of God on earth), but on a broadly humanitarian foundation.

Jesus' work had two parts: calling men into the new society, and legislating for them.

Faith *is the only requirement for entering the society;* love *is the only law.*

Jesus' ideal society agrees in many points with that of philosophical moralists, but whereas their systems have remained abstract ideals, Jesus has brought His into existence by appealing to concrete loyalties.

Ecce Homo is an outline of the life and work of Christ. The author states in the Preface that the book was written to satisfy his own mind concerning a historical character, who, in spite of all the books that had been written about Him, both from the side of faith and from the side of unbelief, remained incomprehensible. The book appeared anonymously, but it was later acknowledged to be the work of John Robert Seeley, who in 1869 became a professor of modern history at Cambridge University.

Seeley rejected the view of certain rationalistic historians, such as David F. Strauss (1808-1874), who maintained that the Gospel account of Christ is an invention of "the consciousness of an age." He took the Gospels as authentic "biographies," and attempted, by the use of constructive imagination, to present Christ as a character of history, setting to one side the claim of the Church that Christ was God Incarnate. Foreseeing the criticism which his work would receive in orthodox circles, Seeley stipulated that in *Ecce Homo* he would deal with only one side of Christ's work, His foundation of a new social and ethical system, and he promised that in a future volume he would treat of Christ as the founder of a new theology and religion. The second work never appeared; and, standing by itself, *Ecce Home* did much to promote the view that Christ was merely the founder of an improved system of morality.

According to Seeley, the life and work of Jesus are easy to understand, once theological assumptions are set aside. "No other career ever had so much unity," he says; "no other biography is so simple, or can so well afford to dispense with details." This is owing to the fact that, from the time of His temptation, Jesus followed a well thought-out plan. Attaching Himself to the prophetic tradition in Israel, He proposed to reinstitute a theocratic society, but to do this with due regard to the altered circumstances of the age in which He lived. Because there was no longer any possibility of recovering Israel's national autonomy, Jesus conceived the idea of constituting God's Kingdom on a broadly humanitarian basis. Contemporary Jewish thought conceived of the Messiah as a new David. Jesus conceived of the Messiah as a new Abraham, and a new Moses. As a new Abraham, He must gather people into the theocratic society; as a new Moses, He must legislate for them. These, according to Seeley, make up the two aspects of Jesus' program. If we keep them in view, all the details fall nicely into place.

At the time of His temptation, Jesus grasped the secret of success. He was conscious, as other great founders have been also, of possessing miraculous powers. But whereas other leaders have thought in terms of their own pre-eminence and used their superiority to enhance their leadership, Jesus resolved to use His powers only for the good of others. "This temperance in the use of supernatural power," says Seeley, "is the masterpiece of Christ. It is a moral miracle superimposed upon a physical one. This repose in greatness makes him surely the most sublime image ever offered to the human imagination. And it is precisely this trait which gave him his immense and immediate ascendancy over men." The mere working of miracles was not enough for His purpose. He won men's loyalty and devotion by combining greatness and self-sacrifice, by dedicating His extraordinary powers to beneficent uses only, and by deliberately disarming Himself when his own interest was attacked. In this way Christ could put Himself forward as "the Founder and Legislator of a new Society," without falling into the traps in which other leaders have been caught.

Christ's "call" for men to join Him in the new theocracy was as original as the method by which He established his sovereignty over them. As Jesus went among men summoning them to enroll in His Kingdom, He did not ask them to disassociate themselves from other groups to which they belonged. Usually founders have been exclusive in their demands; Christ was infinitely comprehensive. He did, however, demand that men "follow him," that they "change all their prospects," and "adopt a new mode of life." Seeley comments: "In this way, without excluding any, Christ suffered the unworthy to exclude themselves."

According to Seeley, the one condition for membership in Christ's Kingdom can best be denominated "faith." Seeley argues, however, that the faith which Christ required is not that which the Church has ordinarily insisted on. Christ insisted on personal loyalty, on faithfulness. The Church has too often misplaced the emphasis and has demanded something more like credulity. The critical mind of modern man, says Seeley, has great difficulty with religious dogma. Indeed, he says, if the important issues of life could be settled by reason alone, one would have to decide in favor of the philosophers rather than Christ. But the philosophers have misunderstood the human condition, for they have failed to effect any worthwhile change, because they have been unable to alter the direction of human motives. It is here that Christ proved wiser than the philosophers. He saw that the only effective way to change men's lives is to encourage them to form concrete, personal attachments to a man of conspicuous goodness. Even the worst of men can be changed into good men by vowing "obedience in life and death to such a person," and by joining their lives with those of "others who have made the same vow."

But besides calling men into a new society, Christ further had the task of legislating for His followers. Seeley points out that with the rise of the Roman Empire, old ethnic moralities had everywhere outlived their usefulness. Not merely Jews, but Greeks, Italians, and other national groups were confused and frustrated by the emergence of an international state. Previous codes had rested upon the distinction between one's friends and one's enemies. Christ minimized this distinction and inculcated in His followers a new "enthusiasm for Humanity."

In the plain sense of the word "law," Christ was no lawgiver, says Seeley. Instead, He gave men "character," instilling into their souls a new governing passion, and holding Himself before them as a model for them to imitate. Seeley acknowledges that, prior to Jesus, virtuous men had on rare occasions risen to the heights which He subsequently demanded; but what had heretofore been regarded as exceptional and praiseworthy was henceforth, among Christians, to become the ordinary mainspring of action. The new word *agape,* translated "love," was brought into existence in order to indicate the law which Christians were to obey. To the question as to how love can be commanded, Seeley replies that, strictly speaking, it cannot. But, says Seeley, love is really native to the human breast; and what can be commanded is that men rid their minds of prejudicial ways of thinking, particularly of the habit, inculcated by natural groups, of regarding outsiders as enemies. If one learns to think of all men as brothers, his kindly fellow-feeling toward them will become habitual, and his character will become like that of Christ.

Seeley distinguishes two aspects in the new morality. The first has to do with the alleviation of physical suffering. Seeley calls it the "law of philanthropy." No other rule is more plainly deducible from the law of love than the duty to feed the hungry and care for the sick. The second, which takes away nothing from the first, is "the law of edification." This law has to do with the moral and spiritual development of mankind, with the duty to raise every man into the society of the humane. Seeley remarks that, while in the earlier stages of the Christian movement, philanthropy consisted chiefly in relieving distress, and edification in preaching the Gospel, the morality implicit in such practices is now obsolete. Christians must, he says, engage in active social reform, investigating and remedying the causes of evil, particularly with a view to "the removal of all such social abuses as destroy natural affection, and by doing so kill Christian humanity in its germ." Nor, he says, is it enough for individuals to contribute financially to a Christian organization; if the Church is to be the representative of Christ's Kingdom in the world, its members must comprise an active society in which each individual is "ready to work in the service of humanity."

As Seeley understands Christ's teaching, it coincides with the utilitarian philosophy of John Stuart Mill (1806-1873). Christ does not censure men for seeking pleasure, but shows them, rather, that "the *summum bonum* of human life, the secret of happiness and of all enduring good," lies in actively promoting the happiness of others. It is a mistake, Seeley thinks, to surround the new society which Christ came to establish with the customary aura of piety. What Jesus intended was merely to institute in actuality what philosophers have often talked about in an ineffective fashion; namely, a community of healthy-minded men, in which the happiness of each would be the happiness of all.

Ecce Homo was roundly condemned by numerous important Church leaders as a repudiation of the divine character of the person and work of Christ. For example, the well-known Congregationalist minister, Joseph Parker (1830-1902), responded with a book called *Ecce Deus* (1868). New Testament scholars, on the other hand, have mostly ignored the work because it does not take account of "Higher Critical" methods. Some churchmen, however, have maintained that Seeley grasped with unusual clarity the essential character of the mission and message of Jesus. Bishop Charles Gore is an example. In *Christ and Society* (1928), he wrote, "There is still no book about the teaching of our Lord which can rival *Ecce Homo.*"

AN EIRENICON

Author: Edward B. Pusey (1800-1882)
Type of work: Ecumenical theology
First published: 1865

Principal Ideas Advanced

The doctrine of the Church of England is Catholic in all points.

Its differences with the Church of Rome are confined to points at which Rome has departed from the teaching of the Apostles and of the ecumenical councils.

The theoretical teaching of the Roman Church is closer to Catholic truth than its practical teaching.

A union of all the Churches could be effected by a new ecumenical council.

In the year 1864, Henry Edward Manning (1808-1892), originally an important figure in the Tractarian Movement, who went over to the Church of Rome in 1851, published an open letter to Edward B. Pusey, charging the Anglican Church with responsibility for the increase of infidelity in England. John Keble (1792-1866), another leader in the Tractarian Movement, celebrated for his poetical work, *The Christian Year* (1827), expressed the view that Pusey should reply to Manning. *An Eirenicon* is, thus, "A Letter to the Author of 'The Christian Year,'" and is subtitled *The Church of England a Portion of Christ's One Holy Catholic Church, and A Means of Restoring Visible Unity.*

To the immediate charge that the Anglican Church is responsible for the spread of rationalism and unbelief in England, Pusey replies that if this is the case then the Roman Church is responsible for the spread of infidelity in France and for the anticlerical movement in Italy. But Pusey declares that he is less interested in assessing blame than in forming a united front against these developments, and he charges bad faith in Romanists who seek to weaken the Anglican position out of a desire to proselyte members. One of the criticisms which Manning made against

Pusey was that, contrary to his Tractarian principles, Pusey had lately been cultivating the friendship of Evangelical Christians. Pusey admits that this is the case. Without sacrificing his Catholic convictions, he has sought to unite with Protestant groups in matters where there is agreement. Such a policy, he argues, has a two-fold advantage: it strengthens the Christian cause; and, by breaking down traditional barriers, it opens the way for better understanding between Catholic and Protestant groups.

Manning had taken up a statement by Pusey to the effect that "the Church of England is in God's hands the greatest bulwark against infidelity in this land," and he had affirmed the contradictory; namely, that it is "the cause and spring of" that unbelief. Manning had argued that the Church of England rejects much of the truth which the Catholic Church receives, and that such truth as it retains it detaches from the authoritative voice of the Church.

Pusey replies, in the first place, that the claim which he made for the Church against infidelity was not original with him, but had been made by "one of the deepest thinkers and observers in the Roman Communion." Pusey is willing, however, to add that he did not intend to say that the Church of England is the best possible bulwark against infidelity, but that, as a matter of fact, it exercises a greater influence against unbelief than either Romanism or dissent.

Pusey then proceeds, in careful detail, to argue that in essential points the English Church does not differ from that of the Roman and Eastern communions. The attitude of the English Church to the sacraments, for example, is entirely Catholic. The English Church affirms the real presence of Christ in the Mass, and it maintains that the sacrifice which the Church presents on the altar is the same as that which Christ pleads in Heaven. Nor does the Church deny that there are seven sacraments, except that it agrees with the Eastern as against the Roman communion as to the proper interpretation of extreme unction.

On certain doctrines, such as the Immaculate Conception, the fires of purgatory, and the efficacy of indulgences, Pusey admits, the difference be tween the Anglican and Roman beliefs is rather wide. But he maintains that even in the Roman communion there are different interpretations of these doctrines, and that often the theoretical teaching of the Church differs widely from her practical teaching. As an example, he cites a Roman devotional writer who says that Christ in the sacrament of Holy Communion is as much disposed to reject sinners as to accept them unless the Blessed Virgin intercedes for them. "We must then go to a sacrament solely of mercy," this Roman writer urges, "wherein Jesus Christ exercises no judgments. This sacrament is the most Blessed Virgin." "So then," Pusey comments, "it seems as if the Roman Church must either advance in her theoretical teaching, or recede in her practical teaching." Pusey finds the same gap between official and popular Romanism when it comes to the subject of images, to prayers for the dead, and to purgatory. The Anglicans, like the Greeks, are willing to accept what is ancient and Catholic in all these doctrines; they reject only abuses which, as a matter of fact, many Roman theologians also reject.

In support of his charge that the Church of Rome practically tolerates what it officially rejects, Pusey cites at length from the *Histoire ecclésiastique,* by the Roman Catholic scholar Claude Fleury (1640-1725). Fleury acknowledges that great changes were introduced into the constitution of the Church after the tenth century, as a result of the acceptance by its leaders of the pseudo-Isidorian Decretals. Most of the prerogatives which modern popes claim, says Fleury, are contrary to the usage of the early Church and have no other foundation than these forged documents, which, at the height of the Middle Ages, were supposed genuine. Since the Renaissance, Fleury says, Roman Catholics have admitted that the documents are false, but they have done nothing to revise the system built upon them. Had they done so, Fleury avers, the Protestant revolt might have been prevented.

Pusey and the Tractarians were, of course, maintaining something very similar to what Fleury says. In general, they argued that the practice of the ancient Church was violated by medieval innovations, and in particular they found fault with the claims of the bishop of Rome (who was supported only by the forged Decretals) to exercise authority over other bishops and over councils. It is on these grounds that Pusey meets the charge by Manning that the Anglican Church has no adequate authority for its teaching. "We ourselves have," he says, "equally with those in the Roman Church, infallible truth, as resting on infallible authority." He has reference to the "infallible authority" of the Scriptures and the ecumenical councils. The Roman Church, on the other hand, has "a tendency to hold cheaply by Holy Scripture, as being comparatively unimportant to them, who have the authority of an infallible Church, forgetting that the authority of the Church depends upon Holy Scripture." Furthermore, in claiming the seal of infallibility for its own rulings, irrespective of the consensus of the Greek and Anglican communions, it is acting on a "quasi-authority."

Pusey entitles his letter *An Eirenicon* because he means it to emphasize those doctrines which Anglicans and Romans hold in common, with a view to an eventual reunion of the two denominations. He says, "I have never expected to see that external unity of intercommunion restored in my own day; but I have felt it to be an end to be wished for, and prayed for." In the interests of this development, he reviews the correspondence which took place in the early eighteenth century between Archbishop William Wake (1657-1737) and the French scholar Louis DuPin (1657-1719). DuPin examined in detail the more controversial of the Anglican Thirty-Nine Articles and concluded "that the controversies between us may easily be settled, if only the fairer Theologians are heard on both sides, if dictating is avoided, and we are led, not by party-spirit, but by love of seeking the truth."

Raising his sights to envisage a possible reunion not only with Catholics but also with Protestants, Pusey agrees that the Anglican communion is in a unique position to bring union to pass. This truth, he says, did not escape the notice of so zealous a Romanist as Joseph De Maistre (1753-1821), who said, "If Christians ever in fact reunite, as everyone urges them to do, it seems that the Church of England must initiate the movement. We [the French] are too far removed from the sectarian groups, and have no way of reaching them; but the Church of England, which touches us with one hand touches with the other those whom we cannot reach; and, although it is condemned by both parties, and in fact does present the slightly ridiculous spectacle of a rebel which preaches obedience, still, it performs a valuable function, and may be compared to a catalyst which is able to bring into combination elements which by their nature have no tendency to unite."

Pusey argues that union could be realized by means of an ecumenical council. At such a council, he says, the Anglican Thirty-Nine Articles, the Roman Decrees of the Council of Trent, and other denominational creeds drawn up at the time of the Protestant revolt, could be retracted, and a new platform laid down on which all could agree. The difficulty with the Greek Church over the expression "filioque" in connection with the doctrine of the Procession of the Holy Spirit is of a different sort; no doubt each party would continue to use the formula to which it has become accustomed, but this could be done at the same time that unfortunate misunderstandings were erased. What is mostly desired, according to Pusey, is public explanations of the sort that are commonly given privately by Roman teachers to converts who have difficulty with some of the popular variants of the Church's faith.

For the most part, Pusey bases his argument with Manning on historical precedents, and he appeals to theological authorities who, if not accepted by Manning, might exercise weight with persons born in the Roman Church. In one place, however, he appeals not to authority but to religious experience. In disputing whether the Anglican sacrament of Holy Communion is real or not, he says, "I do not believe that God maintains the faith, where there is not the reality. . . . Heretics, who are really cut off from the Body of Christ, receive the Sacrament, though not the grace of the Sacrament. We have the witness that we have really the true Body and Blood of Christ and the grace of the Sacrament: 1) from the knowledge of those who receive it. God would not allow His own to be deluded in such a matter as this. 2) In the supernatural lives of grace, led by persons, the life of whose souls is Christ in the Holy Eucharist." Pusey goes on to say that God gives to each according to his faith. He distinguishes the kind of piety which characterizes Presbyterians from that which characterizes Anglicans. "Presbyterians have what *they* believe; we, what *we* believe. But they who have observed pious Presbyterians and pious English Catholics, have discerned among our people a spiritual life, of a kind which was not among theirs; in a word, a sacramental life." He justifies the English practice of confession in the same way. As a clergyman who has seen the change in those whose confessions he has heard, he finds the validity of Anglican absolutions self-confirming: "God, the Author of truth, has set his seal upon them."

Before Pusey's long letter had gone to press, two events took place which prompted him to add a lengthy Postscript. One was the elevation of Dr. Manning to the position of Archbishop of Westminster. The other was the appearance of a new Papal Encyclical which, says Pusey, disclosed "how advanced, above all which was known formerly, is the present theory of Papal Infallibility." There is no use any longer in pretending, he says, that the pope claims infallibility only in matters of faith and morals. As now interpreted, the pope's infallibility includes everything declared by him "to regard the Church's right discipline and general good," such as political judgments, injunctions contained in letters to individual persons, syllabi of errors, and statements of fact unconnected with former revelation. Pusey argues that the extent of the claims can only prove embarrassing to the pope's defenders, and he brings forward numerous historical instances which suggest that popes have erred. Nevertheless, the Encyclical, taken together with the promotion of Dr. Manning, who was noted for his zeal as a champion of papal infallibility, cooled Pusey's hopes for closer relations between the two denominations.

When *An Eirenicon* appeared, it was answered by J. H. Newman (1801-1890), another former Tractarian, who had preceded Manning into the Church of Rome, in "A Letter to the Rev. E. B. Pusey on his recent 'Eirenicon.'" Newman's answer dealt particularly with Pusey's charges of Mariolatry, but it held out little which the Anglo-Catholics could accept. Pusey answered Newman in two further eirenicons, which appeared in 1869. The Vatican Council of 1870, however, which made papal infallibility a matter of faith, and finally denied the possibility of an appeal from the pope to an ecumenical council, made clear to Pusey that union was no longer possible. Pusey continued to work for union with the Eastern Orthodox and with the Wesleyan Churches, but he found little to encourage him.

JOHN PLOUGHMAN'S TALKS

Author: Charles Haddon Spurgeon (1834-1892)
Type of work: Popular moral essays
First published: 1869

Principal Ideas Advanced

A sturdy commonsense allied to a Christian character will bring the greatest measure of durable happiness to mankind.

Proverbial wisdom is the bearer of the experience of the past for the practical affairs of the present.

Charles Hadden Spurgeon, English Baptist preacher, came from yeoman stock, and in his formative years he absorbed much of the homespun lore of the English countryside. His popular *John Ploughman's Talks, or Plain*

Advice to Plain People, was as native to the agricultural scene in the Victorian era as a patchwork quilt. There is nothing complicated or esoteric in the religion his book advocates, nothing scandalous in its proverbial wisdom that would eliminate it from the cottage bookshelf, and nothing so uncouth as to bar it from the library of the manor house. The pithy sagacity of John Ploughman spoke to the follies and foibles of human affairs with a plainness, and even bluntness, that carried its own moral force.

The talks originated in 1869 in the form of penny broadsheets entitled *John Ploughman's Almanack.* After 365 issues with a daily proverb and comment, the series came to a close. The requests for the resumption of the talks were so many and so clamorous that Spurgeon began again, and the series continued until his death in 1892, and then for a few years more on the basis of material which he left. The book known as *John Ploughman's Talks* is a selection from these sources.

Spurgeon, reared as a Congregationalist, but converted to the Baptist Church in his teens, was invited to a London pulpit when nineteen years of age, and he remained in the same church all his ministry. Before he arrived the congregation had been searching in vain for a pastor, and their invitation to an Essex lad seemed a desperate move. But in a matter of weeks the place was crowded, all 1200 seats. Exeter Hall with room for 4500 was taken; then the Royal Sussex Gardens Hall with accommodation for about 12,000. Spurgeon filled them all in succession Sunday after Sunday. For a church home, his congregation erected the Metropolitan Tabernacle with 6,000 capacity, and it was filled several times a week for over thirty years.

C. H. S., as he was familiarly called, was a phenomenon of some magnitude in the world of Victorian oratory. He was not a scholar in the technical sense, nor was he a social prophet calling for justice in the industrial sweat shops, nor did his style of speech or writing achieve linguistic excellence. His strength was in his ability to handle an audience, in his forthright utterances on evangelical themes, and in his ability to use an unsophisticated style with direct decisiveness. The printed editions of his sermons sold by the millions, and an enterprising American literary agency offered him $1,000 in gold for each lecture he would deliver in the United States, but he never could be persuaded to cross the Atlantic.

His output in print added up to some 135 volumes, including the sermon series, *John Ploughman's Talks,* and the companion volume, *John Ploughman's Pictures.*

A sample of the titles of items within the *Talks* sufficiently illustrates the territory within which the book moves: To the Idle, On Seizing Opportunities, Things not Worth Trying, A Good Word to Wives, Men With Two Faces, Tall Talk, Things I Would Not Choose. In each of these essays there is an outpouring of simulated rustic wisdom in an abundance of maxims, analogies, proverbs, and anecdotes. By heaping saying upon saying, a cumulative effect is achieved that compels the reader to do some homework by way of self-examination. The whole is unashamedly didactic, consisting of preachments in favor of an earnest moral character which scorns hypocrisy, sham, waste, sloth, and impiety.

Here is the Protestant Puritan ethic in clear unmistakable form. It is robust, assured, and outspoken, even though at times it rises little higher than prudential morality and a worldly wise sagacity. Many familiar aphorisms are liberally strewn across the pages; thus, we read about cutting one's coat according to the cloth, locking the door when the horse is gone, counting chickens before they are hatched, and the like. We are conducted, as it were, up the village street, invited to enter the local bethel, allowed to overhear the market day conversation, and permitted to sit around the open hearth fire. Much of what we hear is the fruit of experience, the wise counsel that knows the popular sins and their all too common consequences.

John Ploughman uses all the tried and proved devices to communicate his pronouncements. Sarcasm, exaggeration, sharp contrasts, emotionally weighted words, and appeals to religious authority make their appearance without apology. He speaks in utter sincerity and neighborly concern, suspicious of the concrete jungles of the city, and innocent of the technical problems of the statesman.

The ideal in Spurgeon's book is what has been called Victorian respectability—but in the good sense of that ill-used phrase. Moral earnestness, diligence, and honest toil, accompanied by an abhorrence of vulgarity, licentiousness, malevolence, and injustice, are marks of the life that is pleasing to God and beneficial to human welfare. John has a strong preference for England and for Sussex in particular. He asserts with pride, "To keep debt, dirt and the devil out of my cottage has been my greatest wish ever since I set up housekeeping."

Though not a spectator of eternal ideas—as was Plato's philosopher—John Ploughman was a shrewd critic of life as he saw it around him, and as he reflected on it behind his plough. Others might plough a crooked furrow; his was straight. If some of his neighbors preferred to be conformist, he was sturdily independent. "I take my leave," he says, "to look about me and speak my mind, for a cat may look at a king, and a fool may give wise men some good advice."

Biblical precedents, warnings about the miseries of the wicked, and remarks concerning the sheer stupidity of the profligate are used to castigate the drunkard, the shrew, the spendthrift, the character assassin, the homebreaker, and the Judas. "It is not a very good sign," says John, "when the fox walked into the hen roost and said, 'Good morning to you all, my very good friends.' "

For John Ploughman and his friends, "home" is one of the great words in the English language, and it inspires a recurring topic in John's counselling program. Allied to the thought of home are the kindred topics of family, wife, and children. Here personal relationships are most intimate, and emotions most intensely felt for good or ill. "Our lane is the most beautiful for twenty miles around, because our home is in it." It is not the size of it or any other physical property, but the love and understanding that is in it that makes a home so desirable. In a homily called "Home," the ploughman sage is eloquent in his denunciation of all who undermine what makes home so precious to him. The beer shop comes in for rough opposition, for in it, John Ploughman says, men waste their time and money to the detriment of their families. Beer is "so much fools' milk to drown their wits in." Husbands who do not take their share of responsibility receive little sympathy from John Ploughman: "If the father drops the reins, the family coach will soon be in the ditch." Likewise a wife can be a power for good or ill, for she is either wise or foolish in her domestic cares. One of the talks is entitled "A Good Word for Wives," for the author is of the opinion that wives are the subject of injustice in some country sayings. No doubt there are many bad wives who make a bethel into a bedlam, but the Bible can supply only one Jezebel. The cause of a husband's grumbles may often be of his own making: "The rottenest bough cracks first, and it looks as if the male side of the house was the worse of the two, for it certainly has made up the most grumbling proverbs." The foundation of a blessed home is mutual love and piety: "When home is ruled according to God's word, angels might be asked to stay a night with us, and they would not find themselves out of their element."

The cartoons which accompany the text of the *Talks,* as in some other works of Spurgeon, such as the three volume *Lectures to My Students,* add greatly to the power of the sayings they illustrate, and lighten the admonitions with a touch of humor. The drawing of two optimistic souls trying to pour water into a sieve raises a smile, and one showing the credulous friend who tries to take a bull by the horns, with less than happy results, supplies a useful visual aid to the text.

Hundreds of thousands of copies of the *Talks* were circulated all over the world, and Spurgeon compiled a companion volume called *John Ploughman's Pictures* in which the cartoons were featured. "There is no particular virtue," he wrote, "in being seriously unreadable." It was this quality of semi-humorous and folksy common sense that made the *Talks* so popular. Spurgeon was deliberately making use of a medium other than the pulpit, and he said of his talks, in the Preface, "I have aimed my blows at the vices of the many and tried to inculcate those moral virtues without which men are degraded."

THE CHRISTIAN DOCTRINE OF JUSTIFICATION AND RECONCILIATION

Author: Albrecht Ritschl (1822-1889)
Type of work: Systematic theology; soteriology
First published: 1870-1874

Principal Ideas Advanced

Christ and His work can be adequately understood only in terms of, and from the standpoint of, the community which He founded.

Based on God's revelation in Christ, the Christian religion resembles an ellipse, one focus of which is redemption from sin, the other of which is the impetus to moral effort in the universal kingdom of God.

Justification, which is equivalent to the forgiveness of sins, means acceptance into God's fellowship; regarded as effective in the life of the believer, justification is to be conceived also as reconciliation.

As the import of theological conceptions lies always in the voluntary activities called forth by revelation in the believer, so the meaning of Chirst is confirmed in the traits of Christian existence: trust in God, peace, patience, humility, thanksgiving, and love-motivated action.

During the last third of the nineteenth century no name was more prominent in Protestant theology than that of Albrecht Ritschl. Professor at Bonn and then at Göttingen for twenty-five years, no one did more than he to shape the characteristic trends of Protestant Liberalism. Son of a prominent churchman in Berlin, Ritschl attended the universities of Bonn, Halle, Heidelberg, and Tübingen. In the early work in New Testament theology he followed the lead of the historical theologian F. C. Baur (1792-1860), who was influenced by the philosophy of G. W. F. Hegel (1770-1831). But by 1857 Ritschl had rejected the Hegelian view and begun developing his own systematic theology on the basis of Friedrich Schleiermacher (1768-1834) and Immanuel Kant (1724-1804), combining the former's method and redemptive interest with the moral stress of the latter. The first volume of Ritschl's major work appeared in 1870, and was translated by J. S. Black in 1872, under the title *A Critical History of the Christian Doctrine of Justification and Reconciliation*. The second volume, published in 1874, concerning the Biblical substance of the doctrine, has not been translated into English. The concluding volume reviewed here, also appearing in 1874, gives Ritschl's constructive statement. Intended as an exhaustive monograph on one theme, the book is, as Ritschl remarked, "an almost complete outline of Systematic Theology, the remaining parts of which could easily be supplied." The formidable style of the work has made it somewhat inaccessible, but through it Ritschl, as a theologian's theologian, has exercised profound influence upon his contemporaries and successors.

In full swing in the 1870's was the so-called "Life of Jesus Movement," which sought to reconstruct objectively the facts about the "real Jesus" as He was prior to the religious interpretations of the New Testament writers. Although Ritschl too had called for a return from the historical development of dogma to the original Christian norm, he rejected the "Life of Jesus" project on the ground that "We can discover the full compass of . . . [Jesus'] . . . historical actuality solely from the faith of the Christian community." Thus the Apostolic—especially the Pauline—witness to Christ is a functional component of the norm. But it is also necessary for the theologian, or anyone who would understand Jesus historically, to share the community's faith. The historical *and* Biblical Christ is the objective ground, and participating, subjective faith is the indispensable means of standing upon it. In striving exclusively for the correlation of these two poles, God in Christ and faith, Ritschl regarded himself as carrying through the intention of the Reformers.

Historical and contemporary theology has allowed rationalistic metaphysics to override the Christian revelation; at least, there has been failure to maintain Christ's authority throughout the theological system. However, Ritschl cannot approve the endeavor of some to return to a theology so purely Biblical as to amount to no more than a concatenation of texts; to follow such a limited course would be to ignore the task of clarifying Christ's relation to human existence in general. Another criticism of preceding theology is that it has almost always presented a biased version of Christianity, sometimes favoring the moral and sometimes the religious-redemptive aspect, despite the fact that, as in an ellipse, these foci equally determine the whole. Furthermore, the theological tradition has been wont to present doctrinal propositions apart from the evaluating will, feelings, and active life of the believer. Ritschl's own theological program aims to avoid the separation of doctrine and life.

Following his introduction, Ritschl undertakes the definition of justification and reconciliation. The two ideas are inseparable, yet complementary. Justification, the Pauline way of putting what for Jesus was the forgiveness of sin, means that God accepts the sinner *in spite of* his guilt. This is the objective basis of reconciliation, which consists of a new life in fellowship with God and in relation to one's fellow men. But justification, as the phrase "by faith" indicates, cannot be construed as absolutely nonsubjective. Like every religious notion, its meaning implies the personal involvement —the value-judgments—of the believer: in this case, a turning to God in trust and penitence. But these subjective conditions are not a law for the sinner to fulfill; they are spontaneously implied in his response to God's gracious offer of pardon. Similarly with respect to the assurance of forgiveness (or of election), such assurance is not something that can be objectively established, as it were, outside the subject. One cannot abstractly prove to oneself that one is sure of God's mercy. Certitude is given only in the spontaneous subjective act of responding to the message of Christ.

Ritschl next develops the presuppositions of the doctrine of justification and reconciliation. Fundamental is the distinctive Christian understanding of the personal God who has created the world and seeks to realize in the world His purpose of righteous love. In the history of theology this understanding has been obscured both by metaphysical notions of God as a neutral ultimate, and by legalistic ideas of God as the indifferent rewarder of good and evil. But Christians worship the "Father of our Lord Jesus Christ." Knowledge of God is not neutrally theoretical but of infinite interest to the knower. And the divine righteousness, when grasped Biblically, means not unconcerned retribution but God's unswerving faithfulness to His loving purpose. The Kingdom of God obtains wherever, and in whatever measure, the purpose is realized. Eternal Life is life in time which shares in the realization of the purpose and is thus everlastingly upheld in the divine will of love.

Justification's negative presupposition is sin, which expresses the felt disparity between man's actual state and God's will. Ritschl stresses the claim that the idea can be developed properly only by reference to Christ as the human criterion under the judgment of which the rest of us stand. To express our own lack of merit was the purpose of the doctrine of original sin, which, however, was like using a "boulder to kill a gnat." Ritschl proposes the "kingdom of sin" as a substitute notion, thereby signifying the collusion in sin by which all are influenced and to which all contribute. Sin is not reducible to ignorance but is conditioned by it, at least in inception. It is forgivable except in the hypothetical case of resolutely conscious defiance of God's will of love—a defiance which is the sin against the Holy Spirit.

The third main presupposition of justification is Christ's person and work. These two aspects of the total meaning of Christ cannot be separated. The description of the person in terms of human ideality and of divinity can be validated only through the effects He has upon us; that is, in terms of His work. That God was active in Him in a unique way cannot be doubted, but in the absence of any theoretic understanding of how this was the case, the practical import of His Godhead is "the worth to be put on those human achievements of His which suffice for our salvation." Ritschl insists that the estimate of Christ is to be based on the Biblical picture of His historical life, not on speculations about pre-existence or postexistence. The exalted Lord who reigns is the man who is victorious on the Cross through unbroken trust in God. Christ's will and purpose so coincide with God's intention that through Christ the sinner receives the word of reconciling pardon as well as the imperative which demands moral action in the Kingdom.

Having developed his presuppositions, Ritschl essays a "proof" of the "necessity" of justification and of basing it upon the work of Christ. He does not envisage a detached rational argument for Christianity. For "the proof is nothing but a demonstration of the harmony of the ideas which are bound up together in the Christian view of the world and the Christian view of the self. The man who altogether rejects this system of ideas will find their proof meaningless too." Ritschl proceeds from the basic fact of man's practical concern for his ultimate worth or meaning. Religion roots in this concern, and the idea of God corresponds to the way in which personal worth is estimated, grounded, and eternally guaranteed. In other words, God, by definition, means that power upon which man's meaning and destiny depend. But sin and guilt vitiate the divine-human relationship; and until they are removed as obstacles to fellowship with God, man's personal worth and destiny stand in jeopardy. Hence the necessity of justification and reconciliation. How, though, were the divine forgiveness and purpose to be made real among men except through their concrete revelation in a historical personal life mediated through community? Without such revelation, forgiveness and purpose would remain, at best, abstract speculations. But in Christ God's gracious pardon and Kingdom-forming purpose have established themselves as practical realities; they have actually been bestowed upon men. The work of Christ in establishing His community has accomplished the archetype, and also the vessel, of God's eternal purpose. In identifying with this purpose, and through being accepted, in spite of sin, into the Body of Christ, the individual finds the answer to his own deepest needs (the guarantee of his ultimate worth and meaningfulness) precisely in and through what Christ has done for him. Thus, in Ritschl's view, the "proof" is completed with the exposition of the integral mediating role of the historical Christ.

The concluding part of the book sets forth the "consequences" of justification and reconciliation. One of Ritschl's constant emphases is that the meaning of theological notions must be manifested in practical life—in the spiritual and moral activity of the personal subject. He isolates the marks of Christian existence which are grounded in and derived from Christ. A key idea is lordship over the world, sublimely exemplified in Christ on the Cross. Through unshakable trust in God the Father, men bear suffering, the world's contempt, and even violent death with patience and humility. Such faith in God, freeing one from all selfish worldly pursuits, issues in spontaneously prayerful thanksgiving and in love-motivated action. One can act "in" the Kingdom of God, for by faith one affirms the universal sovereignty of God; so to act is to partake, in time, of the life eternal.

No brief summary can do justice to the incisiveness, subtlety, and detail of Ritschl's massive tome. With masterful competency in Biblical scholarship and in the history of theology, he sharpens his views against the diversifications of the whole tradition in which he stands. His own central thrust emerges from the interplay of two concerns: the redemptive and ethical normativeness of the Biblical, historical Christ, and the practical character of religious affirmations, both as answering to real needs of human existence and as manifest in the actualities of man's will, feeling, and course of life. A widely influential Ritschlian school flourished for decades after the master's death. More recent theology has seen sharp reactions against him. Yet his greatness is reflected in the fact that so much of subsequent theological discussion, even when explicitly anti-Ritschlian, has proceeded from one or another elements in his combination of themes.

COLLOQUIA PERIPATETICA

Author: John Duncan (1796-1870) [Edited by William Knight]
Type of work: Theological conversations
First published: 1870

Principal Ideas Advanced

God is apprehended within the soul of man; God is the archetype of human existence.

Evil is the privation of the good; although God is the author of all things, He cannot be the author of sin, for sin has no author.

A balanced Calvinism avoids extremes of Arminianism and Antinomianism, for the will of man chooses the good only because of the efficacious operation of the grace of God.

Mysticism is not altogether false; it errs only when it attempts to destroy the logical.

Dr. John Duncan, known to his students and admirers as "Rabbi Duncan," was born at Aberdeen in 1796. Having left the Secession, he entered the Established Church and studied theology at the University of Aberdeen (1817-1821). There, under the influence of his professors, he was brought out of "Spinozism" or any other form of naturalism. Dr. Duncan later told how he "danced on the brig of Dee with delight, when he was convinced that there was a God." In 1825 he was licensed to preach, although he accepted the Westminster Confession only as "articles of peace." Shortly afterwards he experienced a conversion under the influence of Caesar Malan of Geneva and his own biographer, David Brown. Malan sought by syllogism to bring inquirers to assurance of faith. His words to Duncan, "See, you have the word of God in your mouth" flashed through him like a shock of electricity. Duncan says of the outcome: "Next day as I sat down to study, and took my pen in my hand, I became suddenly the passive recipient of all the truths which I had heard and been taught in my childhood. I sat unmoving for hours, and they came and preached themselves to me. There was no investigation, but the presentation of the truth to me passive." Assurance of salvation by syllogism was shattered in Duncan's later experiences of tormenting doubts as to the sincerity of his faith. The influence of the eccentric Dr. John Kidd of Aberdeen and the searching experimental preacher Dr. John Love contributed to the ripening of Duncan's personal piety and doctrinal thought. The writings of the Puritan, John Owen, and the Dutch Master of Federal Theology, Herman Witsius, gave a distinct cast to his theological studies.

In 1836, Duncan was ordained as pastor of Milton Church, Glasgow, and was married the following year. A skilled Hebraist, he was sent by the Church of Scotland in 1841 to minister to Jews in Hungary. After the disruption of the Church of Scotland in 1843, Duncan was appointed Professor of Hebrew in the New College of the Free Church at Edinburgh. Although his absent-mindedness and other eccentricities were not conducive to effective language teaching, his influence on the thought and piety of his students was incalculable. He was himself the "good specimen of the Patristic Scholastic Puritan" which he judged John Owen to be.

Colloquia peripatetica consists of

notes of conversations with Duncan, made by William Knight, Professor of Moral Philosophy in the University of St. Andrews. The colloquia are miscellaneous, ranging over many aspects of philosophical and practical theology. The peripatetic flavor of Duncan's dialectic exemplifies what he says about Aristotle in one of the colloquia: "He is by far the compactest and most precise writer we have, in any literature. He is the *beau ideal* of the precise. Two things I wonder at in Aristotle—the extent of his acquirements and the exactitude of his writing. . . . He could see, I suppose, as far as a mason could see into a wall that he had built, and that is a good deal farther than other people see into it." The charm of the *Colloquia,* however, is due to its Socratic and Platonic as well as to its peripatetic character. Duncan admired Aristotle, but he loved Plato: "Plato goes peering up, often into cloudland; yet I like to follow him into the mist, for when I don't see through it, I generally think *he* does. It is a good thing to go up now and then into the mist, if we do not, like Ixion, embrace the cloud."

The *Colloquia* opens with the remark, "I am a philosophical sceptic, who have taken refuge in Theology." God is the starting point for Duncan's thought, which is deductive from that postulate. Dr. Knight asks, "But as we are not divine, how do you get *up* in the first instance?" Dr. Duncan replies, "I cannot tell you; *only, I am up*. Probably it is by instinct. Say, if you choose, that reason has overleapt itself. I find that I cannot bridge the gulf between the creature and a Creator, the many and the One, in my ascent, so I endeavour to do so in my descent." To the charge of circularity in reasoning, Duncan retorts, "No: there is no circle; for God is apprehended within the soul of man, as the archetype of existence. We do not infer His being from what we are. We cannot rise to Him thus. But He is himself within us. *His* voice, not the voice of consciousness, may be heard."

Duncan believed in reason and respected it as the creature of God, but he was doubtful of the philosophies. Reason is of use to show its own impotence and to welcome a revelation. The results of the Scottish Common Sense philosophy are valid, but not philosophically. Duncan believed in axioms (including the mathematical and logical laws); in the senses which report the external world; in objectivity (including the existence of other minds); in testimony (under which is to be ranked the evidences of a historical revelation); and in the syllogistic nexus. He believed in common sense, but not in a philosophy of common sense which he branded as "can't-help-myself-ism."

Belief in God presses multifariously upon man, Duncan declared. Its origin is neither here nor there, but everywhere. There is a knowledge of God which all men have, and a knowledge possible only to the new creature. The operation of the Holy Spirit must be recognized as the source of a faith in God which is more than parrotism and traditionalism. Consequently, not all conviction can be due to demonstration.

George Berkeley and David Hume, though in error, were profounder than the Scottish philosopher Thomas Reid (1710-1796), Duncan believed. Objectivity reached through the immediate perception of matter may be true for the percipient alone. An absolutely universal truth is needed, Duncan emphatically asserts; "I would despise humanity, were it not so." Plato was on the track of this truth with his theory concerning archetypal ideas, but the final answer is found in the creation of man in the image of God; as cast in the divine image, man possesses a universal element in his nature.

Duncan thought much and deeply on the nature and origin of evil. He stoutly defended the Augustinian thesis that evil, including sin, is a privation. God is not the author of sin, because sin has no author. The privative view of sin enabled Augustine to escape from Manichaeism and supported Samuel Rutherford's strong position that God is the author of all entitive acts. Though sin is positive as well as privative, its privative nature is its profoundest. Sin aims at deicide. It seeks to slay Being at the root.

Whence comes sin? Not from God, but *from naught*. At this point the causal nexus is broken, for sin is causeless and irrational. The causal nexus fails also to bind the will of God *qua* will. As *moral* the divine will is necessarily holy, but it is free *qua* will. The determinism of Jonathan Edwards is rejected, as hazarding a speculation on will *qua* will, and therefore on all will, divine and human. Yet the question of free will may not be dismissed as an insoluble problem of metaphysics. Four ultra theories, two on either side of the controversy, are repudiated: liberty of independence and liberty of indifference, on the one hand, and freedom from co-action without or within the will, on the other. The liberty which is the ground of accountability is more than the latter and less than the former theories maintain. Independency is Epicureanism. God is remotely the cause of the action's causality. The *permission* of sin by God, as Rutherford said, is adorable, while the *actual fact* of sin is abominable. As to the permission, some of God's attributes would not have been displayed had sin not been. Duncan says paradoxically: "In a certain sense I am a tremendous free-willer. My predestination is all free will." There was no necessity that the perfections of God should be displayed. Edwardian determinism leads to the *necessity* of creation. Yet Edwardian theology, despite this metaphysical blot, is steeped in the affections.

Duncan once remarked "There's no such thing as Calvinism." Calvin simply pieced together teachings of St. Augustine, St. Remigius (c.438-c.533), St. Anselm, and Luther. Duncan called himself a *high* Calvinist, while deploring the miserable narrowness of some Calvinists. He also repudiated the "hyper-Calvinism" which he characterized as all house and no door. His breadth included a willingness to turn Thomist commentator on one occasion. He quotes Aquinas as saying, "Deus voluit hoc propter illud, sed non propter illud voluit hoc Deus," and comments: "There is a relation of *propter*ty between the two things as the objects of divine volition. There is much more in this distinction of Aquinas than meets the eye at first glance; though the vulgar mind will call it a distinction without a difference."

The *Colloquia* represents Calvinism as a *juste milieu* between Arminianism and Antinomianism. Arminianism robs God while Antinomianism fanaticizes man. Moral power in the will is to be admitted against the Antinomians, but disowned against the Arminians. That God works half of salvation and man the other half is the Arminian error. That God works all, and man does all, is true. As metaphysicians we are compelled to fall back on the Apostle Paul's statement, "Work out your salvation, for it is God that worketh in you." One colloquium, warning against the loose use of the word "heresy," notes that Amesius in his *De conscientia* discussed the question whether Arminianism is a heresy. Duncan's zeal for the moral law overcame him in another colloquium, in which he suggests that there is only one heresy, and that is Antinomianism. F. D. Maurice's ethical theory is branded as pure illegality, a charge which Maurice repudiated in the preface to his work on conscience, in which he magnanimously paid tribute to Dr. Duncan's learning and worth, in return for the latter's censure on his writings.

Several of the colloquia exemplify what one of them refers to as the attempt to say the unsayable. Two kinds of perplexity are distinguished: one when the theme itself is slippery as an eel and glides from us altogether; the other when, in our attempt to solve a perplexity, or to grapple with it, it gives out its mystery as if it were throwing out a great cuttlefish blackness about itself. Duncan's colloquia studiously avoid the meaninglessness they censure, while they exhibit an abundance of paradoxical expressions in their effort to express the deepest mysteries of the Christian faith. Thus, Duncan says: "Mysticism is not altogether false. Mysticism only errs when it enters into the province of logic to destroy it; as logic errs when it trespasses into the domain of intuition to fetter it. Whenever we worship, we acknowledge that there is a region above us, at once known and unknown, half-clear and half-dark."

SYSTEMATIC THEOLOGY

Author: Charles Hodge (1797-1878)
Type of work: Calvinistic apologetics; soteriology
First published: 1871-1873

Principal Ideas Advanced

Theology is an inductive science in which the systematically arranged data of the Old and New Testament constitute the basis of man's knowledge about God, man, and man's final destiny.

The writers of Scripture exercised their own talents even though the authors were infallible instruments of the Holy Spirit; what the writers of Scripture wrote is the Word of God.

Although our knowledge of God is imperfect and partial, sufficient information has been revealed to insure the possibility of man's redemption from sin and to guarantee man's eternal salvation.

Charles Hodge was born in 1797, and he taught at Princeton Theological Seminary from 1822 until shortly before his death in 1878. His *Systematic Theology* is representative of orthodox Protestant theology as far as doctrine is concerned, but Hodge's views of the nature of theology itself are original and provocative.

In Volume One Hodge defends the thesis that theology is a science. The Bible itself, however, is not a system of theology. Nevertheless, the truths which the theologian has to collect, arrange, and exhibit in their internal relations to one another are contained in the Bible. What nature is to the natural scientist, the Bible is to the theologian. The Bible is a storehouse of facts about God; the theologian applies the inductive method to these facts. Facts are to be carefully collected, and the theologian is to seek the greatest comprehensiveness possible. Theological principles are not to be impressed upon the facts, but are to be derived from the data of the Scriptures. The latter constitute the facts of theology. Theology is, therefore, concerned with nothing other than the facts and principles of the Bible.

Hodge argues that to hold that the task of theology is to exhibit the facts of Scripture is not to rule out the possibility of natural theology, although what nature teaches concerning God and our duties is revealed more fully and more authoritatively in God's Word. The Bible is the sole infallible source of knowledge of things divine. Hodge repudiates the claims of rationalism, mysticism, and Romanism that reason, or an inner supernatural light, or an infallible Church are superior or co-ordinate avenues to theological knowledge.

The Scriptures of the Old and New Testaments are infallible, Hodge declares, because they are the Word of God, and they are the Word of God because they were given by the supernatural inspiration of the Holy Spirit. The latter exerted an influence upon the minds of certain select men so that they became the organs of God; what God said, they said. The sacred writers were not machines, but living men. Their being inspired as the organs of God in no way interfered with the free exercise of their distinctive mental characteristics as individual writers. The writers of Scripture impressed their peculiarities upon their productions as though they were under no special influence. God spoke in the language of men, and He used men as His instruments, each according to his own special gifts, according to his own nature. Although the inspired writer wrote out of the fullness of his own feelings and thought, and used the language and expressions which he found most natural and appropriate, what he wrote was what the Holy Spirit moved him to write.

As a Christian theologian, Hodge is concerned with the doctrine of God, with our knowledge of His nature and attributes, with the Trinity, the divinity of Christ, with the nature of the Holy Spirit, the divine decrees, the doctrines of creation and providence, with miracles and angels. He is concerned further with anthropology and soteriology, the subject matter of Volume Two; with the origin of the soul, the unity of the human race, with man's original state, the fall into sin, and with the divine plan of salvation through the person and work of Christ. He is concerned with regeneration, faith, justification, sanctification, with the moral law, with the means of grace, and finally, in the concluding section of Volume Three, with eschatology, the doctrine of last things, and with the state of the soul after death, the Resurrection, and the Second Coming.

The theologian's task is to study the Scriptures, Hodge writes. The theologian is supported in his efforts by the fact that all men have some innate knowledge of God, for men are sentient, rational, and moral beings. In addition, the traditional arguments for the existence of God, except for the ontological argument, in spite of the objections of Hume and Kant, serve to prove what theists hold to be true concerning God.

That God can be known does not mean that all that is true concerning God can be known. We cannot form a mental image of God, Hodge declares, nor can He be comprehended in such a manner that we can know His essence and all His attributes. Although our knowledge of God is partial and imperfect, it is true as far as it goes. To the extent that our idea of God is determined by the revelation He has made in the constitution of our nature, in His works, in His Word, and in the person of His Son, God is really what we believe Him to be. He is an infinite, eternal, and unchangeable Spirit, whose being includes wisdom, power, justice, goodness, holiness, and truth.

The triune God is the creator of man, Hodge insists. Man's body was formed by the immediate intervention of God, and his soul was derived from God. Man consists, therefore, of two distinct principles, a body and a soul: the one corporeal, the other spiritual. The soul is not a form of the divine life, or a series of acts, or an unsubstantial force; it is, rather, a real subsistence, an entity or substance. Man is a created spirit in vital union with a material organized body.

Man was originally created in a state of maturity and perfection, Hodge writes. The body of Adam was free of disease and the seeds of death. Its constitution contained nothing that was not conducive to the highest happiness and well-being of man. The distinguishing characteristic of man is that he is created in the image and likeness of God. As God is a spirit, so the human soul is a spirit. God thus endowed man with the essential attributes of spirit; namely, reason, conscience, and will. It is because we are like God that we can know Him and are capable of having communion with Him. Man was created in a state of original righteousness, in perfect harmony, and endowed with knowledge and holiness.

After the creation, God made a promise of life to Adam, upon the condition of perfect obedience, and He attached the penalty of death for disobedience. Man's state of probation ended in an act of disobedience, the account of which is neither allegorical nor mythical, but truly historical. Man's Fall resulted in the immediate execution of the righteous judgment of God, in man's expulsion from the Garden of Eden, and in the loss of man's original righteousness.

The sin of Adam and Eve injured not only themselves, but also all their descendants, who are, therefore, rendered incapable of performing any spiritual good. The redemption of fallen man can, take place only because God Himself has graciously accomplished it through the person and work of Christ Jesus.

The incarnation of the eternal Son of God was not a necessary event arising out of the nature of God, Hodge declares, but an act of voluntary humiliation.

Jesus was truly man, with a real material body, in every respect like the bodies of ordinary men. He also had a rational soul; He thought and reasoned like other men. Nevertheless, He was truly God. He was perfect man and perfect God and still one person—two natures united in hypostatic union, but not mingled or confounded.

The name of Christ is the only name by which man can be saved. The design of the incarnation of the Son of God was to reconcile man unto God. Christ is the only Mediator between God and man.

Christ is truly a priest, writes Hodge, in that He alone has liberty of access unto God. Sin could not have been taken away by any sacrifice other than His. For it is only through Him that God is propitious to sinful men. Christ once offered Himself as a sacrifice to satisfy divine justice, and thereby He reconciled us to God. Christ suffered vicariously; He suffered in the place of sinners; He was their substitute. The guilt of the sinner is expiated, and the justice of God is propitiated. For Christ's work was of the nature of a satisfaction; it met all the demands of God's law against the sinner, so that the sinner who believes in Christ is no longer condemned by the law, but is delivered from the power of sin and Satan and from all evil. The sinner is thus restored to the image and fellowship of God. His guilt is removed, and his soul is quickened with a new principle of divine life.

According to Hodge, the success of the whole scheme of divine redemption rests upon the fact that Christ rose from the dead with the same, although a changed, body. The ascended body of Christ as it now exists in Heaven is glorious, incorruptible, immortal, and spiritual, and yet it retains all the essential properties of a body.

Man's salvation is accomplished by the grace of God, which works a subjective change in the soul, thereby causing a spiritual resurrection, and a new birth or regeneration. Regeneration is an act of God, an act of His power, in which God is the agent, a quickening of the soul, a communication of a new principle of life. The first conscious exercise of the renewed soul is faith, the persuasion of the truth of the facts and doctrines recorded in the Scriptures, on the testimony of the Spirit of God.

Christ is the special object of saving faith, says Hodge, since by receiving the testimony of God concerning Him, the salvation of the sinner is secured. For faith is the condition on which God promises to impute unto men the righteousness of Christ, so that when they believe, they are no longer condemned, but are justified by a forensic act, in which God declares that justice has been satisfied so far as the believing sinner is concerned.

The act of justification is followed by a process of sanctification, a supernatural work of grace, whereby the principles of evil infecting our nature are increasingly removed and the principle of spiritual life grows until our acts, thoughts, and feelings are brought under control, and the soul is brought into conformity with the image of Christ. The soul is led to receive Jesus as its Savior, and is delivered from the guilt and power of sin. The soul of the believer is united to Christ; it participates in His merits, and it becomes the abode of the indwelling Holy Spirit, the source of a new spiritual life, a life that bears fruit in good works, in the keeping of God's holy law.

According to Hodge, the ordinary channels of God's grace, of the supernatural influence of the Holy Spirit, are the Word of God, the sacraments of baptism, the Lord's Supper, and prayer. It is by these means that God communicates to the souls of men the life-giving and sanctifying influences of the Spirit.

After death, after the dissolution of the body, the soul continues its conscious existence in an intermediate state, until the resurrection of the body, at the Second Coming of Christ. The Second Coming is marked by the resurrection of the just and the unjust, the Final Judgment, the end of the world, and the consummation of the Kingdom of Christ.

The Final Judgment is a definite event, Hodge declares, when the eternal destiny of men shall be finally determined and publicly manifest. Each person shall be assigned his final abode, in Heaven or in Hell. The righteous will then enjoy the incomprehensible blessedness of Heaven, which arises from the vision of God and which flows from His infinite love. The saints will enjoy the secure and everlasting possession of every good, and they will be entirely exempt from all sin and sorrow. The wicked will enter into everlasting punishment, the sufferings of which will arise from the loss of earthly goods, and the presence and favor of God, from the final withdrawal from them of the Holy Spirit, from the despairful operations of conscience, and from positive afflictions, which, although not literally fire, are nevertheless perpetual. As there are degrees in the glory of the blessedness of Heaven, so there will be degrees in the suffering of the lost.

The theology of Charles Hodge has exercised and continues to exert considerable influence on orthodox segments of the Protestant Church. It is characterized by a thorough treatment of opposing views and by a minimum of speculation upon matters on which there is little Biblical evidence.

LITERATURE AND DOGMA

Author: Matthew Arnold (1822-1888)
Type of work: Critique of theology
First published: 1873

Principal Ideas Advanced

Since the language of the Bible is fluid and literary, a knowledge of culture is necessary to an understanding of the Bible.

Dogmatic theology falsifies the meaning of the Bible, for such a theology rests on the logical development of metaphysical ideas about which there is endless disagreement.

The object of religion is conduct; religion is morality heighened by emotion.

Religious beliefs are not scientific; they are instances of "Aberglaube," or extra-belief, the literary expression of hope.

Jesus showed that righteousness and happiness are one by exhibiting a sweet reasonableness, a method of inner examination, and a secret of self-renouncement.

Matthew Arnold's *Literature and Dogma* is both a plea and a demonstration. It is a plea for a literary reading of the Bible, for an understanding of the Bible as an expression of human aspirations and expectations, and it is a demonstration of such a reading. The result is a sensitive and suggestive interpretation of the Bible, particularly of the New Testament.

Arnold's argument together with his interpretation has relevance in the twentieth century, for a division persists between those who take the Bible literally and build dogmatic theology upon it and those who take the Bible as a literary work and build their lives upon it.

Arnold was disturbed by the decreasing power of influence of the Bible, and he attributed the Bible's decline to the effect of dogmatic theology. He wanted to find an experimental basis for the Bible, a way of verifying its message, and he deplored the theologian's reliance on unverifiable assumptions. He decided that if the Bible were properly read as a literary expression of hopes and ideals, it could then be experimentally tried by putting into action the suggestions to be found within it.

It was not enough for Arnold to declare that the Bible has to be read as a literary work. He had first to consider how a proper reading of the Bible is possible. The answer, it seemed to him, is that one can read the Bible only after having acquainted oneself with "the best that has been known and said in the world"; that is, with culture. If a man immerses himself in letters, he acquires a "flexibility of spirit" which, together with "the judgment which forms itself insensibly in a fair mind" as a result of culture, provides the reader with a new perspective on what he reads.

Armed by culture, a man can recognize the language of the Bible as being literary, not scientific, language. Arnold points out that such terms as "grace," "new birth," and "justification," terms which St. Paul used "in a fluid and passing way, as men use terms in common discourse or in eloquence and poetry, to describe approximately, but only approximately, what they have present before their mind," have been used by theologians "in a fixed and rigid manner, as if they [the terms] were symbols with as definite and fully grasped a meaning as the names *line* or *angle*. . . ." Once one realizes that theologians have misread the Bible, the irrelevance and logical austerity of dogmatic theology can be accounted for.

The term "God" is central in religious writings, Arnold points out, and yet, he declares, no other term is more ambiguous. The difficulties of understanding the word are multiplied when those who use it suppose that it has a definite and precise meaning. Theologians have constructed an elaborate and presumably Biblically justified conception of God as "an infinite and eternal substance, and at the same time a person, the great first cause, the moral and intelligent governor of the universe; Jesus Christ consubstantial with him; and the Holy Ghost a person proceeding from the other two." But, Arnold writes, this "scientific" idea is nothing more than a fanciful construction by men who are not cultured enough to be able to read the Bible. When one considers that religion is concerned primarily with conduct and that conduct is three-fourths of life, when one regards religion as "morality touched by emotion," then one finally realizes that the term "God" has been used to call attention to *"the enduring power, not ourselves, which makes for righteousness."* Arnold attributes the difficulties which come out of theology to the failure of theologians to recognize the moral relevance of the term "God" as used in the Bible. He quotes with approval Luther's definition of God as the "best that we can know."

Arnold claims that Israel's original comment on experience is a true comment: *"Righteousness tendeth to life."* The belief was that the Eternal, the enduring way of things, is such that a man is truly himself, truly lives, and is truly happy, only if he is righteous. As time went on, however, this basic idea —that righteousness tendeth to life —which was more an expression of hope and a comment on experience than it was a metaphysical generalization, tended to be perverted by the expectation that eventually the righteous would prosper in some material and political fashion and that the ungodly would go down to obvious defeat. The idea that righteous living is *living* in the best sense of that term was obscured by the idea that righteousness somehow leads to an *outer* victory, a triumph of the outer and not merely of the inner man. Thus, the idea of the Messiah arose. But the idea of the Messiah is not an experimental idea; it is "a kind of fairy-tale. . . ." Such an idea, the idea of a Messiah, a belief for which there is no justification in experience, Arnold calls "Aberglaube" or "extra-belief." Extra-belief is "the poetry of life"; it expresses human hopes and resolutions, and since it is poetry, it must be understood as poetry.

By the time of Jesus Christ righteousness was no longer associated with happiness; the impulse which emotion had given to righteousness had been lost. Arnold describes Jesus' task, then, as that of restoring to righteousness "the sanction of *happiness.*" To accomplish this end, Jesus had to turn attention to the inner man. Judaism had come more and more to emphasize the outward manifestation of righteousness, the act according to the law, but Jesus turned the attention of His followers to "heart and character," to matters of motive, sentiment, and intention. He taught with such "sweet reasonableness" that by His manner He made righteousness attractive; in finally understanding the reasons behind rules, the followers of Christ found themselves refreshed in spirit and made happy. Jesus also encouraged self-renouncement, a turning from the ways which lead to the destruction of the self, and a turning to the ways of righteousness, a way already exemplified by Christ's mildness and sweet reasonableness and by His concern for the inner self. The sanction for righteousness became, then, not the utility of obedience—if you obey, *then* you will be happy—but the love and happiness which Christ inspired by his presence, by His method of inwardness, and by His secret of self-renouncement. In loving Christ, men loved righteousness, and in the love of Christ and of righteousness they were happy. Happiness became the consequence, but not the motive, for those who followed Him. The motive was love, not happiness, and thus happiness became the sanction of the righteousness which that love encouraged.

But just as the Old Testament idea that to righteousness belongs happiness, or that righteousness brings life, gave way to the *Aberglaube* of the Messiah, so the New Testament idea, which was the sanction of the Old Testament faith, gave way to the *Aberglaube* "of a phantasmagorical advent of Jesus Christ, a resurrection and judgment, Christ's adherents glorified, his rejectors punished everlastingly."

Once Christianity succumbed to the temptation of "extra-belief," it lost the strength that came from reliance on internal evidence. The emphasis then fell on prophecy and miracle. What was wrong with this fall within Christianity was not the introduction of *Aberglaube;* Arnold agrees with Goethe in regarding *Aberglaube* as "the poetry of life." Poetry has its uses; it enables the imagination to construct a possibility to which the heart can give assent. But poetry has its dangers also, particularly for those who forget that it is poetry with which they are concerned, imaginative and not scientific language. The fall was not to *Aberglaube,* but to prophecy and miracle.

Arnold argues that is is a mistake to rely on prophecies for evidence in support of Christianity. Prophetic language is ambiguous; the description of an act is adaptable to the language of prophecy; men sometimes act in full knowledge of what has been prophesied; and translations tend to emphasize, as prophetic, passages which were in all likelihood innocent of prophetic intent. In any case, the truth of predictions has nothing to do with the essential emphasis upon conduct and righteousness. Even if there have been prophets, men able, through supernatural support, to know of the future, the meaning of the Christian religion does not come from them.

Nor can Christianity find its proof in miracles. Men forget—and many never realize—that the idea of God is not a metaphysical but a moral idea; the idea is concerned with the character of conduct, not with the structure of reality. But ordinary minds are very much impressed by events which seem to depart from the natural course of things, and many persons are inclined to suppose that a religion which encourages extraordinary events must somehow be a true religion. Anthropomorphic language suits the sentiments of conventional minds, and the supposition of miracles, a supposition suggested and encouraged by anthropomorphic language, confirms the metaphysical faith which tends to accompany the blind use of poetic language.

But, Arnold declares, there is a persistent and tenacious critic of prophecy and miracle; that critic is the *Zeit-Geist,* the Time-Spirit, the mind of man enlightened by experience. One can understand very well how hope and imagination can combine to foster belief in prophecy and miracle; the creative impulse which moved Shakespeare moved also the writers of the Old and New Testaments. The critical and experienced mind, the mind trained by culture, can find every reason for believing that in the accounts of prophecies and miracles the poetic imagination is at work, but no mind can find criteria by reference to which rival miraculous claims can systematically be tested. The only truth which may reside in the accounts of miracles is the psychological truth that those who err tend to become ill, while those who recognize their crimes and receive forgiveness tend to become healthy again. Jesus was a man capable of freeing others from the sense of guilt. Enlightened by the *Zeit-Geist,* the critic understands that the account of the Resurrection, for example, is not so much a fragment of history as it is an expression of hope. In effect, writes Arnold, the Biblical narrators, for all their simplicity and good faith, are really saying, *"Behold a legend growing under your eyes!"*

Despite the fact that the writers of the New Testament were not aware of their literal acceptance of extra-belief, and despite the possibility that Jesus Himself did not apprehend the full significance of His conduct and was Himself affected by the *Aberglaube* which determined the descriptions of His acts, the meaning of the New Testament becomes clear to one who takes the difficult road of literary criticism. The New Testament record is inconsistent, ambiguous, and puzzling; it is full of the "poetry of life." But, properly understood, it presents Jesus as one who asked men to look into themselves and to renounce whatever is not worthy of the self.

Jesus spiritualized the *Aberglaube* of Israel — the belief in a Messiah—by His method of inner searching and His secret of self-renouncement. But the method and the secret need the support of His "sweet reasonableness," a matter of disposition which He could not bequeath to His followers. When that sweet reasonableness is missing, the method and the secret fail, and what should be read as a call to the Spirit becomes a metaphysical hint to be deciphered by dogmatic theologians. Perhaps the most tragic consequence of the failure to read the Bible properly is the Christian's coming to believe that resurrection from physical death is the final reward of religion. The idea that the "dying" which Christ encouraged is an inner dying of the unrighteous self and that what was demanded by Him was not a physical but a spiritual crucifixion and resurrection—a death of the old spirit to make new life possible—is an idea lost to anyone who takes the language of the Bible literally.

When readers suppose that the Bible is to be read as history or metaphysics, there is the danger of their giving up the Bible altogether, for time will show that much of what the Bible says is either false or improbable—insofar as it is meaningful at all. But if the Bible is read as a literary attempt to endorse the righteous life and to commend the method, the secret, and the sweet reasonableness of Christ, the Bible can survive scientific attack, for such an attack is then seen to be irrelevant.

In taking the Bible seriously as a literary expression of that spiritual reconstruction which Christ made evident, Arnold performed a service to the Christian reader. His work reveals a sophisticated, a *cultured,* awareness of the uses of language. Philosophers and theologians who are coming to the Bible with a fresh appreciation of the varieties of linguistic uses—an appreciation made possible by twentieth century philosophical investigations—can find a fresh and resourceful tutor in Matthew Arnold.

SCIENCE AND HEALTH WITH KEY TO THE SCRIPTURES

Author: Mary Baker Eddy (1821-1910)
Type of work: Principles of Christian Science
First published: 1875

Principal Ideas Advanced

By denying evil and by stressing the primacy of the mind, one can overcome illness and death.

God is Mind; since God is infinite, all is Mind.

Jesus redeemed man from matter, sin, and death by giving man a true sense of love.

Sin and suffering are the result of the false belief in the existence of matter; matter is nothing, an illusion.

Along with its author, Mary Baker Eddy, and the religious body, Christian Science, which is built upon it, *Science and Health with Key to the Scriptures* occupies a unique position in modern religious thought. It is practically impossible to understand any one of the three separately, for to a most unusual degree the lives of the author, the book, and the church are interwoven one with the other. Mary Baker Eddy, who was born in obscurity in rural New Hampshire in 1821 and who was at her death in Boston in 1910 internationally known as the founder of Christian Science, poured into the countless editions of her constantly revised book the totality of her religious, philosophical, and practical world views.

There is no difficulty in understanding Mrs. Eddy's opening statements on the discovery and mission of Christian Science: "In the year 1866 I discovered the Science of Metaphysical Healing, and named it Christian Science. God has been graciously fitting me, during many years, for the reception of a final revelation of the absolute Principle of Scientific Mind-healing. This apodictical Principle points to the revelation of Immanuel, the everpresent God,—the sovereign Omnipotence, delivering the children of men from every ill that flesh is heir to."

The first edition of one thousand copies contained 456 pages divided into eight chapters dealing with the following subjects: Natural Science, Imposition and Demonstration, Spirit and Matter, Creation, Prayer and Atonement, Marriage, Physiology, and Healing the Sick. Later editions were much amended and contained additional chapters on such themes as Animal Magnetism, Christian Science Practice, Teaching Christian Science, together with an important section entitled "Key to the Scriptures" which provides Mrs. Eddy's original interpretations of Biblical teaching and terminology. The variations among the editions not only reflect the progressive refinement and extension of Mrs. Eddy's theological position but also chronicle her reaction to the many and varied responses the public was making to her developing religion.

Promotion of the work was of great interest to the author who insisted that each loyal follower obtain the newest edition and discard the old. An idea of the significance of this is suggested in the fact that just twenty-two years after the first appearance of the book, it had passed into 124 editions. Judgment regarding the nature of the author's indebtedness to writers and thinkers other than herself is influenced by the position taken toward Mrs. Eddy and her movement as a whole. Some reject any suggestion of influence other than divine inspiration; others are convinced that the book reflects quite clearly a direct indebtedness to other writers, among them Phineas Quimby, an itinerant New England mental healer (1802-1866), John Ruskin (1819-1900), and Thomas Carlyle (1795-1881). However the matter is viewed, it is certain that whatever the sources for the extensive work, everything which Mrs. Eddy presents is marked with her own distinctive touch.

The major themes of Mrs. Eddy's work reflect her convictions in three important areas: psychology, philosophy, and theology. Her psychology has as its dominant theme that of mental prophylaxis or mind-healing. By denying evil, by positive thinking, by stressing the primacy of the mind, indeed, by denying the objectivity of the material world, one can overcome illness and death by recognizing them as illusions. Mrs. Eddy writes, "The notion that mind and matter commingle in the human illusion as to sin, sickness, and death must eventually submit to the Science of Mind, which denies this notion." This position receives philosophical and theological support in the identification of God, good, mind, and all: *"God is Mind, and God is infinite; hence all is Mind."*

The fundamental position of *Science and Health* is that "All is Mind and Mind's idea." Since God, perfect goodness and the only reality, is Mind, then sin, sickness, evil, and matter are not real. Matter and evil can thus be identified. The only reality is the world of the mind; there is no objective world. He who would progress in an understanding of these teachings must learn by doing; he must demonstrate that life itself is God. "Hold perpetually this thought," Mrs. Eddy writes, "that it is the spiritual idea, the Holy Ghost and Christ, which enables you to demonstrate, with scientific certainty, the rule of healing, based upon its divine Principle, Love, underlying, overlying, and encompassing all true being." (Present editions of Mrs. Eddy's work conclude with a long chapter of one hundred pages entitled "Fruitage" in which nearly a hundred testimonies are given to the healing effected through acceptance and practice of the teaching in *Science and Health.*)

The first subject presented in the current authorized editions is prayer, which is interpreted as a subjective state whose value is hindered by audible expression. In keeping with this view the only spoken prayer at Christian Science services is the Lord's Prayer accompanied by Mrs. Eddy's verse by verse explanation of its "spiritual sense." The phrase, "Deliver us from evil," is interpreted as "Deliver us from the evil one" which "is but another name for the first lie and all liars." Mrs. Eddy's version demonstrates succinctly the nature of her entire work: "Our Father-Mother God, all harmonious, Adorable One, Thy kingdom is come; Thou art ever-present. Enable us to know,—as in heaven, so on earth,—God is omnipotent, supreme. Give us grace for to-day; feed the famished affections; And Love is reflected in love; and God leadeth us not into temptation, but delivereth us from sin, disease, and death. For God is infinite, all-power, all Life, Truth, Love, over all, and All."

Turning next to the atonement and the Eucharist, Mrs. Eddy presents a moral influence theory of the former, and the latter is seen not as commemorating the evening meal before the day of Jesus' crucifixion but rather the morning meal which Jesus had with His disciples after His resurrection. By giving man a truer sense of love, Mrs. Eddy claims, Jesus redeemed man from the law of matter, sin, and death by the law of the Spirit. Mrs. Eddy rejects both "erudite theology," which is said to provide a ready pardon for all sinners by means of Jesus' crucifixion, and Spiritualism, which uses Jesus' death as a means of proving that spirits can return to earth. Jesus' crucifixion and resurrection are proof that death is a mortal dream, and thus they provide the supreme vindication of the divine Science. The material disappearance of Jesus assisted the disciples to move from belief to understanding, a movement which is the real meaning of Pentecost.

The brief teaching on marriage as a legal and moral temporary provision to be accepted until "it is learned that God is the Father of all" is followed by a refutation of the errors of Spiritualism on the basis of the irreconcilability of mind and matter. In the next chapter animal magnetism is identified with hypnotism and mortal mind, and is soundly rejected. The chapter on science, theology, and medicine contains the central propositions of the book: "1. God is All-in-all. 2. God is good. Good is Mind. 3. God, Spirit, being all, nothing is matter. 4. Life, God, omnipotent good, deny death, evil, sin, disease—Disease, sin evil, death, deny good, omnipotent God, life." Disease is healed by knowledge of or belief in Mind or God.

The chapter on physiology reiterates the lack of affinity between mind and matter and the power of truth to cast out the ills of the flesh. Evil is seen as nothing, as having neither power nor reality, yet as self-assertive. The perspective changes with great frequency from what appears to be true to mortal mind and what is actually true from the standpoint of Science. Thus one finds the author repeatedly claiming that although sin and suffering are real, they are illusions.

In the chapter "Science of Being," Mrs. Eddy further supports the basic teaching regarding the unreality of matter, and she summarizes the teachings of Christian Science. Again, error is defined as illusion having no real existence; since "*Truth is real . . . error, Truth's unlikeness, is unreal.*" Divine metaphysics explains matter away and only "Spirit" is recognized.

The reader must decide when Mrs. Eddy is speaking descriptively and when normatively, as when she states that "As for spiritual error there is none." Hostile critics have heaped scorn upon both style and content in this work, and even the most charitable admit to difficulties in gaining precision of understanding.

The thirty-two tenets offered as the platform of divine metaphysics or Christian Science reiterate the themes already mentioned here. The third one is typical and illustrates both the thorny nature of the problem with which Mrs. Eddy wrestled and the kind of answer she proposed: "The notion that both evil and good are real is a delusion of material sense, which Science annihilates. Evil is nothing, no thing, mind, nor power. As manifested by mankind it stands for a life, nothing claiming to be something—for lust, dishonesty, selfishness, envy, hypocrisy, slander, hate, theft, adultery, murder, dementia, insanity, inanity, devil, hell, with all the etceteras that word includes."

It is easier to point out the ineptness of asserting the nothingness of that for which fifteen words denoting fifteen painfully familiar actualities are available than it is to solve the problem of evil. No reader familiar with the life and work of Mrs. Eddy can escape the poignancy of this representative passage any more than he can escape in his own experience the necessity of coming to terms with the same problem.

After considering various objections to Christian Science, Mrs. Eddy concludes with chapters on the practice and the teaching of Christian Science; she provides a recapitulation of her ideas, and an appendix of commentary on approximately one hundred verses of Scripture, together with a glossary of key Biblical terms.

LECTURES ON PREACHING

Author: Phillips Brooks (1835-1893)
Type of work: Homiletics
First published: 1877

Principal Ideas Advanced

Preaching has in it two elements, the truth preached and the personality of the preacher.

The preacher must be a whole person, able to enter into the most varied relationships with his fellow men.

The truth preached is the divine-human Christ, who said, "I am the Truth";

and preaching is the continuation of His witness that God is the Father of all men.

The goal of preaching, which is that of saving the souls of men, must guide the preparation and delivery of sermons.

Phillips Brooks delivered his *Lectures on Preaching* under the Lyman Beecher Lectureship at Yale Divinity School while he was rector of Trinity Episcopal Church in Boston. Brooks's thesis is that preaching has two essential components: the truth proclaimed, and the personality of the man who proclaims it. Christianity, for Brooks, is a "personal force," stemming from the Jesus who was both human and divine. Christ's loving proclamation of the universal Fatherhood of God transformed the lives of those whom He touched; and, witnessed to by His disciples, Christ's proclamation has been powerful to the ends of the earth. Jesus chose preaching as the method of spreading his Gospel. Preaching would serve for the dissemination of any truth equally well, but, says Brooks, it is especially adapted to the Gospel because "that truth is preeminently personal."

Because Brooks considers the man to be inextricably bound up with his message, he devotes the same number of lectures to "The Preacher" as he does to "The Sermon." The task of the theological seminary, he says, "must be nothing less than the making of a man. It cannot be the mere training to certain tricks. It cannot be even the furnishing with abundant knowledge. It must be nothing less than the kneading and tempering of a man's whole nature till it becomes of such a consistency and quality as to be capable of transmission."

The first task awaiting the potential minister is that of "winning a true self." Brooks warns against the tendency of most ministers to conform to the clerical "type." But he finds equally objectionable the way in which some try to pattern themselves on one or another outstanding preacher. The kind of development necessary is that which comes from a constant openness to God and to man, to divine truth and to human need. The first quality required in an effective preacher is "personal piety, a deep possession in one's own soul of the faith and hope and resolution which he is to offer to his fellow-men for their new life."

Great care should be exercised in the screening of ministerial candidates, writes Brooks. Above all, the ministry requires "whole" men, because it brings a man into almost every conceivable relation to his fellows. There are no specific ministerial duties. A minister has no contract which says what he is to do and where his responsibility ends. He is totally at the service of those who need him.

Brooks repudiates the view that the ministerial functions can be parceled out, so that one man can be a preacher and the other a pastor. Good health, both of body and soul, are of first importance; so are a disciplined mind and cultivated manner: "For a good sermon there must be a man who can speak well, whose nature stands in right relations to those to whom he speaks, who has brought his life close to theirs with sympathy."

Few callings, says Brooks, offer more challenge to greatness or grant more in the way of personal rewards than the ministry, but the dangers of failure are correspondingly great. Because the minister is, in most cases, responsible to no man for the way in which he employs himself, the temptation to sloth and indulgence always besets a preacher. Moreover, he is almost totally exempt from severe and healthy criticism, in spite of the willingness of gossips to find out his little faults and let him hear of them. That the young minister will be self-conceited is altogether likely, and when he gradually learns that men do not share his views concerning his worth, he runs the risk of becoming resentful and blaming the age and its aversion to preaching. There is no deliverance from this fault, says Brooks, except to fall back upon God, who is able to make us as ready to fail for Him as to succeed. However, Brooks adds, success can also have the effect of humbling a man, if it opens to him the deeper meaning of his work and lets him see that more is at stake than his personal ambition.

It is wonderful, says Brooks, to hear a minister talk about "my congregation!" This way of thinking contains much folly, but, at the same time, deep truth. A young minister, especially, is likely to attribute almost mystical qualities to the group which he faces as he stands in the pulpit and to forget that his congregation is composed of individual men, women, and children, whose thoughts are widely variant from one another's, and even further from his own. On the other hand, says Brooks, there is something hallowed in the relation of a preacher and his congregation. A preacher becomes a better man as he stands before the congregation; and the congregation ("this strange composite being"), if it sees that its minister is totally devoted to it, stands devotedly with him, and follows him as far as it is able. Even here, however, lies a danger; for the congregation will spoil the minister by its indulgence if he is not on his guard.

As the messenger must be one whose life is from day to day being molded by the power of Christ, it follows that the message will be nothing more nor less than the witness to others of the love that has transformed the life of the messenger. Preaching, says Brooks, is essentially witnessing: "However the Gospel may be capable of statement in dogmatic form, its truest statement we know is not in dogma but in personal life." The Incarnation itself is the personification of Truth. Jesus said, "As my Father has sent me into the world, even so have I sent you into the world." Preaching is, thus, the continuation of the Incarnation, of His life who said, "I am the Truth."

The minister must never lose sight of the truth that the purpose of preaching is always the salvation of men. The sermon is not intended to be a work of art for men to admire or contemplate—although it comes to be regarded as such both by the minister and by the people whenever it loses its purpose of persuading and moving men's souls. Again, the sermon is not intended to be a lecture in which Christ and the Gospel, faith and the Church, are made the subject of a discussion. Much preaching, Brooks complains, is "preaching about Christ as distinct from preaching Christ."

What salvation means in the concrete may not be the same for every minister; whether it has to do mainly with sin or with suffering, with the individual or with society, with the present world or the world to come, is a matter to be decided. "The first thing for you to do," says Brooks, "is to see clearly what you are going to preach for, what you mean to try to save men from. By your conviction about that, the whole quality of your ministry will be decided." In general, the goal of preaching is always to bring men to Christ and Christ to men: "The sermon is God's message sent by you to certain of your fellow-men." When, as he inevitably must, the minister undertakes to speak on social and political issues, he does so not as an expert in these disciplines, but as "the messenger of Christ to the soul of man." He is ready to speak on any contemporary topic, but his sermon will never be mistaken for a newspaper editorial. The minister is nothing apart from the authority of the Word which he is given to proclaim.

Although the *Lectures on Preaching* are concerned with broad principles and not with homiletical details, the book has much to impart in the way of practical advice on sermon-preparation. As between the practice of preparing intensively for each week's sermon and expending the same industry in wider studies, Brooks favors the latter. A congregation can always tell the difference between a sermon which has been "crammed" and one which is the result of seasoned thought and wide experience. Brooks maintains, however, that sermons ought to be carefully prepared during the preceding week and not gotten up on Saturday night. He is not impressed with the arguments for extemporaneous preaching, and he maintains that if a sermon is genuinely extemporaneous when it is written, it will still have that quality when it is spoken. The main question, says Brooks, is whether the sermon springs freshly from the preacher's heart and mind, and whether it is responsive to its audience. If so, a man's sermon will be "like the leaping of a fountain and not like the pumping of a pump."

Speaking of the selection of sermon topics, Brooks recommends following the calendar of the Church year. It is flexible enough to permit each man all the liberty he needs, while providing the kind of direction which will help him to preserve a proper symmetry. The actual selection of a text or a topic should, says Brooks, arise from a sympathetic and wise perception of what the people need. This, he adds, will not come as a sudden impression resulting from a casual conversation or a parish visit or the need to convince some critic. "It is the aggregate effect of a large sympathetic intercourse, the fruit of a true knowledge of human nature, combined with a special knowledge of these special people, and a cordial interest in the circumstances under which they live." Brooks urges that a minister particularly remember the large group in his congregation who are only loosely attached to the Church. He calls them "seekers." If you preach to these, he says, you will be preaching to all.

Brooks warns ministers against what he calls "the haunting incubus of the notion of great sermons." Pastors who think of sermons as oratorical masterpieces care for their sermons and not for the truth they have to proclaim or for the people whom they have to help. The man who is thinking every day about Christ and man, about the Bible and the world, will not have difficulty each time he enters the pulpit in saying things that are relevant.

Most of the discussion as to the merits of different kinds of sermons (doctrinal, topical, textual, expository) is beside the point. Different things need to be said, and said in different ways. The best sermon, says Brooks, is simply "the time's best utterance." A preacher must be a man of his age, in sympathy with those things in it which are praiseworthy, but aware also of its besetting sins. Even so, if he is constrained by too narrow a conception of the sermon, he is prevented from achieving his full effect as the spokesman of God to his generation.

In a lecture entitled "The Ministry for our Age," Brooks takes account of the anti-religious world-view that was becoming more and more prevalent. He saw clearly that the main difficulty was not the conflict between science and theology but the fact that men had become preoccupied with the machinery of life to the neglect of its ultimate meaning. In particular, they had lost a sense of personal values and of the certainties that are necessary to give direction to life. He counseled preachers against trying to argue down the atheist or the materialist. To argue with them, he said, is to misunderstand their need. They do not really believe these doctrines; their trouble is that they have lost the ability to believe anything else. The only way the minister can help them is by declaring the facts of spiritual life. It is possible, Brooks says, to declare spiritual truths today with as much certainty as in any of the "ages of faith." The truths are as new as ever, and men are as ready as ever to feel their truth. "The world," writes Brooks, "has not heard its best preaching yet."

LECTURES ON GODMANHOOD

Author: Vladimir Solovyev (1853-1900)
Type of work: Christian social philosophy
First published: 1878

Principal Ideas Advanced

Secular humanism is doomed to failure because it does not unite man to the unconditioned, which is the source and end of his being.

The external freedom which Western civilization has brought needs to be supplemented by the internal freedom which positive religion can give.

The union between God and man, which is sought throughout the history of religion, is realized in Christianity, by means of Christ's becoming man.

The *Twelve Lectures on Godmanhood* was originally a series of public addresses given by Solovyev at St. Petersburg in his capacity as a member of the Ministry of Public Education. The lectures were phenomenally successful, filling the large hall where they were given, and drawing such intellectual leaders as Fyodor Dostoevski and Leo Tolstoy. In spite of his youth, the author, who had previously been a fellow at the University of Moscow, and had studied at London and at Cairo, spoke with authority on philosophy and history. A zealous Christian, but not a clergyman, he also impressed men by the ascetic purity of his life, as we easily understand when we learn that Dostoevski used him as the model for Alyosha in *The Brothers Karamazov*.

The *Lectures on Godmanhood* is a synthesis of many strands of thought: Western philosophy, Buddhism, Platonism, the Church Fathers, the Hebrew Cabala, the mysticism of Boehme, and the speculation of Schelling and Hegel. Solovyev was disposed to find truth everywhere, and his great passion was to unify the world in truth and love. Having sensed the growing pessimism and nihilism of Western secular thought, Solovyev had turned to religion to find the organizing principle of life. He maintained that the conception of *Sophia* (Wisdom), preserved in Eastern Orthodoxy, contains the central and all-comprehending revelation which will unify creation by uniting it to God.

Although the reader may be tempted to see in Solovyev's lectures simply a Russian version of the romantic philosophy of Johann Fichte (1762-1814), Friedrich von Schelling (1775-1854), and G. W. F. Hegel (1770-1831), he will do better to begin by viewing it as an emendation of the Positive Philosophy of Auguste Comte (1798-1857). Comte had labored for a new society which should have for its foundations the laws of positive science and for its goal the unity of mankind. It was, in Comte's opinion, one of the positive laws of society that mankind passes through three stages: the theological stage, which is a constructive or positive moment because it possesses a unifying faith; the metaphysical or critical stage, which is a destructive moment, and divorces thought from action; and the positive stage, which is once more constructive, but, unlike the theological stage, promises to be permanent, because it puts man's critical capacities to work in serving society. Solovyev, like Comte, put thought at the service of life and of action, and he regarded it as his vocation to "transform the world." But, in his opinion, positive or empirical knowledge was no more successful than the rationalism it was meant to replace in arriving at the knowledge of reality which is essential for man's spiritual life. Nor did a socialism based on the promise of satisfying man's egotistical wants offer any more hope for unifying mankind than did competitive society. In Solovyev's opinion, socialism and positivism were not new moments in the history of mankind, but closing phases of the godless, humanistic movement which came into existence with the breakup of Catholic Europe. The next, and final, moment in the history of mankind must be a revival of positive religion. Such a revival need not involve a return to the past. It is a law of history that only one function can be developed at a time. Accordingly, in the religions of the world, man realized the divine idea in the realm of spirit; then, in Western secular civilization, he realized the divine idea in the realm of nature. What remains, Solovyev argues, is to bring religion and civilization together in a new synthesis in which truth shall find its foundation in the knowledge of God, and brotherhood shall be realized through the love of God.

According to Solovyev, the failure of secularism is a result of the attempt to comprehend the conditioned world of sense experience while remaining agnostic about the unconditioned being on which the sensible world depends. Nowhere is this failure more apparent than in the secular view of man. Solovyev sums up the new humanism in the mocking formula: "Man is a hairless monkey and therefore must lay down his life for his friend!" There is nothing in secular thought to justify the high value which Western civilization places on human life; nor is this surprising if, as Solovyev holds, the value of human existence lies in the link which it provides between the creature and the Creator. Like Comte, Solovyev was completely devoted to the service of humanity, but the humanity which he served was not an empirical collection of individual men but a transcendent reality, man's ultimate and perfect state, which Solovyev called *Godmanhood.*

Because our active life cannot be divorced from knowledge, we must, says Solovyev, bring philosophy and religion to bear upon the human problem. The result is a novel blend of Hegelian dialectics and gnostic intuitions. Reality, says Solovyev, is organically one, a whole made up of parts. The principle of organization is that of tri-unity. We can discover this principle in the human soul, as Augustine showed, where within the unity the self we distinguish being, knowing, and willing. But the same principle is present in the blade of grass and in the Divinity. Moreover, it is this principle which enables men to understand the relationship which exists between God and the world within the All-encompassing. For, in Solovyev's ontology, the world is the eternal image or counterpart of God, the essence or content which is implied in primal being. The world is God's *alter ego,* necessitated by that logic (Hegelian) according to which "being" implies "essence," and "unity" implies "plurality." Thus, the world must be differentiated from God. But because the identity of being is more fundamental than any diversity, God and the world are bound to each other by ties of eternal love. Once again, the whole scheme can be understood in terms of being, knowing, and willing: God is, the world is God's perception of Himself, and the All-encompassing whole is God's self-affirmation.

As has been suggested, the triunitarian motif may be traced repeatedly, both within the Deity and within the world. The familiar Trinity of Christian theology exemplifies the principle within divine unity, but, unlike the world, God is beyond all diversity, movement, or change. A corresponding trinity may be traced within our world of diversity and change. The first moment, comparable to the being of God, is inchoate matter, the world "without form and void," in which each material particle asserts its own identity irrespective of every other. The second moment, comparable to the Logos or Reason of God, is mind or intellect; it is the world of Platonic essences, but also of angels, who are pure intellects. The third moment, corresponding to the Holy Ghost in the divine Trinity, is the world soul, which in mystical theology is called Sophia. This third moment brings together matter and mind in an organic whole.

Solovyev triumphantly concludes

that man and man alone is the synthesis of the physical and the mental, of chance and logic, of lawlessness and love. But it is not man considered as a collection of empirical individuals who achieves this synthesis; rather, it is man as a corporate whole, of which the individuals are the cells of a greater organism. Man, then, is the temporal image of God, the consummation of the world; in him the whole of creation is recapitulated; and by man's free will, creation makes its movement back toward reunion with God in the All-encompassing.

The estimate of man at which Solovyev arrives has many points in common with the optimism of Renaissance humanism, as shown, for example, in Pico della Mirandola's (1463-1494) famous poem "On the Dignity of Man." But it is modified, in Solovyev's case, by a profoundly Russian sense of the radical character of evil. Man, as the lord and priest of nature, should bring the whole creation into harmony with God. That he does not is due to the freedom which is inherent in the creature and to the consequences of the disobedience of the Adam, the father of mankind. Made in the likeness of God, Adam, "or the world soul in him," was not satisfied with being the passive recipient of God's essence, but strove to become the foundation of his own being; in thus asserting himself, Adam fell away from God. As a further tragic result, man lost the harmony which was natural to his own being, and fell under the domination of matter. For in matter, according to Solovyev, self-assertiveness tends to prevail, and this is the cause of sin and suffering.

Still, with his eternal part, man strives for unity and truth; such is the theme of history, the underlying motif of religion and morality. But, aside from pointing to unity as man's goal, history has been futile and tragic. Only as Christ, in whom Logos and Sophia are joined, "descended into the stream of phenomena" could mankind and the world be restored to harmony with itself and to unity with its Creator. For Christ is not one individual among others; as the Second Adam, He is "the universal being, embracing all the regenerated, spiritual humanity."

Solovyev sought to show that all the wisdom and virtue of previous history came together in Christianity. He denied that there is such a thing as a false religion, although a religion becomes unfruitful when it turns fanatical and exclusive. In every religion, he said, there is a "sudden appearance of truth," partial though it be. Primitive religion, for example, found God in nature, but too exclusively; hence, the religions of India were useful insofar as they freed human personality from nature, but they erred in going to the opposite extreme by denying reality to nature. The failure was the unfortunate result of confusing the world and God. The Greeks and the Hebrews affirmed the transcendence of the unconditioned, but in different ways; the former affirmed God as object; that is, as essence or idea; the latter affirmed Him as subject; that is, as will and personality. Both the Greek and the Hebrew emphases were needed; Alexandrian philosophy brought them together, and developed the idea of the Trinity. Christianity, coming soon after, recapitulated the whole development. Christianity contains the ascetic principle of Buddhism, the idealism of the Greeks, the monotheism of the Hebrews, and the trinitarian understanding of the Alexandrians. To these, however, it added that which brings all the others to their fulfillment, lifting them from the ideal into the actual, inasmuch as it proclaims the Incarnation, or, as the Russians prefer to say, the "inhumanization" of Christ, in whom the disaffected world is effectually reunited with God.

Thus, to the positivism of secular philosophy Solovyev opposes "the truths of positive religion." When he wrote these lectures, he inclined to the view, shared with Dostoevski, that Eastern Orthodoxy holds more promise than Roman Catholicism or Protestantism. He praised the steadfastness with which Rome binds men to the Absolute, but he complained of the use which it makes of force. He praised the Protestant emphasis on freedom of conscience, but he deplored its tendency toward subjectivism and individualism. The Russian Orthodox Church, he maintained, preserves the positive values both of Catholicism and of Protestantism, while avoiding their respective faults. In later years, this judgment was modified, and Solovyev came to place more hope in the Roman than in the Russian Church, so far as the world mission of Christianity is concerned, even going so far as to become a communicating member of the Roman Catholic Church, in an effort to help heal the schism between the East and the West. The most immediate result of his life and labor, however, was the revival, around the turn of the century, of Christianity among young Russian intellectuals. Sergius Bulgakov and Nikolai Berdyaev are prominent examples.

THE GRAND INQUISITOR

Author: Fyodor Dostoevski (1821-1881)
Type of work: Christian ethics
First published: 1880, in *The Brothers Karamazov*

Principal Ideas Advanced

In opposition to Christ, who refused to do anything which would take away from the freedom of men, the Grand Inquisitor maintains that the masses can never be happy until they are relieved of the burden of freedom.

Socialism supposes that once men have bread they can be entrusted with freedom, but the socialist experiment will fail, and the Roman Church, which understands that men must also have miracles and someone to worship, hopes to complete the harmonious ant-society which the socialists have begun.

The Russian Church, which preserves the spirit of Christ, is destined in the long run to win over the socialist and the Roman way.

The Grand Inquisitor relates, in the form of a legend, how Christ was received when he visited Seville during the height of the Spanish Inquisition.

Dostoevski includes the story in the novel *The Brothers Karamazov*, as part of the explanation which the brilliant and sensitive university graduate Ivan Karamazov gives to his younger brother, Alexey, of his rebellious attitude with respect to the human condition. Ivan is incensed at man's cruelty, especially toward children, and on this ground he charges that God ought not to have given man free will. Alexey, a novice at the monastery, protests that before we accuse God of recklessness in giving man freedom, we must remember that God consented to suffer in His own person the consequence of men's cruelty. This prompts Ivan to relate his "legend," of which the purport is that, at least in Western Christendom, the Church has for many centuries been attempting to take away the freedom which God gave men, and for which Christ died.

Ivan's story of the "Grand Inquisitor" is essentially an independent statement, which brings to the highest artistic expression a dilemma which has tormented many minds in our own times nearly as much as it tormented Dostoevski.

The setting of the story is the sixteenth century, when, as Ivan explains, it was not uncommon for authors to describe heavenly personages as coming to earth. Christ's visit is not His promised coming in glory; rather, in answer to the fervent prayers of that century of religious conflict, Christ deigns to come once more in the form of a servant to reassure men of His way. Strangely, for He wears no insignia and has no one to herald Him, everyone recognizes Him as he moves silently in their midst with His gentle smile of compassion. Healing virtue radiates from his garments. The crowd weeps and does homage to him. Then the cardinal, the Grand Inquisitor, approaches and commands his guards to take Him. The people tremble before the Inquisitor, but they make no protest while the guards lead Christ away. Afterwards, they bow before the high churchman and receive his benediction.

That evening, the Grand Inquisitor visits Christ in the prison cell and accuses Him of coming to hinder the Church's work. Christ is to be burned at the stake the next day. Christ is silent throughout the interview, and thus he appears to justify the Church's claim that He has surrendered all authority to the pope. The Inquisitor, an old man of ninety, reveals the secret which he has kept in his heart for many years. Having tried in his youth to follow Christ's teaching, he has long since concluded that such teaching is impractical. A few elect souls can follow Christ's way, but it is too difficult for the masses.

As the Grand Inquisitor understands the Gospel story, the spirit of destruction who tempted Christ in the wilderness was more realistic and practical than any man, than even the Son of Man Himself. In rejecting the Devil, Christ persisted in His high opinion of human nature. He refused to purchase men's obedience by giving them bread, or by accepting the crown which they proffered him, or by bowing to their love for miracles; He hoped, rather, to win their hearts from rebellion by the power of truth and justice and of love freely given. Satan saw this ideal as a cruel mockery. Men want bread more than they want freedom; indeed, they are so weak that if they have freedom they will never have bread. They want someone before whom they can bow down and worship, someone in whose name they can conquer the world and force all men to believe and worship as they do. Moreover, they demand miracles, and they will not believe in a God who disdains miracles; they will shift their loyalty to the first charlatan who will concoct wonders for them to gape at.

The Inquisitor explains that the Catholic Church, having seen the impossibility of Jesus' way, has acted with the insight of a master psychologist. The Church has taken away men's freedom, and men have loved it for that very reason. "I tell Thee," the Inquisitor says to Christ, "that man is tormented by no greater anxiety than to find someone quickly to whom he can hand over that gift of freedom with which the ill-fated creature is born." Men readily bless the Church for giving them a steady objective in life, and they are readily persuaded that their only freedom is to come through submission to religious authority, especially when they are reminded of "the horrors of slavery and confusion" which their former freedom entailed. Leaders of the Church have consented to take upon themselves the freedom which knowledge of good and evil imposes upon men. Like adults in the midst of children, the priests have incurred anxiety and guilt, but in doing so they have allowed the weak and lustful to live out their lives in innocence and happiness. "Judge us," he says, "if Thou canst and darest."

The Grand Inquisitor protests that he too has dwelt in the wilderness and eaten roots. He too has prized the freedom which Christ taught and has striven to stand among the elect. "But I awakened and would not serve madness. I turned back and joined the ranks of those *who have corrected Thy work.* I left the proud and went back to the humble, for the happiness of the humble." Christ, he concludes, in returning to the world, hinders the Church's work; therefore, He deserves to be burned as a heretic. When he has finished speaking, the Inquisitor waits for his prisoner to answer, but Christ, after looking at him intently in silence, approaches in silence and kisses the Inquisitor on his "bloodless aged" lips. The old man is visibly moved and, opening the door, says, "Go, and come no more. . . . Come not at all, never, never!" Christ departs.

In the mouth of Ivan, the story raises the utmost doubt respecting the teaching that man's crowning dignity is the gift of freedom. Even if one supposes that in the distant future men shall learn to live together in freedom and harmony, one cannot justify the wretchedness and torment which freedom has brought in its train. And it is not even certain, especially to one without faith, that eternal harmony is in store. Ivan's lack of faith especially torments him and the Inquisitor. Alexey has said, "Your Inquisitor does not believe in God, that's his secret." "It's perfectly true," replies Ivan, "that that's the whole secret, but isn't that suffering, at least for a man like that, who has wasted his whole life in the desert and yet could not shake off his incurable love of humanity?" Unlike the Inquisitor, however, Ivan has spent no time in the desert. He can only dream of a distant time when men will be happy in a socialist paradise. Meanwhile, to his anguished mind, Satan appears with other proposals. Is not a man who knows that there is no God, himself a God among men? And why is such a man bound to pity his fellows? Such is the further logic of "the spirit of self-destruction and non-existence," which was to prove Ivan's undoing.

There are other dimensions to the story. A theme which interested Dostoevski, together with other Russian writers (for example, Vladimir Solovyev) is the relationship between Eastern and Western Christianity and their respective roles in the future of mankind. Dostoevski belonged to the Slavophile group, which maintained that, despite the glaring incompetencies of the Russian Empire and the corruptions within the Orthodox Church, the spirit of Christ was profoundly at work in the lives of the Russian people, from which it would one day rise up and take the leadership of mankind away from Europe.

The Western Church, Dostoevski held, has long since forsaken the Gospel and has put its hope in the secular power which it inherited from ancient Rome. The Roman Church, says Dostoevski, proclaimed itself a state at the time of Charlemagne; Protestantism never reversed this step. Thus, in the West, a prisoner condemned by the State is condemned absolutely; there is no Christian society, apart from the civil order, which continues to claim the criminal as a member. As a consequence, the criminal rarely repents. Society triumphs over him by force, and he, in turn, considers his crime a legitimate protest against oppressive authority. In the East, according to Dostoevski, the situation is different. The civil power has, indeed, taken into its hands the judgment of men, but alongside the law courts the Church remains, which continues to minister to the criminal as to a precious son; and though, for many centuries, the Church has bowed to the Empire, it cherishes the hope of a time when the Empire will be diminished and all jurisdiction will pass to the Church.

As we learn from *The Diary of a Writer,* which comes from the same period as *The Brothers Karamazov,* Dostoevski was greatly interested in the reforms then taking place within Roman Catholicism, particularly in those reforms suggested by Christian socialism. For Dostoevski, atheistic socialism was merely an expression of denigrated Protestantism. The atheistic socialist had lost his faith in God and in the dignity of man. But, as one of the characters of *The Brothers Karamazov* says, "The socialist who is a Christian is more to be dreaded than a socialist who is an atheist." The reason becomes apparent in *The Grand Inquisitor.* Atheistic socialists have for their slogan, "Feed men and then ask them for virtue!"; with this slogan they draw men away from the Church. Dostoevski predicts that they will have a temporary success. With much bloodshed they will build their tower of Babel, "not to mount to Heaven from earth but to set up Heaven on earth." But they will not succeed. The reason is, they have only the wisdom of men, and the socialists err in supposing that after they have fed men they can give men freedom. The Church of Rome is wiser, having learned that freedom is worse than hunger, and that he who wants to deliver man from his anguish must also give him miracles and someone to worship. In this way, says the Inquisitor, the Roman Church is destined to triumph over socialism and to complete the tower of Babel, "uniting all in one unanimous and harmonious ant-heap. . . . For having begun to build their tower of Babel without us, they will end, of course, with cannibalism. But then the beast will crawl to us and lick our feet and spatter them with tears of blood. And we shall sit upon the beast and raise the cup, and on it will be written, 'Mystery.' But then, and only then, the reign of peace and happiness will come for men."

This triumph of cynical power is, of course, horrible to contemplate; Dostoevski regularly opposes to it what he calls the Russian approach, which is moral and Christian. "In Europe," he writes in *The Diary of a Writer*, "such an approach is inconceivable, although there, sooner or later—after floods of blood and 100 million heads—they will have to recognize it because in it alone lies the solution."

WHAT I BELIEVE

Author: Leo Tolstoy (1828-1910)
Type of work: Christian ethics
First published: 1882

Principal Ideas Advanced

Whereas civilization is based upon the belief that personal life is the true life, Christ taught that this belief is illusory and that obedience to God's will and service of mankind is the true life.

Christ's commandments, including "Resist not evil," are not impossible for man to keep, because they are natural to man and because keeping them will bring general and eternal peace.

The attempt of man to attain and defend personal good, by resisting evil and taking the product of other men's work, is the source of war, poverty, and misery.

When Tolstoy was in his early fifties, he quit writing novels for a number of years and devoted himself to the study of religion, writing his *Critique of Dogmatic Theology* (1880), and his *The Four Gospels, Harmonized and Translated* (1882). These bulky works have little interest for the general reader. But *My Confession* (1879), which serves as a preface to the former work, and *What I Believe,* which sums up the whole enterprise, deserve a permanent, if humble, place in the religions literature of mankind.

What I Believe is sometimes published under the title *My Religion,* not unsuitably in view of the fact that the Russian word *vera,* which appears in the Russian title, connotes a religious creed.

Tolstoy turned to religion in an effort to find the "meaning of life." In *My Confession,* he relates that as he approached the age of fifty he began to be plagued with the questions "Why?" and "What Then?" He possessed six thousand desyatinas of land in Samara. What then? He was educating his children to be gentlefolk. For what reason? A few more literary successes and his name would take its place with Shakespeare and Molière. What of that? At first, he tells us, these questions were merely interruptions; he continued to have enthusiasm for his work, telling himself that, were he to take the time, he could find the answers. But, like the symptom of a mortal disease, the question "What then?" grew more insistent, and Tolstoy was forced to admit that he did not know the answer. This brought his life to a standstill. He could no longer live without being able to give a reason for what he was doing. He consulted science and philosophy, but in vain. The only philosophers who seemed to face up to the problem were Solomon (in Ecclesiastes), Buddha, Socrates, and Schopenhauer, all of whom averred that life is meaningless and that death is a release from suffering. Men of affairs were of no more help, for however vigorously they pursued their respective goals, none of them knew why they were doing so. Because it seemed to him that certain humble folk found in religion a reason for their way of life, he concluded that in the end one must have a faith in order to live. For this reason he returned for a time to the Russian Orthodox Church, performed its rituals, and studied its theology. But the more he learned about official Christianity, the more he was disgusted. It was, he said, like a bag of stinking mud, in which a pearl is hidden, which has always been covered with mud. He was discouraged until, at last, he persuaded himself that the pearl could be had without the mud, and that, cleansed of dogmatic accretions, the Gospel could shine with the same luster that drew men to it in the beginning.

What I Believe presents to us this pearl of great price, with Tolstoy's account of how he managed to find it, and his explanations of how so precious a gem came to be, for all practical purposes, lost to mankind.

The passage in the Sermon on the Mount in which Jesus says, "Resist not evil," first brought home to Tolstoy the force of the original Gospel. Suppose Jesus really meant what he said! If so, His view of life was radically different from what His followers are accustomed to suppose it to be. Civilization and morals, religion and politics, are based on resisting evil. If Jesus meant what these words say, He was demanding a complete revaluation of all values. Suddenly, Tolstoy says, everything in life fell into place, like pieces of a broken statue which one had been trying vainly to reconstruct, when, although the pieces fit, the statue which they form turns out to be a different one from what had previously existed. (Like other sectarians, Tolstoy supposed that he had found the whole truth in a single Biblical passage.)

Whereas men are accustomed to believe that Christ came to bless their personal lives, Tolstoy writes, the fact is that Christ tells us our personal lives cannot be saved. Trying to save our lives, we are quick to resist everything that threatens them and to seize anything that might help to save them. But we cannot save them no matter how hard we try, and our frantic efforts in this direction are the cause of most of the evil in the world today. Tolstoy does not make "nonresistance" the center of Christ's Gospel; he merely says that, in his own case, it was

Christ's teaching of nonresistance, and the bold contradiction between this teaching and the precepts and practice of the Church, which served as a key to open the Gospel to his understanding.

Actually, the command, "Resist not evil," is only one of the five commandments which, according to Tolstoy, sum up the teaching of Christ. They are all found in the fifth chapter of Matthew, in the passage in which Jesus contrasts his righteousness with the righteousness of the Pharisees. "Ye have heard it said by them of old time . . . but I say unto you. . . ." Human laws, says Tolstoy, are always conditional. For example, Moses forbids killing, but he immediately qualifies the command and mentions circumstances in which killing is lawful. So with divorce, and with other prescriptions. Christ, on the other hand, proclaimed divine laws, which admit no qualifications. Thus, He forbade all killing, all divorce, all oath-taking, all vengeance, and all discrimination between one's own nation and other nations. The Jews, especially Paul, failed to understand that Jesus was repudiating their law. They thought that when He said that not "one jot or tittle shall pass until all be fulfilled" he was speaking of the law of Moses. Thus, they glossed His teachings, putting into the text qualifying phrases. For example, when He said, "Be not angry," they added, "without just cause." Similarly, when He forbade divorce, they added, "except for cause of adultery." These changes show that they entirely misapprehended Him. When He said that the Law shall not pass away, he was referring to the Eternal Law laid down by the Creator for the direction of mankind. That Law upsets every maxim of human prudence. For him who has ears to hear, it announces that as long as men seek to satisfy their personal desires, life is futile and evil, and that the only way to diminish suffering and to find peace and joy on earth is to obey the will of God and thereby to serve the good of mankind.

Man must have a faith to live by, yet there are, says Tolstoy, two rival faiths. One is faith in the possibility of personal life, both here and hereafter. This is the faith professed by the Church and by secular culture, in spite of what the world's wisest men have said about the vanity of this way of life. The other faith starts with the recognition that our personal lives are perishable and demands that, forsaking our illusory goals, we obey the will of God and devote ourselves to the well-being of humanity. This is the faith Christ taught. According to Tolstoy, Christ said nothing to encourage the popular belief in the continuing life of the individual after death. He spoke, instead, of the resurrection of the *son of man,* by which He meant, not an individual person, but humanity as such. "The true life," says Tolstoy, "is only the one which continues the past life and which cooperates with the good of the contemporary life and with that of the future life. To be a participant in this life, a man must renounce his will for the purpose of fulfilling the will of the Father of life, who gave it to the son of man. . . . But the will of the Father of life is not the life of a separate individual, but of the one son of man who lives in men; and so man preserves life only when he looks upon his life as upon a pledge, a talent given him by the Father, that he may serve the life of all, when he lives not for himself, but for the son of man."

Tolstoy takes up the objection that this plan is unworkable. Those who suppose this, he says, simply do not realize how hard and unworkable the world's way is. Christianity has had its martyrs, but they are negligible by comparison with the victims of onward-marching civilization. Not without reason did Jesus say that the Christian's yoke is easy and his burden light. Tolstoy calls upon the reader to compare the sufferings endured by Christians with the suffering which the cultured and godless classes perpetuate from generation to generation through their sterile and profitless regimen. If universally practiced, Christ's commandments would mean the return of mankind to a healthy, hardworking life, closely attuned to nature. As to the solitary believer who ventures to turn his back on civilization, Tolstoy counts the suffering such a man must bear as being unimportant so long as the solitary believer's life and death "serve the salvation and the life of all men." But Tolstoy argues that even the enmity of the world is hardly enough to counterbalance the positive gain in peace and joy which comes from forsaking the illusions of civilization and living according to God's will and the principles of nature.

Tolstoy does not rest his teaching upon any authoritative claims for Jesus, as if He were a divine messenger. On the contrary, he maintains that there is a rational clarity to the Gospel which agrees with the truth of nature and with the light of reason in man. In this sense, he maintains that the Gospel is eternal and universal. The Church, which formerly moulded European and Russian life, he believes, has ceased to serve any good purpose. It is, he says, like the umbilical cord which carries nourishment from mother to fetus, but after the infant is born, the cord is fit only to be decently buried. Tolstoy regarded the European world of his day as being like a newborn animal, trying to find its own way; its energetic life was possible only because it was still living on its mother's fluids. Tolstoy hoped that Europe would shortly develop its own conscious spiritual foundation based on the recognition of "the rational teachings about the good life" which Christ first made clear. This teaching, in his opinion, "cannot fail to be accepted by men, not because it is impossible to deny that metaphysical explanation which it gives (everything can be denied), but because it alone gives those rules of life without which humanity has not lived and cannot live, and not one man has lived or can live, if he wants to live like a man, that is, a rational life."

EVOLUTION AND RELIGION

Author: Henry Ward Beecher (1813-1887)
Type of work: Christian evolutionary theory
First published: 1885

Principal Ideas Advanced

Man is not a fallen saint but a risen animal.

Christian religion is the product of a long, divinely inspired, human quest for higher spiritual and moral life; hence, what the theory of evolution discloses about the development of the natural order is true of the realm of the spirit as well.

Orthodox theology has unnecessarily alienated sensitive religious men by insisting upon the centrality of creeds rather than life, and by demanding absolute allegiance to primitive dogmas which are repugnant to man's increased moral and intellectual sensitivities.

A purified religion, focused on life and receptive to God's continuing revelation of truth, would be able to command the allegiance of all good men and thus to resume its place as a dynamic force for human growth.

The Reverend Henry Ward Beecher was eminent for his eloquence, his social concern, and his ability to relate Christian religion to the thought and life of his times. Because of his liberal stands on social issues and because of his considerable ability as a popularizer of the best sort, he was perhaps the most influential preacher of his day. From the pulpit of Plymouth Church in Brooklyn, New York, and in numerous books, he skillfully translated complicated philosophical, theological, and scientific ideas into language which the ordinary man could understand. *Evolution and Religion,* comprised of twenty-six sermons preached over the course of several years "discussing the bearings of the evolutionary philosophy on the fundamental doctrines of evangelical Christianity," is typical of his work.

Convinced that Christianity has been an evolving religion, and that God reveals Himself to man continually through the thought and life of the present day, Beecher was wholeheartedly an expositor of the "new Theology," a liberal theological movement of the late nineteenth century led by Horace Bushnell (1802-1876), and he helped to turn the popular religious mind in the liberal direction by his powerful preaching of these doctrines. A Christianity responsive to the findings of science was his central concern, for he regarded religion as a search for all truth wherever it be found.

The theology which had developed among these liberals in the nineteenth century was such that there was no serious conflict with the new theory of evolution. Liberalism had already made its peace with modern thought. Liberals had come to understand God's revelation in terms of inspired human thought, and they argued that wherever truth be found, God is speaking. Since the voice of science is one of the voices of God, it must be listened to with reverence. The great traditions of religion, the Bible, and later reflections on moral and spiritual truths, are all products of a long and patient human search for truth and life. As man grows, religiously and otherwise, he has to put away childish thoughts, rejecting what he has discovered to be outmoded and accepting new truth, whatever its source. What science discovers is religiously valid and presents to modern man new ways of describing how God has actually worked in and upon mankind. Liberalism as a whole stressed the immanent working of God (God's working *in* things) rather than, as the Orthodox tradition did, His transcendent working (God's working *on* things from outside).

As Beecher saw it, then, he was not engaged in modifying Christianity to fit new scientific ideas of evolution; rather, he was engaged in using new ideas to interpret what religion had already known: that man has undergone spiritual growth. The theory of evolution did not force Beecher to change his ideas of God and man, for early in life he had come to believe in man as a growing being. Beecher writes, "Later I began to feel that science had struck a larger view, and that this unfolding . . . in spiritual things was but one application of a great cosmic doctrine, which underlay God's methods in universal creation, and was notably to be seen in the whole development of human society and human thought." The scientific doctrine, then, merely fit in with the already known facts of spiritual and intellectual evolution, and showed them to be parts of a general cosmic process. The theory of evolution traced, on the natural level, the same patient workings of God to create a higher order of life that religion had already traced on the spiritual level. Hence, the publication by Charles Darwin (1809-1882) of his *Origin of Species* (1859) and *Descent of Man* (1871), works which established the theory of evolution scientifically, and the writing of Herbert Spencer (1820-1903), who presented similar doctrines in philosophical form and who was directly influential on Beecher, served not to weaken but rather to provide confirmation for Protestant liberal theology. Evolution replaced the outworn science which had become so troublesome for modern Christianity and in so doing allowed morality and the true spiritual life to emerge more clearly as the concerns of religion.

Beecher has provided several summaries of his theology, the shortest of which follows: "These four truths—the fact of sinfulness; the fact of regeneration, its need, its reality, its possibility; the life-giving Spirit of God, that helps a man out of this lower into the higher stage; and the fact of the holiness into which man may come by the aid of the Spirit, concurrent with his own will—these are what I call the executive doctrines of Christianity. . . ." Other summaries mention also the redemptive work of Jesus as teacher and inspirer of men, and the achievement of miraculous powers over nature by men whose spirituality has been fully realized. As for the rest of the traditional doctrine, Beecher once said, "If, besides all that, the Church wants to carry baggage and baggage-wagons, and all sorts of furniture and all sorts of ordnance, and is able to do so, it may. There is no law by which a man should not go to battle now with Saul's armor on, but he would be a fool to sweat under Saul's armor on a midsummer's day. So that all of the churches or the people may be just as foolish as they please, if they do not set themselves up for models. . . ."

According to Beecher, much that orthodox Christianity has believed is badly in error. Man did not fall from some primitive paradise; rather, he has risen from primitive animality by a long process of moral and spiritual growth. The orthodox view was that Adam fell, passing on to all his descendants a corrupt nature which rendered all their works odious and left them spiritually unclean, thereby requiring a bloody sacrifice so that God might be free to welcome man again. Moreover, the orthodox view held that God predestined some men to salvation, condemning all others to eternal torment in Hell. According to Beecher, these doctrines are both false and morally repugnant.

The fact of the matter, Beecher insists, is that man did not descend; he *ascended*. Through centuries of gradual discovery and exploration, man has broken free from primitive superstition and moral crudity, and has created for himself, by the inspiration of God, lofty theological ideals and a way of life which leads to true morality and the spiritual life. Jesus did not come to save man by buying man's salvation; rather, He came to inspire men by His teachings and His example, showing clearly to men that there is a spiritual power which can regenerate them by raising them up to spiritual sonship. Sin is man's failure to do the things that he knows he should do: it is his failure to grow in spirit, his willingness to remain fleshly. Regeneration, which is the process of spiritual growth, takes place only as man is inwardly transformed; hence, regeneration is accomplished *in* man and cannot be applied to him from outside by magical rites such as baptism. As men develop their spiritual lives, they rise to such heights of nearness to God that they develop godlike powers over nature which enable them to perform what seem to ordinary men to be miracles. At death, according to Beecher, most men are extinguished, but those who by their efforts to grow in this life have become fit for further growth enter into another stage of life and ascend spiritually.

The view that religion has undergone spiritual evolution is confirmed, according to Beecher, by modern theories concerning the Scriptures and the doctrines of the Church. Scholars have concluded that the Bible is a very human document, the result of gradually growing spiritual insight, rather than an infallible transcription of words which came from God. The Bible, properly interpreted, records man's gradual discovery of moral and spiritual truth. Much of the Biblical writing reflects primitive ideas about man and his universe, and these ideas are consequently not binding upon present generations; the lasting truths of Scripture are its great examples, the power of its ideas and ideals. To achieve a separation of what is false and outworn from what is perennially valid is to liberate religion. As Beecher has eloquently stated it, modern theology will "free the Sacred Scriptures from fictitious pretensions made by men, from clouds of misconceptions, and give to us the book as a clear and shining light, instead of an orb veiled by false claims and worn-out philosophies."

The history of Christianity has been further complicated by the fact that too many theologians have chosen for crucial emphasis doctrines which are primitive and morally crude: use has been made of arbitrary selections of proof texts which are contraverted by the more advanced insights of the Bible itself. Every party to every theological dispute has his own set of texts to appeal to, and "there is scarcely a square league that has not a separate sect in it, and all of them cry, 'Thus saith the Lord!'" Because so many of the doctrines heretofore selected for emphasis have been barbarous, because such quarrels are divisive, and because they result from and contribute to a preoccupation with creeds instead of life, religion has been badly distorted and has lost much of its effectiveness.

Religiousness is to be measured, Beecher writes, in terms of what one does, how one puts into practice moral and spiritual truths, not in terms of what theological creeds, forms of government, or religious rites one believes in. It is by their fruits that men are known to be Christian or not. Beecher even went so far as to say that no church had the right to make *any* rules or regulations which would prevent a man of good religious life from participating in the activities of the church. Rather, churches must change their ways so that all godly men can be included.

Religion is the product of a long spiritual evolution, the creation of a divinely inspired effort to find what is true and noble in life. Orthodoxy has threatened continued growth by its insistence upon the infallibility of the past, and by requiring that men continue to believe things which are not only untrue but religiously offensive. The evolutionary process continues, and a religion which is to be responsive to God must grow; it must listen to the voice of God in the present as well as in the past, in order that it may once again become a vital means to the spiritual growth of mankind. Man stands on the threshold of a new age and he must give himself wholeheartedly to the task of shaping his further spiritual growth, for the Kingdom of God, the seeds of which were planted long ago, is now almost fully come. Thus the theory of evolution, as a statement of a general principle of the cosmos, illuminates man's knowledge of both nature and spirit, contributing to his understanding of both the past and the future. A religion in which this awareness has become articulate can help man to rediscover the regenerative powers which reside in God.

The Church is a necessity for religious life, Beecher agrees, but if it is to meet the religious needs of modern men it must become more spiritual and inclusive, less dogmatically inclined and less factional. In his final sermon, Part I, Beecher gave voice to his hope for the Church, saying ". . . I hope yet to see the day when that proverb will have died out of the memory of man: 'I know they are Christians, they quarrel so.'"

SYSTEMATIC THEOLOGY

Author: Augustus Hopkins Strong (1836-1921)
Type of work: Protestant orthodoxy
First published: 1886; new and enlarged version, 1907 (Volumes I and II) and 1909 (Volume III)

Principal Ideas Advanced

The times call for a defense of the old evangelical doctrines of sin and grace against a growing tendency to deny them.

The key to such a defense is provided by the philosophy of ethical monism, which teaches that reality consists of a single substance, God, whose divine life is partially and progressively manifest in the universe through the agency of Christ the Logos, in and through whom all things are unified.

Such a monistic and idealistic world-view enables the theologian to take into account the scientific theory of evolution, the philosophical emphasis on the immanence of God, and the conclusions of a sane higher criticism, while at the same time preserving the fundamental truths of the Biblical revelation.

Augustus Hopkins Strong's *Systematic Theology* has been the most widely used textbook of theology produced in America by a Baptist theologian. Published originally in 1886, seven editions appeared in the next two decades. In the meantime Strong, president of Rochester Theological Seminary for forty years, underwent a change in his philosophical orientation and issued a new and enlarged version of the system in three volumes during the period 1907 to 1909. A one-volume outline containing all of the major propositions, but eliminating all bibliographical and illustrative material as well as the index, was published in 1908 under the title *Outlines of Systematic Theology*. Strong's *Systematic Theology* continues to be widely read today in conservative circles and has recently been reprinted both in England and in the United States.

Strong believed that he had discovered a way of uniting philosophical and theological truth in a version of metaphysical idealism which he called ethical monism. This outlook is heavily dependent on the personal idealism of the German philosopher Hermann Lotze (1817-1881) and is closely related to the thought of such American idealists as George Trumball Ladd (1842-1921) of Yale University. More fully explained in *Christ in Creation and Ethical Monism* (1899), Strong's view is that there is one basic spiritual substance, God, who is partially and progressively expressed in the various finite and temporal grades of the created world. Strong's metaphysical monism, however, is qualified by the doctrine of psychological dualism which teaches that human personality is distinct from matter, on the one hand, and from the transcendent personality of God, on the other hand. The creator is Christ, the Logos, who is the organ of divine self-consciousness and self-determination. This means that Christ is the ground of unity in the universe and the organizing principle of all truth and reality, thus guaranteeing that reason and Scripture are harmonious though distinct sources of knowledge. Matter is the spiritual product of the divine will manifesting itself in the form of force under the law of necessity; finite mind or personality is the expression of God under the law of freedom. Reality, then, is one organic spiritual life grounded in the eternal transcendent personality and will of God, whose infinite being is partially manifested through the creative agency of Christ, the divine reason, in the various levels and kinds of finite existence.

Strong did his work at a time when the leading theological centers in America were moving toward liberalism, and his writings reflect this struggle. Unable either to give up his modified Calvinism or to turn his back completely upon the newer currents of thought in philosophy and science, Strong attempted to present the old doctrines in a modern intellectual setting. His ethical monism took into account the prevailing idealistic tendencies in philosophy and reflected the growing emphasis on the immanence of God and the progressive development of nature and history; yet his essential loyalties were given to a Calvinistic type of Protestant orthodoxy. Strong accepted evolution and higher criticism in principle but insisted on the historicity of Adam, the plenary inspiration of the Bible, and the Mosaic authorship of the Pentateuch. While maintaining that no scientific or historical error had ever been shown to exist in the Bible, he did leave the door open for Biblical criticism by an admission that inspiration does not necessarily guarantee infallibility in matters not essential to religious truth.

With regard to method Strong was in the scholastic tradition of the older Protestant dogmatists. His system of theology consists of a series of propositions arranged around the main doctrinal headings and outlined to the finest detail. Strong employs a rationalistic and proof-text approach in supporting his views. As an idealist he affirms the organic unity of truth and stresses the power of reason to buttress Scriptural teaching. Natural theology is supplemented by a fuller disclosure of religious truth recorded in the Bible, which is the court of final appeal. Deductive and inferential reasoning is accompanied by numerous quotations from the Scriptures. Strong makes extensive references to opposing views and refutes them systematically. Containing a wealth of homiletical and illustrative material, his presentation abounds with copious quotations from philosophers, theologians, poets, and other writers, whose views support his own or call for counterargument.

Theology, according to Strong, deals with God and His relations to the universe. Its sources are the world of nature as it is apprehended by reason and the Bible. God is an infinite, perfect Spirit, whose existence is a rationally intuited first truth logically prior to all other knowledge. In Strong's opinion, the classical arguments for the existence of God, while not demonstrative, do provide cumulative evidence of a corroborative nature.

A priori reasons suggest the probability of a revelation of God, and the Bible provides such a revelation, attested by miracles and fulfillments of prophecy. Rational considerations prove that the authors of Scripture are honest men, credible witnesses to divinely-given truth; furthermore, the nature and unity of the Bible, the moral superiority of the New Testament, the character and testimony of Christ, and the marvelous success and beneficent influence of the Christian enterprise all point conclusively to the supernatural character of the Biblical writings.

Strong argues that inspiration is the divine influence which makes the Scriptures a source of truth sufficient for salvation. The Bible bears the marks of its human authorship and is not necessarily correct in matters not essential to salvation, but because of its supernatural inspiration it does constitute an infallible rule of religious faith and practice.

The attributes of God fall into two main classes, Strong argues. The absolute attributes (life, personality, self-existence, immutability, unity, truth, love, and holiness) belong to God independently of His relationships with the world. The relative attributes (eternity, immensity, omnipresence, omniscience, omnipotence, and the transitive dimension of truth, holiness, and love) belong to God considered in relation to the creation. Holiness is the supreme moral attribute and the norm of love. God exists as one essence manifested in three eternal and distinct persons; both the tripersonality and the unity of God are essential elements in the inscrutable but not irrational doctrine of the Trinity.

Strong claims that although by the decrees of God certain events of the universe have been made certain, God is in no way responsible for sin or for voiding the free agency of man. Creation is the absolute origination of the universe without the use of pre-existing materials. Preservation is the maintenance in existence of created beings and their powers. Providence is the directing of all events toward the end planned for them. Instances of special providential action, miracles, and regeneration are simply extraordinary cases of God's working among men and are not contrary to his general direction of the universe according to law. Both good and evil angels exist and are, in different ways, agents of the providential agency of God.

While man has a brute ancestry, he appears on the scene as a fully moral and self-conscious being, and the whole human race is a unity descended from a single pair. Strong argues that man consists essentially of body and soul and possesses the moral powers of conscience and will. Created originally in the image of God and thus characterized by personality and holiness, man lost his state of original righteousness and communion with God by his mysterious, self-chosen revolt. Sin is any lack of conformity to the moral law of God, whether in act, disposition, or state, its essential nature being best defined as selfishness. Sin proceeds from a corrupt nature inherited from Adam, whose original transgression constituted the fall of the whole human race, since all men existed in organic unity with and were seminally present in him. Thus, all men suffer the consequences of depravity, guilt, and penalty, although infants are saved by a special act of grace which regenerates them at the point of death.

God wills to save man by the redemptive act performed by Christ, who is one person with a fully human and a fully divine nature. Prophet and king as well as priest, Christ makes atonement by suffering for sinners the punishment demanded by the holiness of God, thus satisfying the demands of justice and making possible the operation of grace. As the creator and the immanent life of the human race Christ is organically one with it. Therefore, He can, as the incarnate Logos, suffer the punishment due to mankind for the racial sin of Adam. This unity of Christ with the race also explains how the benefits of Christ's death can be appropriated by the repentant sinner. The incarnate Christ reveals and completes historically the work of atonement which the eternal Logos accomplishes in the divine realm both before and after Calvary.

According to Strong, the Holy Spirit makes effectual in the lives of men the salvation objectively made available by Christ. God eternally elects certain of the lost to be the recipients of saving grace, and this election is accomplished through the efficacious calling of men by the Holy Spirit and the establishment of a spiritual union between Christ and the believer. The components of redemption viewed from the standpoint of its beginning are regeneration (the divine side of the new birth), conversion (the human side of regeneration and involving repentance and faith), and justification (the divine judicial acquittal of the sinner). The components of redemption viewed from the standpoint of its continuation are sanctification (growth in holiness accomplished by the Holy Spirit) and perseverance (the human side of sanctification).

The universal or invisible Church consists of the whole company of regenerate persons in all ages, while the individual church is a local group of believers who have voluntarily united themselves together. The proper government of the church is congregational, and the proper offices of the church are two: bishop, presbyter, or pastor and deacon. Two ordinances have been given the local church as visible signs of the saving truth of the Gospel. Baptism is the immersion in water of a believer, while the Lord's Supper is the eating of bread and the drinking of wine by baptized believers; thus, the regenerate person is united with Christ by whom the spiritual life is nourished.

The Christian life is not completed in this life but awaits a consummation in the life to come, Strong believed. After death both the righteous and the wicked exist consciously in an intermediate state and experience a foretaste of their ultimate destiny. The final events to occur will be the millennium, the second coming of Jesus, the Resurrection, and the Last Judgment, all of which are outward visible happenings. The Resurrection will reunite the souls of all the dead with appropriate bodies, and the Last Judgment will send the wicked into everlasting though not necessarily physical torment and the righteous into everlasting and unimaginable joy.

In short, what Augustus Hopkins Strong offers in his *Systematic Theology* is a standard Baptist version of a Calvinistic type of theology based on a scholastic method and set within a context of a version of metaphysical idealism. While Strong's ethical monism seems to be only remotely connected with the development of most of his doctrinal convictions, it did function in his own mind as an overall vision of reality which enabled him to incorporate rational and revealed truth into one harmonious system of thought.

A STUDY OF RELIGION

Author: James Martineau (1805-1900)
Type of work: Philosophy of religion
First published: 1888

Principal Ideas Advanced

From the principle of causality, which the intellect employs to interpret external phenomena, the natural world is resolved into the effect of one wise and mighty will.

From the sense of duty, by which the conscience finds a sacredness in life and puts a divine construction on a large portion of internal experience, man's affinity with a supreme omnipresent righteousness is discovered.

From the relation between causality and duty it is evident that the two are separate only in apprehension; in reality, causality and duty meet in one Being, perfect both in thought and holiness.

A Study of Religion by James Martineau is a critical examination of the source and content of religion. The work contains four books, published in two volumes. The limits of human intelligence are discussed in Book One. Book Two is devoted to a discussion of theism; Book Three reviews the opposing system of pantheism, and discusses determinism and free will; Book Four deals with the life to come.

Martineau is unwilling to identify God with nature, but he does not seek to propound a religion without God. The belief and worship of that supreme mind and will which directs the operations of the universe and sustains moral relations to man is the very essence of religion, he claims. Such a supreme mind not only exists, but notwithstanding the skeptical conclusions of Kantian and post-Kantian philosophy, He is also knowable. Martineau challenges the assumption that our intellectual apprehension is limited to the data of sensation and to the *a priori* conditions that lie in the mind itself. A human being is more than a collection of faculties and susceptibilities which coherently treat and interpret phenomena without access to anything beyond. It is logically possible that our cognitive faculties are constituted in accordance with things as they are. Nothing stands in the way of trust in the reliability of our instinctive trust in a world beyond the content of consciousness. Through experience we have access to other persons and to an external world, to objects not to be found within consciousness. The outer world is not merely an illusory postulate of thought; the external world is a complex of actual events which condition experience and are affected by experience.

Religion is concerned with what is higher than man, Martineau suggests. God is conceived as a supreme mind, a mind superior in scope and creativity to all finite minds. What we seek to know of the divine can be subscribed under two relations: the relation of God to nature; that is, God as cause; and the relation of God to man; that is, God as holy.

To understand God as cause, the meaning of the causal relation must first be ascertained. No static thing can ever play the part of cause, except as the seat of change, or as partner in a change. Nor is the causal relation to be resolved into a mere arrangement of feelings and mental images. When God is spoken of as cause, what is meant is that there is but one universal cause, the infinite and eternal seat of all power, an omniscient mind, ordering all things for ends selected with perfect wisdom.

Just as the causal aspect of the divine nature is opened to us by our own will and extended into the sphere of nature, so the moral aspect of the divine nature is disclosed by conscience, and is then applied to human relationships. From knowledge of ourselves, says Martineau, we gain knowledge of God. From our volitional experience, we can infer objective causality; from our moral experience, we can infer an objective authority.

Our knowledge of an infinite and righteous cause of all is the result of an immediate intuition, Martineau claims; such knowledge is on the same footing of certainty as our apprehension of the external material world.

According to Martineau, the conscience supplies the moral nature with a special sphere of cognition. Whenever we are confronted by two incompatible courses of action, our moral intuition provides us with the certainty that one of the alternatives is superior in excellence. The more excellent course is not marked by greater pleasure or advantage, or by greater seemliness or beauty, but its excellence consists in a greater degree of *rightness,* which demands our assent and commands our obedience.

Such superiority may be disregarded by us, but when the lesser course is followed we are haunted by a sense of disloyalty. We accuse ourselves and know that our offense is not a private mistake. We are cast down by guilt. The springs of action are differentiated to the conscience by an element of value. The superior terms in the scale of right claim us by their *authority;* they tell us that we *ought* to follow them, that they are binding on us, that they are presented to us by a Being higher than we, and that we sin in neglecting them. We are in fact responsible for doing our duty; that is, for conforming our voluntary life to the preferential scale of obligation, as its parts emerge into consciousness.

The moral law, writes Martineau, is imposed by an authority foreign to our personality; it may be obeyed or disobeyed. The right is not determined by social vote; the authority which forces itself upon us is not simply the embodiment of public opinion, an ideal aggregate of sentiment which bestows praise and blame on what aids or is detrimental to human interests. Neither self-love nor collective self-interest is sufficient to account for the idea of right. The inherent differences between right and wrong are more than subjective fancies. They are urged upon us by an objective power with which their validity is identified.

According to Martineau, we are introduced immediately in the act of conscience to a being higher than ourselves, which causes us to know the right. There is a perfect analogy between the dualism of perception, which confronts us with an objective world, and the dualism of conscience, which confronts us with an objective higher mind. The integral meaning of the moral law is reached when the latter is seen as implicit in a perfect mind, which communicates to us and by exercising its power over our affections draws us into divine communion. The very constitution of our moral nature is intelligible solely when viewed as a response to an objective perfection pervading the universe with holy law. The moral differences that we feel have their verification in reality, in an eternal holiness. The conscience reveals the living God, an infinite objective perfection, not merely a set of moral ideals.

The theism developed upon the basis of causality was outward, in the cosmos, but the reference now is inward, in the human soul; the divine agency is here seen in the moral law, not in the laws of nature, which are laws of invariable necessity, but in the laws of variable possibility and freedom.

By our conscience, says Martineau, we can apprehend certain attributes of God. God is identical with the *highest,* the supreme term in the hierarchy of spiritual natures; He is the eternal life of moral perfection. By analyzing the elements of ideal perfection, we recognize the attributes that may be ascribed to God. We thus reach conceptions of God by probing our moral nature, for God's attributes are the transcendent forms of human aims and prayers. Benevolence towards sentient beings must, for example, be ascribed to God. From the constitution of our humanity we learn that God its author is loving, merciful, and compassionate. In the infinite disposer we recognize justice toward moral beings. The conscience of mankind refuses to believe in the ultimate impunity of guilt. No objective belief has more than a subjective guarantee, but there is no less reason to accept our conscience as delegate of a sovereign righteousness, than to regard our bodily dimensions as limited from universal space. Since moral effects surely must flow from a moral source, we may discover the reflections of an eternal justice in our own ethical discriminations. However vast the distance between God and man, we may suppose that God is sympathetic to devoted minds. Related spirits are joined by a common creative aim, intent on what is pure and good. Religious experience affirms that the silent soliloquies of the heart are happily interrupted, for divine words flow in and break the loneliness.

According to Martineau, the revelation of the all-perfect is not simply to the individual but to all mankind; one harmony vibrates throughout the universal medium of spiritual existence; God stands in one relation to all, breathes the same inspirations, gives the same warnings, and invites the same affections. Our united human nature constitutes the Kingdom of God; for it has no offenses which are not sins and no penalties which do not express His will. As nature constitutes one intellectual organism, so humanity constitutes one moral organism. The whole domain of knowledge and duty can thus be seen to be suffused with the divine.

Martineau claims that there is a unity of God as cause and God as perfection. While it is possible to find the origin of our primary religious ideas in the two sides of our nature, the intellectual and the moral, God's attributes are inseparable. Intelligence, power, self-existence, benevolence, justice, holiness, and sovereignty over men are attributes of the one causal and holy God.

We ourselves unite in our own persons a subjection to the outward physical order and to the inward moral law, writes Martineau. The moral order and the physical order are organically blended in real existence. External nature is not foreign to the system of moral laws. The moral system to which we belong corresponds to the righteousness of God. A certain range of contingency is surrendered to the free will of finite beings, for God does not necessitate a good; moral evil is thus possible.

Neither pantheism nor determinism is compatible with the theism here defended, since the former invalidates all personal relations, and the latter all moral relations, between the human and divine mind.

The universe presents us with a grandeur that is divine only when we read the causality behind phenomena. And when we find our duty invested with a supernatural light, we are subdued by its sanctity. The embrace of the all-comprehending God transforms each object into a religious object. The same transition, from the empirical to the transcendent, brings the future life under the surveillance of religion.

Martineau suggests that the question of a life to come centers in the interpretation of death as affecting the individual. From the physiological point of view, there is no way of knowing that the individual soul does not survive the dissolution of the body, for the universe may well contain means of individualization other than the present human body. Martineau believes in the immortality of the soul, not as a demonstrable truth of science, but as a supreme article of an abiding faith in the reasonableness of God's work. From the moral point of view, two inferences seem to force themselves upon us, Martineau suggests: first, that there are everywhere indelible marks of a morally constituted world, moving toward righteous ends; and second, that nowhere do we find the fulfillment of the latter, so that the unfinished character of ourselves and of our world implies a justifying and perfect sequel. It is, therefore, reasonable to believe, Martineau concludes, that we stand in divine relations which indefinitely exceed the limits of our earthly years.

THE ASCENT OF MAN

Author: Henry Drummond (1851-1897)
Type of work: Christian evolutionary theory
First published: 1894

Principal Ideas Advanced

The scientific account of evolution is the story of creation as told by those who know it best.

Naturalists err in interpreting nature from the standpoint of the atom; theologians err in separating man from his environment.

Any evolutionary account must consider the place of soul and spirit in the world, for the universe is an expression of God's will.

There is no inherent opposition between science and religion.

Henry Drummond's Lowell Lectures published in 1894 as *The Ascent of Man* are of value today less for their specific teaching than for what they reveal of an important type of response to the challenge the theory of evolution presented to religious thought in the late nineteenth century. The title reflects the theme which is constantly reiterated throughout the book: the theory of evolution supports a positive interpretation of man's progressive *ascent;* the theory need not be castigated as insisting upon the *descent* of man from some primeval ape.

Drummond's purpose was a corrective one: to re-examine the notion of evolution which had been given to the modern world. The impetus for his work lay in the author's deep-seated conviction that a more balanced, broader, and deeper evolutionary theory was needed as a standard for the thought of his day. His aim was to speak to neither the specialist nor the theologian but to an audience of laymen; he wanted to describe the basic phases in the ascent and arrest of man's body, the dawn of mind and language and the struggle for life. Finally, he wanted to offer an interpretation of all these matters.

Henry Drummond, a gifted Scotsman, preacher of a practical Christian religion, and a teacher of science, was a person with a compelling and passionate concern for achieving a reconciliation of science and theology in the service of Jesus Christ. Drummond enjoyed very great fame as a lecturer on religious themes presented in an unconventional manner, utilizing the latest intellectual methods, and permeated with a contagious faith in God and the reality of religious experience. He was possessed of a commanding appearance and a penetrating gaze which caused one who knew him to say: "No man could be double, or base, or mean, or impure before those eyes." He was so influential that Christian work among students in England, America, Germany, Australia, Japan, and Russia owes a direct indebtedness to his inspiration. On tours to college campuses Drummond made deep impressions upon his audience. His most famous and lasting work is the sermon on love, which has become a classic and best-selling work under the title, "The Greatest Thing in the World." Of his other works, *Natural Law in the Spiritual World* (1883), the most widely read religious work in the world in its day, and *The Ascent of Man* are the most important.

The problem of the ascent, or evolution, of man is at once the noblest and most practical of all studies, Drummond asserts. The scientific account of evolution is, after all, simply "the story of creation as told by those who know it best."

The critical modern reader notes in these lectures the absence of any discussion concerning the propriety of associating a cosmological theory of creation with a scientific account of evolution. Drummond accepted the science of his day as providing definitive answers to the problem of man's creation and evolution. Thus, Drummond's work is interesting and informative as much for what it does not say and for what it takes for granted, as for its positive claims.

Despite Drummond's enthusiasm for science, he was not uncritical in regard to it. He points out, for example, that evolutionary theory as an attempt to explain the development of life quite naturally tends to express the predilections of the particular thinkers who contribute to evolutionary theory. But science is self-corrective, for criticism within scientific circles is more severe than the irresponsible charges which come from the outside.

Drummond advises suspension of judgment concerning Darwinism. He describes his age as "the age of the evolution of Evolution," and he suggests that because of the constantly changing content of scientific thought, and in consideration of the humility, tolerance, and lack of dogmatism which often accompany scientific work, evolutionary theory be accepted in general in order that it might continue to emerge ever stronger from its many immersions in "the crucible of criticism." Evolutionary theory for Drummond was no mathematical proposition which may be declared true or false; it is the product of a method of looking upon nature, of a way of intellectual life.

The error of his time Drummond sees as too little rather than too much attention to evolution. The naturalists make the mistake of interpreting nature from the standpoint of the atom, while theologians err in separating man from his environment. Deploring those "defenses" of science and religion which have the effect of removing the rational basis of religion and the legitimate crown of science, Drummond protests unnatural religion and inhuman science. Both scientist and theologian need to enlarge their views, the former to include the whole man in all of his moral, social, intellectual, and religious dimensions, and the latter to include man as human being in a world setting. Drummond's unfailing gift for expressing such notions in an appealing manner is illustrated in the following passage: "The man who is busy with the stars will never come across Natural Selection, yet surely must he allow for Natural Selection in his construction of the world as a whole. He who works among star-fish will encounter little of Mental Evolution, yet will he not deny that it exists. The stars have their voices, but there are other voices; the star-fishes have activities, but there are other activities. Man, body, soul, spirit, are not only to be considered, but are first to be considered in any theory of the world. You cannot describe the life of kings, or arrange their kingdoms, from the cellar beneath the palace." That his admirers appreciated such rhetoric and the ideas it expressed is suggested by the fact that whole blocks of tickets for the lecture series were bought by speculators and sold for fabulous prices and that many persons were turned away. One writer described the published lectures as "the New Testament of the science of evolution, as Darwin's work was the Old."

Drummond would have agreed that the importance of his efforts lay not in the detail which make up the chapters tracing through nature the struggle for life (individualism) and the struggle for the life of others (altruism). It is well that specific detail should be rendered obsolete as new insights develop. What is essential is the recognition of the validity of the evolutionary insight which permits nature to be seen as the garment of God, His revelation and expression of His will. It is not to be supposed that Drummond's work was a facile reconciliation of the very real tensions facing those who were struggling to reconcile the apparent dichotomies between the traditional religious and the new scientific views. He knew the issues in both science and theology. One of his significant contributions was in making articulate the perplexities facing the thoughtful person of his day.

Drummond was very much aware that his was not the time for grand summations. He was cautious with regard to statements about the manner of development of the course of evolution. He doubted that it would ever be possible to determine whether the ascent of man took place in a continuous and uninterrupted rise or by steps abrupt and steep.

Drummond's concern was one which characterizes that of deeply discerning minds in every period: to relate scientific and religious insights in a way which pays honor to them both. Not for Drummond was the practice of giving to religion the left-overs of science with the result that God becomes the symbol for what science has not yet been able to understand. For Drummond, "nature is God's writing and can only tell the truth," while evolution is God's method of creation. The immanent God of evolution "is infinitely grander than the occasional wonder-worker who is the God of an old theology." While readers today may properly take exception to certain aspects of both the science and the theology which Drummond used in his remarkable harmonizing of the two, no one can read *The Ascent of Man* without sensing the appealing enthusiasm and sincerity which were the result of Drummond's having actually achieved for himself the reconciliation of the mind and the heart about which he so eloquently spoke.

IN HIS STEPS

Author: Charles Monroe Sheldon (1857-1946)
Type of work: Novel, or social tract
First published: 1896

Principal Ideas Advanced

Since Jesus is truly an example for mankind, it is possible to follow in His steps but only if one is willing to follow Jesus in making the sacrifices that such a course of action may require.

The task of the Christian who wants to be obedient to Jesus in his present life is defined by the question "What would Jesus do?"

Charles Monroe Sheldon, a successful minister and author of many books, has accomplished what few men have: he has written a book which can truly be said to have helped change the world. It has been estimated that *In His Steps,* subtitled "What Would Jesus Do?" sold at least thirty million copies within the half-century following its original publication in 1896 and that it has been translated into at least twenty-one languages. Originally read chapter by chapter on Sunday evenings to the Christian Endeavor Society of the Central Congregational Church of Topeka, Kansas, and published simultaneously in serial form in the *Chicago Advance,* the book entered the public domain because of a defective copyright, a fact which may have contributed to its popularity among publishers.

In terms of its influence as a social tract, *In His Steps* has been ranked alongside such American classics as *Uncle Tom's Cabin,* and it has been described as having nearly brought on all by itself a national movement for social reform, despite such defects as its highly sentimental and romantic form.

The book is not a literary masterpiece, being neither particularly well-written nor profound in its characterizations. That it was written as a series of Sunday night readings accounts for a somewhat laborious repetition of themes since each episode had to be nearly complete in itself. *In His Steps* is a series of episodes strung together on its subtitle's theme "What Would Jesus Do?" There are too many subplots, many of which seem overly sentimental to modern readers, and many themes are introduced which are never adequately developed; hence it is not its literary perfection which accounts for the power of this book.

What does account for the book's influence is its call to a deepened conception of Christian discipleship. The book proclaims that there is something wrong about the fact that there are Christians who claim to follow Jesus without themselves sacrificing anything, who are able to enjoy all the good things of life, even profiting financially from social evils, without feeling that there is anything religiously wrong about their activities. *In His Steps* consists of a series of episodes involving people who, feeling this wrongness, renounce their ordinary ways, resolving to apply the example of Jesus to their own lives by walking in His steps, doing what Jesus would do were He in their place.

The hero, Henry Maxwell, a minister known for his polished sermons but for little else, is the pastor of the First Church of Raymond. Maxwell is an ordinarily decent man, warm-hearted and sincere, but with typically little social conscience, as is shown by his remark at one point in the book that this is the first time he has ever shaken the hand of a laboring man. The situation, then, is that of a quite ordinary Protestant church at the end of the nineteenth century, undistinguished in every respect. What causes it to become distinguished is the fact that some of its members undertake a radical adventure.

The crisis introducing the story is the appearance of an unemployed printer who raises in a dramatic way the question, "Do ordinary Christians really follow in His steps? Do Christians really apply their Christianity to the problems of society?" This man has lost his job because of the introduction of machines, and although he has looked long for other employment he has found none. His wife is now dead and his child is placed in another's home because of his poverty. Profound questions are raised as to whether our so-called "Christian" society is really what it pretends to be. Maxwell, shaken when the printer dies in his home, proposes to his congregation the following Sunday that they respond to the challenge in the following way: that for a period of one year they try to follow Jesus *completely* by doing what Jesus would do were He they. The story then recounts what happens during the course of that year to a few of those who volunteer to walk in His steps.

Not all sweetness and light ensues, for what Sheldon offers are tales of sacrifices which really hurt. The lovely church soloist Rachel Winslow, refusing an opera career, decides to devote her talents to bringing musical enrichment to the lives of the poor. A railroad superintendent responds by leaving his excellent job, thus alienating his family, because he discovers his company in wrong-doing. A bishop and a prominent minister in Chicago, influenced by Maxwell, leave their prosperous positions to open a settlement house. An heiress and her brother, both socially useless, find meaning in sacrificing their wealth to better conditions among both poor and rich. In most of these cases, families are broken up because there are members who protest these steps as extremist, impractical, and out of step with the requirements of modern social as well as religious life. In a deeper sense, however, there *is* peace and tranquility, as those who follow in His steps find former values fading and new values bestowing character and nobility upon their once rather useless but pleasant lives.

Many of the problems posed are unambiguous, easily solved in terms of simple moral action, such as: Should a Christian rent space for a saloon? Should the college president and minister enter into the practical business of political reform, or should they remain aloof, isolated in their intellectual and spiritual interests respectively? Sheldon also shows at times a realistic wisdom about social and spiritual problems, realizing that they cannot all be disposed of by the exercise of will power. The movement to close the saloons fails. The editor in deciding to create a Christian newspaper is forced by his conscience to stop printing accounts of prize fights, to cancel liquor and tobacco advertising, to refuse to print family scandals, and to drop his Sunday edition—measures which cause his readership to dwindle. His appeal to fellow Christians to support his newspaper arouses some response, but the newspaper is delivered from its financial difficulties only by a large endowment given by an heiress who has joined the volunteers; hence it is never clear whether the author intends to say clearly that such ventures are economically feasible. Lastly, Maxwell's movement awakens some response outside his own congregation, but it does not silence all opposition, nor does it immediately lead to a renewal of the whole church, as might have been expected in a more simple-minded, completely sentimental book.

The novel, in other words, ends ambiguously. Henry Maxwell hoped that the movement would spread, that the knowledge of what is possible for those who fully follow in Jesus' steps would inspire Christians throughout the nation to take up similar work, but he also knew that the task was difficult and that resistance was great. One church, his own, had been radically changed; his community had been alerted to do battle for social betterment, and a few outsiders had been touched, but he had doubts as to whether his movement would ever spread beyond its present level of success, and even as to whether the progress made would in the long run be really significant.

About one form of success, however, the author is quite clear. Those who follow in His steps, carrying out their resolves to do what Jesus would do in their places, find meaning and joy in life. Several dramatic changes are briefly sketched, for example that of Rollin Page, society man, who is at first spurned by Rachel Winslow because he has no purpose in life, and is later converted at evangelistic meetings in the slums at which Rachel was singing. With a new sense of purpose for his own existence he sets to work redeeming his fellow club-men, becoming fully a man, and winning her admiration and love in the process. This is but one of a number of similar tales recounted in the book.

There are failures, also. Jaspar Chase, introduced as a young novelist whose love was also spurned by Miss Winslow, falls into unhappiness. In contrast to Rollin, who found life in following what Jesus would do, Jaspar is unable to carry out his pledge. Having finished a novel which is entertaining but socially useless, and knowing that Jesus would not have published it, Jaspar's will is not sufficient to his need. He falls into a pattern of cynical success. Similarly, in a wealthy family with two daughters divided, one daughter finds happiness and love in teaching cooking to the poor, while her sister, rejecting such a life, turns to security and a loveless marriage. Sheldon thus makes clear his conviction as to the seriousness of the choice between inconsequential worldly success and the deep joy that comes from serving God with all one's heart and strength by plunging into the fight for a Christian society which provides social justice for all.

The ethic displayed can be shown in terms of the following list which states "what Jesus would probably do in Milton Wright's place as a business man": He would engage in business primarily to glorify God rather than to make money; He would regard profits as a trust to be used for the good of humanity; His relations with His employees would be loving and helpful, with their interests, their well-being, the good of their Souls, taking precedence over the making of money; He would do nothing even questionable in His business dealings; and unselfishness would direct His business activities, shaping His relations to employees, customers, and to the general business world. This list fairly represents the type of reform that the author intended to inspire for his times.

The particular social adversaries are the saloon, tobacco, prize fights and billiard halls, slums and unemployment, but the major enemy seems really to be the complacency of churches. The book is primarily an effort to show Christians that to follow in Jesus' steps is to do what Jesus would do about social evils, regardless of personal cost. It is a book written by a Christian pastor for his congregation and Christian readers everywhere in which the author describes a path of active discipleship which could change the world.

Although the book tends toward an individualistic approach to social reform, there are more communal notes sounded at times. Stress is laid repeatedly upon the corporate life of the church as a source of strength and guidance. Weekly meetings of the volunteers help to guide and strengthen those who have undertaken this serious task, and there is a strong sense of mutual help and comfort. The power of the vote is emphasized as a means to social reform. Sheldon's own age was an age of crusades to change society by changing the individuals in it, and although he was a child of his times he sometimes took into account the need for more powerful means of social change.

Recognition of the fact that social conditions shape men and that to transform men one must transform their environments (the "Social Gospel") came relatively late to Christianity, and *In His Steps,* perhaps more than any other book, helped to popularize this insight. It was aimed both at problems created by indolence and wealth and at problems created by habitual vice and degradation. The indictment is primarily directed not at the struggling poor but at the indolent and unconcerned rich who sit in complacent comfort, deriving financial profit from the vices of modern life, yet think of themselves as walking in Jesus' steps. In the tradition of the great prophets, Sheldon challenges the consciences of those who "are at ease in Zion" (Amos 6:1).

THE CHRISTIAN PASTOR

Author: Washington Gladden (1836-1918)
Type of work: Pastoral theology
First published: 1898

Principal Ideas Advanced

The priestly conception of the Church as distinct from society must be replaced by the conception of society as an organism, with the Church as one of its parts.

The old distinctions between sacred and secular, clergy and laity, worship and work must be abandoned.

The pastor's office is that of teacher, leader, and friend to the whole community; his task is to preach the good news that God is organizing a divine society on earth, and to lead the people in social work.

The supernatural power of God's redeeming love works through nature; individual salvation consists in possessing a character harmonious with spiritual laws, but the individual cannot be saved except in relationship with society.

The Christian Pastor is one in the important series of volumes, by different authors, known as *The International Theological Library.* Gladden's book covers the subject of practical theology in all its aspects, but because a separate volume in the series is given to the subject of preaching, Gladden does not dwell at length on that topic.

The full title of the book, *The*

Christian Pastor and the Working Church, indicates the perspective within which Gladden approaches pastoral theology. One of the first advocates in this country of the "social gospel," and active in municipal affairs in Columbus, Ohio, where for thirty-six years he was pastor of a Congregational church, Gladden sought to awaken in his readers a sense of the Church's responsibility "to spiritualize the whole of life." "We have seen," he says, "that the new and higher conception of the church is that it is primarily a working body; that it is formed not mainly of those who seek to be fed and ministered unto, but of those who are working together to extend the Kingdom of God."

Although Gladden's own background was that provided by New England theology, he read widely in the literature of all communions. His book, indeed, abounds in lengthy quotations from such standard authors on pastoral theology as Horace Bushnell, Patrick Fairbairn, J. J. Van Oosterzee, and Alexandre Vinet. In spite of, or we might almost say because of, his conception of "the Working Church," Gladden produced a broad-gauged work which any pastor can read with profit. Many pastoral practices that were new in his day, such as the emphasis on pastoral counseling, have become accepted parts of the pastor's work two generations later. But they are nearly all dealt with in this book, and by one who had the advantage of being able to compare them with the different conceptions of the ministry that prevailed a hundred years ago. The book's chief limitations, from a practical standpoint, stem from the fact that it treats of the pastorate exclusively from the vantage point of the city church.

A main objective in Gladden's book is to break down the antitheses which have grown up in the Church owing to sacerdotalism. The priestly type of church quite deliberately insists on the distinction between sacred and secular, between the clergy and the laity, and between the Kingdom of God and the world. Even the reformed churches, which in principle have rejected most of these ideas, still follow them as a matter of habit. Gladden proposes that these distinctions be done away with. He insists that there must be no division between the Church and the community of which it is a part. The human community, he says, is an organism, with many specialized parts, of which the Church is one. But specialization of function does not mean separation of life. On the contrary, says Gladden, it is the function of the Church to sanctify every department of human life; and, if the Church fails, permitting the community about it to decay, then nothing can preserve the life of the Church.

From this conception of the Church's task, it follows that the minister must be no narrow churchman, but very much a man of the world. The notion that ordination sets him apart from other members of Christ's Church in any sense other than that he is to be their leader, teacher, and friend, Gladden rejects. Of the various names (priest, parson, pastor, minister) that are used to designate his office, Gladden prefers "minister," because, in its original intention, it signifies "one who serves."

What distinguishes the minister's activities from those of other leaders of the community is that all that he is able to do with and for men, as leader, organizer, and fellow worker, has a spiritual basis. Before all else, he is a spiritual teacher, who has the appointed task of awakening in men the desire to serve by means of the truth which it is given him to impart. This truth is the Gospel of the Kingdom of God, the Good News "that God is organizing on earth a divine society; that the New Jerusalem, whose walls are salvation and whose gates are praise, is rising here upon sure foundations." Because it is his task to "discern this Kingdom, to recognize the silent forces which are building it, to interpret its legislation," the pastor must have time for study. But he will be less interested in prying into traditional problems of theology and apologetics than he will in informing himself concerning such subjects as economics and sociology. He has not, it is true, to become an expert in the technical aspects of these subjects, but because industrial and urban developments involve "human relations," he has an active interest in them.

In a chapter entitled "The Pastor as Friend," Gladden says that the minister ought to be one of the most widely acquainted men in a community. Businessmen, teachers, professional men, workers, and school children should recognize him on the street and greet him as a friend. Gladden wishes to be rid of the old image of a parson as a kind of religious functionary, whose visit demands a special decorum, spiritual conversation, and official benedictions. Even when calling upon the sick, he should go simply as a friend, and he should offer prayer only when he is sure that the patient desires it. As a city pastor, Gladden recognized that more and more the pastoral call was being replaced by the demand for personal counseling. "The pastor offers less of personal service because the sacerdotal character of the minister is fading out, and the brotherly character is more strongly accentuated." This was written, however, before the day of the amateur psychologist, and the best thing that Gladden knew for a pastor to say in cases of marital difficulty is: "You two must live together. . . . Separation is not to be thought of. . . . The problem for each of you is to win and compel the respect, the affection, of the other. You can do it if you try. You had better die than fail. Go home and begin today." Such words, he testifies, have saved many a household, and thereby prevented children from growing up homeless.

Just as the sacred is not to be separated from the secular, so the worship of the Church is not to be set over against its work. In worship, as in work, the pastor is one with his congregation; they are priests together before God. Nothing is more fruitful of misapprehension than the supposition that those who sit in the pews form an audience, which has come to hear the preacher and to enjoy the choir. Gladden expresses approval of liturgical forms so far as these help involve the congregation in the service; he regards the choir as existing primarily to lead the congregation in singing the hymns, and he states his opposition to any kind of music which tends to draw attention to the performer and which interferes with the worship of God.

But the Church, as Gladden sees it, exists not merely for worship, but also for work; and he adds that the latter is in no way secondary to the former. In discussing "institutional churches," which were just then coming into prominence, Gladden deplores the tendency on the part of some, even those kindly disposed to the innovation, to speak apologetically of reading-rooms and bowling alleys, as if they were secular additions. "They are not merely means of getting people under religious influences," he says; "they are means of grace, every one of them —helps to a godly life—just as truly as is the prayer meeting itself." Gladden wants these things to be kept in mind when new churches are built. The churchbuilding should be adapted to "the newer conception of the church as a working body," and it should have provisions for class rooms, social rooms, committee rooms, and any special accommodations the particular church's work requires.

Gladden claims that the most important meeting in the church year is the congregational meeting, at which reports from the various organizations are received. In a working church, the organizations are central. Gladden deals with these in appreciative detail, giving separate chapters to the Sunday School, mid-week service, committees, social gatherings, women's work, and youth groups. When a person joins the Church, he should do so with the understanding that he is to take on some responsibility. Gladden was not interested in activity for its own sake. He refers to the familiar complaint of the minister in a growing community of thousands who need to be reached. The minister's first thought, he says, quoting Dean Gott, is that to reach those thousands is impossible; his second thought is, "Through Christ I can do all things"; his third thought is that he can secure help through organization. "Into this teeming multitude, ever coming and going, diffuse yourself that you may concentrate yourself through an army of church-workers, and unite them with your parishioners and yourself in Christ."

Gladden was not unmindful of the importance of pressing home the message of salvation to individual souls, but he construed redemption and regeneration in terms of character building. There are multitudes, he writes, for whom no salvation is possible, unless they completely reverse the whole course of their lives; it is the preacher's mission to bring about this change, wherever possible. The older theology, says Gladden, distinguished between preaching law and preaching grace, but this distinction no longer holds, because we now know that spiritual laws are natural laws, and that love is the foundation of law. The dogma of the "new birth" is no mere mystical extravagance, but a psychological fact. It occurs daily, both within and without the Church, most frequently under the mysterious workings of human love. Gladden had little sympathy with "revivals and revivalism"; he preferred the path marked out by Horace Bushnell in *Christian Nurture,* who, in the chapter entitled "The Out-Populating Power of the Christian Stock," argued that the Church need only "hold its own" to speedily gain possession of the world. Here, as elsewhere, Gladden appeals to the organic principle. Wholesome character can thrive only in a wholesome society.

Gladden advises ministers to accentuate the practical and the positive, and to leave speculation and doubt alone. "When a man begins to preach the Gospel the great underlying verities of the Kingdom of Heaven ought to be settled in his mind beyond questioning; it should not be necessary for him to keep convincing himself that they are true." The minister has as his fundamental postulate the existence of the spiritual realm. He believes that love and not law is at the heart of things, that God is a personal being who loves men and in fellowship with whom men find grace and strength in time of need, and that man is a free spirit who chooses his own destiny. When members of his congregation have difficulties with what they call "the supernatural," the minister will point out that what is supernatural is not *anti*-natural, and that there is no antecedent reason why there should not be a power active in our lives and in the world about us that we cannot understand. He will further point out that the only proof possible that there is a God is the practical test of living in fellowship with Him.

The spirit of Gladden's own ministry, and that of the ideal of *The Christian Pastor and the Working Church* is, perhaps, most perfectly expressed in Gladden's hymn, "O Master, let me walk with thee, in lowly paths of service free."

CHRISTIAN MYSTICISM

Author: William Ralph Inge (1860-1954)
Type of work: Apologetic theology
First published: 1899

Principal Ideas Advanced

The witness of Christian mysticism constitutes the strongest evidence for the truth of the Christian religion.

Christian mysticism, following in the path of St. John and St. Paul, is preserved from the pessimism and nihilism of Oriental mysticism.

There is a mysticism which experiences God in the external world and in sacramental acts, as well as a mysticism which finds Him within the human soul.

Although in the form of a brief history of the subject, Dean Inge's Bampton Lectures on Christian mysticism are in substance "a contribution to Christian apologetics." The author seeks to show that where men's minds are illuminated by the revelation of God in Christ, they have a saner, more profound "sense of the tremendous issues of life in the world wherein we move," and he argues that it is on this ground that Christianity must base its case. On the practical side, he maintains that a return to "the fundamentals of spiritual religion" is required if the theological and liturgical forms of the Church are to meet the needs of our times.

Mysticism, according to Dean Inge, is only one form of man's "consciousness of the *beyond*." What distinguishes it from other types of religious experience, as well as from art and philosophy, is its attempt to "realize" the *beyond* as present in the soul and in nature. In Christian mysticism, where it is true to its New Testament origins, reality is experienced in relation to the image of Christ; in Inge's view, it is this relationship to Christ which has kept Christian mysticism "sound and sober." St. John's teaching that Christ is the Eternal Logos manifest in the flesh has preserved in Christian mystics a due reverence for reason, on the one hand, and for nature and life on the other. Similarly, St. Paul's teaching that a man's "old nature" must be crucified with Christ before that man can rise to newness of life in Christ has made the Christian mystics aware of the supreme worth of human personality.

Historically, however, Western mysticism has suffered incursions from non-Christian sources. One of the worst blights, according to Inge, has been the influence of Indian Pan-nihilism, which infected the philosophy of Plotinus (c.204-c.270) and, even more directly, of Pseudo-Dionysius (c.500), whose works were authoritative for both Eastern Orthodoxy and medieval Catholicism. It was, Inge holds, an error in Plotinus' philosophy when he declared that "the One," which for him was the fount and origin of all things, is beyond distinction. Westerners, world-weary and frightened at the collapse of their own civilization, were too ready to adopt the pessimism of the East; moreover, the doctrine of nirvana received specious support from the deadly seductiveness of the "blank trance" to which Plotinus was subject. According to Inge, this aberration is not required by anything in Plotinus' philosophy, who had himself observed that "he who tries to rise above reason falls outside it."

Inge has little affection for the Middle Ages. The "negative theology" which it learned from Pseudo-Dionysius was, he says, to blame for "nearly all that repels us in medieval religious life": hostility to civilization, contempt for the family, abuse of the body, and absorption in solitary contemplation. However, the mischief attributable to the negative theology must be measured against the vicious consequences of the Roman Church's emphasis on miracles as the basis of belief in God. The more superstitious and magical aspects of medieval religion may be considered simply as survivals from primitive animism, but the fact that they survived in a Christian atmosphere is only to be understood in view of the sharp distinction which Roman theology makes between natural and supernatural, between reason and grace. The distinction is first fully developed by Richard of St. Victor (d.1173), one of the greatest mystics in the Middle Ages, who, although conceding that reason is a useful guide for bringing the generality of men to God, maintained that the supernatural grace which the mystic receives is completely beyond reason. According to Inge, this distinction between the rational and the mystical is both unphilosophical and unscriptural; far from leading to a "truer and deeper view of the actual," it introduces into the lives of men a lawless and disturbing force which threatens every genuinely human interest.

The little-known English mystics of the fourteenth century, Walter Hilton (died 1396) and Julian of Norwich (c.1342-after 1413) finally shook off "the chains of Asiatic nihilism." Of the former, Inge writes, "It is, I think, gratifying to observe how our countryman strikes off the fetters of the time-honoured Dionysian tradition, the paralysing creed which blurs all distinctions, and the 'negative road' which leads to darkness and not light." John ("Meister") Eckhart (c.1260-c.1327) and his successors among the German mystics had, indeed, moved to identify the Divine Logos with the Father. But Inge finds "something wrong with a system which ends in obliterating the distinction between the Creator and His creatures." Julian is a welcome contrast: "I saw no difference," she writes, "between God and our substance, but, as it were, all God. And yet my understanding took, that our substance is *in* God—that is to say, that God is God, and our substance a creature in God."

So far, we have spoken only of those mystics who seek to realize God's presence within the soul. Those are no less mystics, according to Inge, who discover His presence in nature, which they take to be "a world of symbolism, a rich hieroglyphic book," where things visible half conceal and half reveal invisible mysteries. Ancient astrology, the Greek mystery religions, the Jewish cabbala were all expressions of nature-mysticism. Such mysticism has been abused as shamefully as the speculative kind, but in able and devout hands, it is no less fruitful. Among its more creditable exponents are Jakob Boehme (1575-1624), and William Law (1686-1761), who in his mature life was a follower of Boehme. Inge cites with commendation a passage in which Law denies that there is anything supernatural in the whole of Christianity. "All our redemption," says Law, "is only nature set right, or made to be that which it ought to be." Law goes on to affirm that distinctions between right and wrong, truth and falsity, blessedness and misery are ultimate, and that nothing supernatural can change them. Inge does not limit the mysticism of nature to those who follow the path of prayer and mortification. The Cambridge Platonists of the seventeenth century, and several nineteenth century poets (notably, Wordsworth, Tennyson, Kingsley, and Browning) are eminent representatives of this order. Inge ventures to suggest that the task for the twentieth century is "to spiritualize science," which lags behind philosophy and the arts, and has not yet "found her God." He sees no reason why scientific workers who approach nature with the same earnestness and intensity which engage poetic and religious men should not be rewarded with a comparable revelation of God's wisdom and power.

According to Inge, the Christian sacraments are best understood in terms of the mysticism of nature. Although the plain man prefers to believe either that the sacraments are magical rites or that they are commemorative observances, the true view is that they are symbolic acts. For the mystic, the commonest acts of life are sacramental; that is, they enable us to realize our privileges as children of God. The sacraments of the Church are "divinely-ordered symbols, by which the Church, as an organic whole, and we as members of it, realize the highest and deepest of our spiritual privileges." It is, he believes, one of the assets of the Church of England that its teaching on this subject, as on many others, corrects the inadequacies of Romanism and Protestantism, neither of which by itself "possesses enough of the truth to satisfy the religious needs of the present day." In the mysticism of St. John and St. Paul, the Church of England possesses the "fresh springs" of spirituality by which it can retain its eternal youth.

Inge does not wish to maintain that mysticism is the whole of Christianity. The faith of the Church is grounded in historical events, and depends for its continued existence upon religious institutions. A "vague spirituality tempered by rationalism" would not carry men very far, but a proper appreciation of the Church's mystical heritage, Inge believes, leads to three conclusions that should "have a calming and reassuring influence upon those who, from whatever cause, are troubled with religious doubts."

First, there is the high degree of unanimity among those pre-eminent in saintliness that God is a spirit, that human spirits can hold fellowship with Him, that in Him they meet with perfect truth, beauty, and goodness, and that they "come to themselves" in proportion as they draw near to Him. This testimony cannot be set aside, any more than can the testimony of specialists in any other subject.

Second, although the mystical experience cannot guarantee the truth of historical events, such as are attested in Gospel history, still it must be the living experience of Christ which vests sacred events with their eternal meaning. To maintain that the truth revealed in Christ is the very truth of God is, says Inge, to make a statement which, strictly speaking, only God can make. All that we can intelligently mean by such a statement is that, when we read the Gospels, our spirit is persuaded that "here are the words of eternal life."

Third, mystical experience gives us the only satisfactory answer to our questions concerning man's ultimate destiny. That part of our life is bound up with the future of mankind upon earth, Inge gladly concedes, but man's spirit "beats against the bars of space and time," seeking its true home in "some higher sphere of existence." Only through the most inadequate symbols can we represent to ourselves what such a life would be, but the faith is "enthroned in the centre of our being . . . an earnest of a final victory over the grave."

PRACTICAL CHRISTIANITY

Author: Rufus Matthew Jones (1863-1948)
Type of work: Practical ethics
First published: 1899

Principal Ideas Advanced

What is vital in religion is not belief in certain doctrines, participation in certain formal rituals, or obedience to a moral code, but a direct, immediate, personal experience of God which floods the soul with peace, joy, and power, and leads to a new life of holiness and active love.

The heart of Christianity is its witness to a God of love who has manifested Himself among men in the perfect human-divine personality of Jesus Christ and who, as life-giving Spirit, works in the world to transform mankind into the Kingdom of God.

The only real internal proof of Christianity is the soul's immediate awareness of being drawn into a spiritual union with God, and the only real external test of the genuineness of Christian experience is a transformed moral life which overflows with love for the neighbor expressed in helpful deeds of practical service.

The Church is a spiritual organism whose mission is to proclaim the salvation available to men in Christ and to continue the practical ministry of aiding stricken humanity that Jesus began when he was on earth.

Undoubtedly, Rufus Jones is the most outstanding personality, religious leader, and writer the Society of Friends has produced in America during the last hundred years. Jones was the author of fifty-seven books. *Practical Christianity: Essays on the Practice of Religion* was the second book he wrote and the first one to set forth an interpretation of the Christian life. It provides excellent insight into the nature of the practical, experiential Christianity which he so well represented both in his personal life and in his many writings. His concern in this early book, as indicated by the title of his last book written nearly half a century later, is to present "a call to what is vital in religion." He magnifies the importance of the practical application of Christian teachings and of the actual doing of the will of God in human life. Constantly manifesting a disdain for abstract theory and mere talk about Christianity, Jones calls men to "practice the presence of God" in daily affairs and thus to find empirical validation of the claim of Christianity to be an authentic revelation of God. Throughout the pages of this book one encounters a deeply religious personality who has caught the spirit of the sect's tradition and who writes as one who knows at firsthand whereof he speaks as he defines practical Christianity and invites men to respond to its stirring challenge.

Rufus Jones was a mystic in his personal religion and a liberal in theology. The impact of modern knowledge convinced him that new ways of thinking about the Bible and religious authority were necessary, and thus he felt most at home with the exponents of theological liberalism. However, since, as a good Quaker, he stressed the authority of a direct, personal experience of God, he was convinced that no possible development in science, philosophy, or historical research could undermine the abiding essence of Christianity. With his faith grounded securely in the immediacy of experience, he could sincerely urge a free and open spirit before the facts in order that new truth for new situations might be forthcoming. One of his greatest fears was rigidity in belief and the freezing of traditions into hard and fast forms. The only test of orthodoxy, as he saw it, was the quality of man's moral and spiritual life, not the formal creed which he professed intellectually.

Mysticism meant for Jones essentially an unmediated personal awareness of the reality and goodness of God which fills the soul with peace, joy, and love and supplies life with new meaning and moral power. He put the emphasis on the practical, ethical, and social aspects of religious experience rather than on quietistic states of private ecstasy. The Christian life consists of a vital, personal encounter with God in the depths of the inner life, and the Christian spirit manifests itself in the doing of the divine will in the everyday world of people and events. The genius of Christianity is its power to draw men into intimate fellowship with a God of love revealed in the perfect human-divine life of Jesus Christ and to send them out into the world filled with the envigorating Spirit to do battle for a Kingdom of God in which all men will live as brothers. Jones, then, espoused a Christ-centered, ethical mysticism which stressed the practical results of religion in the struggle for human betterment. His was a robust, activistic, optimistic faith centered in a God who works ceaselessly among men to bring them into spiritual union with Himself and to make His Kingdom a reality here and now.

The second edtion of *Practical Christianity* (1905) contains a collection of sixty-six short chapters, the great majority of which are about three pages long. Most of these essays had appeared previously as editorials and are here put together in no apparent order. Various topics ranging from Christian recreation and diversion to the doctrine of the Trinity are dealt with in independent chapters, and no common theme is pursued from one to another. Most of the chapters, however, deal with some aspect of the Christian life. Jones's focus of attention seldom gets away from the practical side of Christian belief, and even when he does occasionally venture to discuss topics such as the Trinity, the Incarnation, or the atonement, he attempts to relate this to the concrete experience of the believer.

Central to any interpretation of Christianity is an understanding of the being and nature of God. Using, with very few exceptions, the ordinary language of the man on the street, Jones states the Christian view of God in practical terms. However, he does dare in a few instances to provide some insight into the meaning of the trinitarian doctrine. God is the Father in Heaven whose inner essence is love. Since love implies a beloved object, God has from eternity generated the Son, who is the express image of His person. This is the Logos, the self-revealing aspect of God. Yet, the Father and the Son, along with the Holy Spirit, are one in the same way that a ray of light exists in indivisible unity though it appears to us as light, color, and energy. This brief and tentative hint as to what the Trinity means is the closest that Jones ever comes in this book to an approach which borders on theological speculation. Since God could not disclose Himself to human beings in any other way, He manifested Himself in person at a particular point in time in the life of Jesus Christ, who is both a perfect man and a partaker of the divine nature. The Incarnation is a mystery beyond comprehension and must not be made into a metaphysical puzzle. However, if human minds could be sufficiently enlightened, it would become apparent that humanity and divinity are not incompatible. The practical meaning of the doctrine is that God has come among men in person and in power to make them sons and eternal heirs of His Kingdom. In confrontation with Christ men come to know who God is and what they are and may become in fellowship with God in Christ.

The Spirit of God is working constantly among men, Jones writes; the Spirit floods into life, drawing persons into spiritual union with Christ and remaking them into new creatures. The Christian is Spirit empowered. Religion is not a burden to be carried by human effort; religion is rather a matter of being lifted up to new heights of joy and moral achievement by a power that breaks into life from without and makes it over from within so that all things are seen in a new light, and love of others becomes the spontaneous expression of a Spirit-filled soul.

Salvation is not a judicial transaction whereby the guilt of inherited sin is removed from the soul thereby making it eligible for bliss beyond death. Instead, salvation is a matter of being transformed here and now so that life becomes patterned after the teachings and example of Jesus. To be saved is to live in direct, immediate fellowship with God and in organic unity with Christ through the power of the life-giving Spirit. Salvation means more than morality, for salvation involves a holy life and obedience to the will of God. Holiness in the Christian life means genuine emancipation from the power of sin, and the perfection of one's deepest motives. To be holy is to hate sin and to love the will of God with such absoluteness that perfection of moral character becomes a reality here and now. The life of holiness is possible because of the intimacy of fellowship between the soul and Christ and because of the flow of the Spirit into the heart of the believer. The believer is organically related to Christ as the branches of a plant are related to the vine. In such union the aims and ideals of Christ are infused into the life of the Christian in such a way that the individual becomes an instrument of the divine purpose in the world. The believer's supreme motive is to serve his Savior by working diligently to relieve the burdens of the oppressed and to make the good life a reality for all.

The Christian life is incomplete without the communion of the soul with God in worship. To worship is to enjoy God in the intimacy of spiritual fellowship. The Friends way of gathering to sit in silence to listen to God is of inestimable value, but it needs to be supplemented by speaking and teaching on the part of those who, having listened, have heard a helpful word from God. The Sabbath should be set aside for such worship and the refreshing of body and spirit.

The Church is an organic community of individual believers who have been drawn into union with Christ through the Spirit. It is not an institution directed by a hierarchy which imposes dogmas and traditions by power and by might. It is a free fellowship of believers animated by the love and spirit of Christ. It exists to proclaim the power of God unto salvation and to invite men to receive new life by becoming a part of the Christian organism. Moreover, it is part of its mission to continue the ministry of practical aid to hurt humanity begun by Jesus himself. The Church should exert its influence to bring about such reform of society as will enable every person to attain his fullest possible development. The only test that can be applied to the Church is that of determining whether it does actually serve as an agency of proclamation of the Gospel and as a center of social action which improves the quality of life on earth.

The brief essays in this volume set forth a view of the practical meaning of Christianity as one outstanding Society of Friends leader sees it. In the longest chapter in the book Jones attempts to interpret the historical significance of the Society of Friends movement itself. Christianity began with the revelation of God in the divine-human person of Christ and with the offer of new life through the grace and power of God. The Friends movement emerged in seventeenth century England as a part of the great emancipation from the tyranny of an ecclesiastical institution which for centuries had smothered the dynamic Gospel of grace by restricting the approach to God to certain defined channels. The original message of the Friends was that salvation is a matter of a personal relationship between a man and God, that Christ brings new life to the soul, and that the witness of this is to be found in the immediate awareness of intimacy with God and in the actuality of a transformed life. Here was a call for firsthand religion based, as was modern philosophy, on the testimony of the immediate self-consciousness of the individual. The movement stressed freedom from external authority and tradition, experiential knowledge of God, the priesthood of all believers before God, and the reality of salvation in this life. The ultimate goal becomes perfected men living in a perfected society ruled by the pervading Spirit of God who draws men into organic union with Christ and into loving fellowship with the total community of believers.

Rufus Jones has presented in *Practical Christianity* an exposition of the message of the Quakers for the present age. The purpose of the sect as Jones sees it is identical with the purpose of this book, which, in his own words, is "not to develop or defend a theory, but to attract persons to a type of life—to set men actually to practising the presence of God."

WHAT IS CHRISTIANITY?

Author: Adolf Harnack (1851-1930)
Type of work: History of theology; liberal Continental theology
First published: 1900

Principal Ideas Advanced

The essence of Christianity is found in the Gospel proclaimed by Jesus Christ, the leading features of which were (1) the Kingdom of God and its coming,

(2) God the Father and the infinite value of the human soul, and (3) the higher righteousness and the commandment of love.

This sublime message, which received its personal realization and its impelling force from Jesus himself, ought not be obscured or perverted by speculative Christological theories about His person; the Gospel, as Jesus proclaimed it, has to do with the Father only and not with the Son.

The greatest transformation and corruption of the Gospel occurred during the early Patristic period, when, under the impact of Hellenism and the threat of Gnosticism, the Christian religion developed into Catholicism; Protestantism represents an attempt to reform the Church and its message according to the pristine Gospel.

Adolph Harnack, Professor of Church History at the University of Berlin from 1889 to 1921, was the most distinguished Patristic scholar of his generation. His *What Is Christianity?*, the book which resulted from a series of open lectures on *Das Wesen des Christentums* during the winter of 1899-1900, attracted an extraordinary response, and by 1927 it had appeared in fourteen editions and had been translated into fourteen languages. The amazing success of the work cannot be attributed simply to the author's immense erudition in the field of history of doctrine or to his ability to present the subject matter in a lucid and interesting fashion. Rather, the book stands as a classic expression of the so-called "liberal" Continental theology, which was deeply rooted in the thought of an earlier German Protestant theologian, Albrecht Ritschl (1822-1889). As an expression of liberal theology, the book aroused bitter opposition as well as eloquent praise.

Harnack's purpose was to answer the pressing question: What is Christianity? His interest was that neither of the apologist nor of the religious philosopher, but of the historian. The materials for his investigation are at once simple and exhaustive: Jesus Christ and His Gospel. However, the focus is not limited to the New Testament period alone, but extends to the differing historical forms assumed by the Gospel during the course of history. Harnack's intention was to discover the permanently valid truth inherent in the Gospel, regardless of the historical form. He of course realized the limitation faced in any such inquiry; namely, the fact that in history absolute judgments are impossible.

The author's first task is to distinguish the leading features of Jesus' own message as set forth in the four Gospels in the New Testament. What is the "Gospel" according to the Gospels? Harnack concedes that the Gospels offer no biography of Jesus, but he believes that they do supply reliable information concerning Jesus' teaching, how His life issued in the service of His vocation, and the impression He made upon His disciples. His teaching, which is really the heart of the matter, can be summed up under three headings, each of which actually contains the whole: (1) the Kingdom of God and its coming, (2) God the Father and the infinite value of the human soul, and (3) the higher righteousness and the commandment of love.

Harnack recognizes that there are two different views of the Kingdom of

God in the Gospels: the external rule of God that is anticipated as a purely future event, and the internal rule of God that is already present. It is Harnack's opinion that Jesus rejected the former, traditional view and proclaimed the latter: the Kingdom that comes to the individual, the rule of God in the heart. As such, declares the author, "it is God himself in his power," which means that the Kingdom is a gift from above that confers a purely religious blessing and is the most important experience a man can have. One's whole existence becomes permeated and dominated by the living God through this inner link.

Another way in which Jesus expresses this truth is by His declaration that God is the Father of all mankind, and that, as the Father, He is infinitely concerned for His children. Every human soul is precious to God. Indeed, declares Jesus, the very hairs of one's head are numbered! Since God is the Father, then all His children are brothers; consequently, Jesus taught men to live the humble life of brotherly love. Ethics in the Kingdom involves far more than attention to external religious forms and technical observance; what is demanded is a "higher righteousness" that stems from man's inmost disposition and intention, the inner motive of love.

Having defined the main elements of the Gospel as Jesus declared it, Harnack next examines certain problems related to that Gospel. Concerning the relation of the Gospel to the world, he argues that world-shunning asceticism has absolutely no place in the Gospel; Jesus teaches that His disciples should live in the world but struggle against three great enemies: mammon, care, and selfishness. What Jesus demands is not ascetic withdrawal, but the self-denying and self-sacrificing love that serves the world. In regard to the social question, or the relation of the Gospel and the poor, Harnack eschews both the view of Jesus as the great social reformer and the view that He had little or no interest in social and economic conditions. Harnack contends that the Gospel is a powerful social message, proclaiming solidarity and brotherliness in favor of the poor, but this message is bound up with what Jesus said about the Kingdom of God and the infinite value of the human soul. It contains no law bidding us forcibly to alter the conditions of the age in which we happen to be living.

How is the Gospel related to the law? Here Harnack reminds us that the Gospel is fundamentally above mundane questions, such as the question of public order, since the Gospel is concerned primarily with the souls of men. Nevertheless, the Gospel is not unrelated to constituted authority and legal ordinance. Jesus did not disparage the law, but He did insist that everyone has certain rights and that His disciples should share in the administering of God's justice. However, the basis for this administering is to be, not force, but free obedience to the good; not legal constraint, but the ministry of love. Harnack claims that the attitude of Jesus toward work, and questions of civilization, is basically the same. While labor and the progress of civilization are precious and worthy of great effort, they do not comprise the highest ideal; namely, the Kingdom of love. We live, not in so far as we work, but in so far as we love and are loved.

Professor Harnack's final pair of questions are the most controversial:

the questions of Christology and of creed. In regard to the first, he contends that what is important is not some doctrine about Jesus' person and dignity, but Jesus' message. Harnack's central claim is this: "The Gospel, as Jesus proclaimed it, has to do with the Father only and not with the Son." However, this circumstance does not mean that Jesus is a merely incidental factor in connection with the Gospel. On the contrary, He was its personal realization and its strength. Nevertheless, His message is the touchstone, a living force that has become efficacious and of critical importance for all time, and it should never be confused with a creed or a system of doctrine or a philosophy of the universe. To place a "Christological" creed before the Gospel, declares Harnack, is to reverse the order of values. No man can think rightly about Christ until he has begun to live according to Christ's Gospel.

The second half of the book is an inquiry into "The Gospel in History." What happens to the Gospel when the Christian religion (which for Harnack means one thing only: "Eternal life in the midst of time, by the strength and under the eyes of God") enters the course of history? The author's investigation begins with the Christianity of the Apostolic Age, traces the development into Catholicism, delineates the characteristics and achievements of the Greek Catholicism of the East and the Roman Catholicism of the West, and ends with a discussion of Protestantism.

Christian religion in the Apostolic Age was characterized, first, by the recognition of Jesus as the living Lord, whose sacrificial death for sinners put an end to all blood-sacrifices and made an atonement that shames and purifies us, and whose resurrection and ascension to the right hand of the Father brings to mankind the certainty of eternal life in and beyond time, and establishes faith in the value of personal life. Second, religion for the members of the new community was an actual experience involving the consciousness of a living union with God through the gift of the Spirit. Finally, the members led a holy life in purity and brotherly fellowship, and in the expectation of Christ's return in the near future. They were mistaken in this expectation, of course, but it nevertheless proved efficacious in lifting them above the world and in helping them to distinguish between what is of time and what is of eternity.

It was also during the Apostolic Age that the Apostle Paul delivered the Christian religion from Judaism. Conceiving the Gospel as the message of effected redemption and present salvation that abolished the religion of the Law and pertained to all individuals, Paul gave the Gospel a new language intelligible to all men, transformed it into a universal religion, and laid the groundwork for the Church. Although Paul did not violate the inner and essential features of the Gospel, his modifications in the realm of ecclesiology, Christology, and Scripture were, according to Harnack, not altogether salutary.

One of the main contentions of the author is that the greatest transformation of the Christian religion took place in the second century, when it developed into Catholicism. With the waning of the original enthusiasm, a religion of law and form arose; with the influx of Hellenism and the union of the Greek spirit with the Gospel, faith was intellectualized as doctrine; in its struggle against Gnosticism, the supreme illustration of the Hellenization of the Christian faith, the Church put its teaching, worship, and discipline into fixed forms and ordinances, and excluded everyone who would not yield them obedience. Thus the Church itself obtained an independent value as an institution and became a religious power.

Greek Catholicism, argues Harnack, is little more than a continuation of Greek natural religion: a Greek product in Christian dress rather than a Christian product in Greek dress. Its characteristic traditionalism, intellectualism, and ritualism have little to do with the Gospel; only its monasticism preserves a Christian element in the Church. The Roman Church of the West shares with the Eastern Church these corrupt features of Catholicism, but it has also been profoundly affected by the Latin spirit and the Roman world empire, on the one hand, and the spirit and religious fervor of St. Augustine (354-430), on the other. The latter proved to be an inward resuscitation of Pauline experience and doctrines, but the former turned salvation into a form of contract under definite conditions, revelation into law, and the Church into a legal institution claiming divine dignity. Although the internal and external elements in this *"complexio oppositorum"* continue to struggle for union, Harnack's judgment is that the inward influence of Augustinianism is overwhelmed by the institutional Church, with its exercise of governmental power under an infallible Pope. In this form, he asserts, Roman Catholicism is simply the transformed continuation of the Roman world empire and, as such, is a total perversion of the Gospel.

Protestantism is to be understood as a reformation in regard to the doctrine of salvation and as a revolution in regard to the Church, its authority and apparatus. Here religion is freed of alien accretions and critically reduced to its essential features: the Word of God and faith. The Church is divested of its priestly system, external authority, sacramentalism, ritualism, and double morality, and becomes again a spiritual community of faith, a universal priesthood constrained only by the Gospel. The Reformation had its bad features, however, especially in the Church's affiliation with the State and in the onesided emphasis on faith to the exclusion of "good works." During the post-Reformation period a Biblical scholasticism and doctrinal orthodoxy further weakened the force of the Reformation. Harnack ends the book with a plea that the Protestant Churches grasp again the Christian religion of the Reformation: the Gospel in its simplicity and purity. He argues that theology alone will not avail; firmness of Christian character will also be required. But his attitude is optimistic, like that of other liberal theologians of his day, and he ends by affirming "the forces and the standards which on the summits of our inner life shine out as our highest good."

THE PHILOSOPHY OF RELIGION

Author: Harald Höffding (1843-1931)
Type of work: Philosophy of religion
First published: 1901

Principal Ideas Advanced

That which expresses the innermost tendency of all religions is the axiom of the conservation of value.

In its golden ages a religion provides its adherents with a comprehensive explanation of existence, but as religion develops it meets challenges which force it to relate to competing value systems and to reassess its own nature.

Essentially, religion is concerned with the valuation rather than with the comprehension of existence.

The criterion for judging religion lies in the ethical sphere: What effect does the religion have on the conduct of the believer?

Neither religion nor science can solve the riddles of existence, but both must proceed vigorously with their critical tasks.

The Philosophy of Religion, by the Danish professor Harald Höffding, has earned a permanent place in the scholarly world for its thoroughness in developing the idea of religion as the conservation of value. Höffding's work may be understood in the context of the discipline that is indicated by the title of his work: the philosophy of religion. This discipline employs the tools of critical analysis and evaluation upon the general subject of religion, without known bias to any particular form religion may take. Religion and its thought comprise the subject matter of the philosophy of religion as Höffding understands it.

The distinction between religion reflecting upon its own problems from its own presuppositions and religion as the object of critical and disinterested investigation is crucial in Höffding's understanding of the philosophy of religion. Only when other aspects of the spiritual life—science, art, moral and social life—begin to emancipate themselves and to claim free independent value does the religious problem in the sense used by philosophers of religion arise. In its great and classic periods of inception and organization, religion has either ignored these other areas or assessed them from its own point of view and its own standards. Only when these other aspects develop their own standards of judgment and value does the opportunity exist for the development of philosophy of religion. Spiritual discord is a pre-condition of the philosophy of religion. This book is addressed neither to the satisfied nor to the anxious, neither to those whose minds are made up, whether positively or negatively, regarding religion, nor to those who are afraid to think about religion. Höffding's work is addressed rather to the seekers after truth.

Höffding's work is an example of that type of scholarly ideal which essays objectivity by renouncing any ready-made philosophical system as the point of departure for the investigation of religion. Acknowledging that internal harmony and consistency are the signs of truth within all spheres, he accepts them for his discipline. His goal, however, is not to bring religion into relation with an already concluded philosophical scheme, but rather to illuminate and elucidate the relation of religion to the general spiritual life of which religion itself is a mode or form. The philosophy of religion has the goal of discovering the means by which religion can continue to deepen and enrich the spiritual life as it develops.

The three main divisions of Höffding's work follow from his interpretation of the history of religious ideas: the epistemological, the psychological, the ethical. In its golden ages religion supplies men with a comprehensive explanation of existence. But when an independent science arises, a new mode of explanation is available and some attempt at harmonization must be made. The attempt to discover the relationship of religion to science involves the consideration of the ways of knowing and of validating knowledge which each employs. This first phase of investigation is the epistemological phase.

If it turns out that religious ideas do not solve the riddles which science faces and, indeed, are made irrelevant by the success of science in its ever-increasing sphere, the question arises as to what significance religious ideas do actually possess. The investigation turns naturally to a consideration of what the ideas mean in the experience of the individual holding them. This phase of investigation is the psychological phase. If religious ideas lose their status as claims to knowledge, their value must lie elsewhere. Höffding discovers their value to lie in the conviction that no value perishes out of the world. Religion in its innermost essence is concerned not with the comprehension but with the valuation of existence. "Religious ideas express the relation in which actual existence, as we know it, stands to that which, for us, invests life with its highest value."

The third phase of the investigation of religious ideas is the ethical phase; the question concerns the ethical significance of the belief in the conservation of value. What effect does the religious idea have upon human conduct? This question is fundamental for Höffding, for the ultimate criterion for judging religion must originate within the ethical sphere where spiritual accounts are finally balanced.

The "problem of religion" rises when faith and knowledge are distinguished from one another. Roman Catholicism does not make a rigid distinction here and thus recognizes no "problem" within the intellectual sphere. A distinction between faith and knowledge implies an interruption of the unity of the spiritual life. The question as to whether any compensating value may be ascribed for the presumed loss of unity indicates the centrality of the question of value for religion. The concern for value is not limited to the human world but extends also to the cosmological level. One has to ask about the relationship between man's highest values and the laws of existence. It does not matter for Höffding's thesis what values are being held and conserved, but that religion is the concern for values is axiomatic. Value is defined as "the property possessed by a thing either of conferring immediate satisfaction or serving as a means to procuring it."

Höffding describes two types of thinking present in human experience: the scientific and the religious. The task to which he sets himself is to investigate the presuppositions and forms which constitute the basis of each. Understanding involves reducing something hitherto unknown to the known. Kinds of understanding comes from identity, rationality, and causality. Scientific causality seeks to relate causes to a series of effects; the longer and more continuous the series, the better. Scientific work is a work of personality. Religious causality does not demand natural causation; its interest lies not in discovering an inner connection between events, but in regarding all events as expressions of one identical power. Though there are thus basic differences in the "explanations" of science and religion, they may meet and unite if their origin in personal experience and their differences in intention are kept in mind. Höffding, a neo-Kantian who was obligated to Kant for the distinction between explanation and evaluation, was well versed in science as well as in religion; he felt it improbable that science and religion would be able in the long run to develop independently of each other, though he was not optimistic about their relationships in the near future. In his opinion, the empirical sciences have not fostered the habit of mind which would make co-operation with religion easy, and religion has been centered on traditional concepts which fail to meet the newer spiritual needs.

In response to the traditional cosmological argument for God as the first cause which is not itself an effect of any antecedent cause, Höffding accepts and extends Kant's criticisms. It is not possible to reason from finite effects to infinite causes. Höffding's theory of knowledge forces him to reject the notion of creation in any sense in which creation is used in scientific thought. The inexhaustibility of experience makes it impossible to arrive at an objective conclusion to knowledge. In contrast to Kant, Höffding states that we have no right to reject the possibility that the inconclusiveness of experience and of knowledge may be attributable to the fact that being itself is not complete but, rather, continually developing. An absolute conclusion to knowledge would involve the annulling of the distinction between knowing and being, subject and object, but it is precisely this distinction which is the condition of all knowledge.

The failure of thought, be it scientific or religious, to reach absolute objectivity does not cause Höffding to despair: "To cease thinking is not the same as to begin understanding." He accepts the analogical method as providing the only auxiliary available, though it is not without considerable problems itself. Science, psychology, religion—all use analogy in the attempt to understand experience, and yet it is clear that at a critical point all analogies fail when an attempt is made to move from the finite to the infinite.

The failure of analogy is especially clear in the arguments as to the personality of God. If the term *personality* is used to describe God, either it is used in a sense quite different from its ordinary use, or else God is necessarily limited in ways which traditional religion finds difficult to accept. It is important to note that Höffding does not move from an acceptance of the impossibility of absolutely objective knowledge to the conclusion that the "unknowable" is entirely different from everything that appears in experience. There is no foundation for this belief, he asserts; on the contrary, there must be some connection between the ground of being and the experience of men who possess being. The very fact of our thinking forms part of existence and must be accounted for in any conclusion. Religious thought is tasked with acknowledging its inherent limitations while proceeding vigorously with critical reflection upon the relation of the part and the whole. This is the task of what Höffding calls "Critical Monism." The function of religious ideas is not to explain special events or to afford conclusions for scientific thought, but to serve as symbolic expressions for the feelings and aspirations of men in the struggle for existence.

Having dealt with the epistemological significance of religious ideas, the book moves to an examination of the actual constitution and origin of religious ideas regardless of their use or validity. The central portion of the work deals with the psychological study of religious experience, religious faith, the development of religious ideas, dogmas, and symbols, the axiom of the conservation of value, and the principle of personality.

In the distinctly religious states of consciousness the quest for knowledge is less dominant than the desire to express and to react, to symbolize. Religious experience ought to be given encouragement and freedom of expression in view of the fact that no conclusion is to be reached. The religious feeling is that which is determined by concern for the fate of values in the struggle for existence. Religious faith involves the struggle to hold fast to the relation between reality and value. Conservation of values is faith's object, and the existence of faith is itself a witness to the axiomatic nature of the concern for conservation of values. The concept of God may be understood as the principle of the conservation of value in reality, and it is the fundamental predicate of all religious judgments and quests.

Höffding concludes the central section of his work with an extensive discussion of the principle of personality, which he terms a necessity within the religious sphere. Since personality invests all other things with value, as centers of value personalities must possess independent and immediate value as ends themselves. No absolutes must be permitted to exercise dominance over personality and its freedom: "It is homogeneity and schematism, not differences and peculiarities which have to justify themselves." The distinctive movement in religion is to personality rather than to dogma, Höffding insists, and Protestantism is the illustration of this truth.

Concluding with an investigation into the relationship between ethics and religion, Höffding shows that it is religion which is based upon ethical ideas. As men discover ethical problems and develop ethical sensitivity, so their gods assume ethical characters. Man's gods grow with him and are symbols of his highest values. The transition from nature religion to ethical religion is the most significant in the history of religion. Mature religious insight assumes an independent human ethic. The "other world" is always derived from this world.

It is not surprising that with this critical emphasis on the human dimension of religion Höffding should arrive at an agnostic attitude toward traditional dogmas and a negative opinion of much popular religion. Where once religion was the pillar of fire showing the way for the human race, it now too often assumes the role of "the ambulance which follows in the rear and picks up the exhausted and wounded." Even though religion cannot solve the great riddles of life any more than can science, it is no less significant, for it is concerned with the "inner experience of the relation between values and reality in conjunction with the need for an emotional and imaginative expression of the content of this experience." It is to the cultivation of this dimension that the Church is called. Each man is tasked to make of his life a work of art, and religion, as faith in the preservation of values, and ethics, as discovery of the principles according to which the discovery and production of values occurs, are two of tools for realizing the art of life. "To live eternal life in the midst of time, that is the true immortality, whether or not there is any other immortality," writes Höffding. He concludes by stressing the point that the idea of the continuity of all forces and values is that toward which each religious movement strives.

THE GOSPEL AND THE CHURCH

Author: Alfred Loisy (1857-1940)
Type of work: Biblical criticism; apologetics
First published: 1902

Principal Ideas Advanced

If Christianity is to meet the intellectual challenge of our times, it must take its stand on the developed Christianity of the Church.

Harnack's attempt to recover the "essence of Christianity" by stripping away historical accretions is mistaken.

The original Gospel was not an ethical doctrine concerning the nature of God and man, but the proclamation of the approaching Kingdom of God.

The organization, creed, and worship of the Church developed naturally from the Gospel as it found a place in the Hellenistic world.

Only through the means provided by the living Church can modern man enter into relation with Christ and with the Father.

Alfred Loisy was a French Roman Catholic priest and Biblical scholar whose modernism led to his excommunication in 1908. *The Gospel and the Church,* which was written in reply to Adolf Harnack's *What is Christianity?* (1900), is an attempt on the part of a progressive Catholic theologian to meet the "great religious crisis" which, Loisy says, Christianity faces as a result of modern developments in the political, intellectual, and economic realms.

Loisy argues that it is a mistake for the Church to try to meet the crisis by a minimizing apologetic, like that of Harnack, which reduces the Gospel to a single principle, more ethical than religious. Instead, one should take his stand on Christianity as we know it and show "how necessary and useful is the immense development accomplished in the Church" to adapt the primitive Gospel to the needs of men in widely different historical circumstances.

Many of the criticisms which Loisy directs against Harnack's book will be supported by modern Protestant scholars, whether liberal or conservative. Loisy charges the German scholar with confusing theology and history when Harnack tries to maintain that the essence of Jesus' teaching is the proclamation that God is a merciful Father to mankind. Warning that "the historian must resist the temptation to modernize" the Gospel, Loisy says, "It is his own religion, not that of the gospel, which Herr Harnack expounds and defends when he announces that 'God and the soul, the soul and its God, are the whole contents of the gospel.' " If there is to be a historical reconstruction of early Christianity, says Loisy, it must proceed without doctrinal commitments. The scholar must not assume at the beginning that what he himself regards as the true religious system will be found in its pristine form on the lips of Jesus.

Harnack's distinction between the "kernel and the husk" seems to Loisy an unfortunate metaphor. It suggests that the Gospel is a fruit, a kind of metaphysical essence, which can be abstracted from the concrete experience of men. Moreover, in identifying the kernel with what is "personal," and the husk with what is "traditional" in the teaching of Jesus, Harnack adheres too closely to outmoded rationalistic conceptions of human nature, as if the individual were independent of society and the soul unaffected by the needs of the body.

Loisy maintains that it is more in accord with the historical outlook to think of the Gospel as a seed than to think of it as a fruit. It is not by peeling away the supposed accretions that surround the Gospel that we shall come to understand Christianity, but by observing its origins, its characteristics, and its developments. "Let us regard the Christian religion in its life, observing by what means it has lived from the beginning and is still sustained; let us note the principal features of this venerable existence, convinced that they lose nothing in reality or importance, because today they are presented to us under colours that are not those of a former time." This means, according to Loisy, that we must first see Christianity in its Jewish setting, and then trace its development as it moves into the ancient and into the modern world, always with a view to finding those features which are recognizable throughout the whole of its career.

Loisy inclines toward the interpretation of primitive Christianity later popularized by Albert Schweitzer, according to which the original Gospel was rooted in Jewish apocalyptic hopes, and consisted in the proclamation of the near approach of the Kingdom of God, together with Jesus' belief that He was the Messiah whose death and resurrection were essential to His future glorification and rule. So far from finding the center of the Gospel in eternal moral truths, Loisy says that the ethical teachings of Jesus and His attitude toward society (the family, wealth, the state) were inseparably bound up with his conviction that civilization was soon to be destroyed and that a new order, divinely constituted would take its place.

Loisy concedes that at this point rationalism and faith part company, and he concludes that rationalizing theologians, who, like Harnack, are disposed to see in Jesus a moral and spiritual teacher, are running counter to plain historical evidence. Harnack places Jesus higher than Socrates. But, says Loisy, on the basis of the record, Jesus cuts a pitiable figure alongside philosophy's greatest martyr. His piety cannot be disentangled from His dreams, and He "died the victim of error rather than the servant of the truth that was in Him." Such, at least, is the judgment at which clear headed rationalism must arrive.

Because it is a closed system, with its own presuppositions and logic, rationalism cannot be refuted by faith. But that, says Loisy, is poor grounds for confusing the point of view of reason with that of faith. Rationalism, religion will maintain, simply breaks down when it attempts to understand the great mysteries connected with "God and the providential destiny of man." These are disclosed only to faith, and they find their expression in symbolic representations. "The concrete symbol, the living image," says Loisy, "not the pure idea, is the normal expression of faith, and the condition of its moral efficacy in man and in the world." Seen in this way, the mission and the message of Jesus are signs not of folly but of wisdom of the highest order. Jesus went voluntarily to death in the confidence that He had chosen the way in which His destiny would be fulfilled. His faith was rewarded in a way and to a degree that no philosophical historian can fail to recognize.

Because the Gospel was a living faith and not a metaphysical teaching, it must find expression in concrete, historical terms. Nothing, says Loisy, could make Jesus other than a Jew, or eliminate from His teaching fundamentally Judaistic modes of thought and expression. By the same kind of necessity, when the Gospel spread outside of the Jewish world, it took on many of the characteristics of its new environment. "The gospel will always need a body to be human," Loisy insists; and when, after a century and a half, we find that the followers of Christ constitute a tightly organized cult, with a priesthood, a law, a ritual, and a creed, we ought not to lament how much the Gospel has changed, but ask rather whether these developments were not inevitable if the Gospel was to achieve its purpose. We do not discover the essential character of a man, Loisy reminds us, by going back to the cradle.

Harnack gives a particularly unsympathetic picture of the development of the Roman Church, which, he says, became merely a political organization. Loisy protests that this is unfair, that the spiritual mission of the Church has always set it off from that of the empire or the state. The fact that the Church is organized along lines comparable to a state is another matter, and the question arises whether it makes any sense to talk about a human society which does not have the characteristics of an organization. Loisy charges Protestants with talking nonsense when they speak of the primitive Christians as forming a purely spiritual fellowship. He points out that Jesus set apart the twelve disciples and that the early churches took over the pattern of the synagogue. He further maintains that if the Church of the second century had not had strong and able administrators, it would almost certainly have been absorbed into the general religious milieu of the times. "Does it not follow," he asks, "that the Church is as necessary to the gospel as the gospel to the Church, and that the two are really one, as the group of believers were during the ministry of Jesus?" There is no point, says Loisy, in attempting to justify the forms which Christianity has taken by making an appeal to Jesus' own teachings or those of His immediate followers. One need only ask whether the Church through the centuries has stood for the "essential elements of the living gospel"; namely, the idea of a heavenly Kingdom, of a divine Messiah, and of a world-wide mission.

Loisy answers in a similar fashion Harnack's complaint that the Gospel has been turned into a dogma. While Loisy admits that the Gospel itself is not dogma, he finds it inevitable that, as men reflect upon their faith, dogma develops out of the Gospel and, henceforth, Gospel lives in dogma. Pauline theology, he says, was essential if Christianity was not to remain essentially Jewish; Johannine theology was essential if it was to make its way in the Hellenistic world. But Loisy denies that, when theologians began to state the faith in Greek terms, Christianity was changed into philosophy. Indeed, he denies that theology is a science in the true sense of the term, maintaining that "the logic of faith," dealing as it does with images, is incommensurate with the logic of science. Such developments as the trinitarian and Christological dogmas were part of an attempt to bridge the gap between the new religion and Greek ways of thought. "It was not erudite research that determined their character, but the instinct of faith in souls otherwise saturated with the Greek spirit."

Pure spirituality in worship, according to Loisy, is as unrealistic as fellowship without organization and Gospel without theology. Harnack has alleged that the kernel of the Gospel became so overlaid with rites, relics, images, and mysteries taken over from pagan religion that it soon appeared "not as a Christian creation with a Greek thread, but as a Greek creation with a Christian thread." But, says Loisy, if Christianity is to be a religion, and not a kind of "mystic philosophy," it must have particular liturgical forms. Loisy argues that the important question is not whether the forms are borrowed from pagan sources, but whether, in being taken over by the Church, the forms are taken into the life of the faith. All worship approaches the Creator through the image of the creature. But in pagan worship, says Loisy, the association of human features with divinity was detrimental to man's understanding of God, because it undermined the sense of God's transcendence. "Christianity," he says, "avoided this confusion, while satisfying, by the worship of Jesus and the sacraments coordinated therewith, that need of deification which seems inseparable from human nature. . . . It has been able to do so without falling into polytheism or man-worship, because it distinguishes, in the object of its adoration, the Eternal God and the human nature in which this God was manifested on earth."

Loisy does not deny that there are many things in the Roman Catholic

Church which stand in the way of modern man's acceptance of the Gospel. He is mainly concerned to argue for what he calls the principle of development within the faith. The Church, Christian dogma, and Christian worship are not deformations of the Gospel, but its natural product; and if, due to the changes in our times, certain traditional ways of thinking must be revised, then let them be revised. But, Loisy maintains, Christianity endures only by the force of its past, nor is there any way in which modern man can enter into communion with Christ and the Father except through the living Church.

Loisy was, undoubtedly, over-optimistic about the readiness of the Roman Church to accept change. (His book was immediately condemned by the Archbishop of Paris.) He maintained that even the conception of "ecclesiastical authority" needed to be further reflected on. In any case, he says, those who have followed the progress of Christianity from the beginning cannot doubt that change will continue to take place. Religious symbolism, by its very nature, is always inadequate, striving after perfection. The historian sees in the teachings of the Church an "interpretation of religious facts, acquired by a laborious effort" through many centuries; although their substance is divine, their structure and composition is human. "It is inconceivable," he says, "that their future should not correspond to their past. Reason never ceases to put questions to faith, and traditional formulas are submitted to a constant work of interpretation wherein 'the letter that killeth' is effectively controlled by 'the spirit that giveth life.' "

THE VARIETIES OF RELIGIOUS EXPERIENCE

Author: William James (1842-1910)
Type of work: Psychology of religion
First published: 1902

Principal Ideas Advanced

A working definition of religion sees it as "the feelings, acts, and experiences of individual men in their solitude, so far as they apprehend themselves to stand in relation to whatever they may consider the divine."

Temperament has much to do with the nature of religion, as the distinction between the optimistic and healthy-minded, and the pessimistic and sick-minded, indicates.

The mystical state is distinguished by the qualities of ineffability, illumination, transiency, and passivity; although mystical experience carries authority only for the mystic, it helps to break down the exclusive authority of rationalistic states.

The traditional metaphysical descriptions of God have no practical significance, but they are important as restatements of religious experience.

From the time of their delivery in 1901-1902 at the University of Edinburgh, James's Gifford Lectures, as collected in *The Varieties of Religious Experience,* have enjoyed both critical and popular acclaim. Scholars have found this pioneering work in the psychology of religion an inexhaustible source of insight and stimulation. Ordinary readers have enjoyed the direct conversational style and the interesting illustrations with which the book abounds.

William James studied physiology at Harvard, but he soon turned to psychology, which he proceeded to change from "mental philosophy" to a laboratory science. His restless mind led him from the laboratory to the study of religious experience and psychic phenomena. The subtitle of the work under consideration, "A Study in Human Nature," reveals the nature of his interest. The choice of first-person accounts of religious experience as sources for his study indicate James's consistency with his own experience-centered philosophy of pragmatism. Through twenty lectures it is personal experience which serves as source of observation and court of appeal.

James begins his lectures with a direct confrontation of current theories which interpreted religion "scientifically" on the basis of its alleged sexual and neurotic origins. Pointing out the fallacy of judging solely on the basis of origins, James insists that the real significance of religious experience is determined by its results. He scorns "medical materialism" which easily disposes of St. Paul's vision as the result of a lesion of the occipital cortex, while St. Teresa of Avila is viewed as a hysteric, St. Francis of Assisi as a hereditary degenerate, and George Fox as simply sick. James argues that if organic conditioning be influential in religious emotion, so it must be in every other sphere including that of scientific theorizing. To single out religion for derision and rejection on this account would be illogical and arbitrary, and James declares that he would not tolerate such action in either science or religion.

A good part of the appeal of James's work is the result of his devotion to personal religion "pure and simple." He largely ignores institutional religion, systematic theology, and philosophy of religion. Cautioning that religion defies exact definition, he interprets "the divine" as "only such a primal reality as the individual feels impelled to respond to solemnly and gravely, and neither by a curse nor a jest." The experience-centered method leads to the conclusion that religion is not only vitally important but actually essential to human life in that it "makes easy and felicitous what in any case is necessary."

Characterizing religion in the most general of terms as belief in an unseen order, and the supreme good as the harmonious adjustment to that order, James examines the "psychological peculiarities" of the belief in the reality of the unseen. Brief references to Kantian and Platonic doctrines and to more personal anecdotes are used to support the thesis that psychological certitude is infinitely more significant in religion than is rationalistic certainty. Reasons are cogent in religion only when one's articulate feelings have already been impressed in favor of the conclusions to which reason leads. "The unreasoned and immediate assurance is the deep thing in us, the reasoned argument is but a surface exhibition," declares James. James intends neither to approve nor to disapprove dependence on feeling, but only to point out that the priority of feeling is a fact.

Since the kind of religion one has is thus determined more by temperament than by intellectual acceptance or rejection of various "proofs," James proceeds to make his famous delineation of two major temperamental types of religious outlook: the healthy-minded (tough-minded) and the sick-minded (tender-minded.) Seemingly unable to write a dull page, James affords the reader a rich diet of fact and opinion as he documents his contentions with vivid first-person accounts of religious experience. Responding to criticism that his work over-emphasizes the bizarre, James notes that his purpose is to emphasize the enormous diversities of the spiritual lives of men. He castigates as stupid those of the "deadly respectable" type who bar phenomena which they are incapable of experiencing themselves.

In his conclusions regarding the sick-minded in religion as opposed to the healthy-minded, James characteristically commends the latter as being splendid provided it works. It ceases to work, however, when inescapable melancholy comes. Thus optimistic healthy-mindedness is charged with inadequacy because the evils it refuses to account for are an integral part of reality. Often it is the evil in life which opens one's eyes to the deepest levels of truth. The universe is more complex than either healthy-minded optimism or sick-minded pessimism alone allows for. Since all verifications are simply experiences which agree with systems of ideas that men's minds have formed, it ill becomes anyone to insist that only one such system of ideas is true. No one view, be it religious or scientific, is exhaustive of reality's riches. Perhaps the method of alternating between various approaches depending upon the seeker's temperament and his goal is most desirable. The religion of the healthy-minded is the religion of the once-born, and a simple algebraic sum of pluses and minuses suffices for their religious accounting. The religion of the sick-minded is far more complex and mysterious. The most complete religion is one in which the pessimistic elements are best developed. Buddhism and Christianity as religions of deliverance in which the person dies to an unreal life before being born into real life—that is, is "twice-born"—are commended.

In their extreme forms healthy-minded religion is naturalism, and sick-minded religion is salvationism. Consideration of the latter leads to a consideration of the divided self and the experience of conversion. James interprets conversion as a normal adolescent phenomenon occurring as one passes from a small universe to the wider intellectual and spiritual life of maturity. Two types of conversion are distinguished: volitional and self-surrender. In response to the question as to whether conversion is a divine miracle or a natural process, James turns to the current field of consciousness theory which stresses the wide variety of individual differences in mental states. The nature of one's religious conversion will depend in large part upon the character of his field of consciousness. Whether or not one interprets the religious experience of conversion in orthodox terms, mere transcendency proves nothing about either the divine or the diabolic. Only the effect of an experience in the life of the individual can attest to its origin. The most significant fact about conversion is not its duration or even its type, but its effect upon the life of the person involved.

His emphasis upon the practical fruits of religious experience prompts James first to describe and then to evaluate the characteristics of saintliness, a state of being which he sees as involving conviction regarding the existence of an ideal power or God, a willing self-surrender to its control, a sense of elation and freedom, and a movement of the emotional center toward loving and harmonious expression. Practical consequences of saintliness are asceticism, strength of soul, purity, and charity. Genuine firsthand religious experience always appears to observers as possibly arising out of madness and as leading to heresy. Ecclesiasticism, which grows up about a primary experience, tends to stifle the spontaneous religious spirit, but the bigotries of organized religion are due less to religion than to its intellectual partner, the spirit of dogmatic dominion. The corruption of excess afflicts the fruits of religion as it does all other human products. James is hesitant to pronounce the saintly type as the "ideal" type for every man, for there are many functions to which men are called. But even though some saints lose their heads and thus become failures biologically, they may be successes in the sense of being leavens of religion and righteousness in the world. Testing religion by practical common sense and through the empirical method, James finds it soundly occupying its towering place in history.

It is not until the sixteenth and seventeenth lectures that James considers those mystical states of consciousness from which personal religious experience springs. He distinguishes the qualities of ineffability, illumination, transiency, and passivity within the mystical state. Following documentation of these characteristics, he observes that while mystic states carry authority for him who has them, they do not do so for anyone else. Since it is not possible to argue from psychic states, it is always necessary to subject positions based on the authority of such states to rigorous scrutiny. Often when psychological certitude is confused with epistemological or rational certainty, one is asked to accept the validity of a proposition solely upon the basis of another's psychic state. But even though one ought to be cautious of knowledge claims based on mystical experience he ought to be appreciative of the tendency of such experience to break down the exclusive authority of rationalistic systems which may overlook man's emotional dimensions. For James, feeling is primary in religion. Mysticism has more affinities with music than with conceptual speech, and in speaking of mysticism James demonstrates a degree of empathy quite remarkable in a scientific examination. He speaks of musical and mystical whispers which hover in the mind and mingle with the operations of our understanding "even as the waters of the infinite ocean send their waves to break among the pebbles that lie upon our shores."

Having found mysticism too private and variable to stand as universal authority for the claim of religion to be objectively true, James then investigates religion's claims from the standpoint of philosophy. Both philosophical and theological formulas are secondary products, whereas feeling is primary in religion. But philosophy's essential role is to redeem religion from the kind of mystery, paradox, and unwholesome privacy which detracts from its objective validity. Myth, superstition, dogma, creed, metaphysical speculation, party rivalry—all are spontaneously and inevitably engendered by religious experience, and all need the ministration of philosophical examination. James hopes that his work will contribute something to this "science of religion." Yet philosophy itself is scarcely a perfect tool, for it fails to banish differences, and it founds schools and sects just as feeling does. The philosopher finds arguments to fit his prior convictions just as the preacher does who writes his sermon and then searches for his text.

After briefly surveying other characteristics of religion, including aesthetic elements, sacrifice, confession, prayer, and the phenomena of automatisms, James concludes his lectures with a recapitulation of the major themes of his lectures. He expresses his dismay at the amount of emotionality which he finds in his manuscript, and he thus proposes to close with the practical question as to the dangers inherent in the religious element of life. Protesting that it should not be assumed that all men should have identical religions, he rejects the notion that modern science should develop a religious creed for all men. Scientific objects are abstractions, too, and only individualized experiences are concrete. Since religion deals with concrete personal experience, it is nearer to truth than those disciplines which deal with the cosmic and the general. A common nucleus of religion may be discerned, however, in the feeling of uneasiness about something wrong and in the desire to seek deliverance from the wrong through connection with higher powers.

Few persons read James without having been enriched through contact with a truly large mind and spirit, as revealed in his edifying, stimulating, and provocative essays.

CHRISTIAN THEOLOGY IN OUTLINE

Author: William Adams Brown (1865-1943)
Type of work: Liberal theology
First published: 1906

Principal Ideas Advanced

Revelation is continuous with reason, and the natural with the supernatural.

Jesus Christ reveals God in Christ's consciousness of divine Sonship, and in His embodiment of God's moral purpose, the Kingdom of God.

The world is adapted to the Christian end, and history is its progressive fulfillment.

Sin is selfishness, and it is overcome by the redemptive power of Christ in history and, ultimately, in eternity.

Christian Theology in Outline gives expression to the Ritschlian theology as modified by American optimism and social idealism. William Adams Brown pays tribute to a former teacher, Adolf Harnack (1851-1930), and to William Newton Clarke (1841-1912), as honored friends in whom systematic theology has reached its freest and clearest expression. But it is William Adams Brown's own capacity to clarify and organize ideas and to give them effectual expression that makes his *Christian Theology in Outline* a permanent point of reference for this form of Christian theology.

Following his own account of it, the theology may be characterized as modern, empirical, idealistic, and progressive. Great confidence is manifested in modern philosophy and science, in "our better psychology," and in the present progress of the Christian ideal in the world. Systematic theology is described as "the philosophy of the Christian life." Consistently with this position, no authority, ecclesiastical, creedal, or Biblical is recognized, although Scripture, the creeds, and traditional doctrines are freely used and interpreted to express the meanings of the new theology. It is a theology which accepts the historic Christian faith in God the Creator, in Christ the Incarnation of God, and in the salvation of man from sin, and translates this faith into terms of the Christian experience, or the consciousness of the Christian.

The place of the historic Jesus is central and primary in this theology. He is the Incarnation of God not in a metaphysical sense, but in His moral character and purpose and in His unclouded consciousness of Sonship to God. There is nothing miraculous or supernatural in the Incarnation. God is immanent in the world and in all men, in the noblest of whom we have the clue to His will and purpose; Jesus Christ is in this sense the supreme revelation of God.

While the Christian's knowledge of God comes to clarity and completeness in Christ, it is broadly based on the whole of human experience. No line can be drawn between reason and revelation, or between the natural and the supernatural. All things reveal God and give some knowledge of God. Both science and philosophy contribute to the idea of God which, however, reaches its ultimate expression in the historic person of Jesus Christ. Christian faith is really faith in the *idea* of God which is given its definitive form in Christ. It is based not on mystical experience or on speculative thought but on the practical needs and nature of man. The idea of God is also the Christian ideal, and belief is complete trust in it. Brown freely accepts the "moral value" interpretation of the idea of God. As will be seen, God is regarded by Brown as being objectively real, but He is the "unseen" reality who is manifested in the personality of Christ and in the religious consciousness of the Christian. Such revelation is possible because God is moral personality; He is a Christlike God.

While all speculative theology is rejected, Brown nevertheless recognizes the validity of the philosophical conception of the Absolute. God is beyond our comprehension as He is in Himself. The doctrine of the Trinity therefore is accepted; God is the Absolute, the ultimate source of all being and life; God is the self-revealing one, known to men through His revelation in nature, in history, and, above all, in Christ; God is the self-imparting one, known through experience in the consciousness of man. The conception of God thus formed through Christian experience, and, more generally, through the experience of the race is empirically verified "partly in the response which the idea meets in the individual consciousness, partly in its growing supremacy over the reason, the conscience and the religious feeling of the race."

The objective reality of the God so conceived is postulated or assumed as are the general assumptions of science or moral theory. God is creator of the world. Creation for the Christian is based primarily upon "experience of the new life in Christ, of which we are daily partakers through his Spirit." Brown claims that creation is best conceived intellectually, in accordance with scientific knowledge, "as a permanent process, expressing that continual relation between phenomena and their spiritual ground which is the form in which the idealistic philosophy conceives of the reality of the world." But the real meaning of creation for the Christian is in the end or purpose of God in creating the world. This end is generally defined as the Kingdom of God; more specifically, it is the "production of beings like the good God, and their union with himself in the fellowship of holy love." The spirit of the time and the whole outlook of Brown are revealed in this statement: "It is because the world as we know it to-day ministers to such a spiritual end that we believe it had its origin in the will of the holy and loving Father whom Christ reveals."

Jesus Christ is both the revealer of God and the redeemer of man. The core of the revelation is the eternal purpose of God which is the Kingdom of God, "the all-comprehending theological conception" of the Christian faith. Jesus revealed this purpose in His own life and character, and He established the Kingdom in history. The Kingdom of God is a society of men living by the ethic of love: this is God's "end." Therefore Christianity is a teleological religion, the perfect ethical religion, and all its meanings are to be determined by this basic conception. The religious form of the Kingdom of God is the consciousness of sonship to God, and its moral form is the life of love and service. The Kingdom is found in history as the progressive realization of the Christian ideal, and the Church is the divinely appointed means for its realization. The world itself is "adapted to the Christian end." This is frequently indicated by the term "the divinity of the world." The Kingdom of God is not, therefore, as with Ritschl, a supramundane reality, but an actual fellowship growing in history and destined to embrace all men. The power of this development finds its historic source in Jesus and in the influences that come from Him through the preaching of the Gospel and through the life and witness of the Christian community.

Christ is also redeemer. The great obstacle to progress of the Kingdom of God is sin, and sin is selfishness with all its by-products in the life of man. By His moral example, through the preaching of the Gospel and the influence of Christian fellowship, Christ calls men to repentance of their sins and to participation in the life of love, which is participation in the Kingdom. Such repentance is salvation. Sin is primarily an individual thing, but it is also a social fact and heritage. There is no such thing as an individual acting independently of social influences; his moral freedom must be understood in the light of his union with other persons, and also of the universal sovereignty of God. Brown rejects the "libertarian" doctrine and accepts the "determinist" view of man's moral development, which is realized only through union with other persons, and which takes place under divine law and control. The freedom which man enjoys in his spiritual life is freedom from the "blind" necessity of nature. But, Brown claims, "spiritual influences, as well as physical, are at God's disposal, and through the use of these he is certain to accomplish his end." Upon the basis of divine sovereignty so conceived, the progress of the Kingdom of God in history is assured, together with its ultimate triumph in the future life.

Implications of Brown's doctrine of divine sovereignty are carried out in several directions. Sin is not the arbitrary misuse of human freedom, for it is included in the purpose of God. Its role in the divine purpose is educational; the experience of sin and the conquest of it through Christ is a way to the highest and richest development of personality. The certainty of God's ultimate victory and the full realization of His Kingdom rob sin of any final power over human life.

Real freedom of choice, or self-transcendence, is rejected by Brown because it would mean a limitation on the power of God in the world. It is always a person who chooses, and a person is what he is in a social context. The idea also of a sheer act of will as such is incomprehensible. But the self-identification of the person which is revealed in choice is involved in sin, and this involves freedom. It is freedom, however, not of a momentary act, but of the total life of the person as exhibited in all his choices. In Brown's words, two things are affirmed in the light of this dilemma: (1) "In the secret places of the human spirit takes place the strange change by which the non-moral is transformed into the moral. . . . It is the mystery of all beginnings"; (2) Christ revealed sin "for the first time in its true nature as an offense against the loving Father who ever seeks the highest good of his children, and in whose love, supremely manifested in Christ, is found the ground for faith that sin shall finally be overcome."

The progressive realization of the Christian ideal in history is one of the proofs of the truth of the Christian religion. The Christian faith is destined eventually to win all men. This expectation is based both on the purpose of God and on the common nature and need of men. But so many influences obstruct the progress of the Kingdom in this world that complete victory will come only in the future life. In this victory the Cross of Christ has a decisive part to play. His suffering on the cross revealed His full fidelity to God, but it also showed that the way to moral victory is through suffering and sacrifice. And it is a revelation of the pain endured by the good God and loving Father because of the sin of men. It is the cost to God of His own forgiveness and of our reconciliation.

So essential to the perfection of moral personality and the realization of the Kingdom of God are the endurance of suffering and the conquest of sin that both suffering and sin will continue in the life to come. That life will not be static goodness, but a life of growth and progressive attainment. However, there remains as certain, Brown claims, the final consummation (I Cor. 15:28) "when Christ, his mediatorial work complete, shall surrender his authority to the Father that God may be all in all."

A MUCH ABUSED LETTER

Author: George Tyrrell (1861-1909)
Type of work: Christian apologetics; pastoral counseling
First published: 1906

Principal Ideas Advanced

One can be a good Christian without giving intellectual assent to the theology of the Church.

The Church "invisible" is not confined by the historical limits of Christianity; yet the Church "visible" is the highest expression of the divine purpose in history.

The life of the Church is a hidden, subconscious force, and is inadequately expressed in theology.

Faith is a kind of divine insight by which each man apprehends Unseen Reality.

The Catholic Church, if it is to continue to witness to Divine Reality, must abandon its reliance on authority and its claims to infallibility.

George Tyrrell went over from the Anglican to the Roman Church in 1879 and became a leading member of the Jesuit order. His counsel was much sought after by educated Catholics who found difficulty in reconciling the teachings of the Church with modern learning. For the help of one of these, a professor of anthropology, Tyrrell composed a long letter, in which he declared that one can be a good Christian—even a good Catholic—without giving intellectual assent to the theology of the Church. Because the kind of problem raised by the anthropologist was one which he met often, he reproduced the letter for private circulation. Contrary to his intention, it was made public in an Italian translation, with the result that he was expelled from the Society of Jesus and excommunicated from the Roman Church. These events led Tyrrell to publish *A Much Abused Letter,* which includes the text of the original letter, an account of the controversy which it occasioned, and numerous explanatory notes.

Tyrrell is careful to explain that the letter was never intended for the general reader, and that those who published it were administering indiscriminately a medicine which was intended for a limited group. He maintains that the advice which he gives in the letter, although it may seem scandalous to those who are strangers to the world of intellect, is the kind regularly given in the confessional by priests who are accustomed to dealing with cases of this sort. Persons who are ignorant of Biblical criticism, of history, and of anthropology are unwilling to believe that there is any conflict between theology and the sciences, but the truth of the situation is well known among educated persons, both lay and clerical. If the conflict causes no concern to the more worldly type of Catholic, it is serious enough to compel those who, like the anthropology professor to whom the letter is directed, consider it their moral obligation to withdraw from the Church.

Tyrrell explains that his method in dealing with such cases is an indirect one. Instead of attempting to resolve the questions which the scientist raises, he undertakes only to show that intellectual doubts need not stand in the way of religious faith. Tyrrell insists that he is not indifferent to truth and that he does not wish to encourage indifference in others, but he points out that as a confessor he has to minister to people who, when it becomes impossible for them to accept the pronouncements of the clergy, imagine that they are guilty of mortal sin. By his indirect method, he frees them from this misconception, trusting in positive spiritual forces to bring about recovery, just as a physician, having removed a foreign particle from the body, trusts nature to heal the wound.

The metaphor of healing is suitable, in view of Tyrrell's general philosophy, which is closer to that of Henri Bergson than to that of Thomas Aquinas. The divine Being, Tyrrell maintains, is a creative force which we feel within ourselves and recognize in humanity everywhere. He approves Matthew Arnold's description of it as the "Power that makes for Righteousness." Although we cannot think of it as other than personal or spiritual, we must not narrow it to the dimensions of our comprehension, as if it were defined by our human aspirations. Men, he says, are free either to resist this divine force or to obey it; but only in obedience to it can they find rest and peace.

Tyrrell holds that we can recognize the operation of this force in all branches of the human race, "whom it binds together into one mystical body and brotherhood and shapes to a collective presentment and revelation of itself, and to a society for the furtherance of its own ends." This mystical brotherhood is the Catholic Church; understood, however, as the invisible rather than as the visible institution; for it is only of the former that the motto holds good, *Extra ecclesiam salus nulla* (No safety outside the Church). "We do not worship Humanity, with the Comtists," Tyrrell explains, "but we worship the Power that is revealed in human goodness of every sort." He suggests that wherever men have sacrificed themselves for what is just and noble, there the mystical Christ is present, "and every member of that society is in his measure a Christ or revealer in whom God is made flesh and dwells in our midst." On the other hand, says Tyrrell, there is much to be said for keeping up communion with the visible Church. In spite of all its defects, Roman Catholicism remains "at once the highest expression or determination and the most effectual instrument of the life of religion." Her creeds embody the religious experience of a great sector of mankind. If we do not take them too literally, but see in them rather the "impression of itself which the Infinite has left" upon men's minds, all her doctrines will appear to us as "determinations of one and the same presentment of the Eternal Goodness," like pieces of stained glass through which the colorless light of God's truth is made comprehensible to our eyes.

Tyrrell insists that his correspondent's quarrel is with the theologians and not with the body of the Church. Drawing upon the distinction between the conscious and the subconscious, he suggests that the statement of doctrine which the theologians are accustomed to give is comparable to the ego's interpretation of the soul's motives, and that, consequently, theological doctrines are often mistaken. Theologians, he says, stand to the Church in the same relation as political leaders stand to a nation; the business of politicians is to bring to consciousness the unformulated mind of the people, and, so far as they do this correctly, they are instrumental in civilizing and improving the masses; but all too frequently the political leaders divorce themselves from the will of the people whom they are supposed to represent and become a separate class whose interests conflict with those of the body politic. In the same way, says Tyrrell, the theologians have mistaken their true function in that they have supposed that the intellectual systems which they devise are the substance of religion. Tyrrell is careful, however, to distinguish between the ecumenical creeds or symbols of the Church, which were a spontaneous expression of the Church's life, and the dogmas of the schools. It is the latter, he maintains, that are the source of such difficulties as those mentioned by the professor of anthropology.

Everything depends, says Tyrrell, upon a correct understanding of what is meant by faith. One must distinguish between "the facts of religious experience" and "their analysis and expression." It is ridiculous to suppose, with the clerical party, that it is the latter which is necessary for salvation. When Christ rebuked men for their lack of faith, He was not accusing them of harboring heretical beliefs, but complaining about their want of "that deeper intelligence which is conditioned by moral dispositions." Faith, then, is man's grasp of that which lies beyond sense and reason. By faith we see God only darkly, to be sure, but nevertheless it is a "seeing for oneself; not a believing in hearsay." Faith is "a rudimentary faculty relating us to a world which is as yet 'future' and 'beyond' in respect to our clear consciousness." In moments of faith, we "gaze with God's eyes and from the standpoint of the whole." A life based on faith is one lived in the light of these moments, in consequence of which a man's horizons are lifted beyond mere selfish goals. It is a life which, united to the divine energy that surges through the world, becomes an instrument in the service of universal ends. Expressed in Christian terms, this is as much as to say that faith gives rise to hope and to love.

Tyrrell maintains that the Roman Church will have to undergo radical changes if it is to continue to be a bearer of divine truth. Its claims to infallibility, its lazy appeal to authority, its practice of hurling anathemas will all have to go. "Already," he says, "their authority-theory is stretched to snapping-point, and self-strangled by inherent contradictions and preposterous consequences." He compares the condition of the Church in our times with that of Judaism at the time of Christ. The Jews quoted the Prophets to show that Judaism would at last conquer the world. They were right, but only in a sense which they did not understand. "Judaism was to live a risen and glorified life in Christianity." Similarly, Tyrrell says, the theologians may be right in another sense than they suppose when they look for the Church to embrace humankind. Catholicism, like Judaism, may have to die in order to live again in a more prefect form.

Tyrrell's *Letter*, together with his spirited stand in the face of Vatican censure, marks the high-tide of modernism within the bounds of the Roman Church. In 1907, Pope Pius X (1835-1914) issued two sharp decrees commanding bishops to "purge their clergy of modernistic infection." Although the movement did not lack other spokesmen, notably Baron Friedrich von Hügel (1852-1925) and Alfred Loisy (1857-1940), Tyrrell's untimely death silenced its most effective spokesman, but not before he had vindicated his stand in two other important books, *Through Scylla and Charybdis* (1907), and *Christianity at the Crossroads* (1909).

THE QUEST OF THE HISTORICAL JESUS

Author: Albert Schweitzer (1875-)
Type of work: History of New Testament criticism
First published: 1906

Principal Ideas Advanced

For 130 years scholarship has been engaged in a quest to discover the historical Jesus obscured by centuries of Christian dogma.

These attempts have generally failed in that they have portrayed Jesus as a man relevant to the modern world rather than as a man holding a vastly different world-view.

Jesus was thoroughly a man of His own time, in that He believed that history was about to come to a cataclysmic end and that the Kingdom of God was to be established.

Although the historical Jesus cannot be adapted to modern conditions, His spirit transcends His time and inspires men today.

Had modesty permitted, Albert Schweitzer could very well have entitled his great book, originally entitled *Von Reimarus zu Wrede, From Reimarus to Schweitzer,* for in it he seeks to trace the eschatological interpretation of the life of Jesus from the time that it emerges in the writings of the deist and Biblical critic Hermann Samuel Reimarus (1694-1768) to Schweitzer's work, *The Mystery of the Kingdom of God,* published in 1901. The original title also alludes to the skeptic William Wrede (1859-1906).

Schweitzer's interest in the history of scholarship concerning the life of Jesus grew out of a course of lectures he delivered in 1905 while a member of the theological faculty at Strassburg. He became so fascinated with the subject that he went on to the full-scale study embodied in *The Quest of the Historical Jesus.*

Surprisingly enough, Schweitzer believes that *hate* was a great motivating force in the historical investigation of Jesus in German scholarship from Reimarus to his own day. It was not that the scholars hated Jesus, but rather that they hated the tyranny of the dogma which surrounded the church's conception of Jesus, and they used historical investigation as a weapon in fighting it. They were anxious to rid Jesus of the "supernatural nimbus," to "strip from Him the robes of splendour with which He had been apparelled, and clothe Him once more with the coarse garments in which He had walked in Galilee."

Even David Friedrich Strauss (1808-1874) whose career was ruined by the persecution which followed publication of his revolutionary *Life of Jesus* (1835-1836) never ceased to be proud of his accomplishment. As Schweitzer points out, the critical work done on the life of Jesus "has been for theology a school of honesty. The world had never seen before, and will never see again, a struggle for truth so full of pain and renunciation as that of which the Lives of Jesus of the last hundred years contain the cryptic record."

The great key to the understanding of Jesus, according to Schweitzer, is eschatology; that is, the belief that God is to intervene in human history by bringing it to a cataclysmic end. It was Reimarus, professor of Oriental Languages at Hamburg (whose theological fragments were published by the noted German author Gotthold Lessing in 1778), who first introduced the question of eschatology into the study of Jesus. Since Reimarus was the first person in eighteen centuries to gain an inkling of the importance of eschatology in the life of Jesus, the scholars of his day were not prepared to realize the importance of his views. After Reimarus another hundred years elapsed before Johannes Weiss (1863-1914) once again brought the problem of eschatology to the fore—where it has since remained.

In the intervening years, the world was treated to various approaches to an understanding of Jesus. Schweitzer patiently works through these schools of thought and isolates those elements which he believes contributed insight concerning the difficult task of separating the historical Jesus from the other elements included in the Gospels.

Each of these schools of scholarship attempted to make Jesus at home in contemporary life. In a real sense Jesus was created in the image of the creators.

Schweitzer produced his record of the history of the quest of the historical Jesus at the very point he believed crucial for the resolution of the problem. By the beginning of the twentieth century two approaches were contending on the field, what Schweitzer labeled "thoroughgoing scepticism," on the one hand, and "thoroughgoing eschatology," on the other. As diverse as these approaches to the problem are, Schweitzer believed that they combined to destroy the "modern view" which was prevalent at the end of the nineteenth century.

The modern view presented Jesus as

an enlightened teacher who sought to spiritualize the earthly, political conception of the Messiah expected by the Jews. According to this view, Jesus attempted to found an ethical Kingdom of God on earth. When, however, He failed in His effort at enlightenment and lost the popular following which was initially His, He resolved to die at Jerusalem to seal his mission and thus carry it to victory.

The modern view of Jesus as the ethical reformer began to crumble with Schweitzer's forceful presentation of the challenge made by the schools of thoroughgoing skepticism and thoroughgoing eschatology.

The thoroughgoing skeptical school is best exemplified by the work of William Wrede. In *The Messianic Secret in the Gospels* (1901) Wrede held that the Gospel of Mark, although it was in time of composition closest to the events it recounts, cannot be accepted as history. Wrede took the position that this Gospel must be approached with great skepticism. The fact that Mark pictures Jesus as a Messiah who kept His messiahship a secret indicates that the historical Jesus never claimed messiahship but considered Himself to be a teacher. The Messianic elements were read back into Jesus' life by the early Christian community. Indeed, the eschatological framework of the Gospel of Mark is the creation of the early Church and is not a valid picture of the world-view which Jesus held. Wrede insisted that the very fact that there is a patent lack of connection between the various sections of Mark's story indicates that the author never really knew the circumstances of Jesus' life but was imposing his own interpretation on material which had come down to him.

Schweitzer attempts to show that, although Wrede presents a serious challenge to New Testament scholarship with his skeptical view of the sources, there is an alternative theory which better explains the material with which the scholar is confronted. Instead of viewing eschatology and the secret messiahship as something imposed on the record by the Gospel of Mark, Schweitzer believes that they shoud be accepted as historical elements. Furthermore, Schweitzer believes that the reliability of Mark should not be questioned because of seeming breaks in the narration, for the Gospel reflects the situation as it was. Schweitzer's view is that Jesus imposed His own dogmatic eschatological interpretation of history on the natural events of His day and that our failure to grasp this fact has kept us from understanding the true impact of eschatology on Jesus. "Eschatology is simply 'dogmatic history'—history as moulded by theological beliefs—which breaks in upon the natural course of history and abrogates it."

If one reads the story with this in mind, what formerly appeared as puzzling actions on the part of Jesus, now become clear. Jesus was not at all concerned with the attitude which the multitudes or, for that matter, other important elements of society, showed toward Him. He was interpreting events in an eschatological manner. Thus when, after His baptism by John, He enjoyed initial success in His native Galilee in preaching the coming of the Kingdom of God and suddenly withdrew to the north for a "period of inexplicable concealment," Jesus was not motivated by the standards of "success" in this world but by His dogmatic eschatological view of what was needful.

Schweitzer, in fact, denies that success as a "teacher" was of any concern to Jesus, for Jesus did not consider Himself to be a teacher. Using the thoroughgoing eschatological approach, Schweitzer argues there is little didactic material truly present in the message of Jesus. Actually, Jesus did not exhort people to prepare for the coming of the Kingdom, but instead He announced its coming. He did not expect to be understood by all but only by those who had been predestined by God for entrance into the Kingdom.

That predestination is an important element in Jesus' interpretation is shown by such statements as. "Unto him that hath shall be given, and from him that hath not shall be taken away even that which he hath" (Mark 4:24-25). "Many are called but few are chosen" (Matthew 22:1-14). Thus, even the Beatitudes are not to be taken as injunctions or exhortations designed to convert people in time for entrance into the Kingdom of Heaven but rather, writes Schweitzer, as statements of fact: ". . . in their being poor in spirit, in their meekness, in their love of peace, it is made manifest that they are predestined to the Kingdom. By the possession of these qualities they are marked as belonging to it." In other words, one cannot earn the Kingdom; one is predestined to it. The so-called "reward" sayings among Jesus' teachings are not really such if set before "a background of predestination."

Schweitzer believes that Jesus' public career lasted just a few months. He points out Jesus' references to sowing and reaping and contends that there is a symbolic and temporal connection between the coming of the harvest and the coming of the Kingdom. The end is truly at hand.

When Jesus sent out the Twelve to announce the coming of the Kingdom, he did not expect to see them again in this life. In sending them forth he fully expected to loose the final woes and strife which were associated with the Parousia (appearance) of the Son of Man (supernatural Messiah). Jesus, however, was mistaken in His expectation. The disciples returned and still the Son of Man and the Kingdom had not appeared. It was this disappointment which motivated Jesus to take a new direction. He no longer expected the preaching of repentance to bring in the Kingdom; thus, He decided to go to Jerusalem to die.

Schweitzer is convinced that Jesus identified Himself with the Son of Man whose appearance on the clouds of Heaven was to usher in the Kingdom. The Messianic consciousness of Jesus, Schweitzer believes, is apparent in all He does. Jesus, however, never revealed His secret to the people. His entrance into Jerusalem was as a secret Messiah. The people were obviously not aware of His belief, and, says Schweitzer, did not greet him as the Messiah. If they had taken Him as the Messiah, the charge would have been brought against Him in His trial—something that was not done. The High Priest could produce no witnesses to say that Jesus claimed messiahship; the attempts to convict Him were based on other grounds. Only when all else had failed did the Priest, using information supplied by the disciple Judas, accuse Jesus of Messianic pretensions. Jesus finally was convicted because of His own admission.

Jesus' death, then, was not the result of historical necessity but, rather, was grounded in dogma—in His own conviction that He had to die for the predestined in order that the Kingdom might come.

So it is, argues Schweitzer, that the figure of Jesus created by nineteenth century scholarship is critically exposed both by thoroughgoing skepticism and by thoroughgoing eschatology. No matter which of these two schools is finally proved to be right, the Jesus of nineteenth century scholarship is destroyed. Just at the point in the history of the quest for the historical Jesus where we "were already stretching out our hands to draw Him into our own time, we have been obliged to give up the attempt and acknowledge our failure." Not only can we not transport Him and make Him a part of our time, we must be prepared "to find that the historical knowledge of the personality and life of Jesus will not be a help, but perhaps an offence to religion."

But although the historical Jesus was captive to His world-view and cannot be adapted to our own time, Schweitzer does not conclude his *Quest* on a note of frustration. On the contrary, he claims that despite the tremendous chasm between the world view of Jesus and our own, despite the fact that "Jesus as a concrete historical personality remains a stranger to our time," the spirit of Jesus transcends His day and reaches out as an inspiration to men in ours.

The old names for Jesus—Messiah, Son of Man, Son of God—mean nothing to us. We are incapable of devising a name that describes His meaning for us: "He comes to us as One unknown, without a name, as of old, by the lakeside, He came to those men who knew Him not. He speaks to us the same word: 'Follow thou me!' and sets us to the tasks which He has to fulfill for our time. He commands. And to those who obey Him, whether they be wise or simple, He will reveal Himself in the toils, the conflicts, the sufferings which they shall pass through in His fellowship, and, as an ineffable mystery, they shall learn in their own experience Who He is."

PERSONALISM

Author: Borden Parker Bowne (1847-1910)
Type of work: Systematic theology
First published: 1908

Principal Ideas Advanced

The knower and the known are not alien to each other in their natures.

The world which is known is the world as ordered by minds.

Nature must be understood as affected by a dynamic cause; such a cause must be a unified and creative Will and Intelligence.

The creative Intelligence is best understood as the ground of ordered experience; He is an infinite Person who provokes a creative response in finite persons.

Borden Parker Bowne's whole scholarly life as a philosopher was immersed from 1876 on in teaching at Boston University, where he became the first dean of the Graduate School. Strongly influenced in his thought by Hermann Lotze (1817-1881), Immanuel Kant (1724-1804), and George Berkeley (1685-1753), he dissented from each significantly. As he said, "I am a Personalist, the first of the clan in any thorough-going sense." The author of several books and many articles, Bowne was constantly concerned to defend the vitality of experience as a whole from the pontifical claims of the Christian supernaturalism, evolutionary naturalism, psychological associationism and materialism, and the ethical utilitarianism of his day.

In *Personalism* (the Norman Wait Harris Lectures at Northwestern University for 1907) Bowne found it possible to summarize and to epitomize his more elaborate studies in *Theism* (1902), *The Theory of Thought and Knowledge* (1897), and *Metaphysics* (1898).

Persons do not make themselves, he claimed, nor do they create the common world of experience they take for granted, or the laws of reason which allow them to communicate in this common world. The world is, to be sure, an orderly world on which persons can depend. But an orderly world need not be a nonmental world. One must not jump to the conclusion, as do realists and naturalists, that this world can exist in entire independence of persons. From the outset it must be clear that science and practical daily living need a trustworthy world, but by no means a self-sufficient realm of nonmental beings.

We must ask what the nature of the trustworthy world is, Bowne writes, and we can do no better than to start with the undeniable datum, the knowing experience of persons. Knowing is itself a unique event unlike any other known fact. For its very nature consists, inscrutably, in referring to something other than itself, a something it does not create by such referring. Once more, however, one must not jump to the realistic and naturalistic conclusion that since knowing refers to something other than itself, it refers to something nonmental.

What knowing presupposes, Bowne suggests, is a not-me (or not-us) that is in interaction with me (or us). But in interacting with the knower the object to be known obeys its own nature. Realization of this fact leads to a far-reaching conclusion. For if the human mind, in knowing the object not of its own making, meets the conditions of that object and knows it, then the object, in turn, evidently meets the conditions set by the nature of the knowing subject. The knower and the known are not alien to each other in their natures.

Still further conclusions must be drawn: "No knowledge, whether of the ideas of another or of anything else, is imported ready-made into a passive mind, but the mind must actually construct knowledge for itself." The object as known and the object to be known are never one or identical. The nature of the mind is to think; the nature of the object is to be. The known object is the thought object. The knower *thinks* the object to be known; he does not "embrace" it. In other words, what happens in the knowing process is not that things as thought pass into a passive mind. Upon the occasion of interaction, the mind responds in accordance with its own laws and "creates" its own known world. Just as the thoughts of a teacher as expressed in his words are read back to a teacher in accordance with the understanding capacity of the student, so what we know as "the physical world" is our human reflective response to the "real" world. Our world is not identical with the real world that supports this humanly known world.

More analytically: each knower is bombarded with a flux of discontinuous impressions which as such certainly are not the world as we know it. If in the midst of this flux there were no abiding knower to interpret these discontinuous impressions, and if the knower had no rational principles in accordance with which he could organize these incoming sense data, there would be no "world" of sense but only the meaningless maelstrom of unassorted sense-impressions: sounds, colors, smells, and other sense data. Thus the world we know, in order to be a world and not chaos, must be a world as organized by the patterns of understanding intrinsic to the knowing mind. The world as we know it, the "phenomenal" world, is not a "material" world, and certainly not the real world. It is the world as ordered by minds that interact with the real world.

Yet this is only one side of the story, the side neglected by realists and naturalists. The other side, neglected in Kant's doctrine that the real world cannot be known, is that the mind cannot impose its phenomenal construct on a reality completely alien to it. The phenomenal world exhibits the rational structure which persons impose upon it, to be sure, but that rational structure does not itself create the real objects with which persons interact. The world as known is the world persons construct on the basis of the reality beyond thought. The phenomenal world is not a mask of the real world; it is that world as manifested to minds which find it cooperative with their natures.

Is the real world made up of nonmental entities and events spread out in nonmental space and time? Bowne finds no reason for introducing nonmental entities in order to explain either persons or their knowledge. He admits that he does not prove beyond a shadow of a doubt that such nonmental beings cannot exist. But he finds them unnecessary, unexperienced supports for the actual phenomenal world as ordered in accordance with human categories and as steadfastly serving human purposes. That nonmental, unintelligent, unpurposive entities would interact supportively with intelligent minds is hard to believe, Bowne suggests. And for intelligent minds to be produced in a world made up of unintelligent entities which in turn can be known by them—this seems the least likely way to explain what one actively confronts in experience; namely, ordered world. Why not, then, postulate, more economically and empirically, a unified Intelligence as the productive cause both of human minds and of the order of events it puts at their disposal?

Again, Bowne does not assert that just because the phenomenal world expresses the structure of the knower, all existents are mental. He insists that there is an order of being beyond human intelligence. But why try to explain the known, knowing beings and their ordered world, by nonmental beings, if to do so creates rather than solves problems? His fundamental contention is that since persons can find identities in and through change in the experienced world, and since persons can find that world meaningful, what is ultimately real must have not only an affinity with persons but also the kind of self-identity and unity that persons exemplify.

What happens to space and time on this view? Bowne would be willing to postulate that the cosmic Intelligence operates via a nonmental space and time world, if he could find evidence for such a world in experience. But, in Kantian fashion, he finds that we do not experience space as an infinite, three-dimensional, all-embracing, nonmental reality, nor time as an infinite, all-embracing being independent of mind. Space, in fact, is the form that pervades all "outer" experience, while time pervades both inner and outer. The objects in dreams are as much "in space and time" as are any others. There is no more experiential ground, then, for supposing that we need an independent "real" space and time "in which" to live than to suppose that the space and time of our dream-objects need "real" space and time.

Does this not mean that space as known is an illusion or a mask that we put on reality? Not for a moment, Bowne insists. If we stay close to experimental fact we note a specific spatial order. There must be something, then, in the dynamic structure of the real that imposes this and not some other order upon us. And the same reasoning applies to time.

We run into trouble, Bowne writes, only when we try to *picture* how a spatial order might "copy" the real, or how a nonspatial Being can manifest itself as spatial in our experience. The facts as known must stand: the space-relations and the time-sequence as known are what they are, and hence they cannot be identical with the nonphenomenal world. Instead of trying to put either finite or infinite mind "in space" why not simply realize that minds are where they act? Minds, by their very nonspatial nature, cannot fill some vacuum with bulk.

If we pass from space and time in general to individual substances such as stones, apples, and chairs—substances which presumably exist independent of persons—we uncover similar picture-thinking philosophy, Bowne claims. For actually we do not bump into solid, unified objects; we sort out our experiences into dependable sequences, and we selectively organize different clusters into a world of things having the continuity which certain sequences of experiences impose on us. Once more, these phenomenal things are not outright creations of persons, but the constructs which persons develop in response to the continuity and structure of the supporting dynamic realm beyond themselves.

What, then, does it mean to talk about nature, if we stay close to experienced data? Nature is the continuous, organized world of objects in spatial and temporal continuity; it is a common world, exhibiting dependable laws of sequence and concomitant change, a world that reflects the interplay of finite minds and a dynamic realm beyond themselves. To call nature a causal world is to emphasize the dependable order and continuity among our experiences. But order and cause are descriptive. If we are to explain the fact that we do not make the continuity and establish the order we find in experience, cause must be given another meaning, namely "productive" or "dynamic" cause.

What shall we conceive such a productive cause to be? We experience a dynamic cause in our own wills, and we experience continuity when our wills carry out one purpose. Bowne, reasoning by analogy, suggests, then, that the order, lawfulness, and continuity we discover in the processes of nature can find no better explanation than that they exhibit the working-out of the purposes of a creative Will. If we postulate a unified Will and Intelligence, we can say that the real world, not the phenomenal world, is the activity of the Creator on a cosmic level; the real world is His thought in action; the Creator is both thought and deed.

The phenomenal world of nature, concludes Bowne, is the world as we construct it in response to the continuity, unity, and variety of the presentations the cosmic Person produces in us in accordance with our receptivity. His cosmic activity is not necessarily restricted to such presentations as we have, for He may well produce a cosmic order without any relation to us. Yet we can trust the connections we have inferred from the past only because this world-order, far from being a mere succession of causes, is the manifestation of one unified, purposeful Creator.

The plurality-in-order that we know as our world is "posited" by the Creator without loss of His own unity. He remains immanent in the world that manifests him, but His nature is not exhausted by it. He is both immanent and transcendent; He is the ground for our system of common experience which testifies to a basic affinity between finite intelligence and deeds and infinite Intelligence and Deed.

The controlling analogy in conceiving the infinite Person is the finite person and his kind of unity. This unity is irreducible; abiding through change and time, it is self-equivalent. Otherwise knowledge such as we have would be impossible. But this unity cannot be explained by the very categories that express its unity. The person, then, is the category of categories, Bowne suggests.

The person also experiences admittedly mysterious self-determination or free-will—a phenomenon that must not be reduced to some form of mechanical order. Freedom and order, rightly conceived, are far from inimical to each other. Freedom is the unity of the person in choice-action: it is not an abstract power unrelated to desire or intelligence. Since the unity of the person is not a collection of will, intelligence, and desire, will is "the power to form plans, purposes and ideals and to work for their realization." As such, freedom initially and always is the freedom to work in relation to order.

The vision of man, world, and God that spreads before us becomes clear only as we see man, with the created autonomy granted him, working out the concrete significance of his freedom in a world order that at once limits him and gives him the opportunity for fulfillment. Freedom would effect nothing did it not live in a realm of order. Freedom does not create rational law but uses it to guide whatever thought and action is open to the individual's nature in a given world order. For the personalist, then, the natural order is not an order in terms of which the individual's intelligence and freedom can be explained away. The natural order is the objectification of interaction of both finite and infinite persons. Finite persons are not reducible to an impersonal order or to a qualityless parade of nonmental events. But the world in which finite persons express their will and intelligence is common ground with the Infinite Will upon whose living will and purpose they depend for the basic form and order of their existence. To try to *picture* this relation of the free creative person to the Creator is to court failure by attempting to think of the person as a part of a larger whole. But the inalienable unity of thought, will, and feeling as found in finite persons cannot be merged into an Absolute One without blurring the fundamental fact that persons live in independence and dependence.

Thus, reversing the argument and moving from God to nature and man, the world-view that emerges can be briefly stated as follows: The infinite Unified Will and Intelligence, or Person, creates finite unities of will and intelligence and allows them relative independence within the larger realm of dynamic order that constitutes His world. The capacities, cognitive and otherwise, of finite persons are not alien to this larger order of thought and will with which they interact, and they depend upon that underlying order for the relative phenomenal world they construct in accordance with their cognitive-volitional capacities.

The phenomenal world of space, time, and things is not a world out of all relation to the constant intelligent willing of the cosmic Person, but neither is it identical with Him. There is no sufficient reason for imposing, between the cosmic Person and finite persons, an orderly realm of nonmental entities. For all we could empirically mean by such entities is certain dependable forms and systems of experience that persons find they can develop in response to the inferred steady activity beyond themselves. Why not, then, asks Bowne, hold that the system of experience presupposed by common sense, science, and philosophy is a system grounded not in impersonal or nonpersonal forces, but in the interplay between the dependable creativity of the cosmic Person's active will and the creative response of free, intelligent, finite persons?

Reality, Bowne concludes, is composed of a purposive system—a whole of purposers, and not a whole of parts without freedom or creativity. The infinite Person manifests Himself in a dynamic order that sustains and directs in basic ways the constructive response of finite persons. They in turn, with their delegated freedom and intelligence, can create within that dynamic order a phenomenal and moral world that expresses in different ways the interaction between man and God.

The concrete world-order at any time is the product of the interplay between the Creator and His orderly activities and the constructive responses of persons who make of the cosmic data what they will, within the limits of their powers. According to Bowne's personalistic world-view, finite persons can fulfill both themselves and the purpose of God only as they will purposes born of reason and love in their relations to one another and to their Creator.

OUR CALLING

Author: Einar Billing (1871-1939)
Type of work: Systematic theology
First published: 1909

Principal Ideas Advanced

The nature of the Christian faith is such that it permits itself to be made contemporary; that is, to become relevant to the modern world.

The Christian's "calling," or vocation, must be seen in relationship to the overall history of the Bible, in which God has made Himself known.

Man is capable of contributing to the building of God's Kingdom on earth.

By means of our calling, that is, in the fulfillment of those tasks to which God has called us, particularly to the service of our neighbor, we participate in the building of His Kingdom.

Man is a participant in the creation of God's Kingdom only by virtue of the fact that he is a forgiven sinner.

Einar Billing, who was professor of theology at the University of Uppsala, in Sweden, as well as Bishop of the Lutheran State Church, was one of the most influential thinkers in his country. His contribution to Swedish theological thought (unfortunately, he is not well-known outside his native land) is based upon an analysis of the Bible and of the thought of Martin Luther. *Our Calling,* which is one of Billing's major theological works, demonstrates his reliance upon the Bible and Luther in the presentation of the doctrine of vocation.

The study of the Bible provided Billing with material for theological works dealing with the nature of ethical thinking in the early Christian Church and with the doctrine of the atonement. In his analysis of the Old Testament Billing discovered in what way the ethic of the Hebrews is continued in the New Testament. In his study of the New Testament and the atonement, Billing considered different theories of the atonement within the Christian Church. The Bible, Billing discovered, proposed a world view, including a concept of history—"history as the drama of revelation"—which was antithetical to the Greek world view. The God of the Bible cannot be compared to the God of Classical Greek philosophy, Billing claims. God is an acting God in the Bible; He is constantly revealing Himself to individuals in history. According to the Old Testament, He led the Jews from Egypt in the Exodus, and He called the prophet into being to bring the immediate knowledge of His will. In the New Testament, Jesus Christ is the bearer of the news that God is ultimately concerned about man. This "good news" takes the form of God's coming into history in the person of Jesus Christ. Thus, the essential element in the Bible is the historical element, by means of which God makes himself known. Revelation is historical.

On the basis of his reflections, the task of theology became very clear for

Billing. Theology must relate the Biblical confessions of faith regarding God's activity in history to the present day and the modern world. It must do so, however, in terms of the reality of the situation. Another distinction between the Bible and Greek philosophy then became clear; the Greeks, unlike the Biblical writers, always became lost in abstractions.

Billing believed that even Luther could be understood only on the basis of the *setting* in which his ideas were expressed. Luther is a part of a period in theological history, and his work is important to the Christian church only if it is analyzed historically. The words Luther used, Billing found, had undergone a change in meaning. This fact alone motivated Billing, the Luther-scholar, to look more carefully at the Reformer in terms of the world in which he lived. Not everything in Luther has equal value, Billing asserted. His teachings do not become normative simply because he uttered them. However, Luther's significance for the Christian Church lies in the fact that in his discussion of the New Testament he gave an insight which is constantly being verified in the experience of believers. Luther's historical significance, according to Billing, lies not in the particular ideas he expressed, but in the fact that he interpreted and preached the Gospel more accurately than anyone else in his time. What does not relate to the central motif of Luther, that God has revealed himself in Christ, is only of *secondary* historical interest. Billing insisted that one can understand Luther solely from this theological point of view and that one is likely to misinterpret Luther if this presupposition is not maintained. Luther, too, Billing felt, was to be the object of the investigations of the theologian, and again the theologian was to make Luther's insight into the nature of the Christian gospel relevant to modern man.

Billing saw a direct line between the Bible and Luther. Luther's theology was simply a reduplication or rediscovery of the Pauline (and early Christian) faith. Just as Luther had taken the Bible and made it come alive in his world (as Paul had done with the Old Testament), so too must the modern Christian make the past come alive, and make the Word of God speak to the present situation.

Billing's methodology is important as a background for his work, *Our Calling*. Into his Biblical-historical view, he introduced the Christian doctrine of calling or vocation.

Billing maintained that there is a continuity between the acts of God in history, the present-day activity of God and the Kingdom of God which is to come. However, Billing maintained that man participates in the construction of the Kingdom. Unlike Luther, who at times insisted that the Kingdom is to be identified with the Church of Christ which shall stand when the world shall fall, Billing believed that man is able to contribute to the creation of God's Kingdom. Man's contribution to the Kingdom involves necessarily the nature of man's *calling*, said Billing. The Kingdom shall not be fulfilled automatically, although God has assured us that it will be consummated. Rather, Christian man is responsible for bringing about its fulfillment. Billing wrote: "God builds his kingdom in time through the centuries. God has by virtue of his forgiveness called us to participate in the building of His kingdom. By means of the orders of our world he has given us our vocation. Very rarely are we given any prior knowledge of how our rather insignificant deed contributes to the kingdom. . . ."

Billing could not, however, find a similar conception of vocation in Luther's theology. The relationship in Luther between faith and works and vocation is very clear: faith evokes love, and love expresses the good deeds which belong to one's calling. There is not in Luther a *final* goal to which these good deeds are directed, and there is no way by which specific good deeds can be related to a larger whole. Billing, however, saw that the relationship of the doctrine of the forgiveness of sins and the doctrine of God's kingdom provided such a unity. He wrote: "In the forgiveness of sins, we experience our escape from the Egyptians. We know, therefore, that God will lead us to his eternal kingdom. The divine ordinances which we encounter during our lifetime show us their intention to carry us towards that goal. Furthermore, deep within each of them is a message of grace. . . . If we faithfully and patiently permit the forgiveness of sins to force us back once again upon the forgiveness of sins, then in the midst of darkness (even a 70 year exile, when all hope was lost) a kingdom shall spring forth. . . . But only the calling, which God himself has given us, makes this possible for us."

Billing observed that the aim of the good deeds of the Christian is "to aid another, that is, to serve one's neighbor." But the good deed, the giving aid to another individual, is related directly to the Kingdom of God. Although Billing could not find within Luther the relationship of the Christian doctrine of vocation to the Kingdom of God, he nonetheless believed that Luther had intended to emphasize such a relationship and Billing regarded himself as simply carrying forth the consequences of Luther's own work.

Our Calling relates the doctrine of vocation directly to the idea of the Kingdom of God. Nonetheless, Billing's conception of vocation is dependent upon the Christian doctrine of the forgiveness of sins. We can understand the relationship between vocation and the forgiveness of sins, said Billing, when we conceive of the forgiveness of sins as the action of the living God in approaching man. But this fact compels each individual to approach another individual. This is the nature of our vocation. God initiates the act of response in relation to our neighbor. As we go to our neighbors, we become co-workers with God. In this way, God molds our lives so that they become related to God's activity in history.

Billing reintroduces his conception of history at this point. Long before most men could rightfully talk about their calling, Billing wrote, a people, the people of Israel, had a specific calling. They received their calling by virtue of God's act of election. The people of Israel knew, therefore, that there was a purpose to their history, and that God would lead them to the fulfillment of His election. Their vocation was to co-operate with God in this fulfillment. Vocation in an individual's life, therefore, said Billing, corresponds to what was the nature of history for Israel. History is always "the message of grace." Vocation is an example of this history, but in a personalized sense. Vocation reveals again that God has entered history on behalf of man, to save him. Billing could say, therefore, that "vocation is the forgiveness of sins." In vocation, "there is the gift of God's son, the forgiver of sins." "In vocation, one finds the gospel." It is clear that faith in the living God of history is the primary element of Einar Billing's conception of vocation.

The doctrine of vocation is therefore closely related to Billing's study of the ethical thinking of the early Christian Church, as well as to his study of the atonement. In contrast to the Jewish ethic, which distinguished between God's righteousness and mercy, the Christian in the early Church unified the concept of the righteousness and love of God. However, Billing said, the nature of the election of the Jews by God excluded forever the possibility that a distinction could be made between God's righteousness and mercy. The prophets saw this clearly, as did Second-Isaiah. The fact of election means that God's righteousness and His love *concur*. The history of the Jews in the desert, the miracle of the Red Sea, all indicate clearly that God's election meant that His love was identical with His righteousness. The tragedy of the Jews, for Billing, was that they made their relationship with God dependent upon what He would do for them. On this basis, they could then make a distinction between the different ways in which it appeared God was dealing with them. Only then could they distinguish between God's love and His righteousness.

Jesus' message attempted to reconcile these divergent characteristics of God. Jesus Himself is motivated solely by the Father. His work is an integral part of God's election. He forgives sins in the name of the Father. He, therefore, has united in His person, (and in His death and resurrection), the themes of the mercy and righteousness of God. Billing found, furthermore, that Paul had seen very clearly this unity in God's nature.

The difference between the Old Testament and the New Testament is therefore simply that in the Old Testament, election (the unity of mercy and righteousness) is of a people, the people of Israel, whereas in the New Testament, election is of an individual, Jesus Christ. In the New Testament, the forgiveness of sins, which Christ offered, corresponds to the Old Testament experience of the Jews' being led through the Red Sea. Because of Jesus Christ, God's revelation is concentrated about a *person* rather than a people. By means of Christ's resurrection, God has extended His activity through the history of all mankind and through every century. God is not changeable, however. He does not act in one way in relation to the Jews and another way in relation to Christ. God's will is a unity of grace and judgment, love and justice, which work together on the basis of the one overarching principle—the *forgiveness of sins*. The central meaning of God's election is that man, sinful man, who does not deserve it, is nevertheless forgiven by God.

The Church is important to Billing in relation to the doctrine of vocation. It is within the Church that God's acts in history are brought into their clearest focus. In the Church, the forgiveness of sins becomes a "present" possibility. For Billing, the Church of Sweden is the promise of God to the Swedish people that their sins are forgiven. The baptism of a child is a witness to the presence of God in the present world. The Church is a reality in the world because it is itself dependent upon the Christ who died for it; God, in Christ, continues to relate Himself to man through the Church. Since in the Church the history of the living, active God, is made known, the Church is "the bridge" which makes Biblical history part of contemporary history. The Church and vocation, Billing says, "seek for an association" with modern man.

Vocation, therefore, is not primarily to be thought of as a *task* given to man by God. Rather, it is a gift which God has given man by virtue of the forgiveness of sins. Vocation "creates man's life" and provides the connection between Israel's history and that of modern man.

THE PERSON AND PLACE OF JESUS CHRIST

Author: Peter Taylor Forsyth (1848-1921)
Type of work: Christology
First published: 1909

Principal Ideas Advanced

Concentrating on the way Christ's person is demonstrated by His benefits, fruitful Christological reflection starts with the conviction that in Christ's action we experience God's action upon us.

The dichotomy between the Jesus of history and the Christ of faith is a false one because even the writers of the Gospels believed in and worshiped a risen, glorified, and redeeming Christ.

When the dogma of the Incarnation is taken out of the realm of the speculative and is made a matter of personally ethical religion, it describes not a union of two static natures into a person, but a moral act which unites God to man and man to God.

Christ's redeeming act consists in the way this God-man and man-God movement is traced by the self-emptying (kenosis) *of the eternal Son and his self-fulfillment* (plerosis), *by which He regains through His human obedience what is His by right.*

Peter Taylor Forsyth studied at the university of his native town, Aberdeen, Scotland, and he spent a semester in 1870 under the theologian Albrecht Ritschl in Göttingen. He held pastorates in London and Manchester before becoming pastor of the important Emanuel Congregational Church in Cambridge. From 1901 to 1921, Forsyth was the principal of Hackney College, a Congregational Seminary. It was in this capacity that in 1909 Forsyth delivered the lectures to the Congregational Union of England and Wales which were subsequently published as one of the most representative statements of Forsyth's thought, *The Person and Place of Jesus Christ.*

According to Forsyth, correct reflection about Christ's person starts with the conviction that in experiencing Christ's actions we experience God's actions upon us. The benefits of Christ demonstrate His nature. The deity of Christ is at the center of Christian truth because it alone makes the Christian experience of redemption conceivable, and redemption in turn is Christianity. Such theology and such thought about Christ is evangelical, lay, and theocentric. "All Christology exists in the interest of the evangelical faith of the layman who has in Jesus Christ the pardon of his sins and everlasting life," writes Forsyth; "We are all laymen here." Yet the lay mind which in these matters everyone shares, must be called back from some deceptive preoccupations. "Lay" has become increasingly not the antithesis of "sacerdotal" but of "theological," as the lay mind has become more and more detached from the Bible. We have become "more concerned with man's religion than with God's salvation," Forsyth claims. It is not enough for Christianity to be merely Christocentric, for it is possible to have a religion which claims Christ's centrality but which actually aims at developing the innate spiritual resource ascribed to a splendid race of mankind. This is an anthropocentric Christianity which is subtly less Christocentric than egocentric. What must be specified is a theocentric faith in which man lives, in Forsyth's terms, "for the worship and glory of God and for obedience to His revelation of Himself; which is not in man, and not in spirituality, but in Christ, in the historic, superhistoric, Christ."

Forsyth elucidates his views about the "Jesus of history" versus "Christ of faith" problem. In this scheme, set forth by an influential part of nineteenth century scholarship, the "Jesus of history" was the religious figure of the Synoptics whose religion involved the "Fatherhood of God and the brotherhood of man." The "Christ of faith" was what the disciples and Apostles made out of the simple Jesus of Nazareth. This view of Christ is recorded most prominently in the Pauline and Johannine literature. In opposition to this dichotomy, which Forsyth believes is a false and impossible one, Forsyth follows the German theologian Martin Kaehler, who is described as the most powerful theological mind on the subject, and says one cannot distinguish between the Jesus of history and the Christ of faith. What may be called Pauline Christianity was the faith of the earliest Church we know of, and it was the faith even of the writers of the Gospels. "Jesus was for the Apostles and their Churches not the consummation of a God-consciousness, labouring up through creation, but the invasive source of forgiveness, new creation, and eternal life," Forsyth writes. In essential matters the Apostolic documents are prolongations of the message of Jesus.

All who extol Christ's greatness affirm some great unity of Christ with God. Forsyth designates three ways this has been done: Socinianism explained Christ's greatness in terms of His being God's perfect prophet, and Arianism did so in terms of His being God's plenipotentiary. Athanasianism, although including the positive aspects of the other two, went on to affirm that in Christ there was God's real presence. If for the first Christ was man, and for the second, superman, for the third he was the Lord from Heaven. At stake was man's salvation, for a mere prophet or a half-God could not redeem the soul created by the whole God. God must be the immediate doer in Christ's saving actions. On this score, the Church decides among these alternatives according to whether or not she counts herself an aided or a purchased people.

Christ, the whole Christ, was mindful of His own divinity and included it within His own Gospel. Leaving aside the Johannine self-testimonies, Forsyth says he is willing to use only the Matthew 11:27 passage concerning the Father's exclusive knowledge of the Son and the Son's exclusive knowledge of the Father. An exposition of this passage leads, according to Forsyth, to the conviction that Christ believed His Sonship to be unique in kind, and it leads further to the doctrine of His pre-existence; that is, His existence eternally as the Son of God. In the Synoptics, Christ's witness to Himself is part of His preaching about the Kingdom. Only in the completion of the Cross did Christ become the object of the preaching recorded in the Gospel, because only then was He perfected as Redeemer. Then the Spirit was released for men even as men were then released for the Spirit. The consequence was that Christ's own preaching about the Kingdom was replaced by the Apostolic preaching about Christ, and he became identified with the Kingdom.

When Forsyth looks at the testimony of the Apostolic inspiration, he distinguishes between the material and formal aspects of revelation. The material aspect of revelation was a person, Christ. The formal aspect of revelation was its completion in the Apostolic interpretation or inspiration. The material revelation took effect in the New Testament, and the New Testament is not solely the product of revelation but is a part of it: the formal element of it, as Christ was the material element.

Both the Bible and the Church are products of the Gospel; both are sustained by the Spirit, the one through faith, the other through inspiration. What Forsyth calls positive revelation has three component parts: the incarnate fact (God entering the world), the interpretive notice of that fact in the Apostles, and the same fact enshrined in the soul of the believing Church. The Apostolic inspiration was, Forsyth writes, "a certain action stirred by the heavenly Christ in the soul, by which his first elect were enabled to see the moral, spiritual, and theological nature of the manifestation with a unique clearness, a clearness and explicitness perhaps not always present to Christ's own mind in doing the act." Insofar as the Bible is witness to revelation but is not revelation itself, it is final but not infallible.

Forsyth reserves an important place for "experience in the Soul." Protestantism is, he says, a blend of two currents: the Reformation and the Enlightenment; or three by another reckoning: "classical Protestantism," emphasizing the objective tendency; "romantic Protestantism," emphasizing the subjective tendency; and the Enlightenment. The goal for Protestantism is not to correlate the views of the Reformation and the Enlightenment, but to correct itself with an emphasis on the practical relations between God and the soul arising not out of reason or romance but out of the "renovation of faith by the piety and genius of men like Spener, Francke, Schleiermacher, and Wesley." The personal experience of Christ, Forsyth claims, is not visionary and mystical but moral, personal, and mutual. Christ works a change in one's life comparable only to birth. This experienced salvation is not a passing, subjective impression, but an objective relationship, even a transaction effected by the Spirit as God in action.

Dogma is "the collective expression of a Church's belief," Forsyth writes, and to moralize dogma is to change it from a speculative notion to a personally ethical religion. Dogma is necessary to the Church, but it has to be revised from time to time to keep pace with the Church's growth as a living body in a living world. The dogma of the Incarnation needs especially to be moralized: a view of the Incarnation is needed which is ethical and dynamic instead of metaphysical and static. The Greek Fathers described the Incarnation too much in terms of cosmic and natural forces, and in terms of the metaphysical and miraculous. "Union" is too physical a term to describe the Incarnation; the Incarnation was not an act uniting two natures into a person, but one uniting two natures through the moral act of the person. Ethical categories (such as society, history, personality) have taken precedence over categories of being (such as nature and substance). Forsyth insists that "The ethical notion of the true unity as the interpenetration of persons by moral action must take the place of the old metaphysic of the union of natures. . . ."

Sketching the outlines of such a moralized Christology, Forsyth shows successively how it involves (1) a doctrine of the pre-existence of Christ, (2) a doctrine of the self-emptying, or *kenosis,* of Christ, and (3) a doctrine of the self-fulfillment, or *plerosis,* of Christ. For Forsyth, the clue to the relation of God and man in the person of Christ is the relation of God's movement toward man and man's movement of active passivity toward God. "On the one hand we have an initiative, creative, productive action, clear and sure, on the part of the eternal and absolute God; on the other we have the seeking, receptive, appropriative action of groping, erring, growing man." This God-man, man-God movement is traced by the self-emptying of the pre-existent Christ and His growing self-fulfillment or "reintegration."

Accounting for Christ's uniqueness in terms of the Virgin Birth is no longer viable, according to Forsyth. Forsyth chooses to handle the problem in terms of another doctrine, that of Christ's pre-existence; and in doing so, he claims to be following the lead of St. Paul. Forsyth's point is that the special relation to the Father could not have arisen in time. Christ's victory in history is the index of a choice and conquest in the Godhead itself; Christ's obedience as a man was only a detail of the supreme obedience by which He became man. Christ never ceased to have a unique relation to the Father. It was this unique relationship which constituted, which was the very essence of, His personality of absolute Sonship: this can be said of none of us. It is clear that Christ saved primarily because He was God.

The reality of Christ's moral conflict as man was ensured by His kenotic ignorance of His inability to sin. This self-emptying was not the renunciation of eternal and divine attributes such as omniscience, nor was it the conscious possession and concealment of them. By this "self-retraction," which term might be better than "self-emptying," the history of Christ's human growth became the history of His recovery by gradual moral conquest of the mode of being from which He came. It was a reconquest: Christ "won by duty what was his own by right." The reason for this *kenosis* was our redemption, Forsyth claims; "He who is the end of all, humbles himself to be the means, that he may win all."

Forsyth opposes his view of the *kenosis* to those views which concentrate on the negative, resigning character of the Incarnation. Besides the subjective repudiation of Christ, we must note, Forsyth writes, "the growth, the exaltation, of his objective achievement, culminating in the perfecting at once of his soul and our salvation in the cross, resurrection, and glory." This positive growth of Christ was the growth of human redemption in which the agent of creation became the very soul it pleased Him to make. By this self-fulfillment, Christ presented as His satisfaction to God the perfect, holy Humanity.

THE RELIGIOUS A PRIORI

Author: Ernst Troeltsch (1865-1923)
Type of work: Philosophy of religion
First published: 1909

Principal Ideas Advanced

Religion is independent of morality and philosophy.

Religion rests ultimately upon certain intuitively apprehended and self-evident truths, which are religious in character; this body of truths is the religious a priori.

The religious a priori *is the regulative, creative, epistemological, and ontological principle of religion.*

The religious a priori *is being realized in the development of the historical religions of the world.*

The Religious A Priori formed the basis for what Ernst Troeltsch called the "science of religion" (*Religionswissenschaft*). Troeltsch was very much dependent upon the philosophy of Immanuel Kant (1724-1804), and in agreement with Kant he argued that values are justified only when they exhibit an immanent rational necessity and can also satisfy the demands of universality. Religion, Troeltsch wanted to show, rested ultimately upon certain intuitively apprehended and self-evident truths, which are religious in nature. To demonstrate this, it was necessary for Troeltsch to employ the critical philosophy of Kant. In the *Critiques*, Kant proposed the idea of the *a priori* character of experience. In the first *Critique, The Critique of Pure Reason* (1781), Kant attempted to discover *a priori* constituents of theoretical knowledge. In the second *Critique, The Critique of Practical Reason* (1788), he performed the same task for practical knowledge; that is, in relation to our knowledge of good and evil. However, when Kant came to the question of religious knowledge, he insisted that the procedure had to be modified somewhat. Religious knowledge, Kant believed, is dependent upon our knowledge of good and evil; that is, it is a product of our practical reason. Because of this, Kant never recognized any separate *a priori* in religious experience; he insisted, rather, that the only genuinely *a priori* element in religion is the ethical element.

Troeltsch was not at all satisfied with Kant's refusal to give an independent place to religion in the *a priori* structure of man's experience. Religion, he insisted, possessed its own existence and could not be subsumed under morality or any other human experience. For this reason, Troeltsch sought to find the religious *a priori*. He sought to demonstrate that the fundamental affirmations of the religious consciousness are ultimate truths of reason which are intuitively apprehended and immediately evident. He wanted to give religious knowledge a firm and independent foundation of its own.

Religion cannot be identified with cosmological speculation, Troeltsch wrote in 1905 (in *Psychologie und Erkenntnistheorie in der Religionswissenschaft*). Consequently, Troeltsch was interested in demonstrating "the nature of truth within the religious consciousness itself." He approached this task in two ways: first, by reference to religion as a psychological and sociological phenomenon; second, by considering the source of religious truth.

According to Troeltsch, in his *Die Absolutheit des Christentums und die Religionsgeschichte,* 1901, the first problem for religion, when one considers religion as a phenomenon of consciousness, lies in an examination of religion as an aspect of empirical psychology. In this study, the religious phenomena are studied as much as possible in their unreflective stage; that is, before they have been influenced by or related to any other experience. It was one of Troeltsch's fundamental assumptions that all vital religion arises in the uncultured classes, where no distinction is made between symbol and reality; the imaginative pictures of religion are entirely unquestioned there. Religion is always born absolute. It necessarily assumes the form of a divine "revelation," absolute in its claims, and everywhere authoritative. Reflective religion is, on the other hand, critical, rational, individualistic, and aristocratic. The "naïve" type of religion shows too that the affective side is the most vivid and intense of all the constituent parts of the religious life. Thus, for Troeltsch, religion is primarily a state of feeling (*Gefühlsgehalt*), although the religious consciousness is found to contain three constituents—conation, cognition, and affection. Real religion for Troeltsch is therefore an identification of the finite with the infinite, but an identification in which the infinite is related to the root of all life, immediate, spontaneous, and unconditioned. The religious "feeling" is a feeling of the infinite, attainable only through the activity of a free agent. The fundamental presupposition of religious experience is, therefore, personal creative faith in the living God.

The second task in Troeltsch's program to determine the independent nature of religion within the consciousness of man deals with the question of the truth of one's religious beliefs. His inquiry is concerned with the validity and objectivity of those experiences one calls religious. We must find an instrument, Troeltsch urged, which will enable us to distinguish the true and the valuable forms of religious experience from the illusory and subjective. The empirical investigation of religion (religious sociology or psychology) must now give way to a rational analysis of religion (religious epistemology). The task of religious epistemology, said Troeltsch, is to find the rational within the phenomenon known as religion, and the valid within the actual religions of the world. Once again, Troeltsch was willing to let Kant define the "true" epistemological method. In every area of experience it was Troeltsch's desire, following Kant, not only to distinguish the genuinely *a priori* elements within experience, but also to apply this method to the religious experience.

Troeltsch insisted that the modern study of religion must follow in principle Kant's critical method. It must seek the *a priori* law of consciousness which finds expression in the phenomena of the religious life. Only in this way can the *truth content* of religion be apprehended. Furthermore, a method or an instrument will thereby be obtained which can be used to criticize further the psychological manifestations of religion.

Troeltsch was, however, critical of Kant's "narrow" definition of the *a priori.* Kant seemed to think that it was possible to offer a complete or "closed" system of the *a priori* conceptions operative in every sphere of experience, but Troeltsch argued that all systems of the *a priori* are provisional and are subject to constant revision on the basis of new experiences. Troeltsch claimed that one can never assert finality for any system of categories.

Troeltsch criticized Kant's conception of the *a priori* structure on one other point. He argued that there was a difference in the way Kant used the *a priori* of the theoretical reason from the way he used it for the practical reason. In the area of morality, Kant represented the *a priori* as the whole of morality. Kant seemed to speak as if the bare abstract formula of the categorical imperative were sufficient by itself and could be equated with the entire moral experience. Furthermore, in the realm of religion, he spoke as if the simple awareness of a moral order were the entire legitimate content of the historical religions of mankind. Troeltsch insisted, rather, that the ethical and the religious *a priori* are both abstractions from the realities themselves. The religious *a priori* served to determine that which is necessary and universal in the empirical religions of the world.

Troeltsch agreed that values are justified only when their rational necessity as universally valid concepts has been demonstrated. On this basis, he proceeded to construct a critique of religion (the religious *a priori*); that is, to find those constitutive principles without which there could be no religious experience. While the religious *a priori* is similar to the *a priori* in logic, ethics, and aesthetics, in terms of the concept of necessity, there are nevertheless essential differences. The major difference may be seen in the association of the ethical, the aesthetic, and the religious *a priori,* as distinguished from the theoretical or logical *a priori.* "I have emphasized," Troeltsch affirmed in *The Religious A Priori,* "the distinction between the *a priori* of science and that of the ethical-religious-aesthetic forms of value judgment." The distinction between "theoretic logic and the practical logic of the ethical, aesthetic, and religious" must be maintained, he continued. The theoretical or logical *a priori* deals with experience in an abstract way; that is, it seeks to unify experience in terms of mechanical causation, which gives a picture of reality that is purely phenomenal. Theoretical science provides laws and concepts which can be used to control the actual empirical qualitative world of experience ("die naturwissenschaftlich-kausalgesetzliche Vernunft"). The ethical, aesthetic, and religious *a priori,* on the other hand, deal with concrete vital powers, with the creative activity of historical personalities ("die geschichtswissenschaftlich-wertgesetzliche Vernunft"). There is in our historical experience, Troeltsch asserted, something which is more than phenomenal, which is in fact, "metaphysical." There is in our historical experience the emergence of a power from within "which realizes an interior whole of spiritual values." Religious knowledge is therefore not merely a description of pious feeling as it was in Friedrich Schleiermacher (1768-1834), but it is metaphysical, proceeding from the epistemological subject, whose judgments of value bring us into association with all reality and with God, who is the absolute worth and root of all life.

The religious *a priori* is, therefore, related to the "unity" of our mental life. As a result of his psychological and epistemological analysis of the religious experience, Troeltsch claimed to have found the *a priori* conditions upon which the possibility and the fact of reality itself must depend. The religious consciousness of union with the infinite is an experience which relates the finite individual to the entire development of life. The "revelations" of the great religious personalities disclose this relationship of the finite to the infinite.

To summarize, Troeltsch's conception of the religious *a priori* may be seen in the following: (1) The religious *a priori* is the *epistemological principle* of religion. The religious *a priori* indicates the fact that there are immanent rational elements in consciousness, which we recognize to be unconditionally valid, and which relate us to God, the source of all value; (2) The religious *a priori* is the *ontological principle* of life. The religious *a priori* gives a basis to the logical, aesthetic, and ethical experiences of life, and relates these to the unconditioned, the absolute consciousness, which is beyond all phenomenal manifestations; (3) The religious *a priori* is an *epistemological* and *ontological principle* which is *being realized* in the historical development of religion; that is, religion is recognizable only through history. The religious *a priori* discloses itself in the religious experience as the norm of the religious experience. It is the standard by which the various historical religions are to be appraised, as well as the criterion by which the prevailing religion is justified and propagated and its vitality critically regulated.

Troeltsch found that his concept of the religious *a priori* gave to the religious state of feeling (*Gefühlsgehalt*), which is itself a purely irrational, alogical, experience, its fundamental quality of rational necessity. In this way, he discovered, the characteristic ideas of religion are born. By means of the religious *a priori* he came upon the epistemological and metaphysical root of the presupposition for all religious experience—the idea of God. This idea, which received its content only in union with the historical religions of the world, is an ontological concept which signifies the reality in which all things exist, the reality "in whom we live and move and have our being."

THE MEANING OF GOD IN HUMAN EXPERIENCE

Author: William Ernest Hocking (1873-)
Type of work: Philosophy of religion
First published: 1912

Principal Ideas Advanced

Whatever is real for man is so by consent of his will, but the universe cannot be defined as merely the fulfillment of man's will.

God is known in experience; the original source of the knowledge of God is the experience of not being alone in knowing the world.

God as the Absolute Other promotes human morality by allowing man to escape reference to himself alone.

The vision of God which is provided by the mystic experience supplies the basic reason for the irrational loyalties which give life value.

Religion aims at producing a prophetic consciousness whereby man is enabled to act by reference to the divine.

William Ernest Hocking's *The Meaning of God in Human Experience* is important as a carefully reasoned attempt by an American idealist to strengthen the idealistic conception of religion by attending to pragmatic criticism and by relating experience to human action. Hocking argues that pragmatism revealed the weakness of classical idealism to be its inability to do the "work" which religious truth must do if it is to be worthwhile to man. It was Hocking's conviction that a new idealism might be fashioned which would finish the task left unfinished by classical idealism; namely, the task of giving direction and content to worship by finding the way to the concrete and the particular.

If the meaning of God can be found in human experience, Hocking argues, the generalizations of idealist philosophers will finally make sense. Hocking attempts to study religion through its effects; he develops the notion that religious truth is a function of the active will; he claims that the experience of God arises originally as the experience of not being alone in the world; and he concludes that it is through the experience of God that man develops a concern for others and a motive for acting on their behalf.

In initiating his pragmatic study of religion, Hocking concedes that there is the danger of reducing all concerns with the "Other-world" to a present concern for men in their social relationships on this earth. But he argues that there is an interrelationship which unites the religious concerns for this and the "Other" world, and he contends that the interrelationship is best understood through experience and human action. History shows that religion begins by giving culture its content; finally, culture becomes the whole of religion. An understanding of this development is provided, Hocking claims, once it is realized that only creativity satisfies instinct, and only religion can call forth a unifying creativity.

Religion can be distinguished from art, according to Hocking, for art undertakes infinite tasks, "infinitely distant," while religion "involves a present possession in some sort of the very objects which the Arts infinitely seek." A religious man acts *as if* what he sought were already present; he conducts himself *as if* the knowledge and the immortality he seeks were already realized; he knows, in present experience, what could be attained and realized were he to confine himself to the course of nature, "only at the end of infinite progression."

Religion could not, through experience, achieve meaning and value, were feeling not an integral part of the religious experience. But Hocking is not content to reduce the religious experience to feeling alone. Although intellect cannot do the kind of work which religion demands, feeling cannot exist independently of theory. In Hocking's words, "a *feeling does no work apart from its guiding idea.*" What is needed, then, is a conception of religion which shows ideas organically unified with feeling.

Proceeding from the central belief which is common to all idealistic theories, namely, the belief that experience alone is real, and that all knowledge of reality is through experience, Hocking advances the idealistic theory of knowledge by maintaining that reality is in part a function of will. He rejects the idea that the objects of religious knowledge are static and wholly independent; on the contrary, he argues that the objects of religious knowledge are in process of development, and that they are responsive in both character and reality to man's will. But although Hocking claims that whatever is real is so by man's consent, he goes on to argue that the real objects of man's knowledge are not merely fulfillments of his will; the objects of religious knowledge are not creations of will, although they would not be real for man were man not actively responding to them in experience. Hocking writes: "The universe fulfills my will; but it is not definable as the fulfilment of my will; it is *That Which* fulfills my will. . . . The universe has its own soul, and its own counsel which is not mine. This is its independence."

Hocking calls attention to man's desire for unity and an absolute. Optimism seems to require a monism; although a unity might be conceived as possibly being bad, an organization of many factors into a unity satisfying to the creative mind is what men require if they are to be content. Man requires the Absolute, Hocking claims, but the Absolute must not be a denial of human experience or a mysterious static entity which is in itself eternally removed from all finite values. The Absolute functions to provide a unity which man ultimately desires; it provides the terminus of man's search for truth; the monism of the world gives meaning to pluralism. Consequently, "God . . . must needs also be the Absolute," and as the Absolute, God can be of worth to man only to the degree that the meaning of God can become clear in human experience.

But how is God to be known in human experience? Hocking calls attention to the feelings of fear and awe with which men have in the past met the changing events in nature; he agrees with other writers who have argued that the experience of God seems sometimes to be provoked by moments in which man regards himself as threatened by nature and as in need of assistance. But the experience of God would not arise, Hocking goes on to argue, were not the negative aspects of experience taken as negative in virtue of the supposition that there is a positive side to be sought. Hocking finds the original source of the knowledge of God to be "an experience which might be described as an experience of *not being alone in knowing the world,* and especially the world of Nature."

In a fascinating passage which anticipates the perspective of later Christian existentialists, Hocking describes religion "as the healing of an alienation between man and his world . . . the healing of a breach which religion itself has made. . . ." In developing the conception of the "Other," who may turn out to be either an enemy or a companion, man develops, through experience, the conception of God. To fear God, to be in awe of God, to seek God—all of these states presuppose the experience of God as the Other.

Hocking does not rest with the conception of God as the Absolute and the Other; he continues by insisting that God is Other Mind. But mind is ordinarily known only through knowledge of body; all that we meet in experience are natural bodies. Hocking does not succumb to skepticism at this point; nor does he allow himself to be satisfied with accepting the hypothesis of other minds (and of Other Mind) *as if* that hypothesis were true. He expresses the desire to show how knowledge of other minds is possible. The answer is that knowledge of other minds, like knowledge of any reality, is partly a matter of the consent of will; we know because we desire to affirm what presses upon us for acceptance.

It becomes relevant for Hocking, then, to examine what knowledge of Other Mind we desire. Knowing what we desire to know, we may find that we already know it through the consent of will. Hocking decides that what any experience of Other Mind must contain is a social experience of a common world. When one person has the conviction of identity with another mind, the conviction is no illusion; the world of experience which the two selves share is a common world; changes within one person's experience of nature are changes for the Other. "I have sometimes sat looking at a comrade," writes Hocking, "speculating on this mysterious isolation of self from self. Why are we so made that I gaze and see of thee only thy Wall and never Thee?" But then the discovery comes: "But I *am* in thy soul. These things around me are in thy experience. They are thy own; when I touch them and move them I change *thee.*" The conclusion is triumphant: "This world in which I live, is the world of thy soul: and being within that, I am within thee."

Hocking argues that the idea of a social experience, the idea of Other Mind, is an idea which rests on the social experience of Other Mind. The epistemological problem concerning other minds arises only because the experience of other minds makes the problem possible. Hocking is emphatic: ". . . my idea of Other Mind is at the same time an experience of Other Mind."

Hocking's next step is to argue that the experience of Other Mind is not to be identified with the experience of the presence of any other individual person or group of persons. The experience which constitutes for any man the knowledge of nature and of other minds is a knowledge of God. Hocking writes, "My current social experience, the finding of any fellow finite mind, is *an application* of my prior idea of an Other; in a sense, an application of my idea of God. It is through the knowledge of God that I am able to know men; not first through the knowledge of men that I am able to know or imagine God." Hocking's ontological argument for the existence of God, then, consists of an appeal to the experience on which any experience of nature or of other minds depends: the experience of the Absolute Other, of God.

The moral value of the experience of God arises from the circumstance that God by presence alone draws man from a self-centered concern. In being Other Mind, God continually challenges man to a self beyond himself; the individual finds himself only through abstraction from a universal social experience. Even the knowledge of the Son depends upon a knowledge, through experience, of the Father. "Without the Father, the Son is a mere man," Hocking writes; "for the incarnate is always bound and infected by the finite thing it touches."

For Hocking, worship or prayer is the attempt to approach God to know through experience the attachment to the Other on whom all experience centers. Through the vision of God—which is to say, through the experience which gives value and being to all experience—man acquires that love which motivates him in all his actions henceforth. "The vision of God must give the reason for all the irrational attachments of life, all the sacrifices of self to brother, state, or cause. It furnishes the answer to the last Why of duty." And because of the pervasive power of that vision, Hocking argues, man finds himself being loyal to God and man; from knowledge and love of the One, man turns to knowledge and love of the many.

The mystic experience which worship engenders (or is) is prophetic, Hocking claims. Since the experience of God is an experience which incites man to creative action, it is anticipatory; it looks forward to experiences yet to be won through action. And since the religious experience is prophetic and creative, it is an experience in which the individual shares in the reality of the divine. Through creative action the individual works toward a unification of history; the religious man discovers or creates a meaning which endows human action with new sense. The religious institution, as Hocking describes it, encourages the individual not only in his social and moral relationships, but in his response to the world. What religion seeks to provide through creative experience, writes Hocking, is a "unified and responsible world, one which cares for the individual in his concrete character, and will bear out his rightful will to endure. . . ."

The influence of William James (1842-1910) is clear in this book during the early chapters in which Hocking refashions idealism according to the pragmatic ideal, and the spirit of Josiah Royce (1855-1916) makes itself felt in the later chapters in which Hocking develops the idea of God from the idea of community experience. Hocking acknowledges his debt to his "honored masters," but the product of his labors is an original work, a unified and responsible view of man's relationships to God; as such, the book contributes to that prophetic consciousness by which the labors of various men come together in a unity which is both enlightening and encouraging.

THE SOCIAL TEACHING OF THE CHRISTIAN CHURCHES

Author: Ernst Troeltsch (1865-1923)
Type of work: Christian ethics
First published: 1912

Principal Ideas Advanced

The Christian Gospel is not primarily ethical but religious.

The churches' ethical and social ideals have developed out of the relationship between the Church and the world.

The two main themes of the Gospel have given rise to two distinct types of Christianity: universalism, which stresses the universal scope of salvation through the Church; and individualism, which holds fast to the sectarian demand for individual perfection.

Because the ethical and social ideals of the churches have been developed in response to varied world-situations, there is no absolute Christian ethic that waits to be applied, but in each age it must be formulated anew.

Social structures rest upon economic and not upon ethical foundations, but men with religious and ethical convictions can change social structures.

As a teacher of theology, Ernst Troeltsch stands in the tradition of Friedrich Schleiermacher (1768-1834) and Albrecht Ritschl (1822-1889), for he holds that Christianity is rooted in the religious feeling which is common to all mankind. In *The Social Teaching of the Christian Churches* Troeltsch argues that the original Christian Gospel contained no explicit ethical or social teachings, but consisted in the purely religious vision of the Kingdom of God, according to which, out of purity of heart, men should seek only to know God and to do His will. The fact that the first disciples came together upon the death of their Master inevitably led, however, to the formation of a social structure, with the consequence that ethical principles and a social philosophy soon made their appearance. It is Troeltsch's contention, moreover, that as the Christian community has moved into different world situations, it has modified its principles to suit changing circumstances. Thus, while Christianity has been a perennial inspiration of ethical and social renewal, the abiding source of its influence is religious. In Troeltsch's opinion, it is a mistake to look to the New Testament, or to any period in the history of the Church, for an absolute Christian ethic. Rather, the Church today, facing an altered world situation, must work out fresh approaches to the problems confronting it. Since in this task much depends upon the correctness with which the Church understands the economic and social needs of the new age, a clear apprehension of the history of its previous successes and failures is necessary.

According to Troeltsch, the original Gospel contained two distinct ideals which have made their presence felt throughout the history of the Church and are mainly responsible for the variety of social expressions within Christianity. These ideals, which find expression in the commandments to love God with all one's heart and to love one's neighbor as oneself, are *individualism,* with its emphasis on inward purity as the prerequisite for the ultimate blessedness of seeing God, and *universalism,* with its insistence on the equality of all men in God's sight. These two motifs, reconcilable in the abstract, have been something less than compatible under the conditions of human existence. Thus, when Christians have been concerned to make salvation accessible to all sorts and conditions of men, they have tended to neglect the requirement for individual perfection. On the other hand, when Christians have concerned themselves with the ideal of personal holiness, they have tended to lose sight of the goal of universality.

Troeltsch maintains that the two motifs of individualism and universalism have given rise to two distinct types of Christian thought, each with its characteristic sociological expression. Church-type Christianity has pursued the goal of universality while sect-type Christianity has emphasized individuality. The sect, as Troeltsch views it, is not a mere schism of the church, nor is it an undeveloped form of church-type Christianity, but it is a rival expression of the same Christian faith. According to Troeltsch, the relation between Church and sect is complementary; each stresses one of the aspects of Jesus' teaching. Christianity requires both if its Gospel is to be fully effective in the world. Moreover, the two forms interact, and they stimulate each other. Historically, the church-type is the more fundamental, whereas the sect-type, which comes and goes, has provided the dynamism necessary to bring the Church into new relations with the changing world.

As Troeltsch understands it, church-type Christianity, with its concern to make salvation accessible to entire populations, has interpreted the Church as an objective embodiment of a supernatural power in the world. It has provided itself with an authoritative clergy, which ministers salvation to all comers through the sacraments and the

Word. Recognizing human weakness, it emphasizes grace rather than law, but it provides men with an other-worldly ethical code, designed to guard them against the more prevalent perils of the flesh. The church-type regularly compromises with "the world," under the theory that the present age is the result of man's Fall and will one day be destroyed. Meanwhile, it tries to keep alive the ideal of inwardness and spiritual perfection by encouraging its members to strive for a higher devotional life. According to Troeltsch, the church-type emerged in Patristic times, and, although the Roman Catholic Church is its most complete expression, the Reformation Churches (Lutheran, Reformed, Anglican) were essentially of the same type. Further, there is a tendency for sects, as their membership grows, to pass gradually into the church-type, as, for example, the Baptist and Methodist groups.

Historically, sect-type Christianity has most often arisen in protest against the abuses of church-type Christianity. Men impressed with the demand of the Gospel for purity of heart are likely to judge that, in its emphasis upon universality, the Church has departed entirely from the spirit of its Lord. Sect-type Christianity, therefore, tends to deny the objectivity of the Church as an institution, to break down the distinction between clergy and laity, and to emphasize the necessity of individual believers working out their own salvation by inward discipline. Sociologically, sects tend to be small, intimate groups, composed of members who have demonstrated in their lives the seriousness of their profession. They interpret the universality of the Gospel in terms of love for the brethren, and they tend to view the world with indifference, if not with active hostility. According to Troeltsch, the spirit of sect-Christianity has been present in every age of the Church's history, from the Donatists and Montanists down to the present time. The beginning of the modern sect-movement, however, is traced to the Gregorian reforms of the twelfth and thirteenth centuries, at which time the Roman see was making its most strenuous efforts toward universality. Numerous sects also appeared at the time of the Protestant Reformation.

Any account of the Christian ethical and social philosophy is bound to be complicated by the fact that church-type and sect-type Christianity emphasize opposite poles of the Christian message (not to mention here the mystical-type, which, in Troeltsch's analysis, constitutes a third important variant). It is further complicated by the fact that the Church has faced different economic and social conditions in each period of its history, and it has responded to them concretely.

In the ancient world, the Christian movement encountered a highly developed social system in process of deterioration. Its response was mainly that of passive acquiescence. Following the way marked out by Paul, it accepted the Roman Empire as a provisional institution of divine justice for sinful man; in the same way, it made its accord with the social structure of the time, including the institution of slavery. The Church looked upon itself as a new society in which the demands of brotherly love and equality must be respected, but the larger social and economic situation, even after Christianity became the official religion of the Empire, was not its concern.

With the rise of new territorial regimes in Europe, the situation was altered. Monarchs, ambitious to bring their peoples the benefits of civilization, welcomed the help and guidance of the Church. Laboring under crude conditions, the Church of the early Middle Ages was offered an unexampled opportunity to mold a civilization according to ethical principles. According to Troeltsch, the Church's lack did not lie on the ethical side, nor did it want the highest motivation; its failure to accomplish more was due to its not understanding economic and social processes and the dependence of ethical achievements upon those processes.

A change took place at the height of the Middle Ages, when Gregory VII (c.1021-1085) and his successors undertook to recover the leadership from the territorial churches. The high catholicism of Innocent III (1160-1216) and of Thomas Aquinas (c.1225-1274) rested upon a historical achievement—the existence in actuality of a Christianized Europe. This made a difference in social theory. No longer was the Church thought of as being in opposition to the world, but as perfecting the world. In the new synthesis, ethical, social, and political foundations were ascribed to natural law; the Church considered that its task was not to criticize or revise these foundations, but to bring them to their intended perfection by means of supernatural grace.

With the passing of the feudal order and the rise of nationalism and an urban economy, the Christianized institutions of the Middle Ages ceased to suffice. At this point, says Troeltsch, following in the main the thesis of Max Weber's *Protestant Ethic and the Spirit of Capitalism* (1905), it was the Calvinistic churches which proved resourceful, taking a constructive attitude toward such problems as urban government, international competition, and a money economy. Lutheranism, in Troeltsch's judgment, faltered before this new undertaking when it accepted on principle a division of function between the Church and the secular order. The sects, on the other hand, commonly representing the lower strata of society and fired with apocalyptic visions, stirred up radical and Utopian movements which continued to gain momentum even after the sects had disappeared. According to Troeltsch, the social ethic of contemporary Protestantism is an amalgam of Calvinistic and sectarian principles; he calls this combined ethic "ascetic Protestantism." It stands for separation of Church and State; for democracy, independence, and love of liberty; for zeal in one's calling, concern for humanity, and the reform (rather than the overthrow) of existing social institutions. Meanwhile, says Troeltsch, the Catholic Church has revised its social outlook, while retaining its medieval foundation. Accepting capitalism and industrialism, it has strived to remedy the impersonality and servitude of modern society by recalling men to the principles of natural law, and by working to restore such features of the organic society of the Middle Ages as the family, the guild, and the social class.

Troeltsch maintains, in opposition to historical materialism, that the spiritual life of man is independent of economic and social conditions. The Gospel preached by Jesus and the early Apostles had a religious origin and cannot be explained in terms of the class struggles and political oppressions of the time. In the history of the West, religious and ethical beliefs have interacted with social and political forces to help determine cultural change. The teachings of the churches have, to be sure, been influenced by economic conditions, but the reverse is also true.

Nevertheless, according to Troeltsch, the Church must learn from modern social science the impressive truth that the foundation of society is always economic and not ethical. This means, on the one hand, that if Christianity is to achieve the fullest moral and spiritual development of men, it must concern itself with the need for changes in the social constitution. On the other hand, it also means that Christian reformers have to divest themselves of many naïve notions about the possibility of achieving the kind of changes which they desire.

Reviewing the situation in 1911, Troeltsch concluded that the churches had lost most of the influence that they formerly exercised. Ascetic Protestantism, which had done so much to shape modern bourgeois society, had ceased to be a source of fertile directives; Catholicism, in seeking to restore an organic pattern of society, was blind to historical actualities; Christian Socialism, the heir to sect-type radicalism, nourished dreams of Utopian transformations, but had no sense of the brute reality of economic and social forces. The prevailing social philosophy of the day, said Troeltsch, was not Christian, but an expression of the new rationalistic individualism which owed its foundations to the principles of Newtonian and Darwinian science. But Troeltsch regarded the situation as unstable. "Radical individualism," he said, "will probably soon be an interlude between an old and a new civilization of constraint. This individualism may be compared with the process of taking the materials of a house which has been pulled down, sorting them out into the actual individual stones, out of which a new house will be built. What the new house will look like, and what possibilities it will provide for the development of Christian ethics and of Christian social philosophy, no one can at present tell. Christian social philosophy will bring to the task both its common sense and its metaphysical individualism; but it will have to share the labour with other builders, and like them it will be restricted by the peculiarities of the ground and of the material."

Troeltsch suggests that five main ethical values have emerged in the history of Christianity; these values will, undoubtedly, find their place in any new formulation of the Christian social ideal. First is the conviction, arising out of its belief in a personal God, that the human personality is worth while; to this is added its conception of a fundamental social relation between man and man, based on its belief in God's all-embracing love; a solution to the problem of equality and inequality, rooted in the voluntary acceptance by man of his responsibility in the social order; a high realization of charity, or the spirit of active helpfulness, without which no social order can long endure; and, finally, a conviction of the validity of human aspirations, not as conditioned by the relativities of earthly life but as founded in the original purpose of creation. Possessing these guiding persuasions, says Troeltsch, the Church has no need of fixed programs or Utopian goals. "The truth is," he concludes, "the Kingdom of God is within us. But we must let our light shine before men in confident and untiring labour that they may see our good works and praise our Father in Heaven. The final ends of all humanity are hidden within His Hands."

THE PROBLEM OF CHRISTIANITY

Author: Josiah Royce (1855-1916)
Type of work: Philosophy of religion
First published: 1913

Principal Ideas Advanced

The central features of the Christian religion are the idea of a spiritual community of the faithful, the idea of the inescapable moral guilt of the individual, and the idea of atonement for the sin and guilt of mankind.

The Christian doctrine of life, understood as the coherent interpenetration of these three essential ideas, is metaphysically grounded as a community of interpretation within the world, which is a universe of signs and interpretation.

This interpretation of Christianity is both faithful to the distinctive essence of the Christian religion and ethically and religiously significant for the modern man.

The Problem of Christianity first appeared as a lecture series delivered at Manchester College, Oxford, in the winter of 1913. This work constitutes the mature reflections of Josiah Royce about those religious problems which first drove him into philosophy and which persistently engaged his attention. These meditations reveal the author's special concern with the Christian faith, and most especially with the spirit of the Church. At the same time, these contemplations are philosophical in character and have their immediate origin in the author's work on the philosophy of loyalty. The philosophy of loyalty is an absolute ethic which implies and depends upon the concept of community as its metaphysico-ethical foundation. Thus, the historic Christian religion has to be interpreted for modern man, while modern religious philosophy needs an interpretation of the historic Christian community. The interpretation of Christianity involves the convergence of the religious and philosophical aspects of our remembered history and, consequently, a method which is neither apologetic, skeptical, nor indifferent in its attitude toward the Christian religion.

The concept of "problem" is an important clue to Royce's method of analysis. It is Royce's intention to interpret to his fellow men a common religious inheritance for the sake of the future. This intention expresses itself in the activity of formulating the historic Christian religion as a "problem" for modern man. The concept of "problem" is connected with grasping the essential Christian ideas in their coherence. A "problem" is formulated in the understanding of these ideas as an interpretation of life, rather than as an empty metaphysical or theological dogma. The question of the philosophical truth of these ideas as an interpretation of life also functions as a "problem." All of these problems are unified in the problem of Christianity, Royce's own venture of interpretation. The concept of "problem" thus indicates the method of Royce's philosophy of religion.

Royce begins his examination of the essential concepts of the Christian religion in their human significance with the idea of a beloved community. Man is naturally a social creature. Furthermore, because the community is an organism making demands upon its members, the individual can be obligated or devoted to the community as such. Devotion to the community is the condition of the ethics of loyalty; the ethics of loyalty, in turn, implies the concept of a beloved community, the community as a source and object of devotion. Human devotion is ordinarily directed toward a particular community, although the social history of man shows the emergence and development of the ideal of a universal community.

The Christian idea of community becomes important in connection with the universalization of the idea of the beloved community. The Christian idea has one of its most important sources in Jesus' idea of an active love based upon the love of God for man rather than upon man's self-abnegation. Hence the ethical significance of the Kingdom of God. Yet the Christian idea of the universal community comes to full expression only in the Pauline doctrine of the Body of Christ. The concept of the Kingdom of God is an incomplete sketch of a universal community because it is lacking in ethical rules for practical decisions.

In the doctrine of the Body of Christ, Paul articulates the concept of a new entity which counsels the love of neighbor as neighbor because the neighbor is a fellow member of the visible community, which is based upon the hope that this community will actually become universal, and which thereby becomes a form by means of which Christian love assumes the ethical aspect of the spirit of loyalty. Thus, the Christian achieved the idea of a beloved community. Still this essential idea must be interpreted for modern man because the idea was originally connected with the expectation of the imminent end of the world.

The second essential idea of the Christian religion is the idea of the overwhelming moral burden of the individual. This idea has its natural origin in the fact that in human nature there are many tendencies which the moral consciousness views as evil. Conduct is learned within the social environment. Social training teaches the individual knowledge of "the law" and at the same time intensifies self-consciousness as opposed to "the law." The dialectic of internalized social tension tends to breed an ever greater sense of guilt and a growing division within the will. The dialectic of moral guilt essentially expresses the Pauline doctrine of "original sin," because it describes that moral situation in which one cannot save himself. The Pauline doctrine of original sin, stripped of its antiquated language, is essentially the idea of the overwhelming moral burden of the individual.

The problem is resolved by means of the doctrine of grace or the idea of a beloved community. The individual cannot of himself effect his own wholehearted union with the natural community. He can be saved from his predicament only through faith or loyalty in the beloved community, a universal community of grace which is both existent and lovable. But a community which is so beloved is possible only by divine grace. We can choose to be loyal only insofar as we find ourselves already within the community of grace and choose to remain loyal. What is the origin of such a community? How can there be an actual universal community which transcends the natural bonds of communities of law? Royce concedes the mystery of the origin of such a community. He can speak only of the miracle of a leader who loves and who has the power to create what He loves. In Pauline language, the beloved community is the consequence of the work of Christ. The spirit of Christ is the origin of the beloved community. Beyond this mystery, this miracle, we cannot penetrate.

A still deeper problem than that of the overwhelming moral burden of the individual faces the beloved community. If it is possible to choose loyalty to the beloved community, it is also possible to choose disloyalty. Disloyalty is shown in the act of betrayal. The problem of the traitor is not merely the problem of social alienation, of an individual's being unable to save himself through the attitude of loyalty. The traitor, remembering his act of disloyalty, finds himself in a kind of spiritual damnation. He has committed a sin which neither he nor the community can forgive. As long as time continues, nothing that he can do will ever erase the deed. He is condemned to "the hell of the irrevocable." Yet, Royce claims, there may be a way in which the traitor can be reinstated within the community. The guilt of the traitor may be atoned, not by denying or seeking to obliterate the traitorous deed, but rather by overcoming it. If a faithful and suffering servant of the beloved community acts in response to the evil deed so as to help create a better world than would have existed if the evil deed had not been done, then atonement is possible. The act of atonement does not remove the evil deed, but rather transforms its meaning by a creative and thereby reconciling efficacy. For every traitorous deed of Judas in the history of the beloved community, there can be an atoning work of Jesus, the suffering servant.

These three doctrines of community, guilt, and atonement, together constitute the Christian doctrine of life. The doctrine of life is both a mode of living and a way of salvation. It involves a creative attitude toward the human will in that it seeks the raising of the human self from its natural level to the level of grace by means of the definition of the ideal community. It implies the creation of a universal community which, throughout its history, realizes new forms of morality within the Christian spirit and seeks continually the triumph of good over evil through deeds of loyalty and atonement.

In the second volume of *The Prob-*

lem of Christianity Royce turns to a consideration of the metaphysical bases of the Christian doctrine of life. This is both an inquiry into the metaphysical foundations of the essence of Christianity and an articulation of the metaphysical aspect of Royce's own method of delineating the essence of Christianity. The metaphysical inquiry thus has both its ontological and its epistemological aspect. Through Royce's ingenuity these two aspects are held together in his account of what might be called the metaphysics of the Holy Spirit.

Consider, for instance, Royce's treatment of the relation of time and community. Individuals are differentiated in their perceptions, feelings, and acts. The fact that people function collectively in a common social nexus does not necessarily mean that they form a community; they may be nothing more than a mob. Community by definition requires a common interpretation of a remembered past for the sake of an ideal expectation. Time is of the essence to community also with respect to the transformation of the irrevocable deed of guilt by the succeeding act of atonement. There is a community only insofar as there is a temporal continuity serving as the foundation for present acts of cooperation.

The concept of interpretation requires further analysis. Why does the community require interpretation? How does interpretation form the basis of community? Royce declares that his theory of interpretation is based upon Charles Sanders Peirce's (1839-1914) theory of signs, but is a novel application of it. Like Peirce, Royce describes interpretation as a triadic function in contrast to the dyadic character of perception and conception. In perception or conception there is merely the perceiver and the perceived, or the thinker and the thought. Interpretation, however, implies that which is to be interpreted, an interpreter, and a society for whom the interpretation is made. The datum of interpretation is thus a sign to be interpreted *by* someone *to* someone. Furthermore, any factor in one triadic order of interpretation may serve as the datum for a further interpretation. Consequently, interpretation as a theory of signs is itself an infinite social process. Interpretation is necessary for community because individuals are unique in the individuality of their perceptions, conceptions, and action. Interpretation arises from the will to interpret, and it has as its aim the ideal unity of community.

Insofar as individuals are real and are characterized by the will to interpret, the theory of signs is also a theory of reality as social process. In this respect the world always appears as a situation requiring interpretation. An interpretation of the world is true in proportion to the adequacy with which the community of interpretation realizes its ideal unity. Furthermore, any interpretation of the world becomes at the same time a sign for further interpretation. Thus, the world as social process consists of signs and interpretation. "The world is the interpretation of the problems which it presents."

The world understood as social process is profoundly connected with the fact of historical change and with the task of interpretation. This task of interpretation Royce takes upon himself when he treats the problem of Christianity, interpreting the essential

Christian doctrine of life to modern man. Modern man, the man who epitomizes the historical education of the human race, is not the same as the man of the New Testament world. The future vitality of the Christian religion depends upon its adequate interpretation to modern man. Yet modern man longs for a universal community, and this search depends for its realization upon the interpretation of the essence of Christianity. In his interpretation of the problem of Christianity, Royce exhibits the ethic of loyalty in the realm of philosophical action.

THE IDEA OF THE HOLY

Author: Rudolf Otto (1869-1937)
Type of work: Phenomenology of religion
First published: 1917

Principal Ideas Advanced

The essence of deity cannot be defined conceptually.

The idea of the holy depends on understanding the features of the experience of the numinous, that which transcends comprehension.

By the feeling of mysterium tremendum *man knows the power and majesty of the holy.*

By the feeling of fascinans *man knows the appealing fascination of God.*

An awareness of the nonrational elements in the deity is found in every religion, for mankind is endowed with a pure a priori *capacity for experiencing the holy; but the numinous has been most fully realized in Christianity, for the holy has been made manifest in the person of Christ.*

The Idea of the Holy endeavors to describe the nonconceptual elements of religion. According to Rudolf Otto, religion is rational in that it ascribes definable attributes to the deity; it is nonrational or suprarational in that the essence of the deity is not exhaustively defined by any such ascription.

The nonrational aspect of religion does not admit of a conceptual definition. The nonrational is the innermost core of religion, the experience that is peculiarly religious, the experience of the holy that can be evoked but not defined. The awareness of deity transcends comprehension in either rational or ethical terms. To describe such awareness Rudolph Otto coined the word *numinous.*

The primary purpose of *The Idea of the Holy* is to analyze the numinous into its elements, and to explore the conditions under which the consciousness of the numinous has arisen.

The numinous is felt to be objective and outside the self. It is more than merely a feeling of dependence. To be understood it must be experienced in oneself, in a creature-consciousness or creature-feeling, when a person feels himself overwhelmed by and responds to an overpowering might.

The nature of the numinous, that aspect of deity which transcends or eludes comprehension in rational or ethical terms, can only be suggested by the way it is reflected in the mind in terms of feeling. The numinous is not identical with feeling; it is rather what evokes certain affective states.

The deepest and most basic element of strong religious emotion is the feeling *mysterium tremendum*.

The adjective *tremendum* connotes more than is usually understood by fear. It implies marking the holy off by a feeling of peculiar dread; it contains an element of awfulness, of awe, of religious dread, evoked by the awe-inspiring object as it is experienced directly. Man feels that certain aspects of the deity are absolutely unapproachable; he is overwhelmed by the absolute overpoweringness, the awful majesty of the deity. He feels submerged and as nothing. He feels the urgency or energy of the numinous object which he expresses symbolically in terms of will, force, wrath, and in the idea of the living God.

The substantive idea *mysterium* refers to more than what is merely an uncomprehended and unexplained secret; it is here the "wholly-other." It places the mind in a stupor and fills it with wonder and astonishment. What is mysterious lies beyond the usual, the intelligible, and the familiar. The character of what is "wholly other" is incommensurable with our own character, and it is in this feeling of the "wholly other" that the numinous is experienced.

The numinous experience is not exhausted by the element of daunting awfulness and majesty; such experience also contains something uniquely attractive and fascinating, the element of *fascinans*. The deity may appear as an object both of dread and of fascination. Man is entranced and captivated by the mystery. The numinous exercises a supreme fascination, analogous to the sublime in the field of aesthetics.

Man's reaction to the numinous is the occasion of his awareness of sin and atonement. As he feels submerged into nothingness, his self is devalued; the holy appears as a category of value. For when the numinous reality is a fact of consciousness, man spontaneously depreciates himself and is aware of his own "uncleanness" and "sinfulness." Such awareness does not arise from the consciousness of a violation of a divine commandment; it accompanies rather the awareness of the deity. It belongs to a special category of valuation: the feeling of absolute "profaneness."

To understand what this profaneness is a person must himself be in the spirit, for profaneness is felt only when a person knows himself to be a creature in confrontation with that which is above all creatures.

Such an encounter enables him to pass upon the deity a judgment of appreciation diametrically opposite to the profane; namely, the ascription of the category of the holy, a category that belongs to the numinous alone.

The recognition of the holy need not be accompanied by the sense of moral demands. The holy is inwardly recognized as commanding our respect; it is extolled as a value beyond all conception, as a power that received praise because it is absolutely worthy of praise. The deity is valued subjectively because of its fascination; it is valued subjectively because it is august.

The awareness of sin and the need of atonement develops when numinous unworthiness or disvalue is centered in moral delinquency. The need of atonement arises when man feels that his profaneness makes him unworthy to stand before the holy, that he might even defile it by his presence. Man's desire for atonement is expressed as a longing to transcend his unworthiness as a creature, as a profane rational being.

Christianity, more than any other religion, has expressed the need for atonement, not because it has developed the conceptual theory that the righteousness of Christ is imputed to the sinner, but because the Christian experiences the atonement as an incomprehensible grace whereby God permits access to Himself.

The essential nature of the consciousness of the numinous can be clarified by examining the way in which it is outwardly expressed and is transmitted from mind to mind.

The numinous cannot be taught, but where the spirit is present and there is an inborn capacity to receive and understand it, it can be directly induced, incited, and aroused.

The sense of the numinous is indirectly evoked by feelings that seem to be opposite to the numinous in significance. Thus, the fearful and loathsome may give rise to genuine feelings of religious awe. Terror and dread may be replaced by a feeling for the grand and the sublime. The terrifying, the baffling, and the miraculous may awaken man's sense of the *mysterium*. The numinous is also evoked by art and by the sublime; it appears in music, in magic, and in silence.

The feelings of the nonrational and the numinous are found in every religion but they are pre-eminently present in the Old and New Testaments.

In the Old Testament, mystery moves in all its potency. In Yahweh the numinous dominates the rational, and in Elohim the rational overshadows the numinous. Moses marks the beginning of a process in which the numinous is rationalized and moralized until it becomes the holy in the fullest sense in the Prophets and the Gospels. In Deutero-Isaiah the stage of a universal world-religion is reached; Yahweh in His pre-Mosaic form is transcended.

The Old Testament champions of the living God, the God of anger, love, and the emotions, unwittingly defended the nonrational core of the Biblical conception of God against excessive rationalization. They erred, however, in that they misconceived the numinous character of such attributes and regarded them literally instead of admitting them only as figurative "indications of something essentially non-rational."

In the New Testament, apprehension of the numinous reaches its consummation in the Gospel of the Kingdom, for the Kingdom is absolute greatness, the wholly other, contrasted to the world of here and now.

The numinous experience is to be found in the garden of Gethsemane and in the Christian confession "I believe in Jesus Christ risen from the dead." To speak of the "Resurrection" is to speak of a mystery. To hold to the mystery of the risen Christ necessitates the rejection of two interpretations; namely, the supernaturalistic notion that the empty tomb was evident to the senses, and the rationalistic notion that the faith in the Resurrection grew out of the subjective impression made by Jesus on His disciples.

Both the rationalists and the supernaturalists ignore the important fact about this experience; namely, that it was a mystery, a mystery which, with the certainty of eternal truth, discloses the numinous.

The numinous is present in the writings of Paul, when he speaks of predestination, and it is also present in the writings of John, when he writes of the Spirit; it is seen in Roman Catholic forms of worship and dogma, and it is also found in the works of Luther and of Schleiermacher.

The permeation of the rational by the nonrational deepens the rational conception of God. To disregard the numinous elements leads to the impoverishment of religion, but when the numinous is permeated by elements signifying rationality, purpose, morality and personality, a fuller idea of the holy emerges. The "holy" now appears as a complex category that combines rational and nonrational components; the "holy" is a purely *a priori* category. Rational ideas of absoluteness, completion, necessity, substantiality—ideas of the good as objective value—are evolved not from sense perception but from an original, underived capacity of the mind implanted in the "pure reason." (Otto's view here is markedly Kantian.) The nonrational elements in the category of the holy are also absolutely pure. The ideas of the numinous and the feelings that correspond to them refer to what is deeper than pure reason, to the *Seelengrund* (the bottom of the soul). Sense impressions are simply the occasion, the stimulus for our awareness of the numinous.

The facts of numinous consciousness point to a hidden substantive source, to a pure reason in the profoundest sense, to a depth beyond the pure theoretical reason and the pure practical reason of Kant.

The discovery that man has an innate predisposition to religion provides the key for an insight into the historical origin and development of religion, from its cruder phases to its most mature Christian form.

Man possesses a faculty of divination, a faculty of genuinely cognizing and recognizing the appearances of the holy. Instances of divination are to be found in primitive Christianity, as, for example, when the disciples of Jesus experienced the holy in His person and life; He became a revelation of the holy. Divination is also to be found in Christianity today, for even modern man recognizes the holy and responds to it. It makes no difference that the records of Christ's life are fragmentary, filled with uncertainties and with legendary elements. Christianity has undergone significant changes since the time when it was simple, unpretentious religion. Nevertheless, contemporary Christianity retains the essence and inner meaning to be found in the religion of Jesus; Christianity continues to be a religion of redemption and salvation, a redemption to be fulfilled by God in the promise of His Kingdom hereafter, and yet to be experienced here and now in the present experience of His Fatherhood.

Otto writes that any man can experience Christ as holiness made manifest, not by demonstration or by applying some conceptual rule but by pure contemplation, by the submission of the mind to a pure impression of the object, out of which there arises the pure feeling of "recognition of holiness," the intuition of the eternal in the temporal.

The holy is thus an *a priori* category of the mind, and yet it is manifest in outward appearance. The ultimate criterion of religion is to be found neither in what a religion has done for a culture nor in any external feature. The innermost essence of religion is the idea of holiness as such. Rudolph Otto argues that holiness is found supremely in Jesus, who is more than a prophet: "He is the Son."

The Idea of the Holy is a part of that contemporary theological tradition which places religious intuitions beyond rational criticism, beyond the results of Biblical exegesis and higher criticism, in the realm of religious feeling. The book has contributed to the widespread tendency of religious thinkers to emphasize the nonrational element of religion. It may be regarded as a modification and outgrowth of the liberal tradition within Protestantism.

A THEOLOGY FOR THE SOCIAL GOSPEL

Author: Walter Rauschenbusch (1861-1918)
Type of work: Christian social ethics
First published: 1917

Principal Ideas Advanced

Just as the social gospel needs theological grounds to be effective, so theology needs social concern to be vital and relevant in the modern world.

The social gospel is neither alien nor new; it exists as an authentic part of the Christian faith and seeks to focus religious interest on contemporary ethical problems.

By its stress on the pervasiveness of sin in the corporate and collective efforts of men and on social salvation, the social gospel is a corrective to the one-sided focus on personal sin and individual salvation.

The doctrine of the Kingdom of God is central in a theology for the social gospel.

Occasionally a book is hailed as the epitome of an entire movement. This is the case with Walter Rauschenbusch's *A Theology for the Social Gospel*. Walter Rauschenbusch was one of the most distinguished leaders of the influential "Social Gospel Movement" which was prominent in American Church life from 1875 to 1930. His name is synonymous with that movement.

Rauschenbusch published his first book in America in 1907 (earlier he wrote *Leben Jesu*, 1895, and three other works in German) in order to discharge a debt. The book was *Christianity and the Social Crisis*, and the debt he owed, in his own words, was "to the working people on the west side of New York City," whose life he had shared for eleven years as pastor of the Second German Baptist Church, on the borders of "Hell's Kitchen."

In his last and greatest work, *A Theology for the Social Gospel,* Rauschenbusch never ceased to feel that he still owed "help to the poor and plain people" who were his friends. This volume consists of lectures delivered under the auspices of the Nathaniel W. Taylor Foundation at Yale Divinity School. The author sought to construct a systematic theology large enough to match and vital enough to back a social gospel. He wanted to furnish intellectual grounds for the social gospel. This meant no less a task than to conceive Christian doctrine in social terms and to relate the Christian message to the regeneration of the social order.

Thus, the book gives the lie to those who charge that the social gospel is without theological foundations and convictions. Rauschenbusch writes with power and passion. Some of the passages in this book read as if they were straight from the prophetic writings of Amos or Isaiah. This modern prophet brought to his task a disciplined intellect, which shows signs of his professorship for twenty-one years at Rochester Theological Seminary. Never turgid in style, his scholarship is blended with the social compassion and zeal which characterized his vigorous ministry.

Many of the issues that the author deals with in this book have a familiar contemporary ring. He stressed the importance of relating theological thought and social concern. Failure to relate theology and social ethics means that the choice is between an "unsocial system of theology and an irreligious system of social salvation." The social gospel without theology is ineffective, but theology without social relevance is dead. The interplay and interdependence of theology and ethics will result in a purifying influence upon theology. When ethics inspires theology, religion is more sensitive to ethical righteousness. But lest it become sterile intellectualism, theology always stands in need of the kind of rejuvenation that ethics can give to it. Hence, the social gospel is a reformatory force within theology.

Often the social gospel is pitted against a personal gospel of individual salvation. This debate between a personal or social gospel remains unresolved today. It is true that the social gospel movement centered attention on the social side, perhaps as a corrective to the preoccupation of conservative Christian thinkers who stressed personal salvation. However, among the best thinkers of the social gospel movement, and particularly in the thought of Rauschenbusch, the social gospel and individual salvation are not mutually exclusive.

Religion seeks nothing less than the wholeness and unity of life, Rauschenbusch claims. It speaks to man's total existence, both personal and social. When the Gospel becomes narrowly individualistic and places excessive emphasis on personal salvation and on the sin in the individual human heart, it fails to comprehend the pervasiveness of sin in man's collective efforts and in the institutions of society. It is against this oversimplified view of individual sin and personal salvation that much of the polemic of the social gospel movement was waged.

Walter Rauschenbusch argued that

theology must be related to the human situation. Great religious thinkers who wrote seminal theological treatises were leaders whose ideas responded to the challenge of specific situations. Thus, St. Paul wrote in the context of a fresh religious experience and of practical problems facing particular Christian communities. Luther's doctrine of "justification by faith" grew out of his profound religious experience and of the great social, political, and religious upheaval of his time. In like manner, the social gospel is a response to the "consciousness of vast sins and sufferings and the longing for righteousness and a new life."

The social gospel concentrates religious interest on the major ethical problems of social life. It despises the tithing of mint, anise, and cumin, and it seeks to deal with the weightier matters of God's law, with justice and mercy. It is neither alien nor new, but authentic as a vital part of the historic Christian faith. It is found in the Old and continued in the New Testament. Far from its being alien or novel, the gospel rests on the most ancient and authentic foundation of the Apostles and Prophets. The social gospel restored the doctrine of the Kingdom of God that John the Baptist and Jesus proclaimed, a doctrine which was obscured and forgotten by theologians who developed their system along individualistic lines.

Rauschenbusch's major aim is to examine theological doctrines to discover how the social gospel affects them and to see how these doctrines could give more adequate expression to the social gospel. He deals extensively with the doctrines of sin and redemption. He also considers such theological topics as the Kingdom of God, God, the Holy Spirit, revelation, the sacraments, eschatology, and the atonement.

In his discussion of sin, Rauschenbusch acknowledges that one of the widespread criticisms of the social gospel is that its exponents fail to appreciate the power of human sin and tend to put the blame for wrongdoing on the social environment. Although he stresses the social reality of sin, Rauschenbusch himself never fails to recognize sin in its personal dimension. Sin is defined as selfishness, sensuousness, and godlessness. It is always revealed in contrast to righteousness. The view that selfishness is the essence of sin is more in harmony with the social gospel than the notion that sin is rebellion against God.

Rauschenbusch explains the nature of sin in the following passage: "The sinful mind, then, is the unsocial and anti-social mind. To find the climax of sin we must not linger over a man who swears, or sneers at religion, or denies the mystery of the trinity, but put our hands on social groups who have turned the patrimony of a nation into the private property of a small class, or have left the peasant labourers cowed, degraded, demoralized, and without rights in the land. When we find such in history, or in present-day life, we shall know we have struck real rebellion against God on the higher levels of sin."

Traditional theology has overworked the doctrine of original sin. Rauschenbusch contends it has overlooked the fact that sin is transmitted through social customs and institutions, through traditions which the individual absorbs from his social group. A theology for the social gospel must argue that original sin is partly social. It is transmitted from generation to generation not only by biological propagation, but also by social assimilation. The result is corporate sin or a "Kingdom of Evil."

Despite our common involvement in a Kingdom of Evil in which we share a collective guilt, the social gospel holds forth the possibility of personal and social salvation, and the necessity of redeeming the historical life of man from social wrongs. Salvation involves a transformation in which man turns from self to God and humanity. Man's selfishness is replaced by a loving spirit in conformity to the loving impulses of the spirit of God. Faith becomes not mere belief or the submission of the mind to affirmations of dogma; rather, faith means prophetic vision, hope in a righteous and fraternal social order, and affirming our fellowship with God and man.

The doctrine of the Kingdom of God is central in a theology for the social gospel. With it, the task of redeeming the social order and of proclaiming and applying social morality has a firm footing. The doctrine of the Kingdom occupied a chief place in the teachings of Jesus, but it was reduced to a pathetic remnant in the course of Christian thought. As a result, the ethical force and revolutionary ferment of Christianity was weakened. The Church was left without a corrective force, and salvation was viewed in terms of an individual's relation to the Church and to the future life, but not in relation to the task of saving the social order.

Contrary to much popular misconception, Rauschenbusch did not hold the naïve view that the Kingdom of God would soon be ushered in on earth by dint of man's own labors. Others in the social gospel movement may have thought in such optimistic terms, but Rauschenbusch wrote that the Kingdom of God was initiated by Jesus Christ and will be brought to fulfillment by the power of God in His own time. He believed that the Kingdom of God is always both present and future: "The Kingdom of God is always coming, but we can never say, 'Lo, here.'" Rauschenbusch did express hope, however, in the progressive development of mankind toward the Kingdom of God. The living marks of the Kingdom are worth of personality, freedom, growth, love, solidarity, and service. He regarded our labor for the Kingdom here and now as preparation for our participation in it hereafter.

Rauschenbusch indicates how the social gospel is related to the doctrine of God by his contention that man's conceptions of God are shaped by the social conditions of his environment. Under tyrannous conditions the idea of God is apt to be tainted with despotism and to stress God's right of arbitrary decision. When Jesus called God "our Father," he democratized the conception of God. As long as economic and political despotisms prevail, the triumph of the Christian idea of God as a loving Father will never be final. The transcendent conception of God as dwelling on high, apart from human life, is a natural basis for autocratic ideas about God. The view that God is immanent in humanity, and that He moves and lives in the life of mankind, is the natural basis for democratic ideas about him. God is the ground of all social unity; He transcends all human barriers so that all become unified by a spiritual oneness and social solidarity.

The work of the Holy Spirit gives

evidence of the social nature of religion. Old Testament prophets were not solitary figures, but were surrounded by religious groups to whom and for whom they spoke in moments of inspired social consciousness. Genuine prophecy arises where fervent religious experience combines with a democratic spirit, a strong sense of social injustice, and free utterance.

Rauschenbusch was convinced that the era of prophetic Christianity had just begun, and that the "social gospel is the voice of prophecy in modern life." American Christianity stands forever indebted to the eloquent and prophetic voice of Walter Rauschenbusch. He made Christian faith relevant to the abuses, injustices, and social miseries growing out of the industrial revolution during the first few decades of the twentieth century.

THE PLAN OF SALVATION

Author: Benjamin B. Warfield (1851-1921)
Type of work: Calvinist apologetics
First published: 1918

Principal Ideas Advanced

The basic issue with respect to the nature of God's plan of salvation is between the naturalists, who hold that man saves himself, and the supernaturalists, who maintain that God saves man.

The entire organized Church—Orthodox Greek, Roman Catholic, and Protestant, whether Lutheran, Reformed, or Arminian—opposes naturalism by confessing that whatever part man plays in the saving process is subsidiary and is itself the effect of the divine operation; it is God and God alone who saves the soul.

The fundamental issue among supernaturalists concerns the immediacy of the saving operations of God: Does God save men by the immediate operations of His grace (as the evangelicals contend), or does He act upon men only through instrumentalities established for that purpose (as the sacerdotalists maintain)?

The Plan of Salvation was written by Benjamin B. Warfield, who was a Professor at Princeton Theological Seminary from 1887 until 1921. During his lifetime Warfield was considered by many to be the leading orthodox protestant theologian in the English speaking world.

The Plan of Salvation is concerned with an examination of those divine activities which center around, and have as their proximate goal, the salvation of sinful man. That God acts upon a plan in all His activities is a presupposition of theism. To believe in a personal God who has immediate control of the world He has made is to believe in a plan underlying all that God does, including what He does to save man. For believers, therefore, there can be no question as to the reality of God's plan. The only question that can arise concerns the nature of God's plan. The latter question has been answered in many different ways, not only by non-Christians, but by Christians themselves. The first chapter of the present work surveys and critically examines views which have been held by large parties in the Church. It is followed by separate chapters on autosoterism, sacerdotalism, universalism, and Calvinism.

The most profound division with respect to the plan of salvation is for Warfield the cleft between the naturalists and the supernaturalists. The issue here is whether God has planned to leave man completely responsible for saving himself, or whether He has planned to intervene and thereby to bring salvation to man. In other words, does God save man or does man save himself?

The naturalists have maintained that salvation is from ourselves. Such a doctrine of autosoterism, self-salvation, is in effect the denial of the true God and the gift of His grace.

The influence of the notion that salvation can be secured by man's own wisdom and power was first systematically presented in the Christian church by Pelagius (c.360-c.420), the British monk and theologian, whose system is characteristic of such ideas of salvation which have succeeded it.

Pelagius built a complete autosoteric scheme upon the central principle of the plenary ability of the human will; since man has been endowed with an inalienable freedom of will, he is fully competent to do all that is required of him. Pelagius denied any "fall" suffered by mankind. Man does not inherit any sin or weakness from his past history. He is born in the same condition of innocence in which Adam was created, and throughout his life he continues in the same condition in which he is born. Adam's Fall is at most a bad example which no one need follow unless he so chooses. Even our own past sins do not in any way abridge our ability to keep God's commandments and to be henceforth free from sin. Man can at any moment cease all sinning and be perfect from that very instant. To this great gift of freedom God has added the gifts of the Law and the Gospel to point to the way of righteousness and to persuade man to walk in it. The gift of Christ supplies expiation for past sins for all who will do God's will, and it sets a good example. Everyone who turns from his sins and acts righteously is accepted by God and rewarded according to his deeds. The grace of God, in the sense of inward help from God, is not needed. The Pelagian meaning of grace refers solely to the fundamental endowment of man with an inalienable freedom of will, together with the inducements God has given man to choose the good.

According to Warfield, the entire Christian Church has taken an official stand against naturalistic Pelagianism. The class of supernaturalists is divided, however, into two main divisions, the evangelicals and the sacerdotalists.

The sacerdotalists and the evangelicals agree that salvation is wholly from God. They differ, however, in that the former hold that God operates indirectly upon the human soul though instrumentalities, as the means by which His saving grace is communicated to men; whereas the latter insist that the welfare of the soul depends directly and solely upon the grace of God.

The sacerdotal principle finds expression in the Roman Catholic Church. The Church teaches that what God does for the salvation of man He does through the mediation of the Church, to which, having endowed it with powers adequate to the task, He has committed the whole work of salvation.

The Roman Catholic Church does not regard itself as having superseded Christ's work, but as having taken over that work. The Church believes itself to be a reincarnation of Christ whereby His redemptive mission is continued and completed. Christ perpetuates His offices as prophet, priest, and king through the Church, which interprets doctrine with infallible authority, mediates between God and man, provides the propitiatory sacrifice of the Mass, and secures the absolute obedience of its members.

With respect to the actual salvation of individual men, the sacerdotalists maintain that God wills the salvation of all men by an antecedent conditional will and that He provides for their salvation in the Church by its sacramental system. The actual work of the Church, however, is accomplished through second causes by which the application of grace is effected. Those who are saved by obtaining the sacraments, and those who are lost by missing them, are saved or lost by the natural working of secondary causes rather than by divine appointment.

Evangelicals refuse to follow the sacerdotalist in their separation of the soul from the direct contact with and immediate dependence upon God the Holy Spirit as the source of all grace. The evangelical is convinced that God deals with each sinful soul directly and for itself. There is in Protestantism, however, a tendency to construe the saving activities of God universally instead of individualistically. Evangelical Arminianism and Evangelical Lutheranism hold that what God does with respect to salvation, He does not for individual men as individuals but for all men alike as men, without distinction. Such a position is, however, fraught with difficulties. For if God alone works salvation and works on all men alike, all men without exception must be saved. However, if salvation depends in part upon man, then evangelicalism must be abandoned in favor of the naturalism of autosoterism. If God's gracious activities are not extended to all men alike, then universalism must give way to particularism. Consistent evangelicalism and consistent universalism are incompatible unless all men are saved. Such a solution, however, contradicts the clear teaching of Scripture that not all men are saved. The attempts that have been made to overcome this difficulty inevitably lead by one path or another to the destruction of the supernaturalistic principle by transferring salvation from God to man.

In opposition to all attempts to understand the operations of God as directed toward universal salvation, Warfield defends Calvinism as the most consistent form of Christianity. Calvinism maintains that the saving operations of God are not directed to those individuals who are not saved. Calvinism is frankly a particularism. The Calvinist insists that in His saving operations God deals solely with those who are actually saved. The acceptance of the supernaturalism of salvation and of the immediacy of the operations of divine grace necessitates the acceptance of particularism; and the denial of particularism is tantamount to the denial of the immediacy of divine grace, that is, of evangelicalism, and of the supernaturalism of salvation, that is, of Christianity. To reject particularism is logically to reject Christianity.

Discrimination is placed by some Calvinists, the Supralapsarians, at the root of all God's dealings with His creatures. The very fact that God has any creatures at all is evidence of discrimination. In fact, everything God decrees concerning His creatures He decrees in order that He may discriminate between them. The decree of "election" by which men are made to differ is therefore placed *logically prior,* in the order of decrees, to the decree of creation, at least insofar as the latter is concerned with man as such. The decree of election is thus logically prior in the order of thought to the decree of the Fall.

Other Calvinists, the Sublapsarians or Infralapsarians hold that election is specifically concerned with salvation, so that the principle of particularism, in the sense of discrimination, belongs in the sphere of God's soteriological, not in that of his cosmical, creation. Election is regarded as logically prior to those operations which concern salvation, but not to those which concern the Creation or the Fall. In the order of decrees, election is placed at the head of those decrees of God which look to salvation, but election falls into position in the order of thought *after* the decrees of Creation and the Fall. The latter refer to all men alike, since all men have been created and all have fallen. The decree of election precedes the decree of redemption and its application, but it follows logically after that of the Fall.

Still other Calvinists are post-Redemptionists. Because of the Scriptural teaching concerning the universal reference of the redemption of Christ, and because of their desire to base the universal offer of salvation on an equally universal provision, the post-Redemptionists postpone the introduction of the particularistic principle to a point within the saving operations of God. They therefore introduce the decree of election, in the order of thought, after the decree of redemption in Christ.

Post-Redemptionists, who are also called Amyraldianists or Hypothetical Universalists, differ among themselves in that some hold to a Congruism or Pajonism, that is, to the principle that grace comes to those upon whom the Holy Spirit operates in His gracious suasion in a fashion that is carefully and infallibly adapted by Him to secure their adhesion to the Gospel. It can thus be said that men voluntarily come to Christ and are joined to Him by the free act of their own unrenewed wills, even though only those come to Christ whom God has selected so to persuade to come to Him that they certainly will come of their own free wills.

Warfield recognizes Supralapsarians, Infralapsarians, post-Redemptionists, and Pajonists as Calvinists insofar as particularism is concerned, but he rejects the post-Redemptionists as inconsistent Calvinists who turn away from a substitutive atonement by holding that Christ died to open the way of salvation to sinners rather than to die in their stead. Pajonists depart even further from pure Calvinism in that their view also denies the whole substance of that regeneration and renovation by which, in the creative work of the Spirit, we are made new creatures.

There is for the true Calvinist no antinomy in saying that Christ died for His people and for the world. Unless it is Christ who actually saves His people, there is no reason to believe that there will ever be a saved world. His people may be few today, but the world will be His tomorrow.

It is the Calvinist alone who has warrant to believe in salvation, whether of the individual or the world. Both rest upon the sovereign grace of God, and for Warfield all other ground is shifting sand.

THE EPISTLE TO THE ROMANS

Author: Karl Barth (1886-)
Type of work: Biblical commentary
First published: 1919

Principal Ideas Advanced

The voice of the Apostle Paul has relevance in our times.

Paul's theme of the "power of the resurrection" is a sign of judgment upon all things temporal, and a sign of hope in the Coming World of God.

Christian religion and morality fall under judgment with all things temporal, but they direct us to God's grace and to man's obligation in response to grace.

There are two reasons why Karl Barth created a stir in theological circles with his Biblical commentary *The Epistle to the Romans*. In the first place, he challenged the theological specialists by venturing to write a commentary with a different aim from the one usually pursued by those devoted to modern objective, historical scholarship. Barth did not reject the methods of Biblical criticism, as conservative scholars do. But he was inclined to treat lightly the notion of historical objectivity, and he denied that there is any theological worth in commentaries which have no higher goal than to reconstruct the minutiae of the Biblical period. Especially he deplored the practice of making modern liberal humanism the criterion for judging the contents of Biblical writings. Turning his back on the professional exegetes, he declared it his purpose to let the Apostolic message break with full force upon our age, which, in his opinion, needed to hear once again the Gospel message.

The second reason why Barth's commentary attracted attention is that the message which he discovered in Romans turned out to be a violent attack on the whole nineteenth century spirit of liberalism, progressivism, and humanism. It is true that voices had been raised against these optimistic notions before Barth's work appeared, and, following the first World War, many voices joined his. But Protestantism, which had in many quarters become simply the official expression of the spirit of the age, could remain complacent as long as these troubled liberal spirits and "enemies of the people" remained outside the Church. But Karl Barth was a promising young theologian, a member of an eminent family of scholars, and the pastor of a rural church in Switzerland; when he ventured to suggest that Western culture is no more acceptable in God's sight than that of Nineveh and Rome, theologians had to stop whatever they were doing and answer him. His book rapidly went through several editions, and its author, appointed to a professorship, shortly became the dean of Protestant theologians.

Barth's *The Epistle to the Romans,* although it bears little resemblance to the technical commentaries of modern research, is nonetheless in the great tradition of Biblical exegesis. The author has written with a host of works at his hand, and he is in a position to report not merely what Paul says but also what others have understood by the Apostle's words. But he never allows the details of scholarship to dull the edge of his exposition. Perhaps the reader marvels most that a man can sustain a single theme over so many pages without exhausting the resources of language and imagination. For, in a sense, Barth's *The Epistle to the Romans* is a *tour de force*. Barth, in writing as if Paul had only one message, has displayed no little genius, not merely in the singleness of mind with which he holds to a paradoxical thesis, but also in the subtlety with which he implements this theme by reference to the Apostle's writing. Much of the power of the work derives from the relentlessness with which it presses its one astonishing claim. Yet Barth, in a later preface, his *Shorter Commentary on Romans,* acknowledges that there is greater variety (though also greater monotony) in his *Romans* than he had acknowledged, and that were the commentary to be rewritten, many threads then unnoticed would have to be unraveled.

The theme of the Biblical book of Romans, according to Barth, is "the infinite qualitative distinction" between time and eternity, or between man and God. Wherever God's revelation appears, it will appear as judgment (*krisis*) upon the world. Consequently, eschatology is central to Christian theology. At least, such is Barth's assumption in regard to the theme; in answer to objectors, he appeals to the work for confirmation: "If Paul was not primarily concerned with the permanent *krisis* of the relation between time and eternity, but was dealing with some other theme, the absurdity of a false assumption will become clear in the course of a detailed examination of the text."

The key, perhaps, to Barth's reading of Paul lies in his identification of Paul's "gospel" with the Resurrection of Christ from the grave. "The Gospel of the Resurrection is the action, the supreme miracle, by which God, the unknown God dwelling in light unapproachable, the Holy One, Creator, and Redeemer, makes himself known." But the Resurrection is not to be viewed as an ordinary miracle, a "supernatural" event; that is, as an event which, although exceptional so far as our experience is concerned, is nevertheless relative to it. On the contrary, the Resurrection brings us to the ultimate limit of human experience; it confronts us with "the Primal Origin" in the presence of which all our creaturely notions and expectations are dissolved and reconstituted on a different foundation. For the Resurrection of Christ is the intersection of eternity and time, a moment in which the absolute antithesis between man's righteousness and God's righteousness becomes manifest.

The power of the Resurrection manifests itself in two ways. First, it condemns all human "possibilities," shatters all human hopes, and shakes the foundation of every human enterprise. In the light of God's eternity, all human light is darkness. There is, indeed, what Barth calls the "wisdom of night," an awareness of the tragedy of man's condition. But no advantage comes of such awareness because it lacks the power of grace; hence, despairing of every "possibility," men resign their humanity and plunge themselves into sensuality and greed; or they fasten determinedly upon science, morality, statecraft, or religion in order to secure for themselves an island in the sea of despair and thereby to preserve at least one "possibility." Even religion, which Barth calls the "last human possibility," the one to which man flees when all else has failed, stands under eternal judgment, for religion attempts "with criminal arrogance" to mix together the temporal and the eternal.

There is a second way in which the power of the Resurrection manifests itself. Besides condemning all human "possibility," the Resurrection also discloses the divine "impossibility." That Jesus of Nazareth should rise from the dead is, in Barth's words, "*the* possibility which possesses all the marks of impossibility." Thus, instead of leaving mankind to perish in the hopelessness of his temporality, as does the "wisdom of night," the Resurrection awakens in man "the memory of Eternity." Christ's resurrection was not the first occasion of eternity's breaking into time; history shows different points at which men were enabled to take the divine perspective on themselves. Even in paganism, there were those who saw in the corruptible a "parable of the incorruptible," and concluded that, "though the world is incapable of redemption, yet there is a redemption for the world." The Resurrection does not overthrow these "signposts"; rather, it establishes them and gives them direction. For here is proclaimed the invisibility of God and the reality of that "new creation," uninhabitable by flesh and blood, for which our whole creation groans. In His death, Christ is completely at one with our tragic condition; in His resurrection, He foreshows God's "decision to erect His justice by the complete renewal of heaven and earth."

Barth warns us against holding either of these ways without the other. For man, the truth of Eternity must always be dialectical. Barth finds a dialectical movement in Romans itself in that a chapter devoted to the righteousness of men is followed by a chapter devoted to the righteousness of God; a chapter devoted to history is followed by one devoted to the Coming Day; a chapter devoted to the ambiguity of religion is followed by one devoted to the decisiveness of Grace. For this reason, one should not read the commentary by snatches. Indeed, a person needs to know the substance of the whole book in order rightly to assess the meaning of any part, which, in a sense, is as true of Paul as it is of Barth. As every Bible student knows, Romans falls into two parts; the former part (Chapters 1 to 11) dealing with doctrine, the latter (Chapters 12 to 16) dealing with ethics. Barth is especially concerned lest his readers try to understand his commentary on

Paul's doctrine without his commentary on Paul's ethics, or vice versa.

We have seen something of the ambiguity which, according to Barth, is characteristic of religion. As the "last human possibility" it speaks both a "yes" and a "no"; that is, it partly affirms the world and denies God, and it partly denies the world and affirms God. Genuine religion, according to Barth, always bears the impress of revelation. In every oracle, rite, or sanctuary is some vestige of an erstwhile manifestation of eternity. Such religious appurtenances are, however, no more than burned-out craters or empty canals. They belong entirely to this world; though religious persons depend on the appurtenances of religion, nothing transcendent or eternal is to be found there. Should we, then, abandon religion? Yes, in the sense that we must not have any faith in it. But, in another sense, we must never abandon religion; as the "last human possibility," religion bears witness of our sinfulness and rebellion and prompts us to call out for forgiveness. Contrary to what many suppose, religion brings uneasiness and dread, not peace and contentment. Its ultimate expression is a nameless fear, together with the question, which it can never resolve, "What are we then to do?" In this sense, religion is a proper attitude for man. The difficulty lies in sustaining it without becoming self-righteous and supposing that God is obliged to visit us because we wait on Him.

Christianity, it must be remembered, is a religion, and falls under the same judgment as the rest. Because the Church is the place where the invisible was once and for all transformed into a visible thing, its members and particularly its leaders are under constant temptation to suppose that the divine presence tabernacles here in time. Barth was greatly impressed by Dostoevski's story "The Grand Inquisitor" (in *The Brothers Karamazov*, 1880). In the sinister churchman there represented, Barth saw the Church's perennial effort to "humanize the divine," and its ambition to substitute a kingdom of this world for that Kingdom which flesh and blood cannot inherit. Thus, the Church is guilty of "criminal arrogance." On the other hand, those who attack the Church ordinarily do so on the assumption that they possess some righteousness or hope which is superior to that which the Church holds out, and this is even more arrogant. We must, says Barth, hold the Church and the Gospel in tension. In condemning the Church, we must preserve our solidarity with it, realizing that we condemn ourselves. This is the real tribulation of the Church, to know its guilt, and to recognize its guilt as unavoidable. But precisely in tribulation there is hope—the hope of the Resurrection in which God justifies himself by justifying the ungodly.

Barth finds much the same kind of ambiguity in ethics and in politics as he finds in religion. The keynote of Christian ethics, as he reads Romans, is "disturbance." The Resurrection disturbs life, because obedience to the power of grace therein revealed demands that one attack the world, one's fellowmen, and one's own self. On the primary level, revelation discloses to man the dominion of sin over his life, and also the fact that sin's dominion has no other foundation than man's freedom. With this discovery it becomes impossible for man to live, either as a conservative or as a revolutionary, either in the world or in flight from it. In ethics, as in dogmatics, the only conclusion is *soli deo gloria.* One can only sacrifice his life and wait for God's judgment. On the secondary level, there is, according to Barth, a positive and a negative "possibility" set before the Christian. On the positive side, obedience to the Resurrection demands that, while living under the conditions of this world, man shall bear in his body the marks of the divine transformation of the world; that is, his life must become legible as a protest against human *eros* and as a parable of divine *agape.* This requirement, however, issues in no scheme of reform and gives no ground for moral indignation. Our love for men, says Barth, is itself trivial, but it is a parable of God's love for men. On the negative side, obedience to the Resurrection demands of man that he live humbly and that he avoid the pretense and ambition, and, in a word, the "titanism" which characterize the wisdom of this world—taking all care, however, lest he become arrogant and in warring against the titan make himself a titan.

Following Paul's words about ruling power, Barth has a word concerning the believer's duty toward the state. He calls the state "the great negative possibility." It is "great" because it gathers to itself the totality of human pretension, and it is "negative" because it arrogates to itself the possibility that belongs only to God. Barth says that revolutionaries are justified insofar as they find intolerable the pretenses of any existing order, but they are condemned when they raise their hand against it, because in doing so they are presuming to execute a judgment that belongs to God. What the revolutionary actually intends, according to Barth, is to obviate the necessity of the Resurrection and to actualize the "impossible possibility" by man's strength alone. It is better, says Barth, to choose the "possible possibility" which is proportionate to our situation, the possibility of living in contentment under the usurpation and of leaving judgment to God. This view, however, is far from justifying the legitimist, who seeks to identify God's justice with the existing order. The ultimate antithesis to the "great negative possibility" is not the "possible possibility" of the political reactionary, but the "great positive possibility" of love. The possibility of this "possibility" places the reactionary in the wrong, along with the revolutionary; in loving, one cannot wish for either the old or the new, but only for The Coming World.

Barth finds an interesting contradiction in the ending of Paul's Romans. Where the Apostle enjoins his followers from making their Christian freedom a stumbling-block to weaker brethren, Paul is, says Barth, letting Romans "dissolve itself." This ultimate perception of the ambiguity of man's condition forbids any man, even the Apostle, setting up a scheme of dogma and ethics. Nothing is to be done but to point to the Resurrection. Thus, there should be no Paulinism—and *a fortiori* no Barthianism, as Barth is the first to acknowledge.

THEOLOGY AS AN EMPIRICAL SCIENCE

Author: Douglas Clyde Macintosh (1877-1948)
Type of work: Scientific theology
First published: 1919

Principal Ideas Advanced

Religious experience at its best provides the empirical ground for a scientific theology.

The presupposition peculiar to theology is the assumption that God exists; it is left to scientific theology to determine the properties of the divine object.

The empirical data for scientific theology come from revelations of the divine, as in the person and work of Christ, and in the Christian experience of salvation.

The one fundamental attribute of God, from the point of view of empirical theology, is absoluteness; theology also discovers God to have such moral attributes as holiness, justice, love, and mercy.

The theologian has always been eager to justify his profession, but the urge was especially strong in the early twentieth century when the growing eminence of science threatened to put theology into the shade forever. Douglas Clyde Macintosh, who at the time of writing *Theology As an Empirical Science* was Dwight Professor of Theology at Yale University, attempted the defense of theology not by maintaining, as theologians often do, that the attempt to understand God, although unscientific, is the most significant effort to be made by the mind and spirit of man, but by insisting that theology is itself, or at least *can* be, an empirical science. To be sure, Macintosh did not suggest that the data of theology are of the same sort as those which provide the physical sciences with their content and starting-point; he maintained, rather, that the data of an empirical theology come from "religious experience at its best," but he did regard religious experience as reliable and as subject to formulation and development through use of the inductive method.

Although nontheological scientists might quarrel with Macintosh's use of the term "science"—and, indeed, he anticipated such criticism—no one who has read Macintosh can deny that he has made every reasonable attempt to clarify and organize religious experience and to realize its implications. Perhaps the data of a "scientific" theology are not as hard as Macintosh supposed, but given the sorts of experiences which Macintosh regarded as indicating the presence of the divine, whether or not fashioned by the faithful expectations of the believer, it is reasonable to conclude that knowledge about the implications of religious experience is possible. It was to much the same systematic development of religious ideas, on the basis of religious experience, that the British philosopher H. D. Lewis was later to devote his effort in *Our Experience of God* (1959).

Macintosh begins his inquiry with an analysis of theological method. He discusses traditional theology, with its emphasis on ecclesiastical and Biblical sources; rationalistic theology, with its emphasis on *a priori* truths to be developed deductively; mystical theology, paradoxically attempting to derive knowledge from ineffable experience; eclectic theology, drawing upon various sources and experiences which more limited theologies count on exclusively; and, finally, scientific theology, the "new" theology, not yet born, but the voice of the future.

Macintosh quotes with approval T. H. Huxley's remark, "If anyone is able to make good the assertion that his theology rests upon valid evidence and sound reasoning, then it appears to me that such theology must take its place as a part of science." Macintosh also assents to the words of William James: "Let empiricism once become associated with religion . . . and I believe that a new era of religion as well as of philosophy will be ready to begin."

The problem, then, is not *whether* theology should be empirical, but *how* it is to be empirical. Macintosh suggests that a scientific theology is possible if theology turns from religious pragmatism to a scientifically critical pragmatism. He distinguishes between a partial working-out of an idea and "that working which constitutes full verification. . . ." To use James's terminology, which Macintosh does not adopt in this context, religious pragmatism can become scientific only if it becomes "tough-minded." To be tough-minded the theologian must be content with nothing less than the rigorous procedures of the empirical scientist; like the physical scientist, the theologian must identify his data and frame his inductive generalizations in such a way that they can be justified by reference to the data.

A scientific theology will begin, Macintosh suggests, with an examination of the presuppositions of theology. The fundamental assumption which the scientific theologian makes is that God exists; he justifies his presupposition by reference to revelations of the divine to be found in religious experience; his central effort becomes that of discovering the properties of God, and he does not, like the agnostic or skeptic, waste time attempting to prove what only religious experience can make convincing. Just as the physical scientist assumes the existence of material substance, and has some basis in experience for his belief, so the theologian assumes the existence, but not the nature, of God.

Having examined the presuppositions of his science, the theologian then turns to the task of collecting empirical data on the basis of which his laws will be constructed. Finally, on the basis of the laws, theological theory will be devised. Theory construction involves taking advantage of those intuitions provoked by religious experience, taking as a practically necessary hypothesis whatever man's religious and moral needs demand, and framing theories as to the nature of the religious object—God—whose existence prescientific experience insisted upon.

According to Macintosh, sciences other than theology may provide theology with well-established results which can serve as theological presuppositions. Thus, the physical facts of the universe, as established by the physical sciences, may be taken for granted; the immensity of the universe, the conservation of energy, the evolution of man and society—these discoveries become the presuppositions of theology. Of special relevance to theology, however, are the findings of those scientific activities we may call the history and psychology of religion. The central historical claim on which Christian theology depends is the proposition that Jesus of Nazareth lived and that He regarded Himself, at least on occasion, as a Messiah sent by God to prepare for the Kingdom of God. Macintosh regards this claim as probably true, relative to the evidence of history; there may be disagreement as to the precise influence of the Messianic idea on Jesus, but the arguments of all parties appear to come together when the claim is made that Jesus lived, that He acted compassionately, that He preached the love of God and man, and that He died for His beliefs.

Other presuppositions of theology, according to Macintosh's account, are the beliefs that man is a free agent (that is, that his acts are not completely determined by heredity, environment, character, and ideas), the belief that immortality is possible (which is to be presupposed together with the idea that immortality is morally imperative), and the belief that sin (wrong-doing) has evil consequences.

A scientific theology must be based on empirical data, Macintosh insists; and the empirical data for theology are those experiences which may reasonably be taken as revelations of the divine. The author rejects primitive, traditional, and rationalistic accounts of revelatory experience. Like Lewis (whose *Experience of God* has been mentioned), Macintosh begins with the experience of the *presence* of the divine; the divine is revealed to the individual, and only after the revelation of the divine is it possible to frame normative notions, ideas of value.

The divine has been most clearly revealed in the person and works of Christ, Macintosh asserts. A critical examination of historical evidence, together with a consideration of what religious experience suggests in regard to the interpretation of the evidence, leads one to the empirical conclusion that Christ exhibited a divine quality of personality; He was deeply religious, and He depended on God for moral support and received reinforcement in response to prayer. Macintosh does *not* believe that a scientific theology can justify the further claims that Jesus, because of His essentially divine nature, can be identified with God; that the spirit of Jesus existed before Jesus the man began his earthly trials; that it is possible to be in direct communication with Christ through prayer; and, finally, that Jesus could not be equaled or transcended in spiritual quality by another man. (Earlier in his discussion of empirical theology Macintosh declared the belief in the Virgin Birth to be scientifically indefensible.)

Macintosh describes the atoning work of Christ as a revelation of the divine through the moral and religious teaching of Christ and through His acts; Jesus revealed the divine in that He was Himself saved from sin through religious dependence, and He was moved by holy love.

The Christian experience of salvation provides further empirical evidence of the divine. A man knows through experience that his dependence on God is not merely emotionally satisfying; it is practically effective.

In framing the laws of empirical theology, Macintosh writes, one is able to rely on certain "constants." What he calls "the Constant" of empirical theological laws is God Himself, "the necessary objective Factor in religious experience, . . . the Object of active religious dependence, . . . the Source of salvation, i.e., of religious deliverance from evil." Certain variables also must be taken into account: the quality and degree of the individual's responsiveness to the divine, and the religious adjustment involved.

Macintosh then offers as the principal laws of empirical theology two sets of laws: primary theological laws, which he defines as "the laws of volitional experiences," and secondary theological laws, which include the laws of emotional, intellectual, physiological, and social experience. The laws may be described in general as indicating the responsiveness of God to the efforts and reasonable petitions of men; one receives moral power, victory over temptation, peace, joy, and love from Christian effort and success.

It now becomes possible for Macintosh to proceed to the *a posteriori* definition of God's nature. Having begun with the presupposition of the reality of the divine object, and having won through empirical investigation a knowledge of certain laws having to do with the exercise of divine power, it becomes possible to theorize in regard to the divine nature. Macintosh's theories are concerned with the moral and metaphysical attributes of God, with the relation of God to the universe, with eschatological matters, and with the problem of evil.

The fundamental moral attribute of God, according to Macintosh, is *absoluteness*. By "absoluteness" Macintosh does not mean what the absolute idealist means; namely, the completely nonrelational, nonrelative, nonconditioned character of the divine. Macintosh uses the word "absoluteness" in what he calls a "pragmatic and empirical sense" to mean "absolute satisfactoriness as Object of religious dependence, absolute sufficiency for man's religious needs." Empirical theology justifies the claim that God is morally ideal, that He is perfect relative to human needs.

Macintosh analyzes the moral absoluteness of God into the "immanent" attributes of holiness and love, and the "transitive" attributes of justice and mercy, or righteousness and grace. These attributes entail God's granting to man the opportunity for working toward the moral ideal. Since the moral struggle involves freedom, man is free and God becomes both judge and redeemer.

An empirical theology shows that God is not only good, but great. To make His greatness clear, it is necessary to determine God's metaphysical attributes. Once again, the fundamental attribute is God's absoluteness, His being the "absolutely dependable Object of dependence and Source of salvation." But God is known empirically not only to be what man needs Him to be, but also *not* to be what man needs Him *not* to be. Thus, there are negative attributes as well as positive attributes to be determined. The mystics and rationalists have been in error, or at least have not been empirical, in uncritically assigning to God such negative attributes as incorporeality, invisibility, incomprehensibility, immutability, and infinity. An empirical theology shows that the matter is by no means so simple. God cannot be thought of in purely corporeal terms, but since the physical universe may be an expression of the divine spirit, it is possible that there is a divine body. God is invisible considered as spirit, but considered as body, as the physical universe which is moved by His spirit, He may be considered to be visible. God is not completely comprehensible, but it does not follow that He is in no way comprehensible. The situation is much the same as regards other negative attributes; there is no need to think of God as completely impassible (without feeling), as in no way mutable, as completely out of time, and as absolutely unconditioned. In fact, if God is to be the absolutely dependable object of religious devotion, He must be responsive in feeling to man's needs, and He must be able to work within the limits of time and space.

Turning to the positive metaphysical attributes, Macintosh insists upon God's aseity; that is, on His ultimate self-dependence. But God need not be considered to be in every way omnipotent; all that is needed is divine power sufficient to meet the needs of man; it would be idle, as well as empirically meaningless, to assign the power to resolve contradictions to God. God's knowledge is absolutely sufficient relative to man's needs, but it need not be supposed that God possesses useless knowledge. God is immanent to the extent that His presence is needed; He is transcendent in that He is a real source of spiritual power. He is a personality in that He is a rational being, self-conscious and self-directed. He is almost certainly a unity, for no more than one absolute God is necessary. God is a trinity relative to the attempt to conceive the divine One from the practical Jewish point of view (as the Father), from the mystical-philosophical Greek point of view (as the Son), or from a point of view which emphasizes spirit (as the Holy Ghost). Finally, it is possible to know that God exists, whatever His complete nature might be, if one proceeds scientifically from religious experience at its best and most revealing.

Once the attributes of God are agreed upon, it becomes possible to draw certain conclusions concerning the relation of God to the universe. Empirical theology, as Macintosh conceives it, justifies the claim that God preserves and creatively controls the universe He created. But creative control does not involve divine interruption of natural order; a scientific theology is not likely to be sympathetic to the idea of miracles.

Certain eschatological conclusions also follow deductively: a future life is necessary to the consummation of Christian salvation; God's justice and mercy will continue to affect the spirit of man; Heaven is the transcendent reality which makes realization of the moral ideal possible.

Finally, an empirical theology has something to say about the problem of evil. Macintosh asserts that "a world of human free agency is the best possible kind of world." Yet a world of free agency is one which permits suffering through sin and error. Order in the world would seem to entail sensation, thought, free will, and moral salvation; thought corrects sensation; freedom makes creative thinking possible; salvation corrects the errors of thought and action. But salvation demands development of the spirit beyond the present life; thus, immortality is morally necessary. The conclusion seems to be that evil is a necessary accompaniment of the best possible state of affairs, but there is no empirical justification for claiming that the Devil exists.

ON THE ETERNAL IN MAN

Author: Max Scheler (1874-1928)
Type of work: Phenomenology of religion; social criticism
First published: 1921

Principal Ideas Advanced

Religion is an autonomous activity of the mind, an activity independent of conscience and reason; by means of this faculty man knows God as personal Creator and Redeemer.

The collapse of European culture is due to the loss of religious knowledge, a loss which has resulted in an inverted sense of value.

The hope for the future lies in repentance and renewal, in the recovery of objectivity in ethics and in philosophy, and in the emergence of a new hierarchy of value, with Christian faith in the highest place.

The essays which make up *On the Eternal in Man* were written by Max Scheler in the closing years of the first World War. Three of them are technical investigations in the same phenomenological vein as the author's celebrated studies on "resentment" and on "sympathy." They are entitled: "Repentance and Rebirth," "The Nature of Philosophy and the Moral Preconditions of Philosophical Knowledge," and "Problems of Religion: The Renewal of Religion." These studies are followed by two popular lectures, entitled "Christian Love in the Twentieth Century," and "The Reconstruction of European Culture," which serve to point up the relevance of the foregoing investigations to the crisis in contemporary civilization. The relevance is never far to seek, for, as was the case with Augustine, Pascal, and Newman, Scheler's intelligence was always at the beck of his restless heart, and few thinkers were more deeply concerned than he with the sickness that had plunged Europe into war.

Scheler's thesis is presented in the central essay, "Problems of Religion," a book-length study which deserves to be set alongside Rudolph Otto's *The Idea of the Holy* (1917) as a major contribution to the phenomenology of religion. Scheler protests the inadequacy of the genetic accounts of religion which have been put forward by anthropologists and psychologists; he denies that their way is the only scientific way of viewing religion. He likewise denies that the truth of religion can be assimilated either to ethics or to metaphysics. It is his claim, rather, that religion is an autonomous activity of the human spirit, with its own evidence and logic, and with a distinct kind of object. For the most part Scheler's findings agree with those independently arrived at by Otto, for whose work he has unstinted praise. There is, however, this important difference between them, that Otto, laboring upon the foundation of Kantian subjectivism, traces the formal elements of religious thought to the constitution of man's mind, whereas Scheler takes his stand in the older, Augustinian tradition, and maintains that in religion, as in other kinds of knowledge, man discovers the *a priori* in the world of objects.

Scheler holds that Augustine was correct in stating that man has his knowledge of essential being by divine illumination, but that Augustine was prevented from doing justice to this truth because he possessed no philosophical technique other than that of the Neoplatonists. Because of Neoplatonism, Western thinkers have tended to look upon religious and philosophical truth as, either wholly or partly, identical. What is needed, Scheler argues, is a new philosophical technique which will enable reflective men to recognize the uniqueness of religious insight without taking anything away from the independence and authority of reason and conscience, and *vice versa.* It is Scheler's opinion that philosophical phenomenology, as developed by Edmund Husserl (1859-1938), provides a method by which Augustine's insights can be fully exploited.

Following Husserl's method, Scheler has developed, in a separate volume, *Der Formalismus in der Ethik und die materiale Wertethik* (1913-1916), a phenomenology of morals, maintaining the point of view best known to the English-speaking world through Nicolai Hartmann's *Ethics* (1926). According to Scheler and Hartmann, values constitute an objective hierarchy, disclosed to man by means of conscience. Within this hierarchy, says Scheler, the *summum bonum* or highest value is personality; but, because it is no function of the moral judgment to disclose reality to us, conscience is silent on the question whether Ultimate Being is personal.

The faculty by means of which man knows reality is reason or intelligence. But, Scheler argues in the essay entitled "The Nature of Philosophy," one must distinguish carefully between the conditional knowledge given to us by common sense and experimental science, and the unconditional knowledge which is proper to philosophy. The former, for all its practical value, does not reveal to us the nature of reality, because of limitations such as those imposed by our physical make-up, the limited purpose to which it is directed, and the presuppositions which it borrows from its cultural era. Man can, however, free his mind from these limitations by means of the phenomenological technique of "bracketing" them. When he does this, his reason is in a position to investigate essential Being, and to discover certain ultimate truths, notably the following: that there is something, that there is knowledge of it, that some beings are dependent on others, that there is a Being which is not dependent on any other. Philosophy, viewed in this manner, is knowledge of reality. Still, it is a limited knowledge, restricted by the nature of the intellectual act, which can apprehend only essences and their relations. Thus, although philosophy apprehends being, it is unqualified, in the nature of the case, to apprehend being as personal.

Religion, says Scheler, arises out of a third noetic capacity in man, as natural to him as conscience and reason, and even more fundamental; for, in the religious act, man discerns the lineaments of mind and will in the world about him, and, at the same moment, knows that he possesses mind and will himself. Thus, through religion we are able to make existential judgments which intellect and conscience, limited as they are to beholding static essences, cannot make. Philosophy, for example, distinguishes between absolute and relative being, but it is religion which, through the sense of dependence, enables us to affirm that the world is in fact dependent upon God's will and purpose. Or, to return to what was said above concerning the *summum bonum,* through conscience we can see that personality is the highest value, but only through the religious response to divine revelation can we affirm that the Supreme Being is personal.

On these foundations, Scheler proceeds to show the validity, not merely of a natural theology, based on the evidences of mind in man and in nature, but also of a positive theology, based on the revelation of God's will through the disclosures of *homines religiosi,* who, according to Scheler, comprise an important class of leaders, distinct from geniuses, but in many ways comparable to them. Scheler writes as a Roman Catholic, and his purpose at this point of the work is to make intelligible the submission to authority which is fundamental to Christian orthodoxy. Persuaded of the actuality of man's Fall and his dependence for restitution upon divine grace, Scheler tries to do, in modern terms, substantially what Anselm (c.1033-1109) attempted in *Cur deus homo,* even going so far as to offer proof of the necessity for an infallible Church and the impossibility that Christianity should ever be superseded. There are marks of amateurism, however, in Scheler's discussion of theological matters; and the reader is not especially surprised to learn that, in subsequent years, Scheler moved away from many of these traditional notions.

Scheler's efforts to recover objectivity in the realm of spiritual truth is the major thesis of his work, but what he has to say by way of diagnosing Europe's trouble and prescribing for its cure is important as an application of his ideas to the needs of the times.

The horror of World War I was sufficient evidence to sensitive minds that European culture was in deep trouble. Those who wanted to place the blame on Prussia, or on monarchism, or on the armament makers were, in Scheler's opinion, mistaking the symptoms for the disease. The real blame rested on Western civilization, a blame shared in by the Allies and the Central Powers alike. Spokesmen from the Far East were inclined to lay the fault at the feet of Christianity. Scheler's reply is that Christianity cannot be blamed because, since the Middle Ages, Christianity has not determined European culture. On the contrary, humanitarianism has been in revolt against theism, welfarism has taken the place of love of man, and class spirit has disrupted the communal tie. Fundamentally, the trouble is a breakdown in world-order. When modern man dethroned God, he lost his "world" at the same time. Scheler traces the deterioration from century to century, laying the blame partly on Renaissance secularism, and partly on Protestant subjectivism. The eighteenth century, according to Scheler, still revered many Christian values, but these gave way in the nineteenth century to "realism" and "historicism." Thus, according to Scheler, although Christianity was still on many lips at the beginning of the War, Machiavellian policy dominated European life and thought.

Such, in Scheler's diagnosis, is the apostasy of Europe which resulted in world war. The only hope for the future lies in *repentance*. For, says Scheler, contrary to much modern psychology, repentance is a positive act, by means of which guilt is disposed of and past happenings are constructively integrated into a new life-purpose. Without repentance, deterministic despair will paralyze an individual or a society; but by means of repentance, advance to new spiritual levels is possible. Such, we may say, is Scheler's theodicy. Sin and guilt are very much a part of human history; but where these are followed, as they can be, by grace and remission, man emerges a higher being than before he sinned. Scheler claims this is especially the case where the guilt and the repentance are corporate, and he expresses the belief that a new European community will be born if the world crisis issues in collective repentance.

Believing as he did in the objectivity of moral and philosophical truth, Scheler assigned to conscience and to intellect important roles in the reconstruction which lay ahead. Much depended on man's ability to overcome the debilitating effects of French positivism and German transcendentalism. The objective hierarchy of values must be rediscovered, and, so far as possible, made the basis for a new social order, with the economic man subordinated to the citizen, and with the citizen duly respectful of the genius and the *homo religiosus*. Human society, says Scheler, must rest on spiritual foundations, and if it is to flourish, its development cannot be left to economic forces or to political necessity.

Scheler thought, in the months following the Armistice, that the self-knowledge gained during the war might be sufficient to arouse in men the determination necessary to rebuild civilization. Among youth groups and in new political unions, there were signs which he read as pointing toward an authentically human order; and, at the same time, there were signs that the Church might throw off its subservience to bourgeois interests and exercise the leadership needed to bring these secular movements into a living relation with God, whose redeeming grace can alone release from guilt and malice. The war had, in addition, taught many the spirit of sacrifice, and it had showed the possibilities of co-operative activity, which, he hoped, would lead to a kind of guild socialism; guild socialism, in turn, combined with mutual disarmament and political federalism could bring about a new society, based *on the eternal in man.*

CHRISTIANITY AND LIBERALISM

Author: John Gresham Machen (1881-1937)
Type of work: Orthodox Protestant polemics
First published: 1923

PRINCIPAL IDEAS ADVANCED

An examination of the teachings of liberalism in comparison with those of Christianity shows that at every point the two movements are in direct opposition.

Liberalism differs from Christianity in its view of God, of man, of the seat of authority, and of the way of salvation.

Whether it is true or false, liberalism is no mere heresy—no mere divergence at isolated points from Christian teaching; it proceeds from a totally different root, and it constitutes, in essentials, a unitary system of its own.

J. Gresham Machen was on the faculty of Princeton Theological Seminary from 1906 until 1929. From 1929 until his death in 1937, he was Professor of New Testament in Westminster Theological Seminary, an institution that he helped establish. Machen devoted his life to the scholarly defense and exposition of orthodox Protestantism as contained in the Westminster Confession of Faith. Machen's *Christianity and Liberalism,* first published in 1923, sets forth the difference between historic Reformation Protestantism and liberalism or modernism. The book is the clearest and most able statement of the conflict between historic redemptive Protestantism and the modern non-redemptive "liberal" religion.

Machen compares the liberal and the orthodox views of doctrine, of God and man, the Bible, Christ, salvation, and the Church to show that modern liberalism has in fact relinquished everything distinctive of Christianity.

Liberalism frequently regards differences in doctrine as unimportant; it argues that creeds are simply the changing expression of a single Christian experience. From the liberal point of view, creeds are all equally true, if they express Christian experience. Christianity is not a doctrine but a way of life. The liberal puts his trust in the person of Jesus, rather than in what Jesus did; in Jesus' character rather than in the message of His death and resurrection.

Orthodoxy, in contrast to liberalism, contends that Christianity has a doctrinal basis. What Christianity is can be determined by looking at its beginnings. At its inception the Christian movement was not just a way of life, but a way of life based upon a message, upon an account of facts; that is, upon doctrine. The Apostle Paul, for example, certainly did not advocate an undogmatic religion. To remove Paulinism from Christianity is not a solution, the orthodox believer argues, because Paul was not an innovator, as is clear from his relationship to the church at Jerusalem and to the original companions of Jesus. The primitive Church was concerned with what Jesus had done. It was the proclamation of an event that was to redeem the world. Two elements are contained within the Christian message: the narration of the facts, that is, history, and the narration of the facts together with the meaning of the facts; that is, doctrine.

Jesus' disciples did not distort Christianity by basing it upon an event, for Jesus Himself did the same thing. The message Jesus proclaimed in Galilee was the coming of the Kingdom, an event, or a series of events. Jesus not only announced an event, but He announced the meaning of the event. Jesus' teaching was rooted in doctrine because it depended upon the presentation of Jesus' own person, in His Messianic consciousness.

To maintain the doctrinal basis of Christianity does not mean that Christianity is irrelevant to life, nor does it mean that all points of doctrine are equally important, nor does it mean that conservatives and liberals must live in personal animosity, although specifically Christian fellowship between them is impossible, Machen insists.

The rivalry between Christianity and liberalism is further in evidence in the contrasting views of God and man. Modern liberalism frequently is indifferent to any conception of God; it would merely feel His presence. Some liberals would become acquainted with God only through Jesus. Some liberals, though perhaps a decreasing number, think of God as a personal God, as a Father. Liberalism as a whole, however, has broken down the sharp distinction between God and the world, and when it is not consistently pantheistic, it tends toward pantheism.

The liberal view of man follows quite naturally from its doctrine of God. Liberalism has lost the awareness of sin and has supreme confidence in human goodness. Liberalism is rooted in the predominant pagan spirit of present-day Western civilization, a spirit which finds the highest goal of human existence in the harmonious development of existing human faculties.

Orthodox Christianity, in contrast to liberalism, holds that the knowledge of God is the very basis of religion. Theism, the knowledge of one Supreme Person, Maker, and active Ruler of the world is at the very root of the religion of Jesus. Jesus believed in the real existence of a personal God. Neither Jesus nor the New Testament supports the modern view of the Fatherhood of God, and its corollary, the brotherhood of man. What is distinctive in the New Testament teaching about the Fatherhood of God concerns only those who have become followers of Christ. Liberalism has lost sight of the very center and core of Christianity by eradicating the distinction between the creature and the Creator. Liberalism denies the transcendence of God, but orthodox Christianity holds that God is immanent in the world not because He is identical with the world but because He has created it and continues to uphold it.

According to the views of Machen, Christianity regards man as a sinner; unlike liberalism it begins with the consciousness that man is under the just condemnation of God and that his condition can be changed solely by the grace of God, after which change the Christian can proceed to develop every faculty in a higher Christian humanism founded not upon human pride but upon divine grace.

The two great presuppositions of the Christian message, the fact of sin and the presence of the living God, are disregarded by modern liberalism. The divergence between Christianity and liberalism is, however, not limited to presuppositions, but it affects the message itself. This is not surprising when it is remembered that the Bible is the Book through which the Christian message is delivered, and that the modern liberal rejects the notion that the Bible is a true revelation from God, free from error, and that it is an infallible rule of faith and practice. The liberal does not regard the Bible as trustworthy. He may at times give the false impression that Jesus is his authority in religious matters, but the words of Jesus which are regarded as authoritative are only such words as the liberal is willing to select. Jesus is not the real authority, then; the real authority is the liberal principle by which the selection within Jesus' recorded teaching is made. The real authority for liberals, Machen contends, is "Christian experience," and since individual experience is diverse, such authority is no authority at all.

The foundation of liberalism is the shifting emotions of sinful men. Christianity, on the other hand, is founded upon the Bible. Some Christians accept the central message of the Bible although they believe that the message itself rests upon the authority of reliable witnesses without the supernatural guidance of the Spirit of God.

The view which Jesus Himself seems to have had of the Bible not only holds that the contents of the Bible are unique, but that the writers have been preserved from error. The Spirit of God did not dictate the Bible in a mechanical fashion. The doctrine of plenary inspiration, espoused by Machen, does not deny the individuality of the Biblical writers; nor does it ignore their use of ordinary means of acquiring information; nor does it involve a lack of interest in the historical situation which gave rise to the books of the Bible. It simply holds that the Bible is free of error; the account that the Bible gives is true, Machen argues, because the Spirit of God kept the writers from falling into error.

Christianity and liberalism are also sharply opposed in their attitudes toward Jesus, Machen points out. Christians stand in a religious relation to Jesus; liberals do not. To the liberal, Jesus is an example for faith; to the Christian, Jesus is the object of faith. Liberalism regards Jesus as an example and guide; Christianity, as a Savior. Liberalism regards Jesus as the fairest flower of humanity; Christianity regards Jesus as a supernatural Person, indeed as a person who was both God and man. Liberalism rejects the Jesus of the New Testament; it rejects His miracles, and finds in Jesus the highest type of humanity, a man who made such an impression upon His followers that after His death they could not believe He had perished but experienced hallucinations in which they thought they saw Him risen from the dead. The Jesus of the New Testament, in which Christians believe, performed miracles; He is the Savior who voluntarily entered into this world for our salvation, suffered for our sins on the cross, rose again from the dead, and continues to make intercession for us. The imitation of Jesus has a basic place in the Christian life, the orthodox Christian agrees; but the Jesus who can serve as an example is the Jesus of the New Testament, not the Jesus of modern liberal reconstruction. The New Testament Jesus, the Jesus accepted by Christians, primarily offered man, not guidance, but salvation.

To the extent that liberalism is willing to speak of salvation at all, it finds salvation in man; Christianity finds it in an act of God. The message of the Christian Gospel is that God has saved man. A cardinal doctrine of modern liberalism is that the world's evil may be overcome by the world's good.

Christianity teaches that Jesus is the Savior, not because of what He said, not even because of what He was, but because of what He did, because He took upon Himself the guilt of man's sins and bore it, on the cross, in his stead. The atonement taught in the New Testament is a vicarious atonement.

The liberal view of the death of Christ is that it had an effect upon men, not upon God. The liberal is correct in holding that the death of Christ is an example of self-sacrifice which may inspire self-sacrifice in others; it is also true that it shows how much God hates sin and how much He loves men, but these truths are swallowed up in a greater truth, a truth which liberalism denies; namely, that Christ died for man in order to present him faultless before the throne of God.

Christianity is dependent upon history, Machen insists; it is based upon something that happened; it offers tidings of something new; it is exclusive in its claim that Christ is the only means by which man can be saved, so that the Church has the responsibility of proclaiming the Gospel to everyone. Liberalism denies that a person can suffer for the guilt of another, but in so doing it forgets that Jesus was no ordinary person, no mere man, but the eternal Son of God.

Liberals persist in speaking of the sacrifice of Christ as though it were made by someone other than God, thereby forgetting that according to the Christian doctrine of the Cross, it is God Himself, and not another, that makes the sacrifice for sin. The atoning death of Christ, and it alone, makes sinners righteous in God's sight. On the basis of Christ's redeeming work, the Christian dies unto sin, and lives unto God. The work of Christ is applied to the individual Christian by the Holy Spirit. The believer is thus regenerated, and stands in a new relation to God by an act of justification.

The Christian is saved by the object of his faith, by Christ, so that an act of God becomes the beginning of his new life. The regeneration and justification of the sinner is followed by sanctification. In principle the Christian is free from the present evil world, but in practice the battle has just begun.

According to Machen, the liberal regards religion as a means to a higher end; his program has little place for Heaven, and this world is really all in all. The liberal believes that applied Christianity is all there is to Christianity; the Christian believes that applied Christianity is the result of an initial act of God, that man exists for the sake of God, and not conversely.

True Christians are united into the brotherhood of the Christian Church; the true brotherhood of man is the brotherhood of the redeemed, the

Church invisible, which finds expression in the Church visible.

The greatest menace to the visible Church, Machen concludes, comes not from its external enemies but from the presence within its membership of a type of faith and practice which is anti-Christian to the core. It is highly undesirable that liberalism and Christianity should be propagated within the same organization.

THE FAITH OF THE CHRISTIAN CHURCH

Author: Gustaf Aulén (1879-)
Type of work: Theology
First published: 1923

PRINCIPAL IDEAS ADVANCED

Systematic theology can be a descriptive science, though the nature of the description must be adapted to the faith being described.

The holy God saves, judges, and creates, as His love overcomes His wrath and other powers hostile to man, and thus establishes its sovereignty.

In Jesus Christ the love of God was incarnate, became triumphant on the Cross, and thus delivered man, who, under the dominion of the risen Christ, is incorporated into fellowship with God.

The Church, in which Christ continues to be present and active on earth through word and sacrament, will ultimately be transformed into God's perfected Kingdom of glory.

Gustaf Aulén first wrote *The Faith of the Christian Church* in 1923 while professor at the University of Lund, Sweden. The book has since undergone several revisions reflecting the development of Aulén's thought during his professorship and his subsequent episcopate. The book begins with a discussion of faith and theology, after which sections on the doctrine of God, the doctrine of redemption, and the doctrine of the Church follow. Aulén points out that no particular section is exclusively devoted to eschatology (the doctrine of the last things), since eschatology as an essential dimension is implicit throughout the system.

The task of systematic theology, according to Aulén, is not to demonstrate the truth of the Christian faith, nor to prescribe what Christians must believe. It is rather the critical scientific task of describing the Christian faith, which Aulén insists is a given objective reality which can be made the object of scientific study. It is therefore not God Himself who is being described, but the relationship between God and man characteristic of the Christian faith, and the concept of God presupposed in that relationship.

The correlate of faith is revelation. God is revealed in nature and history, but the decisive revelation is in Jesus

Christ. This revelation must be understood in a broad context. No limits may be drawn about it, but no God is recognized other than He who reveals Himself in Christ.

In defining the content of the Christian faith, Aulén distinguishes between "motifs" and "forms of expression." There is a primary meaning (motif) of the Christian faith to which one must penetrate, a meaning which remains the same though forms of expression change, and is not to be identified with any particular form of expression, whether ancient or modern.

The primary meaning of the Christian faith is Biblically determined. Nevertheless, Aulén affirms, the Spirit of God has continued its activity after the closing of the canon, so that tradition has a legitimate place in so far as it expresses and interprets anew what is manifest or latent in the Biblical message. Tradition can be understood as a series of confessions, the first of which, namely, the New Testament confession of the resurrection of Jesus Christ, has been canonized. The two other primary confessions of the Church, according to Aulén, are the ancient Church's confession of the Incarnation, and the Reformation confession of justification by faith and grace alone.

Since our language is necessarily spatiotemporal, faith affirmations must be symbolic. Such affirmations involve inescapable tensions. The Christian faith affirms that although God is involved in history, He is above all change; although He is sovereign, evil is real; although sin is a human condition, it is voluntarily entered; although faith is divine, man can attain it. Such tensions must neither be eliminated nor embraced for their own sake; they reflect the tension-filled unity of divine revelation.

Aulén divides his discussion of the doctrine of God into two sections. He first discusses how God is conceived in the Christian faith, and then he discusses the activity of God. Holiness provides the background against which God is conceived. God is wholly other, unconditionally majestic, the one upon whom man is unconditionally dependent. The most fundamental thing, however, that can be said about God is that God is love. God's love is spontaneous, creative, self-giving, and unfathomable. This love must in turn be related to God's justice and power. Aulén is critical of theologies in which the tensions of love, justice, and power in God are rationally resolved. On the other hand, sheer irrationalism, whereby contradictory divine attributes are affirmed, is equally inacceptable. According to Aulén, tensions are resolved only as love itself struggles with opposing forces, asserting its predominance over wrath, and defining the meaning of divine sovereignty.

Just as three fundamental ideas, love, justice, and power, are involved in the concept of God, so also God's activity is threefold, in that He saves, judges, and creates. God saves through establishing fellowship between Himself and a sinful and lost humanity. To achieve fellowship God must overcome the hostile power of man's egocentricity. The possibility of salvation lies entirely in the divine will and not in any human quality. The decisive encounter between God and the forces opposing Him has occurred, but the battle continues. Each individual Christian experiences fellowship here and now, but remains a sinner. The

Kingdom of God, in the sense of God's perfect dominion, therefore transcends history.

The love which saves also judges those who refuse to tolerate it. Yet there is no punishing activity which does not ultimately serve the saving activity. Aulén states that the ultimate destiny of those who stand under judgment lies beyond "the boundary line of faith." Faith is unable to decide between condemnation, annihilation, or the final return of all things to God (*apokatastasis*).

When one speaks of God's creative activity, one is not primarily concerned with a theory of origins. Creation has a beginning, but it also continues, and it has a goal. God's redemptive activity is continued creation. Creation is therefore that work of divine love through which God manifests His sovereignty in relation to existence. Since providence is continuous creative activity, providence cannot be distinguished from creation.

God as creator opposes all that ruins and destroys. The law of creation (of which natural law is a reflection) is nothing other than the law of love revealed in Christ. While moral evil is always in radical antithesis to the divine will, physical evil cannot be wholly separated from the divine will. God does not will everything that happens, but since He is sovereign in grace and judgment, He wills something in everything that happens.

Aulén's discussion of the doctrine of redemption divides into a section devoted to the act of God in Christ, and a section devoted to God's work in us. The meaning of the Incarnation, according to Aulén, is that the divine love, and thus God Himself, is incarnate in Jesus Christ. The Incarnation is perfected on the cross. Aulén states that the Virgin Birth is not to be used as a rational explanation of the Incarnation.

The work of Christ, with which Aulén is primarily concerned, is the reconciliation Christ achieved by destroying and subjugating the hostile power of evil separating God and the world. The Cross is therefore understood in terms of struggle and victory. The emphasis is placed not on satisfaction offered on man's behalf to God, nor upon the sufferings of Christ that are to move man to repentance. Aulén speaks rather of Christ's victory over powers, such as sin and death, which are opposed to God, and also of Christ's overcoming of God's wrath itself.

The work which Christ finished on the cross does not need to be repeated. His exaltation in the resurrection, ascension, and session at the right hand of God unveils, reveals, and realizes the victory contained in his finished work. There is no significant difference, according to Aulén, between this continuing work of Christ and the work of the Spirit.

Aulén's discussion of God's work in us deals with sin, forgiveness, and faith. Sin, according to Aulén, has no meaning apart from reference to God, for sin is whatever separates God and man. Sin may be defined positively as egocentricity, negatively as unbelief. Aulén maintains that all sin is original sin, with actual sin as its external manifestation. Sin cannot be explained by reference to the Fall, for the original estate and the Fall belong to each individual. Faith, however, is more concerned about the nature of sin and its subjugation than about its origin.

Forgiveness of sin is that act of divine love through which sinful man is subdued and incorporated into fellowship with God. Though man is forgiven, his unworthiness remains. Indeed, forgiveness makes for a more acute consciousness of sin. Man then participates through forgiveness in the eternal life of God, and thereby he gains power to struggle against sin and to serve his neighbor; he becomes an instrument of the divine love.

Faith is a work of God, but it also involves unconditional trust on man's part. Aulén points out that it is important that the divine and the human not be regarded as being independent; man's activity can never be separated from God's activity. Struggle is necessary even for man sustained by faith; hope is therefore the eschatological dimension of faith.

Aulén contends that the Christian Church, which appears as a living reality in and through the exaltation of Christ, is not to be understood as a society of qualified persons, but as a fellowship created by the Holy Spirit. The Church exists wherever faith discovers the dominion of Christ.

The Church is one, holy, ecumenical, and apostolic. Christ working through the Word and the sacraments is the source of its unity. This unity must be acknowledged and the divisions created by men must be overcome. However, there can be differentiation in structure of organization, in the way the faith is described, and in patterns of religious life; such differentiation does not destroy the basic unity which is of the essence of the Church. The holiness of the Church can be seen only by faith. The Church is holy because Christ is present in it, but the Church is also sinful. It shares with its individual members the ambiguity of being both holy and sinful. The Church is ecumenical (the word Aulén prefers to express the catholicity of the Church), because the finished work of Christ is universal. No boundaries can be drawn to limit the activity of the Spirit. The Church is finally apostolic in the sense that it constantly needs new messengers to proclaim the living Word, who in turn must stand in continuity with the first authorized messengers of the Lord, and with the fundamental work they accomplished.

The Church, in Martin Luther's words in his *Large Catechism,* may be described as "the mother who bears and fosters every individual Christian." Though there is a direct and immediate relation between each individual and God, individualism in the sense of isolation is a sin from which the individual must be delivered. Here the Church becomes "a solidary interrelationship of blessing which is opposed to and struggles with the solidary interrelationship of sin."

In identifying the means of grace, means which are constituent factors of the church, Aulén with Friedrich Schleiermacher (German theologian, 1768-1834) adds prayer to the Word and the sacraments. Prayer, Aulén insists, is not solely a human act; it is also God's approach to us and may thus properly be regarded as a means of grace.

The Word of God is best understood as a message whereby the divine love is self-imparted. There is no standard by which the Word can be judged, but the Word itself convicts man through its own content and character. This Word, which is incarnate in Christ, is anchored to the Bible. The Bible's authority does not depend upon theories of its inspiration, but upon "the fact that the Christian faith is Christocentric, that Christ is the central content of the Scripture, and that every message about the act of God in Christ is derived from and determined by the message of Scripture."

The divine love can be self-imparted not only through the Word, but also through actions. The Church has several holy actions, two of which, baptism and the Lord's Supper, have been identified as sacraments because they comprehensively express the central content of the Gospel and are organically connected with the Christ event.

Aulén calls baptism the sacrament of prevenient grace, since baptism makes it evident that God's love seeks man before man seeks God; the validity of infant baptism is thereby established. In this way also all man-made hindrances to membership in the Church are removed. Yet the fellowship with God given in baptism must be actualized. The Church is obligated to sustain fellowship; at the same time each individual member should spend his entire life living out the implications of his baptism.

In the Lord's Supper Christ actualizes the sacrifice which began with the Incarnation and was completed on the cross. The significance of this sacrament depends entirely on the real presence of Christ. This presence must neither be unduly spiritualized nor unduly materialized, for the former misconception obscures the Cross, while the latter obscures the Resurrection. The primary gift of this sacrament is communion with Christ, in which gift other gifts, such as forgiveness, life, and salvation, are included. In this sacrament Jesus Christ is the true celebrant, using human servants as means. At the same time, the Lord's Supper is the Church's most important act of prayer, while those who participate are consecrated for a life of loving sacrificial service.

Prayer, according to Aulén, is both man's turning to God and God's approach to man. The purpose of prayer is not to change God's will, but to be a means through which God's will is done. Such a view does not, however, imply resignation, but rather a militant and conquering faith.

Aulén regards the ministry as also one of the constituent factors of the Church, because the ministry is a necessary instrument in the activity of the Word and the sacraments which establish the Church. All Church members have a dual obligation, to make use of the means of grace and to practice neighbor love, both of which obligations are also privileges.

Aulén concludes by discussing the Church in the light of the Christian hope. The life of the Church is ultimately eschatological in character, since the fellowship with God experienced in the Church is eternal in nature. Faith therefore looks forward to the ultimate perfection of the Church in the Kingdom of Glory. There is continuity between the militant Church and this Kingdom of Glory, in the sense that the struggling Church is transformed into the finished dominion of God, but there is also discontinuity, since God's perfect dominion will be accomplished by an act of God's eternal power which will involve radical transformation of the present order. Thus, the Christian hope avoids both world-denying pessimism and evolutionary optimism.

I AND THOU

Author: Martin Buber (1878-   )
Type of work: Religious existentialism
First published: 1923

Principal Ideas Advanced

Man finds fulfillment through personal encounters, but to become a person, he must also relate himself to an objective world.

To know a thing, a person, or a proposition, as an object is to know it as nothing more than an it *to which one is related.*

To know a thing or a person, not as an object, but through a direct, mutual encounter, is to have established the I-Thou *relation.*

Since, whenever we stand in the relation of I and Thou, *the* Eternal Thou *speaks to us through the temporal instance, true religion involves discovering what God demands of us in the present moment.*

Martin Buber's *I and Thou* is one of those exceptional works which know no ordinary boundaries of classification. Although Buber is a Jewish philosopher, his work has so illuminated the Christian faith—by providing an existentialist account of what he calls the "I-Thou" relation—that more than many works written by Christians, *I and Thou* can properly be called a masterpiece of Christian literature.

Buber is more interested in tearing down barriers than in erecting them, as is shown in the following instance which he recounts in *Between Man and Man,* a later work which particularly supplements *I and Thou.* At an international meeting early in 1914, when a delegate arose to protest that too large a proportion of the representatives were Jewish, Buber rose to the defense. "I no longer know," he writes, "how . . . I came to speak of Jesus and to say that we Jews knew him from within, in the impulses and stirrings of his Jewish being, in a way that remains inaccessible to the peoples submissive to him. 'In a way that remains inaccessible to you'—so I directly addressed the former clergyman. He stood up, I too stood, we looked into the heart of one another's eyes. 'It is gone,' he said, and before everyone we gave one another the kiss of brotherhood."

The anecdote sheds light on Buber's attitude toward Christianity. His Judaism is of the unorthodox kind which, through the centuries, has turned a deaf ear to rabbinical authority. This appears from the emphasis he places on the prophetic voice in his Old Testament studies, and in his appreciation of the eighteenth century Jewish pietistic movement known as Hasidism. Even today, living in Jerusalem, he makes no pretense at keeping the ceremonial law. It is, therefore, not surprising that Buber is disposed to listen to the Christ of the Gospels, and to find in Christian writers, from the Apostle John to Søren Kierkegaard, authentic witnesses to divine truth. Indeed, to many Christians it appears that Buber's most characteristic teachings are directly derived from the New

Testament. In any case, it is difficult not to agree with Buber's English translator, R. G. Smith, when he says, "In *I and Thou* the two traditions interact and illuminate one another in a remarkable and moving way."

It is, however, to be noted that the point of the anecdote of 1914 is not that Jew and Christian found in Jesus a common ground of meeting, but that when Buber directly addressed his opponent, so that they looked deep into each other's eyes, a meeting took place which could not have been achieved on the secondary level of argument and discussion. Communication gave way to communion. In Buber's words, "The discussion of the situation between Jews and Christians had been transformed into a bond between the Christian and the Jew. In this transformation dialogue was fulfilled. Opinions were gone, in a bodily way the factual took place." Here we have a good illustration of the two fundamental dimensions of human experience, delineated by Kierkegaard, but brought to a new clarity by Buber; namely, the relation between *I* and *It* and the relation between *I* and *Thou*. The "change from communication to communion" is a transition from the *I-It* relation to the *I-Thou* relation. The former, according to Buber, is not, in the full sense of the word, a relation; he uses the term "experience" for the *I-It* type of knowing. When I know a thing, a person, or a proposition, in the mode of an *it,* I make it an object; I am related to it, I experience it, but it is unaffected by the relation. When I know any of these in the mode of *thou,* neither is an object for the other, but each "has to do with" each in a living mutuality. Ordinary communication between man and man is indirect, inasmuch as that which passes between them is an object for each one. But in a moment such as that described by Buber, when the object and its relations are allowed to fall to one side and one self encounters another self, direct relation or communion is established.

Although the *I-Thou* relation is recognizable by most of us in the encounter between man and man, Buber maintains that essentially the same relation can exist between man and nature, and between man and spirit.

The word "nature," of course, stands to civilized man for the ordered cosmos, for the world of *It.* Our technical reason has laid hold of nature's uniformities and has taught us to regard the whole as a complex of identifiable things. But this has not always been the case. For the primitive, as for the child, nature is perceived much more directly, not as a complex of things but as expressions of a *Thou.* Moreover, in favorable moments, even civilized man is able to recover that elemental relation. Buber uses the example of a tree. One can classify it, analyze it, and subdue it to one's practical and scientific schemes; on occasion, however, without giving up any of this hard-earned knowledge, one finds oneself and the tree caught up into an unspeakable union. The experience is never more than a fleeting one, but it is qualitatively the same as that closer union between man and man made possible by speech. For this reason, Buber calls the sphere of our relation with natural entities the "prethreshold" or "preliminal" stage.

When Buber speaks of our relation with spirit, he has reference not to angels or to disembodied souls but to creative works which embody form. Since at this stage the relation is not directly man to man, but beyond such a relation, Buber calls the stage "superliminal." A saying of some old master, when it is not the object of critical inquiry but that which is received in "the indivisible wholeness of something spoken," is an example of that which allows man to encounter spirit. Buber tells of confronting a Doric pillar in a church wall in Syracuse. He encountered the pillar as "mysterious primal mass represented in such simple form that there was nothing individual to look at, nothing individual to enjoy," and he reports that he did all that could be done; he "took [his] stand, stood fast, in the face of this structure of spirit, this mass penetrated and given body by the mind and hand of man."

Of course, the spoken word and the carved column readily harden into things, thereby becoming objects alongside other objects in the world of *It*. But they are unlike most things in that they have built into them a disposition to "change back again and again" and to draw man out of the world of *It* and into the world of *Thou*.

There is something melancholy about the human situation, Buber comments; the melancholy arises out of the fact that man cannot dwell for more than a fleeting instant in the union of pure relation. At the same time, the key to man's greatness is that he is able to move back and forth between the exclusiveness of *I-Thou* and the inclusiveness of *I-It*. The history of civilization, as well as the growth of individual persons, is dependent upon the "progressive augmentation of the world of *It*." Both our technical knowledge and our awareness of ourselves as individuals as distinguished from the group and as persons as distinguished from other kinds of being depends upon the primary distinction between subject and object and upon the fixed relational order which we discover in both the external world and the private world of the self. The human situation is melancholy, according to Buber, because the more articulation we introduce into the world of *It*, the farther we remove ourselves from the unity of the world of *Thou*. On the other hand, without this differentiation, neither the *I* nor the *Thou* can come to its highest realization; while relation cannot arise between two independent *Its*, neither can it arise in an undifferentiated *One*.

It is the primacy of relation and the fact that genuine relation can take place only between two persons that distinguishes Buber's religious philosophy from mysticism. As an example of the perfect union between man and God, he cites Jesus' words in the Fourth Gospel, "I and my Father are one." Here is no mystical absorption, no declaration of identity between the self and the divine One, but the exclusiveness of personal encounter. "The Father and the Son, like in being—we may even say God and Man, like in being—are the indissolubly real pair, the two bearers of the primal relation, which from God to man is termed mission and command, from man to God looking and hearing." According to Buber, mysticism is the end-product of the false kind of spirituality which results when man lives entirely in the dimension of *I* and *It* and loses touch with the dimension of *I* and *Thou;* the world of *I* and *It* tends to fall into two parts, the objective world of matter and causality and the subjective world of feelings and ideas.

In Buber's opinion, much of what passes for spirituality, including religious feeling, is a kind of subjectivism, which exists in alienation from nature, from society, and from the everyday world. (Buber himself passed through the mystical stage, which he regarded as a necessary step on the way to the *I-Thou* philosophy.) Mysticism is an attempt to recover unity, but it is spurious because it denies the world and seeks salvation "within the self-sufficient interior life of man." Only when man recovers the other dimension of *I* and *Thou* is he delivered from subjectivism and solipsism. The *I* of the *I-Thou* relation is not an individual, isolated from other individuals and from the world of events; he is a person, whose life consists in the relations of faith, hope, and love. He lives in community with other man, but the relation which binds him to other *thous* also binds him to the *Eternal Thou.*

Buber agrees with Søren Kierkegaard that, as between man and man, the *I-Thou* relation is exclusive; but he denies that this is the case between man and God. In this manner he hopes to remedy the one-sidedness (as he views it) of Kierkegaard's teaching. The Danish philosopher seemed to be saying that in order to serve God one must break off every relation that binds Him to the world, whether it be ties of marriage, vocation, or politics. Buber, on the contrary, wants to show that love to God is inclusive of all other loves. He uses the example of the relation of a poet and his reader. The reader does not meet the *whole* of the poet in any poem, but he nevertheless meets him in each poem. Similarly, while we do not meet God *in His entirety* in any one of our encounters, in each meeting we encounter the *Eternal Thou.* God "speaks" to us through natural events, through history and biography, through situations which demand of us that we act. Hence we should not turn away from the creature, for through fulfilling our responsibilities to the creature we perform our service to the Creator.

Because we are as likely to meet God at the workbench as at the altar, Buber finds much religion inadequate. Once, he tells us, he was much given to religious exercise. One day, after having spent the morning in his devotions, he was visited by a youth whom he had never met. The young man asked several questions and went away. Only later did Buber learn that his visitor had come to him in despair and had gone away with his deepest questions unasked. Buber thereupon concluded that he had failed the young man. Had he given himself fully to this meeting, he would have guessed the questions which his visitor was not able to ask. Henceforth, he renounced that kind of religion which draws one's attention away from the ordinary, and he resolved to occupy himself at all times with whatever occupation he had at hand. He calls this incident his "conversion."

Not only religion but also morality is taken up in this new point of view, which calls us to live intensively in the present moment and to recognize each new moment as a gift fresh from the Creator which lays on us the responsibility of making of it the best we can. This acceptance of responsibility is, from one point of view, what Buber understands by faith. Each situation in which we find ourselves is a new one. There are no rules to guide our action, as moralists, with their reliance on custom and reason, are accustomed to suppose. Each enterprise involves the risk of novelty, and calls for faith. But he who accepts his responsibility from God does so with hope. He who lives in the present is conscious of freedom and creativity. Necessity, the twin of intelligibility, belongs to the world of *It*, which is always past, and never exists. Necessity does not govern the present, and he who dares live in the present and to choose the way that is momentarily opened to him by God does so with hope. Furthermore, he who willingly responds when God speaks to him does so with love; in Buber's language, love is responsibility for a *thou*, whether a dog, a child, or one's fellow in a crowd. Love involves awareness of the other in the concreteness of his being and dares to wish the being of the other for just what he is. This, indeed, is the meaning of the commandment, "Love thy neighbor as thyself." The commandment does not mean that one should love one's neighbor as one loves oneself; it does mean that one should love one's neighbor by encountering him as one like oneself. In making oneself responsible for others, one performs the sacrifice of love: "A newly-created concrete reality has been laid in our arms; we answer for it. A dog has looked at you, you answer for its glance, a child has clutched your hand, you answer for its touch, a host of men moves about you, you answer for their need."

LOVE, THE LAW OF LIFE

Author: Toyohiko Kagawa (1888-1960)
Type of work: Christian ethics
First published: 1924

Principal Ideas Advanced

The experience of sacrificial love, which Jesus awakens in men's hearts, enables men to understand the nature of God, the world, and man.

Love is the principle underlying organic and social evolution; physical love tends to develop into psychical and, finally, into ethical love.

Love of individuals is an expression of a Cosmic Will.

The individual can realize his potentialities only as part of an organic whole to which he is bound by a social will.

When Toyohiko Kagawa was a high school boy he discovered, through personal conversation with a missionteacher, the transforming power of divine love in his heart. Turning his back on a family inheritance and on his former Buddhist faith, he gave up studying for a diplomatic career and attended a Presbyterian seminary in Kobe (from 1905 to 1908), where he began his lifelong practice of living and working in slum districts. In the midst of a busy life as evangelist, labor organizer, and youth leader, Kagawa found time to write dozens of books, including several novels and volumes of poetry. The present work, which, literally translated, is entitled "The Science of Love," was begun with a view to counteracting the lax views of marriage that were then finding a vogue in Japan; but as the book unfolded in his hands, it turned into a comprehensive philosophy.

Kagawa does not claim that Jesus himself had any "philosophy of love." "Jesus," he says, "loved men without formulating any theory of love." Nevertheless, says Kagawa, it is the concept of sacrificial love which Jesus awakens in men's souls that provides the means for understanding the world and man's place in it. By creating a new dynamic within the heart, love enables man for the first time to recognize his kinship with his Creator, according to the principle expressed by the Apostle John, "Everyone that loves is born of God, and knoweth God; he that loves not does not know God, for God is love."

Nineteenth century vitalistic philosophers, such as Schopenhauer, were, in Kagawa's opinion, on the right track when they maintained that an unconscious Universal Will surges through nature, goading it on by an irresistible passion. However, Kagawa finds Schopenhauer too theoretical in his account of love, because he viewed love from the outside, as it manifests itself in evolution and in art, and did not experience it practically in his heart.

Kagawa credits Kant with first making clear the distinction between "two kinds of perception, the external and the internal," and with showing that it is only through the latter, conscience, that the Absolute is revealed. But Bergson, in Kagawa's opinion, gives an even more adequate account of the Absolute, because he grasps better than Kant the fact that the Absolute is "pure continuity" and is perceived only through an intuition of the inner self. It is Kagawa's reliance upon a kind of Bergsonian intuition that has led some writers to speak of him as a mystic.

Kagawa identifies God with evolution. "The man who says he believes in evolution but not in God, deceives himself," says Kagawa; "for it is a matter of difference in terms, not of variation in essence." When we speak of God we are using the language of subjective experience; when we speak of evolution, we are using the vocabulary of objective science. But, according to Kagawa, there is no ground for believing in evolution, in the sense of progress, except the experience of God which man has in his soul. "Thus," he says, "the idea of progress is subjective effort reflected objectively. When man begins to glimpse the first rays of the dawning hope of progress, he for the first time becomes assured that there is evolution in the cosmos; but when this hope is wanting, he thinks of the changes tending toward complexity in the cosmic structure merely as fetters binding mankind." The theory of evolution, he says, is a faith —"the greatest faith since Abraham." Theoretically expressed, it is the "belief that the God who is from the beginning becomes the final God."

To maintain that God is love is to believe that the evolution of the world manifests the effort of a cosmic will to "lift all and save all." Kagawa cites the argument of the Russian revolutionist Pëtr Kropotkin (1842-1921), to show that evolution could never have taken place if the struggle for existence had not brought forth a mutual aid on the part of individual creatures. This "unreasoned impulse" found in the animal world is not yet love, but love grows out of it; for example, love between the sexes, and the love of parents for their children.

Kagawa distinguishes three grades of love on the human level: physical, psychical, and ethical love. These are not exclusive, and, in the natural order of things, the first tends to develop into the second, and the second into the third. For example, sexual attraction tends to become refined into passionate love, which, because it overlays sexual desire with ideal elements, must be accounted psychical. Moreover, as passionate love develops, it may reach a point at which the sexual element disappears, as in the romantic love of St. Francis and St. Claire. The latent presence of this sacred love in physical attraction is, according to Kagawa, merely one instance of the presence throughout the cosmos of the higher, divine love, which found its perfect expression in the life and death of Jesus. For, as Kagawa understands it, the essential characteristic of this higher love is its readiness to sacrifice itself for others.

In Kagawa's philosophy, the theory of evolution finds its counterpart in an organic theory of nature and of society. Defining society as "the assembling of imperfect individuals for the purpose of securing something more nearly perfect," he says that there are as many kinds of societies as there are kinds of love. From physical affinities based on race and the struggle for survival, men tend to pass to psychical affinities based on economic and cultural wants, and then on to moral affinities based on the recognition of the divine life in every creature.

Kagawa's discussion of law and government presupposes this theory of society. In an organism, different parts have different functions, which, if they are not defined, may lead to conflict and disorder. Law exists to expedite the functioning of the social organism. As society evolves from one stage to another, law too evolves; and because evolution is gradual, different kinds of law exist side by side. Criminal law is an example. Kagawa finds that, while both physical and psychical societies are intolerant of nonconformists, ethical societies, because they value every person for his own sake, seek to reclaim social failures. Kagawa recognizes a similar development in international law, and he looks forward to the emergence among civilized peoples of a free society based on moral affinity. Kagawa's philosophy is not that of an "absolute optimist." He denies that there is any economic or political solution to the problems of war and crime. These can be solved only step by step, as more individuals experience inner awakening, and as sacrificial love replaces physical and psychical love.

Kagawa criticizes the individualism of representative nineteenth century ethical thinkers. Tolstoy, for example, had declared that the doctrine of social organism is injurious to the dignity of the ego; but Kagawa argues that blindness to the "supra-egoistic elements of self-consciousness" prevented Tolstoy from understanding the nature of love. Love, says Kagawa, does not begin in individuals; it is a social will, which comes to consciousness in individuals; ultimately, it is an expression of the cosmic will; that is to say, of God. Kagawa criticizes the perfectionist ideal of T. H. Green, the utilitarianism of John Stuart Mill, and the hedonism of Walter Pater on similar grounds. One and all, they fail to see that, apart from his fellows, the individual is a fragment, and that personality is total only in society. "Society," he says, "is an aggregation of individuals who supplement each other and cooperate in order to become stronger, more nearly perfect. It is the hundreds of millions of human beings who would share in striving after God-like perfection."

Kagawa's profound sense of social mission has its basis in his organic view of the world. Just as the cooperation of many has brought about all the beauty and excellency in the world, so it follows that the weakness of the few is a threat to the well-being of all. "It is a fundamental principle," says Kagawa, "that if there is anywhere in the universe a single flaw, the whole universe suffers. . . . If there were only one sinner in the universe, all creation would suffer sorrow and pain—God and I alike would suffer, and thereupon would be born spontaneously the energy which lifts up the sinner." Kagawa uses the example of a blood cell which spontaneously sacrifices itself to heal a wound; similarly, he says, men in whom a sense of moral affinity has been awakened are stirred to devote their lives to sacrificial labor whenever they find evil and pain. Such was the divine love which took Jesus to Calvary and prompted the parable, "Unless a grain of wheat falls into the earth and dies, it remains a single grain; but if it dies, it bears much fruit."

Redemptive love constrained Kagawa to spend most of his life with people in the slums. Studying the needs of the poor at close range, he found that those who worked could be helped by labor organizations, but that those who were physically or spiritually disqualified from working could be helped only by neighborhood movements. Kagawa divided his energies between the two. It was through his efforts that the first labor unions were formed in Japan. Labor organizing was illegal at the time, and Kagawa and his associates were put in prison; but they persisted, and the laws were changed. Kagawa also carried on settlement work in Tokyo, Osaka, and Kobe, making each project an experiment in some aspect of social betterment. He stressed the fact, however, that no program and no amount of financial support can succeed in neighborhood work except where men and women of moral force are willing to sacrifice everything and to live among the persons whom they are trying to help. "These folk," he says, "do not have the health that the laboring classes have." Their trouble, he claims, is a kind of moral bankruptcy, and hence anyone who tries to help them must endure threats, misunderstanding, and even bodily harm. But the task is simple, at least, in principle: "It is simply being kind to one's neighbors." It may mean nursing a castaway child, teaching an old man to read, teaching a woman to sew, or giving advice in personal matters.

The possibility of reclaiming adult slum dwellers seemed to Kagawa very slight. While ministering to them as to the incurably ill, he placed his hope in salvaging the young (those under twelve) by emphasizing health and nutrition, mental therapy, and education. Kagawa's theories of education are based on the principle of "unfolding the child's whole nature." Education, he argues, is a psychological activity, and consists in "calling forth the original nature of man." Kagawa looked in this direction, rather than toward economics and politics, for the "socialization" of the world. He believed that capitalism must be abolished, and that government must be based on love instead of on the interests of special groups. But he maintained that this change can never be realized while the souls of men are famished and in distress. The proletariat must be emancipated "through the spirit of love and mutual aid," and enabled to live "always with its ideals firmly in mind" if society is to be reconstructed and a higher type of humanity created.

The strength of Kagawa's convictions and his unflagging zeal come from his deeply religious persuasion that the love which he finds in his own breast is "the motion of the unseen cosmic will." "It is not the *ego* which loves others," he says; "love is rather the motion resulting from the prior winding up of the mainspring." For Kagawa, the desire which draws the whole creation forward is the "wish to become divine." God is, in his view, the absolute value, and the morality of self-sacrifice and nonviolence is an absolute and eternal rule: "For those who eternally evolve there is an eternal cross."

RELIGION IN THE MAKING

Author: Alfred North Whitehead (1861-1947)
Type of work: Philosophy of religion
First published: 1926

Principal Ideas Advanced

Religion in its profoundest aspect, manifested clearly and fully only at the level of rationalization, consists of the intuitions of the individual in his solitariness.

The intuitions of rational religion, while they constitute the sources of religious insight, are not self-evidently authenticating but require metaphysical criticism for the verification of their truth.

The idea of God as the source of all actual order in the world and as the measure of the ideal harmony of the world is the metaphysical correlative of the intuitions of permanence and the hope for the realization of values experienced in rational religion.

Religion in the Making marks a transition in Whitehead's thought. Previously he had written works dealing with the philosophy of science. Subsequently he was to write metaphysics. *Religion in the Making* is a reflection of the older epoch in Whitehead's written thought inasmuch as it is an examination of the role of religion in the development of Western thought, an examination parallel to his analysis of the role of science in the Western tradition in *Science and the Modern World* (1925). *Religion in the Making* is at the same time an anticipation of the new epoch in Whitehead's thought because it contains a sketch of a religious metaphysics which finds its most systematic statement in *Process and Reality* (1929).

That this transitional work is Whitehead's most sustained treatment of religion shows that a religious factor plays an important formative role in the shaping of his thought. Because his efforts were those of philosophic thought, the focus of his analysis is upon religion as a constitutive factor in human experience rather than upon Christianity as a religious faith. He writes as a philosopher of religion rather than as a theologian. He writes, furthermore, as a philosopher of religion eager to arrest the development of what he sees to be the erosion of the traditional religions.

Nevertheless, numerous aspects of Whitehead's thought make it clear that he is chiefly, though not exclusively, concerned with the Christian religion. His analysis of the evolution of religion from ritual to emotion, myth, and reason is most relevant to Christian history. His criticism of dogmatism in religion is obviously applicable to Christian theology. The special attention paid to the metaphysical functions of God shows a Christian rather than a Buddhist interest. His plea for a search for ever more rational theological formulations expresses a feeling of the importance of Christian theology. His espousal of the idea of persuasion, which admittedly finds one of its most winning expressions in the New Testament picture of Christ, discloses an inheritance from Christian ethics. In all of these aspects, Whitehead's philosophy of religion reveals its Christian bias. It is no accident that Christian theologians have seen in Whitehead's thought new modes of expressing their faith more adequately.

The essence of religion, according to Whitehead, does not become apparent until religion has evolved to its rational expression. Only at the stage of rational religion does the inwardness of religious intuition stand sharply against collective emotions. Only at this point are the intuitions of religion themselves tempered by ethical insight. Only then do religious intuitions become fully capable of intellective elaboration. Indeed, to speak of religious intuition at all implies the context of rational religion. If Whitehead defines religion as "what the individual does with his own solitariness," he also makes clear that it is "not until belief and rationalization are well established that solitariness is discernible as constituting the heart of religious importance." Not until man's historical development allows him a genuinely cosmopolitan experience can a world-consciousness be produced and can religious intuitions be disengaged from the confining bonds of communal religion.

With the advent of rational religion religion's essential solitariness and its universal relevance become apparent. The source of religious insight becomes the direct intuitions of the individual, intuitions which claim to be universally valid. "Rational religion appeals to the direct intuition of special occasions," Whitehead writes, "and to the elucidatory power of its concepts for all occasions. It arises from that which is special, but it extends to what is general." Religion is peculiarly that type of human experience by which the juxtaposition of particularity and universality is understood. Religious intuition, insofar as it is genuinely intuitive, is the product of special moments of extraordinary insight. Yet religious intuitions, insofar as they are genuinely religious, are intuitions of what is permanent in the world. Religious intuition "brings into our consciousness that permanent side of the universe which we can care for."

Nevertheless, one cannot move simply from the special insights of religious intuition to their universal validity. The solitary individual may be the occasion of religious insight, but religious truth is not the self-evident product of such moments. Religious intuitions require metaphysical criticism because they must be correlated with other kinds of intuitions, because they cannot guarantee the adequacy of their own statement, and because they are inevitably infected by the historical circumstances of their origin. Furthermore, it is a primary metaphysical conviction of Whitehead that no single occasion is self-explaining. Rational religion originates from the intuitions of the solitary individual; but without reference to the world of other individuals, a solitary person cannot be uniquely individual nor can his intuitions be truly rational.

One other crucial factor enters into Whitehead's understanding of rational religion: the concept of value. Rational religion is that level of growth in religion characterized not only by a rational coordination of beliefs, but also by a purified understanding of the good. The world-consciousness of rational religion "rises to the conception of an essential rightness of things." Religion, in its earlier forms particularly, Whitehead argues, "is by no means necessarily good. It may be very evil." Only in rational religion does a purified and generally impartial view of value become possible.

Value pertains first of all to the self-valuation of the individual in his solitariness, then to the value of different individuals for each other, and finally to "the objective world which is a community derivative from the interrelations of its component individuals, and also necessary for the existence of each of these individuals." Hence, the intuitions of rational religion are intimately bound up with valuation and the realization of value. Hence, too, the intuition of permanence in rational religion is the intuition of a permanence which, as Whitehead states, "provides a meaning, in terms of value, for our own existence, a meaning which flows from the nature of things."

The social character of realized value is another reason why the individual in his solitariness and self-valuation may not simply accept his own intuitions and valuations normatively. For instance, he cannot legitimately appeal to a direct intuition of an omnipotent personal deity. If God is believed to be personal, this belief, for rational religion, must be inferential and not intuitive. Otherwise, God's person appears as an intuition incapable of generalization; God's existence becomes an essentially unverifiable supposition; and the goodness derivitive from God's person is arbitrary. The belief in a direct intuition of a personal deity is a relapse of religion into a prerational form.

With respect to the concept of value, Whitehead argues that the simple trust in individual self-valuation cannot explicate the problem of evil. Insofar as the world, seen as a social whole, exhibits a lack of complex self-consistency, it is evil. Hence, evil must be understood as the thwarting of intense social harmonies by recalcitrant realizations of partial values. Insofar as an actual entity is considered in itself, it is the realization of value. But insofar as it functions socially as a destructive agent with respect to greater possible realizations of value, it is evil. Appeal to the self-evidence of private intuitions, then, is no guarantee of the value of these intuitions.

At the same time, the intuitions of the individual are not necessarily arbitrary, and the self-valuation of the individual's solitude is not unqualifiedly evil. Evil is not intrinsic to the self-realization or self-valuation of the individual; evil arises from the maladjustment of this realized value to what might have been achieved in its world. Thus, self-valuation can also be the way in which a more complex harmony is introduced into the world. At any rate, it is Whitehead's conviction that evil is unstable and self-stultifying and that evil can be overcome by good.

A more complete account of the nature of the permanence discerned in religious intuition and of the possibility of the social harmony sought by rational valuation requires reference to Whitehead's view of the metaphysical functions of God. The idea of God is one of the three concepts Whitehead believes necessary for the elucidation of the world. The world consists of a multiplicity of temporal-spatial epochal occasions, each of which reflects in itself the other proximate occasions. This world requires the concept of creativity to explain the temporal succession of these occasions as being such that the succession exhibits the character of transition. Creativity is that characteristic of temporal success whereby one occasion can become a creator of a new creature. Whitehead says that the creatures exhibit the quality of creativity, though creativity cannot be conceived as an epochal occasion. Second, the world requires reference to a realm of ideal entities or forms in terms of which one epochal occasion can be relevantly related to other occasions. This ideal realm is itself a multiplicity of possibilities, any one or group of which is relevant to the relation between epochal occasions. The realm of ideal entities is not the same as the actual world because the epochal occasions in their creativity determine the way in which the ideal entities qualify the creative process. Third, the world requires reference to an "actual but non-temporal entity whereby the indetermination of mere creativity is transmuted into a determinate freedom." This is the function of God. Apart from God there would be no explanation of the actual order which the world does exhibit. Neither the principle of creativity nor the realm of ideal entities can explain this order because they are principles of potentiality and not powers of actuality. The succession of epochal occasions cannot explain this actual order in the world because epochal occasions are limited realizations of actuality which precisely in their multiplicity call for explanation.

These metaphysical functions, however, precisely correlate with the intuitions of rational religion. If religious intuitions are intuitions of the element of permanence in the world, God, in Whitehead's metaphysics, is that nontemporal actuality upon whom all actual order in the world depends. Nor is this metaphysical function lacking in its implication for values. As the nontemporal actuality upon whom order in the actual world depends, God partly determines the possibility of ideal entities for epochal occasions and partly conditions the creativity of the creatures. This is why the self-valuation of any epochal occasion is not wholly arbitrary. In its freedom of self-valuation, any creature exhibits a possibility which is never ultimately incompatible with God's harmony of apprehension. In religious language, as Whitehead explains it, "the kingdom of heaven is not the isolation of good from evil. It is the overcoming of evil by good. This transmutation of evil into good enters into the actual world by reason of the inclusion of the nature of God, which includes the ideal vision of each actual evil so met with a novel consequent as to issue in the restoration of goodness."

Though Whitehead's idea of God diverges significantly from important aspects of the Western religious tradition, Whitehead belongs to this tradition as its critic. He belongs to the Christian tradition because he does not fear to criticize what he believes to be its failures. He belongs to the Christian tradition also because he constructs a complex alternative to some of its chief doctrinal problems. Consequently, Whitehead's philosophy of religion must be considered an important event in the history of Christian thought.

FREEDOM AND THE SPIRIT

Author: Nikolai Berdyaev (1874-1948)
Type of work: Philosophy of religion; existentialism
First published: 1927

Principal Ideas Advanced

Spirit can never be understood in terms of a philosophy which accepts the categories of nature as ultimate.

Spirit reveals the freedom of its inner life in the symbolism of myth and religious dogma.

The Christian dogmas of the Creation, Fall, and redemption of the world represent the true life of Spirit.

The incarnation of God in a human nature and His resurrection from the grave contain the promise of man's victory over nature.

This spiritual hope is realized, not in technical progress nor in political union, but in the corporate experience of the Church.

In *Freedom and the Spirit,* Nikolai Berdyaev does not undertake to discuss either spirit or freedom in the traditional manner. His contention is that both philosophy and theology have erred in treating of spirit as if it were part of nature, subject to the categories of reason. If this error is to be corrected, an entirely new philosophy is needed which will start with spirit's knowledge of itself. Spirit knows that it does not derive its freedom from the world of nature; on the contrary, nature derives whatever meaning it has from the freedom which is spirit's very being.

According to Berdyaev, spirit represents a "breach in the structure of the psycho-corporeal monad." Spirit is not observable outwardly by scientific observation, but only inwardly, by reflection on the moral and religious experience of mankind. Refusing to be confined by the repetitious patterns which dominate matter, spirit is always striving to realize its own life more completely; and because spirit is essentially dynamic, it cannot make use of the static concepts of reason, but must devise a symbolism of its own. Thus, spirit invents the language of religious dogma and myth.

Religious symbolism, according to Berdyaev, makes possible a "revelation" of the secret inner life of spirit. The subconscious potencies of spirit disclose themselves in terms of the surface contents of mind, taking such natural and historical forms as lie near at hand. For example, the Biblical account of man's creation, his fall, and his redemption reveals to man that he is a child of two worlds: man is made of dust, but also he is fashioned in God's image; he is condemned to death, but also he is appointed to an eternal destiny. The Creation, Fall, and redemption, says Berdyaev, all transpired within the life of spirit itself; and it is a false philosophy which questions whether such spiritual events correspond with reality. Spirit *is* reality, and the symbols through which it comes to know itself are as real as anything in our experience.

Without denying that there are profound insights in all the world religions, Berdyaev holds that the Christian religion is the one through which free spirit has preserved its most authentic witness. Berdyaev considers "the mystery of the theandric humanity of Christ" to be the key to understanding both man and God; according to his view, the central reality of the religious life is the mutual interaction of God and man. The "humanizing of God" and the "divinizing of man" are both essential to spiritual development, and nowhere is this twofold movement so perfectly realized as in the coming of Christ, the God-man.

Nikolai Berdyaev's attachment to Christianity was "spiritual" and "free." He was not reared in the Church, and when he declared himself a Christian it was through no compulsion or authority. "I have come to Christ through liberty and through an intimate experience of the paths of freedom," he wrote in the introduction to *Freedom and the Spirit.* "Nor am I the only one who has passed through this experience. . . . Those whose religion is authoritarian and hereditary will never understand properly those who have come to religion through freedom, and through the tragedy immanent in their life's experience." Passionately engaged in Russian revolutionary activity, Berdyaev came to the conviction that secular humanism, which had prevailed from the time of the Renaissance, was no longer tenable, and that its collapse left no foundation for a belief in man's personal worth. Gradually he came to rely upon Christian revelation.

The Christ whom Berdyaev embraced was the silent figure who, in Dostoevski's *The Brothers Karamazov,* confronted the Grand Inquisitor. In this parable for our times, the Grand Inquisitor represents the socialist impulse (whether secular or clerical) which tries to relieve men's suffering at the expense of their liberty. The Inquisitor's professed love for the masses is a degrading pity. Christ refuses to palliate men's sufferings at the expense of their spiritual dignity. He shows his love by dying for them so that they may share in His resurrection. For it is only by participating in the risen Christ, whose human life is transfigured by the divine, that man can realize the life of free spirit.

The natural man, Berdyaev writes, knows only two kinds of freedom: the freedom of indeterminacy and the freedom of organized control. By the former he affirms his independence of nature and becomes, in fact, a spirit; however, as the story of Adam's Fall makes clear, man all too soon finds himself once again in bondage to the forces of nature. By bringing his life under regulations and social authority, he recovers a kind of independence; but in organized society his activity tends to become automatic, and regulation degenerates into tyranny. When the oppression becomes intolerable, man revolts and reaffirms his initial liberty. Thus, history is a "fatal dialectic" between two freedoms, a struggle from which there is no escape except that offered in Christ, "the new Adam." Through Him a third kind of liberty is offered to us in which the other two are reconciled. Christ saves man's initial and God-given freedom from bondage to nature, not by means of the kind of human engineering favored by the Grand Inquisitor, but by uniting man's spirit to the Father of spirits, in the fellowship of all free spirits.

Berdyaev describes Christ's work as having universal scope. In His resurrection, the forces of nature are brought under the sway of divine love; all nature, like man, acquires the capacity of "divinization." Because He took true humanity upon Him, the whole race may be said to participate in His victory. On this account, Berdyaev is impatient with the historical churches, which, in his opinion, have been too apt to lapse into the freedom of organized control, and too little willing to claim the fruits of Christ's victory. Recognizing with St. Paul that not all men stand at the same spiritual level, Berdyaev concedes that the Church must accommodate its ministry to the "carnal" as well as to the "spiritual"; it must dispense milk to those who are unable to digest more substantial food. His complaint is that throughout the centuries the Church has catered exclusively to those weak in faith; thus, the Church has become authoritarian, rationalistic, and legalistic. At the same time, the Church has been singularly insensitive to the needs of the spiritually elite, with the result that great numbers of them have been excluded from its fellowship, to their loss, but also to the loss of the Church and of the non-Christian world. Thus, in the interests of preserving the authority of its doctrines, the Church has driven from its midst numerous gnostics, theosophists, and mystics, simply because they have claimed new knowledge of God. A similar rigidity in its social and political attitude has alienated from its fellowship progressive and liberal spirits whose genius has disclosed new depths in man's understanding of himself.

Impatient with the narrowness of institutional Christianity, Berdyaev broadens his definition of the Body of Christ to include such men as Goethe and Nietzsche. The actual Church, the Church Universal, is a spiritual company, never truly represented by "the visible historical church." But Christians ought not to be indifferent to the historical Church nor ought they to slacken their efforts to heal its schisms and to make it more representative of the Church Universal.

Berdyaev finds that in the history of the Church two classes of persons have been the bearers of revelation to their fellow men. He employs the term "mystic" to include them both. There are those whose calling is to holiness, persons ordinarily thought of as mystics; but besides these, there are mystics without any claim to holiness, whose calling is to prophecy. Among the holy mystics, Berdyaev believes, those who have experienced God within the compass of human experience are more truly Christian than those whose union with God has meant leaving their humanity behind. He cites with favor the saying of the German mystic and poet, Angelus Silesius (1624-1677), "I know that without me God could not endure for a moment. . . ." Among the prophetic mystics, Berdyaev includes an array of men whose "feeling for life and understanding of it" has been mystical, although they have not brought their persons under religious discipline. Dostoevski is cited as a leading example; the list also includes Joseph de Maistre (1753-1821), Søren Kierkegaard (1813-1855), Vladimir Solovyov (1853-1900), and Leon Bloy (1846-1917).

As may be expected in one who stresses the dynamic quality of spirit and the community of God and man, Berdyaev is especially concerned with the problems of eschatology. He warns that secular progress, which involves the materialization and rationalization of human life, is purchased at the expense of spiritual freedom. Spirit develops only where changed circumstances, such as those in which modern man finds himself, call forth new revelations from the potential depths of spirit.

Berdyaev claims that spiritual gains are made and consolidated. For example, Christianity has impressed upon the Western soul a new compassion toward suffering in man and beast. God is no longer to be described as inflicting torment on brutish creatures. In fact, says Berdyaev, the notions of Heaven and Hell were never Christian, but pagan and naturalistic; and a true eschatology is not concerned with an afterworld but only with our "present spiritual orientation and moral will."

Berdyaev's ideas are those of an Eastern Orthodox Christian, particularly his conception of the corporate nature of redemption, called by the Russians *sobornost.* The Western Church, he believes, has overstressed the individual character of salvation. "The spirit of *sobornost,* the idea of the collective character of the ways of salvation, is opposed to this sort of individualism. In the Church we are saved with our brethren, all together." The universalism which Berdyaev calls for is qualitative, not quantitative. The Western experience of Christ differs from that of the East because of different historical circumstances, but variety is compatible with unity. Ecumenicity requires that the historical consciousness be subordinated to the eschatological and that the past be reinterpreted in terms of the future universal reign of Christ.

PHILOSOPHICAL THEOLOGY

Author: Frederick Robert Tennant (1866-1958)
Type of work: Natural theology
First published: Volume I, 1927; Volume II, 1928

Principal Ideas Advanced

Religious experience is experience interpreted from a religious point of view; such experience may be a source of intellectual, moral, and aesthetic inspiration.

The wider theological argument leads to belief in a purposive intelligence as the world's source and sustainer.

The world-ground is not infinite in the sense of being an indeterminate being; God is changeless in His self-identity and self-consistency; He is not to be described in terms of such static concepts as completeness, immutability, and timelessness.

The highest ideal we can conceive is that of a developing moral order; there must be the possibility of moral evil in the world.

Christ is the religious genius of theism; Christianity is the climax of the historical development of natural religion.

Since its appearance in two volumes in 1927 and 1928 Frederick Robert Tennant's *Philosophical Theology* has been recognized in the scholarly world by admirer and critic alike as a major contribution to natural as contrasted to dogmatic theology. Tennant, who taught science before becoming a priest in the Church of England, found in philosophy a means of reconciling the demands of science and theology. From 1913 to 1931 he was Lecturer in Theology at Cambridge University.

The nearly seven hundred pages of the *Philosophical Theology* are so uncompromising in their demands upon the reader that they have daunted many who might otherwise agree with the philosopher C. D. Broad that theologians and candidates for the ministry could not be better employed than in studying Tennant's work. He who makes the effort of following Tennant through the development of the argument will be rewarded for his effort, for he will have been guided through the intricacies of theological and philosophical problems by a most able teacher. Tennant's classical erudition influenced his literary style; and a subtle humor enlivens the pages at unexpected moments. An unrelenting concern for scientific accuracy, a philosophic judiciousness, and a mellow wisdom characterize the work.

The purpose of *Philosophical Theology* is twofold: to present the studies required for serious discussion of the grounds upon which theology rests, and to present the developed theistic interpretation of the world, man, and God toward which the examination of basic studies led. Volume One begins with a detailed examination of the major issues in psychology and philosophy, their data and method, the subject of consciousness and its elements, what is in the senses and what is in the mind itself, perception, imagination, memory, and ideation. Tennant acknowledges an indebtedness to James Ward (1843-1925), the English psychologist. Other chapters deal with theories of personality, value, thought and knowledge. The first volume concludes with considerations of induction and probability with reference to knowledge, belief, and faith. Only at the end of his investigation does Tennant turn to religious experience and to the nature and limitation of scientific knowledge.

Sensory experiences are the "humble beginning" of all human knowledge, according to Tennant. From the irreducible data of the senses, the *qualia* of sense which are not reducible to activity of the mind, man receives the opportunity for knowledge. Each man's experience begins with that consciousness which is prior to self-consciousness, the experiencing (*erleben*) of his embodiment. From this experience man becomes aware; he knows the fact of his being and in this knowledge being and thinking meet. From this experience comes the conviction regarding embodiment, the notion of "having" a body which "has" experience.

The mind has both passive and active characteristics; it receives the stimulation of that which is over against it, but it responds, retains, assimilates, fuses, and differentiates the data in distinguishable manners. It is from the private (psychic) world of sense experience that the individual emerges in his quest for knowledge (epistemology) and for satisfaction regarding the nature of ultimate reality (metaphysics.) For Tennant it is extremely important to realize that the private world of the individual is the prerequisite of knowledge.

From the private world of certainty (psychological) one moves to communicate and to share meaningful observations about the realms of knowledge and truth. The presence of an ultimate or metaphysical reality underlying the phenomenal world is a postulation directly related to man's efforts to gain knowledge. This metaphysical reality cannot be known as the immediate private world of sense data is known, but reasonable speculation concerning its nature is permitted.

Tennant's theory of value is in harmony with his empirical approach to reality. He rejects value realism (the view that value is inherent in objects) and value absolutism (the view that values are nonrelational) just as he rejects metaphysical realism and absolute idealism. Values relate to persons and their individual experiences. A value is experienced as the object of desire. As desires are met, pleasure and pain result, and verdicts of "good" and "bad" are given. But as experience continues, life is discovered to have rewards other than mere pleasure, and pleasure itself becomes subject to a more discriminating assessment. The experiencing person begins to form concepts of value, to see goods become evils and evils become goods. He reaches a stage in which over-individual values are recognized and sought.

Concepts of values may be found to be at variance one with another, and the experient finds others who hold antithetical values. He becomes concerned with the truth; he wonders about the nature of supreme value; he aspires after a universal standard. The concepts may be manipulated in a way that ascribes metaphysical status to them, but here Tennant demurs. Perhaps, as in the knowing process one passes from a private world to a reality beyond, so in the process of valuation one may pass from over-individual values (those of a society) to the supreme value, but the experient cannot know that such progress is possible. He may not rightly hypostatize individual values into absolutes. One must be content with a psychological value-certainty which may indeed be reasonable and in harmony with the ultimate truth about value. Thus, Tennant concludes that there is no *a priori* absolutism in values. He offers instead an empirical ethics.

For Tennant, religious experience has as much cognitive value as any other experience rightly understood. He recognizes the emotional impact of religious experience, but he cannot grant to it status as an independent basis for belief in God. He argues that both science and religion have keys to reality and that both may be correct within their spheres. It is always the lock which determines whether the key shall fit. He rejects the mystical version of religious experience as confusing psychological certainty with epistemological certainty. He insists that the mystic inadvertently confuses these two, though Tennant admits the freshness, power, and sense of illumination that the mystic experiences. While there might be a mystical way of illumination, we cannot know that there is. No ineffable experience can be described. Every experience combines a given element and an interpretation of it. Tennant thus rejects views which describe religious experience as self-validating encounters with the numinous or the wholly other.

Tennant clarifies the cognitive value of religious experience by pointing out that even as science develops certain theories to account for facts of human dealings with matter and "nature," so religion develops theoretical constructs to account for human experience with factors in the "spiritual" realm such as value, beauty, goodness, and truth. Both science and religion require faith and belief.

In his second volume of *Philosophical Theology* Tennant moves from consideration of mental processes and knowledge into the realm of more strictly theological studies. His general problem is the validation of theistic belief. He presents two principal demonstrations of the truth of theism. The first is its essential continuity with the faith-venture in science and religion. He demonstrates this continuity from the reflective, the psychogenetic, and the analytic standpoints.

Tennant begins by defining law as a summary of past experiences which provides a basis for the prediction of future experiences. Law renders intelligible the manifold variety of nature. Any assertion of immutable and all-pervading law is logically and scientifically unwarrantable. Thus, Tennant rules out *a priori* law, and on the same ground he denies the *a priori* conclusion that all is ungrounded coincidence, that there is no law.

Tennant goes on to observe that science has not been successful in interpreting the world in totally mechanical terms. Indeed, the more developed science becomes, the more complex and varied are the explanations offered in hypothetical terms: "Every attempt thoroughly to mechanise Nature has involved resort to the mysterious and unknowable."

Continuing with an analysis of "explanation" in terms of the human desire for simplicity, changlessness, and rationality, Tennant sees it as human prejudice that men should hope for immutability in the real. He claims that to regard immutability as an attribute of deity is to prefer the material to the spiritual, for activity is as much a part of the soul as rest.

The world is such as to demand explanation in terms of purpose and design, Tennant claims. Theism as reasonable belief and as a philosophical theory of the world is a position which is based on facts of experience. Theism postulates an integrative and directive mind, and it thereby unifies the diversity of phenomena.

Tennant's teleology is new in that it seeks completion in a moral argument by which man is regarded as needing to work with nature. In contrast to the traditional form of "proving" the being of God by seeking to demonstrate a real counterpart to a preconceived idea, Tennant follows the empirical approach. He will, he says, take the world as it is and attempt from it to read its message for better or for worse. If someone should protest that this is scarcely a lofty method for an elevated science such as theology, Tennant replies that, after all, we know other selves about whose existence we have unshakable conviction on similar grounds. No immediate (unmediated) knowledge either of other selves or of God is possible. Objects, be they other selves or God, are mediated inferences "provable" only by cumulative pragmatic verification.

According to Tennant, there are outstanding features in the world which call for a cosmic explanation: the world as an order amenable to thought, an order of progressive organic changes, an order of inorganic adaptations, an order which evokes beauty, an order instrumental to morality, an order of interconnected causes.

After examining in detail each of these features, Tennant is convinced that the only alternative to cosmic teleology "is to regard the self-subsistent entities of which the world is constituted, as comparable with letters of type which have shuffled themselves not only into a book or a literature but also into a reader commanding the particular tongue in which the book utters its unintentional meaning. If the inference from cumulative adaptiveness to design be non-logical, as is admitted, it at least is not unreasonable."

While we need not (and cannot) go further back than a creative spirit, we must go further back in explanation than the world because our minds are not satisfied with the notion that a nonintelligent world can create purposive beings. A purposeless world's producing the purposeful is scarcely a reasonable possibility. We are a part of the evolutionary process; we are of the world, and the purposeful demand we make is one the world itself has raised.

Through a complex synthesis of analogical discovery and ejective inference built out of the rapport of a socialized self and the ontal world and used by the self to interpret the experienced world, one gains an insight into the nature and being of God, Tennant claims.

According to Tennant, God is the creator whose being is transcendent to the world but who posits the constituents of the world. Creation is seen in terms of responsible volition. God is also viewed as the designer who constrains creatures in the general direction of evolutionary growth toward an environment suited to goodness, beauty, and truth. And if God's aim is to develop finite moral personalities, He must Himself be moral and thus respect the freedom of His creatures. One is able to read in the natural world the revelation of God's existence and purpose.

God's nature may truly be as superior to man's nature as scientific knowledge is to a worm's knowledge, but God's nature is like man's in that it involves intelligence, valuation, and volition. "God" is no generic term for universal reason, absolute morality, or a tendency making for righteousness. God is rather a determinate spirit, the source of beauty and love, as well as of the natural world.

There is only one method of reasonable inquiry concerning the knowledge that can be attributed to the supreme being, Tennant writes. The method is to begin with analogy, without which no discussion is possible, and then to eliminate from human knowledge such characteristics as are known to be humanly conditioned, subtraction of which will still leave what can legitimately be called knowledge. Tennant goes on to demonstrate this method which leads him to view God as the creator who gives His creatures freedom.

It is in this context of limited human freedom that Tennant offers his view of evil as inevitable in a world in which God permits authentic personal growth in human individuals. Final and unshakable answers are not possible. Indeed, God's purpose for us is to seek and to question rather than to have full light and certain knowledge.

Theism cannot countenance any doctrine of God's presence or man's life which destroys man's individual responsibility, Tennant insists. Any theory of God's relationship to man which appears to make that relationship personal is emphatically rejected.

For Tennant there is no discontinuity between religion and philosophical theology. The message of Christ, though grounded on other insights, is found to be identical with the world view reached by the indirective teleology Tennant employs.

Theistic belief is taken as the essence of Christianity, which is thus on a par, intellectually, with science. Christ is the religious genius of theism. Christianity is the climax of the historical development of natural religion. The theistic view to which Tennant has been led permits him the concluding observation that the cosmos is not a logico-geometrical scheme but rather "an adventure of divine love." For many readers Tennant's name is revered precisely because through his work they have been led to the same conclusion.

SELECTED LETTERS

Author: Baron Friedrich von Hügel (1852-1925)
Type of work: Devotional letters
First published: 1927 (written 1896-1924)

Principal Ideas Advanced

Religion is adoration by the creature of the Creator.

God as perfect personality is not finite but the absolute, unconditioned, ultimate reality, a being of joy, pure and undefiled.

Mysticism needs to be inclusive of the three elements of religion—the institutional, the rational, and the experimental-mystical—and the three corresponding forces of the human soul—the sensational, the intellectual, and the volitional.

Suffering is the greatest grace; it deepens religious sensitivity and assists in transforming the human personality.

As friend, father, spiritual director and critic, Baron Friedrich von Hügel reflects within the *Selected Letters* of 1896 to 1924 his unique response to the religious life. The letters are personal and yet candidly direct about the life of the spirit in its quest for God. The theme and mood of each letter reveals the writer as a man passionately involved in this quest.

Friedrich von Hügel, Baron of the Holy Roman Empire, was born in Florence, Italy, May 8, 1852. His father, Baron Karl von Hügel, a member of a noble Catholic Rhineland family, was appointed by the Emperor of Austria as ambassador to the Grand Ducal Court of Tuscany. After several years of service in Tuscany and Brussels, the elder von Hügel moved his family at the time of his retirement to Torquay in England. This country became the permanent residence for Friedrich von Hügel, although his thoughts and many of his letters were directed toward friends and associates living on the Continent.

Friedrich von Hügel's education was informal. Private tutors were appointed for his education. In England young von Hügel was tutored to some extent by the schoolmaster-geologist, William Pengelly. The influence of this tutoring and the natural inclination of von Hügel toward geology and scientific research are evident in his great regard for the discipline of both science and religion. In a letter to Mrs. Lillie, dated April 20, 1922, he compared science to a coral reef; like the constant interaction between reef and water, there is within science a process of ceaseless search, an effort to discover error, and to substitute for error something which is nearer to the truth. Religion, on the other hand, is like a golden shower from above, bestowing like rain the affirmation of belief in a definite God, a definite future life, and a definite loyalty to the Church: "Assimilate Religion to Science and you have levelled down to something which, though excellent for Science, has taken from Religion its entire force and good; and you have shorn Samson of his locks with a vengeance. On the other hand force Science up to the level of Religion or think that you have done so and Science affirms far more than, as such, it can affirm, and you, on your part, are in a world of unreality."

During his late teens, Baron von Hügel contracted typhoid fever, which left him with an extremely nervous and delicate physical constitution and with a deafness that increased through the years. Along with the disease came the death of his father. These two events temporarily shattered the bright world of the young von Hügel. However, it also provided the time and inclination to enter the circles of religious thought and devotion influenced by a Dutch Dominican friar, Father Raymond Hocking, and the Vicar of Saint Augustine in Paris, Abbé Huvelin. Special advice—short and concise—was given by Abbe Huvelin to von Hügel, which he in turn later included in some of his letters to friends in need of spiritual direction.

Von Hügel's marriage to Mary Herbert, daughter of Sidney Herbert (Gladstone's friend and ministerial colleague), opened the doors to the Catholic social-clerical world of London. It also afforded the opportunity for meeting the leading thinkers in English society interested in the religious and scientific issues of the day. Later, in writing to many of these leaders, von Hügel expressed his own reactions to their opinions.

Three daughters, Gertrud, Hildegaard, and Thekla, were born to Baron von Hügel and Lady Mary. All of them received letters which may be found in this collection. They received their formal and religious education from their father. One letter in particular reflects this religious training. Thekla is quoted as being very insistent upon describing religion as primarily an "is-ness" not an "oughtness." Her father was sympathetic and most likely responsible for this concept which found religion to be essentially evidential; he wrote that religion "intimates, first of all, that a superhuman world, a superhuman reality *is*, exists." Thus, the first and essential act of religion would be to adore, to proclaim this sense of God.

The death of the eldest daughter, Gertrud, resulted in the fine personal meditations on suffering included in *Selected Letters*. "Suffering can be the noblest of all actions," he wrote; "How wonderful it is, is it not, that literally only Christianity has taught us the true peace and function of suffering. The Stoics tried the hopeless little game of denying its objective reality, or of declaring it a good in itself (which it never is) and the Pessimists attempted to revel in it, as a food to their melancholy, and as something that can no more be transformed than it can be avoided or explained. But Christ came, and He did not really explain it; He did far more, He met it, willed it, transformed it; and He taught us how to do all this, or rather He Himself does it within us, if we do not hinder the all healing hands. In suffering, we are very near to God."

Von Hügel's daughter Hildegaard

writes about her father as one who considers suffering to be a splendid school, for it teaches one more than any amount of learning. It provides the opportunity for being near to the great realities, and from this, one can gain strength for work. Thus, suffering is the greatest grace.

Baron von Hügel's first scholarly effort in the field of religion was to study Greek and Hebrew in order to do research in the historical criticism of Biblical documents. "Certainly I have myself noticed in the Old Testament," he writes, "of which criticism is so much older, how stable and persistent is its general orientation, how more and more of detail are the questions which still arise. And I do not see why this principle, so universal in all the sciences, should turn out not to be operative in New Testament criticism also."

The weakness of Roman Catholic scholarship in New Testament criticism became apparent to him. He worked to obtain real respect for Catholic research, and from this task the principal struggle of his life emerged: "the defense of Catholic enlightenment in the face of obscurantists in the Church on the one side and her non-Catholic critics, especially in university circles, on the other." This struggle for Catholic enlightenment brought von Hügel into contact not only with the foremost English minds of the day such as William George Ward (1812-1882), John Henry Newman (1801-1890), James Martineau (1805-1900), George Tyrrell (1861-1909), Clement Webb (1865-1954), A.E. Taylor (1869-1945), Claud Montefiore (1858-1938), Evelyn Underhill (1875-1941), and Norman Kemp-Smith (1872-1958), but also with such Continental leaders as Archbishop Söderblom (1866-1931), Ernst Troeltsch (1865-1923), Rudolph Eucken (1846-1926), and Alfred Loisy (1857-1940). Von Hügel was interested in the intellectual endeavors of those men and others who were writing in the religious and philosophical fields. Thus he became involved in a large correspondence—a great deal of which is found in the *Selected Letters* —with men and women of various countries to whom he wrote usually in their own tongues—German, French, Italian, or English. Into these letters he put the "most minute and conscientious labor."

This correspondence and personal acquaintance with the astute minds of Europe placed von Hügel in the center of the "Modernist Movement." Within the Roman Catholic Church, this movement produced several groups which opposed the authority of the Church in matters of criticism, scientific and historic. It also caused a division within these circles themselves when some members advocated extreme measures. Baron von Hügel, for example, supported the stand of Tyrrell and Loisy for Biblical criticism, but he diverged from them and from the "Modernist Movement" in general on the immanental view of religion. The Papal Encyclical of 1907 would have confronted von Hügel with excommunication if he had been forced to sign the anti-Modernist pledge which condemned all the efforts of Modernism. However, he was a layman and this fact spared him from signing the pledge. The fear of being excommunicated from the Roman Catholic Church remained with him throughout this period and this anxiety permeates some of his letters as he persuades and argues for the pure and ideal form of his Church: "Yet I cannot but note that Catholicism, *at its best,* still somehow produces saints of a depth of other-worldliness, of a delicate appealing heroism, and of a massiveness of spiritual wisdom, greater than I can find elsewhere."

Concepts concerned with the nature of God and the nature of religion permeate the majority of von Hügel's letters. In a letter to Maude Petre, von Hügel describes God as personal in nature. He rejects the charge of anthropomorphism and its resulting limitations when applied to the Infinite. To classify anything personal as rank anthropomorphism while accepting such concepts as thought, love, law, and substance as being above the anthropomorphic condemnation is, according to von Hügel, an illogical conclusion. All concepts knowable to man have the specific characteristics of the human thought which formulates them.

The necessary condition involved in this personalistic conviction regarding God is the distinction sensed within man between himself and God. This is realized especially by man in the religious experience of adoration and worship. Religion is adoration to von Hügel, adoration by the creature of the Creator: "And by religion I mean not some vague sentiment, or some beautiful thought, not even, though this is getting nearer to it, moral striving as apart from faith in, and realization of the great Spiritual Reality, God in Whose presence, and as Whose will, we thus strive to grow and be: but by and in self-donation, such self-commitment to a, to *the* Reality other than, yet immensely near to, ourselves."

God as perfect personality is not finite. Von Hügel writes to Maude Petre that the belief in a finite God is contrary to the affirmations of a whole-hearted religion. Von Hügel's discussions concerning suffering and God are now classical expressions of the divine impassibility. According to von Hügel, suffering if correctly transformed by religious sensitivity may help in the development of human personality. There is no reason for ascribing suffering to the eternally perfect personality of the realized ideal. The serious difficulties, von Hügel insists, arising from divine impassibility are less than those connected with the concept of a suffering God. The only value derived from the concept of a finite God is that it points to the likeness between God and man. Beyond this conviction the value of the suffering God ceases. God is limited only by His relationship to creation. Ever beyond this relation, He remains the absolute, unconditioned, ultimate Reality, "as Being, as Joy Pure and Undefiled."

Von Hügel's total approach to religion indicates that the nature of God is apprehended by man's normal faculties of knowledge when these are properly directed to that end and suitably trained and assisted by divine grace. God's nature is not apprehended solely by means of intuition, nor is it grasped by some unique mystical faculty. A matured concept of God involves a keen sense of the objective, given, full reality of God which is obscured by the normal cognitive faculties of man.

Central to all von Hügel's letters is a mystical quality with which the author is usually identified. He carefully describes this mysticism in one letter to Father Tyrrell as having a place for the ingredients of the contingent world. It safeguards its own health by continual reference to the institutional and intellectual elements of religion. Von Hügel describes this type of mysticism as inclusive; that is, it stresses the inevitable mutual necessity and interaction among the three elements of religion and the three corresponding forces of the human soul. The institutional, rational, and experimental-mystical elements of religion and the corresponding sensational, intellectual, and volitional forces of the soul are indispensable to one another and to religion as a whole. It is extremely difficult to maintain the correct balance among these elements and forces. The problem of controlling one element and its corresponding force has appeared throughout the historical account of man, illustrating first the element's corrective dominance and then its dominant weakness. The only corrective to the wrong type of mysticism is another type—the inclusive—which brings into harmony the elements and soul-forces of the religious life.

Inclusive mysticism is religion at its best. Von Hügel describes it further in a letter to the Reverend H. Handley. All religion must have a world-fleeing and a world-seeking element, he writes. The spiritual life, often labeled the mystical life, cannot be measured by the world-fleeing element alone. There is rather the necessity of maintaining the two-fold movement of the spiritual life. This creates the true paradox and thereby the "divinely intended tensions" of the mystical way: "The two movements together —the tension thus generated between what thus conjointly produces a true paradox—are, I submit, of the very essence of our training, our testing, and our trail. . ."

It is this training, this testing, and this trial which Baron von Hügel reveals so intimately in his letters. As a man of faith and an independent thinker, von Hügel, in attempting to answer questions of universal religious importance, provides spiritual direction for all Christians.

CHRIST AND SOCIETY

Author: Charles Gore (1853-1932)
Type of work: Christian social ethics
First published: 1928

Principal Ideas Advanced

Christ's mission of salvation included the establishment of a new social order.

The ethics of the Gospel was partly provisional, having regard to the initial stage of Christ's program, and partly permanent, having regard to a continuing community.

Historically, the Church never lost sight of its social mission until modern times when, confronted with the problems of the industrial age, it narrowed its concern to the salvation of individuals.

Contemporary churches are in no position to recover their social mission, but concerned Christians in various denominations should form associations for achieving political and social reforms.

Christ and Society is a series of six lectures delivered under The Halley Stewart Trust, which was founded in 1924 to further "research toward the Christian ideal in all social life." Bishop Gore, a member of the Anglo-Catholic wing of the Church of England, had for many years made his influence felt in behalf of the social message of the Church. In *Christ and Society* he reaffirms his conviction that Christ's mission was to establish a new social order in the world, and that the ultimate goal of history is the realization of the reign of God on earth. The Church, as Bishop Gore understands it, was instituted by Christ to be a spiritual brotherhood, with rigorous ethical standards, commissioned to bring God's Kingdom into being. Unfortunately, in our day the nominal churches have ceased to have the character of a spiritual elite; hence, small informal societies of persons who have a passion for humanity and for reform must be assembled to carry on the proper work of the Church. It is Gore's hope that such activity may do much to restore the fabric of the Church itself, permitting it to resume its leadership in world affairs. In *Christ and Society*, the next to the last of Gore's major works, the author presents the best summary of his thought on the "social gospel."

Gore wrote at a time when the ethical teachings of Jesus were being subjected to criticism. He mentions in particular the doubts raised in the minds of many by the "consistent eschatology" of Albert Schweitzer, according to whom Jesus' teachings provide only an "interim ethic" suited to those who are expecting the end of the world. Gore admits that many of Jesus' moral teachings have a heroic quality which makes them unsuitable for a settled Christian community, but he explains this characteristic of Jesus' teaching as representing only one stage of His program. For, in Gore's opinion, Jesus deliberately planned His ministry, taking account of the historical situation within which He had to work. The radical self-denial demanded by many Gospel precepts was asked of the chosen band of disciples, whom He selected, tested, and organized to be the nucleus of the redeemed society. This was only the first stage. The second stage, which would be instituted after His death and resurrection under the influence of the Pentecostal Spirit, was the formation of the Church. His apocalyptic utterances with respect to the destruction of apostate Jerusalem referred to a third stage. After this, in the uncharted future, would come "the complete and final victory or vindication of God" against the cosmic background of "a great final world-catastrophe, world-judgment and world renewal."

Gore devotes the greater part of his book to reviewing the social attitudes of the Church through history. He was justified in undertaking this task because Ernst Troeltsch's *Social Teaching of the Christian Churches* (1912) had not yet been made available in English. (The translation was published in 1931, also under the Halley Stewart Trust.) Gore has made some use of Troeltsch's work, but his standpoint is different from that of the German scholar. Troeltsch denied that the Gospel contains any recognizable ethical or social teaching, and his account of the Church's social teaching was meant to be an objective survey. Gore, on the other hand, holds that the Gospel does provide normative ethical and social principles, and he uses these as a standard for judging the Church's performance. Generally speaking, he gives the early Church high marks for its faithfulness to the Master's purposes. The early Church made fellowship fundamental, and it insisted that its members live up to the ethical and social principles of the New Covenant. After the Edict of Milan, the situation was changed for the worse: membership in the Church became more and more nominal; in its new position as a civil religion, the Church bowed to expediency on every hand, particularly in resorting to compulsion. But, Gore points out, almost as soon as the Church proved unfaithful to the teachings of the Gospel, monasticism gave a new and far-reaching expression to Christian social ideals.

Bishop Gore has no special enthusiasm for the Middle Ages. While not inclined to minimize the importance of the Church as a civilizing medium, he wonders that it fell so completely away from the principles of the New Covenant, while returning to those principles that governed the Old. Little could be expected of a Church which availed itself of the services of a Clovis and a Charlemagne, and into which men were "baptized in platoons." Still, Gore acknowledges, it never occurred either to the popes or to the scholars of the Middle Ages that it was not the task of the Church to build the Kingdom of Christ on earth. They were unfaithful, in many instances, to the Master's goals, and they disregarded this appointed means, but at least they insisted that no aspect of life ought to be carried on without reference to Christian principles.

The abandonment of "the idea of the Church as the representative of the kingdom of God and the lordship of Christ on earth," says Gore, occurred only in modern times. The breakup of medieval culture and the rise of nationalism and of the new urban economy brought about momentous social changes with which the Church was increasingly unable to cope. Gore rejects the view that the Reformation, with its emphasis upon individualism, destroyed the old moral order and opened the way for the moral chaos of the industrial age. On the contrary, he says, the Reformed Church tried, much in the same manner as the medieval Church, to impose religious controls on commerce and on politics. It failed because it went about the task in the wrong way, trying to enforce regulations on institutions even though it was unable to exert any real influence on the lives of men. Conscious of this failure, and faced with the fact of a secular state and a self-regulating economy, the churches (Catholic and Protestant alike) turned their backs on society and concentrated on the "salvation of the individual." An anti-Christian philosophy, based on the theory that man's only ultimate motive is the pursuit of his own self-interest, was, thus, permitted to dominate the whole new industrial order; and such protests as were launched against it came not from the churches but from individuals like Charles Dickens, and from groups like the

Chartists and the Christian Socialists.

Gore recognizes that modern secular culture has done a great deal for the improvement of the human condition. One can point to the higher living standard and to the spread of political democracy; these, to some degree, offset the evils of wage-labor, colonialism, and war. Still, he maintains, the present system is so unsatisfactory as to demand complete revolution; and, for this reason, he is pleased to join hands with a wide range of social crusaders, so long as they are not pledged to violence. Christians share their desire to give every individual a chance to make the best of himself, and their belief is that this can come to pass only when the present capitalistic and nationalistic system is replaced by one in which the wealth of the world is placed at the disposal of humanity and not usurped by any one class or race.

But, although Christians can join with liberals in many projects, they cannot surrender their distinctive faith. Modern emancipatory movements ordinarily proceed upon the same basic assumptions as does bourgeois individualism, differing only in their determination to distribute to the many the advantages hitherto enjoyed by the few, whereas Christians are committed precisely to the task of reversing "the inner spirit of selfish individualism." The new society which Christ came to establish presupposes that men's lives have been radically changed, that they live in fellowship with God the Father and with the brotherhood of Christians, and that they have become fellow workers with Christ in the labor of extending His dominion throughout the world. In a very important sense, says Gore, Christianity is "other-worldly." It is not otherworldly in the sense of being indifferent to "this" world, but in the sense of maintaining that "this" world needs another world to complete it. "This world is not the goal nor the end," says Gore, "nor can we rely on progress being maintained in this world. But history has a goal. One day God is to come into His own. One day Christ is visibly to reign in all the universe. One day we are to see the City of God; and the Church of here and now, which is the vestibule of the kingdom of God, will pass into the kingdom realized in its perfection."

Gore carefully avoids any distinction between natural and supernatural agencies. He sees in Christianity the fulfillment, not merely of spiritual forces which were previously at work in Israel, but, in a broad sense, of principles struggling to be born in all the great world religions. Moreover, he insists, the Church must have "its ears open to the moral ideals of each age and country," for these, at their best, are also "real expressions of the divine purpose and the divine wisdom." If we believe in "a permanent Gospel which speaks through all unchanging ages to the unchanging heart of man," we must, he says, "be able to recognize also a fresh 'movement of God' in each age." Gore tends to see in the widespread demands of people everywhere for "liberty, equality, and fraternity," such a movement of God. But he distrusts large scale mass movements and violent attempts to rectify wrong. "If we accept the teaching of past experience," he says, "we should expect the general alteration to arise from the influence in our society of groups of men, inspired probably by prophetic leaders, who have attained to a true vision both of the source of our evils and the nature of the true remedies; and who have the courage of faith to bind them together to act and to suffer in the cause of human emancipation until their vision and their faith come to prevail more or less completely in society at large."

Gore has confidence in the ability of small groups to alter the course of history. "There must," he says, "be thirty or forty or a hundred in every town, who are both believers in the Name of Jesus as the true redeemer of man, and are also sure that this redemption requires for its free course social and industrial reform and reconstruction of a radical kind." Let them organize, cutting across denominational lines, and not claiming to be representative of any church but "only of a state of mind and determination of action." They should join forces with others who are working for political and social reform. But they must never forget that change of laws and redistribution of wealth are not to be sought as ends, but have value "only so far as they are means toward the expression of the kingdom of God."

AGAPE AND EROS

Author: Anders Nygren (1890-)
Type of work: History of Christian ethics
First published: Volume I, 1930; Volume II, 1936

Principal Ideas Advanced

The meaning of Christianity as a system of thought is best understood by determining its fundamental motif.

The fundamental motif of Christianity is Agape, God's spontaneous and unconditional gift of love to mankind.

Agape is incompatible with any other motif, but the history of Christianity reveals many attempts to synthesize it with Nomos and with Eros.

Nomos (law) is the fundamental motif of Judaism and Eros (man's egocentric and acquisitive love of the divine) is the fundamental motif of Hellenism.

St. Augustine determined the basic character of medieval piety by synthesizing Agape and Eros into Caritas, which is man's divinely inspired love of God.

Martin Luther attacked the Caritas piety of the medieval Church, broke the medieval synthesis of Agape and Eros, and returned to the motif of Agape as expressed in the New Testament.

Bishop Anders Nygren of the Church of Sweden, a former professor of theology at the University of Lund, is one of the foremost representatives of the so-called "Lundensian theology." Others in the movement are Bishop Gustaf Aulen, formerly a Lund professor, and Ragnar Bring and Gustaf Wingren, presently Lund professors.

The Lundensian school is distinguished by its theological method rather than by any novel theological conclusions. The Lundensians take seriously Immanuel Kant's attacks in *The Critique of Pure Reason* (1781) against the metaphysical presuppositions with which Christian theology had become associated. They see Kant's strictures as a reminder to the theologian that his task is to set forth objectively and descriptively a religion's understanding of how God and man come into fellowship with each other. The theologian's task is neither to defend the validity of religious experience nor to interpret this experience according to preconceived categories of philosophical or scientific analysis. The Lundensian method reflects also the influence of Martin Luther's belief that the Christian Gospel is its own authority. The theologian shows greatest respect for the freedom and authority of the Gospel when he limits himself to describing how the Gospel has been understood in its history.

The Lundensians in general, and Nygren in particular, hold that religions can be classified according to their answers to the question of the nature of the divine-human relationship. The study of these answers is called "motif research." The way to understand a religion is to determine the fundamental motif which it expresses through its thought and cultic practices. The method of motif research is appropriate for the study of any religion and not just for Christianity. Indeed, *Agape and Eros* is a comparative study of Judaism, Christianity, and various currents of Hellenistic religious thought. Still, the emphasis in this book is upon Christian thought, and the method has been used very largely for the investigation of Christian theology.

Part I of *Eros and Agape* is a comparative treatment of the two motifs of Agape and Eros as these motifs are exhibited in their classic expressions.

"Agape" is the Greek word used in the New Testament for describing the unique character of Christian fellowship with God, a fellowship which depends completely upon the unconditional divine love. Nygren's analysis of the New Testament Agape distinguishes four main characteristics: (1) It is spontaneous. (2) It is indifferent to the value of its object. God does not love the good man for his goodness nor the wicked man because of his wickedness. (3) Agape creates worth in its objects. (4) Agape initiates fellowship between God and man. Neither through merit nor repentance nor any other avenue is man able to come to God. Rather, God comes to man.

Nygren contends that the thought of both Jesus and St. Paul is controlled by the Agape motif. The chief difference between them is the latter's reluctance to speak of Agape as a human response to God, a reluctance which Nygren explains in terms of St. Paul's belief that human love can never be as completely unmotivated and spontaneous as divine love. St. Paul did, however, use Agape to refer to the Christian's love for his neighbor, for he saw the Christian as the instrument and bearer of Agape which flows out of God.

Plato (427-347 B.C.) and Plotinus (c.204-c.270) stated the Eros motif in the forms which most seriously challenged Agape, although there were numerous other Hellenistic religions and religious philosophies which also expressed the Eros motif. In Plato's thought Eros is the force which drives the soul upward from the material world to the world of absolute truth and beauty, the world of pure rational essences, or Ideas.

Plotinus, whose thought contains many Platonic elements and is described as Neoplatonic, sharply separated God and the physical world but provided for continuity between the two realms of being in the form of intermediate beings who emanated from God. The emanations represent a divine descent, but God in His essence remains aloof from the material world so that man by the power of Eros must ascend to God.

Eros is, in summary, that acquisitive, egocentric love by which man attempts to enhance the quality of his own being by possessing God. It is the upward movement by which man makes his way to God, whereas Agape is the downward movement by which God makes His way to man.

In Part II Nygren traces the seesaw history of the Agape motif once it had lost its initial clarity and depth and had begun to encounter the Jewish Nomos motif and the Hellenistic Eros motif.

The Apostolic Fathers and the apologists of the post-Apostolic period subordinated Agape to Nomos by picturing man's salvation as dependent upon his obeying the divine law of love.

Eros, however, was to present a more serious and persistent threat, and Nygren pictures Gnosticism as the form in which Eros presented its earliest serious challenge to Christianity.

The Gnostic interpretation of Christianity, an interpretation which reached its peak of influence in the first half of the second century, provided for a divine descent in the form of Christ. Still, the Gnostic Christ descended from Heaven mainly to give men esoteric knowledge and an inspiring moral example which would enable them to save themselves from the lusts of the body. The Gnostic Christ was religiously significant in stimulating Eros rather than in giving rise to Agape.

Nygren sees the Agape motif coming to the fore again in the thought of Marcion (died c.140), but finally receding because of Marcion's heretical views. In the thought of Tertullian (c.150-c.230) Agape was subordinated to Nomos. After having been under suspicion because of its association with the Gnostic heresy, Eros was prominent in the thought of the Alexandrian theologians, Clement (c.150-c.215) and Origen (c.185-c.254). Irenaeus, writing late in the second century, affirmed the centrality of Agape, but in a form mixed with Eros. The Eros motif gained strength in the thought of the fourth century theologians Methodius of Olympus, Athanasius, and Gregory of Nyssa, and in the thought of these men Eros and Agape were related in a situation of compromise, without achieving a true synthesis.

True synthesis was to come in the thought of St. Augustine (354-430). Just as Agape seemed in prospect of disappearing from Christian thought it experienced a powerful renewal, but not without undergoing a transformation which was to be crucial in the history of Christianity. Nygren argues that Augustine's doctrine of love as Caritas effectively superseded the New Testament concept of Agape. Caritas was a uniquely new motif which was similar to but different from its two components of Agape and Eros.

Because Eros was the chief attraction for him in Neoplatonism, Augustine readily detected the centrality of love in Christianity. Nygren contends that Neoplatonism prepared Augustine to achieve deeper insight into the meaning of Christian love but that it also imposed limits on his understanding of Agape.

Eros alone, Augustine contended, is insufficient because the ascent to the divine which it inspires results in pride, and this pride prevents further ascent. The function of God's Agape is to break the power of pride. Caritas results when man's inherent Eros is combined with and transformed by the divine grace. Thus Agape enters the Caritas synthesis in the form of divine grace which enables man to ascend to God. Although it is primarily man's God-given love of God, Caritas may also have the neighbor as its object. Caritas includes self-love, but a self-love which is sublimated and spiritualized in love of God and neighbor.

Augustine's Caritas synthesis dominated medieval Catholic piety and held unchallenged dominion for a millennium. Gradually, however, tension between the two elements in the synthesis became so powerful that disintegration set in, with the Renaissance expressing the Eros motif and the Protestant Reformation expressing the Agape motif. Martin Luther (1483-1546) led the Protestant assault against Caritas. He objected to all egocentric features of medieval piety and insisted upon a radically theocentric fellowship with God. Luther taught that the great stumbling block to fellowship with God lies in man's temptation to strive for goodness and holiness in order to win this fellowship. This temptation is rooted in prideful unwillingness to live wholly upon God's forgiving mercy as freely given in Christ. Thus Luther returned to the New Testament motif of Agape and its emphasis on a divine-human fellowship which occurs on the human level to which God descends. Caritas piety pictured this fellowship as occurring on the divine level to which man must climb.

Luther's return to an unmodified Agape motif stemmed largely from his own religious difficulties with the idea of Caritas as the sublimation of self-love into pure love for God. His efforts to love God led him to the despairing conclusion that self-love lay behind these efforts. Thus Luther broke with Augustine's distinction between sinful self-love (which expresses *cupiditas*) and proper self-love (which is present in sublimated form in Caritas). Any scheme of salvation which depends in any degree upon any kind of self-love is egocentric.

It is a mistake, Nygren affirms, to say that faith stands at the center of Luther's thought whereas love stands at the center of Catholic piety. Fundamentally, Luther was concerned to establish Agape against Caritas because he saw in the latter a subtle expression of Eros. Eros blocks fellowship with God because—no matter how high-minded it may be—it is acquisitive and self-seeking. But through faith man becomes open to divine Agape and serves as a medium through which Agape touches the world.

Nygren's picture of Agape as radically opposed to all forms of natural human love, while widely influential in Protestant circles, has met challenges from both Protestant and Roman Catholic theologians. The Protestant theologian Paul Tillich, in his book *Love, Power, and Justice* (1954), distinguishes between Eros and Agape as two *qualities* of love rather than as two *kinds* of love. The English Jesuit scholar M. C. D'Arcy, in his book *The Mind and Heart of Love* (1945), takes issue with Nygren's characterization of Eros and Agape, claiming that the two forms of love are complementary, with Eros as the possessive love which belongs to the essential side of the self and Agape as the sacrificial love which belongs to the existential side of the self.

CHRISTUS VICTOR

Author: Gustaf Aulén (1879-)
Type of work: History of doctrine
First published: 1930

Principal Ideas Advanced

In addition to the "objective" (Anselmian) and "subjective" (Abelardian) types of the idea of the atonement, there is a second objective type which may be called the "classic" idea of the atonement.

In the classic type the atonement is wholly the work of God and is achieved as God in Christ overcomes hostile powers which hold man in subjection.

Because of its predominance in the New Testament, in patristic writings, and in the theology of Luther, the classic type may be called the distinctively Christian idea of the atonement.

Gustaf Aulén's *Christus Victor*, which is a historical study of the three main types of the idea of the atonement, is an example of the application of the method of "the history of ideas" to historical theology. This theological method flourished during the past four decades at the University of Lund, Sweden, where Aulén taught until he was named a bishop. In using this historical method in *Christus Victor*, Aulén seeks to distinguish various "types," "ideas," or "views" of the atonement. He is primarily concerned that the reader should be able to recognize these types as they reappear in various periods of Church history. While some suggestions are given as to the origins of these ideas of the atonement, Aulén is less concerned with origins than with content. He holds, however, that it is significant to know which type is most characteristic of the teaching of the early Church.

In traditional histories of the doctrine of the atonement only two views have usually been presented, the "objective," or Anselmian, and the "subjective," or Abelardian, views. According to Aulén, however, there is another type of atonement doctrine in which Christ fights against and triumphs over evil powers (hence the expression "Christus Victor"), at the same time that God in Christ reconciles the world to Himself. This dualistic view Aulén calls the "classic" idea of the atonement, since it was dominant in Christianity for the first 1000 years of its history and was not displaced until the Middle Ages. The classic view was later restored by Luther, though his insights on this point were not accepted by his followers. Since the classic view is also objective, Aulén prefers to call the Anselmian view the "Latin" idea of the atonement. There are, then, two objective types (the classic and the Latin) as opposed to one subjective (or humanistic) type.

Aulén attributes the neglect of the classic view in recent times to the fact that both the orthodox and the liberals, although for different reasons, have failed to appreciate it. The classic view is not rational enough for the orthodox, while it is too mythological for the liberals, who react against its dualism and trace the idea to Zoroastrian sources.

Since the classic view can be clearly seen in the patristic period, and since our preconceptions do not blind us in studying the Fathers of the Church to the extent that they do when we read the New Testament, Aulén begins his study with the patristic writings. While Irenaeus, Bishop of Lyons (c.130-c.200), the first patristic writer who gives a clear and comprehensive doctrine of the atonement, places chief emphasis on the Incarnation, Aulén points out that in the classic view the atonement and the Incarnation are inseparably related. The Incarnation is necessary since only God can overcome the powers of sin, death, and the Devil. Through the life, death, and resurrection of Jesus Christ, whereby the life of man is recapitulated, these powers are overcome and God both reconciles man to Himself and is Himself reconciled. This recapitulation continues in the work of the Spirit in the Church and has an eschatological dimension.

Variations on this theme are found in the other patristic writers, though it is essential to understand correctly the imagery such writers use. Some say that the Devil, because of man's sin, has rights over men; others insist that the Devil is a usurper. All say the Devil is deceived. Some say a ransom is paid to the Devil, but that he is unable to retain it. Others prefer the thought of sacrifice. All are trying to say that God does not save man by almighty fiat, but participates by self-oblation in the drama by which men are freed. Those who say that the Devil is a usurper, yet has certain rights, are defending a limited dualism. The Devil is God's enemy, but the Devil is also the executant of divine judgment. To say that the Devil is deceived, is to say that the power of evil ultimately overreaches itself when it is in conflict with good or with God Himself.

The atonement, however, does not involve simply defeat of the Devil, for God is reconciled. Thus, the Devil and death are executants of the divine judgment. The emphasis on endurance of punishment and sacrifice shows the cost of victory for God. The paradoxical nature of this interpretation of the atonement prevents complete rational clarity, but Aulén suggests that there may be theological wisdom in not seeking to achieve complete rationality at this point.

After surveying the patristic period Aulén turns to the New Testament. He writes that we may assume it likely that the atonement view which dominates the patristic period should also be set forth in the Apostolic writings. One finds the Apostolic works are no more logically articulated in their ideas of the atonement than were the patristic. Nevertheless, one finds also a recurring theme of deliverance from hostile powers. Paul, in speaking of the powers which oppress man, emphasizes the Law more than do the Fathers, and he speaks of demonic *powers* rather than of the Devil. The Law is a hostile power not because it condemns sin, but because in so far as it contributes to legalistic religion it leads away from God. Divine love cannot be confined by the categories of merit and justice; it breaks through them. (Aulén attributes the early Church's failure to understand the hostile power of the Law to the controversy provoked by Marcion, a second century Christian heretic who wanted to exclude the Old Testament from the Christian canon.) Throughout the New Testament, in which it is emphasized that divine love itself is the agent of redemption, dualistic, or classical, concepts are prominent. In the Synoptic Gospels the exorcisms express the theme of triumph over evil powers, and the passion narratives tell how Jesus ultimately triumphs over the great adversary by succumbing to him and by giving His life as a ransom for many.

If the classic idea of the atonement is predominant in the New Testament and during the patristic period, how then is the origin of the Latin idea of the atonement to be explained? Aulén traces its beginnings to the Roman theologian Tertullian (c.160-c.220) and to Cyprian (c.200-258), who, in connection with their interpretation of the institution of penance, developed the ideas of satisfaction and merit. The characteristics of the Latin theory of the atonement are that it is legalistic and that it emphasizes what Christ did as a man. Anselm of Canterbury (c.1033-1109) gives the Latin theory its most complete systematic formulation, emphasizing that because of man's sin satisfaction must be made by man, and this requirement is met by Christ's atoning deed. The earlier dualism, which held that there were hostile powers from which man needed to be delivered, was discarded. The atonement was interpreted in such a way as not to infringe upon the order of law and justice. The alternatives for God are either forgiveness, which would mean that sin would not be treated with sufficient seriousness, or satisfaction, which can only be achieved through the death of Christ, the God-man. In one sense, God's attitude is not changed in the process of the atonement, for it is His will that Christ should on man's behalf make the satisfaction divine justice demands. Yet Aulén argues that if satisfaction can make amends for sin, God's radical opposition to sin is compromised. Aulén also points out that when the atonement is so understood sin itself remains unremoved.

In the later Middle Ages the Latin doctrine of the atonement was dominant, though Anselm's insistence on its rationality was no longer maintained. Yet the fact that this Latin view of the atonement is so fully in accord with the medieval emphasis on penance and the sacrifice of the Mass causes it to remain as authoritative doctrine. Peter Abelard (1079-1142), on the other hand, represents a different point of view. According to Abelard, Christ is both a teacher and an example exciting meritorious love in man. But

Abelard saw no special significance in the death of Christ. However, his view does not exert any great influence during the Middle Ages, and it was not until later that his more subjective approach to the atonement was given much attention.

The next major development, as far as the doctrine of the atonement is concerned, was the revival of the classic idea in Martin Luther (1483-1546). Many interpreters of Luther have regarded Luther's teaching with respect to the atonement as being simply a continuation of the medieval Anselmian tradition. Aulén insists, however, that Luther's realistic imagery must be taken seriously. Luther speaks of sin, death, the Devil, Law, and wrath as tyrants that must be overcome. He refers also to the deception of the Devil, which is his way of saying that the God who reveals Himself and delivers man is at the same time hidden in that which is lowliest and most despised. This is God's "deceit," which leads evil to assail the good to its own undoing. According to Aulén, the three typical characteristics of the classic idea of the atonement are present in Luther's interpretation of the work of Christ. Luther stresses (1) the continuity of the divine operation, so that the atonement is wholly the work of God, (2) the close connection of the atonement with the Incarnation, and (3) the dualistic and dramatic aspects of Christ's sacrifice.

Aulén finds in Luther not only a restoration of the classic idea of the atonement, but also a deeper development of this idea. This can be seen in Luther's interpretation of the Law and the wrath of God as enemies which are overcome in the atonement. Because the demands of the Law are deepened to include not merely external commands but also the spontaneous obedience of love, legalism becomes impossible and the Law can be clearly recognized as an enemy. Since the Law can never provide the basis for man's relationship with God, it must give way to grace. The emphasis on the wrath of God as one of the enemies brings the conflict by which man is redeemed almost within the divine nature itself. The wrath is real, yet love must prevail. Aulén suggests that the wrath of God may be understood as transcended, so that though it is overcome by divine love it still remains latent in and behind the divine love.

Luther's view of the atonement, however, was not fully understood by his successors, and thus in Protestant orthodoxy the atonement continues to be interpreted in medieval terms. Later, during the periods of Pietism and the Enlightenment, the humanistic and subjective ideas earlier expressed by Abelard were emphasized. It was then believed that due to God's benevolence no atonement is necessary, as far as God is concerned; all that is needed is that man repent. Friedrich Schleiermacher (1768-1834), a German theologian who, according to Aulén, represents a subjective approach to the atonement, distinguishes between salvation and atonement, emphasizing the former. According to Schleiermacher, it is man's salvation that makes the atonement possible. Thus, the emphasis shifts from what is done by God to what is done in and by man.

Aulén concludes his study by contrasting the three types which he has distinguished. When they are compared as to structure, Aulén finds that in the classic type there is continuity in the divine operation, with discontinuity in the order of merit and justice. God saves man, but to do so He must do violence to the just demands of His own Law. In the Latin type there is continuity in the order of merit and justice, with discontinuity in the divine operation. In order that the demands of the Law might be justified, Christ suffers as man. Thus, at this crucial point the atonement is man's work rather than God's. In the humanistic type the whole emphasis is on man's approach to God, rather than on God's approach to man. There is accordingly no attempt to view the atonement as a divine achievement.

With respect to the problem that sin poses, Aulén claims that in both the Latin and the classic types sin is taken seriously, while in the humanistic type the power of sin is not so strongly emphasized. In the classic type forgiveness, however, has a positive meaning, implying the restoration of fellowship, while in the Latin type forgiveness implies only the removal of guilt. With respect to salvation, in the classic view justification and atonement are identified, and atonement and salvation coincide. In the Latin view, atonement makes salvation possible, but justification and sanctification are separate acts having no organic connection. In the subjective type, salvation makes atonement possible and the change which takes place in man is emphasized.

As far as the Incarnation is concerned, in the classic type Christ is set forth as the man in whom God reveals Himself, carrying out His work of deliverance and atonement. In the Latin type, the connection between the Incarnation and the atonement is not as evident, while in the subjective type the whole emphasis is on the humanity of Christ. With respect to the concept, the classic type affirms dualism, yet insists that God is sovereign. In the Latin type, there is rational compromise of the opposition between God and evil, while in the humanistic type, God's opposition to evil is obscured.

Aulén finally reminds his reader that his intent in this book has been historical rather than apologetic. He has sought to describe three main types of the idea of the atonement, and he has not intended that his study should be a defense of the classic view. Yet Aulén does admit that in so far as the classic view is recognized as the authentic Christian understanding of the atonement, it is also in his opinion to this extent vindicated.

THE FAITH OF A MORALIST

Author: Alfred Edward Taylor (1869-1945)
Type of work: Moral theology
First published: 1930

Principal Ideas Advanced

Ethics has important metaphysical and theological implications, for what is and what ought to be may be distinguished but not divided.

The goal of the moral life is marked by a tension between the temporal and the eternal, and involves diminishing identification with the temporal and increasing participation in the eternal.

The historical religions have developed institutions to mediate and preserve their beliefs, and these institutions need not be regarded as irrational or scandalous by philosophers.

The prejudice against the historical and the individual on the part of many philosophers is unfortunate and, hence, the emphasis by Christianity on the historical as a real sphere of divine action is to be commended.

In the two volumes of his Gifford Lectures, *The Faith of a Moralist,* A. E. Taylor covers a wide territory of culture, philosophy, and theology. His vast scholarship produced a richly woven tapestry of mature learning. His stance in the first volume, entitled "The Theological Implications of Morality," is that of a professional teacher of ethics probing into the presuppositions and implications of the moral life to discover what, if anything, it has to say about the assertions of theology. Three issues, Taylor believes, are critical; first, how the moral ideal is related to time and the supratemporal; second, how it is related to human effort and the claim of divine grace; and third, how the question of autonomy should be handled in ethics and related disciplines.

His argument on the distinction between value and fact is fundamental. Ethics, some have said, has to do with values, ideals, and obligations and not with existences as such. Its sphere is that of the goodness or badness of what is. If this is so, the moralist would seem to be straying from his subject when he pronounces on what is, rather than on what ought to be. Ethics, it is argued, cannot be made to say anything about existence. Religion, however, if it is anything at all, certainly does say something about reality, for its object of worship must be taken as a reality; its god cannot be known to be an illusion.

A. E. Taylor will have nothing to do with such a sharp disjunction between fact and value, and he asserts, "I regard it as the most important problem in the whole range of philosophy to examine this alleged want of connection between reality, actuality, existence or being, and goodness or value in a spirit of thorough criticism." Values, he argues, are always resident in persons, are more than mere ideas, and are always given together with facts. Therefore what they say is by no means unimportant to theology and metaphysics.

Human life is embedded in history, but this specter of the transitoriness of time need not be a frustration. The concept of time is a different thing in mathematics and morality. Mere before and after is one thing; past, present, and future is another. Man is unique in that he can survey the past, form expectations for the future, and respond to an ideal good which is present in all his moral striving. It is here that morality makes contact with religion, for God as "the absolute and final plenitude of good" can relieve our frustration. If the moral life is taken seriously, it involves aspiration and progress; and both imply time and its transcendence, attachment and detachment, in which the very salvation of the soul is at stake. Man in his pilgrimage may choose to follow the desires of the moment, or even to improve on the present and to tie his hopes to the march of history; but so long as he conforms himself to the temporal, the full ethical implications of the good will not be realized, for these implications point to the eternal, the goal of deiformity.

To argue thus is not to say that the moral end is clear and distinct after the manner of René Descartes (1596-1650), the father of modern philosophy. The moral ideal is not available to men through introspection; men come to know the good only as they are faithful to whatever light is already present. Morality involves faith.

Some reinforcement of the thesis that the moral life has religious ties comes from the experience of evil—a topic, says Taylor, that is often handled inadequately in ethical discussion. The experience of evil is exclusively human. Explanations in terms of environment, inefficiency, or outworn superstition will not do. The awareness of guilt and pollution can be evaluated adequately only in intrapersonal terms, as a breakdown of, indeed as an outrage against, an ideal which is actualized in God, the fount of all goodness.

How does a person go from badness to goodness? Moralists have tended to discuss both, but they have been less than satisfactory on how the transition is to be made. For religion, motivation is related to the grace of God, the divine initiative; and here again ethics leads up to theology. It would be a mistake, of course, to regard grace as eliminating human effort. Ethics can never permit the surrender of personal decision and striving. The position is rather one of response to the divine action so that, even in natural theology, there are directional signals toward God as redeemer, lover, and self-revealer.

Has the moral nature of man anything to say about the destiny of the individual? We do not have a blueprint of Heaven, and inferences have to be made with caution. At least, Taylor argues, we can note as of some interest that mankind as a whole believes in some kind of continuance of life after death. This ordinary belief is, however, limited in impressiveness. Kant's sophisticated argument that the balance of virtue and happiness demands immortality appeals to many, but does the moral imperative actually set up such a demand? If a convincing case can be made out for obligation as valid only within history in terms of an increase in individual happiness and social betterment, then obligation cannot be used as a witness to any life beyond history. Taylor prefers to argue, however, that the moral end is not exclusively concerned with a better world, but centers about the task of making better people, and this, in history, involves man's becoming less dependent on fluctuating circumstances, less identified with the temporal, more concerned with the eternal.

In fact, the concept of another world, if properly defined, is indispensable to moral endeavor in this world. The belief in eternal life has profound effects on the conduct of life. A moral person dare not make society, nation, or family his supreme loyalty. The alternative end may lack clear definition, but at least it can be said to be both present and future, immanent and transcendent, truly human and truly divine.

Great care must be taken to avoid defining morality in such a way that its end negates it. For example, if goodness is the result of successful conflict with evil, overcoming temptation, righting wrongs, putting the Devil to flight, then the struggle against evil would be an essential ingredient in the good life. When this fight is over and the victory won, goodness would vanish also. The correction needed here is to refuse to accept evil as necessary to good. The element of activity, adventure, and progress can still be present without the presence of evil. There can be progress *in* goodness as well as progress *toward* it. A life of service to God could mean the continual enrichment of personal life in moral activity.

A. E. Taylor proceeds to confront the positive religions in the second volume of his series. There is, he asserts, no philosophical religion, only religions that are historical and institutional, and these have four features: (1) they originate in some historical founder, (2) their message is believed to be revealed rather than discovered, (3) there is an authoritative medium of interpretation for the message, and (4) institutions are developed to sustain belief. All of them incorporate the three factors discussed in the first volume; namely, the existence of God, the grace of God, and participation in the life of God.

Many philosophers recoil from such religions and prefer to remain detached, because a historical religion is committed to association with contingent factors. Historical and empirical involvement creates tensions for the rational mind. As a matter of fact, however, these very philosophical critics, Taylor points out, are deeply in debt to institutional religion for some of their own perspectives and may be in danger of discarding in the name of reason what in fact may be true by revelation.

The assault on the claims of the great religions, it must be admitted, has been impressively argued. Furthermore, Judaism, Christianity, Islam, Buddhism, and the like are in strong disagreement, and none seems to be able to establish its claim to be an exclusive medium of truth. In any case, the critics assert, the claim to revelation is incredible, and any pretension to finality is impossible where fallible human recipients are included. What really matters, it is said, is the practical function of religion in society and the moral quality of the life it stimulates, not its absurd doctrines which, as a matter of record, abound in scientific and historical errors.

These are serious charges, and Taylor is most anxious to give them their due while at the same time refusing to concede all that is claimed for them. A reasonable case can be made out for revelational religion, he believes, even in the face of such radical criticism. A conflict of claims between religions for example, does not mean that they cancel one another out. It could be that one is actually true. With regard to revelation, could it not be argued that genius is in the same vulnerable positions, for its appearance is also associated with insights into truth? In fact, the objections are too sweeping. It is not unreasonable to claim that revelation could be contextual and also final; the kernel and the husk can still be distinguished. Again, with regard to the contribution made by religion to morality, it is certainly true that religion has had an important moral effect, but this is true because of the theology behind religion. Indeed, the proper order is to make theology primary, and ethics derivative. Finally, the fact that proponents of religion have propagated some scientific and historical errors from time to time can be quite fairly charged to the fallible agents involved and need not imply the falsity of the religious truths they represent.

A really sore point of contention is the assertion, especially on the part of Christianity, that certain events of history are also facts of the faith by which one must be saved. This has been a sensitive point from earliest times. How can a faith claiming finality rest securely on a basis which is open to historical criticism? What if the records should prove to be false? Indeed some have argued that the mythical outweighs the historical in the Gospels.

Honest criticism, Taylor admits, must have its day in court. In fact, when its story is told, the divine Incarnation in a historical person is not weakened. On the contrary, the conviction that this is the strength of Christianity can be defended. The Apostolic message was never tied to biographical details; in fact, the message seems never to have made use of these details; it concentrated on the Crucifixion and Resurrection. Christians have never concealed the necessity of faith involved in the assertion of the Incarnation as divine revelation. "It is not the part of wisdom, which is always humble," Taylor writes, "to pronounce too confidently that there is 'nothing in' any conviction which has fed the spirituality of generations."

A special case of the historical factor is the matter of miracles, and this factor has provoked strong criticism. Undoubtedly miracles abound in religious literature, and few will dispute that great quantities of these stories of miracles are apocryphal. Must we say all?, Taylor asks. If reality were a closed system of natural law, Taylor says, this would end the argument; but, in fact, it is not so, as far as we know. Nature has its surprises as well as its regularities; and, if God exists, then He may very well act in ways that appear unusual and even startling to men. Such actions cannot be ruled out by a theist as either impossible or improbable. Miracles can be significant communication. Mistaken identification of the "numinous" quality of some events should not lead to a blanket rejection of all claims in regard to miracles.

Another feature of the positive religions with which A. E. Taylor deals in an incisive section is the assertion of an authority to which all must submit. This appears to be "treason to reason." All pronouncements, philosophers aver, should be scrutinized by rational analysis and their credentials evaluated. Undoubtedly, it must be granted, there have been so many utterances by religious persons that are highly questionable that discrimination is inevitable. On the other hand, the authoritative force of some experiences is common enough, such as in everyday sense perception of the natural world. Religious authority is the force with which religious experience is compelling independently of the mind's own action. The reports of such experiences, Taylor believes, are not necessarily accurate, and where asserted as authoritative these reports need scrutiny. Yet the sense of authority itself defies analysis. No better illustration of the paradoxical features of religious authority is available than in the function of conscience where the old rule holds true, that though conscience is not infallible it should always be followed.

Those who resent the authoritarian stance of the positive religions generally also object to the sacred procedures and structures which religions have developed to express their mission and to stabilize the approach to the supernatural. There are, of course, degrees of formality and convention all the way from the spontaneous Spirit-filled Apostolic fellowship to the elaborate liturgical spectacles of some modern churches. Support for or against forms and ceremonies has oscillated back and forth throughout Church history. Surely, however, there is nothing either religious or nonreligious about conventions as such. Life in general without habits would be intolerable. The true issue, Taylor argues at length, is neither fixed forms or spontaneous formlessness, but finding a mean that will be effective without being artificial. The aim of institutional procedures is to create an impression adequate to the theme, to contribute to significance. Human beings need orderly ways of doing things to channel affections and to sustain them. Thus, conventions appear in family life, in social and political action, in the administration of justice, as well as in religious activities. But conventions should never be so inflexible or so uniform as to prevent worship rather than promote it.

A special cause of scandal to some rationalists is the ritual of sacraments; that is, the use of objects of sense as media of spiritual benefit. To many this is nothing less than a relapse into magic. Taylor is insistent that this is not so, or not necessarily so. Belief in sacraments need not clash with the rational principles of metaphysics, for their present meaning is not tied to the more crude and primitive forms which engross the attention of the anthropologists. Again, it is not the material elements used that produce grace, but the divine will and the condition of the participant. Nor is it usual to hold that this is the only way the help of God can be found. Magic enters in only when some manipulation of material is believed to be automatically productive of some favor or curse. Such practices are certainly to be repudiated. Taylor is also opposed to precise enumeration of sacraments. "The effect on the Western Church of the hard-and-fast dogmatising of the divines of Trent, and the Reformers alike, about the number of the sacraments of grace and their immediate institution by Christ seems to me to have been wholly unfortunate," he writes. While the great moments of worship may come in sacramental acts, it is not in the power of man to tie God to a fixed number of ceremonies.

Again and again in the lectures the tension between the temporal and the eternal appears as the key problem. The historical and the superhistorical confront but do no oppose one another, and Christianity at least demands that neither be taken as illusory. The Incarnation demands time as a real element, though not necessarily as an ultimate element, in the divine purpose; dogmatism here, where knowledge is partial, would be reprehensible. A sane agnosticism befits an honest man. What we do know, however,

Taylor insists, we should try to make intelligible, and theology has its contribution to make to the search for truth just as much as do science and philosophy.

THE DESTINY OF MAN

Author: Nikolai Berdyaev (1874-1948)
Type of work: Christian ethics
First published: 1931

Principal Ideas Advanced

Ethics can be understood only in the context of man's created nature and ultimate destiny.

The suffering God alone can answer the problem of evil by revealing human creativity as of ultimate meaning in the completion of creation.

Ethics has beauty as its goal, the content of which must emerge through creative entry into the uniqueness of each situation.

For centuries, Eastern Orthodoxy has been of only historic interest to the West, even among Christian thinkers. The reasons for this isolation are two-fold. First, Eastern theological reflection has been ingrown and static. Second, there has been little interest in or capacity for creative dialogue with Western thought.

Consequently, the translation of the works of Nikolai Berdyaev into English, and particularly his chief work, *The Destiny of Man: An Essay in Paradoxical Ethics,* is to be heralded as a monumental first step in the establishment of creative theological dialogue between East and West. The results thus far have been considerable, both in fact and promise. For a Western Christianity thoroughly grounded in the emphasis of the Western Fathers on personal guilt and the atoning answer of Crucifixion, Berdyaev's reformulation of the emphasis of the Eastern Fathers on cosmic transformation through Incarnation and Resurrection comes as a welcomed addition. Immersed both in Western and Eastern philosophy, Berdyaev creatively relates Eastern process-thought and Western existentialism within a Christian framework shaped by the Kantian critiques.

For a contemporary theology presently obsessed with culture, Berdyaev must be recognized as one of the most original Christian thinkers on the meaning of culture and the arts. Finally, in the present social crisis, Berdyaev appears as one of the most outspoken critics of both Capitalism and Communism.

For Berdyaev, the modern dilemma has its basis in epistemology. "Man has lost the power of knowing real being, has lost access to reality and been reduced to studying knowledge." There can be no return to pre-critical metaphysics, but neither can man rest with the epistemological dualism made absolute after Immanuel Kant (1724-1804).

The only solution is an existentialist understanding of knowing: knowledge is a sympathetic penetration into the existence of the known. The error of modern philosophy was the attempt to become a science, to reduce all reality to phenomena, under the category of necessity. True knowledge is participation in the noumenal dimension. Theology is concerned with this realm, but its results are forced on it from without, through dogma accepted on authority. For the philosopher, however, such revelational facts are part of the world to be known and thus are true only if they become an inner experience. Philosophical knowledge, then, "is not revelation, but man's free cognitive reaction to revelation." Because philosophy deals with the mystery of being and life, it rests in spiritual experience.

Berdyaev's methodology is thus Augustinian, as opposed to the Thomistic method which he sees as thoroughly pagan: "Philosophy knows being in and through man and finds in man the solution of the problem of meaning, while science knows being as it were apart from man and outside him." Epistemology must discover who the knower is; and the intuitive discovery of the noumenal, spiritual self is the key to all knowledge; it is the penetration into being from within.

It is from this methodology that the nature of ethics, Berdyaev's primary concern in this volume, is to be derived. Like philosophy as a whole, ethics must rest on intuitive moral experience. It must be part of a living ontology centered in the interior knowledge of the doer. Since ethics involves all values (moral, aesthetic, cognitive), it embraces everything connected with human freedom; and since human freedom can be understood only in its relation to divine freedom, ethics can be understood only in terms of a total philosophical world view. "Ethics must be the theory of the destiny and vocation of man, and must inquire in the first instance into the nature of man, his origin and his goal."

It is at this point that the most difficult but fascinating portion of Berdyaev's understanding emerges. The primary problem of ethics is the feud between creature and Creator. Atheism is the honest attempt to come to terms with the fact of evil; there can be no transition to theism without an adequate theodicy. The traditional Christian understanding Berdyaev finds inadequate, for while it affirms human freedom as the cause of evil, this freedom is affirmed to be determined by God. Foreseeing that man would fall, God consents to create man. Likewise, in awaiting man's response, God is awaiting Himself, for even the response is predetermined.

For Berdyaev, the Christian understanding of God must begin not with Greek philosophical ideas of impassivity, pure actuality, and the like, but with an immanent awareness of the God of the Incarnation. From this perspective, the traditional theodicy is inadequate and stands in living contradiction to the suffering God of the Cross. Certain insights of the Christian mystics seem closer to the truth. Out of the Divine Nothing, the Holy Trinity is eternally being born; that is, God is not complete actuality, but He who acts. Because God exists, nonbeing takes on infinite possibilities in the creative imagination of God, and its fulfillment enriches God Himself. While God did not create nonbeing, whatever God creates must be created from nonbeing; that is, it must be created with freedom.

Consequently, man is the child both of God and freedom (nonbeing). While nonbeing consented to this creative act by God, man in his freedom rejected the Creator, yearning for nonbeing and thereby mixing being with nonbeing. This is man's tragedy, but also God's, for God longs for His friend, for man, to share in completing creation by bringing being from nonbeing through freedom.

God is all-powerful over being, but He is powerless over uncreated freedom. God cannot avert the Fall without destroying man. After the Fall, God does all that He can do. He appears not as Creator but as Redeemer. The Cross must not be understood juridically, as recompense for an autocratic deity, but as the supreme act of the suffering God, who descends into the abyss of nonbeing and participates in the world of demonic freedom. Evil can be enlightened only from within, or the positive possibilities of freedom are destroyed; redemption cannot be coercion.

The Fall itself points to this sublime destiny of creativity intended by God for His creatures. While the theologians use the Fall to humiliate man, Berdyaev sees it testifying to man's power, for man can rise against God Himself, transforming the world into an evil chaos. What belittles man is not his nature, but his evil use of freedom. In the Incarnation man is restored to his sublime nature, the image of the *Creator* God. Through spiritual experience, the Incarnation becomes living fact. The God-man is not only a revelation of God, but also an anthropological revelation. This restored self is man's noumenal self, Kant's free self, which in the noumenal depths participates in the very life of God as well in the noumenal depth of all created reality. Thereby, through the inspiration of the Holy Spirit, man is opened in each new situation to its creative possibilities, transfiguring its nonbeing into being.

The Christian God is the Trinity, corresponding to the three-fold aspect of man's spiritual experience. When one ascribes to an Unmoved Mover all the attributes which one despises in man, man cannot help but revolt; only in the God of suffering love, yearning for his human "other," is human rebellion won over from within and freedom brought to its full creative possibilities.

It is from this understanding of man's destiny that ethics takes its meaning. Creativity is the divine-human vocation; and creation *"means transition from non-being to being through a free act."* The Fall created the distinction between good and evil. Good comes into being—and disappears—with evil. Thus, although the beginning and end of history is existence beyond the distinction, history is a tragic circle unless beginning and end are far from identical. Although Eden was the life of bliss, of instinct, the realm of the unconscious, man chose to abandon this ignorance in order to explore his destiny. Knowledge in itself is good, not sin, but man's choice was for nonbeing rather than a positive response to God's creative call. Once this choice is made, man must follow his destiny to its end.

The image of God in man could

have been preserved through limited consciousness, although consciousness is purchased at the price of the noumenal-phenomenal distinction. The real fall occurs when man makes this distinction absolute, surrendering to the necessity of the phenomenal realm. To do so is to forfeit freedom, the true self, and man's destiny as creator. This risk God cannot avoid; He must allow evil for the sake of the good of freedom.

This is the root of the tragedy of ethics. To legislate the good is to destroy freedom and to undermine the very good which one is intent on realizing. Ethics must correspond to the dynamism of existence; it must transfigure evil by enlightening freedom from within. True freedom is not in obeying laws but in creating new realities, in creating the good, not just in fulfilling it.

Such creativity is possible, Berdyaev believes, because the worlds of nature and spirit intersect in man. This is the existential meaning of the Incarnation, exposing "personality" as *the* moral principle. The "individual" is fallen; it is hardened selfhood. Personality is the melting away of the individual in communion with reality. The human task is thus to sublimate and reorient man's biological base through a revelation of man's spiritual, noumenal nature; this is to answer in freedom the divine call to creativity. Freedom is liberated creative energy.

Berdyaev's view is in radical opposition to much Christian ethics. Man is called not to reject his own self, but to love it as the image of God. The egoist is the one who has an aversion to the self. To love others as ourselves means to love the divine possibilities in our nature and to fulfill them; such fulfillment is through the mutuality of love.

In mutuality, the source of creativeness is revealed—the imagination. Through imagination, God created the world; through loving imagination, man enters into its completion, creating out of nonbeing images of beauty that have never before existed. In living dialogue with these images, the self and the other are mutually fulfilled. In ethics, imagination plays the part of talent.

Man is sick because he does not do what he wants to do. Not seeing this, Christian ethicists have seen only two possible ethics: the ethic of law (the Old Testament ethic of the Father) and the ethic of redemption (the New Testament ethic of the Son). A legal ethic cannot change human nature, for it only represses the unconscious. An ethic of society imposed on the individual renounces sin, but it cannot conquer it. In the primitive stages of humanity, such an ethic was necessary, and aspects of it are still necessary against demonic exploitation in the social sphere. Its highest achievement, however, is the concept of justice.

Once the distinction between good and evil appears, man thirsts not only for escape from evil, but also for escape from the very distinction. He thirsts for redemption. With redemption, morality is based not on ideas of the good but on the power of grace. The only law is that every moral action demands its own individual solution. Berdyaev writes, "Every moral act must be based upon the greatest possible consideration for the man from whom it proceeds and for the man upon whom it is directed." This is the heroic ethic of love, following the line of the greatest resistance to the world. It is to accept suffering positively, as the "fundamental law of life," for through suffering comes love and in love evil is illuminated from within.

These two ethics expose the dualism of man, in that they show that he belongs to the order of nature and spirit, law and grace. The Gospel and the world are utterly incompatible, and in this tragic tension the call to a third ethic is felt, the ethic of creativeness (the ethic of the Holy Spirit). In speaking ot talents that must be returned with profit, Christ spoke of man's creative vocation. Gifts from God are not to be passively awaited and received, but are to be performed actively as tasks. Genius feels that he is a means by which God works His own ends; he is a man possessed. Grace is inspiration, and freedom is response; their interaction is creativity. In creative work, the self is forgotten; one passes beyond good and evil and participates in the freedom of the Holy Spirit. Redemption, although utterly necessary, is negative; it is deliverance *from* sin. It is not an end but a means; it is *for* creativeness, for self-justifying fullness.

The ethic of creativeness neither destroys nor binds, but transfigures. Its stress is on motive, Berdyaev says, on the "selfless and disinterested love of God and of the divine in life. . . ." Each person must act as himself in the uniqueness of each situation, and not as one would have him act. Man must rise to divine creativeness, or the dynamism of his being will drive him into the destructive womb of nonbeing. Empty evil cannot be crushed; it must be reoriented. Sex, for example, can never be eliminated, but it can be creatively transfigured into the loftiest of values.

An ethic of negativity is self-destructive and existentially impossible, for it mistakes man's fallen condition for his ontic nature and ultimate destiny. The fallen creature desires, but on acquiring the object of desire, he tires of it; life is a continuous frustration. But in redemption the real nature of receiving is made known; in giving is the receiving real. Thus the true end of life is seen as not being the good, for good rests in dualism with evil. The final end is *beauty*. "Beauty is the image of creative energy radiating over the whole world and transfiguring it," writes Berdyaev. Creative intuition alone is an escape from sin, from necessity, from time; it is a momentary glance into eternity from which true beauty is inspired and to which in the end it will return with interest, to be completed as the enrichment of God Himself.

Because all ethical attainments are incomplete, ethics must ultimately rest in eschatology. The ethical vision of beauty shows that meaning is found only in terms of eternity, in that which conquers the nonbeing of death. Thus the fundamental principle of ethics is so to act as to conquer death by affirming the eternal possibility in every aspect of life. Christ's love means love for everything that lives, down to the very blades of grass. Either all must receive eternal life, or the world cannot be accepted and justified. Nothing is immortal in itself, but in the resurrection of Christ the hope witnessed to in life becomes a divine promise. This end to be, however, involves a demand. Berdyaev regards human creativity as having ontic significance; creativity makes possible "eternal, permanent, immortal goods and values which further the victory of eternity and prepare man for the end."

THE GROWTH OF THE IDEA OF GOD

Author: Shailer Mathews (1863-1941)
Type of work: American Protestant liberal theology
First published: 1931

Principal Ideas Advanced

Originating in the quest for security and moral direction through personal relations with the cosmic environment, the idea of God always reflects the prevailing social patterns of an era, and thus it must be understood through a study of its development in the light of the various mind-sets through which it has passed.

The evolutionary process described by modern science manifests something akin to purpose in its production of personality, and this fact provides the clue to a view of God viable for contemporary men.

God is the human conception of the personality-evolving and personally responsive factors in the universe upon which men are dependent for their fulfillment and with which religiously satisfying relations are possible.

Shailer Mathews's *The Growth of the Idea of God* is an excellent example of a widespread movement in twentieth century American theology which attempted to employ the methods and conclusions of empirical science in order to reinterpret the ancient Christian Gospel for the present age. One of the strong centers of this scientific modernism in the years following 1915 was the University of Chicago. Here Mathews and others constituted what has been called the Chicago school of theology, a group of men holding a variety of views but characterized generally by a socio-historical, empirical, and pragmatic approach to the study and interpretation of religion. Some of the other representatives of this left wing of liberalism were Shirley Jackson Case (1872-1947), Gerald Birney Smith (1868-1929), Edward Scribner Ames (1870-1958), and John Merlin Powis Smith (1866-1932). All agreed that traditional Christian teaching had to be radically rethought if it were to compete for the minds of contemporary men. The present work attempts just this sort of modernizing with regard to a particular doctrine. It begins with an effort to discover by historical analysis the pragmatic meaning of the idea of God in human experience, and it concludes with a view of God which is thought to be relevant to the religious and intellectual needs of the scientific era.

Underlying this book is Mathews's conviction that religious doctrines are functional formulas which interpret the human experience of God in terms derived from the dominant social patterns of the age. This orientation leads him to affirm that the idea of God must be studied from the historical, social, and practical religious point of view and not from the standpoint of metaphysics. Philosophy has rationalized the idea of God but did not originate it. Religion, the human quest for aid, peace, and moral control through personal relations with the cosmic environment, has led men to speak of God, and society has provided the patterns in which this experience has been expressed. Since social patterns change, the forms of religious doctrines likewise change. God, then, is not an absolute metaphysical term with an unchanging content but is relative to the needs and the dominant social "mind-sets" of various cultural epochs. In short, the meaning of the idea of God is to be found in the history of the religious uses of that idea and in the study of the underlying social patterns which have structured it during the course of its development. Since through a combination of fortunate circumstances the idea of God has attained its most complex development in the Christian religion, Mathews concentrates on the background and growth of this social tradition.

The thesis of Mathews is that the ultimate origin of religion among primitive men is not to be found in fear but in the desire to establish help-gaining relationships with the mysterious powers on every hand on which human welfare was felt to be dependent. These relationships were initiated by approaching the gods in the socially approved ways of dealing with other persons, especially those held in high esteem. Certain persons were set aside as being experts in bringing about proper adjustment to the gods; desire for reality in worship led to the representation of the venerated powers in various art forms; and finally the Gods were assigned the task of protecting and directing the mores of the group. In this way religion was born. The further development of religious ideas followed upon the increasing complexity of society and the emergence of civilization.

Hebrew religion, according to Mathews, had its roots in primitive practices, but over a period of one thousand years it underwent a remarkable growth and emerged with a high ethical monotheism. Lacking a philosophical spirit and the capacity for metaphysics, the Hebrews developed their unique religion by virtue of the special factors which characterized their social history. The distinctive faith of the Hebrews began to emerge when they adopted one god to be worshiped in exclusion to all others. The entrance into Canaan tore Jahveh loose from His mountainous home in the Sinaitic peninsula; the adoption of agriculture as a way of life led to an extension of His power over nature; the union of the tribes into a monarchy gave rise to a corresponding growth in the majesty and power of God; and finally the impact of other nations upon Israel suggested the idea that Jahveh is an international deity directing the destinies of all men. Thus, monotheism emerged and was given its classic statement in the writings of Deutero-Isaiah.

A cosmology adopted from the Babylonians explained the relationship of God to nature as that of Creator, and a pattern derived from Israel's political life interpreted the relationship of Jahveh to His people as that of Sovereign King, while the unusual insight of the Prophets gave rise to a view of God as a completely moral being. The emergence of the wisdom literature as a commentary on the practical problems of life, the development of legalism in an attempt to be obedient to the last detail of the divine law, and the emergence of apocalypticism under the pressure of persecution completed the major elements of the tradition into which Jesus appeared with His idea of God as a loving Father who desires all men to be brothers.

Mathews finds that the Graeco-Roman world had a quite different development. The Aryan peoples produced a popular polytheism and a philosophical monotheism. The latter was the product of the speculative genius of the great Greek and Roman thinkers who spoke in various ways of a unity of being and of a rational order underlying the multifarious processes of ordinary experience. While no clear-cut religious monotheism ever emerged to win universal adherence, a trend in this direction was furthered by the sense of power and unity generated by the Roman Empire, typified by the worship of the Emperor. It remained for Christianity to effect a union of Greek philosophical monotheism with Hebrew religious monotheism.

It is the view of Mathews that this union was accomplished by the widespread interpenetration of peoples throughout the Roman Empire and the transition of Christianity from Jewish to Hellenistic membership. A modification of Hebraic monotheism took place as Jesus was exalted to a divine status, and a complex struggle ensued in which the precise relationship of the divine Christ to the Creator-Father God of the Old Testament was worked out. The outcome was the formulation in the fourth century of the classical doctrine of the Trinity, which spoke of one God-substance existing in three persons. Mathews sees this orthodox formula not so much in terms of a triumph of superior logic or theological reasoning over alternative perspectives as in terms of a power struggle in which the strongest party was able to enforce its views on the whole Church. Although the doctrine of the Trinity contains insoluble philosophical difficulties due to the impossibility of treating analogies, symbols, and patterns such as paternity, sonship, generation, and procession as metaphysical truths, it did serve the important religious function of preserving a genuine though complex monotheism in which the same personal God is confronted in nature, in the life of Jesus, and in personal experience.

Mathews sees the growth of the idea of God from the fifth to the twentieth centuries as a reflection of the underlying changes which took place in the social structure of Western civilization. The theology of the Middle Ages took over the pattern of political sovereignty and presented God as an exalted feudal Monarch who orders all things by His omnipotent will. The Renaissance of the fourteenth and fifteenth centuries introduced an approach to God which saw Him immanent in the processes of nature, but, more importantly, it generated a line of development outside the Church regarding the idea of God which was to parallel from that time forward the theology within the Church. The Reformation, reflecting both political and economic factors, produced at its center a theology based on the absolute sovereignty of God patterned after the political absolutism of the emerging nation states. However, growing democratic tendencies in England and Holland were reflected in the gradual modification of the absolute divine decrees as, for example, in the rise of Arminian theology. The final triumph of democracy and a changed conception of God came about because of the demand of the bourgeoisie for economic freedom. In the last half of the nineteenth century God took on a humanitarian character and was presented in a growing liberalism as a loving Father, and adjustments to the patterns suggested by modern science were seen to be forthcoming in those social orders where freedom had made creative thought possible.

The contemporary era has been marked, according to Mathews, by the emergence of new religious patterns suggested by sociology, science, and philosophy. Out of a sociological background has come a humanism which stresses devotion to human values but which neglects the relationship of men to the cosmos which produced them. Numerous scientists have spoken of the reality of religion as the response to the mysterious spiritual powers which pervade the world of purposeful activity open to empirical observation. Present-day philosophers are characteristically oriented by scientific modes of thought and tend either to define religion as the pursuit of values or to speak of some sort of cosmic purpose based on the facts of creative evolution. All these conceptions abandon the patterns of traditional theology and make clear that any contemporary view of God must be based on the scientific outlook.

At the conclusion of this study, which has attempted to illustrate the thesis that all ideas of God are relative to the social mind-sets of the various cultural eras through which it moved in its growth, Mathews sets forth his own conception of God. The many patterns in which the idea of God has appeared express relations between persons and their cosmic environment and therefore point to something real, although the reality does not correspond literally to the pattern. The problem, then, is to express this reality in contemporary terms. Mathews begins with the scientific description of a world process which has produced and continues to sustain personalities existing in organic relationship with the cosmos. The only explanation of this fact, Mathews urges, is that there are personality-producing factors in the universe. Moreover, these creative forces continue to function in the environment in which men live and offer aid to human fulfillment when proper adjustment is made to them. God is the conception men have of these personality-evolving elements in the cosmic environment upon which men rely for their fulfillment. The term includes both pragmatic and metaphysical elements in that it refers both to the functional concept and to objectively real activities in the cosmos. God viewed in this fashion cannot be thought of as a super-individual or as a metaphysical personality. However, since the fulfillment of human life requires the furtherance of such personal activities and relations as love, prayer, and worship, the cosmic environment which makes this kind of adjustment necessary must be thought of as personal in nature. Thus, it is legitimate to speak of God as Father, Great Companion, King, or even Almighty. The advantages of the conceptual view of God are that it (1) gives men confidence that their struggle for the good life is aided by the cosmos itself, (2) provides an objective foundation for morality in the dynamic structure of the world process, and (3) shows religion to be a means of gaining personal value through proper adjustment to the creative factors in the universe.

To summarize, Mathews argues that the socially-conditioned patterns used throughout human history to refer to God stand for something real in the very nature of things, and while the patterns change, God is forever the Cosmic Friend.

LECTURES ON CALVINISM

Author: Abraham Kuyper (1837-1920)
Type of work: Calvinistic apologetics
First published: 1931 (Stone Lectures, 1898)

Principal Ideas Advanced

Calvinism meets the requirements of furnishing Protestants with a world and life view because its principles provide a unique answer to the question concerning man's relation to God, to his fellow man, and to the world.

Calvinism provides the basis for political justice, and it insures the independence of the Church, the family, and other segments of life, from the encroachments of the state.

Each aspect of human society derives its authority from the sovereignty of God, rather than from the will of the people, or from the state; under God's grace, science, art, commerce, and politics will benefit from the exercise of the principles of Calvinism.

These lectures on Calvinism were delivered as the Stone Lectures in 1898 at Princeton University by Abraham Kuyper, who as a philosopher, theologian, and statesman successfully devoted his life to making the impact of Calvinism felt in the religious, political, and scientific life of his own country, the Netherlands.

Kuyper's *Lectures* are a battle cry against the advance of the spirit of the French revolution that regarded Jesus Christ as a scoundrel, and heralded the overthrow of the tyranny of the Bourbons as an emancipation from the authority of God. As an alternative to such an anti-Christian *Weltanschauung,* Kuyper sets forth the life-system of Calvinism, and applies its principles to religion, politics, science, and art.

Calvinism is not here equated with the dogmatic beliefs of any particular church or with any specific doctrine. It refers, first, to the historical course taken by the Reformation, so far as it was neither Lutheran, nor Anabaptist nor Socinian; second, to the system of conceptions that arose under the influence of Calvin in various social spheres; and third, to the political movement which brought political liberty in constitutional statesmanship, in Holland, England, and the United States.

Calvinism, an all-embracing system of principles, is able to do more than create a different Church-form. Calvinism can provide human society with a different form of life, with a unified *Weltanschauung,* or life-system, for it offers a peculiar insight, derived from a special principle, into three fundamental relations, our relation to God, to man, and to the world. Kuyper's lectures proceed to an analysis of these relations.

First, how does Calvinism interpret our relation to God? Calvinism does not seek God in the creature, nor does it isolate the creature from God, nor does it impose an ecclesiastical middle-link between God and man; it proclaims rather that God the Holy Spirit enters into immediate fellowship with man. There is no divine grace other than that which comes immediately from God to man. The Church is not an office or an independent institute; it is identical with the believers that constitute its membership. Every single believer can have the assurance of eternal salvation and live his life in the immediate fellowship with God, fully persuaded that his entire life is to be lived in the divine presence.

Calvinism's unique view of man's relation to God and God's relation to man is augmented by its own interpretation of the relation of man to man. By regarding human life as the immediate concern of God, it views all men, regardless of social or economic status, as lost sinners, who, as equal in the sight of God, are in consequence equal among themselves. No distinctions among men are to be recognized, except such as are imposed by God Himself, in that to some He gives authority and greater talents that they might serve those with lesser talents, and thereby also serve God. Calvinism could result only in a democratic view of life, in which nations are free, and every man, because he is a man created in the image and likeness of God, ought to be treated fairly, both politically and socially. Man is here placed on a footing of equality with man, not against God, but on his knees before God.

The third basic relation which determines the Calvinistic life-system is man's relation to the world. Calvinism rejects any dualism between a sanctified Church and a demonic world that must be taken into the protective custody of the Church. Calvinism honors man because of his likeness to the divine image; it honors the world as a divine creation. Particular grace works salvation; common grace arrests the corruption of the world and allows our life to develop outside the institutional Church to the glory and honor of God the Creator.

Under the influence of Calvinism, the institutionalized Church is nothing more than the assembly of believers; every sphere of life is emancipated from the dominion of the Church, but not from the sovereignty of God. Family life, trade, commerce, politics, science, and art are restored to their positions of independence. Man is not required to retire from the world in a monastery; his duty is to flee from sin alone. His task is to serve God in the world, in every phase of worldly life. Man is duty bound to discover and to develop the potencies hidden by God in nature and in human life. To do so is to keep the divine command given in Paradise: "Subdue and replenish the earth."

Calvinism is a life system and as such it is offered by Kuyper as the completed evolution of Protestantism, as providing principles which, when embodied in a form suitable to the requirements of our own century, can restore unity to Protestant thought and action. The benefits of Calvinism are to be found in every sphere. Its influence on religion, as such, stresses the fact that religion exists not for man, but for God; it operates directly from the heart, without human interposition; it is not partial in its operations, but affects the whole of our existence, and its character is soteriological, springing from the new man in Christ Jesus.

Calvinism regards the Church as a spiritual organism, with the starting point and center of its action in Heaven and not on earth. The Church on earth manifests itself in the form of local congregations of believers, living together in obedience to the ordinances of Christ; it is not an institution for the dispensation of grace. Its purpose is not human or egoistic; it exists merely for the sake of God, for the glory and honor of His name, to which end its members are called to conversion, worship, and moral purity.

Calvinism places the believer before the fact of God, not only in the Church, but also in his political life, in the domain of the state. The influence of Calvinism on political conceptions springs from its dominating basic principle: the sovereignty of the Triune God over the whole cosmos, including the state. For the magistrates derive their power by the institution of God, by reason of sin. Because of sin they are indispensable, on the one hand, and because of sin, the people must ever guard against any assumption of power by the magistrates which would deprive the people of their personal liberty.

Sin alone has made the institutions of governments necessary, but the right to rule over men is a right possessed by God and by Him alone. Such authority does not belong to any man or to the people, nor does it originate in a social contract. The authority of earthly governments originates solely in the sovereignty of God, so that every magistrate rules solely by God's grace; the final duty of obedience to civil powers, no matter what form they take, is imposed by God Himself.

The sovereignty of God in the political sphere, recognized in the American revolution, is equally opposed to popular sovereignty, manifested in the French revolution, and to state sovereignty, propagated in Germany as a result of philosophical pantheism. To the Calvinist there is a court of appeal beyond that of the whims and desires of men, and whenever men have usurped the power that rightfully belongs to God alone, the Calvinist has not hesitated to appeal directly to the King of kings, and to overthrow the pretender to earthly power, by force, if necessary.

The sovereignty of God is in no way limited to its manifestation in the state. It is equally present in society as a whole, in the family, in business, science, and art, and in all other social spheres.

These social structures do not derive their existence from the state, Kuyper claims, but are endowed with their own form of authority; an authority which rules by the grace of God, not by the grace of the state. The individual social spheres possess their own individual sovereignty; they have nothing above themselves but God. The state cannot properly intrude; each social sphere is sovereign in its own domain.

The state bears the power of the sword of justice, to mete out punishment to the criminal; the sword of war, to defend its rights and interests against its enemies; the sword of order, to thwart rebellion at home. But state authority cannot properly be extended into any other social sphere. The life of science, of the family, or of commerce may never properly be enclosed by the stultifying tentacles of the state. This does not mean that the state can never interfere in these autonomous spheres of life. When the different social spheres clash, the state must compel mutual regard for the boundary lines; when power is abused, the state must defend the weak; and it must use coercion to see that each sphere bears its proper personal and financial burden for the preservation of the state. The state, however, must never forget that the source of authority for the social spheres of society is the same as that from which the state derives its own authority; namely, the absolute sovereignty of God.

The Calvinist, in fact, has not always been clear in his conception of the relationship between the sovereignty of the Church and the sovereignty of the state and has invoked the power of the state to defend the truth of his confessions. In principle, however, Calvinism recognizes that the magistrate has a spiritual duty towards God, in that he must recognize that it is from God that he derives his power, and that it is according to God's ordinances that he must rule the people. It is, however, the duty of the government to suspend its judgment concerning which temporal manifestation of the body of Christ is to be found most perfect in the eyes of God. The government must honor the complex of Christian churches as the multiform manifestation of the Church of Christ on earth. The sovereignty of the Church and the sovereignty of the state must both be recognized. The government is to see that the individual liberty and conscience of its citizens is respected, so that every man may serve God according to his own convictions. For the sovereignty of the Church is limited by the sovereignty of the free personality.

The benefits of Calvinism are not limited to the political sphere, Kuyper contends. With respect to science and learning, Calvinism has fostered, and could not but foster, a love of investigation. For its doctrine of the divine decree of God means that the entire cosmos, instead of being the plaything of chance, obeys law, a fact which permits science to ascend from the empirical investigation of phenomena to the laws and principles which rule them. Calvinism placed science in its proper domain by acknowledging that nature is God's handiwork; it delivered it from its unnatural bondage to the state and to the Church. Calvinism also provides an answer to the alleged conflict between faith and science by showing that such a conflict is not possible. The real point of dispute is between the assertion that the cosmos as it now exists is normal, that it moves by means of an eternal evolution from its potencies to its ideal, and the assertion that it is abnormal, that a past disturbance has taken place, and that a regenerating power alone can bring it to its final goal.

Kuyper contends that in the sphere

of art Calvinism did not produce a general art style because Calvinism reached such a high stage of religious development that its very principles prevented it from expressing religion in visible and sensible forms. In principle, however, Calvinism offers an interpretation of art which frees it from any slavish interpretation of nature. Art is a gift of the Holy Spirit, and it has as its vocation the task of disclosing to man a higher reality than he can find in this sinful and corrupted world. By releasing art from the trusteeship of the Church, Calvinism encouraged and advanced the development of the arts, especially in the fields of music and painting.

The significance of Kuyper's call to a return to Calvinism is not to be minimized. It has been more than sixty years since he delivered his lectures. The Free University of Amsterdam, which Kuyper founded, one of the six universities in the Netherlands, continues to flourish along the lines suggested by Kuyper in 1898. Outside the Netherlands, the Calvinists of the world still look to Kuyper and to his spiritual successors, to such men as Herman Bavinck, G. Berkouwer, and Herman Dooyeweerd, for leadership as they continue his struggle to bring the world to a recognition that God is sovereign in every sphere of life.

THE NATURAL AND THE SUPERNATURAL

Author: John Wood Oman (1860-1939)
Type of work: Philosophy of religion
First published: 1931

Principal Ideas Advanced

The natural is the environment as apprehended through the senses; the supernatural is the environment as apprehended through religious feeling.

Human progress has been made possible through man's apprehension of the supernatural, which, as eternal, provides him a footing amidst the flux of the natural.

The religions of mankind may be classified according to the manner in which they conceive of the natural and the supernatural.

Mysticism denies the natural and affirms the supernatural as undifferentiated unity.

Ethical and ceremonial legalism opposes the supernatural to the natural in an other-worldly fashion.

Prophetic monotheism discerns the supernatural in the natural and seeks a means of reconciling the ideal and the real.

The Natural and the Supernatural, as John Oman explains to the reader, is not a theological work, but merely "an attempt to lay a foundation for theology, by considering its method and its problems." Oman views the history of religion as the progressive victory within human experience of the supernatural over the natural. He maintains that the victory is most complete in Christianity, with its belief that God is personal and its confidence that "all things work together for good to them that love God."

Writing at a time when Anglo-Saxon religious thinkers were preoccupied with the problem of providing a spiritualistic alternative to naturalistic evolution, Oman reflects their concerns in his book. His work shows the influence of Friedrich Schleiermacher (1768-1834), whose *Discourses on Religion* he translated.

One of the most fruitful parts of Oman's work, still worth careful study, is his account of cognition, in the course of which he criticizes philosophical naturalism for too readily abandoning experience in favor of abstract principles of explanation. Abstract ideas are necessary, he says, as providing the framework within which reality is perceived, but they must never become a substitute for perception, as they are likely to do when one refuses to view the world except in causal terms. The child and the artist, says Oman, are on much firmer ground, because they constantly explore reality in its concreteness, thereby finding that it rewards their highest expectations. Naturalism, however, is no more culpable in this regard than traditional religion, and Oman finds it one of the striking features of Jesus' teaching that the truths which He discloses to us do not require the dead hand of authority to make them convincing. Higher religion, from Oman's point of view, is synonymous with higher truth.

Oman maintains that religious experience is just as much a part of the knowledge which we have of our environment as sense experience, and that it is equally important to human progress. Through the experience of the senses we know our environment only as a flux of varying impressions, but through religious experience we discover the abiding character of the whole. In Oman's terminology, the temporal world given us through the senses is the natural, while the eternal world given us through religious feeling is the supernatural. Our environment, says Oman, always includes both the natural and the supernatural: "the seen and temporal," on the one hand, and "the unseen and eternal," on the other.

Following upon this theory of cognition, Oman develops a spiritualistic account of the evolution of culture. In contrast with the prevailing naturalism of his day, which sought to explain all origins in terms of physical forces, Oman maintains that evolution involves a positive effort on the part of a creature to find a place for itself in its environment. If this thesis seems obscure when applied to organic evolution, it is plain enough when applied to the development of civilization. Progress, Oman maintains, depends on meaning, not on physical impulse; the history of civilization is the story of man's struggle to achieve more perfect relations with reality.

Oman explains the development of human culture through man's capacity to entertain free ideas. All perception includes fixed ideas, otherwise known as sensations and feelings, but man is unique in being able to engage himself with ideas which are not immediately given. These free ideas, says Oman, have made it possible for him to distinguish between the permanent and the changing in his environment, the eternal and the evanescent. Specifically, the idea of the sacred, apprehended through religious experience, enabled primitive man to rise above the determination of the natural, by providing him with "firm footing in the flux of experience," and by making it possible for him to "escape from mere immediate impression and natural desire." Primitive man sensed the numinous quality in birth, death, sexual union, and the more exceptional events of nature; his mind was awakened, as those of lower creatures were not, and he invented myths and rituals in response. So it has been with every advance in history; progress always involves the extension of the claims of ideal values over ephemeral ones, and only religion has the power to enforce these claims over the clamor of appetite and the fear of strife.

Because he conceives of religion as man's effort to win and hold faith in the supernatural in the face of the natural, Oman finds a basis for classifying religions in the manner by which these two are related. "When the Supernatural is submerged in the Natural, we have idolatry; when the Natural is submerged in the Supernatural, we have pantheism; when they are set sharply apart, we have deism; when they are related by some kind of moral victory, we have at least some kind of theism."

Primitive religion, says Oman, tends to find the supernatural diffused as an animistic force throughout the natural. Polytheism is an advance over animism, in that it introduces individuation into man's experience of both the supernatural and the natural; polytheism, thus, is associated with the rise of agriculture and of cities, and it constitutes a most important step in the development of civilization. Pantheism, on the other hand, is regressive. In its cosmic form, it identifies the supernatural with the natural, under such notions as fate and karma; in its acosmic form, it denies the reality of the natural and regards the supernatural as a self-sufficient unity. Deism, in Oman's sense of the terms, is the theory underlying the ritualistic and ethical dualism of Judaism, Zoroastrianism, and Islam. It is an advance over polytheism, in that it affirms the unity of the supernatural on the one hand and of the natural on the other, without sacrificing the concrete individuality of either; but because it distinguishes sharply between the sacred and the secular, deism represents an uneasy truce between the natural and the supernatural rather than a progressive victory of the supernatural over the natural. Theism resembles deism in affirming the unity of the supernatural and of the natural, but it differs in the way in which it brings these into relation. As expressed by the Hebrew Prophets, by Christ, and by the Apostles, theism opposes the ceremonial and legal outlook of deism, and it insists that the supernatural must find expression in the daily lives of men. It recognizes, as fully as deism, the presence of evil in the world, but it insists that the reality of the natural is dependent on the reality of the supernatural, and that faith in God gives victory over all evil.

According to the way in which they relate the natural and the supernatural, religions are either mystical or apocalyptic. Oman insists on reserving the term "mystical" for those religions which deny the reality of the natural. "A mystical religion is, as it always should be understood scientifically, one that seeks the eternal behind the illusion of the evanescent." Since, for mysticism, the natural is a delusive veil, and the concrete individual is a fiction derived from the senses and the appetites, the way to redemption for anyone lies in pressing toward absolute unity with the undifferentiated, unchanging Real. Oman maintains that, rightly speaking, there is no such thing as Christian mysticism; he argues that the whole apparatus of "negation, darkness, void, unknowing," and of "visions, raptures, ecstasies, physical manifestations, the large role assigned to the Evil One, and . . . of special cultivated emotions" is remote from theism and appropriate only to acosmic pantheism.

Those religions are apocalyptic, in Oman's sense of the term, which expect the Eternal to be revealed in the evanescent. Oman calls attention to the root meaning of the word *apocalypsis,* which literally signifies "revelation." As used by Oman, the term describes both deistic and theistic religions, since both affirm the reality of the world, and both look for manifestations of God's will and purpose in the lives of concrete persons. The difference is that deists, because they draw a qualitative distinction between the supernatural and the natural, think of these manifestations as special, miraculous interventions. Thus, deists believe in a special priesthood, a sacred literature, and a revealed code of conduct to arm the faithful for their journey through the world, while expectation of future judgment and heavenly reward gives them hope despite the presence of the world's evil. The theists, on the other hand, find God revealed in ordinary human relations and in great public events. Not only is nature obedient to God's voice, but history manifests His purpose toward mankind. Prophets and apostles have recognized the presence of evil in their own lives and in the lives of others, but they have considered evil to be the result of a failure to achieve positive righteousness rather than as the consequence of transgression of divine law, and they place their hope, not in their ability to achieve ethical or ceremonial perfection, but in the reconciling love of God, and in the response, however imperfect, which divine love finds in the human heart.

While Oman is inclined to describe the world in terms of progress and to see religion as the growing edge, he recognizes also the tendency for a culture, after it has achieved material prosperity, to fall away from its best insights. Religion, he says, is to be thought of not as a ladder which, once climbed by civilization, can be discarded, but as a pillar, on which civilization rests. "Some religion man must have," says Oman, "and when he fails to maintain a higher religion, he falls back on polytheism, meaning by that whatever gods there be that protect his body, his family, his property and his state, without exacting much self-denial in their protection." This fall within religion occurs even within Christianity, whenever, instead of sharing in God's perfection by forgiving others, men place their trust in "judicial ideas of pardon, mystical mechanical ideas of grace, and rules of belief and action which are ceremonial, in the sense of rules imposed from without and enforced by fear." A regressive religion is a "bad religion," Oman insists, and although he concedes that such religion has some use in conserving past gains, he maintains that it is an obstacle to further progress. A vigorous civilization, he says, must be striving for ideals that are beyond it, and these ideals, to be valid ones, must represent a truer apprehension of reality than has been possible before. High civilization depends upon high religion; for us, this can be nothing less than the increasing realization in our lives of the spirit of Jesus and the Apostles.

What Oman finds central in the teaching of Jesus is the conception of the universe as "in some sense personal." Against deism, which conceives of God as a potentate and proprietor who stands over the world and demands man's obedience, prophetic religion conceives of Him as a friend who, by means of the environment, seeks to manifest Himself to us in order to win our love and trust. Such, says Oman, is the best way to account for man's evolving experience of his environment. When ideals run beyond facts, and then, suddenly, facts comport with ideals, what is this, asks Oman, but a kind of personal intercourse? To those who are responsive, the world has never appeared dead or hostile; seeming chaos turns to order; obstacles prove a means to further advance, and even suffering can turn to joy. Such a world, says Oman, is "a realm of free children of God, and not a theater of even the most admirable puppets." Thus, the world cannot adequately be understood as anything less than an expression of a personal God.

THE VISION OF GOD: THE CHRISTIAN DOCTRINE OF THE *SUMMUM BONUM*

Author: Kenneth E. Kirk (1886-1954)
Type of work: Theological foundations of Christian ethics
First published: 1931

Principal Ideas Advanced

Worship, as the means by which men experience the vision of God and respond to it, is the central path to understanding and to the acceptance of Christian moral responsibility.

Self-fulfillment is an unsatisfactory motivation for Christian goodness; the search for pleasure, mystical ecstasy, or religious salvation turns the attention of the self inward and excludes devotion to God.

While formal codes embraced for their own sakes destroy the vision of God by robbing morality of its true center of attention, a spirit of reasoned orderliness is essential to the highest kind of service to God.

A Christian ethic should exhibit an element of rigor and devotion and be marked by some renunciation and sacrifice.

The Vision of God is the published form for the Bampton Lectures for 1928. To the lectures as delivered has been added extensive documentation. It is a historical and theological study of the relationship between worship and morality expounding the thesis that "the principal duty of the Christian moralist is to stimulate the spirit of worship in those to whom he addresses himself, rather than to set before them codes of behaviour." The book is not to be understood, however, as an antinomian tract, for it allows a place for lawful orderliness providing it is subservient to the vision of God. It is well to remember that its author earlier penned an introduction to casuistry entitled *Conscience and Its Problems* (1927).

The Vision of God defends the central thesis that worship, by focusing attention upon God, creates the only kind of disinterestedness which can enable the self to pursue the ethical life in creative abandon to God. Philosophical hedonism is not a sufficient foundation for Christian behavior because the effort of the self to achieve happiness may be just as fully an expression of selfishness as is crass worldly egoism. Formalism, which advocates obedience to rules for the sake of the soul's eventual reward, is equally unable to achieve the desired God-centeredness symbolized by worship. Only when obedience to rules becomes a means of expressing gratitude to God does it constitute an adequate Christian expression of moral concern. Such gratitude flows naturally and freely from the vision of God experienced in worship. Here lies the central significance of the beatitude in Matthew 5:8: "Blessed are the pure in heart, for they shall see God."

The argument of the book employs the juxtaposition of three terms: formalism, rigorism, and humanism. Formalism expresses itself as obedience to codified rules; rigorism prescribes for its adherents mortification and self denial, and is frequently a branch of formalism; humanism emphasizes possibilities for attainment, growth, and achievement through moral action. Formalism is an enemy of true Christian morality because it forces men into legalistic molds. Humanism is also unsatisfactory because it sometimes proceeds towards its goal without a sense of dependence upon God and it frequently makes the self central to ethical concern. Seeking to avoid humanism, Christians have sometimes embraced rigorism, especially at times when the Church has felt called to emphasize its distinctive separation from the world. But none of these alternatives to Christian morality can be adequate for one who would love God; Christian morality cannot be based on some generalized human ideal for such a foundation places a subordinate principle in the prime place reserved for the highest human experience of devotion to God.

A good proportion of the book is a detailed exposition of historical materials illustrating its main theme. Beginning with Old Testament and Hellenistic backgrounds which prepared the way for the vision of God as proclaimed in Christianity, the problems of New Testament interpretation receive early attention, and especially the sharp differences that have arisen over the interpretation of the teachings of Jesus. These differences are said to arise because rigorism and humanism stand side by side in the teachings of Jesus, so that even the Gospel writers themselves portray them differently. By focusing men's attention upon God and His Kingdom Jesus opened for His hearers a path leading to humility and purity; in doing so, He portrayed God's power and active concern for all the humanly meaningful aspects of experience. In the early Apostolic period the rigoristic elements in the teachings of Jesus became the foundation for an ethic in which the formalistic element was dominant, but the codes which expressed such rigorism were compatible with disciplined life in the world. Later the humanistic aspect was submerged to the rigoristic one and asceticism found its way into Christian practice.

It is clear that Kirk discerns a major gulf between the writers of the New Testament and the ethical thinking that followed soon thereafter. His sympathies are with the teachings of Jesus, the outlook of Paul, and the orientation of John. In Jesus he finds the centrality of the vision of God. In Paul the relationship of the believer to Christ is treated in much the same way in which Christ relates the believer to God. St. Paul was convinced that the vision of God was most perfectly given in Christ. John makes the vision of God a perpetual experience realized, not by individual mystical ecstasy, but through participation in the corporate vision of the Church. But soon after these early and creative Christian writings appeared, the Christian life was codified into a formal system. Both the way of life and the way of death are portrayed by the *Didache* (c.150), which gives a list of detailed prescriptions for behavior, obedience to which means salvation while violation means doom. Rabbinical patterns of teaching as well as the catalogued form of Orphic and Pythagorean ethical instruction undoubtedly influenced the development of this formalism and thereby eclipsed much of the creative originality of the earlier material. Kirk's objection to formalism is based upon the fact that it permits and even encourages a complacency concerning one's obedience to ethical standards, whereas the vision of God as given in the teachings of Jesus and the perspective of Paul gives no comfort to those who feel they have attained a sufficient level of virtue to merit a reward.

The rise of monasticism within the Christian tradition gave expression to the rigoristic impulse that frequently skirts the edges of the Christian ethic, most strongly so when the surrounding culture is at a low level of moral attainment. St. Jerome (c.342-420) was driven to monasticism in reaction to the excesses of fourth century Rome, and his converts renounced domestic responsibility. St. Antony of Egypt (c.251-356) undertook the same renunciation in individual terms and his attention focused on "holy ones" rather than on God. The anchorite thrust for ecstatic experience stands in sharp contrast to St. Paul's preference for love and knowledge rather than for mystical experience divorced from disciplined responsibility. Gradually the Church came to see that monastic renunciation was valid only for a few, a fact which Kirk uses to reinforce his conviction that domestic responsibility is a legitimate channel for the rigoristic impulse. Once this channel of responsibility is accepted it cannot be renounced, since to turn one's back upon family duties once they have been accepted is to violate duty to God. The book gathers several anecdotes from early monasticism which warn the family man against turning to monasticism.

Attempted reforms within monasticism are interpretated by Kirk as the effort of the Church to hold the rigoristic impulse in proper bounds. In its effort to set life in the ordinary world on an equal basis with monastic discipline the Church created a double moral standard of equally honored alternatives, even though the struggle to emphasize the equality was long and difficult. Even with the addition of manual work and practical service to the monastic way the assumption persisted that the monastic life was superior as a path to the vision of God. The fourth, fifth, and sixth centuries sought to bring monastic life into closer kinship with the life of ordinary Christians, but the efforts at reform had difficulty breaking through the rigoristic assumptions of the monastic impulse.

The author observes that even monasticism cherished the beauty of the world it sought to reject. Theological minds sought valiantly to reconcile the rigoristic impulse of monasticism with the humanistic concerns to be found in the Gospel. It was St. Augustine (354-430) who saw the implications of faith for social existence, and even though he was personally involved in the monastic system, his doctrine of the two cities created a theoretical foundation for Christians who were concerned about the cares, responsibilities, and achievements of the earthly city as well as for the good to be achieved on a higher level in the city of God. Influenced by historical conditions that placed him between the rigorist and the humanist alternatives, Augustine made his major contribution to Christian thought with a doctrine of grace which proved incompatible both with the earned salvation postulated by rigorism and with the trust in human achievements implicit in humanism. Kirk honors Augustine for this achievement and also St. Bernard of Clairvaux (1090-1153), who did much the same thing in devotional rather than theological terms.

In the demands which arose in the twelfth century for lay participation in Church life on the basis of full significance and equality as well as the development of mystical piety Kirk finds reinforcement for the idea that life can be disciplined without resort to monastic withdrawal, and he also finds confirmation of the contention that man's thrust to know God has a perennial place in the Christian tradition. St. Thomas (c.1225-1274) found meaning in the natural order, but only when that natural order was embraced in the cradle of a supernatural realm. Thomas placed reason above asceticism and opened the devotional life to all men. The latter achievement was carried even further by St. Ignatius Loyola (1491-1556), and St. Francis of Sales (1567-1622).

Kirk's treatment is predominantly concerned with Christian experience and thought prior to the Protestant Reformation. Modern Catholicism and Protestantism receive brief treatment. Kirk's distrust of the radical liberty which he attributes to the leadership of the Reformers is clearly apparent. He suggests that the Reformers instituted iron discipline in their own churches to offset the decline of inward discipline created by their radical theory of freedom. The rise of the radical left is treated as a protest against the same trend. The predominance of petitionary over adoration prayer in Luther is considered to show that Luther's vision of God was less adequate than it should have been. But post-Reformation Catholicism revived the invalid form of the double standard and likewise diminished the true vision of God in modern Christendom.

The treatise ends with a plea for a valid vision of God, in which worship and service are united, in which the corporate dimension of the search saves it from self-centeredness, and in which the nature of service to God is truly disinterested. The self can be taken out of the center of its own experience only by a vision of God. When the vision is clearly apprehended reasoned orderliness replaces formalism and vital devotion to the crucified and risen Christ becomes the channel of a dedicated service replacing the false kinds of rigorism which otherwise abound.

CHURCH DOGMATICS

Author: Karl Barth (1886-)
Type of work: Dogmatics; Christian ethics
First published: 1932 (unfinished)

Principal Ideas Advanced

Knowledge of God is totally dependent upon God's making Himself known; God has revealed Himself in Jesus Christ, His incarnate Word, to be triune—the one Lord who exists eternally in the three modes of Father, Son, and Holy Spirit.

The one Word of God, which is heard and obediently acknowledged by man through God's gift of faith, has a threefold form: "revealed," "written," and "preached."

Dogmatics is the theological science in which the Church critically tests the content of its proclamation by the standard of the Word of God; it thereby asks for the "dogma" in the "dogmas."

Creation and redemption are inextricably conjoined in God's one work of grace; creation is the external basis of God's covenant with man, just as the covenant is the internal basis of creation.

The Church consists of those who, through the power of the Holy Spirit, participate in Jesus Christ—His life, death, and resurrection—and who, gratefully living the life of reconciliation in the light and truth of God, witness to Jesus Christ as the Savior of the world.

Karl Barth has become a legendary figure during his own lifetime. Initiator of the revolution against liberal theology, one of the leaders of the "Confessing Church" in its struggle against the Germanized Christianity advocated by the Nazi regime, and writer of what many consider to be the greatest dogmatics in the history of the Church, this life-loving Swiss theologian has been acclaimed by his admirers to be "the Church Father of the twentieth century." Whether Roman, Protestant, or Orthodox, no responsible theology can hereafter be written without taking into account the theological position which has been expounded by Barth in his monumental *Kirchliche Dogmatik* (*Church Dogmatics*).

Karl Barth was born in Basel, Switzerland, on May 10, 1886, the eldest son of Fritz Barth, who was a pastor of the Reformed Church and later Professor of New Testament at the University of Bern. Karl Barth received his theological education at Bern, and then in Germany at the Universities of Tübingen, Berlin, and Marburg. The teachers who influenced him most were Adolf von Harnack (1851-1930) and Wilhelm Herrmann (1846-1922), two outstanding exponents of liberal theology. Though possessing a mind that was never uncritical, Barth began as an advocate of the theological liberalism espoused by his teachers.

The foremost characteristic of liberal theology is its anthropocentrism. Attention is focused upon man—to be sure, pious, ethical, religious, Christian man—but, nevertheless, man. In such a theology God is not forgotten, of course, but even the divine is to be found through His essential connection with the human: in man's reason, in his innate sense of ethical obligation, and in the depths of his feeling. It is hardly surprising that, even in the nineteenth century, Ludwig Feuerbach (1804-1872) charged that liberal theology is really nothing more than anthropology, and Friedrich Nietzsche (1844-1900) proclaimed that God is dead. These keen-witted philosophers detected that the "liberal" theologians, in their attempt to accommodate Christianity to the modern world views, were, at bottom, pseudo-philosophers. Nor is it surprising that at the beginning of the twentieth century theologians had turned their attention to such subjects as the history of dogma, the history of religions, and the communion of the individual soul with God. Anthropocentric theology foundered in a sea of historicism and psychologism.

The time was ripe for revolt. All that was needed was an incendiary occasion and someone to strike the match. The First World War (1914-1918) provided the occasion; it smashed man's illusions of grandeur and inevitable progress, and starkly revealed his tragic involvement with sin and evil. Karl Barth, who in 1911 had become a pastor in the Swiss village of Safenwil, lit the fire whose flames rapidly spread into a conflagration designed to purify and reform the Church according to the Word of God.

The book which catapulted Barth into the center of the arena of public theological controversy was his commentary, *The Epistle to the Romans*, a work he undertook in order to clarify his own thinking. Published in 1919, and in a second, completely rewritten edition in 1922, this volume, in which the author tried to interpret the message of the Apostle Paul for twentieth century man, marked the turning point from liberal theology to a theological movement which was loosely designated during the 1920's as the "Theology of Crisis" or "Dialectical Theology." This theology emphasized the "otherness" of God, or what Søren Kierkegaard (1813-1855) had called "the infinite qualitative distinction between time and eternity," the eschatological nature of salvation, the dialectic of God's "Yes" and His "No" to sinful man, and the paradoxical character of the Incarnation. Against liberalism's tendency to allow God and man to coalesce, the watchword of the new theology became: "Let God be God!"

On the basis of his *Römerbrief*, Barth, who had now spent ten years in the pastorate, was invited in 1921 to assume the chair of Reformed Theology at the University of Göttingen. Here he launched an academic career which was marked by moves to the University of Münster in 1925, to the University of Bonn in 1930, and, finally, after being dismissed from his post at Bonn by the Nazi authorities, to the University of Basel in 1935, where he continued as Professor of Systematic Theology until retirement in 1962. Barth is an indefatigable worker, and his literary output has been prodigious, embracing almost every discipline within the realm of theology.

The first half-volume of his *Church Dogmatics* appeared in 1932, and by 1959 the yet unfinished work had grown to twelve large books. The overall plan is simple. The author has designed the *Dogmatics* as a five volume work, although the length of his treatment has necessitated the subdivision of each into part-volumes for publication. Volume I is entitled "The Doctrine of the Word of God"; Volume II, "The Doctrine of God"; Volume III, "The Doctrine of Creation"; Volume IV, "The Doctrine of Reconciliation"; Volume V, "The Doctrine of Redemption."

The extraordinary length of the *Church Dogmatics* can be attributed to several factors. First, because this is truly a *Church* dogmatics, the author has incorporated extensive commentaries on Scripture and on the history of doctrine, in which churchmen of all ages and persuasions enter into critical dialogue concerning the truth of the Gospel. Second, because of his conviction that ethics and theology are inseparable, Barth has included major treatises on general and special ethics. The treatment of general ethics appears in Volume II under the heading "The Command of God," whereas a chapter on special ethics accompanies each of the volumes on creation, reconciliation, and redemption, elucidating the command of God from the viewpoints, respectively, of order, law, and promise. Finally, mention must be made of this theologian's circuitous style of writing, whereby he moves round and round a subject, relentlessly asking ever new questions and delving into different aspects in the belief that this procedure will finally allow the truth to disclose itself. In this way he seeks to serve the truth, rather than to master it.

Karl Barth begins his *Church Dogmatics* by defining the task he is undertaking: "Dogmatics," he states, "is the scientific test to which the Christian Church puts herself regarding the language about God which is peculiar to her." The material to be investigated is the present proclamation of the Church, pre-eminently in the form of preaching and sacrament, and the criterion to be used is the Word of God, which assumes a threefold form: the "revealed" Word, which was originally and conclusively uttered through God's revelation in Jesus Christ; the "written" Word, which is the attestation of the Prophets and Apostles in Holy Scripture; and the "preached" Word, which is the proclamation of the Church. The latter two forms are dependent upon the first, but in the hearing of the Word of God today all three forms are inevitably interrelated. The function of dogmatics within the Church is to test its proclamation by the standard of Holy Scripture and under the guidance of its confessions. The task is made necessary because of the fact that heresy arises in man's attempt to proclaim God's Word.

Barth insists that the Word of God is God Himself in His revelation, and that man's knowledge of God is utterly dependent upon God's revelatory action. There is no way from man to God, only the way of God to man. God has chosen to reveal Himself on the plane of human history in the man Jesus of Nazareth, and He continues to reveal Himself through the Church's witness to Jesus Christ. In the act of God's self-disclosure, to which there is a corresponding act of faith on man's part, God makes Himself an "object" for man, albeit an object unlike any other, since He remains indissolubly Subject and Lord. The reason of the man of faith is bound to and determined by this object, and thus revelation prescribes its own "epistemology."

"Prolegomena" is that part of dogmatics in which an account is given of its pathway to knowledge, and since the theologian must follow the way God Himself has taken to make Himself known, prolegomena becomes essentially the exposition of the revelation of God in His Word. Here Barth expounds the doctrine of the Trinity, for in Jesus Christ God reveals Himself to be the triune God; namely, the one Lord who exists eternally in the three inseparably related but distinguishable "modes" of Father, Son, and Holy Spirit—or, in terms of the special activity appropriated to each: Creator, Reconciler, and Redeemer. It is the doctrine of the Trinity that distinguishes the Christian God from all falsely conceived gods.

In Volume II Barth discusses in succession God's knowability, reality, election, and command. He reiterates that man has no innate capacity for knowing God; the possibility of the knowledge of God cannot be discussed apart from its actuality. Since God has chosen to reveal Himself in the "sacramental objectivity" of the humanity of Jesus Christ, the Word made flesh, any idea of a "natural" knowledge of God is rejected. The triune God discloses His being in the act of His revelation, which means that God's being and action are inseparable. The living God, declares Barth, is He who loves in freedom, and His perfections are those of the divine loving (grace and holiness, mercy and righteousness, patience and wisdom) and those of the divine freedom (unity and omnipresence, constancy and omnipotence, eternity and glory). These perfections of His being are manifest in the freedom and love in which He elects Himself for fellowship with man, and man for fellowship with Himself. The doctrine of election, declares Barth, is the sum of the Gospel, for it is the Good News of the reconciliation between God and man that has been accomplished in Jesus Christ, who is at once the electing God and the elected man. In Jesus Christ God says "Yes" to sinful mankind and takes upon Himself the reprobation which man deserves. In this election of grace God makes known His claim upon man, revealing His eternal will and command, and this is the foundation of all theological ethics.

Volume III concerns the doctrine of creation, that is, the existence of a reality other than God, and Barth emphasizes that this doctrine, too, is a doctrine of faith. Creatureliness cannot be known in abstraction from the Creator, God the Father, whose overflowing love is revealed and actualized in the Incarnation. God's election of grace inseparably conjoins creation and redemption, and the author illustrates this by an exposition of the creation sagas in Genesis 1 and 2. In the first, creation is shown to be the external basis of the covenant, whereas in the second, the covenant is shown to be the internal basis of creation.

Man is the creature who is determined by God to be His covenant-partner, and the essential humanity of man is found in his togetherness as I and Thou, male and female. Barth finds in this togetherness the *imago Dei,* for it corresponds to an analogous relationship of I and Thou in the triune God Himself. Because the Word of God reveals man to be a sinner who perverts his own true nature, knowledge of the real man is disclosed solely in Jesus Christ, in whom the existence of man in his proper relationship with God is actualized. While natural sciences can provide much interesting and useful information concerning human phenomena, theological anthropology, stresses Barth, must be grounded in Christology.

The doctrine of reconciliation, which is the heart of the *Church Dogmatics,* receives masterly treatment in Volume IV. Barth endeavors to present all aspects of this doctrine, from Christology to ecclesiology, in their intrinsic relatedness, so that the wholeness of the work of reconciliation shines through. Thus he expounds the person and work of Christ in conjunction with the nature of sin, the objective results of the atonement, and the work of the Holy Spirit in the Christian community and in the life of each believer. Reconciliation, he declares, occurs in two great movements that take place simultaneously in the life, death, and resurrection of Jesus Christ, who in His own person is truly God and truly man. The first is a movement from above downwards: Jesus Christ is the Lord who humbles Himself and becomes a servant in order to do the work of atonement (His priestly office); the second is from below upwards: Jesus Christ is the servant in whom man is exalted into fellowship with God (His kingly office). The material content of the doctrine of reconciliation is exhausted in these two movements, but there is a final fact that must be emphasized; namely, that both are combined concretely in the person of Jesus Christ, who is the God-man, the eternal Mediator. Thus He Himself is the Guarantor and the true Witness of the reconciliation that has been accomplished conclusively (His prophetic office).

The Church is composed of those persons who, through the power of the Holy Spirit, acknowledge in faith God's saving action in Jesus Christ, gratefully live reconciled lives in the light of this truth, and assume the responsibility of witnessing to the whole world that Jesus Christ is its Lord and

Savior. Indeed, Barth calls the Church Christ's own earthly-historical form of existence.

Volume V, which deals with the doctrine of Redemption, has not yet been written. In it the author intends to discuss questions about the "Last Things," the final judgment, and the consummation of the world. If Karl Barth is able to complete his *Church Dogmatics,* we can be sure that this doctrine will be illuminated by the same Christocentric focus that has characterized all his theology.

THE DIVINE IMPERATIVE

Author: Emil Brunner (1889-)
Type of work: Christian ethics
First published: 1932

Principal Ideas Advanced

Christian ethics is the reflective examination of human conduct as this conduct is determined by the creating, judging, and redeeming will of God.

The ethical element is inseparable from the revealed element; the good is based on the Holy; and ethics becomes a part of dogmatics.

Legalism in ethics must be rejected, for it displaces the proper object of man's ultimate allegiance and violates the center of human personality.

The ethical meaning of God's revelation in history is that man is designed for community; the individual cannot be understood apart from the community, and the community cannot be understood apart from the individual.

Christian ethical responsibility becomes effectual in the various divine orders which constitute the human community: marriage and the family, the economic order, the state, culture, and the Church.

Emil Brunner's *The Divine Imperative* was published in German under the title: *Das Gebot und die Ordnungen: Entwurf einer protestantisch-theologischen Ethik* (The Command and the Orders: An Outline of a Protestant Theological Ethic). The present English title was used only after consent and approval were given by Professor Brunner. The work was undertaken by the author because it was his belief that since the time of the Reformation no single work on ethics had appeared which made the Christian faith central. To formulate such an ethic is the projected task in *The Divine Imperative.* Only in the Christian faith, argues the author, do we find the final answers to man's ethical problems. This faith has its source in God, concretely known as Creator, Judge, and Redeemer. It is the contention of the author that during the development of Christianity this faith has received one of its most decisive historical expressions in Luther's formula: "Justification by faith through grace." Consequently, Brunner concludes that "the Christian ethic is not based upon a principle, but upon this process of Divine restoration, whose meaning is disclosed in 'justification by grace alone.'"

The pivotal point in any theory of ethics is the problem of the good. The major varieties of philosophical ethics in the Western tradition have been determined by their conceptions of value. Brunner examines these varieties—naturalistic ethics, idealistic ethics, ethics of self-realization, and utilitarianism—and finds that none achieves a real synthesis. Each approaches the problem of value in a different way, emerging with insights that are valid up to a point, correcting the errors and weaknesses of rival views, but falling into embarrassments of its own. Thus each version of philosophical ethics has its own particular contribution to make but so also does each have its special weakness. Brunner claims that the deficiencies of ethics point up the natural limits of the philosophical approach; at best philosophy is critical and regulative, but it can offer no final ethical perspective.

Kant's position in this tradition of moral philosophers is in some respects an exception for Brunner, and there are some evident similarities between Kant's "categorical imperative" and Brunner's "divine imperative." In both cases we find an "ethic of duty" in which responsibility is understood in terms of an obligation to a specified command or commands. But this structural similarity does not conceal significant differences as regards both the intention and final norm of the two approaches.

Brunner's criticisms of Kant are basically two. First, Brunner argues that Kant overlooked the Pauline and Lutheran teaching on the "enslaved will," and thus he fell into the error of Pelagianism. The author does recognize the import which Kant attached to the notion of "radical evil," but this radical evil is seen to be ultimately subordinated to a moralism and rationalism which attenuates the tragic implications of evil and precludes the necessity for divine grace. If the moral law commands that "thou *shalt* become a better man," for Kant the conclusion follows that "thou *canst.*" Brunner's second criticism is that Kant's ethic fails to give content to the "good will," and thus his ethic remains purely formal. Insofar as any ethical content is implicit, it must be understood in terms of the principle of well-being as the material principle which governs action. In the formulation of his theological ethic Brunner is able to avoid these errors of Kant's idealism. Human sin is taken most seriously as a fundamental fracture in human existence, requiring for its atonement an act of divine restoration, and the content of ethical action is supplied by revealed commands. The will of God becomes the basis and the norm of the good.

Although the basis for ethics is the divine imperative, this divine imperative should not be legalistically formulated, Brunner warns. The command of the will of God cannot be condensed into a tablet of moral laws without doing violence to the personal and existential relationship which should obtain between God and man. The Christian ethic requires the obedience of faith, but the obedience of faith is different from that of the obedience of law. The obedience of faith replaces all spurious claims for human autonomy and self-sufficiency. Man cannot live the good life on the basis of his own resources. His ethical independence is thus denied and he becomes dependent—but he becomes dependent on God and God alone. In turn this dependence on God frees man from the bondage to any religio-moral law. The Christian ethic thus leads to a life of freedom. This freedom, however, has a paradoxical quality. It is a freedom from external, legal constraints, a freedom which is rendered possible through man's absolute dependence on God. In the last analysis freedom means being rooted and grounded in God. To be free means to be able to enter into a relationship with God, who alone is sovereign. Ethical legalism vitiates this movement of freedom and surreptitiously introduces an ethic of self-righteousness (Pharisaism). Legalism, in teaching that man becomes good by following the law, neglects the basic sinfulness of man and instills a false confidence. An ethic based on justification by grace alone shatters this false confidence with its acknowledgment of the tragic fact of sin and the need for divine restitution. The ethical question is thus not simply a question in the sphere of conduct but is relocated in the sphere of personality as personality is defined in light of the structures of sin and grace.

An ethic based on the evangelical faith is indelibly social, Brunner insists. The ethical meaning of God's creating and redeeming activity is that man is designed for community. The concrete response to the divine imperative is a response by individuals in the life of their community. It is in the life of the community that we see the concrete realization of the moral commands. The essential structure of this community is a complex of I-Thou relationships. Its essential directive is love. This structure and this directive provide the basis for authentic communal responsibility. Responsibility is determined by the fact that the "I" is always confronted by the "Thou." The distinctive quality of man's communal existence is that the other can be addressed as a "Thou." The directive which gives this "I-Thou" existence its final meaning is love. "The *meaning* of this existence, however, as a responsible reciprocal existence, is *Love,*" Brunner writes; "Every human relationship which does not express love is abnormal. In Jesus Christ we are told that this love is the whole meaning of our life, and is also its foundation. Here the Creator reveals Himself as the One who has created us *in* love, *by* love, *for* love. He *reveals* to us our true nature, and He *gives* it back to us."

The communal significance in Brunner's Christian ethic is made explicit in his doctrine of the divine orders of creation. He defines five forms or orders which constitute the communal topography of human existence: the order of the family, the order of economic life, the political and legal order, the order of culture, and the ecclesiastical order. The distinctive character of these orders is that they are orders of creation essentially based on nature. They exist because of the psychological nature of man. Their structure is recognized not by faith but by reason. Although Brunner is openly and sharply critical of the classical notion of natural law because of its tendencies toward legalism, his own theory of the natural orders exhibits a formal similarity to the classical idea. Insofar as God is the creator of nature, religiously and morally binding directives can be deduced from nature. The author formulates the argument that monogamy is the "natural" marriage relationship and is therefore sanctioned by the divine imperative. Two primary considerations lead him to this conclusion: (1) every human being is irrevocably the child of one man and one woman, and (2) genuine natural love is in its essence monistic, instinctually reactive against the intrusion of a third person. These factors indicate the intrinsically "monos" quality of the marriage relationship.

Man's economic institutions, like the institution of marriage, are founded upon a natural ordering of nature. God created man as a being needing economic organization. The provision of material goods is necessary for the preservation of life itself. Part of man's nature is thus that he is an economic creature, inextricably involved with various forces of production and exchange that structure his communal existence. A specific ethical implication of this fact is the assignment of dignity to economic activity. Economic activities, in that they arise from a natural order, are not "low" or "unspiritual." One of the contributions of Luther, the author maintains, was the restoration of the dignity of labor through his doctrine of the "calling" after this dignity had been obscured by the monastic ethic of the Middle Ages. However, there is another side to the natural orders which must not be neglected—the pervasive reality of sin. The natural orders, good by virtue of their grounding in the divine creativity, are nonetheless subject to the distortions and ambiguities of a sinful existence. This sin expresses itself as pride, and its effects can be seen in the economic order in the instances of exploitation and the false tendencies of specific economic programs to become ends in themselves, become absolutized, and demand ultimate allegiance. So whereas God as Creator requires of man that his first duty is to adjust himself to the natural orders, God as Redeemer requires of man that his second duty is to transform the existing state of affairs in view of the redemptive action of Christ and the coming of the Kingdom of God.

The state, like the community of labor, is a God-given order. The state arises from the self-consciousness of a people (*Volk*), united by a spatial environment, blood relationships, and a common destiny. Now the state, although equal in importance, is supplementary to the family and to the economic order rather than prior to them. With this insight Brunner purports to reject the idealistic view of the state (elaborated by Hegel in particular), a view which has an explicit emphasis upon centralized supremacy. The state as an empirical political unit is morally neutral. Hence, one cannot speak of a Christian form of the state, nor is there any justification for the institution of Christian political parties. However, man's relationship to the state does take on moral meaning when viewed in the religious context of creation, judgment, and redemption. Like all natural orders the state must be understood as an expression of the goodness of God's creation, as corrupted by the Fall, and as subject to the process of divine restoration. This implies a regulative principle by which two unfortunate extremes can be avoided: (1) a false secularization which views the state as intrinsically evil, and (2) a sentimental radicalism which obscures the state's bondage to sin.

The community of culture, as the fourth natural order, includes man's activities in the area of science, art, and education. Like the others, this order also is part of the divine purpose, comprising areas in which God's creativity expresses itself in human creativity. But the cultural creations of men and women not only manifest the rational nature created by God; they also exhibit the tendency to transform intellectual and artistic forms into absolutes which become idols and threaten both personal life and the life of the community. It is in the realm of culture that the temptation to erect a "Towel of Babel" becomes strongest. It is for this reason that faith must always take a critical attitude toward culture and attack all demonic claims for absoluteness in the fields of science, art, and education.

The Church constitutes the fifth communal order. A church is a place where two or three meet in the name of Christ to hear the preaching of the Word of God. According to the author, this definition constitutes the heart of the evangelical faith. A father expounding the Gospel to his family affords us an instance of the Church in action. Nothing else is necessary to make a house a real church. However, in the development of the worshiping community there is an increasing institutionalization required to enable it to realize its central purpose. This institutionalization may take the form of a state church, national church, or free church. Each of these forms meets special conditions and poses special problems. But in any of its institutional forms the Church must be understood as the earthly and historical manifestation of the Kingdom of God. It is thus that the divine mission of the Church becomes explicit. Nonetheless, the Church is not immune from error and corruption. As an expression of the Kingdom within history, the Church is subject to the conditions of sinful historical existence. The Church and perfection are mutually exclusive ideas. Those who comprise the community of the Church are still sinners, and therefore the Church like all other orders of creation remains an imperfect community, permeated with the distortions of sin. The Church, like the redeemed man, is *in* the world, although not *of* it.

THE TWO SOURCES OF MORALITY AND RELIGION

Author: Henri Bergson (1859-1941)
Type of work: Philosophy of religion
First published: 1932

Principal Ideas Advanced

Customary morality and static religion take their rise in a closed society understood as an extension of nature; creative morality and dynamic religion take

their rise in an open society which transcends the structural permanence of nature.

The principle of obligation in customary morality functions primarily as a force of social cohesion; the principle of obligation in creative morality constitutes an aspiration toward an ideal through which the given social order is refashioned and vitalized.

Static religion provides the sanction for customary regulations, resists the individualizing and dissolving power of intelligence, and is riveted in the spatial determinations of nature; dynamic religion transcends the spatially bound spirits and deities of a religion of nature and finds its culmination in the mystical vision and action of exceptional personalities, such as the Christian mystics, who make the vital impetus (élan vital) *effectual as a force of creative and transforming love.*

Henri Bergson's approach in *The Two Sources of Morality and Religion* to the problem of the nature and origin of morality and religion is an empirical one; however, his empiricism must be understood in the broadest sense of the term. He appeals to experience, but this experience includes both the findings of scientific research and the records of the insights of the mystics. He makes use of the genetic approach in his description of morality and religion as universally given phenomena, and consequently he draws heavily from the discoveries in modern anthropology and sociology. Yet he is well aware of a possible misuse of the genetic approach insofar as it leads to the genetic fallacy. The genetic approach does not provide a criterion of evaluation. A description of origins cannot produce value judgments. Facts should not be confused with values.

The author begins his essay with a discussion of the nature of moral obligation. Moral obligation has been expressed in two ways in the history of mankind. On the one hand there are the obligations which arise out of a customary morality; on the other hand there are those which arise from a creative morality. In customary morality moral obligation functions primarily as a force of social cohesion. The directives which issue from it seek to perpetuate the existing social order, thus maintaining a given structure and equilibrium. This customary morality presupposes a "closed society" which in the author's words comes "fresh from the hands of nature." Customary morality is thus rooted in nature. Man was made for society just as the ant was made for the antheap. The distinctive feature of such natural phenomena as anthills and beehives is that each member is riveted to the given natural structure, and the task of each member is that of perpetuating the structure. The organization is fixed and invariable. A society of ants constitutes a "closed society." Although the author cautions the reader about overworking the analogy, he finds that it does convey a fundamental point. A "closed society" of human beings is similar to that of the ants in that the original structure of organization is perpetuated without consideration of critical questions concerning the need and nature of this structure. The preservation of society becomes the chief end of man. The morality of such a society must of necessity be a customary morality, one which finds its directives in the already established customs and mores. The power of motivation in such a morality comes from what Bergson calls "the totality of obligation." Obligation cannot be reduced to any one thing. Instinct and intelligence, passion and reason, habit and reflection interpenetrate in a proliferous configuration which in its totality defines the requirements of social life. The essence of obligation is thus quite clearly different from any requirements of an isolated and abstracted reason. Nonetheless, intelligence and reason are ever present, and specifically they are present in the task of legalizing the accumulated customs and habits. Customary morality thus becomes a morality of law.

Creative morality has its source in the aspiration toward an ideal rather than in the accumulated customs and habits which form the basis of obligation in customary morality. Such a creative morality requires an open rather than a closed society. In an open society the given organizational complexes are constantly subjected to critical questioning and evaluation. Instead of simply perpetuating the existing social order, creative or ideal morality seeks to change it. Customary morality is static, resistant to change and innovation; creative morality is dynamic, constantly striving to refashion and transform the given. The two moralities thus differ in essence; yet, at the same time, they are not wholly discontinuous.

The open society cannot dispense with customary regulations entirely. This would lead to chaos. Thus, it must seek to appropriate the stabilizing norms of customary morality and to find a place for them in its program of creative transformation. "Current morality is not abolished; but it appears like a virtual stop in the course of acutal progression. The old method is not given up; but it is fitted into a more general method, as is the case when the dynamic reabsorbs the static, the latter then becoming a mere particular instance of the former."

The dialectical relation between the old and the new, the static and the dynamic, is exemplified in the development of the concept of justice. Justice was first a social category, used as a norm to order the existing elements of a given society. But gradually justice emerged from social life and soared above to a transcendent and universal plane. Through this process of development its specific social function is not abolished, but this function receives its final definition through a principle which transcends the particular society. Morality thus becomes a "human" morality and is no longer simply a "social" morality.

Whereas customary morality becomes solidified into a morality of law, creative morality remains the morality of exceptional men. It is the exemplary life of the mystic, in particular, which supplies the touchstone. It is in the personality of the mystic that the *élan vital,* the fundamental principle of life itself, receives its most decisive expression. Creative morality is thus founded on the vital impetus, the dynamo in the process of creative evolution, which electrifies and inspires exceptional men in history.

Bergson's discussion of the nature of static and dynamic religion proceeds with an eye to this previously made distinction between customary and creative morality. Static religion and customary morality are coupled, as are creative morality and dynamic religion. The first function of religion, as that of morality, is social preservation. In primitive society morality is coextensive with religion. The whole of morality is custom, and religion provides the final sanction for customary regulations. Primitive religion thus takes precautions against any tendencies toward individualization by which the human intelligence may threaten the cohesion of the group. It is in light of this that primitive religion can be understood as "a defensive reaction of nature against the dissolvent power of intelligence." Primitive religion fights all forces which threaten group solidarity. This accounts for its static character. Like customary morality primitive religion is but an extension of nature, and such religion strives to maintain the structural and organizational permanence exhibited by anthills and beehives. Closely allied with the first function of static, primitive religion is the second function. This is its function as "a defensive reaction of nature against the representation, by intelligence, of the inevitability of death." Intelligence, through the process of generalization, discloses the universality and inevitability of death. Life is transitory and marked for destruction. Religion resists the implications of this generalization and instinctively affirms a belief in an afterlife. The idea that men live on as phantoms or shadowy replicas of what they were in this life is a natural belief present in all primitive cultures.

The static character of primitive religion can also be seen in its close alignment with magic, in spite of the essential difference between the two phenomena. In religion the individual seeks a relationship with a power conceived to be intrinsically personal; magic has to do with a mechanical manipulation of impersonal forces. Magic and religion thus go their separate ways and there can be no reduction of one to the other. Yet, the anthropological fact remains that in primitive religion the two phenomena are intertwined, and as a result of this mixture magic confers upon religion a static quality. This becomes evident through an inspection of the governing formula of magic, "Like is equivalent to like," which is itself convertible to the formula, "The static can replace the dynamic if it traces the pattern of the latter."

The more basic factor, however, in determining the static character of primitive religion is its bondage to space. Each spirit is bound to the spatial locality where it manifests itself. The multiple spirits in animism as well as the plurality of gods in polytheism are riveted to space. In the various religions this spatial quality is expressed in different ways. The gods depicted in the Vedic poems have their spheres of influence in the heavens, earth, and middle air respectively. Babylonian cosmology designates the sky as the realm of Anu, the earth belongs to Bel, and the sea is the dwelling place of Ea. In Greek religion we find again that the world is spatially dissected according to divine regions. Zeus is the god of heaven and earth, Poseidon is the god of the sea, and Hades is sovereign over the underworld. Static religion gives priority to the category of space.

Dynamic religion is a religion of time rather than of space. The vital impetus, which provides the ultimate basis for dynamic religion as it does for creative morality, permeates the entire evolutionary process and thus transcends every given spatial region. It thus supplants both animism and polytheism. The apex of this dynamic religion, as the author has suggested earlier, is mysticism. It is in the great mystics, particularly those of the Christian tradition, that dynamic religion attains its highest expression. The great mystic is defined by the author as that individual who is capable of transcending the limitations imposed on him by nature (matter and space), uniting with a divine reality, and transforming the given through the efficacy of human love and action. It is in Christian mysticism that such a movement is most illustriously exemplified. Greek and Indian mysticism never came to full fruition. The Greeks were too intellectual to be capable of mysticism. Plotinus, remaining faithful to this Greek intellectualism, never reached the final stage—the stage in which contemplation drives beyond itself to action. In Plotinus there is no union with a divine will and no consequent transformation of the human will. In Indian religion, mysticism is thwarted by a philosophy of pessimism which seeks not only to quench the fires of the will-to-live but also to depreciate everything finite and earthly. Complete mysticism is achieved only by the great Christian mystics. St. Paul, St. Teresa, St. Catherine of Siena, St. Francis, and St. Joan of Arc are listed as some of the most illustrious examples. Christian mysticism is a dynamic mysticism, a mysticism of action. It strives for a baptism of the will. The ecstatic union is not the point of culmination. The "vision of God" leads the Christian mystic to decisive action. The all-pervading directive in this decisive action is love. "God is love, and the object of love: herein lies the whole contribution of mysticism."

The mystic vision and the ensuing action evince an interrelated complex which is suprarational in character. Dynamic religion, like creative morality, transcends the merely rational and intelligible. This is why the author expresses some far reaching reservations regarding the religious significance of the "God of philosophy" (as had Pascal three centuries earlier). The God of the great mystics is not the God of the rational philosophers. Yet, according to the author, there is no complete break between reason and the mystic vision. Reason is transcended but not vitiated. Dynamic religion itself, although differing in essence from static religion, retains images and symbols borrowed from static religion which it then uses for its own propagation. Static religion is deepened with the new directive of love as expressed in the exemplary mystics, but its social function is not denied. It is transfigured but not abrogated.

THE LIVING GOD

Author: Nathan Söderblom (1866-1931)
Type of work: Philosophy of revelation
First published: 1933

Principal Ideas Advanced

Religious research indicates that the religion of revelation, of divine self-communication, is a definite type within the history of religions.

The Bible distinguishes between a general revelation of God and a special unique revelation of God in Christ.

The uniqueness of Christianity consists in the fact that God has chosen to reveal Himself in a special person of history, Jesus of Nazareth; the historic person of Jesus is, therefore, the full revelation of God on earth.

God's revelation is never finished, however, and can be seen in nature, history, and in the moral life; the continued revelation of God in Christianity is the continued action of the living Christ in the Church and in the experiences of men.

Nathan Söderblom in his Gifford Lectures of 1931, entitled *The Living God,* concerns himself with the problem of revelation. He believed in a general revelation of God. "There is a living God," he asserted on his death bed; "I can prove it by the history of religions." This idea of a general or "common" revelation is the integrating factor of his entire theological system, of which *The Living God* is the most mature expression. Söderblom believed that the Bible told of a general revelation of God to all men and of a special revelation of God to Israel and the Christian Church. A revelation of God could be found wherever real religion was found; that is, "wherever we find religious sincerity." Wherever God is known, no matter how imperfect and distorted the knowledge may be, it is God who has made himself known. Söderblom writes in *The Living* God, "Religious research distinguishes the religion of revelation as a definite type within the history of religions, and in the same way the Christian faith marks off a special sphere of revelation. . . . But a measure of revelation, i.e. of divine self-communication, is present wherever we find religious sincerity. That has been expressly declared by the belief in revelation within and without Christianity."

Revelation is defined as the action of the divine making Himself known. Therefore it is obvious, Söderblom argues on the basis of his research in the history of religions, that Christianity is not the sole depository for "the divine self-disclosure." Real religion is not a product of culture, but must depend upon a revelation of God. Belief in a general revelation of God is forced upon us, claims Söderblom, when we make a serious study of the non-Christian religions, no matter how debased, degraded, or "ignorant" they may be, and however loudly they may call for the Gospel of the Cross. The same God revealed himself to the Buddha, to Socrates, to Epictetus, to Christ, and to Mohammed. The originality and uniqueness of Christianity consists in the fact that "unique and absolute truth has in Christianity the form not of a rule, a law, Dharma, nor of ideas or theologies; Christian revelation has the form of a *man.*" Söderblom continues, "God reveals himself in a human life. In Buddhism Gotama Buddha, the Revealer, reveals the truth about suffering; he reveals a rule or doctrine, Dharma, and the result is an order of monks, the Samgha. In Christianity Christ reveals not a doctrine, but his own heavenly Father."

With the myriad savior gods, hero cults, and divine beings found in the history of religions, why did the Christ gain such an important historical position among all the other saviors of antiquity? Söderblom, in *The Living God,* gives three reasons for the ascendancy of Christ: (1) the Israelitic-Jewish tradition and the Bible with its monotheistic exclusiveness and the overpowering experience of the zeal of God; (2) the personal character of Jesus Christ and His supreme religious power, both in His dramatic and pathetic death and also in the strength of His personal gifts; (3) the historical reality of Jesus Christ. Söderblom uses I John 1:1-3 in this reference: "That which we have heard, which we have seen with our eyes, which we have looked upon, and our hands have handled . . . declare we unto you."

In all religions there is revelation, but not everything in religion is revelation. The miraculous is not what we cannot understand, but that which only faith understands. A miracle, like revelation, is an indication of a "divine interference," an act of God. Growth in faith, Söderblom asserts, means seeing more of God's acts in history; that is, seeing more miracles. Revelation as divine self-disclosure is a miracle. It is not found in the realm of science, which is concerned only with causal events and relationships. God never appears as a *secondary* cause; that is, as a cause which the senses can perceive. Religious wonder does not consist in an external miracle, a break in the chain of causes, but is rather an interpretation of the natural connection as caused by God; it consists in the experience of divine guidance and in the belief in a meaning and a goal for that which happens. Therefore the explanation of an event by science and an explanation by religion represent "two different ways of seeing." The former looks for causes; the latter, for divine purposes.

Söderblom suggests an agnostic position in reference to our understanding of revelation. We can never say, "Here is God and revelation!, There is man and Nature!" Even in the perfect revelation of God in the person of Christ the divine and human are commingled.

Söderblom's conception of revelation leads directly to the problem of whether God is personal or impersonal. The author makes a distinction between two kinds of mysticism—the mysticism of infinity and the mysticism of personality. Söderblom suggests that we compare Jesus with Buddha. Jesus is a prophet, Buddha a mystic; that is, Buddha defines communion with the eternal as a union, in pure ecstatic enjoyment, of all personal, conscious selves in a beatific state of Nirvana. Söderblom calls this view the "mysticism of infinity." Jesus, on the other hand, reveals communion with God to be a "prophetic experience." Knowledge of God is of a living, active, personal or superpersonal almighty power, of God as the Lord of life and history. This mysticism is the "mysticism of personality."

The difference between the two types of mysticism lies in the role which the person plays in each. Is the person repressed or extinguished in order to attain to the higher stages of the religious experience? Or is the person re-created and an eternal loving union with God realized, the person growing into a new man? Is the way to knowledge of the divine the *via negationis,* which leads, as Plotinus said, to the other side of existence, to where the "soul without being good or evil or anything," without consciousness of body or spirit, receives the divine? "Must we, with Hierotheus, reach the mysterious, silent stillness, which dissolves consciousness and form?", Söderblom asks; must we with the Areopagite, or Eckhart, or Ruysbroeck, arrive at the "divine darkness," "the nameless, formless nothing"? Or, is the way to God a way of affirmation (*via positionis*), a way which leads through complete self-renunciation and self-denial to a richer and stronger personal life, to the revelation of the divine will of love in the most glowing, most perfect, and most nobly formed personal life, Jesus Christ? The highest endowment of life is a personal love built on the foundation of a living trust in God. Such love is a warm, human reality, whether in suffering or in jubilation. Emphasis upon such love is entirely different from the motif of self-sacrifice in mysticism, which is the renunciation of all human relationships. The life of Christ demonstrates in a manner never surpassed how man may live confidently in relation to his fellowman and to God. The Christ of the Bible, however, does not become truly a revelation until the veil has been lifted from our eyes and we are led to see the divine life; that is, when we are able to see "the will of God beneath all of existence."

Söderblom maintains that religion is always a personal matter. The only effective answer which can be given to the religious question is found in the "discovery of the real sources and conditions of revelation in the life of the human spirit." However, the relation of one person to another in the mysticism of infinity becomes at best something impersonal and is associated with an illumination, or knowledge. The influence of personalities upon one another is fundamentally antagonistic to a mysticism which transcends time and history. Therefore, society and history are hindrances to the religious life and must be rejected in favor of the inner life. Mysticism, Söderblom claims, eludes the ancient and fundamental Christian question: How can we reconcile the fact that Christianity is indissolubly joined to a phenomenon in time, with the claim that Christianity is the absolute religion? Within revealed religion the person is an integral part of religion and is recognized as such. Revelation exists for the person. The unexpected has happened in the history of religions. Revealed religion has reached its perfection, not in doctrine or as a guide to salvation, but in a person, Jesus Christ. He is "the perfection of divine love and of human faithfulness."

Ethical relevance is not lacking in the mysticism of infinity, Söderblom concedes. On the contrary, the ethical is given a prominent place in the process of "purification," and in those means by which communion with God is attained. But in the mysticism of infinity the actual communion with God is affected "beyond good and evil." The individual's personal life is repressed rather than fulfilled in the communion with God. In the religion of the monks, which is an example of the mysticism of infinity, writes Söderblom, personality entirely disappears. The moral life becomes an ascetic practice, a self-discipline for the purpose of transcending every "creaturely" thing. It is not service of God with the positive "ideal," the Kingdom of God, in mind.

Furthermore, Söderblom writes, it is important to recognize that the mysticism of personality still contains unusual and abnormal physical and psychical phenomena, such as visions and ecstacies. God permits His power and love to be revealed in heavenly visions and raptures. Important religious experiences can be clothed in such strange forms.

Within that complex religious creation which is called Christianity, the mysticism of infinity has always remained, Söderblom claims. Historically, the mysticism of infinity is seen in the idea of the "consciousness of God," an idea which tended toward pantheism and abstract idealism. It is also seen in a conception of a Christ who is detached from history and becomes part of the mystic's inner life. Martin Luther, who for Söderblom was an example of a personal mystic, described "the communion of the Christian with God" according to the character of revealed religion, as contrasted with the sublime mysticism of infinity. Faith and confidence are expressions of personal relations. Basing his faith on Christ, on the revelation of God in Christ, not on any ambiguous or uncertain experiences of his own, Luther found his certainty of salvation. In the subsequent new life, resulting from faith in Jesus Christ, Luther found the distinguishing mark of personal religion. This, Söderblom remarks, was Luther's victory over mysticism.

Luther was able to identify the psychological experience which belonged to the mysticism of personality. The experience is the *terrores conscientiae,* (the "fear and trembling" of Søren Kierkegaard). The mysticism of infinity, however, seeks to unify man with God by destroying the creaturely nature of man. Only in this way, when the distinction is transcended between existence and nonexistence, between being and nonbeing, can union with God be achieved. The mysticism of personality, as expressed by Luther, cries out with the words, "Lord, spare me, depart from me! My guilt!" Here is man who cannot escape God—a God who is active, a God who crushes, but who also saves.

As we study the peculiar and distinctive forms of communion with God both within and outside revealed religion, Söderblom writes, we cannot escape the strong impression that in the mysticism of personality God conducts Himself in a manner entirely different from that observed in any other kind of religious orientation. God is active, intervening, self-communicating, attacking, revealing, standing forth in the life of the soul as in the world of history.

The "higher" religions represent a one-sided conception of the divine reality. Söderblom holds that the proper religion of revelation provides a richer knowledge of God. The religion of revelation, that is, the religion of the revealed God, the religion founded on Christ, knows much more of God. Therefore the Christian Church builds upon the experience of forgiveness of every regenerate soul.

Söderblom believes that the positive contribution of the mysticism of infinity is that in such a mysticism the divine is conceived to be other than that which is able to be expressed in conceptual terms. We cannot, asserted Söderblom, form an adequate conception of God. The God of Christianity is the "concealed God, revealed in

Christ." Christianity is communion with God through Christ. God can be conceived concretely only in the form of the Son. When Christ came, He had the power of making man's whole search for God an "antecedent of himself." The revelation of God in Christ complements what others have found, but it is this revelation which is the complete disclosure of the one God.

In conclusion, Söderblom makes the sincere piety of the individual the criterion for religious truth. Conviction about God, Söderblom claims, must build on an overwhelming personal experience of his reality, not on an accumulation of facts accessible to all. Religious knowledge is therefore subjective. Real piety is always "in its essence a secret of the soul, a revelation." In the sincerity of a heart in need of help there is something of God's revelation. The capacity to seek and find God is dependent upon the sincerity and seriousness of the seeker. Revelation requires a medium of expression, and the quality of the revelation depends on the quality of the personality receiving it.

NATURE, MAN AND GOD

Author: William Temple (1881-1944)
Type of work: Natural theology
First published: 1934

Principal Ideas Advanced

The emergence of mind in the process of nature suggests the hypothesis that the process itself needs Mind as its explanation.

The beauty and intelligibility of the world, and the phenomenon of morality are further evidence that the world derives from a transcendent Mind.

Transcendent Mind is personal; that is, it is governed by ideal purpose.

If the world is produced by Divine Personality, it is revelatory of Divine Character.

Like the angels which ascended and descended Jacob's ladder, the argument of Archbishop Temple's Gifford Lectures (Glasgow, 1932-1933, 1933-1934), follows a two-fold movement from nature to God, and from God to nature. In the first part, entitled "The Transcendence of the Immanent," Temple argues from the presence of mind in nature to the existence of a personal God in terms of whose purpose the world may be understood. In the second part, entitled "The Immanence of the Transcendent," he argues that only on the hypothesis that a personal God is revealing Himself in the world are the higher reaches of human experience meaningful. The title, *Nature, Man and God,* is well chosen, for it indicates what the author calls the "dialectical transitions of the argument": it is the problematic position of man in nature which leads our thoughts to God; and it is the revelation of God in the experience of man which at last enables us to understand and appreciate nature.

Nature, Man and God is a work in natural theology inasmuch as it does not rest its argument on the authority of revelation. The Archbishop was keenly aware of the tension which exists between the devotional and the critical frames of mind, or, in his language, between religion and philosophy. How shall we criticize that which, by its very nature, comes to us as authoritative? Temple's answer is, in effect, to take the notion of "criticism" in the Kantian sense. Given the higher religions, as part of human experience, what principles and categories are necessary in order to make them intelligible? Temple's argument is that the hypothesis of an Eternal Logos present throughout nature and history does make intelligible, not merely Christian beliefs, but the hopes and aspirations of all the religions of the world.

Although Temple calls himself a realist and is at pains to make clear his acceptance of "the new situation" in philosophy, his main argument, from the organic character of nature, and especially from the continuity between man's mind and nature, to Mind as first principle, has its roots in neo-Hegelianism. Temple follows emergent evolutionism in his account of the origin of mind, and he stresses the fact that in the beginning mind consisted simply in the organism's "responsive adjustment" to its environment. But, he argues, eventually there arose in consciousness a distinction between the self and the not-self; so that, while from one point of view minds are mere "episodes within the process," from another they transcend the process. Man "knows it while it does not know him."

But, the argument continues, that which transcends so much of nature can hardly be accounted for in terms of natural processes; yet, because minds are part of nature, if their origin is not explained, the world itself is not understood. Thus, it becomes reasonable to "test the hypothesis that Mind contains the explanation of the World-Process." This result marks Temple's first "dialectical transition." It is the hypothesis of "Immanent Theism."

The next step in the argument, which is to explore the extent to which Mind is immanent within nature, leads to an examination of values. In the pursuit of truth, beauty, and goodness, Temple argues, mind finds that the world is akin to itself and vindicates its interests and activities. Knowledge comes to have intrinsic value when, in addition to any instrumental use it may possess, mind discovers "its own principles in the world of its environment." The same is true in the mind's search for beauty; the aesthetic apprehension of nature and the appreciation of works of art both have as their foundation the meeting of mind with mind.

But the claims of truth and beauty, in which mind is related only indirectly to other minds, are secondary to those of moral goodness, for which the object is literally another mind. Obligation or duty, which in Temple's view is the foundation of morality, arises in social relations, and usually appears to the moral consciousness as a conflict between the interests of the self and the interests of the community. Moreover, this community does not admit of being sharply limited: as man progresses, "his mind finds what is akin to itself in the object, and he is on the way to learning that it is not only of a human community that he is a member, but also of a society which includes the myriad tribes of nature, animate and inanimate, because through all there lives and moves that Mind or Other akin to mind, with which in his Science and his Art man enters into fellowship." Thus, it is argued, man's most characteristic pursuits, which on the principle of the continuity of nature have to be viewed as immanent in the world, lead us to the view that the world owes its origin to a transcendent Mind.

In order to explain how mind can transcend process and create values, Temple examines the human personality, which, arising out of the flux, achieves a measure of self-determination by means of "free ideas." What chiefly characterizes man is that he is not determined by purely mechanical causes, but is guided by ideal considerations. Action determined in this way is called "purposive." In it lies man's "freedom," which is not indeterminism but "spiritual determination." "It is determination by what seems good as contrasted with determination by irresistible compulsion." Every organism is self-determined in the limited sense that it reacts to stimulation as an entirety; however, as Temple points out, nothing transcendent is involved, since the reaction is determined by the circumstances which exist in the present moment. Purposive action, possible only to personality, transcends the present and is determined by that which can have existence only in the future. Joining these considerations, then, to the previous conclusion, Temple affirmed that the world owes its origin to the purpose of a personal deity, or, in the language of religion, of a living God. So he concludes the first series of lectures, "The Transcendence of the Immanent."

In the second series, entitled "The Immanence of the Transcendent," Temple develops his philosophy of revelation. His method is to employ the concept of Divine Personality as an explanatory hypothesis, one to be tested in terms of its ability to render intelligible the religious experience of mankind. Although Temple claims that a spiritual interpretation of the universe is more acceptable to general science in modern times than formerly, he holds that truth is better served when religion and science operate each within its proper province.

From the hypothesis that the world is the handiwork of a personal God, it follows that everything in nature is a "self-communication" of a purposive being, first of all to Himself, but also, because personality "exhibits itself supremely in the purposes of fellowship and love," to created persons. But although all of God's acts, as expressions of His freedom, are to some degree revelatory of His character, there is no reason to suppose that they are all equally revelatory. The Divine Logos, universally effective in the world, might act for centuries without disclosing the more personal aspects of His being; then, when the time is suitable, God may manifest Himself in more intimate ways. General revelation is thus the ground for special revelation which, according to Temple, need involve no breach with the ordinary processes of nature. For example, the birth of Christ from a virgin "is due to the same cause as other normal births, namely, the Will of this same Logos, now aiming at a special and unique result." The particularly revealing purpose of the one act does not make it any *more* God's act than other births, but merely makes it more fully expressive of Himself.

Temple distinguishes, even in the sphere of special revelation, between the revelation itself and the record of the revelation. The essence of revelation is "the intercourse of mind and event, not the communication of doctrine distilled from that intercourse." God reveals Himself in events, but an event is revelatory only when another person responds to it. For example, God spoke to the prophets of Israel through historical events; their words serve as the expression of their "personal apprehension of the Divine Character and activity as disclosed." And this apprehension is as much a submission of the will as it is an informing of the mind. Although it is true that many who read the words of the prophets are convinced that through those words God has spoken to their own souls, still "what is revealed is not truth concerning God, but God himself." Thus, revelation is not conceptual. Temple says, "I do not believe in any creed, but I use certain creeds to express, to conserve, and to deepen my belief in God."

Although God is not communicated through concepts, what is revealed is, according to Temple, intelligible. God is incomprehensible in the sense that what is Infinite can never be grasped by the finite, but this does not mean that His nature is unintelligible. Temple claims that there is "an impassable distinction between Creator and creature, Redeemer and redeemed," but he maintains nevertheless that "in so far as God and man are spiritual they are of one kind; in so far as God and man are rational, they are of one kind." Thus Temple guards against superstition and fanaticism; in the long run, revelation must satisfy the deep-seated demands of human reason and conscience.

The claim that a transcendent purpose is manifest in nature and history raises a profound philosophical issue; namely, how the eternal can be understood as present in time. Temple discusses three traditional views. The first, which he attributes to Plato, holds that there is a one-way dependence of the temporal on the Eternal. The second, which is presumably that of Spinoza, is that Eternity is the totality of temporal events apprehended simultaneously. The third is the view, more appealing to imagination than to the reason, which conceives the Eternal as outside the world and time, and yet as persisting through it, so that time makes a difference to Eternity. Since none of these views was satisfactory to Temple, he developed a synthesis of his own.

Temple suggests that we be guided by what we know of human creativity and that we think of the world and history as grounded in God's will. God's thoughts are expressed not only in nature but also in the lives of men whom, however, He must control "according to the law of their being which he has imposed upon them"; that is, through what appears good to their unforced will and affection. Only in some such manner, Temple writes, is it possible to preserve the importance of the temporal and its characteristic meaning without surrendering "the complete and all-controlling supremacy of the Eternal." Temple calls this the "sacramental" view of the universe, because, like a sacrament, the world is viewed as "the effectual expression or symbolic instrument of spirit," yet in such a way that the natural order of things is given full cognizance. The Incarnation is the outstanding and unique instance of a direct expression of spirit through embodied existence. Christianity is the most "materialistic" of religions, Taylor suggests, in that it does justice to embodied existence.

BEING AND HAVING

Author: Gabriel Marcel (1889-)
Type of work: Christian philosophy
First published: 1935

Principal Ideas Advanced

Man's capacity for thought sets him over against himself and the world.

In his anxiety to recover wholeness, he seizes upon the objects of thought and by their means tries to have the world.

Because thoughts are abstractions from being, a genuine recovery must come through concrete approaches, such as faith, prayer, and sacrifice.

The only way in which we can know being is by addressing it in the second person.

Metaphysics, like religion, is concerned not with a problem but with mystery.

The most direct paths for approaching mystery are through such spiritual means as fidelity, love, and hope.

Being and Having is a metaphysical diary, covering a period of five years, beginning in the Fall of 1928, shortly before Marcel's conversion to Christianity and his baptism into the Roman Catholic church. Besides the diary, Marcel has included several short essays, addresses, and book reviews which further develop the themes dealt with in the diary.

The title is taken from the two contrasting themes which appear as the author's thought unfolds itself. At the beginning of the work, Marcel is mainly exploring the problem of *being* (ontology); but as the investigation proceeds, he finds himself asking why modern man has characteristically avoided the problem of *being* in favor of the problem of knowledge and the problem of value. His answer to this question comes midway through the work when it occurs to him that the anti-ontological bias of modern thought is an expression of a fundamental attitude which he calls *having*.

Marcel's philosophy is unsystematic by its very nature, a chain of reflections rather than a set of conclusions, so that it is in his journals, dramas, and other occasional writings that one finds his ideas most authentically expressed. The present work, which is a continuation of his longer *Metaphysical Journal* (1914-1923), is a nuclear work; and if it lacks the organization of a system, it possesses the kind of unity which characterizes a successful improvisation.

Marcel was reared outside the Church. His philosophical training was mostly in the Neo-Kantian and Neo-Hegelian tradition. But his original work in philosophy, beginning as early as 1914, led him, with many of his contemporaries, away from idealism toward realism. Following his own line of development, Marcel found himself approaching more and more closely to religious faith. In time, partly due, no doubt, to the influence of such confessing Christians as Nikolai Berdyaev (1874-1948), Jacques Maritain, and François Mauriac, men of note who moved in the same intellectual circles as his own, Marcel declared himself at last "hemmed in" by Christianity; and, after submitting to instruction, he was baptized on March 23, 1929.

Even before he was converted, Marcel believed that the direct communion with reality called "faith" is experienced by some men, although he counted himself as one who was denied this experience. After he was converted, it seemed to him that to believe in the faith of others is itself a kind of faith. "The fact is," he told a group of Christian students in 1934, "that when we have already come as far as this, we are in an open and expectant state of mind which either implies faith or is faith." In his opinion, many who think of themselves as unbelievers are in this condition. He contrasts their unbelief with that of those persons whose minds are closed and unexpectant because they have embraced a set of preconceptions which on principle exclude faith.

Openness and expectancy characterize quite well Marcel's philosophical outlook. As he views the human predicament, man's capacity for thought poses a threat to his integrity. Descartes and his followers were mistaken, he says, in believing that thought is identical with being. On the contrary, thought abstracts from being, both as respects the thinker and the thought. In this sense, thought is "a sort of lie, or rather a sort of fundamental blindness." Knowledge, if it is based on a recognition of this initial blindness, is a return to being and a recovery of man's integrity. But none of us is disposed to begin with this recognition. In our anxiety at being alienated from being, we seize upon the abstractions of thought as if they were things, and then we fix them in a framework of ideal relations which we call the "world." Therefore, what we commonly call knowledge rests on self-deception, and it places a permanent barrier between man and reality.

These two ways of knowing are, however, merely expressions of two fundamental modes of responding to the ambiguities of the human situation. The kind of knowing which abstracts the ego and the object from reality and sets man up as a spectator of the world is, according to Marcel, a subtle form of the mode of *having*. To *have* anything implies, on the one hand, a kind of egotism. If I have knowledge, wealth, or power, my self is enhanced in its own eyes. On the other hand, to have implies a dualism between the ego and that which it calls the "world." What I have comprises a different order of being from myself, a world of things which are either objects of my passion or instruments for my exploitation. Marcel maintains that man's attempt to realize himself in the mode of *having* is self-defeating. "Having as such," he says, "seems to have a tendency to destroy and lose itself in the very thing it began by possessing, but which now absorbs the master who thought he controlled it. It seems that it is of the very nature of my body, or of my instruments in so far as I treat them as possessions, that they should tend to blot me out, although it is I who possess them."

As Marcel sees it, if man is to recover his identity and a fruitful relation to reality, he must find another way of responding to his environment. Instead of viewing it as a spectator, he must become a participant; instead of seeking to manage it, he must commit himself to the "creative intention that quickens the whole."

Man's relation to his own body is a ready example. I can either say, "I have a body," in which case I think of it as an instrument to be used for certain purposes; or, by diminishing the sovereign pretensions of the ego, I can say, "I am my body," and make this recognition the starting-point for finding my way back to *being*. For, says Marcel, "incarnation" is "the central 'given' of metaphysics." He continues: "To say that something exists is not only to say that it belongs to the same system as my body (that it is bound to it by certain connections which reason can define), it is also to say that it is in some way united to me as my body is."

To Marcel, the way of participation in being is what mankind has always known as religion. Like everything else in man's experience, religion is subject to ambiguity, and it easily slides into an object of *having*. But in its genuine expressions (faith, prayer, sacrifice) religion is the way in which man overcomes his alienation from *being*.

As early as 1918, Marcel argued, in the *Metaphysical Journal,* that what sets the religious frame of mind over against the scientific is that the religious man, like the lover, apprehends the Other as *thou*. The scientist, when he investigates a man, regards the object at hand in the "third person," grammatically speaking. This, says Marcel, does not exclude the possibility of a shift in perspective enabling the scientist to know the man in the "second person" as a friend. But, Marcel maintains, a contradiction enters when we try to apply the scientific attitude not simply to other entities, be they persons or things, but to the total environment, as if we ourselves were not involved in the very thing we try to reduce to the status of an *it*. "I would be prepared to say dogmatically," writes Marcel in the *Metaphysical Journal,* "that every relation of being to being is personal and that the relation between God and me is nothing if it is not a relation of being with being, or, strictly, of being with itself." This leads Marcel to declare that "God is the absolute *thou* who can never be converted into a *him,*" and to conclude that the only knowledge man can have of God is through prayer.

In *Being and Having,* Marcel points out that the same distinction which we make between a *him* and a *thou* is preserved in the distinction between *thinking* a thought and *thinking of* a person or thing. In the former case, thought deals with ideas, which are abstractions from being. The error of the idealist or the essentialist consists in overlooking this fact. In the latter case, thought is engaged with concrete entities, and it stands in direct relation with aspects of reality which cannot be intellectualized.

With this new distinction in mind, Marcel returns to the subject of prayer. When we pray to God, he says, we *think of* God in a manner analogous to thinking of a person. Marcel writes, "When I think of a finite being, I restore, in a manner, between him and myself, a community, an intimacy, a *with* (to put it crudely) which might seem to have been broken." Something similar takes place in prayer: "To ask myself how I can think of God is to enquire in what sense I can be with him." There are obvious differences, says Marcel, between our relations with other persons and our relations with the One in whom we have our being. But he points out that even in the former case, to *think of* someone is an "active denying" of space and time, in the sense in which they involve separation. Thus, common experience points the way in which thought overcomes the fragmentation which, in its utilitarian mode, thought introduces into being.

Marcel observes that one of the characteristics of *having* is to view what lies beyond its current limit as a problem to be solved. It is a mistake, however, to carry over into our concrete relations with *being* the notion of a problem or the expectation of a solution. Here, he says, we are "in the realm of the metaproblematic, that is, of mystery." Whereas a problem lies before me as something that I can "lay siege to and reduce," a mystery is "something in which I am myself involved." There is, says Marcel, a temptation to reduce a mystery to a problem, as philosophy has traditionally done in speaking of the problem of being or the problem of evil. This, however, he claims, is "a corruption of the intelligence." A truer way of proceeding is to recognize that every genuine problem "conceals a mystery"; that is, implies something which cannot be reduced to a problem or treated as an object. For example, "the act of thinking cannot be represented and must be grasped as such." It is a mystery, and lies outside every explanatory system; but it is not, for this reason, unthinkable. We can *think of* it, even if we cannot *think* it.

Marcel concludes that the "mysterious" is the proper province of metaphysics, just as the "problematic" is the proper province of science. He further holds that, at bottom, metaphysics and religion, the way which leads to Being and the way which leads to Holiness, are in some hidden way identical. The approaches to "the ontological mystery," are, therefore, not principally to be found in exploring the presuppositions of science, but "in the elucidation of certain data which are spiritual in their own right, such as fidelity, hope, and love, where we may see man at grips with the temptations of denial, introversion, and hard-heartedness."

Marcel's account of these Christian "virtues" is perhaps the most illuminating part of his study. Faith, he says, presupposes fidelity, which, in turn is based upon commitment, an act of freedom by means of which man affirms his own being together with that of the Other. Love, Marcel interprets as a process of "decentralizing" the self, of becoming more completely "disposable," more open to others, more at one with the Other, less "autonomous," and more "free." Hope, he sees as the courage to turn away from the false promise of *having;* like the latter it yearns for salvation, for healing, for the re-establishment of order and peace; but it places its confidence not in programs and techniques, but in divine power and beneficence.

Religion would, of course, be no more than a delusion if it were merely a readiness on man's part for a response that never came. The believer "witnesses" that the Other is responsive. He can do no more than witness; because his whole person is involved, he cannot ask another to stand in his place and verify his experience. Witnessing, says Marcel, is a kind of fidelity. As such it involves a "mysterious union of necessity and liberty." At its root lies the recognition of something given. "In attesting," he writes, "I really proclaim, *ipso facto,* that I should be going back on myself, and —yes—even annulling myself, were I to deny this fact, this reality of which I have been the witness."

For many years Marcel wrote about the religious experience without being able to witness to it. On February 28, 1929, he says, "I at once fear and long to commit myself." The next entry, five days later, is: "I have no more doubts. This morning's happiness is miraculous. For the first time I have clearly experienced *grace.* A terrible thing to say, but so it is. I am hemmed in at last by Christianity—in, fathoms deep. Happy to be so! But I will write no more. And yet, I feel a kind of need to write. Feel I am stammering childishly . . . this is indeed a birth. Everything is different."

Marcel records experiencing "heavy weather" while studying the catechism preparatory to being baptized. He also confesses the misery he felt when confronted with the claims of Thomist philosophy. After having looked at Christianity from the outside for so long, he found it difficult to get used to seeing it from within. His main support was "the desire not to be on the side of those who betrayed Christ. . . . It is that part of the Gospel which is the spring of inspiration in my present state." He had the feeling, however, that each resistance which he made was cauterized away: "Is this an illusion?" he asks. At his baptism, he was tranquil. "My inward state was more than I had dared to hope for," he writes; "no transports, but peaceful, balanced, and full of faith and hope."

Five years later, he looks back on the experience. "Is faith an escape?" he asks, in an address to a group of students. An objective answer to the question is, of course, precluded. Marcel can only testify that in many cases it does not seem so. "For instance," he says, "I can assure you from my own experience that my faith was born at a time when I was in an exceptional state of moral stability and personal happiness. Otherwise I might have been suspicious of it."

Marcel's faith, in spite of his submission, remains free, however, in the same sense in which the faith of his friend Nikolai Berdyaev remains free. (See Berdyaev's *Freedom and Spirit,* 1927.) He declares that he has no interest in denominational religion, and he goes so far in one passage as to say that if his conviction (that God does not demand to be loved *against* Creation but rather *through* Creation) is heretical, "so much that the worse for orthodoxy." What he appreciates in the Roman Church is certainly not its exclusiveness, nor its claims to possess a universal and objective truth, but "the interdependence of spiritual destinies" which there becomes a reality. "That," says Marcel, "is the sublime and unique feature of Catholicism."

JESUS THE LORD

Author: Karl Heim (1874-)
Type of work: Christian existentialism
First published: 1935

Principal Ideas Advanced

Except for Christ, all men are prevented by the relativity inherent in human experience from knowing God, who is Ultimate Reality.

The Christian claims that by surrendering his will to Jesus as Lord, he comes to know God.

If man refuses to surrender his will to Christ, he tends to regard Christianity as an illusion; if he surrenders to Christ, he tends to explain man's natural predicament as the product of a Satanic will.

Karl Heim has spoken of the development of his theological career under the figure of a stream which must flow past a mountain. The stream of his thought flows in the direction of trying to make experience intelligible; the reality of Christ, like a mountain, alters the course of the stream but does not choke it off. It is Heim's opinion that contemporary Protestant theologians, in their zeal to recover the uniqueness of the Christian revelation, have too often failed in their responsibility to make intelligible the relation between faith in Christ and the remainder of human experience. In an effort to bridge the gap, Heim has written a series of volumes entitled *Christian Faith and Contemporary Thought.* The present volume is the second in the series, and it is central to the project inasmuch as it is here that the reader is placed most directly at the juncture of revelation and reason.

Heim argues in the first part of the book that left to his own resources man is in a hopelessly contradictory situation. Both in his efforts to understand the world and in his practical pursuits, he requires some kind of absolute; but due to the structure of empirical experience, he can never find it. Heim uses classical mechanics to illustrate his point. Leibniz is his authority for saying that rest and motion are essentially the same: were we to conceive of all the bodies in the universe remaining at the same distance from each other, it would be indifferent whether we said they were at rest or in uniform movement. To arrive at the conception of rest and motion as opposites, we must posit an original "state of indifference," and then destroy it. Thus, rest and motion are in polar relation to each other. But, Heim maintains, what is true of rest and motion is true of all the terms of our mundane experience. Polarity is an original relation which is basic to every other, and our sensible world is a breaking-up of an original "state of indifference" to which thinking endeavors to return. This is true of light and dark, sound and silence. It is also true of the fundamental relations of time (now and then) and of space (here and there). Everything in our world *is* because of something else. There are no ultimate causes or final goals.

Requiring, as he does, some absolute, man has proceeded in one of two ways to escape from his relativity. The usual way is to affirm the reality of the phenomenal world and arbitrarily to declare that some part or parts of it have original status. For theoretical purposes, man takes certain truths as self-evident and certain kinds of experience as primary; and, as a basis of conduct, he maintains the authority of certain axioms and the primacy of certain ends. According to Heim, this procedure is essentially idolatrous in that it accords to that which is relative an independence which could belong only to a Reality standing outside the relation of polarity; and, in fact, the dynamics of existence being what they are, men's idols are constantly being overthrown. But not their idolatry: even self-styled realists, such as Oswald Spengler (1880-1936), who mock the claims of philosophy and morality, and attempt to explain reality in terms of will, race, instinct, and power, are merely substituting new gods for old.

Such is one alternative—to affirm the reality of the phenomenal world and to deify some portion of it. But in times of widespread doubt and despair, sensitive individuals have discovered the other alternative, which is to deny that the phenomenal world is real, and to force thought back in the direction of the unitary "state of indifference" implied in our manifold experience. This, according to Heim, is the significance of mysticism, both Eastern and Western. However, because the "state of indifference" is implicit in our experience of the phenomenal world, it too is involved in the relation of polarity. Hence, as an attempt to escape relativism and to find the ultimately Real, mysticism must also fail.

There is, according to Heim, no way in which man can escape the absurdity of his situation. The curse of polarity makes it impossible for him ever to bridge the abyss between phenomena and transpolar Reality. He cannot even speculate how this abyss might be bridged from the other side. Yet man cannot live without an ultimate.

This is the background against which Heim invites us to consider the claims of Christianity. The early Christians, whose testimony has come down to us in the New Testament, professed an experience of God which transformed their view of the world, brought joyous calm into their hearts, and gave them victory over death. Unlike other religions, early Christianity made no claims within the phenomenal world, set up no sanctuaries, proclaimed no laws, ordained no priesthood. Its faith consisted purely and simply in the surrender of men's whole lives to Jesus as *Lord.* In this way, it opened up a radically new perspective.

Heim acknowledges that the "category" of lordship was already present in the experience of the Hellenistic age, even as it has been revived by such twentieth century "lords" as Lenin, Gandhi, Mussolini, and Hitler.

But leaders of this sort remain within the sphere of the relative. Only in Christ does "lordship" find its fulfillment, for His leadership, unlike that of the others, "encompasses our whole existence, not only the fate of our body but also all our volition and cognition, not only our life until death but our entire future destiny for everlasting." In the experience of absolute surrender to Jesus as the "one true Leader," the early Christian found himself beyond polarity, face to face with God, the ultimately Real.

Whether obedience to Christ does in truth enable a man to transcend polarity poses a difficult question. Since the claim which Christians make is incompatible with our ordinary view of the world, it can be neither established nor refuted by argument, but only in practice. Thus, in Heim's terms, the fact of Christianity confronts man with a radical either-or. Either he surrenders himself totally to Christ, which involves surrendering his cognition along with everything else; or, he remains under some other leadership (perhaps his own) and refuses to surrender his mind to Christ. In the latter case he will never know whether the claim of the early Church was true. Only if he takes the step and surrenders wholly to Christ can he know the truth of the claim.

Heim, of course, has taken the step and is persuaded that the claim is true. But his aim in *Jesus the Lord* is not so much to persuade others to take the step as it is "reflectingly to develop and describe the content of faith in Christ." Accepting Christ, he maintains, gives rise to a wholly new world view. The Christian can only fall into confusion and error if he first embraces a system of philosophy and then seeks to enthrone Christ in it. On the contrary, he must start with the experience of Jesus as Lord, and then employ his reason in discovering "what this fact entails for an understanding of the world and of human existence."

According to Heim, the first question for the Christian philosopher is why mankind is estranged from Reality. Is it man's fault, or is it due to his creaturely condition? Other religions say, in effect, that man is not to blame, and their salvation consists in an attempt to deliver him from suffering, misfortune, and finitude. Instead of regarding man as the victim of evil circumstances, Jesus regarded him as enslaved by a Satanic will, which He came to destroy.

Here, then, is the Christian's clue for understanding the human predicament. Satan stands for a will that is more fundamental than any of man's particular wants and wishes, for it is the will which originally prompted the act of enmity against God. By yielding to Satanic temptation, man freely declares his independence of his Creator, and this fundamental choice determines how he henceforth apprehends the world. Heim agrees with the thesis of existentialist philosophy, that the will or intentionality of the observer determines the structure of his world. Heim's special contention is that all men have been seduced into rebellion, and that what is for man the ordinary world of objective experience, with its polarity, relativity, aimlessness, and uncertainty, is the result of this rebellion. On this view, man is to blame for his predicament; and the choice by which he became imprisoned within it is so fundamental to his being that he cannot, by an ordinary act of will, reverse it.

Meanwhile, through surrender of his will to Jesus as Lord, the Christian sees the world in a wholly new light. "If our heart is with God while we are watching the object, then we can see it with pure childish eyes. Then all that we experience, do and suffer is in the light of fellowship with God." Actually, however, no man except the sinless Christ is able steadily to behold the world in its true light. The condition of the Christian is that of a man in whom two world-views are in constant tension. Original sin remains to plague him. No more than unbelievers can he escape the curse of polarity. But for the believer a new polarity has arisen which embodies hope: the polarity between our world of sin and death and the heaven and earth of God's intention. The Christian has experienced them both and knows that they are contradictory; but he also knows that God, who has revealed Himself in Christ, will finally resolve the contradiction; and he lives in the burning expectancy of that consummation.

A second question for the Christian philosopher is how God is able to reveal Himself within the compass of man's experience. In the first volume of this series, Professor Heim analyzes the nature of speech, making use of the distinction between *I-It* and *I-Thou* relations which the Jewish philosopher Martin Buber has explored in *I and Thou* (1923). The "word," according to Heim, is the means by which one self encounters the dynamic resistance of another "eternally foreign" self and seeks to change its world. The possibility of such an encounter presupposes a common "dimension," just as the meeting of two infinite lines presupposes the dimension of a plane; hence, speech takes place in the world of objects, although the word itself is not an object but an act. It is in this manner, according to Heim, that the early Christians conceived of God's revelation in Christ. God speaks to men, they said, through His Son Jesus Christ. It is important says Heim, that God speaks through a *Thou*. For, although Jesus enters our world of experience, and takes His place as a creature in the same frame with other creatures, the believer does not behold Christ simply as a figure of history. But, just as the spoken word is heard against the background of meaningless noise (and silence), yet is not heard merely as a sound, so Jesus, while intersecting our ordinary world of objects, is experienced not as an object but as an act by which God's will impresses itself upon ours.

Heim describes his world-view as essentially dynamic. Man's existence is constantly being renewed. He is in flight between the past, which is the world of "it," the objective world of our polar experience, and the future, which is determined only insofar as it is willed. What the future shall be depends upon a battle between wills, a battle not merely between the competing wills of men, who are all alike doomed to destruction, but between Satan and God, and correspondingly between those who are in rebellion against God and those who have submitted their lives to Christ.

THE PARABLES OF THE KINGDOM

Author: Charles Harold Dodd (1884-)
Type of work: Theory and interpretation of parables
First published: 1935

Principal Ideas Advanced

The Kingdom of God, as presented in the parables of Jesus, was not intended as a future, eschatological event, but as a present fact, a realized eschatology.

In the ministry of Jesus the sovereign power of God had come to effective operation as a historical happening to which men should respond by repentance.

Christian thought finds a supreme crisis in the ministry and death of Jesus Christ, when history became the field within which God confronted men in a decisive way and placed before them a moral challenge that could not be evaded.

As one of the leading British Biblical scholars, Charles Harold Dodd examines the treatment of the theme of the Kingdom in recent scholarship and argues in *The Parables of the Kingdom* that the New Testament parables refer not to some esoteric future event but to a contemporary reality. The older world closed with the ministry of John; the new world begins with the Gospels and with the ministry of Jesus. Until the end of the nineteenth century the parables were treated as elaborate allegories, as teachings clothed in unintelligible forms. Instead, Dodd argues, the allegories are the natural expression of a mind that sees truth in concrete pictures. The parables are not esoteric doctrines but are metaphors or similies drawn from nature or from common life; as used by Jesus, the parables were vital parts of the proclamation of the Kingdom. (The break in the tradition of allegorical interpretation came with the publication of *Die Gleichnisreden Jesu* by the German scholar Adolf Jülicher in 1886.)

The typical parable presents one single point of comparison. Details are kept strictly subordinate to the dramatic realism. What we must assume is that Jesus meant to point to an inward affinity between the natural order and the spiritual order. Nature and the supernatural are one order, we must suppose. The sense of the divineness of the natural order, then, is the major premise of all the parables, Dodd is convinced. A parable is an argument, enticing its hearer to a judgment upon the situation depicted. In each parable there is a challenge, Dodd claims, to apply that judgment to the matter at hand. The way to an interpretation lies through a judgment of the imagined situation and not through the decoding of the various elements of the parable. We should expect the parables to bear upon the actual and critical situation in which Jesus and his hearers stood. How are we to apply the parables? The clue for the application must be found in such ideas as we may suppose to have been in the minds of the hearers of Jesus.

The Kingdom is a present fact. But the King is to be King of all the world. Israel looked for a temporal and political messiah, but instead, in an unsuspected way, God's sovereign power became manifest in Jesus. For him, sovereignty is something other than the scrupulous observance of the Torah. The Kingdom is a present fact, but not in a sense which could be recognized in the then current Jewish usage. Despite Israel's inability to recognize the Kingdom in this form, something critical had happened: the sovereign power of God had come to effective operation as a historical happening which men should respond to by repentance. In the very earliest tradition discernible in the New Testament, Jesus understood Himself as proclaiming that the Kingdom had at last come. The final Kingdom has moved from the future to the present.

Dodd's analysis yields the conclusion that in the ministry of Jesus the divine power was released in conflict with evil. The parables of the Kingdom must be taken as realized eschatology, as the impact of powers of a world-to-come manifest in a series of events, unpredictable and unprecedented, in actual process. What is new is that this Kingdom is to be revealed on earth, not in some later transformed age. Jesus conceived His ministry as moving rapidly to a crisis, one which would bring about His own death, the acute persecution of His disciples, and a general upheaval in which the power of Rome would make an end of the Jewish nation. His foresight was primarily insight. His predictions were primarily dramatizations of spiritual judgments. Jesus declared that the Kingdom of God had come. His words suggest, not any readjustment of conditions on this earth, but the glories of a world beyond this. Even before His death Jesus declared the Kingdom to have come, so that it was not uniquely connected even with His death.

The Kingdom is God exercising His kingly rule among men, writes Dodd. Divine power is effectively at issue with the evil in the world, making an end to the enemy's kingdom. Judgment is the primary function and weapon of the Kingdom. In rejecting Jesus the Jewish nation was rejecting the Kingdom of God, and thereby it brought itself under the judgment of that Kingdom.

Paul understood that the death of Jesus fell within the Kingdom of God, as a part of the effective assertion of God's sovereign rule in the world. The course of events which outwardly was a series of disasters holds within itself, for those with insight, a revelation of the glory of God. That this could be so, that apparent disaster could actually be the coming of the Kingdom, is the mystery of the Kingdom of God. The final state is now a matter of actual experience, but it is experienced in the paradoxical form of the suffering and death of God's representative. Thus the Kingdom has come, but in a strange and unexpected guise.

The Scriptures also refer to the Day of the Son of Man, and it is not made clear that this Day is identical with the Day of Judgment. Yet in all our primary Gospel sources, Dodd writes, Jesus is identified with the Son of Man. "The Son of Man" must have been at some stage a current Messianic designation for Jesus. In the Gospels themselves the term is never used except in the mouth of Jesus. Interestingly enough, the term most familiar in the early Church, "Messiah," is recognized to be inappropriate in the mouth of Jesus. To apply the term "the Son of Man," with its apocalyptical and eschatological associations, to a living man is no doubt a paradox; but it is also a paradox to say that the Kingdom of God, itself an eschatological fact, has come in history. Both the death and the resurrection of Jesus, Dodd writes, are eschatological events.

Dodd contends that we are confronted by two diverse strains in the teaching of Jesus, one of which appears to contemplate the indefinite continuation of human life under historical conditions, while the other appears to suggest a speedy end to these conditions. A drastic criticism might eliminate the one strain or the other, but both are embedded in the earliest form of the tradition known to us. We must face the issue, and it may be possible to find a place for both strains, if we make full allowance for the symbolic character of the apocalyptical sayings. The symbolic method is inherent in apocalyptic sayings. Thus it is open to the reader to take the traditional apocalyptic imagery as a series of symbols standing for realities which the human mind cannot directly apprehend. However, in the teaching of Jesus the traditional apocalyptical symbolism is controlled by the central idea of the Kingdom of God. But Jesus declares that this ultimate, the Kingdom of God, has come into history, and He takes upon himself the eschatological role of the Son of Man. Thus, the absolute, the wholly other, has entered into time and space. And as the Kingdom of God has come, so also has judgment and blessedness come upon human experience.

According to Dodd's account, the imagery retains its signficance as symbolizing the eternal realities, which though they enter into history are never exhausted in it. The Son of Man has come, but it is also true that He *will* come. The Day of Man stands for a timeless fact. So far as history can contain this fact, it has become embodied in the historic crisis which the coming of Jesus brought into the world. Whether the subsequent span of the Day will be long or short, men will henceforth be living in a new age, an age in which the Kingdom of God, His grace, and His judgment stand revealed. Jesus points his hearers directly from the historic crisis in which they are involved toward the eternal order of which the crisis is only a mirror.

The ministry of Jesus cannot be regarded as an attempt to reform Judaism, Dodd declares; His ministry brings something entirely new into the world, which cannot be accommodated to the traditional system. But what of the group of parables which refer directly to the expected second advent of Christ? Did Jesus Himself teach His disciples to anticipate His second advent after a long and incalculable interval? The idea of this group of parables is really that of alertness and preparedness for any emergency, Dodd's examination suggests. We may then ask, what was the emergency which Jesus had in mind? We know that He saw in His own ministry the supreme crisis in history. But there is nothing in the parable itself against the view that the emergency He contemplated was in fact the crisis created by His own coming, and it is this view which Dodd adopts and urges as the best interpretation of the parables of the second coming. It was not to be some expected crisis in the more or less distant future, but simply His own first advent which brought the emergency for which men needed alerting.

The crisis which Jesus brought about was not a single momentary event but a developing situation. He did not speak these parables to prepare His disciples for a long though indefinite period of waiting for a second advent, but to enforce the necessity for alertness in a crisis then upon them. The growth of the interest in the expectation of the second advent, then, must have begun as soon as even a few years had elapsed since the Resurrection without bringing the expected consummation. The Kingdom of God had actually come, unexpectedly, incalculably, and Israel was taken by surprise. In all of these parables, Dodd suggests, there is the suggestion of complete unpreparedness for a sudden disaster. The predictions of the coming of the Son of Man or of That Day are to be regarded as running parallel with the predictions of historical disaster then upon them.

The coming of the Son of Man, then, in its aspect as judgment, is realized in the catastrophe which Jesus predicted as lying immediately in store—the persecution of Himself and His disciples, the destruction of the Temple and of the Jewish nation. It seems possible to give to all these eschatological parables an application within the context of the ministry of Jesus as it has been recorded. They were intended to enforce His appeal to men to recognize that the Kingdom of God was already present and that the day of judgment meant that, by their conduct in the presence of this tremendous crisis, they would judge themselves as faithful or unfaithful, wise or foolish. Then when the crisis had passed, the parables were adopted by the Church to enforce its appeal to men to prepare for the second and final world-crisis which it believed to be approaching. Thus the early Church transformed the original intent of the parables and set our present problem of interpretation.

The predominant interpretation of these parables makes them refer to future history and to the coming of the Kingdom of God in the world. If this is the way the parables are usually taken, and if Jesus declared that the Kingdom of God had arrived, these parables indicate that the Kingdom was present only in germ, and they allow for an indefinite period of development before consummation. This is one way of solving the problem, and yet, Dodd contends, the interpretation of the parables depends upon the view taken of the Kingdom of God. The view which he takes is that the Kingdom is neither an evolutionary process nor yet a catastrophic event in the near future, but a present crisis. Dodd argues that it is not that the Kingdom of God will shortly come, but that it is a present fact, in the sense that something has now happened in the ministry of Jesus which has never before happened. The parables would suggest, Dodd feels, that a crisis which had then arrived was the climax of a long process which prepared the way for it.

The parables represent the interpretation which our Lord offered of His own ministry, Dodd concludes. Jesus used parables to enforce and to illustrate the idea that the Kingdom of God had already come upon men, there and then. The inconceivable had happened. History had become the vehicle of the eternal; the absolute was clothed with flesh and blood. In the events before their eyes, then, God was confronting them in His Kingdom, in His power and in His glory. This world had become the scene of a divine drama, in which the eternal issues were laid bare. It was the hour of decision; it was realized eschatology.

The parables proclaim: this is the hour of fulfillment. Yet the Kingdom of God does come with judgment, it is still true to say. The disciples forsook Him and fled; but afterwards they rose out of failure into a new life and understood only then how the mystery of the Kingdom of God had been finally revealed in Jesus' death and resurrection.

The preaching of the Church is directed towards reconstituting in the experience of the individuals the hour of decision which Jesus brought, Dodd concludes. The Kingdom of God had come, and he who receives it as a little child shall enter in. The thought of Jesus had passed directly from the immediate situation to the eternal order lying beyond all history, of which the spoken word was clothed in the language of apocalyptic symbolism. The pattern of history, so far as its spiritual values are concerned, is exhibited in crisis rather than in evolution. Christian thought finds this supreme crisis in the ministry and in the death of Jesus Christ with its immediate sequel. The supreme significance of the crisis lies in the fact that here in history the historical process became the field within which God confronted men in a decisive way and placed before them a moral challenge that could not be evaded. We have warrant, Dodd is convinced, for affirming that God comes to meet us in history and sets before us the open but narrow door into His Kingdom. This is the present significance of the Gospel parables concerning the Kingdom of God and its coming, and they in turn serve as the central fact in the interpretation of Jesus, His person and His ministry.

A NEW CRITIQUE OF THEORETICAL THOUGHT

Author: Herman Dooyeweerd (1894-)
Type of work: Christian philosophy
First published: 1936

Principal Ideas Advanced

Philosophy presupposes a religious commitment concerning the origin of the world, the nature of its unity and diversity, and the origin and the nature of the laws that govern it.

The alleged autonomy of theoretical reason is unmasked by an analysis of the theoretical attitude of thought and by a careful investigation of the history of philosophy which discloses various motives at work, ranging from that of form and matter in ancient Greece, to the motive of nature and freedom in modern humanism.

The Christian philosopher is properly guided in his philosophical investigations by the open acceptance of the Biblical motive of Creation, Fall, and Redemption in Christ Jesus in the communion of the Holy Spirit.

A New Critique of Theoretical Thought, in four volumes, is the major work of Herman Dooyeweerd, the founder of a new school of Christian philosophy in the tradition of St. Augustine. The work first appeared in Dutch in 1936.

Volume I deals with the necessary presuppositions of philosophy. Volume II develops a theory of modal spheres and treats problems of epistemology. Volume III is devoted to an elaboration of the structure of individuality within temporal reality and to the development of a Christian view of society. The fourth volume is an index of the entire work.

The central thesis defended by Dooyeweerd is that a religiously neutral philosophy is impossible. Philosophy can furnish a theoretical insight into the coherence of the aspects of our temporal world, if, and only if, the philosopher answers questions concerning the origin of the world and concerning his own relationship to that origin. Such a decision with respect to the origin of the world, both in its diversity and unity, is nontheoretical; it is religious, the result of an act of faith; it arises out of a religious community. The Christian philosopher is guided by the motive of Creation, Fall, and Redemption by Jesus Christ in the communion of the Holy Ghost. The spirit of apostasy from the true God, in contrast, leads the human heart in an apostate direction, towards the deification of the creature, to the absolutizing of the relative.

The classical Greek world was dominated by the motive of form and matter, which originated in the encounter of the pre-Homeric Greek religion of life with the later cultural religion of the Olympic Gods.

According to Dooyeweerd, the second manifestation of apostasy in Western thought has been guided by the motive of nature and freedom. Modern humanism has consciously or unconsciously absolutized the theoretical attitude of thought and has secularized the Christian idea of creation and freedom, thereby emancipating human personality from its religious dependence upon the God of Biblical revelation. Humanism has given rise to a polar tension between a "Faustian" passion to dominate reality by the method of science and the "Titanic" notion of practical freedom, expressed in the idea of the absolute sovereignty of human personality. Humanism is, therefore, characterized by a struggle between pessimism and optimism: individualism opposes an irrationalistic trans-personalism; universal validity opposes individuality; form opposes matter; theory opposes life; speculative metaphysics opposes skepticism; and the concept of function opposes the concept of substance.

Within humanism reason is made the origin of our world. Reason becomes the giver of law. At times the laws of the world are hypostatized. Under the primacy of the ideal of science, the result is a freedom-idealism which hypostatizes the categorical imperative. When reason is the law giver, the ideal of science leads to the absolutization of special forms of scientific thought (such as the mathematical, mechanical, biological, and psychological). When the ideal of human personality is given primacy the result may be the direction of transcendental thought, in its *a priori* syntheses, toward the idea of freedom. In Kant, for example, in relation to the experience of nature, transcendental thought is the formal origin of the laws of nature; but as practical reason, transcendental thought is the origin of the norms of moral freedom. In speculative metaphysics reason receives its final hypostatization and is identified in a theoretical or in a practical sense with the Deity.

Humanism leads to irrationalism when it hypostatizes individual subjectivity, Dooyeweerd claims. It may end in a biologistic vitalism, or in an irrationalistic dialectical spiritualism and historicism. An aspect of reality may then be absolutized, and the conception of general laws may be rejected.

The idea of the totality of our temporal world is conceived in many different ways by humanism, writes Dooyeweerd. The laws governing the external world may be absolutized. When the ideal of science is absolutized, a particular mathematical or natural scientific system of functional relations within an absolutized aspect of the temporal world may be made the common denominator in terms of which all other aspects of reality are then interpreted. When the ideal of personality is absolutized, the totality of the world may be interpreted in terms of the *homo noumenon*, or in terms of a totality of values, in which both theoretical and a-theoretical values are unified into a hierarchical order, established by the autonomous freedom of human personality. The totality of the world may also be conceived in terms of an infinite succession of individual forms, in terms of feeling, or as the historical stream of experience. The absolute idealist conceives of the world in terms of the dialectical development of the absolute Idea through the totality of creative individuality, viewed, for example, in terms of an absolutized moral or aesthetic aspect.

According to Dooyeweerd, the interrelationship between the various aspects of reality is also regarded in such a manner that the modal laws of the world are absolutized. An absolutized aspect is then made the basic denominator of reality, and the result is mathematicism, mechanism, biologism, or psychologism. The laws governing the cosmos are at times regarded as a general concept of function, in which theoretical thought creates the genetic coherence of reality, and individual subjectivity becomes a dependent "exemplary" or particular function of this law. At other times the law in the sense of the universal law of nature is reduced to a transcendental thought-form, which determines the sensory material of experience, while at the same time the law in the supersensuous realm of freedom is identified with the pure will of human personality, thereby leading to an unbridgeable dualism between the laws of nature and the norms of freedom.

The laws of the cosmos may also be regarded as technical symbols which enable man to adapt biologically to nature. Man is then regarded as a creative individual who is not subject to a universally valid law, but is a law unto himself in nature, in culture, and in ethics.

Dooyeweerd asserts that the many forms of humanism seek their starting point immanently within the created world and are, therefore, irreconcilably opposed to Christian philosophy. Any attempt at synthesis between Christian and non-Christian thought is doomed to failure. A genuine Christian philosophy requires a basic presupposition which is the theoretical expression of the pure Biblical *Grundmotif*.

The neo-Augustinian recognizes the priority of faith and unmasks the alleged neutrality of theoretical reason as a dogma which masks the religious foundations of theoretical thought. But the Christian philosopher, writes Dooyeweerd, chooses Christ as the Archimedean point of his philosophy. The *cogito ergo sum* and the irrationalistic *vivo in fluxu continuo, etiam cogitans* is replaced by: *Ego, in Christo regeneratus, etiam cogitans ex Christo vivo.*

Christ is the new religious root of the entire temporal cosmos, Dooyeweerd states. From this foundation regenerate mankind derives its spiritual life, always subject to the central religious meaning of the law; namely, to love God and one's fellow men with all one's heart.

The Archimedean point of Christian philosophy is freed of the obscuring effects of sin, but this does not mean that the Christian philosopher is freed of error. The freedom of the Christian against errors is guaranteed solely by the constant subjection of his work to the Word of God which reveals us to ourselves.

As Dooyeweerd sees the Christian situation, the regenerate human heart is the center out of which Christian philosophy proceeds. The heart, in its Biblical sense, is the religious root and center of human existence. The heart is the fullness of the selfhood. It is within the heart, Dooyeweerd claims, that our temporal functions find their religious concentration and consummation of meaning. The heart transcends the boundary of cosmic time. Although the heart transcends the diversity of the aspects of temporal reality, and although it transcends temporal thought, within this diversity the heart is not to be identified with a complex of functions such as the metaphysical concept of the soul found in Greek and humanistic metaphysics. As the fullness of selfhood the heart is alien to any dualism between the body, conceived of as a complex of natural functions, and the soul, conceived of as a complex of psychical and normative functions.

Christian philosophy is emancipated from the polar tensions characteristic of non-Christian philosophy. By belonging to Christ, says Dooyeweerd, the Christian wages a daily battle against the temptation to absolutize temporal reality and to withdraw it from God. The basic religious motive which directs the labors of the Christian philosopher, the Biblical motive of creation, fall into sin, and redemption in Jesus Christ in the communion of the Holy Ghost, implies a conflict at the very root of our cosmos, the conflict between the kingdom of darkness and the Kingdom of God. It implies further that common grace checks the disintegrating activity of sin, because of the regenerate members of the human race, but it does not lead to antinomies in philosophy. It does result in an absolute antithesis with all philosophy dominated by apostate motives, and it leads also to a grateful recognition of the gifts and talents left by God to a fallen humanity.

With respect to the ultimate origin of the world, the Christian philosopher finds that origin in God's holy, sovereign, and creative will. All laws, and all things which are subject to law, originate in God's creative will. The cosmos is subject to God who stands above the cosmos as the sovereign Lawgiver. His law is the absolute boundary between Himself and His creation. All creatures are subject to it.

The Christian philosopher finds the totality of meaning in its direction of philosophical thought towards Christ, who provides the root and fullness of meaning of the cosmos. The Law is fulfilled in Him, and all subjective individuality is concentrated in Him. Nothing is indifferent; nothing in our temporal world is withdrawn from His dominion.

The very coherence in the modal diversity of our cosmos owes its origin to the divine world order. The intermodal coherence of our world, its unity, is not a construction of philosophical thought, but an enduring effect of God's sovereign power. Each mode, each aspect of our cosmos is under divine law. Each aspect of our world is a sphere of law, sovereign under God in its own domain. The structure of each aspect points toward and is an expression of the temporal coherence of meaning which points beyond itself to Christ. The integral coherence of meaning between the modal aspects of our cosmos is guaranteed by a cosmic order of time. There is no pre-logical natural reality *an sich,* separate from the normative aspects of reality.

The universe is ruled by God's laws, Dooyeweerd insists. In their modal diversity, God's laws constitute the universal valid determination and limitation of the individual subjectivity subject to them. Therefore, Dooyeweerd concludes, the Christian philosopher cannot tolerate any theoretical conception of cosmic reality which is emancipated from a Biblical starting point, for all such conceptions are dominated wholly or in part by apostate religious motives.

TRUE HUMANISM

Author: Jacques Maritain (1882-)
Type of work: Philosophy of culture
First published: 1936

Principal Ideas Advanced

Man is a spiritual being who can find fulfillment only as he is completed by God; hence, a true humanism must be a theocentric (God-centered) humanism.

The tragedy of modernity is that in its discovery of man and the temporal order it turned gradually to anthropocentricity, a process which led inexorably to man's descent into sheer materiality and subjectivity and from which there is no escape except by a rehabilitation of man in God.

The hope of humanity lies in the creation of a new social order designed to preserve genuine human values which, although Christian in spirit, have autonomy from the Church and will thus elicit the co-operative working together of all men of good will, in order that all men can find fulfillment through God.

In *True Humanism* Jacques Maritain shows, by the depth of his analysis of the plight of modern Western society, the intellectual wisdom which has made him one of the most widely read of all modern Catholic thinkers. Originally a student of Henri Bergson (1859-1941), the vitalistic philosopher of creative evolution, Maritain was converted to Roman Catholicism in 1906. After pursuing an intensive study of St. Thomas Aquinas (c.1225-1274), the architect of modern Catholicism, Maritain began a prolific writing and teaching career as a Christian philosopher. Primarily a philosopher, Maritain has been wide-ranging in his interests, even serving at one point in the diplomatic corps, and the topics of his books range from the most difficult metaphysical philosophy to devotional treatises on the liturgy. His own position is that of a Neo-Thomist, one who attempts to apply and interpret St. Thomas's teachings in such a way as to take account of what has happened since St. Thomas's day. Perhaps no one has done more than Maritain in showing the continuing intellectual vitality of the Thomist tradition.

He writes primarily as a philosopher, and an appreciation of his work requires some training in Thomistic philosophy. *True Humanism* presupposes, and does not really adequately supply, a general knowledge of the basic principles of Thomistic philosophy; hence, the reader would be well advised to acquaint himself with Thomistic notions of revelation, man's Fall, supernatural grace, and natural law, prior to a reading of this book.

Humanism is defined as that which "tends to render man more truly human and to make his original greatness manifest by causing him to participate in all that can enrich him in nature and in history. . . ." True humanism, Maritain contends, is theocentric (God-centered), not anthropocentric (man-centered). The only true way to find man is to seek God, for man is the creation of God and can find his fulfillment only as he is led by God, filled with divine power, and illuminated by divine truth. Without God man is overcome by his defective nature and falls victim to error and selfish concerns. With God man is able to overcome his defects and to be raised to true knowledge and service. This theological insight can also be validated in terms of the cause of modern history. Modern society has proved to be destructive of what is best in man, and thus it provides historical testimony as to what happens to man when he loses God.

The historical side of Maritain's argument consists in his tracing the decline and fall of modern man from that moment when a separation of the supernatural from the natural first began. Ignoring the truth that grace bestows freedom, man began to think that he is free and glorious in himself. What began as a glorification of man degenerated in time into a denial of human dignity. The Renaissance celebrated the glory of man, the grandeur of truth, and the worth of the temporal order, but succeeding ages such as the age of liberalism chronicled man's descent. Liberalism, which Maritain describes as "a philosophy of freedom which makes of each abstract individual and his opinions the source of all right and truth," showed by its subjectivity and unchecked individualism that man had lost his moorings in objective truth and nobler strivings.

Developments in the late nineteenth century, especially the evolutionary hypothesis of Charles Darwin (1809-1882) and the psychoanalytic theories of Sigmund Freud (1856-1939), reduced man to the merely animal and degraded his nobler strivings toward higher values by presenting these as merely manifestations of basically animal instincts. His dignity and nobility surrendered, his nature interpreted by views which contradicted religious conceptions, modern man has been driven to the desperate expedient of sacrificing himself to the state in the false hope of receiving once again a meaning for life.

Maritain claims that a true philosophy of man knows that man as a child of God can be fulfilled only by divine grace. Grace is not some additional quality which merely crowns man's natural goodness; rather, it is a healing power which makes man whole, protecting him against his sinful propensities, guiding him toward truth, and bestowing the freedom and value which make man truly human. Only as man is vivified by grace can he become truly man.

Protestantism is not a tenable alternative, Maritain suggests. Protestantism is so much affected by man's depravity that it is unable to realize that grace liberates and transforms man. Protestantism understands grace and freedom to be antithetical; hence, in affirming God and grace Protestantism repudiates man's freedom and genuine dignity. Liberalism draws the opposite conclusion, that for man to be free he must reject God. Both positions in forcing an "either/or" instead of a "both/and" deprive man of his real fulfillment through grace.

Pure atheism is only in theory an alternative, for a pure atheism cannot be lived. Every will, whether it knows it or not, desires God when it desires the good, since all good is in God. To avoid God, then, one would have to cease to desire or affirm any values whatsoever. Citing the example given by Kirilov in *The Possessed* (a novel by Dostoevsky), who says just before his suicide that if God exists then all things depend upon Him and nothing can be done which is outside His will, Maritain observes that Kirilov's suicide is the logical outcome of his attempt to deny God completely.

Pure atheism, metaphysical atheism, cannot be lived, Maritain insists, but it is possible to have a social order which *believes* that it is radically atheistic when in its actual life it is not. In Russia, for example, there is an official atheism but nevertheless there is a practical involvement in genuine human problems. Russian life as it is lived is another form of the sin of idolatry, which is the refusal of man to regard obedience to God as the final aim of human life, and it is not, therefore, the radical opposite of Christianity. Because God is active in human life, and because man cannot escape seeking God in seeking the good, Maritain hopes that gradual modification of Marxist theories can be achieved. Because God offers grace in moments of crucial choices whether man believes in God or not, as the Russian people genuinely face practical problems and decisions a new truly human order may gradually emerge. Perhaps the Communist movement in Russian history, like liberalism in the West, marks a discovery of values which have been submerged, but a discovery which has been wrong-headed.

The tragedy of modern man is that the decline of man was not necessary. The concern for man and the temporal order, a concern which was implicit in Medieval Christendom, could have been made explicit within the Christian context. St. Thomas provided a proper way, and had modernity not departed from his synthesis a true humanism could have been created.

What man must do now, suggests Maritain, is to create a synthesis based on the insights of St. Thomas. A new Christian synthesis would include several points of difference from the medieval one. First, instead of the stress on conformity, there would be provision for a pluralism of communities and of interests within the wider whole. Second, instead of the temporal order's being primarily a *means* to the spiritual order, the temporal order would be regarded as autonomous, for although the temporal order is inferior in value to the spiritual, the temporal order has a legitimate sphere of its own; its concern is with the conditions which provide for the well-being of man. Third, coerced obedience would be replaced by persuasion. Instead of using secular power to enforce the claims of the spiritual, that power would be used to protect the freedom of persons. The freedom of the individual includes freedom of belief, expression, and practice, which means also the freedom of religion to integrate its own work with that of the state by assisting in public charity and providing Christian instruction. Maritain stresses also the freedom to own property and the freedom of women to return to their proper place in society, to the home and family. Fourth, instead of a diversity of social races (according to the aristocratic notions of past times) there would be a unity of social race, an equality of essence. Blood and wealth would not be the basis for hierarchy; rather, ability alone would determine whatever hierarchies there need be. Fifth, rather than viewing the purpose of society as being that of building an empire for Christ, the aim of the new Christendom would be that of realizing a genuine fraternal community, which Maritain conceives as a kingdom of men built upon "the dignity of human personality and its spiritual vocation, and of the fraternal love which is its due. The task of the commonwealth will be the realisation of a common life here on earth, of a temporal system truly in conformity with that dignity, that vocation and that love."

Such an ideal of a new Christendom, allowing as it does the presence and interests of both believers and unbelievers, but allowing also the proper functioning of religion that is demanded by man's very nature, can provide a common program for all men of good will whether they have religious beliefs or not. Such a Christendom gives ample scope for the genuine discoveries of modern thought and life, the explicit concerns for man, his dignity, and his place as a temporal being, which medieval Christendom lacked, while at the same time re-establishing man on his proper basis. A true humanism is a theocentric humanism. It is humanistic in contrast to the humanism which was only implicit in the old Christian order; it is theocentric in contrast to the atheism and anthropocentricity of the modern secular order.

Such a new Christendom enables the Church to be free to carry out its own proper function, that of bringing man to God and thus bringing man to his own fulfillment. Maritain writes: "It is not for the Church but for Christians as temporal members of this temporal organism to strive directly and immediately to transform and act upon it in the spirit of Christianity." The Church, by its work, inspires the Christian citizen, but the Church as Church cannot be tied to specific social programs and still be loyal to its purpose. Christians as citizens must enter into the political and social arena, striving through united action to create a truly human social order.

Maritain was convinced, in writing this book in 1936, that the present order of civilization is dying: "Modern civilisation is a worn-out vesture: it is not a question of sewing on patches here and there, but of a total and substantial reformation, a trans-valuation of its cultural principles; since what is needed is a change to the primacy of quality over quantity, of work over money, of the human over technical means, of wisdom over science, of the common service of human beings instead of the covetousness of unlimited individual enrichment or a desire in the name of the State for unlimited power." Were St. Thomas living today he might very well urge such a Christian philosophy, a philosophy free from what is outmoded in order to be true to that wisdom of the past which is imperishable.

WORSHIP

Author: Evelyn Underhill (1875-1941)
Type of work: Liturgical theology
First published: 1936

Principal Ideas Advanced

Worship is the response of the creature to the revelation of the Creator.
Man's worship is part of the praise which the whole universe brings to God.
Because man is body as well as soul, his worship must involve physical and psychical dimensions.
Only trinitarian worship adequately responds to the revelation of God as transcendent, as incarnate, and as the sanctifier of the race.
In the sacraments, creaturely acts are endowed with divine grace and power.
The perfect sacrament is the sacrifice of Christ, offered to God in the Eucharist.

Evelyn Underhill's *Worship* is an important contribution to the liturgical revival which began with the Oxford Movement in the Church of England and has gradually found its way into most of the major Protestant Churches. Miss Underhill writes from the standpoint of Christian theism, having moved from the vaguely Bergsonian philosophy of her earlier work on *The Essentials of Mysticism* (1920) to the view of Neo-Scholasticism. Her book is not an anthropological investigation of worship the world around, but a loving exposition of Christian forms of devotion, forms which she finds foreshadowed, indeed, in the rites and sacrifices of other cults, but fully realized only in the services of the Church, specifically in the Divine Office and Holy Eucharist as observed in the Orthodox, Roman, and Anglican traditions.

For Miss Underhill, there are only two candid attitudes that one can take toward worship. One can regard it either as a tragically mistaken expenditure of human effort, or as the ultimate meaning and purpose of creation. Taking the latter alternative, she suggests that the deliberate praise which most peoples of the world accord to God must be extended until it envelops the whole of man's life. Nor is worship limited to man. As the angels and archangels pour out their lives in perpetual worship, so, if the world is of a piece, the lower forms of life must also be understood as rendering silent and unconscious praise to their Maker.

Christians, in attempting to understand their own religion, must not forget their bond with all creation. If, in virtue of our spiritual part, we claim kinship with the heavenly host, we must, on account of our physical aspect, recognize our affinity to lower forms of life. For this reason, Christians should not quarrel with the barbaric origins of many Christian practices. The history of sacrifice, for example, is replete with fear and cruelty. But, according to Miss Underhill, the important thing to remember is that ancient men, by the light that was given to them, were sincerely responding to "the impact of the Eternal." Although there is a tendency for the spirit of worship to degenerate into superstition and magic, worship initially is disinterested, an expression of man's desire to give back to God that which he has received; to be worthy of this high office, the gift must be costly. Old Testament worship includes many dreadful elements; for example, the binding of Isaac, and the institution of the Passover. Moreover, these very elements are taken up and sublimated in the Eucharist, where the unbloody sacrifice of the Son of God is daily celebrated. Christians must acknowledge the primitive roots of the Gospel, says Miss Underhill, in order that their worship will not become something thin, intellectual, and humanistic.

Worship, to achieve its full expression, must involve the entire psychological powers of man. Whatever truth the James-Lange theory of the emotions may have in general, it accurately describes the activity of worship, says the author, who quotes in support of her view a statement by the liberal Catholic theologian, Ulrich von Hügel: "I kiss my child because I love it," said von Hügel; "and I kiss my child in order to love it." Physical attitudes, rhythmical motions, sensible stimulants, unconscious associations are all part of the worship experience. This is true of single elements, such as kneeling or chanting; and the highest forms of worship are those in which the maximum of effective elements are brought together. It is a specious spirituality which, in the name of inwardness, would do away with ritual, lavish display, and apparently useless dedication of wealth.

Worship, however, is not merely a human invention, nor is its purpose the satisfaction of human needs. Worship, we are told, is the response man makes to the revelation of the Eternal. In one aspect, worship is the acknowledgment of the transcendence of God over everything that partakes of succession and change. But God is not merely transcendent; in the language of Neo-Scholasticism, He is "one who Acts," who discloses Himself to man in Christ and in the Church. Highest worship, therefore, must be trinitarian. While adoring eternal reality, it will also lay its gifts at the feet of Him who gave Himself on Calvary, and will offer up its praises to the Holy Spirit who transforms mankind into a holy community.

Miss Underhill discusses four main characteristics of worship, all of which, in her opinion, achieve their highest expression in Catholic worship: ritual, symbolism, sacrament, and sacrifice. Of these four, the notion of "sacrament" has especially interested Anglo-Catholic thinkers, involving as it does an extension of the "incarnational philosophy." A sacrament differs from a symbol, according to Miss Underhill, just as a significant deed differs from a significant image. Symbols are static; sacraments are dynamic. By means of the sacrament, "the Supernatural draws near to man in and through the natural." Common acts of daily living easily acquire sacramental significance, and by their means one after another aspect of creaturely existence is taken up into "the fabric of the worshipping life." Miss Underhill is inclined to favor a sacramental outlook on life over an ethical one, since the goal of Christ's redemptive act is not so much to change man's outward behavior as it is to sanctify the whole of life and to offer it to God. Christ, she says, is Himself "the major sacrament," and the Church, His Body, receives its life from the specific sacraments recognized by all the Catholic Churches. Miss Underhill notes that some people want to embrace the notion of sacramentalism in a vague and diffused fashion, without acknowledging such high doctrines as baptismal regeneration and the real presence. But, she says, it is only by being canalized through special acts "held sacred, and kept for Himself alone," that God is able to make His grace and power felt by the religious soul.

Sacrifice, the fourth main aspect of worship, is both symbolic and sacramental. It is a token act, by which, out of pure love and gratitude, man seeks to make a gift to the One from whom all gifts come. Human charity responds to divine charity; and, like sacramental worship, it finds its perfect expression in the Mass, "the eternal movement of charity whereby the Son is self-given to the Father, and in union with Him, His Mystical Body, the Church—which is represented, but not repeated, under the conditions of time and space, in every Eucharist."

One of the most important aspects of worship, according to Miss Underhill, is its social dimension. The ideal is for the human worshiper to place himself in the company of "every creature which is in heaven and on earth and such as are in the sea"; and this sense should be preserved in the liturgy itself. For the rest, it is of utmost importance that Christians worship God in the congregation of the redeemed, and that, through corporate silence and various liturgical devices, such as the response, the whole body unite in one act of worship. Atomistic and subjectivistic piety are to be rejected, and so are those practices, such as the Low Mass, which permit the clergy to carry on the ceremony at the altar while the worshipers engage themselves in private prayers. Miss Underhill does not suggest that "personal" worship is by any means to be neglected, but personal devotion is not to be understood as a "private" affair. Plato's *Laws* are cited as showing that God "has ordered all things with a view to the excellence and preservation of the whole," and that the life of the individual exists "in order that the life of the whole may be blessed." The individual cannot achieve a deep and satisfactory devotional life in any other way than by repeating within his own daily life the great rhythms which are sacramentally achieved in the life, death, and resurrection of Christ, and which are repeated daily and annually in the worship of the Church.

In the second part of her book, Miss Underhill turns from the principles of Christian worship to consider different types of worship in the history of God's Church. Chapters are given to Judaism, to the Apostolic community, to Catholicism (East and West), to the Reformed Churches, to the Free Churches, and to the Anglican tradition. In the Preface, she notes that some of her friends criticized her for giving "too sympathetic and uncritical an account of types of worship" which are full of shortcomings. She explains, however, that her "wish has been to show all these as chapels of various types in the one Cathedral of the Spirit; and dwell on the particular structure of each, the love which has gone to their adornment, the shelter they can offer to many different kinds of souls. . . ." She tries generously to respond to the positive aspects of nonliturgical groups. Even those groups which repudiate the sacraments altogether—groups such as the Quakers—have, she says, something sacramental in the very austerity and bareness of their worship, "a positive witness to the otherness of God, which may be more impressive, more suggestive of the unseen Holy, than the veil before the tabernacle or the sanctuary lamp." Moreover, she acknowledges the abuses which perennially accompany liturgical worship, and she understands the zeal, though she cannot help but lament the intemperance, of those who reject the ceremonies of the Catholic Church. It is a consolation to her, she writes, that Luther, Calvin, and Knox did not reject the liturgy as completely as did some of their followers, and she expresses satisfaction with attempts which are being made in Scandinavia, in Scotland, and elsewhere, to recover this aspect of their heritage.

Worship is one of the volumes of a series known as *The Library of Constructive Theology,* to which various authors have contributed. In the General Introduction, the editors remark that the present age is in revolt against authority, and that few people are content to rest their faith on dogma. We observe that this is the case with Miss Underhill. Her Neo-Scholastic philosophy does not lead her to accept the Roman doctrine of authority as the basis for her belief in the efficacy of the sacraments. Her case rests, instead, on the self-authenticating character of the Christian experience. The worship of God through the Eucharist proves itself to be the richest, most rewarding experience known to man. Other ways of worshiping God are not thereby repudiated but, rather, established in their various degrees; hence, a way is held open for all churches and all religions to join at last in one great divine society, at once prophetic and priestly, evangelical and eucharistic, historical and eternal.

THE COST OF DISCIPLESHIP

Author: Dietrich Bonhoeffer (1906-1945)
Type of work: Christian ethics
First published: 1937

Principal Ideas Advanced

The deadliest enemy of the Church is "cheap grace"; that is, grace understood as a general truth requiring only intellectual assent and used surreptitiously to justify a life void of discipleship.

Faith and obedience are inseparable; only he who believes is obedient, and only he who is obedient believes.

Discipleship means exclusive allegiance and bodily adherence to the person of Jesus Christ; it involves an obedient response to Jesus' call to follow Him and denotes both a breach with the world and a joyful sharing in His suffering love for the world.

The same Jesus Christ who called the first disciples into visible communion with Himself is alive and present today in the Church through the ministry of Word and Sacrament; as the crucified and risen Lord, He now calls us through the preaching of His Word, incorporates us into His earthly Body through baptism, and fosters and sustains our communion in that Body through the Lord's Supper.

Dietrich Bonhoeffer, a Christian whose life and thought are closely interwoven, lived during the tumultuous period of Adolf Hitler's Third German Reich. Son of a prominent psychiatrist and reared in the best liberal tradition, Bonhoeffer pursued his theological studies at the Universities of Tübingen and Berlin and at Union Theological Seminary in New York City. He enjoyed a brief career as Lecturer in Systematic Theology at the University of Berlin, but when Hitler came to power, Bonhoeffer soon became involved in the "German Church Struggle," in which he actively supported the "Confessing Church" in its opposition to the Nazi-backed "German Christians." At the height of the struggle, when he was the leader of a clandestine seminary in the Pomeranian village of Finkenwalde, Bonhoeffer wrote and published *The Cost of Discipleship,* which firmly established his reputation as a talented theologian. Later Bonhoeffer joined the underground resistance movement, which worked for the overthrow of Hitler's regime; his resistance activities led to his imprisonment in 1943 and to his execution on April 9, 1945, at the age of thirty-nine.

In his introduction to *The Cost of Discipleship* Bonhoeffer questions whether the modern Church has so obscured the pure Word of Jesus (by adding man-made dogmas, burdensome rules, and irrelevant demands) that to make a genuine decision for Christ has become extremely difficult. He proposes to tell how Jesus calls us to be His disciples, and his intention is not to impose still harder demands on already troubled and wounded consciences, but to show how anyone who follows the command of Jesus single-mindedly and unresistingly finds His yoke to be easy. Discipleship, asserts Bonhoeffer, means joy, and it is not limited to a spiritual élite, but is for every man.

The book is divided into two parts. The first is an exposition of the conception of discipleship that is to be found in the Synoptic Gospels, together with an interpretation of the Sermon on the Mount. The second part consists of Bonhoeffer's attempt to show how the terminology used by the evangelists has been translated into the language of the Church of the Apostle Paul.

Bonhoeffer opens *The Cost of Discipleship* with a powerful polemic against cheap grace, which he calls the deadly enemy of the evangelical Church. Cheap grace is grace as a doctrine or a principle, the forgiveness of sins proclaimed as a general truth, the justification of sin without the justification of the sinner. Cheap grace is the grace we bestow on ourselves, the grace by which we calculate in advance that our sins are forgiven and then conclude that there is no need for a life of obedience, no need for discipleship. The followers of Luther have turned his saying, "Sin boldly, but believe and rejoice in Christ more boldly still," into a *carte blanche* for sin. What for Luther was his very last refuge and consolation, after a lifetime of following Jesus Christ, has been perverted into a premise for obtaining grace as cheaply as possible. Happy are they, declares Bonhoeffer, who discover the truth that grace is costly just because it is the grace of God in Jesus Christ. "Such grace is *costly* because it calls us to follow, and it is *grace* because it calls us to follow *Jesus Christ.* It is costly because it costs a man his life, and it is grace because it gives a man the only true life."

The call of Christ to discipleship demands the spontaneous response of obedience. Discipleship means adherence to Christ, and its only content is to follow Him. That is, discipleship offers no intelligible program for a way of life, no goal or ideal to strive after, no cause which we might deem worthy of our devotion. It offers only exclusive allegiance to the person of Jesus Christ, the living Son of God who became man. There can be no faith without following, no believing without obedience. Indeed, stresses Bonhoeffer, only he who believes is obedient, and only he who is obedient believes; it is unbiblical to hold either proposition without the other.

The single-minded obedience of the faithful disciple means self-denial and submission to the "law of Christ," which is the law of the Cross. The Cross is laid on every Christian, which means that he must expect to share in the suffering of Christ. There is a suffering entailed in the disciple's abandonment of attachments to the world and in the daily dying of the "old man" as a result of his encounter with Christ, but the more significant suffering is found in his bearing the burdens of others and thus participating in Christ's work of bearing and forgiving the sins of men. The disciple discovers that Christ's permission to share His suffering is really a token of His grace, for it becomes the way to communion with God. Suffering is overcome by suffering; the Cross brings forth joy.

The call of Jesus makes one an individual, for each man must decide and follow alone. Nevertheless, the disciple, who has broken all natural ties and relationships for the sake of following the Master, finds that he does not remain alone; through Christ he enters into a new fellowship that far surpasses what was lost. Christ is the Mediator, not only between God and man, but between man and man and between man and the world. Through His mediation the individual disciple is incorporated into a community, the community of the Cross. It is primarily to this community that Jesus addresses the Sermon on the Mount. The disciples are they whom He calls "blessed" in the Beatitudes, who by bearing the Cross in the life of grace are the salt of the earth and the light of the world, who live the extraordinary life of utter love, self-renunciation, absolute purity, truthfulness, and meekness. Yet the "extraordinariness" of this life is hidden from the disciples and becomes visible for the world alone. That is, the disciple never sees his "good works" and "better righteousness," because his eyes are directed solely to his Lord. He seeks merely to do His will, and therefore what seems extraordinary to the world appears to the disciple as the natural thing to do.

The life of the disciple is one of carefree simplicity: carefree because his trust is wholly in the Lord, and simple because his obedience is to only one Master. He need not look for complicated or hidden meanings in Christ's commands, nor is he given any special vantage point from which to judge the neighbor who is not a disciple. Since his righteousness is a gift deriving from his association with Christ, he can approach the unbeliever only as one to whom Christ comes, and therefore the disciple approaches others with an unconditional offer of fellowship and with the single-mindedness of the love of Jesus.

Following his expositions of the Sermon on the Mount and of the commissioning of the disciples as messengers equipped with the gracious sovereignty of the creative and redemptive Word of God (Matthew 10), Bonhoeffer raises the question of the possibility and meaning of discipleship for the Church, which no longer knows Jesus in the flesh. Does Jesus call men today to follow Him, just as He called Levi the publican? Bonhoeffer asserts that there is something strange about this question, for in the very asking "we are retreating from the presence of the living Christ and forgetting that Jesus Christ is not dead, but alive and speaking to us today through the testimony of the Scriptures." It is not the case that we who live today are worse off than the original disciples; indeed, we have a distinct advantage, for our call comes from the victorious and glorified Christ, who is present in the Church in bodily form and in His Word. The Church is indeed the Body of Christ, and through the ministry of Word and Sacrament the call of Christ goes forth and His gracious will is made known. Of course, our recognition of the Christ must be solely by faith, but this was precisely the same for the first disciples. "*They* saw the rabbi and the wonderworker, and believed on Christ. *We* hear the Word and believe on Christ."

Bonhoeffer points out that, whereas in the Synoptic Gospels the writers speak of the relationship between the disciples and the Lord almost exclusively in terms of following Him, St. Paul in his Epistles employs a new set of terms that depict the presence of the risen and glorified Lord and His work in us. It is Bonhoeffer's conviction that this difference in terminology involves no break in the unity of the Scriptural testimony and that neither set of terms is preferable to the other.

Where the Synoptists speak of Christ calling men and their following Him, St. Paul speaks of baptism. In baptism man suffers the call of Christ and becomes His possession; baptism betokens a breach with the world and the death of the "old man." Baptismal death means a daily dying in the power of the death that Christ died once and for all, and as such it is a death full of grace, for it means justification from sin and the gift of the Holy Spirit.

Just as the first disciples lived in the bodily presence and communion of Jesus, we are made members of the Body of Christ through baptism. "The word of preaching," emphasizes Bonhoeffer, "is insufficient to make us members of Christ; the sacraments also have to be added." Baptism incorporates us into the unity of Christ's Body, and the Lord's Supper fosters and sustains the fellowship in that Body. The Body is the Church, which is not to be thought of as an institution but as a person in a unique sense. The Church is essentially One Man, the new humanity of the risen Christ, and yet this one body of Christ includes all those members who through the Spirit are united with Christ and who participate in His suffering and glory.

Unlike truths or doctrines or religions, which are disembodied entities, the Body of Christ takes up space on earth. The Church is made up of living men and women, and this means that it is a visible reality. Bonhoeffer explains that the Body of Christ becomes visible in the preaching of the Word, in the sacraments of baptism and the Lord's Supper, in Church order, and in the daily life of the members in the world. The Christian gives the world a visible proof of his calling, not only by his sharing in the worship and discipline of the Church, but also by the new fellowship of brotherly love.

Where the Synoptists speak of the self-denying life of discipleship, St. Paul tells of Christians being drawn into the image of Christ crucified. In the life of suffering love they recover their true humanity and at the same time find a new solidarity with the whole human race. The new life in Christ is a life of joy, since those who share in His cross also share the glory of His resurrection. But, Bonhoeffer reminds us, the members of Christ's Body are oblivious to their own lives and to the new image they bear, for they look solely to their Head. Nevertheless, whether they realize it or not, in patterning their lives after that of their crucified Lord they have become "imitators of God."

THE PHILOSOPHICAL BASES OF THEISM

Author: George Dawes Hicks (1862-1941)
Type of work: Philosophy of religion
First published: 1937

Principal Ideas Advanced

All consciousness, including the religious consciousness, has an element of knowledge or interpretation.

Self-consciousness reveals the self or mind as a subject; things in nature are objects.

Minds and things are existences; qualities, ideas, and ideals are subsistences or essences.

We know existences through essences, the symbolized through the symbol.

God is known through the higher ideas, truth, goodness, and beauty, and through the sense of a presence that inspires reverence and trust.

George Dawes Hicks's *The Philosophical Bases of Theism* represents the Hibbert Lectures, delivered in 1931, as revised for publication in 1937. The author, who was one of the founders of the *Hibbert Journal*, develops the argument for a nontheological theism in its most cogent form. The philosophical point of view is that of post-Kantian idealism. Religion in its highest form is presented as belief in a supreme living and personal Mind. It is the business of philosophy to validate and interpret this belief. Religious experience is held to be the basis of the knowledge of God, and the revelation which comes through experience is described as a developing thing. Reason is present in all experience as interpretation, Hicks claims, and is therefore continuous with revelation. Philosophy carries this interpretation on in systematic and critical form. Philosophy is to religion what science is to common sense

As Hicks uses the term, religious faith is fundamentally a matter of knowledge, for all aspects of experience are elements of consciousness which is essentially knowing. "The transition from consciousness to self-consciousness is by far the greatest, by far the most momentous, advance ever made in the history of mind; or, indeed, for a matter of that, in the whole course of organic evolution." Man's knowledge of himself as subject, as even dimly distinguished from his knowledge of objects, is the key to his knowledge of spirit. The argument for a distinctive kind of knowledge upon which religious belief is based begins with this contrast between the subject and the object. Natural science deals with the relations of physical objects. But the knowing subject is not an object among other objects. The relation of the subject to the object is different in kind from the relation between objects in nature, which is a causal relation.

Even in physical science the idea of a purely mechanistic relation between objects in nature has been abandoned, Hicks argues. Physics has gone beyond the idea of simple efficient causation, and the doctrine of evolution has introduced a dynamic and developmental factor that suggests, if it does not prove, the presence of purpose. The organic character even of the atom means that there is an influence of the whole on the parts and their relations that is not mechanical. These developments strongly suggest the freedom and purposive presence of a divine Mind.

The affirmation of theistic faith is that we are in the presence of a spiritual environment as well as of a physical environment. We become aware of the latter through sense perception, and we are aware of the former through the religious consciousness which is native to consciousness of self. But basically all knowledge is the same. Consciousness involves interpretation as well as sensation and feeling. We see a tree as a tree; we see red as red (not blue) because implicit in our seeing is the idea of tree and red. It is the same in religious experience. Friedrich Schleiermacher (1768-1834) resolved religion into the feeling of absolute dependence; but feeling is never pure feeling, and the feeling of dependence involves an idea; namely, that the feeling is a feeling of dependence. Religious consciousness thus always has an element of interpretation, or knowing. Our knowledge of nature, however, is a knowledge of qualities as well as of quantities. The color and other qualities are objectively real; they are *in* the complex of objects and events that we perceive. Thus, the world of nature is not merely a collection of quantities; it has the qualities that we perceive it to have. The mind is not composed of those qualities, although it apprehends them. The elements of the divine, the spiritual elements of experience, truth, beauty and goodness, are also objective. They are elements in the spiritual environment which is the world of religious belief.

Religious experience, or the religious consciousness, gives us knowledge of the supernatural environment. The supernatural is known through the natural. Almost any event can be the medium or the occasion of the disclosure of the spiritual, but the form of apprehension is symbolical; we know the symbolized only through the symbol. This is not proved or demonstrated knowledge, but it is nevertheless genuine knowledge. The divine is not an element in our own consciousness, as claimed by Schleiermacher. Knowledge of the divine is not gained through the sense of the numinous, as Rudolph Otto (1869-1937) claimed; completely nondivine objects produce not only awe and a sense of the uncanny, but also other responses which create the feeling of the holy. Knowledge always involves intellectual form, for it is through interpretation of experience and events that knowledge is acquired of the objectively existent divine. Thus, religious knowledge is essentially like all other knowledge; religious knowledge is, in fact, the most comprehensive kind of knowledge.

Hicks's theory of knowledge, and of religious knowledge in particular, arises out of and expresses a certain metaphysics, which includes conceptions of (1) existences, (2) subsistences, and (3) essences. There are two kinds of existences, physical, and mental or spiritual. It is characteristic of both kinds that they are individual and concrete, and also that they are active. Objects in nature are physical existents; they are individual and active. Minds are spiritual existents; they too are individual and active. They exist in time, and are unique and changing. Minds are subjects; physical entities are objects. Human minds are individual existences; the divine Mind is also an existent being. Subsistences are realities that do not exist, such as laws of nature and ideals, especially the ideals of goodness, beauty, and truth. Goodness, beauty, and truth are eternal realities, as Plato declared them to be. But they are not God; neither are they merely subjective aspects of our consciousness. They constitute a realm of essences. But they are the true *via media* between minds, and between minds and objects. We know existences through essences. We know the natural world by a direct perception of its qualities as found concretely in individual objects. This is also the way we know the spiritual existence that we call God. The essences are spiritual, that is, mental; nature can be known because it is intelligible, or rational. But by that very fact nature points beyond itself to the intelligible source of its existence. Our knowledge of God, however, is enhanced by our apprehension of the higher aspects of experience, the values of truth, goodness, and beauty, and the sense of a presence that inspires reverence and trust. Thus, both directly and indirectly our knowledge of the divine Mind comes through the mediation of essences.

Ultimate interest in this philosophical essay is in the existent called God. It is noteworthy that Hicks does not himself speak of God as Spirit, but always as Mind. Reason and intellect are essentially instruments or forms of knowing, and while knowledge is taken to include the full range and depth of religious experience, such knowledge still has the essential character of rationality. God is Mind. As a spiritual or mental existent God is individual, active, and distinct from all other minds; He is not the absolute. Pantheism, wherever found, is rejected; for if God is the whole, then other minds are parts of Him. But the definition of mind excludes this possibility. Each mind is a distinct and separate subject. Minds have knowledge of, and regard for, each other; but "other minds do not, therefore, enter into my being in any other manner or in any other respect," writes Hicks; "There is no such thing as confluence or overlapping of selves as existents." The same is true in the relation of the divine mind to human minds. Minds are essentially external to each other. The medium of their regard for and knowledge of each other, either man for man, or man for God, and God for man, is the world of essences; the truths, qualities, and values that are intelligible but not minds; such truths are subsistences but not existences.

God is the supreme personal Mind, Hicks writes, "a consciousness that knows all that we cannot know, that loves beyond our power of loving, that 'realizes' the good where our faltering efforts fail." The knowledge of God is not a "privileged experience," different from the normal rational experience of man. Hicks concludes, "The fuller the individual's life is of all that goes to constitute rich human experience the better equipped will it be for attaining knowledge of God. . . . If (man) brings to bear upon what is offered in experience his whole personal life in its concrete completeness,—intellect, reason, feeling, aspiration and love,—what ground is there for assuming that the divine reality will escape his ken?" It is Hicks's basic contention that in this wholeness of human experience and in its rational unification our knowledge of God is actually attained.

THE WISDOM OF GOD

Author: Sergius Bulgakov (1870-1944)
Type of work: Theology of culture
First published: 1937

Principal Ideas Advanced

The modern world faces the problem of recovering the religious meaning of culture, lost between secularist humanism and otherworldly religion.

The ancient doctrine that Sophia, or Wisdom, is the essence of God and also the essence of the creature provides a basis for this recovery.

In human culture, creation becomes aware of its sophianic character and its oneness with the Creator.

Secular humanism, having repudiated Sophia, must give place to the "true humanism" of God-manhood.

The Church must correct its dogmatic foundations in order to overcome its Manichean attitude toward the world.

Sergius Bulgakov was a priest of the Russian Orthodox Church, who was forced, because of the Revolution, to carry on his theological teaching in exile. *The Wisdom of God,* a brief outline of his theology, is a work which was prepared at the request of ecumenically oriented Western churchmen. Bulgakov is one of a group of Russian intellectuals who embraced Christianity after experimenting with its modern alternatives. Originally destined for the priesthood, he lost his faith, left the seminary for the gymnasium and the university, and became a Marxist, and eventually a professor of economics. Under the influence of Vladimir Solovyev (1853-1900), he made his way from materialism to idealism, then from idealism to Christianity. His ordination to the priesthood came in 1918, after many of his important works had already been published. Bulgakov, therefore, is hardly a conventional representative of Orthodoxy; he explains that "sophiology," his doctrine of Divine Wisdom, is merely a development within Eastern Christianity, comparable to New-Thomism or Barthianism in the West.

According to Bulgakov, the great problem facing Christendom today is to recover the religious meaning of culture. In Europe, the problem dates from the time of the Renaissance and the Reformation, when the creative impulses of modern civilization became independent of the Church, and the Church withdrew from worldly concerns in order to preserve fundamental religion. In Russia, the problem became acute only in the nineteenth century, when the national culture was taking shape. Representatives of art and literature, confronted with the secularism of the West, were made deeply conscious of their own religious roots; but the Eastern Church was as unsympathetic toward their undertakings as were the Reformation and Counter-Reformation churches in the West. In Bulgakov's opinion, the problem still remains unsolved, for the liberal wing of Christendom has embraced the secularist solution and has abandoned God, while the conservative wing has continued to "excommunicate the world." Nor, according to Bulgakov, is there any possibility of a dialectical resolution of the antithesis: "We must discover how we can overcome the secularizing forces of the Reformation and of the Renaissance, not in a negative way or 'dialectically,' which is in any case merely theoretical and powerless; but in a positive way—through love for the world."

Bulgakov maintains that the "sophianic interpretation" of the world offers the only solution to the difficulty. Sophia, or Divine Wisdom, is, according to Bulgakov, the mediating principle which binds the world to God. On the one hand, Sophia is the very *ousia* or being of God, the divine substance which is one in all three persons of the Trinity. Not itself a person, or hypostasis, it is the divine nature, hidden in the Father, revealed in the Son, and beloved in the Spirit. But as Sophia is the life of the Godhead, so it is the hidden reality of the world, which was created "out of nothing," and has both its nature and existence from God. Since Sophia is not a person in the Godhead, but the nature common to the three persons, it can be realized outside the Godhead; and that is precisely what is effected in creation. Without being identical with God, the world is fundamentally divine in its nature. Bulgakov writes, "Wisdom in creation is ontologically identical with its prototype, the same Wisdom as it exists in God."

Although the principle of Sophia has deep roots in Christian devotion, as witnessed by the name of the famous church in Constantinople, and by its appearance in mystical literature and in Orthodox liturgy, Christian theology has failed, until recently, to take it into account. For example, the Nicene formulation of the Trinity makes use of the abstract and empty term *ousia* to designate the divine nature, and it makes no mention of Sophia, probably because early theologians mistakenly identified Sophia, the true name for God's nature, with the Logos, which is one of the divine hypostases. Similarly, the Chalcedonian formulation of the Incarnation, according to which Christ is a divine person with a divine and human nature, is content with a purely negative account of the hypostatical union between the two natures (*inconfuse, immutabiliter, indivise, inseparabiliter*), whereas an adequate understanding of the divine and creaturely Sophia would have made this union intelligible. So it is, according to Bulgakov, with all the main doctrines. For want of the key notion of Sophia, the Church has but rarely understood the doctrines which it affirms.

Of particular importance for the present crisis is the relation of Sophia to the question of human nature and destiny. Because man is a hypostasis, a person, like the members of the Trinity, it would not be correct simply to identify Sophia and humanity. But, just as Sophia is the nature which the divine persons share, so in humanity, Sophia is the essence which human persons share. On the creaturely level, where divine perfection is worked out imperfectly in time, the divine image in man is not realized at the beginning. When, at the creation, the Father made man in His image by His Word and Spirit, the divine perfections were present only potentially;

their actualization has been achieved through the entrance of the second and third hypostases into history, at the time of Christ's birth, and when the Spirit descended at Pentecost. Thus, the history of mankind, according to Bulgakov, is the history of the perfecting in man of his likeness to God. Bulgakov stresses the divine agency in history, but at the same time he seeks to preserve man's freedom. He does this by means of the doctrine of *kenosis.* According to the New Testament, Christ "emptied himself" (*heauton ekenosen*) of His divine glory when He became man. Similarly, says Bulgakov, the Spirit emptied Himself of His power when he gave himself to the Church at Pentecost. Thus, the three persons of the Godhead are active in the world, but in such a way that the world is not lost in the Infinite. Bulgakov underlines this point by calling his doctrine "pan-entheism," in contrast to pantheism. But though insisting that man's will is independent of the divine, Bulgakov argues that the divine efficacy and "the compelling attraction of Wisdom" will win out over the willfulness of the creative. After all, says Bulgakov, evil is parasitical; essentially it is nothing, and it must "wither before the radiance of Wisdom."

Bulgakov holds that all human creativity, in thought, art, economics, and society, is the working out of Divine Wisdom on the creaturely level. He writes, "In man creation is to become aware of its own sophianic character and recognize it in intelligence, the seminal reason of creation, and its flower. And therewith man will recognize the likeness of the wisdom of God in himself." This development is, of course, not limited to Christendom; but with the coming of Christ, man found new freedom and reached levels of culture undreamed of in the pagan world. For this reason, special attention must be given to the divorce between culture and religion in the Christian world. Supposedly advancing under the banner of humanism, modern culture has, in Bulgakov's opinion, surrendered the better part of humanity, and has fallen under the retrogressive forces of pagan sensuality and Satanic pride. For this, however, the Church is itself mainly responsible. With an inadequate doctrine of God, and an even less adequate doctrine of man, it has too frequently assumed an ascetic, almost Manichaean, attitude toward history and culture, and either sought to dominate the world through artificial constraint, or condemned it outright as a peril to men's souls. Modern civilization, in Bulgakov's opinion, is headed toward sterility and death unless it discovers some way to heal this breach, some mode of creativity which is both churchly and free. With Jacques Maritain, Bulgakov calls for another kind of humanism, the "true humanism," wherein man's potentialities find their fulfillment in God. But unlike the Catholic philosopher, who desires to see human nature complemented by supernatural graces, Bulgakov maintains that human nature is essentially divine, and his wish is to see that potentially divine come to its proper fruition. True manhood is God-manhood, says Bulgakov, borrowing Solovyev's expression; that is, it is manhood become conscious of its oneness with God.

Like others who draw their inspiration from Solovyev, Bulgakov holds that the Church is the center of human history: "God created the world for the sake of the Church. That is as much as to say that it is at once the ground and goal of the world, its final cause and entelechy." In the Church man finds true society, which eludes him in other kinds of association, and he realizes something comparable to the perfect love and communion of the Godhead. On the other hand, Bulgakov describes the state as "a kind of callosity on the skin of the social body—the Great Wen." Founded upon force, the state denies human nature and deals with man according to the principles of material necessity. Thus, although the Church is the best friend of culture, she is the sworn enemy of politics; and any concordat between them can be only a compromise, "embarrassing to the Church, which must always remain in relation to the State an anarchic force."

The Church, as Bulgakov thinks of it, is not to be identified with any of its historical manifestations. Though it has its visible embodiment, it transcends our empirical mode of knowledge. Thus, although Bulgakov was very much interested in "the several Oecumenical Movements of our modern religious world," it can hardly be said that he expected them by themselves to effect any important change; whatever change occurs must first take place within the churches themselves, suffering as they do from the abiding antinomy between an acosmic affirmation of God's transcendence and an atheistic affirmation of the world. It is futile, according to Bulgakov, to suppose that any external "pact" between denominations can remedy so fundamental a fault. The first concern of the Church must be to find its own foundations, which it cannot do on the canonical or liturgical, but only on the doctrinal, level. But, according to Bulgakov, efforts to lead the churches back to the old creeds are foredoomed, because the creeds themselves are unstable. Even "incarnationism," which many churchmen seek to make the central affirmation of Christianity, is, says Bulgakov, not a primary doctrine, for it presupposes dogmatic assumptions about the nature of God and man which must first be dealt with. These presuppositions, long latent in Christian faith, have now been unfolded in sophiology. "The creaturely world is united with the divine world in the Divine Sophia . . . ," Bulgakov writes; "God-manhood represents a dogmatic call both to spiritual ascesis and to creativity; to salvation from the world and to a salvation of the world. This is the dogmatic banner which should be henceforth unfurled with all power and glory in the Church of Christ."

THE CHRISTIAN MESSAGE IN A NON-CHRISTIAN WORLD

Author: Hendrik Kraemer (1888-)
Type of work: Theology of missions
First published: 1938

Principal Ideas Advanced

Contemporary culture and the Christian Church are in crisis, both undermined by relativism; consequently, the Church must rediscover its absolute foundation if it is to have a mission to the modern world.

Christianity is utterly unique, founded in the revelation of divine forgiveness in Jesus Christ; all other religions are unaware of the permeation of all things by sin.

The fundamental need of man is for conversion to the new life of forgiveness; all missionary effort must thus be motivated in evangelism, however much such a call may issue in works of social service.

From the beginning of Christianity, Christian life has been characterized by the dialogue of worship and witness. Questions concerning the meaning of the Church and the mission of the Church are inseparable. It is not surprising, then, that the radical transition in Protestantism from Reformation orthodoxy to nineteenth century liberalism effected a radical revision not only in the understanding of the Church, but also in the conception of the Christian world mission.

In like fashion, it is to be expected that the emergence of neo-orthodox theology in the twentieth century would stimulate an equally radical reappraisal of "the Christian message in a non-Christian world." The liberal tended to understand Christianity as being a higher, purer form of a universal religious consciousness; consequently, the world mission was less a matter of evangelism and more a moral effort to better the social and physical state of the underprivileged.

Hendrik Kraemer's *The Christian Message in a Non-Christian World* is the most important single attempt to challenge this liberal understanding by vigorously insisting that the entire missionary enterprise be thoroughly evangelistic. Under Kraemer's influence, theologian, missionary, and indigenous Church leader alike are being forced to rethink the entire missionary enterprise, from undergirding theology to practical program.

Kraemer's argument begins by appraising the condition of the contemporary world to which the Church is called to witness. The outstanding characteristic of our time is "the complete disappearance of all absolutes, and the victorious but dreadful dominion of the spirit and attitude of relativism." The problem of religious certainty, consequently, is the ultimate problem of modern man.

The spirit of secularism and relativism began as a courageous and exhilarating discovery of man's power, worth, and destiny to conquer the mysteries of nature and life. Yet, glorious and important though this process was, it has ended in the self-destruction of man. "Man, being rooted in God, destroys himself by destroying God." Man has not really abolished God, however, for every effort to do so has resulted in the creation of another god. The need for the divine Word belongs to the very essence of man. Even though the conscious hunger of our time is for a more untrammelled enjoyment of life, an unconscious but deep spiritual hunger is gradually making itself known.

To the degree that the modern plight is seen, to that degree is man's craving for an absolute bearing witness to two things. First, man's prime obligation is to seek for the "absolute Truth and Ultimate Reality" in which he was created; second, "he cannot produce it by his own efforts." If God has placed the eternal within man's heart, man can never create Ultimate Truth, but can be only its humble receiver. The problem is that this truth is not seen. Relativism remains the decisive reality in modern life, and where relativism is not dominant, man is threatened by flight from it through such self-made absolutes as Communism, Fascism, and National-Socialism. This contemporary situation is universal, the only difference being that in the West the crisis is the result of an inner development, while in the East the primary cause is the penetration of West into East.

The Christian Church is also in a state of crisis. But since there should always be a tension between the Church's essential nature and its empirical condition in the world to which it belongs, its real crisis today is its blindness to its true critical nature. The representatives of religion, because of their diluted conception of religion, have contributed to the contemporary notion of God's irrelevance. There is hope, however, for the contemporary Church is beginning to sense the crisis caused by its capitulation to culture. Out of this awareness is growing a theological revolution that is driving the Church back to the basic Christian revelation. What has been lost and must be regained is "the vision of what God in Christ meant the Christian community to be—a fellowship of believers, rooted in God and His divine redemptive order, and therefore committed to the service and the salvation of the world." The Church must live in opposition to evil by a fundamental identification with the sufferings and needs of the world.

This loss of the meaning of the unique Christian revelation has led to a wholesale confusion concerning the missionary enterprise, so that now there is a cry for reorientation and clarification. The Christian mission has represented either escapism, on the one hand, or, as is more often the case, a reflection of modern society "with all its respectabilities, entrenched interests, prejudices and hypocrisies. . . ." Because of this identification of Christianity with Western civilization, much of the rejection of Christianity has been political.

With the breakdown of Western culture, however, is coming the awareness that the missionary movement must work by purely religious and moral persuasion. Ironically, crisis is drawing the Church away from the cultural atmosphere of its history back to its true nature and calling. Secondary arguments for missions, such as social or political enlightenment, often usurped the primary motive; now the primary motive alone can remain, for the "spell of the erroneous identification of Christianity and the progressive West is broken, and, still deadlier, the prestige of Western culture has decreased enormously." To promise that Christianity will cure economic and social problems is to court disillusionment, for these are caused and cured by many factors outside the Church's mission. The real motive and purpose of the Christian mission is founded not on anything that men ask for, but exclusively upon "the divine commission to proclaim the

Lordship of Christ over all life," whether there are "results" or not.

No matter how important the task of translating Christian faith to modern man, the fundamental task, as Kraemer sees it, is to recapture the original Christian faith whose only source is the Bible. Christianity is utterly unique; its origins are irreducible. Christianity offers no moral or religious philosophy, no theology or world-view. The whole content of the Bible is the living, eternally active God, revealed redemptively in the crucified and risen Lord. Christ is the crisis of all religions and philosophies, for all others evade *the* problem: how sinful man can walk with the holy God. There is only one answer: "Jesus Christ and the forgiveness of sins are the divine elements; repentance is the human element. . . ." The joy which is at the heart of the Christian mission is rooted in the miraculous forgiveness coming from God's free and sovereign grace in Jesus Christ, creating a new life in the Spirit. On this basis alone can the Christian "stand in the world, the object of God's saving and renewing activity, as His co-worker in service and love."

Kraemer understands Christian ethics in like manner. All other ethics are forms of eudaemonism, the search for the highest value. The goal of the Christian ethic, however, is "the fulfilment of God's will from which various values derive as fruits and results." This will is intensely concrete and eternally changing according to the situation, yet absolute, for it is *God's* will. One must love another, not because the other is of value, but because God wills every man as His creature. Consequently, we can love only because God first loved us in Jesus Christ. From this base, no political or social programs can be derived, for the Kingdom of God is beyond human realization. Instead, the Christian must work as *"a ferment and an explosive"* in every relative human sphere. Only openness to God's holy will in loving freedom brings moral sensitivity to the utmost intensity where the depths of the relative may be plumbed for absolute direction, without falling into nihilism.

The Christian atttiude toward non-Christian religions is governed by two poles of the revelation in Christ: a knowledge of God that upsets all other conceptions of the divine, and a knowledge of man that is revolutionary in comparison with all other views. The issue here is not one of pragmatic value, but of truth. The Christian must insist that "God has revealed *the* Way and *the* Life and *the* Truth in Jesus Christ and wills this to be known through all the world." This is a matter of faith, never of rational argument. Yet there is no room here for arrogance or the feeling of superiority, for the Christian stands always as a forgiven *sinner*.

There is a universal religious consciousness among men of all ages, but man's sin corrupts all his religious creations and achievements. The same is true of all attempts at natural theology, for "to reject the God of revelation inevitably means to erect man in some form as god." Nor is there such a thing as general revelation, for, by nature, revelation is special. "The real Christian contention is not: 'We have the revelation and not you,' but pointing gratefully and humbly to Christ: 'It has pleased God to reveal Himself fully and decisively in Christ; repent, believe and adore.' " God shines through man's yearning for truth, beauty, goodness, and holiness, but in a broken and troubled way. The highest and loftiest religious and moral achievements in the non-Christian religions, Kraemer insists, need Christian regeneration.

The point of contact for the Christian message is the perverted human quest for God. Consequently, such a point is not the agent that makes possible missionary results. "The sole *agent* of real faith in Christ is the Holy Spirit." In the end, the only real point of contact is the genuine and continuous interest of the missionary in the total life of the people.

Kraemer's book divides non-Christian religions into naturalist religions of self-realization (primitive, Hinduism, Buddhism, Confucianism, Taoism) and the prophetic religions of revelation (Christianity, Judaism, Islam), attempting to show by a general summary of these religions how each stands in fundamental contrast to Christianity. The difference is not one of grade or richness of religious experience; it is a difference of kind in regard to the understanding of God and man.

It follows, for Kraemer, that the Christian mission cannot be understood as the attempt to permeate other religions and cultures with Christian ideas and ideals. Under the influence of Christianity, Gandhi became not an "unbaptized Christian" but an "invigorated Hindu." What is necessary is a *decision* for Christ; this means not a sympathetic attitude toward Jesus, but a break with one's religious past. The Christian Church must stand firm against the present aversion to evangelizing, proselytizing, and conversion. For the Christian understanding, the primary need of man is conversion. Adaptation and social service, although a necessary part of the Christian witness, must find their basic motivation in evangelism.

So understood, adaptation becomes not assimilation but vital involvement for the sake of exposing the intrinsic inadequacy of man's religious efforts. This dare not mean that the missionary's own theological approach and forms of ecclesiastical life and worship are normative for African or Asiatic Christians. Christian adaptation emerges as the challenge to express the religion of revelation in vigorous indigenous forms in such a way that it is true to its real character. To do this is to expose the relevance of Christianity to all concrete social situations. This is not a matter of relating Christianity to the thought of a society, but a matter of expressing Christianity through this thought. Understood in this fashion, social and cultural activities are not accessories to the Church's witness, but are expressions of it.

Kraemer attempts in the latter portions of his work to suggest how regenerative work can be done in the concrete situations of key missionary fields today. His underlying understanding of such work is that the main aspects of Christianity are worship, witness, and ministry, in integral relation. If any of these elements is given priority, if service, for example, is favored over against evangelism, the meaning of Christianity is lost. To understand these ingredients in their interrelatedness is to grasp the meaning of the Church. Missions in the past have made the mistake of being either evangelical-minded, cultural-minded, or church-minded, according to the dominant interests of their supporters. Each of these attempts has made significant contributions, but today the weakness of each is becoming manifest. That goal toward which these weaknesses point as corrective is the indigenous Church. Such a goal, Kraemer believes, both calls for and results from radical rethinking concerning missions. Such rethinking emerges in the call to take seriously the Church as a radically theocentric community, united in common faith, common love, common worship, and common witness, brought into being by the divine miracle which is the forgiveness of sins.

Such considerations, Kraemer insists, are not a matter of theory, but a matter of the life or death of the Christian Church. Missions are not an optional matter; the introverted Church is without a future. In the end, Kraemer's prophetic call is not for a lessening of Christian permeation; it is a call for even greater scope and influence by a purifying of motive and spirit through a return to the unique foundation of Christianity.

THE IDEA OF A CHRISTIAN SOCIETY

Author: T(homas) S(tearns) Eliot (1888-)
Type of work: Christian social philosophy
First published: 1939

Principal Ideas Advanced

Because of its concern that every man achieve both his natural and his supernatural end, the Church must interest itself in the problems of society.

But reforms which do not alter fundamental social attitudes fall short of what Christianity demands.

Since the neutral society which characterizes the Western democracies does not favor the true ends of man, Christians must work to replace it with a society based on Christian principles.

Moreover, since a neutral society will be unable to hold its own in competition with the new pagan states, a Christian society is the only plausible alternative to the totalitarian degradation of man.

In *The Idea of a Christian Society,* T. S. Eliot presents a thesis which, although familiar from the writings of Roman Catholics such as Christopher Dawson and Jacques Maritain, is bolder than we are accustomed to hear defended by Protestants; namely, that Christians ought not content themselves with a neutral society in which the practice of religion is merely permitted, but ought rather to work for a society worthy to be called Christian. For Eliot, who became a Christian and joined the Anglican Church after having given classic expression to the despair of the "lost generation" in the 1920's, it is not enough that Christians work with non-Christians in seeking to remedy the injustices of the present order; they must seek a new social order "in which the natural end of man—virtue and well-being in community—

is acknowledged for all, and the supernatural end—beatitude—for those who have the eyes to see it."

Eliot defends the thesis, further elaborated in *Notes towards the Definition of Culture* (1949), that religion is fundamental for the formation and preservation of any culture. Without religion, he says, there is nothing to give meaning to life, nothing to protect the masses from boredom and despair, and nothing to direct the artist and the philosopher or to counteract the ambition of entrepreneurs and politicians. Eliot nevertheless rejects the pragmatic contention that the truth or falsity of a religion consists in the benefits which it confers upon a people. "To justify Christianity because it provides a foundation of morality, instead of showing the necessity of Christian morality from the truth of Christianity is," Eliot writes, "a very dangerous inversion."

Christian teaching, Eliot reminds us, is that man has an eternal destiny, that his proper goal is the knowledge and love of God, and that what really matters in our earthly life is whether, when one leaves this earth, he enters fully into God's presence or is excluded from it. The world in which the Church finds itself is constantly changing, but the Christian faith does not change; thus, the task of Christianity in every age is to evangelize the world. This task, Eliot argues, has no bounds. A philosophy of co-existence with the world is contrary to the whole spirit of the Gospel, which wants everybody to be saved and to make the greatest possible progress in things of the spirit. The Church does not exist merely for those who are temperamentally suited to attend its services while the rest of mankind goes on its way. Indeed, says, Eliot, it is folly to think that pious exercises on Sunday are in any way sufficient for the spiritual development even of those who want to be Christians while devoting their lives to a society in which industry, politics, and education are dominated by a secular scheme of values. The Church has no choice but to interest itself in social problems; it "must struggle for a condition of society which will give the maximum of opportunity for us to lead wholly Christian lives, and the maximum of opportunity for others to become Christians." One might suppose that because the Christian holds man's temporal welfare to be merely a means to an eternal goal, he will have less concern than worldly philosophers for the betterment of social conditions. The contrary is the case, says Eliot; precisely because "they are means and not an end in themselves, Christians are more deeply committed to realizing these ideals than are those who regard them as ends in themselves."

For these and similar reasons, Eliot argues that Christians are not doing their full duty when they team up with secular reformers in an effort to remedy particular injustices. Such reforms are worthwhile insofar as they bring about changes which make it possible for persons to live a more fully Christian life, but in most cases the possible benefit of any reform is lost because our culture does not favor Christian pursuits. Nothing will do, Eliot insists, but to alter our whole social enterprise so that, instead of impeding the life of devotion, society will foster it.

Eliot's idea of a Christian society is by no means utopian. A Christian, he says, will not make the mistake of the secular reformer who thinks that he can convert society without being himself converted. Christians believe that the Kingdom of God, although it is continually being realized, can never be consummated in history. Aware that a society will be no more just or humane than are its members, Christians are resigned to the fact that in any society which they can hope to achieve, immorality and hypocrisy will still appear in high places and in low, and that the majority of people will continue to devote most of their attention to their work, their families, and their recreations. Nonetheless, it would be a marked gain if the average man, no matter what his personal interests, were to be grounded in the teachings of the Church and to acknowledge the rightness of its precepts; however slight his own inclination toward things of the spirit, he ought to respect the religious vocation in others.

Such a society, Eliot maintains, can be the foundation for a Christian state; that is to say, for a state of which the laws and policies are based on Christian principles. There is no need for the rulers of a Christian state to be saints; they need not even be professing Christians. But they should be men of statesmanlike vision, and they must be masters in the art of government. As such, they will be ruled by the ethos of the people and compelled to temper their policies to Christian teachings. Even when they perform un-Christian acts, they will have to defend them on Christian grounds.

Because religion remains for most people a matter of habit, we must distinguish within the Christian Community, which comprises all believers, that part which Eliot calls the "Community of Christians." The latter consists of "consciously and thoughtfully practicing Christians, especially those of intellectual and spiritual superiority." They will not form a separate social class. Some of them will choose to live in cloisters; but others will lead an active life as teachers, artists, scholars, and priests. This is not to say that all who are engaged in intellectual callings or ministering to men's souls will belong to the "Community of Christians." But there will be a sufficient number of these keener Christian spirits, and they will have enough identity of belief and purpose, of background and culture, to "enable them to influence and be influenced by each other, and collectively to form the conscious mind and the conscience of the nation."

Eliot is writing chiefly with the old Christian countries of Europe in mind, which have the tradition of an established Church. (In America and other countries where variety of races and religion has long prevailed, the problem of a Christian society is, says Eliot, vastly more complicated.) In Eliot's opinion, the principle of establishment must be reinforced. Churches must come together again into one body, under a hierarchy standing in official relation to the state, and with a parish system reaching down to the smallest units of society. The "Community of Christians," forming a kind of "Church within the Church," will help to keep the Church spiritually alert and make it effective in matters of public policy and in the daily lives of the people. The Church must be Catholic both in the sense that it is the guardian of the high Christian culture of former ages, and in the sense that it is part of a world-wide Christian communion. Thus, it will serve as a counterpoise to hasty opportunism and to narrow nationalism wherever these appear in society. Eliot does not suppose that dissident sects will cease to exist; in fact, he is quite sure that besides sectarians there will be outright skeptics and unbelievers; but, in a society such as he has imagined, the positive culture will derive from the establishment, and the contributions of others will remain marginal—though not necessarily unimportant.

Eliot knows as well as anyone how unpopular his proposal must be, not merely with secularists but also with modern Christians, who have come to take for granted the freedom of a neutral society and are suspicious of any kind of social discipline or restraint. But the author of *The Waste Land* (1922) and *The Hollow Men* (1925) finds little to commend in the present order. He argues that the little that is positive in it, such as its feeling for social justice, is rooted in Christian faith, and that the more Christianity loses its effectiveness, the farther the Western democracies will sink into apathy and despair, "without faith, and therefore without faith in themselves; without a philosophy of life, either Christian or pagan; and without art." A second possibility, which Eliot regards as more likely, is that, spurred to compete with the new pagan civilizations (Fascism and Communism), the Western nations will unintentionally transform themselves into totalitarian states: "a state of affairs in which we shall have regimentation and conformity, without respect for the needs of the individual soul; the puritanism of a hygienic morality in the interest of efficiency; uniformity of opinion through propaganda, and art only encouraged when it flatters the official doctrines of the time."

Most people, Eliot complains, do not have enough imagination to believe that the world will ever be any different from the way it is at the present time; and almost no one would be able to feel at home in any future age, no matter how it turns out. But the harsh realities are that the world is changing at a rapid pace, and that powerful new economic and spiritual forces are at work which, if Christians do not stand up to them, seem destined to organize society along pagan, that is, idolatrous, lines. Even non-Christians, Eliot thinks, when faced with the bankruptcy of liberalism and the alternative of aggressive paganism, will not hesitate to throw their energies into the recovery of a Christian society. It will not be a paradise; it will involve "discipline, inconvenience and discomfort"; it will, in a word, be purgatory; but this, says Eliot, is the only alternative to hell on earth.

Paganism has sometimes been identified with the life of nature and thus has been thought to contrast favorably with Christianity. Eliot is sympathetic with the sentiments which give rise to this view. The attempt of D. H. Lawrence (1885-1930), for example, to recover the sense of man's relation to nature and to God, seems to Eliot important, even though it was ill-conceived. But truly understood, says Eliot, Christianity recovers the natural life more fully than primitive paganism ever did, and today it is the only force in the world which refuses to bow down to the idol of unregulated industrialism. The "deformation of humanity" and the "exhaustion of natural resources" are part of the ritual of the neo-paganism of our times. What we can learn from the pagan civilizations of the past, says Eliot, is that in order for human powers to flourish, art, religion, and society must function together. The error of modern Western civilization has been to suppose that man can enjoy the advantages of new material knowledge and power without raising himself to a higher plane of spiritual knowledge and power. The error must be corrected by Christianity if technological society is not to destroy itself.

A PHILOSOPHY OF RELIGION

Author: Edgar Sheffield Brightman (1884-1953)
Type of work: Philosophy of religion
First published: 1940

Principal Ideas Advanced

Religion descriptively defined is an attitude of devotion to the source and sustainer of the highest values; religion normatively defined is co-operation among human persons and the Divine Person for the realization of individual and social values.

The conception of God as a conscious and creative person immanent both in nature and in values provides the most coherent interpretation of all the facts of experience taken synoptically.

The problem of good-and-evil requires a revision of the traditional theistic conception; the power of God is limited by given, nonrational conditions, which God's will neither created nor approves; hence, God is viewed as the finite-infinite controller of the Given.

During the second quarter of this century Edgar Sheffield Brightman was the leading proponent of personalism (or personalistic idealism) in America. Brightman had studied at Boston University under Borden Parker Bowne (1847-1910), the first philosopher in America to develop the personalistic position. Brightman occupied the chair of Borden Parker Bowne Professor of Philosophy at Boston University from 1925 to his death in 1953. Under his leadership a flourishing graduate department of philosophy grew up.

A Philosophy of Religion contains Brightman's mature, systematic, and controversial formulation of the distinctive conception of God for which he has become widely known. Two earlier books, *The Problem of God* (1930) and *The Finding of God* (1931) had prepared the ground for his approach and argument in the 1940 book. A crisp statement of his position was also given in Brightman's presidential address, "An Empirical Approach to God," to the Eastern Division of the American Philosophical Association in December, 1936.

The personalistic perspective, according to Brightman, provides the strongest philosophical foundations for theism. In *A Philosophy of Religion,* Brightman starts by advocating a radically empirical method; that is, a method which considers the whole field of experience, "all that is at any time present in consciousness," including value experience as well as sense experience. He, therefore, rejects three other methods; namely, (1) the method which grounds the truths of faith on *a priori* principles which are independent of experience; (2) the method of logical positivism which restricts the meaning of experience to sense experience, thus eliminating statements about religion (non-sense) as meaningless discourse; and (3) the method associated with the theology of the Swiss Karl Barth, a theology which identifies vertical revelation, uncontaminated by human reason or experience, as the source of salvation.

On the basis of a consideration of "Religion as a Fact" (in a lengthy but illuminating chapter presenting the basic results of the various sciences of religion), Brightman offers the following descriptive definition: "Religion is concern about experiences which are regarded as of supreme value; devotion toward a power or powers believed to originate, increase, and conserve these values; and some suitable expression of this concern and devotion, whether through symbolic rites or through other individual and social conduct." Philosophy of religion is a *"rational interpretation of religion"* which seeks to determine *"the truth of religious beliefs and the value of religious attitudes and practices."* Since religion is rooted in value experience, Brightman devotes the third chapter to analyzing religious values, emphasizing both their uniqueness and their coalescence with other values. Since religious values are related to other dimensions of life, the problem of relating ideal values to existence, and of reconciling conflicting religious value-claims and beliefs, is a problem which calls for a philosophy of religion.

Brightman accepts empirical coherence as the criterion of religious truth. A principle of verification by coherence does not claim to provide theoretical certainty for religious belief, but it does give a basis for commitment (risk-taking action), and it keeps one open to new truth. Coherence is a better way of gaining knowledge of—that is, of understanding—the nature of God than immediate experience of God (mystical intuition), revelation, faith, *a priori* principles (rationalism), or action (pragmatism).

Having established his descriptive foundations and his methodological principles, Brightman turns to the substantive questions, the most important of which is the problem of God.

The generic *religious* meaning of the idea of God is "objective source and conserver of values." "Only the source of value is God," Brightman writes. The question is not whether there is a source of value (that is, whether God exists), but rather, how are we to *conceive* the source of value? As a background for answering this question, in the fifth chapter Brightman canvasses the major alternative available conceptions. He defines and analyzes polytheism, henotheism, monotheism, pantheism, agnostic realism, humanism, deistic supernaturalism, impersonal idealism, religious naturalism, and theism. In the seventh chapter Brightman evaluates these conceptions and develops his case for the superior adequacy of theism, the belief that God is "a conscious mind (spirit or person), immanent both in physical nature and in value experiences."

It is misleading to think of this case for personalistic theism as an "argument" for God. Brightman does not cast his argument in the form of traditional proofs. Indeed, he makes only the most cursory mention of the ontological, cosmological, teleological, and moral arguments. The basic thesis is essentially this: the hypothesis of a personal God provides the most coherent interpretation of all the available evidence; it gives the most adequate account of all the facts of experience taken synoptically. Consequently, the "argument" consists in presenting the following supporting evidence: (1) conscious experiences constitute all of the actual first-order data; (2) all physical entities are known only to the extent that they produce and affect conscious experience; (3) evidence of law and order suggests, though it does not logically entail, a cosmic ordering mind; (4) evidences of purpose, whether psychological, biological, or in evolution, point to a personal God; (5) the evidence supplied by history of religion, psychology of religion, and sociology of religion is best explained "by the hypothesis that one supreme personal God is at work in all religious experience"; (6) the entire range of value experience is most adequately grounded by this same hypothesis. Brightman concludes that the superiority of personalistic theism to impersonalistic naturalism is shown by its "more inclusive coherence."

In another connection, Brightman develops a theme which can be viewed as an argument for a personal God. This theme is what is called "the dialectic of desire." Dialectic is "the mind's search for completeness and coherence," and desire is the most universal psychological fact. The progression of the dialectic of desire leads, in a way that can only be barely outlined here, from the desire for pleasure (enjoying), to the desire for physical things (having), to the desire for activity (doing), to the desire for other persons (sharing), to the desire for ideals (planning), which leads to desire for the Supreme Person as a resolution of "the antinomy of the ideal."

The core of Brightman's case for a personal God becomes clear, however, only in his grappling with the problem of evil. It is really, Brightman maintains, the problem of good-and-evil. Naturalism can give no satisfactory explanation of value, nor can traditional theism account adequately for evil. The seriousness with which Brightman confronts the problem (in Chapter 7) may be indicated in two ways: (1) He makes a careful analysis of value and disvalue, intrinsic and instrumental, moral and nonmoral; there is a realistic recognition of the factuality of evil which is epitomized in his view of surd evil, "a type of evil which is inherently and irreducibly evil and contains within itself no principle of development or improvement"; (2) Brightman takes an inventory of ten possible and prevalently proposed solutions of the problem of evil and finds them singly and collectively not worth further consideration.

Brightman's constructive proposal for dealing with the problem of evil involves significant modifications in the theistic conception of God. His distinctive analysis of the nature of a personal God is elaborated first by a critique of traditional theism (or as Brightman calls it, "theistic absolutism"). Theistic absolutism is defined as "the view that the will of God faces no conditions within the divine experience which that will did not create (or at least approve)." The chief objections to it are that (1) it appeals to ignorance; (2) it ascribes surd evils to the divine will; (3) it tends to make good and evil indistinguishable; (4) it cuts the nerve of moral endeavor; and (5) it is unempirical.

The position which Brightman accepts and advocates is theistic finitism, the view that "the will of God does face conditions within divine experience which that will neither created nor approves." It is easy to misunderstand what Brightman means by speaking of God as finite. Brightman does not mean (1) that God is dependent on anything other than His being, or (2) that God, though personal, is human. God, according to Brightman's conception, is in legitimate and prevalent senses *infinite* (uncreated and unending), *eternal* (everlasting), *absolute* (ultimate reality, unconditioned by any external environment), *omnipotent* (having all the power there is except that which He delegates to created beings), and *perfect* in His complete and continuous commitment to the highest values.

What differentiates theistic finitism from theistic absolutism is the insistence of the former that the divine nature includes a nonrational aspect. This aspect Brightman calls the "Nonrational Given"; it refers to refractory data, brute fact, such as sensation. A second aspect of God's nature Brightman calls the "Rational Given"; it corresponds very closely to the traditional notion of the divine reason. The third aspect of the divine being is the divine will. God's will does not, according to Brightman, create either the Nonrational Given (brute fact) or the Rational Given (rational norms). God's will does, however, control the Nonrational Given according to His rational principles, giving significant form to what is otherwise meaningless content. Although God is never absolutely in control, He never loses control and is always at work overcoming obstacles. New values are continually being created through heroic struggle and sacrificial love. God is thus, in Brightman's terms, the "Finite-Infinite Controller of the Given."

The basis for this characterization of God is Brightman's analysis of the structure of experience. All persons are complex unities of experience consisting of rational form, activity (purpose), and nonrational content, inextricably interwoven. (The problem of human personality is dealt with separately in Chapters 10 and 11.) If God is personal, it is more intelligible to think of Him in this fashion. Furthermore, such a conception would be more consistent with the facts of evolution and surd evil. Brightman denies that the traditional notion of God's absolute power is a presupposition of the religious consciousness.

The last major issue which Brightman treats is that of personal immortality. Weak arguments both against and for immortality are considered and rejected. The crucial argument against immortality is physiological psychology. The answer to this consists in a critique of the naturalistic assumptions of the argument. The crucial argument for immortality is the goodness of God. The case for immortality is thus seen to depend on the general theistic position which Brightman has developed.

The last two chapters of the book seem more like appendices, but they are most interesting. One (Chapter 15) deals with internal criticisms of religion; that is, with religion's self-criticism. The other considers external criticisms of religion; for example, the criticism that religion is a device in the class struggle.

For Brightman, religion normatively conceived is "cooperation with God and man for the realization of individual and of shared values."

Personalistic theism represents an effort to go between traditional supernaturalism and current naturalism. Brightman would claim that personalism is more adequately empirical than positivism and more genuinely person-centered than existentialism.

CHRISTIAN DOCTRINE

Author: J. S. Whale (1896-)
Type of work: Systematic theology
First published: 1941

Principal Ideas Advanced

All Christian doctrines are the doctrine of God.

The doctrine of creation affirms a divine purpose for man, and the doctrine of the Fall expresses the conflict between man's will and the divine purpose.

Belief in the Resurrection is the Christian faith.

Since the Church belongs to Christ, it is more than an earthly society; it is the visible institution that gives expression to the Word of God.

Christian Doctrine includes the eight lectures which J. S. Whale, president of Cheshunt College, presented to the faculties of the University of Cambridge during the Michaelmas Term of 1940. The lectures provide an analytic exposition of the central features of Christian doctrine, and they have been well received as offering a clear modern statement of Christian ideas as developed from a Protestant viewpoint.

Whale considers, in the order named, the following Christian doctrines: the Christian doctrine of Creation, of the Fall, of history, of the atonement, of the Trinity and the Incarnation, of the Church, of the Word and the Sacraments, and of Last Things.

Whale's presupposition, which is an expression of his faith, is that all Christian doctrines are concerned with the reality and nature of God. No doctrine can be made clear unless reference is made to God by whom, or by reference to whom, all problems are resolved. "Christian doctrines," he writes, "presuppose and illustrate the fundamental doctrine that God is, and that man's chief end is to know him."

The claim that all doctrines reduce to the fundamental doctrine of God's reality is illustrated by reference to six common Christian ideas. The Christian conception of man, for example, is the conception of that being made in the image of God; thus, man cannot be understood unless God is known. The idea of sin involves the idea of moral evil relative to God's will. Redemption cannot be conceived except by reference to God's grace. Jesus is the Savior only if He is regarded as divine. The Church is nothing more than a moral society if it is not an expression of God's will. Finally, the Christian doctrine of history is without content unless God is considered to be the beginning and the end of all things.

Thus, God's reality is central to Christian doctrine. But how is God to be known? Whale points out that there have been three types of answers to that question: God is known through the authority of the Church; God is known through reference to the Bible; and God is known through mystical experience. Many persons have had the tendency to emphasize one source of knowledge at the expense of the others, but Whale argues that the three sources of knowledge about God interlock and are not mutually exclusive.

The author considers the place of reason in the effort to appreciate the reality of God, and he maintains that the proofs of God's existence are important as providing testimony of God's presence; only through revelation, however, is it possible to know *"who* God is. . . ." To pass from rational argument to the "living awareness of God" entails being ready to know God "experimentally" and with the heart. Christian doctrines, such as that of the Creation, are best understood not as cosmological theories but as expressions of faith in a transcendent God.

Having described the Christian doctrine of Creation as an expression of man's trust in the primacy of God, Whale turns to the doctrine of the Fall. He first of all rejects two views of human nature which are not compatible with the Christian faith; namely, naïve optimism and cynical pessimism. The former view is unrealistic, even sentimental, in regarding man as marked for continued progress and happiness; the fact is, Whale asserts, that the tragic view of human nature, a view which regards man as liable to sin, is closer to the truth than is the bland philosophy of naive optimism. Cynical pessimism, however, is equally mistaken in its extreme portrait of the human condition; to suppose that man is utterly abandoned and that his sin is without any hopeful issue is unchristian. The Christian view of man's Fall, a view customarily described as "Christian anthropology," is that man is God's creature; man sins by denying God and rebelling against Him; he is alienated and incurs the wrath of God; and each man is guilty with his fellowmen: no man stands alone in his sin. The doctrine of the Fall, like the doctrine of Creation, is important as symbolism; just as the doctrine of Creation calls attention to God's existence and the primacy of His being, so the doctrine of the Fall calls attention to man's "recalcitrant will" and to man's tendency to misdirect his life by turning himself from the divine.

A Christian doctrine of history is necessary if there is to be any satisfactory understanding of the relation of man in time to an eternal God who is "above history." The Greek and Hebrew attempts to resolve the problem of history failed, claims Whale; only the Christian answer succeeds. Christian doctrine presents God as infinite and eternal, ineffable and *"totum simul"*; at the same time, God makes finite man's worship possible by bridging the gap between the eternal and the temporal; the miraculous resolution of paradox was accomplished when "The Word was made flesh, and dwelt among us." Christian doctrine, then, regards history as a divine instrument; God has taken certain events out of history and has made time a part of eternity. It may be supposed by some persons that every event in time is equally significant, but in opposition to this claim Whale calls attention to the central fact in all history: the "redeeming activity of God." But the Redeemer cannot logically be considered apart from the fact of the Resurrection. "Belief in the Resurrection is not an appendage to the Christian faith," writes Whale; "it is the Christian faith." The Resurrection "explains the Gospels," Whale insists, and he adds that the Resurrection, which is "the mightiest of the mighty acts of God" provides the foundation of the Christian doctrine of history.

Whale describes atonement as "the creation of the conditions whereby God and man come together." Man needs to be reconciled to God because through his sin man has destroyed the harmony between himself and the source of all being. The Christian doctrine of the atonement, as Whale analyzes it, is the doctrine that the divine sacrifice is a revelation of God's love, a revelation which calls for a human response which will make reconciliation possible. There are theological problems which arise from the doctrine of the atonement—in particular, the problem of explaining the triune being of God and the motivation for the sacrifice of Christ—but it is clear, asserts Whale, that the atonement was that decisive act by which man, despite his weakness, was allowed to draw close to God.

The problem of explaining the Trinity and the Incarnation arises because the intellect demands a philosophical resolution of such a paradox as that God, although one, is three. But Whale begins his exposition of the Christian doctrine of the Trinity and the Incarnation by calling attention to the historic evidence which the Gospels provide, evidence which establishes both the humanity and the divinity of Jesus Christ. In a striking pair of sentences Whale explains the distinctive power of the idea of Christ: "He is what God means by 'Man.' He is what man means by 'God.'" Liturgical testimony also implies that Jesus is to be identified with God. Finally, theological dogma includes the Christian doctrine that Christ is unique; if no problem arose because of His uniqueness, the claim of His uniqueness would not survive.

Whale insists that man must serve God not only with the heart but also with the mind, but he concedes that to describe that which is finally unique is to end in paradox. The effort which theologians have put into the attempt to clarify the idea of the Trinity is worth while as a "monument" to what must remain a mystery to the intellect, but like the doctrine of the Incarnation the idea of the Trinity expresses the faith in God's unity and love, together with the belief that God came into—not out of—history in order that man might once again be in harmony with God.

Whale begins his consideration of the Christian doctrine of the Church by agreeing with those who maintain that religion is a personal matter. But religion cannot be a private matter, he adds, for "redemption must mean the restoration of that community of sons which God wills eternally." The Christian life is "necessarily corporate," Whale insists; the Church is the Body of Christ. It is true that the Church is divided and that the pure Church is with God, but the pure Church is one in spirit; it is more than an earthly society; it is the visible expression—through the Scriptures, the sacraments, the rites, the offices, the buildings—of the Word of God. Thus, the Church as an institution makes a new life possible through its corporate life. The Church provides finite man with the opportunity to attend now to the infinite and the eternal; through the Church man looks beyond the limited and beyond death to those final spiritual matters that ultimately concern his most personal being.

The Church provides two elements which are commonly called "the means of Grace": "the preaching and the hearing of the Word" and "the Sacrament of the Eucharist." These two elements are not two in spirit, for the Word which is spoken is the very Word which is shown in the Eucharist, the breaking of the "Bread."

The sacraments perpetuate the natural symbols which Christ made meaningful through His acts. Whale insists that the symbols which the Church utilizes were not chosen arbitrarily, for they call attention to the means of grace which Christ Himself employed; and when the sacraments are taken seriously, they continue to serve as means of grace. Thus, they are not merely symbolic acts; the sacraments are "signs of God acting."

It is important to be clear about death, Whale claims in his concluding chapter, because to understand life one must consider its end, and to consider the end of life is to consider death and the purpose of death. Death is certain, tragic (in that man alone knows that he is mortal), universal, and inescapably compelling (in that it forces man to choose between despair and faith). To choose faith is to make life meaningful; the end of life is not the dissolution of the body but the realization of eternal life. Thus, the Christian eschatology calls attention to the end already realized in Christ, but at the same time Christian eschatology reminds man of his mortality and of the possibility of his refusing to accept the eternal. Although God is gracious, man is responsible for making the effort to realize the end for which he was created.

THE MEANING OF REVELATION

Author: H. Richard Niebuhr (1894-1962)
Type of work: Confessional theology
First published: 1941

Principal Ideas Advanced

All human knowledge and action, revelation included, is radically conditioned by historical relativism.

Since to act is to decide in the face of objective uncertainty, faith is necessary at every stage; to become a self is to have a "god" as the orienting value which makes existence meaningful.

Man has dual perspectives regarding all things: objective appraisal in terms of "external history," subjective appropriation in terms of "internal history."

Since "internal history," the realm of revelation, is known only through participation, there can be no defense of one revelation against another; the only viable theology is confessional, a recital of one's inner history for the sake of sharing.

The year 1781 serves well to divide modern Protestant theology from its orthodox foundation, for in that year Immanuel Kant published his *Critique of Pure Reason.* From this point on, the awareness that emerged to unify the efforts of Protestant theologians was that, for perhaps the first time in the history of Christianity, the theologian no longer knew what revelation was.

The Reformers, such as Martin Luther (1483-1546), not only rejected the excesses of Roman Catholic ecclesiastical practices, but also found in both the Pauline view of human sinfulness and in the nominalist insistence on the finitude of reason a firm basis for challenging the ambitious attempts by Scholastic philosophy to reach the divine by human effort.

Although the Reformers distinguished between the revelatory Word grasped through Scripture by faith and the actual words of Scripture, irrational subjective interpretation of the Bible in the post-Reformation period forced theologians to make an unqualified identification of Scripture with revelation. "Protestant scholasticism" substituted an infallible Scripture for an infallible Church. Under the further influence of rationalism, the personal, experiential aspects of revelation were minimized in favor of propositional belief, thereby shifting reliance to natural, philosophical knowledge of God in order to defend, supplement, and often to interpret Scripture.

During the generations that followed, Biblical literalism was subject to the impact of literary criticism extended to Scripture, and to the challenge of natural science in regard to miracles and the Biblical account of creation. Studies in the history of religions showed similarities between supposedly "unique" religions. With the publication of Kant's *Critique of Pure Reason,* the questioning of revelation was complete, for the claim that reason can support revelation by framing proofs for God's existence was critically weakened.

For over a century, liberal Protestant theology attempted to answer the question of revelation, developing answers along lines established by the three Kantian *Critiques.* Friedrich Schleiermacher (1768-1834) developed religious knowledge in terms of feeling (*Gefühl*), a unique but universal "faculty" of man. Albrecht Ritschl (1822-1889) interpreted revelation in terms of moral consciousness. G. W. F. Hegel (1770-1831) understood revelation in terms of rationalism, within the confines of Absolute Idealism.

With the beginning of the twentieth century, it became clear to many scholars that in interpreting and judging revelation from the perspective of finite categories, liberal theologians had reduced the uniqueness of Christianity to a series of "universal truths."

It is within this context that twentieth century Protestant theology must be understood. While such neo-orthodox theologians as Karl Barth have returned through Kant to a radical Reformation understanding of revelation, H. Richard Niebuhr stands as one of the leading "mediating" theologians of the present. He is concerned in *The Meaning of Revelation* not only with the uniqueness of Christian revelation, but also with both the finality of the Kantian critique of human reason and the effect of revelation on all human knowledge and action. Revelation must be true to its uniqueness, but this uniqueness, if it is to be relevant, can be understood only in terms of the situation of *modern* man. Niebuhr's answer is the development of a "confessional" theological methodology.

Niebuhr's underlying problem is this: "We are aware today that all our philosophical ideas, religious dogmas and moral imperatives are historically conditioned and this awareness tempts us to a new agnosticism." There can be no denying the Kantian dictum that there is no universal knowledge of things in themselves; *all* knowledge is conditioned by the standpoint of the knower, whether the subject is ethics, political theory, or revelation. Knowledge emerges through experience, and experience is limited by space and time; that is, by the historical. Even language, the communicator of experience, bears radically the marks of the flux permeating all things finite.

It is the burden of Niebuhr's work to show that it is not the case that "the man who is forced to confess that his view of things is conditioned by the standpoint he occupies must doubt the reality of what he sees." In the midst of universal relativity man must still act. Action is thus always in the face of objective uncertainty; it is a faith risk. Yet the object of action is truth, for its justification is in its fruits.

The case is similar in regard to revelation. Religious faith is circular in the sense that statements about God can be made only from the point of view of faith in Him, but such circularity the Christian holds in common with every man. Theology, then, because of the nature of the human situation, must be resolutely confessional. Its function is to confess "what has happened to us in our community, how we came to believe, how we reason about things and what we see from our point of view." Anything less than confession robs religion of its distinctive personal involvement; anything more than confession is the idolatry of substituting human categories, conceptions, and institutions for the living God to whom one is confessing.

It is confessional theology that is loyal to the human situation, for it has as its task the determination of "what revelation means for Christians rather than what it ought to mean for all men, everywhere and at all times." Such an inquirer realizes that what he sees is from a limited point of view, yet his faith is an orienting acceptance of that truth as true for him *in that situation.*

This understanding, Niebuhr insists, is not a retreat for a Christianity threatened with extinction, but a rediscovery of the original Biblical witness. The early Christians neither argued for the existence of God, nor attempted any defense of absolute moral norms. The proclamation of the Christian was no more, *but no less,* than a "recital of the great events connected with the historical appearance of Jesus Christ and a confession of what had happened to the community of disciples."

The motive for Christian declaration must be that underlying the early disciples' recital of their lives; there must be an inner compulsion to share that which is possessed only in sharing. Thus revelation is history, and its communication is historical. To understand Christian revelation is to look out at the world of history and nature through the eyes of the believer and from his particular perspective. The Scriptures are revelation only when read from the perspective of the community of which the Scriptures are a record.

What becomes clear is that Niebuhr's analysis is based on the Kantian distinction between pure and practical reason, between objective and subjective necessity. According to Niebuhr, all things, even history itself, can be interpreted from two perspectives. The first is the mode of objectivity, of externality, accounting for events environmentally, concerned with pure, uninterpreted facts. It is this perspective when made exclusive that leads to skeptical relativism.

But such pure objectivity is existentially impossible, for in the process of acting, one necessarily imbues facts with meaning. In so doing, history is discriminately appropriated as "inner history." Thus history has two dimensions, established by the dual types of human relation. There is "history as contemplated" and "history as lived." Niebuhr illustrates this distinction brilliantly by comparing the events of July 4, 1776, from the "objective" perspective of spectatorship characterizing the *Cambridge Modern History* and the "subjective" perspective of involvement reflected in Abraham Lincoln's Gettysburg Address. These are two different orders. For one the subject is "Congress," and for the other it is the reality known as "Our Fathers." For one it is a matter to be described; for the other it is an idea to be defended to the death. All events can be so appraised from without or from within. Every individual and every community lives in the midst of two histories so drawn.

This difference in perspective is in no way a distinction between true and false. It must remain a matter of perspective, and a dual perspective is unavoidable, for no man nor group nor society can escape the search for a normative knowledge that transcends the purely descriptive, for value beyond pure fact, for meaning beyond mere information. One must study history not only with scientists, but with poets; that is, in terms of persons, purposes, and destinies.

It is Niebuhr's insistence that man has no option but to engage in this faith-dimension. At the most basic level, man is a creature of faith, for external reality is life lived in trust of repeated experiences. Likewise, on a higher level, either man must believe in something that makes life worth living or he cannot exist. Man as a practical, living being never exists without a god or gods. To be a self is to have a god; to have a god is to have history. To have one god is to have one history. Thus, belief in a god is a necessity founded in man's nature. The only question left to man is to ascertain which God is loyal in everyday existence. This can be known only by appropriating external history internally.

The traditional distinction between nature and supernature, then, must be seen as pertaining not to the type of thing perceived, but to the perspective employed. "We can speak of revelation only in connection with our own history without affirming or denying its reality in the history of other communities into whose inner life we cannot penetrate without abandoning ourselves and our community." Only a leap of faith can lead from observed to lived history. In no way can objective inquiry create faith, for no event is ever known as it really is. God alone knows in one act what something is from within and without. One must think *with* Isaiah and Paul rather than *about* them in order to verify their visions; so to participate in thought is to share their history. For man, there is no metaphysical solution to historical dualism. The solution is a practical one.

Yet, external history is important, for it is the medium in which internal history rests and comes to life. The alternation which is life is the dialogue of internal and external history. Internal history rests upon Pascal's "reasons of the heart," but rather than conflicting with the "head," such revelation becomes the base by which reason detects the meaning of all history through the spectacles of illuminating pattern, of image.

For the Christian, this image is Jesus Christ, for through Him history as a "tale told by an idiot, full of sound and fury, signifying nothing" becomes a grand epic. Even more, inner history makes past and present a living whole, exposing in our presence both those who are corrupted for thirty pieces of silver, and those whose bodies this moment are being broken for our sake.

Thus, by nature, revelation is dynamic; as the starting point for the interpretation of past, present, and future history, revelation is subject to progressive validation. For the Christian, the God revealed in history continues to reveal Himself through history in all times and places.

Jesus Christ is not the only divine self-disclosure that the Christian knows, for there is the echo of conscience, the numinous in nature, the craving of reason for a beginning and end. Yet, through Christ, all is radically transvalued, for what is revealed is not what was expected, and our expectations are put to shame. "We sought a good to love and were found by a good that loved us." It is the value and meaning of the world, grasped through an inner history, molded by him who makes all things new, that provides the existential answer to the problem of revelation in a world of relativities, and the answer is a confession. Niebuhr concludes his account of the meaning of revelation with the following comment: "Whatever other men may say we can only confess . . . that through our history a compulsion has been placed upon us and a new beginning offered us which we cannot evade."

THE NATURE AND DESTINY OF MAN

Author: Reinhold Niebuhr (1892-   )
Type of work: Philosophical theology
First published: Volume I, 1941; Volume II, 1945

Principal Ideas Advanced

Man is the created conjunction of spirit and nature.

Sin consists in man's self-centered refusal to recognize his creaturely limits.

In contrast to two other perspectives, namely, the Greek view of man as a rational animal, and the modern view of man as ever-progressing, the Christian or Biblical view defines man as image of God, creature, and sinner.

In contrast to views which reduce history to nature and also to those in which history is swallowed up in eternity or supernature, the Christian view of man is indefeasibly historical; the Christian view of historical destiny may be characterized as a drama which begins at Creation, rises to climax at the coming of Christ, and moves on to conclusion at Judgment Day.

The Nature and Destiny of Man is the most definitive and comprehensive statement of Reinhold Niebuhr's theology. It consists of his Gifford Lectures delivered at the University of Edinburgh in 1939, and historically it marks the clear and forceful emergence in American religious thought of the new theological viewpoint which originated in Germany with Barth's *The Epistle to the Romans* in 1919. Niebuhr's formulation of this theology consists of a study of man in what the subtitle of the present work terms "a Christian interpretation." Throughout both volumes runs a comparison of the Christian interpretation of man with alternative schemes of interpretation, Greek classical views in the ancient world, and naturalism and idealism in the modern world. The viewpoint of Christian faith upon human nature and destiny is also frequently contrasted with that of Marxism and of secular liberalism which are its contemporary alternatives. Niebuhr's enterprise is apologetic in the classical sense of offering an *apologia,* though not an apology, for the Christian view. Believing that this view is more adequate to all the facts of human existence than alternative views, Niebuhr proposes and undertakes a comparative study. Yet it is a study which appeals to facts and avoids defensiveness and special pleading. Indeed, Niebuhr is sharply critical of forms of Christian thought which exhibit these latter traits.

Niebuhr's viewpoint may be characterized as Christian existentialism, in that it centers upon the question of man and seeks a Biblical or Christian answer to this question. While he has much to say of God and other basic religious matters, they enter discussion as answers to the question raised by human nature and destiny. Among other existentialist features of Niebuhr's thought are his emphasis upon man's actual being, prior to any rational theory concerning the human essence, and also his emphasis upon the self-alienation of man in sin. In contrast to many other types of existentialism, Niebuhr emphasizes man's social being as well as his solitude.

The Christian character of Niebuhr's thought is based upon the Protestant Reformers, the Church Fathers, particularly Augustine, and most of all upon the Bible. It may thus be said to have a pronounced Protestant character. Niebuhr's thought as illustrated by *The Nature and Destiny of Man* has both influenced and been influenced by the current revival of Biblical studies.

Among current forms of Neo-Protestant theology, Niebuhr's shows both similarities to and differences from other formulations. Along with Karl Barth and Emil Brunner, Niebuhr emphasizes the radically transcendent character of the God of Biblical and Christian tradition, and the consequent creatureliness and sin of man. The influence of Brunner's *Man in Revolt,* a work which was published in 1939, on *The Nature and Destiny of Man* is particularly apparent. Yet the differences from the work by Barth, Brunner, and other contemporary theologians appear in Niebuhr's freer and more critical approach to traditional theology as well as in his lifelong concern with the issues of a responsible and functioning social ethic.

The two volumes of *The Nature and Destiny of Man,* entitled respectively *Human Nature* and *Human Destiny,* are so closely interrelated that neither can be considered apart from the other without serious distortion of the author's purpose. Human nature defines for Niebuhr the structures of created freedom, sin, judgment, and redemption which find application in the historical process. Conversely, human destiny is the drama of history in which man's nature is acted out.

The argument begins with man as a problem to himself. According to the author, all the various views of man, ancient and modern, may be observed to raise radical problems for themselves. If we seek to define man in terms of mind, rationality, or spirit, we are immediately confronted with his involvement in nature. If, on the other hand, we define man as an aspect of nature or natural process, the question arises of how we shall understand his self-conscious and self-transcendent freedom.

Greek philosophical views in Plato and Aristotle tend to define man in terms of his rationality, though Niebuhr notes in passing a sharply contrasting view of man in Greek tragedy. Distinctively modern views of man, while moving between philosophic idealism and naturalism, have in common an optimism regarding human good and evil which generates the characteristically modern view of progress with its confidence in human autonomy, reason, and virtue.

In sharpest contrast to both ancient and modern alternatives, Niebuhr's Christian view of man finds the source and also the key to man's fulfillment in his relation to God. This view emphasizes in Biblical fashion the integral unity of body and spirit, and of freedom and creatureliness, in human nature. Thus, according to the author, the Christian view combines the truths and avoids the failures and errors of the alternative views of man. This thesis concerning the Christian view is maintained throughout the work.

Chapter 2 of the first volume analyzes the elements of form and vitality in non-Christian views of man, ranging from the classical rationalism of Plato to the apotheosis of vitality in modern romanticism. Again the argument is that the Christian view is best able to hold together these contrasting aspects of man's nature. The third chapter devotes similar arguments to the idea of individuality in modern culture. While individuality has a basis in physical and biological nature, it finds expression in various cultural forms. The modern West exhibits forms of individualism ranging from the economic individualism of liberal democracy to the romantic individualism of a Goethe or an Emerson. Yet by a curious dialectical process, this trait so proudly and so characteristically asserted by modern thought is asserted by Niebuhr to be "lost" in conclusions which subordinate the individual person completely or totally to the state or to society. Idealist social philosophies like that of Hegel are offered as illustrations. Modern totalitarianism is cited as a practical manifestation of this loss of the individual in a modern culture originally dedicated to individualism. In contrast to the extremes of individualism and collectivism in practice, the Christian view of man is asserted to maintain a viable balance between individuality and community.

If there is a single pervasive trait of the modern mind which embraces all the many conflicting varieties of modern thought and life, it is, according to Niebuhr in the words of the title to Chapter IV, "The Easy Conscience of Modern Man." From Pico to Dewey, and from Helvetius to Hegel, modern man has thought well of himself and has refused to take seriously the traditional Christian doctrine of original sin. Indeed, one of the primary motivations of modern thought has been a criticism of the Christian idea, and a contrary or opposite assertion that man has in his own nature sufficient virtue and intelligence to solve his problems and master his fate. This modern viewpoint has tended to diagnose existent human evil as inertia or ignorance which may be conquered by improved education and social reform. Such characteristically modern ideas of good and evil give birth to the idea of human progress and also to the utopian strain of thought from Thomas More to Condorcet, Comte, H. G. Wells, and the Marxists. From Niebuhr's viewpoint, all such views represent a radical misreading of the nature and extent of evil in man. History wreaks its vengeance upon such inadequate ideas.

The Biblical view of man is asserted to be rooted in the idea of the God who reveals Himself to man, and in whose presence alone man sees himself as he truly is. Niebuhr argues for a general revelation or disclosure of God in the structure of creation. Thus, in the ordered and determinate structure of the world and in the freedom and conscience of man are to be found significant intimations of the same God who speaks through the Bible.

Niebuhr's view of man comes to explicit formulation in the exposition of the idea of man as the image of God and as the self-venerating sinner. What is the image of God in man, and where is it located? Speaking historically, many of the early Church Fathers who were under the influence of Greek philosophy sought to identify the image of God with human reason. Niebuhr disagrees. Following Augustine, he sees the image of God as the self-conscious and self-transcendent character of the human mind and self. It is this trait of man's nature which drives him to push beyond every fixed context or structure, forcing the distinctively human questions: Who am I?, Why am I alive? It is this trait which constitutes man as a self-conscious and centered self with the capacity of self-determination. Yet this freedom of self-transcendence is inextricably and integrally related to man's finite, mortal nature as a part of God's creation.

Man, who is both image of God and creature, is also, according to Niebuhr, a sinner. By sin is meant the human tendency to egotism or self-centeredness. It is, in Niebuhr's phrase, man's attempt "to play God"; that is, to make himself the center of all things. Such arrogant self-deification is the content of the traditional Christian vice, pride. The Genesis story of the Fall of man resulting in original sin is regarded by Niebuhr as a mythical statement of this aspect of man's observable behavior. There is no absolute necessity for a human self to be self-centered, for he is still free to find his proper center in God, yet the combination of man's freedom and creatureliness constitutes a situation of temptation which makes self-centeredness overwhelmingly probable. In the vertical relation of man to God, egotism manifests itself as self-deification, while in the horizontal relation of man to man, its consequence is injustice.

One of the most trenchant and original features of Niebuhr's thought is his fresh development of the social implications of such traditional theological ideas as sin. Thus, Chapter 8, entitled "Collective Egotism," is for the author completely in character. He argues that egotism is an even more pronounced and significant feature of social than of individual behavior. All human groups, whether states, nations, races, classes, or churches, exhibit an inevitable tendency toward self-centeredness which is then rationalized by an identification of group interest with that of civilization, humanity, God, or whatever is taken as ultimate. Such efforts "to put God on our side" are by no means limited to traditional religious groups; Marxist parties and nations exhibit a similar belief in the absolute rightness of their cause, rationalized by science and Marxist dialectics. Such a belief, wherever it occurs or however rationalized, constitutes a kind of final expression of pride.

Similar tendencies are exhibited in the higher life of man's mind and spirit. Righteousness, perverted by pride, becomes self-righteousness. Human reason is degraded—and becomes intellectual pride or arrogance. Man's vision of God can similarly become pride of religion, amounting to individual or collective self-deification.

By these lines of thought Niebuhr is led to a reassertion of a Pauline or Augustinian view of human nature which attempts to deal realistically with the extent and nature of evil in man. Final chapters in the first volume seek to relate sin to guilt, and both sin and guilt to human responsibility and to the doctrine of *justitia originalis,* which asserts the originally good character of man.

The second volume, dealing as it does with the problem of human destiny, begins with a basic distinction between historical and nonhistorical views of man. The latter include views which, like ancient or modern naturalism, subsume history to nature, and at the opposite pole, those faiths and philosophies in which history is swallowed up in eternity, as is the case in Neoplatonism and in philosophic Hinduism.

A clear characteristic of the historical type of faith is held to be the expectation of a Messiah, a figure in whom the meaning of history is fulfilled or realized. While various types of national messianism are mentioned, Niebuhr devotes most of his analysis to the development of Biblical or Hebrew messianism from the prophetic period to the first century, A.D. Against this background he proceeds to analyze the Messianic claims and significance of Jesus, arguing that, while in some respects Jesus fulfills Hebrew messianism, in others, such as in His rejection of Jewish legalism and particularism, He rejects or radically reforms it.

The figure of Christ is interpreted by Niebuhr in the Pauline phrase, the wisdom and power of God. That is to say, Christ is to be understood as God's decisive word to man concerning the nature of human life; Christ is God's power at work reconciling man to Himself. The human figure in whom this wisdom and power are manifested is a man utterly dedicated to sacrificial love, of which the Cross is the climactic expression.

The figure of the crucified Christ also defines the limits and possibilities of history. For love is a human possibility, yet no man or group does in any total or realistic sense live by the sacrificial love of the Cross. To this extent historical existence is involved in sin and must be saved by the divine grace revealed in Christ's sacrifice.

God's grace is understood by Niebuhr as the divine love toward man which is able to fulfill and perfect man's fragmentary and corrupted life. He compares and contrasts the two main theological interpretations of grace, the Catholic idea of grace *in nobis* (in us) and the Protestant idea of grace *pro nobis* (for us), coming to strongly Protestant conclusions. Against the Catholic view of infused grace, Niebuhr points to the continuance of sinful, egotistical behavior on the part of presumably regenerate men.

The Reformation is understood by Niebuhr as a powerful assertion of the Protestant view against the problems and perversions of the late medieval church. Yet the Reformation took place at a historical time when, due to the Renaissance and its new and optimistic estimate of man, it was being widely suggested that man does not really need divine grace at all. To summarize Niebuhr's conclusions, it may be said that the Renaissance, with its views of the goodness and self-sufficiency of man, won a victory over the Reformation in the battle for men's allegiance. So it is that modern thought has in this respect followed the Renaissance rather than the Reformation.

Yet, in another sense, the debate between these two views of the nature and destiny of man has continued throughout modern history. The Renaissance viewpoint assumes the virtue and self-sufficiency of man and affirms the infinite possibilities of progress that lie ahead, whereas the Reformation viewpoint asserts the finitude and corruption of man and concludes that man's only hope lies in God's grace. Niebuhr proposes a synthesis of these two viewpoints in which man's life in the course of history will be seen to stand before ever new possibilities of both good and evil.

Two aspects of this resultant synthesis are developed in detail; namely, the idea of tolerance, in Chapter 8, entitled significantly "Having and Not Having the Truth," and the idea of justice expounded in Chapter 9, "The Kingdom of God and the Struggle for Justice." The former chapter turns upon the paradoxical problem of holding a truth in genuine conviction, yet without the arrogant finality or absoluteness which generates intolerance. The test of tolerance comes not in ideas to which there is no real attachment, but rather in those believed with deep and genuine conviction. The solution in the view that man has truth and not final Truth. Absolute Truth must be affirmed as an aspect of God rather than as a human achievement. Historically, the origin of religious toleration may be seen to lie in the leftwing sects of the Protestant Reformation.

The Kingdom of God remains Niebuhr's statement of ideal society to which he relates the various structures and achievements of human law and justice. All such structures must accordingly be placed "under" the Kingdom of God. This means that their validity derives from their capacity to point toward the Kingdom. But it also means in full realism that all actual human structures and achievements fall short of the perfection of the Kingdom of God. They do so because man is both creaturely and sinful.

These considerations place limits on man's historical actions to achieve justice, but they have the more affirmative significance of freeing man from static absolutism for free historical action in the service of God. Niebuhr is critical both of Christian social conservatism from Paul and Augustine to Luther, and of the utopian illusions of much radical thought. Between the two lies Christian realism.

A final character develops the significance of the doctrine of Judgment Day as the end of history. Here, as elsewhere, Niebuhr's viewpoint is that one must take the Bible seriously but not literally. Hence, Judgment Day is to be taken no more literally than is Creation. Rather, it must be taken seriously as the final fulfillment of history's meaning.

PRAYER

Author: George Arthur Buttrick (1892-)
Type of work: Devotional philosophy
First published: 1942

Principal Ideas Advanced

The chief theoretical obstacle to prayer is an unexamined conception of natural law which leaves no place for God's action in the created order; the chief practical obstacle is a sense of sufficiency that presumes no need of His help.

Without prayer morality becomes hollow, knowledge reaches an impasse, science turns to destructive use, and religion grows flat and lifeless.

Our truest knowledge of prayer comes from the example and teaching of Jesus.

The path to success in prayer is a discipline that combines form with freedom.

Prayer by George Arthur Buttrick is a carefully written discussion of the obstacles to prayer, of its nature and practice, and of the fruits that come from its faithful performance. The approach of the book ranges from weighty argument against philosophical and psychological criticisms of prayer to simple and practical advice concerning the cultivation of the prayer life. The book repeatedly contends that prayer is the central feature of a deep religious life and that if prayer falls before the assaults of objections to it, all religion is lost. These modern objections are both theoretical and practical in character, involving both scientific agnosticism and temperamental nihilism. Written with urgency and vigor, the argument sets allegiance to prayer in the sharpest possible contrast to the contemporary rejections of prayer, especially to the unexamined conception of natural law which leaves no place for God to act in His creation. In prescribing the practice of prayer, however, the tone of the book is melioristic and its suggestions varied. Throughout his book Buttrick emphasizes the creativeness of prayer.

Beginning with a brief discussion of the absence of prayer in modern life and the corrosive consequences, the book turns to the contribution made toward our understanding of prayer by the teachings and example of Jesus. Jesus' teaching about prayer is scanty, yet ultimate. It is terse yet demanding. Prayer may be lonely and hard; it is to be humble and done in secret; it must be pursued with untiring persistence. Calvary teaches us that prayer must not expect to issue in selfish gain; it must be undertaken at great risk. But the spirit of Jesus also shows us the genuine possibility of radiance as the issue of prayer, even amidst trial. Above all else, according to Buttrick, from Jesus we learn that prayer is the path by which we find God and become related to Him in surrender and in trust.

The world has many criticisms to make of prayer. The criticisms can be refuted by argument but practice alone is the confirmation for prayer itself. The world accuses prayer of originating in fear, but origins alone do not condemn a current reality which has enlarged and grown since its inception. The world considers prayer a form of auto-suggestion or wishful thinking, but the same judgment is not applied to the criticism itself. The scientific world-view does not enlarge its borders to take in prayer, but confines its discussions to the external, fractional, and analytical sides of life. With its vision thus limited, it has no right to consider the reality of prayer.

No discussion of prayer is possible, according to the author's thesis, without presuming both human freedom and divine providence. The first is crucial because prayer involves the consent of will acknowledged in doctrines of human freedom, while the second is necessary because a God enmeshed in a mechanistic order could never qualify as Friend and Father. The freedom of man is experienced in life, not defended with logic. Even the logical arguments made against human freedom are cited by Buttrick as proof of this fact, for the men who make such arguments act as though others are free to accept them as true. In assuming, but never arguing, the existence of God, the man who prays acts as though God is faithful as well as flexible. The dependable quality of the universe witnesses to God's faithfulness. The flexibility of God presupposes that the same universe is subject to His controlling activity.

The activity of God is a mystery. He cannot do everything, but the limits to His power, like the limits to the scope of prayer, are difficult to define with precision. The sharpest issues concerning the relationship of prayer to the lawful order seen in creation arise with respect to petitionary prayer. Its religious validity is not in doubt since it is right and proper to ask God in candor to meet human needs. But its consequences are less easy to consider, for we must acknowledge God does not always give men what they ask for. Intercessory prayer, less prone to selfish yearning, is also religiously valid. Its fulfillment depends upon God and therefore defies prediction. Any telepathic theory of intercessory prayer would put too much control in human hands, hands not properly trusted with such power.

In a section on "Prayer and Personality" Buttrick explores the psychological and behavioral implications of prayer. In his constructive argument he builds a case largely independent of technical matters, but he does take pains to refute what he regards as false conclusions drawn from contemporary theories of personality. Where psychology is critical of prayer Buttrick is critical of psychology and accuses it of being recent, fractional, dogmatic, and limited in understanding. Where conscience is attributed to mere conditioning, Buttrick takes pains to explore its larger meaning of "knowing with" God. But the criticisms are not all aimed at the aberrations found in secular points of view. The description of faith as mere assent to propositions or as unfounded credulity must give way to a conception of faith as the axiom of the spirit which engenders expectancy and bestows a quiet confidence in self, in neighbors, and in Creation itself. To those who argue that prayer must be considered a matter of pure spirit, Buttrick retorts that form and body are essential to experience and to the practice of prayer. In contrast with the plea for unfettered freedom in the spiritual life Buttrick suggests that habit has a place in our devotions. To those who would regard prayer as a purely individual matter Buttrick has much to say about its corporate and communal possibilities.

The functions of prayer in relationship to personality seem twofold in the author's mind, though many variations of each function are explored in the several chapters. The chapters deal with the roles of instinct, memory, imagination, and conscience, among other topics. On the one hand Buttrick holds that prayer directs attention to proper objects of loyalty and into constructive moods of life; on the other hand prayer cleanses and purges human attitudes of the poisons which plague the spirit.

The directing and releasing functions of prayer are many and varied. Prayer creates a fundamental honesty in man, which enables man to put his inner house in order. True prayer and hypocrisy are incompatible. Prayer focuses the conscious mind upon God and provides a proper focus for man's attention. The focus carries over to the subconscious. The new orientation thus given to man makes him ready to receive events and to meet them with poise. It gives a standard against which to measure alternatives and thus it guides decision. It gives man power to act after a decision has been properly reached. Prayer enables the spirit to break out in spontaneous joy as it acknowledges the providence of God. Prayer turns the attention of the self toward others. Prayer trains the conscience. It prepares men to meet crises.

The cleansing function of prayer is equally important and complex. Confessional prayer enables the soul to purge itself of guilt. It lances the infected wound of the inner life so that healing can take place. Buttrick is appreciative of the concern of the Roman Catholic church to provide such a cleansing process through its confessional, and he pleads that each man must have some means of experiencing the release which such a practice intends. Confessional prayer must not become excessive, however, since men then become morbid and self-centered in a negative way. Prayer cleanses and purifies the motives of men; it purges, redeems, and trains the memory; it provides, through intercession for others, an outflow from the stagnant pool of our own thinking.

The concluding several chapters of the book are a pleasant and surprising contrast to the main argument. They discuss in very practical terms the ways and means of prayer. Consistent with Buttrick's strong contention that prayer must have body and form, the book surveys the actual forms that prayer can take. Buttrick admits that forms are subject to both use and misuse and deems them "inevitable, dangerous, and precious." Thus the suggestions he offers are intended as guides and not as prescriptions and they draw upon many sources from both private diaries of prayer and the liturgies of the Church.

Buttrick argues that the Church has been remiss in its failure to provide men with specific instruction in the way of private prayer. Seeking to set right the scales Buttrick proffers specific advice about the life of personal prayer. He suggests that such prayer should be undertaken in a quiet and a private place which becomes an accustomed place as a result of regular use. Evening seems to Buttrick the best time for regular prayer, though ejaculatory utterance throughout the day is commended to the reader. The merits of silent and uttered prayer are weighed, but there is no preference expressed for one to the exclusion of the other.

In the discussion of corporate prayer Buttrick provides a brief yet helpful discussion of public worship. Prayer is the central feature of such worship, as he sees it, and much is said in criticism of traditions in which the prayer is relegated to a secondary place, either in position or in preparation. Worship is related to the realms of work and education, to which its moods and resources should be carried. The family altar, the weekly prayer meeting, and other forms of group worship are urged in revived and recreated forms.

The final chapter recapitulates without summarizing. It restates the case without merely rehearsing the arguments. A short paragraph from near the end of the work will introduce the reader better than extended commentary to both the gist of the argument and the flavor of its presentation: Speaking of the loneliness of man in a vast cosmos, Buttrick writes:

"Always that loneliness, to which the new astronomy has added a dismay. But in other ages the yearning was endurable; for then men by faith and prayer caught glimpses of a homeland, and were sure that at death they would live at home. Their paradox of loneliness and at-homeness had a certain smart of tension which gave tang to life. But now mankind no longer accepts orthodoxy—which the church has often made angular and narrow—and can find no hope or nourishment in the nihilism of natural law. Behind our wars is the loss of ultimate Sanction: the wars will not end until the Sanction is recovered. Behind our weariness, which is not disproved but only underscored by our insistence that we are 'having such a good time,' is the loss of Horizons; the play will be boring until there is some background of mountains and sky. Behind our restlessness and nervous breakdown is a fear we dare not face—the fear that there *is* no Home, and that we are only driven fugitives of time and dust: the fear will vex us until we find God!"

THE SCREWTAPE LETTERS

Author: C(live) S(taples) Lewis (1898-)
Type of work: Christian ethics
First published: 1942

Principal Ideas Advanced

Modern man is confronted by serious obstacles in the effort to become and to remain a Christian; the chief obstacle is man's failure to utilize his reason in the acquisition of the virtues of faith, hope, charity, justice, temperance, and courage.

The young convert to Christianity is beset by temptations of the body and mind, by the enticement to illicit sexual activity, by fear, anxiety, pride, and flippancy; in his struggle to lead the Christian life, the young convert receives little assistance from the Church or society.

The faithfulness, love, and mercy of God are, however, sufficient to overcome the wiles of the Devil and to bring the Christian safely to his eternal home.

The Screwtape Letters is a profound analysis of the pitfalls that confront a Christian living in the twentieth century. The book is an application of such virtues as justice, courage, temperance, faith, hope, and love to the life of the Christian. The literary form of the work is an imaginary correspondence between Screwtape and Wormwood. The former, a devil in Hell, is entrusted with the task of instructing the latter, a devil on earth, in the art of successfully luring a particular human being from the path of virtue into the pseudo-pleasures of vice. The activity of the devils is hampered by their "enemy," God, who loves the human creatures.

The work of the devils has been made easier because many human beings either have come to disbelieve in their existence or to take an excessive and unhealthy interest in Satan. Both attitudes are beneficial to Wormwood's success.

Screwtape's instruction to Wormwood may be divided into two parts; the first is designed to prevent the "patient," the human being entrusted to Wormwood's care, from becoming a Christian; the second is designed to destroy the faith of the patient if he has accepted Christianity.

A few centuries ago, Screwtape points out, argumentation might have been used to keep an intelligent human being out of the Christian fold, for in the past people knew when a proposition was proven and when it was not, and if it was proven, they accepted it. Thinking was connected with doing, and a chain of reasoning could lead to the altering of a way of life. Today, however, modern man is more sophisticated. He can entertain a dozen incompatible philosophies. Doctrines are no longer thought of as true or false, but as conventional or ruthless, contemporary or outworn, academic or practical. Therefore, it is jargon, not argument, that can best keep a man from becoming a Christian. Argumentation is dangerous because reason is on the side of Christianity. It is not necessary to argue that materialism is true; it is sufficient to create the attitude that materialism is the philosophy of the future, that it is strong, courageous, and somehow connected with real life. Attitudes are created by practical propaganda, by attending to the stream of immediate sense experiences, by the ordinariness of things. The real sciences in no way support a defense against Christianity, for they encourage reflection upon what cannot be seen or touched. The belief to be encouraged is that whatever ideas the patient has casually picked up are the findings of scientific investigation. In this way materialism is accepted unchallenged and without proof. But in spite of the merit of the advice given by Screwtape, Wormwood's initial efforts to prevent his patient from becoming a Christian were unsuccessful.

The second course of instruction, as Screwtape presents it, makes it clear that not all is lost. For hundreds of converts have been reclaimed after a brief stay in the Enemy's camp. The mental and physical habits of the patient are not readily overcome. In fact the visible Church is one of Satan's greatest assets. The liturgy used in worship is unintelligible, the lyrics are poorly composed, and many Church members are hypocrites. The patient is encouraged to look around for the church that suits him. He may then join a faction and become a critic when he should be a pupil. He may find a minister who has watered down the faith and has deserted the liturgy. Or he may find a minister who preaches only what is calculated to shock, grieve, puzzle, or humiliate.

The prayer life of the patient must also be rendered innocuous. This can be accomplished by making his prayers so spiritual that they are far removed from his daily problems. They should be made spontaneous, inward, informal, and unregularized, aimed at producing a devotional mood, without real concentration of will and intelligence. His gaze should be turned away from God towards himself. His efforts should be directed towards the manufacturing of feelings. Instead of asking God for charity, he should be encouraged to arouse charitable feelings; instead of praying for forgiveness, he should feel forgiven. The value of each prayer should be measured by the success in attaining the desired feeling.

The outbreak of a war may be of use in the destruction of the Christian faith, but it is not necessarily Satan's ally. Whether the patient is a pacifist or an ardent patriot can be put to good use by Wormwood. Wars can create anxiety and hatred, but there is also the danger of the growth of benevolence. What is most important for the Devil's purpose is that the patient adopt an extreme position. Every extreme, except devotion to God, is to be encouraged. Our age is unbalanced and prone to faction. Any small group which is bound together by an unpopular interest tends to make its members proud and hateful of outsiders. Whether the patient is a conscientious objector or patriot is unimportant as long as he can be made to make his pacifism or patriotism a part of his religion, for then he can be led to make it the most important part, until finally it becomes the whole of his belief.

The spiritual life of the young Christian can be expected to hit a series of troughs and peaks: periods of emotional richness will alternate with periods of numbness and poverty. The periods of depression provide ample opportunity for temptation. The patient must never be permitted to know that ups and downs are normal. Rather he should be made to feel that the first ardors of his conversion should have lasted forever. He may then be led to despair, or he may be made to feel content with a low-ebb religion which is as good as no religion at all. In such periods of despondency his faith is open to direct assault. From the feeling that he is losing interest, he may be led to the conclusion that his faith is false, merely an adolescent phase in his development.

The young Christian can further be distracted from the path of righteousness by being brought into the company of rich, smart, superficial intellectuals who are skeptical about everything. Such people can appeal to his social, sexual, and intellectual vanity, and with encouragement they can destroy temperance, chastity, and sobriety and arouse cynicism, skepticism, and self-satisfaction.

The patient is to be encouraged in mistaking flippancy for humor and joy. The Devil would have him discover that he can do almost anything with approval, if it can be treated as a joke. To make a real joke is difficult, but to be flippant about virtue and to treat it as if it were a joke is quite easy. Flippant people always assume that the joke has been made, without anyone actually making it. Every serious subject can then be discussed as if a ridiculous side to it had already been found. Genuine joy, fun, and laughter which arise from a sudden perception of incongruity are of no aid to Satan, for such delight can actually promote charity, courage, and contentment.

The patient must be kept from the genuine enjoyments of the Christian life. It is quite proper if he keeps the habits of a Christian externally, as long as he gradually becomes inattentive to their real meaning. He need not commit spectacular sins; little sins will do. Positive pleasures, doing what he really likes, ought never to be allowed. Above all, the young Christian ought never to be allowed to hope for the daily and hourly grace to meet the daily and hourly temptations. Let him expect grace for life; let him hope for perpetual virtue. Should he become humble, the Devil's purpose is best served by implanting the awareness of his own humility, so that humility will then be transformed into pride; pride at his own humility will appear. The true end of humility, namely, self-forgetfulness, must be concealed from the young Christian. The latter must not be allowed to turn his attention away from himself to God, and to his neighbors; he must be made to be concerned only with himself, and to have contempt of himself so that he can then have contempt for others. He will become gloomy, cynical, and cruel. He must be made to feel that humility consists in trying to believe that his talents are of no value. This will breed dishonesty and will prevent him from loving himself in such a way that he can love his neighbor.

The young Christian is to be encouraged in intemperance, not only in the sphere of sex, but also in regard to food. Gluttony of excess is, however, of no more value than gluttony of delicacy, where no large quantities are involved. By enslaving the young Christian's life to this form of sensuality, the gluttonous appetite for food can be used to produce querulousness, impatience, uncharitableness, and self-concern.

In the area of sex, the Christian is enjoined by his faith to complete abstinence or unmitigated monogamy. The foundation of the latter is undermined by inculcating the notion that the usually short-lived experience of "being in love" is the only respectable basis for marriage. A marriage that does not render this excitement permanent is, therefore, no longer binding. Loyalty to a partnership for mutual help, for the preservation of chastity, and for the transmission of life must be made to be regarded as something less worthy than a storm of emotion.

When sexuality cannot be transformed into brutal cynicism or unchastity, a marriage can be used to serve the Devil's purposes equally well. The desires of men can be carefully directed so that husbands will desire what is not attainable. If a man should happen to marry a real Christian, it is still possible to use her family and friends for Satanic purposes. A proper Christian atmosphere, a Christian family, and Christian friends may even be used to awaken in the young Christian a feeling of spiritual pride. It may be used to arouse the feeling that the outsiders who do not share his new-found belief are stupid and ridiculous.

The new Christian is to be encouraged to add something to his Christianity. Mere Christianity threatens the Devil's purposes, but if it be coupled with something else, such as Christianity and social crises, or Christianity and the new psychology, then Christianity can be made to be a means to something else. The Devil wants men to treat Christianity as a means—preferably as a means to their own advancement, but if necessary even as a means to social justice. If social justice is valued as something God wants most of all, it is then easy to value Christianity because it produces social justice.

The young Christian is to be encouraged further to despise the same old thing, to look for novelty. Novelty produces heresies in religion, folly in counsel, infidelity in marriage, and inconstancy in friendship. It diminishes pleasure and increases desire, and it distracts attention from real danger.

It matters not whether the patient is in physical danger; the Devil's concern is with his spiritual state. Courage can be turned into pride, and cowardice can be turned into hatred. What is to be encouraged is the feeling that man has something other than God to fall back on. Man's fears and fatigue can be turned into anger, malice, and impatience, but they can also lead to trust in God, to kindness, and courage. Physical death by no means serves Satan; it can in fact spell defeat. For it is the spiritual state of the believer at the time of his death that is important. The soul of the Christian who dies in a state of grace passes into the presence of his Savior, and the Devil is defeated. The soul of the believer escapes the torments of Hell and passes on to its eternal reward.

CHRIST AND TIME

Author: Oscar Cullmann (1902-)
Type of work: Christology
First published: 1946

Principal Ideas Advanced

Because of the Biblical understanding of time, Christian theology ought to be, fundamentally, a recital of Biblical history, all speculation being based upon and controlled by it.

History is an ascending time-line, moving forward purposefully to its predestined completion in a new creation.

Christ is the center of history, the absolute revelation of God in terms of which all of history and nature are to be understood: everything was created to be subjected to the Lordship of Christ, and to be reconciled to God through Christ.

To understand time as meaningless and eternity as opposed to time is to substitute an alien philosophy for the New Testament faith which sees time as the locus of God's actions and eternity as continuous with time.

Oscar Cullmann, author of *Christ and Time* and a leading Protestant New Testament scholar, is one of a group of theologians who have been given the name "Biblical theologians." This group, in its two-fold battle against fundamentalism (insistence upon the infallibility of Scripture in every detail) and modernism (the replacing of Christian faith by modern philosophy), has as its defining characteristic an effort to be Biblical without being bound, to derive controlling insights from the Biblical view of God and history without at the same time accepting the whole Bible as eternally binding.

Cullmann has attempted in *Christ and Time* to determine "what is central in the Christian proclamation." Attention must be given to both halves of this statement, for he tries both to isolate what is central and to find it within and because of the Christian past. Thus, one of his major adversaries has been the author Rudolf Bultmann, the controversial Continental theologian, who, according to Cullmann, has used the method of modern existentialist philosophy and has reduced all theological statements to symbols about the meaning of human existence. Bultmann, recognizing with Cullmann that the Biblical proclamation centers upon the activity of God, nevertheless has rejected the time-structure of the Bible as being important for modern Christianity.

An example of proper theologizing, according to Cullmann, is provided by Karl Barth, the most forceful and eminent of the "neo-orthodox" theologians, who has attempted to base his theology upon the Bible historically considered and to present a Christ-centered theology which incorporates the basic elements of the Biblical view of God, history, and nature. Cullmann's only criticism is that Barth's work has been marred by an un-Biblical view of eternity, a view which Barth derived from Greek philosophy. *Christ and Time* is the result of an attempt to carry Barth's views to their correct conclusion by developing the Biblical understanding of eternity as continued time.

Christ and Time embodies the results of Cullmann's exploration of the basic presupposition of New Testament theology; namely, its conception of time and history. In opposition to philosophies which have *cyclical* views of history and which devaluate time as meaningless or evil and therefore as something to be escaped by means of a salvation which lifts one "above" history, Biblical man believed that history and nature are the deliberate creation of a God who intended to manifest His revelation and salvation in history. History is not meaningless but meaningful; history is not a circle but a straight line. God rules over history and acts in history, creating all things to be subjected to the Lordship of Christ, bringing to pass the crucial events leading up to the first manifestation of that Lordship, and manifesting that Lordship fully through a new creation which, for us, is still to come. Thus the ages of pre-creation, creation, and new creation are segments of an ascending time-line, each age being higher in value than the preceding one.

History is, then, the locus of the revelation and redemptive activity of God. The time-line is a redemption line, and the meaning of that line is to be found in the moment when redemption takes place. Jesus of Nazareth is the decisive point in the time-line, His death and resurrection is the manifestation of that Lordship for which creation was intended and is the *"absolute divine revelation* to men." Both creation, as the creation of that over which this Lordship is to be manifested, and new creation, as the age of the full manifestation of that Lordship, are thus to be understood only in terms of this absolute divine revelation. The whole time-line takes its meaning from its midpoint, the revelation of God in Christ. History is thus decisively Christ-centered, as our modern system of reckoning time counting forward and backward from the date of Christ's birth can be used to symbolize.

Judaism shares with Christianity the view that the ascending time-line has three ages, pre-creation, creation, and new creation. The difference is that Judaism still looks forward to an event to come, whereas Christianity looks back upon an event which has already taken place. According to the early Church, the decisive battle in the new creation has already been won. Although mankind still remains in the age of creation and will continue to remain there for an undisclosed period of time, the crucial event for salvation has taken place in the death and resurrection of Christ, which accomplished His victory over the evil powers and the manifestation of His Lordship over the whole of creation. It was because the early Christians knew that the decisive event *had* happened that they were not dismayed when the end of the age did not come as quickly as they had originally anticipated.

The "scandal" of Christianity is this, that it proclaims that in a particular moment of time salvation was affected for the whole temporal order. The act of faith that was demanded of the early Christians was thus enormous, for they were called upon to accept as fact that a man who dressed and spoke as they did had, just a few days before, won salvation for all mankind. They were confronted by the necessity of believing that a man with whom they had been acquainted was God's appointed means for redeeming the world.

That this belief has been perennially difficult is shown by the fact that the first great heresy, still quite active, was Docetism (from the word *doceo,* "to seem"; thus, the teaching that Christ only *seemed* to have a body and only *seemed* to die). Cullmann uses this name broadly to denote all those who deny that redemption takes place in history and who therefore look for salvation apart from history. Docetism understands salvation spatially, in terms of the removal of man from the temporal realm of being to a nontemporal realm of eternity which lies alongside this realm, whereas Christianity understands salvation temporally, finding salvation in the death and resurrection of an actual historical being and finding it to involve continued temporal activity. For Christianity, salvation is measured in terms of then and now, not here and there.

The most controversial feature of *Christ and Time* is its insistence that eternity and time are continuous with each other. Eternity must be taken in neither the Platonic nor the modern philosophical sense, but, rather, as merely endless time. "Thus in the New Testament field," Cullmann writes, "it is not time and eternity that stand opposed, but limited time and unlimited, endless time. . . . This latter time is not different from the former. The difference consists only in the fact that it is not limited." The future age, the age of the new creation which is yet to come, is also temporal in character, not timeless. Biblical expressions such as "the first and the last," "the beginning and the end," ought to be interpreted as they actually read; namely, as temporal concepts rather than as symbols for some nontemporal eternity.

The New Testament, as Cullmann shows through abundant citation, does contain an understanding of past, present, and future in terms of Christ. Christ is presented as the creative Word, the Mediator foreordained from before the foundation of the earth. He is the one toward whom the whole creation and all of past history has pointed, the one for whom the whole earth has longed. The Old Testament portrays redemptive history, a history which points forward to His coming, and is to be understood "as preparation for the incarnation and the cross." The various events portrayed in this revelation are part of redemptive history, but they are not complete in themselves; they require Christ for their completion.

Present time is also understood in terms of Christ. The Apostles knew themselves to be persons commissioned to carry on the redemptive work of Christ by proclaiming the fact of salvation to the Gentiles. That which was promised to Israel had come; the decisive manifestation of God's power and purpose had taken place, and the Gentiles had been included. The Church was created in order to preach to the rest of the world that Jesus Christ is actually Lord. It is Cullmann's claim that the New Testament Church believed that the Lordship of Christ has actually been manifested over the Gentiles, the supernatural powers, the state, the whole of creation. All things have actually been subjected to Christ, but since they do not know it, it is necessary to proclaim what has taken place.

The future time, the age of the new creation, is also understood in terms of Christ. Christ will come again, bringing to a close the present segment of the time-line, manifesting his authority absolutely over the whole of creation, and every tongue will then confess that Jesus Christ is Lord. The Lordship of Christ which was accomplished in His death and resurrection, but which is now largely unrecognized by those who are really his subjects, will become fully obvious when He comes again.

Thus the meaning of all of history and nature is to be understood by reference to Christ. Cullmann writes: "In the three decisive stages of the Christ-line of salvation the general process is drawn into the redemptive process. It is so in Creation: everything is created through Christ. It is so in Christ's death and resurrection: everything is reconciled through him. It is so in the eschatological completion: everything is subjected to God, who is all in all." Time is an ascending line, with creation, reconciliation, and the subjection of the whole of creation to God, as its segments, and all points of this redemptive line are related to "*one historical fact* at the mid-point, a fact which . . . is decisive for salvation."

This book is primarily descriptive, being an inquiry into the meaning of New Testament texts in an effort to discover what is central in them, but it is also obviously prescriptive. Cullmann intends to suggest that the New Testament view of time be normative for Christianity; he does not (some critics maintain) consider concepts of time which can be found in the Bible but which differ from his own. Rejecting not only modern attempts to base theology upon non-Biblical concepts of time and eternity, but also classical Christian deviations from Biblical doctrine, Cullmann criticizes some of the Church Fathers for their neglect of history and their preoccupation with nontemporal views of eternity. Because his conception of Christ and time stands at variance with the classical Christian tradition at so many points, Cullmann's thesis has been severely criticized as overstated. From the standpoint of the classical tradition his view is a radical one, for he defends the claim that the Bible had no sense whatsoever of a nontemporal eternity, that, as a matter of fact, Biblical man thought *only* in terms of a temporal eternity continuous with present temporal process. The oft-encountered "paradox" of time and eternity results, in Cullmann's view, from the illegitimate union of the Biblical idea of time with an idea of eternity drawn from an alien philosophy. There is a scandal connected with Christianity, the scandal that in a particular segment of time the meaning of the whole temporal process is revealed, but this has nothing to do with the "paradox" of the eternal entering time.

In addition, some interpreters see in the views expressed in *Christ and Time* radical implications for traditional doctrines of divine impassibility (the doctrine that God is neither acted upon from without nor emotionally affected) and election (the doctrine that only some are elected to salvation), although Cullmann does not raise either of these questions for discussion. That God's time is also man's time seems to imply that God is not impassible, and the fact that Christ reconciles both history and nature suggests the possibility that *all* men are saved.

DOGMATICS

Author: Emil Brunner (1889-)
Type of work: Systematic theology
First published: Volume I, 1946; Volume II, 1950; Volume III, 1960

Principal Ideas Advanced

The dogmatic task of the Church is to understand the contemporary relevance of the confession, "Thou art the Christ, the Son of the Living God."

Dogmatics is based upon the revelation of God in Christ: God, who by His nature cannot be known, makes Himself known in revelation.

Jesus Christ, as the final revelation of God, is the revelation of God as a person, "The Word became flesh."

God has not permitted any man to be without some knowledge of Himself; a knowledge of God forms part of the creaturely existence of every man.

The world as it has been created by God is the "proper" sphere of natural knowledge, although it too, must be understood "Christologically."

Three volumes of Emil Brunner's *Dogmatik* have appeared. Volume I is entitled *The Christian Doctrine of God (Die christliche Lehre von Gott)*; Volume II, *The Christian Doctrine of Creation and Redemption (Die christliche Lehre von Schöpfung und Erlösung)*; and Volume III, *The Christian Doctrine of the Church, Faith, and Fulfillment (Die christliche Lehre von der Kirche, vom Glauben und von der Vollendung*).

Brunner believes that the Christian Church stands or falls on the basis of the confession, "Jesus Christ, the same yesterday, today, and forever." The revelation of God in Jesus Christ is the central feature of any Christian dogmatic system. Brunner asserts that at all times in history, if faith is to be true and genuine, it must become "contemporary" with Jesus Christ, with His Cross and with His resurrection. The Church, however, can never make the claim that it is identical with revelation; nonetheless, it is a *form* of revelation. It is through this "form" that the Christian Gospel is propagated to the world.

The task of dogmatics is therefore an essential one for the Christian Church in the modern world. Dogmatics is, for Brunner, the fundamental "function" of the Church. The Church must at all times be clear about the content of her message. But dogmatics presupposes the life *within* the Church. Brunner writes, "Dogmatics is itself a function of the Church. Only one who is a genuine 'believer' and, as such, believes in the Church and its teaching, can render to the Church the service which is implied in the idea of dogmatics. The presupposition of dogmatics is not only the existence of the Church and its doctrine, but life *within* the Church, and *in* its doctrine. Dogmatic thinking is not only thinking *about* the Faith, it is *believing* thinking."

Dogmatics points beyond itself to a reality which it cannot contain. Christian dogma deals with God, and God by His very nature is far beyond all human doctrinal conceptions. A doctrine of God, Brunner maintains, cannot be taught, because God is not a "something"; He is not even a "concrete reality." God is, rather, Absolute Subject. Since man is competent to deal only with the world, God stands outside the area in which human knowledge and experience are relevant. How then, asks Brunner, can man come to a knowledge of God, which would be the proper subject matter for dogmatics? The answer is that the knowledge of God exists only in so far as there is a self-disclosure, a self-manifestation of God; that is, only in so far as there is revelation. Brunner writes, "There is a doctrine of God, in the legitimate sense of the words, only in so far as God Himself imparts it. The human doctrine of God—which is undoubtedly the doctrine of the Church—is thus only legitimate, and can only claim to be 'truth,' in so far as the divine revelation—that which God teaches about Himself—is validly expressed by it."

Christian dogma, therefore, is merely a pointer to something outside itself; that is, to the God who is beyond human conception, but who discloses something about Himself. Dogma (dogmatics) and revelation are, for Brunner, categories which are inextricably bound together.

In the New Testament the idea of *revelation* is clearly oriented to the historical event of Jesus Christ. "The Word became flesh" is the central affirmation of the original Christian witnesses in the New Testament period. It is obvious, however, says Brunner, that the "Word" or the "Word of God" has nothing to do with a human conception of a word. Jesus Christ is more than all of the words man can put together regarding Him, His person, or His works. Furthermore, the "Word of

God", the divine self-communication, is in the form of a person, a human being, a man in whom God Himself comes to us and "encounters" us. Revelation has therefore one meaning for the Christian: Emanuel, God with us. In Brunner's words, "It is the same Son of God who in Jesus Christ became man, whom the Prophets discerned dimly from afar; He is the same in whose image man has been created, and in whom lies both the meaning and the foundation of the Creation of the world. It is He who constitutes the secret or manifest centre of all the testimony of Scripture; He it is whom the Word of the Church has to proclaim and to teach, whom the Holy Spirit attests in the heart of the believer, and through whom the 'new man' is created. It is also for that complete revelation at the end of the age that the Church waits, in whom the 'faithful will see God face to face.' "

Revelation, therefore, becomes the key theological category for Brunner; revelation originates with Jesus Christ and only in the light of God's revelation in Christ is it possible for man to know God's creation, and subsequently to know himself as part of God's creation.

The Holy Scriptures testify to the revelation of God in Christ. The Old Testament testifies to this revelation as promise, the New Testament as fulfillment. The New Testament is called the New Covenant for a reason, says Brunner, for it is in the New Testament that God is "with us." When, in the Prologue to the Gospel of John, the author asserts that "The Word became Flesh," he means, argues Brunner, that "He who could only be foretold previously in human language through the speech of the Prophets, is now present in His own Person." The message of the Prologue to John is that Jesus Christ, the Son of God, is the *principle of creation* to which the Old Testament could refer only in the form, "God spoke." The revelation of God in Christ, so Brunner claims, is no longer a provisional, indirect form of speech, a pointer, but the *form* of revelation itself. The word about God is now translated into God himself, who becomes part of the historical setting.

The revelation of God in Christ is never completed, writes Brunner, until it is made manifest in a human life; that is, until a human being knows Jesus to be the Christ. Revelation is objective in the Incarnation of the Son in history, but it is also subjective—in the inner witness of the Spirit to man. Brunner argues that it is important to localize the revelation within man. The divine Spirit confronts the human spirit, and the human spirit responds as it is illuminated by the divine Spirit. This confrontation, Brunner indicates, is a necessary factor in the New Testament conception of the knowledge of God.

Because the "Word became flesh," the story of Jesus had to be told. The New Testament witnesses performed this function, and their report is found in the Four Gospels. But, in addition to this intimate, personal account of the revelation, Brunner writes, there is further need for doctrinal testimony: "It is the task of the doctrinal testimony to make the subject of these deeds and words, of this suffering and victory, visible, which is invisible in the narrative as such. While this is only suggested in the narrative of the Gospels, it comes out clearly in the doctrinal testimony. Just as the narrative moves deliberately, in order to show who He is, and what is His secret, within the sphere of time and space, so the doctrine develops gradually, within the sphere of thought, in order to make the meaning of the mystery clear."

The original confession of faith, which Brunner calls the "Thou" form of faith, is widened into dogmatics where one speaks about God by the use of the term "He." Now, in the development of doctrine, reflective speech *about* God replaces the spontaneous, personal response, which is the most primitive and original witness to the revelation of God in Christ. Dogmatics is therefore concerned primarily with right thinking; as the logical function of the Church, it is concerned to define clearly the teaching of the Church. Dogmatics, however, is necessarily confessional (and Brunner very clearly labels his dogmatics as Reformed), but it must also be related to a truly ecumenical spirit, which believes that the knowledge of divine truth is present in many churches.

The concept of revelation occupies much of Brunner's concern in *Dogmatics.* It is clear for Brunner that God is known only "where He Himself makes Himself known." Apart from this self-manifestation, He is unknowable and therefore remote and inaccessible. God can never be discovered, says Brunner; He can only make Himself known; that is, He gives knowledge of Himself to man.

But even the man to whom God has not made Himself known is not without a certain knowledge of God, Brunner argues. A knowledge of God forms part of the creaturely existence of every man.

The world as it has been created by God can be the proper sphere of natural knowledge. This knowledge, Brunner insists, which is acquired through the senses and the intellect, is not something profane, but sacred knowledge. Brunner writes, "Through the Creator, the world, and the knowledge of the world, are destined for each other. Both are rooted in the Logos of Creation; from it they derive both the objective basis of existence and the subjective basis of knowledge. This Logos of Creation, however, is no other than He who in Jesus Christ became Man and thus revealed to us His secret."

Creation, therefore, for Brunner, is also to be understood "Christologically." All revelation in creation is derived from the Eternal Son (or the Logos). All of the "orders of creation" which became norms of action have been created through the Logos-Son, and are related to His plan and purpose for the world.

The capacity of man to know is an aspect of his being made in "the image of God." Man is distinguished from the rest of creation by the fact that he can "grasp" natural knowledge. This fact, too, gives man a particular dignity and a special destiny. Natural knowledge is, of course, never a final and complete truth, for this truth belongs to God alone, but natural knowledge is a real possibility for modern man. Indeed, Brunner claims, natural knowledge of God's creation is necessary for the achievements of modern civilization and technics.

Brunner does not believe that to affirm that there is natural knowledge in creation permits a natural theology to come into being. It is certain, he says, that the Creator leaves some signs of His Spirit upon His creation. However, one can never deny the reality of sin and its negative effect upon perception.

Sin not only perverts the will; it also "obscures" the power of perceiving truth of the knowledge of God. On the one hand, Brunner insists, the reality of the revelation in creation is to be admitted, but on the other hand, the possibility of a correct and valid natural knowledge of God is to be contested. (In this context, Brunner in his *Dogmatik* refers the reader back to his *Natur und Gnade* where he asserted (a) that the revelation in creation is a reality; (b) that natural theology, as a legitimate possibility, does not exist; (c) that the fact of natural theology as an empirical fact, as something which belongs to the nature of the natural man, is understood in its ambiguity.) Brunner feels that in this way he relates the question of the knowledge of God in creation to anthropology, or to a doctrine of man. He refers to Paul and Romans 1:19ff., and to the fact that man has knowledge of God in creation. Man is, therefore, responsible for his sin and idolatry, even though man has a *distorted* vision of God in creation. Human responsibility is, nevertheless, based upon this general revelation. The quality that makes man "human" is derived from the revelation in creation; that is, from the relation which God established at the very outset between man and his Creator. Responsible existence, that is, the existence of man in contrast to that of every other creature, is his existence as *person.* No sinful man ceases to be a responsible person, for his responsibility as a person, which is grounded in creation, cannot be lost.

THE IDEA OF CHRIST IN THE GOSPELS

Author: George Santayana (1863-1952)
Type of work: Christology
First published: 1946

Principal Ideas Advanced

The Gospels are not historical records but are products of inspiration.

Behind the eschatological figure of the Christ a new and more complete image of man was revealed.

Uniting in His person the divine and the human, Christ marks out the tragic path which man must travel in order to achieve spiritual victory.

Although never an orthodox believer in Roman Catholicism, Santayana maintained all through his life that there is more wisdom in the creeds and precepts of the Roman Catholic Church than in most secular philosophies. His book *The Idea of Christ in the Gospels,* written toward the end of his life, is a devout exposition of this viewpoint. As is indicated by the alternative title, *God in Man,* Santayana maintained that the Christ presented by the authors of the Gospels is first, last, and always, the incarnate Son of

God. The Christ of faith is no mere moralizing teacher; neither is He a god in human disguise. In one person He combines essential divinity with essential humanity; in so doing, He becomes the architect of man's redemption.

There is no point, according to Santayana, in trying to discover in the four Gospels the lineaments of the Jesus of history. The Christ in whom the early Christians trusted was the risen Lord, who dwelt in the hearts of believers by His spirit. Because He was the promised Messiah or Christ, the true meaning of His earthly career was to be found in the Old Testament. Because He lived and reigned at God's right hand, His mercies and ordinances were daily renewed in the experience of the Church. To have known Christ "after the flesh" was no special advantage to missionaries or evangelists who, like inspired preachers of every age, identified themselves so completely with their Master that they freely read their own experience of redemption into every report of Jesus' ministry and teaching that came down to them.

The writers of the four Gospels had no account of Christ to draw from other than that which lived in the faith of the Church, and two of them, at least, were themselves in the living Apostolic tradition. Mark's account is the most lifelike, so much so that it has misled modern critics into thinking that they could there recover the Jesus of history. On the contrary, Mark's portrait of Christ is a powerful image of the Son of God in the flesh, a man leading a "double life." As Mark represents him, Christ has human moods and a human memory and foresight; yet He knows that He is more than human, and the drama of the story arises from the way in which His divinity now conceals and now boldly reveals itself. John's account, on the other hand, emphasizes the inward life of the Son of God and the tensions and paradoxes which result from His dwelling amidst the conditions of sin and death. His humanity is genuine and unethereal, but it is recognizably an instrument for spiritual graces which Heaven seeks to bestow upon earth. The other two Gospels, according to Santayana, are somewhat removed from the living stream of Christian tradition. In the case of Matthew, a didactic purpose has taken the place of the initial impulse to confront men with the image of Christ; Luke seems to have regarded his task as a literary one. Still, the image which they preserve is in conformity with that of the community of believers.

Santayana attributes this common image of Christ to "inspiration," by which he means a perfectly normal activity of man's psyche. Our image of the world, according to Santayana, always includes a large mixture of fancy. But in moments of special inspiration, the psyche "remakes the image of the world, or unmakes it, according to the mood of the soul." External circumstances are sometimes especially propitious to inspiration, but they contribute merely "by stimulating the organism to fuse scattered impressions, to revive and transform forgotten images, to invent, as in dreams, scenes that justify ripening emotions, and to feel affinities or equivalence in apparently disparate things." In themselves, inspirations are neither true nor false, neither helpful nor harmful. They become such when they are adopted as clues for understanding the world, or as goals toward which we must aspire.

The Christian inspiration, according to Santayana, had its origin in the lively Jewish nationalism of the time. The ancient prophetic hope of a political kingdom, to be achieved through the prowess of some future son of David, had given place in the Hellenistic age to apocalyptic dreams of a heavenly Kingdom, which would bring a cataclysmic end to gentile world-rule and establish the rule of God on earth by the hand of a divine Messiah. Exoterically, according to Santayana, the Christian Gospel was simply the claim that, in a cryptic manner, the Messiah had been revealed and that the heavenly Kingdom had begun; the humiliation and death of the Anointed One was part of the terrible drama by which the powers of sin and death must be broken before the new heaven and earth could be manifest. But behind the myth of world-redemption subtler motifs were being worked out. The substitution of a crucified Messiah in the place of a Joshua-style deliverer betokened a fundamental conversion from physical to spiritual goods. At the heart of the Gospel, never entirely lost behind the eschatological symbols, was the conception of a new and higher humanity which, having died to sin, was raised to newness of life in fellowship with Christ. This esoteric strain, which brought consolation to saddened and disillusioned spirits throughout the Roman world, makes the image of Christ in the Gospels, in Santayana's opinion, the soundest ideal that has been offered to humankind. That ideal constitutes a revaluation of values, as Nietzsche said, but, according to Santayana, Nietzsche was wrong in thinking that the ideal subverted the essential human image. On the contrary, the idea of Christ expresses the judgment to which wise and mature men must ever and again return.

What impressed Santayana in the figure of Christ was the degree to which the natural and the spiritual sides of man's nature were rendered compatible within a single image. It was a standing complaint of Santayana against mysticism that it violates the legitimate aspirations of the human spirit; its ecstatic vision of the whole is an impoverished one which, although legitimate, has nothing to recommend it over many other partial ideals. On the other hand, Santayana objected to any ethics which, when worked out to its ultimate conclusions (as, for example, by Marcus Aurelius or Benedict Spinoza), sacrifices everything specifically human and personal to the inexorable laws of nature. Classic Christianity reaffirms the human good, so transfigured as to be both faithful to the Church and compatible with the conditions of man's existence. The Christian ideal is an ascetic ideal, and it enjoins man from much that is instinctive and habitual to the race, but it does this without violating human nature.

What is distinctive of human nature, according to Santayana, is the dualism introduced into animal life by the presence of consciousness. As a physical organism, man is continuous with the material world, but as consciousness, man transcends nature, including his own body, and new worlds of truth and value are opened to his view. The true philosophy must, therefore, embrace a diversity of principles, even at the sacrifice of unity and completeness. But an ultimate pluralism such as Santayana calls for is more congenial to poetry and myth than it is to speculative philosophy and systematic morality. Thus, in Santayana's view, the Hebrew conception of a monarchical deity squares better with the facts of moral life than does the rationalism of the Greeks.

The idea of Christ, combining as it does the divine and the human natures in one person, has, in Santayana's judgment, proved uniquely suggestive of true insights into nature and life. The divine in Christ is for the most part tempered to our understanding. As the Son of God, Christ opens the way for all men to call God "Father"; through His miracles and parables, He exhibits the presence in nature of a kindly, ministering presence; by the victory of His resurrection, He removes the last doubt concerning man's favored place in creation. Still, God is not made over in the human image; there remain hard sayings, arbitrary judgments, acts that from a human point of view are inappropriate and cruel. (For example, the parable of the laborers in the vineyard; the miracle of cursing the barren fig tree.) As revealed in Christ, God's ways remain higher than our ways, and His thoughts higher than our thoughts.

The human nature of Christ, according to Santayana, differed from that of mankind generally in that it was free from ordinary desire (*eros*) and was governed by divine love (*agape*). Christ sought nothing for Himself, but desired the good of every natural thing with the love which the Creator has for His creatures. Such an extension of the affections demanded, however, a profound renunciation of man's normal purposes, the tragic quality of which appears in Christ's agony in the Garden. Charity, when perfect, is the loving submission of man's will to the will of the Heavenly Father. Not merely for Christ, but for all who would be His disciples, divine love demands the way of self-denial and cross-bearing.

According to Santayana, the union in Christ of the divine and the human is a parable of the union of the spiritual and the physical in man. "The Incarnation is the palmary instance of God uniting himself with man at the human level. Yet the whole life and teaching of Christ, and especially his Passion and death, show that this descent was not accomplished for its own sake, as the creation was. It had an ulterior object: the salvation of man, his elevation from the human to the divine level. This demands a tragic transformation in man himself, who must sacrifice his animal will and a great part of his nature in order to assimilate his spirit to that of God. No wonder that mankind is recalcitrant: nor do I think we could blame them if *all* the sweets and *all* the virtues proper to our nature had to be renounced in honestly following Christ. But that is not the case. There is nothing more human or more satisfying than self-transcendence; and the liberation and light that comes of renouncing the will seem, when really attained, the fulfillment, not the surrender, of our inmost powers."

THE SOURCE OF HUMAN GOOD

Author: Henry Nelson Wieman (1884-)
Type of work: Naturalistic theology
First published: 1946

Principal Ideas Advanced

The ultimate reality is a creative event which transforms persons so as to enrich the qualitative meanings of their appreciable world.

The creative event is immediately and fully accessible to man through perception and is open to observation and experiment.

The central creative event is God, and a naturalistic theism can best interpret and make available the resources of the Christian faith.

Henry Nelson Wieman's "naturalistic theism" is one of the most provocative successors to the liberal period in American theology. Wieman's major critical thrusts have been directed against a liberalism which, emphasizing the moral values in Jesus' teaching, tended toward humanism, and also against a Neo-Protestantism which abandoned liberalism on the grounds of divine-human discontinuity and stressed the ambiguous and paradoxical nature of the human situation.

The Source of Human Good contains Wieman's fullest statement. It furnishes the outline of the theological system that has emerged in his other writings. The touchstone of the work is an analysis of value experiences in terms of a "newer naturalism" which takes the basic reality accessible to men as "events, their qualities and relations (structure)." This contextualistic definition is deemed to be the best definition of value as well as the only one sufficient for discussion of matters pertaining to philosophy of religion. Wieman also contends that such an analysis of value is more consonant with the Jewish Christian stress upon divine creativity in history as opposed to the Greek Christian emphasis of transcendental form.

Rejecting interpretations of value as goods, as satisfaction, as quality, or as human control, Wieman focuses on "qualitative meaning," defined as "that connection between events whereby present happenings enable me to feel not only the quality intrinsic to the events now occurring but also the qualities of many other events that are related to them." This is "created good," and it depends upon a prior "creative good."

The "creative event," Wieman's process-synonym for creative good, may be analyzed empirically into four classes of subevents (also processes): (1) the "emergings" of the awareness of qualitative meaning communicated from another organism; (2) the "integratings" with previous meanings, usually done in solitude; (3) the "expandings" of qualities and possibilities of the appreciable world; and (4) the "deepenings" of community based upon previous subevents.

Creative good, thus defined, may be distinguished from both instrumental and intrinsic good, although it contains elements of both. The most significant element for Wieman is the dialectic between creative and created good. Whenever the latter has emerged there is the danger that men will hold it to be final. When this is done, it becomes "demonic," blocking and excluding further creativity. In similar fashion, qualitative meaning can erroneously be preferred to its source in the creative event.

For new goods to emerge, continual transformations of the organism are required. The danger in religion is that it tries to conserve previous structures of transformation at the price of precluding future ones. Our contemporary situation, dominated by science and technology, is releasing vast new human powers. These will destroy us unless they can be guided to increase the growth of creative good. Wieman argues that current religious attacks on "reason" move in precisely the opposite direction, one "fatal to man in the days of his power."

Were any religious revelation to transcend reason, as is often asserted, it would be indistinguishable from its opposite. A similar problem arises from religious appeals to an "eternal" reality, in that we are thrust back into the temporal realm helpless to find creativity there.

The proper source of human devotion is the creative event, working in history and accessible to empirical analysis. Such was the originating event of Christian faith. The fellowship around Jesus of Nazareth experienced transformations characteristic of the creative event. Jesus' death ended the possibility of interpreting these transformations in traditional Jewish terms. Subsequent experiences of continuing transformation led the disciples to speak of "resurrection," but, Wieman writes, "what rose from the dead was not the man Jesus; it was creative power."

"Faith" is therefore an act rather than a belief. It presupposes fellowship with men of faith, and dissatisfaction with present purposes. It is characterized by the giving of the self to that which will creatively transform the self. The only "authority" of any religious teaching is the evidence, produced by inquiry, that the teaching can sustain creative changes.

The creative event, which operates in history, is also operative at the subhuman level, Wieman claims. Evolution depends upon increasing sensitivity and diversified responsiveness. The price of specialized protective mechanisms has been degeneration.

Of even greater importance is the supra-human quality of the creative event which "cannot be caused by human intention and effort, because it can be produced only by a transformation of human intention and effort." Previous mythologies, for this reason, have often described the creative event as "supernatural." Since it is not beyond all our appreciation, however, the creative event is best treated as a part of the "temporal, spatial, material world."

Creative good may be regarded as "absolute good" in that it is not relative to human desire; its demands are unlimited; its value is infinite; it is unqualified by any perspective; and it is "entirely trustworthy." It must not, however, be termed all-powerful.

Events which negate created good are characterized by Wieman as "destructive" evils, while opposition to creative good is termed "obstructive" evil. This second form is absolute in that it is universal, unqualified, ultimate, and unconfined. Neo-orthodoxy is criticized at this point for its historical pessimism (which overlooks the increase of qualitative meaning in the evolution of life) and for its ultimate romanticism (based on the "overbelief" in an ultimately all-powerful goodness).

Pain and suffering are to be distinguished in that suffering is a meaningful, communicable event. It is inevitably related to increases in qualitative meaning. Emotional maturity is precisely the willingness to incur suffering in order that creative good may emerge. The mature man does not seek suffering, but he recognizes it as the concomitant of transformation.

Certain evils are rooted in the nature of things. One is "inertia," which Wieman describes as "insensitivity and resistance to creativity." The most serious modern form is that "tolerance" which has characterized much of secular and religious liberalism. A person's ultimate commitments are arbitrary and trivial if they are simply determined by birth; that is, by class or national or religious origin. There is a sovereign, absolute goodness, which may be demonstrated "rationally and empirically." Unless this is done, our increasing control over nature simply aggravates our sense of futility.

A second class of natural evils is composed of the "protective hierarchies" of sensitivity, prestige, control, and intimidation. These are necessary, but subject to change. "Progress" in history may be measured by the widening of the upper levels of the hierarchies accompanied by increased communication, apprehension, and integration.

A third class of evils is more specifically human. "Sin," for instance, Wieman writes, is "any resistance to creativity for which man is responsible." Like creativity, it is always social. It is not always the result of pride; sometimes it grows from a prideless frivolity.

The second half of the book illustrates the general thesis by examining specific values. "Beauty" is similar to qualitative meaning, but it operates within a sharply delimited whole. Aesthetic form stresses the quality of events. It cannot, and does not, point "beyond existence," although the richness of qualities is often such as to evoke this claim. Folklore and myth convey these qualities which are determinant of history.

Our difficulty lies in the maladjustment of our two cultural structures. The traditional matrix which in medieval times could sustain rich communication through aesthetic and other noncognitive forms is increasingly unable to sustain intercommunication within the supertechnological matrix. An effective "proletarian art" is needed to guide industrial workers toward the good inherent in the new technology and to enable them to avert its evils.

Tragedy is the contrast between the actual and the possible, a contrast from which creativity may spring. Art can mediate this to us symbolically in many cases where a direct encounter would be more than we could survive. The Cross of Christ is such a symbol.

Art also supplements our quest for truth by reminding us of the qualitative richness of events that is always sacrificed in our drives toward clarity and precision.

Truth cannot be the goal of life since life rests on value. Wieman defines truth as "any specifiable structure pertaining to events and their possibilities." Truth is infinite since the totality of all structures is infinite. "Knowledge" is "structures specified." Our knowledge of truth rests initially upon our "noncognitive feeling-reactions." Western thought has impoverished itself, Wieman claims, when it has tried to depart from its feeling-matrix. Our intellects move more comfortably among "linguistic events" rather than "heavy events," but both must be preserved. Prophetic Judaism emphasized those rich structures which give value to our lives. Much of our religion, however, has reflected the partiality of the Greeks toward clarity of form.

"Heavy events," so often depicted mythologically, remain only possibilities until "observation and experiment" have rendered them actualities. A proper analysis of the perceptual event furnishes us with all the necessary metaphysical categories. "Mind" is meanings as "generated, communicated, and received by an organism." "Intuition" is simply a dramatic instance. "Mystical experience" is simply a form of intuition.

Knowledge is related by Wieman to human cultural development and to linguistic structures. But since certain basic meaning-structures characterize the world of the human organism, his epistemology is not a complete relativism. Both "mind" and "world" are ultimately determined by the creative event. The knowledge of the sciences supplements rather than supplants common sense, and "religious knowledge" is a branch of philosophical knowledge. The teachings of Jesus, for instance, do not represent any special knowledge. Instead, Wieman writes, "the total impact of events gives power to the teachings." All knowledge is certified by the same tests: observation, agreement between observers, and coherence.

Morality is conduct guided by principles which facilitate creative interchange. This is "obligatory," Wieman insists, in that "we cannot continue to be human if we do not act morally." Modern men cannot hope to eliminate all barriers to communication between cultures and specialists. We can, however, all discuss the creative event since it concerns each of us.

Sexuality functions pre-eminently in rendering us capable of indefinite transformations by the creative event. Recognizing this, an adequate sexual morality will be constructive and point us toward creativity.

"Christian love," which embraces that which is hostile, is possible only for the unselfish person. It retains a certain mutuality, however, in that it expands the appreciable world of the lover.

A society is "just," Wieman writes, when each member may seek and find "what he most needs for the creativity of life." Love increases the dynamic toward such a society. Our need for restoration and our despair over the limits and failures of our own righteousness point us toward religion.

Western man has no effective alternative to the Judaeo-Christian religion, Wieman believes. The "Christian myth" in the past has functioned to turn men away from lesser, created goods, and toward the source of good. Myth "known to be myth," however, loses its power unless its representations can be established as actualities. Wieman reinterprets the metaphysically transcendent Christian level in functionally transcendent terms as the creative event. Only psychologically may this God be understood as "personal." Theologically, Christianity has proffered a "revelation of God, forgiveness of sin, and the salvation of man—these all by way of Jesus Christ." Interpreting nature from the standpoint of the creative event, we may discern its three "triumphs" to date: the living cell, man, the living Christ. Subsequent transformations are anticipated in eschatological mythology.

To worship is to practice ritual which, Wieman says, "loosens the coercive grip of fears and desires" obstructing the creative event. The main duty of the Church is to demand those human relations which release this power.

The major influences upon Wieman's thinking have been Henri Bergson (1859-1941), John Dewey (1859-1952), and Alfred North Whitehead (1861-1947). He sees naturalism as affording the best method for interpreting the central realities of Christianity to a modern world. Wieman's ideas are theistic in the sense that he believes that the creative event is a determinant of man rather than that it is determined by man, and that in this sense man is incapable of foreseeing the structures of the future. God, so described, is the proper name for that creativity which is the dynamic part of reality.

THE DIVINE RELATIVITY

Author: Charles Hartshorne (1897-)
Type of work: Metaphysics, theology
First published: 1948

Principal Ideas Advanced

Classical theology affirmed that although God is absolute, He causes, knows, and loves His creation; such a doctrine is obviously self-contradictory since to know or to love is to be related and thus not to be absolute.

Contradiction can be avoided by distinguishing between those aspects of God which are relative and those aspects which are absolute.

A God who is relative is required by both metaphysics and religion, whereas a God who is absolute in every respect is compatible with neither.

A relation between two things can be internal to one and external to the other; hence such a relation relativizes the first and leaves the second absolute.

Charles Hartshorne, author of *The Divine Relativity,* stands firmly within the classical metaphysical tradition at least in one sense. He is one of the few contemporary philosophers who still find compelling cosmological and ontological arguments for the existence of God. He holds that the existence of God can be rationally demonstrated either by proceeding from the nature of the world to a necessary Creator or by proceeding from the definition of what it is to be God.

In another sense, however, Hartshorne is not within the classical tradition; his metaphysical ideas follow closely those of Alfred North Whitehead (1861-1947) and not those of past Western metaphysicians. Hartshorne, following Whitehead and others, conceives of reality as social (not individual) and in terms of process (not static substance). So-called "individual" entities are not simple, independent substances; they are processes which are intimately interrelated with other processes. Stated simply, all that anyone meets or has met is really part of him. He is a spatio-temporal process, made up of all of the relations which he has with other things including his own past. He is an ever-changing personal process, ever growing by the addition of new experiences and relationships which literally alter his being so that it constantly becomes something new.

All reality is social process, undergoing constant change and growth; hence, God, who is the all-inclusive reality, is also a growing social process. God, then, cannot be described in an unqualified way as immutable, simple, or absolute, for, in Hartshorne's terms, God is supreme *yet indebted to all,* absolute *yet related to all.* In short, God is divinely relative. The major claim in this book, originally presented in the form of lectures delivered at Yale University as the twenty-fourth series of Terry Lectures, is that it is both possible and necessary to describe God as *divine* (that is, as absolute and supreme), but also as *related* (involved in relativity).

Classical metaphysics and theology mistakenly maintained that God is purely absolute, nonrelative in every respect. God was said to be timeless, changeless, related only to His own self and therefore not really related to His creatures, and gaining nothing from His creatures. However, it was also claimed, inconsistently, that God is Creator, and that He knows and loves the creatures that He has made. Theology certainly affirmed this, and so did metaphysics inasmuch as metaphysics used as its basic argument for the existence of God the argument that God is first cause.

Hartshorne observes that it is an intolerable contradiction to assert both that God is related and that He is absolute and hence not related in any respect. If it is said that God creates, then it must be admitted that God is related; if it is said that God loves, then it must be admitted that God is related to and receives from the objects of His love; if God really knows, then God is really related; and a God who is really related cannot be absolute in every respect. Hartshorne analyzes some of the ways in which the classical tradition attempted to evade this dilemma and he concludes that the attempt failed.

It is Hartshorne's contention that the doctrine of God can be stated in such a way as to avoid this self-contradiction by distinguishing those aspects of God by which He is absolute from those aspects by which He is relative. There is no contradiction in holding that God is both absolute and relative, provided that these contraries are applied to different aspects of God. As to the relation which holds between these aspects, "the main thesis . . . is that the 'relative' or changeable, that which depends upon and varies with varying relationships, includes within itself and in value exceeds the non-relative, immutable, independent, or 'absolute,' *as the concrete includes and exceeds the abstract.* From this doctrine . . . it follows that God, as supremely excellent and concrete, must be conceived not as wholly absolute or immutable, but rather as supremely-relative, 'surrelative,' although, or because of this superior relativity, containing an abstract character or essence in respect to which, but only in respect to which, he is indeed strictly absolute and immutable."

Chapter 1 develops the notion of God as relative, presenting the case, both metaphysical and religious, for a God who is all-inclusive, supremely relative, indebted to and enriched by all. Chapter 2 shows that a related God is also absolute and shows what the relation between relativity and absoluteness in God is. Chapter 3 discusses the attributes of God, particularly the attributes of omniscience, omnipotence, and goodness, showing exactly in what way both relativity and absoluteness must be specified with respect to each of these, and concludes with an account of the beneficial consequences which would flow from a notion of divine relativity.

A conception of God as both absolute and relative is both logically sound and metaphysically necessary according to Hartshorne. In three earlier works, *Beyond Humanism* (1937), *Man's Vision of God* (1941), and *Reality as Social Process* (1953)—the latter composed of articles most of which were written before 1948—Hartshorne presents his full metaphysical argument, and much of this groundwork is presupposed in *The Divine Relativity.* In all these books Hartshorne tries to show that modern metaphysical theory requires the existence of God, the sort of God who is Himself the supreme exemplification of the categories of metaphysics, and who Himself, while involved in process, exists necessarily and persists eternally in time. Many arguments are presented, including forms of the cosmological and ontological arguments, which take into account developments in modern metaphysics and which prove the existence of a God who is Himself a being in process rather than the timeless absolute being of classical metaphysics.

But more than metaphysics is at stake, Hartshorne argues, for the moral and religious needs of mankind can be satisfied only by a God who is related and who includes within Himself all value. Morality and religion both demand an ultimate value which is unrestrictedly worthy of worship, and thus a value which contains all value and which is unrestrictedly good in its own actions, always working for good. Such a God, because He literally includes all actual values, is enriched as new values and combinations of value are added to His experience; hence He is a God who is really served by man. Classical theology, however, Hartshorne observes, could not allow that God be served. To allow this would be to admit that God profits from something outside Himself and, hence, is not in all respects absolute. But if creation added nothing to God, added nothing to the fullness of His value, it could not be said that creation was a good. Only if creation *adds* to value can it be a good. God must profit from creation and from everything which takes place within it. Such a God can be served by men and can satisfy their moral and religious longings.

God is perfection, but He is self-surpassing or growing perfection; God is the greatest conceivable being, but He is able to surpass His present states as He grows into richer, fuller states. God is the greatest conceivable being because only God includes all value, but God can surpass His own present state by creating and including more values, by bringing novel values and richer relationships among values into existence and including them in future states of His being. As men create richer social orders, as artists create and share new art works and forms, as human sensitivities are increased, new values come into existence and the state of God which includes those values surpasses the state of God before those values were actual.

What does it mean, after all, to say that something is good, or what does it mean to say that something is better than something else? Hartshorne argues that higher levels of existence, such as the level of human existence, are said to be higher levels because such beings as men are more related, more sensitive to other things, more dependent upon other things, than are lower forms of existence. A stone is "impassible," but a person receives richly from other things. God as highest or best or supreme being is, then, the maximal case of dependence. Classical theology made the word "best" mean the absolutely independent and unrelated, but it is not at all clear that the independent is what is really best. Rather, that which is maximally related, related to and considerate of all values, is best.

Hartshorne's central claim is supported by typical analogies used in religion. To speak of God as "father" is to use a social analogy to describe the nature of God, an analogy which suggests that just as a human father is related to his children, so God is related to His, the difference being that God is a perfect Father and His relationships to all creation are much more intimate and rich. It would be an equivocation, not an analogy, to say God is a father *but* one who is absolutely independent of His children, one who neither knows nor loves His children. To be a father is to love, to enjoy, and to share. Classical theology equivocates in affirming that God is Father but denying that He is related to His children.

One must begin first with the notion of God as social being, as love, intimately related to all, and only then ask about the ways in which such a being can be absolute. An "immutable" *person* is a person who is not subject to death or degeneration and who is not vacillating because of fear or weakness; he is not unchanging in every respect. A *person* who exists necessarily is a being who persists endlessly in time and cannot not exist, yet as a person he may change in some respects and hence in those respects be contingent, not necessary. A being that is absolute in all respects cannot be related, but a being who is related can still be absolute.

The idea that God is supreme, yet indebted to all, and that God is Absolute, yet related to all, is in marked contrast to the ideas of classical theology and humanism. Classical theology drew the conclusion that God is the Absolute Being who is related to and indebted to none. Humanism has maintained that because all being is related to and indebted to other things there is no absolute. Both are wrong, for a being can be related to all yet be in some respects absolute.

The classical view, in its way of conceiving of the eminence of God, the perfection of God, was one-sided. It affirmed perfection of only one of equally legitimate opposites. Similarly, modern views as a rule are one-sided, affirming only the alternative one of each pair of opposites. Hartshorne affirms both in each case. Classical thought conceived God as eminently absolute; Hartshorne adds eminent relativity; to eminent permanence he adds eminent change; to eminent simplicity he adds eminent complexity; to eminent activity he adds eminent passivity (God is not merely cause; He is also effect). In each pair it is the term which emphasizes relativity which must be stressed as the more significant, for what is relative is the fullness of God, while what is absolute is merely His abstract essence.

A basic distinction, Hartshorne claims, can save the doctrine of God from internal self-contradiction. In *essence,* in terms of His kind of being, God is absolute; in *actuality,* in terms of His concrete actual being, God is relative. For example, all instances of knowing share an abstract essence, but this abstract essence is not itself an instance of knowing, just as twoness is not itself a pair. The abstract characteristic by means of which one defines instances of knowing is absolute and independent, even though every concrete being which embodies this characteristic is relative and dependent. Similarly, then, it can be said that God in essence is abstract and independent, whereas in concrete being, as an instance of Godness, He is relative.

In a knowing relation, such as a subject-object relation, the object is absolute, the subject relative. God as object of all subjects is absolute; God as subject of all objects is maximally relative.

Similar observations hold with respect to the cause-effect relationship. A cause is absolute and independent, whereas its effect is relative and dependent. God as first cause, then, is absolute; God as effect, God as including all that is, is maximally relative.

In His completeness, God is the divine relativity, for the relative includes the absolute as a mere aspect of the relative, just as an actual entity includes its essence, as a knower includes the known, as the concrete includes the abstract, as a whole includes its parts, and as an effect includes its cause. In each of these cases a relation is specified which is internal to (that is, relativizes) the first, but external to (that is, leaves absolute) the second. Such a solution of the problem of God, then, is intimately related to the problem of relations and occupies a great deal of Hartshorne's discussion. He argues that since relations can be external to one term and internal to the other, this solution to the problem of God is possible, for externality is absoluteness, and internality is relativity.

God exists necessarily, Hartshorne claims; He knows all and does all that is possible to do consistent with His nature; He loves all things literally and knows all things fully, whereas men neither love nor do anything fully. God is above the battle, independent in the sense that nothing that happens can threaten His being, for He necessarily exists. Because God includes and harmonizes all value, past and present, nothing can take place which would destroy the divine blessedness. God experiences tragedy (as He must if He really loves and enters into the experience of his creatures), but tragedy cannot overwhelm Him. In all these respects God is metaphysically different from all other beings. God *is Supreme, yet indebted to all; Absolute, yet related to all.* By means of a logical distinction and a conception of reality as social process Hartshorne is able to provide a God who is both metaphysically necessary and religiously satisfactory.

GOD WAS IN CHRIST

Author: Donald M. Baillie (1887-1954)
Type of work: Christology
First published: 1948

Principal Ideas Advanced

Traditional understandings of Christ tend to undercut the humanity of Jesus; modern Christological thinkers, while recognizing His humanity, tend to make it irrelevant.

The dogma of the God-man is a confession based on Christian experience; consequently, the clue to the meaning of this paradox is the experience of the paradox of grace.

Jesus is the Incarnation of God, for in every moment His self-consciousness was sacrificed to the will of God and was dependent always on divine grace.

The doctrine of the Trinity is the confession that the union of Jesus with God is available after Jesus' death through the Divine Spirit: the doctrine of the atonement is the declaration that forgiveness is costly for God, occurring within the divine life itself.

Three basic creeds which were forged during the formative days of Christianity have served almost every major strand of Christianity as theological guidelines. These are the Apostles' Creed (developed from c.160 to c.650), the Nicene Creed (325), and the Chalcedonian Creed (451). These creeds have been of central importance not because of the depth of their theological penetration into major doctrines of faith, but because of their utility as channel markers for theological reflection concerning the essence of Christianity.

Despite its usefulness, the Chalcedonian Creed in particular has been the cause of perennial dissatisfaction. Few theologians will question the worthy intent of its formulators in insisting upon Jesus Christ as "fully God and fully man." Yet, in trying to give meaning to this confession of faith, the resulting creed bristles with many statements which are either contradictory or meaningless for faith.

Most difficult of all is the declaration that Christ was "made known in two natures, inconfusedly, immutably, indivisibly, inseparably, the differences of the natures by no means annulled through the union, but rather the peculiarity of each nature being preserved and concurring into one person and one substantial individual, not divided or separated into two persons, but one self-same and only Son. . . ." The difficulty here is not simply linguistic; it goes far deeper, for such a statement rests heavily on a Greek metaphysical understanding that is little accepted or understood today.

In nineteenth century liberal Protestant theology there were many attempts to make the person of Christ understandable, but almost always in a manner that sacrificed Christ's uniqueness for his "perfect humanity." Donald M. Baillie's *God Was In Christ* is thus perhaps one of the most important works in contemporary Christology, for in a manner both original and suggestive Baillie attempts to give meaning to the orthodox Chalcedonian understanding. His approach is an attempt to mediate the truths of liberalism and neo-orthodoxy.

For Baillie, the attempt by nineteenth century theologians to recover the historical Jesus helpfully countered the tendency from the beginning of Christian thought toward Doceticism; that is, the view that Jesus is fully divine, although He appears to be human. There can be no denying the humanity of Jesus. The Bible clearly witnesses to the fact that since Jesus was human, His knowledge was limited; His miracles were possibly only through the power of God, a power available to every man; He had temptations that were real struggles; He prayed to God as would any other religious human being.

Contemporary theologians have accepted the unqualified humanity of Jesus without question, certain theologians even declaring that, historically regarded, Jesus was not even a remarkable man. Such an awareness of the humanity of Jesus is regarded by Baillie as a real gain, but many theologians render Christ's humanity irrelevant by contending that Jesus is the Christ, not through His humanity, but in spite of it. The "Jesus of history" thus takes second place to the "Christ of faith." Thus the Resurrection becomes the revelation of the divinity of Christ. Protestant theologian Karl Barth, for example, insists that we know no more about God through Christ than was known through the Old Testament; we know through Him only that the promise of God has been fulfilled. Baillie's task, consequently, becomes that of showing how, *in* and *through* His humanity, Jesus was "the very life of God Himself." If God's nature is not revealed in Jesus, there is no meaning to the affirmation that God became man.

Much of the loss of interest in the historical Jesus stems from the position fostered by form criticism, which holds that the historical Jesus cannot be known because Scripture is the creation of the faith of the early Church rather than an objective account of the historical Jesus. The mistake such thinkers make, according to Baillie, is the mistake of forgetting that "the story may have been handed on simply or primarily *because it was true,* because the incident had actually taken place in the ministry of Jesus. . . ." The quest for the historical Jesus becomes impossible only for those who radically prejudge Scripture from their own perspectives. Such persons refuse to admit that the Biblical writers were probably interested in reporting everything Jesus said and did; Scriptural interpretation may very well be more the effect of selection than of imagination.

Yet Baillie is fighting not only against those "who wish to sacrifice the Jesus of history to a high Christology," but also against "those who wish to sacrifice Christology to the Jesus of history." It is not sufficient to say with the liberals that Jesus is the climax of man's search for God, nor even that He is "the living Way, through whom alone we can surely come to the Father." The neo-orthodox have rightly seen that the God "discovered" by Jesus is the God who acts, who seeks His creatures before they seek Him. If we are to believe what Jesus tells us of God, "we must pass beyond words like 'discovery' and even 'revelation' to words like 'incarnation.' " The idea of the Incarnation is the only idea by which the Christian understanding of God becomes either credible or expressible. The center of Baillie's insistence is that "a true Christology will tell us not simply that God is *like* Christ, but that God was *in* Christ. Thus it will tell us not only about the *nature* of God, but about His *activity*. . . ." Theology, as Baillie insists, must be Christology, for the New Testament writers regarded every act that Jesus did as an act of God.

Quite clearly, the Incarnation is a paradox, but it becomes a contradiction unless restated in the language of each generation. The creeds are only signposts against heresy; the meaning of their affirmations must be thought out in every age. There are three lines of Christological thinking in modern theology. The anhypostasia understanding maintains that Christ is a divine Person who assumed human nature without assuming human personality. The kenotic theory holds that the Second Person of the Trinity laid aside His distinctively divine attributes and lived on earth within the limits of humanity. Both of these explanations Baillie finds unacceptable, for in each case the humanity of Jesus is undermined. Finally, Karl Heim's highly original understanding of Christ in terms of the political category of "Leader" (Führer) is rejected by Baillie as avoiding the Christological question altogether.

Baillie's attempt at a new approach to the problem begins with the assertion that the only justification for and reconciliation of paradox is experience. The experience which is the heart of Christian life is thus the illuminating clue to the Incarnation. This clue is the experience of grace. (Here Baillie shows the influence of Augustinian thought.) The Christian experiences all good things to be the product of God, and yet human action is never more truly personal, responsible, and free than when the divine foundation of all is affirmed. The key paradox of Christian experience is the lived truth stated by St. Paul: "I laboured more abundantly than you all; yet not I, but the grace of God which was with me."

There is no boundary that can be drawn between God's work and our own; both sides of the paradox of grace must be affirmed. Nor can the boundary be drawn in Jesus' case; He claimed nothing for Himself. "I, . . . yet not I, but the Father." Jesus' sinlessness consisted in denouncing all claim to ethical heroism, in throwing

Himself totally on God's grace. He attempted to bring others into His own close union with God, into a life in which self-consciousness is swallowed up in God-consciousness. The Fourth Gospel states boldly that all Christ's people should achieve the same kind of unity with God as did Jesus. Jesus' choices were human choices, but like all human choices they were dependent upon God's grace. It was because what Jesus did was always pleasing to God that this prevenience of grace "was nothing short of Incarnation. . . ."

Is this simply to say that any perfect man would be God Incarnate? For Baillie, to ask such a question is to take a far too optimistic view of human nature; it is not to take divine prevenience seriously. "When we really accept the paradox of grace, when we really believe that every good thing in a man is wrought by God . . . and have taken that divine priority in earnest, the question loses its meaning, and . . . fades away into the paradox of the Incarnation."

Such a view of Incarnation, Baillie insists, sheds light on the related doctrine of the Trinity. In Jesus Christ human selfhood came fully to its own because it was wholly yielded to God. Thus Jesus' life *was* the life of God; the initiative was always God's. After His death, Christ's divine presence returned. It was "independent of His actual presence in the flesh, though not independent of His *having* lived on earth in the flesh." Christ now drew believers into His union with God, even those who had not known Him in the flesh. This experience was interpreted as the "era of the Holy Spirit"; it provides the experiential basis for the doctrine of the Trinity.

Throughout history, God was continually pressing through into human life. But He became incarnate only when at last a man was perfectly receptive. The Father's love for the Son was conditional on Jesus' fulfilling His vocation as "Son." When the Christian speaks of the "pre-existent Son," Baillie declares, he does not refer to Jesus of Nazareth but to the divine priority in the total life of Jesus.

Likewise, the meaning of the ascension must be taken radically. "If we believe in the Incarnation, we cannot possibly say that Jesus ceased to be human when He departed from this world." This means that the divine presence that came into the world in Jesus continues through the Holy Spirit to dwell in us. Our knowledge of God is not like Christ's knowledge, but it is dependent on that knowledge.

Baillie's understanding of the atonement is developed by the same method as that which led to an understanding of the Incarnation. Through an analysis of human experience, Baillie attempts to show that moral failure, disobedience of conscience, is at the heart of psychic disorder and is something concerning which the individual himself is powerless. Sin is self-centeredness, the refusal of divine and human community; it is an absorption in oneself which kills true individuality and destroys the soul. Such a self cannot change itself, for the more it tries, the more its concentration is focused on the self. Divine forgiveness is the only possible instrument for fulfilled existence.

Yet divine forgiveness is impossible without atonement, for there is a great difference between "a good-natured indulgence and a costly reconciliation." Neither God nor man can be moral and still take sin lightly. Since sin is disloyalty to God, such "ultimate betrayal" can be rectified only by divine action. The atonement is God's act, and its meaning is that forgiveness takes place "in the very heart and life of God. . . ." Divine forgiveness involves Divine suffering. Such Divine forgiveness is not the result of the Crucifixion; the Crucifixion occurred because God loved the world. The love which led Jesus to the cross is the love of God Himself coming to man in Christ.

Yet divine sin-bearing is not confined to the moment of Crucifixion, for God "has a direct 'vertical' relation to each moment. . . ." The Cross "is actually a part (the incarnate part) of the eternal divine sin-bearing." There has never been an age when God was not carrying the sins of His people and thus making atonement and offering forgiveness.

THEOLOGY OF THE NEW TESTAMENT

Author: Rudolf Bultmann (1884-)
Type of work: Exegesis of the New Testament
First published: 1948-1953 (3 fascicles)

Principal Ideas Advanced

Faith is man's response to the Word of God that encounters him in the Church's kerygma, which proclaims the crucified and risen Christ to be God's eschatological act of salvation.

Theology is the unfolding of the thoughts of faith; it is necessarily existential in character, since the Christian's new understanding of God, the world, and man involves inseparably a new understanding of himself in his concrete existence.

New Testament theology is the scientific endeavor to set forth the thoughts of faith found in the New Testament writings.

The message of Jesus is a presupposition for, rather than a part of, the theology of the New Testament.

The theologies of Paul and John form the center and apex of theological interpretation in the New Testament; within the framework of Hellenistic Christianity they historicize the Jewish apocalyptic eschatology of the earliest Church, so that the eschatological occurrence of salvation is interpreted in existential-human categories rather than natural-cosmic categories; in the later development toward the ancient Church the eschatological tension is relaxed, and the Church more and more conceives of itself as a sacramental institution of salvation.

The publication in Germany of *Theologie des Neuen Testaments* marked the crowning achievement of one of the truly creative and challenging theologians of the twentieth century. The author was Rudolf Bultmann, Professor of New Testament Studies at the University of Marburg from 1921 to 1951. His work combines rigorous historico-critical analysis with a passionate desire to interpret Christian faith in a way meaningful for modern man. Bultmann is firmly grounded in the research into early Christianity conducted by the "history-of-religious school," and he became one of the first New Testament scholars to apply the historical method of "form criticism" to the material of the Synoptic Gospels. Moreover, Bultmann joined Karl Barth in repudiating the anthropological basis of "liberal theology" in favor of a "dialectical theology" that recognized what Søren Kierkegaard (1813-1855) had called "the infinite qualitative distinction between time and eternity." Fruitful study of the philosophy of the early Martin Heidegger, which is strongly oriented on Kierkegaard, led Bultmann to call for an existentialistic interpretation of the New Testament texts; finally, he instituted his controversial program of demythologizing the proclamation of the New Testament. In his work, mythological concepts are interpreted according to the self-understanding which is operative in them. In this way Bultmann intends to carry through the Pauline-Lutheran doctrine of justification in the realm of knowledge.

In his *Theology of the New Testament* the author attempts to set forth the theological thoughts of the New Testament writings, not in a systematically ordered unity but in their variety, by indicating the locus of each in the historical development of the early Church. In opposition to orthodoxy's method of collecting Biblical quotations to confirm dogmatic propositions, as well as to rationalism's method of formulating concepts of doctrine in accordance with rational truth, Bultmann explicates theological thoughts in their connection with the "act of living"; that is, he regards theological ideas as expressions of faith's self-understanding in response to the kerygma (proclamation) as God's personal word spoken to man in his concrete situation. Because of this inevitable involvement of the believer's self-understanding, the theological task of unfolding the understanding of God, the world, and man, a task which arises from faith, can never be accomplished once and for all, but requires ever-repeated solutions.

Bultmann has divided his work into three parts: (1) "Presuppositions and Motifs of New Testament Theology," (2) "The Theologies of Paul and John," and (3) "The Development toward the Ancient Church." The second part is the central and most detailed part of the book, and it is considered to contain the most profound understanding of Christian faith available in the New Testament. Parts One and Three present, respectively, a progression toward and a regression from the outstanding theological achievements of Paul and John.

In sharp contrast to "liberal" interpretations, Bultmann boldly affirms that "the message of Jesus is a presupposition for the theology of the New Testament rather than a part of that theology itself." If theology is an unfolding of the thoughts of faith, and if faith is response to the Christian kerygma, and if the kerygma proclaims the crucified and risen Christ to be God's eschatological act of salvation, then Bultmann's affirmation is a logical conclusion. Jesus' eschatological message of the imminent inbreaking of the reign of God, and His call for decision between God and "the world" sets the stage, as it were, for God's saving act; but faith affirms Jesus and His coming. His crucifixion and resurrection are to be the saving event. He who was *bearer* of a message became the essential *content* of the message of the early Church.

The earliest Church, however, conceived Jesus as the *coming* Messiah, the "Son of Man" whose impending advent would bring an end to world history and inaugurate the perfect reign of God. The "end of days" was near, and the Church believed itself to be the "eschatological congregation" which would finally be saved. The Easter faith declared the crucified Jesus of Nazareth to be the Messiah who will come, and in this sense there is attributed to Him a power to determine the present. All of this, of course, remains within the context of Jewish eschatological expectation, with its apocalyptic picture of the future.

The Jewish Christianity represented by the earliest Church in Palestine presupposed an understanding of the history of salvation embodied in the Old Testament-Judaic tradition, with its emphasis on the centrality of the Law for the People of God. When Christianity, under the impetus of the missionary movement, moved into the Hellenistic (Greek) world, it inevitably met with difficulties that forced the transformation of the form of its proclamation. First, there was the difficulty that arose from Hellenistic Christianity's acknowledgment of the authority of the Old Testament, while at the same time denying the validity of the Old Testament Law for Christians. Thus, Christians were brought into conflict with the Jews of the Hellenistic synagogues. A second difficulty emerged in the problem of communicating the kerygma in the Hellenistic cultural and religious milieu, with its popular Greek philosophies, its mystery religions, and its Gnostic myths of salvation.

Bultmann contends that pre-Pauline Christianity is by no means a unity, so that there were various solutions to the above-named difficulties. Christian preaching in the Gentile world could not have been simply Christological; it had to begin with the proclamation of the one God, who is both Creator and Judge of a world which has fallen into the sin of idolatry. However, beside God, or even in His place, Jesus Christ appears as God's plenipotent representative who will judge the world and save those who belong to the Congregation of the faithful. This eschatological Judge and Savior is none other than the *crucified* Jesus of Nazareth whom God raised from the dead and exalted to his eschatological role at the time when the dead shall be raised for judgment. Indeed, Bultmann declares that first in Hellenistic Christianity is Jesus Christ (now a proper name) given the title "Lord" and decreed worthy of cultic worship. In addition, the title "Son of God," which for the earliest Church denoted the Messianic king, came to mean in Hellenistic Christianity the divinity of Christ, by virtue of which He is differentiated from the human sphere. Christ is now the pre-existent Son of God who became man, the "Logos" or "Word" who was also the agent of creation. The terminology of the mystery religions, with their dying and rising "divinities," and that of Gnosticism, with its mythological figure of the "Redeemer," is now employed to interpret Christian faith, and this represented at once a danger and an opportunity. The critical question, emphasizes Bultmann, is whether the newly interpreted eschatological event of salvation inaugurated by the history of Jesus Christ will be conceived as natural process or as genuinely historical, that is, as existential, happening.

It is the remarkable service of Paul and John, contends the author, that they, standing in their different ways *within* Hellenistic Christianity and using its terminology, were able to demythologize the Gnostic cosmological-dualistic conceptuality and to present the eschatological occurrence of salvation as taking place in the present. The salvation-event is not a cosmic-natural occurrence, but is present solely "in the proclaiming, accosting, demanding, and promising word of preaching." Judgment and salvation are no longer considered to be in the indefinite future, but to be present now in the response of men to the kerygmatic word of Jesus.

Bultmann considers Paul to be the real founder of Christian theology. Unlike a Greek philosopher or a modern theologian, Paul did not theoretically and systematically develop his thoughts in an independent scientific treatise, but he lifted the knowledge inherent in faith into the clarity of conscious knowing. His theology, then, is not speculative; he does not deal with "God in Himself" nor with "man in himself," but with them only in their relation to each other. Thus, "every assertion about God is simultaneously an assertion about man and vice versa," and it is in this sense that Paul's theology is, at the same time, anthropology. In like manner, Paul is not concerned with the metaphysical essence or the "natures" of Christ, but with Him as the one through whom God is working for the salvation of the world and man. Thus, Paul's Christology is simultaneously soteriology.

Pauline theology is dealt with under two main headings: "Man Prior to the Revelation of Faith" and "Man Under Faith." Bultmann thereby indicates his intention to present Biblical theology as an anthropology, by means of an existentialist interpretation. Man's existence prior to faith is an existence "according to the flesh," in which he sinfully tries to live out of his own resources and consequently falls into the power of death. The man of faith, however, surrenders his self to God and receives the gift of salvation which God has wrought in the crucifixion and the resurrection of Jesus Christ. He now lives "according to the Spirit," made righteous by God's act of grace and set free from sin, death, and the tyranny of the Law. In faith, which comes from hearing the word of preaching and which primarily involves obedience, God's eschatological salvation-event becomes a present reality but never a possession, so that the decision of faith must be made again and again. The life of faith, then, is understood as a dialectic between "no longer" and "not yet," between the indicative and the imperative.

The historicizing of eschatology that begins in Paul, who, nevertheless, still retained terminology relating to the Old Testament-Judaic conception of the history of salvation, is carried through in radical fashion by John, in whom the history-of-salvation perspective is missing altogether. The central topic for discussion for John is not, as for Paul, the way to salvation, but, rather, salvation itself. Jesus Christ is understood as the Revelation of God, the Son or Word of God whose very coming brings salvation to the fallen world. In the Son's own person man is given life and truth as the reality out of which he can exist, and faith means transition into eschatological existence, which, at the same time, involves a turning away from the world, desecularization. The believer is in the world, but not of the world. All this is made possible, of course, by the word of preaching, in which the saving event of the "Word made flesh" becomes present reality through the activity of the Spirit.

Bultmann sees in the development toward the ancient Church a gradual transformation of the Church's understanding of itself. The eschatological tension relaxes, and the Church begins to organize itself as a new religion. The constituting element of the Church changes from the activity of proclaiming the Word to the congregational office and the sacrament. The Church conceives itself as an institution of salvation; thus, the Church is able to mediate transcendent powers in the present through its sacramental cultus and priestly office. The Lord's Supper becomes the "medicine of immortality." Right doctrine, rather than faith, comes to distinguish Christians from Jews and heathen. An ideal of moralistic piety begins to replace the eschatological consciousness and the consciousness of being endowed with spiritual gifts. The keeping of commandments becomes the condition for salvation, and a radical understanding of sin gives way to a conception that differentiates between "light" and "grave" sins. Baptism is thought to secure forgiveness only for those sins committed prior to its administration, so that post-baptismal sins become a problem. The genuine understanding of "grace" is lost, and the Church moves ineluctably toward the legalism of the Catholic penitential system.

ETHICS

Author: Dietrich Bonhoeffer (1906-1945)
Type of work: Christian ethics
First published: 1949

Principal Ideas Advanced

To meet the opposition of anti-Christian forces, Western man must recover a totally Christian world view.

Taking the revelation of God in Christ as central, Christianity has the task of "conforming" the world to Christ.

In this undertaking, it must avoid the extremes of compromising with the world and of radically denying the world.

While respecting natural law and rationality, the Christian is not guided by abstract principles but is directly responsible to Christ.

The Christian's responsibility is not confined to "religious" concerns but embraces labor, marriage, and government.

During the first three years of the second World War, before he was imprisoned, Dietrich Bonhoeffer spent whatever time he could find while engaged in underground activities against the Nazis in writing what he intended to be a full-length theological work concerning Christian ethics. Bonhoeffer was executed by the S. S. Black Guards, in the concentration camp at Flossenburg, on April 9, 1945. The present work comprises those parts of his projected book which have been recovered from the places where they were hidden. Some parts are in nearly finished form; others are little more than sketches. For the most part, the editors have been able to follow Bonhoeffer's outline, so that the work reads consecutively.

The task which Bonhoeffer sets for himself in *Ethics* is to recover the foundation and the structure of a totally Christian way of life. As Western man has moved away from the foundations of his faith, his life has become increasingly meaningless. The Church is to blame, because it has failed in its responsibility to make the reality of God visible everywhere. There is only one recourse, to take Christ as the absolute revelation of God's will toward men, and to bring every aspect of life under that revelation.

Thus, Bonhoeffer's *Ethics* is Christ-centered. But, unlike the liberal gospel (see Adolf Harnack's *What is Christianity?*, 1900), it does not find its basis in the teachings of Jesus. Rather, like the Gospel of Paul, it sees in the incarnation, death, and resurrection of Christ, God's purpose to form man according to His eternal will. For Bonhoeffer, Christian ethics is "formation." It is the concrete, historical working out of divine redemption in the whole length and breadth of creation, beginning with the Church, but embracing labor, marriage, and government as well. The Christian's duty is to implement the will of God, and in every situation God's will is that the world may be "conformed" to Christ.

Bonhoeffer contends that in and of itself the world of time and change is meaningless. Only as time and change are seen in relation to divine reality do they become significant. The one place where time and eternity meet is in Christ Jesus. Hence, it is to Christ that we must look if our lives are to be redeemed from futility and death. By the Incarnation, God took upon Himself the nature of man, raised that nature from the level of brute creation, and established its dignity. By the Crucifixion, He bore our guilt, making it possible for us to accept ourselves and to live with our past. By the Resurrection, He broke the chains of death and evil and proclaimed that Christ is Lord over all the world. The wisdom of life, says Bonhoeffer, is all present here; the simplest man, by submitting his life to Christ, finds all that he needs for performing God's will. The Church exists to confront persons with Christ. Its members, when conformable to Christ, become the agents of God to bring society into conformity with Him.

Bonhoeffer intended his theology to be free from the errors of what he called compromise and radicalism. The problem is, What shall be the attitude of the Church to the wisdom of the non-Christian world? The compromisers, symbolized by Dostoevski's Grand Inquisitor, destroy the ultimacy of Christianity by subordinating its demands to things as they are. The radicals, symbolized by Ibsen's Brand, make an exclusive commitment to the ultimate the basis for denying their responsibility toward the world. Each of these positions, says Bonhoeffer, contains elements of truth as well as of falsity. The truth is that *ultimately* it is only in Christ that the will of God is manifest, even though *penultimately* God's will is manifest in the world and in society. In other words, God's redemptive purpose finds its realization only in conforming the world to Christ; however, as means to that final condition, subordinate realms have been established by God and have been given relative validity. Nature, the state, reason, and natural law thus exist as means; they must not be taken as ultimate, but neither may they be ignored. The state, for example, must respect the rights with which the Creator has invested every living thing. Specifically, the rights of individual men and women must not be contravened in the name of communal rights. On the other hand, the state as an instrument of order is ordained of God and must be obeyed except when, as Bonhoeffer believed true of Hitler, the ruler openly repudiates the state's legitimate function.

Christian ethics, then, does not go against nature and reason but vindicates them even as it surpasses them. For, according to Bonhoeffer, ordinary morality, with its distinction between what is and what should be, shows man at odds with God and with himself. Like the Mosaic law, a rigid morality is likely to lead to Pharisaism. But the ethics of civilized man is on the way to Christ. Good, honest, honorable men are working toward Christianity. The Church should raise no barrier against such men but should take them in, in the hopes of bringing them the rest of the way.

The Christian, having received the forgiveness and renewal which God offers to sinful man in Christ, no longer judges his duty in terms of abstract right and wrong. Although he respects the penultimate order, he is free from complete obedience to its requirements because he is directly responsible to Christ.

The concept of responsibility was to have been an important one in Bonhoeffer's system. Responsibility depends on the tension between obligation and freedom, a tension which, in Bonhoeffer's experience, constituted the life of Christian discipleship. On the one hand, following Christ means the negation of our "apostate life," the life which as children of the world we seek to live apart from the will of God. On the other hand, it means affirming the new life which God has constituted everywhere—not just in believers—through the incarnation, death, and resurrection of Christ. "This concept of responsibility," says Bonhoeffer, "is intended as referring to the concentrated totality and unity of the response to reality which is given to us in Jesus Christ, as distinct from the partial responses which might arise, for example, from a consideration of utility or from particular principles."

Christian ethics, according to Bonhoeffer, has no need for rules or principles. As abstractions, principles are not adequate to disclose God's will for particular situations. On the contrary, they are apt to frustrate God's purpose, as Bonhoeffer declares was actually the case with conscientious but rule-venerating Christians under Hitler. To the Christian, it is the revelation of God in Christ which gives any situation its meaning. This is not to imply that the Christian relies on intuition. Bonhoeffer uses Paul's words; the Christian must "prove the different situations." Bonhoeffer writes, "The heart, the understanding, observation and experience must all collaborate in the task." But the crucial condition for knowing one's duty is the change in one's being which comes from "conformation with the form of the new man Christ." Intelligence pervaded by prayer beholds each new situation through the eyes of Christ. In thus seeing what is, the Christian sees what is to be done.

Bonhoeffer was particularly concerned to bridge the chasm, which has widened in recent decades, between the Church and secular society. As against the view, prevalent in Lutheran circles, that the Church and the world are exclusive spheres, he maintains that through Christ's work the world is already redeemed; the Church is even now confronting the world with its Redeemer. Bonhoeffer did not favor the "activist" approach to "worldly problems"; the world's problems, posed in terms of the penultimate order, are incapable of solution. His view is, rather, that those who make up the "body of Christ," or the Church, will carry out Christ's mandates in every sphere of human activity.

In a penetrating analysis of our times, Bonhoeffer maintains that the void which threatens to swallow Western civilization is "a specifically Western void, a rebellious and outrageous void, and one which is the enemy of both God and man." Nations and civilizations have declined before without leaving men's souls in such desperation. But because Western civilization owes its special character to Christ, its loss of faith has assumed a peculiarly virulent quality. "It is not the theoretical denial of the existence of a God. It is itself a religion, a religion of hostility to God." Ostensibly the West proclaims the deification of man, his natural goodness, his new-found freedom; in fact it proclaims nihilism, an unrestrained vitalism, and a negation of order and law which can lead only to self-destruction. For the West, in particular, Christianity is healing and reconciliation. The West can recover its historical and political form only in returning to justice, order, and peace, but it can scarcely hope to regain these virtues unless the form of Christ is renewed in its midst, through a revival of faith in the Body of the Church.

FAITH AND HISTORY

Author: Reinhold Niebuhr (1892-)
Type of work: Christian apologetics
First published: 1949

Principal Ideas Advanced

The Christian interpretation of history makes the claim for an eternal Gospel which has universal application amidst the changes and relativities of the historical process.

The Christian view is contrasted with the classical Greek view, which seeks a meaning for history by seeking within a changeless realm of ideas; the Christian view is also contrasted with the modern view which sees both time and history as self-explanatory.

The Christian view, based on a Biblical interpretation, begins with the sovereignty of God as this sovereignty expresses itself in creation, judgment, and redemption.

The sovereignty of God finds its most decisive revelation in Jesus as the Christ, who is the center of historical meaning, who discloses the divine love which transfigures historical justice, and who reconciles the antinomies and ambiguities of human existence.

In *Faith and History* Reinhold Niebuhr formulates a Christian theology of history and develops its unique contrast with rival views. The basic presupposition of the Christian view is that the Gospel of Christ is true for all men and is thus relevant to the historical process in all ages. The peculiar relevance of the Christian Gospel to history is discussed in detail and the idiosyncracies which distinguish the Christian view from classical and modern conceptions are delineated. The method of argumentation is that of apologetics, tacit if not explicit. Although it is clearly stated by the author that there is no simple Christian "philosophy of history," the validity of which can be rationally demonstrated as it is set over against the classical and modern conceptions, nonetheless it is argued that an indirect defense is possible by showing that the alternative views do not account for nor give meaning to the complexities of historical experience. "The Christian philosophy of history is rational, therefore, only in the sense that it is possible to prove that alternatives to it fail to do justice to all aspects of human existence; and that the basic presuppositions of the Chrisitan faith, though transcending reason, make it possible to give an account of life and history in which all facts and antinomies are comprehended."

The classical conception, informed primarily by the philosophies of Plato and Aristotle, advances a consistent rationalism in which it is affirmed that life and history have a rational intelligibility by virtue of their relation to a world of changeless and eternal ideas. Since the world of temporal and historical becoming was understood as merely a corruption of the eternal world, it was ultimately devalued and negated. The basic presupposition of the Greek view is that of an otherworldliness which negates the vitalities and possibilities of history itself. Correspondingly, historical time is regarded as an extension of natural time. The temporal world is a cycle of natural-historical recurrences ever coming to be and passing away. Meaning is attained only in a liberation from this cycle through a participation in the eternal ideas.

The modern view rejects the other-worldliness stressed in the Greek conception and also the equation of historical time with natural time. Proponents of the modern view agree with the Greeks that there is a rational intelligibility which explains the historical process, but unlike the Greeks the moderns argue that this rational intelligibility is within the historical process itself rather than localized in a supra-temporal world. The growth of reason in the historical process is affirmed to be limitless, and history becomes the story of man's ever increasing rationality, power, and freedom. Unlike the Greek conception, the modern conception advances a linear rather than a cyclical view. History is a process of linear development, ever moving onward and upward. The religious expression of such a view is that God is made wholly immanent and becomes a symbol for history itself, which in the last analysis is self-derived and self-explanatory; and redemption is equated with the progressive realization of freedom. The modern view thus emancipates history from its dependence upon nature and recognizes the unique significance of historical development.

In granting history its autonomy and intrinsic "laws" the modern view, according to Niebuhr, is subject to a most grievous illusion in affirming that history is self-explanatory and self-redemptive. This illusion itself rests upon two miscalculations: (1) an exaggerated estimate of the quality and growth of human freedom and power, and (2) the easy identification of freedom and virtue. In its extravagant estimate of historical freedom the modern conception loses sight of the irreducible finitude of man which imposes multitudinous restrictions upon his freedom. Man is subject to biological limitations, surveys the world from a particular perspective, is restricted by the particularity of his speech, conditioned by his social institutions, and unequivocally limited by his death. In its identification of freedom and virtue the modern view conceals the inevitable moral ambiguities which arise from the actualization of freedom. It fails to recognize that human freedom and power contain destructive as well as creative possibilities and thus it fails to do justice to the tragic antinomies and discontinuities which recur throughout the historical development.

The Christian interpretation, although in some respects similar to both the Greek and modern conceptions, differs from these two views both in its general presuppositions and in details of doctrine. It rejects the criterion of rational intelligibility as the final court of appeal. History is rationally intelligible neither by virtue of its participation in eternal ideas nor by virtue of its intrinsic laws of development. It derives its meaning through the revelation of Biblical faith which centers around the rationally offensive "scandal of particularity." It is a scandal for all rationalistically oriented interpretations of history that the final meaning of the historical process should be rooted in a particular and concrete historical event, whether it be the event of a covenantal bond between God and Israel or the event of a man who is received and acclaimed as the Christ. More specifically, the Christian view rejects the non-historical classical approach with its equation of history and nature and its otherworldliness through which historical events are deprived of existential significance. It rejects the modern view because of its abortive effort to localize redemption within the historical process itself, inviting an unwarranted optimism as to the possibilities of human reason and human freedom.

Founded on a Biblical faith, the Christian approach affirms the sovereignty of God over man's individual and collective historical destiny. God as Creator, Judge, and Redeemer is the Lord of history, providing history with the only universalism which can give it meaning. History is conceived as a meaningful unity because all historical destinies are under the governance of a single divine sovereignty. Although the idea of a divine creation of the temporal world is not a uniquely Biblical concept, it does distinguish Christian thought both from classical thought with its idea of the temporal world as a corruption of the eternal world and from modern thought with its idea of a self-explanatory time and history. Divine judgment plays a peculiarly important role in Christian thought in that it displaces the locus of historical meaning as an extension of relative and finite goods, such as national purposes and human reason. These relative and finite goods are constantly subject to divine judgment. All moral, political, and cultural claims are seen as relative and contingent, partial and parochial; and every attempt to confer absolute and final significance upon these claims is condemned to historical disappointment as an abortive defiant rebellion of the creature against the Creator. It is thus that the divine judgment entails a continuing protest against any and all false absolutes which intermittently arise in history. The author is aware of the tragic tendency in Christian civilizations to fall into the error of worshiping such false absolutes. It is for this reason that Christian interpretations of life and history must be constantly re-examined in light of the truth of divine judgment.

The sovereignty of God finds its most decisive revelation in the Biblical faith of redemption, as this faith proclaims the foolishness of the Cross in its denial of the "wisdom of the world." Reason is scandalized by the claim that a particular event in history can be the locus of the final revelation of God's redeeming activity. This events unites within itself two decisive movements—Crucifixion and Resurrection. These movements not only climax the whole series of previous revelations but also disclose the unique relationship which obtains between man and God. The Crucifixion and Resurrection incomparably express the decisive obligation of dying to sin with Christ and arising with him to newness of Life. The Crucifixion and Resurrection elucidate the drama of sin and redemption as these unfold in historical experience. The Christian interpretation alone takes sin and guilt seriously; thus, the Christian view is able to take full account of the moral ambiguities, tragic cross-purposes and abuses of power which emerge throughout man's actualization of his freedom. But the Biblical faith does not rest with these tragic implications of human sin. It receives its final expression in the conviction that man's fragmentary historical existence is completed by a power not his own, and that the ambiguities of his moral existence are forgiven by a love which purges and heals the effects of his sinful pride.

Eschatology plays a dominant role in the Christian interpretation of history. History has an end in the sense of *Telos*. There is a point of reference which marks history's moral and spiritual culmination and confers upon the historical process its final meaning. This point of reference, symbolized by the final judgment and general resurrection, is not localized within history itself. *Die Weltgeschichte* is not *das Weltgericht*. There is no possibility of a final judgment within history, only at the end of it. But this *Telos,* prefigured in the Resurrection, must not be confused with a quantitative spatio-temporal point in chronological time. It indicates a qualitative judgment which is imminent every moment. This is why the New Testament introduced a note of urgency and emphasized that "the time is short" (I Corinthians 7:29). The eschatology of which the Christian Gospel speaks teaches an existential urgency in which one experiences the impingement of divine judgment in each moment of time as this moment becomes the locus for historical decision. Although judgment and redemption are not contained within nor derived from history, they are at every moment relevant to it. The symbol of the Last Judgment paradoxically expresses the tension between the historical and the trans-historical both by claiming a point of reference beyond history and by affirming the existential relevance of divine judgment as it becomes effectual in the historical process itself. It thus rejects both the utopian dreams of the optimistic modern interpretation of history and the Platonic flight from the historical process into a realm of eternal forms. Although the eschatological symbols point to that which transcends time and history, they also indicate the eternal dimensions within man's historic existence.

GOD'S GRACE AND MAN'S HOPE

Author: Daniel Day Williams (1910-)
Type of work: Christian ethics
First published: 1949

Principal Ideas Advanced

A better world can be made by men who are devoted to God, for God is present and working in human history.

The thought categories of process philosophy are better able to indicate the nature of God than are the thought categories of static being.

Protestant theological liberalism has been overly optimistic about the human contribution to historical change, and Neo-orthodoxy has been too pessimistic. Therefore, neither has adequately understood the redemptive activity of God.

Man's hope is rooted in the realization and affirmation of the divine activity; such hope cannot be based upon what man can do for himself or upon what God will do without man.

God's Grace and Man's Hope was first delivered as the Rauschenbusch Lectures at Colgate-Rochester Divinity School in the spring of 1947. It is widely appreciated as a thoughtful attempt to find a meaningful synthesis between Protestant liberalism and Protestant Neo-orthodoxy, both of which were prevalent schools of thought at the time of its delivery. In the book, Williams argues that a better world can be made since God is present and working in human history. According to its author, the book's chief problems can be described as follows: ". . . the nature of God's working and our knowledge of Him; the conflict between Christian love and power politics; the mystery of time and its relation to the idea of human progress; the meaning of the Christian's 'calling' in the making of moral choices; the question whether there is a Christian ideal for society, and how such an ideal is to be stated; and finally the query which searches the human heart, whether and how it is possible for a man to love his neighbor as himself."

Throughout most of the book a contrast is drawn between theological liberalism and Neo-orthodoxy. Seeking to incorporate and preserve valid insights from each, the author threads his way to a position sometimes between and often beyond each of these dominant theological outlooks. These two theological perspectives agree in claiming that history is the place where God is working out the redemption of the world, though they have contrasting ways of interpreting how God works in the world. Liberalism sees the work of God evidenced in man's progress toward the coming of the Kingdom of God on earth. This Kingdom is understood in terms of universal brotherhood and peace and is advanced when men respond to God with reasonableness and moral earnestness. Neo-orthodoxy places its reliance upon the justifying love of God for sinful men and it replaces the progressive view of history with a tragic view. In this tragic view the Kingdom of God is understood as coming suddenly and in the indefinite future whereas in the liberal view it is described as possible only by means of a gradual shift from evil to goodness brought about as a consequence of human endeavor. According to Williams, neither formulation makes a sufficient place for the fact of God's redeeming activity, since liberalism sees no need for it and Neo-orthodoxy postpones it to the "end." What is needed is a vision of the goodness of creation coupled to an acknowledgement that evil has invaded that goodness and overarched with a realization that God is redemptively at work to restore the goodness.

In making his case for the redemptive activity of God, Williams relies upon the categories of process philosophy. God is said to be at work in the world, encountering the sinner with His mercy. The activity of God may be experienced in human life just as much as real objects are experienced, though in different ways. To be sure, God is above all, and hence we speak of His transcendence, but He is known in Christ and in other manifest evidences of His love for man. Evil is real, but it is met and finally overcome by the redemptive activity of God, who ". . . does transform rebellious and self-sufficient men into persons who can begin to love their fellows." This process is described by the traditional term "grace."

Love is central to the idea of grace and is the symbol of God's unity. This love expresses itself in the continual divine process of urging men to live in universal, free, and genuine community. Love must be conceived in terms of a viable relation to the actualities of human history. Williams chides those commentators who define love in terms so absolute as to remove it from possible contact with the everyday realities of human life. Selfless love is not full love, since the Kingdom of God does not exclude any good, even the good of the individual self.

Williams discusses the social as well as the personal expression of love. He acknowledges that it is initially more difficult to reconcile the harsh facts of power conflict with the idea of love than to see the evidence of love in personal relations. Again, he criticizes liberalism for oversimplifying the role of love and Neo-orthodoxy for seeming to deny the place of love within the impersonal structure of human life. He affirms that God's redemptive work in human history will express itself through both the personal and the social instrumentalities of life, never finding complete expression, yet always present in a profound and important degree.

This central thesis is explored in relationship to the idea of time. Time itself does not heal, nor is it redemptive apart from God's power. Time itself is a threat as well as a potential aid to the achievement of value, and there is a deep and persistent rent in human history. Neo-orthodoxy, following the thought of Søren Kierkegaard (1813-1855), stresses time as being both an individual and existential source of meaning, and the view loses sight of historical time. In order to avoid the errors inherent in the idea of progress, Neo-orthodoxy makes the movement toward God alien to any common human experience. Even though subsequent interpreters have been less extreme than Kierkegaard, they have sometimes lost sight of the fact that life is process and that our present history proceeds under the reign of Christ. Because Christ reigns, and only because He reigns, can we serve one another in love. In the light of this reign the author feels it is wrong to imply that the love of God cannot overcome the obstacles that beset the expression of love in history even though we must not expect the love of God to find a quick and easy expression.

Two-thirds of the way through his argument Williams changes both his problem and his categories. The new problem is the problem of law and grace, a problem to be illuminated by a consideration of the Catholic and Protestant understandings of the moral imperative. Williams claims that the problem of knowing the good, difficult as it is, is secondary to the great need of man for power to do the good. Even so, the problem of knowing the good is difficult and contains many perplexing dilemmas. Williams is dissatisfied with Catholic sources of ethical guidance since they falsely absolutize a human institution and prevent the individual from speaking a prophetic word against the Church. The Reformation doctrine of vocation, on the other hand, has been stunted by its identification with the ethos of success and worldliness. The Christian will not be totally transformed nor will he totally transform the life of the world when he responds to the vocation of God, but this does not mean that he is to acquiesce in the given sinfulness of the world. He is to do whatever is possible to effect a positive good, reckoning all the time with the grim necessities that seem to hinder the achievement. Williams says, "The divine call to us men, and our response to it, means that we are responsible for doing here and now in the situation in which we stand whatever will serve the work of God who is seeking to bring all life to fulfillment in that universal community of love which is the real good of every creature."

Perfectionistic withdrawal and unbothered subservience to the *status quo* are contrasting mistakes which must be avoided by the Christian who would adequately serve God in the realities of the world. In serving God the specific injunctions of moral law are to be taken as guides to responsible action and cannot be dispensed with even though the Gospel appears to supersede all law. Williams does not embrace antinomianism in order to escape legalism. Moreover, the faithful Christian can be reinforced in his vocation by the community of faith and the life of prayer.

The concluding portion of the book addresses itself to the grounds of Christian hope. Rightly understood utopian impulses are given a place in the Christian life because they contribute great social dynamism even when they fail to achieve their objectives. They spring from the thirst for a better life, a thirst which is one of the continuing signs of God's image in man, and they keep alive the trust that society can be transformed through God's active involvement in history. Christians are to hope for a good society and to focus their attention on the pragmatic possibilities of improving the conditions of existence for all men, keeping the exchange of work and ideas between men free and orderly, preserving the right of voluntary groups to make their contribution to social good and the healing of broken lives, and insisting that men have a voice in the making of those decisions that affect their own lives and destiny. There is no place in Christian thinking for a kind of fatalism that destroys the zest for new and more fruitful achievements of social betterment.

Williams is especially critical of those thinkers who insist that Christian love must be defined in perfectionistic and selfless terms. No man possesses perfect or completely selfless love, but all men can grow in grace. The proximate achievements of men who are faithful to God, even when that faith itself is imperfect and the achievements are limited or ambiguous in character, can be both genuine and fruitful. But Williams also guards against every easy identification of particular achievements with the divine fullness. He asserts that every stage of new life is open to the possibility of new temptation, particularly if men forget their dependence upon the divine mercy or let pride creep into their lives. When men grow in grace they grow in response to the action of God made known in Christ and learn to serve Him fruitfully without presuming to regard the human achievements made in such service as the basis of hope. The source of man's hope lies in the divine power and grace, yet the two are kept in living and dynamic relationship with each other.

Williams states, "The God we serve is the giver of this life with its obligations and possibilities. There is no situation in which the Christian cannot find meaning and hope. There is no social wrong which need remain unattacked, unmitigated, unreformed. There is no private desperate struggle with anxiety and bitterness and failure which cannot yield new hope when we discover that God does not leave us forsaken. But those who know this, while they are released to spend themselves in doing what needs to be done, live with a certain divine carelessness concerning earthly fortunes. Their hope sees beyond the years and they live in this demanding present under the everlasting assurance of God's love."

THE LIVING WORD

Author: Gustaf Wingren (1910-)
Type of work: Homiletics
First published: 1949

Principal Ideas Advanced

Preaching is proclamation of the Biblical message of the death and resurrection of Jesus Christ by which life and freedom are offered to men who are in bondage to sin and death.

Through faith man is called to share Christ's death and resurrection, dying in his earthly calling and ultimately completing the resurrection of Christ's Body, the Church.

Until Christ's final victory over Satan and death, man cannot separate the law which kills from the Gospel which gives life.

The Living Word by Gustaf Wingren, professor of systematic theology at the University of Lund, Sweden, is a study of preaching viewed from the vantage point of systematic theology. The purpose of preaching, according to Wingren, is to create an encounter between man and the word of God. This word is a message centering about the death and resurrection of Jesus Christ through which the hearer is summoned also to die and rise, in order thereby to be created and to live.

Since, according to Wingren, the congregation is already present in the text, the preacher's problem is not that of making a subjective application to an objective message. Since, furthermore, man is a prisoner of Satan, the primary opposition with which preaching must reckon is not between God and man, but between God and Satan. Deliverance for man through Jesus Christ is to be proclaimed, which deliverance takes place in the context of the congregation, as man recovers the humanity God intended he should have.

The Bible, which provides the texts the preacher uses, is a book about the acts of God. These acts continue in preaching as the history the Bible records, namely God's victory over Satan, continues. In this way the Bible through being preached receives a unity it would not otherwise have.

Christ is the Lord of the Scriptures. The Old Testament looks forward to Him, while the New Testament interprets His death and resurrection as the defeat of man's enemy, the Devil. The decisive victory over Satan has been won, but the struggle continues in the hearts of men. Christ's victory is heard but not seen. As the word which proclaims this victory is heard again and again man is created.

Man is created by God's word, Wingren writes, but God works against opposition. Prior to being reached by this creative word man is subject to sin, death, and guilt. Only in the final resurrection will he be completely free from these enemies.

Though man has been conquered by Satan he belongs to God. Therefore Christ in the Incarnation did not come to an alien world, but to creatures who had been alienated. The central theme of the Bible is not, accordingly, that God meets man in the Incarnation (at this point Wingren is criticizing Karl Barth, the eminent Swiss theologian), but that there is victory over death in the Resurrection. Barth regards it natural for man not to believe and interprets faith as a paradox. Martin Luther (1483-1546), on the other hand, held that unbelief was demonic. When God is said to be life, this means that man receives authentic existence from God. When Satan is said to be death, this means that man loses his humanity under Satan's dominion, for Satan is a murderer.

Through the creative word mediated through preaching, which is the link between Christ's resurrection and our own, Satan is forced to let go his grip on us. Those who are ministers of the word are sent into the camp of the enemy, as "sheep among wolves." Man is to be delivered from sin through forgiveness and from death through resurrection.

Since the Bible presupposes unity between the messenger and the sender of the message, he who hears preaching hears Christ. In sending the Apostles Jesus appears as Lord of the whole world, making claims on all peoples. Through the ascension Jesus achieves the divine attribute of omnipresence. Thus the basis for preaching is the ascension and the outpouring of the Spirit which follows. Through the ministry Christ, the Word, moves among men till the end of the world. To insist upon a particular kind of ecclesiastical succession implies doubt as to the reality of the living Christ, and is similar to the doctrine of the verbal inspiration of the Bible. It is to hold that God once lived and acted, but does so no longer.

The authority of the ministry rests upon the fact that the meaning of the message is clear. Those who insist it is unclear then need authorities to interpret it, who in turn become judges of the Scriptures. But the lordship of the word must be affirmed. The ministry receives its validity from the word; the word does not derive its validity from the ministry.

The ministry of the word belongs to the interim of struggle between Easter and the return of Christ, and will end when Satan is destroyed. Christ will eventually reign visibly, though now His lordship is preached. Christ's resurrection is being completed as His Body, the Church, rises through the mediation of word and sacrament.

The New Testament presupposes a conflict between God and Satan in which man is necessarily involved. The only alternatives are faith or unbelief, both of which imply activity. Unbelief is not natural, but demonic. Faith is freedom from that which destroys, fellowship with the source of life, the Creator. In this relationship one can, accordingly, speak unreservedly of both human and divine activity.

According to Wingren, faith and the word belong together. God creates through the word. To believe is to receive the life God gives. Faith belongs to the present, as one awaits the time that Christ's victory will be fully visible. This time of faith is the time of conflict with sin, but thereby creation also takes place. By faith authentic man frees himself from all alien controls. Faith is our death and resurrection by which the word is given freedom to accomplish its destroying and life-giving work.

The question of the truth of what is preached must now be considered. Wingren states two theses: The only valid ground for preaching is the factual death and resurrection of Jesus Christ, for faith is not valid apart from the fact which it believes. But the fact which faith believes does not remain the same fact if faith is absent.

Although the necessary foundation for preaching is the resurrection of Christ, this cannot be treated as simply a matter of scientific truth. We must approach this question as men who are in bondage. If Christ is not risen, we are still in our sins, but if He is risen, we are freed from sin and thus also from death. Our own resurrection is therefore involved. Christ's body arose from the grave, but Christ's Body is the Church, ourselves. This is not to say that the resurrection of the body of Jesus that was laid in the grave need not be affirmed. Faith in creation is absent when one can leave the body outside of Jesus' resurrection.

Wingren points out that in the sixteenth century it was hard to understand that God could forgive. Now the difficulty is accepting the fact that He can create life. The guilty conscience finds it hard to believe in forgiveness, while the intellectual conscience finds it hard to believe in resurrection. To reaffirm Christ's resurrection as an external event is, however, to strengthen both the faith in God's creation of the external world and our eschatological hope.

The message of death and resurrection has implications for an understanding of the relation between law and Gospel. The law does not represent a message which is in addition to the Gospel. There is but one message, the message of death and resurrection. The law serves this message, exercising its function together with the Gospel so that man can die and rise. The law is God's defense against sin, and it was already functioning in the world to which Jesus came. Through Christ's death and resurrection the law began to come to an end. This process continues in the death of the "old man" in each Christian; it will culminate in the final fall of Satan in the last times. Until this consummation is complete, however, law and Gospel belong together.

Thus the Christian conscience is free from the law, Wingren declares, and the conscience may be said to be in Heaven, but the Christian as a sinner in this bodily existence lives under the discipline of the law, his body having not as yet risen. Through the law God creates life by demanding that duties be performed. It is the law that calls man's attention to his neighbor and directs him to labor for his neighbor's welfare. This process of sanctification, in which the old man is crucified and the new man is born, is not to be regarded as peculiarly religious, as though there were a special law for Christians. Life even for Christians in this world is to be left as it is, hard and honorable labor, a journey through death's valley listening to the word, with the forgiveness of sins as our only piety and the resurrection at the last day as our only ultimate hope.

The message of death and resurrection is also proclaimed in the sacraments. These sacraments are rooted in the history of Israel. Israel received its "baptism" in the Red Sea and thus became a people. But Israel was chosen to die. Only in the role of the Suffering Servant does Israel become a light to the nations. This is anticipated in the Old Testament, but is fulfilled only in the death and resurrection of Jesus Christ, which in turn is identified as Jesus' "baptism" (Luke 12:50). This is also a baptism which Jesus' disciples may share (Mark 10:38). To pass through baptism, then, is to die and rise again.

If Jesus was baptized in order to fulfill the role of the Suffering Servant, becoming in this way identified with sinners, the Christian in being baptized is identified with Christ, sharing His death and resurrection. The Christian's baptism is fulfilled in his earthly calling and ultimately in bodily death, when the true life of the resurrection is finally gained. So also Jesus' resurrection is not complete until His Body, the Church, has died and risen again. Thus in each baptism the power of the Resurrection enters into this world and the dawning of the last day becomes nearer.

In the Lord's Supper the fulfillment of Israel's calling through death and resurrection is also central. The food of this sacrament is sustenance as the Church wanders through the present wilderness toward the eschatological consummation. Now Christ's real presence is heard; then it will be seen. This interim of listening to the word in preaching and sacrament is the Church's place in the history of redemption.

Just as the sacraments rest upon events that have occurred, writes Wingren, so also they point to events which are to occur. The resurrected body to which they point, however, is not supernatural; the resurrected body is a liberated and purified body. Thus also the sacramental elements are not supernatural substances, but are water, bread, and wine, with the power of the word to expel unbelief and create anew human life.

Baptism like birth occurs only once, but the Lord's Supper, which gives food for the journey, is repeated. If the imagery of conflict is used, baptism is deliverance from the land of darkness, while the Lord's Supper provides strength for continued conflict with sin. That the sacraments point to the eschatological consummation is another way of saying that through them man receives a life which begins here and now, but is fulfilled in the final resurrection.

Satan has been defeated and he will be defeated. Victory has begun, but its final completion has not yet taken place. This means, Wingren claims, that man now has the forgiveness of sins and that he awaits the resurrection of the dead. Death and sin are both enemies of God, but sin is attacked first and is overcome by means of death, for to kill the "old man" is really to produce life. But death also will finally be destroyed. Then Satan's whole tyranny will be broken, and man will be completely free.

Until this consummation takes place man lives in the Church. Yet Christians are also to remain in their earthly callings, where sanctification is to take place. The Church is to be bound to word and sacrament, but it is to be open to the world, losing its life in its ministry to all men. The Church does not so much draw men to itself, as it sends them out with the forgiveness of sins into the world. Just now it is not important to determine who belongs and who does not belong to the Church. This division will take place at the Last Judgment. The Church's present task is to go out into the world with the word it has received.

This word is heard, a bit at a time, by men who are on a journey, and who are thus led on their way towards life. The Christian life was originally lived in terms of the week, in which both the Cross and the Resurrection were celebrated. In a similar way the Christian year developed, with Easter as the feast about which the others were grouped. The addition of many martyrs' days did not in principle change this emphasis of the Christian year, Wingren suggests, for these days pointed to the mystery that life in the Body of Christ rises out of death. In the Middle Ages, however, many more saints' days were added and the concept of merit changed the structure of theology. Thus Luther's reform of the Christian year was needed to restore its earlier character.

The Christian year indicates that the history of salvation continues. The emphasis on the order of salvation in pietism, however, suggested that the work of salvation was finished, the only problem being man's appropriation of it. Thus the individual rather than Christ and the congregation became the center of reference. If one is to speak of an order of salvation, writes Wingren, one must say that the Christian year is the order of salvation in which we live, move, and have our being, just as the local congregation is the place in which we find our calling.

The concept of an order of salvation has been related to attempts to structure preaching so as to adapt it to different groups of people, such as the unconverted, the awakened, and the converted. Wingren states that it is the word rather than the congregation that is to be divided, and that the word is to be divided into law and Gospel. But this division cannot really be made either by the preacher or the hearer. The text is to be preached and the Holy Spirit then divides the word in such a way that it is adapted in each particular situation, either as law to put to death the "old man," or as Gospel to bring to birth the "new man."

This problem of the division of law and Gospel is related to the Lutheran doctrine of "the sharing of the attributes" (*communicatio idiomatum*), a doctrine which affirms that in Jesus Christ human and divine attributes are shared in such a way that God suffers and dies, while man is raised to Heaven. Wingren states that those who criticize this doctrine presuppose a fundamental cleavage between God and man. Luther, however, knew God only in Jesus Christ. Therefore he saw God's glory revealed in the humiliation of the Cross, and the man Jesus exalted in the Resurrection.

Just as law and Gospel are intermingled in the word, so the attributes of death and resurrection jointly characterize the present existence of the Christian, and we are unable to separate them. Thus one arrives at the two rules of preaching: Christ who is both God and man must be preached, and the plain sense of the text must determine what is said. The doctrine of the sharing of the attributes points to our incapacity to speculate at this point and our need simply to accept the word and proclaim it, believing that the word is God and is even now becoming flesh. Such a nonspeculative approach, Wingren finally affirms, is needed not only in preaching but also in systematic theology.

BASIC CHRISTIAN ETHICS

Author: Paul Ramsey (1913-   )
Type of work: Christian ethics
First published: 1950

Principal Ideas Advanced

Christian morality is an expression of religious and theological commitments and cannot be understood apart from knowledge about the nature and righteousness of God.

Christian ethical obligation is best described by reference to "obedient love"; obligation based on love transcends the rules of code morality without diminishing the rigor of morality itself.

God is the only legitimate object of unqualified allegiance; He alone creates and sustains virtue in the individual and in the community.

Christian ethical considerations are rooted in the nature and activity of God as portrayed in Biblical material and elaborated by the great thinkers of the Church. Starting from this conviction, Paul Ramsey opens his discussion of *Basic Christian Ethics* with a study of the righteous nature of a loving God and the presence of God's righteousness in His Rule, or Kingdom. According to Ramsey, the righteousness of God is expressed both in His judgment and in His faithfulness to the convenantal bond. Hence, it includes elements of steadfast mercy and even of sure love. Moreover, the righteousness of God is normative for the justice of man. The God who shows mercy to His people, even to the widow, the outcast, and the resident alien, expects His people to show similar mercy to their neighbors. Justice, righteousness, and mercy are interrelated in the activity of God; hence, God requires of men a special bias toward the needy and the outcast and not mere equality before the law of abstract fairness. The moral duty of men must be expressed in active concern for those who stand in greatest need of such concern. In the teachings of Jesus the obligation to meet human need is rooted in response to God's loving work, and hence both the old and the new covenants put primary emphasis upon a concerned and outpouring righteousness and mercy.

The reign of God in His Kingdom is the crucial focus of Christian morality and explains both the eschatological thrust and the radical demands upon the believer which are found in the teachings of Jesus. The terms of this teaching are so strenuous that some commentators, such as Albert Schweitzer, have come to regard them as valid only for a limited interim while other thinkers, such as Martin Dibelius (1883-1947), regard them as intended for an eventful future situation. Ramsey suggests that the teachings of Jesus are intended as an absolute portrayal of the nonpreferential and uncalculating love ultimately demanded of the Christian. Such a nonpreferential element means that the Christian must treat as neighbor the immediately encountered fellow man. Moreover, it effectively removes self-regarding motives from the ground floor of Christian love since love is required even when no return is assured.

While Ramsey understands the source of Christian morality to be rooted in the righteousness of God, he suggests that the nature of Christian morality combines binding and strenuous obligation with freedom and liberty of action. Code morality, illustrated by Ramsey with several colorful examples from the Pharisaical legal system at the time of Jesus as well as from much subsequent moralism in the Christian movement itself, endlessly expands the law by minute descriptions of specifically required or forbidden acts until the major intention of a moral ideal is buried under a mountain of detailed prescriptions. The life and teachings of Jesus are interpreted as a significant break with legalism. Partly by His overt disregard for the provisions of the law and primarily because He taught that allegiance to God transcends all the codification devised to describe it in detail, Jesus provided "an ethic of perfection which transcends any possible legal formulation." St. Paul is primarily responsible for showing in his letters what the Christian does without a code. Paul nullified laws that even Jesus did not question, but in doing so he remained true to the intentions of his Lord and elaborated a moral understanding basically the same as that which Jesus Himself displayed. According to the Apostle Paul, freedom from the law sets men in bondage to the whole need of the neighbor.

With these basic understandings set forth as the foundation of discussion, Ramsey devotes the remainder of his work to a discussion of Christian morality in relationship to religious and philosophical systems both outside and inside the Church of later centuries as well as to the social problems of the contemporary scene. The first part of this discussion revolves around issues raised by philosophical ethics, particularly those concerning the place of self-regard in the ethical life. The Christian, says Ramsey, embraces love that is uncalculating and disinterested, nonresisting and nonpreferential. Such love is poured forth before it is merited, expressed before being sought. "No more disastrous mistake can be made than to admit self-love onto the ground floor of Christian obligation, however much concern for self-improvement, for example, may later come to be a secondary, though entirely essential, aspect of Christian vocation." The higher virtues sought by philosophical morality are entirely compatible with Christian ethics when they are sought for the good of the neighbor. "Whose good?" is prior in the Christian ethic to the question "What is the good?" Even the love of God must be understood, not as the aspiration of the soul for union with the supernatural, but as the love shed by God into the heart of the believer, turning the believer's heart toward the need of the neighbor. Salvation must not be the motivation for doing good works, as in many religious patterns of the Middle Ages, since good works thus motivated are means for achieving selfish ends rather than for serving other men.

When Christian duty becomes involved with the service of the neighbor, problems of conflicting claims arise which can be solved only in terms of Christian vocation. Christian duty to others may involve duties to the self. Concern about the self is permissible to the extent that it results in such prudence as to render a contribution to the neighbor more profound and adequate. The self may, for example, protect itself if by such protection a contribution to the neighbor is preserved or enhanced. Moreover, the Christian may need to employ physical resistance to evil and is even required to do so in forceful defense of the neighbor if such means are available to him. Nonviolent resistance is not preferable to violent resistance nor can it be defended merely because it employs different, and supposedly "spiritual," techniques in the exercise of its function. The Christian, however, will guard against a rationalization by which he justifies duties to the self as a service to the neighbor when in reality he is largely pleasing his own fancies. The Christian becomes virtuous only when he bends all his energies to the service of the neighbor's needs.

Elaborating upon his doctrine of Christian virtue, Ramsey draws heavily upon historical example. Augustine is credited with one facet of a complex truth because he insisted that virtue is elicited when love bends the personal will to the service of the neighbor; Aquinas is also commended for his view that grace, operating primarily but not exclusively in the sacraments, infuses virtue; while the Aristotelian view that virtue should be cultivated and developed is credited with yet another partial contribution. The Reformation view of Christian virtue as the grace which flows from God in the relationship of justification is considered by Ramsey to be the most adequate view of the matter, despite the fact that Protestant morality has not always made a place for some of the partial truths noted in Augustine, Aquinas, and the view that virtue is to be cultivated. The Protestant view of virtue precludes any autonomy in the virtues themselves, but insists that only in relationship to God can the Christian come to his fullness. Unlike virtues sought for their own sakes, which must be held in moderation, Christian virtues may embrace the dimensions of intemperance when the service of God is enhanced by abandoning a philosophical ideal of the mean in favor of an unconditional commitment.

The relationship of Christian love to the social philosophies of the nineteenth century is treated as a problem in the creating and sustaining of human community and in the valuing of human personality. Ramsey shows that the philosophical consideration of values does not function well to create community because the pressing issue of *whose* value overshadows the question of *what* value. The Christian may need to treat similar cases differently rather than similarly, since the needs of the neighbor and the particularities of each situation defy the generalizations created by abstract rules and by philosophical efforts to define the general good. It is Christian love which prompts men to regard the value of one another. Therefore, Christian love should be honored as the source rather than as the derivative of regard for human personality.

In this chapter on the nature of man Ramsey begins by considering how the doctrine of God's image in man should be understood. He first considers those philosophies which have found the divine spark in reason. He is more sympathetic with personal idealism and its view that the moral will represents the divine element in man. But he rejects both theories in favor of the contention that it is the relationship between man and God rather than some capacity innate to man which most adequately symbolizes the idea of the image. Naturalism as a theory of man's relationship to reality is examined and found wanting, even though its pragmatic elements are considered valuable. While Ramsey is more inclined to make common cause with an idealistic metaphysic, he never compromises his basic insistence that only insofar as man is related to God may he be considered important and valuable.

Christian moral theory must face the problem of sin. Sin involves willful decision and causes disruption in the relationship between man and God. It occurs as idolatry, or self-love, even when that self-love is unconscious and takes the form of loyalty to false goals which really serve the self while supposedly serving others. The will remains the source, or origin, of sin. Anxiety is the occasion, since the self is prompted to sin when it is in dread concerning its own status. In the discussion of these matters Ramsey draws upon contemporary theological and literary writings, thus remaining faithful to the covertly historical framework of his discussion.

Contemporary issues occupy the final part of the book, but as theological considerations and not in terms of practical suggestions for action. The role of love in restraining sin is considered in relationship to the place of statutory law and the role of the state. Statutory law cannot embody all that love requires, but love must employ for its purposes the instrumentalities of justice which such law represents. Love remains to prompt and criticize all social ideals and policies and must never subordinate itself in order to co-operate with them. It is to remain dutiful, yet free; co-operating, yet independent of all vitalities with which it makes common cause for the rendering of its service to God.

The fundamental orientation of the book is theological in the best sense of the term. It explores the nature of the covenantal relationship between God and man which forms the basis of all Christian behavior and action. It therefore furnishes the perspective out of which all Christian moral decision must spring, and it leaves to the reader the making of such decisions in the many complex and practical issues of life.

CHRIST AND CULTURE

Author: H. Richard Niebuhr (1894-1962)
Type of work: Christian social ethics
First published: 1951

Principal Ideas Advanced

The relationship between Christ and culture is an enduring one which finds different expression under varying historical circumstances.

The relevance of Christ to the human world of time and history may be understood in terms of five major types of relationship between Christ and culture.

The two polar positions are "Christ against culture" and "the Christ of culture."

The three median positions are "Christ above culture," "Christ and culture in paradox," and "Christ transforming culture."

Although each position contains validity and there can be no one "Christian answer," each Christian makes an individual answer in the dialogue he carries on between Christ and culture in his own life.

Christ and Culture by H. Richard Niebuhr is frequently cited as the best single volume in the field of Christian social ethics. It deals with the all-important theme of the interaction between faith and culture. The study of the relationships between religion and society has become the concern of the theologian and the social scientist as well as of the thoughtful Christian layman.

H. Richard Niebuhr considers a pivotal and perennial question of Christian life and thought. Every Christian carries on a dialogue in his own life between Christ and culture. Each person's conception of "Christ" influences his participation in culture, and his involvement in culture shapes his understanding of faith in Christ.

Niebuhr's incisive study of the problem is the product of nearly a lifetime of reflection and teaching of the subject to many grateful generations of seminary students at the Divinity School of Yale University. Not one to rush rapidly into print, the author has written three earlier books, each of which stands as a seminal contribution to literature in the field of religion: *The Social Sources of Denominationalism* (1929), *The Kingdom of God in America* (1937), and *The Meaning of Revelation* (1941). In *Christ and Culture,* he contributes a polished and precise essay that is at once a work of art and a reflection of mature scholarship.

One of the influential scholars at the turn of the present century to whom Niebuhr is most indebted is Ernst Troeltsch (1865-1923), author of the monumental two volume work, *The Social Teaching of the Christian Churches.* Niebuhr acknowledges that his *Christ and Culture* seeks "to do no more than to supplement and in part to correct" Troeltsch's great work. It is a correction in the sense that Niebuhr is more explicitly theological and theocentric than Troeltsch in dealing with the relativities of history. Niebuhr's account supplements Troeltsch's analysis in that Niebuhr discerns five main types of relationship between Church and world in contrast to Troeltsch's three: Church, sect, and mysticism.

Before he sets forth the five types, Niebuhr defines what he means by "Christ" and by "culture." There are different views of Christ, but they are all based on the historic Jesus with His several virtues. Often one of these virtues is extolled at the expense of the others—*love* by the liberals, *humility* by the monastics, and *obedience* by contemporary Christian existentialists —but the real key to understanding Christ is His Sonship to God. The Christian virtues can be understood only as they are related to God, and Christ is the intermediary between man and God. Niebuhr uses the term "Christ" as a kind of theological shorthand by which one may refer to one's faith in the entire Christian tradition.

"Culture" is "that total process of human activity and that total result of such activity to which now the name *culture,* now the name *civilization,* is applied in common speech. Culture is the 'artificial, secondary environment,' which man superimposes on the natural." Culture is the social heritage which is received and transmitted through either written or oral tradition. Culture is a purposive human achievement, aimed toward the preservation of values. Culture is also pluralistic in that it sustains many values.

The five major theological positions or "ideal types" which Niebuhr delineates are as follows:

(1) *Christ Against Culture.* The first theological position gives all authority to Christ and rejects culture's claims to authority. *God* and the *world* are opposed and the Christian can love only the former. Corruption and sin are equated with civilization. This position is epitomized by the sectarian viewpoint, the monastic movement, and is found in men like Amos, Tertullian, and Tolstoy. Tolstoy sees Christ as the giver of laws which are to be literally interpreted and which force us to reject the institutions of the world, such as property, church, and state.

Niebuhr considers the "Christ against culture" view as necessary for its own witness and as a balance to other positions, but he finds serious fault with it. Primarily, persons adopting this first position are mistaken in thinking they can depend solely on Christ and thus can reject culture, for a man's very habits, language, and reason are culturally derived. Even when a "perfect society" is set up it is governed by cultural rules. The problem here is that this group relates itself only to Christ and not to God the Creator and hence, in effect, rejects the creation as evil and unnecessary. Moreover, there is a tendency to legalism and an unawareness of sin as a vital force in all human nature.

(2) *The Christ of Culture.* The second solution stands at the opposite pole from the first. It identifies Jesus with what is best in one's particular culture and sees Him as the one who fulfills and perfects that culture's best. Though there is selection in both realms of Christ and culture, what is enduring in each is in agreement (and what does not agree is therefore not enduring). Thus there is no tension felt between the demands of the two. The "Christ of culture" position characterizes those who feel no conflict between Church and world. The Christian Gnostics interpreted Christ solely in the terms of their own culture. In the era of liberalism the emergence of "culture-Protestantism" moved in this direction and Albert Ritschl is a prime example of one who holds the "Christ of culture" view. Ritschl saw man's problem as the conflict with nature and he found Christ to be man's ally in this struggle.

"The Christ of Culture" answer does help any culture to accept and to understand Christ, and it does show that Christ is relevant to cultural concerns, but it has serious faults. It accommodates Christ to culture only by distorting the historic Jesus. Moreover, while its advocates wish to rely on reason to the exclusion of revelation, they are dependent on the historic but nonrational fact of Jesus. Furthermore, unlike the first approach, the second view does not involve the realization that all culture is pervaded by sin. Finally, while it relates well to the Immanent God, the idea fails to apply to the God who is Lord and Creator.

(3) *Christ Above Culture* (Synthesist). To argue that Christ is above culture is to adopt the median answer of synthesis. The final three approaches agree on demanding *both* Christ *and* culture. They see the way in which Christ's demands run counter to culture and yet they see culture as a good, arising from God the Creator and thus containing objects of loyalty and laws which must be obeyed. These three viewpoints, seeing the universality of sin and the values of culture, cannot easily oppose Christ and culture, but rather must center on the opposition between God and man.

The "Christ Above Culture" position combines the opposing elements in a single system so that a synthesis between Christ and culture is possible in which both are affirmed. Clement of Alexandria realized that a man must be good in the cultural sense before he can go on to the Christian graces. Thomas Aquinas saw such a hierarchy in all areas. Reason is necessary as far as it goes; then revelation appears. Natural law exists but only with the divine law above it. The goods of culture have their place as do the divine goods.

The major objection to this position is that there is no recognition in it of the pervasion of the natural world and its value by sin. Also, when Thomas Aquinas examines natural law, he fails to see that he cannot escape his culture and that he therefore sanctifies a particular cultural system.

(4) *Christ and Culture in Paradox* (Dualist). This position involves a radical dualism. The dualist sees sin in all of man's works. Before the holiness of God there is no distinction between what we call good and evil. The dualist attacks all culture, yet he realizes that he is a sinful part of it and must

live in it. He sees the radical demands of God but knows his inability to obey. St. Paul viewed the institutions of culture as of negative value only in restraining sin. Luther's dualism is quite clear. God's forgiveness affects the inner man but social life cannot be redeemed.

This position represents a more realistic view, but since it merely describes our situation, it gives us no viable solution. Moreover, it tends toward antinomianism or at least toward cultural conservatism.

(5) *Christ the Transformer of Culture* (Conversionist). The final position, like the dualist one, takes sin seriously but places greater emphasis on the Incarnation and on the present creative work of God. The emphasis is not merely on restraining sin, but on overcoming it. Creation and the Fall tend to be confused by the dualist but not here, for the Fall is a corruption of creation. Creation may be redeemed and all things are possible for God in history. Eschatology is, at least in part, already realized. F. D. Maurice is important here for emphasizing both Christ the King and sin, and for regarding the conversion of men and society as a universal possibility. Culture is under the governance of God, and Christians must be socially responsible in obedience to God. Their duty is to make Christ the Lord of culture.

These five major types of relationship between Christ and culture are found manifested in different periods of history. In a concluding chapter ("Concluding Unscientific Postscript"), Niebuhr refuses to choose one or another of the types as representing *the* Christian answer. While some scholars have praised this relativistic and objective approach, many have criticized the author for not making his personal point of view explicit. Niebuhr maintains that knowing the five alternatives and knowing our own limited perspective, we must make a particular choice in the existential moment of decision. But to do this is not to be relative or individualistic or independent, for we rely at all times on the Christian community, on history, and, by faith, on God.

THE CHRISTIAN UNDERSTANDING OF GOD

Author: Nels F. S. Ferré (1908-)
Type of work: Philosophical theology
First published: 1951

Principal Ideas Advanced

God is best understood as personal spirit who is sovereign love.

This uniquely Christian concept, if taken seriously enough for thought, can provide both a more coherent explanation of philosophic problems arising for Christians and a more adequate interpretation of the true claims of Christianity than can traditional approaches premised on alien notions of God.

God as sovereign love eternally creates for the sake of fellowship.

Through His loving providence and self-revelation, God ultimately wins all His children to free acceptance of never-ending joy and growth in love.

The Christian Understanding of God represents the first thoroughgoing attempt to derive consistently the substance of Christian doctrine from Christianity's central affirmation, "God is love." The author, Nels F. S. Ferré, was impressed by the systematic consistency and coherence of his professors in philosophy, Edgar S. Brightman (1884-1953) and Alfred North Whitehead (1861-1947), but he remained unconvinced of the adequacy of the central concepts around which their thoughts were structured. Later Ferré found his professors in theology at Lund University in his native Sweden correct in pointing to *agape* (other-centered love) as the dominant and fully adequate motif of Christianity, but he was dissatisfied at the incompleteness with which implications of this motif were made normative for Christian thought by nonphilosophical Lundensian theologians like Anders Nygren, author of the classic *Agape and Eros.*

Consequently, in a series of books importantly typified by *The Christian Understanding of God,* Ferré has engaged in the formidable task of joining the theoretical strength of philosophical rigor to the saving adequacy of Christian content. This proposed marriage is not, however, to commit Christianity to accepting into its household philosophy's ancient Greek dowry. Theology's own insights are not to be dominated or diluted by alien presuppositions—however familiar—about the nature of the ultimate.

With this motive, Ferré turns in *The Christian Understanding of God* to consider the explanatory potential of sovereign love when it, rather than being, is rigorously taken as the key concept for ultimate reality. Beginning from the master motif of cosmic *agape,* Ferré finds that the traditional philosophic puzzles of being and becoming dissolve within his analysis. Being, first, is itself to be understood in terms of the intrinsic stability of love, that concrete total concern which is supremely self-sustaining and self-directed; love is only mistakenly conceived under the rubric of the abstract category, "being." Thus correctly defined, being is discovered to be intimately related to—not, as is usually supposed, in radical opposition to—nonbeing; creative love, even as being, requires nonbeing as the bottomless abyss of potentiality thanks to which it may endlessly increase its self-sharing through new creation. Another traditional difficulty, understanding how ultimate reality, or the Absolute, can remain absolute and yet have relations to beings other than itself, disappears once the notion of absolute being is viewed in the light of cosmic love. Relations are not alien to, but are required by, love; it is a a false conception of the Absolute which would force it logically into an abstraction from all relatedness.

Although being is best understood in terms of love, love is not comprehended in being. Of equal or greater importance is the illumination that love throws on the nature of becoming, inasmuch as love is that which can *be* what it most truly is only by *becoming*. Standard philosophical problems in relating being to becoming are thus transcended: "Only by becoming can being become what it is." Change, in terms of growth and fulfillment, is as intrinsic to love as is stability; the form of love's stability, indeed, is found precisely in such controlled and constructive change. The concept of becoming thus subordinates that of being, while at the same time presupposing it, when both are seen in terms of the primacy of love. "Start with being as ultimate, and arrive at no adequate doctrine of becoming; start with becoming as ultimate, and find no real interpretation of being. Start with love as ultimate, and being and becoming are both inherent within His nature; being and becoming are then abstractions from the fullness of reality."

A long step toward concreteness from the abstractions of beings and becoming is represented by the concept of personality. It is only in the personal, not in sheer being-in-becoming, that we find love. Taking love seriously as our starting point, therefore, strongly suggests the legitimacy of considering God as personal. Besides including concretely both being and becoming, the concept of the personal indicates the complex truth about God: that He is being-in-becoming who is characterized by self-transcendence (relating to others), self-consciousness, self-direction, self-perpetuation, and creative purpose. The concept of the personal, further, may aid us in conceiving of those elements in His nature analogous to the bodies through which all persons we know express their capacities for overt manipulation of the impersonal, for communication with other persons, and for objectifying the past in memory.

God, for Ferré, is not basically to be described even in such terms, however, despite their essential place in our understanding of sovereign love. The personal cannot be the ultimate form of love, first, because love may work (analogously to bodily functions) in impersonal ways and, second, because personalities—however intimate —never "interpenetrate" one another in that spiritual harmony which is the essence of completely realized fellowship and the goal of creative love. *Agape,* then, no less than "spirit," is the principle (as Ferré defines it) of union or cohesiveness. This concept of spirit, including but transcending the concepts of personality, becoming, being, and nonbeing, is alone adequate to the master motif of sovereign love.

The understanding of God as personal spirit who is creative love brings a solution to the traditional philosophic problem of "the One and the many." How can God, if infinite, exist together with a world of change and multiplicity that is somehow not Himself? If He is really infinite, is it not a contradiction to suppose that there exists anything *besides* the infinite? Does this not make of God merely one being alongside other beings—beings which must inevitably limit His infinitude simply by existing as other than Himself? Supposing God to be infinite, then, would seem to entail holding "the many" to be mere illusion; while taking "the many" of our experience as real would seem to require believing "the One" to be finite, merely one being among others, and without unique status. Ferré's answer to this dilemma is to point out that once again a needless puzzle has been generated by the false adoption of the abstract notion of being as the essence of God. Infinite being *qua being* cannot permit the coexistence of rival beings, but infinite being *qua love* has no such difficulty. God's unique identity is established by His uncreated status as infinite creative love and by the constancy of love's purposes and activities. The situation of "the One and the many" is not a contradiction, therefore, but a consequence of the distinctively Christian concept of the ultimate who creates and enters into relations with His world.

The relational character of the Christian God not only fails to pose a problem for consistent thought on Christian premises but also undergirds the otherwise vexing doctrine of the Trinity. Love is not relational by accident; God's very essence is social. The fellowship of the Persons of the Godhead is the model and ground for all created fellowship. Considered thus, instead of in terms of alien substance-philosophy, the Christian understanding of Trinity makes irrelevant many of the problems that have so often obscured it.

If social relations and the mutual interplay and successive experiences of personal love are present within God Himself, then the otherwise thorny metaphysical concept of time and its relation to eternity is illuminated by Ferré's account. God's successive experience is what we mean by eternity, "God's time." The specific nature of such time we are unable to imagine; but we may know of its character in principle through our own experience of time, the function of which is essentially the same for us and for God: to make fellowship possible. Time is the means and medium for learning, for growth, for coming to love. Time itself, Ferré shows us, is best interpreted through the primacy of *agape*.

In like manner, space serves love. Just as time is the condition for becoming in fellowship, so space is most basically the condition for "simultaneous otherness" without which fellowship would be inconceivable. Space-time, therefore, is in its broadest sense not accidental in the structure of things but an eternal element in a universe created by and sustained for *agape*.

If time is real, even for God, can God know the future? Ferré's answer requires us to make a distinction between "knowing the future" in the general sense of knowing confidently the outcome of all God's ultimate purposes and "knowing the future" in the specific sense of knowing precisely the details of that which is not yet real. In the former sense God knows the future, for He knows that He is sovereign and competently in control of all times; in the latter sense God does not know the future, since He permits His children, for the sake of free fellowship in love, to have genuine power to determine the specific future. Knowledge of what is not yet determinate would be false knowledge. God's omniscience is complete inasmuch as He knows all there is to know; His knowledge is not limited by His not knowing what is not yet real.

Does God's sharing of power with His children for the sake of their freedom limit His nature? Not in the slightest, answers Ferré. Power is not the essence of God; power is properly defined in terms of "the capacity of love to effect its end." If the end of love is the free fellowship of responsible persons, it is not a limitation but an expression of God's nature to provide power enough to His children for freedom and learning in love. God must remain in ultimate control, of course, if His sovereign love is to be responsible. His creatures' powers are never infinite, as the world with its blend of predictability and precariousness constantly reminds us. The rebellious creature may call such a world "evil" and formulate a "problem of evil" with regard to the pedagogical precariousness of the world; but God's love remains responsible, and His benevolence remains great enough even to cause us pain for a time to remind us that ultimate fulfillment is not to be found in our own power—real and responsible though it is.

Even this stern holiness of God is no contradiction to His essence as love. Holiness, above all, is "the infinite purity of love or internal self-consistency of its nature." *Agape* is far from sentimentality. The demands of holy love may, Ferré thinks, cause God to suffer; but even if this is so (and it is by no means certain), the sufferings of the Sovereign can never have the quality of despair that would make His suffering incompatible with supreme joy in present fellowship and the certainty of future joy in still wider fellowship.

With this developed concept of the nature of God, Ferré turns to an examination of the work of God in creation and redemption. God as love is inevitably creator, not out of blind necessity but as a free expression of cosmic *agape* itself. Creation, then, is as much an expression of God's love as is redemption. The nature of His creations, too, reflect God's sovereign concern. He has made, in our particular "cosmic epoch" (and it would be unthinkably parochial to suppose that our own universe, however vast, is God's only creation), an "open" universe, open to His providential purposes as well as to our lesser purposes. Even general providence, God's permissive way of allowing things to happen as they normally do for the sake of our growth in freedom, is best understood through reference to love. All providence, whether general or "special" (in which God takes a more personally active part in events through suggesting ideas to His children or influencing directly chains of causation), remains "the patient guidance by God of all His creation toward the best possible end for it."

Redemption involves revelation. As love, God wants to be known, but as personal spirit, God must reveal Himself (as must any person) if He is to be known by others. Ferré discusses God's self-revelation in nature, or the possibility of a natural theology, and finds that while some general revelation must be present even in nature, God cannot be found in His full character of *agape* in nature or in history. Only through His working in the Holy Spirit is God present with us as personal spirit who is love; hence, Christian thought should focus not on natural theology but on a theology grounded in study of the Church and Incarnation, where, and nowhere else, God is to be found as He most reliably is.

God's work in Incarnation is thoroughly and supremely redemptive. Jesus, whose much controverted "virgin birth" has no essential bearing on biological fact, was the Christ through the unprecedented initiative of the love of God. To this dependence on an extraordinary act of God the doctrine of "virgin birth" symbolically attests, whatever the historical facts (now unascertainable one way or the other) surrounding Mary's impregnation. The doctrine of atonement must, Ferré holds, also be seen consistently in the light of love; God was working through the whole atoning life of Jesus (not just through His death) to bring men back into fellowship with Himself, a fellowship without which there is no fulfillment for man. Resurrection, on the other hand, illustrates the sovereignty of eternal love. In the doctrine of the resurrection of Jesus is symbolized, Ferré believes, God's inevitable victory over the forces of evil, destruction, and despair. The resurrection may well be more than a symbol; it may be—Ferré thinks it probable—a historic fact, a foretaste of God's triumph over all lovelessness and self-defeating rebellion.

A theology based on sovereign love will, Ferré insists, uncompromisingly stand for universal salvation. Anything less would be inconsistent with God's sovereignty and would impugn God's love. Such a universalistic position presupposes an afterlife, of course; and Ferré does indeed strongly maintain that life after our physical death is an absolutely essential tenet of Christian faith. Without providing further opportunity for the expression of His pedagogical concern beyond the present life, God would have to be supposed either not to care enough about His children to pursue their welfare after the grave or not to be sufficiently in control of events to carry out His aims. Neither supposition is compatible with the distinctive motif of Christianity. Also clearly incompatible with sovereign love is the vicious doctrine of eternal Hell. It may be that "hell" exists as a post-mortem condition of unrepentant self-separation from loving fellowship with the holy God, but the "gates of hell" must always be hinged so as to open outward at the touch of the penitent child. Only so can there be joy in Heaven. "Heaven, to those who truly love all, can be heaven only when it has emptied hell." Even Judgment and Hell, therefore, and the consequent preaching of fear or of life's seriousness, need definition in terms of love's aim. Life is earnest and sin has consequences; purgatory, Ferré believes, may exist as a state in which the repentant and forgiven sinner works willingly toward repairing the destructive effects of his sin on himself and others. God is too good a Father to spoil His children but God is the one Father who "has no permanent problem children." He never coerces, but infinite love is the one reality strong enough and patient enough to be sure of winning all, not despite our freedom but through our freedom.

Thus Ferré's final vision is of God, love constantly beyond limit, as He surges from victory to greater victory in sharing Himself with the countless myriads of creatures for each of whom He has unlimited individual concern. Before this cosmic vision Ferré stands —and asks us to stand—in amazement and adoration toward Him who offers us out of sheer love the prospect and the certainty of unceasing adventure from joy to joy, fulfillment beyond creative fulfillment, worlds without end.

Ferré's vision and his entire enterprise of rethinking theology (and much of philosophy) demand time for assimilation; and although the contemporary theological and philosophical communities in general have not yet fully felt the radical impact of *The Christian Understanding of God,* it may with justice be supposed that a work of this kind, whose influence is already noteworthy, has been addressed not merely to our own decades but to generations still to come.

INTRODUCTION TO THE PHILOSOPHY OF RELIGION

Author: Peter Anthony Bertocci (1910-)
Type of work: Philosophy of religion
First published: 1951

Principal Ideas Advanced

The core of religion is the personal belief that one's most important values are sponsored by the enduring structure of the universe.

Neither strict logical consistency nor immediate religious experience is an adequate foundation for religious knowledge; reason as a method of gaining coherence in our total experience can lead to reasonable faith.

The wider teleological argument supports the hypothesis of a Personal Source of Value as the most comprehensive and coherent explanation of the interconnectedness of physical nature, life, and human experience, and of man's intellectual, moral, aesthetic, and religious values.

Excess evil is due to a recalcitrant aspect of God's own nature; God nevertheless creates and preserves values through never-ending heroic struggle and sacrificial love.

Since mid-century, Bertocci's *Introduction to the Philosophy of Religion* has become the best-known philosophical treatment of religion from the point of view of personalism (or personalistic idealism). In America personalism was first elaborated by Borden Parker Bowne (1847-1910). Bertocci has been Borden Parker Bowne Professor of Philosophy at Boston University since 1953. Two thinkers have had a notable influence on Bertocci's philosophic position. One was Edgar Sheffield Brightman (1884-1953), the leading proponent of personalism during the second quarter of the century, and Bertocci's predecessor at Boston University. The other major influence on Bertocci's thought has come from F. R. Tennant (1866-1957), British philosopher and author of the two volume work, *Philosophical Theology* (1930).

In general, Bertocci develops what may be called a broadly empirical philosophy of religion in the tradition of personalistic idealism. He proceeds on the assumption that religious beliefs must be examined and understood in "the light of the believer's total experience." The essence of religion, Bertocci maintains, is "the personal belief that one's most important values are sponsored by, or in harmony with, the enduring structure of the universe," even if they are not supported by society. After exploring briefly some of the factors that affect religious belief, Bertocci raises the question: Can reason justify or repudiate religious beliefs? That is, is reason competent to judge among religious beliefs in the complex of human experience? To answer this question, Bertocci finds it necessary to distinguish between two conceptions of reason. He argues that reason as *logical consistency among premises* is indispensable to the life of thought, but it is not sufficient to interpret the concrete concerns of religion; while reason as *empirical coherence* (the finding of connections among the experienced facts) may not provide logical certainty, but it can provide growing though probable truth when applied to religion.

A major alternative to this approach is the view that faith has unilateral access to indubitable religious truth, that religious experience contains its own warrant for the absolute knowledge it reveals. Bertocci takes sharp exception to this position. He seeks to show that religious experience is not cognitive, that no immediate experience can give indubitable guarantee to religious belief. He emphatically denies "the *independent* validity of religious experience as a source of knowledge." Bertocci's criticism is based on the general epistemological argument that all immediate experience requires interpretation before it will yield knowledge, and on the "instability" and "vagueness" of the nonsensory qualitative content of religious experience. Bertocci criticizes William James (1842-1910), Rudolph Otto (1869-1937), and Henri Bergson (1859-1941) for maintaining in different ways that religious experience is directly cognitive. Religious experience, Bertocci concludes, makes whatever contribution it does only within the total context of life.

Reason as a method of gaining coherence in experience can lead to reasonable faith. Reasonable faith, according to Bertocci, has a close affinity to scientific method. Religion and science are, therefore, not incompatible; they both involve the conception of reason as empirical coherence. But what about the conflict between the religious and scientific perspectives? Bertocci holds that this clash reflects the tension between two contrasting but not irreconcilable intellectual motives. The first is expressed in the desire to know the "how" of things. In the developed scientific perspective this motive takes the form of mechanical explanation; that is, understanding the causal sequences of the parts or elements in the natural world. The second motive is expressed in the desire to know the "why" of things. In the developed religious perspective this motive takes the form of teleological explanation; that is, understanding the purposes and plans which give order to the whole. According to Bertocci, the conflict between these two modes of explanation becomes a problem only when either is taken as final, exclusive of the other.

Consistent with the contextual approach characterized above and preparatory to the synoptic outlook of his argument for God, Bertocci devotes a section of five chapters (6-10) to scientific questions (facts and issues) about the physical, biological, psychological, and moral orders. The most distinctive feature of these chapters is found in Bertocci's discussion of the moral dimension and particularly in his treatment of the problem of free will.

Bertocci draws a distinction between "will-agency" and "will-power." Will-agency is an innate, not acquired, property of a person in virtue of which he chooses among alternatives. But will-agency is not an autonomous faculty; will-power refers to the "actual efficacy . . . of the willing to reach a chosen objective." The capacity to choose (will-agency) is affected by other facets of the personality and by environmental factors. The concept of will-power is thus used to acknowledge limits on free-will but without jeopardizing the reality of choice.

Bertocci's treatment of the standard arguments for God in the Western tradition is appreciative, yet critical. The ontological argument, given its classic formulation by St. Anselm of Canterbury (c.1033-1109), maintains that the idea of perfection, possessed by every human being, implies the existence of a perfect being. Unfortunately, the existence of God cannot be deduced from the idea of God. Nevertheless, the emphasis on perfection is a distilled though perhaps vague intellectual transcription of the central religious affirmation; namely, the relevance of the highest values (perfection) to reality (God).

The cosmological argument, associated classically with Aristotle (384-322 B.C.) and St. Thomas Aquinas (c.1225-1274), maintains that the changing world requires an unchanging First Cause. Dissatisfaction with the infinite regress of finite causes shows a commendable interest in the metaphysical ultimacy and unity "behind" the order of change. Ambiguity as to the meaning of "cause" seriously vitiates the argument. Is the First Cause an uncaused cause wholly other than the series of causes it initiates, or is the First Cause "a productive power initiating change" and "the basic continuant in all change"? Furthermore, what is it that allows us to identify the First Cause with the God of faith?

The classic teleological argument infers the existence of a providential God from evidences of design, from "the *adaptive* order of the world." This argument is implicated in the issues raised regarding the cosmological argument. In addition, it suffers from a static pre-Darwinian formulation and from the tendency of its advocates to overlook the purposeless and disharmonious in nature.

The moral argument for God is based on the contention that the existence of God is a presupposition of man's moral consciousness and of an objective realm of ideal values to which this consciousness gives access. Since moral values figure prominently in Bertocci's argument for God, no further comment is needed here.

The difficulties in the traditional arguments are underlined by Bertocci's analysis of the attributes traditionally ascribed to a personal God. Bertocci raises the issues that arise when God is conceived as a supremely good creator who is immutable and eternal, transcendent and/or immanent, omnipotent, and omniscient. For example, is God's omniscience consistent with human freedom?

The residue of truth in each of the traditional arguments needs to be reformulated and coordinated. This Bertocci attempts to do in what he calls "the wider teleological argument for a personal God," an argument influenced by Tennant's work. The wider teleological argument differs from the traditional arguments in that it does not claim to be definitive or demonstrative; rather, it offers a tentative and probable hypothesis. Thus the wider teleological argument is less rationalistic and more empirical than the traditional arguments. It rests its case on a comprehensive and cumulative interpretation. It appeals to a wide range of evidence, insisting "on the interconnectedness of physical nature, life, and human experience" and blending intellectual, moral, aesthetic, and religious values into the texture of the hypothesis. The wider teleological argument is metaphysical in maintaining that the theistic hypothesis (that is, the "hypothesis of a Personal Source of Value") provides the most intelligible and coherent explanation of all the contextual interrelations adduced. This hypothesis, Bertocci argues, gives the most adequate account of both the continuity and the development in the total process.

In detail, the wider teleological argument consists of seven links. Link One stresses "the purposive interrelation of matter and life." Life is dependent on but cannot be reduced to matter. That a cosmic creative Intelligence is at work in the natural order is, Bertocci holds, the best explanation of the collocation of matter and life. Link Two draws attention to "the relevance of thought to reality." Knowledge depends on reliable interaction between man and nature. Mind is thus relevant to its world. Indeed, reality seems to put a premium on the development of moral disciplines.

Link Three discusses "the interrelation of the moral effort and the order of nature." "Unless man is free, there is no real point to moral effort," *but* unless there is also a dependable natural order, there is no significant moral effort. Link Four broadens the scope to emphasize "the interrelation between value and nature." This theme, in conjunction with Link Five, which interprets "this world as good for man," constitutes the heart of the wider teleological argument. Here Bertocci seeks to weld the positive features of the cosmological and moral arguments. Human values are not merely man-made but are a joint product of man and his world. Human values disclose "what nature can be." For Bertocci, "that human beings should be co-creating values in his universe is *the* value attending all other values." Thus, "the value of values is character." The fact that the universe promotes and sustains moral growth is best explained by a conscious cosmic sponsor of value. This fact is also the basis for believing in the goodness of God. "The world in which man lives can best be understood as a moral order in which God purposes creative love as the source of all goodness and happiness."

Link Six adds "the significance of aesthetic experience" to the argument. The aesthetic dimension reflects another creative interaction between man and the universe. Link Seven is now able to treat "religious experience as confirmatory." Although religious experience taken independently is an insufficient basis for belief in a personal God, it reinforces and is reinforced by other aspects of our experience.

Bertocci now turns to the problem of evil. The traditional explanations of evil are not convincing. To say that evil is the result of man's abuse of his freedom overlooks the superfluous sufferings that human existence so often brings. To say that evil is ultimately part of the divine plan overlooks the evidence "that God is not omnipotent." Bertocci concludes that the weight of moral guilt and natural evil cannot be squared with the traditional theodicy.

How, then, is excess evil to be explained? Is it due to divine ill-will or neglect? No, Bertocci answers, there is too much positive evidence (already adduced in support of the wider teleological argument) of ultimate goodness. Then there must be some limitation on God's power, some impediment to God's good purposes. Bertocci expounds three conceptions of the nature of an impediment which partially frustrates God's plan and leads to excess evil.

First is Plato's view that God is a cosmic artist who shapes a raw material he did not create. In other words, the impediment (to use Plato's term) is the "receptacle of becoming," an environment external to God, unshaped and obdurate, but subject to control. The second conception of the impediment which Bertocci considers is that of the American philosopher, W. P. Montague (1873-1953). Montague holds that the impediment is within God, an internal environment which is the world. That is, the world is part of God's being but is external to His infinite mind.

The third explanation of excess evil which Bertocci examines is that of his teacher and predecessor, E. S. Brightman. Bertocci holds that Brightman corrects weaknesses in Plato's and Montague's conceptions of the impediment. Bertocci therefore adopts Brightman's position. In *A Philosophy of Religion* (1940), Brightman argues forcefully that excess evil is due to "a recalcitrant aspect of God's own nature." This aspect Brightman calls the "Nonrational Given"; it refers to refractory data, brute fact such as sensation. A second aspect of God's nature Brightman calls the "Rational Given"; it corresponds very closely to the traditional notion of the divine reason. The third aspect of the divine being is the divine will. God's will does not, for Brightman, create either the Nonrational Given (brute fact) or the Rational Given (rational norms). God's will does, however, control the Nonrational Given according to His rational principles, giving new significant form to what is otherwise meaningless content. Although God is never absolutely in control, He never loses control and is always at work overcoming obstacles. New values are continually being created through heroic struggle and sacrificial love. God is thus the "Finite-Infinite Controller of the Given," in Brightman's terms. Bertocci believes that Brightman's view preserves more adequately the integral unity and rich complexity of a supreme personal God than does that of either Plato or Montague. It is also, Bertocci maintains, a firmer basis for the religious consciousness than the traditional theodicy.

Bertocci now concludes: "Religion is the faith that God is the ultimate Personal Creator and Sustainer of all values, and that human beings realize the utmost in value when they join him, conscientiously and joyously, in the creation of value." It follows from this that prayer occupies a central place in the religious life. For prayer is "the conscious attempt of the individual to commune with God for the purpose of fellowship." Furthermore, the urgency of establishing an open and growing world community is rooted in such a faith. Finally, Bertocci's moving justification of personal immortality (in the concluding chapter) draws the consequences for man's destiny of the religious hypothesis which the book develops.

Whether Bertocci's personalistic philosophy of religion will continue to be a viable alternative to the competing contemporary perspectives of naturalistic humanism and theological existentialism only time can determine.

SYSTEMATIC THEOLOGY

Author: Paul Tillich (1886-)
Type of work: Philosophical theology
First published: Volume I, 1951; Volume II, 1957

Principal Ideas Advanced

Theology is a systematic and disciplined investigation of that which concerns man ultimately; the method of theology is the "method of correlation," correlating man's basic questions about himself and his world with the symbols of the Christian message which provide the answers to these questions.

Revelation provides the answer to the questions implied in the existential conflicts of reason; revelation does not destroy reason, but is continuous with the depth of reason.

The symbol of God provides the answer to the question implied in human finitude; the question of human finitude arises in the awareness of the possible disruption of the essential structures of finite being—the shock of possible non-being; the answer to this question is God, who is Being-itself, living, creating, and related.

The symbol of the Christ provides the answer to the question implied in man's existential estrangement and self-destruction; the reality element of this symbol is the New Being disclosed in the unique event of Jesus as the Christ who conquers estrangement through His power of salvation.

Systematic Theology comprises Paul Tillich's effort to formulate a theological system which is at the same time universal and peculiarly relevant to contemporary man. The projected system consists of five parts: I. Reason and Revelation, II. Being and God, III. Existence and the Christ, IV. Life and the Spirit, and V. History and the Kingdom of God. In all of the five parts the method of correlation provides the guiding methodological motif. Revelation comes as an answer to the conflicts of reason; God is the answer to the question of the finitude of being; Christ is the answer to the question of human finitude under the conditions of estrangement; Spirit provides the answer to the ambiguity of life; and the Kingdom of God constitutes the answer to the question of the meaning of history. Only the first three parts of Tillich's system are contained in Volumes I and II, discussed here.

Tillich has appropriately characterized his theology as an "answering theology," thus indicating both the method and content of his theological system. In its general form the problem is presented in terms of the relation between philosophy and theology; in one of its specific forms the focus is upon the relation between reason and revelation. On the one hand, philosophy and theology diverge; on the other hand, they converge; in the last analysis they are understood as being mutually dependent. They diverge in their respective cognitive attitudes. The attitude of philosophy towards its subject is theoretical; the attitude of theology towards its subject is existential. In the theoretical attitude the distance between the knower and the known is decisive; in the existential attitude the unity of the knower and the known is decisive. Yet the convergence of the two must be acknowledged insofar as philosophy always arises in a concrete situation and therefore has existential presuppositions, and theology in dealing with the logos of being has theoretical implications. The two thus become mutually dependent. Insofar as it has existential presuppositions philosophy is dependent on theology; insofar as it has theoretical implications theology is dependent on philosophy.

The problem of the relation between reason and revelation arises as an instance in the wider relation which obtains between philosophy and theology generally. Reason and revelation are distinct but not discontinuous. Tillich finds it necessary to distinguish between an ontological and technical concept of reason. The former, expressed predominantly in Greek rationalism and German classical idealism, indicates a structure in which mind is related to the reality which it grasps and transforms. The latter, expressed predominantly in British empiricism, has to do with methodological tools and logical procedures which determine the means in a given means-end relationship. Although Tillich sees ontological and technical reason as companions, the relation of reason and revelation arises only on the level of ontological reason. This does not mean that ontological reason and revelation are to be identified (the mistake of idealistic philosophy). Such an identity is present only in the realm of essential perfection. Ontological reason as actualized appears under the conditions of finitude, existential estrangement, and the ambiguities of life and history. Actual reason moves in and through finite categories and self-destructive conflicts. Nonetheless, in spite of its finitude and estrangement, reason is aware of its infinite depth, and the quest for revelation proceeds by virtue of this relatedness of reason to the infinite; and the quest culminates in the reintegration of the existential conflicts and historical ambiguities of reason. It is thus that revelation constitutes an answer to the questions which arise in the actualization and conflicts of reason.

The fundamental theological issue has to do with the idea and reality of God. God is the answer to the question implied in the finitude of being. The question of finitude is most decisively posed in the experience of "metaphysical shock"—the shock of possible nonbeing. To be finite is to be limited by nonbeing. Nonbeing makes its appearance as the "not yet" of being and the "no more" of being and indicates an irreducible dialectical constituent of finitude. The question initiated by the metaphysical shock leads to an interest in the structures of being. These structures are discussed by the author on four levels of ontological analysis: the self-world correlation as the basic ontological structure; the polar elements of individualization and participation, dynamics and form, and freedom and destiny as the constituents of the ontological structure; the duality of essential and existential being; and the categories of time, space, causality, and substance as the basic forms of thought and being. In the finitude of being these structures, elements, and forms are threatened with disruption and self-destruction. This threat gives rise to ontological anxiety on various levels. There is the anxiety of the possible loss of self and world. There is an anxiety of not being what one essentially is as one confronts the possible disruption of the polar elements of individualization and participation, dynamics and form, freedom and destiny. There is the anxiety of nonbeing arising from the possible dissolution of the categories or forms of thought and being. Expressed specifically, the anxiety of nonbeing is the anxiety of transitoriness because of one's having to die, the anxiety of insecurity because of the loss of one's space, the anxiety of formless change and becoming because of the loss of one's substance, and the anxiety of contingency because of the dissolution of causality. In these threats of disruption and self-distruction the duality of essence and existence is of paramount importance. Being is not essentially in a state of disruption. The breaking of the polarities, as an implication of freedom and destiny, occurs only in the transition to existential actualization. Finitude must thus be understood in terms both of its essential being (as potential perfection) and of its existential actualization. Religiously speaking this distinction is that which holds between the created and the actual world.

God is the answer to the question implied in the finitude of being as this being is threatened with nonbeing in the possible disruption of its structures, giving rise to ontological anxiety. The reality of God is described by the author as Being-itself, living, creating, and related. Only God thus understood can provide the answer to the question of finite being. *God is Being-itself*. This is the only statement about God which is nonsymbolic. God is neither *a* being nor the totality of beings. He transcends the basic ontological structure which underlies every definition of finite being. Although both self and world are rooted in God as Being-itself, they are in no sense constitutive of God nor can they provide symbolic material for the understanding of the being of God. Being-itself infinitely transcends every finite being.

God as Being-itself is also *living*. Life, however, as applied to God must be understood in its symbolic sense, and this can be done through the symbolic use of the elements which constitute the basic ontological structure —individualization and participation, dynamics and form, freedom and destiny. These elements can become symbols because they do not speak of kinds of being (self and world) but rather of qualities of being which can be applied universally to all beings and symbolically to being-itself. God is symbolically the "absolute individual" and the "absolute participant." The divine life is the ground of everything individual and personal as well as the principle of participation in everything that is. The polarity of dynamics and form also applies symbolically to God. A living God is one in whom these two elements remain in tension.

According to Tillich, the classical definition of God as *actus purus* is misleading, for it involves a neglect of the dynamic side of God. God is symbolically structured by both form and dynamism. The polarity of freedom and destiny likewise can be symbolically applied to the divine life. Freedom points to the aseity of God; there is nothing given in God which is not at the same time affirmed by His freedom. Destiny as attributed to God means that God is His own destiny. His freedom is not limited by a destiny imposed from the outside; in God freedom and destiny are one.

The third general description of the reality of God is *creativity*. The doctrine of creation constitutes the answer to the question implied in man's experience of his creatureliness. This divine creativity is expressed in an originating creativity, sustaining creativity, and directing creativity (purpose and providence).

Finally, God as *related* comprises the symbols of holiness, power and love. God as Being-itself is the ground of every relation. The holiness of God describes His unapproachable character—His majesty and glory. The divine power of God describes his ultimacy by virtue of which He can properly be understood as the "object" of man's ultimate concern. The courage through which man is able to conquer the anxiety of finitude is founded upon participation in God as the ultimate power of being. Divine love (*agape*) describes God's acceptance of the creature in spite of his resistance and is thus the final answer to man's finitude.

In Part III of his system Tillich examines man's existential estrangement and the reality of Jesus as the Christ as an answer to the questions implied in this estrangement. Already in part II of the system we have been made aware that there are two sides to the finite being of man—the essential and the existential. Man's essential being is his created being, mythologically expressed in the Biblical story of man in Paradise. Man's existential being is his being as subject to estrangement and self-destruction, mythologically expressed in the Biblical story of the Fall of man. Demythologized, the story of the Fall of Adam expresses the truth of man's transition from his essential unity with God to his condition of existential estrangement. This is the meaning of sin (*suendo*)—a cutting off or estrangement from God. This estrangement from God comes about through man's actualization of himself as finite freedom, which is always in a polar relationship with destiny. Insofar as sin is an expression of freedom it becomes a matter of personal responsibility; insofar as it is an implication of destiny it is a matter of tragic universality.

The marks of estrangement, as implications of the Fall, are fundamental and pervasive. They are unbelief, *hubris,* and concupiscence. Unbelief is the movement whereby man removes his center from the divine center. *Hubris* is the movement of self-elevation whereby man seeks to establish himself as the center of creation. Concupiscence indicates the unlimited desire of man to draw the whole of reality into himself. These three movements of estrangement lead to existential self-destruction, which manifests itself in the various forms of existential anxiety—the anxiety of fate and death, guilt and condemnation, spiritual loneliness, doubt and meaninglessness, and despair. Despair is the final index of the human predicament. It constitutes man's final boundary situation; it is that limit beyond which men cannot go, for in despair all of his possibilities are obliterated. Man in despair exists "without hope." This experience of despair is indicated in the symbol of the "wrath of God."

It is the awareness of man's existential estrangement and self-destruction which motivates the quest for the New Being and for the meaning of the Christ. The New Being in Jesus as the Christ provides the answer to the questions implied in human existence, just as, in Part II of the work, God provided the answer to the questions implied in human finitude. The formulation of the symbol for the conquest of estrangement, *Jesus as the Christ,* is not accidental. Both sides of the symbol, the humanity of Jesus and the divinity of Christ, must be maintained. Jesus as the Christ is both a historical fact and a subject of believing reception. To conquer estrangement the New Being must become historical and be subjected to the anxieties of finitude and existence, but also He must retain an unbroken unity with God for only thus does He have the power to conquer estrangement. Jesus as the Christ is subject to all the consequences of existential estrangement. He has to die and to experience the anxiety of death. He must experience the anxiety of physical and social displacement, the anxiety of uncertainty and doubt ("My God why has thou forsaken me?"), and the anxiety of guilt. But through His courageous faith, His perfect obedience, and His unbroken unity with God, He is able to conquer the estrangement of existence and thus to fulfill His Messianic vocation.

This picture of the New Being in Jesus as the Christ becomes the basis for the Church's doctrine of salvation. Salvation means healing, and healing means the reuniting of that which is estranged. The doctrine of the atonement is the description of the effect of the New Being in Jesus as the Christ on those who are grasped by Him in their state of estrangement and thus experience His healing power. Through His atoning work the split between man and God is healed and man receives the power to face courageously the tragic implications of his existence. The anxieties of death, loneliness, guilt, doubt, and meaninglessness are not removed, but man in the state of salvation has the power to accept them and to affirm himself creatively in spite of them.

TIME AND ETERNITY

Author: Walter T. Stace (1886-)
Type of work: Religious metaphysics
First published: 1952

Principal Ideas Advanced

All religious and theological language is symbolic.

God is nothing to the conceptual intellect.

Religious symbolism becomes meaningful when the symbol is related by mystic intuition to God.

God is utterly other; His mystery is absolute; all ideas of relations between God and the world are metaphorical ideas.

In September 1947 Professor Walter T. Stace of Princeton University published an article in the *Atlantic Monthly* entitled "Man Against Darkness." The article was a defense of philosophic naturalism and a call for courage and creative action in the face of the unconcerned void which naturalism presents as the true picture of reality. The article provoked a considerable amount of controversy, and Professor Stace was accused of being atheistic. Less than five years later *Time and Eternity* appeared, and the critics were surprised to discover that Stace had made what appeared to be a definitive about-face, for *Time and Eternity* is certainly a defense of theism, of supernaturalism, of mysticism, of religion and theology, and of the evocative effect of religious discourse. But Stace himself regards his book as making complete a description that told only half the story. One must of course recognize time and the particular, he writes, and naturalism can handle the assignment of making conceptual sense out of the finite and temporal world; but there is also eternity and the divine, and naturalism is unable even to make sense of these aspects of reality. *Time and Eternity* is a philosopher's attempt to argue that both naturalism and religion are on the track of the truth; the conceptual intellect, Stace maintains, orders the world for limited, practical purposes, but only the mystic consciousness, through union with the divine, transcends the intellect and acquires knowledge of God and eternity.

Stace argues that all religious discourse and thought is symbolic. To take religious discourse literally is to try to conceptualize what is beyond all distinction. Paul Tillich, Friedrich Schleiermacher (1768-1834), and St. Thomas Aquinas (c.1225-1274) are mentioned as prominent theologians who, from different ages and perspectives, came to much the same conclusion. The author also acknowledges an indebtedness to Immanuel Kant (1724-1804) and to Rudolf Otto (1869-1937); the latter's *Idea of the Holy* and Sri Aurobindo's *The Life Divine* (1914) are mentioned as having had, after Kant, considerable influence on Stace's thought.

Religion is described by Professor Stace as "the hunger for the non-being which yet is." Religion is the attempt to get beyond the ordinary world of experience and thought to the ultimate Being which is Non-Being, or nothing, from a nonmystical point of view. The fact that over the centuries men of great intelligence and sensitivity have supposed that such an effort should be made suggests to Stace that the experience of the divine is a common, although often unappreciated, feature of ordinary life.

Stace agrees with Dean William Ralph Inge (1860-1954), who argues that it is an error to take the negative divine as the whole truth. To think of God as nothing but emptiness and the void is to give priority to the conceptual and to eliminate the possibility of appreciating the positive divine.

Although no conceptual understanding of God is possible, it is possible, Stace maintains, to use certain terms which more than others which might have been chosen prepare the mind for an intuitive recognition of God. He mentions such positive terms as "spirit," "mind," "person," "love," "power," and "bliss."

Not only is it not possible to conceive of God intellectually, but also any attempt to understand the divine by reference to relations is bound to fail. God transcends all relations; He is not simply an additional term to be related to other terms which the mind can isolate. Since all relations attributed to God are attributed to Him metaphorically, and since even the idea of relation is metaphorical, any attempt to conceive of God in relation to time, even when He is identified with the eternal, cannot bring man closer to the truth. Only in a moment of mystical illumination is it possible to understand that time and eternity are somehow united in the divine.

Nonreligious symbols can be translated into literal symbols, Stace writes, but religious symbols do not permit such reformulation. An even more important distinction between nonreligious and religious symbols is that the former "mean" what they symbolize, while religious symbols "evoke" their significance through intuitive experience. An utterance in religious language evokes an experience by which a nonconceptual understanding of the divine is made possible.

Stace refers with approval to Rudolph Otto's description of the experience of the divine as "numinous," that is, as having to do with the ineffable and nonnatural. But Stace objects to Otto's analysis of the mode of symbolism exhibited by religious language. It is an error, Stace maintains, to suppose that similarities constitute the basis of religious discourse. Such terms as "awful" (awe-full) and "fascinating," used to describe the numen, are effective not because it is possible to draw analogies between the natural and the divine, but because in the mystic moment there is an "intersection of the natural order by the divine order. . . ." The relation between the religious symbol and what it symbolizes "is not that of resemblance," Stace writes, "but that of greater or less *nearness* to the full self-realization of God." There are degrees of adequacy in the use of religious symbolism: "Thus it is truer to say that God is a mind or a person than that He is a force." It is Stace's contention that predicates taken from language about persons and minds tend to be more adequate in evoking mystic awareness than are predicates used to describe physical forces and lower forms of life.

Although a distinction may be drawn between ethically neutral predicates—such as "mind," "person," and "power"—and value predicates—such as "love," "pity," and "mercy"—and although one may discern both an order of being (within which the first set of predicates applies) and an order of values (which calls for the predicates of the second set), one must realize, Stace writes, "that what is lower in the one scale is also lower in the other scale, and that what is higher in the one is also higher in the other." Only the mystic is able to discover the scale of values within the order of being which points to the divine.

The belief that there are higher and lower pleasures and that the higher pleasures are those of the mind or spirit is a belief based on an almost universal intuitive discovery that results from the intersection of the natural and the divine. Stace fills out his natural-supernatural theory of values by maintaining that values are both absolute and relative: "There is an absolute scale of values, but it does not belong to the natural order. It is revealed only in the supreme moment of mystical illumination. . . . But if we look at these value revelations from the outside, from that standpoint in which they appear as successive moments of time, they are then relative, temporal, and subjective."

Stace describes God as "the Truth" and as "the Supreme Reality," but he points out that God cannot be true in the sense in which propositions, or sentences, are true. The term "Truth" is a value term; to say that God is the Good, the True, and the Beautiful is to emphasize His status as the supreme value. God is Truth in the sense that "He is the content of revelation."

Naturalism insists that the divine is illusory and that discourse about God is meaningless. Stace suggests that the naturalistic view is true—given the naturalistic method of experiencing and conceiving the world. But the claim that ultimate reality is divine is also true—from the mystical point of view. Confusion results when the conceptual language of the naturalist is used in the interpretation of the symbolic language of the mystic.

Naturalistic critics cannot be satisfied with a view like the one presented by Professor Stace. The naturalist wants to be given a method for determining the difference between the divine and the natural; if there is no observable difference, says the naturalist, there is no distinction in meaning. But Stace rejects a theory of meaning which cannot encompass the world which is "other" than the natural world. He argues that the religious consciousness "lies in a region which is forever beyond all proof or disproof."

All attempts to prove the existence of God must fail, Stace maintains, because there is no logical passage from the natural order to the eternal order. However, the divine order, like the natural order, is self-contained, and it is possible to find arguments for the divine within the divine order itself. By seeking within himself, by using his intuitive powers, a person may learn of the divine.

To the objection that intuitions are variable, Stace responds by arguing that it is the rational element, which is introduced in the act of interpretation, which is responsible for differences—not of intuition, but of opinion. He compares disagreement in intuitive matters to disagreement in the aesthetic sphere. Despite differences in reports based on intuitive experiences, there is considerable agreement among those mystics who claim to have known the divine immediately. Finally, Stace asserts, there is no conflict between faith and intuition; the two are "one and the same thing."

Stace concludes his book by examining the relations between mysticism and logic. Logic cannot be applied to mystic truths, he argues, for logic is the instrument of the conceptual mind. Intuitive experience is not analyzable, and it does not afford man with any basis for logically consistent descriptions of the divine. If logic is used to express intuition, the result is contradiction. Stace concludes by reasserting his claim that "God is utterly other" and that "the mystery and incomprehensibility of God are absolute and irremovable. . . ."

Time and Eternity is a cogent and responsible defense of the intuitive method of grasping religious truth. Unfortunately—perhaps by the very nature of the case—no analysis of intuition as a method is offered by Professor Stace. It would not be possible, by reading this book, to discover what intuition is. Thus the naturalist who does not admit the divine side of reality cannot possibly be converted to Stace's view.

NATURAL RELIGION AND CHRISTIAN THEOLOGY

Author: Charles E. Raven (1885-)
Type of work: Natural theology
First published: 1953

Principal Ideas Advanced

Contemporary science is moving toward a unified vision of the universe and man which makes a natural theology possible even as current neo-orthodox theology rejects the possibility.

The organismic, evolutionary universe now presented to us can be adequately interpreted only in terms of its present highest emergent—human personality.

The historical understanding of Jesus shows Him to be the best exemplar of human emergence, and such an understanding renders a liberal Christian theology again relevant.

In the 1951-52 Gifford Lectures, *Natural Religion and Christian Theology,* Charles Raven, a distinguished theologian, scientist, and educator, calls for a "New Reformation" which will place "natural theology" in the center of Christian thinking. The contemporary nature of the sciences makes this feasible. The first series of lectures, "Science and Religion," reviews the scientific scene; and the second, "Experience and Interpretation," is devoted to a reassessment of Christian doctrine in scientific terms, by the use of which, Raven contends, the central affirmations of orthodoxy can be maintained.

Raven criticizes historians of science as having created a "papal succession" from Copernicus to Newton. Such a view took present successes (in physics, for example) as normative, and it stressed only those thinkers and trends which led to success as being significant. Science has thus been seen as quantitative and mathematical. Raven claims that this historiography resembles the treatment of Christian doctrine, which took the fourth century Nicene formulation as orthodoxy and judged earlier tendencies which did not support it as heretical.

Classical Greek and Jewish thought were in fact coming together in their treatment of nature, and the New Testament reflects this "intimate and fruitful union." Jesus typically used illustrations from nature; and Paul, too, emphasized the evidences of divine plan in the creation. Raven sees both Jesus and Paul as less dualistic than Augustine, Luther, or Calvin.

In the early Church, the Logos-theology developed at Alexandria emphasized the immanence of God; consequently, science and philosophy were held in high regard as sources of Christian truth and as evidences to be used in controversy. Later theologians, especially in the West, rejected this position. In place of a real concern for nature and history, they turned to allegorization and hagiography. The imagery of ancient fable and bestiary was deemed an adequate source of natural knowledge.

In the medieval period, Franciscans like Robert Grosseteste (c.1175-1253) and Roger Bacon (c.1214-1292) moved toward a more positive view of nature, but the dualism of Dominicans like Albertus Magnus (c.1200-1280) and Thomas Aquinas (c.1225-1274) prevailed. The natural world, uncritically viewed, yielded a minimal natural theology, but the central doctrines of Christianity rested upon a "supernatural" revelation. The final medieval chapter was the skepticism of Johannes Duns Scotus (c.1264-1308) and William of Ockham (c.1300-c.1349).

The first thinker to suspend the tradition and to publish detailed field investigations of natural history (fish, birds, Alpine flora) was Konrad von Gesner (1516-1565). "Before Copernicus had been appreciated enough to be condemned," biological studies, through Gesner's efforts, had reached a high level, Raven claims. In fact, he writes, "the modern scientific movement began" in biology.

The role of the British Royal Society in spreading the New Philosophy of the seventeenth century is well known, as is Francis Bacon's utilitarian emphasis upon the power created by knowledge. What is often overlooked is Bacon's equal insistence upon the correlation of knowledge, which would provide a surer foundation for living than religion. The Cambridge Platonists sensed this and initially felt greater affinity with Descartes. The position they ultimately achieved, however, was of great significance in tempering Cartesian dualism and mechanism. Benjamin Whichcote (1609-1683) spoke of two books, Creation and Scripture, as showing forth the same God. Ralph Cudworth (1617-1688) went on to describe a "plastic nature" that was clearly organic and nonmechanistic. John Ray (1627-1705) endorsed Cudworth's thesis, illustrated it, and asserted the existence of intelligence on the animal level. His rejection of "spontaneous creation," in spite of Scripture and the classics, was a major step toward a uniform conception of nature.

From the seventeenth century until quite recent times, Raven claims, the mainstream of scientific development flowed necessarily, but unfortunately, through narrowing, mechanistic channels. Newtonian physics had no place for human values, and its very success revived theological dualism and a wide range of romantic protests. Biological science was similarly diverted by the influence of Linnaean classifications which were theoretically trivial, thus leaving conceptual formulations to the chemists, physicists, and astronomers.

Mechanism was, thus, a real challenge to the traditional religious interpretation of man and his world. One of the ironies of the nineteenth century was that the battle of science and religion took place in biology and geology. The Bridgewater Treatises of 1829 reflect the bewilderment of eight eminent British scientists commissioned to defend Christianity. Yet they also reflect the consensus among Christians and nonbelievers as to the orderliness of nature.

It was this teleology that received Darwin's bombshell. Did the universe evolve by chance or by design? Charles Darwin (1809-1882) confessed himself in "an utterly hopeless muddle," but many of his followers, especially after the results of work by Gregor Mendel (1822-1884) were confirmed, took natural selection and heredity to be the ultimate proofs of the mechanistic hypothesis.

Under such circumstances, an uneasy truce prevailed between science and religion in Britain. Elsewhere the battle lines were sharply drawn. Everywhere the dilemma seemed to be: "an agnostic humanism or an authoritarian supernaturalism." With the advent of relativity and quantum, however, a "new situation" emerged. The determinate, closed, predictable universe passed into limbo. Variability, the keystone of biological theory, was in some measure also found in suborganic realms.

Finally it was psychology and psychiatry that climaxed the new understanding of the scientific enterprise. The inadequacy of simple, reductive analysis became apparent; and the stress upon objective, general, ponderable facts, already suspect in physics, was ended. This larger view outmoded previous distinctions between science, on the one hand, and history and theology on the other. The universe was one, and it included persons. Organismic thought appeared in writers like Alfred Whitehead (1861-1947), Samuel Alexander (1859-1938) and Lloyd Morgan (1852-1936). Religious thinkers such as William Temple (1881-1944) and John Oman (1860-1939) developed a similar yet more specifically Christian interpretation.

By the middle 1930's, however, dualism came to be reasserted in religious circles. Just as the scientists were reaching for new syntheses that would include man and his values, the theologians retreated to what Raven calls "their ivory towers, cells and catacombs."

Raven calls for a "new Reformation" which will reverse this trend in theological circles and make full use of the new scientific situation. This theology would be clearly in the "liberal" tradition, which in Britain sprang more from the Cambridge Platonists than from the Enlightenment. British liberals have been characterized, Raven says, by "an insistence upon a reasonable faith, a regard for scientific studies and an emphasis upon history." Liberalism is a tradition which correlates well with the new scientific attitude that a problem is answered only "as it is related to the whole body of knowledge." Scientists and theologians alike should now agree, Raven argues, that "the whole story of our universe is a serial and that the volume dealing with the evolution and character of life on this planet begins (perhaps) with the amoeba and ends (at present) with the saint." Both the general and the particular, order and uniqueness, atoms and history, fall within the scope of the new kind of inquiry. The creative process in history embodies continuity and novelty. Adequate explanation must start from the end. Our universe "cannot be explained in lower than personal categories," Raven insists. The new liberal theology will therefore make no claims of a special preserve of knowledge, but will culminate and integrate the whole.

Raven's theological construction begins with an analysis of "experience," which always precedes "interpretation." Our encounters with the universe as a whole are the raw material of religion, and they display an inescapable polarity of self-consciousness and contemplation. Interpretation of the primal experience as "dread" or "shame" overlooks the companion aspect of "wonder." Historical religions have sought to integrate these modes in two ways. The negative way of most mystics proceeds by "subtraction," a concentrating and narrowing of attention. Some success may be achieved this way, but it seldom yields much energy or inspiration. A more positive approach is by "sublimation," the disciplining and training of attention. The positive approach is preferable, Raven says, because it leads to "world-acceptance" and "world-redemption," whereas the negative approach typically results in "world-rejection." No symbolism is sufficient to describe the sublimation process—it can be "shown" but not "said."

As we pass from the unitary experience of the ineffable to its interpretation, we become aware of attractions and repulsions, the ground of our value experiences. By selection and examination, we scrutinize our attitudes, thereby introducing a certain limitation on adequacy. Our interpretations are expressed in emotive, cognitive, and conative activities. In religion, these are epitomized by cult, creed, and morality.

It will not do, however, Raven argues, to insist on the simple subjectivity of all resulting interpretations. The commonality of categories is too great. The Johannine "Light, Love, Life" could, for instance, subsume Christian and Buddhist interpretations. It is then but "a short step" to agreement on the "perfect Son of Man."

Raven reviews the records of Jesus of Nazareth, rejecting both the miraculous affirmations of the conservatives and the historical skepticism of the neo-orthodox. What we can learn shows that Jesus was "one of ourselves" and yet is able "to awaken and quicken our sensitiveness" as no other man has done. This conclusion, Raven notes, agrees with that of traditional orthodoxy.

The fact of agreement does not mean, however, that the traditional interpretations will be valid for us today. The period in which the creeds emerged was permeated by a conditioning social despair that makes the traditional formula "unreal and to many of us a stumbling-block." We moderns would do better to turn from controversial doctrines of Incarnation, which are often dualistic and speak of a divine intruder, to a fresh statement of atonement. Each previous epoch has worked this out in terms of its deepest needs. Our need, and here we resemble the third-century Alexandrians, is for a comprehensive image of the personal culmination of the creative process in the universe.

Our problem is to understand man —the creature emerging in a universe of infinite size, possibly doomed by entropy, surrounded by a measure of natural ruthlessness, enmeshed in sin, suffering, beauty, and freedom. We must not say, with Emil Brunner and Neo-orthodoxy, that this creature is a "sinner." Man is both "sinful and redeemable," Raven writes. Evil has a reality, and much of it is created by us. Unless men are to be automata, however, evil is the price a loving God must pay for human freedom. Progress in eliminating evil is possible, though neither inevitable nor automatic. God is involved, Raven says, "not as spectator or judge but as partner and guide."

How does such a world come into being? By evolution, in the broadest sense. Raven rejects the idea that mutation alone can account for variation and he notes that botanists never accepted the doctrine of an isolated germ plasm, a doctrine advanced by August Weissmann (1834-1914). Organism and environment are related more intimately than such a doctrine allows. Although our theories are still imperfect, we can affirm, Raven suggests, that "the world is so ordered that life and life more abundant prevails in it." If we reject the Cartesian mind-body dualism which generated the debates of mechanists and vitalists, we can outline an immanental teleology. There is a Nisus, a Model, and a Being that we encounter in our "fullest experience." This interpretation corresponds rather closely to that involved in the Nicene faith.

The key doctrine in the new reformation will be the indwelling Holy Spirit (the most neglected aspect of traditional theology). This doctrine can preserve Christianity from gnostic dualism and make it possible to see deity reflected in each stage of an evolutionary process whose goal, Raven says, is "the attainment by mankind of its true status and significance." In psychological terms, the doctrine of the Holy Spirit will remind us that sensitivity precedes perception.

The Spirit is seen in the operation of true communities where an "integrative loyalty" appears. The primitive Church is a prime example. While we can affirm a "divine initiative," this is always present and must be "voluntarily conditioned" by man's response. The Church should be such a community, Raven insists; in our day it can exist only by creating full social reform. The nature of nuclear warfare makes it impossible to retreat from the world's problems.

Raven's natural theology thus leads him to a kind of panpsychism, in which to all intents and purposes he identifies the Spirit and the Logos, although traditional theology has separated them.

No theology can ignore the persistent human desire for immortality. The eschatological expectancy of early Christianity has, however, been overemphasized. Raven rejects any idea of an "immortal soul," and he interprets the "eternal life" taught by Paul and the Fourth Gospel as a way of facing and mastering death. We are, Raven writes, "to behave in this work-a-day world as if the Kingdom of Heaven was already here, as in some sense indeed it is." Man is what he loves, and "we abide so far as we love what is real and abiding."

CHRISTIAN THEOLOGY: AN ECUMENICAL APPROACH

Author: Walter Marshall Horton (1895-)
Type of work: Ecumenical theology
First published: 1955

Principal Ideas Advanced

An ecumenical approach to the central problems of Christian theology is most likely to lead to satisfactory resolutions.

There is a consensus of Christian opinion concerning the following claims: God is known through the specific revelation in Christ; God is both Creator and Redeemer; He is holy, good, and powerful; the world is dependent on its Creator and is adapted to God's purposes; man is a sinner who is regenerated by God's redemptive grace; Jesus is the divine-human Savior of the world; the Church is the Body of Christ; the Christian hope is in the coming of the Kingdom of God.

Walter Marshall Horton, professor of theology at Oberlin College, argues in his *Christian Theology: An Ecumenical Approach* that "a sectarian theology is something just as absurd as the 'Baptist astronomy' which a devout Baptist trustee of the University of Chicago wanted to have taught there in the early days." Horton's conviction that if God is one, theology should also be one, led him to pursue his theological studies at Union Theological Seminary, where the ecumenical approach is endorsed and practiced. Subsequent experience as a teacher and as a student of theological reform through ecumenical conferences strengthened his faith in the value of the ecumenical approach.

Horton describes his book as an exercise in systematic theology, and he uses the ecumenical approach to seven areas of theological concern: (1) The knowledge of God, (2) the nature of God, (3) God and the world, (4) God and man, (5) Christ the Savior, (6) The Church and the means of grace, and (7) the Christian hope (God's Kingdom).

He asks, in regard to each of the seven topics, "What is the universal ('ecumenical') human problem which underlies this topic in theology? . . . What is the universal ('ecumenical') Christian answer to this problem, so far as the Christian churches and schools of thought are now agreed? . . . What are the principal disagreements and conflicts which obscure the clarity of the Christian answer to this particular problem?" He warns that the ecumenical approach is not likely to resolve the problems once and for all; in fact, he argues, a "flat uniformity" would make progress in theology through honest dissent impossible. But the ecumenical approach is valuable in that it centers attention upon the central issues and illuminates the areas of agreement.

Before proceeding to the specific discussion of the seven problems with which the body of the book is concerned, Horton attempts to resolve the ambiguity of the term "ecumenical" by asking, "Does 'ecumenical' imply a literally world-wide perspective on the theological thought currents of our age?" and "Does 'ecumenical' imply a literally universal perspective on all denominations claiming to be Christian?" His answer to the first question is that the present ecumenical effort must center on the theological views being developed in Continental Europe, the British Commonwealth, and the United States. But the ideal ecumenical effort, an ideal which suggests lines of development for the future, would be one which encompassed Christian theology wherever in the world it is developing. The answer to the second question is that since Roman Catholics, Unitarians, and Jehovah's Witnesses do not participate in the World Council of Churches, they cannot participate in the parliamentary effort to achieve ecumenicity. But, once again, although there are practical limitations to a universal effort, the ideal would be to devise a theology which would achieve, among other objectives, "a vital union between the Catholic sacramental principle and the Protestant prophetic principle"—an ideal suggested by Paul Tillich.

According to Horton, the human needs which religion must satisfy are the need for an object of trust, the need for a final goal of hope, and the need for divine salvation as a means to the satisfaction of both trust and hope. The historic religions have incorporated these three elements of trust, hope, and salvation. Religion is needed as a unifying activity by which material means are adapted to moral or spiritual ends and controlled by a concept of man in relation to God. Christianity attempts to satisfy the needs of man by acting on the truth claim that through the reconciling love of Christ man can achieve the salvation which vitally connects his trust and his hope. Horton summarizes the ecumenical definition of essential Christianity by stating that Christianity "presents the God and Father of Jesus Christ as the Ground of trust, his everlasting Kingdom as the Goal of hope, and Christ himself as 'the Way, the Truth and the Life.' "

Systematic theology cannot be considered in a linear fashion, Horton claims. Although consideration of God, the world, man, Christ, the Church, and the Kingdom are necessary, that consideration cannot proceed by beginning with some basic matter and then developing, in a logical way, the remaining topics. Horton insists that "each topic presupposes what follows, as well as what precedes it. . . ." Systematic theology, then, must be circular in the sense that it cannot consider the discussion of any one topic adequate which has not received correction from the discussion of the remaining topics.

The first topic which Horton discussed ecumenically is the problem of religious knowledge: How can God be known? The Christian answer is that a purely rational approach is not adequate; revelation is necessary. Revelation is achieved through historical events and personages. The central figure in the historical revelation of divine purposes is Jesus the Christ, who is not merely the Messiah, Israel's answer, the fulfillment of Hebraic prophecy, but also God's Son, the Word made flesh. The problem for the Christian Church, Horton writes, is to interpret and to apply God's central revelation in Christ.

But although Christians are agreed in claiming that the revelation in Christ is central, there remain questions concerning the relation between the revelation in Christ and the general revelation in nature, history, and other religions; and there is disagreement, also, concerning the value of tradition as a source of revelatory knowledge. Horton considers with careful attention the Catholic positions (Roman and non-Roman), the Protestant positions (Conservative, Liberal, Radical, and Neo-Orthodox), and the Anglican positions, on these questions concerning revelation; he comes to the conclusion that some specific, concrete revelation is needed if general experience is to serve as a source of illumination concerning religious matters.

An ecumenical approach to the problem of God's nature yields, first of all, the conclusion that God must possess the attributes of holiness, goodness, and greatness. The universal necessity to men of faith in a deity, "an Object of ultimate trust and devotion," involves attributing holiness to God, for without holiness He would not be able to draw men to Him in wonder and awe; and without goodness and greatness, He could not adequately respond to men's trust and hope. The Christian answer to the question concerning God's nature is that He is the God of Israel, the Creator and Judge; He walked with men in the person of Jesus the Christ; He abides as Holy Spirit in the community of believers, the Church. Power, judgment, and love are the divine attributes by which God's holiness manifests itself. God is both Creator and Redeemer.

The central unresolved issue concerning the nature of God is whether the Absolute Being of Greek metaphysics can be reconciled with the conception of God as Father and Creator. Another issue concerns the sense in which God is personal. Horton discusses the various views, philosophical and theological, which center about these issues.

What is the relation between God and the world? Horton argues that the Christian answer, insofar as there is a consensus of opinion, is that the world has real existence; it is dependent on its Creator; and it is adapted to God's purposes. (This particular formula, involving reference to the reality, dependence, and adaptation of the world, is derived by Horton from William Adams Brown's *Christian Theology in Outline,* which appeared in 1906.)

For theologians there is still the problem of reconciling the Biblical conception of the world with the modern scientific conception. And the problem of evil continues to provoke conflicting resolutions. Horton's discussion of these controversial problems is both cogent and provocative.

The next question which is considered is the relation of man to God. Horton suggests as the consensus of Christian opinion the view that man, who is made for fellowship with God, must honor God by loving his neighbor; man is a sinner who opposes the divine will; man is regenerated by God's redemptive grace through Christ. In other words, man is created by God, judged by God, and redeemed by God.

Unresolved issues having to do with the relation between God and man center about the doctrines of the Fall and Original Sin. The Augustinian view of the Fall as making all men sinners has always provoked opposition, and the controversy continues. Horton reviews Pelagian and Arminian views, and he turns his attention to the contemporary opinions of such outstanding theologians as Reinhold Niebuhr and Paul Tillich. It is Horton's hope that the assertion of human freedom can be balanced with the Augustinian view.

Christology arises in response to the problem of mediation. How can God be ultimate and yet concretely in touch with human needs? The Christian consensus of opinion is that Jesus is "the divine-human Savior of the world, the Man in and through whom God turned the course of history and reconciled a rebellious world to himself."

The two contemporary issues concerning Christ as Savior are raised by those who question the doctrine of the Trinity and the doctrine of the Virgin Birth. The Unitarians are the most forceful exponents of the view that Christ was not God, while Protestants are often among those who challenge the belief, to which the Roman Catholics hold firmly, that Christ was born of the Virgin Mary. As Horton points out, even "neo-orthodox Christians like Brunner and Aulén express the most ardent and unwavering faith in the Incarnation, while remaining skeptical or unconcerned about the Virgin Birth." If Christians who believe in the Trinity would insist upon the unity of God, while nevertheless regarding Christ as "the Word made flesh" and the Holy Spirit as God's activity in the world, the tensions between the Unitarians and the trinitarians might be reduced, even if differences of opinion remained. The conflict between the Protestants and the Roman Catholics concerning the Virgin Birth is even more serious, but again there is some possibility of a reduction in the tension of disagreement, Horton suggests, if Catholics admit the danger of idolatry in the veneration of the Virgin and if Protestants admit the danger of losing the sense of "God with us" if they reject mediators other than Christ.

There are various Christian churches or sects, Horton points out, precisely because there is disagreement concerning the Church and the means of grace. Yet there is agreement centering about the claim that the Church is the community of those chosen by God; it is the Body of Christ; and it is the community of the Holy Spirit. Christians are also agreed that the Church is "positively related to the Kingdom of God," but they disagree as to the precise nature of that relationship.

Unresolved issues concerning the Church are considered by Horton by reference to three questions suggested by C. T. Craig in his book *The One Church* (1951): "(1) What are the limits of this one Church which alone can exist? (2) Is there a prescribed form for the Church? (3) How is continuity to be maintained within this Church?" Only "ecumenical conversation" among the conflicting churches can make possible the realization of a Church which men can recognize as the Body of Christ.

Horton concludes his ecumenical examination of issues central to Christianity by examining the Christian hope. Earlier in his book he had analyzed "the logic of monotheism" as involving man's hope, man's trust, and man's salvation through a vital relation to God. The problem of hope is the problem of finding an object of hope that will be trustworthy and will actually fulfill man's highest desires.

The Christian answer is that man's hope is in the Kingdom of God. Many Christians have answered that man's hope is in Christ, but since Christ may be understood to have come to establish God's Kingdom, there need be no difference of opinion, other than verbal, concerning the answer to man's hope. The Kingdom of God is not yet realized in every respect; although a Christian becomes a son of God through Christian love, he has not yet received that spiritual fulfillment which will come when Christ brings the redeemed together, and all men will be "like him" (I John 3:2).

Unresolved issues concerning the Christian hope include, according to Horton, the question of the Second Coming, the question of eternal punishment, and the question of progress: Will Jesus literally come again to establish the Kingdom of God on earth? Will some men receive eternal punishment, or will all men be saved? Is it any longer sensible to speak of human progress? Once again, rather than attempt to force definitive answers to issues best resolved through "ecumenical conversation," Horton discusses the various positions involved, and he suggests the strengths and weaknesses of the alternatives.

As a systematic and clearly expressed account of issues of first importance within Christian theology, as a source of information concerning areas of Christian consensus and disagreement, and as a persuasive but reasonable plea for an ecumenical approach to the central issues, Walter Marshall Horton's *Christian Theology* has won a modest but useful place within the company of books which illuminate the Christian faith.

THE DIVINE MILIEU

Author: Pierre Teilhard de Chardin (1881-1955)
Type of work: Devotional theology
First published: 1957

Principal Ideas Advanced

Organic theories of the universe find their complement in the doctrine of the Mystical Body of Christ.

Because the Incarnation has as its goal the perfection of the human race, Christians are bound to exercise their capacities in active human undertakings.

The growth of Christ's Body in the world has only begun, and it will continue until this earth has been changed into a paradise; afterwards, Christ will return and will translate His Body from time to eternity.

Teilhard de Chardin was both a priest of the Jesuit order and a paleontologist, best known for his part in the discovery of Peking man. In a book called *The Phenomenon of Man,* written in 1940, Father Teilhard viewed the whole scheme of cosmic evolution in the light of the Christian doctrines of Creation, Incarnation, and Resurrection. In *The Divine Milieu,* written in 1927, he dealt more intimately with the life of Christian obedience. The two books supplement each other in that, according to Teilhard, to live as a

Christian is to participate in the divine work of creation, to be co-creator with God, and to die as a Christian is to be united with the Mystical Body of Christ, which is the Omega-point, the goal toward which the whole creation moves.

The Divine Milieu is a deeply meditated work of the sort that rewards careful and repeated reading. It is the record of Father Teilhard's own struggles with the Christian faith, of his intimate discussions with believers and unbelievers, and of certain mystical experiences which came to him. With a nod to his scientific background, Teilhard introduces the book as "a simple *description* of a *psychological* evolution observed *over a specified interval.*" He says that all he has tried to do is note down "a possible series of inward perspectives gradually revealed to the mind in the course of a humble yet 'illuminating' spiritual ascent." But in spite of the calculated objectivity of presentation, it is impossible to doubt that the experiences here recorded are the author's own. Consequently, the book is for the advanced Christian who has himself struggled with his faith.

Teilhard says that there is nothing in his writings that is not in accord with the "eternal lesson of the Church," and that he has sought merely to reinterpret Christianity in a modern idiom. "Is the Christ of the Gospels, imagined and loved within the dimensions of a Mediterranean world, capable of still embracing and still forming the centre of our prodigiously expanded universe?" Teilhard asks. For his answer, he draws copiously from the more mystical and eschatological parts of the New Testament, particularly from the writings of Paul and of John; but he interprets these Biblical teachings in terms of a hierarchical world-view, patterned upon that of Aristotle, but including also the fundamental assumptions of modern developmentalism.

Teilhard views the evolution of the cosmos as the gradual gain in complexity and individuality of its multiple components. "Organization" and "organism" are notions fundamental to his understanding of development within the cosmos, but these ideas are no less fundamental to his understanding of the cosmos as a whole. Holding that the distinction between matter and spirit is only relative, Teilhard argues that man, in virtue of his reflective powers, is the terminus of physical evolution; that each human being, as the center of an independent perspective, recapitulates and sums up the whole world in a unique and incommunicable way. But the ultimate end of creation is not a multiplicity of separate minds, each forming an independent milieu; it is, rather, "a unitive transformation" by means of which the monads are brought together into eternal harmony with the mind of the Creator. By the Incarnation, God introduces into the world the ultimate organizing principle, in terms of which the universe becomes truly one. "What," Teilhard asks, "is the supreme and complex reality for which the divine operation moulds us? It is revealed to us by St. Paul and St. John. It is the quantitative repletion and the qualitative consummation of all things: it is the mysterious Pleroma, in which the substantial *One* and the created *many* fuse without confusion in a *whole* which, without adding anything essential to God, will nevertheless be a sort of triumph and generalisation of being." The efficacy of this higher principle of organization is what Teilhard means by "the divine milieu."

The reader who is interested in Teilhard's speculation must turn to *The Phenomenon of Man.* The present work is chiefly devoted to the practical problem of following the Christian way of perfection. Teilhard identifies two main objections which modern unbelievers bring against the Christian ideal. The first is that it introduces a duality into a man's soul, setting the claims of God over against the claims of the world. The second is that, instead of teaching men to resist evil, it teaches submission to the will of God. Teilhard admits that these objections are all too valid against the greater part of the Church's traditional teaching. Christians ought, he maintains, to be more concerned than secular humanists with the tasks of increasing the sum of knowledge about the world and of improving the conditions for human living; but, too often, because they have failed to keep in view the scope of Christ's dominion, Christians have allowed these tasks to pass by default into the hands of unbelievers.

Teilhard finds it helpful to distinguish between man's "activities" and his "passivities," and to explore the significance of the Christian's commitment with respect to each of these.

Applying his conception of creative evolution to man's *active* life, Teilhard seeks to recover a true sense of the spiritual significance of work. In theory, he says, there has never been any doubt but that a believer is serving God when he tills the soil, or builds a house, or writes a book; but, in practice, nine out of ten devout Christians think of their work as a "spiritual encumbrance." Teilhard calls, therefore, for a rethinking of the distinction between the sacred and the profane. "Everything," he says, "is sacred to those capable of distinguishing that portion of chosen being which is subject to the attraction of Christ in the process of consummation. Try, with God's help, to perceive the connection—even physical and natural—which binds your labour with the building of the Kingdom of Heaven; . . . then, as you leave church for the noisy streets, you will remain with only one feeling, that of continuing to immerse yourself in God."

Teilhard is mindful, however, that in most of the relations which go to make up our lives, we are not active but *passive.* Our current energies are almost entirely beyond our control, and we had nothing at all to do with the chain of events which gave us being in the first place. We can form all sorts of projects in the mind, but we have little to say about whether they will come to pass. Teilhard finds the situation frightening to contemplate. He is reminded of the Patriarch Jacob who wrestled with the angel of the Lord; and, like Jacob, he too ends by adoring that against which he struggled.

On the one hand, says Teilhard, there are the "passivities of growth," those salutary circumstances which silently minister to our health and our development. These "blessed passivities," as Teilhard calls them, ("the will to be, the wish to be thus and thus, and the opportunity to realize myself according to my desire") are all manifestations of God's organizing energy, to be received by the Christian with gratitude and humility. We must never trifle them away; but, confiding in God's universal Providence, we must make the most of every opportunity to realize our several beings.

More perplexing are the other kind of passivities, those which stand in the way of our growth and rob us of our happiness. Teilhard calls them "the passivities of diminishment." Often, because they have too static a concept of God's omnipotence and perfection, Christians are inclined to accept these passivities with an air of resignation. In a world that is progressing from imperfection toward perfection, there must necessarily be these "shocks and diminishments," says Teilhard; but by his power and wisdom, God is able to turn every defect to some advantage and to make "all things work together for good to them that love him."

Teilhard suggests that it will help the Christian determine his practical attitude towards evil if he distinguishes two phases or periods in dealing with it. In the first phase, he must struggle to overcome all circumstances which threaten to diminish his being. He may say confidently, "God wants to free me from this diminishment." He has a right to see the working of Providence in the arts and sciences, and he has the duty to avail himself of every means presently known to man for removing his ill. But he has no assurance that his struggles will succeed; therefore, in the event of failure, he must be prepared for the second phase, that of defeat and its transfiguration. Now, he may ask God to convert his evil into good, and he may rest in the confidence that God never fails to do this, even in the most difficult case of all, that of death. For, says Teilhard, every diminishment can be used by God to spiritualize desires and ambitions, and thus to unite our lives more closely to Christ. "God must, in some way or other, make room for Himself, hollowing us out and emptying us, if He is finally to penetrate into us. And in order to assimilate us in Him, He must break the molecules of our being so as to re-cast and re-model us. The function of death is to provide the necessary entrance into our inmost selves."

The Christian, says Teilhard, is both the most "attached" and the most "detached" of men. He is as interested in this world as it is possible for anyone to be, and he finds the fullest development of his own being in engaging in the work of the world. But his interest in *things* derives from their absolute dependence on God, and the goal of his striving does not lie in his own personal advantage but in the fulfillment of the Creator's purpose. Teilhard finds in the Cross of Christ the proper symbol of this tension between the active and the passive elements of the Christian's life. The disciple must achieve something with his life; otherwise, he has nothing to bring to Christ in the way of an offering.

So far, we have spoken only of the individual believer and of the divinization or supernaturalization of his milieu; for, according to Teilhard, "there are as many partial divine milieux as there are Christian souls." A few words remain to be said about the way in which these individual milieux are integrated into a single, comprehensive milieu; how, in the words of the Fourth Gospel, many mansions are joined together to form the Father's house.

Like certain existentialist philosophers, Teilhard holds that every man naturally tends to regard every other man as a threat to his own being. "Would I," he asks, "be sincere if I did not confess that my instinctive reaction [to the 'other'] is to rebuff him? and that the mere thought of entering into spiritual communication with him disgusts me?" Through the influence of Christ, however, the envelope in which each one tends to isolate himself is broken. In proportion as men's lives are centered in Christ, they converge in a community; their "partial rays" merge into "the principal radiance of Christ."

Teilhard believes, of course, that the Mystical Body of Christ, in which Christians are linked together by the bond of charity, is an actuality in the present state of things. But, accustomed as he was to think in geological epochs, Teilhard describes the unification and divinization of the human race as having but just begun. In time to come, he writes, the greater portion of the race will be united to Christ, and, having at its disposal resources of knowledge and skill as yet undreamed of, mankind will make of this world the holy paradise envisaged by the Hebrew prophets. One day, however, man will have exhausted his possibilities on this planet; then, says Teilhard, will take place the great consummation of the universe, the *Parousia,* when Christ will suddenly be revealed, and humanity be translated to its eternal habitation.

Teilhard has some difficulty with the doctrine of Hell. A prospect of universal salvation might seem to accord better with his thesis that the world is progressing toward the unity of a perfect whole. Nevertheless, he accepts the existence of Hell on the authority of Scripture, and prays for strength of mind to see how it fits into the structure of the universe. That conscious elements or souls possess the freedom to set themselves in opposition to the beneficent forces of creation and to separate themselves eternally from the Mystical Body does, he ventures, add "an accent, a gravity, a contrast, a depth" to the historical process.

When *The Divine Milieu* was written, evolutionary philosophies were more common than they are today. Teilhard's outlook, however, remained unchanged through the remainder of his life, probably because it owed less to philosophical fashions than to the eschatological outlook of the New Testament. In the year of his death, he wrote: "Today, after forty years of constant reflection, it is still exactly the same fundamental vision which I feel the need to set forth and to share." It is the vision of humanity united, master of its potentialities, and reflecting in its consciousness the perfection of the Creator.

FAITH AND KNOWLEDGE

Author: John Hick (1922-)
Type of work: Apologetics; philosophy of religion
First published: 1957

Principal Ideas Advanced

The traditional association of "knowledge" with objective infallibility is logically mistaken; human knowledge can in principle aspire to no more than subjective rational certainty.

Although volition, moral experience, and general epistemological principles are relevant to a correct understanding of religious faith, the latter is not to be interpreted merely as a voluntary "will to believe," or merely as a theoretical implication of moral experience, or merely as parallel to ordinary judgments of fact.

In an ambiguous universe where all cognition requires interpretation, faith's true epistemological status is the free interpretative apprehension of all experience as religiously significant.

In *Faith and Knowledge* John Hick attempts to bring to bear on theistic religion in general and on Christian faith in particular the methods and epistemological findings of contemporary analytical philosophy. Born and educated in Britain, the homeland of analytical philosophy, Hick is well situated to provide what he calls a "bridging operation" between current movements in philosophy and theology.

If such a bridge is to be built, the general character of "knowledge" first requires Hick's philosophic scrutiny. Traditionally, and even within much contemporary analytical theory, the concept of knowledge is inseparably joined to the notion of infallibility. If one *knows* (so the standard argument runs) one cannot—logically cannot—be wrong. The propositions one "knows" *must* be true, or they do not constitute genuine knowledge. It simply fails to make good sense ("It is a misuse of language," say many analytical philosophers) to assert that one *knows* something but that one might be mistaken about it. In this respect "knowledge" differs from mere "belief," which entails nothing with respect to the truth or falsity of the propositions believed. Such an account of "knowledge" Hick firmly rejects.

First, the "infallibilist" theory maintains that when one "knows" one must also "know that he knows." Knowledge unaware of itself as knowledge is a contradiction. In this requirement, however, Hick finds a fatal flaw. It all too frequently happens that what we claim to know turns out to be false; evidently there exists no mark within cognitive experience itself that infallibly indicates when one is "truly knowing" and when one is only "seeming to know." Without such a mark, however, one can never—even in principle—*know* that he knows, and the entire theory falls to the ground.

Second, every supposed item of "infallible knowledge" that is actually put forward as such either fails to achieve perfect *certainty* or is unable to provide real *information,* the hallmark of genuine knowledge. Sense experience is notoriously uncertain; the immediate awareness of one's sense field or of one's bodily states offers no information about the world; and, similarly, analytic truths of logic or mathematics purchase their icy certainty at the cost of informational content. The class of infallible truths turns out to be empty, to the discomfiture of those who hold to the infallibilist theory.

Given, then, that "knowledge" as defined by infallibilism is an unattainable ideal, it becomes Hick's task to show what it is that constitutes knowledge in actual cognitive practice. There is no cause for despair, as though the forced abandonment of infallibilism destroyed all hope for genuine knowledge; on the contrary, a way is now opened to bring our understanding of the term into greater contact with the real situation of the human knower. This situation has always been such that those beliefs are claimed as "knowledge" of which men are most certain. Certainty, though inevitably subjective, need not, however, be arbitrary; and Hick maintains that knowledge as *rational* certainty will involve a degree (a degree which in principle defies specification) of critical examination. For the rational man, then, knowledge will consist in the psychological "sense of intellectual satisfaction, of security, or immoveableness, achievement, finality" which follows inquiry. If his inquiry has taken all relevant evidence into account and has not violated the rules of correct reasoning, the rational man is entitled to assume confidently that any other person in his position would agree that his certainty is well grounded; Hick finds that such certainty provides an objective element even when knowledge is defined subjectively.

The subjective definition of knowledge accords well, Hick believes, with the general analysis of cognition which recent philosophical debate has helped to clarify. Belief, as the genus of which knowledge is a specific mode, involves a fourfold subjective movement: ". . . the entertainment of a proposition in thought; assent to this proposition, or the adoption or embracing of it as true; a resulting disposition to act, both in thought and in overt deed, upon the adopted proposition; and a disposition to feel an emotion of conviction toward the proposition whenever its truth is challenged." Knowledge is distinguished from other beliefs only by the certainty with which the proposition believed is "embraced" as true, as we have seen; and with respect to the other elements of the cognitive situation, items of knowledge no less than other propositions believed to be true have an intimate bearing on action and emotion. Among the claims to knowledge most profoundly relevant to feelings and behavior are religious beliefs, and it is to an analysis of this domain of cognition that Hick next turns his attention.

Adopting as his acknowledged starting point the nearly universal rejection of the standard theistic arguments, Hick proceeds to examine the cognitive status left to a religious faith shorn of its proofs. Can an adequate analysis of this status be given in terms of volition alone? Is it possible adequately to understand faith as a "will to believe," a deliberate gamble, in the absence of coercive theoretical arguments for or against theism? Hick doubts that such an analysis can succeed in revealing the epistemological structure of faith: first, because an appeal to pure volition licenses too much, any number of mutually exclusive religious options being open to "cognitive justification" on such a theory, and, second, because a volitional analysis (modeled after a game of chance) is unable to account for the sense of immediate personal acquaintance with numinous reality—an attitude quite different from the gambler's—actually reported by religious persons.

A second theory, allegedly better suited to the recognition of the believer's sense of experiential involvement with the object of his belief, attempts to analyze the cognitive status of faith in terms of moral experience. On the basis of one's sense of obligation one can know that a moral order exists and, consequently, a moral orderer or lawgiver, God. Hick, however, is unconvinced by this theory, at least as long as God remains for it a mere unapprehended postulate of the moral life (once again religious experience is unaccounted for) or of ethics (a logically coercive argument from ethics to religion has yet to be advanced). If moral experience is taken as a channel for the direct apprehension of God, there may be value in the moral theory, but no claims of logical "proof" or "demonstration" from ethics are allowable.

Finally, a theory may be advanced to account for religious cognition by appeal to the existence of data so plentiful and pervasive as to defy clear and exhaustive articulation. Religious knowledge may be compared with other common beliefs of which we are justly certain without absolute or indisputable evidence. We rightly accept as knowledge many propositions concerning which doubt, though farfetched, would be logically possible: our knowledge, for example, that the earth is approximately a sphere. The justification for such cognitive practice is found in the infinitely complex concatenation of bits and pieces of evidence the drift of which points to the same conclusion and undergirds our informal inference, even though we may not be able to express this inference formally in such a way as to overcome the doubts of an obstinate skeptic. Religious faith, on this theory, shares such a logic of informal inference. Hick, though accepting the justice of this analysis within many departments of ordinary knowledge and agreeing that the religious believer is able to *know* what he cannot formally prove, remains unable to accept the theory's applicability in questions of religious belief. The assumption of this theory is that judgments of religious faith are of the same logical type as judgments referring to limited and particular facts of the empirical world. This assumption, however, is false. Religious belief is logically far more complex than this theory is equipped to recognize.

In what, then, does the logical complexity of religious faith consist? Hick reminds us that all cognition rests ultimately on interpretation; religious faith, in a hierarchy of interpenetrating interpretive schemes, functions as man's ultimate interpretation of the significance of reality as a whole.

Defending this theory, Hick shows that even on the level of our cognition of *nature* knowledge is not free from the need for interpretative decision for which there can be no logically coercive justification. It requires an act of interpretation, he points out, to hold that one's sense experience is of a world existing independent of oneself. Solipsism, the position that nothing but one's self exists and that the apparent world is no more than a figment constructed by one's own experiences, is logically irrefutable. The fact that nearly all men make the same free act of interpretation, rejecting solipsism and finding in experience a significance that goes beyond the self, should not blind us to the fact that interpretation is actually present. That such an interpretation is cognitively meaningful despite positivist doubts is shown by the fact that solipsism has a different "cash value" in experience from that of our normal interpretation; sense experiences would have a different quality if they were apprehended as self-manufactured illusions; one's behavior toward other persons would differ if he "saw" them as mere appearances reducible to fictional products of his own psyche instead of as independently real centers of consciousness and value.

Mention of *value* brings us to another level of apprehension on which agreement about the significance of our world is far less uniform and on which interpretation is consequently more often noticed *as* interpretation. We may, or we may not, apprehend scenes in the world as beautiful; we may, or we may not, apprehend events in the world as laying moral obligations upon us. Just as all men seem to have an innate tendency to interpret experience as signifying an objectively existing world, so all men seem to have a tendency to interpret their world in value terms, aesthetic and moral. The parallel, however, is not exact. The former interpretation is a precondition for the latter, since for a solipsist there could be neither beautiful *objects* nor moral obligations toward other *persons*, but value interpretations are not a requirement for an interpretation of nature as an independently existing world. As such, apprehending values is more clearly voluntary than is apprehending the world as objectively real—an interpretation on which survival may depend! Still, seeing the world as aesthetically and morally significant in general, despite specific differences of interpretation, is a normal part of human life.

Another normal characteristic of human existence is the apprehension of the totality of things as *religiously* significant. As an interpretation, once again, religious faith is no more open to coercive proof than is the apprehension of the world *as* a world or *as* aesthetically or morally significant. Just as the logic of a determined solipsist or amoralist may be impeccable, so may an atheist's reasoning be formally valid. For the religious believer, however, such considerations are quite literally beside the point, since he has seen nature, beauty, and morality as mediating for him an apprehension of reality that puts all earlier levels of significance into an ultimate context of meaning and truth. The theist puts his trust in no argument that will lead him securely from facts of nature or of value to certainty about the existence of God. Instead, he finds all experience freshly illuminated by his certainty; and this kind of certainty, as we have seen, equals knowledge. The theist genuinely knows, therefore, what he cannot prove, just as the informal inference theory of religious cognition maintained; he finds that moral experience as a dimension of interpretation is deeply relevant to his faith, as the moral theory insisted; and he discovers that his faith is a matter not of theoretical necessity but of responsible decision in an ambiguous world, as the voluntarist theory (stripped of its abstract "wagering" overtones) correctly taught.

Hick now needs to meet two possible objections to his theory of religious knowledge. First, what in experiential terms does theism *mean?* Any allegedly cognitive assertion that means anything specific at all must somehow inform us that, if it is true, we may expect to have certain experiences (the assertions "cash value") and expect *not* to have other specifiable experiences. If an alleged assertion is compatible with *every* conceivable experience, it is uninformative, but we have seen that a hallmark of knowledge is that it must be informative; therefore, religious belief must be incompatible with *some* expectation of experience before it can qualify as a candidate for belief or knowledge. Hick's theory, however (so the objection continues), maintains that theistic faith is a total interpretation of *all* experience as religiously significant. If we take this seriously, then any experience whatever will be "apprehended" as compatible with theistic belief, but this consequence entails that theism is uninformative; hence, religion is ruled out as a cognitive enterprise. Hick acknowledges the force of the requirement that genuine cognition entail determinate experiential expectations, but he rejects the assumption that theism offers no specifiable expectations of its own. On the contrary, theism maintains that after death certain experiences will be available which, if theism is correct, should verify adequately for rational certainty the truth of the religious assertions made in this life. Thus theism's eschatological dimension, together with the experiences of new qualities of life and power in this world, provides quite enough promise of significant experience to establish the total theistic interpretation as cognitive.

A second objection might hold that the religious interpretation of experience is altogether too much a matter of personal choice to be compatible with the actual existence of a supposedly all-powerful God eager to make Himself known to men. Why, if God exists, does He make it so easy for men to decide against their (supposed) natural inclination to apprehend Him? Hick's answer is that a loving God should be expected, if He exists, to permit cognitive freedom to His children. If men are to be genuinely free rather than automata, if they are to turn to God in responsible fellowship rather than in coerced slavery, a gracious God must veil Himself from their immediate vision so that they may come to Him of themselves, not as overawed sycophants, but as grateful children.

Such a concept of God is not without its historical origins, of course, and it is to the religious total-interpretation of Christianity that Hick alludes in concluding *Faith and Knowledge.* In the person of Jesus is seen a *man* who at the same time is apprehended by Christians as the revelation of *God.* Faith in Christ is a seeing of divine significance in His loving life and teaching, through which faith apprehends the world afresh under the God known in Jesus. Is this an interpretation which defies proof? Yes, Christian faith never becomes less than a matter of responsible choice; but from that choice springs an apprehension of a significance in all experience of nature, beauty, and morality, a significance which confirms and reconfirms the Christian's certainty that in his faith he has found unparalleled knowledge.

THE FORM OF THE PERSONAL

Author: John Macmurray (1891-)
Type of work: Philosophic reconstruction; philosophy of religion
First published: Volume I (*The Self as Agent*), 1957; Volume II (*Persons in Relation*), 1961

Principal Ideas Advanced

Modern philosophy is in a state of crisis due to two initial errors: first, the error of considering man as primarily thinker rather than agent, and, second, the error of considering man in solitude rather than in social relation.

Questions insoluble by traditional philosophy are freshly illuminated by considering the self as agent.

The nature of morality, politics, and religion may be clarified through an approach which makes central the concrete situation of rational agents in personal relation.

The two volumes which constitute the published version of John Macmurray's 1953-1954 Gifford Lectures, entitled *The Form of the Personal,* are pioneering ventures aimed at redirecting current thought toward greater philosophic adequacy and consequently towards greater appreciation of the nature, importance, and truth of religious belief. Since the time of René Descartes (1596-1650), the "father of modern philosophy," the direction of philosophic thinking has been toward atheism, Macmurray holds; but that this should be so is *prima facie* odd in view of the overwhelming tendency of men at all times and of all conditions to find religious expression a natural and enormously significant element in life. Religious belief, on the evidence, is no aberration. If, then, modern philosophy, on its premises, can find no theoretically valid place for religion, may it not be that the theories and premises of modern philosophy are themselves aberrant and in need of re-examination?

Macmurray in *The Self as Agent* (1957) finds that he is not alone in raising radical questions as to the foundations of traditional philosophy in a revolutionary age. Contemporary analytical philosophy, with its accent on new and rigorous techniques, has thrown in doubt the propriety of many of the problems which are traditionally considered the stock in trade of philosophy. Existentialism, on the other hand, has with equally radical impact tended to put in question the traditional methods of philosophy for the sake of heightened emphasis on basic human problems. Both radical movements, however, are for Macmurray unsatisfying because one-sided. Analysis dismisses the problems for the sake of technique; existentialism scorns technique for the sake of the problems: both recognize the urgent need for re-evaluation of traditional thought, but neither in itself offers constructive adequacy, and neither identifies the nature of our current crisis with sufficient clarity to go to its root.

The crisis of our age, Macmurray

insists, is the crisis of the *personal*. Existentialism is aware of the threat to personality, but it lacks the techniques needed to meet this threat with philosophic rigor. Analysis, by the very rigor of its techniques, exposes the depth of the threat through its inability to deal constructively with such deeply personal questions as morality, metaphysics, and religion. In practical terms, likewise, the crisis of the personal is represented by the growth of the state and the consequent decline in personal responsibility in favor of the collectivism of fascism and communism. The same crisis is further manifested in the widely noticed decline both in the power of religion and in the general level of sensitivity to human values within a world of massive industry and inconceivably destructive warfare.

Although the overwhelming problem of our age is the crisis of the personal, traditional philosophy is ill-equipped even to form an adequate concept of the person. What is the self? Macmurray points out that this question defies answer for those who approach it with the usual categories of thought fashioned for dealing with impersonal forms of being. The British empiricist philosopher David Hume (1711-1776), for example, showed the impossibility of constructing a concept of self out of substantial categories relevant to the "form of the material." On the other hand, Søren Kierkegaard (1813-1855), "father of existentialism," showed the inadequacy of the attempt by the idealist philosopher G. W. F. Hegel (1770-1831) to describe the self in terms of the "form of the organic," concepts drawn from living things on the subpersonal level. Only by developing concepts adequate to the subject matter, only by constructing and applying a new form—the "form of the personal"—will the crisis in philosophy, and in our culture, be resolved.

The difficulties which have prevented modern philosophy from creating an adequate form of the personal begin at the birth of modern philosophy itself, with Descartes's *Cogito ergo sum*. His "I think, therefore I am" has involved its philosophic heirs in two egregious mistakes: first, in the false supposition that the self may be conceived as being in isolation from other selves; and, second, in the mistaken identification of the self as primarily a thinking thing. Neither of these assumptions can withstand examination: the first leads to the absurdities of solipsism and the second leads to the irrelevancies of subjectivism and thus to abstraction from real life and experience.

Turning first, in *The Self as Agent*, to the second assumption, that the self is essentially a thinking thing, Macmurray first acknowledges the obvious—that the self is capable of thought and is in this sense a subject. Such acknowledgment is not, however, tantamount to accepting thought as the essential constitutive characteristic of the self. On the contrary, pure thought is seen, if we examine our experience, to be negative, a remainder left when we deliberately abstract ourselves from our full existence as thinking *agents*. We are rational agents first; we are inactive thinkers only derivatively. Pure thought, the self as subject, is over against the world. Only as agent does the self have existence in the world. For the "I think" of traditional philosophy Macmurray substitutes the "I do."

If we take such a substitution seriously, what light may we expect to find shed on traditional problems in philosophy? The problem of perception, first, is shown to be misconceived if put (as it too often is) in terms of a theory of vision. Vision is far from an appropriate standard for perception if the self is correctly understood as primarily agent. Touch, rather, is the agent's paradigm for perception; touch is the one sense which is not merely contemplative but does something to—acts against—the object perceived. The other senses then may be interpreted in terms of touch. Vision, for example, can be understood as a form of symbolism in which present experience (the sight of an object) signifies a possible future tactual experience in which the object will be given immediately to the perceiver rather than mediately through the fallible images of sight.

The nature of space and time, second, are illuminated by Macmurray's proposed shift. Space, for an agent, is best understood as the possibility of movement. Logically prior even to space is time, the very presupposition for action, and thus for space. Reference to our own most concrete experience shows that these great sources of metaphysical puzzlement become, for agents, direct implicates of action.

Other major problems for philosophy have been posed by the interpretation of "cause" and the status of the "world." From Macmurray's starting point, however, the concept of cause can be seen to be reducible to an abstraction from the agent's personal experience. If cause is best described in terms of a recurrent pattern of change, the experience of *habit*—that domain of activity from which the element of thought has been abstracted—can best ground our understanding of causality. Similarly, the physical world, as the realm of causes, can best be interpreted as an abstraction from personal experience of activity.

Science, as the deliberately abstract study of the physical world, is shown from Macmurray's perspective to be the mode of reflection in which the causal regularities of the world are objects of reflection in order that agents may discover what is to be counted on toward furthering action. As such, science is interested in the world as means; it deliberately limits its attention to the general and ignores the unique. Art, on the other hand, is that form of reflection which, from the point of view of the self as agent, is primarily interested in the intrinsically valuable, the unique which may be worthy of the agent's valuation in its own right. Art, therefore, is considered by Macmurray to be a higher form of reflection than science; from attention to the unique one may be able to recognize general features of things, but from exclusive concentration on the general one is never able to appreciate the unique.

History, finally, is interpreted by Macmurray as neither art nor science. In terms of the philosophy of the "I do," history's role is illuminated as reflection on action itself. History is interested both in the particular and unique (thus resembling art) and in the general and lawful (thus resembling science), but its primary task is the provision of a social memory. This social memory, interested in all action, exhibits the form of the personal as a whole; and, in so doing, it finds a continuity within all past actions, revealing the world as an intentional unity of personal activity.

At this point, however, the focus of Macmurray's attention has begun to move from the isolated self to the broader subject of selves in society. For the most part *The Self as Agent,* while shifting the concept of self from a thinking thing to an actor, has left unchallenged the solipsistic assumption implicit in Descartes's *Cogito ergo sum.* It has therefore remained incapable of interpreting essentially social phenomena like morality, political theory, and religion. To this cluster of subjects Macmurray next turns in his second volume, *Persons in Relation* (1961).

The first necessity is to establish fundamental categories through a formal examination of the fully personal in its simplest manifestation, which Macmurray finds in the initial condition and development of the human infant. A baby, the author points out, finds himself from birth within the field of the personal; the infant's original situation is within an environment dominated by personal intention; his one naturally given adaptive capacity is for communication of feelings of comfort and discomfort to agents who deliberately care for his needs; his first knowledge is of the personal Other. It is only when the developing child learns to discriminate within the Other that he is forced—as an agent—to acknowledge the nonpersonal, "that in the Other which does not respond to my call." The form of the personal, consequently, is originally and irremediably social. The "It" comes second, temporally and logically. The baby is constituted as a person by the Other, the You, with whom he communicates.

In the simple case of the infant, the motive consciousness which directs his communication exhibits a fundamental polarity, as we have seen, between discomfort (the "negative" phase) and comfort (the "positive" phase). Developing his thesis, Macmurray finds the positive and negative poles—love and fear, broadly understood—basic to the personal at all levels of development. If the child is to grow, his mother must deliberately disappoint his well-grounded expectations and at some point refuse to do for him what he must learn for himself. This experience of the withdrawal of the personal Other cannot fail to arouse fear, the negative phase, which by its essential egocentric character may smother the positive and heterocentric pole of love, without which real personal relation is impossible. The goal of the mother is to reinstate the dominance of the positive phase, without sacrificing the increasing capacities of the child to do for himself, by convincing him of her love despite all appearances. If she succeeds, love is more and more richly possible through the cycle of withdrawal and return; if she fails, the child's personal consciousness may more and more be dominated by the negative pole, which may express itself in either of two basic forms: aggressiveness (overcoming fear by forcing the Other to conform to one's will) or fantasy (overcoming fear by escape to an ideal world of imagination where there is no conflict between the Other and one's will).

Equipped with the model provided by this description, Macmurray turns to the philosophical task of giving an account of morality, political philosophy, and religion in terms of the person.

Morality, first, falls into three modes corresponding to the one positive and two negative personal responses outlined above. Each of the three moves the person in whom it may be dominant to select differently what he shall notice about the Other and himself. These three modes of apperception are the communal (positive pole), the pragmatic (negative-aggressive pole), and the contemplative (negative-escapist pole). Each mode of apperception leads to a mode of morality. The goal of morality for philosophy based on the form of the personal is given as realizing personal relation; but though morality is to "intend" community, community may be differently intended depending on one's mode of apperception. One may intend community pragmatically, taking ends for granted and finding the primary moral problems in aggressively developing means for achieving the good in actual life; one may, on the other hand, intend community contemplatively, finding the moral good in fantasies of an ideal realm and considering spiritual life as the only *real* life; or, Macmurray hopes, one may intend community communally, taking the Other as the center of loving concern and finding the primary moral problem in the overcoming of egocentricity and fear.

Political philosophy, too, is believed to be more adequately illuminated by the form of the personal than by means of other conceptual models. Once again Macmurray finds the two ambivalent negative possibilities standing over against the one positive pole of the personal. The views of the philosopher Thomas Hobbes (1588-1679) on the state, for example, reflect the negative-aggressive mode of apperception; the theories of the French philosopher Jean Jacques Rousseau (1712-1778), on the other hand, illustrate in this field the negative-escapist mode. But neither can find true *community*, which goes beyond mere *society* in being founded on the positive heterocentric mode of apperception and intention.

True community is the concern of religion. Religion, interpreted through the form of the personal, is a reflective activity engaged, on the one hand, in symbolically celebrating the achievement of community in so far as community is actual and, on the other hand, in strengthening the will to community by helping to overcome the negative pole in the personal, substituting the motive of love for the motive of fear in social relations. These two complementary functions require, Macmurray believes, the symbol of a personal Other who (1) stands in personal relation to each member of the community (this symbol, God, focuses joyful attention on the achieved community and helps withstand fear of losing this community through eventual relapse into mere society) and who (2) is the Agent for whom nature stands as his action (this symbol helps to overcome not only the fear of losing community but also the fear of the impersonal Other). Religion, as the reflective activity of community itself, can be recognized as the primary form of reflection from which art and science are derived. Art, reflection on what is worthy for its own sake, and science, reflection on how to attain given ends within the (abstract) impersonal Other, are both specialized limitations drawn from religion's fully concrete concern for both ends and means.

Persons in Relation ends with a defense of the intellectual right of the religious person to represent the universe in personal terms. We not only *may* conceive of the Other in its totality as personal, we *must* do so if our conception is to be adequate. Alternative conceptions of the universe are logically possible, of course, but a philosophy based on the form of the personal will expose them all as abstractions—legitimate, perhaps, within the context of their own subordinate (personal) intentions, but culpably partial when taken as the model for our conception of all things. The form of the Personal, the only model of the cosmos which can strengthen our full capacity to act as what we most surely know ourselves to be—persons—is the one which alone has the capacity to include ourselves in the universe, which alone makes possible an understanding of personal activity, and which alone reflects our original and most incorrigible knowledge.

In these volumes Macmurray, it is evident, has offered a major challenge to modern philosophy and has demonstrated a creativity of thought and breadth of conception for which he is widely respected. It will be both surprising and unfortunate if his ideas—both critical and constructive—are not widely debated in the years to come.

THE REALITY OF FAITH

Author: Friedrich Gogarten (1887-)
Type of work: Existential theology
First published: 1957

Principal Ideas Advanced

Implicit within Christian faith—understood as creaturely existence-in-relation made possible by the reception of the creative Word of God—is a two-fold freedom: for God and toward the world.

This freedom born of faith, which was discovered by Paul in his understanding of the believer's release from the soteriological claim of the Jewish law and the Hellenistic cosmic powers, and rediscovered by Luther as justification by faith, guarantees the secularity of the world which it turns over to man, the steward-son, for examination and responsible mastery.

Subjectivism, the historical source of modern man's freedom toward the world at a time when freedom was denied him by the Church, proves inadequate to provide meaning and unity to a technologically fragmented world.

In Christian faith this unity is made available, not as a metaphysical world view but as an existential reality in freedom for God and toward the world.

The Reality of Faith is one of several works emerging out of Friedrich Gogarten's later period. In this book he seeks to come to grips with contemporary technologically oriented secularism from the standpoint of Christian faith. Far from being antithetical to faith, secularism is implicit in the Biblical understanding of man's relationship to God and the world, claims Gogarten. As the "image" and the "son," man is that creature entrusted with a peculiar responsibility for the world. He is steward over a world which, according to the Biblical writers, has been purged of the numinous power and soteriological value which the world has for religions generally. The "principalities and powers" have been defeated by God through His victory in Jesus Christ, writes the Apostle Paul. Whereas previously man was victimized by worldly powers claiming divine authority, he now participates through faith in the victory of God as freeing him to live in a world depopulated of controlling spirits and demons, a secularized world. Genuine faith guarantees the preservation of this secularity, for in faith man receives his meaningful existence as a son from the Father. Since the world provides him with no ultimate meaning, it can make no ultimate claim upon him. The world remains properly secular.

This understanding of man's relationship to the world was not and could not have been adequately preserved in the medieval Church, Gogarten writes, because the understanding by faith which would have made it possible was obscured. Rather than a quality of being created in the relationship with the Father, faith became trust in and assent to a certain kind of world, the world of the Church. Divine reality was merged with ecclesiastical reality, and the fear and reverence which medieval man felt in the presence of natural and cosmic forces was redirected toward this Church-world. Admirable though the unity achieved by the medieval world may have been, it was doomed to be broken by two developments which sought to restore to man the freedom which is his according to the Christian Gospel: the Reformation, with its emphasis on justifying faith, and the Renaissance and Enlightenment, with their emphasis on reason.

Understanding faith not as assent to doctrines or as adherence to a world view of the Church but as a trusting response to the Word grasped as the intention of God directed toward man, Luther reintroduced the Biblical view of the relationship between man and God as dependent upon the event of revelation. Wherever revelatory communication takes place, in which God gives himself to man as man's God, the creature is freed from the necessity of releasing himself from the world and is freed for a responsible interaction with the Creator. Unfortunately this freedom for God was soon obscured even within the Reformation churches themselves as they fell back into medieval scholasticism, thereby transforming Christian faith once again from direct responsibility to a living God into adherence to certain doctrines; that is, into conformity to a certain kind of world view which was supposed to assure salvation. The implications of Luther's position as freeing man for independent and responsible investigation of the world as unencumbered by doctrinal limitations—as seen for instance in Luther's own relationship to his colleague on the Wittenberg faculty, Rhaeticus, who championed the views of Copernicus—never had a chance to develop, for the Reformation churches soon reaffirmed the medieval tradition of the Bible as the canon of the natural sciences. It remained for forces outside the Church to bring about the revolution which would make available to man the freedom toward the world which is rightly his in genuine Christian faith.

With the high valuation placed upon reason by the Renaissance and Enlightenment, man was given a principle by which he could stand over against his world and examine it in a way hitherto impossible—dispassionately and without religious anxiety. The assumed correspondence of reason within man to reason without gave man a position of pre-eminence as that being "who gives all being its measure and applies the plumb line," as Martin Heidegger has written. This development provided man with a degree of control over his world which steadily has been enlarged through the growth of the empirical sciences, until today man's control over his world is simply taken for granted—if not as a present attainment, at least as a future certainty. Not with cosmic spiritual powers and demons does the responsibility of the maintenance of the world lie, but with man.

The orientation which has accomplished this revolution is the "subjectivism" with which Gogarten wishes to enter into dialogue, as he indicates in the subtitle of the book, "The Problem of Subjectivism in Theology." The designation of this development as "subjectivism" may seem strange, especially since the concern of so much of the movement is for objective reality. Yet Gogarten sees, from the standpoint of the whole history of thought, the dominant motif as subjectivistic; that is, as that way of thinking which regards the thinking subject as the center of that which is thought, as the one who holds the plumb line to all reality. Contemporary scientific relativism only intensifies this orientation. Subjectivism succeeded where the Church did not in freeing man from religious worship of his world and in turning him toward the scientific control of it. Thus the initial point of contact between theology and subjectivism lies in the fact that subjectivism has brought to realization the second part of the two-fold freedom (freedom toward the world) which is available in the Christian faith. In order to draw the parallel and contrast between subjectivism and theology as sharply as possible, however, Gogarten proceeds to describe Christian faith in such a way as to make it appear closely akin to subjectivism, calling faith a "fully reflected self-consciousness," and quoting Luther to the effect that man's faith is the presupposition (*Voraussetzung*) of the reality of God's revelation. Man's faith "creates deity," as Martin Luther (1483-1546) wrote. What does this mean?

The first thing which must be said is that the faith here described is not the product of man but of God. Indeed, Gogarten interprets Luther's whole discussion of "the bondage of the will" as an attempt to make plain the fact that faith is the result of God's activity. And apart from this activity God cannot be known. But if this be the case, how can one say that man's faith is the presupposition of God's revelation? Precisely because God is known in his "creative power and deity" only when He is known as one's own Creator; that is, only as one receives one's very being, one's meaningful historical existence out of the encounter with Him. God is not God as a metaphysical hypothesis but only as one's own Lord in an actual faith relationship. It follows that one cannot speak meaningfully—that is, in a way which corresponds to an existing reality—of God without speaking of this kind of involvement with Him, for to speak without involvement is at best to use an unknown cipher and, at worst, a word, "God," which becomes a hoax, a subterfuge for a human longing or desire which has no external referent. The being which the believing man is given in the creative encounter with God, on the other hand, is the presupposition of everything he knows, not only concerning God but his world and himself as well; his being is fundamentally conditioned by this encounter, and therefore his knowledge reflects this same conditioning and is inseparable from it. Thus it can be said that Christian faith is "fully reflected self-consciousness" in the sense that the self-consciousness (*Selbstbewusstsein*) of the man in faith is the product of the encounter with God in which the being with which man entered into the encounter is reflected back as a new image "conformed to the image of His Son" (Romans 8:29), conditioned fundamentally by the revelation of God in Jesus Christ. Therefore faith is the presupposition of God in the only sense in which it is appropriate to speak of God at all, in speech which is the product of historical involvement and relativity. Thus Christian faith, analyzing itself, can see certain similarities to subjectivism's understanding of the nature of knowledge and reality.

Having come—to borrow a phrase from John Wesley—"within a hairsbreadth" of subjectivism, Gogarten now turns to point out the basic difference between Christian faith and the subjectivism of the modern era. Modern subjectivism began as the result of the discovery within man of an autonomous principle which provided direct access to the world and made the supernaturally given medieval metaphysical view of the world quite irrelevant (including the theology constructed thereupon). The locus of subjectivism's initial strength is the source of its eventual bankruptcy, however, for the ever present temptation to which the human reason again and again succumbs is the temptation to pull the world together into some kind of unity and wholeness which seems to be necessary to sustain meaning, a unity and wholeness lost with the dissolution of the heteronomous unity of the medieval world. Yet the technological mastery of the world can proceed only by breaking down one by one these unifying constructs of the human mind, with the ironic result that the successive failure of these attempts at meaning has insured the continuing success of man's ever expanding technological control and responsibility, making it appear ever more necessary to have an overall system, a universal scheme of things, to bring order and integration to a technologically fragmented life. The quest for unity is doomed to frustration, however, as long as it continues to go back to that source which is already known to be relative, man's mind, while seeking to find something absolute. World views do not become more absolute as they become more pretentious and grandiose. They cannot complete man's world but can only curve it in upon itself, thus rounding off the sphere of meaning within its own source. What is the alternative to this built-in frustration in subjectivism?

The Christian faith, claims Gogarten, does not seek to complete the world in terms of a scheme of the world, a metaphysic, to which the world must conform. Instead, the two-fold freedom given in faith not only turns the world over to man's reason for examination independently of metaphysical limitations, apart from the sheer givenness of the world itself, but it demands that the secularity of the world be maintained. This secularity is of course qualitatively different from the secularism of subjectivism. It not only rids the world of gods but refuses to allow other gods to be put in their places. It is secularity born of faith in the one God, not as a metaphysical theory but as the one source of existence in freedom. Delivered from "the horrible delusion" that the world will have meaning only if he can give it one, man is freed to examine the world as his rightful object as "son" and steward. Nor is it necessary, Gogarten concludes, for man to squeeze ultimate meaning out of the world, for he has his being and meaning from the Father.

CHRISTIANITY AND PARADOX

Author: Ronald W. Hepburn (1927-)
Type of work: Critique of theological methods
First published: 1958

Principal Ideas Advanced

Philosophical analysis shows that certain essential Christian claims about God and our knowledge of God embody conceptual confusion rather than legitimate paradox.

Attempts by contemporary theologians to base assertions about God on immediate acquaintance through "encounter" experiences or knowledge of Jesus Christ are doomed to failure.

Equally futile as justifications for theological claims are appeals to history, morality, or the world as a whole.

Despite the conceptual weakness of their theology, Christians need not fear that the only alternative to Christian faith is life without ethical or religious meaning.

Ronald W. Hepburn's *Christianity and Paradox* throws down a challenge to theology—a challenge offered by a contemporary analytical philosopher who characterizes himself as a critic with a "naturally religious mind." To what extent, Hepburn asks, are the long-recognized peculiarities of Christian language legitimate paradoxes, justifiable by the unique subject matter of theology, and to what extent are these oddities attributable to logical confusion? Can the sympathetic philosopher find satisfaction, without violating his rigorous critical standards, in the answers given by modern theologians? If not, must intellectual integrity be paid for at the cost of personal meaningfulness?

A possible objection, that philosophy has no business meddling with questions of faith, is quickly turned aside by Hepburn. The moment a theologian engages himself in scrutiny of his own concepts, terming them "symbols" or "analogies" or the like, he is engaged in philosophic endeavor. There can be no bar, therefore, against an acknowledged philosopher's examining the theologian's philosophical theories or offering theories of his own. In like manner, a theologian who ventures to judge any viewpoint incompatible with Christian faith, any morality at variance with Christian ethics, has thereby entered the philosophical arena and cannot object when his ideas attract the professional attentions of his colleagues. Even if the theologian refrains (as he usually does not) from the foregoing activities, his assertions are fair grist for the philosopher's mill to the extent that theological utterances are supposed to carry meaning and truth. There is no side-tracking the enterprise of *Christianity and Paradox* by demanding that the philosopher mind his own business; any claim to meaning or truth *is* the philosopher's business.

How can meaning or truth be expressed by language which characteristically takes the form of apparent contradictions, as in the statement cited by Hepburn from *De trinitate,* in which Augustine writes that God is "good without quality, great without quantity, a creator though he lacks nothing, ruling but from no position, eternal yet not in time"? How can it be maintained that God is both three and one, that God acts in the world but is in neither time nor space? How can such paradoxical claims be defended as anything other than confused or meaningless utterances?

One popular defense proposed by contemporary theologians is to claim that the language of Christian faith is abnormal because of the abnormality of its subject matter, and that the resulting verbal difficulties are resolved in immediate experience of Him to whom they refer. Given such experience, the apparent contradictions of Christian language should be no more philosophically troublesome than are the apparent contradictions in the physicist's talk about light, with respect to which he speaks as though his subject matter were at the same time a wave and a particle. We do not doubt the existence of light or the propriety of physical theory, despite this logical oddness, because light can be given an "ostensive definition" (it can be pointed to in experience); similarly, if God can be defined ostensively, we must not cavil at the inevitable peculiarities of speech about Him. Hepburn agrees that *if* an ostensive definition can be provided for the word "God," the theologian is standing on firm ground, but is such a definition actually possible with respect to Him who is beyond the reach of our senses? The philosopher's duty is to examine the theories of theologians who answer affirmatively.

One theological school of thought, much influenced by the Jewish philosopher-theologian Martin Buber (*I and Thou*), claims that the required ostensive definition of "God" is available in experiences of encounter with a personal *"Thou"* who transcends the sense-bound "impurities" inherent in personal relations with human beings.

Hepburn is unable to agree. The basis of this theological position is the assumption—plausible at first—that personal encounters are in principle independent of any objective test or check-up procedure. Is it not the case that there is a spectrum of personal encounter ranging from radically "impure" meetings in which the other person is reduced to an observable thing to be studied, manipulated, or used, to the comparatively "pure" personal encounters in which objective factors, those features of one's friend which are open to observation, are of much diminished importance? Hepburn agrees, but he points out that such a spectrum does not in the least entitle the theologian to maintain that somewhere *off* the spectrum exists the possibility of a personal encounter with *no* observational or objective characteristics. Quite the opposite, the relative unimportance of objective characteristics when a profoundly personal relation is achieved itself depends on the objective features being so well known, so intimately understood, their significance so often confirmed by experience, as to be taken for granted. The fleeting gesture, the unconscious twitch of a muscle, even the pregnant silence—all contribute to the sense of encounter. What, however, of the radically different theological claim that personal encounter can be experienced without any gestures, without any breaking of silence to discover that both persons have been following similar trains of thought, without any indication at any time that there even exists a *Thou* brooding behind the objectively unbroken stillness? "Personal encounter" of this sort has torn itself free from the essential moorings of our universal experience of genuine "encounter," and in so doing it has been emptied of any meaning which might be of use to theologians in offering an ostensive definition of the divine *Thou*. In an age made aware by Freudian psychology of the tricks constantly being played on our minds by unconscious factors, the theologian cannot hope to rest his case on a peculiar sense of personal presence that shares none of the objective characteristics of real meetings between persons. If he wishes to found the peculiarities of his speech on the nature of an ostensively definable reality, he must look elsewhere.

A second school of Christian thought relies for its answer not on feelings of personal communion but exclusively on Jesus Christ. The doctrine of Incarnation, it is claimed, licenses the Christian to point to the God-man as the ostensive definition of God. Hepburn, however, doubts the logical strength of this move, at least when taken by itself. Certainly statements about Jesus cannot be made logically equivalent to statements about God without heretical departure from Christian faith. According to orthodox belief Jesus died, Jesus was limited in knowledge, Jesus was bounded by time and space; but God cannot be considered finite or mortal. Even a Christocentric theology must remain within certain bounds. Jesus fails to provide "God" with an adequate ostensive definition, nor is it possible to evade this verdict by insisting that it is to the Christ, to the Second Person of the Trinity, that reference is given by such a theory: such a move simply pushes the problem back one step to the notorious difficulty of describing intelligibly the relation between Jesus, the man of Galilee, and the eternal Christ.

No escape is offered by this route, and the enterprise of offering ostensive definitions for God seems fruitless.

Another way of justifying problematic language, however, is to show that for all its peculiarities such language is required to explain certain features of experience. Can theological statements be defended on the basis of their explanatory power?

Hepburn turns first to claims that the events of history are best interpreted in terms of God's activity. He detects an unfortunate logical conflict, however, between the contemporary theologian's assertion that "history matters" and the insistence of many theologians that Christian faith does not stand or fall on any events open to the probing of the historian. If Christianity is to claim historical roots and explanatory value, it must take the risks of falsification by growing historical knowledge, but theologians who demand a faith imperturbable by fact undermine the very basis of their explanatory claim.

A second area of alleged explanatory power is found by some theologians in the domain of morality. Apart from Christian faith, they contend, the fullness of moral experience can neither be illuminated by thought nor achieved by life. Hepburn agrees that secular ethical thought may be arid and shallow, but he challenges the claim that this *must* be the case when ethics is separated from theology. A "man-centered" ethic need not be equivalent to egotistic meanness; Christian doctrine is not the only avenue to the recognition of human corruption or human possibility; and, most significantly of all, Christian faith cannot in any event obviate the need for making a human moral judgment—that God's will is good and that it is right to obey His commands—which judgment must inevitably precede the adoption of any theological ethic. Theology is neither a necessary nor a sufficient explanation for morality.

At last it may be urged by the theologian that the world as a whole requires explanation in terms of God. Why should there be anything rather than nothing? Surely the cosmos demands a ground beyond itself, a causal source and sustainer, who is God. For Hepburn such an argument has an appeal, reflecting both a sense of wonder at the cosmos as a whole and a sense of "ontological anxiety" at the recognition of our own precarious place in existence, but as a rational proof for the existence of God and thus for the legitimacy of theological language it has serious shortcomings. The argument presupposes that every event must have a cause, including the world, the totality of all observable events. The "certainty" of the argument depends, however, (1) on its proponents shifting illicitly from making an uninformative statement (true by definition) about the mere meaning of "cause" and "effect," and (2) on the dubious suppositon that the world as a whole can meaningfully be talked about in language applicable primarily to things *in* the world. Even granting that the statement "Everything must have a cause" is informative and true, the causal argument defeats itself, since on this premise God must also have His cause; and even granting that the world as a whole can meaningfully be spoken of, it is not clear that causal language is ever applicable to the universe itself. That it is so applicable must be shown, not merely assumed.

Hepburn offers an alternative both to traditional Christianity and to blank frustration of the religious impulse. The alternative is a recognition of the importance of parable and of imaginative construction within a life sensitive both to the values of religious experience and to the seriousness of the moral pilgrimage. Within profoundly evocative parable may be found the basis for an imaginative response to one's fellows and one's world that will furnish the religiously sensitive skeptic with support in his moral endeavors and integration for his life—but without violating his intellectual integrity. Even religious experience, for such a person, can be valued for its high worth independent of such dogmatic interpretations as, offending the mind, too often have been allowed to stultify the experience.

CHRISTIANS AND THE STATE

Author: John Coleman Bennett (1904-)
Type of work: Christian ethics
First published: 1958

Principal Ideas Advanced

The Christian faith places the state under the providence, judgment, and redeeming love of God.

The government of the United States is neither secular nor neutral regarding religion; it officially recognizes theism.

The negative religious freedom of the minority ought not to outweigh the positive religious freedom of the majority.

The Christian ethic stands in an objective moral order broader than the Judeo-Christian tradition.

Absolute judgments regarding the state are inappropriate for the Christian whose proper relationship to it is compounded of judgment and responsibility.

The Christian Church ought not to be identified with any particular social or political order.

In *Christians and the State,* John C. Bennett develops his views of the theological basis of the state, the nature of the state and its functions, and the problems of political ethics. The work is important for three reasons: its themes are perennial perplexing issues of vital significance, its author is qualified to speak authoritatively for much of mainline Protestantism in the mid-twentieth century, and it is written so clearly that it demonstrates that a work of responsible scholarship can be made available to the general reader.

Dealing with the Christian faith in a religiously pluralistic society, Bennett presents in Part One the very basic questions to which his work is addressed: (a) How should Christians in such a society express their faith that both nation and state stand under the providence, judgment, and redeeming love of God? (b) How should they cooperate with those of other faiths or with those who reject traditional religion? and (c) How should they conceive of the relationship of their own faith and its ethic to the more general moral convictions present in the culture?

Restricting his discussion to the United States, Bennett notes that its heritage is vitally Christian but is not committed to any one faith. Though the state is friendly toward organized religion, American Christians cannot participate in the "advantages and illusions" of a formal Church-state relationship. Yet, Bennett argues, the state is not in principle secular, nor is it even neutral as between religion and the rejection of it. There is an officially recognized theism in the United States as evidenced in various of our state documents, the Constitution, official prayers, and the like. The criticisms leveled against the vagueness of this national theism are important, but they are only part of the truth, as is illustrated so well by Abraham Lincoln's genuine worship of God without the use of divisive Christian symbols. Bennett advocates a clear understanding that while the state is neutral as between faiths, it is not secular or indifferent to religion. It does not profess a common-denominator religion, nor act as a teacher of religion. The state uses symbols and provides for acts of religious recognition which "refer to the Reality which the churches and other religious bodies alone are competent to interpret."

Naturalistic humanists, atheists, and agnostics who reject traditional religious symbols advocate an absolutistic version of separation of Church and state. Bennett feels that while their protest against obscurantism and clericalism is important, one has to weigh the negative religious freedom of this small minority with the positive religious freedom of the majority. Restraint and consideration are needed on both majority and minority sides.

Especially noteworthy in the light of the theological environment with which Bennett is familiar is his explicit repudiation of that rejection of a natural theology which leads to rejection of general revelation. He thinks of the religious responses to God that are broader than distinctively Christian when he observes that "the rejection of general revelation represents a theological austerity that denies deep human realities." The Christian who believes that Christ fulfills and transforms the ideas of the Deity cannot deny that there is much in the broad religious response of mankind to be fulfilled and transformed.

The distinctively Christian ethic needs to be set in the context of moral convictions whose base is broader than the Judeo-Christian tradition. Such moral convictions may be defended as true apart from Christian revelation, Bennett claims. There is an objective moral order which includes both Christians and non-Christians. The objectivity of the ethical notion of love is demonstrated by the suicidal effects of hatred as shown internationally in war and individually in the mental illness of the person who is driven by hate. The real unity of the human race, the common fate of humanity, the concern for justice, freedom, honesty, integrity, and personal discipline —all have more than narrowly Christian dimensions, Bennett insists. Dedication to the goals of the common morality are often present outside the Christian community, but it is within the Christian understanding that one finds the most adequate context for such goals.

Considering characteristic Roman Catholic and Protestant views in the light of New Testament warnings against anarchy and the absolute state, Bennett expounds his own constructive position in which the state's coercive power is viewed as a necessary factor in but not the definition of the state's role. The power of evil is greater than either Roman Catholic or Protestant Liberal thought has understood. The Fall of Adam is best understood in a dynamic way which removes the emphasis from the condition of Adam before the Fall as contrasting with the condition of humanity since and places it rather on the experience of sinfulness in every man. Sin rooted in spiritual pride reaches to all areas of human life, and it is in this sense that the traditional notion of total depravity is to be understood. Toward human sin the state has the complex relationship of simultaneously restraining it, embodying it, and being limited by it. Theological realism of the type which Reinhold Niebuhr represents has shown the limitations of moral idealism which is so often preoccupied with inapplicable solutions and is frequently used as the basis for rationalizations of tyranny.

In view of the presence of both the negative and positive aspects of the state, what can the Christian position be regarding resistance to the state? Absolutistic judgments are not appropriate, but when, as in a democracy, the government provides for its own correction, the Christian has the responsibility of respect for the government. The Christian must insist that the state be seen as a limited instrument of society and not as the all-encompassing social reality itself. There is a high degree of agreement between Protestant and Catholic on this point.

Though the characteristic movement in the modern period has been the loosening of the relationship between the law of the state and the law of God, the government of the United States was set in the context of belief in a higher or divine law. The influence of this higher law remains in American constitutional law. Natural law, of which God is the Author and which is known to reason and confirmed by revelation, is accepted as the criterion of all positive law for Roman Catholic thought. Protestants have tended to have reservations about natural law in view of man's fallen state, for fallen man is not able to know or properly to apply such law. The rise of the totalitarian state has provoked renewed concern for the criteria of justice above the law and the state. Consistently Bennett counsels moderation and restraint in situations in which the state and individual conscience collide. He argues that absolutes are inappropriate in the area of Church and state discussions.

Cautioning repeatedly against the danger which the state poses to freedom, Bennett sees the role of the state as essential in certain spheres such as the economic. Only the state has sufficient scope to deal effectively with national problems, and there is nothing morally or socially wrong in the state's participating in economic affairs. It is, in fact, the state which often stands as the one effective guarantee of freedom for much of the population. Discussions associated with the ecumenical movement have featured a helpful scrutiny of economic ideologies which has resulted in rejection of rigid thinking regarding either capitalism or socialism. Capitalism as unfettered free enterprise has received especially serious scrutiny. Bennett makes it clear that insofar as capitalism presents many centers of power and initiative in society and regulates large segments of the economy by the market, and takes seriously the problem of incentive, Americans can well preserve it and recommend it to other nations. Yet only the great changes in capitalism in the past decades have made it morally tolerable. The Christian must avoid identifying his Christianity with any economic system, be it capitalist or socialist. The same is true with identifying Christianity with any form of government, though Bennett shows the affinity of Christianity with the responsible democratic society whose government is based upon the consent and participation of all elements in the population and which has constitutional safeguards for freedom of expression and minority rights.

Central to the final third of Bennett's work are his presuppositions regarding the nature of the Church. He stresses the Church as a human institution whose purpose is to relate man to the redeeming acts of God. Community itself is an essential part of the Gospel. The Church is a universal community having responsibility for the total society. Its authority rests not in itself but in the Word of God. It ought not to be confused with any particular social order. In his discussion of the meaning of separation of Church and state, the author recalls that the word "separation" never appears in the Constitution, and that the First Amendment was a compromise which ought not be subjected to too rigid an interpretation. The state and local communities ought to be given the benefit of the doubt when they are experimenting with solutions of the very difficult problems involved when the positive and the negative forms of religious liberty are brought into heightened tension. Genuine misunderstanding often exists when those whose faith is secularism take an extreme view of separation as it involves the system of public education. They see their position as a valuable concern for fairness and freedom. It may be such for the minority but not for the majority whose rights must also be considered. Bennett approves the government's going out of its way to encourage voluntary associations, such as churches, which are important for the general welfare of the community.

In the perplexing and frequently rancorous area in which Church and state meet in concern for education, Bennett succeeds in presenting a balanced view of various interests. He advocates the encouragement of experiments rather than unyielding rigidity of movement within narrow limits. The only generalization he permits is that all proposed solutions create difficulties and none apply universally. Teaching the "common-core" of the Judeo-Christian tradition has value, but such instruction easily becomes sectarian and encourages a public school "doctrine." Teaching about religion has merit but is often less than many want in the way of direct religious education. Released time has been tried and found wanting by many Protestant leaders, though it still offers a significant area for experimentation. Noting that the idea of parochial schools is hardly un-Protestant, Bennett cites the almost universal Protestant opposition to direct government aid to such schools. He accepts the view that public financial encouragement of parochial schools would be destructive not only of public schools but of the level of education generally. Bennett is less rigid than many, however, and he advocates experimentation in this area. The welfare of the pupils and the harmony of the community receive strong emphasis in his thinking.

Bennett's presentation of the Protestant view of Roman Catholic power in America is distinguished not so much by the thoroughness of its rehearsal of the fears of Roman Catholic dogmatic intolerance and its frequent companion, civil intolerance, as in its insistence that it is an error to project such fears indiscriminately into an indefinite future. No attempt is made to deny that Protestants fear a powerful Church which suffers or tolerates a pluralistic democracy only as an expediency on the way to its goal of a Church-dominated confessional state. There is real tension between an authoritarian, centralized hierarchical Church and the spirit of an open, pluralistic, democratic society. Yet Protestants need to be aware that some of their fears stand in need of scrutiny.

The Roman Catholic Church is not without variation among the various nations and cultures where it is found. "The difference between French Catholicism and Spanish Catholicism almost belongs to the study of comparative religion," Bennett writes. The Roman Catholic aggressiveness in the United States which offends so many Protestants has its roots in the cultural situation which was alien to it. Further, Roman Catholicism is far more divided on matters of principle than is generally understood so far as the proper view of religious liberty and social policy are concerned. Bennett hopes that exaggerated fear may be allayed, that Protestants will stress their own positive teaching more, and that both religious groups will exhibit greater understanding and share more in striving for common goals.

Most churches have spoken out regularly on public issues. When the cry is heard that the Church ought to stay out of politics, the objection is more likely to be against what the Church is saying rather than that it is speaking forth. Self-restraint is advisable in technical and strategic issues lying outside the specific competence of Christian wisdom, but the Church's nature is such that its interests are inclusive. What must be guarded against is making the ethos of one part of the community the basis of the law of the whole community. Protestants and Roman Catholics alike have need to exercise great care here as the experience with Prohibition and with birth-control legislation suggests. Bennett advocates that the Church should affect the state through emphasis upon the spiritual values of the society and its individual members, by being true to itself, by refusing to yield to forces of political manipulation, and by teaching its members about the relevance of Christian faith for the great public issues. Indirect forms of action are more important than the direct. Any direct action needs to be most thoroughly scrutinized and should represent an overflow from the indirect action. Christians may be expected to differ on political matters, and Christian political parties and movements generally misrepresent Christianity as implying a particular political program. The area of politics is one of moral ambiguity because real alternatives are so limited that compromise must be achieved. Compromise and corruption ought not be identified, for compromise can be a legitimate expression of Christian concern.

It is not difficult to understand why John Bennett's book received an excellent reception, for it is marked by comprehensiveness and clarity, and its critical passages are presented with an irenic concern for balanced positive solutions.

COMMENTARY ON GALATIANS

Author: Ragnar Bring (1895-   )
Type of work: Exegetical theology
First published: 1958

Principal Ideas Advanced

The law, according to Paul, must be recognized as a part of the redemptive history of the Old Testament, and interpreted in the light of the fulfillment of this redemptive history in Jesus Christ.

Christ fulfilled the law by accepting its curse on the cross, thus revealing the law's true function of revealing man's sin, but also freeing all men from condemnation by the law.

The Christian's freedom from the law expresses itself as faith active in love: thus, the righteousness that the law could not create is realized.

Commentary on Galatians by Ragnar Bring, professor of systematic theology at the University of Lund, Sweden, is intended to be neither philological nor popular and devotional; it is, rather, an attempt to present the content of thought and the context of ideas to be found in Paul's Letter to the Galatians.

According to Bring, Paul's letter shows how the early Church differentiated itself from Judaism, though this differentiation did not mean emancipation from the Old Testament and the law. The letter was occasioned by a controversy in congregations established by Paul. Some congregations were insisting that Christians, in addition to responding in faith to the Gospel of salvation through Christ as preached by Paul, were also obligated to keep the Old Testament law. Paul answered these critics, establishing his Apostolic authority and defining the proper understanding of the Old Testament, and more particularly its first part, the Pentateuch or the law, in the light of the revelation in Christ.

The Gospel for Paul was not a human doctrine but a divine revelation, a renewal of the prophetic interpretation of the Scriptures. Thus the message was the same whoever proclaimed it. There was not complete clarity in the Church, however, as to the implications of the Gospel message for the Gentile mission, especially in so far as the law was concerned. Included in the Old Testament law were required observances by which the Jew separated himself from the Gentile. According to Paul, since the law had been fulfilled in Christ these observances were no longer necessary, and it was now possible to see that the real function of the law was to reveal man's sin. In the old age prior to Christ's coming the demands of the law had been misunderstood to mean that man through keeping them could achieve righteousness. But with Christ a new righteousness had been revealed, and the condemning function of the law could now be freely recognized.

The Jews claimed to be Abraham's children, but Paul insisted that Christians are the true children of Abraham. The concept of election as Paul interpreted it excluded any emphasis on human qualities as providing the basis for the divine blessing. Instead election pointed forward to the fulfillment of the promise made to Abraham, which fulfillment had now come. Thus for Gentiles to be circumcised in order to separate themselves from other Gentiles involved a denial of the covenant with Abraham, for Abraham had not received the promise on the basis of his circumcision. Nor was God's election to be limited by such efforts to separate men from one another.

Whereas Jews drew a line from Abraham to Sinai, Paul drew a line from Abraham to Christ, in whom the law was fulfilled and brought to an end. According to Paul the law is holy and good, but it condemns man. The law is fulfilled only in the righteousness revealed in Christ. Until Christ came the purpose of the law was to put man under a curse, to demand of man what man was unable to perform.

In order to explain Paul's understanding of the fulfillment of the law in Christ, Professor Bring paraphrases a crucial passage, Galatians 3:11-12: "Righteousness is connected with faith. It does not say in Scripture that righteousness comes through observance of the law. It says rather, he who does what is written in the book of the law shall thereby receive eternal life." The law is to be fulfilled. This fulfillment is not contrasted with faith, but comes with the Messiah. Christ fulfilled the law in that He submitted to God's will to the extent of going the way of the cross. To gain life through the law is therefore to gain it through the fulfillment of the law wrought by Christ. The right relation to the law is to submit in faith to its judgment and to believe in Christ. Thus "the just by faith" and "he who does the law" are not opposites, but mean the same thing, since for Paul even the commandments of the Old Testament witness to Christ. In the light of the Gospel, Paul sees a deeper meaning in the Old Testament references in Leviticus 18:5 and Deuteronomy 30:11-20 which speak of life coming through fulfilling the law, for these passages, according to Paul, may now be interpreted as referring to Christ.

The law came because of transgressions and was a judgment on sin, not a guide to a righteous life. Thus true obedience to the law was to submit to its judgment, while to try to make oneself righteous through the law was to disobey it. Christ, on the other hand, identifying Himself with sinful humanity, accepted death on the cross, thereby showing himself to be righteous, and fulfilling the law. This judgment could be accepted only by one who was Himself personally free from judgment. The judgment was actually the curse of God, but Christ's encounter with this condemnation had cosmic dimensions. Blessing could now come to all, for all who were in any way bound by the curse of the law were now freed by Christ. The self-righteousness of the Jews, on the other hand, reached its ultimate expression in their rejection of Christ. Yet the result of this act was that Israel was itself freed from the curse of the law, and the Gospel could also now be proclaimed to Gentiles. If the Gentiles, however, were to accept the necessity of circumcision and other law observances, this would be to identify themselves with the concept of law that had led to the rejection of Christ.

Paul held that if the promise to Abraham was correctly understood, there could be no ultimate opposition between the law and the promise. To think that righteousness according to the law was a condition for sharing in the fulfillment of the promise in Christ was to fail to see salvation in Christ as the fulfillment of the promise. Paul did not criticize the Jews for valuing the law too highly, but for making it something God had not intended it to be. Instead of the law being a part of God's redemptive history, it had become an idol worshiped by the Jews in the interest of their own self-righteousness. But to idolize the law, Paul insisted, was to dishonor the law.

Since the law was given because of trespasses, it was not present prior to the creation, nor was it a complete expression of God's nature. The law could demand righteousness, but the law could not create righteousness. While the law therefore had a place in God's pedagogy, the law was not the goal divine. When the law, furthermore, led to legalistic righteousness, the law could no longer reveal sin. The depth and meaning of sin thereby became hidden. The law increased sin and thus drove people from faith in the one God which the law proclaimed. The Galatians accordingly were led away from Christ to Moses, though Moses was to lead to Christ.

Paul saw that through Christ God was to be the one God of all people, as all men became one, with no distinctions whereby some among them could claim more merit than others. Thus belief in Christ, according to Paul, was no threat to monotheism. On the contrary, through faith in Christ faith in the one God was fully realized.

Christ through the Spirit was now at work in the believer, and thus the goal of creation was being achieved, for Christ was the origin and goal of creation. Through baptism all shared in Christ's death and resurrection, becoming united with Christ and with other Christians. No distinctions between men were here insignificant. Since at the most basic point all Christians were alike, other differences between them could not be degrading. Some of these differences were even to disappear, while others were to be gratefully acknowledged as making possible the many and varied ministries which the welfare of the Christian fellowship required.

Bring points out that in this letter

Paul is not primarily concerned to tell people to change their ways of thinking. He is more interested in proclaiming an objective fact which has changed the human situation and has made possible a new religious orientation. That Christ came with life and righteousness, which can come only from God, manifests His divinity. Since the law had divine validity, freedom from the law could not be achieved through teaching. The law could be set aside only if God, who gave the law, now allowed it to be fulfilled.

Paul strongly emphasized that those who had been made free must not return to bondage. The powers to which one was subservient in legalistic righteousness had been made powerless by God in Christ, but apart from Christ they were real powers. Yet to worship temporal powers was fraudulent, for in the deepest sense they lacked real existence. Paul writes to the Galatians as if he were a mother who in travail had given them birth. Now new labor was necessary that Christ be formed again with them. Paul wishes that he could present the Gospel so clearly that the Galatians would at last be firmly rooted in it. The allegory of Sarah and Hagar may represent such an attempt.

Sarah and Hagar represent two covenants, one which is to terminate, the other which is to continue. In their emphasis on physical descent from Abraham, the Jews were like Ishmael, the son of Hagar and Abraham, who had physical descent but no promise. So also Hagar had prided herself over Sarah, just as the Jews did over the Gentiles. Hagar thought her son would be the only heir, and the Jews had similar opinions of their privileged status. The promise to Abraham that he would have many descendants in terms of redemptive history looked forward to the coming time when righteousness would be realized through the Messiah. This is the understanding of Scripture that Paul presupposes. Bring suggests that though Paul's interpretation of the story of Sarah and Hagar appears allegorical, it might better be called typological, for it is this understanding of the Scriptures in terms of redemptive history which determines the meanings Paul finds in the story. Bring also points out that Paul may during his stay in Arabia have heard of Arab legends about Ishmael. Thus he could say that Israel's claims to descend from Abraham were like the claims of the Arabs. What distinguished Isaac was the promise, now fulfilled in Christ, but the Jews rejected the promise. Thus the Jews through their use of the law had become like those outside the covenant of promise.

The Christian's freedom from the law according to Paul, however, is to be a freedom in the spirit expressing itself as faith active in love, and not a freedom in the flesh. Fleshly freedom would simply be a new form of bondage. Love for Paul is not egoistic desire and its satisfaction, but a willingness to serve. The freedom of which he speaks is not the freedom of fulfilling one's own desires and asserting one's own interests against others, but a freedom which naturally realizes itself in a selfless love. Yet this new behavior is possible only through the Spirit given through Christ. Thus Paul's ethical exhortations are implications of his doctrinal exposition.

In the eagerness of the Galatians to add various law observances to faith, they had ceased to love one another.

The opposite of love is that men destroy one another. Christ revealed the truth that men are created to love and to serve one another.

Paul does not teach sinlessness, Bring concludes, for although sin is a power overcome in Christ, as long as man lives on earth he continues to feel the power of sin. Man is, however, not wholly passive in this struggle. He can turn away from the flesh and toward that which belongs to the life of faith. Christians are not to judge one another, but to share one another's burdens. To live by sharing is to live in accord with the love of Christ. At the same time one is to see one's own faults and thus to be spared from the self-righteousness that comes from comparing oneself to others. This carrying of one's own burdens will in turn make one more willing to carry those of others.

THE NATURE OF FAITH

Author: Gerhard Ebeling (1912-)
Type of work: Systematic theology
First published: 1959

Principal Ideas Advanced

The Christian Church can no longer proclaim its faith by means of the traditional language of Bible and creed, nor can it rely on contemporary language.

Christian faith is not religious allegiance to creeds and doctrines or intellectual assent to the conclusions of historical research, but a mode of existence through the witness of faith in the words and actions of Jesus.

Christian faith is a summons and a gift that comes to man out of history and places the individual in a new relationship to the world (the sphere of faith), endowing the present with the power of reconciling love, and filling the future with hope.

Das Wesen des christlichen Glaubens, by the Protestant theologian Gerhard Ebeling, contains a course of lectures given in the winter of 1958-59 at the University of Zürich for students of all faculties. It was not the author's intention "to present complete dogmatics, but to give an introduction to the understanding of Christian faith." Thus the work is clear in its structure, avoids technical language as much as possible, and does not involve discussion with alternate points of view through extended footnotes.

Gerhard Ebeling began his academic career at Tübingen as a Church historian. In 1942 he published a study of Luther's hermeneutics, a study entitled *Evangelische Evangelienauslegung: Eine Untersuchung zu Luthers Hermeneutik.* His studies in the problem of hermeneutics (which is the problem of the character of historical knowledge and, in particular, the problem of understanding historical documents delivered by tradition) led him into the field of systematic theology. In 1956 Ebeling joined the faculty of Zürich as professor of dogmatics. In 1959 *Das Wesen des christlichen Glaubens* was published, and in 1960 a volume of collected essays appeared under the title *Wort und Glaube*. Since 1950 he has been the editor of one of the leading German theological periodicals, *Zeitschrift für Theologie und Kirche*.

The free English translation of the title *Das Wesen des christlichen Glaubens* as *The Nature of Faith* is misleading. In this work Ebeling is not concerned with either a psychological analysis of religious experience (as was William James) or with a phenomenological and ontological analysis of the dynamics of faith (as Paul Tillich has been); Ebeling is concerned, rather, with the "essence" (*Wesen*) of Christian faith; that is, with the peculiar nature of Christian religious experience as an exercise of faith which involves one's total existence, and with the relevance of such a conception of faith to man's existence in the contemporary scene. With the Marburg theologian Rudolf Bultmann (*Theology of the New Testament*) and Karl Heim (*Jesus the Lord*), Ebeling shares an acute awareness of the irrelevance of formalized Christian faith to most churchmen. He writes as follows: "Christians have become accustomed to existence in two spheres, the sphere of the church and the sphere of the world. We have become accustomed to the co-existence of two languages, Christian language with the venerable patina of two thousand years, and the language of real life round about us. Certainly, it may happen that the spark of understanding leaps across the gap. But there are no comprehensive rules for translating from the one language to the other. . . . It is not a matter of understanding single words, but of understanding the word itself, not a matter of new means of speech, but of a new coming to speech."

It is the problem of a "new coming to speech," of "understanding the word itself," that is, the word of "faith" that concerns Ebeling. He is fully aware, with Bultmann, that the cosmology of the first century and the language appropriate to it are foreign to twentieth century man and that the distinction of "kerygma" (the Gospel which the Church proclaims) and "myth" (the historically relative language and forms of expression employed in proclaiming the Gospel) must be made. But this distinction, the product of literary and historical criticism of the Biblical text, must not be translated into a distinction between "faith" and "history."

It is central to Ebeling's theological program that "faith comes to us out of history, and takes us into its history." Faith is "event," "movement," "happening." Faith comes to a man in his existential situation, informing and transforming it. Faith comes to him in and through the witness of others (the historical tradition) as they, like the figure of the evangelist in the Grünewald altar painting of the Crucifixion, point to *the* witness and ground of faith, Jesus Christ.

Given this initial definition of the essence of Christian faith, Ebeling proceeds to examine the traditional themes of theological discourse: Jesus Christ, God, the Word of God, the Holy Spirit, man, justification, love, the Church, the world, temptation, and hope; and he seeks to rediscover and to disclose the significance of these theological themes in delineating the nature of faith.

Prior to pursuing the major theological themes Ebeling treats briefly the historical sources of faith: "tradition," which he calls "the history of faith," and "Scripture," "the record of faith." Faith is not an idea or a mode of existence that an individual can create for himself. Faith is received, constantly received. Faith "comes into being as the consequence of the witness of faith. And it depends for its nourishment on the constantly renewed witness, the Word of faith. That is to say, faith comes into being, and continues in being, when it is handed on, in tradition." By "tradition" Ebeling is not referring to the deposit of creeds and doctrines found in theological libraries. "Tradition," understood as "the history of faith," refers to the preaching of the Church through the ages. It was this ancient and continuous witness to the Word of faith that Martin Luther received and to which he appealed in his attacks upon a static and foreign conception of Christian faith in the sixteenth century. Tradition therefore is the ongoing, changing, and cumulative witness of the Church throughout the ages. It is the history of faith and thus reflects the changes that the proclamation has undergone as the Church witnesses in diverse places and eras. What, then, is the constant, the norm for judging the history of faith? Like Luther, Ebeling refers to Scripture, "the record of faith," for it is Scripture that "bears witness, in its witness to Christ, primarily to that on which faith lives, namely the creative power which summons faith out of unbelief. . . ." The Bible is not a document of law, but a document of preaching; it does not provide answers to the questions how or what one is to believe or what once was believed. The Bible is a document of preaching, and as such it suffers all the limitations and inadequacies of human creation. But the decisive thing about the Bible is its witness to Christ, to that which Christian faith must cling to, and its peculiar, original relation to the historical person and event Jesus Christ.

It is at this point that Ebeling's departure from Rudolf Bultmann, and especially from Fritz Buri, is most evident. In Chapter 4, "The Witness of Faith," Ebeling asserts that to speak of Christian faith is to speak of faith in Jesus Christ, and this is to have to do with a historical figure. Ebeling accepts fully the task of historical criticism, but he rejects the use of it that seeks to make Jesus the awkward object of faith by establishing certain "facts" concerning Jesus as objects of faith; as, for example, the fundamentalist beliefs in the Virgin Birth and the miracles. Ebeling also rejects the claims of those who assert that few, if any, historical facts are ascertainable and that the Biblical kerygma is concerned not with a historical Jesus, but primarily with a self-understanding that requires a personal decision. Ebeling has persisted in his support of what James M. Robinson has called "a new quest of the historical Jesus." There is, Ebeling believes, "a historically reliable general impression of Jesus," an impression which is preserved in the Synoptic Gospels. There is the essential structure of the narrative of events concerning Jesus' ministry and death. More importantly, there is the message of Jesus, which "cannot be separated from his Person." It is clear that Ebeling shares with Gunther Bornkamm (author of *Jesus von Nazareth,* 1956) and Ernst Fuchs (author of *Zur Frage nach dem historischen Jesus,* 1960) the conviction that the secret of Jesus' being is enclosed in His words and that being and speaking cannot be completely separated. Thus the historical Jesus may be approached most significantly through the message of Jesus. The historical Jesus to which Ebeling is referring is, therefore, not a figure whose deeds and words become objects of faith. On the contrary, what is known of the deeds and words of Jesus refer beyond themselves. Jesus is "the witness of faith." His message, proclaimed in deed and word, is "the nearness of the rule of God, the clarity of his will, and the simplicity of discipleship, with joy, freedom, and lack of anxiety." In this proclamation Jesus is the witness of faith. He is faith, which calls to faith and shares faith with him who hears. As He is heard and known, He becomes the historical ground or "the basis of faith." This, in fact, is the Easter witness of the early Church; it is knowing Jesus as the basis of faith, as the author and originating power of faith, as the one who discloses God's will for men. The Resurrection is not an object or article of faith among others to be believed. "Rather," according to Ebeling, "faith in the Resurrected One simply expresses faith in Jesus."

James M. Robinson notes that in his formulation of the relationship of the Jesus of history and the Christ of faith Ebeling has returned to Wilhelm Herrmann's "distinction between the historical Jesus as the ground of faith (upon which it falls back in moments of trial) and Christology . . . as the content of faith (in terms of which faith expresses itself)." However, while it is true that Ebeling is indebted to both Wilhelm Herrmann (author of *Der Verkehr des Christen mit Gott,* 1886) and Adolf von Harnack (author of *Das Wesen des Christentums,* 1900), it is important to observe that Ebeling does not separate the words of Jesus from the mystery of His being and thereby efface the character of Jesus as Christ either by a psychological concern with Jesus' "inner life" or by making Jesus primarily a teacher. The point of shared conviction of Ebeling and the nineteenth century theologians is that Christ is correctly preached not where something is said about Him, but only where He Himself becomes the proclaimer.

What is known in and through Jesus Christ, the witness and basis of faith, is "the truth of faith"; namely, God. What the word "God" means apart from Jesus Christ can be expressed only as a question, "as a pointer to the radical questionableness which touches everyman." This questionableness is portrayed most fully in the Crucifixion, for it would appear that for man death is his sole destiny. It would appear that man is without a future and, hence, without an answer to the problem of guilt, which is the "sting of death" (I Corinthians 15:55). But the Biblical question: "Adam, where art thou?" (Genesis 3:9), which raises the question of man's nature and destiny, receives its answer in Jesus Christ. In the witness of faith one encounters God as the provider of man's future and the redeemer of his present. It is Jesus Christ who is "the communication of faith," the Word of God to man. In His life, death, message, and the Church's experience of His resurrection Jesus Christ makes clear what is essential about human existence: that man is created for community with God and with other men.

It is the act of making man's nature and destiny clear that is expressed in the term "God's Word." The communication of faith does not refer to knowledge about faith. It refers to knowing as "an event in the event of speech." Communication takes place where the content of the word and the fulfilling of the word, its reaching its goal, are identical. Faith, the experience of grace and love, the firm hope of a future free from what Kierkegaard called "a sickness unto death," is the fulfilling of the Word of God, the receiving of God's promises in and through the words and actions of Jesus Christ. When men respond in faith to the words of one who witnesses to the truth of faith, there is the Word of God. God himself is communicated. Such is the humanity of God.

As God is the truth of faith (Father) who addresses man in and with His Word (Son), so it is the same God who awakens the heart of man and upholds him with "the courage of faith" (Holy Spirit). The happening, the realizing, the knowledge of God's presence in His Word, the courage to hear and respond to God's Word is the work of God as Holy Spirit. While the primacy of the Christological theme is preserved by Ebeling, the doctrine of the Holy Spirit is not given an auxiliary role as in Reformation thought. In the tradition of Friedrich Schleiermacher and Wilhelm Herrmann, and later of Karl Heim (author of *Jesus der Herr,* 1935), Ebeling's thought has a polar character. It is at once both theocentric and Christocentric. For Schleiermacher and Herrmann, God is the culmination of religious experience and Christ is the means to the culmination. So too for Heim and Ebeling. But whereas the nineteenth century theologians could speak in a rather positive way of man's "God-consciousness" or "pious self-awareness," which is enlivened or informed and brought to completion in Christ, and which reflects the "primary relationship" between the Spirit of God and the spirit of man, Heim and Ebeling speak of the presence of God to man as the awakener of man's conscience to an awareness of man's *Gottesferne* ("distance or estrangement from God"). Man does not possess a prior knowledge of God which is then "completed" by the revelation in Christ. Man is estranged from God. But in the midst of and in spite of his estrangement God stands present to man as the One who encourages faith and bestows the courage of faith.

To speak of faith is not only to speak of God, but also to speak of man, the believing subject, "the I of faith." For as the true knowledge of God is of God who is for us and with us, so the true knowledge of man is of man in his relation to God. Ebeling affirms the priority of God's grace, for faith has the character of being a gift. It is the gift of freedom. In his *Gottesferne* man is caught up in the concern about himself—his guilt and death. His whole life is thus spent in clinging to himself in resolute despair or concealed self-loathing. The gift of grace is freedom from the bondage of such concern. It is not something added to man's being, but a transformation of his mode of existence; from existence projected to death (slavery) to existence projected to life (history or purposeful existence). Faith, as God's gift, discloses a new view of reality in which the future is opened and is seen as belonging to God. The knowledge of the future as salvation, as belonging to God, is the knowledge of justification, which is "the reality of faith."

To speak of the reality of faith is to speak of its power. Apart from God, man's situation is one of powerlessness. He is limited and determined physically and intellectually. He is powerless over the past which contains his guilt and helpless in his guilt before the relations and decisions facing him in the future. The gift of a transformed existence, of the reality of faith, is the gift of "the power of faith."

So concerned is Ebeling to preserve the antecedent reality of God throughout his theological exposition of Christian faith that rather than speak of the Church in such traditional terms as people, community, fellowship, or congregation, he employs the phrase "the summons of faith." For Ebeling the Church is not understood in terms of its place, structure, or the extent of its representation of peoples. These are secular bases of definition. What constitutes the reality of the Church is the summons of God. The Church exists solely in virtue of God's call to men to be his people in faith through Jesus Christ. The life of the Church therefore is service in the summons of faith; service to God in worship and to man in witness.

The "sphere of faith," writes Ebeling, is the world. Christian faith is not life removed from the world in ascetic withdrawal, mystic flight, or speculative thought in quest of the perfection of being. Faith is lived in the immediate temporal order with all its ambiguities and disteleological features. The language of "beyond" so often employed regarding the sphere of faith is appropriate only in so far as it witnesses to the fact that faith and the community of faith do not have their origin, their power of being, from the world. Nonetheless the Church is summoned to be in the world and for the world and to affirm it in word and action as the creation of God. But since the world is fallen creation, living in the world is living perilously in the confrontation of temptation with only "the steadfastness of faith."

According to Ebeling, eschatology is not an appendix to faith. Faith and the future belong together. Faith means letting the future approach. It surrenders the future to God, acknowledging that He alone can and shall have the last word.

OUR EXPERIENCE OF GOD

Author: H. D. Lewis (1910-)
Type of work: Christian epistemology
First published: 1959

Principal Ideas Advanced

Unless religion is supported by conviction as to the truth of certain religious statements, it cannot be taken seriously.

Intellectual arguments for the existence of God attempt to demonstrate by a series of logical steps what is basically a single insight.

God is the incomprehensible, unconditioned, and transcendent source of all reality.

Religious experience is the response, in the course of ordinary experience, to the presence of the transcendent "Other."

In moral action, finite experience is transmuted into the disclosure of the transcendent.

Professor H. D. Lewis of King's College in the University of London, who has held chairs in philosophy and in the history and philosophy of religion, concerns himself in *Our Experience of God* with answering the question, "How are particular religious assertions justified?" The author expresses his conviction that this question is urgent because of the spread of religious indifference and the fear that it is not possible to be religious without suffering a loss of intellectual integrity.

Lewis begins with a point which the pragmatic interest in religion has obscured; namely, that unless a religion is supported by a conviction as to the truth of certain central beliefs, it cannot be taken seriously as religion. The question, then, as to how religious beliefs are to be justified, becomes a crucial one. It is not enough for the religious devotee to believe that he possesses the truth in regard to religious matters; he would also like to know how he can defend his beliefs against criticism. If it be maintained that religion must be true in the sense that it must be faithful in answering the needs of the devotee, Lewis responds by insisting that religious beliefs must be true in the ordinary sense in which statements are said to be "true," as distinguished from "false" or "meaningless": "A religion must stand the test of truth and falsity in the normal sense . . . there must be at the core of a religion something significant to which the distinction of true and false in the normal or literal sense applies. . . ."

Lewis insists that true belief is essential in religion not only because a religion without belief would be, at the most, an emotively motivated moral effort, but also because religious beliefs are "of the most momentous nature, and if sound and acceptable . . . could hardly fail to make an overwhelming difference to our outlook." The belief in the survival of bodily death, for example, has implications concerning the present behavior of man.

Lewis refers to recent empiricist and linguistic trends in philosophy. He agrees that a great deal of religious language has been so used that what the religious believer tries to say is either meaningless or confusing. But Lewis cannot accept the generalized conclusion that all religious discourse is meaningless or emotive, and he resists with religious fervor the claim made by Professor R. B. Braithwaite, who has argued that "religion is no more than a moral policy and that whatever there seems to be over and above this are mere stories."

The author agrees with the linguistic philosophers insofar as they maintain that a critical examination of language is almost always helpful in the process of clarifying ideas. He thinks that religious apologists are mistaken who attempt to defend religious claims by arguing exclusively for their "peculiarity" or by calling attention to the open texture of language and to the various types of discourse. Lewis's own predilection is to attempt to make a positive defense in support of certain notions the empiricist objects to: for example, the idea of an abiding self, or the belief in moral principles which are independent of human sentiments. The problem of clarifying religious discourse and of supplying evidence in support of religious claims is a difficult one, Lewis asserts, because religion, by its very nature, is concerned with matters that are beyond the scope of ordinary intelligence. The problem of justifying religious claims is best handled, Lewis concludes in his initial statement, not by giving way to unreason, but by making reasonable the claim that our examination of nature leads us to believe that "the world cannot be an ultimately random one" and that there is something incomprehensible, a positive mystery, which must somehow be posited as "accounting for" the world of our experience.

Lewis's criticism of the intellectual arguments for the existence of God is that the arguments attempt to demonstrate by a series of logical steps what is basically a single insight. A study of the traditional arguments has value, however, in calling attention to the basic conviction that some single unconditioned Being is somehow the source of the conditioned and incomplete reality which men encounter in ordinary experience.

The problem which positing God as the incomprehensible and unconditioned source of reality presents is that if religion rests on mystery, it would seem inevitable that religion be without content. The problem is not to be solved, writes Lewis, simply by talking in the existentialist manner about "encountering" God, as if it were possible to encounter a being about whom one had no knowledge. The only hopeful line of development involves making sense out of the claim that religion concerns both what is beyond man and what is altogether within. Although there is a sense in which one cannot know God by an appeal to evidence, there is, nevertheless, an experience of God which provides abundant evidence "of what God is like and what He does."

Lewis makes it clear that he does not intend to prove the existence of God by an appeal to religious experience; nor does Lewis argue that religious experience consists in a literal union of God and man; finally, he denies that reflection on what has been called "the human situation" is sufficient to the kind of knowledge he seeks.

The word "religion" is notoriously ambiguous, Lewis points out; he suggests that the term be reserved to mean an activity or attitude which involves some awareness of a transcendent being, and by a "transcendent" being, Lewis means a being "beyond" or "other than" man in that He is perfect and absolutely complete. A consideration of primitive religions shows, Lewis claims, that the religious experience of those who have lived close to nature bears striking affinities to the religious experience of modern and civilized man; in fact, a consideration of primitive experience may very well serve to emphasize and bring out the experience of the "beyond" in one who, because of the cultural complexity of his life, has forgotten or tended to ignore his own religious experience.

Idolatry begins, Lewis explains in a particularly striking passage, when men are overwhelmed by the consciousness of the transcendent and, sensing the demands that God makes upon them and the inescapable power of His reality, attempt "to resist God, to be in conflict with Him or try to escape Him, *just because He is God.* But they will not do this in the first instance by merely forgetting or disregarding God. For they are also drawn to Him and need Him. They will thus try to limit or restrict their own consciousness of God by containing it within the media and symbols which are needed for its articulation. This seems to me the essence and beginning of idolatry."

(In a note on Ronald Hepburn's *Christianity and Paradox* (1958), Lewis rejects Hepburn's suggestion that religion can provide the myths for a life pilgrimage, and Lewis also objects to Hepburn's claim that the experience of the numinous is not necessarily a religious experience.)

As Lewis continues his examination of religious experience, it becomes more and more certain that he means to limit religious experience to the sense of the presence of the God. The religious experience is not simply an awareness of power and mystery in nature; such a feeling might very well be a function of human ignorance and frailty; the religious experience is, rather, an undeniable sense of wonder which accompanies the conviction that an absolute and unconditioned being is the source of all reality. Although the religious experience is a response to the transcendent and mysterious "Other," it is an experience which is vitally related to other experiences in life.

Religious imagery may play a significant role in religious experience, but unlike the basic sense of the presence of the transcendent—an experience mediated by what Lewis calls "first-order symbols"—the experience which depends on imagery is not a direct experience of the divine. Nor is the historian able to report on the influence of religious ideas if he is not finally grounded in the religious experience itself.

Dogma has a place in the religious life, says Lewis, only to the extent that it makes possible "the constant renewal of personal experience of God and the sense of His presence." Ritual acts and the material objects which figure in them form another class of religious symbols, other than first-order symbols, by which the religious experience can be provoked and enriched. It is possible, Lewis suggests, that certain physical disciplines, or the use of certain drugs, may initiate physical conditions which make first-hand religious experience possible, but he reminds the reader that not all kinds of physical excitation, for example, sexual stimulation, are conducive to religious experience. There is always the danger that an absorption in physical practices or the uses of the instruments of worship may lead to the degenerate practice of magic and an idolatry which is incompatible with true religion. Symbolism and tradition may become sentimentalized, and the strenuous moral demands of Christianity may be forgotten; when joy is expressed because of Christ's triumph over the Cross, it is possible that the symbol of the Cross loses its element of horror and thus fails to remind the Christian of the strenuous kind of struggle which Christianity demands.

Preternatural experiences, particularly abnormal experiences such as those the mystics report, or those which accompany the exercise of such powers as levitation, precognition, and clairvoyance, are not necessarily religiously significant, Lewis warns. Going beyond ordinary experience is not enough; to be religious, an experience must provide a sense of the presence of the absolute and unconditioned Being who lies at the center of all reality.

Lewis devotes two chapters to a consideration of the problems which arise in connection with petitionary prayers. He argues that a belief in the efficacy of petitionary prayers is compatible with the belief in the presence of a concerned God. But the independence of the divine will must be insured, and it may be that the most illuminating answer to any petitionary prayer is an enlivened sense of the presence of God.

According to Lewis, morality supplies "the sphere *par excellence* where finite experience is transmuted into the disclosures and operations of the transcendent within the world we know." It is on the moral or ethical level that the personal character of the relation of man to God is completed. In his freedom and dignity man prepares himself, in his moral moments, for the most significant of his encounters with God.

Lewis concludes his work by emphasizing once again the point that God is a transcendent being and that a finite being cannot hope to resolve the mystery of the divine being by enjoying any momentary contact or unity with God. It is through responsible and devoted response to the challenges which arise in the ordinary course of social and cultural experience that man comes to experience God and to acquire the inspiration which strengthens him in his religious life. The vision of Jesus is possible, Lewis insists, "if we diligently seek it where God ordained that it should be found, in the live and continuing witness to what Jesus was and did."

AUTHOR INDEX